THE
SIMON AND SCHUSTER
BOOK OF THE OPERA

THE
SIMON AND SCHUSTER
BOOK OF THE OPERA

A Complete Reference Guide — 1597 to the Present

Over 400 Illustrations

SIMON AND SCHUSTER · NEW YORK

Copyright © 1977 by Arnoldo Mondadori, Editore, S.p.A., Milano
English Translation copyright © 1978 Arnoldo Mondadori Editore, S.p.A., Milano

Published by Simon and Schuster
A Division of Gulf & Western Corporation
Simon & Schuster Building
Rockefeller Center
1230 Avenue of the Americas
New York, New York 10020

Printed and bound in Italy
By Officine Grafiche,
Arnoldo Mondadori Editore, Verona

2 3 4 5 6 7 8 9 10

Library of Congress Cataloging in Publication Data

Main entry under title:

The Simon and Schuster book of the opera.

   Translation of L'Opera : repertorio della
lirica dal 1597.
   Includes indexes.
   1. Opera—Dictionaries.   2. Opera—Chronology.
3. Operas—Stories, plots, etc.   I. Mezzanotte,
Riccardo.
ML102.06063   782.1′03   79-1317
ISBN 0-671-24886-3

Translated from the Italian by Catherine Atthill, Judith Elphick, Mary Fitton,
John Gilbert, Virginia Renshaw, Judith Spencer, Pamela Swinglehurst.

The following have contributed to this book:

Antonio Bertelé (ABe), Rossella Bertolazzi (RB), Lorenzo Bianchi (LB)
Antonio Bossi (AB), Simonetta Columbu (SC), Renata Leydi (RL)
Riccardo Mezzanotte (RM), Giovanni Palmieri (GPa),
Fabio Parazzini (FP), Edgardo Pellegrini (EP), Guido Peregalli (GP),
Matilde Segre (MS), Maria Simone Mongiardino (MSM).

Editor-in-chief: Riccardo Mezzanote
Editors: Francesca Agostini, Franco Paone
Photograph research: Adriana Savorani
Layout: Bruno Lando
English-language editor: Nicholas John

As an art form, opera has existed for more than 380 years. Proof of its enduring popularity are the many thousands of scores and librettos which have been produced during this time, first in Italy, then in other European countries, and finally in America. Many have achieved fame, even in some cases immortality, others falling at the first hurdle or, at best, failing to win posterity's favour.

It was not our intention to attempt a comprehensive review of opera over the centuries; what we have done is to select nearly 800 operas which, because of their historical importance, public acceptance and acknowledged artistic quality, command a special place in the history of musical presentation.

The task has not been without its hazards, especially as regards source material referring to the earliest periods. While we can only crave the reader's forbearance for any omissions or inaccuracies, we offer this volume in the earnest hope that it will lead to a greater understanding of individual operas and to a keener awareness of the marvellous world of musical theatre.

Colour drawings by Bernardo Buontalenti for an intermedio *to* La Pellegrina, *produced in Florence in 1589. Such* intermedii, *dumbshows with scenery and music, were staged between the acts of a play and may be considered the immediate precursors of opera.*

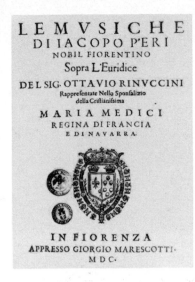  

LA DAFNE

Dramatic fable in a prologue and six scenes by Jacopo Peri (1561–1633) with text by Ottavio Rinuccini (1562–1621). First performance: Florence, Jacopo Corsi's palazzo, during the 1597 carnival.

SYNOPSIS. Based on Ovid's *Metamorphoses*, the fable is preceded by a prologue, in which the character representing the Latin poet greets the audience. As the first scene opens, the chorus introduces the god Apollo who, proud to have killed the monster Pitone (Python), declares his immunity to the wiles of the god of love, Amore. The latter swiftly has his revenge. Dafne, a beautiful nymph, appears in the act of hunting a deer. Apollo, overwhelmed by the girl's beauty, falls in love with her. She flees and is pursued by the god. Amore sings of his triumph and the chorus echoes his song. A messenger arrives, saying that Dafne, on the point of falling into the god's clutches, has sought divine assistance and has been changed into a laurel. Thereafter the tree is to be sacred to Apollo and its leaves will be used to crown poets and kings. The fable ends as the chorus extols love and hopes that the feelings of every lover will be reciprocated by the beloved.

■ The music written for this short composition has been entirely lost. Nevertheless, a reading of the libretto makes it quite clear that *La Dafne* represents a very important development in the history of music and the theatre. The elaborate theories of the group of writers and musicians known as the Florentine Camerata, which during the last quarter of the sixteenth century met first in the house of Giovanni Bardi and then in that of Jacopo Corsi, found their first practical realization in *La Dafne*. The members of the Camerata initiated a new form of music – monody – and aimed to revive the spirit of ancient Greek tragedy by using a kind of musical recitative which they called 'recitar cantando'. The conviction that Greek tragedy had been sung, and its dramatic quality expressed through music or, more specifically, by means of words

intoned musically, provided the basic impetus for the birth of opera; and, in the view of many musicologists, *La Dafne* was its first example. It would seem that Giulio Caccini and Jacopo Corsi also wrote settings of the libretto. Caccini's music is also lost, but two fragments of Corsi's reveals a strophic pattern in that the same melody is repeated through all the stanzas of an ode. An enlarged version of Rinuccini's play was later set to music by Marco da Gagliano (1608) and produced at the court of Mantua. A German version partly translated from Rinuccini by Martin Opitz was set to music by Heinrich Schütz and first produced on 23 April 1627 in Torgau. It was among the first operas to be written in Germany.

L'AMFIPARNASO, or LI DISPERATI CONTENTI

'Harmonic comedy' for chorus of four and five voices by Orazio Vecchi (1550–1605), with text probably by himself, performed in Venice in 1597.

SYNOPSIS. The 'opera' consists of a sequence of episodes devised in the spirit of the *Commedia dell'Arte*; they are not connected with one another, although they do have some themes in common. At the beginning, the aged Pantalone is captivated by the beauty of the courtesan Hortensia, who, however, does not return his love. Another love story is enacted in the second scene, but of rather a different nature, involving Lelio and Nisa. In the third scene Graziano seeks the hand of Pantalone's daughter and the old man, after a formal discussion about dowry and prospects, gives his consent. In the next scene Isabella arouses the jealousy of her suitor Lucio by pretending to respond to the advances of the captain Cardon. At first the joke threatens to backfire, but a little stage trickery soon puts the situation right and all ends happily in marriage. The final scene, somewhat different from the previous ones, illustrates the activities of Jewish pawnshops and the part they played in sixteenth-century domestic economy.

■ *L'Amfiparnaso* is regarded as one of the master-pieces of the polyphonic style and is sometimes considered, though wrongly, to be one of the earliest examples of lyric opera. It comprises short songs, dances, madrigals and dialogue. The maskers talk in dialect, the other characters in a particularly elegant, polished Italian. It was composed in 1594, three years before its first performance, and was possibly introduced to the public, though not in stage form, around that time in the Sala Spelta in Modena.

LA PAZZIA SENILE (The Madness of Old Age)
Musical comedy or madrigal drama by Adriano Banchieri (1568–1634), with verse text by himself. First published in Venice in 1598.

SYNOPSIS. The action takes place in Rovigo, the period being unspecified. The old merchant Pantalone is madly in love with Lauretta, who does not return his passion. His daughter Doralice loves Fulvio and he, in turn, adores her. Pantalone, however, does not take kindly to this show of ardour and summons the elderly doctor Graziano, offering him Doralice's hand. The two old men do everything they can to further their plan but in the end they are forced to admit defeat, and Doralice finally marries her Fulvio.

■ The comedy, although similar in many ways to traditional music melodramas, is in a sense a hybrid, something between a true opera and a collection of songs and madrigals. It has often been described as one of the forerunners of comic opera; and Banchieri was certainly one of the first composers to set comic situations to music. The complete title of the work is *La pazzia senile – Ragionamenti vaghi et dilettevoli, a tre voci, di*

Graziano and Pantalone. Illustration for Act I, Scene 3 of the Venetian edition of L'Amfiparnaso *by Orazio Vecchi (1597).*

Adriano Banchieri, bolognese. The text is in verse and of mediocre poetic quality. The dialogue between the characters (the so-called ragionamenti) alternate with intermezzi, in which the actors impersonate chimney-sweeps and match-sellers. There is a prologue, recited by Whimsical Humour, and the work ends with a dance of country girls. It is not really suitable for stage presentation because, among other things, the parts of the individual characters are written for several voices, in madrigal style.

The characters are for the most part the maskers from the *Commedia dell'Arte*. In Doctor Graziano, for example, it is possible to recognize the character who became the archetypal doctor from Bologna, Doctor Balanzone.

The comedy was probably staged with actors miming the parts, while the singing was entrusted to a hidden chorus. The first edition of 1598 was followed by others in the early part of the seventeenth century. A complete version of text and music has recently been published.

EURIDICE
Dramatic fable in a prologue and six scenes by Jacopo Peri (1561–1633), text by Ottavio Rinuccini (1562–1621). First performance: Florence, Palazzo Pitti, 6 October 1600, on the occasion of the marriage of Maria de Medici to Henri IV of France.

SYNOPSIS. Following the pattern of Politian's *Orfeo*, the plot differs only in that this version has a happy ending. After a prologue, in which the spirit of Tragedy announces the subject of the opera and greets the royal spectators, a chorus of shepherds and nymphs celebrate the marriage of Orfeo and Euridice. They are joined by Euridice herself in a joyful dance. Orfeo prays that the gods will preserve her, and Arcetro and Tirsi wish the pair good fortune. Euridice leaves. Dafne reports that the bride has died from the bite of a snake. The shepherds express their grief. In the following scene Arcetro describes to the chorus Orfeo's despair and how in his misery he wished to kill himself. But Venere, appearing from Heaven, has comforted him and urged him to go down to Hades and to request Plutone gives back his beloved. Orfeo descends to the Underworld and by virtue of his piteous lament moves both Plutone and Proserpina to pity. Euridice is allowed to go free, without any conditions. A chorus of shades accompanies the lovers as they return to the light of earth, where the nymphs and shepherds are anxiously waiting. A shepherd, Aminta, now brings the joyful news that Orfeo is on his way back. The bridal couple enter and their restored happiness is celebrated with singing and dancing.

■ Since the music of *La Dafne*, also composed by Peri and performed three years previously, is lost, *Euridice* is the first complete opera to have survived. It gives us a valuable insight into the nature of the new art form devised by the Florentine intellectuals towards the end of the sixteenth century. Rinuccini's concise libretto,

Jacopo Peri in the part of Orpheus in the first production of his opera Euridice.

EURIDICE
Dramatic fable in six scenes by Giulio Caccini (1546–1618), nicknamed Romano, libretto by Ottavio Rinuccini (1562–1621). First performance: Florence, Salone di Antonio de' Medici, Palazzo Pitti, 5 December 1602. Composed in 1600.

■ The opera was based on the libretto by Ottavio Rinuccini which had earlier been set to music by Jacopo Peri (see Peri's *Euridice*, p. 8). Some passages from Caccini's opera were introduced in the first performance of Peri's *Euridice* at Florence in 1600. Caccini managed to anticipate his rival, if not in staging his opera, at least in publishing his version in January 1601. It appeared under the title *L'Euridice composta in musica in stile rappresentativo di Giulio Caccini detto Romano*. With the loss of Peri's *La Dafne* (see p. 7), the two versions of *Euridice* are, in effect, the oldest known examples of opera.
Like Peri, Caccini was a member of the Florentine Camerata, and, because of his gift for melodic invention, his version is perhaps the more pleasing to the ear. But Peri was considered a more skilful technician and a more accurate exponent of the new movement in music.

ORFEO
Musical fable in a prologue and five acts by Claudio Monteverdi (1567–1643), libretto by Alessandro Striggio (c. 1573–1630). First performance: Mantua carnival, 24 February 1607. First performance in U.S.A.: New York, 14 April 1912; in U.K.: London, 8 March 1924 (concert performance).

SYNOPSIS. Prologue. La Musica greets the spectators, announces the subject matter of the drama and tells of the wonderful effect that the art of music has on the human spirit. Act I. A shepherd tells how Orfeo has found happiness in his ardently returned love for Euridice, and invites his companions and the nymphs to share in the bridegroom's joy. Orfeo, too, sings of his rapture and Euridice echoes him. All then proceed to a temple to give thanks to the gods. Act II. Returning to the familiar places of his childhood, Orfeo movingly recalls the course of his love, when Silvia, the Messenger, appears, bearing terrible news. Euridice has died while gathering flowers for her wedding crown. Grief-stricken by the calamity, Orfeo does not seem to hear the laments of the shepherds. Suddenly, however, he announces his decision to descend to the kingdom of the dead to regain his bride. Act III. In Hades, Orfeo reaches the banks of the Styx, the river dividing the kingdom of the living from that of the dead. He is accompanied by Speranza (Hope), who leaves him to continue his desperate mission alone, for she cannot enter the realm of shadows. Although moved by Orfeo's sad song, Caronte, the boatman who ferries souls across the dark river, will not grant him passage. But the gods intervene, making the guardian of Hades fall asleep so that Orfeo can enter the kingdom of the dead. Act IV. Proserpina, wife of the king

consisting of 790 verses, is not without literary merit and dramatic force, and in setting it to music, Peri employed a strict monodic line which, rejecting the complexities of polyphony 'so that the words can be properly understood', was flexible enough to express the emotions of the characters. The writers and musicians of the Florentine Camerata hoped that they were reviving the spirit of Greek song with their 'recitar cantando'; but this did not prevent Peri indulging himself in passages which exploited the virtuosity of the human voice. There are sections which, although not yet taking on the attributes of an 'aria', have an unprecedented beauty of line, and dramatic conviction is conveyed by the effective matching of music to words. According to Massimo Mila, it is hard to know what to admire more in this opera, 'the innocent but somewhat rough, primitive quality or the civilized refinement'. The score shows a style of notation that was to become very common: only vocal parts are precisely and completely indicated, while figured bass is given with no indication as to the instrumentation. We know, however, that at the first performance the continuo instruments consisted of a harpsichord, a chitarrone, a lyra viol and a lute, all placed behind the stage. Peri, nicknamed Zazzerino because of his red hair, was an expert player of the organ and the harpsichord in addition to having a fine voice. He himself sang the role of Orfeo.

of Hades, pleads with her husband, Plutone, to give back Euridice to the grieving Orfeo. Plutone agrees but makes one condition. Orfeo may lead his wife out of Hades but should he look back he will lose her for ever. Orfeo, overjoyed, departs; but he is unable to check his impatience. Hearing a sudden noise, and fearing Plutone has tricked him, he turns round, thus condemning Euridice to remain eternally in the Underworld, despite all his desperate pleas. Act V. In the woodlands of Thrace, Orfeo weeps for his lost wife, while Eco echoes his lament. Apollo, his divine father, descends from Heaven and offers him immortality. They rise together to the heavens, where Orfeo will be able to gaze everlastingly on his beloved Euridice.

■ After attending the first performance of Peri's *Euridice* in Florence, Vincenzo Gonzaga, Duke of Mantua, commissioned Monteverdi to take the legend of Orfeo, revived in the previous century by Politian, and to set it to music. Alessandro Striggio, son of the famous madrigalist, prepared a libretto which provided the composer with a story full of dramatic situations. Under Monteverdi, the recitative style originating with the Florentine Camerata was given true dramatic impetus. His setting of Striggio's libretto, by virtue of its dramatic tension, its eloquent and moving expression of human passions, and its formal variety, has been the earliest opera to take its place in the standard repertoire. The score of *Orfeo* remains a landmark in the history of opera.

Orfeo is undoubtedly the first great opera. Monteverdi obviously knew and had assimilated the style and implications of the early Florentine operas, but in every respect his work represents an immense broadening of scope in comparison with his predecessors. The basis of *Orfeo* is still the recitative style of Peri and Caccini, yet Monteverdi's recitative is at once more controlled and more dramatic than that of the Florentines. Its harmonic language, too, is more advanced, frequently going beyond even the most extreme sections of Peri's score. The duets and choruses are more interesting than the simple dance-songs of the first operas: while the ensembles in the first act of the opera have an unrivalled freshness and gaiety, the chorus of shepherds in Act II, lamenting the death of Euridice or the long chorus of spirits in Act III look forward to the best of the Sixth Book of Madrigals of 1614. Perhaps the most striking feature of the score is the important role allotted to the instruments. Peri's and Caccini's operas had included virtually no purely instrumental music: a small number of keyboard and plucked instruments supported the voices. Cavalieri's *Rappresentatione del anima e di corpo* required a larger ensemble, and includes some fairly extended instrumental sinfonias. Monteverdi, too, introduces and concludes scenes with similar pieces, notably the famous opening toccata, and also interposes shorter ritornelli between the verses of the strophic choruses and arias throughout the opera, and as a foil to '*Possente spirto*', Orfeo's impassioned plea to Caronte in Act III. The instruments not only shape the music flow of the recitative and choruses, they further the opera's

The room of the ducal palace at Mantua where the first performance of Monteverdi's Orfeo *was probably given.*

dramatic impact with their tone-colours. The score of *Orfeo*, published in 1609, gives a list of instruments which are probably those used in the first performance. It includes both chordal instruments (harpsichords, a double harp, two chittarone, pipe organs) and melodic instruments (strings – viols and violin family; brass – cornets, sackbuts and trumpets; recorders). Printed in the score itself are some indications of instrumentation. These do not tie up precisely with the list of instruments given but they show how the continuo instruments were varied according to the dramatic situation, which also dictated the choice of melodic instruments in the ritornelli and sinfonias, the pastoral atmosphere of Act I being conveyed by the recorders and a pair of *violini piccoli* (small violins tuned an octave higher than the normal violin), while the cornets and sackbuts mirrored the gloom of the infernal regions in Act IV. It is due to this felicitous combination of recitative, ensemble and instrumental writing that *Orfeo* not only holds its exalted position in operatic history but is also the earliest opera to take its place in the standard repertoire.

There have been a number of modern transcriptions, including those by Gian Francesco Malipiero (1929), Vincent D'Indy (1904), Carl Orff (1923), Ottorino Respighi (1935), Paul Hindemith (1954), Bruno Maderna (1967), Denis Stevens (1967) and Raymond Leppard (1967).

LA DAFNE
Opera in one act by Marco da Gagliano (1572–1643), libretto by Ottavio Rinuccini (1562–1621), an expanded version of his text of 1597. First performance: Mantua, February 1608. First performers: Francesco

Rasi (Apollo), Antonio Brandi, detto il Brandino (Tirsi), Caterinuccia Martinelli (Venere).

SYNOPSIS. Prologue. Ovidio (the Latin poet Ovid, from whose *Metamorphoses* the plot is drawn) introduces himself and announces the subject matter of the opera – the dangers awaiting those who scorn the power of love – as well as flattering Vincenzo Gonzaga, Duke of Mantua, and his wife Eleanora.

The action takes place in Arcadia, and opens with the nymphs and shepherds lamenting the havoc wrought by Fitone, a horrible, fire-breathing dragon. They pray for divine assistance; Apollo manifests himself, finally descending and slaying the monster (chorus, *'Ohimè, che veggio?'*). After a chorus in praise of the god, Venere and her son Amore enter. Apollo, puffed up with pride at his deed, taunts the young archer, who swears vengeance. In the aria *'Chi da lacci d'Amore'* Venere warns of the dangers of incurring the wrath of Cupid. Dafne enters, and rejoices at the news that Fitone has been slain. She is joined by Apollo, who has been hit by one of Amore's golden darts, and has thus fallen helplessly in love with her. Dafne, however, was the target for a leaden arrow, which has the opposite effect, and remains indifferent to Apollo's advances. Eventually, Apollo becomes over-insistent and she flees, closely followed by the god, much to Amore's amusement. He exults over his triumph, and returns with his mother to heaven. The shepherd Tirsi enters and narrates Apollo's pursuit of Dafne, and her transformation into a laurel tree. Nymphs and shepherds mourn her fate in an extended scene. At length Apollo reappears and laments his lost love in a long aria, full of brilliant coloratura. He ends each verse with three

The theatre built in Bologna for an opera-torneo by Francesco Rivarola, known as Il Chenda. Miniature from Insignia. *Bologna, Archivio di Stato.*

chords on his lyre, imitated by four offstage stringed instruments. The final chorus again points the moral.

■ Marco da Gagliano had already completed the score of *La Dafne* when he was called to Mantua from Florence late in 1607 to assist in the preparations for the festivities surrounding two important events scheduled for early the next year: the marriage of Francesco Gonzaga, Vincenzo's eldest son, to Margherita, Infanta of Savoy, and the installation of Ferdinando, Francesco's younger brother, as Archbishop. For political reasons the wedding was postponed and the celebrations with it, so *Dafne* was instead staged as part of the carnival, apparently with much success. It was the last time that the Mantuan court singer, Caterinuccia Martinelli, was to appear. Although only 17, she was already famed for her ability, but shortly after singing Venere she was taken ill of smallpox and died a month later.

In its pastoral setting *La Dafne* is reminiscent of the first two acts of Monteverdi's *Orfeo*. Love (albeit unrequited) plays its part here, too, and the action also includes the narration by a messenger of the heroine's off-stage tragedy, a mourning scene for the nymphs and shepherds and a final lament for the hero. Gagliano does not manage to advance the drama with his music as felicitously as Monteverdi. Instead of a subtle interplay of solo, ensemble and instrumental items, the music proceeds, as in the very first operas, by means of solo recitative periodically interspersed with choruses. Gagliano's recitative is fresh and lyrical, but usually lacks the harmonic tension of Monteverdi's, although Tirsi's narration of Dafne's transformation and the solo sections in the mourning scene contain dissonances as striking as any in *Orfeo*. The later sections – Tirsi's narrative, the mourning scene and Apollo's lament – are musically the most considerable. The high point of the whole work is undoubtedly the superb mourning scene with its recurring refrain *'Piangete, ninfe, e con voi pianga Amore'* ('weep, nymphs, and let Love weep with you') and well-managed deployment of solo, duet and choral textures. The central section is especially effective, a miniature madrigal for six voices. A small instrumental ensemble of four stringed instruments and continuo is called for to provide short ritornelli and a *ballo* alternating with the final chorus. The chorus *'Ohimè, che veggio?'*, though, contains the first operatic use of obbligato instruments with chorus.

La Dafne was published in score in 1609 and is prefaced by a long introduction by the composer in which he not only informs us that several portions of the work, including Apollo's lament, were in fact written by someone else (most probably his friend Ferdinando Gonzaga), but also gives detailed information on the staging and production of the first performance. It is thus a valuable musicological document.

ARIANNA (Ariadne)
Tragedy in a prologue and eight scenes by Claudio Monteverdi (1567–1643), libretto by Ottavio Rinuccini

(1562–1621). First performance: Mantua, Teatro della Corte, 28 May 1608, during the festivities for the marriage of Prince Francesco Gonzaga and Margherita of Savoy. Principal performers: Virginia Ramponi Andreini (Arianna); Settimia Caccini (Venere); Antonio Brandi, nicknamed 'Il Brandino'; Sante Orlandi; Francesco Rasi.

SYNOPSIS. The action takes place against the background of 'a wild rocky place in the midst of the waves' representing the island of Naxos. Venere announces that Arianna has been abandoned by Teseo and calls on Amore to protect the unfortunate girl. Teseo, indeed, is about to return to Athens and has left Arianna, alone and weeping, on the deserted island. At this moment she sings her famous Lament. The chorus then relates how Bacco, seeing Arianna, has come down and comforted her. Venere returns and celebrates the marriage. Arianna is made a goddess and joy dispels the sadness of her lost love. It is a thin plot, without many events or much action, conforming faithfully to the dictates of the unities of time and place. The chorus is used to describe the sequence of the action and to express the feelings of the characters – their hopes, doubts and dilemmas. At the end, a group of sixteen dancers, the armed companions of Bacco, perform a 'capering dance' to emphasize the happy conclusion.

■ Preparation for staging the opera began in December 1607. In March of the following year the young Caterina Martinelli, known as La Romanina, who was to have sung the main role, died of smallpox. After many enquiries and rehearsals with famous singers of the day, a substitue was found – the actress Virginia Ramponi Andreini ('La Florinda'), whose acting and singing surpassed all expectations. The opera was a tremendous success. The audience (6,000 people according to Follino, official chronicler of the events, 4,000 according to later estimates) applauded and cheered. The theatre, especially built for the occasion, is now completely destroyed. There were at least three copies of the score but they have been lost, except for a part of the sixth scene – the *Lamento d'Arianna*, a dialogue with Dorilla and the chorus, the justly famed *Lasciatemi morir*, in which Arianna bewails her cruel fate. This was transcribed by Monteverdi himself in his sixth book of *Madrigali*. This fragment, 'sublime in its movingly true expressiveness' (M. Mila), and described by Monteverdi himself as the 'most essential part', is exceptionally powerful and deeply felt. Contemporary composers came to regard it as an unrivalled expression, in musical terms, of human grief and hopeless passion. It is very probable that Monteverdi was here pouring out his own grief for the recent death of his wife Claudia. He was to make two later versions of this exquisite fragment from the opera, one as a madrigal for five voices, and another in monodic style with a Latin religious text entitled *Pianto della Madonna sopra il Lamento di Arianna*. The opera was revived in Venice for the opening of the Teatro di San Moisè, in 1639, when Monteverdi held the post of *maestro di cappella* at St Mark's.

IL BALLO DELLE INGRATE (The Dance of the Ungrateful Souls)

Music by Claudio Monteverdi (1567–1643), text by Ottavio Rinuccini (1562–1621). First performance: Mantua, Teatro della Commedia, 4 June 1608, during the festivities for the marriage of Prince Francesco Gonzaga and Margherita of Savoy.

SYNOPSIS. The scene represents the mouth of a dark cave, within which appears a chasm belching fire and smoke. At the beginning of the opera Amore and Venere request Plutone to bring up from Hades the spirits of the ungrateful women who had rejected love when alive, so that they can act as an example to others and urge them to treat their lovers with yielding gentleness. The spirits arrive, escorted by shades from Hell, and perform a sad dance expressing 'great grief by means of movements, their steps being accompanied by the music of a large number of instruments playing a melancholy and tearful dance air'. Then follows a monologue by Plutone (*Tornate al negro chiostro, anime sventurate*), and as the spirits move off, one of them pauses to sing a deeply moving lament for lost life and love (*Ahi troppo, ahi troppo è duro*).

■ The dramatic action is slight, but there are particularly penetrating musical touches, well integrated with the words and the action. The *Ballo* itself follows the style of the 'court ballets' that Monteverdi came to know in the course of his stay in Flanders in 1599. At

Title-page to Dafne, *set to music by Heinrich Schütz (1627). Dresden, Sächsische Landesbibliothek.*

the first performance, twice as many dancers appeared on the stage as originally planned. They included the duke himself, the princely bridegroom, six other nobles and eight ladies from high Mantuan society. They were accompanied by 'a large number of musicians with different string and wind instruments', although Monteverdi had only called for 'five viole da braccio, a clavicembalo and a chitarrone'. The opera was also staged in Vienna in 1628 and was transcribed, probably in amended form, under the title of *Ballo delle ingrate in rappresentativo*, in the eighth book of *Madrigali guerrieri et amorosi*, published in Venice in 1638. The report of the first performance mentions that at the end the audience was so moved that it proved necessary to follow it with a festive scene of nymphs and shepherds singing happy songs and madrigals in order to drive away the gloom.

IL COMBATTIMENTO DI TANCREDI E CLORINDA (The Duel of Tancredi and Clorinda)

Madrigal in stage form by Claudio Monteverdi (1567–1643), based on the twelfth canto of Gerusalemme liberata *by Torquato Tasso (1544–95). First performance: Venice, Palazzo Mocenigo, 1624.*

SYNOPSIS. The subject of the twelfth canto of *Gerusalemme liberata* is the death of Clorinda, a Moslem heroine. Tancredi, a Christian warrior, meets Clorinda, whom he loves secretly but does not recognize in her suit of black, rusty armour. He challenges her to a duel and in the ensuing encounter Clorinda is fatally wounded. She requests baptism and Tancredi hastens to fetch water from a nearby stream. Raising her visor, he recognizes the girl he has loved and she is transfigured as she 'dies happily'. The third character introduced by Monteverdi is Testo (Narrator), the composer himself, who announces the theme and comments on the important parts of the action.

■ The *Combattimento* is included in the eighth book of madrigals, *Madrigali guerrieri et amorosi* (1638). Apart from its undisputed poetic merit, certainly equal to that of the libretto, this work is also important from the viewpoint of compositional technique. The action is dramatized in monodic style and the score contains the earliest example of the *stile concitato*, or 'agitated style', theoretically described two thousand years earlier by Plato but thus far never given actual musical expression. In the preface of his book, Monteverdi also treats the subject theoretically and explains how he has come to devise and apply it: '. . . for I had two contrasting passions to represent in song, namely war and love'. In order to represent the dramatic vibrancy of these two contrasting sentiments, he introduces the string tremolo. The writing for the voices is simple and spare, the music faithfully following the realistic and psychological components of the text. As in *Arianna*, *Orfeo* and Monteverdi's other works, the music brilliantly reflects the human drama of love and death. The score calls only for four *viole da brazzo*, and a continuo of harpsichord and *contrabasso da gamba*.

LA DAFNE

Pastoral tragi-comedy in a prologue and five acts by Heinrich Schütz (1585–1672), libretto by Martin Opitz (1597–1639). First recorded performance: Hartenfels Castle, Torgau, 23 April 1627.

■ The libretto is a free translation of Ottavio Rinuccini's *La Dafne*, already set to music by Jacopo Peri (for synopsis see under Peri's *La Dafne*, p. 7). Composed and staged on the occasion of the marriage of George II of Hesse-Darmstadt, the libretto was adapted and rewritten so that the bride and bridegroom could recognize direct allusions to themselves. It was among the first attempts to transplant Florentine opera to Germany. The text was by Opitz, the greatest German poet of the time, who had made a profound study of Italian and French verse forms, on which he modelled his German version. Schütz's score was lost and has never been recovered.

LE NOZZE DI TETI E PELEO (The Marriage of Thetis and Peleus)

Opera in a prologue and three acts by Francesco Cavalli, real name Pier Francesco Caletti-Bruni (1602–76), libretto by Orazio Persiani. First performance: Venice, Teatro Tron di S. Cassiano, 24 January 1639.

SYNOPSIS. Jupiter wishes to marry the nymph Teti to Peleo, but Juno persecutes her with jealousy. Hell arouses Discordia against the lovers, but is finally conquered by Amore.

■ This was Cavalli's first opera and it is the oldest Venetian opera whose music has been preserved. The choruses play a very important role.

LA DIDONE (Dido)

Opera in a prologue and three acts by Francesco Cavalli, real name Pier Francesco Caletti-Bruni (1602–76), libretto by Giovanni Francesco Busenello (1598–1659). First performance: Venice, Teatro Tron di S. Cassiano, carnival of 1641.

SYNOPSIS. The prologue tells of the fall of Troy and attributes it to the revenge taken by Juno for the judgement of Paris. The rest of the action more or less follows the classical story, except for the unusual ending. Here, when Dido decides to kill herself after being abandoned by Aeneas, she is restrained by Iarbas, the Moorish king whom she had previously rejected. He now manages to console her and win her love, so that the opera closes with their love duet.

■ This was Cavalli's second opera, following *Le nozze di Teti e Peleo*, and in it the composer made his real mark in this field. The libretto was the best he ever set to music and, in fact, this was the most successful of Busenello's plays. The composer is often criticized for not giving enough attention to texts and for setting

Stage design for Cavalli's Le Nozze di Peleo e Teti. *Paris, Bibliothèque de l'Opéra.*

them to music without consultation. This work established one of the characteristic styles of Venetian opera, that of decorative melodrama. This type of opera was to become increasingly important in the next few decades; it is notable for the large number of characters, the close link between scenes and episodes, the scope of the choruses and the lavish quality of the staging. *Didone* was revived and produced again in Florence on the occasion of the sixteenth Maggio Musicale in 1952.

IL RITORNO DI ULISSE IN PATRIA (The Homecoming of Ulysses)

Opera in a prologue and five acts by Claudio Monteverdi (1567–1643), libretto by Giacomo Badoaro (1602–54), based on the last Books of the Odyssey. *First performance: Venice, Teatro Tron di S. Cassiano, February 1641. First performance in U.K.: B.B.C. broadcast, 16 January 1928.*

SYNOPSIS. Act I. Penelope (contralto) laments her husband's prolonged absence at the siege of Troy; Ulisse (tenor), however, has been abandoned on a seashore, but does not recognize it as Ithaca, his own homeland. Minerva (soprano) offers to assist him in his return to the palace, which is overrun with suitors for Penelope's hand, by giving him an impenetrable disguise. Act II. The old swineherd Eumete (tenor) compares the troubles of a princely life with the happiness of a countryman; when Ulisse hears him sadly recall that his master has deserted Ithaca, he comes forward and tells the old man that Ulisse is sure to return. Eumete becomes Ulisse's guide, and next recognizes Ulisse's son Telemaco (mezzo-soprano), who has just landed in Ithaca. Telemaco orders Eumete to inform Penelope of his return and of the stranger's news concerning Ulisse; when they are alone, Ulisse reveals his true identity and they warmly embrace. Penelope, meanwhile, refuses each of the suitors who, when they hear of Ulisse's possible return, determine to delay no further in compelling her to select one of them. Act III.

Antinoo (bass), one of the suitors, ridicules the old beggar (Ulisse in disguise) but he (Ulisse) easily defeats Iro (tenor), the suitors' boasting jester, in a wrestling match. Penelope compliments him before she reluctantly agrees to marry the man who can draw Ulisse's bow. The 'beggar' asks to take part, although agreeing not to claim the prize. The 'beggar' succeeds and shoots each of his rivals. Iro miserably resolves to kill himself since his masters are dead. Neither the arguments of Telemaco and Eumete nor Ulisse's appearance without disguise can convince Penelope that the 'beggar' is her husband. It is the evidence of Ericlea (mezzo-soprano), Ulisse's nurse, which finally resolves her doubts and the opera ends in a great love duet as husband and wife are reunited.

■ The score of the opera, in manuscript and unsigned, was discovered in 1881 by A. W. Ambros in the National Library of Vienna. It contains several differences in structure compared with Badoaro's libretto, and this led to some uncertainty and much debate, which was eventually silenced by a close examination of the musical style and in view of the numerous changes and adaptations to which Monteverdi subjected his texts. The opera, the first to have reached us from the period after the Venetian interlude when the composer was employed in St Mark's, shows traces of the structural novelties that gave new life to opera during that period – a renaissance furthered by the opening of private opera houses to a paying public, as well as by changes in popular taste and stage techniques. The libretto is mediocre but Monteverdi's artistic genius adds depth to the conventional sentiments and gives new dimension to the characters, in a constant stream of musical variety and invention.

L'INCORONAZIONE DI POPPEA (The Coronation of Poppea)

Opera in a prologue and three acts by Claudio Monteverdi (1567–1643), libretto by Giovanni Francesco Busenello (1598–1659). First performance: Venice, Teatro di SS. Giovanni e Paolo, autumn 1642; then throughout the carnival in the following year. First performance in U.K.: Oxford, 6 December 1927; in U.S.A.: Northampton, Mass., 27 April 1926.

SYNOPSIS. In the prologue, the goddesses of Virtue and Fortune are unable to contradict the claim of the goddess of Love to have the most power over mankind and to control history. Act I. Ottone, recently returned from war, looks forward to a reunion with his mistress, Poppea, until he notices that two imperial guards are outside her house and realizes that she must have taken Nerone, the Emperor himself, as a lover. Nerone and Poppea are then seen together before he reluctantly leaves, having almost promised her the throne. Poppea delights in the success of her ambition while her nurse, Arnalta, reminds her to watch out for the jealousy of the Empress, Ottavia. Ottavia desperately begs the gods for vengeance on Nerone; Seneca's stoic advice to bear misfortune with dignity and restraint falls on deaf ears. Seneca in vain tries to persuade Nerone not to follow the dictates of his heart and to honour his wife's feelings, but Nerone furiously announces his intention of marrying Poppea and leaves. Poppea is overjoyed at the prospect and convinces him that Seneca alone is the obstacle to his successful reign. Nerone orders his execution. Ottone turns to Drusilla for consolation. Act II. Seneca receives the death sentence and takes a dignified leave of his pupils. Two scenes of extreme contrast follow; a page begs a pretty girl for a kiss, and Nerone celebrates the death of Seneca with songs in praise of Poppea. Ottavia persuades Ottone to kill Poppea, and he borrows some of Drusilla's clothes in order to gain admittance more easily. Drusilla happily agrees to help him in every way. Poppea talks to Arnalta about Seneca's death until she falls asleep in the garden, to Arnalta's lullaby. She is protected by Venere, goddess of Love, from Ottone's murder; Drusilla is naturally suspected. Act III. Drusilla is arrested and, despite her protestations of innocence, is about to be executed when Ottone discloses his guilt. The Emperor orders his immediate banishment and Drusilla announces that she will share his exile. Poppea learns of these events and that because Nerone suspects Ottavia of instigating the plot, she will be banished immediately. Ottavia laments her departure from Rome and Nerone and Poppea exultantly celebrate the power of love.

■ There are two musical manuscript versions of *L'Incoronazione di Poppea*, which differ from each other quite significantly. One is in the Library of St Mark's, Venice, the other in the Library of the Conservatoire of S. Pietro a Majella in Naples. Likewise there are two manuscript versions of the libretto, and a printed libretto, prepared by Busenello himself, dated 1656, from which several parts, including the love duet from the third act, are missing. This was Monteverdi's last opera, written when he was seventy-five years old. It denounces with bitter realism, yet with touches of affectionate indulgence, the fickleness of the typical man of the Renaissance. The music reaches unprecedented, sublime heights. The subject matter of the libretto is derived from Tacitus, whose story was considered, in this baroque age, morally and politically justifiable. But, because of stage demands, the facts related by Tacitus were complicated by all manner of fantastic and mythological additions and given an interpretation consistent with the views of a liberated, utilitarian society which was emerging from the shadows of the oppressive morality that had prevailed in the last decades of the sixteenth century. The characters are swayed and motivated by two dominant passions – political ambition and love. Victory goes to those – Nero and Poppea – who personify these passions. The losers – Seneca, symbolizing traditional ethical values, Ottavia, the betrayed queen, and Ottone the conventional lover – seem to exist merely to point the contrast. The libretto is the first to deal with a historical subject and for this reason the opera is an archetype. But the historical narrative is 'filtered as through a prism, which diffracts it and isolates all the significant hidden meanings, the ideological and ethical implications, as well as the different psychological

Elevation for stage set at the Théâtre des Machines in the Tuileries, Paris, designed by the architects Gaspare and Carlo Vigarani for Cavalli's L'Ercole Amante.

attitudes, motivations and patterns of behaviour personified by the characters'. (G. Gallico.) The opera is a genuine masterpiece and testifies to the exceptional creative powers of the composer at a time when he might have been expected to bask in his past glories. It was revived in Venice in 1646 and in Naples, by the company of the *Febi harmonici*, in 1651. It fell into neglect until it was rediscovered in the present century and now forms part of the international repertory.

EGISTO (Aegisthus)
Opera in three acts by Francesco Cavalli, real name Pier Francesco Caletti-Bruni (1602–76), libretto by Giovanni Faustini (1619–51). First performance: Venice, Teatro Tron di S. Cassiano, autumn 1643.

■ The work was the composer's seventh opera but the first written expressly for soloists, this being a new trend in Venetian opera, which now tended to do away with choruses. There seems to be no substance in the frequent claim that it was first performed in the autumn of 1642 at the Hoftheater, Vienna.

ORFEO (Orpheus)
Opera in a prologue and three acts by Luigi Rossi (1598–1653), libretto by Francesco Buti. First performance: Paris, Palais Royal, 2 March 1647. First performance in U.K.: Belfast, Queen's University, 11 February, 1976.

SYNOPSIS. On the eve of her marriage to Orfeo, Euridice consults a soothsayer, who terrifies her with black prophecies. Aristeo, son of Bacco, is passionately in love with Euridice and prays Venere to help him and to prevent the wedding. The goddess, who hates Orfeo, grants his prayer and brings about Euridice's death. Juno (Giunone) intervenes advising Orfeo to go down to the Underworld to regain his bride. In order to help this plan succeed, she arouses the anger of Proserpina, making her jealous of her husband's attentions to Euridice. Moved, as are the other inhabitants of Hell, by Orfeo's laments, she persuades Plutone to let the lovers return to earth. But on their way back they break the laws imposed by Plutone, and Euridice is compelled to return to the Underworld. Aristeo, grief-stricken at her death, and feeling guilty for having caused it, goes mad and kills himself. At the instigation of Venere, Bacco and his followers avenge him, tearing Orfeo to pieces. The opera ends with an exaltation of love and fidelity.

■ The court performance of *Orfeo* was requested by Cardinal Mazarin, who obtained the services of the singers in Rome and Florence, through his secretary E. Benedetti. The autocratic minister would not even change his plans when the composer's wife died, and because of the preparations for the opera, Rossi was unable to go back to Rome to see her for the last time. Although the text is somewhat static, the music is lively and inventive. Rossi also introduces comic characters

Scene from Act II of Cavalli's L'Hipermestra: *the destruction and burning of Argos. Engraving by Ferdinando Tacca. Munich, Theatermuseum.*

in the Venetian and Neapolitan tradition, better suited perhaps to the taste of a rowdy public than to that of a cultured aristocracy.

IL GIASONE (Jason)
Opera in a prologue and three acts by Francesco Cavalli, real name Pier Francesco Caletti-Bruni (1602–76), libretto by Giacinto Andrea Cicognini (1606–60). First performance: Venice, Teatro Tron di S. Cassiano, 5 January 1649.

SYNOPSIS. This is the classical legend of the journey of the Argonauts, with special emphasis on the love of Jason and Medea. The text is rather poor but fully representative of seventeenth-century taste. Many of the scenes have little relevance or sense, and the attempted wit merely descends to vulgarity. The finale is cheerful and departs completely from the traditional ending of the story. Here, Jason marries Hypsipyle, Queen of Lemnos, thus assuaging the wrath of Jove, while Medea, Queen of Colchis, returns to an old suitor, whom she had previously disdained and abandoned but who has now rescued her from death.

■ *Il Giasone* was Cavalli's most famous and most frequently performed opera. For more than twenty years it did the rounds of the principal European opera houses. The libretto was published some three times during the first two years and again in 1654, 1664 and 1666. In 1671 the opera was revised by Alessandro Stradella, who added a prologue and three arias. It was performed in this new form in Rome, and then taken on tour in various countries. *Giasone* belongs to the mainstream of Venetian opera, in which recitative, arias and short orchestral interludes are all intermingled.

IL XERSE (Xerxes)
Opera in three acts by Francesco Cavalli, real name Pier

Francesco Caletti-Bruni (1602–76), libretto by Niccolo Minato (died 1698). First performance: Venice, Teatro SS. Giovanni e Paolo, 12 January 1654.

SYNOPSIS. This is a fantasy associated with the marriage of historical characters – Xerxes, grandson through his mother of Cyrus the Great and heir to the Persian crown, and Amastris, daughter of a Persian nobleman named Othar, a follower of King Darius. For the purposes of this story, Darius, wishing to reward Othar for services rendered, has given him the kingdom of Sufia. The Moors attack the capital of the small kingdom when Othar refuses to let his daughter Amastris marry their king. Othar calls on Xerxes for aid and the hero arrives with an army. After defeating the Moors, he falls in love with Amastris and she with him. Then follow a number of events, including the famous crossing by Xerxes of the Hellespont over a bridge of boats. In the end the two lovers celebrate their wedding.

■ To celebrate the nuptials of Louis XIV and the Infanta Maria Teresa, Cavalli was requested to produce his *Ercole amante* (q.v.), but because the theatre built for the purpose (Le Théâtre des Machines) was not ready and Cardinal Mazarin was ill, Cavalli suggested performing *Xerse* instead. So the work was performed in the Louvre, in the Salle des Caryatides, on 22 November 1660, as part of the wedding festivities. After this performance *Xerse* was never again staged. The same libretto was set to music by Bononcini in 1694 with slight modifications, and later also served as the text for Handel's *Serse* (see p. 49).

L'HIPERMESTRA

Theatrical entertainment in three parts by Francesco Cavalli, real name Pier Francesco Caletti-Bruni (1602–76), libretto by Giovanni Andrea Moniglia (1624–1700). First performance: Florence, Teatro degli Immobili, via della Pergola, 18 June 1658.

■ A glittering opera, staged with no sparing of expense. It was commissioned by Cardinal Giovanni de' Medici to celebrate the birth of a son to Philip IV of Spain and was a great success.

ERCOLE AMANTE (Hercules in Love)

Opera in a prologue and five acts by Francesco Cavalli, real name Pier Francesco Caletti-Bruni (1602–76), libretto by the abbot Francesco Buti. First performance: Paris, Théâtre des Tuileries, 7 February 1662, with Louis XIV, dressed as Sun King, himself taking part.

SYNOPSIS. The allegorical prologue added for the occasion by Camille Lilius paid homage to the fifteen most important royal families in the West, among which the French was naturally prominent. They were presented by Diana in Heaven *ex machina* and were portrayed by ladies of the court, together with the King and Queen. Diana commands Ercole to continue his labours and promises him Beauty as his bride. The action then unfolds, with a great coming and going of machines in Heaven, describing the events connected with the love of Ercole and Iole, the intrigues of Giunone, and the love of Hyllo, Ercole's own son, for Iole. In the finale Ercole receives Beauty as his wife

Stage set by Ludovico Burnacini for Cesti's Il Pomo d'Oro. *Engraving. Dresden, Kupferstichkabinett.*

and Hyllo marries Iole. The fourth act takes place on the high seas. The opera lasted six hours.

■ Cavalli went to Paris at the invitation of Cardinal Mazarin, who had tempted him with the promise of an extremely high fee. The composer was asked for an opera that was to be performed during the marriage festivities of Louis XIV and the Infanta Maria Teresa (1660); it was also to inaugurate the Théâtre des Machines at the Tuileries, designed by the architect Gaspare Vigarani especially for Italian opera. Because of construction delays and the illness of Mazarin, the production of the new opera was postponed and in its place there was a performance of *Xerse* (q.v.), which the composer had already staged at Venice in 1655 (or 1654). *Ercole amante* was first performed in 1662, by which time Mazarin had been dead one year. The music was not received as well as had been hoped and the audience had difficulties in understanding the words, which had not been translated into French. But the ballets added by Lully and the stage production by Vigarani were enthusiastically applauded. The main reasons for the disappointing reception were a bias against Italian opera as a whole – a prejudice being fanned by French composers – and the detestation in which Cardinal Mazarin was held even after his death. In May of the same year, Cavalli returned to Venice a disappointed man; he never managed to stage the complex opera in his native land.

ACHILLE IN SCIRO
Opera in three acts by Giovanni Legrenzi (1626–90), libretto by I. Bentivoglio. First performance: Ferrara, Teatro del Conte Bonacossi da Santo Stefano, 1663 or 1664.

SYNOPSIS. Teti, mother of Achille, hoping to enable him escape his destiny, places him in the care of Chiron, who hides him on the island of Scyros under the disguise of a girl named Pirra. Deidamia, daughter of King Lycomede, is aware that the stranger is really a man, but does not know his identity. She falls in love with him and he with her. Lycomede, however, had

A performance of Lully's Alceste *in a courtyard of the Château of Versailles.*

decided to marry his daughter to Teagene. The latter, for his part, upset by her coldness, shows himself more interested in Pirra. Meanwhile another visitor arrives on the island – Ulisse, ostensibly seeking allies for the war against Troy but actually trying to find Achille, whose help is indispensable if the Greek army is to defeat the Trojans. He considers various ways of getting Achille to betray himself. The latter, on catching sight of a splendid suit of armour, starts up, but succeeds in hiding his excitement. Lycomede promises aid and Achille does all he can to persuade Deidamia to accept Teagene as her husband. He senses that he cannot oppose his destiny any longer and confesses to Nearco that he is unable to continue the deception. A banquet is arranged to celebrate the coming marriage of Deidamia and Teagene, and during the festivities a fight breaks out among the soldiers, subtly provoked by Ulisse. Achille can no longer stand aside. He puts on the armour and reveals his identity. It is agreed that he will depart with Ulisse, while Deidamia abandons Teagene and obtains her father's permission to follow the young hero.

■ This was the last and highest achievement of Venetian opera in the late seventeenth century. It is a sumptuous spectacle based on a mythological subject, yet at the same time it preserves links with everyday life, for a vein of lively humour maintains a difficult play of contrast between the heroic and the comic characters.

IL POMO D'ORO (The Golden Apple)
Theatrical entertainment in a prologue and five acts and sixty-seven scenes by Marc'Antonio Cesti (1623–69), libretto by Francesco Sbarra (1611–68). First performance: Vienna, Hoftheater, carnival 1666/1667.

SYNOPSIS. The action revolves around the myth concerning Paris's golden apple of discord. At the end Jupiter took the apple from Venere and gave it to the Empress.

■ This is a typical example of the theatrical entertainment composed for a court theatre and invited guests. It was staged for the Viennese court on the occasion, so it is said, of the marriage of the Emperor Leopold I to the Infanta Margherita Teresa of Spain, daughter of Philip IV. The date of the performance is uncertain; the wedding took place on 12 December 1666. It is known that the opera was revived, again at the Viennese court, for the Empress's birthday. At that time Cesti, having been released from his priestly vows, was *maestro di cappella* at the Austrian court. His opera was the most sumptuous and elaborate ever staged. The cost of the staging alone amounted to 100,000 royal thalers; nor was any expense spared for the ornate costumes, the crowds of extras, the complex stage machinery, the dances and the fights. Everything was glittering and gaudy; and the music, too, matched the baroque scenic designs of Ludovico Burnacini. The Viennese composer Schmeltzer added ballets to the work. The language of the text is conventional and

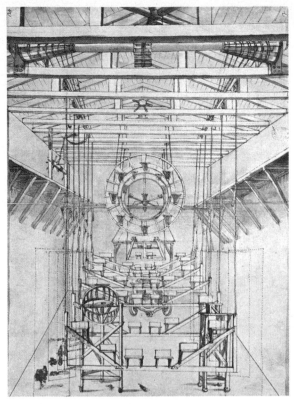

Scene with moving clouds in Legrenzi's Germanico sul Reno, *and at the left a sketch of the machinery used to produce the movement.*

courtly, full of mythological and allegorical allusions, but with comic episodes in the popular style. In the prologue a chorus of eight voices personified the Emperor's domains. *Il pomo d'oro* was probably never again staged. There is a recent critical edition of the opera, but the third and fifth acts have been lost. In the course of the Viennese wedding celebrations another opera by Cesti, *Le disgrazie d'amore*, was given, with a prologue personally composed by the Emperor Leopold.

SEMIRAMIDE
Opera in three acts by Marc'Antonio Cesti (1623–69), libretto by Giovanni Andrea Moniglia (1624–1700). First performance: Vienna, Hoftheater, 9 June 1667.

SYNOPSIS. The story is based on the mythical figure of the terrifying and beautiful queen of Babylon, about whom there were many marvellous and horrific tales.

■ Cesti, then in the service of the court at Innsbruck, intended to compose this opera for the marriage of the Archduke Sigismund Francis, but in 1665 the latter suddenly died. The entire Innsbruck *cappella* was then transferred to the imperial court at Vienna, where the opera received its first performance. It was revised and produced in Italy under the title *La schiava fortunata, ossia Le risembianze di Semiramide e Nino*.

LES FÊTES DE L'AMOUR ET DE BACCHUS (The Feast of Amor and Bacchus)
Pastoral opera in a prologue and three acts by Jean Baptiste Lully (1632–87), libretto by Philippe Quinault (1635–88), in collaboration with Molière and I. de Benserade. First performance: Paris, Académie Royale de Musique (Opéra), 15 November 1672.

■ The solemn tone and mythological atmosphere prevailing in opera were sometimes sacrificed in favour of a popular, idiomatic style, considered better suited to an audience unfamiliar with classical mythology. This was Lully's first opera and was clearly derived from the *ballets de cour*, a point perhaps over-emphasized by critics claiming that these spectacles were the sole historical antecedents of French opera. *Les Fêtes de l'Amour et de Bacchus* was performed six times between 1672 and 1678.

CADMUS ET HERMIONE (Cadmus and Harmonia)
Opera in a prologue and five acts by Jean Baptiste Lully (1632–87), libretto by Philippe Quinault (1635–88). First performance: Saint-Germain-en-Laye, 1674.

SYNOPSIS. Cadmus is in love with Hermione, daughter of Mars, already promised in marriage to the terrible giant, Draco. To win her, Cadmus challenges and kills the giant's dragon, but risks death fighting against Draco himself. Fortunately the latter is turned into a statue by Pallas, so that Cadmus's life is saved. When he is about to be united with Hermione, she is snatched away by Junon. At the end, however, the constancy of the two young people is rewarded. They are married and feasted by all the gods of Olympus.

■ The opera was an enormous success. Louis XIV, who attended the first performance, was, according to contemporary accounts, 'extraordinarily satisfied with this superb spectacle'.

ALCESTE, or LE TRIOMPHE D'ALCIDE (Alceste, or the Triumph of Alcides)

Opera in a prologue and five acts by Jean Baptiste Lully (1632–87), libretto by Philippe Quinault (1635–88). First performance: Paris, Académie Royale de Musique (Opéra), 12 January 1674.

SYNOPSIS. Alceste, who is being sought in marriage by King Licomède, is in love with Admète and plans to wed him. Hercule is also in love with her. During a feast she is abducted by Licomède and taken to the island of Scyros. Hercule and Admète pursue Licomède. Hercule succeeds in rescuing Alceste but Admète, in the course of combat, is gravely wounded. Apollon announces that he will grant Admète his life if someone is found to die in his place. When she hears of this, Alceste kills herself in order to save the life of the man she loves. Hercule then confesses his love for her and promises Admète to go down to Hades to recover her, on condition the young man gives her up. He takes Charon's boat and crosses the Styx. Then he chains Cerbère and presents himself to Pluton during an infernal feast. Having found Alceste, he takes her by the hand and leads her back to the world above. There is a heart-rending meeting between Alceste and Admète, and Hercule, deeply moved, decides to renounce her. A sub-plot added to the opera involves Céphise and her lovers. It is really no more than a pretext to introduce short 'songs', which found great favour with the public.

■ The opera was very well received both by the public and the critics. Madame de Sévigné attended a performance and wrote: 'On Thursday an opera of extraordinary beauty was performed. Passages in the music moved me to tears . . .' Louis XIV saw it for the first time at the Palais Royal on 14 April 1674, and it was later performed at Versailles, Fontainebleau and Saint-Germain. Lully's orchestration of *Alceste* was regarded by contemporary visitors from abroad as the most interesting new feature of his operatic style. His orchestra varied in tone to match the voices, evoked the emotions of the story and introduced the work with an overture of majestic proportions.

CIRCÉ

Tragic opera by Marc-Antoine Charpentier (1634–1704), libretto by Thomas Corneille (1625–1709). First performance: Paris 1675.

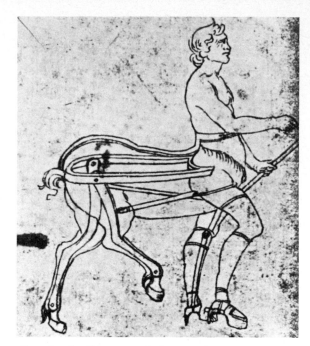

Drawing by Francesco di Giorgio for a stage centaur.

■ The production, inspired by the mythical story of the sorceress Circe, who transformed the comrades of Ulysses into swine, made use of elaborate stage machinery at its first performance.

LA DIVISIONE DEL MONDO (The Division of the World)

Opera by Giovanni Legrenzi (1626–90), libretto by Giulio Cesare Corradi. First performance: Venice, Teatro di San Salvatore, 4 February 1675.

■ This was one of the most important operas, now unfortunately lost, written by the brilliant master of the Venetian Baroque. As in all his operas, much of its success was due to the splendid scenery and the wonderful machines, so beloved by audiences of the time, built by the designers and engineers. As an example of contemporary taste, here is the introduction to the work: 'The curtain rises on a crash of thunder and we see the stage full of clouds which, after various movements, form a crowned lion in the centre. Then they gradually fade to reveal Jupiter seated on an eagle, together with Neptune and Pluto escorted by various deities, drawn up to defend Heaven against the Titans, who are struck down by lightning on the summit of Olympus.'

GERMANICO SUL RENO (Germanicus on the Rhine)

Opera in three acts by Giovanni Legrenzi (1626–90), libretto by Giulio Cesare Corradi. First performance: Venice, Teatro di San Salvatore, 27 January 1676.

SYNOPSIS. The opera relates the story of Julius

Caesar Germanicus, son of Drusus, adopted by Tiberius, who was despatched to the Rhine to quell a revolt. He then embarked on a series of expeditions in Germany, where he defeated Arminius, avenging the latter's victory over Varus.

IL TRESPOLO TUTORE (The Tutor)

Comic opera in three acts by Alessandro Stradella (1642–82), libretto by G. C. Villifranchi. First performance: Rome, Teatro in Borgo, carnival of 1676.

■ Originally produced by Prince Colonna, the opera casts ridicule on a poor tutor and provides a lively glimpse of contemporary customs.

PSICHÉ (Psyche)

Opera in a prologue and five acts by Jean Baptiste Lully (1632–87), libretto by Thomas Corneille (1625–1709) and B. de Fontenelle. First performance: Paris, Académie Royale de Musique (Opéra), 19 April 1678.

■ The libretto is based on the ancient love story of Eros and the beautiful girl, Psyche. Of all Lully's operas, this was the least successful. It was revived only twice in Paris, on 8 June 1703 and 22 June 1713.

LA FORZA DI AMOR PATERNO (The Strength of a Father's Love)

Opera in three acts by Alessandro Stradella (1642–82), libretto by Rodolfo Brignole Sale. First performance: Genoa, Teatro del Falcone, carnival of 1678.

SYNOPSIS. After the death of his first wife, who has borne him a son Antioco, King Seleuco, now advanced in years, decides to remarry. But his intended bride, the princess Stratonica, is loved by Antioco. The young man's passion is so intense that he falls ill. He is unable to sleep at night because his feelings are in utter turmoil and he can find no peace. The king gradually begins to suspect that his son, to whom he has never mentioned a word about the matter, is in love with Stratonica, and he is prepared to give her up in order to see his son happy. But the youth, out of respect for his father, will not disclose his real feelings when questioned. Stratonica, who feels her own affection for Antioco growing, also manages to repress her thoughts and desires, which she regards as illicit and impure, and makes the difficult decision to keep her promises to Seleuco and to turn her back on love. But just as the marriage is about to be celebrated, Antioco, unable to conceal his grief, admits his true sentiments. The king makes the sacrifice of giving Stratonica in marriage to his son.

■ A major influence in seventeenth-century music, precursor of Torelli and Corelli in the development of the *Concerto grosso* and a vigorous composer of oratorios and cantatas, Alessandro Stradella was also a significant figure in the revival of the melodrama. *La forza di amor paterno* (commissioned by the Marquis Rodolfo Brignole Sale, who was also the librettist, and first presented in his castle before its official opening) brings together the trends developing in the various Italian schools. The conventional division of the music into separate sections was abandoned in favour of a greater continuity, which extended even to recitatives. The expressive force and the musical variety of these recitatives, the rapid changing in the arias from an impassioned atmosphere to dramatic accent, the blending of the tragic and the comic, serve to show Stradella as a precursor, in many ways, of ideas which came to maturity in the following centuries.

ACIS ET GALATÉE (Acis and Galatea)

Opera in two acts by Marc-Antoine Charpentier (1636–1704). First performance: Paris, Théâtre Comédie-Française, 1678.

SYNOPSIS. Based on the legend of the Cyclops Polyphème, hopelessly and ridiculously in love with the beautiful nymph Galatée, who prefers the shepherd Acis.

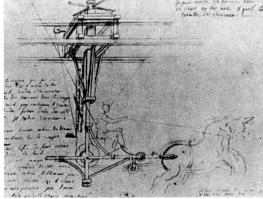

Drawing of a scene from Lully's Phaéton, *produced in Paris in 1683. At the right, a drawing of the machinery for the chariot of the sun in the same opera.*

IL RATTO DELLE SABINE (The Rape of the Sabine Women)

Opera in three acts by Pietro Simeone Agostini (born 1650), libretto by Francesco Bussani (c. 1640–after 1680). First performance: Venice S. Giovanni Crisostomo, carnival of 1680.

SYNOPSIS. The story deals with a famous event that occurred during the early history of Rome.

■ The opera is important for the way it handles mass movement on the stage; and the music gives precedence to this feature of the libretto. It is the only one of Agostini's operas to have survived.

PROSERPINE

Opera in a prologue and five acts by Jean Baptiste Lully (1632–87), libretto by Philippe Quinault (1635–88). First performance: Saint-Germain-en-Laye, 5 February 1680.

SYNOPSIS. During the prologue the poet sings the praises of peace. The scene represents the cave of Discord, in which Peace, Abundance, Games and Pleasures appear in chains. Victory arrives, followed by a crowd of heroes. She unties the chains of the prisoners and in their place puts fetters on Discord and all her attendants. Then begins the story proper. Proserpine is abducted from her mother Ceres by Pluto. Jove, surrounded by all the gods of Olympus, in order to satisfy both Ceres and Pluto, decrees that Proser-

The destruction of the palace of Armida, from Lully's Armide. *Drawing by Jean Bérain, 1686. Paris, Bibliothèque de l'Opéra.*

pine must spend six months of each year in the infernal regions and six months on earth.

■ In this opera Lully made use for the first time of accompanied recitative. The instrumental writing is no longer restricted to pieces preceding the dances and to changes of scene but skilfully woven into various stages of the action.

PHAÉTON

Opera in a prologue and five acts by Jean Baptiste Lully (1632–87), libretto by Philippe Quinault (1635–88). First performance: Versailles, Théâtre de la Cour, 9 January 1683.

SYNOPSIS. The drama derives from the story in Ovid's *Metamorphoses*, of how Phaethon, son of Apollon, tries to prove his divine origin to the skeptical Epaphus. He asks his father for permission to drive the chariot of the Sun for a single day but being unable to control the excited horses, he brings about fire and destruction both in heaven and on earth, until he is finally killed by Jupiter's lightning flash.

■ The story lent itself to the use of numerous spectacular scenic effects, which have helped to make the opera famous. They include the temple of Isis, the palace of the Sun, the chariot course of Phaethon and his downfall, and the transformations of Proteus into a lion, a tree, a sea monster, a fountain and flames. All of these strongly appealed to audiences, so much so that the work became known as the 'people's opera'.

AMADIS

Opera in a prologue and five acts by Jean Baptiste Lully (1632–87), libretto by Philippe Quinault (1635–88), based on one of the most famous of the Spanish knightly romances by Garcia Ordoñez de Montalvo. First performance: Paris, Académie Royale de Musique (Opéra), 14 January 1684. First performance in U.K.: London, Twentieth Century Theatre, 14 June 1938.

SYNOPSIS. Amadis, illegitimate son of Perion and Elisena, is set adrift in a boat and left to the mercy of the waves. For identification purposes he is given a ring and a sword. He is rescued by Gandales, who brings him up at home as his own son. In due course he is taken to the court of King Langrines, where he meets the Princess Oriane, daughter of Lisuarte, king of Great Britain. The two fall in love and swear lifelong faithfulness to each other. Through the intercession of Oriane, Amadis is dubbed a knight, and with her to inspire him, sets out in the name of all womanhood on his chivalric adventures. He succeeds in conquering the giant Abies, enemy of King Perion, at whose court he is received with all the honour due a knight of his rank. Because of the ring he wears, he is recognized by his parents. But his journey is not yet finished and his adventures continue. A spell leads him to the castle of Arcalaus, where he is eventually freed by Urgande, his

A scene from Il fuoco eterno custodito dalle vestali *(The Eternal Fire Guarded by the Vestals) by Antonio Draghi, produced in Vienna. Munich, Theatermuseum.*

mysterious protectress. Without being aware of the identity of his adversary, he finds himself forced to fight his brother Galaor, but in the end the two men are reconciled and become companions, undertaking further feats of chivalry together. After many tests of valour they manage to free both King Lisuarte and his daughter Oriane, who have been imprisoned by Arcalaus in his enchanted castle. Falling victim to a further spell, Amadis is in turn liberated by Oriane, who offers herself to him. Later he arrives in the kingdom of Sobradisa, where he is warmly received by Queen Briolanja; but his thoughts are ever with Oriane and he sets out again on his travels to be reunited with her. During his journey he finds himself unexpectedly in front of a castle where a number of noble knights are being held prisoner; overcoming all obstacles, Amadis frees them. Meanwhile he receives a letter from Oriane informing him that she wishes to break with him, for she suspects that he has fallen in love with Briolanja. In desperation, Amadis retires to the Peña Pobre, calling himself 'il Beltenebros'. But his fantastic adventures are still not done; and once again he has occasion to come to the aid of Oriane and Lisuarte. He soon becomes virtually conqueror of the whole world, victorious not only in his native land but also in Germany, Bohemia, Italy and Greece. Once again he rescues Oriane from the Emperor of the West, who is holding her prisoner, and finally the two are united for ever.

◼ A product of the already successful and prolific partnership of Quinault and Lully, and based on a subject specifically chosen by Louis XIV, who wanted the well-known Spanish novel (published in 1508) to be set to music and staged, the opera was an unqualified success. The sudden death of the queen prevented the opera being immediately presented at Versailles where, however, it was staged the following year.

ROLAND
Opera in a prologue and five acts by Jean Baptiste Lully (1632–87), libretto by Philippe Quinault (1635–88). First performance: Versailles, Théâtre de la Cour (in the presence of Louis XIV), 8 January 1685.

SYNOPSIS. In the course of the prologue there is an exchange of love vows between Angélique, queen of Cathay, and Medoro, the officer of an African king. In the first act Roland, nephew to Charlemagne and the most renowned of all his knights, sends Angélique a valuable bracelet as token of his love. In the second act the scene changes to the enchanted fountain of love in the midst of a forest. Roland approaches in order to see Angélique, but she puts into her mouth a magic ring which has the power of making her invisible. Roland, disappointed and dejected, does not attempt to conceal his sorrow. Medoro arrives, despairing of the queen's ever accepting his love and marrying him. Unable to bear the anguish, he seizes his sword and is on the point of killing himself; but fortunately Angélique intervenes just in time to stay his hand. Her only concern now is to defend the man whom she loves from the fury of Roland. The latter, in fact, still nurses his illusions, not realizing, or not wishing to realize, Angélique's true feelings.
The third act is given over to the chorus, which invites Angélique and Medoro to taste the sweet pleasures of life and love. It predicts that Medoro will shortly become king and that he will make happy all those who

obey his laws. In the fourth act Roland's desperate situation becomes even worse when, instead of finding Angélique at a rendezvous, he reads a note attached to a tree expressing her feelings of love for Medoro. When he approaches a group of shepherds to allay his suspicions and doubts, they show him the bracelet he had sent her, which the queen has given them in gratitude for services they have rendered the two lovers. Roland is mad with fury when he recognizes his gift. In the final act Roland dreams of old heroes who urge him to forget the pains of love and to concentrate his thoughts on the glory that awaits him when he liberates his homeland. He awakes and decides to follow the wise counsel of his illustrious predecessors.

■ The opera, which was a tremendous success occasionally rises to inspired heights, notably in Roland's invocation to night, the chorus of shepherds and the scene of Roland's madness. The action is dominated for most of the time by Angélique and Medoro, Roland's part being comparatively short. Between 1685 and 1743 there were six revivals of *Roland*.

ARIANNA (Ariadne)
Opera in three acts by Bernardo Pasquini (1637–1710), librettist unknown. First performance: Rome, Teatro di Palazzo Colonna, carnival 1685.

The opera relates the adventures of the mythical figures of Arianna and Teseo.

ARMIDE
Opera in a prologue and five acts by Jean Baptiste Lully (1632–88), libretto by Philippe Quinault (1635–88). First performance: Paris, Académie Royale de Musique (Opéra), 15 February 1686.

ORIGINAL CAST. Rochois, Moreau, Desmatins, Du Mesny, Dun, Frère.

SYNOPSIS. In the prologue Glory and Wisdom extol the virtue of Renaud and declare that, notwithstanding all temptations, he will know how to follow the path of honour. At the beginning of the opera Armide, who has managed to seduce all the other crusader knights, nurses her wounded pride, for Renaud has failed to respond to her charms. With the help of her uncle Hydraotes, king of Damascus, and a crowd of nymphs, shepherds and shepherdesses, who are really infernal spirits, she succeeds in abducting the hero and carrying him off to an enchanted island. Hydraotes, by means of his magic arts, manages to make Renaud fall in love with Armide, but the enchantress is herself torn between love and hate, for she realizes that she has captivated the knight only by magic and not by her beauty. Love nevertheless gains the upper hand and Armide persuades Renaud to stay on the island. Here the knight abandons himself to a life of pleasure, completely forgetting his duties as a crusader. Meanwhile, two of his friends have gone to search for him.

Armide's magic initially thwarts their efforts, but they eventually find the knight and prove to him that he has been the victim of illusions. The hero, ashamed of his weakness, decides to resume his travels. Armide is desperate and pleads with him to stay, but the knight has made up his mind to follow his friends. The enchantress then calls upon the gods of the Underworld, who cause the enchanted island to sink to the depths of the sea.

■ This was Lully's last but one opera and there are some sublime moments in it. Renaud's dream is alone enough to give an idea of the composer's stature.

ACIS ET GALATÉE
Heroic pastoral opera in a prologue and three acts by Jean Baptiste Lully (1632–87), libretto by Jean Galbert de Campistron. First official performance: Paris, Académie Royale de Musique (Opéra), 17 September 1686. (The opera was, however, first performed at the castle of Anet, on 6 September of that year, in the presence of the Dauphin.) First performance in U.K.: B.B.C. broadcast, 29 March 1937.

SYNOPSIS. The action is based on the love of the Cyclops Polyphème for the beautiful Galatée who, however, prefers the shepherd Acis. The latter is killed by the jealous giant with a rock and then transformed into a river.

■ The opera was an enormous success, a further stage in the glittering career of the composer.

DIDO AND AENEAS
Opera in three acts by Henry Purcell (1659–95), libretto by Nahum Tate (1652–1715), based on the Fourth Book of the Aeneid. *First performance: London, Hosiah Priest's Boarding School for Girls, October or December 1689. The singers were Priest's girl pupils, but it is not certain who took the parts of Aeneas, the sailor and the male members of the chorus. First modern performance in U.K.: London, R.A.M., 10 July 1878; in U.S.A.: New York, Town Hall, 13 January 1924.*

SYNOPSIS. Act I. The royal palace at Carthage. Belinda (soprano) urges Dido (mezzo-soprano) to be calm, but in vain, for Dido's heart is tormented by love for the newly arrived stranger from overseas, as brave as his father Anchises and as beautiful as his mother Venus. Belinda assures Dido that Aeneas (tenor) returns her love, and the chorus exhorts the queen to marry the prince. Aeneas enters with his followers, confesses his love to Dido and begs her to accept him, even though she pleads with him to forget his feelings for her and continue his travels, following his destiny. Belinda calls upon Love, who intervenes to bring about the union, and the act closes with a chorus and stately dance. Scene II. The cave of the witches. A Sorceress (soprano) summons the witches and reveals her plan to separate Aeneas from Dido and bring about the ruin of Carthage. To accomplish this she sends her elf (soprano), disguised as Mercury, to Aeneas, carrying a false message from Jove to the effect that Aeneas must leave Carthage and Dido in order to pursue his conquering destiny. Act II. A grove near the city. While Aeneas, Dido and Belinda are out hunting with their retinue, they are caught in a storm raised by the Sorceress so as to get the prince to return to the palace. Belinda urges the company to hurry back and the chorus echoes her appeal. They all leave the wood. Aeneas, too, is about to depart when he is met by the elf in Mercury's guise, who instructs him to leave the city that very night. Aeneas realizes with anguish that obeying such an order will entail terrible sacrifices. At first he says he would prefer death, cursing the gods who are condemning him to nights of sorrow before he has been able to enjoy even one night of joy. Act III. The harbour with the rough, simple sailors of Aeneas's fleet. They have received orders to hold themselves ready for departure and happily prepare to set sail. After a dance the Sorceress and witches enter, celebrating delightedly the imminent ruin of Dido and the impending destruction of Aeneas's fleet. The moment of farewell has arrived. Dido confesses to Belinda her deep suffering in having lost her loved one for ever. Aeneas, upset by Dido's rebukes, thinks momentarily of staying and obeying the dictates of Love rather than the orders of Jove; but eventually he summons up his will-power and reproves himself for being weak. Heartbroken with grief, the Queen declares herself ready to submit to her fate and haughtily tells him to go. The chorus solemnly comments on the strange contradictions of human passions. Left alone with Belinda, Dido, dying, sings her funeral song; in a supreme gesture of love, she prays that her errors will not cause grief to Aeneas. The opera ends on a note of tragic calm, as the chorus calls on Love to scatter rose petals on the body of the unhappy Queen.

■ *Dido and Aeneas* was Purcell's only full-scale operatic work. But it had a strange history. During his lifetime it was given no other performance apart from the occasion for which it was specifically written. There were two productions in 1700 and in 1704, in the form of masques, and with the emphases on the text, at the Theatre in Lincoln's Inn Fields. Then, except for occasional productions which were unauthentic, the opera was not revived in London until 10 July 1878, when it was given at the Royal Academy of Music. The circumstances of its composition were unusual. The libretto was rewritten by Tate from a previous text, *Brutus of Alba*, and took account of the fact that the opera was to be performed at a girls' boarding school. The theatrical resources were thus modest and the opera lasted for little more than one hour. In no respect did it conform to popular conceptions of seventeenth-century opera in England. Written when Purcell was thirty years old, *Dido and Aeneas* is undoubtedly the masterpiece that many critics claim, though not free of defects. Events and scenes cluster too hurriedly upon one another, without the intervals for rest that a longer opera would normally provide. The character of Aeneas is sketchy and his feelings are not adequately explored except in a few bars of recitative. Dido, on the other hand, possesses real psychological depth, and her two arias, one in the first act when she comes onto the stage, the other in the third act when she is about to die, are especially moving. The work stands midway between English masque and Italian opera proper. The influence of the latter is undeniable, even though we do not know with which opera Purcell was familiar. In any event, *Dido and Aeneas* opened the way to fresh experiments in the field. Its chief virtue is the mastery with which the composer, virtually prior to anyone else, satisfied the requirements of a serious opera, overcoming the limitations imposed by the subject and fitting it both with regard to duration and action into the equivalent of a single operatic act.

THE PROPHETESS, or THE HISTORY OF DIOCLESIAN
Semi-opera with dialogue by Henry Purcell (1659–95), libretto by Thomas Betterton (c. 1635–1710), based on the play by Massinger and Fletcher. First performance: London, Dorset Gardens Theatre, June 1690.

SYNOPSIS. The prophetess Delphia predicts to the soldier Diocles that he will one day be emperor of Rome, when Aper, assassin of the previous emperor, has been executed. The prophecy is fulfilled when Diocles kills Aper and is hailed as emperor. But Diocles is no longer in love with Drusilla, Delphia's niece. He now loves Aurelia who, in turn, is loved by Maximian, his own nephew. Aurelia has sworn to marry the man who kills Aper. Meanwhile war breaks out with Persia. Diocles emerges victorious thanks to Delphia who, after first taking sides with the enemy, forgives Diocles for abandoning her niece and comes to his aid. The conqueror shows himself magnanimous. He gives his defeated Persian enemy his kingdom back and hands over the empire to Maximian. The young man treacherously repays him by attempting to kill him; but the watchful Delphia intervenes and wards off the blow. Finally, to fill all hearts with joy, the prophetess organizes an extraordinary Country Masque, which is attended by the gods, goddesses, nymphs, heroes, fauns, Graces and Pleasures.

■ Although the music plays an important part in this work, the principal actors do not sing. This was a characteristic feature of the semi-opera of Purcell's time, owing to the tradition and popularity of the masque. The opera, nevertheless, is fresh and inventive in comparison with conventional works of the age, and typifies Purcell's pastoral style.

KING ARTHUR, or THE BRITISH WORTHY
Semi-opera with dialogue by Henry Purcell (1659–95), libretto by John Dryden (1631–1700). First performance: London, Dorset Gardens Theatre, May or June 1691. First performance in U.S.A.: New York, 24 April 1800; modern revival 24 April 1935. Modern British revivals began in 1897 (Birmingham).

Costume of a condottiere for a heroic melodrama, first half of the eighteenth century.

Costume of Diana as huntress. Watercolour attributed to Jean Bérain. Paris, Bibliothèque de l'Opéra.

SYNOPSIS. Arthur, king of the Britons, and Oswald, Saxon king of Kent, both hope to marry Emmeline, daughter of the duke of Cornwall. On St George's day there is a decisive battle between the two rivals. The magician Osmond and two spirits, one of the earth, Grimbald, and one of the air, Philidel, support Oswald, while Merlin sides with Arthur's forces. Philidel is persuaded to join Arthur. Oswald abducts Emmeline but she repels his advances. Meanwhile Arthur, who has resisted the temptations of two sirens, breaks the spell that binds him. In the last act the two armies confront each other. Arthur challenges Oswald to man-to-man combat and after disarming him spares his life. Emmeline promises herself to the victor and Merlin, describing Arthur as the foremost of the 'Christian worthies', uses his magic to summon the islands of Great Britain out of the sea. The opera ends with hymns to St George and a general dance.

■ This is the only Purcell opera (apart from *Dido and Aeneas*) of which the original libretto has survived. Actually what Dryden wrote was not an opera, but rather a play with incidental music, modelled on a genre that was then popular with the English public.

The score was published only after the composer's death and has not survived in its entirety. Despite this, the music, consisting of choruses, dances and numerous arias, plays an important part in this patriotic spectacle.

THE FAIRY QUEEN

Opera in a prologue and five acts with dialogue by Henry Purcell (1659–95), libretto by Elkanah Settle, based upon Shakespeare's A Midsummer Night's Dream. *First performance: London, Dorset Gardens Theatre, April 1692; in U.S.A.: San Francisco, 30 April 1932.*

■ This opera, the longest of Purcell's works for the theatre, consists of a series of arias and dances. It is a suite of masques so much lacking in theatrical or dramatic character that it would be difficult to see it as an adaptation of Shakespeare if the splendid score did not magnificently capture the spirit of the play. In fact, in their enthusiasm for stage spectacle, those responsible for adapting the original text could not refrain from introducing a horde of characters that had nothing to do with Shakespeare's play – gods and goddesses, spirits, nymphs, shepherds, monkeys, Chinese dancers, the four seasons and so on. The opera was virtually transformed into a kind of revue containing a gallery of strange characters, in which brief episodes from the original comedy were inserted as part of a much grander and splendid spectacle.

The writer of the libretto is not known for certain, but is generally assumed to have been Elkanah Settle. The opera was sumptuously produced at Dorset Gardens, without any expense spared for costumes, scenery and decorative effects. It was a great success but the score was lost. After more than two hundred years it was rediscovered. Although not the complete autograph version, there is no doubt that it represents the music played at the first performance.

MÉDÉE

Opera in a prologue and five acts by Marc-Antoine Charpentier (1636–1704), libretto by Thomas Corneille (1625–1709). First performance: Paris, Académie Royale de Musique (Opéra), 4 December 1693.

ORIGINAL CAST. Marthe Le Rochois (Médée),

Moreau (Créuse), Dun (Créon), Dumesny (Jason).

SYNOPSIS. Based on the myth of the sorceress who, after helping Jason to obtain the Golden Fleece, fled with him. Abandoned by him, she took revenge by killing the two children she had borne him and poisoning his wife.

THE TEMPEST, or THE ENCHANTED ISLE

Opera with dialogue by Henry Purcell (1659–95), libretto by Thomas Shadwell (1640–92), based on Shakespeare's The Tempest. *First performance: London, Drury Lane Theatre, 1695.*

THE INDIAN QUEEN

Opera with dialogue by Henry Purcell (1659–95), libretto by John Dryden (1631–1700) and Robert Howard (1626–98). First performance: London, Drury Lane Theatre, 1695.

SYNOPSIS. When the Inca King offers his general, Montezuma, a reward for the capture of the Mexican prince Acacis, Montezuma asks for the hand of the Inca's own daughter, Orazia, in marriage. The Inca is

Watercolour by Filippo Juvara for Alessandro Scarlatti's Giunio Bruto. *Vienna, Nationalbibliothek.*

outraged at this presumption and Montezuma flees to the Mexicans. Orazia and the Inca are themselves subsequently captured by the Mexicans and Montezuma, with whom Zempoalla, the Mexican Queen, has fallen in love, becomes unpopular with his new allies for trying to save the couple from their enemies. Zempoalla consults a magician, Ismeron, in vain about her passion. Acacis commits suicide to stop the sacrifice of the Inca, Montezuma and Orazia, with whom he also was in love. Then the Inca is discovered to be the King of the Mexicans. Zempoalla then kills herself and the Inca consents to the marriage of Montezuma with Orazia.

■ Although the music does not play such an important part in this opera as it does in Purcell's other works (such as *King Arthur* and *The Fairy Queen*), it is, nevertheless, of very high quality. In it Purcell, as in *The Tempest*, which was composed around the same time, shows his complete mastery of musical expression. Indeed, the music for *The Indian Queen* was so warmly acclaimed that the score was immediately published, without Purcell's authorization or knowledge. In the preface the publisher justified his action in a direct address to the composer.

L'EUROPE GALANTE
Opera-ballet in a prologue and four acts by André Campra (1660–1744), libretto by Antoine Houdar de la Motte (1672–1731). First performance: Paris, Académie Royale de Musique (Opéra), 24 October 1697.

SYNOPSIS. The main thread of the narrative is the story of the Frenchman Silvandre, who abandons Doris and goes off in pursuit of Céphise. In the course of the opera, which may be best described as ethnographic, the composer compares the romantic attitudes of various nations – France, Spain, Italy and Turkey. The French lovers are represented as inconstant, tactless and flirtatious, the Spaniards are shown as loyal and romantic, the Italians as jealous, calculating and violent. Finally, there are the Turks – proud men and fiercely passionate women.

■ In *L'Europe Galante*, André Campra has brought to perfection the *opera-ballet*, a genre that, according to some authorities, had had a precedent in the production of *Les Saisons*, based on an idea of the abbé Pic and set to music by Lully and Collase. This genre, which enjoyed enormous popularity in eighteenth-century France, was usually made up of a prologue, announcing the theme of the play, followed by four acts or *entrées*, short self-contained operas linked by a slender thread of continuity. In the *opera-ballet*, sung parts were interwoven with dancing parts. *L'Europe Galante* is one of the 43 *opera-ballets* and *tragédies lyriques* of André Campra, who as *maître de chapelle* of Notre-Dame was forced to hide under the name of his brother Joseph, a counter-bass, because of the incompatibility inherent in his roles as a man of the cloth and

a man of the theatre. After the success of his first operas, he left Notre-Dame in order to devote himself entirely to music, thus revealing his true calling. *L'Europe Galante* is composed of a prologue, *Les Forges de l'Amour*, and four entrées: France, Spain, Italy, Turkey.

LE CARNAVAL DE VENISE (The Carnival of Venice)
Opera-ballet in a prologue and three acts by André Campra (1660–1744), libretto by Jean François Regnard (1655–1709). First performance: Paris, Académie Royale de Musique (Opéra), 28 February 1699.

SYNOPSIS. The story takes place in Venice during carnival time. Isabelle and Léonore both love Léandre, a French knight. Léandre, forced to make a choice, decides in favour of Isabelle. Léonore plots her vengeance with Rodolphe, a noble Venetian, who is also in love with Isabelle. They attempt to kill the French knight, of whom they are both jealous. But the hired assassins mistake their victim and Léandre survives. The work ends with an opera within an opera – a one-act work in Italian entitled *Orfeo all'Inferno*.

ARMINIO
Opera in three acts by Alessandro Scarlatti (1660–1725), libretto by Antonio Salvi. First performance: Pratolino, Villa Medici, September 1703.

SYNOPSIS. Arminio, a German prince, and his wife Tusnelda are the prisoners of the Roman general Varo. They manage to escape but are recaptured by her father Segeste, who has gone over to the Romans. Their return gives new hope to Varo, who loves Tusnelda and plans to make her his wife. Segeste orders Arminio's death in spite of Tusnelda's pleas; his doubts are quelled by the threats and promises of the Romans. He also opposes the love of his son, Sigismundo, for Arminio's sister Ramise. Arminio, well aware of Varo's feelings for Tusnelda, proposes that Varo should wed her after his own execution but Tusnelda angrily refuses, preferring death instead. Varo stops the execution, because he fears Tusnelda's lasting hatred. After Varo has died, Arminio – now a conqueror – returns in time to prevent Segeste from killing Sigismundo and Ramise. Magnanimously, he spares the old man's life and offers Sigismundo the hand of his sister in marriage.

■ The same libretto, with a few modifications, was set to music both by Handel in 1737 and Hasse in 1730. Scarlatti's score was not among his best; but there are some lyric passages and rhythmical touches that prepare the way for his later and better operas. The story is based on Tacitus and inspired by the historical figure of the barbarian prince who defeated the Roman legions, bringing about the death of their general.

IL MITRIDATE EUPATORE (Mithridates Eupator)
Tragedy in three acts by Alessandro Scarlatti (1660–1725), libretto by Girolamo Frigimelica Roberti. First performance: Venice, Teatro San Giovanni Crisostomo, carnival of 1707.

SYNOPSIS. The action takes place in the city of Sinope in the year A.D. 150. Act I. Mitridate Euergete has been killed by his wife Stratonica (mezzo-soprano) and Pharnace (baritone), her cousin and lover. His children, Laodice (soprano) and Mitridate Eupatore (tenor), have been banished, the former being married to the shepherd Nicomede (tenor), the latter having taken refuge at the court of the Egyptian king Ptolemy. Years pass, and Pontus and Egypt are about to sign a pact of alliance. Laodice, intent upon avenging her father, is called back to court, where she has a stormy interview with her mother and step-father. Eupatore and his wife Issicratea (mezzo-soprano), in male dress, arrive, posing as Egyptian ambassadors. Stratonica asks the youth for news of her son, while Pharnace cold-bloodedly demands his execution. Laodice, pretending to be a servant, promises to help the supposed ambassador if he will save the life and throne of her brother, whom she believes to be far away. Act II. A courtyard in front of a temple. Spurred on by Pelopidas (tenor), Pharnace's minister, and by Pharnace himself, the people demand the head of Mitridate. Stratonica, gripped by demonic fury, inflames the passions of the crowd. Eupatore agrees to give way to public will and promises to return with the head of the legitimate heir to the throne. Act III. A deserted spot. Nicomede brings Laodice information about the Egyptian ambassador's decision. The girl urges him to gather together armed followers to await an opportune moment. Eupatore returns with the urn which is supposed to contain his own head. He and his sister joyfully recognize each other. When Pharnace takes the urn he tries to kill Eupatore, who kills him instead. Issicratea prevents Stratonica from killing her own son and in turn kills her. Mitridate Eupatore, acclaimed by the crowd, is crowned king by his sister. Then he proclaims Issicratea queen and she throws off her male disguise. Mitridate Euergete is avenged and Pontus once more finds peace.

■ *Il Mitridate Eupatore*, undoubtedly one of Scarlatti's most important operas, was discovered and transcribed by Giuseppe Piccioli (1905–61). The original had five acts with eleven changes of scene. Piccioli simplified the score, some parts of which were in any event missing. The transcription did not alter the Scarlatti style, which permeates the entire work. Produced in Venice in 1707, the opera was not well received – a hard blow for the composer, now approaching fifty, who was also weighed down with money troubles because of his large family. *Il Trionfo della Libertà*, also performed in Venice in the same year, was, judging from the parts that remain, hardly up to the same standard; yet it was received with enormous enthusiasm because it was more to the public taste. It is probable that in *Mitridate* Scarlatti was trying to express his deepest personal feelings and the audience found his music difficult listening and hard to understand. Although much admired as a musician, Scarlatti was never loved; and it is perhaps for that reason that so much of his work has been lost and that in spite of his name his operatic writing remains virtually unknown.

RINALDO
Opera in three acts by George Frederick Handel (1685–1759), libretto by Giacomo Rossi, from a sketch by Adam Hill, after the famous episode in Tasso's Gerusalemme Liberata (1562). First performance: London, Queen's Theatre, Haymarket, 24 February 1711.

SYNOPSIS. The story takes place during the period of the Crusades. The hero is the young, brave knight of the Templars, Rinaldo, who is in love with Almirena, daughter of Godfrey of Bouillon, leader of the First Crusade to the Holy Land. The sorceress Armida uses her craft to bewitch Rinaldo who, under her spell, falls in love with her. In an attack of violent jealousy, the sorceress takes vengeance on the innocent Almirena, capturing her by witchcraft in her enchanted garden. Argante, a pagan king, falls in love with the young Almirena, and this complicates the plot inasmuch as he is also the lover of the jealous Armida. Fortunately Rinaldo frees himself from the spell, flies to the rescue of Almirena and saves her. In the end Armida and Argante become the prisoners of the young knight and the opera ends happily as both are converted to Christianity.

■ Handel wrote this opera during his first London visit, composing the entire score in two weeks. It was performed for fifteen successive nights, which, by eighteenth-century criteria, marked it as a major triumph. The production at the Haymarket Theatre was extremely elaborate and sumptuous. For the scene in the enchanted garden real birds were introduced – a completely novel device.

IL PASTOR FIDO (The Faithful Shepherd)
Opera in three acts by George Frederick Handel (1685–1759), libretto by Giacomo Rossi, after a poem of the same name by Battista Guarini. First performance: London, Queen's Theatre, Haymarket, 22 November 1712; in U.S.A.: New York, Town Hall, 2 November 1952.

SYNOPSIS. The land of Arcadia, with woods and fountains. Myrtillus confesses to nature his love for the nymph Amaryllis. She returns his love, despite the fact that Diana has promised her to Silvius, but in his presence, she appears cold and disdainful. Dismayed at her attitude, Myrtillus confides in Eurilla, who secretly loves him. She promises, but in fact merely pretends, to sue Amaryllis on his behalf. Silvius now enters, having decided to dedicate himself to the goddess of the hunt

Scenery by Giuseppe Galli Bibiena for Angelica, vincitrice di Alcina *by Fux. A rock splits open to reveal a huge monster, which then vanishes, destroying several ships. Vienna, Nationalbibliothek.*

and resolved never again to fall into the clutches of the god of love. Dorinda, who declares her passion for him, is rejected. Eurilla cleverly arouses the hopes of Myrtillus and the jealousy of Amaryllis by leaving a wreath of flowers beside him while he is asleep; Silvius once more repulses the unfortunate Dorinda, but in the end changes his mind and swears eternal love for her. Myrtillus and Amaryllis likewise confess their mutual love. Tyrrhenius, Diana's high-priest, presides over the double wedding.

■ The opera was seen in at least three versions. It was revived, with modifications, in May 1734, and again in November of the same year, when a ballet accompanied by song was added as a prologue. The libretto is undoubtedly inferior to the poem by Guarini on which it was based; but Handel's music gave the work dignity, transforming it into a notable opera.

IFIGENIA IN AULIDE (Iphigenia in Aulis)
Opera in three acts by Domenico Scarlatti (1685–1757), libretto by Carlo Sigismondo Capece, after the tragedy by Euripides. First performance: Rome, Palazzo Zuccari, 11 January 1713.

SYNOPSIS. The action takes place in ancient Greece. Agamemnon and his army are about to sail for the ten-year siege of Troy. He learns from Calchas that he has angered the goddess Artemis and she will not allow the fleet to sail unless he first sacrifices his daughter Iphigenia. He is thus torn between his paternal love, which shrinks from the dreadful deed demanded by the goddess, and his duty as supreme commander, which would compel him to silence his deepest emotions. Iphigenia believes that she is to be married to Achilles and is quite unaware of the fate that awaits her. Everything is ready for the sacrifice when the truth comes out. Achilles and Clytemnestra, Agamemnon's wife and the girl's mother, protest, but the Greeks, who are keen to embark, insist that Iphigenia must not escape her fate. Calchas is about to kill the victim when the goddess, forgetful of her wrath, intervenes at the last moment and saves Iphigenia.

■ The score has not survived, nor have any contemporary opinions. Judging, however, from *Tetide in Sciro*, an operatic work by Domenico Scarlatti which has survived, it is fair to assume that the great keyboard composer was not greatly attracted by the genre, and that his contribution to the development of opera was slight.

IL TIGRANE, or L'EGUAL IMPEGNO D'AMORE E DI FEDE (Tigrane, or the Equal Pledge of Love and Fidelity)
Opera in three acts by Alessandro Scarlatti (1660–1725), libretto by Domenico Lalli (1679–1741). First performance: Naples, Teatro San Bartolomeo, 16 February 1715.

SYNOPSIS. A long-standing and bitter hostility exists between Tigrane, king of Armenia, and Mitridate, king of Pontus. Unfortunately, the Armenian king loves his enemy's daughter Cleopatra. To see her he presents himself at the court of the king of Pontus, under an assumed name, and offers his services as a soldier. Because of his courage Tigrane rises to the post of supreme commander of the army, and has soon conquered vast areas of territory, including Bithynia and Cappadocia. Despite all opposition and intrigue, the love of Tigrane and Cleopatra triumphs.

■ The events underlying the libretto are based on actual fact, as related in the epitome by Marcus

Junianus Justinus (2nd or 3rd century A.D.) of Pompeius Trogus's *Historiae Philippicae*. In reality Mithridates was a sworn enemy of Rome and fought against her, with varying fortunes, for almost forty years. He sought Tigranes as an ally, and gave him his daughter Cleopatra as wife. This was one of Alessandro Scarlatti's most successful operas. The rhythmic pattern is original and concise, strongly emphasizing the dramatic parts of the narrative. The melodies are fairly well developed and boldly conceived, the technique being more advanced than that previously used by the composer.

AMLETO (Hamlet)

Opera in three acts by Domenico Scarlatti (1685–1757), libretto by Apostolo Zeno (1668–1750) and Pietro Pariati (1665–1733). First performance: Rome, Teatro Capranica, carnival of 1715.

■ The libretto goes back to the same source material that Shakespeare probably used. Only one aria, now in the library of the Bologna Conservatoire, has survived.

AMADIGI DI GAULA (Amadis of Gaul)

Opera in three acts by George Frederick Handel (1685–1759), libretto by John James Heidegger (1659–1749). First performance: London, King's Theatre, 5 June 1715.

■ Inspired by the famous romance from the Spanish knightly cycle, the opera was among the first written by Handel for the English court. For the story see Lully's *Amadis* (p. 22) and Massenet's opera staged in 1922.

ANGELICA, VINCITRICE DI ALCINA (Angelica Victorious over Alcina)

Opera in three acts by Johann Joseph Fux (1660–1741), libretto by Pietro Pariati (1665–1733). First performance: Vienna, on the lake of the imperial villa 'La Favorita', 1716.

■ The libretto is based on Ariosto's *Orlando Furioso*. Pariati was the Viennese court poet, predecessor to Metastasio. Fux was then court composer. His theatrical works included eighteen operas, all in the Viennese Italianate tradition.

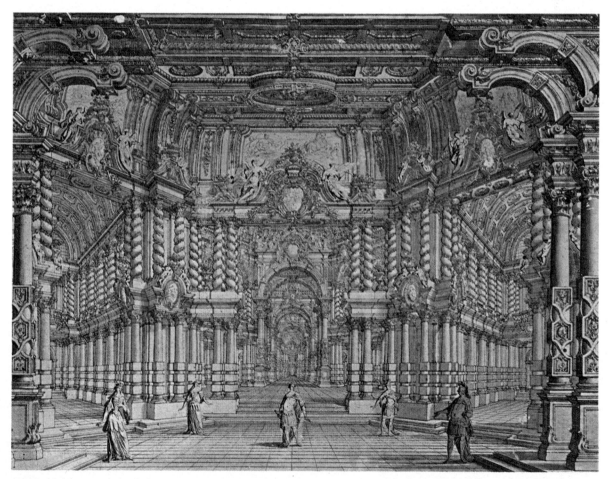

A typical example of baroque staging. Sketch of an enormous room, by Ferdinando Bibiena. Cesarini Sforza Collection.

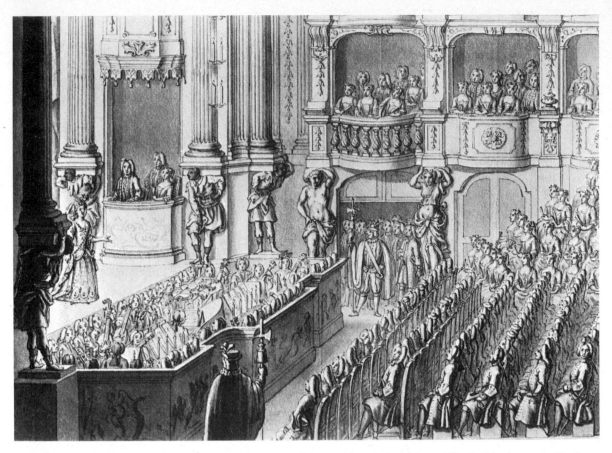

The performance of Lotti's Teofane *on the occasion of the wedding in Dresden of Frederick Augustus II of Saxony, 13 September 1719.*

IL TRIONFO DELL'ONORE (The Triumph of Honour)

Comic opera in three acts by Alessandro Scarlatti (1660–1725), libretto by Francesco Antonio Tullio. First performance: Naples, Teatro dei Fiorentini, 26 November 1718. First production in U.K.: Loughton (Essex), 1937.

SYNOPSIS. Riccardo, a dissolute youth, and his companion, Captain Rodimarte Bombarda, present themselves at the home of the young man's uncle, Flaminio. Flaminio is a rich merchant, who is engaged to a wealthy old landowner, Cornelia, but nevertheless very interested in the charms of Rosina, the maid. One of Riccardo's past conquests, Leonora, is still in love with him and looks to Cornelia and Rosina for comfort in her distress. She recognizes Doralice, who had once loved and been loved by her brother, Erminio, but who is now her rival in love for Riccardo. Riccardo asks his uncle for money but the old man astutely brushes him aside. While the faithful Rodimarte pays court to Rosina, Erminio discovers that his loved one has transferred her affections. After a series of complications, highlighted by a quarrel between the old merchant and Cornelia, Riccardo and Erminio burst onto the scene, duelling. Riccardo is wounded, and his injury prompts him to realize the errors of his ways. Everyone calms down and common sense in the end prevails: Riccardo marries Leonora, Flaminio weds Cornelia, Doralice gives her hand to Erminio and Rosina accepts Rodimarte.

■ The opera is a comic masterpiece. It has its Don Giovanni and, in the bragging captain, its Leporello; but the ending is certainly happier than in Mozart. The humorous atmosphere prevails throughout and Scarlatti's female characters are far less tormented and much shrewder than Mozart's heroines.

TEOFANE

Opera in three acts by Antonio Lotti (1666–1740), libretto by Stefano Benedetto Pallavicini (1672–1742). First performance: Dresden, Hoftheater, 1719.

■ The story is based on the figure of Theophanes, the Byzantine historian and monk (c. 752–817) who was persecuted by the iconoclasts. The libretto was written by Pallavicini, a Dresden court poet, and set to music by Lotti during his stay in that city where, at the invitation of the elector Frederick Augustus, he directed an Italian opera company. While in Dresden (1717–19), Lotti composed three operas, two of which survive in manuscript form. Faithful to the canons of the Venetian school, though not immune to the Neapolitan influence of Alessandro Scarlatti, Lotti was a gifted musician with conservative leanings. After his return to Venice, he abandoned opera and devoted himself mainly to sacred music.

IL RADAMISTO
Opera in three acts by George Frederick Handel (1685–1759), libretto by Nicolò Haym (c. 1679–1729), based on a work by Domenico Lalli. First performance: London, King's Theatre, 8 May 1720.

SYNOPSIS. Pharasmenes, king of Thrace, has married his son Radamistus to the princess Zenobia, and his daughter Polyxena to Tiridates, king of Armenia. The latter, madly in love with Zenobia, throws caution to the winds and declares war on Pharasmenes. He captures the Thracian capital. Radamistus and Zenobia escape through a tunnel leading to a river bank. She, terrified at the thought of falling alive into enemy hands, throws herself into the river, followed by her husband, who is ready to die with her. They are saved by Tiridates's soldiers and Zenobia is led before the enemy king. Radamistus, meanwhile, finds an unexpected helper in an enemy captain – Tigranes. Dressed as a slave, he finds his way to the court, where he is only recognized by his wife, and unsuccessfully attempts to kill Tiridates. Husband and wife are thrown into chains until set free by Tigranes, who has organized a rebellion. Tiridates is himself now a prisoner and finds refuge with his wife Polyxena, Radamistus's sister; Radamistus shows mercy to him and the opera ends in general rejoicing.

■ *Radamisto* is an opera which shows the composer's skill in handling dramatic situations. The text, by the capable librettist Haym, contains a rich variety of climactic events and sudden reversals of fortune; and Handel grasped the opportunity to compose a series of arias in different moods, expressing sadness and joy, melancholy and impetuosity, holding the audience's attention throughout.

LA GRISELDA
Opera in three acts by Alessandro Scarlatti (1660–1725), libretto by Apostolo Zeno (1668–1750). First performance: Rome, Teatro Capranica, January 1721.

■ The opera, an effective work, goes back to the traditional tale of the noble Gualtiero, who falls in love with the peasant girl Griselda and subjects her to the harshest tests in order to be convinced of her love for him.

GIULIO CESARE IN EGITTO (Julius Caesar in Egypt)
Opera in three acts by George Frederick Handel (1685–1759), libretto by Nicolò Haym (c.

The main stage set of Lotti's Teofane, *with libretto by Stefano Benedetto Pallavicini.*

1679–1729), who adapted and translated into English a libretto by Giacomo Francesco Bussani. First performance: London, King's Theatre, 20 February 1724. Modern British revivals began in London in 1927; first performance in U.S.A.: Northampton, Mass., 1927.

ORIGINAL CAST. Bernardi, Robinson, Durastanti, Berenstadt, Cuzzoni, Boschi, Bigonsi.

SYNOPSIS. Act I. Egypt, the banks of the Nile. Decisively beaten in the battle of Pharsalus, Pompeo seeks refuge with the king of Egypt. His wife Cornelia (mezzo-soprano) and son Sesto (contralto) throw themselves on the mercy of the conqueror, Giulio Cesare (bass). Achillas (baritone), a captain of Tolomeo, the Egyptian king, arrives, bearing the head of Pompey. Cesare orders hero's honours to be conferred upon the remains of his enemy, so barbarously assassinated. While Cesare displays kindness towards Cornelia and her son, Archillas falls in love with the widow. Sesto swears to avenge his father. Meanwhile Cleopatra (soprano) requests the conqueror's help in securing her succession to the throne. Tolomeo (bass), her brother, comes to an agreement with Achillas whereby, in exchange for Cornelia as wife, he is to kill Cesare. During a banquet Sesto challenges Tolomeo but is arrested, while his mother is locked up inside Tolomeo's harem. Act II. The terrace of Cleopatra's palace. Cesare has been informed that there is a plot to kill him. While he converses with Cleopatra, the Egyptian assassins break in, and Cesare has to leap into the sea to save himself. Achillas reports the death of the Roman general to his king, but Tolomeo now refuses to give him the hand of Cornelia, for in the meantime he himself has fallen in love with her. Act III. A plain on the seashore near Alexandria. The Egyptians and Romans are locked in battle. The Romans, believing their general to be dead, flee, When Cesare, who has escaped drowning, reaches shore, he finds his army defeated. From a hiding place he overhears a conversation between Sesto and Achillas. Mortally wounded, the latter confesses to having killed Pompey and gives the young man a gold seal which will enable him to muster a hundred of his men, eager to kill Tolomeo.

Playbill for The Beggar's Opera. *Drawing by William Hogarth, engraved by J. Sympson, Jr.*

Cesare, taking possession of the seal, leads the revolt in person. In her brother's tent, Cleopatra is overjoyed to see her lover again. Cesare wins the battle. Sesto kills Tolomeo and avenges his father's death, and, to the jubilation of the populace and the army, Cleopatra is crowned queen. The two lovers exchange vows of faithfulness and love.

■ The opera, begun at the end of 1723, was given for the first time on 20 February 1724 and revived in the following year. The plot is extremely complicated, with many dramatic situations. In England, during performances, it became customary for the lights in the theatre to be raised or for candles to be given out to the audience, so that they could follow the complex libretto. Haym, son of German parents resident in Rome, helped introduce Italian opera to England. Although, in the course of translation, he changed and simplified Bussani's text, he firmly renounced the melodramatics of Metastasio, in whose operas the themes of love and politics, jealousy and heroism, revenge and ambition, are all intermingled. Handel's score, in the popular Italianate style, alternated recitative and arias, heightening the dramatic impact of the action. The arias are particularly notable, far excelling the static, conventional forms of the period, and it is largely thanks to them that the opera achieves remarkable dramatic and stylistic unity.

SEMIRAMIDE, REGINA D'ASSIRIA (Semiramis, Queen of Assyria)
Opera in three acts by Nicola Porpora (1686–1768), libretto by the abbot Francesco Silvani. First performance: Naples, Teatro San Bartolomeo, spring 1724.

TAMERLANO
Opera in three acts by George Frederick Handel (1685–1759), libretto by Agostino Piovene (adapted by Nicolò Haym). First performance: London, King's Theatre, 31 October 1724.

SYNOPSIS. Tamerlane, emperor of the Tartars, having conquered Bajazet, emperor of the Turks, and made him prisoner, falls in love with Bajazet's daughter Asteria. But the girl loves Andronicus, a Greek prince allied to Tamerlane. Andronicus is torn by conflicting feelings – love for Asteria and loyalty to Tamerlane. The latter unwittingly confides in Andronicus his plans to marry Asteria and to give Andronicus in marriage to Irene, previously engaged to Tamerlane. Asteria agrees to marry Tamerlane, to the dismay of Andronicus and her father's fury. She is foiled however in her attempt to kill the tyrant and it becomes clear that she intended to murder Tamerlane from the beginning. She is imprisoned with her father, who kills himself. Irene, still in love with Tamerlane, prevents a further assassination attempt on him; in the conclusion it is she whom he marries, and he permits Andronicus to marry Asteria.

■ The opera was a considerable success and helped to re-establish the reputation of Handel in London, where for a time he had been eclipsed by the triumphs of his rival Giovanni Bononcini. In *Tamerlano* the influence of Italian opera and of Scarlatti in particular is very marked. The dramatic intensity of the action inspired Handel to compose music which, in certain passages, looks forward to the innovations of Gluck.

ARIANNA (Ariadne)
Music drama in two acts by Benedetto Marcello (1686–1739), libretto by Vincenzo Cassani. Composed in 1727. First stage performance: Venice, Liceo Benedetto Marcello, 27 April 1913.

SYNOPSIS. The story takes place on the island of Naxos, where Teseo, having arrived with the daughters of Minos, Fedra and Arianna, abandons the latter while she is asleep. He sails away with Fedra, who is torn between loyalty to her sister and love for the hero. Bacco, with his following of satyrs, bacchantes and fauns, discovers Arianna and falls in love with her. When she wakes to find herself alone she breaks into laments and tries to throw herself into the sea. Bacco woos her, and forcing her to submit to his desire, he raises a violent storm, which drives the fugitives' ship onto the island. Jealous of her sister, Fedra now fears that Teseo will rediscover his love for Arianna, while Bacco, in his turn, doubts whether the hero will be able to resist the pleas of the abandoned girl. Teseo promises the god that his feelings will not change, and also reassures Fedra. Indeed, Arianna's imploring is to no avail. More infatuated than ever, Bacco declares his love for Arianna and the chorus urges her to have pity on the 'god who prays'. She now feels attracted to him and moved by his sentiments; but she remains shy, unsure of his identity. So Bacco performs marvels for

The singers Senesino, Puzzoni and Berenstadt in Handel's Flavio, *at the Italian Opera House in London. Cambridge, H. R. Beard Collection.*

her, and the opera ends happily. Arianna accepts the love of the god while Teseo and Fedra return joyfully to Athens.

■ This opera was discovered and published in 1885 by the musicologist O. Chilesotti. It was described by Marcello as a 'mixture of play and music', and was his only venture into the operatic field, probably performed for the first time at the Casino dei Nobili Accademici in the year of its composition, 1727. The libretto, modest enough by poetic standards, nevertheless offered the composer an opportunity to display his skill in writing expressively for the human voice. Although some passages follow the traditional forms

of Venetian opera, the opening *sinfonia* in three movements and the participation of the chorus in the action are novel, interesting features.

THE BEGGAR'S OPERA
Opera in three acts with music arranged and composed by John Christopher Pepusch (1667–1752), text by John Gay (1685–1732). First performance: London, Lincoln's Inn Fields, 29 January 1728. First production in U.S.A.: New York 1750. Modern revivals began in London in 1878.

SYNOPSIS. In the prologue, the Beggar, pretending to be the author of the work, presents the comedy in which actors, thieves, fences, lawyers, prostitutes and gaolers clash and squabble with the common objective of worming money out of all and sundry. The highwayman Macheath has married Polly, daughter of the fence Peachum. When her father finds out, he is on his guard against the son-in-law, who knows too much about his activities. So he decides to denounce him and have him arrested. Macheath is a popular rascal, particularly with the women. Lucy, the gaoler's daughter, has succumbed to his charms and now, after a promise of marriage, helps him to escape. Further accusations by other women, egged on by Peachum, land him in prison once more and he is sentenced to be hanged. The Beggar now intervenes to reprieve Macheath, at the author's request, and the opera ends in a general dance for, as the Beggar proclaims, 'Nothing is too absurd in this kind of play', and 'Had the play remain'd, as I at first intended it, it would have carried a most excellent moral. 'Twould have shown that the lower sort of people have their vices in a degree as well as the rich: And that they are punish'd for them.'

Satirical print by William Hogarth showing discussions and quarrels between supporters of masquerades and of opera at Burlington Gate. Engraving by I. Cook.

■ *The Beggar's Opera* is the first and most famous of ballad-operas, a work in which prose, verse and music are freely mixed. The first performance was warmly received and ran for 62 successive nights. It remained popular in all English-speaking countries and was still in vogue in 1878, when the part of Macheath was taken by Sims Reeves. The work is really a lively satire on contemporary theatrical conventions, but also on political behaviour. Among recognizable public figures of the time are the Prime Minister Walpole (Peachum) and Lord Townshend (the gaoler, Lockit). Obviously such references have lost their edge over the centuries. Gay had in mind a comedy staged by beggars for beggars, which might come to the notice of some theatrical personage who would give it a wider showing. The characters would be dignified with operatic costumes and sets, but the ambience of thieves, prostitutes and criminals would remain unaltered, as would the roughness and brutality of the action and the coarse, sometimes vulgar language. On 5 June 1920, at the Lyric Theatre, Hammersmith, there was an adaptation of *The Beggar's Opera* by Frederick Austin which ran for 1,463 consecutive performances, an all-time record for an opera. On 22 May 1944, an adaptation by E. J. Dent was staged in Birmingham. Since the town had been badly damaged by bombing, the opera was given in a circus tent. Sir Arthur Bliss adapted the work once more for a film version in which Laurence Olivier played the title role (1953). Finally, Benjamin Britten revised it entirely, creating what was virtually a new opera, far removed from the original, first put on at the Arts Theatre, Cambridge, in 1948. Weill's and Brecht's version of 1928, *The Threepenny Opera* (see below), bears only a remote kinship to Gay's work. The original music contained 69 pieces, which Papusch derived almost wholly from popular songs of the time – 28 English, 15 Irish, 5 Scottish, 3 French, and 18 from other sources. Pepusch gained no advantage from the success of the opera. His name was not even mentioned in the earliest notices of the work, nor did it appear in the first edition of the score. In the second edition he was merely mentioned as the composer of the overture. It is therefore somewhat difficult to decide how big a part he played in the work; possibly his contribution was limited to writing out the bass parts and providing variations, admittedly skilful, of the most popular tunes of his time.

SEMIRAMIDE RICONOSCIUTA (Semiramis Recognized)

Opera in three acts by Nicola Porpora (1686–1768), libretto by Pietro Metastasio (1698–1782). First performance: Venice, Teatro Grimani di San Giovanni Crisostomo, 26 December 1729.

For the story see p. 51 (Jommelli, 1741).

ARTASERSE

Opera in three acts by Johann Adolph Hasse (1699–1783), libretto by Pietro Metastasio (1698–1782). First performance: Venice, Teatro San Giovanni Crisostomo, February 1730. First performance in U.K.: London 1734.

SYNOPSIS. Act I. Arbace, the son of Artabano, has been exiled for having dared to fall in love with the King Serse's daughter, Mandane. Artabano kills Serse, with a view to winning the succession for his son, and gives Arbace, who has returned secretly to see Mandane, the sword with which he killed Serse and which is still stained with blood. When the assassination is discovered, Artaserse, Serse's son and the new King, is persuaded by the true regicide to suspect his brother Dario and anticipating Artaserse's wishes, Artabano has Dario killed. Arbace is then discovered with the incriminating sword. Only the fact that Artaserse is in love with Arbace's sister, Semira, saves him from an immediate sentence of death. Act II. Artabano has to sentence the assumed assassin who, rather than betray his father, declares himself innocent but refuses to say who the murderer is. Mandane, although in love with Arbace, struggles with her feelings and demands justice. Semira, however, begs for compassion. Artabano tries to persuade his son to flee but the latter refuses. Act III. Artabano passes the death sentence on his own son, but now attempts to raise a revolt, hoping to overthrow Artaserse. Arbace, always loyal to the crown and contrary to his own interests, puts down the rebellion. The King, moved by this gesture, frees him and offers him a drink from his own cup. Before he drinks his father has to confess that he has poisoned the goblet and also that he murdered Serse. Arbace has now twice saved the King's life and nobly offers his own life for that of his father. Because of his son's pleas, Artabano is only exiled. Artaserse takes Semira for his queen and gives his sister to Arbace.

■ The libretto, splendidly contrived and full of theatrical tricks and devices, contains many dramatic situations. Its spectacular nature attracted the attention of many leading composers of the time; there are, in fact, 107 different musical scores, testifying to its unbelievable popularity. One of the finest scores is that of Hasse, 'the dear Saxon', as he was called in Italy. Trained in the Neapolitan school, a pupil of Porpora and the great Alessandro Scarlatti, the German composer showed himself aware of the merits of the narrative, which cleverly alternates plain recitative and arias to keep the action moving. He also recognized how admirably the text lent itself to musical treatment, and provided it with a masterly score. He managed to overcome the major problem of contemporary opera – breathing life into the characters. The hero, the noble and incorruptible Arbace, is inevitably a somewhat conventional figure, but the wily Artabano, who sets the entire plot in motion, is vividly portrayed, affection for his son being poised against self-love, rampant ambition held in check only by paternal sensibility. Although by modern standards the work may appear overcomplicated and weighed down by conventional features, there is no denying that words and music are perfectly matched – an all too rare phenomenon in the history of opera.

Performance of an opera in the royal palace at Turin, 1722. Drawing by Filippo Juvara, engraved by Antoine Aveline. Dresden, Kupferstichkabinett.

ARMINIO
Opera in three acts by Johann Adolph Hasse (1699–1783), libretto by Antonio Salvi (with modifications). First performance: Milan, Teatro Ducale, 28 August 1730.

■ The libretto had already been set to music by Alessandro Scarlatti in 1703 (see page 28 for plot). *Arminio* was one of Hasse's better operas. During his long residence in various Italian cities he was able to acquire increasing familiarity with the vocal and instrumental techniques then in vogue, and especially to become acquainted with Alessandro Scarlatti, becoming his pupil and following in his footsteps. His own musical style was stimulated by this Italian influence.

In this opera Hasse handles dramatic events in an original manner, avoiding the conventionalities of sentiment and attitude that characterize so many operas of the period. The music admirably echoes the voiced passions of the characters, and the arias are thrown into relief by the frequent passages of recitative. In addition the composer succeeds in establishing a perfect balance – seldom found even in later theatrical works – between the score and the stage action. This is ample compensation for the weaknesses of the work. The gravest fault of *Arminio* – and it was something Hasse never managed to resolve – is the excessive variety of sources and styles, which detract from the homogeneity and compactness of the score.

CATONE IN UTICA
Opera in three acts by Johann Adolph Hasse (1699–1783), libretto by Pietro Metastasio (1698–1782). First performance: Turin, Teatro Regio, 26 December 1731.

SYNOPSIS. Catone and Cesare are at war, and the city of Utica is besieged. Catone's daughter, Marcia, who secretly loves Cesare, refuses to marry Arbace, her father's ally. Cesare offers peace but Catone retorts that Rome must first be freed of his dictatorship. Marcia tries to argue with her father in Cesare's favour, while Emilia, Pompey's widow, knowing that Fulvio, one of Cesare's generals, is in love with her, tries to persuade him to assassinate Cesare. Catone is horrified to discover his daughter's sympathies. Emilia's attempt to kill Cesare are foiled by Fulvio. When the Roman army breaks into Utica, Catone commits suicide rather than fall into the tyrant's hands. But Cesare refuses to honour the occasion with a triumph because the price was too high: Catone's death signals the removal of an implacable enemy but Cesare recognizes that Catone was the last to embody all the traditional virtues of a Roman citizen.

■ The text is rather feeble, veering between the epic and the sentimental. But the story was very popular, its theme being the celebration of liberty, and it was frequently set to music. Hasse's score, in particular, came close to the spirit of Metastasio's text, so that this version of the opera has a solemn dignity of feeling and expression.

SALLUSTIA
Opera in three acts by Giovanni Battista Pergolesi (1710–36), libretto by S. Morelli. First performance: Naples, Teatro San Bartolomeo, December 1731.

Scene from a performance of Francesco Feo's opera L'Arsace *in the Teatro Regio, Turin, in 1741.*

SYNOPSIS. Giulia wants her son Alessandro to repudiate his wife Sallustia. She slanders her daughter-in-law, which provokes Adriano, Sallustia's father, to try to kill her. He is unsuccessful and sentenced to fight wild animals in the arena. He survives and Giulia pardons him, bringing about the reunion of husband and wife.

■ *Sallustia* was Pergolesi's first attempt at opera, but was not a great success.

LA FIDA NINFA (The Faithful Nymph)
Opera in three acts by Antonio Vivaldi (c.1675–c.1740), libretto by Scipione Maffei (1675–1755). First performance: Verona, Teatro Filarmonico (for its opening), 6 January 1732.

ORIGINAL CAST. Giovanna Gasperini (Licori), Gerolamo Madonia (Elpina), Francesco Venturini (Oralto), Giuseppe Valentini (Morasto), Stefano Pasi (Osmino), Ottavio Sinalco (Narete). Scenery by Francesco Bibiena, dances by Andrea Cattani.

SYNOPSIS. The complicated story involves the two daughters, Licori (soprano) and Elpina (contralto), of an old shepherd from Scyros, Narete (tenor). They have been kidnapped by Oralto (bass) and brought to Naxos, where he tries to take Licori by force. Oralto's lieutenant is now known as Morasto but he is, in fact, Osmino (male contralto), the boy Licori was intended to marry before he was captured by enemy soldiers. Oralto's brother Tirsi falls in love with Licori but pays more attention to her sister to make her jealous. Eventually Osmino reveals his identity to Licori and the two former lovers are reunited; they (and her father and sister) escape. A storm blows up but a shipwreck is arrested by Juno, who has been impressed by the fidelity of the young couple during their long tribulations.

■ Originally the commission of setting this libretto to music was given to the Bolognese composer Giuseppe Maria Orlandini, chapel master to the grand-duke of Florence (and, after 1732, of Santa Maria del Fiore). It

Playbill for Pergolesi's La Serva Padrona *for the Paris production of 1752.*

is not known why the commission was later entrusted to the 'red priest' of Venice, but he agreed to carry out the work in 1729. He completed the opera in the following year, but even so *La Fida Ninfa* was not performed as arranged. One has to look to the historical events of the time to understand the reason for the delay. German troops were massed on the borders of the Serenissima and a number of German officers had asked permission to travel to Verona to attend the first performance. It would not have been diplomatic to deny their request but it would have enabled them to see just how few troops Venice had on the mainland at that time. Certainly it could not be expected that a mere opera should necessitate a redeployment of the entire army.... So Vivaldi had to be patient but he had the satisfaction, two years later, of seeing the new theatre in Verona open with his opera. Maffei himself took charge of the production, spending the enormous amount of 20,000 ducats to stage it. In setting the text to music, Vivaldi had classic precedents in *Aminta* and *Il Pastor Fido*; he alternated arias and recitative continuo, expertly matching melodies to sentiments and words. Each principal character was associated with a particular style of music, so attaining dramatic and expressive individuality.

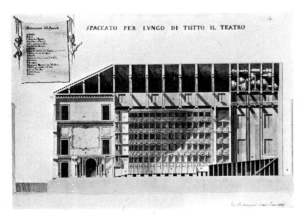

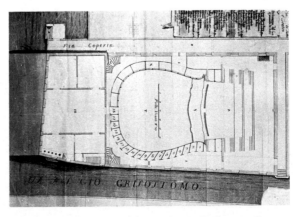

Cross-section and ground plan for the Teatro S. Giovanni Crisostomo in Venice, drawn by F. Pedro.

In this opera Vivaldi extended himself to the limit, creating vocal parts that were extremely effective but very difficult to perform, making it quite clear what singers he required – male, female and castrati. The orchestral music was also of rare quality. The *sinfonia* in the third act (the 'sea tempest') and the interlude are still performed today as separate pieces and are worthy examples of Vivaldi's art.

IL DEMETRIO

Opera in three acts by Johann Adolph Hasse (1699–1783), libretto by Pietro Metastasio (1698–1782). First performance: Venice, San Giovanni Crisostomo, January 1732.

SYNOPSIS. Demetrio Soter, king of Syria, driven out of his kingdom by the usurper Alessandro Balas, dies in exile in Crete. Before leaving he entrusts his young son Demetrio to the faithful Fenicio, with instructions to bring him up and prepare him for revenge. Knowing nothing of his origins, the boy grows up under the name of Alceste. As a young man his bravery gains the recognition of Alessandro, whose daughter Cleonice falls in love with him. Meanwhile Fenicio spreads the news that Demetrio is alive. The Cretans rise in revolt and Alessandro, attempting to put down the rebellion, is killed. Alceste, too, fights against the Cretans and for a while there is no further news of him. Cleonice, now heir to the throne, must find a husband, delaying matters as long as she can in the hope that Alceste will return. He reappears when the queen has almost despaired of his being still alive and is on the point of accepting another suitor. Fenicio now reveals the young man's true identity. Alceste, hailed as Demetrio, marries Cleonice and takes possession of his father's throne.

■ Metastasio's text was set to music by a number of composers, including Antonio Caldara, who staged his opera in Vienna a year before Hasse. The latter's score, however, is better suited to the spirit of the work, brilliant and well constructed, although without much depth of characterization. But Hasse took full advantage of the typically eighteenth-century features of the text, with its dramatic scenic effects and conflicting emotions of love and duty.

EZIO (Aetius)

Opera in three acts by George Frederick Handel (1685–1759), libretto by Pietro Metastasio (1698–1782). First performance: London, King's Theatre, 15 January 1732.

SYNOPSIS. Rome is celebrating the triumph of Ezio, who has defeated Attila. Massimo, his false friend, wants his daughter Fulvia to marry the emperor in order to eliminate him and leave the throne open to Massimo's influence. He tries to convince Ezio that the emperor (Valentiniano), desires to marry Fulvia, who was previously promised to Ezio. Ezio rejects Honoria, the emperor's sister, and pledges his love for Fulvia. Massimo lays an ambush for Valentiniano, who escapes unharmed, but the blame is attributed to Ezio. The prisoner has a stormy meeting with the emperor and his fate is sealed. Honoria is now to be married to Attila and Fulvia to Valentiniano himself. Ezio is sentenced to death but Varo, an old friend sent to kill him, cannot bring himself to carry out the emperor's orders. All Massimo's intrigues are revealed to the emperor who, believing his general already dead, is in despair, until the truth is made clear. Then he consents to the marriage of Fulvia and Ezio, who then obtains pardon both for the treacherous Massimo and for the faithful Varo.

■ This is a typically Metastasian melodrama. The ramifications of the libretto and the excessive number of stage tricks and devices now seem overcomplicated. But Handel's music redeems the artificiality of the sentiments and situations, including, as it does, moments of supreme delicacy and beauty.

LO FRATE 'NNAMORATO (Two Sisters and their Brother)

Opera in three acts by Giovanni Battista Pergolesi (1710–36), libretto by Gennaro Antonio Federico (died c. 1745). First performance: Naples, Teatro dei Fiorentini, 23 September 1732.

ORIGINAL CAST. G. D'Ambrosio, Giambattista Ciriaci, Girolamo Piano, Marianna Ferrante, Maria Negri, Teresa Passaglione.

SYNOPSIS. Act I. The story takes place at Capodimonte in 1730. Carlo (tenor) and the elderly Marcaniello (bass) have made wedding plans; Don Pietro (bass), Marcaniello's son, is to marry Nena (soprano), one of Carlo's nieces. Vannella (soprano) and Cardella (soprano), the maids, gossip about their respective masters. Don Pietro asks Vannella to summon Nena and his sister, Lucrezia (contralto), who is engaged to Carlo. The girls refuse to appear. When Nina (mezzo-soprano) and Nena go out for a walk, they meet their uncle, who scolds them for not treating him with proper respect, and warns them that their prospective husbands have arrived and that the weddings are imminent. The girls receive this news with little enthusiasm. Nena's intended husband is vain and stupid, but at least young; Nina, on the other hand, is even more unlucky, for she is to be married to old Marcaniello. Both girls are secretly in love with Ascanio (tenor), a young man who has grown up in Marcaniello's home. Lucrezia too has a fondness for Ascanio and begs her father not to be made to marry Carlo. When Ascanio, on Marcaniello's advice, tries to persuade Lucrezia to wed Carlo, she frankly confesses her love for him. Ascanio is in torment. He does not wish to deceive his benefactor and he has confused feelings for Nena and Nina. Don Pietro is still looking for Nena, but runs into Vannella, with whom he starts flirting. Marcaniello rebukes him and Nena takes advantage of the episode to express doubts concerning her future husband's serious intentions. Nina ostentatiously ignores Marcaniello and pretends to be overcome by Pietro's charms. Act II. All the wedding plans have gone up in smoke. Don Pietro tells Ascanio that Nena, jealous of Vannella, is in a frenzy and that, judging from certain hints, he believes Nina to be in love with him. Nena enters, takes Ascanio aside, and asks him what his true feelings are, for she fears he prefers her sister Nina. Ascanio is even more disturbed. Meanwhile Nena informs Don Pietro that she has no intention of marrying him. The two sisters are much relieved at having finally got rid of their unwanted husbands, but as far as Ascanio is concerned they are still jealous of each other. He, with his back against the wall, has admitted to being fond of both of them. This confession has been overheard by Lucrezia and makes her furious. Carlo passes by while the irate Lucrezia batters noisily at the windows; affronted by the rude behaviour of his future wife, he tells Marcaniello that he will break his engagement with her unless she learns some manners. Act III. Nena and Nina contine to sigh for Ascanio. The desperate Lucrezia also tells her father of her love for the youth. On the spur of the moment Marcaniello threatens to kill the young man, cause of so much confusion, but eventually compassion for his daughter gains the upper hand. In the meantime Nena and Nina, from the window, tease their suitors. Don Pietro, determined to get rid of Ascanio, follows him, brandishing his sword, and wounds him in the arm. Fortunately the injury is slight. While tending Ascanio, Carlo notices on his arm a mark similar to one borne by his four-year-old nephew, who had been abducted many years ago. This discovery means that Ascanio is brother to Nena and Nina. At last he is free to marry Lucrezia.

■ This was Pergolesi's second opera, composed when he was only twenty-two. Featuring popular but not mannered characters, it is rooted in comedy rather than farce, and was warmly received by the public. It undoubtedly contains passages of lively naturalism and the music is delightfully fresh and expressive.

LA SERVA PADRONA (The Maid Mistress)
Intermezzo in two parts by Giovanni Battista Pergolesi (1710–36), libretto by Gennaro Antonio Federico (died c. 1745). First performance (as an intermezzo between acts of Pergolesi's opera Il Prigionier Superbo): Naples, Teatro San Bartolomeo, 28 August 1733. First performance in U.K.: London 1750. First performance in U.S.A.: Baltimore 1790.

ORIGINAL CAST. Gioacchino Corrado and Laura Monti.

SYNOPSIS. Uberto is an elderly bachelor whose household is ruled by the maid Serpina. Tired of submitting to her whims, he declares that he is going to find a wife, and sends off his servant Vespone to look for a woman who, no matter how ugly, must be submis-

sive. Serpina, knowing full well that the testy old man is secretly fond of her, decides to get her way and become Uberto's wife. With Vespone's encouragement, she announces in her turn that she intends to marry a certain Captain Tempesta. The description she gives of the terrifying soldier she has conjured up in her imagination is such that the old man, concerned for her future, asks to meet him. Serpina promptly introduces Vespone in disguise. Then, taking the old man aside, she tells him that her bad-tempered suitor has agreed to marry her only if her master pays a colossal dowry. Should this be refused, the captain will insist that Uberto himself marry her. Greatly relieved, Uberto joyfully agrees to the second solution. Serpina, who has engineered the whole affair, is now no longer a servant, but mistress of the house.

■ The roots of comic opera can be found in *La Serva Padrona*. The genre continued to develop in the second half of the eighteenth century and culminated in the masterpieces of Rossini. Pergolesi's score sparkles with satirical, witty inventiveness and the characters are boldy portrayed. Comprising both spoken and sung passages, the latter made up of arias and duets, *La Serva Padrona* became the subject of heated controversy when, in 1752, it was produced in Paris by the Bambini company, giving rise to the famous 'Guerre des Bouffons'. This divided musicians and music-lovers into two camps, those in favour of French music (as represented by Lully and Rameau) and those carrying the flag for Italian opera. Among the latter was Jean Jacques Rousseau, who openly declared his support for the imported music both in his *Lettre sur la Musique Française* (1753) and by himself composing *Le Devin du Village*, modelled on *La Serva Padrona*, which was staged at Fontainebleau in 1752. (See page 58 below.)

HIPPOLYTE ET ARICIE
Lyric tragedy in a prologue and five acts by Jean Philippe Rameau (1683–1764), libretto by Simon Joseph Pellégrin (1661/3–1745). First performance: Paris Opéra, 1 October 1733. First performance in U.S.A.: New York, 11 April 1954.

SYNOPSIS. In the prologue, Diane and Amour fight for the allegiance of the forest-dwellers, Jupiter acting as arbiter. Hippolyte declares his love for Aricie. The love of the two young people arouses the anger and jealousy of Phèdre, wife of Thesée and herself in love with her stepson Hippolyte. Phèdre wishes Aricie to consecrate herself to the cult of Diane. Thesée descends to the Underworld and returns, thanks to the protection of his father Neptune; but everyone believes him dead, and Phèdre, considering herself a widow, declares her love for Hippolyte, who spurns her. During the games held in honour of Diane, a terrible monster emerges from the sea. Hippolyte challenges it and disappears amidst flames and smoke. Phèdre, grief-stricken, commits suicide. But Diane comes to the rescue of Hippolyte, who is borne by the

Zephyrs to his beloved Aricie. The couple are married, amid general rejoicing.

■ The production of *Hippolyte et Aricie* in 1733 marked the stage début of the fifty-year-old Rameau. Parisians were divided in their opinion. Rameau's somewhat cerebral approach to operatic composition posed difficulties for the singers, so much so that, after a few rehearsals, he seriously considered scrapping the work. But the performance took place, thanks partly to the insistence of the librettist Pellégrin and to the solid support of the financier Le Riche de la Pouplinière.

L'OLIMPIADE (The Olympiad)

Opera in three acts by Antonio Vivaldi (c. 1675– c. 1740), based on the play by Pietro Metastasio (1698–1782). First performance: Venice, Teatro Sant'Angelo, carnival of 1734.

SYNOPSIS. Aristea, daughter of Clisthenes, king of Sicyon, has been promised in marriage to the winner of the Olympic Games. Aristea loves and is loved by Megacles. Lycidas desperately desires the prize but, knowing that he has no chance of winning the games, asks Megacles to compete in his place. Megacles, who has just returned from Crete, does not know the situation and gladly takes his friend's place. When he discovers the nature of the prize he is torn between friendship and love. Aristea is distressed by the behaviour of Megacles, who tries to persuade her to accept Lycidas as husband and leaves her, intending to kill himself. In the meantime Argene, to whom Lycidas had sworn his love, arrives from Crete but, when she learns what has happened, realizes that he has always meant to betray her. In revenge she reveals the trickery to Clisthenes, who sentences Lycidas to exile; Lycidas thereupon tries to assassinate the king, and is sentenced to death. As he is about to be executed, Argene asks that she, his promised bride, be allowed to take his place. To prove her case, Argene shows the king a necklace that Lycidas had given her as a love token. Clisthenes recognizes it. It was worn by his own son when he was thrown into the sea many years ago, after the oracle had declared that the boy would one day try to kill his father. The opera ends with a double wedding – Megacles and Aristea, Lycidas and Argene.

■ This opera was Vivaldi's answer to the Neapolitan composers of Metastasio's libretti, with whom he had been in dispute and who had been enjoying much success at the theatre of San Giovanni Crisostomo in

Production of the theatrical entertainment La Contesa de' Numi *by Leonardo Vinci (1690–1732), with libretto by Pietro Metastasio, composed to celebrate the birth of the Dauphin and performed on 27 November 1729 at the palace of Cardinal Melchior de Polignac in Rome. Painting by Giovanni Paolo Panini in the Musée du Louvre, Paris.*

Venice. Vivaldi maintained that one had certainly to consider the demands both of performers and public, but that the Neapolitans were ruining Metastasio's plot and characters. The 'red priest' was particularly at issue with Antonio Caldara, whose version of *L'Olimpiade* had been produced in Vienna on 28 March 1733. In 1739 Vivaldi prepared a new version for the Teatro dell'Accademia dei Rozzi in Siena, adding in it arias taken from *Dorilla in Tempe*, an opera he had written in 1726.

LIVIETTA E TRACOLLO
Opera comica by Giovanni Battista Pergolesi (1710–36), libretto by Tommaso Mariani, in two parts, which served as interludes to Pergolesi's opera Adriano in Siria. *First performance: Naples, Teatro San Bartolomeo, 25 October 1734. First performance in U.K.: Edinburgh 1763. Modern revival: London 1933.*

SYNOPSIS. Tracollo, a vagabond thief calling himself Baldracca, goes about the village disguised as a pregnant woman, committing all kinds of petty thefts. He is aided and abetted by his companion Faccenda. Livietta resolves to catch the two rascals and lies in wait for them, disguised as a man, together with Fulvia, in the dress of a peasant girl. While the two women pretend to sleep, Tracollo enters and tries to steal Fulvia's necklace. Livietta unmasks the scoundrel, and the pair indulge in a long dialogue of threats and pleas. Tracollo is ready to do anything to avoid arrest and declares his love for Livietta, swearing to marry her. She remains unmoved by his protestations. In the second intermezzo, Tracollo, disguised as an astrologer, pretends to be mad, still hoping to win over Livietta. She, in turn, pretends to be dead. The grief he displays seems so sincere that she is genuinely moved. Rising from her 'death-bed', she agrees to marry him, after he has promised to change his way of life.

■ These two intermezzi, like Pergolesi's *La Serva Padrona*, are very important historically for their influence on the development of eighteenth- and nineteenth-century Italian comic opera. They contain a number of delightfully happy, melodious arias, like the one accompanying Livietta's first disguise. There are also some engaging comic touches in the part of Tracollo.

ADRIANO IN SIRIA (Hadrian in Syria)
Opera in three acts by Giovanni Battista Pergolesi (1710–36), libretto by Pietro Metastasio (1698–1782). First performance: Naples, Teatro San Bartolomeo, 25 October 1734.

■ In this opera, performed in public for the birthday of the Spanish queen, Pergolesi provided a more important role for the instrumentalist, although still adhering to the pattern of alternating recitative and aria.

POLIFEMO
Opera in three acts by Nicola Porpora (1686–1768), libretto by Paolo Antonio Rolli (1687–1765). First performance: London, King's Theatre, 1 January 1735.

L'OLIMPIADE (The Olympiad)
Opera in three acts by Giovanni Battista Pergolesi (1710–36), libretto by Pietro Metastasio (1698–1782). First performance: Rome, Teatro Tordinona, 8 January 1735. First performance in U.K.: London 1742.

■ There are conflicting contemporary reports of this opera, including those of Charles De Brosses. After Pergolesi's death the opera had a marvellous reception in Venice, as did the individual performance of Faustina Bordoni-Hasse (1738). Metastasio's text was set to music by other composers, including Caldara and Vivaldi (for the plot see *L'Olimpiade* by Vivaldi, page 42).

TAMERLANO
Opera in three acts by Antonio Vivaldi (c. 1675–c.1740), libretto probably by Agostino Piovene. First performance: Verona, Teatro Filarmonico, carnival of 1735.

SYNOPSIS. Tamerlane (Timur) was regarded as the new Genghis Khan. Legends have been woven around the figure of the great tyrant, including the one about the ring he possessed, which changed colour if anyone told him a lie. Tamerlane began his career as a brutal plunderer and after a succession of unexpected victories took prisoner the emperor Bajazet, whom he tortured at length, together with his wife. To escape further torment Bajazet killed himself by striking his head repeatedly against the bars of his prison cage.

■ There is no available information about Vivaldi's score, which has been lost. It is known, however, that the opera contained a *sinfonia* at the beginning and a chorus at the end, for the music of the latter has been rediscovered. When Vivaldi composed the work he had been re-engaged at the Pièta in Venice, with an annual salary of 100 ducats. He was to undertake the duties of his post 'without any intention of leaving again', in the words of the contract, 'as he had done in former years'. The theme of the opera was very popular at that time. Handel's *Tamerlano* had been given in London in 1724, and Porpora's opera on the same subject in Dresden in 1730. It seems that Vivaldi also wrote a second version entitled *Bajazet*. In any event, he and his colleagues based themselves on the version of the Castilian ambassador Ruiz Gonzalez de Clavijo (who died in 1412), apparently ignoring the two-part play by Christopher Marlowe, *Tamburlaine the Great*, published in 1590. In Italy, too, there had been two stage versions of *Tamerlano*, one by Giacomelli, the other by a certain signor Sassone.

ACHILLE ET DEIDAMIA

Opera in a prologue and five acts by André Campra (1660–1744), libretto by Antoine Danchet (1671–1748). First performance: Paris, Académie Royale de Musique (Opéra), 24 February 1735.

■ Both composer and librettist were well on in years when they wrote this opera. It was inspired by the myth of Achilles, the prologue being a homage to Philippe Quinault and Jean Baptiste Lully, who had already used Achilles as a character in French opera. Campra's work was not a success.

DEMOFOONTE

Opera in three acts by Leonardo Leo (1694–1744), libretto by Pietro Metastasio (1698–1782). First performance: Naples, Teatro San Bartolomeo, 20 December 1735.

SYNOPSIS. Demophoön, king of the Chersonnesus in Thrace, is compelled every year to sacrifice a virgin from his people. Upon asking the oracle of Apollo when he will be allowed to end this cruel tribute, he receives the answer 'When the innocent usurper of a kingdom is recognized by himself'. The development of the story provides the solution to this riddle. Demophoön has daughters but has sent them away so that they cannot be chosen for sacrifice. His minister Matusio, who has a daughter named Dircea, intends to do the same. The angry king condemns the girl to be sacrificed, refusing to draw lots. He does not know that she is secretly married to Timante, his own son and heir, and has decided that the prince shall marry Creusa. The latter, however, is loved by Cherinto, Demophoön's second son. Timante rejects Creusa who, deeply hurt, wishes to go away, also refusing Cherinto's suit. Meanwhile Demophoön discovers that Timante and Dircea are married; on the spur of the moment he condemns them both to death, but later pardons them. Matusio, in the meantime, discovers from a document left by his late wife that Dircea is not his daughter but the king's. She is therefore both wife and sister to Timante. Fortunately Timante also learns from a document written by his mother that he is not the son of the king and that his true father is Matusio. All obstacles to love are thus removed, but he is no longer heir to the throne. So the prophecy is fulfilled, because the innocent usurper is now aware of his unintended crime. The sacrifice of virgins can now cease and Demophoön gives Creusa in marriage to his sole heir Cherinto.

■ This opera was a great success both with the critics and the public. Indeed, it was the most popular of all Leo's serious operas. The text was later set to music by other composers.

ACHILLE IN SCIRO

Opera in three acts by Antonio Caldara (1670–1736), libretto by Pietro Metastasio (1698–1782). First performance: Vienna, Court Theatre, 13 February 1736.

SYNOPSIS. The mother of Achille, Teti, endeavouring to help her son escape the destiny that awaits him in the Trojan War, has asked Chirone to conceal him on the island of Scyros. He does this by disguising him as a girl, going under the name of Pirra. On the island Pirra becomes very friendly with Deidamia, daughter of king Lycomede. Because of his fiery temperament, Achille continually risks revealing his true identity. Lycomede promises Deidamia to Theagene, who has a high regard for Pirra, whom he is encouraged to woo all the more when he recognizes Deidamia's cold reception of his advances. Ulisse arrives, ostensibly to seek help from Lycomede for the Greeks in the Trojan War, but in reality to find Achille, who is indispensable to the Greeks for victory. He lays all kinds of plots to make Achille give himself away, but in vain. Achille, however, is keenly conscious of the conflicting shame, ambition and love for which he can find no solution. During a banquet to celebrate the forthcoming marriage of Deidamia and the impending departure of Ulisse, Achille cannot dissemble any longer and joins in a brawl among the soldiers, which Ulisse has provoked. Deidamia is promised to Achille as his future wife. The opera ends with the appearance of Glory, Love and Time, who sing the praises of the happy pair.

■ The married couple being honoured were really the archduchess Maria Teresa and Francis, duke of Lorraine and future German emperor. The opera was, in fact, composed for the occasion of their wedding in 1736.

LES INDES GALANTES

Opera-ballet in a prologue and four entrées by Jean Philippe Rameau (1683–1764), libretto by Louis Fuzelier (1672–1752). First performance with three entrées: Paris Opéra, 23 August 1735; first performance with four entrées: Paris Opéra, 10 March 1736. First performance in U.S.A.: New York, 1 March 1961.

SYNOPSIS. Prologue. The youth of four allied nations (France, Spain, Italy and Poland) are dragged into war by Bellona and forced to abandon Hebe and Amor. The Amores, disappointed at being so neglected by the Europeans, depart for distant lands. First *entrée*: 'The Generous Turk'. Osman, pasha of a Turkish island in the Indian Ocean, loves Emilia, his Provençal slave girl, whom he has abducted from her lover Valère, a naval officer. As a result of a storm, Valère is also taken captive by the pasha. But the latter, recognizing the officer as the man who once saved his life, frees the two lovers, giving up Emilia. Second *entrée*: 'The Incas of Peru'. A mountainous desert in Peru, with a volcano in the background. Don Carlos, a Spanish officer, loves Phani, a young Peruvian princess, who returns his passion. The Inca high priest, Huascar, is jealous, and during a banquet causes the volcano to erupt; but he

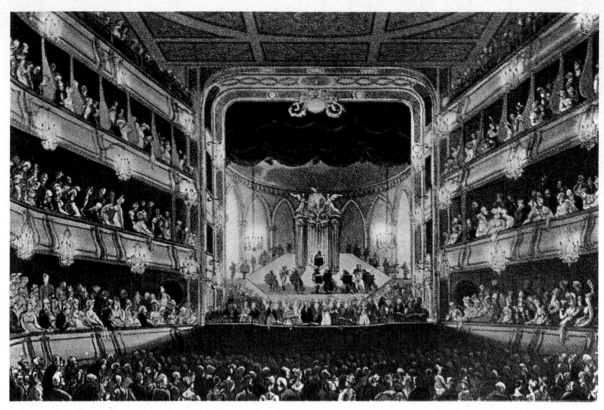

Interior of the first Covent Garden Theatre, London, showing Handel's organ. After an aquatint by Pugin and Rowlandson. London, Victoria and Albert Museum.

himself dies, while Don Carlos arrives to free his beloved Phani. Third *entrée*: 'The Flowers; Persian Festival'. On the day of the Flower Festival, Tacmas, a Persian prince and king of India, arrives, disguised as a merchant, in the garden of his favourite, Ali. He is in love with Ali's slave girl, Zaire. Fatima, the king's slave, is, in turn, in love with Ali, and she arrives, dressed as a Polish male slave. Tacmas, mistaking her for an enemy, attacks her. Eventually everything is sorted out. Tacmas and Ali exchange slaves and take part in the festival together. Fourth *entrée*: 'The Savages'. A wood in America, close to the French and Spanish colonies. The native American warriors, led by Adoro, prepare to make peace with their European conquerors. Two officers, the Frenchman Damon and the Spaniard Don Alvar, are rivals for the favours of Zima, who does not love either of them and chooses Adoro as her future husband. Don Alvar's rage at this slight is cooled by Damon. Eventually all take part in the peace festivities, symbolized in the 'pipe of peace' dance.

■ *Les Indes Galantes* is undoubtedly one of Rameau's masterpieces. Although much of the libretto is banal, it contains a large number of varied situations and provides scope for dramatic scenic effects. Even though the opera is subtitled a 'heroic ballet'', it owes nothing to mythology or the supernatural, apart from the allegorical allusions in the prologue. It is likely that Rameau was attracted to the project by the very diver-

sity of scenes, preceded by the fanciful prologue, thought up by the librettist. The music is adapted to the situations portrayed in the *entrées* with an astonishing measure of insight and technical skill. The opera can certainly not be described as dramatic or profound, yet the individual qualities of the characters, strikingly differentiated and contrasted, are subtly underlined. The opera was not an immediate success. The public complained about the text, and one *entrée* ('The Flowers') had to be completely revised a month later. In the following year the opera was performed again, this time with the addition of the fourth *entrée* – a happy decision. From then on *Les Indes Galantes* was a guaranteed success. Such was the influence it had both on public taste and contemporary musical style that very soon parodies and new versions of many of the arias began to circulate throughout Europe.

ARMINIO
Opera in three acts by George Frederick Handel (1685–1759), libretto by Antonio Salvi (with modifications). First performance: London, Covent Garden Theatre, 12 January 1737.

■ The libretto had already been set to music by Scarlatti (for plot see page 28), and by other composers. Handel's version is not of great merit. It was one of seven operas which he composed for Covent Garden.

Probable portrait of the singer Teresa Lanti. Oil painting of the Bolognese School, 18th century. Milan, Museo Teatrale alla Scala.

CATONE IN UTICA
Opera by Antonio Vivaldi (c. 1675–c. 1740), libretto by Pietro Metastasio (1698–1782). First performance: Verona, Teatro Filarmonico, spring 1737. Conducted by the composer, in the presence of Charles Albert, Elector of Bavaria.

■ Metastasio's *Catone* was set to music by Leonardo Vinci nine years before Vivaldi's version, and had enjoyed considerable success. Another version had been scored in 1731 by Hasse (for plot see page 37). While working on his opera, Vivaldi had many other problems. He had been present, in 1738, in Amsterdam for the centenary of that city's local theatre. This had involved him in much preparatory work, for in the course of the celebrations he had conducted some nine symphonies by various composers as well as a *concerto grosso* of his own. It is perhaps for this reason that *Catone in Utica* shows signs of carelessness and cannot be regarded as one of his finest works.

CASTOR ET POLLUX
Tragédie lyrique in a prologue and five acts by Jean Philippe Rameau (1683–1764), libretto by Pierre Joseph Bernard (1710–75). First performance: Paris Opéra, 24 October 1737. First performance in U.K.: Glasgow 1927; in U.S.A.: New York Vassar College, 6 March 1937.

SYNOPSIS. Prologue. Crumbling porticos, mutilated statues, ruined temples. Minerva (soprano) and Love (tenor) entreat Venus (soprano) to chain the god of war. Venus appears on a cloud, with Mars (bass) enchained at her feet. The world seems beautiful and everyone rejoices in the return of peace. Act I. A place destined for the tomb of the king of Sparta. Preparations are afoot for the funeral of Castor (tenor). Telaire (contralto) weeps for the loss of her lover and is consoled by Phoebea. Pollux (bass) is immortal and will certainly avenge Castor's death. But this does not comfort the unhappy woman who, when alone, prays to her father, the Sun, to allow her to share Castor's fate. Pollux arrives, triumphantly announcing that he has avenged his brother's death and confessing to Telaire that he loves her. She implores him to go down to Hades and bring back Castor alive. Torn between love for his brother and love for Telaire, Pollux decides to sacrifice the latter. Act II. Hall in the Temple of Jupiter (bass). The high priest (tenor) announces Jupiter's arrival. Pollux appeals to him for the life of his brother, but not even the greatest of the gods can violate the laws of the Underworld. The only condition on which Castor will be allowed to return to earth is that Pollux takes his place in the kingdom of shadows. Act III. Phoebea does all she can to prevent Pollux descending to Hades. But then she discovers his love for Telaire and, in despair, incites the demons to bar his entrance to the lower regions. Act IV. The Elysian Fields. Groups of shades walk to and fro, and Pollux searches for that of his brother. Eventually they meet and engage in a contest of generosity. Castor refuses the

gift of life if Pollux has to die instead. Pollux then tells Castor of his love for Telaire and informs him that she is sadly awaiting Castor's return. For her sake Castor accepts the offer of life, but only for a single day. Act V. The neighbourhood of Sparta. Phoebea sees Mercury, who tells her that Castor is alive. Jealous of his love for Telaire, the cause of her own grief, she asks Jupiter for vengeance. The meeting of the two lovers is equally dramatic, since Castor anounces that he is back only for one day. But Jupiter makes his appearance, having released his son Pollux from Hades. He now frees Castor from his promise. Marvelling at the love and virtues of the two brothers, he gives them a place among the constellations of heaven.

■ This was Rameau's third opera, and the success of his first two (*Hippolyte et Aricie* and *Les Indes Galantes*) virtually guaranteed that of the new work; and so it proved. *Castor et Pollux* was a triumph, as shown by the fact that it was performed 254 times between 1737 and 1785, a formidable number of revivals for that time. The opera owed some of its success to its text, which, although somewhat slight, is gracefully written, with a succinct, passionate plot. It was a particularly happy notion to make Pollux fall in love with Telaire; by virtue of bringing his brother back to the land of the living, he is compelled to renounce his love for ever. The opera, when revived in 1754, was completely revised, which resulted in a general improvement, the music being strengthened and the whole made even more compact. *Castor et Pollux* is widely regarded as Rameau's dramatic masterpiece.

L'OLIMPIADE (The Olympiad)
Opera in three acts by Leonardo Leo (1694–1744), libretto by Pietro Metastasio (1698–1782). First performance: Naples, Teatro San Carlo, 19 November 1737.

■ *L'Olimpiade* was given in Naples at the opening of the San Carlo theatre, together with *Demofoonte*. It was one of Leo's most famous and committed works. The same subject, again with Metastasio's text, had already been set to music by Vivaldi in 1734 (for the plot see page 42) and by Pergolesi in 1735 (see p. 44).

ALESSANDRO NELLE INDIE (Alexander in India)
Opera in three acts by Baldassare Galuppi, known as Il Buranello (1706–85), libretto by Pietro Metastasio (1698–1782). First performance: Mantua, Teatro Arciducale, carnival of 1738.

■ The play written by Metastasio in 1727 was very popular with composers; it was used by Corselli, Galuppi, Pérez, J. C. Bach, Sacchini and Piccinni amongst others. Consequently it was one of the most frequently staged eighteenth-century works. This was Galuppi's fifteenth opera, and his first major success, being performed extensively in Italy up to 1762. (For details of the plot, see the opera by Gluck, page 53.)

Prison scene for Rameau's Dardanus. *Engraving by Machi, inspired by Piranesi. Paris, Bibliothèque de l'Opéra.*

This fine work is typical of mid-eighteenth-century *opera seria* and of both the librettist's and composer's style.

SERSE (Xerxes)

Opera in three acts by George Frederick Handel (1685–1759), libretto partly adapted from Niccolò Minato (1654). First performance: London, Haymarket Theatre, 15 April 1738. First performance in U.S.A.: Northampton, Mass., 1928.

ORIGINAL CAST. Maiorano, known as Caffarelli; du Parc, known as La Francesina; Marighi; Montagnana.

SYNOPSIS. On hearing Romilda (soprano) singing, Serse, King of Persia (soprano/tenor), falls hopelessly in love with her, quite forgetting Amastre, to whom he is to be married. But Romilda loves Arsamene (soprano/tenor), the king's brother, and so repels the persistent advances of Serse. The king is prepared to win her by force, if necessary, and resolves to get rid of his rival by sending him into exile. Meanwhile Amastre, discovering this piece of treachery, becomes so desperate that she sees death as the only solution to her suffering. The 'travesty' of this *castrato* role is emphasized by the soldier's disguise which Amastre adopts. The plot is further complicated by the appearance of Atalanta (soprano), Romilda's sister, who is also in love with Arsamene. Atalanta's plan is simple – to encourage the marriage of Serse to her sister so that she can become the wife of Arsamene. She intercepts a letter from Arsamene, sent to Romilda through the servant Elviro (bass), and persuades the king that she is the intended recipient. She urges him to arrange the date for her marriage to Arsamene without delay. Serse, for his part, uses the letter to try to convince Romilda that her lover has betrayed her. In Act II the conspiracy is unmasked. Arsamene and Romilda vow mutual fidelity. But Serse will not admit defeat and uses every means in his power to break down the girl's defences. Finally she agrees to a compromise. She will marry the king if he obtains the consent of Ariodate (bass), her father. Serse talks to Ariodate, but he describes the situation in such an ambiguous fashion that Ariodate is given to understand that it is Arsamene whom Romilda wishes to wed. By the time the king realizes what has happened, in Act III, the two lovers are married. Despite his anger at this humiliation, Serse is compelled to resign himself to the new situation. He now returns the love of Amastre, who has loyally been awaiting him. Atalanta, however, has to look for a new lover to console her in her cruel disappointment.

■ *Serse* does not scale the heights of other Handelian operas and, indeed, is something of a departure in its mixture of serious and comic elements. However, it may be regarded as the most significant opera of the composer's third period. It was written at a time of physical and artistic crises when the composer was becoming increasingly absorbed in oratorio. The first complete performance of the work, as an oratorio, took place in London on 28 March 1738. The libretto, originally written by Minato and set to music by Cavalli in 1654 (see p. 16), was set almost unaltered by Handel. The beginning of the first act is especially noteworthy in musical terms. The *largo* from the opera, *Ombra mai fu*, became famous all over the world, even during the lengthy period when the opera itself vanished from the stage. In fact, there was no revival of *Serse* until 5 July 1924, when it was staged by Oscar Hugen in Göttingen. It is surprising that there were only five performances in Handel's time as there are many arias and the entire opera bears the hallmark of his originality. The theme might well have spurred him to write an epic theatrical work, with ample opportunity to depict, as was then fashionable, the passions of people of high rank. In effect Handel treated the subject in a much freer manner, appealing in large measure to sentiment and introducing various comic touches, such as the character of the servant Elviro.

DARDANUS

Tragédie lyrique in a prologue and five acts by Jean Philippe Rameau (1683–1764), libretto by Charles

Antoine Leclerc de La Bruère (1715–54). First performance: Paris, Opéra, 19 November 1739.

SYNOPSIS. In the prologue, Vénus (dessus *i.e.* soprano) invites the Pleasures to reign at the court of Amour (soprano). They do this with such success that they and Amour fall asleep. Vénus calls Jalousie (played by a dancer) to wake them. Amour then banishes Jalousie, and the Pleasures perform the tragedy. It relates the story of Iphise (soprano), daughter of Teucer, King of Phrygia, who, against her father's wishes, loves Dardanus, an enemy of her country and eventual founder of the city of Troy. Teucer (bass) intends her to marry Prince Anténor. In her anguish Iphise decides to consult the magician Isménor (bass). Dardanus (haute-contre i.e. high tenor), who returns her love, obtains from Isménor a magic wand, with which he himself assumes the guise of the magician. Thus he listens to the confessions of Iphise, including her love for him. Overjoyed, he reveals his identity, but the girl, in confusion, runs away. Dardanus is then captured by his enemies; but Jupiter causes a monster to emerge from the sea, which terrorizes the land. Anténor (bass) goes off to fight it. He is saved from death by Dardanus, who has been freed by Vénus. Not recognizing his saviour, Anténor swears eternal friendship, giving him his sword as a pledge. Neptune's oracle has predicted that Iphise will be married to the man who slays the monster. Thus Dardanus,

A castrato singing a heroic aria. Caricature by Rowlandson.

brought before Teucer and his rejoicing people, is rewarded for his feat; and Anténor, faithful to his promise, renounces his love.

■ The opera was revised on several occasions, necessitating a second edition in 1744 and taking on definitive form only in 1760. The plot summarized here relates to the original version. In the later draft some of the more fantastic episodes were removed. The loss of some delightful melodies from the original version is compensated by the tighter dramatic quality of the music in the final draft.

RICIMERO RE DEI GOTI (Ricimer, King of the Goths)

Melodramma by Niccolò Jommelli (1714–74), libretto by Apostolo Zeno (1668–1750) and P. Pariati (d. 1745). First performance: Rome, Teatro Argentina, 16 January 1740.

SYNOPSIS. The story is based on the narratives of Procopius and Paulus Diaconus, the action taking place in Rome in the fifth century A.D. Ricimero, the barbarian chieftain, has conquered Rome and liberated his sister Theodolinda, who was held captive there. He enslaves the daughter of the Emperor Valentinian III, Placidia, with whom he is in love. The girl, however, loves the Roman general Flavius Anicius Olibrius, with whom Theodolinda is also secretly in love. She hopes that her brother will help to remove her rival but Placidia, spurning Ricimero, incites Flavius to revolt. He becomes Emperor, frees the girl and marries her. He spares his rival's life, yet exiles him from the city.

■ The opera, belonging to the early 'Neapolitan' period of the composer's career, is characterized by many scene changes and interludes. Although one of Jommelli's first compositions for the stage and revealing the influence of Hasse, whom Jommelli greatly admired, its musical structure shows a more intense and personal handling of the dramatic elements than was customary in the *opera seria* of Hasse.

EZIO (Aetius)

Melodramma in three acts by Niccolò Jommelli (1714–74), libretto by Pietro Metastasio (1698–1782). First performance: Bologna, Teatro Malvezzi, 29 April 1741.

■ A second version of Jommelli's opera was staged in Naples in 1748. Metastasio's text was set to music by many other composers, including Galuppi, Gluck, Graun, Handel, Hasse, Leo, Porpora and Scarlatti. (For the plot see under *Ezio* by Handel, page 40.)

ARTASERSE

Dramma musicale in three acts by Christoph Willibald Gluck (1714–87), libretto by Pietro Metastasio

Scene from Rameau's La Princesse de Navarre, *staged at Versailles in 1745. Drawing by C. N. Cochin fils. Paris, Musée de l'Opéra.*

(1698–1782). First performance: Milan, Teatro Regio Ducale, 26 December 1741.

■ Based on the libretto previously set to music by Hasse (for plot see *Artaserse* by Hasse, page 36), Gluck wrote this, his first opera, in Milan. He had arrived in the city four years earlier with Prince Melzi, and studied composition with Sammartini. It was partly as a result of these friendships that he was able to make his successful debut on the Milanese stage.

SEMIRAMIDE RICONOSCIUTA (Semiramis Recognized)
Melodramma in three acts by Niccolò Jommelli (1714–74), libretto by Pietro Metastasio (1698–1782). First performance: Turin, Teatro Regio, 26 December 1741.

SYNOPSIS. Semiramide, queen of Babylon, disguises herself in male attire as her own son Nino, whose upbringing has made him soft and effeminate, to participate at the presentation of suitors for the hand of Tamiri, daughter of the King of Bactria, one of her tributaries. Tamiri has a choice of three possible husbands – Scitalce, Prince of the Indies, Mirteo, Prince of Egypt and brother to Semiramide, and Ircano, Prince of the Scythians. Of these Tamiri prefers Scitalce. Semiramide recognizes this man as her former lover Idreno, who abducted her and then, as a result of lies spread by her adviser Sibari (who was also in love with her), had her thrown into the Nile, where she narrowly escaped death. Sibari himself is now present and recognizes Semiramide. After a complicated series of misunderstandings, Semiramide reveals her identity to the people, justifies her ruse, on the pretext that her son is a coward, extols her own virtues and is confirmed as Queen. Scitalce is not only pardoned but wins the hand of Semiramide, while Tamari marries Mirteo. The opera ends with a vision of the palace of Jupiter. Iride descends from Olympus in a chariot drawn by peacocks and pronounces an epilogue in honour of Ferdinand of Spain.

■ Although the plot is extremely complicated, the opera made its mark with its magnificent staging. Metastasio's text, already set to music by Leonardo Vinci and performed in Rome in 1729, was later scored by many other composers. The music avoids excess of any kind, and it is not surprising that Jommelli enjoyed

Metastasio's approval at this time. Yet there is already an increasing emphasis on *arie accompagnate* and an instrumental independence which was to characterize Jommelli's mature style.

DEMETRIO (or CLEONICE)
Opera in three acts by Christoph Willibald Gluck (1714–87), libretto by Pietro Metastasio (1698–1782). First performance: Venice, Teatro di San Samuele, 2 May 1742.

■ As was the case with so many other texts by Metastasio, *Demetrio* attracted the attention and talents of many composers, including Caldara, Hasse, Jommelli, and Piccinni. Metastasio's verse, here particularly brilliant and inspired, was conceived in theatrical terms most suitable for musical treatment; and Gluck's operatic score did full justice to the lofty ideals of the characters and the poetic beauty of the text. (For the plot see *Demetrio* by Hasse, page 40.)

DEMOFOONTE
Opera in three acts by Christoph Willibald Gluck (1714–87), libretto by Pietro Metastasio (1698–1782). First performance: Milan, Teatro Regio Ducale, 26 December 1742.

■ Metastasio's play hinged on a favourite theme: conspiracy. It was set to music not only by Gluck but also by other composers, including Caldara, Leo (for the plot see under *Demofoonte* by that composer, page 45). Hasse, Jommelli, Piccinni and Paisiello. *Demofoonte* was Gluck's third opera, still written in the Italian style, and at its first performance was an instant success, helping to establish his reputation well before he began introducing his innovative operatic ideas.

DEMOFOONTE
Melodramma in three acts by Niccolò Jommelli (1714–74), libretto by Pietro Metastasio (1698–1782). First performance: Padua, Teatro Obizzi, 13 June 1743. First performance in U.K.: London, 9 December 1755.

■ Jommelli's opera, not one of his best compositions, was twice revised. One version was given in Stuttgart, 2 February 1764, and the other in Naples, at the Teatro San Carlo, 4 November 1770, with little success despite Mozart's presence in the audience. (For the plot see *Damofoonte* by Leonardo Leo, page 45.)

ANTIGONO (or PORO)
Opera in three acts by Johann Adolph Hasse (1699–1783), libretto by Pietro Metastasio (1698–1782) written especially for Hasse. First performance: Hubertusburg Castle near Leipzig, 10 October 1743.

SYNOPSIS. Act I. At the Macedonian seaport of Thessalonica, Antigono Gonata, King of Macedonia, has persuaded Berenice, Princess of Egypt, to marry him; but his son Demetrio and the young princess are secretly in love with each other. Demetrio is banished by his suspicious father. Meanwhile, Alessandro, King of Epirus, previously spurned by Berenice, decides to take revenge by beginning a campaign against the Macedonians. In the royal palace, Ismene confides in Berenice that she is in love with the enemy general, Alessandro. A battle takes place between the two armies. Demetrio disobeys his father's orders in order to ensure the safety of Berenice, but has to announce the Macedonian defeat. Antigono appears and, still mistrustful of his son, exiles him again. Berenice is taken prisoner by Alessandro and once more rejects his protestations of love. Antigono and Ismene are also taken captive. Only Demetrio remains at liberty, thanks to Clearco, his close friend. Act II. Demetrio appears before Alessandro and requests that his father be spared, in exchange for his own life. The nobility of his bearing and words so impress the victorious King that he undertakes to forfeit his conquests on condition that Demetrio persuades Berenice to marry him. In a passionate meeting, the two young people vow their mutual love. Demetrio, for love of his father and despite his inner torment, obtains Berenice's reluctant consent to marry Alessandro. Antigono furiously denounces his son for agreeing to the plan but then receives the news that his reorganized army has destroyed the enemy forces. He, nevertheless, remains Alessandro's hostage. Act III. Antigono, refusing to hand over Berenice to his rival, is locked in a prison cell, which can only be opened by a person bearing Alessandro's ring. Demetrio compels Alessandro to give him this ring and he frees his father. He then resolves to commit suicide so as to be his father's rival no longer. Antigono returns to his palace and generously gives Ismene in marriage to Alessandro. Eventually, after Demetrio has fortunately been prevented by Clearco from committing suicide, Antigono, moved by his son's virtue, gives Berenice to him, restoring peace to the kingdom.

■ *Antigono* is perhaps the best example of the perfect community of feeling between Hasse and Metastasio, combining as it does musical craftsmanship and elegant *bel canto* with an understanding of the undercurrents and ideals which motivate the characters. The German composer was familiar with Italian music, having studied with Porpora and Alessandro Scarlatti. 'Il caro Sassone' as he was affectionately called in Italy, did not attempt to add psychological depth to Metastasio's conventional and, above all, rational characters, and the essentially traditional quality of his music was designed to provide ample scope for vocal display rather than aiming for dramatic effect. The dry recitative, sometimes almost pedestrian, nevertheless has the merit of underlining the intrinsic musicality of the verse. Furthermore, the arias are conceived on a grand scale and are unfailingly easy on the ear, handled with extreme delicacy of taste and formal elegance. The excessive complexity of the plot may not commend itself to modern audiences and gives the music insufficient scope to explore the motivations and feelings of the characters. The formal variety within Hasse's operas is slight and it is not surprising that radical changes in musical taste led to a gradual decline in his popularity. However, both contemporary singers and their audiences found this elegant accomplished music much to their liking.

CIRO RICONOSCIUTO (Cyrus recognized)
Melodramma *by Niccolò Jommelli (1714–74), libretto by Pietro Metastasio (1698–82). First performance: Ferrara, Teatro Bonaccossi, 1744.*

SYNOPSIS. Astiage, King of Media, has been warned in a prophetic vision that he will lose his throne. He has exiled Cambise, the husband of his daughter Mandane, and has commanded his minister Arpago to kill their small son Ciro. But Arpago, pitying the child, arranges for a shepherd Mitridate to take him in and raise him as his own son, under the name of Alceo. The events of the opera take place fifteen years later. News has filtered through that Ciro is still alive and a false pretender claims the throne in his name. Astiage, terrified, summons Arpago, who confesses his disobedience, at which news the king orders his minister's son to be killed. Arpago, eager for vengeance, provokes a rebellion among the leading nobles and brings back Cambise from exile. Astiage pretends that he is anxious to see his grandson again, but really plots to do away with him. After a series of complicated events, the false Ciro is killed and the real one proclaimed king. Ciro then saves his grandfather from the wrath of Cambise.

LA SOFONISBA, or SIFACE (Sophonisba, or Syphax)
Opera in three acts by Christoph Willibald Gluck (1714–87), libretto by Francesco Silvani (1660–?), with extracts from various works by Pietro Metastasio (1698–1782). First performance: Milan, Teatro Regio Ducale, 13 January 1744.

■ The plot revolves around the figure of the Carthaginian heroine Sofonisba, daughter of King Siface, and wife of Masinissa, who poisoned herself rather than be taken to Rome by Scipione as a prisoner of war.

PORO, or ALESSANDRO NELLE INDIE (Porus, or Alexander in India)
Opera in three acts by Christoph Willibald Gluck (1714–87), libretto by Pietro Metastasio (1698–1782). First performance: Turin, Teatro Regio, 26 December 1744.

SYNOPSIS. The central figure is Poro, an Indian king, who was defeated on several occasions by Alessandro Magno (Alexander the Great). Taken captive, he was eventually set free by the Macedonian king, who also restored his kingdom. The plot begins at the time of Poro's second defeat, concentrating on the character of Cleofide, queen of another part of India and Poro's mistress, who succeeds in winning Alessandro's favours and thus retaining her throne. Cleofide and Poro are finally reunited, thanks to the magnanimity of Alessandro, who brings the sufferings of Poro to an end with these words: '. . . He who can keep his spirit untarnished amid so many cruel strokes of fate is worthy of his throne. I give you a kingdom, a wife and your freedom.'

■ *Alessandro nelle Indie*, which Metastasio wrote in 1727, was set to music and performed many times, becoming one of the most popular of eighteenth-century libretti. It provided the basis for scores by Porpora, Hasse, Galuppi, Jommelli, Piccinni, Cimarosa and Cherubini, amongst others. Gluck's opera, one of the composer's exploratory works, was not especially successful at the time. There are, however, a number of features in it which are characteristic of the early Gluck – the male soprano, the *da capo* aria, the *recitativo secco* and the tendency to present the drama in a succession of solo arias and recitatives. Gluck modified Metastasio's text in order to achieve a more satisfactory blend of poetry and music and to give more depth to the character of Poro himself.

ERACLE (Hercules)
Dramma musicale in three acts by George Frederick Handel (1685–1759), libretto by Thomas Broughton after Sophocles and Ovid. First performance: London, King's Theatre, Haymarket, 5 January 1745.

SYNOPSIS. Deianira, Queen of Trachinia (soprano), who does not know the fate of her husband Eracle, is disturbed by the strange forebodings voiced by her son Illo (tenor) during a sacrifice, and persuades him to go out into the world to find his father. At this moment Lica (alto) arrives, announcing the return of the hero, with prisoners from Ecalia, including the princess Jole (soprano). The return of her husband arouses irrational and unfounded jealousy in Deianira's mind. She suspects that Eracle loves his beautiful captive, despite their joint denials, and resolves to make use of the shirt of Nesso, the centaur, for she believes that by persuading Eracle to wear this garment she will regain his love. The hero, however, dies as a result of the poison with which the shirt is smeared. Deianira, mad with grief and realizing that she has been the victim of a cruel ruse, curses Jole, the unwitting cause of all these misfortunes. The Priest of Zeus now arrives to confer divinity on the hero and take him to Olympus. He announces Zeus's will that Jole should marry Illo. The opera ends as the young couple rejoice and the chorus celebrates the divine status of the hero.

■ Broughton's text is derived from the *Trachiniae* of Sophocles and the ninth Book of Ovid's *Metamorphoses*. Rather than an opera, *Eracle* is Handel's only oratorio with classical as well as religious overtones, conceived for stage performance. The score, full of

Performance of an intermezzo, *a short comic opera, usually requiring two singers, given between the acts of an* opera seria. *Painting of the 18th-century Venetian School. Milan, Museo della Scala.*

dramatic passages and rich in emotional expression, still has a powerful musical effect whenever the music is performed today.

LA PRINCESSE DE NAVARRE (The Princess of Navarre)

Comédie-ballet *in three acts by Jean-Philippe Rameau (1683–1764), libretto by François-Marie Arouet (Voltaire) (1694–1778). First performance: Versailles, Théâtre de la Grande Écurie, 23 February 1745.*

SYNOPSIS. Constance, Princess of Navarre (soprano), is held prisoner by the cruel King of Castille, Don Pedre (haut-contre, i.e. high tenor). She manages to escape, taking refuge in disguise with Don Morillo (bass), a baron at whose court is a youth named Alamir (haute-contre), to whom she is immediately attracted. He is really Gaston de Foix, a scion of a family of hereditary enemies of Constance's family. Alamir, for his part, falls hopelessly in love with her, but says nothing, and for that reason rejects the advances of Sanchette (soprano), the baron's daughter. During a banquet Alamir discovers that messengers from the king have arrived to escort Constance back to imprisonment. He declares that he is ready to defend her and learns her true identity. Constance feels herself falling in love with him, but assuming his rank is too humble, and knowing that Sanchette also loves him, she prepares herself to lose him. When he reveals that he has a title and that he has played a major part in the recent defeat of Don Pedre by the French, she forgets her family's traditional feud and agrees to marry him.

■ This sumptuous opera was given to celebrate the wedding of the Dauphin Louis and Maria Teresa of Spain. It was Richelieu who persuaded Rameau and Voltaire to collaborate, hoping that the two great artists would produce a combination of comedy, opera and tragedy. The work is on the whole rather literary and it is the music itself which has survived, independently of the elaborate theatrical scheme, in the form of a few interludes.

PLATÉE, or JUNON JALOUSE

Comédie-ballet *in a prologue and three acts by Jean-Philippe Rameau (1683–1764), libretto by Jacques*

Performance of an opera seria. *Painting of the 18th-century Venetian School. Milan, Museo della Scala.*

Autreau (1656–1745) and Adrien Joseph Le Valois d'Orville. First performance: Versailles, 31 March 1745.

SYNOPSIS. Prologue. The birth of Comedy. In a Grecian vineyard Thespis (haute-contre, or high tenor), inspired by satyrs and maenads and assisted by Thalie (soprano), Amour (soprano) and Momus (bass), proposes the creation of a stage spectacle that will mend human defects and show up the absurdities of the gods themselves. The action proper takes place in a rural setting near a pool full of reeds. To vex Junon (soprano), Jupiter pretends, with the connivance of King Citheron (bass) and Mercure (haute-contre), to be in love with Platée (haute-contre, role de travesti), the silly, vain nymph of the pool. Junon, furious, watches from a hiding-place while Jupiter and Platée celebrate their wedding. In the course of the comic banquet, satyrs, naiads and peasants join in the procession, headed by a coach drawn by two frogs, in which Platée rides, her face covered with a veil. Just as Jupiter is about to swear his vow, Junon appears and, angrily hurling herself of Platée, rips off her veil and . . . falls into a helpless fit of laughter. Jupiter and Junon make their peace while Platée, a victim of general mockery, returns to her pool.

■ *Platée* occupies a unique position in eighteenth-century opera, both with regard to words and music. The libretto, written by the talented Autreau, was subsequently revised so that the opera was transformed into a genuine comic ballet. Rameau, who composed it shortly after *Dardanus*, provided it with vocal and instrumental parts of true operatic scale, and as a result was credited with creating the genre in France.

DIDONE ABBANDONATA (Dido abandoned)

Melodramma in three acts by Niccolò Jommelli (1714–74), libretto by Pietro Metastasio (1698–1782). First performance: Rome, Teatro Argentina, 28 January 1746.

SYNOPSIS. Act I. The audience chamber of Didone's palace at Carthage. Enea enters with Selene (Didone's sister), who is secretly in love with him, and Osmida (Didone's adviser). Driven by his father's ghost, he has decided, in spite of his love and gratitude, to abandon Didone, Queen of Carthage, but he has not yet dared to reveal his plans. Meanwhile Jarba, King of the Moors, arrives, disguised as Arbace, his own minister. Reminding the queen that she rejected Jarba's suit on the pretext of remaining faithful to her husband's memory, he points out that she is now planning to wed Enea, and offers on behalf of the king a peace agreement, in return for her hand and the life of Enea. Didone contemptuously refuses, and Jarba plots revenge, using Osmida, who secretly hopes to become King of Carthage, as his accomplice. Jarba instructs his minister Araspe to kill Enea but Araspe, while protesting his loyalty to the king, refuses. Jarba himself then

attacks Enea but Araspe holds him back. Araspe, however, is discovered with Jarba's dagger and is arrested by Didone. Alone with the queen, Enea tells her that he has decided to leave but, when she furiously accuses him of treachery and ingratitude, he falters and changes his mind. Act II. The royal apartments. Araspe, who has been set free, declares his love for Selene, but she in her turn confesses that she loves another man. Enea begs Didone to be merciful to Jarba; she continues to accuse him of betraying her. Selene prevents Araspe and Enea from fighting a duel. In Enea's presence, Didone pretends to agree to Jarba's proposal of marriage but, when she sees Enea's jealous anger, she goes back on her word. Jarba realizes that he has been deceived and swears vengeance. Act III. The harbour. Spurred on by the Trojans, Enea is preparing to sail when he is surprised by Jarba and his followers. Jarba challenges him to a duel, and this precipitates a general brawl between Trojans and Moors. Jarba is struck down but Enea spares his life. Selene enters and, making a last attempt to prevent Enea's departure, she admits her love for him. Now, however, he is deaf to all pleading; all his thoughts are turning to future glory. Events move to their tragic climax. After Enea's fleet has sailed, Araspe announces that Jarba's troops have set fire to the city. The palace itself is in flames but Didone still rejects the Moorish king's offer. Discovering the treachery of Osmida and the secret love of her sister for Enea, the Queen, bewailing her sad fate, hurls herself into the burning ruins of her palace. The opera ends with the appearance of the god Neptune.

■ Metastasio's text was set to music three times by Jommelli. The first version was notable for the dramatic intensity of the recitative accompanying the final suicide scene. The second version was given for the first time at the Vienna Hoftheater in December 1749. In a letter, Metastasio praised the production for its 'charm, novelty, harmony and, above all, its expressiveness'. The third version dated from the Stuttgart period, where it was first performed in February 1763. All that remains of this score is the incomplete part for harpsichord. From this, it is possible to recognize how typical of the German musical school this opera must have been, with its rich counterpoint and harmony.

DEMOFOONTE

Melodramma in three acts by Johann Adolph Hasse (1699–1783), libretto by Pietro Metastasio (1698–1782). First performance: Dresden, Hoftheater, 9 February 1748.

■ (For the plot, see *Demofoonte* by Leonardo Leo, page 45.) The story is full of twists and turns – accusations followed by repentance and pardon, unexpected recognitions and revelations – all lending themselves to dramatic confrontations but leaving little room for depth of characterization. Hasse's musical sensibility is everywhere evident; but his score fails to provide a genuine feeling of drama and does nothing to disguise the artificiality of the libretto.

SEMIRAMIDE RICONOSCIUTA (Semiramis Recognized)

Opera in three acts by Christoph Willibald Gluck (1714–87), libretto by Pietro Metastasio (1698–1782). First performance: Vienna, Burgtheater, 14 May 1748.

■ Composed for the birthday of Empress Maria Theresa, this opera compensates for the lack of historical information about the legendary Queen, Semiramide, by inventing a complicated and dramatic story of love and intrigue. (For the plot, see the opera of the same name by Jommelli, page 51.)

ARTASERSE

Melodramma in three acts by Niccolò Jommelli (1714–74), libretto by Pietro Metastasio (1698–1782). First performance: Rome, Teatro Argentina, 4 February 1749.

■ Metastasio's libretto was set to music by various composers, including Hasse (for the plot see his *Artaserse*, page 36), Gluck (p. 50) and J. C. Bach (p. 62). Jommelli anticipates the reforms of Gluck in his avoidance of the *aria da capo* and even Rossini in his fondness for the orchestral crescendo.

ACHILLE IN SCIRO

Melodramma in three acts by Niccolò Jommelli (1714–74), libretto by Pietro Metastasio (1698–1782). First performance: Vienna, Burgtheater, 30 August 1749.

■ Jommelli wrote fourteen arias for Vinci's opera of the same name, given in Rome in 1747. His own opera, however, shows the influence of the Viennese environment in which it was produced. Here Jommelli introduced orchestral pieces and an opening *Sinfonia*. Imitative arias of exceptional melodic purity contrast strikingly with the drastic intensity and expressiveness of the recitative. A revised version was also given in Rome in 1749. (For the plot see the opera of the same name by Caldara, page 45.)

ATTILIO REGOLO

Dramma in three acts by Johann Adolph Hasse (1699–1783), libretto by Pietro Metastasio (1698–1782). First performance: Dresden, Hoftheater, 12 January 1750.

SYNOPSIS. Act I. Palace of the consul Manlio. All Rome is concerned about the fate of Attilio Regolo, who has been a prisoner of the Carthaginians for five years. Attilia, his daughter, comes to Manlio, grieving for her father, accompanied by her lover Licinio, but he cannot give them any comforting news. Then she is overjoyed to hear from Barce, the African slave of her brother Publio, that Amilcare, an ambassador from Carthage, accompanied by her father, is expected to arrive soon. In the temple of Bellona, Attilio tells the Roman senators that he has promised the Carthaginians to remain their prisoner if Rome does not accept their peace proposals. To the consternation of the Senators, he advises them not to accept. Act II. A palace in Rome. Attilio Regolo faces the other principal characters of the drama, who oppose his heroic decision. Publio is the first to urge him not to go back to Carthage. Manlio and Licinio proffer the same advice. The final confrontation with his daughter affects him deeply, such is his love for her and his grief at having to leave her again. Nevertheless he has made up his mind to keep his pledge. Friends and family alike are moved by his noble, truly Roman sentiments and realize that further argument would be in vain. Barce and Amilcare, however, are astonished at his heroic attitude, which they find incomprehensible. Act III. Attilio Regolo, preparing to depart, entrusts his two children to the care of Manlio. When Publio reports that the people are rioting and clamouring for him to stay, Amilcare suggests a secret departure. Manlio and the hero's children, although broken-hearted, are proud of him as a citizen and a father, and they try to appease the crowd. It falls to Attilio himself to convince the people, reminding them of the example of ancient Rome, where a glorious death was preferable to a life of shame. The opera ends with a chorus which sings the praises of the hero as he sets sail for Carthage.

■ *Attilio Regolo* was written by Metastasio in Vienna at the request of the Empress Elisabeth for the birthday of Charles VI in 1740, but it was not given because of his unexpected death. The première took place ten years later in Dresden, at the request of Augustus III, King of Poland. Although the epic content of the play might not seem to be suited to Metastasio's poetic talents, the character of the hero is strongly drawn. In the dialogues with the other main figures of the drama, his firmness and resolution of purpose in the face of their arguments are powerfully emphasized, and his agony and turmoil as he listens to the anguished appeal of his daughter are movingly conveyed. Hasse brought out the dramatic features of the story with amazing success, and there are passages which strike even the modern listener; some of them ruggedly powerful, others deeply lyrical. Hasse's fertile invention brought to life what could otherwise have been mere convention and empty rhetoric. Although set to music by many other composers, Metastasio's libretto found in Hasse its most faithful, sensitive interpreter.

EZIO (Aetius)

Dramma musicale in three acts by Christoph Willibald Gluck (1714–87), libretto by Pietro Metastasio (1698–1782). First performance: Prague, carnival of 1750.

■ *Ezio*, like other plays by Metastasio, was set to music by numerous composers. As with all his libretti the course of events is complicated by the ideals and emotions of numerous characters, especially in the last act. Having been invited to write an opera for the new theatre in Prague managed by Locatelli, an Italian impresario, Gluck and his wife, the wealthy widow Marianne Pergin, moved from Vienna to the Bohemian capital in 1750. Here the opera was produced for the carnival of that year. Gluck reworked part of Metastasio's text, in order to make it more suitable for stage presentation and better adapted to his music, eliminating some repetitive passages, tightening up the blank verse and giving more flesh and blood to some of the characters, notably Valentiniano and Ezio. In December 1763 Gluck presented a second version of the opera at the Vienna Burgtheater, incorporating operatic innovations that he had personally just introduced. (For the plot, see *Ezio* by Handel, page 40.)

ISSIPILE (Hypsipyle)

Opera in three acts by Christoph Willibald Gluck (1714–87), libretto by Pietro Metastasio (1698–1782). First performance: Prague, carnival of 1752.

■ Metastasio's text, set by a large number of composers, tells the story of Hypsipyle, daughter of Thoas, King of Lemnos, and bride of Jason.

LE DEVIN DU VILLAGE (The Village Soothsayer)

Intermède in one act by Jean-Jacques Rousseau (1712–78) to his own libretto. First performance: Fontainebleau, Court Theatre, 18 October 1752; first performance in U.S.A.: New York City, 21 October 1790. The great success of this pastoral called forth numerous parodies including Charles Burney's The Cunning Man *(London, Drury Lane, 21 September 1766) and, eventually, Mozart's* Bastien und Bastienne *(see page 70).*

SYNOPSIS. Colette weeps at being abandoned by Colin and laments the happy times they have spent together. She decides to visit the local fortune-teller to find out whether she can expect her lover to return to her. Hesitantly, she offers a few coins and asks if there is any hope. The fortune-teller says that Colin has left her for another woman but that he still loves her; eventually he will return to her and kneel for her forgiveness. Colette would be best advised, meanwhile, to pretend she no longer loves him. When, after all, Colin does tire of the other woman, the fortune-teller informs him that it is too late. In desperation, Colin demands a magic charm but the encounter between the two young people seems unpromising for Colin. Finally, however, love triumphs. On his knees before his beloved, Colin throws down the expensive hat given to him by the other woman and puts on a simpler one handed to him by Colette. The fortune-teller and the villagers join in the general rejoicing.

■ In *Le Devin du Village*, the influence of Italian opera buffa, especially of Pergolesi's *La Serva Padrona*, given in Paris at the beginning of 1752, is very marked. The production of Pergolesi's masterpiece sparked off the celebrated 'guerre des bouffons' between the supporters of French opera (in the style of Lully and Rameau) and those of Italian opera. Rousseau sided with the latter group, explaining his reasons in his *Lettre sur la Musique Française* (November 1752) and putting them into practice by writing this *intermède*. It is charming, elegant and almost naïve, set to his own text, and it was much admired by his friend Moussard, with whom the Swiss philosopher was staying at Passy. He completed the opera in Paris, orchestrating it in three weeks, but did not dare offer it to the Opéra, after the recent failure of his *opéra-ballet*, *Les Muses Galantes*, composed in 1745. The academician Duclos volunteered to act as go-between and the opera was accepted. The court at Fontainebleau heard of the work first and it was there that it received its première. Shortly afterwards, on 1 March 1753, it was given at the Opéra with great success.

The work is especially significant in that it marks the first steps in the rapid rise of *opéra-comique* as a genre worthy of the talents of professional composers and as an international art form transcending social barriers in its humour and realism.

IL FILOSOFO DI CAMPAGNA (The Country Philosopher)

Dramma giocoso in three acts by Baldassare Galuppi, known as Il Buranello (1706–85), libretto by Carlo Goldoni (1707–93). First performance: Venice, Teatro San Samuele, 26 October 1754. First performance in U.K.: London, Haymarket Theatre, 6 January 1761. First complete performance in U.S.A.: Boston, 26 February 1960.

ORIGINAL CAST. C. Baglioni (Lesbina); G. Baglioni (Eugenia); F. Baglioni (Nardo); Masi (Rinaldo); Carattioli (Don Tritemio).

SYNOPSIS. The action takes place in Italy in the seventeenth century. Eugenia (soprano) is the charming daughter of Don Tritemio (bass), a rich citizen who has retired to live in the country. He has promised her in marriage to Nardo (baritone), a well-to-do farmer, who is regarded as a 'philosopher' because of his proud detachment from the everyday passions of ordinary folk. Eugenia is actually in love with Rinaldo (tenor), a young landowner, but her father holds Nardo's 'wisdom' in high esteem and refuses his permission for her to wed the man of her choice. Eugenia, angry at his stubbornness, enlists the help of her maid Lesbina (soprano), who is anything but disinterested in the situation. When Nardo arrives to meet his future wife, Lesbina pretends to be Eugenia and allows him to fall in love with her. When Nardo learns from Rinaldo that Eugenia is being forced by her father to marry him, but that she really loves the younger man, he puts aside all

Stage set, with orchestra and audience, at the Comédie-Italienne, Paris. 18th century. Paris, Bibliothèque de l'Opéra.

thoughts of marriage and promises protection and support for the two young people. He then learns, to his joy, that the girl he has been wooing is Lesbina. Don Tritemio is at first mad with rage to see all his carefully-laid plans thus wrecked; but even he recovers his senses and takes a new wife: Nardo's sister, who has always dreamed of having a husband with a house in town.

■ Unlike the bulk of Galuppi's operatic work, which remained well in the mainstream of *opera seria*, his few comic operas and *Il Filosofo* in particular played a decisive role in the development of the new *opera buffa*. Triumphantly received all over Europe, this, Galuppi's most popular work, was numbered among the most famous comic operas of the age, along with Pergolesi's *La serva padrona* (1733) and Piccinni's *La buona figliola* (1760). The date of the first performance is uncertain; the one mentioned above is the première coinciding with the publication of the libretto. Some writers claim that the first performance took place at the Teatro Regio Ducale in Milan in the summer of 1750, but the earliest libretto to appear in Milan dates from 1755. There is also a reference to a performance in Bologna in 1754, but in this case there is no trace even of a libretto. As frequently occurred at that period, *Il filosofo di campagna* was adapted and produced under various other titles, such as *La serva astuta* (Rome, 1757), *Il tutore burlato* (Brussels, 1759), *The guardian trick'd* (Dublin, 1762), *Der Philosoph auf dem Lande* (Vienna, 1770), *Il filosofo ignorante di campagna* (Stockholm 1780), *Il tutore e la pupilla*, etc. After the composer's death the opera was forgotten. T. Wiel discovered the score by accident in the British Museum, London, and brought it to the attention of Ermanno Wolf-Ferrari, director of the Liceo Benedetto Marcello in Venice. Wolf-Ferrari revived it for the bicentenary of the birth of Goldoni, presenting it at the Liceo on 28 February 1907, with a few cuts and alterations. In 1927 the version known as *La serva astuta* was staged in Treviso. Finally, an authentic version edited by Virgilio Mortari was performed in the garden of the Ca'Rezzonico in Venice on 28 July 1938.

IL RE PASTORE (The Shepherd King)
Dramma per musica in three acts by Christoph Willibald Gluck (1714–87), libretto by Pietro Metastasio (1698–1782). First performance: Vienna, Burgtheater, 8 December 1756.

■ Metastasio's play was set to music by several composers, most notably by Mozart in 1775 (for the plot see the opera of the same name by that composer, page 78). Gluck's setting does not appear to have suited the melodramatic unity and intensity of Metastasio's libretto.

ZENOBIA
Opera in three acts by Niccolò Piccinni (1728–1800), libretto by Pietro Metastasio (1698–1782). First performance: Naples, Teatro San Carlo, 18 December 1756.

SYNOPSIS. The story revolves around Zenobia, daughter of Mithridates, king of Armenia, and wife of Radamistus. Unjustly accused of being unfaithful, she is the embodiment of conjugal loyalty, triumphant over all manner of snares and temptations.

■ The opera was composed after Piccinni had left his native Bari and settled in Naples. Here his works met with considerable popular success, despite the competition of established local composers.

ALESSANDRO NELLE INDIE (Alexander in India)
Opera in three acts by Niccolò Piccinni (1728–1800), based on the play by Pietro Metastasio (1698–1782). First performance: Rome, Teatro Argentina, 21 January 1758.

■ The opera was revived twice: in Florence (1776) and in Naples (1792). The Naples production, in which the opera was conceived on a larger scale and more firmly structured, achieved much more success. (For the plot see the opera of the same name by Gluck, page 53.)

CECCHINA, or LA BUONA FIGLIUOLA (Cecchina, or The Good-natured Girl)
Opera in three acts by Niccolò Piccinni (1728–1800), libretto by Carlo Goldoni (1707–93) after Samuel Richardson's Pamela. *First performance: Rome, Teatro delle Dame, 6 February 1760. First performance in U.K.: London, Haymarket Theatre, 25 November 1766; in U.S.A.: Madison, Wisconsin, 6 January 1967. A notable revival was also given at Bari, Italy, 7 February 1928, to celebrate the bicentenary of the composer's birth.*

SYNOPSIS. Cecchina (soprano) is a poor girl who has grown up since childhood in the house of the marquis of Conchiglia (tenor), where she carries out simple domestic duties. She is in love with the marquis and he with her. The match does not win the approval of Lucinda (soprano), sister to the marquis, who fears that the girl's humble origins will be an obstacle to her own marriage to the knight Armidoro (soprano). Therefore, she does everything possible to prevent Cecchina's love for her brother reaching fruition, exploiting the jealous feelings of the two maids, both of whom spread lies about Cecchina's virtue. Matters are brought to a head by the arrival of the cuirassier Tagliaferro (baritone). He has been sent by a German baron to find his daughter, abandoned as a baby after his wife's death during a war. It is soon clear that Cecchina is none other than the young baroness Marianna. There can now be no objection to the wedding of the marquis and the girl or to that of Lucinda and Armidoro.

■ Piccinni responded more eagerly to comedy (of which *Cecchina* is a splendid example) than to any other theatrical genre. With the help of Goldoni's fresh, realistic libretto the composer breathed life into the traditional comic types. There are also tender, almost sentimental passages which, together with a new naturalistic style of recitative, give his opera a greater measure of human warmth and feeling. As is common in this new, emerging genre, no opportunity is lost to parody the portentousness of *opera seria*. Yet, there is considerable advance in musical technique as is shown by the extension and elaboration of the finale of each act. Piccinni is reputed to have composed the opera in only eighteen days. It was enormously successful and continued to be so until the end of the nineteenth century. In Rome it was so famous that local shops and taverns and even dress styles and wines were named after it (*alla Cecchina*).

L'IVROGNE CORRIGÉ, or LE MARIAGE DU DIABLE (The Reformed Drunkard, or The Devil's Marriage)

Opéra comique in two acts by Christoph Willibald Gluck (1714–87), libretto by Louis Anseaume (1759), based on La Fontaine's fable L'Ivrogne en Enfer. *First performance: Vienna, Burgtheater, April 1760. First performance in U.K.: London, Birkbeck College, 12 March 1931 (as* The Devil's Wedding*); in U.S.A.: Hartford, Connecticut, 26 February 1945 (as* The Marriage of the Devil*).*

SYNOPSIS. Mathurin, a drunkard, wants to marry his niece Colette to Lucas, his ever-faithful drinking companion. Colette loves Cléon, and the couple, encouraged by Mathurin's wife, Mathurine, concoct a plan to foil this arrangement. One night, when Mathurin and Lucas are drunk and sound asleep, the young people drag them down to the cellar; and there, with the help of some actor friends, they simulate a scene in hell. Mathurin and Lucas, waking up in this strange place, soon come to believe that they have been transported to the lower regions, surrounded as they are by the terrifying figures of masked persons, ghosts and devils. 'Pluton', actually Cléon himself, commences by judging Mathurin's soul, yet, heeding the pleas of his wife, he announces that he will be merciful. However, Mathurin must apologize to his wife for the drunken life he has led and for the terrible way he has treated her; he must also permit his niece to marry Cléon. A notary is conveniently on hand to seal the marriage contract of the young couple; Cléon throws off his disguise and the farce draws to a conclusion. The young lovers are united and Mathurin, still trembling, vows that he will drink no more and terminate his empty friendship with Lucas.

■ *L'Ivrogne Corrigé* is, along with *La Cythère Assiégée*, composed the previous year, Gluck's most interesting and amusing comic opera. Although not a major work, the score contains many graceful and tongue-in-cheek passages which allow the composer to break away from the conventional Metastasian pattern

of historical and mythological characters and branch out in the direction of new melodic and stylistic experiments.

L'AMANTE DI TUTTE (The Universal Lover)

Opera in three acts by Baldassare Galuppi, known as Il Buranello (1706–85), libretto by Ageo Liteo (a pseudonym of Antonio Galuppi, the composer's son). First performance: Venice, Teatro Giustiniani di San Moisè, 15 November 1760.

SYNOPSIS. Old Don Orazio is jealous of his wife Lucinda. He goes into hiding in the home of the farmer Mingone, pretending to have been called away to town. Count Eugenio, reputedly a lover of all womankind, appears together with the down-at-heel, arrogant Marchese Canoppio and Donna Clarice, a snobbish and affected woman. Lucinda, who has taken advantage of her husband's absence, invites them for dinner, but when they are seated at the table, Don Orazio bursts in unexpectedly and drives them all out. But when he cannot find his coachman the plot thickens. Lucinda threatens to leave. Meanwhile Eugenio flirts with all the women, including Dorina, the chambermaid, who begs him for assurances of love. Orazio catches him *in flagrante* both with his own wife and with Donna Clarice. He threatens bloodshed but finally agrees to pardon everyone. The farmer Mingone, who had hoped to wed Dorina, having witnessed these alarming events, decides to go back on his word and renounce his marriage plans.

■ *L'Amante di Tutte* was highly successful, especially in Italy. It was given under various other titles such as *Il matrimonio in villa*, *La moglie bizarra* and *Il vecchio geloso*.

ARMIDA

Opera in one act by Tommaso Traetta (1727–79), libretto by Giacomo Durazzo (1717–94) and Giovanni Ambrogio Migliavacca. First performance: Vienna, Burgtheater, 3 January 1761.

SYNOPSIS. The opera is based on Tasso's legend and, more directly, on the *Armide* of Philippe Quinault. For the plot see *Armide* by Lully, page 24.

■ The opera, one of Traetta's most successful works, made his reputation and launched him on his career. He owed his good fortune in large measure to Durazzo, who presented him to the Viennese court and introduced him to the cultural circles of the Austrian capital. Here, among others, he met Gluck, whom he revered most, and whose reforms Traetta's music anticipates to a certain extent. Yet it must be said, in all justice, that until about 1762 it was Gluck who followed Traetta's musical theories. Gluck's operatic masterpieces, particularly *Orfeo ed Euridice*, were inspired, but the latter work shows the influence of

Traetta's *Armida* and *Ifigenia*, wherein Italian and French developments are united in a new, experimental fashion. In *Armida*, there is a dramatic use of the chorus and expansion of full-scale instrumental movements quite unusual before this date. *Armida* was, in due course, revised by the composer and given in its new form in Venice at the Teatro San Salvatore on 27 May 1767.

ARTASERSE
Opera in three acts by Johann Christian Bach (1735–82), libretto by Pietro Metastasio (1698–1782). First performance: Turin, Teatro Regio, 26 December 1761.

■ Metastasio's text had already been set to music by other composers, including Hasse (for the plot see the opera of the same name by that composer, page 36) and Gluck. This was J. C. Bach's first opera, composed in Italy while he was organist at the Duomo in Milan. Having been commissioned to write a work for the Teatro Regio in Turin, Bach visited Parma and Reggio Emilia to find singers capable of doing justice to Metastasio's play. At the first performance, in the presence of the Sardinian royal family, the opera was enthusiastically received, and its success spurred the composer to write other operas, first in Italy, later in London. By virtue of its literary quality and numerous dramatic and emotional passages, Metastasio's play is considered his masterpiece; yet Bach's opera shows signs of immaturity and has seldom been given since. The ballet music in it was composed by Giuseppe Antonio Le Messier.

ARTAXERXES
Opera in three acts by Thomas Augustine Arne (1710–78), libretto by the composer after Pietro Metastasio (1698–1782). First performance: London, Covent Garden, 2 February 1762. First performance in the U.S.A.: New York, 31 January 1828 (but orchestrated by C. E. Horn).

ORIGINAL CAST. Brent, Tanducci, Peretti, Beard, Mattocks, Thomas.

■ This, Arne's most famous work, based on the Metastasio text also set by J. C. Bach (see previous entry) is possibly the most significant English opera of the eighteenth century. It occasioned the first presentation to the English public of an opera in the Italian style, with recitatives in place of spoken parts. The role of Mandane (soprano) was written expressly for Arne's pupil Charlotte Brent, to whose remarkable singing the opera in part owed its success. This success is not surprising, for the work is a unique blend of Italianate display, gallant stylishness and English lyricism. After its première at Covent Garden, the opera was revised by Arne, with the text translated into English and produced several years later at the Theatre Royal, Drury Lane, London. The new version was subsequently given in Edinburgh and in various European

Frontispiece for Gluck's Orfeo ed Euridice, *in the Paris edition of 1774.*

cities and along with Arne's *Love in a Village* remained popular for more than fifty years.

ORFEO ED EURIDICE (Orpheus and Eurydice)
Azione teatrale *in three acts by Christoph Willibald Gluck (1714–87), libretto by Ranieri Calzabigi (1714–95). First performance: Vienna, Burgtheater, 5 October 1762. First performance in U.K.: London, King's Theatre Haymarket, 7 April, 1770, with additional music by J. C. Bach and P. A. Guglielmi. First performance in the U.S.A.: Charleston, South Carolina, 24 June 1794 (see Sonneck,* Early Opera in America, *p. 206).*

ORIGINAL CAST. Gaetano Guadagni, Marianna Bianchi, Lucia Clavereau. A new version, described as *tragédie-opéra ou drame héroïque*, with revisions to the score and a French text was given in the Paris Opéra, 2 August 1774. First performance in U.K.: London, Covent Garden, 27 June 1860 (Berlioz's version, but sung in Italian); in U.S.A.: New York, Winter Garden, 25 May 1863 (in English).

SYNOPSIS. Act I. Beside a tomb in a grotto, shaded by laurel and cypress, shepherds and nymphs mourn the death of Eurydice (soprano), wife of Orpheus (alto in first version, later tenor). He wishes to be alone with his grief, takes leave of his companions and sadly announces himself ready to go even to Hades in order to find his loved one, without whom he can no longer live. Amor (soprano), Jove's messenger, appears. Touched by his grief, the father of the gods allows the musician to go down to the kingdom of the dead. If his singing can melt the heart of the infernal demons, he can have Eurydice back, although one important condition is imposed: while leading his wife back to the sunlight, Orpheus must not turn round to look at her, nor must he reveal this secret condition to her; should he break his word, he will lose Eurydice for ever. Overjoyed, although aware how difficult it will be for him to keep this promise, Orpheus sets off on his journey. Act II, Scene I. In the shadowy haunts of Tartarus, beyond the river Cocytus, Furies and Shades perform a gruesome dance and try to block the passage of the daring mortal. The singing of Orpheus is so sweet, as he tells of his desperate yearning, that the infernal spirits gradually fade away, and he continues his journey. Scene II. Having reached the Elysian Fields, Orpheus stands amazed at the beauty of the scene, admiring the green woods and meadows. Here Blessed Spirits, heroes and heroines, live serenely without pain, and a radiant and exquisite dance is performed before him. He is unable to enjoy their happiness, however, because his only desire is to find Eurydice. Eventually she is led before him. Without looking at her, he takes her by the hand and guides her on the path back to earth. Act III. Scene I. Having led Eurydice through a tortuous maze, Orpheus is anxious to leave Hades as quickly as possible, but Eurydice, having recovered from the initial shock of finding herself alive once more, cannot understand her husband's strange behaviour and bombards him with questions. How did he reach the kingdom of the dead? Why does he not give her a single glance? Does he no longer love her? Orpheus cannot restrain himself when she confesses that she would rather die than live without his love. He turns round and, at the same instant, Eurydice falls dead at his feet. In despair, he calls out her name, crying that he is ready to die so as to be with her (*'Che farò senza Euridice?'*). Once more Amor intervenes. The gods, greatly moved, are prepared to give Eurydice back to her husband so that the two may once more live together. Scene II. Before the temple dedicated to Amor, Orpheus and Eurydice, surrounded by heroes, heroines, shepherds and nymphs, celebrate Eurydice's return to life and the victory of love over death (*'Trionfi, Amore'*).

■ In 1761 Gluck met the Italian writer and adventurer Ranieri Calzabigi in Vienna. The meeting turned out to be a landmark in the history of opera, heralding a fundamental 'reform' of the genre. Metastasio and Hasse had been the first operatic influences on Gluck but already by 1758 he was writing music for *opéras-comiques* depicting human characters in an altogether new vein. Gluck was convinced that eighteenth-century opera was sadly flawed, smothered by the vocal excesses of singers and reduced to a succession of melodies that had little or no relevance to the words concerned. In Calzabigi he found a poet who gave him

the chance, with an Italian libretto, to devise a musical score embodying totally new principles of expression in 'energetic and touching music' (the composer in a letter to the *Mercure de France*, 1781). According to both the composer and the librettist, opera should ideally rely for dramatic impact on naturalism, stripped of the empty refinements which were so much to the fore in Metastasian opera – the stock situations, the arias laden with metaphor. With the object of putting this theory into practice and using his experience acquired in the composition of comic-opera numbers in the later 1750s, Gluck filled the score with a succession of melodies notable for their simplicity and close adherence to the words and the action. He did away with the traditional distinctioon between recitative and aria, combining them to create a single, harmonious musical entity. The orchestral writing, never commonplace, is perfectly adapted to action and situation, and frequently plays a completely independent role in expressing moods and emotions, apart from providing accompaniment for the voices. *Recitativo accompagnato* is a strong factor in creating this new dramatic fluency. As Massimo Mila has written: 'For the first time eighteenth-century *opera seria* found the composer faithful to the sentiments expressed in the play, giving strong musical shape to the characters and reflecting the simple, solemn spirit of Hellenism in interpreting the ancient myths.' Even though the arias and duets in *Orfeo* are sometimes inferior to those of contemporary Italian composers, notably (the later work of) Piccinni, with whom Gluck had engaged in a protracted dispute, there can be no denying the

Some representatives of the 'Italian style of bel canto'. 18th-century engraving.

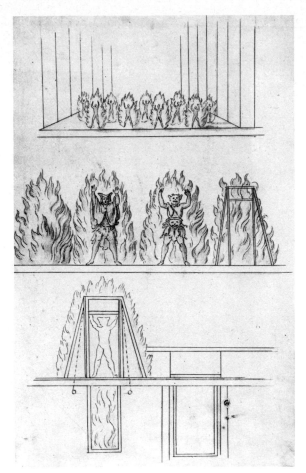

Sketch for a machine to make devils appear on stage. Watercolour by Jean Bérain. Paris, Bibliothèque de l'Opéra.

concision, the dramatic feeling, the unity of conception and the genius of orchestral writing.

The première in Vienna with the *castrato* Guadagni as Orpheus was followed by some hundred repeat performances but the opera was not an unequivocal success, for its novelty was not to everyone's taste and inevitably strong feelings were aroused amongst the devotees of Metastasio. At the second performance the Empress Maria Theresa presented to Calzabigi, chamber councillor to Her Majesty's Exchequer in Vienna, a ring set with a huge diamond; to Gluck she gave a purse with one hundred ducats. A few years later, the composer staged *Iphigénie en Aulide* in Paris. The enormous success of this opera induced him to revise the score of *Orfeo*, adapting it to a French text written by Pierre-Louis Moline, elaborating the vocal parts and adding some new dances (Première, Paris, Opéra, 2 August 1774). In the revised version, the role of Orpheus was given to a tenor. Modern producers have favoured another approach in giving the part of Orpheus to a female contralto, a voice which suits the pure and elegiac melodies characteristic of the opera.

SOFONISBA

Opera in three acts by Tommaso Traetta (1727–79), libretto by Mattia Verazi. First performance: Mannheim, Hoftheater, 4 November 1762.
(For the plot, see Gluck's opera of the same name, page 53.)

ORIONE, or DIANA VENDICATA (Orion, or Diana Avenged)

Opera in three acts by Johann Christian Bach (1735–82), libretto by G. G. Bottarelli. First performance: London, Haymarket Theatre, 19 February 1763.

SYNOPSIS. The opera centres on the deeds of Orione, the mythical giant hunter, to whom the Greeks gave a place among the stars. Aurora (Eos), Goddess of the Dawn, is captivated by his strength and beauty but eventually Artemide (Diana), Goddess of the Hunt, jealous of the handsome hunter's skill, transfixes him with her arrow.

■ This was one of the composer's most notable works and the first that he composed in London, where he was patronized by Queen Charlotte. It exemplifies his view of opera as 'a refined musical treat' to be played with dramatic illusion 'without taking it seriously' (C. S. Terry, *John Christian Bach*, 2nd ed., London, 1967). At the first performance both King George III and his Queen were present. The opera with its flowing and captivating melodies and its euphonious orchestration was a great success, being 'extremely applauded by a very numerous audience' (Burney, IV, p. 481) and was often repeated. Significantly, for the first time clarinets were included in an English operatic orchestra. The work fell into neglect in the nineteenth century and, unfortunately, does not appear in modern repertoires.

ALESSANDRO NELLE INDIE (Alexander in India)

Dramma per musica *in three acts by Antonio Sacchini (1730–86), libretto by Pietro Metastasio (1698–1782). First performance: Venice, Teatro San Salvatore, Spring 1763.*

■ The story tells of the generous action of Alessandro towards Poro, an Indian King. The text was one of the most famous of eighteenth-century plays. Sacchini's note on the score ('entirely new' music) indicated that the play had already often been scored by other composers. An amended version was performed in Naples, 22 May 1768. (For the plot see the opera by Gluck, page 53.)

IFIGENIA IN TAURIDE (Iphigenia in Tauris)

Opera in three acts by Tommaso Traetta (1727–79), libretto by Marco Coltellini (1719–77). First performance: Vienna, Schönbrunn Hoftheater, 4 October 1763. First performance in U.K.: according to Burney (IV, p. 505), London 'at Mrs. Blaire's lately' (i.e. before 1789).

SYNOPSIS. The story has its source in the *Iphigenia in Tauris* of Euripides and tells of Iphigenia, daughter of Agamemnon and Clytemnestra, who is condemned by her father to be sacrificed to propitiate the goddess Artemis before the Trojan War. Artemis, however, mercifully substitutes a hart on the altar, saving the girl's life and then sends her secretly to Tauris where, as priestess, she is compelled to offer every stranger to that shore to Artemis in sacrifice. When Orestes, her brother, arrives, after murdering Clytemnestra, their mother, and Aegisthus, their step-father, she is able to save him from the sacrifice which awaits him.

■ Recent authorities have suggested that this *Ifigenia* preceded Gluck's *Orfeo* and that it was first given in 1761. It was the first of the composer's operas to incorporate his principles of reform – principles which to some extent influenced Gluck himself (although as applied by Gluck such reforms were of greater significance than those of Traetta). Thus there is an abundance of fresh musical ideas. The aria is partially freed from its schematic form; there is a large amount of dramatic declamation and heightening of orchestral coloration and several large choruses emphasize the grandeur of the tragedy. The opera was successfully given at many European courts and was performed in Florence on 21 March 1782 as an oratorio entitled *Sant'Ifigenia in Etiopia*.

EGERIA

Festa teatrale in one act by Johann Adolph Hasse (1699–1783), libretto by Pietro Metastasio (1698–1782). First performance: Vienna, Burgtheater, 24 April 1764.

SYNOPSIS. On a hillside near Rome, before the fountain of the nymph Egeria, Venere (Venus), Marte (Mars) and Apollo meet in a sacred wood dedicated to the nymph to seek her advice in the choice of a king who will govern wisely. The gods are unable to agree among themselves. Venere is in favour of a peace-loving monarch whereas Marte prefers a warlike sovereign. They both advance good reasons; she detests war and its horrors, while he nurses contempt for the gentle activities of peace. Apollo now intervenes in the dispute. If all men were to live in peace, how, he demands, would he be able to sing the praises of brave heroes? Marte ironically points out that if Venere has her way and a pacific king is placed on the throne, the German people will become soft and impotent. Egeria, having listened to the arguments of the contenders, now proposes her solution. Clearly the answer is to find a peace-loving ruler who will, if necessary, be prepared for war; and who better fitted than Joseph of Hapsburg, who combines these qualities?

■ Metastasio was given the opportunity to write this work for the coronation of Joseph II as Holy Roman Emperor, the text making explicit reference to the occasion in several places. Although not one of his best scores, Hasse succeeded in achieving a happy balance of German and Italian musical styles. The sentiment is measured and refined; the music a constant and solid support to the text.

SEMIRAMIDE RICONOSCIUTA (Semiramis Recognized)

Melodramma in three acts by Antonio Sacchini (1730–86), libretto by Pietro Metastasio (1698–1782). First performance: Rome, Teatro Argentina, Summer 1764.

■ The opera, well-received at its first performance, focuses on the legendary figure of Semiramis, queen of Babylon. Sacchini was a fellow student in Naples of Piccinni and Jommelli and was later to move to Paris, where he was described as 'a graceful, elegant and judicious composer' by Burney. (For the plot see the opera of same name by Jommelli, page 51.)

TELEMACCO, or L'ISOLA DI CIRCE (Telemachus, or The Island of Circe)

Opera in three acts by Christoph Willibald Gluck (1714–87), libretto by Marco Coltellini (1719–77), from the play by Carlo Sigismondo Capece. First performance: Vienna, Burgtheater, 30 January 1765.

SYNOPSIS. The story tells of the brave hero Telemacco, who manages to rescue his father, Ulisse, from the seductive clutches of Circe, aided in his task by a beautiful girl of unknown origin, Asteria, and by prince Merione, son of the Cretan king Idomeneo. Circe, compelled to free Ulisse, conjures up spirits from hell to show Telemacco, in a nightmare, the death of his mother. Ulisse shrewdly realizes that this is one of Circe's tricks, and he eventually manages to escape from the island with his son and with Merione and Asteria (who turns out to be the prince's sister). Circe can do no more than curse Ulisse and transform her island into a desert.

■ *Telemacco* is a strange opera. Appearing after *Orfeo* and before *Alceste*, it does not appear to be much influenced by the spirit of 'reform' that characterized these works. Yet it does contain both the bold simplicity which was later to endear him to Parisian audiences and other notable innovations. The libretto was based on an older play with music by Carlo Sigismondo Capece, and was performed in Rome in 1718 to a score by Alessandro Scarlatti. This version was adapted by Marco Coltellini, who had a similar view of theatre as Ranieri Calzabigi. The work was divided into two acts (a form previously allowed only in *opera buffa*), and Gluck's score introduces a number of new ideas, especially in the 'instructions to singers', the treatment of the chorus and the dances.

LA CANTARINA (The Songstress)

Intermezzo in musica in two acts by Joseph Haydn

Throne room with cloud effects for Gluck's Alceste. *Scenery by François Joseph Bélanger for the first Parisian production in 1776. Paris, Bibliothèque de l'Opéra.*

(1732–1809), libretto by Carlo Goldoni (1707–93). First performance: Schloss Eszterháza, carnival of 1767.

SYNOPSIS. Don Ettore (soprano, rôle de travesti) tells the lady Gasperina (soprano), the ward of Apollonia (soprano), the songstress of the title, that his master, the marquis Pelegrio (tenor?) is about to visit her. Don Ettore, who loves the lady, is persuaded by her to assume the guise of her brother. Actually she loves him in return, but since he is penniless, she has too much common sense to reject a wealthy suitor. The marquis arrives to court Gasperina and offer her a ring. Not being sure of her feelings, however, he withholds the gift, on the pretext of wishing to give her a more beautiful one. Then, disguised as a German soldier, he goes through the courtship ritual again. Gasperina once more accepts a ring and is fobbed off with the promise of a more valuable one. In this way Don Pelegrio manages to discover her true feelings. The same procedure is repeated, with Pelegrio disguised as a Gascon. In the meantime, Don Ettore comes into a sizeable inheritance. Perhaps Gasperina will now marry him; and, indeed, he has little difficulty in winning her assent. The marquis, disguised as an astrologer, returns once more with his servant. Despite Ettore's protests, she shows herself ready to accept the proffered ring. The astrologer reads the lady's hand and mocks her. Eventually the two lovers confess their true feelings to Don Pelegrio, who generously hands over the ring to Gasperina and the closing quartet celebrates a general reconciliation.

■ The opera was written one year before *Lo Speziale* (see p. 69) and was in some senses a preparation for this work. The choice of a libretto by Goldoni was not accidental. *La Cantarina* was, in fact, purely Italian in influence, and Haydn adhered completely to the *opera buffa* style. Haydn said 'I prefer to see the humorous side of life' and it is the wit and humour of ordinary folk that his brilliant music spotlights. Here he prefers ensembles to *da capo* arias and swiftly-moving action to detailed characterizations.

APOLLO ET HYACINTHUS, or HYACINTHI METAMORPHOSIS (Apollo and Hyacinth, or The Metamorphosis of Hyacinth)

Commedia *by Wolfgang Amadeus Mozart (1756–1791), Latin text by Rufinus Widl. First performance: Salzburg, University, 13 May 1767. First performance in U.K.: London, Fortune Theatre, 24 January 1955.*

SYNOPSIS. Oebalus rages against Apollo, unjustly accusing him of murdering his son Hyacinthus. Zephyrus, the real murderer, is transformed by the god into a breeze and Hyacinthus becomes a flower. In this way Oebalus is reconciled to Apollo, who marries Melia, Oebalus's daughter, in return.

■ This is not really an opera, but a series of nine intermezzi, for 2 sopranos, 2 altos, tenor and bass, designed to be performed with Widl's play *Clementia Croesi*. The work, one of several dramatic works written in the composer's early years was performed when he was just over eleven years old. The music shows the influence of Ernst Eberlin and indicates how important the Salzburg baroque tradition was to the young Mozart's development.

ALCESTE

Dramma per musica *in three acts by Christoph Willibald Gluck (1714–87), based on the tragedy* Alcestis *by Euripides. First performance: Vienna, Burgtheater, 26 December 1767. The French version with the text adapted and translated by F. L. G. Lebland du Roullet and important changes to the score, was first given at the Académie Royale, Paris, on 23 April 1776. This is the version that has frequently been revived ever since. First complete performance in U.K.: London, 30 April 1795 (a selection was previously given in London, King's Theatre, 10 April 1780, with Bernasconi singing the part of Alceste, which Gluck had written for her). First performance in U.S.A.: Wellesley, Mass., 11 March 1938.*

ORIGINAL CAST. Antonia Bernasconi, Giuseppe Luigi Tibaldi, Domenico Poggi, with Antonio Salieri at the harpsichord.

SYNOPSIS. Act I, Scene I. The action occurs some years after the Trojan War. Before the royal palace of Pharae in Thessaly, the people call on the gods to cure

18th-century engraving for Gluck's Alceste.

the illness of their king, Admète (tenor); but a herald announces from the terraces that the king is actually close to death. Alceste (soprano) comes down into the crowd with her children. Touched by the people's concern for her husband, she gives vent to her grief, asking the gods to show pity and declaring that she is prepared to offer sacrifices to Apollon. Scene II. Inside the temple of Apollo, the High Priest (bass) invokes the god. Suddenly, as the temple is shaken as if by an earthquake and flames leap up from the altar, the voice of the oracle is heard, to the terror of all present. It declares that the king will die unless someone is sacrificed in his place. Left alone, despairing and torn between love for her husband and tender feelings for her children, Alceste finally offers to give her life to save her husband. The High Priest, interpreting the will of the gods, tells her that they accept her sacrifice and that when the day draws to a close she must descend to Hades. Act II. In a room of the royal palace, Evander (tenor) and some of the citizens rejoice at Admète's recovery. The king is saddened to learn that his miraculous cure is due to the sacrifice of a generous stranger. He does not yet know that the victim is his own wife; but seeing signs of distress on her face, he immediately questions her, asking for the name of the person to whom he owes his life, until the queen finally confesses the truth. In desperation, Adète exclaims that if this is what the gods demand, he too will suffer the same fate as his loyal wife. Alceste, in love and aware that she is loved in return, feels the torment of the fate that awaits her. In vain the citizens beg her to abandon her plan; she is determined to resign herself to the will of the gods. Act III. Scene I. In front of the royal palace Hercules learns from the crowd of Alceste's fate and swears to rescue her. Scene II. Alceste has reached the entrance to Hades, but is driven back by the spirits of the Underworld, for the oracle has decreed that she must wait until night falls. Admète joins her, having decided to kill himself as well, so as not to be separated from her. Thanatos (bass) appears, accompanied by infernal spirits, and declares that only one of the pair shall enter Hades. As Alceste and Admète express their desire to die for each other, Hercules appears and confronts the shades, who fade away before him. The son of Jupiter has thus violated the decrees of fate. Apollon (baritone) knows that love, both for gods and men, is the greatest of blessings. He points to the royal pair as the perfect example of conjugal love, decrees that both shall live and exhorts the people of Pharae to celebrate the miraculous event.

■ *Alceste* was the second occasion on which Gluck and Calzabigi collaborated, and it marked a further advance in the musical development of the 'reforming' composer after the bold experiments of *Orfeo ed Euridice*. In the dedication of the first version of the opera to Leopold II, Gluck outlined (although the text of the famous preface was probably written by Calzabigi) the principles that had guided him throughout and his words are as significant in the context of eighteenth-century opera as Wagner's were in the nineteenth century. It was his intention to restore to opera the simple purity of expression that had inspired the members of the Camerata de' Bardi (the Florentine Camerata). The need to make the stage action ring true meant that there must be the closest possible harmony between the music and the libretto so that, in a sense, music should 'serve poetry'. This was an attitude wholly opposed to the ideas of the contemporary Italian opera, which gave absolute priority to pure musical beauty, quite independently of literary content. It entailed the abolition, not only of superfluous ornamentation and embellishment on the part of the singers, but also of virtually all current conventions, such as repetitions. Less emphasis was placed on the distinction between aria and recitative, which, if not disappearing completely, were mingled, by means of expressive declamation, with the accompaniment either of orchestra or harpsichord. In short, all idiosyncratic gestures which might arrest the action and hinder the audience's appreciation of the work were rejected. The opera was tremendously successful in Vienna, and to a lesser extent even in Italy. For the later Paris versions, Gluck made a thorough revision of the score, involving a number of scene changes, a rewritten finale, additional chorus and a new character, that of Hercules. Despite this, the reception was not altogether favourable and considerable energy was expended in partisan debates, Gluck versus Piccinni – a conflict which came to a head in 1777, when both composers were deliberately given the libretto of Quinault's *Roland* to work on.

FETONTE (Phaethon)

Dramma per musica *in three acts by Niccolò Jommelli (1714–74), libretto by Mattia Verazi. First performance: Ludwigsburg, Hoftheater, 11 February 1768.*

SYNOPSIS. The events described in the libretto are taken from the second Book of Ovid's *Metamorphoses*. Fetonte, son of Il Sole and Climene (soprano), asks his father for evidence of his divine parentage, which has been challenged by Epafo (bass), King of Egypt, and persuades him to be allowed to drive the chariot of the sun for one day. Unable to control the impetuous horses, he sets fire to heaven and earth. Il Sole (soprano/tenor) punishes the reckless charioteer by destroying him with a lightning flash and hurling his body into the River Eridanus. Fetonte's mother, Climene (a character to whom Verazi gave some prominence in his libretto), throws herself into the sea to die like her son, while Libia (contralto), the girl loved by Fetonte, dies of grief.

■ The opera was composed while Jommelli was Court Conductor in Stuttgart and to celebrate the birthday of Charles Duke of Württemberg. The work, with its complex but tightly-knit structure, was a success, achieving Jommelli's ambition of discarding melodic elaboration for its own sake in favour of a deeper vein of dramatic expression. *Fetonte* shows Jommelli's sixteen years' experience in Stuttgart and the influence of French opera in its frequent use of choral and orchestral passages, as well as in extra-musical elements such as pantomime, which were much cultivated in Stuttgart. The opera, of which Jommelli had written an earlier version, based on a libretto by Villati, which was performed in Stuttgart in 1753, was preceded by an overture of a cohesiveness which demonstrates Jommelli's influence on the rise of the *Sinfonia*, linked to a powerfully expressive opening scene, which evokes the dramatic atmosphere maintained throughout. Jommelli had, by now, moved so far from the Metastasian operatic ideal that the poet criticized him for his artistic treatment of the orchestra and his neglect of sheer vocal power. Moreover, Mozart's comment in writing to his sister from Naples is penetrating: 'his style is beautiful, but too clever and old-fashioned for the theatre'.

LE HURON (The Huron)

Opéra-comique *in two acts by André Grétry (1741–1813), libretto by Jean François Marmontel (1723–99), based on Voltaire's story* L'Ingénu. *First performance: Paris, Comédie-Italienne, 20 August 1768.*

SYNOPSIS. Square in a French village. Gilotin, son of Le Bailli, meets the daughter of Saint-Yves and tells her that their respective parents have decided that the two shall marry. The girl refuses, for she does not love Gilotin and therefore cannot submit to her father's wishes. While Gilotin tries to persuade her, a stranger appears. He is a Huron Indian who has just arrived in Europe. He offers the girl a gift of game he has just caught. The two fall in love immediately. Gilotin does not fear his rival, a stranger without family or status, for his own father is wealthy and important. But Abbot Kernabon and his sister recognize the young man as the son of their brother who died with his wife during an expedition against the Red Indian tribe of Hurons

The cathedral and the archbishop's palace in Salzburg at the end of the 18th century.

(literally 'ruffians' or 'bristle-heads'). The youth's real name is Ercule de Kernabon, and now that he is discovered his uncle endeavours to persuade him to adopt the dress style and behaviour of the society in which he now finds himself, although they are totally alien to him. He is impatient to marry the girl he loves and will not be bound by convention, which includes the customary rites associated with the marriage ceremony. His attitude angers Saint-Yves who, taking advantage of the Huron's absence (he has gone to defend the village against an English attack), places his daughter in a convent. The Huron is grief-stricken but fortunately the Abbot intervenes and the girl is freed from the convent, thanks to an officer who admires the young man's courage. In the end Saint-Yves has to give in.

■ *Le Huron* was Grétry's first major success. The music was dedicated to the Comte de Creutz, as recognition for the favours bestowed by this wealthy patron on the composer after his arrival in Paris. Grétry's debut in the theatre stemmed from a meeting with Voltaire in Geneva. There he had requested Voltaire to give him a text to set to music and, although the latter had refused, realizing perhaps that librettos were not his forte, Grétry was eventually satisfied with one of the great writer's stories, as a basis for Marmontel's libretto. The action which contrasts the Huron's innocence with the artificiality of French manners is early evidence of the impact of Rousseau's ideas about the 'noble savage'.

LO SPEZIALE (The Apothecary)
Dramma giocoso *in three acts by Joseph Haydn (1732–1809), libretto by Carlo Goldoni (1707–93). First performance: Schloss Eszterháza, Autumn 1768. First performance in the U.K.: London, King's Theatre, Hammersmith, 3 September 1925. First performance in U.S.A.: New York, 16 March 1926.*

SYNOPSIS. Act I. Young Mengone (tenor), in love with Grilletta (soprano), finds a job with Sempronio (tenor), a village apothecary, so that he can be near his mistress, who is Sempronio's ward. Without any knowledge of chemistry, the new apprentice prepares medicines, mixing all sorts of ingredients at random. Meanwhile, Sempronio reads his paper. Among other news, he sees an item about a guardian marrying his ward; so he decides to wed Grilletta. There now arrives Volpino (soprano), an elegant and rich gentleman, who is also in love with Grilletta. He manages to find an excuse for sending Mengone away, but when the latter returns it is Volpino who finds himself humiliated, for Grilletta openly mocks him. When Sempronio is out, the girl encourages Mengone to ask for permission to marry her. Sempronio comes back and settles down to his books again while Mengone supervises the medicaments. The apothecary, announcing he will marry Grilletta without further delay, surprises the young couple exchanging kisses and angrily sends them to their respective rooms. Act II. When Volpino offers Sempronio the chance to become apothecary to

The fire at the Théâtre de l'Opéra, Paris, on 6 April 1763. Contemporary coloured print.

variations in mood and action. The composers were friends and admired each other deeply. In *Lo Speziale* Haydn reserved his duets for comic passages, whereas the trios tended to be more serious in tone; but in both instances he far transcended the Italian tradition, which he had completely assimilated. Thus the serious parts of the opera display none of the rather formal solemnity which characterized so many operas of the period; the music flows freely and brilliantly, in Haydn's liveliest style, even exploring unusual orchestral sonorities in the Turkish music of Act III. By choosing only a few characters, Haydn gave the work a more compact structure; but he also proclaimed quite clearly his adherence to the theories of Gluck and Traetta in rejecting the old operatic tradition of cluttered plots and laboured contrivances in favour of a simpler story line. Here there are natural characters and a close correspondence between the colloquial libretto and music of folksong-like clarity.

the Sultan, he lamely refuses, vowing that he will marry Grilletta. She now accepts Sempronio's proposal, hoping that by so doing she will spur the timid Mengone to action. Two notaries arrive – actually Mengone and Volpino in disguise. Very meticulously they draw up the marriage contract whereby Grilletta declares that she is marrying her guardian of her own free will and makes over to him all her property. Act III. Each of the fake notaries has inserted his name in place of Sempronio's; and the fraud is soon discovered. Volpino takes himself off, but Mengone swears he will do anything to win Grilletta's hand. Preceded by a letter of introduction, a Turk now arrives. It is Volpino in another disguise. He maintains that he represents the Sultan, who intends to purchase Sempronio's complete stock of drugs. The Sultan himself now arrives (Mengone in disguise) and there is much turmoil as Volpino, recognized by Grilletta and once more turned down by her, begins wrecking Sempronio's pharmacy. The poor apothecary can only stand by helplessly until Mengone promises to stop the destructive activity, if the apothecary will agree to his marrying Grilletta. What can the unfortunate man do? He needs little persuasion and hastily agrees to the suggestion.

■ This opera belongs to a more mature period of Haydn's career. Situations and characters, although still somewhat conventional, are conceived in greater depth than in his preceding comic operas. The score is more elaborate, now humorous and now serious, anticipating Mozart, whom Haydn acknowledged to be superior in the operatic field. Karl Geiringer has described the finale of Act II as 'one of the most effective ensemble numbers in the pre-Mozart *opera buffa*', with its frequent tempo changes reflecting

BASTIEN UND BASTIENNE
Singspiel *in one act by Wolfgang Amadeus Mozart (1756–91), libretto by Friedrich Wilhelm Weiskern (1710–68), based on* Les Amours de Bastien et Bastienne *by Charles Simon Favart (1710–92), a parody of the pastoral comedy by Jean-Jacques Rousseau,* Le Devin du Village. *First performance: Vienna, in the home of the hypnotist Dr Anton Mesmer, October 1768. First performance in U.K.: London, Daly's, 26 December 1894; in U.S.A.: New York, 26 October 1916.*

SYNOPSIS. Bastienne (soprano), a shepherdess, complains to Colas (bass), the village soothsayer, that Bastien (tenor) has given her up. Colas consoles her, saying that although her lover's taste for finery is more easily gratified by the Lady of the Manor than by a simple shepherdess, his true love for her will soon return. He advises her to affect indifference to Bastien when they meet, in order to provoke his jealousy. Bastienne hides when Bastien approaches to tell Colas that he has decided to marry Bastienne. Colas sadly reports that his decision has come too late, for Bastienne has now a wealthy suitor. Bastien is quickly reduced to despair, which Colas offers to dispel by making Bastienne appear by magic. The true sadness of Bastien's lament, *Meiner Liebsten schöne Wangen*, is unmistakable, and although Bastienne seems to be indifferent to him when she 'reappears', they have an extended argument, at the end of which Bastien threatens to jump in the river. They are eventually reconciled. They sing of their love for each other and of Colas's excellence as a magician, when the old shepherd joins in to congratulate them on their happiness.

■ The opera is made up of simple, graceful arias and duets in *Lied* form, but there are already signs of the young composer's confidence in handling his small orchestra (strings, two oboes or flutes and two horns)

Interior of the Teatro Ducale at Milan in the 18th century. Engraving by M. A. Dal Re. Milan, Museo Teatrale alla Scala.

Interior of the Teatro San Carlo, Naples, in the second half of the 18th century. Naples, Museo Nazionale di San Martino.

and an instinct for the theatre. In the prelude there are, surprisingly, several short passages that seem to anticipate one of the themes of Beethoven's *Eroica* Symphony. The work is faithful to the *Singspiel* form and is perhaps the only one of the master's compositions to reflect the influence of Gluck. It was chosen to open the 1976–77 season at La Fenice (Venice).

LA FINTA SEMPLICE (The Pretended Simpleton)

Opera buffa in three acts by Wolfgang Amadeus Mozart (1756–91), libretto by Carlo Goldoni (1707–93), adapted by Marco Coltellini (1719–77). First performance: Salzburg, Archbishop's Palace, 1 May 1769. First performance in U.K.: London Palace Theatre, 12 March 1956; in U.S.A.: Boston, 27 January 1961. Viennese performance never happened.

SYNOPSIS. Donna Giacinta wants to marry Fracasso, an Hungarian officer, and her maid Ninetta has set her cap at Simone, Fracasso's sergeant. Both matches are opposed by Giacinta's elderly brothers, Don Cassandro, who is a miser, a grumbler and a woman-hater, and Don Polidoro, a half-wit. The lovers resort to a trick and ask Rosina, Fracasso's sister, who has come to visit them, to make the two old men fall in love with her. The clever and lively girl quickly succeeds, and eventually all ends happily.

■ For some time the libretto was attributed to Coltellini alone, he being regarded virtually as the successor of Metastasio. In 1794, however, one year after his death, Goldoni was revealed as the true author. The text had already been set to music by Salvatore Perillo and performed at San Moisè in Venice in 1764. Undeniably the libretto does not show Goldoni at his brilliant best. The characters are closely linked to the types of the Commedia dell'Arte. There is no attempt to analyse their minds or to explore deeply into their feelings, nor does the music contribute very much in this respect. The thirteen-year-old Mozart composed a series of musical set pieces for this, his first comic opera. Certain arias, especially those given to Giacinta, have a sentimental tone, indicating that Mozart might have been familiar with some of the music written by Paisiello, a composer who introduced the sentimental into *opera buffa*. It was originally composed for performance in Vienna but was not produced there because of a series of unfortunate accidents (not, as Leopold Mozart claimed, as a result of Gluck's intrigues).

ARMIDA ABBANDONATA (Armida Abandoned)

Opera in three acts by Niccolò Jommelli (1717–74), libretto by F. Saverio De Rogatis (1745–1827). First performance: Naples, Teatro San Carlo, 30 May 1770.

SYNOPSIS. The events in the opera do not vary much from those narrated by Tasso in *Gerusalemme Liberata*, taking place in the castle of Armida. Here,

'so as to give the play the right tone', the author of the libretto decided, in addition to the warriors imprisoned by the witch, should be found Erminia, whom Tancredi has followed there. De Rogatis exercised his imagination still further ('with a view to showing such interesting scenes in a single play') by having Rinaldo fell the trees of the forest on the same day as he fled from the island.

■ The opera, dating from the composer's second Neapolitan period after his return, now famous, from Stuttgart in 1769, was an enormous success, whereas others of the same period were received coldly by a public accustomed to having their taste flattered. In the audience were Charles Burney and the fourteen-year-old Mozart who, in one of letters, mentioned Jommelli's opera. Although he found it 'too cautious', Mozart's judgment was quite favourable. A first version of the opera was staged in Rome in 1750.

MITRIDATE RE DI PONTO (Mithradates, King of Pontus)

Dramma per musica in three acts by Wolfgang Amadeo Mozart (1756–91), libretto by Vittorio Amedeo Cigna-Santi (1725–85), after Racine's Mithridate. First performance: Milan, Teatro Regio Ducale, 26 December 1770.

ORIGINAL CAST. Guglielmo d'Ettore (Mitridate), Antonia Bernasconi (Aspasia), Pietro Benedetti, known as Sartorino (Sifare), Giuseppe Cicognani (Farnace).

SYNOPSIS. Nymphaeum. Act I. Both Mitridate's sons (by former wives) have fallen in love with Aspasia (soprano), their father's betrothed. Arbate (male soprano), the Governor of the city, tells Sifare (male soprano) that his elder brother, the villainous Farnace (male soprano), has returned to the city in Mitridate's absence and assures Sifare of popular support and Aspasia's favour. Sifare protects Aspasia from his brother, who tries to force her to marry him; at that moment, Mitridate's return is announced. The king (tenor) has been defeated and is accompanied by Ismene (soprano), a princess already betrothed to Farnace. Arbate reveals Farnace's conduct towards Aspasia and the father compares this to Sifare's loyalty. Act II. Mitridate comforts Ismene and suggests that she should marry Sifare; Aspasia and Sifare declare their love for each other; Mitridate imprisons Farnace for conspiracy with the Romans. He incriminates his brother, who is ordered to withdraw while Aspasia is questioned. Mitridate is soon satisfied that she only loves Sifare and he curses them both. They contemplate suicide together. Act III. Ismene, however, stops Aspasia from killing herself and begs the king to forgive both her and his sons. A Roman attack begins, but Sifare is able to prevent Aspasia from trying to kill herself once again before himself setting off for battle. Farnace is rescued by the Romans, but has a

The theatre at Versailles. Engraving by Marmontel. Paris, Bibliothèque Nationale.

sudden change of heart; Mitridate is then reconciled to both sons and begs Aspasia to forgive his past unkindness to her.

■ This was the most accomplished *opera seria* text that Mozart ever set to music, not because of the librettist's special ability, but because of the power of Racine's tragedy, on which Cigna-Santi freely based his own work. This play had already attracted the attention of Alessandro Scarlatti and Nicola Antonio Porpora as composers and, not many years before, Apostolo Zeno. The nobility, sincerity and grandeur of Racine's characters had, in each instance, been modified in various ways. Mozart himself, barely fourteen at the time, was too young to be able to take full advantage of the opportunity. He had obtained the commission from Count Firmian, governor-general of Lombardy, who had been struck by the exceptional talent of the boy prodigy when, at the beginning of that same year, Mozart had appeared in his house. Hasse, too, had spoken most enthusiastically of him. Mozart's main concern when starting work on the score was to satisfy the singers; but, since he did not yet know who they were, he began by composing the recitative and then the arias. The latter are, for the most part, stylized but nevertheless possess considerable dramatic strength and genuine feeling, as, for example, the aria written for the entry of Mitridate. Another problem for the young composer was to differentiate the characters and styles of the four singers with similar voices (two female and two male sopranos) who had the main parts. The opera was a great success and Firmian commissioned a further work for the following year – *Ascanio in Alba*.

ASCANIO IN ALBA

Serenata *or* festa teatrale *in two acts by Wolfgang Amadeus Mozart (1756–91), libretto by Giuseppe Parini (1729–99). First performance: Milan, Teatro Regio Ducale, 11 October 1771.*

ORIGINAL CAST. Giovanni Manzuoli (Ascanio), Gertrude Falchini (Venere), Antonia Maria Girelli-Aguilar (Silvia), Giuseppe Tibaldi (Aceste), Adamo Solzi (Fanno).

SYNOPSIS. An idyllic landscape, the site of the future city of Alba Longa. Venere (soprano) and Ascanio (male soprano), her grandson, fathered by Enea, descend from the sky and she tells him that he is to rule the region and to marry a beautiful nymph, Silvia (soprano), before the day is over. She forbids him to tell the girl who he is until later, however, and he does not reveal his identity when he meets the Arcadian shepherd and nymph, who arrive to pray to Venere. A priest, Aceste (tenor), introduces Silvia, who tells sadly how she has fallen in love with a man of whom she dreamt; despite this, she vows to be a faithful wife to Venere's grandson, their future sovereign. Ascanio has watched her unseen and Venere reassures him that he will soon be able to declare his love for her. There is a vision of the future city before Silvia and Ascanio meet: the nymph does not realize his identity until Venere descends once again to celebrate the marriage ceremony between them. All ends in rejoicing when Silvia recognizes that the man in her dream was none other than the man whom Venere intended her to love and to marry.

■ This theatrical entertainment was given to celebrate the wedding of the Archduke Ferdinand of Austria and Maria Ricciarda Beatrice d'Este, and his entry to Milan as governor and captain-general of Lombardy, and was intended to display an allegory. Ferdinand's mother, the Empress Maria Theresa, is represented as Venus, the married couple are depicted as Ascanius and Silvia, and the city of Milan is reflected in the mythical Alba. Mozart was not yet fifteen when asked to compose the opera, which is basically an act of courtly homage, interwoven with Metastasian verses suitable for singing. The whole atmosphere is not Arcadian, and it is hard to detect in these conventional lines any hint of the poet who wrote *Il Giorno*. Intended as an intermezzo to Hasse's opera, *Il Ruggero*, it was eventually performed on its own for an entire evening, while Hasse's work was given on the following nights.

IL SOGNO DI SCIPIONE (The Dream of Scipio)

Serenata drammatica azione teatrale *in one act by Wolfgang Amadeus Mozart (1756–91), libretto by Pietro Metastasio (1698–1782). First performance: Salzburg, 1 May 1772.*

SYNOPSIS. The *serenata* opens with Scipione asleep in the palace of Masinissa. He dreams that two goddesses,

Costume design for Gluck's Iphigénie en Aulide, *as performed in 1774. Drawing by Boquet or a member of his School. Paris, Bibliothèque de l'Opéra.*

La Costanza (Constancy) and La Fortuna (Fortune), insist that he choose which of them he will allow to guide his life. Scipione is told that he is in the temple of heaven and he is delighted to recognize among the dead heroes his adoptive father, Publio, who speaks of the soul's immortality and of the reward that awaits the blessed after death, and his real father, Emiliano, who shows him the earth far away and the frailty of mortals. Scipione is eager to join them in paradise immediately, but both heroes and goddesses assure him that he must return to the world to suffer and to conquer before he deserves a place among them. He then chooses to follow Constancy despite Fortune's threats, and awakes.

■ Metastasio's text, based on Cicero's *Somnium Scipionis*, was one of the poet's minor works and had been written for a previous occasion, the Empress Elisabeth's birthday. The play was revived when Hieronymus von Colloredo was installed as archbishop and Mozart was commissioned to set it to music. He made little or no attempt to give psychological depth to the characters. The work concluded with a suitable *licenza* (epilogue), addressed to the archbishop, pointing out the moral of the story.

ANTIGONA

Opera in one act by Tommaso Traetta (1727–79), libretto by Marco Coltellini (1719–77). First performance: St Petersburg, Imperial Theatre, 11 November 1772.

SYNOPSIS. The opera is directly based upon *Antigone* by Sophocles, telling the story of Oedipus's daughter, Antigone, who wishes to bury the body of her brother, Polynices, contrary to the will of Creon, tyrant of Thebes. The king has commanded that the body should be left outside the city walls in view of Polynices's attempt to attack Thebes. Antigone has no hesitation in defying this unjust decree and is duly condemned to be buried alive. She is joined in the tomb by her lover, Haemon, son of Creon, who decides to die with her.

■ The opera was performed in the presence of the Russian court and was well received, although it is not one of the composer's best. It was recently revived, under the baton of Nino Sansogno, for the Maggio Musicale in Florence on 15 May 1962.

LUCIO SILLA (Lucius Sulla)

Opera seria in three acts by Wolfgang Amadeus Mozart (1756–91), libretto by Giovanni de Gamerra (1743–1803), with alterations by Metastasio. First performance: Milan, Teatro Ducale, 26 December 1772. First performed in U.K.: London, Camden Town Hall, 7 March 1967; in U.S.A.: Baltimore, 19 January 1968.

ORIGINAL CAST. Anna De Amicis (Giunia), Veneziano Rauzzini (Cecilio), Bassano Morgnone (Lucio Silla), Felicita Suardi (Cinna), Daniella Mienci (Celia).

SYNOPSIS. The dictator Silla (tenor) loves Giunia (soprano), daughter of his old enemy, Mario. She does not return his love, being already promised to Cecilio (male soprano), now in exile. Cecilio is determined to claim his bride and returns secretly to Rome and surprises her by her father's monument in the catacombs. He intends to organize a conspiracy against Silla, in which he hopes to involve Cinna (soprano), who is in love with Silla's sister, Celia (soprano). The plot is, however, discovered and Cecilio is condemned to death. Giunia immediately appeals to the Senate and boldly rebukes Silla for his arrogance and abuse of power. In a sudden change of mood, Silla is transformed into a wise and understanding citizen. Cecilio and his colleagues are released and a double wedding is celebrated, one between Giunia and Cecilio, the other between Cinna and Celia.

■ The author of the libretto was a beginner in the literary field, having previously been a priest and then a soldier. To be safe, therefore, he submitted his text to the great Metastasio, who approved it in spite of the fact that it did not amount to much. In 1774, Pasquale Anfossi composed another *Lucio Silla* for Venice, and Gamerra adapted it again for Michele Mortellari in 1779. This was the last opera Mozart composed for Italy. At the first performance, the title role was sung

Typical baroque stage design for Italian opera. The theatre of this period made use of complicated machines, concealed behind the backcloth and in the wings, to produce astonishing scenic effects.

by the tenor Bassano Morgnone, who lacked experience and was far from convincing in the part. Mozart, therefore, wrote him only two fairly conventional arias, giving more prominence to the characters of Giunia and Cecilio, interpreted by two fine singers. One of the most impressive passages is the meeting of the lovers at Mario's tomb. The libretto abounds in artificial heroics, quite alien to the composer's taste and interests; yet even here he poured out a wealth of musical material which, it has been said, would have been sufficient for a dozen symphonies. Nevertheless, the opera was not as successful as had been hoped, causing Mozart's father, Leopold, to explain (in a letter dated 2 January 1773) that the first performance had been given under an unlucky star. Mozart himself had arrived in Milan in September 1772 and remained until the end of March of the following year, hoping, in vain, to find regular employment in the city.

THAMOS, KÖNIG IN AEGYPTEN (Thamos, King of Egypt)
Heroic drama by Tobias Philipp, Freiherr von Gebler, with stage music by Wolfgang Amadeus Mozart (1756–91). First performance: Vienna, 4 April 1774.

■ Mozart worked on this music for the stage, consisting of two choruses and five instrumental entr'acte pieces, in 1773, while he was in Vienna with his father. Later, he allowed the music, which he had revised and readapted, to be used by Johann Böhm's travelling company for a comedy by Karl Martin Plümicke, entitled *Lanassa*, based on A. L. Lemierre's *Veuve de Malabar*, on an Indian theme. In this guise, Mozart's music was performed in many cities of southern and western Germany. The original score, particularly the first chorus, is a wonderful example of Mozart's masterly orchestration.

L'INFEDELTÀ DELUSA (Infidelity Disappointed)
Burletta per musica in two acts by Joseph Haydn (1732–1809), libretto by Marco Coltellini (1719–77). First performance: Eszterháza, 26 July 1773.

SYNOPSIS. Tuscany. In the opening quintet all the characters are introduced: old Filippo (bass), who wants to marry his daughter Sandrina (soprano) to Nencio (tenor), a wealthy farmer; Sandrina and Nanni (tenor), who are in love; and Vespina (soprano), Filippo's sister, who is in love with Nencio. Nanni contemplates suicide suspecting that Sandrina prefers Nencio.
Sandrina does not see how she can defy her father. Vespina realizes, however, that if Sandrina and Nanni are married, Nencio will still be single and arranges matters to suit herself. Her intrigues involve her in many disguises – she appears alternately as a wife abandoned by her husband, as a man, a marquis and a notary. Her schemes are successful and all ends happily.

■ The amusing text was by the famous librettist, Coltellini, following in the footsteps of Calzabigi as a reformer, using, in this instance, only a few characters. Coltellini also worked for Mozart, Gluck, Salieri, Hasse and Paisiello. Haydn's music, composed in the tranquil surroundings of Esterhaza Castle, is intentionally satirical, pointing the way to the comic operas of later composers.

CÉPHALE ET PROCRIS, or L'AMOUR CONJUGAL (Married Love)
Lyric ballet in three acts by André Grétry (1741–1813), libretto by Jean François Marmontel (1723–99). First performance: Versailles, 30 December 1773, then Paris Opéra, 2 May 1775.

■ In this 'heroic ballet', which was coldly received by the public, Grétry tried to oppose the musical style of Gluck, then paramount at the Opéra.

IPHIGÉNIE EN AULIDE (Iphigenia in Aulis)
Lyric tragedy in three acts by Christoph Willibald Gluck (1714–87), libretto by F. L. G. Lebland du Roullet (1716–86), after the play (1674) by Racine. First performance: Paris Opéra, 19 April 1774. First performance in U.K.: Oxford, 1933; in U.S.A.: Philadelphia, 1935.

ORIGINAL CAST. Sophie Arnould, Rosalie du Plant, Rinalde Legros, Ubalde L'Arrivée, conducted by the composer.

SYNOPSIS. The island of Aulis, where the Greek army has been delayed on its journey to Troy. The oracle has declared that the anger of Diana may only be appeased and the Greeks allowed to embark if Agamemnon, the Greek king (bass-baritone), sacrifices his daughter Iphigénie (soprano). Agamemnon has reluctantly agreed to summon his wife, Clytemnestra (mezzo-soprano), and his daughter to Aulis on the pretext that her marriage to Achilles is to be celebrated. Act I. Calchas (bass), the high priest, and the king despair over the unnatural crime he has been ordered to commit. Agamemnon has, unknown to Calchas, sent a message to Clytemnestra countermanding his instructions to land at Aulis, but the message is miscarried and mother and daughter arrive in the camp. While the Greeks hymn Iphigénie's beauty, the queen has an interview with Agamemnon in which, in a further attempt to avoid the prophecy by removing Iphigénie from Aulis, he makes out that Achilles has been false. Clytemnestra is appalled, but just as she has told Iphigénie, Achilles himself appears, and his fidelity is proved. Act II. Iphigénie has forebodings about what will happen when Achilles, furious at the insults spread about him by Agamemnon, meets her father. The wedding rejoicings are interrupted, however, by the words of Arcas (bass): he tells them of Agamemnon's vow and that the king intends to kill Iphigénie as she approaches the altar. Agamemnon and Achilles meet and abuse each other: in anguish the king once again orders Clytemnestra to leave the island with their daughter. Act III. The Greeks clamour for a victim and Iphigénie bids farewell to Achilles, who objects violently to her decision to submit for sacrifice. She takes leave of her mother, who is left alone to imagine the horror of her daughter's death. The Greeks begin the ceremony of sacrifice, but are stopped by an attack led by Achilles and his followers. The battle ceases when Calchas announces that Diana's pity has been aroused by the heroism and suffering of everyone concerned. Iphigénie is to be restored to her lover and her parents, and fair winds will blow the Greek ships onward to Troy.

■ One of Gluck's masterpieces, *Iphigénie en Aulide* was an important landmark in the musical career of the composer, who had already given notice of his 'reforming' tendencies in 1762 with the appearance of *Orfeo ed Euridice*. The opera was, in fact, preceded by an article in the *Mercure de France*, in which Gluck attacked Rousseau and his followers, who were staunch supporters of Italian opera. Algarotti and Diderot had already recognized that Racine's play was ideally suited for an opera, but Gluck alone deserves credit for putting the idea into practice; indeed, *Iphigénie en Aulide* is one of those rare examples of a perfect blend of words and music. Although the libretto occasionally displays the absence of true theatrical feeling, the music compensates for this by its sheer dramatic power, its grandeur and its delicacy, displaying to the full Gluck's technical ability and genius for innovation. It is not surprising that the splendid overture should have impressed both Mozart and Wagner. Both composers, in fact, adapted it for concert performance; and Wagner then revised the entire work. *Iphigénie en Aulide* left its mark on Paris. Princess Marie Antoinette, at one time Gluck's singing pupil, wrote to her sister, Maria Cristina Josepha, after the first performance, as follows: '... What a great triumph, my dear Cristina! ... I was captivated by it and can talk of nothing else. Everyone is enormously excited as a result of this event. It is incredible how many arguments and disputes are raging, as if it were some religious controversy. At court ... people take sides and there are lively discussions about it, while in the city the criticism is even more intense ...'

LA FINTA GIARDINIERA (The Pretended Gardener, or Sandrina's Secret)

Opera buffa *in three acts by Wolfgang Amadeus Mozart (1756–91), libretto by Ranieri de' Calzabigi (1714–95). First performance: Munich, Hoftheater, 13 January 1775. First performance in U.K.: London, Scala, 7 January 1930; in U.S.A.: New York, Mayfair, 18 January 1927.*

ORIGINAL CAST. Rosa Manservisi (Sandrina), Tommaso Consoli (Ramiro), Teresina Manservisi (Serpetta).

SYNOPSIS. The land of Lagonero. The podestà (baritone), a stupid old man, is in love with Sandrina (soprano), a gardener. She is really the Marchesa Violante, disguised in this manner in order to discover the whereabouts of her true love, Count Belfiore (tenor), who, in a burst of jealousy, had wounded her and left her for dead. The situation is complicated by Serpetta (soprano), the podestà's maid who, because she is firmly set on marrying her master, although certainly not for love, spurns the attentions of her suitor, Nardo (bass-baritone), who is really the Marchesa's servant but is now in disguise as a gardener, like his mistress. Arminda (soprano), the podestà's niece, spurns her admirer, Ramiro (mezzo-soprano), in favour of Belfiore, who for his part has rejected Violante for her. In the second act, the confusion is cleared up when Violante reveals who she is to save Belfiore from being accused of murdering her. Immediately afterwards, she resumes her part of Sandrina, however, stating that her confession was mere insanity and the act ends in even more confusion. Only in the final act are they reunited, bringing about a happy ending, in which Arminda accepts Ramiro and Serpetta takes Nardo.

■ The opera was composed partly in Salzburg and partly in Munich, between September 1774 and January 1775. According to a letter which Mozart wrote to his mother, the first performance was reasonably suc-

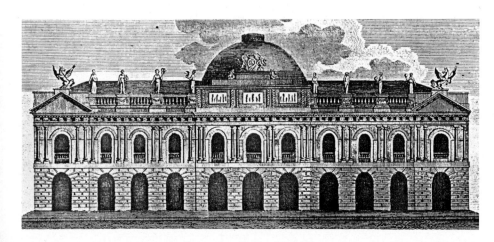

The King's Theatre, Haymarket (London), where many of Handel's operas were performed. It was destroyed in 1789.

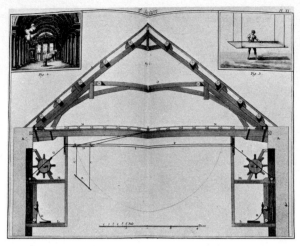

Theatrical machinery, from Diderot's Encyclopédie. *The illustration shows a machine for lifting and lowering actors and scenery, a sketch of a temple and the flying Mercury, and another for a device to produce thunderclaps.*

Theatrical machine for representing a stormy sea. From the Encyclopédie *by Diderot and d'Alembert.*

cessful, but the opera was then forgotten for a while, being revived by Johann Böhm's travelling company in 1779, when it was produced in the form of a *singspiel*. The text of *La Finta Giardiniera* had already been set to music a little earlier by Pasquale Anfossi, the score being familiar to Mozart, who used it as a framework to his own composition. A novel feature of the work was the division into serious and comic parts, but this innovation failed to bring about the miraculous, perfect blend of styles that is to be found, for example, in *Don Giovanni*. Mozart felt himself compelled to write a series of arias, some of them very beautiful; but there are few effective concerted numbers, partly because the characters are not too well defined, nor sufficiently distinctive. The opera, however, makes for pleasant listening and is yet another example of the master's creative genius.

IL RE PASTORE (The Shepherd King)
Serenata *in two acts by Wolfgang Amadeus Mozart (1756–91), libretto by Pietro Metastasio (1698–1782). First performance: Salzburg, Archbishop's Palace, 23 April 1775. First performance in U.K.: London, St Pancras Town Hall, 8 November 1954.*

ORIGINAL CAST. Consoli (Amintas) and singers from the Court Chapel.

SYNOPSIS. Alexander the Great has freed the city of Sidon from the tyranny of Strato and decides to restore the throne to the legitimate heir. Act I. Alexander is intrigued to discover that the heir is Amintas, who leads a quiet and happy life as a shepherd, loved by a girl of noble birth, Elisa, who needs her parents' consent before she can marry him. Alexander and a Sidonian nobleman, Agenor, visit Amintas to test whether he is truly fit to be a king and he impresses them.

Agenor then meets his own beloved Tamiri, daughter of Strato and now in hiding. He promises to intercede with Alexander on her behalf. Elisa is happy telling Amintas that her parents approve their marriage when Agenor returns to reveal Amintas's royal birth and to summon him before Alexander. Act II. Elisa and Tamiri have followed their lovers to the camp and Alexander decides that for reasons of state, to reconcile the factions, Tamiri should marry Amintas. Agenor believes that this will benefit Tamiri, so he does not oppose it. While both women assume that their men are unfaithful to them, Amintas struggles with his conscience before deciding to bow to Alexander's policy and to marry Tamiri. All four appear before Alexander in turn to declare their anxieties and the king resolves to abandon his scheme and to unite the true lovers. He restores the throne to Amintas and promises to conquer a new country for Agenor.

Gluck's Iphigénie en Tauride, *at the Teatro alla Scala, Milan, in 1956–7, with Maria Callas. Scenery by Nicola Benois, produced by Luchino Visconti.*

Coming out of the theatre. 18th-century painting of Venetian School. Milan, Museo Teatrale alla Scala.

■Metastasio's libretto, unashamedly sentimental, extols the idyllic life and introduces elegant characters who argue at length about such topics as wise government, but who do not give the action any real dramatic impetus. Written in 1751, it was one of Metastasio's last works and not one of his best. It was selected to celebrate the visit of the archduke Maximilian Franz, younger son of the Emperor, to Salzburg in 1775. Given this static text, Mozart supplied a score which was largely instrumental. In that same year, he had composed his five violin concertos, and many of the principal arias for *Il Re Pastore*, written for three sopranos and two tenors, are really minature concertos in form. In two of them, solo instruments (flute and violin) are equally important as the voices. The style of the opera was much more robust and concise than that of the Milanese operas, from *Mitridate* to *Lucio Silla*, revealing the composer as a musical personality of note, seeking to do away with the long-winded operatic style so dear to the hearts of the Salzburg public.

IL SOCRATE IMMAGINARIO (The Imaginary Socrates)
Opera buffa *by Giovanni Paisiello (1740–1816), libretto by Ferdinando Galiani and G. B. Lorenzi. First performance: Naples, Teatro Nuovo, October 1775.*

ORIGINAL CAST included Gennaro Lucio (Tammaro).

SYNOPSIS. Don Tammaro has gone mad while studying classical philosophy and now believes he is a second Socrates and imitates the ancient Greek in every detail. He claims, for example, that all he knows is that he knows nothing and therefore, like Socrates, he must be a philosopher. He submits to his wife's anger without complaint, as Socrates did, and implores her to empty a chamber-pot over his head. He has even persuaded his barber, Antonio, to act the part of Plato, and decided to marry him to his daughter, Emilia. She, however, is in love with Ippolito, who is in despair because Tammaro will never give his consent to their marriage. Then Tammaro has a new fancy, that he will take a second wife and he will serve his country by increasing the birthrate. His choice falls on Cilla, the barber's daughter, who is loved by Tammaro's servant, Calandrino. All sorts of schemes are now devised to settle matters satisfactorily, since Tammaro has gone out of his mind, but nothing works, partly because Emilia cannot bear to see her father duped. Calandrino, for example, pretends to be the devil (who, according to the historian Diogenes Laertius, advised Socrates), in an effort to persuade the madman to give his daughter to Ippolito. When this misfires, Calandrino tries to

Play-bill for the first performance of Mozart's Die Entführung aus dem Serail.

make Tammaro drink a sleeping draught, pretending that it is hemlock, so that he can help Ippolito and Emilia to elope and hide Cilla. Tammaro reluctantly takes the potion for 'love of Greece', but it has the surprising effect of restoring his wits, making it possible for everything to end happily.

■ The opera, with a libretto partly written in Neapolitan dialect, was banned in Naples for some years by Ferdinand IV 'for being too daring'. The whole thing was, in fact, a leg-pull, devised by D. Saverio Mattei and his followers, as a reaction against the love, often carried to ridiculous extremes, of many fellow citizens for classicism. In spite of it, Paisiello remained in favour with the Bourbons.

THE DUENNA, or THE DOUBLE ELOPEMENT

Opera in three acts by Thomas Linley the Elder (1733–95). The music was largely composed in collaboration with his son, Thomas (1756–78), based on a libretto by Richard Brinsley Sheridan (1751–1816). First performance: London, Covent Garden, 21 November 1775; in U.S.A.: New York, 10 July 1786.

■ This was one of the most successful of eighteenth-century English operas. During its first season, it was given some 75 performances, as against 63 for *The Beggar's Opera*. In 1915, it was staged in Calcutta (translated into Bengali) and in 1925, a Marathi version was produced in Bombay.

POLLY

Ballad opera in three acts with music by John Christopher Pepusch (1667–1752), libretto by John Gay (1685–1732). First performance: London, Little Haymarket Theatre, 19 June 1777; in U.S.A.: New York, Cherry Lane, 10 October 1925.

■ This opera was designed to be a sequel to *The Beggar's Opera*. The preface to the libretto is dated 15 March 1729 and both text and music were published in

that year. But for political reasons the opera only received a licence to be staged 48 years later. In all probability, the Prime Minister, Sir Robert Walpole, placed a ban on it, angered by having been satirized in the previous opera. In 1777, however, the opera was produced with modifications to the text by George Colman the Elder and some new arias by Samuel Arnold. The work was not a success and was only performed a few times.

IL MONDO DELLA LUNA (The World of the Moon)

Opera buffa in three acts by Joseph Haydn (1732–1809), libretto by Polisseno Fegejo Pastor, adapted from the comedy of the same title by Carlo Goldoni (1707–93). First performance: Eszterháza, 3 August 1777; first performance in U.K.: London, Scala, 8 November 1951 (in complete form); in U.S.A.: New York, Greenwhich Mews Playhouse, 7 June 1949.

SYNOPSIS. Act I. House of Dr Ecclitico. Ecclitico (tenor) loves Clarice (soprano), and his friend, Ernesto (soprano), is in love with her sister, Flaminia (soprano), but the girls' father, Bonafede (bass) is opposed to both matches. Ecclitico decides to play on Bonafede's credulity, enlisting his friend's help and that of his servant, Cecco (tenor), who is in love with Lisetta (mezzo-soprano), Bonafede's maid. Ecclitico pretends to be an astrologer, presenting to Bonafede a magic telescope through which the wonders of the moon can be clearly seen. When Ecclitico announces that he has been invited by the imaginary emperor of the moon to visit the planet, Bonafede begs to be allowed to accompany him. Ecclitico promptly puts him to sleep with a strong potion. Lisetta, Clarice and Flaminia fear that he is dead but are soon reassured and agree to join in the game. The act ends with a stately dance allegorically representing the world of the moon. Act II. Ecclitico's garden, transformed into lunar landscape. Bonafede, waking up, believes that he is really on the moon. The emperor (actually Cecco) arrives in great pomp, seated in a chariot. Lisetta even begins to believe her master's fantasies as well. Now the two sisters, carefully coached by their lovers, arrive and when Cecco claims Lisetta as his bride, at the same time linking Ecclitico with Clarice and Ernesto with Flaminia, the gullible Bonafede happily agrees to the arrangements. He is furious when he realizes he has been tricked and everyone begs his forgiveness. Act III. Ecclitico's house. All the efforts made by the three men to pacify Bonafede have been in vain and he is as furious as ever. Yet he has to recognize the *fait accompli* and grant a general pardon; now that his daughters and his maid are wed, he is ready to give them a generous dowry. Thus all three couples are made happy and the opera ends in joy and celebration.

■ *Il Mondo della Luna* is delightfully entertaining. Haydn took his subject matter from Goldoni and brought the various stock characters to life with bold, unambiguous strokes. When Cecco, for example, sings his aria, *Un avaro suda e pena*, dressed as the emperor of the moon, one is left in no doubt as to the real identity of the man, who possesses no royal dignity at all. The opera was written with meticulous attention to detail and gave Haydn a marvellous opportunity to exploit his gift for parody, the result being far superior to the brand of stereotyped comedy then in vogue, thanks in large measure to the liveliness of Goldoni's text. Apart from its comic and ridiculous situation, *Il Mondo della Luna* retains the fairy-tale atmosphere that Goldoni created in certain parts of his libretto. The illusion of magic is so effectively conveyed in some of the lovely arias (such as Bonafede's *Che mondo amabile*), by technical devices in the score such as the use of echo and, above all, by means of the dances in the second act, that the duped father's reactions seem all the more credible. Haydn, in fact, brought the full wealth of his experience to the composition of this work, which was influenced by contemporary Italian music, by the so-called Mannheim School, by Gluck and by themes and cadences from folk music. The extraordinary freshness and vitality of many of the comic passages are undoubtedly due to Haydn's familiarity with popular music of his day.

ARMIDE

Heroic opera in five acts by Christoph Willibald Gluck (1714–87), libretto by Philippe Quinault (1635–88), freely adapted from Tasso's Gerusalemme Liberata. *First performance: Paris Opéra, 23 September 1777. First performance in U.K.: London, Covent Garden, 6 July 1906; in U.S.A.: New York, Metropolitan Opera House, 14 November 1910.*

ORIGINAL CAST. Rosalie Levasseur, Rinalde Legros, Gélin, Ubalde Arrivée.

■ Written in 1777 – fifteen years after Gluck had initiated his reform of Italian opera – *Armide* was to some extent an act of provocation by the composer, who dared set to music the text by Quinault which had already been used by Lully to create an operatic masterpiece. The first performance, which took place during Gluck's fourth visit to Paris (May 1777 to February 1778), gave rise to a series of arguments in which the composer himself joined, rendered all the more bitter by the fact that the supporters of Italian opera invited Niccolò Piccinni to Paris, as a deliberate challenge to Gluck. Although the opera contained many characteristic innovations, it lacks the unity of *Orfeo ed Euridice*. Despite some ineffective writing for chorus and soloists, the character of Armide is strongly drawn and her beautiful arias are among the finest of Gluck's musical accomplishments. (For the plot, see the opera of same title by Lully, page 24.)

EUROPA RICONOSCIUTA (Europa Recognized)
Opera in two acts by Antonio Salieri (1750–1825), libretto by Mattia Verazi. First performance: Milan, Teatro alla Scala, 3 August 1778.

SYNOPSIS. Europa, daughter of Agenor, king of Tyre, is promised in marriage to the young prince Isseus. Asterius, king of Crete, abducts her, and all efforts by her brothers to find her are unsuccessful. Agenor, having no news of her fate, chooses his niece,

Mozart's Die Entführung aus dem Serail, *scenery by Damiani, production by Giorgio Strehler, for the 1971–72 season at the Teatro alla Scala, Milan.*

Semele, as heir to the throne, but he forbids her to marry until the blood of the first stranger to reach Tyre has been shed in vengeance for Europa's abduction. After Agenor's death, Asterius sets out to conquer Tyre but a storm scatters his fleet and only he, his wife and his small son survive. They are captured as soon as they reach shore by Aegisthus, who hopes, by this exploit, to win Semele's hand. Europa, now Asterius's queen, is recognized and Isseus persuades her to renounce her right to the throne in exchange for her husband's life. Isseus then kills Aegisthus and marries Semele.

■ This opera was composed in 1778, when Salieri obtained permission from the Emperor Joseph II to stay in Italy for a year, and it was the opening production at the Teatro alla Scala. *Europa Riconosciuta* was a big success and was performed many times. To be truthful, apart from a very expressive second-act aria for Asterius, the fame of the opera and its success are disproportionate to its real musical merits.

IPHIGÉNIE EN TAURIDE (Iphigenia in Tauris)
Lyric tragedy in four acts and five scenes by Christoph Willibald Gluck (1714–87), libretto by Nicolas-François Guillard (1752–1814), based on the play by Euripides. First performance: Paris Opéra, 18 May 1779; first performance in U.K.: London, King's Theatre, 7 April 1796; in U.S.A.: New York, Metropolitan Opera House, 25 November 1916.

SYNOPSIS. Act I. A sacred wood near a river. Iphigénie (soprano) has become priestess to Diana in Tauris, and is compelled by Thoas, king of the Scythians (bass), to sacrifice all strangers. She prays to the goddess to be allowed to leave this barbarous place. She has a vision of her mother, Clytemnestra, and of the sacrificial knife turned against her brother, Oreste. The Scythians, led by Thoas, cry out for the blood of a victim to appease the gods. Two strangers have been captured and Thoas bids Iphigénie to prepare for a sacrifice. They refuse to identify themselves; they are in fact Oreste (bass) and Pylade (tenor), and it is Pylade who is chosen to be the victim. Act II. The Temple of Diana. Oreste laments that he is the cause of his friend's death. He is haunted by avenging Furies and the ghost of Clytemnestra. He is terrified and when Iphigénie enters, she believes that it is her presence which frightens him. When she learns that he comes from Mycenae, she questions him and he tells her of the death of her parents and that Oreste himself is dead. Act III. Iphigénie's room. Iphigénie wishes to save Oreste, but he entreats her to be allowed to die. She decides to send one prisoner with a message to her sister, Electre, and to sacrifice the other. At first, she chooses Oreste as the messenger, but when he swears to immolate himself if Pylade is killed, she reverses her decision. Act IV. Before the altar, Iphigénie prays to Diana to give her strength to carry out the sacrifice. Oreste urges her not to delay but at the last moment, brother and sister recognize each other. Pylade's

escape is discovered and Thoas's fury is redoubled when he hears Iphigénie's pleas for her brother. He threatens to kill them both himself, but at this crucial moment Pylade reappears with a band of Greeks to save Oreste. Thoas is killed, Diana intervenes to order the Scythians to restore her image to the Greeks and to cease their barbaric rites and Oreste and Iphigénie return to Mycenae.

■ This was the last but one of Gluck's operas, followed only by *Eco e Narciso*, which was performed on 24 September of the same year. *Iphigénie en Tauride* was a great success, setting the seal on the triumph of the reform movement and signalling the victory of Gluck over his great rival Piccinni. Guillard, a young Parisian playwright and poet, took great pains with the libretto, reworking the famous tragedy of Euripides; and the text attracted Gluck so much that he wrote the entire first act without interruption. He was particularly successful in adapting his score to suit a text in which the human qualities of the mythological characters were strongly underlined. The opera dispensed with ballet and achieved the structural ideal to which Gluck had aspired for many years, representing the synthesis and crowning point of his career as a composer. In it, he triumphed not only as a 'reformer', but also as a classical musician in the fullest sense of the term, achieving a perfect blend of form and content. *Iphigénie en Tauride* truly enshrines the aesthetic ideal for which Gluck had been striving ever since 1762, based on a conception of beauty, expressed in musical terms, that was derived from the canons of simplicity, truth and naturalism.

L'ISOLA DISABITATA (The Uninhabited Island)
Opera seria by Joseph Haydn (1732–1809), libretto by Pietro Metastasio (1698–1782). First performance: Eszterháza, 6 December 1779.

ZAÏDE
Singspiel in two acts by Wolfgang Amadeus Mozart (1756–91), libretto by Johann Andreas Schachtner, based on the singspiel by Franz Joseph Sebastiani, Das Serail oder Die Unvermutete Zusammenkunft in der Sklaverei zwischen Vater, Tochter und Sohn, performed at Bolzano in 1779, with music by Joseph von Friebert. Mozart's score, composed in 1779, was unfinished and the opera was never performed.

SYNOPSIS. A young nobleman, Gomatz, has been taken prisoner by the Sultan Soliman. Another slave, Zaïde, is much more attracted by him than by the Sultan, who is wooing her, and she resolves to escape with him. This plan is foiled and they are at Soliman's mercy. (It is not clear whether the story was intended to end quickly with a few more numbers or another complete act.)

■ This Mozartian manuscript has a strange history. It was rediscovered after the composer's death by his

Wolfgang Amadeus Mozart with his sister Nannerl at the piano, and his father Leopold. Painting by Giovanni Nepomucemo della Croce, 1780. Salzburg, Mozartmuseum.

wife, Constanze, who at that time found herself in financial difficulties. Believing that it might be an important find and hoping to exploit it, she had a notice published in the *Allgemeine Musikalische Zeitung* to the effect that 'whoever had any information as to the title of the *singspiel* or of the place where it had originally been published should get in touch with the editors of the newspaper'. It is not known whether there was any response to this appeal; but soon afterwards, in 1838, J. Anton André, who had taken possession of all Mozart's manuscripts, also published this work under the title of *Zaïde*. Mozart had composed the music for Johann Böhm's travelling company, secretly hoping that the opera would be performed in Vienna. This would have given him an excuse to escape from Salzburg, but unfortunately the death of the Empress dispelled this hope. Leopold Mozart wrote to his son on 11 December 1780 as follows: 'As for Schachtner's work, at this moment I can do nothing because the theatres are closed and it is impossible to get anything out of the Emperor. . . . It would be better to abandon the project, seeing that the music is unfinished. . . .' Mozart was attracted to the subject for several reasons. The story was set in Turkey and this background gave the music a special Oriental flavour. The only comic part is that of Osmin, guardian of the harem, but all the characters are firmly delineated. The plot gave a composer scope for lively and sentimental scenes. There is ample justification for regarding *Zaïde*

as a preparatory exercise for the later masterpiece, *Die Entführung aus dem Serail*.

ANDROMAQUE (Andromache)
Lyric tragedy in three acts by André Grétry (1741–1813), libretto by Louis Guillaume Pitra, based on the tragedy by Racine (1667). First performance : Paris Opéra, 6 June 1780.

■ This opera, composed in 30 days, is rather feeble despite the composer's attempt to emulate the new style of opera devised by Gluck. Even so, it was performed 25 times, and the run only came to an end because the theatre was destroyed by fire.

IDOMENEO RE DI CRETA (Idomeneo, King of Crete)
Opera seria *in three acts by Wolfgang Amadeus Mozart (1756–91), libretto by Giambattista Varesco. First performance: Munich, Hoftheater, 29 January 1781; first performance in the U.K.: Glasgow, 12 March 1934; London, Sadler's Wells, 1962; in the U.S.A.: New York Town Hall, 1951.*

ORIGINAL CAST. Anton Raaf (Idomeneo) V. dal Prato (Idamante), Dorothea Wendling (Ilia),

Elizabetha Wendling (Elettra), Domenico de'Panzachi (Arbace), Giovanni Valesi (High Priest).

SYNOPSIS. Act I. Idomeneo, King of Crete (tenor), is shipwrecked on his return from the Trojan War and vows to Neptune to sacrifice the first person whom he meets on landing in Crete if he should be saved. The sight of his ship near Crete has been a sign for Idamante (soprano), Idomeneo's son, to declare a general amnesty to free the Trojan prisoners, including his beloved Ilia (soprano), daughter of King Priam. This affection is mutual although they have not yet declared this to each other, but Elettra (soprano), a refugee from the troubles of her doomed family, is also in love with Idamante. Idamante is the first to greet his father, who is horrified when he recognizes him and although he does not declare the truth about his vow, he turns away, to Idamante's astonishment. Act II. In an attempt to avert the course of fate, Idomeneo orders Idamante to escort Elettra to the mainland. Ilia unhappily suspects that this shows Idamante does not love her. As the ship is about to leave, however, a storm blows up and a terrifying sea monster approaches. The High Priest commands that the person who has wronged Neptune should come forward. Idomeneo announces that he is the guilty one. The people flee from the monster. Act III. Idamante resolves to kill the monster which is ravaging the island. Elettra, mad with jealousy, and the king, who is anxious for his son's safety, interrupt him as he confesses his love to Ilia. News of his triumphant slaughter of the beast comes just as the wretched islanders have forced Idomeneo to reveal the whole truth of his vow. The High Priest hesitates to sacrifice the young hero who, for his part, is ready to offer himself, while Ilia demands that she be taken in his place. Suddenly the oracle is heard pronouncing the resolution: Idomeneo is to abdicate in his son's favour. With Ilia as his bride, Idamante ascends the throne amid general rejoicing.

■ The subject of the opera, based on the legend of Troy, had been handled by other writers; and Varesco himself made use of a libretto by Antoine Danchet with the same title which had been set to music in 1712 by André Campra. Even after Mozart, a number of distinguished composers returned to it, including Gazzaniga (1790), Paër (1794), Farinelli (1796) and Federici (1806). The success of the first performance in Munich finally led Mozart to leave his native city of Salzburg for good. He had already made various journeys abroad so as to escape from the city's stifling, provincial atmosphere, seeking a freer, more cosmopolitan environment such as existed in Vienna, which he later made his permanent home.

LA SERVA PADRONA (The Maid Mistress)
Intermezzo in two parts by Giovanni Paisiello (1740–1816), libretto by Gennaro Antonio Federico (d. 1748). First performance: Tsarskoe Selo, St Petersburg, 10 September 1781; first performance in U.K.: London, 29 May 1794; in U.S.A.: New York, 13 November 1858.

■ This opera was composed during Paisiello's stay at the court of Catherine II, who had summoned him to St Petersburg and appointed him her Maestro di Cappella. The visit began in 1776 and ended in 1784. *La Serva Padrona*, based on the libretto by G. A. Federico, had previously been set to music by Pergolesi in 1733. (For the plot see the opera by Pergolesi, page 41.)

IFIGENIA IN TAURIDE (Iphigenia in Tauris)
Opera in four acts by Niccolò Piccinni (1728–1800), libretto by Alphonse Du Congé Dubreuil. First performance: Paris Opéra, 23 January 1781.

For synopsis, see Gluck's opera of the same name on page 82.

■ This opera was produced two years after that of the same title by Gluck, which had been an overwhelming success. It was composed with the express intention of making a practical protest against the reforms instigated by Gluck, but the fame of the latter's version completely eclipsed Piccinni's opera.

GIANNINA E BERNARDONE
Opera in two acts by Domenico Cimarosa (1749–1801), libretto by Filippo Livigni. First performance: Venice, Teatro San Samuele, November 1781.

ORIGINAL CAST. Francesca Buccarelli, Benedetto Bianchi, Vincenzo del Moro, Teresa Gherardi, Rosa Garbesi, F. Bussani.

SYNOPSIS. The action takes place in Gaeta in the eighteenth century. Act I. A square. Bernardone (bass), a bailiff, is very jealous of his wife, Giannina (soprano), and is particularly suspicious of her behaviour with Captain Francone (tenor), so he buys a lock that will enable him to keep her permanently indoors. Orlando (tenor), an Hungarian officer resident in Naples, arrives in town, accompanied by his niece, Aurora (mezzo-soprano). They are looking for Captain Francone, who had disappeared without trace after promising to marry Aurora. Orlando meets Giannina and pays her graceful compliments but she takes advantage of the occasion to grumble about her marital troubles. Bernardone then draws his sword on Orlando for pestering his wife, but he returns home to find the door open and his wife gone. She, in fact, has gone to ask advice of her brother; on her return, she finds that she is locked out. Pretending that she is going to kill herself, she throws a large stone into the well. When Bernardone hears the splash and rushes out, crying to his neighbours for help, she takes advantage of the commotion to slip back into the house. Captain Francone meets Aurora in the crowd and swears to marry her. When Giannina appears at a window, ask-

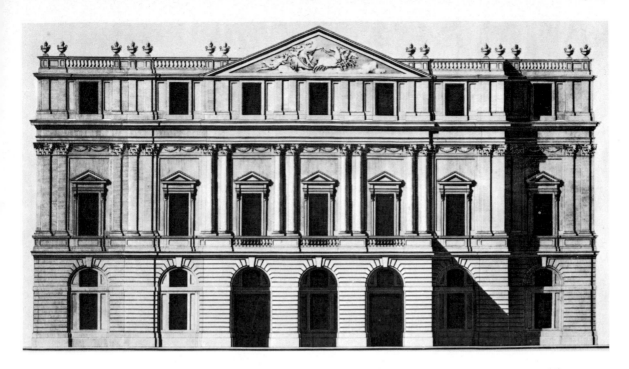

ing what is going on, the crowd accuse Bernardone of being drunk. Next morning, Orlando is still looking for Francone, whom he finds with Giannina, to challenge him to a duel, but Aurora fortunately arrives to explain the situation. Among the guests at the wedding are Giannina and Bernardone who, as usual, begin an argument, which the other guests have to calm down. Giannina promises her husband that she loves him and he vows never to be jealous again. The opera ends in singing and dancing.

■ *Giannina e Bernardone* won great acclaim both in Italy and abroad. Although he did not give much depth to the characterization, Cimarosa was highly successful in revealing each character's state of mind. The music, in fact, cleverly stresses the themes of Bernardone's jealousy, in contrast to the patience shown by his wife, Giannina.

DIE ENTFÜHRUNG AUS DEM SERAIL (The Abduction from the Seraglio)

Singspiel *in three acts by Wolfgang Amadeus Mozart (1756–91), libretto by Gottlieb Stephanie, based on Christoph Friedrich Bretzner's* Belmont und Constanze. *First performance: Vienna Burgtheater, 16 July 1782. First performance in U.K.: London, Covent Garden, 24 November 1827; in U.S.A.: New York, Brooklyn Athenaeum, 16 February 1860.*

ORIGINAL CAST. Caterina Cavalieri, Therese Teyber, Valentin Adamberger, Ludwig Karl Fischer, J. Ernst Dauer, Dominik Jantze (speaking part).

SYNOPSIS. Act I. The palace of Pasha Selim on the coast. Belmonte (tenor), a Spanish nobleman, has just landed intent on discovering the whereabouts of his beloved Constanza (soprano), who has been captured

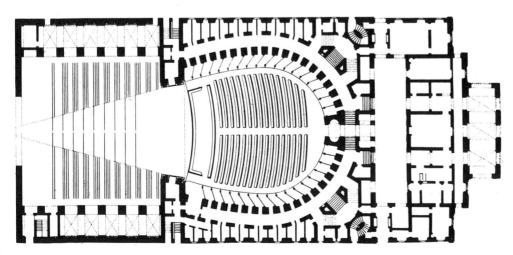

The façade (above) and the ground plan of the Teatro alla Scala, Milan, built in 1778, by the architect Giuseppe Piermarini.

*The Théâtre Royal
Italien (Salle
Favart) in Paris at
the end of the 18th
century.*

by pirates and sold into slavery. He questions Osmin
(bass), the Pasha's overseer, about the inhabitants of
the palace, but Osmin leaves angrily at the mention of
Pedrillo's name – for Pedrillo (tenor) is Belmonte's
own servant, who accompanied Constanza and is now,
as the Pasha's gardener, the bane of Osmin's life. He is
delighted to see his master again and suggests that he
should introduce Belmonte to the Pasha as a famous
architect to gain admittance to the palace and thus help
them in their escape plans. The Pasha (speaking part),
who is in love with Constanza, gives her one further
day to make up her mind whether to submit to his
desires by consent or by force. He welcomes Belmonte
to the palace. Act II. The palace garden. Osmin has
been unable to persuade Constanza's English maid,
Blonde (soprano), to be agreeable to him – she sternly
lectures him on her rights as a subject of King George
III and on the propriety of drinking tea. Blonde then
tries to console her mistress, who has resolved to die
rather than be unfaithful to Belmonte; the Pasha is
amazed at her strength of will. At last, Pedrillo finds a
chance to let Blonde know that Belmonte and his ship
are ready for an escape that night. He invites Osmin to
experiment (despite his religious scruples) with the
taste of wine, which he has drugged; Osmin is soon
incapable of staying awake. Belmonte is then reunited
with Constanza and the two couples sing of their happiness, but only after the ladies' fidelity has been questioned and proved – in Constanza's case by her tears,
and in Blonde's by a slap on Pedrillo's face. Act III.
That night. Pedrillo sings a serenade as a signal for the
escape to begin. At last, Constanza and Blonde appear,
but there are delays caused by further expressions of
ecstasy and the problems of luggage, and the fugitives
are discovered. Osmin drags them before the Pasha,
who is further incensed when he realizes that Belmonte
deceived him and that he is the son of the Pasha's most

hated enemy. He bitterly recalls how Belmonte's
father abducted the woman he loved and was the cause
of many years of grief for him. The four Europeans
seem doomed until the Pasha nobly resolves not to
behave as his enemy would have done, but to set the
lovers free. Osmin is horrified, but everyone else joins
in a chorus of praise and gratitude to the Pasha.

■ The *Singspiel*, a typically German form of stage
entertainment, had its origins in Italian *opera buffa* and
French *opéra-comique*, reaching Vienna around the
middle of the century. This type of music gradually
acquired more importance, being divided into serious
and comic sections and necessitating considerable
vocal dexterity on the part of the singers. *Die
Entführung aus dem Serail* is a particularly significant
example of the genre, as was noted by Goethe during
the period when he was writing texts for the minor
composers of Weimar. 'The appearance of *Die
Entführung*,' he wrote, 'put everything else in the
shade.' Although the Viennese public was particularly
demanding, Mozart's opera was a huge success.
Twenty or so performances in Vienna were exceptionally profitable and there were hundreds of performances in all the main German cities during the composer's lifetime. Mozart had anticipated some of the
themes in the never-performed opera, *Zaïde*, which
had a similar plot and Turkish setting. The libretto for
the new opera was provided by Gottlieb Stephanie,
adapting a play by Christoph Friedrich Bretzner who
lodged a violent protest in the *Leipziger Zeitung* to the
effect that 'a certain Mozart in Vienna has dared to
profane my play, *Belmont und Konstanze*, using it as a
text for an opera. I here make a strong protest against
this violation of my rights, reserving the privilege of
taking any measures that are necessary to safeguard
myself.' Contrary to his usual custom, Mozart spent a

long time, almost a year, composing this opera, partly because for various reasons the first performance was repeatedly delayed. He managed to write music that evoked the true mood of fairy-tale, brilliantly blending the elements of fable, comedy and tragedy. The protagonists are characterized inimitably, especially Osmin, a real rogue, vulgar, ill-tempered, comic as far as his attitude to women is concerned and when in his cups, but truly evil and dangerous. An exotic Oriental atmosphere is brilliantly conveyed by the addition to the orchestra of timpani, triangles, trumpets, flutes and cymbals. This was very much in accordance with fashions of the time, having also provided Montesquieu with the idea for his *Lettres Persanes* (1721).

FRA DUE LITIGANTI IL TERZO GODE (When Two Argue the Third Benefits)

Dramma giocoso in three acts by Giuseppe Sarti (1729–1802), libretto by Carlo Goldoni (1707–93), entitled Le Nozze. *First performance: Milan, Teatro alla Scala, 14 September 1782. First performance in U.K.: London, 6 January 1784 (as* I Rivali Delusi*).*

SYNOPSIS. The Count and the Countess disagree over who shall marry their maid, Dorina, he favouring the servant, Titta, she, the gardener, Mingone. Masotto, a farmer, who is in love with Dorina, puts himself forward as a contender as well, but his proposal comes on the night that the Count has tried to arrange a surprise wedding for Dorina, to the man of his choice. The Countess, for her part, plans a ruse by substituting herself for the maid. Matters become more tangled as nobody is prepared to give way; and, in the meantime, Dorina, who fancies neither of the two suitors, runs away. After a frantic hunt, she is brought back. Her suitors and employers come to blows and are separated by Masotto, who resolutely claims Dorina for himself. Mingone is reduced to stupefied silence, and Titta is persuaded to marry Livietta, another maid. The Count and Countess, reconciled, give their consent to the double wedding.

■ This was one of Sarti's most famous and accomplished operas. The success it achieved at the time is shown by the number of performances it received and by the numerous printed editions under such different titles as *I Pretendenti delusi, Le Nozze di Dorina, I Rivali delusi, Dorina contrastata, Wer's Glück hat führt die Braut heim oder Im Trüben ist gut fischen, Hélène et Francisque.* A vital contribution to its popularity was Goldoni's witty libretto. The work was also performed abroad. In Vienna, the Emperor Joseph II handed over the takings of one performance to the composer, expressing himself well satisfied with the money that the opera had already earned.

IL BARBIERE DI SIVIGLIA, or LA PRECAUZIONE INUTILE (The Barber of Seville)

Opera buffa in four acts by Giovanni Paisiello (1740–1816), libretto by Giuseppe Petrosellini, based on the French comedy of the same name by Pierre-Augustin Caron de Beaumarchais (1732–99). First performance: Ermitage, St Petersburg, 26 September 1782. First performance in U.K.: London, Haymarket, 11 June 1789; in U.S.A.: Philadelphia, 1794.

SYNOPSIS. Act I. A square in Seville. Count Almaviva, a Spanish nobleman (tenor), is waiting under a window of Dr Bartolo's (bass) house, hoping to see Rosina, Dr Bartolo's ward (soprano). Figaro, a barber (baritone), enters and the Count tells him of his love for Rosina, complaining that her guardian watches her so closely that he cannot get near her. Rosina, meanwhile, has come to the window and dropped a note, in which she asks him to identify himself. The Count improvises a serenade, describing himself as a student named Lindoro, but his song is rudely interrupted when a servant slams the window shut. They plan that Almaviva shall gain admittance by pretending to be a soldier billeted on the doctor and that he should appear belligerently drunk. Figaro then acts as a go-between for Rosina and 'Lindoro'. Bartolo, who plans to marry Rosina himself that very day, has been put on his guard by Rosina's music teacher, Basilio (bass), and pesters his ward about the letter she has written. Almaviva enters, pretending to be a drunken soldier looking for a billet. The old man, after a furious row, manages at last to get rid of him, but not before Rosina has received a love note from 'Lindoro'. Act II. Almaviva once more succeeds in getting into the doctor's house, pretending this time to have come instead of Basilio, who has been suddenly 'taken ill', to give Rosina her music lesson. He dismisses Bartolo's suspicions while Figaro manages to pocket the key to the balcony as he shaves him. Basilio unexpectedly turns up, but after a moment's confusion, he is silenced with a bribe. Bartolo nevertheless suspects a trick and rushes out to fetch a policeman to arrest Lindoro. He also asks Basilio to bring a notary for his marriage to Rosina. When he returns, he discovers that the notary has been forcibly persuaded to marry Rosina to Lindoro, who now reveals his true identity as Count Almaviva.

■ This opera was composed when Paisiello was in St Petersburg at the Court of Catherine II, having been appointed her Chapel Master in 1776 and remaining until 1784. The work was very successful in many European opera houses, being notable for the elegance of its score and its charming melodies. Paisiello had the great disadvantage of working on a libretto which, although ostensibly faithful to the original play, had lost the characteristic wit and spontaneity of Beaumarchais's comedy. Indeed, after its initial triumph, the opera was virtually forgotten.

L'OCA DEL CAIRO (The Cairo Goose)

Dramma giocoso in two acts by Wolfgang Amadeus Mozart (1756–91), libretto by Giambattista Varesco. Composed in 1783, the opera was left unfinished.

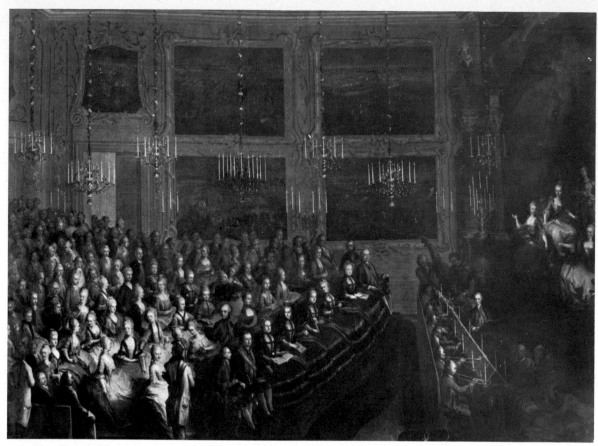

An operatic performance in the Schönbrunn Palace, Vienna, in 1765.

SYNOPSIS. Don Pippo (bass), Marquess and absolute ruler of the seaport of Ripasecca, has exiled his wife Pantea (soprano) and spread a tale that she has since died. He has promised his daughter, Celidora (soprano), to a certain Lionetto. She is actually in love with Biondello (tenor), and her companion, Lavina (soprano), who does not return Don Pippo's affection for her, is in love with Calandrino (tenor). Don Pippo has laid a bet with Biondello that if, during the year, he can penetrate the fortress in which he has imprisoned the girls, he may marry Celidora. Calandrino and Pantea agree to assist Biondello by building a mechanical toy goose in which he can hide. The first act deals, however, with the failure of another possible escape route – a bridge which the lovers cannot finish building before they are discovered. (The goose was to arrive in the market place in Act II.)

■ In the case of some libretti set to music by Mozart, critics have wondered how he came to overlook the inherent nonsense of certain situations and the superficiality of the characters involved. This undoubtedly applies to *L'Oca del Cairo*. It appears from the composer's letters that he discussed the libretto at some length with Varesco without realizing how absurd the whole venture was. He set to work enthusiastically, completing the first act very quckly. His initial enthusiasm led him, somewhat rashly, to remark that 'the funnier an Italian opera, the better it is' (6 December 1783, in a letter to his father), and helped him to overcome the doubts which began to arise in his mind. In another letter he described *L'Oca del Cairo* as 'a stupid business'. Eventually, there comes a point in his correspondence where no further information about the work is volunteered. Either Varesco did not complete the libretto or Mozart himself decided that the whole thing was a waste of time and energy, all the more since he had been offered a new libretto entitled *Lo Sposo Deluso*. Although the plot also begins with a wager, there is a world of difference between this and *Cosi fan Tutte*! Nevertheless, even in this unfinished work, Mozart composed some beautiful passages, such as the finale to Act I, where the comic structure is perfect. In addition, there are sketches of two duets, some arias and a quartet.

LO SPOSO DELUSO, or LE RIVALITÀ DI TRE DONNE PER UN SOLO AMANTE (The Disappointed Husband)
Opera buffa *in two acts by Wolfgang Amadeus Mozart (1756–91), libretto attributed to Lorenzo Da Ponte (1749–1838). The opera, begun in 1783, remained unfinished and was never performed.*

SYNOPSIS. The action revolves around a young Roman noblewoman, Emilia (soprano), in love with a brave Tuscan officer, Annibale (bass). She believes that Annibale is dead and decides, against her will, to marry the elderly Sempronio (bass). Annibale reappears in Leghorn, pursued by Sempronio's niece, Laurina (soprano), and an actress called Metilde (soprano). Annibale, after many adventures, returns to the girl he has always loved, Laurina marries the surly misogynist, Fernando (bass), and Metilde marries Emilia's guardian, Geronzio.

■ The libretto of *Lo Sposo Deluso* was offered to Mozart in 1783, while he was still working on *L'Oca del Cairo*, with which he was probably far from satisfied. It is not certain that the libretto was by Da Ponte, but several critics have attributed it to him even though he did not mention it in his autobiography, possibly because he had little reason to be proud of it. A promising start was made and could well have been developed successfully. Mozart tried to give his characters flesh and blood, and some passages pave the way for arias in later operas. While writing the music for *Lo Sposo Deluso*, Mozart evidently had certain singers in mind, because, alongside the list of characters, he jotted down, in his own handwriting, the names of his ideal interpreters – Benucci and Nancy Storace, his first Figaro and Susanna, Mandini, later to sing Count Almaviva, Cavalieri, Teyber, Bussani and Pugnetti. His driving need to work obviously encouraged him to take on this experimental project, but as a preparatory exercise for the next great phase of his career, now reaching maturity.

RENAUD (Rinaldo)
Lyric tragedy in three acts by Antonio Maria Sacchini (1730–86), libretto by Jean Joseph Lebout, from Giovanni di Gamerra's Armida. *First performance: Paris Opéra, 25 February 1783.*

Le Nozze di Figaro *by Mozart: two stage sets designed by Filippo Sanjust for Luchino Visconti's production at the Opera, Rome, in 1965.*

■ The primary source for this tragedy was Tasso's poem, the opera *Renaud* being the final result of two successive adaptations. The first version, entitled *Armida*, was given in Milan in 1772 and the second, *Rinaldo*, in London in 1780.

LE CORSAIRE (The Corsair)

Opera in three acts by Nicolas Dalayrac (1753–1809), libretto by A. E. X. de Lachabeaussière. First performance: Paris, Théâtre Italien, 17 March 1783.

■ This was Dalayrac's second opera and its success decided the composer to devote himself to this form of composition.

DIDON

Opera in three acts by Niccolò Piccinni (1728–1800), libretto by Jean François Marmontel (1723–99). First performance: Fontainebleau, 16 October 1783.

SYNOPSIS. The story, derived from the Fourth Book of the *Aeneid*, tells of Dido and Aeneas, the Trojan hero destined to found the Italian race, who has landed by chance on the shores of Carthage. The Queen commits suicide when Aeneas leaves her and Carthage for Italy.

ARMIDA

Dramma eroico in three acts by Joseph Haydn (1732–1809), libretto by Jacopo Durandi, based on an episode from Torquato Tasso's Gerusalemme Liberata. *First performance: Eszterháza, 26 February 1784.*

SYNOPSIS. Armida is a sorceress who, by means of her beauty and magic arts, can conquer the hearts of all mortal men. Among the Crusaders to the Holy Land, there is only one who can withstand her charms – Rinaldo. With the aid of infernal powers, she entices him to an enchanted island, where she falls genuinely in love with him. It is not enough that she has him in her power; she is determined that he will return her passion. The conflict between Rinaldo's firm resolution to resume his soldierly duties and the despair of the woman who has deliberately renounced her magic arts for love forms the climax of the opera. It ends by extolling the virtues of chivalry.

■ In the seventeenth and eighteenth centuries there were many works inspired by this passage from Tasso's poem. Durandi's libretto was closely based on the most famous of such adaptations, by Philippe Quinault. Haydn was certainly attracted by the subject – not only the conflict between love and duty, but the contrasting forms of love, one achieved by artifice and the other spontaneous and free. The romantic content of the plot undoubtedly lent novelty to the master's score. With *Armida*, Haydn ranged himself with the so-called reformed *opera seria*, as conceived by Gluck and Traetta.

LES DANAÏDES (The Danaïds)

Lyric tragedy in five acts by Antonio Salieri (1750–1825), libretto by F. L. G. Lebland du Roullet (1716–86) and Louis Théodore Tschudy, partly translated from the Italian libretto by Ranieri de' Calzabigi (1714–95). First performance: Paris Opéra, 26 April 1784.

SYNOPSIS. Danaus, hunted and persecuted by his brother Aegyptus, seeks vengeance and instructs his fifty daughters, engaged to marry the fifty sons of Aegyptus, to be the cruel instruments of his revenge. After the wedding ceremonies, the daughters, obeying their father, kill their husbands. Only one daughter, Hypermestra, defies him and helps her beloved husband, Lynceus, to escape. Incited by their father, the Danaïds pursue the fugitive relentlessly over Mount Thyrsus; in the meantime Lynceus, with a group of trusted men, returns to the palace. Danaus, who has no escape route, looks for Hypermestra in order to take revenge on her, but he is killed by Pelagus. Lynceus flees with his wife to Memphis in Egypt. A flash of lightning destroys the palace of Danaus. The earth opens and there, in Tartarus, surrounded by a sea of blood, Danaus appears, chained to a rock. Lightning flashes continually over his head and a vulture gnaws his entrails. The Danaïds, all chained together, are tormented by demons, serpents and Furies, amidst a downpour of fire.

■ This opera, Salieri's masterpiece, with its emphasis on dramatic expressiveness, heralds the arrival of romanticism. Its production in Paris owed much to the support and enthusiasm of Gluck, so much so that at the première, in honour of the French Queen, Salieri was listed only as Gluck's collaborator. After the opera's enormous success, however, he received his due as its composer.

OLIMPIADE (The Olympiad)

Opera in three acts by Domenico Cimarosa (1749–1801), libretto by Pietro Metastasio (1698–1782). First performance: Vicenza, for the opening of the Teatro Eretenio, 10 July 1784. First performance in U.K.: London, 8 May 1788.

■ In this opera, Cimarosa for the first time introduced an ensemble finale, previously associated with *opera buffa*, so as to make the ending more effective. (For the plot, see the opera by Vivaldi, page 42.)

IL RE TEODORO IN VENEZIA (King Theodore in Venice)

Dramma eroi-comico in two acts by Giovanni Paisiello (1740–1816), libretto by Giovanni Battista Casti (1724–1803). First performance: Vienna, Burgtheater, 23 August 1784; first performance in U.K.: London, 8 December 1787.

The soprano Barilli in Mozart's Le Nozze di Figaro. *Milan, Museo Teatrale alla Scala.*

SYNOPSIS. Trying to alleviate his patron's problems, King Theodore's steward undertakes to bring about an advantageous marriage for him with the daughter of a rich innkeeper. The innkeeper is delighted at the prospect of having a king as a son-in-law, but the girl already has a lover, who is determined not to lose her. He eventually succeeds in having the king locked up in a Venetian goal.

■ The opera was commissioned by Emperor Joseph II. The libretto is based on an episode from Voltaire's *Candide*. Although the plot is entirely fictional, the title part has a basis in historical fact in Baron Theodor von Neuhoff, who proclaimed himself King of Corsica in 1736. Casti's brilliant text and lively characterization made a profound impression on Mozart, who attended the first performance. *Il Re Teodoro in Venezia* had enormous success and was restaged in Dresden under a new title, *The Adventurers*, and with a libretto modified by Caterino Mazzola.

RICHARD COEUR DE LION (Richard Lionheart)
Opéra-comique *in three acts by André Grétry (1741–1813), libretto by Michel-Jean Sedaine (1719–97). First performance: Paris, Comédie-Italienne, 21 October 1784; first performance in U.K.: London, Covent Garden, 16 October 1786; in U.S.A.: Boston, 23 January 1797.*

SYNOPSIS. On his return from the Crusades, Richard has been secretly made prisoner in the castle of Linz. Blondel, Richard's faithful page, is searching for his master and has adopted the disguise of a blind minstrel. When he arrives in Linz, he suspects that the prisoner whose identity no one can tell him is none other than his King. On the same day, Marguerite, Countess of Flanders and Artois, and Richard's beloved, also reaches the castle. Blondel confirms his suspicion about the prisoner by playing on his lute a melody composed for Marguerite by Richard. The King takes up the tune and sings the next verse. Blondel and Marguerite work out a plan to free the King. The governor of the castle invites them to a ball and they hold him captive long enough for Marguerite's knights and soldiers to surround the fortress. Amid general rejoicing, Richard is released and reunited with Marguerite.

■ *Richard Coeur de Lion* is one of Grétry's most interesting and significant compositions. This work, in fact, stands out among other examples of late eighteenth-century *opéra-comique* for its musical excellence. The music is unusually varied and deeply expressive. Thus the choruses of the peasants are delightfully fresh and tuneful, the arias of Richard and Marguerite more pointedly sentimental, almost pre-romantic in tone, and the instrumental parts full of variety and melodic invention.
The aria, *Une fièvre brûlante*, inspired Beethoven to compose a set of variations, while the other famous aria, *O Richard, ô mon roi, l'univers t'abandonne*, pro-

vided an ironic portent of historic events soon to come (as at Versailles on 1 October 1789). Grétry was already highly esteemed by Voltaire and the Encyclopaedists, and this opera assured his popularity with the public at large. It was expanded from three to four acts and performed at the Comédie-Italienne on 21 December of the same year, 1784.

ADONE E VENERE (Adonis and Venus)
Opera by Gaetano Pugnani (1731–98), libretto by G. Boltri. First performance: Naples, Teatro San Carlo, November 1784.

■ The opera is based on the myth about the love of the goddess for a mortal youth.

LA GROTTA DI TROFONIO (The Cave of Trophonius)
Opera comica in two acts by Antonio Salieri (1750–1825), libretto by Gian Battista Casti (1724–1803). First performance: Vienna, Burgtheater, 12 October 1785.

SYNOPSIS. The action takes place in Boeotia, partly in the country house of Aristone, partly in the nearby wood, where the cave of Trofonio is situated. Aristone, father of twin daughters, consents to their marriage to the two men they love: Ofelia to Artemidoro, both inclined to be sober and thoughtful, Dori to Plistene, who are more happy-go-lucky. In the meantime, however, Artemidoro and Plistene have found the cave where Trofonio calls up spirits, and emerge with their characters altered – Artemidoro is now carefree and Plistene serious and pensive. Because they are so changed, both suitors are rejected by the sisters. In despair, they return to Trofonio and have their original characters restored. The two girls have meanwhile also visited the wood and discovered the cave, and they, too, undergo a reversal of character; so the double wedding has to be postponed again. All ends happily, however, because Artemidoro persuades the sorcerer to return his daughters to their own personalities.

■ One of Salieri's major successes in Vienna, this opera has an Arcadian plot with the customary twists and turns. Gluck's influence is strongly pronounced. From the musical viewpoint, the most interesting feature is the overture, which in complexity and depth is comparable to the mature Mozart.

OEDIPE À COLONE (Oedipus at Colonus)
Dramma per musica in three acts by Antonio Sacchini (1730–86), libretto by Nicolas-François Guillard (1752–1814). First performance: Versailles, 4 January 1786.

SYNOPSIS. Polinice, son of Oedipe, asks Thésée, king of Colonus and Athens, for help against the usurper of the Theban throne, which is rightly his. Thésée agrees

Scene from the first act of Le Nozze di Figaro, *Salzburg Festival 1972, designed and produced by Jean-Pierre Ponelle. Left to right: Michel Sénéchal as Don Basilio, Tom Krause as Count Almaviva, Walter Berry as Figaro and Teresa Berganza as Cherubino.*

and gives him his daughter Erifile in marriage. When, however, they approach the temple to pray for divine assistance, the altar bursts into flames as a sign of the gods' anger with Polinice for having approved the expulsion of his father from Thebes. Oedipe and his daughter Antigone have found their way, meanwhile, to Mount Cithaeron. He reflects on his miserable existence and, when the people recognize him, prepares to be driven out once more. Thésée rescues them, however, and Antigone meets Polinice again. She pleads with her father on his behalf so that eventually Oedipe forgives his son and consents to his marriage to Erifile.

■ Sacchini composed his opera in Paris, where he had arrived in 1783, under the patronage of Marie Antoinette. The première took place in the presence of the monarchs, but the composer's hopes that it would be performed on the Paris stage were dashed, for jealousy and political manoeuvres blocked his path. By the time it was put on at the Opéra in the following year, Sacchini was dead. It is undoubtedly his finest work, strong in dramatic impact, yet at the same time full of tenderness. The duet for Oedipe and Antigone, in particular, is one of the most beautiful set pieces in all eighteenth-century opera.

DER SCHAUSPIELDIREKTOR (The Impresario)
Komödie mit Musik *in one act by Wolfgang Amadeus Mozart (1756–91), libretto by Gottlieb Stephanie. First performance: Vienna, Schönbrunn, 7 February 1786; first performance in U.K.: London, St. James's, 30 May 1857; in U.S.A.: New York, 9 November 1870.*

ORIGINAL CAST. Aloysia Lange, Caterina Cavalieri, Valentin Adamberger.

SYNOPSIS. An impresario, after suffering heavy setbacks during a theatrical season, is given the job of building up a new opera company for Salzburg. He gathers together actors and singers. Two sopranos, Madame Herz and Madame Silberklang, show off their talents to him. An argument breaks out between the two women concerning their fees and they begin yelling as loudly as they can. The tenor, Monsieur Vogelsang, has to intervene and calm them down. In the final vaudeville, peace is restored.

■ Mozart composed an overture, two arias, a trio and a vaudeville for this comedy. The theme had already been handled by other authors – Metastasio for his intermezzo to the *Impresario delle Canarie*, Goldoni for the *Impresario delle Smirne*, and by several librettists including Bertati (*Capriccio*) and Calzabigi (*Critica Teatrale*). Stephanie's text, coarse and often bordering on vulgarity, was certainly not one of the best and was hardly calculated to inspire the composer. Nevertheless, Mozart wrote very charming arias for the two sopranos and did his best to provide suitable music for the rather clumsy vaudeville. The best piece of music is the buffo-style overture. The opera was commissioned by Emperor Joseph II and staged for a festival organized at Schönbrunn to honour the governor-general of the Netherlands, Duke Albert of Saxe-Teschen, and his wife, the Archduchess Cristina. The opera was subsequently performed on 18 and 25 February for the public. For the same occasion Salieri was given a much more important and stimulating

Domenico Cimarosa. Portrait by Francesco Candido, 1785. Naples, Museo di San Martino.

commission – setting to music a libretto by Gian Battista Casti, entitled *Prima la Musica e poi le Parole*.

PRIMA LA MUSICA E POI LE PAROLE (First the Music And Then the Words)

Melodramma giocoso *in one act by Antonio Salieri (1750–1825), libretto by Gian Battista Casti (1724–1803). First performance: Vienna, Schönbrunn, 7 February 1786.*

SYNOPSIS. The opera opens with an argument between a court poet (baritone) and a maestro di cappella (baritone) concerning a play that they have been commissioned to write by their employer, the count, which is to be given before an invited audience at a banquet. The composer has discovered a beautiful, ready-made score among some old manuscripts; now it is up to the poet to provide a suitable text. Another problem is the choice of performers, in particular for the principal female role, as between the poet's candidate, a charming comedienne (soprano) and the composer's requirement of a famous prima donna (soprano). All is finally resolved by a clever adaptation of the opera to satisfy both singers, who agree to share the role, one performing the tragic parts, the other the comic sections.

■ Salieri wrote this opera at the command of the Emperor Joseph II, who at the same time had commissioned one from Mozart. Both were staged in the Orangery of the Imperial palace at Schönbrunn.

LE NOZZE DI FIGARO (The Marriage of Figaro)

Commedia per musica *in four acts by Wolfgang Amadeus Mozart (1756–91), libretto by Lorenzo Da Ponte (1749–1838), based upon* La Folle Journée, ou Le Mariage de Figaro *by Pierre-Augustin Caron de Beaumarchais (1732–99). First performance: Vienna, Burgtheater, 1 May 1786; first performance in U.K.: London, Haymarket, 18 June 1812; in U.S.A.: New York, 10 May 1824.*

ORIGINAL CAST. Stefano Mandini, Francesco Benucci, Michael Kelly, Dorotea Bussani, Luisa Laschi, Nancy Storace, Maria Mandini, Marianna Gottlieb.

SYNOPSIS. Act I. In a room of Count Almaviva's castle near Seville, his valet Figaro (baritone) and the Countess's maid, Susanna (soprano), are preparing for their wedding later in the day. Susanna considers it extremely suspicious that the Count should have chosen to give them this room, which adjoins the apartments of both master and mistress, because she knows he wants to seduce her. Figaro is furious when he hears this and resolves to make sure that it is he, and not his master, who calls the tune where Susanna is concerned. The appearance of his ex-landlady, Marcellina (mezzo-soprano), and her lawyer, Dr Bartolo (baritone), introduces another obstacle to his happiness, because he has never settled a debt which he rashly contracted on the understanding that if he could not pay he would marry Marcellina. Susanna is annoyed to find the old woman in her room and teases her unmercifully before she leaves. Cherubino (soprano), a page boy, now joins her and explains that the Count is very annoyed with his impertinent behaviour, particularly in respect of all the females in the castle, and that his latest passion is the Countess herself. When they hear the Count he hides in order to avoid being caught once again alone with a woman, and the Count thinks Susanna is alone when he enters the room. He immediately begins making advances to her until he is in turn interrupted by the arrival of the music master, Don Basilio (tenor). He conceals himself behind the same chair as Cherubino, who hastily creeps around it and kneels on it while Susanna covers him with a rug. Basilio gossips about the goings-on in the castle and in particular about Cherubino's infatuation with the Countess. The Count is so angry that he comes out of hiding to hold forth about the page's latest iniquities, and in doing so he pulls the rug off the chair to reveal Cherubino. Aware that the boy has overheard his own indiscretions, he vents his anger by summarily despatching him to join the army. Figaro ends the Act by mockingly describing the glories of war. Act II. The Countess's bedroom. Figaro and Susanna persuade the Countess (soprano), sad because she feels she is not loved as she once was, to teach her husband a lesson and put an end to his

Scenery by Henry Moore for Mozart's Don Giovanni, *produced by Gian Carlo Menotti for the 1967 Spoleto Festival.*

flirtatious behaviour. Basilio is to be sent to the Count with a note to the effect that the Countess is having an affair with his page, while Susanna will arrange a rendezvous with the Count, at which Cherubino, dressed as a woman, will take her place. They call in Cherubino and start trying on his disguise. The Count arrives, at the worst possible moment, and his wife, in confusion, hides Cherubino in the dressing-room. The noise of Cherubino upsetting a stool awakens the Count's suspicions and he angrily demands to know who is hiding there. When the Countess refuses to tell him, he compels her to accompany him in a search for tools to break down the door. Susanna takes advantage of their absence to take Cherubino's place and he jumps out of the window. When the Count prises the dressing-room door open, the Countess is astonished to see an innocently smiling Susanna emerge. The gardener, Antonio, bursts in, complaining that someone has just jumped out of the window, and although Figaro tries to assume the blame, the Count gets the strong impression that he is being duped. Marcellina and Bartolo come in to complicate matters still further with their claims for satisfaction of Figaro's debts. Act III. A hall in the palace where the wedding is to be held. The Countess dictates a letter for the Count in which she purports to make an assignation for him with Susanna. Before he receives it the Count overhears a whispered phrase from Susanna to Figaro which arouses his suspicions that he is being tricked. Determined now to marry Figaro to the elderly Marcellina, he is nonplussed when Marcellina suddenly recognizes Figaro as her long lost son by Dr Bartolo. Once this turn of events has been explained, a double wedding can be celebrated: Figaro to Susanna and Bartolo to Marcellina in a belated move to legitimate their union. Cherubino approaches, disguised as a village girl among the group offering flowers to the Countess, but he is unmasked by Antonio. The Count's fury is averted by Antonio's daughter, Barbarina (soprano), who embarrasses him by recalling the times when he promised her anything if she would love him – she now asks to marry Cherubino. His spirits rise when he receives, in the course of the wedding ceremony, the note – apparently from Susanna – inviting him to meet her later that evening in the park. Figaro notices that his master is preoccupied with a billet-doux, but cannot guess who has sent it. Act IV. Figaro does not know that the Countess has herself been stung by her husband's behaviour into making a plan of her own. When he discovers that Susanna appears to have suggested a secret meeting with the Count, he is furious; not knowing that the Count is to meet, not Susanna, but the Countess in Susanna's clothes. He conceals himself at the rendezvous point and watches with increasing jealousy as his master makes free with his new bride. Susanna and the Countess realize that their exchange of costumes has deceived not only the Count but also Figaro, and the appearance of the 'Countess' gives the Count an opportunity to hurry his supposed 'Susanna' away and for the real Susanna to play the Countess to Figaro's protestations of adoration. Recognizing her voice, he realizes his mistake and they are reconciled.

He begs her to forgive him, as does the Count of his wife when the trick is revealed, and all ends happily in celebration.

■ Mozart's collaboration with Da Ponte, which proved to be so fruitful and successful for both men, began with *Le Nozze di Figaro*. It was actually Mozart who suggested to Da Ponte that they adapt their work from Beaumarchais, whose play was famous throughout Europe and the object of lively arguments and discussions. Other librettists had already been attracted by it; and three operas had been staged at the Vienna Burgtheater around the same time, all dealing with the difficult and delicate relationships between different social classes. None of them, however, began to measure up to Mozart's version. For reasons of prudence, Da Ponte was forced to eliminate most of the witty French political allusions, so that the work more closely resembled Italian opera; but here and there he underlined the satirical purpose with a number of sharp and biting references. Yet if Da Ponte was constrained to compromise in order not to offend fashionable society, Mozart had no such qualms. The characters of Beaumarchais seemed to feel and suffer as he did, and he used them as mouthpieces to express his own instincts of resentment and disillusionment. The sad, bitter, ironic tone of this self-revelation was not to the liking of the less perceptive sections of Viennese society, who much preferred the lighthearted temperament of a composer such as Cimarosa. Nevertheless, the first performances of *Le Nozze di Figaro* were an enormous success, so much so that Joseph II was compelled to issue a decree forbidding encores of the ensemble passages. The principal themes of the opera are love and duty; and in the characters of Almaviva and Figaro two conflicting forces, symptomatic of that troubled age, are reflected – the aristocracy, unswervingly committed to the status quo, and the third estate, soon to grasp the reins of power. The analysis of the inner feelings of the characters, hinted at by Da Ponte, is completely realized by Mozart in his marvellous score, and nowhere more successfully than in the part of the Countess.

L'IMPRESARIO IN ANGUSTIE (The Harassed Impresario)

Opera in one act by Domenico Cimarosa (1749–1801), libretto by Giuseppe Maria Diodati. First performance: Naples, Teatro Nuovo, autumn 1786.

SYNOPSIS. There is no plot in the accepted sense, the opera consisting mainly of short scenes ironically commenting upon the vanity and petty squabbles of prima donnas and impresarios, so common in the theatres of that time.

■ The opera was revived at the Teatro Valle, Rome, on 31 July 1787, in a revised version. In the audience was Goethe, who commented favourably on it in his travel diary; and one evening a little later he invited the cast to give him another chance to hear the best arias in

Title-page of the first edition of the score of Mozart's
Don Giovanni, *Leipzig, 1801.*

the opera. *L'Impresario in Angustie* cannot, however, be numbered among Cimarosa's finest works, for there are signs that it was written in some haste and not all of the themes are original. It is worth recalling that during that same year Cimarosa staged three more operas (*Le Trame Deluse*, *Il Credulo* and *La Baronessa Stramba*). Yet *L'Impresario in Angustie*, written shortly before Cimarosa's great masterpiece, *Il Matrimonio Segreto*, heralds the latter work in some fine concerted passages, in the charm of its melodies and in the sprightly mood that is evident throughout.

TARARE
Opera in a prologue and five acts by Antonio Salieri (1750–1825), libretto by Pierre-Augustin Caron de Beaumarchais (1732–99). First performance: Paris Opéra, 8 June 1787; first performance in U.K.: London, Lyceum, 15 August 1825.

SYNOPSIS. Atar, a malevolent tyrant, discloses to his confidant Calpigi his hatred for Tarare, a brave captain, who is much loved by his troops. Envy drives the king to try to murder Tarare and when he is unsuccessful, he abducts his wife Aspasia. Tarare has a variety of adventures before rescuing her by defeating the abductor, Altamorte, in a duel. The people rebel and Atar commits suicide. Tarare, acclaimed by the populace, is urged, against his will, to accept the throne.

■ *Tarare* was described by the composer himself as 'an opera in the tragi-comical style'. Beaumarchais, in his libretto, had already declared his intention of weighing 'the virtue of the poor' and 'the influence of public opinion' against the despotism and corruption of those in power. It is probably Salieri's best opera and it was immediately successful. The following year Salieri received from Emperor Joseph II a command to adapt it for the Italian Opera Society in Vienna. Translated

by Da Ponte, it emerged as a completely new opera, *Axir, Re d'Ormus*. Performed for the first time at the Vienna Burgtheater on 8 January 1788, it likewise won popular acclaim.

DON GIOVANNI, ossia IL DISSOLUTO PUNITO
(Don Giovanni, or The Libertine Punished)
Dramma giocoso in two acts by Wolfgang Amadeus Mozart (1756–91), libretto by Lorenzo Da Ponte (1749–1838). First performance: Prague, Tyl Theatre, 29 October 1787; first performance in U.K.: London, Her Majesty's, 12 April 1817; in U.S.A.: Philadelphia, 1818; New York, Park Theater, 23 May 1826.

ORIGINAL CAST. Luigi Bassi, Teresa Saporiti, Caterina Bondini, Caterina Micelli, Antonio Baglioni, Giuseppe Lolli.

SYNOPSIS. Act I, Scene I. The action takes place in a Spanish town. In front of the Commendatore's house, Leporello (bass) waits for his master, Don Giovanni (baritone), who has entered the house to seduce Donna Anna (soprano), daughter of the Commendatore. The Commendatore (bass) pursues the intruder, and Don Giovanni kills him before escaping. Scene II. Don Giovanni then makes advances to a lady who turns out to be a past 'conquest', Donna Elvira (soprano), who has followed him to entreat him to return to her. He leaves Leporello to describe to the unfortunate woman his master's real character, but this only reduces Elvira to disgust and despair. Scene III. Near an inn, Don Giovanni encounters a country wedding. Struck by the charms of the bride, Zerlina (soprano), he instructs Leporello to invite everybody, especially the bridegroom, Masetto (bass), to a banquet at his expense. The girl, flattered by the attentions of the nobleman, is about to succumb to his advances, when Elvira intervenes. Anna and Don Ottavio (tenor) arrive, and beg Don Giovanni's assistance in hunting down the Commendatore's murderer. Don Giovanni dismisses Elvira's accusations as mere madness, but Anna and Ottavio are not wholly convinced, even when he agrees to offer them his assistance, and, when he leaves, Anna recognizes him as her father's murderer. Scene IV. Garden of Don Giovanni's palace. Zerlina is confused because she genuinely loves Masetto but finds it hard to resist Don Giovanni. Masqueraders appear – Elvira, Anna and Ottavio – and Don Giovanni bids Leporello invite them also to his banquet. Scene V. The maskers enter the ballroom and are received by the master of the house with a toast to freedom. During the dancing, Don Giovanni entices Zerlina into an adjoining room. She shrieks for help and the masked figures reveal themselves in turn, openly accusing Don Giovanni of his crime and invoking punishment from heaven. Act II, Scene I. A street in front of Elvira's house. Leporello is tired of the life he is leading, but a bribe persuades him not only to continue in service, but even to dress in his master's clothes for yet another amorous adventure. The target is this time Elvira's maid, and Leporello is to distract

Cesare Siepi (right) as Don Giovanni in Mozart's opera, produced at the Metropolitan Opera, New York.

the mistress. Their change of clothes gives rise to two parallel scenes. In the first, Don Giovanni is mistaken by Masetto for Leporello, and manages not only to escape his due reward, but also to administer a thrashing to the unlucky bridegroom. In the second, Leporello is taken for Don Giovanni and only just succeeds in saving his life, pursued as he is by Masetto, Zerlina, Anna, Ottavio and Elvira. Scene III. A cemetery with the statue of the Commendatore. Don Giovanni, once more on the prowl for victims, has climbed the cemetery wall to escape his pursuers. All the excitement has put him in high spirits and he laughs as he describes to Leporello what has been happening. A sinister voice suddenly rings through the darkness. Don Giovanni hunts among the graves, until he finally realizes that the voice must have come from the statue of the Commendatore. On his master's instruction, Leporello invites the Commendatore to dinner; the statue nods assent and the two men steal away, hardly believing the evidence of their eyes. Scene IV. Anna and Ottavio declare their love for one another, but she asks him to wait for a year before their marriage. Scene V. A room in Don Giovanni's palace. The table is laid and musicians are playing. Don Giovanni is eating dinner, when Elvira interrupts in a desperate attempt to persuade him to repent, He ridicules her and she runs off when there is a loud knock on the door. She shrieks when she sees the statue of the Commendatore,

who has arrived for dinner. Don Giovanni displays no fear, however; he even accepts the Commendatore's return invitation and as a pledge grasps the extended right hand of the statue. The grip is ice-cold, but even as his limbs begin to freeze, Don Giovanni refuses to repent. The obstinate word 'No' is the last he ever utters, and he is hurled down into the flames of hell. The other characters now enter and sing the moral of the story.

■ On 1 January 1787 Mozart and his wife journeyed to Prague to be present at the triumphant première of *Le Nozze di Figaro*; and when he left, about a month later, he had with him a new contract from Bondini's company for another opera, the fee being 100 ducats. Da Ponte hit upon the popular story of Don Juan probably because around the same time three operas on this theme had appeared, one of which, with a libretto by Bertati, had been a fair success. There are certainly some resemblances between the two libretti, but they are confined to external structure and a few minor points of detail. It was planned to perform the opera at a special performance in honour of Joseph II's sister, who was passing through Prague in mid-October of 1787, but as it was not ready, *Figaro* was given instead and *Don Giovanni* first appeared on the stage a few days later. Mozart and Da Ponte were both in the city from the beginning of October to supervise the production and to complete the score, namely the parts (Masetto and the Commendatore) which were to be sung by Giuseppe Lolli, whose vocal talents Mozart did not know. From the manuscript, too, it can be seen that the overture was written in a hurry, although not, as legend has it, on the night before the première.

The audiences at those first performances, which included Giacomo Casanova, gave the opera an ovation comparable to that for *Le Nozze di Figaro* in Prague; and the passage of time has not diminished its popularity. By 1887, the date of its centenary, the opera had been performed 532 times in Prague, 491 times in Berlin and 472 times in Vienna. The legend of Don Juan, like that of Faust, appears throughout European literature and popular folklore. This conception of vice and sacrilege first found poetic and literary expression in Spain at the beginning of the sevententh century in Tirso de Molina's *Burlador de Sevilla*. Mozart had rarely composed a score that so abounded in swift contrasts of mood, ranging from gentle love duets to sinister fulminaticns of divine retribution. The anti-hero of the opera is Don Giovanni himself. Leporello, who embodies many comic characteristics, is an admirable foil for his master. The anxieties of the two women, Anna and Elvira, are drawn with extraordinary feeling; and the Commendatore is the personification of the powers above. These diverse qualities are brilliantly fused in a work which is rightly regarded as one of the greatest operas of all time.

IFIGENIA IN AULIDE (Iphigenia in Aulis)
Opera in three acts by Luigi Cherubini (1760–1842), libretto by Ferdinando Moretti (d. 1807). First performance: Turin, Teatro Regio, 12 January 1788; first performance in U.K.: London, 24 January 1789.

SYNOPSIS. The opera is based on the tragedies of Euripides and Racine, but differs from them mainly in the ending: the heroine commits suicide, exhausted by the fate which persecutes her.

■ *Ifigenia in Aulide* was the last opera that Cherubini wrote in Italy. It was performed in Turin during the composer's brief stay in that city from December 1787 to January 1788. He personally supervised the staging of the first performance.

AMPHITRYON
Opera in three acts by André Grétry (1741–1813),

The oval auditorium of the Royal Opera at Versailles, built by the architect Gabriel in 1770.

A riot outside the Théâtre de l'Opéra, Paris, 12 July 1789.

libretto by Michel Jean Sedaine (1719–97), based on the comedy (1668) by Molière. First performance: Versailles, 15 March 1786; first public performance: Paris Opéra, 15 July 1788.

SYNOPSIS. Jove, in love with Alcmene, comes down to earth with Mercury. Arriving at Thebes, he assumes the likeness of Alcmene's husband Amphitryon, abroad on a campaign, while Mercury takes on the guise of Amphitryon's servant Sosia. Alcmene receives Jove as if he were Amphitryon, and Bromia, her maid, welcomes Mercury, believing him to be Sosia. When the real Amphitryon and Sosia return, there are continual mistakes over identities, beginning when the false and real Sosias meet. The double game ends when a divine messenger tells Alcmene that she will bear twins, one the son of Amphitryon, the other the son of Jove, and the complications are resolved when Jove and Mercury reveal their true identities.

■ This comedy of identities goes directly back to Molière and through him to the original source, Plautus. Perhaps because of its distinguished literary background, the opera did not prove as successful as hoped. Comparison with Molière's play could only show up the deficiencies of Sedaine's libretto, and the opera was coldly received both by the court and by the public. The musical structure was extremely conven-

tional and Grétry, a man of his own times, seemed to be uncomfortable in handling a story placed in ancient Greece. He himself, possibly because of the opera's failure, had little complimentary to say of *Amphitryon*; in his autobiography he merely mentioned the title, without troubling to analyse the work in any detail.

DÉMOPHOON

Opera in three acts by Luigi Cherubini (1760–1842), libretto by Jean-François Marmontel (1723–99), based on the play of the same name by Pietro Metastasio. First performance: Paris Opéra, 1 December 1788.

■ *Démophoon* was the first French opera scored by Cherubini, soon after his decision to move permanently to Paris. In writing it he gave up the Italian style which had characterized his earlier works, performed both in Italy and in London. He did his utmost to utilize his gifts for melody in the service of dramatic expression. The public of his day was not yet ready for this radical change in operatic style, however, and the opera did not win the acclaim it deserved. It was only put on for eight performances and has not been revived, except for some parts which were given a concert performance at Coblenz in 1926. (For the plot, see the opera of the same title by Leonardo Leo, page 45.)

LA MOLINARA, or L'AMOR CONTRASTATO
(The Mill-owner, or The Rivalry of Lovers)

Dramma giocoso *in two acts by Giovanni Paisiello (1740–1816), libretto by Giovanni Palomba. First performance: Naples, Teatro dei Fiorentini, summer 1788; first performance in U.K.: London, Pantheon, 21 May 1791.*

SYNOPSIS. In the house of the baroness Eugenia (soprano), near Naples, the notary Pistofolo (bass) is drawing up a marriage contract between the baroness and her cousin Caloandro (tenor). The project is doomed, however, because the baroness has gone off with her lover Luigi (tenor). Rachelina (soprano), a wealthy and beautiful mill-owner, who has captured the heart both of the notary and of Caloandro, now appears. The former proposes marriage to her, and she tells him she cannot make up her mind, although hinting that she is not ill-disposed towards him. Then the elderly Governor Rospolone (bass) enters, instructing the notary to take a message containing a marriage proposal to Rachelina; and shortly afterwards Caloandro sends him off on the same errand. The notary, in order to rid himself of his rivals, tells them that Rachelina has pronounced one of them to be mad and the other an ass. Fearing reprisals, he then seeks refuge in Eugenia's house, pursued in due course by Caloandro and Rospolone, both uttering threats. His flight is followed by several lively scenes in front of Rachelina's mill. The notary and Caloandro dress up respectively as a miller and a gardener to avoid pursuit by Eugenia and the Governor. In the wood, Rachelina decides she will marry the notary because, unlike Caloandro, he is prepared to become a miller for her sake, admittedly motivated in part by hope of profit. This decision sends Caloandro mad and, in the belief that he is Orlando, he tries to kill the notary, thinking him to be Medoro. The Governor then pretends to be a doctor so as to bring Caloandro to his senses, and at the same time, seeking revenge, suggests to Rachelina that the notary too is mad. She now has to make her choice between a real madman and a feigned lunatic, and wisely decides to remain a spinster.

■ The opera contains many tuneful arias, simple and graceful in form. One of them, *Nel cor più non mi sento*, was used by Beethoven for a set of piano variations.

NINA, or LA PAZZA PER AMORE (Nina, or Mad For Love)

Opera semi-seria *in two acts by Giovanni Paisiello (1740–1816), libretto by Benoît Joseph Marsollier de Vivetières entitled* Nina, ou la Folle par Amour, *translated by Giuseppe Carpani with additions by Giovanni Battista Lorenzi. First performance: Naples, Caserta, Giardini San Leucio, 25 June 1789; first performance in U.K.: London, 27 April 1797.*

SYNOPSIS. Act I. Susanna, Nina's nurse (soprano),

Silhouettes by H. Löschenkohl showing the principal singers in the première of Così fan Tutte *– Francesco Benucci, Dorotea Bussani, Vincenzo Calvesi and Francesco Bussani.*

tells Giorgio, the Count's old bailiff, and the assembled countryfolk, about the girl's recent adventures. The Count, her father, once promised her in marriage to Lindoro (tenor), but then changed his mind, in preference for a wealthy, noble suitor. Lindoro, surprised in Nina's company by his rival, has been killed by him in a duel. Nina (soprano), who loved Lindoro, has gone mad and now seems to be waiting for her dead lover's return, raving every time she hears her father's name. The Count is truly repentant and, torn by remorse, asks Giorgio for the latest news of his daughter. The bailiff assures him that she will eventually be cured and that she really loves him. When the Count tries to approach her, however, she fails to recognize him and runs off to look for Lindoro. Susanna patiently counsels her to go down to the village, following a shepherd (tenor) playing the bagpipes. Act II. While the Count is thanking Susanna for the loving care she has shown for his daughter, Giorgio brings the joyful news that Lindoro has recovered from his wounds. He has, in fact, been arrested by the gamekeepers for trying to climb the wall into the Count's garden. When the young man arrives in person he is naturally anxious about his reception by the Count, and is delighted to be embraced as a son before he hears that Nina has lost her wits. He is advised to take off the waistcoat embroidered for him by Nina, so as not to excite her unduly, before she is brought in. She does not at first recognize him and seems very disturbed, but little by little, by means of recalling past conversations, she recovers. When at last she realizes that she is with her

The Vienna Hofburgtheater in a print from the end of the 18th century.

lover, and that her father is no longer opposed to their marriage, she shares her happiness with everyone, including all the countryfolk who have anxiously been following the events.

■ The opera was inspired by French sentimental domestic comedy, and it immediately brought renewed fame for the composer. In *Nina*, he showed his ability to heighten the drama of a situation by the musical accompaniment of syncopated rhythms and various recurring animated themes. The huge success which the opera had on its first appearance lasted all over Europe into the early nineteenth century, and Nina's lament, *Il mio ben quando verrà*, was especially famous.

CLEOPATRA

Opera in two acts by Domenico Cimarosa (1740–1801), libretto by Ferdinando Moretti. First performance: St Petersburg, Hermitage Theatre, 8 October 1789.

■ Inspired by the story of Cleopatra, Queen of Egypt, this is one of the few *Opere serie* written by Cimarosa. It was composed during his three years at the court of Catherine the Great, where he also wrote *La Vergine del Sole* (The Virgin of the Sun).

COSÍ FAN TUTTE, ossia LA SCUOLA DEGLI AMANTI (They All Do It, or The School For Lovers)

Dramma giocoso in two acts by Wolfgang Amadeus Mozart (1756–91), libretto by Lorenzo Da Ponte (1749–1838). First performance: Vienna, Burgtheater, 26 January 1790; first performance in U.K.: London, Haymarket, 9 May 1811; in U.S.A.: New York, Metropolitan Opera House, 24 March 1922.

ORIGINAL CAST. Francesco Benucci (Guglielmo), Dorotea Bussani (Despina), Francesco Bussani (Don Alfonso), Adriana Ferraresi (Fiordiligi), Louise Villeneuve (Dorabella), Vincenzo Calvesi (Ferrando).

SYNOPSIS. Act I, Scene I. The scene is set in Naples around 1790, and the events are sparked off by a bet. Two officers, Ferrando (tenor) and Guglielmo (baritone), seated at a café table, boast to Don Alfonso (bass) of the faithfulness of Dorabella (mezzo-soprano) and Fiordiligi (soprano), the girls they are engaged to marry. The old bachelor cynically contradicts them and says he is prepared to make a bet that, given the chance, both girls will forget the promises they have given and take new lovers. The two young men confidently accept the wager and, in accordance with Alfonso's conditions, place themselves at his disposal for twenty-four hours. Scene II. A garden overlooking the sea. Dorabella and Fiordiligi gaze at the portraits of their lovers and pour out their fond feelings. Alfonso enters, announcing that the two young officers are coming to take their leave, because they have suddenly been called to the wars. This make-believe parting has been devised by Alfonso to test their fidelity. Ferrando and Guglielmo enter to bid their loved ones goodbye. The melting music of their farewells is punctuated by Alfonso's cynical comments. Scene III. A room in the sisters' house. Despina (soprano), the maid, tries to console her mistresses. Her concepts of morality are similar to those of Don Alfonso and she uses the same types of argument. Why weep over the parting? Why not spend the period of separation as happily as possible, seeing that their absent lovers will certainly not remain faithful to them? The sisters go out and Alfonso arrives. He asks Despina to help him in his plan, promising a reward, and she agrees to introduce two new suitors into the house. These are none other than Ferrando and Guglielmo, disguised as Albanians. Dorabella and Fiordiligi react angrily to the declarations of love professed by the two strangers and flounce haughtily out of the room, while the two young officers, more than ever convinced of the fidelity of the girls, are beside themselves with joy. Nevertheless they agree to carry on, according to the terms of the bet, and for the full twenty-four hours to play the parts Alfonso and

Despina have devised. Scene IV. The garden. Dorabella and Fiordiligi, inconsolable, lament the absence of their lovers. The two Albanians, apparently desperate, enter, followed by Alfonso, who tries to talk to them. Before the sisters' eyes, the Albanians drink from small bottles of poison and fall to the ground. Despina rushes off to fetch a doctor and the two girls, left alone with their new suitors, who have tried to commit suicide for love, are moved for the first time by feelings of tenderness. Despina returns, disguised as a doctor, reviving the men with a magnet. Immediately they resume their declarations of love, thanking them for their recovery. Act II. Scene I. A room in the house. The sisters, encouraged by Despina, allow themselves to be persuaded to meet the new suitors that evening in the garden. Scene II. The garden by the sea. The two Albanians appear on board a sumptuously decorated boat. Alfonso and Despina arrange that the 'wrong' couples are formed. Fiordiligi and Ferrando wander off down the garden, while Dorabella, not unreceptive to Guglielmo's wooing, agrees to exchange tokens with him. Fiordiligi, however, refuses to give in. When Ferrando and Guglielmo meet to compare progress, Guglielmo is delighted to learn that Fiordiligi has not yielded to his friend, whereas Ferrando is in despair at

Design by Alessandro Sanquirico for Mozart's La Clemenza di Tito. *Milan, Museo Teatrale alla Scala.*

Frontispiece and title-page of La Clemenza di Tito *by Mozart, 1795 edition.*

Dorabella's betrayal. Scene III. A large room in the house. Dorabella tells Despina what has happened in the garden. Fiordiligi enters, announcing that she is going off to join her fiancé so as not to be further tempted by improper thoughts and feelings. Dressed as a soldier, she is about to depart when Ferrando enters. His arguments are more successful this time, and she eventually falls into his embrace. It is now Guglielmo's turn to despair, as Alfonso claims his victory. Nothing now remains but to prepare for the weddings. Scene IV. A room with a table prepared. The wedding banquet is about to commence and the deception reaches its climax. Before a notary, who is actually Despina in another disguise, the two couples sign the marriage contracts; but the ceremony is interrupted by a distant rolling of drums announcing the return of the army. The two Albanians hide in the next room and return in officers' uniform. The marriage contracts are handed over by Alfonso to the two young men, who refuse to listen to their fiancées' excuses for their behaviour. Guglielmo and Ferrando draw their swords and burst into the next room to avenge themselves on their rivals, only to emerge half-dressed as the Albanians. The trick is finally disclosed. Don Alfonso calms the girls down and the couples – but which ones? – are united.

■ Probably as a result of a successful performance of *Le Nozze di Figaro* in Vienna in 1789, Mozart was commissioned by Joseph II to write a new opera in collaboration with his librettist Da Ponte. The story, apparently suggested by the emperor himself, was supposed to have been based on something of the kind that had really happened around that time in Trieste and was the subject of much gossip in Viennese drawing-rooms. The score was completed in an amazingly short time, almost wholly during the month of December 1789. An evidence of this is the fact that Mozart frequently used abbreviations, something he normally never did. On 31 December, at his house in the Juden-platz, Mozart presented his opera to a few friends, including the loyal Puchberg (who had so often come to the composer's aid when in financial trouble) and Joseph Haydn. On 21 January there was a first rehearsal with orchestra. The Viennese public gave the opera a rapturous reception and there was a run of five performances before the end of January, cut short by the death of Joseph II. The action of *Così fan Tutte* is extremely simple, and, in contrast to the traditions of *opera buffa*, is shorn of all irrelevant episodes that are likely to hold up the story. The entire plot has an intentionally symmetrical structure adapted from Italian comedy. At the centre is Don Alfonso, cynical and rational, a man of the world all too well acquainted with human failings, who arranges the couples in new, diverting poses, as if they were puppets. He is the anti-conformist who denies everything, who strips away all illusions and always appears in ensemble scenes as if he were conducting an orchestra. The music skilfully conveys the message that underneath the masks and the artifice there are real people with genuine emotions. The climax of this amusing interplay of sentimental relationships comes in the final duets for the pairs of lovers, the words of which suggest a sober return to the realm of reason and a sweeping away of illusions, human nature being as it is – fragile, unstable and vulnerable. It may have been this rather cold, intellectual tone which prevented the opera from achieving wide popularity in the nineteenth century. It is said that Beethoven criticized it rather severely, judging the subject to be too frivolous. The libretto was readapted many times during the course of the nineteenth century, the moral being more sternly underlined to make it more acceptable; and it was only in the early years of the present century that Mozart's original version again took the stage, soon to be hailed as a masterpiece all over the world.

GUILLAUME TELL (William Tell)

Drame lyrique *in three acts by André Grétry (1741–1813), libretto by Michel-Jean Sedaine (1719–97), based on the work by Antoine Lamierre. First performance: Paris, Comédie-Italienne, 9 April 1791; first performance in U.S.A.: New Orleans c. 1817; New York, 12 August 1831.*

SYNOPSIS. In the Swiss village of Altdorf, in the canton of Uri, the Austrian governor Gessler has set up a pole with his hat on top and ordered the villagers to bow down to it in token of their submission as they pass. William Tell, a simple, peaceable man, passing by with his son, refuses. Gessler angrily accuses him of insubordination, and as punishment commands him to shoot an arrow at an apple placed on his son's head. Tell, a marksman with the crossbow, obeys the cruel order and splits the apple in two, declaring that had his son been killed, he would have avenged himself on Gessler. For this he is imprisoned, but as he is being ferried across Lake Lucerne a storm breaks enabling him to escape. He returns to take vengeance on the governor and kills him. This was the signal for the revolution to begin which would liberate Switzerland from the oppressor.

■ The opera, which was triumphantly received in 1791, owed much of its success to the fact that the public identified closely during this French revolutionary period with the Swiss patriots. To be fair, however, the music is not without merit, strongly evoking the atmosphere of mountain life and making good use of Swiss folk themes. Grétry mentioned in his memoirs that he had met a Swiss officer at Lyons and asked him to sing some of the most popular songs of his homeland. *Guillaume Tell*, which held its place in the repertory throughout the revolutionary years, was later banned by order of the Emperor; only in 1828 did it reappear at the Opéra-Comique, even though by this time both the libretto and music had been drastically mutilated.

LODOÏSKA

Opera in three acts by Luigi Cherubini (1760–1842), libretto by Claude-François Filette-Loraux, based on the romance Les Amours du Chevalier de Faublas *by Jean-Baptiste Louvet de Couvray (1760–97). First performance: Paris, Théâtre Feydeau, 18 July 1791; first performance in U.S.A.: New York, 4 December 1826.*

SYNOPSIS. The action takes place in Poland in 1600. It tells the story of the young Count Floreski (tenor) who, accompanied by his squire Varbel (bass), is desperately searching for the girl he wishes to marry, Lodoïska (soprano), princess of Altanno, although the match has been turned down by her father. He finds that she had been imprisoned in the grim castle of Dourlinski (baritone), who also desires to marry her. Floreski risks his life in challenging Dourlinski but, when the castle is attacked and burned down by the

Scene from Mozart's Die Zauberflöte, *designed by Marc Chagall for a production at the Metropolitan Opera, New York, in 1967. In the foreground are Sarastro, Tamino and Pamina.*

Design by Simon Quaglio for Mozart's Die Zauberflöte, *for a production in 1818 in Munich.*

Tartar chieftain Tizikan (tenor), Dourlinski forgets about his prisoner, who is rescued by her lover.

■ This was the second opera written in Paris by Cherubini. It was an overwhelming triumph and had two hundred performances in succession. In fact, it was the great operatic showpiece of the French revolutionary period, more than compensating Cherubini for the failure of his first Parisian opera, *Démophoon* (page 100). Fifteen days after it was produced at the Théâtre Feydeau, another opera based on the same libretto, with music by Rodolphe Kreutzer, was staged at the Comédie-Italienne, but the third act borrowed much of Cherubini's music. In subject matter and in style, *Lodoïska* was a forerunner of romantic opera.

LA CLEMENZA DI TITO (The Clemency of Titus)

Opera seria *in two acts of Wolfgang Amadeus Mozart (1756–91), libretto by Caterino Mazzolà, based on a play of the same name by Pietro Metastasio. First performance: Prague, Ständetheater, 6 September 1791; first performance in U.K.: London, Her Majesty's, 27 March 1806; in U.S.A.: Tanglewood, 4 August 1952.*

ORIGINAL CAST. Antonio Baglioni (Tito), Maria Marchetti-Fantozzi (Vitellia), Domenico Bedini (Sesto), Carolina/Anchulina Perina (Annio), Gaetano Campi (Publio), Antonini (Servilia).

SYNOPSIS. Ancient Rome. Vitellia's palace. Vitellia (soprano) is jealous that Tito (tenor), Emperor of Rome, has chosen to marry Berenice and she schemes with Sesto (soprano, originally castrato) to kill him and set fire to the Capitol. Sesto is reluctant to overthrow his friend, who is now a model ruler, but he would do anything to please Vitellia, whom he loves. Annio (soprano, 'travesty' role) tells them that Tito has sent Berenice away because the marriage would not have pleased his subjects, so Vitellia asks Sesto to postpone execution of the plot. Annio then asks Sesto to obtain Tito's permission for his marriage to Servilia (soprano), Sesto's sister. The forum. The Emperor receives ambassadors and announces his intention of marrying Servilia himself. Annio bravely compliments him on his choice and is commanded to tell Servilia of the decision. He tries but cannot bring himself to do so. The Imperial garden. Tito refuses to look at a list of conspirators but praises Servilia for confessing her love for Annio and gives his permission for their marriage. Vitellia misconstrues Servilia's happiness to indicate that she is already enjoying the prospect of being the next Empress and orders Sesto to go through with their plot. She then learns with dismay that Tito has resolved to ask for her own hand. Sesto returns from carrying out the arson and assassination and would almost confess to Tito's murder if Vitellia did not stop him, for fear of being implicated. The chorus bewails the destruction of the Capitol. Act II. Sesto is amazed to hear that Tito has survived and while Annio urges him to remain in Rome, Vitellia encourages him to leave before the plot, and her part in it, is discovered. Sesto is arrested by Publio, who later reports to Tito that the Senate has condemned him to the arena. Annio makes a last plea for his friend. Tito interviews Sesto before signing the warrant and eventually decides to tear it up. He lets Publio think, however, that he has signed it. When, on the way to the arena, Annio and Servilia tell Vitellia that as the future Empress she alone can save Sesto, she realizes that although she has not been betrayed her remorse compels her to confess her crimes. In the arena, therefore, when Tito announces that Sesto's fate has been decided, Vitellia rushes forward and clears him with her own confession. Tito is exasperated to find further evidence of conspiracy, but he pardons them both, and all the other conspirators.

■ Mozart had composed no serious opera for ten years when, towards the end of the last summer of his life, the impresario Guardasoni asked him to write an opera to celebrate the coronation of Emperor Leopold II as King of Bohemia. He was given only four weeks to write the music and had no choice as to the libretto. This was *La Clemenza di Tito*, written by Metastasio in 1734, and now, as Mozart himself noted, '. . . abridged as an opera by Signor Mazzolà, court poet to the

Papageno in Mozart's Die Zauberflöte. *Engraving by Pistrucci. Milan, Museo della Scala.*

The trials of fire and water in Mozart's Die Zauberflöte. *Design by Simon Quaglio, 1818. Munich, Theatermuseum.*

Sketch by Camillo Parravicini for the first act of Cimarosa's Il Matrimonio Segreto, *as performed at La Scala on 1 January 1936.*

Elector of Saxony'. The reason for this reworking of the text was that in 1791 it was no longer possible to orchestrate a Metastasio libretto without modifying entire acts by introducing ensemble scenes, notably, in this case, three duets, two trios, the final quintet to Act I and the final sextet in Act II. The characters in the libretto were pretty dull and lifeless, and Mozart had great difficulty in providing them with flesh and blood. Because of the short time at his disposal Mozart entrusted his pupil Süssmayr with the composition of the recitatives. The first performance was moderately successful and as a result of later revivals, audiences gradually warmed to the work. *La Clemenza di Tito* was the first Mozart opera to be performed in London.

DIE ZAUBERFLÖTE (The Magic Flute)

Singspiel in two acts by Wolfgang Amadeus Mozart (1756–91), libretto by Johann Emanuel Schikaneder (1751–1812). First performance: Vienna, Theater auf der Wieden, 30 September 1791; first performance in U.K.: London, Haymarket, 6 June 1811; in U.S.A.: New York, 17 April 1833.

ORIGINAL CAST. Johann Emanuel Schikaneder (Papageno), Josepha Hofer (the Queen of the Night), Benedict Schack (Tamino), Franz Xaver Gerl (Sarastro) Anna Gottlieb (Pamina).

SYNOPSIS. The action takes place in an imaginary ancient Egypt. Act I. A mountain landscape, with a temple in the background. Tamino (tenor), dressed as a hunter, enters, pursued by a snake. Exhausted, he falls unconscious. The doors of the temple open and three Ladies (two sopranos, one contralto) emerge. They kill the snake, admire the handsome youth and retire to warn the Queen of the Night (soprano). Tamino, recovering consciousness and seeing the dead serpent, is astonished, believing he owes his life to an odd-looking person who has just appeared, the wandering bird-catcher Papageno (baritone), dressed in feathers and playing on a pipe. Papageno does not deny having performed the feat, but is immediately punished for his lie by the three Ladies, who close his mouth with a golden padlock. Meanwhile they show Tamino the portrait of the Queen of the Night's daughter Pamina who, they say, has been kidnapped by an evil magician called Sarastro. Struck by her beauty, he at once falls in love with her. The Queen (soprano) then appears in person and Tamino swears to rescue her daughter. The Ladies hand the prince a flute with magic powers and free Papageno of his padlock, instructing him to accompany Tamino to Sarastro's palace, and giving him a magic set of chimes. They promise that three Genii will guide them on their journey. In Sarastro's palace Pamina (soprano) has tried to escape from the amorous advances of Monostatos

Ball at the Teatro San Carlo, Naples. Opera houses were centres of social life where people met, gambled and attended dances and masked balls.

(tenor), but he has recaptured her. Monostatos runs away, terrified, when he sees Papageno who thus has time to tell Pamina that, under her mother's instructions, he has come with a young prince to save her. They steal away together. The scene changes to a wood. Tamino enters, led by the three Genii (two sopranos, one contralto). They reach the temple of Isis. Two of the doors, those of Reason and Nature, are closed. The third, the door of Wisdom, opens to reveal a priest, who explains that Sarastro is not a cruel magician and that the most compelling motives have led him to take Tamina away from her mother's evil influence. Tamino is relieved to learn that the girl is still alive. Left alone, he plays his flute and wild animals come forward to listen. Then he hears Papageno's chimes and runs off to look for his companion. Papageno and Pamina, in the wood, are then caught by Monostatos but he and his followers are bewitched by the sound of the magic chimes and release them. Immediately, Sarastro's approach is heralded. Pamina asks his pardon for trying to run away and explains her reasons. Sarastro says he is prepared to let her marry a noble youth who is worthy of her, but cannot allow her to return to her mother. Tamino is dragged in by Monostatos. The two young people, meeting for the first time, fall into each other's arms, while Monostatos, begging to be rewarded, is punished instead. Act II. A palm grove outside the temple. Sarastro instructs his priests (one tenor, one bass) to take charge of Tamino, who is prepared to face the ordeals prescribed for the temple initiates, thus enabling him to marry Pamina. In the porch of the temple Tamino and Papageno, both hooded, also prepare themselves, one resolute, the other shaking with terror. The first ordeal to be faced is that of silence. Left alone, they are confronted by the three Ladies, who do all they can to make them fail the test, but in vain. Meanwhile Monostatos furtively approaches Pamina, while she is sleeping in a garden, intending to seduce her. The Queen of the Night appears in order to protect her daughter and Pamina happily embraces her, seeking consolation for the fact that Tamino has apparently abandoned her. The Queen makes her promise to kill Sarastro with a dagger. Monostatos, who has overheard everything, threatens to reveal the plot unless she gives herself to him. She refuses in horror, but Sarastro enters in time to save her. He reassures her that love, not vengeance, will lead to happiness. In the hall of the temple, Tamino and Papageno continue their ordeal. An ugly old crone talks to Papageno, saying that she is in love with him but before she can tell her name she vanishes to the accompaniment of a loud clap of thunder. The Genii descend with a table of food, which Papageno is consuming when Pamina enters. Tamino, sworn to silence, will not speak to her and she is overcome with misery. Sarastro then initiates them into the final mysteries, assuring Pamina that Tamino's feelings for her are unaltered. Papageno meanwhile has been thinking about wine and women. The old crone has made him swear to be faithful to her and been transformed into Papagena (soprano), a young woman dressed in feathers exactly like him, but a priest immediately orders them to separate. The Genii stop Pamina from committing suicide and lead her to the place where Tamino has to go through the final ordeals of fire and water. They greet each other tenderly and by playing the flute they come through the ordeals unscathed. Papageno, in despair, contemplates death since he seems to have lost his girl, but the Genii bring her in and they are joyfully reunited. In a vault beneath the temple, the Queen of the Night, accompanied by Monostatos and her three Ladies, plot to kill Sarastro but the ground, convulsed by an earthquake, opens wide to engulf them. The last scene in the temple of the Sun sees Sarastro on his throne, surrounded by priests who, with Tamino and Pamina, celebrate the victory of the sun over darkness.

■ The disturbing news arriving from France in 1790 had augmented the gloom and suspicion pervading the Austrian capital, currently adapting to the rule of the new sovereign Leopold, who had succeeded his brother Joseph II. Many people were especially attracted by the ceremonies of freemasonry, Mozart himself having joined the ranks of an order which preached the spirit of universal brotherhood. It was a difficult period for the composer. His health was beginning to decline, his finances were in a precarious state and his friend and collaborator Da Ponte had been dismissed from the court theatre. At this critical time, both materially and psychologically, Mozart was asked to compose the music for a *singspiel* by Schikaneder, manager of a small theatre in the suburbs of Vienna, the Theater auf der Wieden. Schikaneder was an odd individual. In his role as impresario he delighted in spectacular effects, with much splendid scenery and plenty of complex mechanical devices. As an actor he was considered to be the finest living interpreter of Shakespeare, and in everyday life he shunned all rules and conventions. Mozart found all these aspects of Schikaneder's character appealing. He also happened to be the author of the libretto offered to Mozart. It was based upon the story *Lulu oder die Zauberflöte*, by August Jakob Liebeskind, published in Wieland's famous collection. The text had originally incorporated, with varying success, elements of fairy-tale, then much in vogue (as it was, too, in Italy, where Gozzi had ushered in a similar revival); but in Mozart's hands it was completely transformed by the introduction of ideals and rituals inspired by freemasonry, which heightened the inner significance of the work. The *singspiel* or German operetta was a fairly recent genre, the origin of which went back, in fact, to the French *opéra-comique* which had been warmly received in Vienna since 1752. It contained a miscellany of diverse ingredients ranging from French-style romances to Italian arias and German *lieder*. Mozart's score united these disparate elements and left the world this musical testament to the ideals of humanity. The public acclaim for the opera, which increased with each performance, made Mozart very happy. On 7–8 October 1791 he wrote: 'What pleases me most is the silent assent!' In the first year alone *Die Zauberflöte* was performed more than one hundred times, but barely a month after the première Mozart died. Even his rival Salieri immediately realized that here was a truly important opera; and Goethe declared that only this music would have been of sufficient stature to provide an accompaniment to his *Faust*.

IL MATRIMONIO SEGRETO (The Secret Marriage)

Opera buffa *in two acts by Domenico Cimarosa (1749–1801), libretto by Giovanni Bertati (1735–1815), based on the comedy* The Clandestine Marriage *(1766) by George Colman the Elder and David Garrick, and on the comedy* Sophie, ou le Mariage Caché *(1768) by M. J. Laboras de Meziers-Riccoboni. First performance: Vienna, Burgtheater, 7 February 1792; first performance in U.K.: London, King's Theatre, 11 January 1794; in U.S.A.: New York, Italian Opera House, 4 January 1834.*

SYNOPSIS. A room in the house of Geronimo, a rich merchant from Bologna. His younger daughter Carolina (soprano) has secretly married Paolino (tenor) and they are waiting for a convenient moment to reveal the situation. Geronimo is far from happy about her choice of suitor, for he wishes both his daughters to marry into the nobility. Paolino, hoping to bring Geronimo (bass) round to his way of thinking, arranges for Count Robinson (bass), a needy English nobleman, to ask for the hand of the elder daughter, Elisetta (mezzo-soprano). Geronimo is delighted. Elisetta interprets Carolina's lack of interest in the prospect as jealousy and this provokes a squabble between the sisters, Geronimo seeking to calm things down by promising Carolina that she too will have a good match. When Count Robinson arrives he promptly makes for Carolina, who decides that the time is now ripe to disclose the truth. She and Paolino consider asking the Count for his cooperation, but when Paolino tries to do so the Count anticipates him by saying that he plans to marry Carolina and not Elisetta. Elisetta surprises the Count declaring his feelings for her sister and angrily calls him a traitor and her a flirt. Act II. The same room as in the first act. Old Geronimo, who is deaf, cannot keep pace with events, but the Count manages to explain that he intends to marry the younger daughter rather than the elder, and obtains his consent, though with only half the promised dowry. The Count informs Paolino, who decides to ask for the assistance of Fidalma (contralto), Geronimo's widowed sister. As he is about to broach the subject, Fidalma tells him she wants to remarry and that he is her choice! Paolino promptly faints. The young couple decide that the only solution is to run away, but Carolina suggests trying once more to enlist the Count's aid. They leave, and the Count enters with Elisetta. He lists his many defects in an attempt to

Madame Scio, who sang the leading role at the first performance of Cherubini's Médée.

dissuade the girl from marrying him, but she will not take the hint and manages to persuade Geronimo to place Carolina temporarily in a convent. As Paolino and Carolina get ready to run away, Elisetta hears whispering in her sister's room. Thinking it is the Count, in a fit of jealous rage she summons everyone to catch the guilty pair red-handed. But while the Count enters from another room, Paolino and Carolina emerge from hers, kneeling before Geronimo and confessing the truth. Once the surprise and expressions of grief are over, they receive Geronimo's forgiveness, while the Count resigns himself to marrying Elisetta.

■ *Il Matrimonio Segreto* was Cimarosa's most representative and successful work, a perfect example of eighteenth-century Italian comic opera. After staying for three years at the Russian court, from 1789 until 1791, Cimarosa, on his way back from St Petersburg to Naples, stopped for three months in Warsaw and for rather longer in Vienna, where Leopold II offered him a lodging and an annual salary. It was here that he composed *Il Matrimonio Segreto*, first performed on the day Leopold signed a treaty of alliance with Prussia against the revolutionary French government. The opera was a huge success. The Emperor, who was in the audience, invited the composer and the entire cast to dinner when it was over. After dinner he asked them all to go back into the theatre and repeat the whole work – an unprecedented occurrence in the annals of opera. In 1793 *Il Matrimonio Segreto* was staged in Naples with a few alterations and the addition of some new pieces. The enthusiasm was so great that it was given 110 successive performances. The opera became famous all over Europe and is still as popular as ever. As a rule the last scene, in which Count Robinson goes back on his word and abandons Elisetta, is omitted.

PAUL ET VIRGINIE

Opera in three acts and six scenes by Jean-François Lesueur (1760–1837), libretto by Alphonse Du Congé Dubreuil, based on the novel by Bernardin de Saint-Pierre. First performance: Paris, Salle Favart of the Opéra-Comique, 13 January 1794.

SYNOPSIS. The story tells of the love of two young people, Paul and Virginie, who live far from civilization, on the remote Île de France (Mauritius) in the Indian Ocean. One day, however, Virginie is forced to leave this island paradise, having been summoned back to France by a rich aunt who wants to provide her with a suitable education. It is not long before the girl has grown melancholy and quite changed character, until one day she resolves to return to her lost island and her love. She boards a ship but, when almost at her destination, dies during a storm at sea. Paul helplessly watches her dead body washed ashore.

■ The opera, at its first performance, was not very successful, but the storm scene was greatly praised, influencing the stage design of many later operas.

LE ASTUZIE FEMMINILI (The Cunning Women)

Melodramma giocoso in four acts by Domenico Cimarosa (1749–1801), libretto by Giovanni Palomba. First performance: Naples, Teatro dei Fiorentini, 16 August 1794; first performance in U.K.: London, 21 February 1804.

ORIGINAL CAST. Carlo Casaccia, L Martinelli, Antonio Benelli, Giovanna Codecasa, Marianna Muraglia, Luisa Negli.

SYNOPSIS. The action takes place in Rome. Act I. Bellina's house. Romualdo (baritone), her guardian, tells Bellina (soprano) that her father has stipulated that she can only inherit his property if she marries Giampaolo (bass), an elderly landowner from Naples. Giampaolo, although received mockingly by the girl, is enchanted by her. Bellina, with the approval of her duenna Leonora (mezzo-soprano) and her friend Ersilia (soprano), decides to do all she can to avoid marrying the old man because she is in love with her cousin Filandro (tenor). To create confusion, Leonora tells Giampaolo that both Romualdo and Filandro hope to marry Bellina. The elderly suitor prepares for battle, and has a few tricks up his sleeve. He informs Filandro that Romualdo is due to marry Bellina and tells Romualdo that Filandro is in love with the girl. Act II. The garden of Leonora's house. Bellina and Filandro express their mutual love and resolve to play a joke on Giampaolo. The old man surprises them embracing and draws a gun. Bellina asks his forgiveness and Giampaolo replies that he is ready to get married immediately. He goes into the house, brandishing his pistol, but Leonora pretends to mistake him for a criminal and starts yelling from the window. People gather, there is general confusion and plans for the wedding go up in smoke. Act III. Bellina's house. Leonora tells everyone that Bellina has left home. A Hungarian officer, speaking a strange language, appears (it is Filandro in disguise), and says he is looking for his fiancée, who has run off to find a certain Filandro, with whom she is in love. The officer has already arrested Filandro but cannot trace the girl. Bellina arrives, likewise dressed as a Hungarian, and indicates that she is searching for her fiancé, who has run away to be with a certain Bellina. The latter has been apprehended but there is no sign of her man. The two eccentric foreigners are introduced and promise in exchange to find Bellina and send her home. Act IV. A veranda, with a view over Rome. Giampaolo and Romualdo are discussing the question of marriage between old men like themselves and a young girl such as Bellina. The two 'Hungarians', just married, appear, amid general rejoicing. The old men then recognize Bellina. At first they are furious, but resign themselves to a *fait accompli*, forgive the couple and join in the celebrations.

■ Written for the imperial court of Vienna in 1792, this opera is a mature work, full of freshness and originality, despite the banality of the plot. Cimarosa provided it with a delightfully melodious score and instead of making caricatures out of such conventional figures, as was usual in comic operas, allowed them to express their deepest feelings in singing of their joy and grief.

ALZIRA
Opera lirica *by Nicola Antonio Zingarelli (1752–1837), libretto by G. Caverta, based on* Alzire, ou Les Américains *by Francois-Marie Arouet de Voltaire (1694–1778). First performance: Florence, 7 September 1794.*

■ This was the year when Zingarelli became maestro di cappella at Loreto, and he did not care much whether or not the opera was a success. The only aria which is sometimes performed is *Nel silenzio i mesti passi.*

GIULIETTA E ROMEO (Romeo and Juliet)
Opera lirica *by Nicola Antonio Zingarelli (1752–1837), libretto by Giuseppe Maria Foppa*

(1760–1845). First performance: Milan, Teatro alla Scala, carnival of 1796; first performance in U.K.: London, 21 June 1824; in U.S.A.: New York, 26 July 1826.

ORIGINAL CAST. Adamo Bianchi, Giuseppa Grassini, Girolamo Crescentini, Angelo Monassi, Carolina Dianand, Gaetano De Paoli. Conductor: Luigi De Baillou.

SYNOPSIS. The opera follows closely the tenth chapter of the second volume of Girolamo Della Corte's *Storie di Verona*, without recourse to any of the later versions of the story, including that of Shakespeare.

■ This was the most important opera written by the prolific Neapolitan composer, who was highly esteemed by contemporaries. The first performance was given in honour of the Archduke Ferdinand and the Archduchess Maria Beatrice of Austria.

LODOÏSKA
Melodramma *in three acts by Giovanni Simone Mayr (1763–1845), libretto by Francesco Gonella, based on an anonymous poem. First performance: Venice, La Fenice, 26 January 1796.*

SYNOPSIS. The action takes place in Poland in medieval times. In the castle of Ospropoli, on the border with Tartary, Lodoïska is the prisoner of Boleslav, who has abducted her and wishes to force her to marry him; but she loves and is faithful to the young paladin, Lovinski. Meanwhile the Tartars threaten to invade Poland, war breaks out and Boleslav departs to challenge the Tartar forces commanded by Giskano. Lovinski, who has been searching for Lodoïska, is trapped by the Tartar army and fights a duel with Giskano, defeating him and, by sparing his life, winning his friendship. Narsemo, Lovinski's friend, tells him where to find Lodoïska and who has imprisoned her. When Lovinski meets Boleslav, he does not reveal his identity, and offers to help him persuade Lodoïska that her lover Lovinski is dead. The pair arrive at the castle, while Sigeski, Lodoïska's father, is warned of his daughter's perilous situation. Then, as Boleslav prepares to marry Lodoïska publicly, Lovinski casts off his disguise and, aided by Giskano, Sigeski and other companions, frees Lodoïska and punishes the evil Boleslav.

■ *Lodoïska*, along with *Ginevra di Scozia*, was one of the most famous operas written by Donizetti's German teacher, Johann Simon Mayr. The knightly theme stimulated him to compose music that is epic in style, with a wealth of rich, stirring tunes. The love duets provided an opportunity for music in a softer, more lyrical vein, sharply underlining conflicting feelings and passions. In the triumphant finale all the strands of the story – the violence and heroism of action and the tenderness of passionate love – are woven together as the music reaches a dramatic climax.

TÉLÉMAQUE DANS L'ÎLE DE CALYPSO, ou LE TRIOMPHE (Telemachus on the Island of Calypso)
Opera in three acts by Jean-François Lesueur (1760–1837), libretto by A. F. Dercy, based on Fénélon's romance Télémaque *(1699). First performance: Paris, Salle Favart of Opéra-Comique, 11 May 1796.*

■ The opera recounts some of the adventures of Telemachus, inspired by the first four books of the *Odyssey*, especially his visit to the island of Calypso. This idyll ended abruptly when the young man, loved by Calypso, but himself in love with the nymph Eucharis, had to flee the isle. The overture to this typically neoclassical opera was composed, according to Lesueur himself, 'in a hypodorian mode and spondaic rhythm'.

GLI ORAZI E I CURIAZI (The Horatii and the Curiatii)
Opera seria in three acts by Domenico Cimarosa (1749–1801), libretto by Antonio Simeone Sografi (1759–1818). First performance: Venice, Teatro La Fenice, 26 December 1796; first performance in U.K.: London, 2 May 1805.

The singer Giuditta Pasta in Cherubini's Médée.

ORIGINAL CAST. Giuseppe Grassini, Carolina Manaresi, Girolamo Crescentini, Odoardo Caprotti, Antonio Mangini.

SYNOPSIS. The action takes place in Rome. Act I. Scene I. Porch of the temple of Janus. Alba Longa is at war with Rome. Sabina (soprano), a member of an important family of Alba Longa, the Curiatii, has married a Roman, Marcus Horatius (tenor). She finds that she is unable to hide her concern for her brothers, who are now engaged in the war against her homeland. Her brother-in-law Publius Horatius (tenor) informs her that a truce has been arranged between the two cities. When she also hears that another marriage is to be celebrated between the rival families (between Horatia (soprano) and Curiatius (baritone)), she is much relieved and leaves to prepare for the wedding. Scene II. At the house of the Horatii. The marriage ceremony has commenced and the two young people express their hope that they will never again be separated for political reasons. Licinius (tenor) brings news that the King of Rome Tullius Hostilius, and the King of Alba Longa, Mettius Fufetius, have agreed to settle the outcome of the war by combat between three warriors on either side. The contestants are to be three Horatii and three Curiatii – to the dismay of Sabina and Horatia. Act II. Scene I. On the Campus Martius all is ready for the combat when Horatia and Sabina arrive with the chief soothsayer (bass), priests and people. They claim that the gods may be unwilling to see a fight between relatives, and insist that the oracle be consulted prior to the battle. The combatants reluctantly agree, which gives the women a spark of hope. Scene II. A cave beneath the Aventine Hill. The background opens up to reveal the temple of Apollo. The voice of the oracle (bass) proclaims that the contest between the rival factions must proceed. Act III. Scene I. Outside the Circus Maximus. Horatia remains alone after being left by Curiatius. Voices from inside the stadium announce that two Horatii are dead. Horatia leaves with her attendants. Scene II. A large square in Rome. Marcus Horatius, on a triumphal chariot, is hailed by a joyful crowd. At his feet are the dead bodies of the three Curiatii, one of whom was Horatia's husband. Crazed with grief, Horatia curses her brother, who rebukes her for showing so little love for her country. When she invokes the curses of the gods upon him. Horatius strikes her down with his sword.

■ At its first performance the opera was a complete failure, but later it became popular enough to be performed 48 times in succession.

LE CANTATRICI VILLANE (The Singing Countrywomen)
Opera giocosa in two acts by Valentino Fioravanti (1764–1837), libretto by Giovanni Palomba. The date of the first performance is uncertain, but was between 1796 and 1801; first performance in U.K.: London, 27 May 1842.

Maria Callas in the part of Medea in Cherubini's opera at the Teatro dell'Opera, Rome.

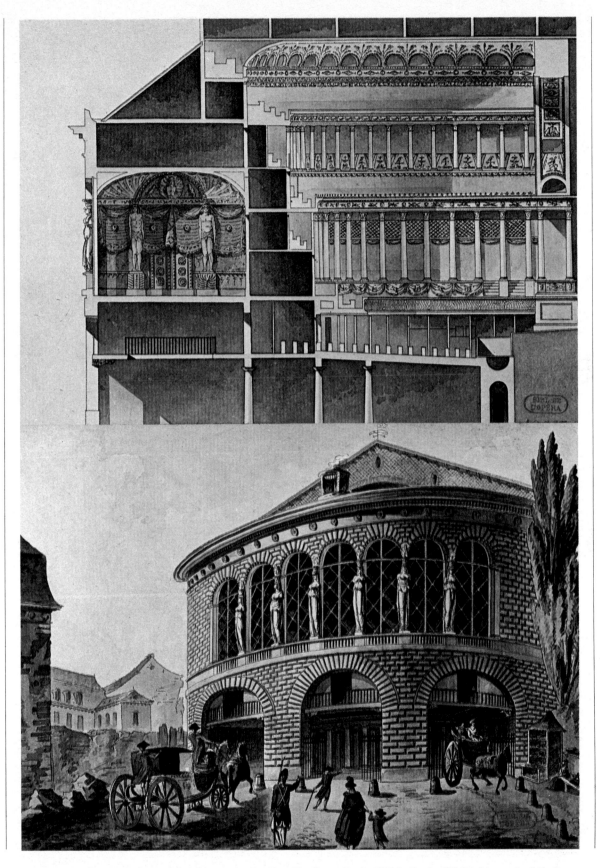

Cross-section and exterior of the theatre in the Rue Feydeau, Paris, 1791. Paris, Bibliothèque de l'Opéra.

SYNOPSIS. Act I. At Frascati, the innkeeper Agata (soprano) and two countrywomen, Giannetta (mezzo-soprano) and Rosa (soprano), have decided to become singers. Bucefalo (bass), a poor, ignorant musician, promises to teach them to sing. The three women immediately begin squabbling over the best parts and their respective talents. Agata and Giannetta are also jealous because their teacher seems to prefer Rosa. He asks Marco (bass), a foolish and benevolent music-lover, to lend him his harpsichord so that he can take it to Rosa's house. Marco, because he is in love with Rosa, agrees. Rosa is, in fact, the supposed widow of Carlino (tenor), a young soldier missing in Spain. At this point in the story he returns, sporting large moustaches so that nobody recognizes him. Hearing the country gossip, he suspects that his wife has been unfaithful, forgetting him all too quickly. His suspicions light on Bucefalo and Marco, and he vows to avenge himself. In order to achieve this, he pretends to be billeted in Rosa's house, on his quartermaster's orders. She objects at first but is gradually persuaded to agree, when Carlino threatens to smash everything in sight. Act II. Marco, to ingratiate himself with Rosa, decides to become an opera impresario so that he can sing duets with her. A group of musicians arrives from Rome and he borrows them for the evening for a full-scale rehearsal in Rosa's house. This arouses the jealousy of the other women still further, but when Rosa and Marco sing, they stumble over both the words and the music. Carlino and some peasants arrive with pistols drawn. In the confusion Giannetta runs off to fetch the police. Now Carlino reveals his identity to everyone and begs forgiveness, claiming that he has been motivated by jealousy and love. Marco sends the police away and all ends happily.

■ The date of the first performance is not certain. Some critics believe that the opera was staged at Reggio Emilia in 1796, others that it was given in Turin (1795) or Naples (1798), etc. The libretto bears the date 1798. Fioravanti, in his memoirs, wrote that it was performed at the Carnival of 1798 at the beginning of 1799. In any event, a shortened one-act version (with the libretto adapted by Giuseppe Maria Foppa) was given at Venice, in the Teatro di San Moisè, on 28 December 1801. Of the 75 operas written by Fioravanti, all of them popular at the time, *Le Cantatrici Villane* was greatly acclaimed and performed throughout Europe, remaining in the repertory to this day.

MÉDÉE (Medea)
Opera in three acts by Luigi Cherubini (1760–1842), libretto by François Benoît Hoffmann, based on the tragedy (1635) by Corneille, itself inspired by Euripides and Seneca. First performance: Paris, Théâtre Feydeau, 23 Ventôse of Year V (13 March 1797); first performance in U.K.: London, Her Majesty's, 1865; in U.S.A.: University of Hartford, Conn., 1970.

ORIGINAL CAST. Mme J. A. Scio in the role of Médée.

SYNOPSIS. The story takes place in Corinth. Act I. Entrance to the palace of Créon, King of Corinth (bass). It is the eve of the wedding of his daughter Glauce (soprano) to Jason (tenor), the hero who had brought back the Golden Fleece from Colchis. This task had been achieved with the aid of Medée (soprano), the sorceress who, for Jason's sake, had betrayed her father and the people of Colchis, and had killed her brother Absyrtus. She had then followed Jason to Corinth and borne him two sons. Now Jason has abandoned her in order to wed Glauce, who fears the vengeance of Médée. Jason and Créon are unable to calm her. A mysterious, veiled woman presents herself at the palace gate. It is Médée, uttering sinister threats. Créon drives her away. She vainly tries to entice Jason back, but he spurns her and she angrily curses him, threatening terrible vengeance. Act II. A wing of the palace next to Juno's temple. Médée is desperate and her maid Neris (mezzo-soprano) is unable to drag her away from the palace. Créon enters and orders the sorceress to leave the city immediately. Médée, already resolved to kill her children to avenge herself, requests him to allow her one last day to spend with her boys, and Créon agrees. She pretends to be resigned and instructs Neris to take as a wedding gift to Glauce a nightgown and a magic diadem, given to her by Apollo. Act III. The area between Créon's palace and the temple. Neris comes out of the palace with Jason's children, who embrace their mother. Médée is still torn between her love for them and the desire to avenge herself on Jason. She draws a dagger and clasps her children close. Just then there is a great cry of lament from the palace. Glauce is dead, killed by the gifts of Médée. Jason grieves for his lost love, while the infuriated crowd bays for the blood of the sorceress. She takes refuge with her children in the temple, but reappears soon afterwards, followed by Neris, who is screaming in terror. Médée is surround by the Furies as she brandishes the bloodstained dagger with which she has just killed her sons. She promises that her shade will follow Jason even to the Underworld. Setting fire to the temple, she vanishes in the flames.

■ Generally considered Cherubini's most successful opera, *Médée* is also the most complex and compelling. When first performed in Paris, it was not particularly successful and was not staged again there. In the same month, March 1797, two parodies of the work were performed, in two different theatres – *La Sorcière* by Charles Auguste Sewrin and *Bébée et Jargon* by Pierre Villiers and Pierre Adolphe Capelle. Nevertheless, with *Médée*, Cherubini pointed the way to nineteenth-century tragic opera, far removed from eighteenth-century models. The atmosphere of tragedy which pervades the entire work is evoked in masterly fashion. Following the traditions of the Théâtre Feydeau and of the Opéra-Comique, Cherubini was not permitted to provide music for the recitative, which remained as spoken dialogue. These passages were later set to music by Franz Lachner for a performance at Frankfurt-am-Main (1 March 1855), and from then on recitative accompanied by music became an integral part of opera. In the German-speaking countries *Médée* achieved considerable popularity. The first German version was staged in Berlin in 1800, and the opera was praised by Beethoven, Weber, Schumann, Brahms and Wagner. In Italy, the composer's homeland, it was not performed until 1909, at La Scala, Milan. It was revived in 1952 at the Florence Maggio Musicale, and the stupendous performance of Maria Callas in the title-role brought the opera vividly to life.

L'HÔTELLERIE PORTUGAISE (The Portuguese Inn)
Opera in one act by Luigi Cherubini (1760–1842), libretto by Étienne Aignan (1773–1824). First performance: Paris, Théâtre Feydeau, 25 July 1798.

SYNOPSIS. Portugal, about 1640. The scene is a courtyard of an inn, near the Spanish frontier. Two women, Gabriella (soprano) and her maid Ines (soprano), arrive. Gabriella has fled from her home to escape from her hated guardian Roselbo (baritone), who wants her to marry him. She is trying to reach Lisbon, where she hopes to find her lover Don Carlos (tenor). Rodrigo (bass), the innkeeper, who is instinctively suspicious and tends to see intrigues where they do not exist, has read casually in a paper that the governor's wife has fled from Lisbon with a lady friend and is trying to reach the frontier. Rodrigo at once identifies his customers as the fugitives and resolves to help them. When Carlos arrives with his groom Pedrillo (baritone), searching for Gabriella, Rodrigo mistakes them for secret rebel agents hot on the tracks of the governor's wife, and turns them away, saying that the ladies have departed for the frontier. Roselbo, the guardian, also turns up at the inn, in pursuit of his missing ward. Once more Rodrigo is completely mistaken, and believing that he can trust Roselbo, informs him that there are two very important ladies inside who need help. Roselbo pretends to agree to protect them. The innkeeper triumphantly calls out the two women but when he sees how they react to seeing the old man, he realizes that there has been a mistake. Carlos and Pedrillo return unexpectedly, however, carrying a decree annulling the will of Gabriella's father, by which she became Roselbo's ward. The enraged guardian departs and the lovers embrace.

■ This opera was not a great success when first performed. The subject was judged unsuitable and this alone decided the public against it.

LES DEUX JOURNÉES, ou LE PORTEUR D'EAU (The Two Days, or The Water-Carrier)
*Opera in three acts by Luigi Cherubini (1760–1842), libretto by Jean Nicolas Bouilly. First performance: Paris, Théâtre Feydeau, 16 January 1800; first perfor-*mance in U.K.: London, Covent Garden, 14 October 1801; in U.S.A.: New Orleans, 12 March 1811.

ORIGINAL CAST. Mme J. A. Scio, P. Gaveux, Juliet.

SYNOPSIS. Paris, about 1640. A water-seller, the Savoyard Daniel Micheli (baritone), has concealed in his house Count Armand (tenor) and his wife Constance (mezzo-soprano), who are wanted by the police for having offended Cardinal Mazarin. Old Daniel has recognized Armand as the man who once, in Berne, saved him from dying of starvation, and wishes to repay the debt. His children, Antoine (tenor) and Marcelline (soprano), appear, having just obtained passes enabling them to travel to the village where Antoine is to marry Angélique (soprano), a farmer's daughter. Together they concoct a plan to get the two fugitives out of the city. A captain of the guard arrives, with orders to requisition the house. Daniel immediately puts the Count to bed and pretends that he is his old sick father. The next day Constance manages to get through the cordon by using Marcelline's pass. She is joined by Daniel with his cart and water-barrel, inside which the Count is hiding. The water-seller tells the guards he has seen the fugitives elsewhere and then opens his barrel so that the Count can leave his hiding place and escape. In the village where his fiancée lives, Antoine helps Count Armand to conceal himself in the hollow trunk of a tree, while Constance takes refuge in Angélique's house. Some soldiers appear and settle down at the foot of the very tree where Armand is hidden. Constance, who has brought her husband food, is arrested for her suspicious behaviour and faints. When she recovers she calls to her husband by name, causing him to be recognized and arrested. Fortunately, Daniel arrives with a royal decree which exonerates and frees Armand.

■ *Les Deux Journées*, *Médée* and *Lodoïska* were the three greatest operatic successes of Cherubini. The first of these established the composer's reputation in Europe, and its success compensated him for the failure of preceding works. The opera was given 200 successive performances; and it was staged in translation in the German-speaking countries. Later it was almost completely forgotten. The libretto is complex and rather threadbare, but Cherubini's music stems from his greatest creative period. Beethoven and Weber both admired the work.

LE CALIFE DE BAGDAD (The Caliph of Baghdad)
Comic opera in one act by François Adrien Boïeldieu (1775–1834), libretto by Claude Godard d'Aucour de Saint-Just. First performance: Paris, Opéra-Comique, Salle Favart, 16 September 1800; first performance in U.K.: London, Her Majesty's, 11 May 1809; in U.S.A.: New Orleans, 2 March 1806.

SYNOPSIS. The caliph of Baghdad, Isaaum, wishes to be loved for his own sake, In disguise he pays court to the charming Zeltubé but he is mistaken by many

The Theater an der Wien, Vienna. Coloured print, c. 1815.

people, including Lémaïde, Zeltubé's mother, for a brigand who has been roaming the district and terrifying the people. Despite all the people who denounce him and all the tests to which he is subjected, the girl's tender feelings are unchanged. The characters of the opera include a highly ridiculous cadi and a mischievous servant girl.

■ The theme is derived from Arabic stories, presenting an Oriental world as viewed through European eyes. A well-contrived plot and a fresh, melodious score guaranteed that the opera would be popular. It was, in fact, one of Boïeldieu's greatest successes, although contemporaries judged its popularity undeserved. It is said that Cherubini, after a performance, rounded on the composer, saying: 'Aren't you ashamed of such an undeserved success?' In the eight years that he stayed at the court theatre in St Petersburg, Boïeldieu worked hard to perfect his technique, well aware of his shortcomings.

GINEVRA DI SCOZIA (Ginevra of Scotland)

Opera by Giovanni Simone Mayr (1763–1845), libretto by Gaetano Rossi (1774–1855), based on Ariosto's Orlando Furioso. *First performance: Trieste, Teatro Nuovo, 21 April 1801.*

SYNOPSIS. Ginevra, daughter of the king of Scotland, and Ariodante, a brave Italian knight, are in love. Polynesso, duke of Albania, is the young man's rival. He spreads the rumour that he is the princess's lover and, with the connivance of Dalinda (her maidservant) manages to convince Ariodante that Ginevra is being unfaithful to him. Dalinda, in fact, shows herself, in her mistress's clothes, on the balcony in a secret meeting with Polynesso. Ariodante, in despair, throws himself into the river. According to Scottish law, a duel be-

tween two knights must be fought to decide whether Ginevra is innocent or guilty. Her champion Rinaldo defeats Polynesso, accusing him of calumny and treason. Ginevra is declared innocent and Ariodante, who has been saved from drowning, marries the princess and succeeds the evil Polynesso as high constable of the kingdom.

■ The opera has considerable dramatic power, and the music, especially in some of the more romantic scenes, is poignant and expressive, giving the work a genuine feeling of modernity.

SCHERZ, LIST UND RACHE (Jest, Cunning and Revenge)

Singspiel in four acts by Ernst Theodor Amadeus Hoffmann (1776–1822), libretto by Johann Wolfgang von Goethe (1749–1832). First published: Poznan, 1801.

SYNOPSIS. Scapino and Scapina are a married couple who plan to extort money from a rich, miserly doctor by setting a trap for him. Scapino pretends to be poor and lame, introducing himself to the doctor and asking for employment. The doctor agrees and meanwhile tries to seduce the charming young Scapina. She pretends to be poisoned and accuses the doctor of trying to kill her. He is terrified of being charged with homicide and decides that his only chance of evading discovery is to get rid of the inconvenient body as soon as possible, For this, he enlists Scapino's help, offering him fifty sequins as reward. The cunning servant carries his wife into the garden, where she begins to weep and complain, a sign, at least, that she is not yet dead. Hearing the noise, the doctor, scared that she will now accuse him of attempting to poison her, offers her another fifty sequins to hold her tongue. The opera ends in the

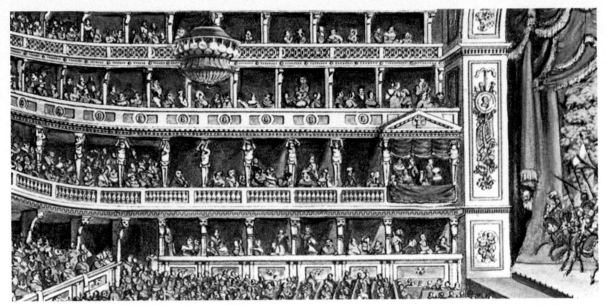

Interior of the Theater an der Wien.

complete triumph of the artful pair and the discomfiture of the duped old miser.

■ The play was written by Goethe in about 1790, on the invitation of the composer Kayser who, after a journey to Italy in 1784, had been much impressed with Italian comic opera. Goethe, too, seemed happy with the work and wrote a libretto based on the traditional characters of the Italian *commedia dell'arte* (the figure of the doctor is clearly derived from the Bolognese Doctor Balanzone), creating a variety of amusing situations. But the opera, although furnished with a score by Kayser and published in 1790, was never staged. The same libretto came to the notice of Hoffmann when, as a young man, he was a government official in Poznan, and he used it to compose a *singspiel*, one of his first musical exercises. Neither Goethe's text (which the author himself later criticized severely, for although containing many comic touches it lacked coherence) nor Hoffmann's somewhat immature and unoriginal music is of great interest, and the *singspiel* is seldom performed today.

ANACRÉON, ou L'AMOUR FUGITIF (Fleeting Love)
Opera in two acts by Luigi Cherubini (1760–1842), libretto by R. Mendouze. First performance: Paris, Opéra, 4 October 1803.

SYNOPSIS. The opera takes place at Teos in Ionia. The poet Anacréon is now old and preparations are being made to honour him. He meditates sadly on his physical disabilities, for mentally he still feels young and alert. Corinne, a young singer, loves him and he returns her love; when he sees her, he becomes more cheerful and sings, to the accompaniment of his lyre, in praise of Amor and Bacchus. A violent storm breaks

out and amid the uproar he hears the voice of a boy begging to be admitted to his house. Anacréon readily agrees and the youth tells him of a family intrigue which has forced him to run away. There is no truth in this tale, for the boy is really Amor in disguise. During the festivities the god fills all the participants with ardent passion. Meanwhile a messenger arrives from the island of Cythera, sent by Vénus to ask for the return of her son. She is prepared to grant any wish to the person who sends him back to her. In Anacréon's house a lengthy discussion ensues as to whether it would be right for Amor to return. Then Vénus herself appears in her chariot. To reward Anacréon for his hospitality, she allows him to live for the rest of his days with his loved one.

■ This opera marked the composer's return to the theatre during a period of grave anxieties. But the work was unsuccessful, the main criticism being that the music was too typically German. It was not given again after the première; but in 1805 several passages were performed at a concert in Vienna.

LEONORA, or L'AMORE CONIUGALE
Opera in two acts by Ferdinand Paër (1771–1839), libretto by Giacomo Cinti. First performance, Dresden, 3 October 1804.

■ This opera was staged several months before Beethoven's *Fidelio* on the same subject. In Paër's composition there are certain similarities with Beethoven's style, which are also evident in various other works of that period. In 1798 an opera of the same title *Léonore, ou L'amour Conjugal* had been performed, with a libretto by Jean Nicolas Bouilly and music by Pierre Gaveaux.

Scene from the third act of Beethoven's Fidelio, *performed in Vienna in 1970.*

FIDELIO, oder DIE EHELICHE LIEBE (Fidelio, or Conjugal Love)

Lyric drama in two acts by Ludwig van Beethoven (1770–1827), libretto by Josef Sonnleithner after Jean-Nicolas Bouilly's Léonore, ou L'Amour conjugal *for Gaveaux; reduced to two acts by Stefan von Breuning (1806); final form by Georg Friedrich Treitschke (1814). First performance: Vienna, Theater an der Wien, 20 November 1805; [final two-act version, Vienna, Kärntnertor Theatre, 1814]; first performance in U.K.: London, Haymarket, 18 May 1832; in U.S.A.: New York, Park, 9 September 1839.*

ORIGINAL CAST. A. Mildner, L. Müller, F. Demmer, S. Meyer, Caché, Rothe, Weinkopf, conducted by the composer.

SYNOPSIS. A state prison near Seville during the eighteenth century. Leonora (soprano) in disguise as a youth, calling herself Fidelio, has entered employment as an assistant to Rocco (bass), the chief jailer, in order to discover whether her husband Florestan (tenor) is imprisoned there. When Florestan disappeared two years earlier a rumour spread that he had died, but in fact he had been secretly captured by Don Pizarro (bass), the prison governor, who hates him. Only Leonora suspects this. Act I. Scene I. Marcellina (soprano), Rocco's daughter, now favours Fidelio with her attention rather than Jaquino (tenor), the porter. Rocco is delighted with his new assistant and promises to give him Marcellina as a bride, to his daughter's joy and Fidelio's distress. Fidelio asks to be allowed to help Rocco more in his duties and the old jailer agrees, saying that there is only one prisoner, held in the lowest dungeon for two years, whom he must not visit. Scene II. Don Pizarro gives orders for more sentries to be posted and receives an anonymous warning that a

Minister of State, Don Fernando, is to make a surprise inspection of the prison the next day. He resolves to have Florestan murdered, but Rocco refuses to kill a prisoner and agrees only to dig the grave. Fidelio overhears this scheme; when Pizarro has left to read his dispatches, she reminds Rocco that it is the day when he permits the prisoners a brief walk in the open air. Fidelio eagerly scans each prisoner as he emerges into the sunlight, hoping in vain that one may be her husband. Rocco tells her that Pizarro has agreed to the wedding of Fidelio and Marcellina and that Fidelio may accompany him to the dungeon to dig the grave. Pizarro re-enters, angrily objecting that the prisoners should not have been allowed out without his express permission, but Rocco justifies himself by replying that it was to celebrate the King's birthday. As the prisoners return to their cells, Fidelio and Rocco prepare to descend to the dungeon. Act II. Scene I. A dungeon. Florestan, exhausted by starvation and delirious, thinks that he hears Leonora calling him to heaven. Rocco and Fidelio enter and begin to dig the grave; Leonora cannot immediately see whether the prisoner is her husband or not, but resolves in any case not to let him be murdered. When she gives him food, however,

Illustration for Beethoven's Fidelio.

La Vestale *by Gaspare Spontini. Scenes and costumes by Piero Zuffi, production by Luchino Visconti, at La Scala on 7 December 1954. Cast: Maria Callas (Giulia), Franco Corelli (Licinio), Ebe Stignani (high priestess), Nicola Rossi Lemeni (pontifex maximus).*

she recognizes him; Florestan begs Rocco to send a message to his wife that he is still alive but Rocco refuses; Leonora tries to calm his mounting hysteria. Pizarro enters and prepares to stab his victim when Leonora reveals her true identity and threatens him with her pistol; a trumpet announcing Don Fernando's arrival sounds. Pizarro realizes that he must greet the Minister, and husband and wife sing a joyful duet. Scene II. Fernando (bass) promises to right the wrongs of all those unjustly imprisoned and is horrified to see that his old friend Florestan, whom he believed dead, stands before him. The story is explained and Pizarro is arrested; Leonora unlocks her husband's chains amidst general rejoicing.

■ Initially Beethoven was commissioned to write a fantastic-heroic opera entitled *Vestas Feuer*, to a libretto by Schikaneder, manager of the Theater an der Wien. He had already begun work on it when news arrived that Schikaneder had been replaced; so he had to abandon that project and choose another subject, eventually accepting a new work suggested by the composer and writer Sonnleithner. This was a 'rescue-opera', of a type that was very fashionable at the time, entitled *Léonore, ou L'Amour Conjugal*, previously set to music by Gaveaux, Paër and Mayr, and based on Bouilly's *Léonore*. The work was a tragedy with a happy ending, such as was very popular in France, but the librettist provided new, original versions of certain pieces, making substantial alterations to the plot. The composer worked on the music from 1803 until 1805; but when the opera was finally staged, the audience pronounced it a failure. The lack

of enthusiasm was due mainly to the weakness of the singers and to the presence of many Frenchmen in the audience who did not understand German. A modified version of the libretto was used by von Breuning for a production, entitled *Leonore*, given at the Theater an der Wien on 29 March 1806. On this occasion the opera was reduced from three to two acts, but it still met with little success. After a few performances, the embittered Beethoven revised the score. A third version was staged at the Kärntnertor Theater in Vienna on 23 May 1814. This time the text – with the plot much simplified – had been adapted by Treitschke; and once more the score was reworked by Beethoven himself. This complicated chain of events is largely explained by the fact that this was the great composer's first excursion into the field of opera. Commenting on this, both Wagner and Berlioz gave the highest praise to the purely symphonic parts of the score or, more precisely, to passages not conditioned by the stage action. This was borne out clearly by the third, definitive version of the opera, in which the demands of the plot were sacrificed, in large measure, to the concern for emphasizing the inner significance of the opera. Sternly moralistic in outlook, Beethoven saw in Leonora's heroism a striving towards the highest ethical and civilized ideals. For this reason *Fidelio*, although acknowledged to contain passages of sublime beauty and pure musical genius, is often criticized for being too static and somewhat lacking in dramatic coherence. That is probably why it was only a modest success in the nineteenth century. Today, however, *Fidelio* is regularly performed (almost always in its third version) all over the world.

Design by Alessandro Sanquirico for the temple of Vesta in Spontini's La Vestale.

JOSEPH EN ÉGYPTE
Drame mêlé de chant *in three acts by Etienne Nicolas Méhul (1763–1817), libretto by Alexandre Duval (1767–1842). First performance: Paris, Opéra-Comique, 17 February 1807; first performance in U.K.: London, Drury Lane, 7 April 1841; in U.S.A.: Philadelphia, 15 October 1828.*

ORIGINAL CAST. Elleviou (Joseph), Solie (Jacob), Mme Gavandan (Benjamin), Gavandon (Siméon).

SYNOPSIS. Memphis, at the time of the Biblical famine. Joseph (tenor), governor of Egypt, has saved the country from starvation, as a result of having stored quantities of grain during the seven 'fat years'. He wishes his father Jacob (bass) and his brothers to join him, in order to save them, too, from the famine. They arrive by chance and, unaware of his identity, ask for hospitality. Joseph consents, without telling them who he is. Siméon (tenor), the brother responsible for selling him into slavery, unknown to his father and brothers who have assumed him dead, is overcome by remorse. Unable any longer to bear the weight of his guilt, he confesses his deed to Jacob, who angrily curses him. Joseph, however, begs for the father's forgiveness and then reveals his identity. Pardon is given in an atmosphere tense with emotion, and the opera ends in songs of peace and honour to God.

■ The music to this opera, Méhul's most famous work, is lyrical and melodious, although the tone is at times too gentle and unenterprising to do full justice to the subject. On the whole, however, the opera, rich in harmony and counterpoint, contains many pages of simple but happily inspired music.

LA VESTALE (The Vestal Virgin)
Tragédie lyrique *in three acts by Gaspare Spontini (1774–1851), libretto by Victor Joseph Etienne de Jouy. First performance: Paris Opéra, 16 December 1807; first performance in U.K.: London, King's Theatre, Haymarket, 2 December 1826; in U.S.A.: New Orleans, 17 February 1828.*

ORIGINAL CAST. E. Lainé, F. Lays, H. E. Dérivis, A. C. Banchu, M. T. Maillard.

SYNOPSIS. Act I. The forum in Rome, near the temple of Vesta. The city is preparing for the triumph of Licinio (tenor), a young general who has returned victorious from Gaul. He is, however, deeply troubled, confiding to his friend Cinna (tenor) that he is in love with Giulia (soprano) who, in obedience to her dying father, has become a priestess of Vesta, vowed to chastity. Giulia, too, is perturbed at the hero's return but the chief priestess (mezzo-soprano) encourages her determination to resist profane love and selects her to crown Licinio with the laurel wreath. As she performs this ceremony, Licinio tells her of his love and his hopes. Act II. The temple of Vesta. Giulia is left alone to watch over the sacred flame, which must never be extinguished. At first she prays for strength to withstand Licinio, but when he enters they sing an impassioned love duet, forgetting to attend to the holy flame, which dies out. Cinna warns them of the arrival of the priests and Vestals. Licinio escapes to seek help. Giulia refuses to give his name to the pontifex maximus (bass) and prays that he may be spared the fate which is decreed for her – stripped of her priesthood she is to be buried alive. Act III. Near the tomb where Giulia is to be buried alive. Licinio confesses his guilt to the pontifex maximus, but to no avail. Giulia's black veil of shame is placed on the altar and she bids farewell to life and her companions. Suddenly the sky darkens and lightning strikes the altar upon which Giulia's veil has been placed. Vesta's will is clear: the sacred flame has begun to blaze again and the goddess has forgiven the girl. Giulia is now free to marry Licinio and in a grove of roses, before the temple of Venus Erycina, the young couple are welcomed by a joyful chorus of Vestals.

■ This was Spontini's most ambitious opera and the most important neo-classical work of the First Empire. The opera worthily enshrines the artistic ideals of its day in endeavouring to reestablish measure and balance, characteristic features of classical art. Although the characters seem a bit lifeless and contrived, being incapable of independent action and at the complete mercy of events, the opera has much solid merit. The score is inventive, the music well structured and the tonal combinations often bold and original, pointing in the direction of Beethoven's symphonic works. In this sense the opera aims at combining Italian melodic genius with German symphonic ideals.

FERNAND CORTEZ, ou LA CONQUÊTE DU MEXIQUE (The Conquest of Mexico)

Tragédie lyrique in three acts by Gaspare Spontini (1774–1851), libretto by Victor Joseph Etienne de Jouy and Joseph Alphonse Esménard, based on a tragedy by Alexis Piron. First performance: Paris Opéra, 28 November 1809; first performance in U.S.A.: New York, Metropolitan Opera House, 6 January 1888.

Costume for the character of Joseph, as sung by Jean Elleviou in Méhul's Joseph en Égypte. *Paris, Bibliothèque de l'Opéra.*

Costume design by Hippolyte Lecomte for Spontini's Fernando Cortez, 1809. *Paris, Bibliothèque de l'Opéra.*

ORIGINAL CAST. A. C. Banchu, E. Lainé, F. Lays, Laforet, P. Dérivis, J. H. Bertin.

SYNOPSIS. Act I. Mexico City. Temple of the god of evil. The high priest (bass) is about to sacrifice some Spanish prisoners including Alvaro (tenor), brother to Cortez (tenor). On the advice of the Mexican prince Telasco (baritone), whose sister Amazily (soprano) is a captive of the Spaniards, king Montezuma (bass) decides to interrupt the sacrifice. Amazily enters with an offer of peace from the Spaniards, who are almost at the city gates. Cortez has fallen in love with her and she has been converted to Christianity. The oracle which the Mexicans have consulted gives inauspicious replies. Act II. The Spanish camp. Cortez is unable to raise the morale of his soldiers. Moralez (baritone), his friend and confidant, warns him that Amazily may be a spy, but Cortez, certain of her loyalty, receives her lovingly when she returns to the camp. She tells him what has happened and stresses the cruelty of the Mexican priests. Cortez swears to save Alvaro and when Telasco arrives, with rich gifts and a proposal to exchange Alvaro for his country's safety, Cortez persuades his men not to accept. He orders the Spanish fleet to be burnt so that nobody can leave and that Telasco be held hostage. Act III. The funeral monument of the Mexican kings in the city. The Spaniards advance and Cortez releases Telasco. Telasco, however, unyielding in his hatred of the enemy, swears to return Alvaro and the other prisoners only in exchange for Amazily. Cortez reluctantly allows Amazily to go back to her people and she brings them another offer of peace from the Spaniards. The Mexicans have prepared to die, along with their prisoners, in their besieged and ruined city, but Montezuma, finally convinced of Cortez's sincerity, agrees to his marrying Amazily and becomes his ally.

■ Strange things happened to this opera at its earliest performance. It had been commissioned by the Emperor Napoleon I, who had suggested the subject as if to celebrate his own victories in allegorical style. He had just declared war on Spain. The public, however, fascinated by Spontini's music, ignored the propaganda intended by Napoleon and read a completely different meaning into the work. So although *Fernand Cortez* was extremely popular and successful, it was promptly banned from the stage. The composer revised it, and when it was performed again in 1817 it was far more dramatic and had an unexpectedly happy ending. Spontini himself was far from satisfied with the finale, so much so that he sketched out four different versions. Today there is no way of knowing which of these scores he regarded as definitive. There is a yawning gulf between his story, with its happy conclusion, and historic reality. Montezuma was, in fact, assassinated and his people wiped out. Although judged to be inferior, both in dramatic power and expressiveness, to *La Vestale, Fernand Cortez* is an opera on a large scale, with moments of extraordinary beauty. Particularly memorable, among modern revivals, was the one at the Naples San Carlo in December 1951, with Renata Tebaldi as Amazily.

PIMMALIONE (Pygmalion)
Opera in one act by Luigi Cherubini (1760–1842), libretto by Stefano Vestris, partly based on an Italian version by Antonio Simone Sografi of Rousseau's Pygmalion. *First performance: Paris, Théâtre des Tuileries, 30 November 1809.*

SYNOPSIS. The story is based on the Greek legend of the Cypriot sculptor who, falling in love with his statue of the beautiful Galatea, brings it to life, with the help of the goddess Aphrodite.

■ Cherubini was going through a period of severe depression, coupled with financial difficulties and the hostility of Napoleon, when he was persuaded to write a one-act opera to be presented anonymously at the private theatre in the Tuileries. The suggestion came from the singer Crescentini and the soprano G. M. Grassini, two Italian artists who enjoyed the Emperor's favour and who believed that this might be a way for the composer to regain Napoleon's regard. The text was Italian and the opera did not displease the Emperor; but it achieved nothing for Cherubini. It was performed twice in 1809, and again in 1812.

SILVANA, or DAS WALDMÄDCHEN (The Girl of the Woods)
Romantic opera in three acts by Carl Maria von Weber (1786–1826), libretto by Franz Karl Hiemer based on the play entitled Das stumme Waldmädchen *by Carl Franz Goulfinger von Steinsberg. First performance: Frankfurt-am-Main, 16 September 1810; first performance in U.K.: London, Surrey, 2 September 1828.*

SYNOPSIS. Act I. During a bear hunt in a forest, Silvana (soprano), a dumb girl, hides in her cave. Rudolf (tenor), who is betrothed to Adelhart's daughter Mechtilde (soprano) though he cannot love her, catches Silvana. He falls in love with her and takes her back, drugged, to the castle. Act II. Adelhart (bass) vainly tries to persuade his daughter Mechtilde to accept Rudolf, whom she does not love. She is in love with Albert (tenor), the son of the man who stole her sister Ottilie to revenge himself on their mother, who had rejected him in favour of Adelhart. Meanwhile Silvana has awoken in Rudolf's room in the castle and indicates that she loves him and that she has left her father behind in the forest. Rudolf sends Krips (bass) to find him. A tournament is held and an unknown knight carries off the prizes; when he is revealed as Albert, Mechtide and Rudolf defend him from arrest by Adelhart's men. Act III. Silvana's 'father' Ulrich (spoken) turns out to be a squire who disobeyed orders to kill Ottilie, Adelhart's other daughter, and brought her up in the woods instead. At his command, 'Silvana' speaks again and she is reunited with her father and married to Rudolf in a double wedding with Albert and Mechtilde.

■ Written during a stormy period of Weber's life (he had been expelled from Württemberg for an alleged fraud, of which he was probably innocent, and for an affair with the singer Margaret Lang), *Silvana* is a brilliant example of the composer's 'second period'. The première was not well attended because on the same day people were more interested in watching Mme Blanchard making a balloon ascent. The Berlin revival, however, was a great success.

LA CAMBIALE DI MATRIMONIO (The Marriage Contract)

Farsa comica *in one act by Gioacchino Rossini (1792–1868), libretto by Gaetano Rossi (1774–1855). First performance: Venice, Teatro San Moisè, 3 November 1810; first performance in U.K.: London, Sadler's Wells Theatre, 23 April 1954; in U.S.A.: New York, 8 November 1937.*

ORIGINAL CAST. R. Morandi, N. De Grecis, L. Raffanelli, T. Ricci.

SYNOPSIS. A room in the house of the elderly agent, Tobia Mill (bass). He is satisfied because a rich American businessman named Slook (baritone) has made him a good offer – a large sum of money for a beautiful young wife. Tobia immediately thinks of his own daughter Fanny (soprano) who, in turn, quickly hears of the scheme from her father's cashier, Norton (bass), and her chambermaid, Clarina (soprano). She is secretly in love with the handsome young Edoardo Milfort (tenor) and is distressed by her father's decision, but her two friends promise to help her. When the American arrives, he cannot but be aware of the frigid reception she gives him – she threatens to put out his eyes if he marries her – yet is nevertheless pleased with her. Edoardo then arrives, asserting his own right to marry Fanny. Slook is impressed by the determination of the two young people, so he gives Edoardo the marriage contract and names him his heir. He then takes Tobia aside and, though expressing approval of the girl, declares he will not marry her. The old man is furious and reminds him that he has signed the marriage contract, but the American cannot be moved and accepts when Tobia challenges him to a duel. On the duelling ground Slook informs Tobia that his daughter is deeply in love with Edoardo, and Tobia, knowing that the young man is now heir to all Slook's property, agrees to the marriage. The generous benefactor then takes his leave, returning to his own country, and the opera ends amid general rejoicing and congratulations.

■ *La Cambiale de Matrimonio* was composed when Rossini was only eighteen years old. Although not a success, it was well received. According to newpapers of the day, it was repeated a dozen or so times, not at all discouraging for a beginner. The story was based on a five-act comedy by Camillo Federici, which had provided a libretto that Carlo Coccia had set to music two years previously. Both texts did scant justice to the original, but Rossi's at least had the merit of introducing some comic episodes which enlivened the rather banal plot. Rossini, moreover, recognized the amusing possibilities of other passages and turned them to good account. Clearly he still lacked the knowledge and experience to create a new and original opera, and the methods he used for *La Cambiale* were derived from the contemporary Italian school. It must not be forgotten, either, that Rossini wrote the overture for the opera when he was still at the Liceo Musicale. It is interesting to note that this first operatic overture closes with the same chords and the same rhythm as his last, that of *William Tell*. The trio *Quell'amabile visino* seems to be the work of a master rather than that of a beginner. The aria *Vorrei spiegarvi il giubilo* contains a motif that recurs in the aria *Dunque io son la fortunata* in the *Barber of Seville*. Also worth noting is the final sextet *Vi prego un momento*. So there is a mixture of comic and sentimental features which already give a hint of the originality marking Rossini's later style. His special fondness for *opera buffa* was certainly demonstrated from the very beginning.

ABU HASSAN

Singspiel *in one act by Carl Maria von Weber (1786–1826), text by Franz Karl Hiemer from a story from the* Arabian Nights. *First performance: Munich, Hoftheater, 4 June 1811; first performance in U.K.: London, Drury Lane, 4 April 1825; in U.S.A.: New York, 5 November 1827.*

SYNOPSIS. Abu Hassan (tenor) and his wife Fatima (soprano) are besieged by creditors, notably Omar (bass). Hassan hits upon a scheme by which they each claim that the other is dead in order to claim the funeral money and a silk shroud. The trick succeeds and meanwhile Omar has been persuaded by the promises of Fatima's charms to settle the bills. When the Caliph arrives to discover which spouse has died and is confronted with two apparently lifeless bodies, he offers a large sum of money to any who can say who died first. Hassan immediately jumps up, claims that Fatima died first, and explains the story to the Caliph's amusement. Omar is conveyed to prison for immorality and Hassan is promoted to a higher salary.

■ The *singspiel* was a resounding success. Written in collaboration with Abbé Wogler, it is in an Oriental style following in Mozart's footsteps. During his stay in Munich Weber met the famous clarinettist Bärman, with whom a fruitful working relationship later developed.

L'INGANNO FELICE (The Happy Stratagem)

Farsa per musica *in one act by Gioacchino Rossini (1792–1868), libretto by Giuseppe Maria Foppa (1760–1845). First performance: Venice, Teatro San Moisè, 8 January 1812; first performance in U.K.: London, 1 July 1819; in U.S.A.: New York, 11 May 1833.*

SYNOPSIS. A valley, with the entrance to a mine, and the house of Tarabotto, leader of the coalminers. Ten years previously Tarabotto took into his home a poor young girl, Nisa, who he pretended was his niece, but who is really Isabella, wife of the Duke who owns the mine and who believes that she is dead. Ormondo and Batone, in fact, were responsible for a plot to make her disappear. The Duke then remarried but his second wife has since died. The Duke arrives with Ormondo and Batone (who almost recognizes Nisa) and Tarabotto arranges things in such a way that the Duke sees her, and they both become uneasy. Tarabotto then overhears Ormondo and Batone planning to abduct his 'niece', who so strangely resembles the duchess they had believed dead. Batone is on the point of repentance but does not wish to give himself away to Tarabotto, who plies him with pointed questions. Eventually Tarabotto tells the Duke that someone is trying to harm his 'niece'. Ormondo is ready to kill himself to expiate his crimes. Isabella, finally recognized as the duchess, prevents this. The opera ends in general rejoicing.

■ The opera, although described as a 'farce', only contains one minor episode that can be called amusing. It did, however, provide Rossini with a chance to show how cleverly he could handle characters, alternating comedy and drama. In this very youthful work, the characteristics that were to emerge so triumphantly in Rossini's later operas can already be recognized. The work was a great success, and none of his operas, prior to *Tancredi*, enjoyed a larger number of performances.

CIRO IN BABILONIA (Cyrus in Babylon)
Dramma *in two acts by Gioacchino Rossini (1792–1868), libretto by Francesco Aventi. First performance: Ferrara, Teatro Municipale, 14 March 1812; first performance in U.K.: London, Drury Lane, 30 January 1823.*

SYNOPSIS. Baldassare, King of Babylon, is attracted by Amira, wife of Ciro, King of Persia, whom he has defeated in battle. While she and her small son are his prisoners, the Babylonian king tries to persuade her to yield to his desires. She resists him. Ciro, disguised as an ambassador, tries to rescue her but is discovered and imprisoned. Baldassare is determined to have Amira, even against her wishes, and orders a wedding banquet to be prepared. Suddenly a violent storm erupts and in the midst of the thunder and lightning a mysterious hand traces on the wall, in letters of fire, an obscurely menacing message. The Babylonian king, much perturbed, summons his magicians and the prophet Daniele, who interprets the words as a sign of divine wrath. The magicians counsel the king to sacrifice his three illustrious Persian captives. As Ciro, Amira and their son prepare for execution, news arrives that the Babylonian defences have been breached by the Persians. Ciro is set free and assumes Baldassare's throne. The people pay homage to their new king.

■ *Ciro* can be regarded as an experimental work pointing to the mature masterpieces of Rossini's later years. He himself judged it a failure. In fact, the libretto is pretty weak, full of banalities and commonplaces. Yet the score contains some original arias, which gave the opera a certain popularity at the time.

LA SCALA DI SETA (The Silken Ladder)
Farsa comica *in one act by Gioacchino Rossini (1792–1868), libretto by Giuseppe Maria Foppa (1760–1845) after Planard's L'Echelle de soie for an opera by Gaveaux. First performance: Venice, Teatro San Moisè, 9 May 1812; first performance in U.K.: London, Sadler's Wells Theatre, 26 April 1954.*

SYNOPSIS. Giulia's apartment. Her guardian, Dormont, is unaware that his ward is secretly married to Dorvil, and wishes to marry her to Blansac. The latter is loved by Giulia's cousin Lucilla. Every night Dorvil joins his wife, climbing to her room by means of a silken ladder. One evening, coming away from their secret meeting, he meets Dormont and Blansac in front of the house, and they invite him in to see Giulia. Thus the husband is forced to watch Blansac pay court to his wife, who does not appear to be all that unwilling. Germano, the servant, hints to Blansac that Giulia will be waiting for him that night. Lucilla, discovering the assignment, hides in order to catch the couple; and the servant, too, prepares to eavesdrop. The silken ladder affords entry, as usual, to Dorvil. Then Blansac, the optimistic suitor, clambers up by the same route; and finally Dormont climbs the ladder into Giulia's room, surprising Lucilla, Germano and Blansac. The only solution would seem to be a quick wedding; but Dorvil, who has hidden himself on Blansac's arrival, now reveals the true state of affairs. The young couple are forgiven by Dormont, who also agrees to the marriage of Lucilla and Blansac.

■ The libretto was based on a French farce of the same name, already set to music by P. Gaveaux. Foppa, a noted writer, produced on this occasion a dull, feeble libretto, redeemed only by an amusing finale. Certainly it was a poor imitation of Cimarosa's *Matrimonio Segreto*. At the Venetian première, the reception was mixed; yet the opera held the stage until mid-June, an evident sign of approval. But it is not among Rossini's best works.

LA PIETRA DEL PARAGONE (The Touchstone)
Melodramma giocoso *in two acts by Gioacchino Rossini (1792–1868), libretto by Luigi Romanelli (1751–1839). First performance: Milan, Teatro alla Scala, 26 September 1812; first performance in U.K.: London, St Pancras Town Hall, 19 March 1963; in U.S.A.: Hartford, Conn., College of Music, 4 May 1955.*

SYNOPSIS. The wealthy Count Asdrubale (bass) invites a number of friends to his country home, among

Design by Alessandro Sanquirico for Rossini's Ciro in Babilonia, *1818.*

them the widowed marchioness Clarice (contralto), whom he loves. Two other ladies, Aspasia and Fulvia, are determined to marry him, so he decides to put them to the test. Disguised as a Turkish merchant, he arrives at the villa, claiming that the count owes him a large sum of money. His servant informs him that the debt will never be paid, so the Turk threatens to confiscate all the count's possessions. Most of his 'close' friends, not wishing to get involved in this affair, deny having anything to do with Asdrubale. Only Giocondo (tenor) and Clarice remain loyal to him. The count then reveals the trick and pardons them all. Meanwhile Clarice, determined to turn the table and test the count, dresses up as a soldier and introduces herself at his home as Lucindo, Clarice's twin brother, who is determined to remove his sister from an unsuitable environment which is causing her considerable distress. The count asks the stranger for his sister's hand in marriage. Clarice abandons her disguise and the two swear their mutual love. Aspasia and Fulvia, disappointed, have no choice but to find other lovers.

■ *La Pietra di Paragone* was received with great acclaim, and there were fifty performances after the première. The score is, in fact, one of Rossini's most graceful compositions.

IL SIGNOR BRUSCHINO, or IL FIGLIO PER AZZARDO (Mr Bruschino, or A Son By Chance)

Farsa giocosa *in one act by Gioacchino Rossini (1792–1868), libretto by Giuseppe Maria Foppa (1760–1845). First performance: Venice, Teatro San Moisè, end January 1813; first performance in U.K.: Orpington, Kentish Opera Group, 14 July 1960; in U.S.A.: New York, Metropolitan Opera House, 6 December 1932.*

SYNOPSIS. Florville (tenor), on the death of his father, tells Sofia (soprano) that he is finally able to marry her. Her guardian, Gaudenzio (bass), however, a bitter enemy of Florville's father, has promised the girl in marriage to a certain Bruschino (tenor), a stranger to everyone. Florville, for his part, refuses to accept this situation and goes to the inn where Bruschino is lodging. He discovers that the young man is in debt to the landlord, Filiberto (baritone). Florville pays off part of the debt and obtains in exchange a letter from Bruschino to his father, expressing regret for his folly and asking for help. Florville, letter in pocket, now goes to Gaudenzio, and impersonates Bruschino, getting into the old man's good books. When Bruschino senior arrives (bass), he does not recognize Florville as his own son but everyone

Rear façade of the Teatro La Fenice, Venice. 19th-century engraving.

assumes that he is deliberately denying him, because he does not really believe that he is repentant. When young Bruschino does appear, however, the father pretends that Florville is really his son and marries him off to Sofia in order to cancel the marriage contract with Gaudenzio. The guardian, enraged by the hoax, has to accept the *fait accompli*.

■ *Il Signor Bruschino*, also known as *I Due Bruschini* and *Il Figlio per Azzardo*, is another of Rossini's youthful works, but this is not why it failed to win the favour of audiences with conventional taste. Although the libretto was weak, Rossini's bold score scandalized his contemporaries. Thus the overture at one point has the violinists tapping their bows on their stands.

TANCREDI

Melodramma eroico in two acts by Gioacchino Rossini (1792–1868), libretto by Gaetano Rossi (1774–1855), based on Voltaire's tragedy and Tasso's Gerusalemme Liberata. *First performance: Venice, Teatro La Fenice, 6 February 1813; first performance in U.K.: London, 4 May 1820; in U.S.A.: New York, 31 December 1825.*

ORIGINAL CAST. A. Malanotte, E. Manfredini, P. Todran, L. Bianchi, T. Marchesi.

SYNOPSIS. Syracuse, in the ninth century. Act I.

Argirio (tenor), lord of the city, has promised his daughter Amenaide (soprano) in marriage to the leader of a rival faction, Orbazzano (bass) with a view to uniting all groups against the common enemy, the Saracens, who are besieging Syracuse. Amenaide is in despair, however, for, as she confesses to her friend Isaura (mezzo-soprano), she loves Tancredi (contralto), son of the deposed King of Syracuse; and she sends him a message. In the park of Argirio's palace, Amenaide warns Tancredi that he is suspected of being an ally of the Saracens and urges him to flee, without telling him about her father's marriage plans. When Tancredi discovers that the girl is about to wed another man, he reproaches her bitterly for her treachery. The girl confronts her father and proudly refuses the hand of Orbazzano. Orbazzano then produces a letter sent by Amenaide to her lover, which was intercepted accidentally near the Saracen camp. Because it does not bear the name of the intended recipient, it is assumed that it was intended for their chief, Solamir. Amenaide is thrown into prison, accused of having shamefully betrayed her people. Act II. Amenaide's prison. Argirio laments the fate of his daughter, for he has the duty of condemning her. Tancredi, unrecognized in disguise, challenges Orbazzano to a duel to prove the girl's innocence, although even Tancredi believes her guilty. Orbazzano is killed in the combat and Isaura reveals to Amenaide the true identity of the youth who has saved her. Tancredi still believes that she has betrayed him and despite her entreaties, he rushes off to defend the city against a fresh Saracen assault. His forces defeat the enemy and lift the siege of Syracuse. The message thought to have been sent to Solamir is discovered to have been meant for Tancredi and so, while the people celebrate the victory, he is finally united with Amenaide, with her father's blessing.

■ Whereas in Voltaire's tragedy Tancredi died in battle, not believing in Amenaide's innocence, the librettist's adaptation provided a happy ending, bowing to public taste. When, during Lent of the same year, the opera was staged at Ferrara, the book was partially rewritten, and the work ended with the hero's death. The audience showed its disapproval and the first version was restored. *Tancredi* was not an immediate success, for the Venice première had to be broken off half-way through the second act because of the sudden illness of one of the cast. But when staged again in Venice, the opera was a triumph, so much so that the aria *Mi rivedrai, ti rivedrò* was sung in the streets and on the canals. Making sparse use of 'dry recitative', Rossini filled his score with bold touches. The freshness and originality of the music justified the work's popularity, which was the first to establish the composer's fame.

L'ITALIANA IN ALGERI (The Italian Girl In Algiers)
Dramma giocoso *in two acts by Gioacchino Rossini (1792–1868), libretto by Angelo Anelli (1761–1820). First performance: Venice, Teatro San Benedetto, 22 May 1813; first performance in U.K.: London, Haymarket, 26 January 1819; in U.S.A.: New York, 5 November 1832.*

ORIGINAL CAST. M. Marcolini, S. Gentili, F. Galli, P. Rosich.

SYNOPSIS. Act I. Algiers. A room in the palace of Mustafa, the bey of Algiers. Mustafa (bass) no longer loves his wife Elvira (soprano) and plans to get rid of her by marrying her to Lindoro (tenor), a young Italian slave. He orders his henchman, Haly (bass), to find him an Italian wife. By chance, an Italian ship is shipwrecked on the coast and Haly congratulates himself on finding a beautiful girl, Isabella (contralto), suitable for the bey. She is, in fact, looking for Lindoro, whom she loves, and travelling in the company of an old admirer, Taddeo (baritone), whose niece she pretends to be. Isabella immediately impresses Mustafa with her beauty and, recognizing Lindoro, she arranges matters to her liking: she insists that Mustafa should retain Elvira as his wife and takes Lindoro as her personal slave. Act II. Haly, Elvira and Zulma (mezzosoprano), her confidante, are astonished to see the terrible Mustafa become so docile, while Isabella and Lindoro confirm their love for one another and plan an escape. Mustafa nominates Taddeo as Grand Kaimakan of Algeria in honour of his niece. In Isabella's apartment, she is dressing herself in the Turkish style and invites Elvira to join them. When the

Marietta Marcolini (Isabella), Filippo Galli (Mustafa) and Serafino Gentili (Lindoro), who sang at the first performance of Rossini's L'Italiana in Algeri *at the Teatro San Benedetto, Venice, on 22 May 1813.*

First act of Rossini's L'Italiana in Algeri *in the version given at La Scala, Milan, during the 1973–4 season. Designed and produced by Jean-Pierre Ponnelle.*

bey arrives to have coffee with her, Mustafa, anxious to be alone with Isabella, tells Taddeo that he will sneeze as a signal for his Kaimakan to get everyone else to leave. Isabella, however, intends to avoid being alone with him, and despite all his sneezing, everybody stays. Mustafa is overjoyed when Lindoro explains to him that the only reason Isabella delays in marrying him is that he does not belong to the noble order of 'Pappataci' (those who shall eat and be silent), because he can be initiated by Lindoro and Taddeo. Dressed in Italian clothes Mustafa is prepared for the ceremony by all the Italians in his household – Isabella has prepared escape for them all in return for their help. The guards are given too much to drink and the ceremony begins. Lindoro and Isabella pretend that the arrival of the ship is part of the ritual and it is only when all the Italians are on board and it is safely underway that Mustafa is brought to realize he has been tricked. Thankfully, he returns to Elvira and all ends happily.

■ Although the composer modestly described it as 'my pastime', *L'Italiana in Algeri* is one of Rossini's masterpieces, and was an immediate success with the Venetian audience, which insisted on the singers encoring almost all the numbers and gave Rossini a tremendous ovation. The composer, who had not thought his music would be understood, was so amazed that he exclaimed: 'Now I am happy. The Venetians are madder than I am.' The subject was probably based on a newspaper story. Anelli's libretto, commissioned by the Teatro alla Scala, was originally intended for Luigi Mosca, a Neapolitan composer, whose version had been staged in Milan five years before Rossini's own. Rossini took the same libretto, making minor alterations, and orchestrated it in the summer of 1813, taking only about twenty days. The pace of the action was determined by the rhythmic movement of the music; and although the characters are caricatures, they are drawn with considerable psychological perception and sympathy, emerging as completely original comic creations.

IL TURCO IN ITALIA (The Turk In Italy)

Dramma buffo in two acts by Gioacchino Rossini (1792–1868), libretto by Felice Romani (1788–1865). First performance: Milan, Teatro alla Scala, 14 August 1814; first performance in U.K.: London, Her Majesty's, 19 May 1821; in U.S.A.: New York, 14 March 1826.

SYNOPSIS. A gypsy camp, near Naples. Prosdocimo (baritone), a poet, is looking for a plot for a play. He comes across two runaway Turks, and Zaida (mezzosoprano) tells him that she left the service of one Selim Damelec because her love for him could not be fulfilled. A Neapolitan, Don Geronio (bass), then appears to have his palm read and complains that his wife Fiorilla is very temperamental, an observation that is borne out by her behaviour when she sees a handsome Turk (none other than Selim (bass)) arrive in the harbour. Prosdocimo is delighted by the turn of events for his purposes, but narrowly avoids a beating when the participants notice that he is making fun of them. From the moment when Fiorilla (soprano) confronts Zaida, the complications build up to a suitably hilarious climax of a masked ball, after which Selim takes Zaida back to Turkey, Fiorilla returns to

Geronio, Narciso (Fiorilla's young admirer) learns from his experience and Prosdocimo goes off to write his play.

■ *Il Turco in Italia* was not an immediate success. One reason was that it followed on the heels of *L'Italiana in Algeri*, and many people persisted in regarding it merely as a pale imitation of the more famous opera. Another was that the public could not adjust to Rossini's brilliant and novel idea of creating the action on two levels, one devoted to the comic intrigues and misunderstandings involving the main characters, the other isolating the figure of the poet, at once inside and outside the main action, but virtually pulling the strings. The charm of the opera was immeasurably increased by Rossini's sparkling score.

IL BARBIERE DI SIVIGLIA (The Barber of Seville)
Melodramma buffo in two acts by Gioacchino Rossini (1792–1868), libretto by Cesare Sterbini (1784–1831), based on the comedy by Beaumarchais. First performance: Rome, Teatro Argentina, 20 February 1816 (with title of Almaviva *or* L'Inutile Precauzione*); first performance in U.K.: London, Haymarket, 10 March 1818; in U.S.A.: New York, Park Theater, 3 May 1819.*

ORIGINAL CAST. L. Zamboni, G. Giorgi-Righetti, M. García, B. Botticelli, E. Vitanelli.

SYNOPSIS. Act I. Scene I. Seville, a square at dawn. Count Almaviva (tenor) is in love with Rosina (mezzo-soprano), ward of Dr Bartolo (bass). With his servant Fiorello (tenor) and a group of musicians, he sings a serenade to the girl, *Ecco ridente in cielo*, but with no result. A joyful song from offstage announces the entrance of Figaro (baritone), city barber and jack-of-all-trades. Carefree and confident, he is an old friend of the count and a regular visitor to Bartolo's house. He promises to help Almaviva in his courtship. Bartolo comes out of the house and the pair overhear him mentioning a plan to marry his ward as soon as possible. Following Figaro's advice, the count sings another serenade, introducing himself as a certain Lindoro, since he does not wish to win the girl's heart with the aid of his noble rank. Now she replies. Almaviva is happy, and resolves to get into Bartolo's house by pretending to be a slightly tipsy soldier with a fake billeting order. Scene II. A room in Bartolo's house. Rosina is impatient to send back a love message to Lindoro, *Una voce poco fa*, and also asks Figaro for his assistance. But their conversation is interrupted by the return of her guardian. Then her music master, the hypocritical, obsequious Basilio (bass), enters, announcing the arrival in Seville of Count Almaviva (who he knows has been making eyes at Rosina, but whom she does not know). He advises Bartolo to use calumny to compel this potential rival to leave the city.

Design by Francesco Bagnara for an early Venetian production of Rossini's L'Italiana in Algeri.

Bartolo and Basilio go out and Rosina gives Figaro a note for Lindoro. Bartolo, on his return, suspects something is wrong and scolds his ward. Now the count enters, disguised as a soldier and pretending to be drunk; but he tells Rosina that he is actually Lindoro. When the doctor persuades the girl to hand over what he assumes to be a letter, he discovers that it is a laundry list which she has cleverly substituted. He vents his anger on Lindoro, and the uproar attracts the city guard (bass). Figaro vainly tries to pacify the old man, but eventually the count is placed under arrest. He shows a card to the officer, who immediately snaps to attention and lets him go free. Everyone is dumbfounded. Act II. A room in Bartolo's house. Bartolo is very suspicious of the billeted soldier; but now the count comes in again, this time in the guise of a music teacher, introducing himself as Don Alonso, Basilio's pupil. He says he has come because Basilio is ill. Bartolo immediately mistrusts him, and to allay his suspicions, Almaviva hands him the note he has received from Rosina, pretending that he has intercepted it before it reached Count Almaviva. He advises the doctor to dash the hopes of his ward by telling her that the count has given it to one of his mistresses to play a joke on her. Bartolo is convinced and summons Rosina. While the old guardian snores, the two lovers pretend to have a music lesson. Figaro, arriving at an opportune moment, begins shaving Bartolo and astutely extracts the key to the balcony so that the lovers can get away from the house that night. But now Basilio makes an unexpected and unwelcome appearance. He is on the point of revealing the truth, when Almaviva bribes him to feign sickness. Bartolo finally realizes that he is being duped. Everyone rushes off and he mounts guard at the door. Berta (soprano), the housekeeper, comments on the stupid things that are going on. Scene II. Bartolo sends Basilio to look for a notary to witness his marriage to Rosina; then he shows her the note from Lindoro, and convinces her that the young man is not really in love with her, but is merely a go-between who is trying to get her to marry Count Almaviva. The girl falls into the trap and in her disappointment confesses her plans for running away that night. Bartolo goes off to call the military. A storm breaks out, and through the balcony window come Figaro and Lindoro. The latter explains to Rosina that he is actually Almaviva. By the time they have reaffirmed their love for each other and are ready to escape they find that the ladder has been removed. Basilio enters with the notary, and, with great presence of mind, Figaro pushes forward the young couple as the prospective bride and groom. Basilio needs some more persuasion, a ring and a brandished pistol being strong arguments. When Bartolo bursts in with the police, it is all over. The count reveals his true identity. The old man, at first furious, is finally resigned, especially when he understands that he can keep Rosina's dowry. The opera ends in general rejoicing.

The Opéra audience applauds Rossini. French lithograph from the middle of the 19th century.

Il Barbiere di Siviglia *in a production at La Scala on 22 April 1933. Cast: Salvatore Baccaloni (Bartolo), Benvenuto Franci (Figaro), Feòdor Chaliapin (Basilio), Toti Dal Monte (Rosina), Tito Schipa (Almaviva).*

■ Cesare Sterbini was given the job of writing the text by Rossini himself, after the famous librettist Jacopo Ferretti had failed to produce a suitable comic text for the Teatro Argentina. Despite every precaution, including the alteration of the title, Rossini was violently attacked by the supporters of Paisiello, who had composed an opera based on the same play of Beaumarchais in 1782 (see above, p. 87). The six hundred pages of *Il Barbiere* were composed, according to Rossini, in a mere eleven days; certainly the opera did not occupy him for more than twenty days, but he indulged in his usual habit of borrowing from his other operas suitable music for the task in hand. The overture, for example, had been heard several times before. What is especially striking about *Il Barbiere di Siviglia* is its marvellously balanced and compact structure. The action never comes to a standstill, the orchestral accompaniment supporting the singers in a steady, melodious flow from beginning to end. There are innumerable subtle and inventive touches, and, more

than anything, a pervasive atmosphere of joy throughout the opera, which has delighted audiences all over the world for more than a century and a half. The score bubbles with freshness, charm and high humour. In writing it, Rossini had the example of many illustrious predecessors, but although he availed himself of various models he blended everything so perfectly that there are no conflicts of style. It is as perfect in its way as Mozart's *Le Nozze di Figaro*, based on the second play of the Beaumarchais trilogy. Rossini's characters have an entertaining attitude to their affairs which is realistic and unsentimental. The music is familiar even to those who have never seen the opera on the stage. The most famous aria is Figaro's *Largo al factotum* at the end of Act I, which, together with the sparkling overture, immediately establishes the comic atmosphere which pervades the whole opera. But it is a pity to take any single part out of context, so closely knit are words, music and action from start to finish. A point worth special mention is that the role of Rosina,

Luigi Lablache in the part of Figaro in Rossini's Il Barbiere di Siviglia.

originally written for contralto, is nowadays generally sung by a light soprano.

UNDINE
Opera in three acts by Ernst Theodor Amadeus Hoffmann (1776–1822), libretto by Friedrich Heinrich Karl de la Motte-Fouqué (1777–1843). First performance: Berlin, Schauspielhaus, 3 August 1816.

SYNOPSIS. Undine, a mysterious girl born in a palace of crystal on the bed of the ocean, is brought up by a fisherman and his wife to replace their own daughter, lost as a baby at sea. When she grows up she falls in love with the handsome knight Uldibrand, who marries her. In her husband's castle lives the wicked Bertolda, the real daughter of the fisherman and his wife, who had been abducted by one of Undine's uncles, a marine demi-god; she captivates Uldibrand's heart. The despairing Undine is dragged down to the bottom of the sea by the water spirits who watch over her; they decide that her faithless husband must die. When Undine, beautiful and in tears, appears on the wedding day of Uldibrand and Bertolda, the remorseful knight goes to embrace her; but as soon as he comes into

contact with her body, he turns to ice and dies. A stream of water, fed forever by the tears of Undine, forms around his grave.

■ *Undine* is the composer's recognized masterpiece. After the enormous success of its première in Berlin, there were fourteen performances until the theatre was destroyed by fire on 27 July 1817. After that (apart from an unsuccessful production in Prague in 1821) the opera was not staged until performed at Aachen more than a century later, on 30 June 1922, with a libretto adapted by Hans von Wolzogen. *Undine* was thus restored to the operatic stage and was performed, though infrequently, throughout Germany. The opera is of interest because it reflects the German romantic spirit after the Napoleonic wars, which sought refuge in a magic world populated by the divinities of nature and by knightly heroes – a world skilfully reproduced by Hoffmann in his score.

FAUST
Opera in two acts by Louis Spohr (1784–1859), libretto by Joseph Karl Bernard. First performance: Prague, 1 September 1816; first performance in U.K.: London, Prince's Theatre, 21 May 1840.

SYNOPSIS. The young Rosina is in love with Faust. Cunegonde, loved by Ugo, languishes in prison, guilty

Adelina Patti dressed as Rosina in Rossini's Il Barbiere di Siviglia.

Design by Karl Friedrich Schinkel for Undine *by E. T. A. Hoffmann (1816). Berlin, Nationalgalerie.*

of refusing the advances of Faust, who loves her. She is freed by Ugo, but Faust, resolved not to lose her, seeks the aid of Mephistopheles, asking him for the power to be loved by her and to reject Rosina. Having drunk the magic love potion, he appears to Cunegonde while she is celebrating her marriage to Ugo. Gripped by a mysterious force, she now responds to Faust's amorous advances, which she had previously spurned. Ugo, unaware of the diabolical power which compels her to act in this way, believes he is betrayed and furiously hurls himself at Faust, killing him. Rosina, whose love for Faust has been unalterable, drowns herself. Mephistopheles, satisfied with his work, drags the dead Faust down to Hell.

■ Conducted for the first time by Carl Maria von Weber, the opera enjoyed great popularity all over Europe for some decades. Nowadays it is never performed, although it contains some of the composer's finest music and has moments of great romantic warmth. Nevertheless, it is very uneven in quality. This was the first attempt to present a musical version of the Faust legend.

OTELLO, or IL MORO DI VENEZIA (The Moor of Venice)
Opera in three acts by Gioacchino Rossini (1792–1868), libretto by Francesco Berio di Salsa, based on the tragedy by Shakespeare. First performance: Naples, Teatro del Fondo, 4 December 1816; first performance in U.K.: London, Haymarket, 16 May 1822; in U.S.A.: New York, 7 February 1826.

SYNOPSIS. Venice, sixteenth century. Otello, after defeating the Turks, is welcomed by the people and by the doge. But Rodrigo, who fears that Desdemona, promised to him in marriage, loves the brave Moor, is plotting against him. The girl confides to her maid Emilia that she does indeed love Otello. Rodrigo and her father, Elmiro, hasten their plans for the wedding. But during the ceremony itself Otello bursts in, and Desdemona is unable to conceal her love for him. The furious father locks the daughter in her room. Later, Iago manages to persuade the Moor that she is deceiving him with Rodrigo. Otello challenges Rodrigo to a duel and is exiled for this act. When he returns secretly to Venice, he goes to Desdemona but, in a fit of jealous rage, kills her. Iago, overcome by remorse, commits suicide, after confessing his plots. When the doge and Elmiro, not knowing of the tragedy, inform the Moor that his banishment is revoked, Otello, frantic with grief and despair, confesses his crime and kills himself.

■ Berio di Salsa's adaptation did little justice to Shakespeare's original, which is virtually unrecognizable. The first performance saw Isabella Colbran in the role of Desdemona. Later the part was associated with the name of the famous Spanish singer Maria Malibran, Desdemona being one of her best known roles.

LA CENERENTOLA, ossia LA BONTÀ IN TRIONFO (Cinderella, or Virtue Triumphant)
Melodramma giocoso in two acts by Gioacchino Rossini (1792–1852), libretto by Jacopo Ferretti (1784–1852). First performance: Rome, Teatro Valle,

Caricature of Rossini by H. Mailly on the occasion of his 75th birthday in 1867, which appeared on the cover of the French literary magazine Le Hanneton.

25 January 1817; first performance in U.K.: London, Haymarket, 8 January 1820; in U.S.A.: New York, 27 June 1826.

ORIGINAL CAST. Giorgi-Righetti (Cenerentola), Mariani, Rossi, De Begnis, Guglielmi, Vitanelli.

SYNOPSIS. Act I. The house of Don Magnifico, Baron of Mountflagon. Angelina, known as Cenerentola (Cinderella) (contralto), lives with Clorinda (soprano) and Thisbe (mezzo-soprano), the daughters of the baron (bass), who is her step-father. She is treated as a servant and humiliated by everybody, despite her gentle nature. It is she who gives hospitality to a beggar (actually the philosopher Alidoro (bass), counsellor to Prince Ramiro (tenor)), whereas her step-sisters chase him from the house. A group of nobles announce that the prince is to give a ball at which he will choose a wife from the ladies present. The prince himself, who has exchanged clothes and roles with his valet Dandini (bass), arrives at the baron's house to escort the ugly sisters to the palace. He notices the lovely Cinderella and at once falls in love with her, but her family tell him that she is only a servant. She is left at home when everyone departs for the ball. At the palace, the festivities are at their height when a beautiful stranger enters. Everyone admires her, noting how much she resembles Magnifico's step-daughter. The step-sisters are busy trying to attract Dandini's attention thinking that he is the prince. Act II. Cinderella refuses the advances of Dandini, posing as the prince, and confesses her love for his valet, the real prince. She gives him one of a pair of bracelets so that he can identify her. Ramiro is overjoyed. The real Dandini, meanwhile, has told Magnifico that he is not the prince, and the baron returns home, deeply disappointed, with Thisbe

and Clorinda. Cinderella is already back, having changed her clothes, busy with her domestic chores. During a storm, conjured by Alidoro, the prince seeks refuge, recognizes her, and asks her to marry him. In the throne-room of the palace, Cinderella and the prince receive the congratulations of the nobility, among whom kneel her step-father and his daughters. She forgives them and all live happily ever after.

■ Based on the fairy-tale by Charles Perrault, the libretto for *Cenerentola* lacks the magic, fanciful elements of the original, because Ferretti claimed that the public would not have accepted a mere fireside story on the operatic stage. The words were written in twenty-two days, the music in twenty-four days. Thus, like other works by Rossini, this opera was composed in a great hurry. The première, before a Roman audience, was not a great success, possibly because the singers gave inadequate performances. Rossini, who had experienced the same lukewarm reception at the première of *The Barber of Seville*, was not discouraged; and the very next evening, in fact, saw a much more enthusiastic audience. *Cenerentola*, with its extraordinarily lively and brilliant score, is still frequently performed. It is full of delightful and richly expressive music, and the characters created by Rossini are remarkably fresh and original. The structure of *Cenerentola* is not as balanced as *The Barber of Seville* because the second act is not as musically effective as the first.

LA GAZZA LADRA (The Thieving Magpie)

Opera in two acts by Gioacchino Rossini (1792–1868), libretto by Giovanni Gherardini (1778–1861). First performance: Milan, Teatro alla Scala, 31 May 1817; first performance in U.K.: London, Haymarket, 10 March 1821; in U.S.A.: Philadelphia, October 1827.

SYNOPSIS. In the house of a wealthy merchant Fabrizio (bass), in a village near Paris, everyone is waiting for the return from military service of Giannetto (tenor), particularly his parents, Fabrizio (bass) and Lucia (mezzo-soprano) and the maid Ninetta (soprano), who loves him. Lucia finds fault with Ninetta, believing, wrongly, that she is responsible for the disappearance of a silver fork. When Giannetto returns, he declares his love for Ninetta. She has managed to help her father Fernando (baritone), who is wanted by the authorities as a deserter, to escape, by reading to the mayor the description of the deserter in which she has inserted false details. The mayor, Gottardo (bass), takes the opportunity to make advances to her. Before leaving, Ninetta's father asks her to sell a silver spoon for him, telling her to hide the proceeds in a hollow of a chestnut tree. She eventually sells it to Isaaco (tenor), a wandering pedlar. Lucia has now noticed the disappearance of a spoon and accuses the girl. When Lucia hears that a spoon has been sold, she assumes that it was hers and she makes the mayor take Ninetta to prison. He once more tries to profit from the situation but is again put in his place. Lucia begins to doubt her guilt but the judges condemn her to death. Fernando is arrested when he tries to save her. At the last moment, the true thief is discovered – a magpie. Ninetta is released and free to marry Giannetto. Her father receives a royal pardon and all ends happily.

■ The subject of Gherardini's libretto, based on a French play by J. M. Th. Baudouin d'Aubigny and Louis Charles Caigniez, entitled *La pie voleuse*, was inspired by a newspaper story. *La Gazza Ladra* was very successful in Milan and was even more enthusiastically received when performed in Paris.

MOSÈ IN EGITTO (Moses in Egypt)
Opera seria *in three acts by Gioacchino Rossini (1792–1868) to a text (*azione tragico-sacra*) by Andrea Leone Tottola. First performance: Naples, Teatro San Carlo, 5 March 1818; first performance in U.K. as* Pietro l'Eremita: *London, King's Theatre, Haymarket, 23 April 1822; in U.S.A.: New York, 2 March 1835. Enlarged, revised and renamed by Giuseppe Luigi Balochi and Victor-Joseph Etienne de Jouy*

(1764–1846) Moïse et Pharaon, ou Le passage de la mer rouge *(Moses and Pharaoh, or the Crossing of the Red Sea). First performance: Paris, Opéra, 26 March 1827; first performance in U.K. (as* Zora*): London, Covent Garden, 20 April 1850; in U.S.A.: New York, 7 May 1860.*

ORIGINAL CAST. of the first version included Isabella Colbran (Anaïde), Benedetti (Mosè) and Nozzari (Aménophis), and of the second version Laure Cinti-Damoreau (Anaï), Adolphe Nourrit (Aménophis) and Nicholas Levasseur (Moïse).

SYNOPSIS (of the extended French version). Act I. Egypt, camp of the Midianites. The Hebrews, enslaved by Pharaon (bass), pray for their liberation. As Moïse encourages the crowd, his brother Eliézer (tenor) arrives with his wife Marie (mezzo-soprano) and their daughter Anaï (soprano). Eliézer announces that Pharaon has decided to free the Hebrews. Marie tells how Pharaon's son, Aménophis (tenor), has fallen in love with Anaï, who is torn between love and the duty

Design for the Wolf's Glen in Weber's Der Freischütz. *Weimar, Kunstsammlung.*

Maria Malibran in the role of Desdemona in Rossini's Otello. *Painting by Henri Decaisne. Paris, Musée Carnavalet.*

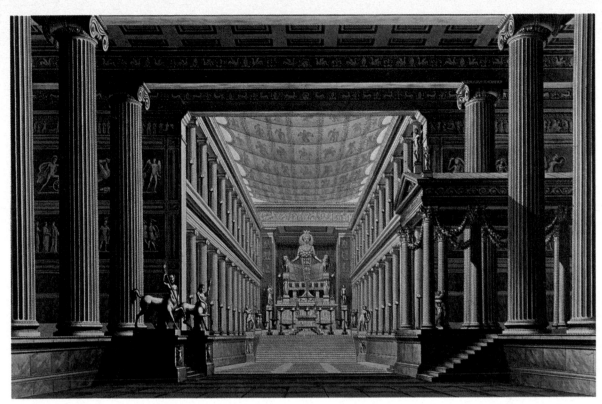

Design by Schinkel (1819) for first act of Spontini's Olimpie. *Engraving by Gügel. Paris, Bibliothèque de l'Opéra.*

to follow her people. Moïse takes heart on hearing a mysterious voice (bass) that predicts that the Jews will at last see the Promised Land. Aménophis, however, threatens to keep them in Egypt so as to prevent his separation from Anaï who, although she loves him, bows before the necessity of obeying the laws of her people. Indeed he then reports that Pharaon has reversed his decree and now forbids them to go. Momentarily disheartened, Moïse angrily defies Pharaon and demonstrates the power of his God by causing the sun to be obscured. Act II. Palace of Pharaon. In despair at the terrible darkness, Pharaon renews his promise to Moïse and Eliézer and the sun returns to the heavens. Pharaon, alone with his son, proposes that he marry the King of Assyria's daughter and tries in vain to discover the reason for his son's distress. Aménophis then confides in his mother Sinaïde (soprano), who counsels him to resign himself to his fate. They leave for the Temple of Isis. Act III. Portico of the Temple of Isis. The Egyptians sing praises to their goddess. Moïse asks for the promised freedom, but Oziride (bass), the high priest, demands that the Hebrews pay homage to Isis before their departure. Moïse refuses. Ophide (tenor), an Egyptian officer, reports the appalling effects of the plague on Egypt: the Nile has turned red and the land gives off a noxious vapour, causing death. The Egyptians want to attack the Hebrews. With a gesture, Moïse extinguishes the flame on the altar of Isis. Pharaon expels the Jews from Memphis. Act IV. The flight of the Jews into the desert takes them to the shores of the Red Sea.

Having abducted Anaï, Aménophis returns her to her people as supreme proof of his love. He tries to persuade her once again to stay, but she refuses. The Hebrews are about to be overtaken on the shore of the Red Sea by the Egyptians, when Moïse exhorts them not to be afraid. As he intones a solemn prayer, the waters part miraculously and the Hebrews pass safely along the seabed. Aménophis and his troops pursue them, but the waves close over them with a thunderous crash and they drown. The sun then shines once again on the peaceful waters.

■ With the title *Mosè in Egitto* and a libretto by Tottola, this work was performed on 5 March 1818 at the Teatro San Carlo in Naples and aroused much enthusiasm. Extensive changes were then made to the score and the text, resulting in the final version in French. The opera was subsequently given in both versions throughout the century all over Europe. Rossini's style is often majestic and at times reaches sublime heights. The gracefulness and liveliness of the music enhances the diversity of characters and situations.

APOTEOSI DI ERCOLE (Apotheosis of Hercules)
Opera in two acts by Saverio Mercadante (1795–1870), libretto by Giovanni Schmidt. First performance: Naples, Teatro San Carlo, 19 August 1819.

ORIGINAL CAST. Isabella Colbran, Giovanni

David, De Bernardis (the Elder), Nozzari, Pesaroni, Benedetti.

SYNOPSIS. Ercole returns victorious from the war and finds that Iole, the girl he loves, is among the prisoners. His son Illo is also in love with Iole. Deianira, Ercole's wife, hopes to regain her husband's love and asks his permission for the two young people to marry. Ercole, in anger, imprisons all three. His friend Philoctete intercedes for them and Deianira, once free, in order to please her husband, gives him a shirt she had been given by Nesso, the centaur. The shirt is poisoned and Ercole dies in frightful agony. Jove decrees his apotheosis, surrounded by a heavenly retinue.

■ This was the young composer's first opera, given on the birthday of the heir to the throne of Naples, Prince Francis of Bourbon. The audience, breaking a tradition whereby in the presence of royalty they were required to show neither approval nor disapproval, broke into great applause. The opera does not depart from eighteenth-century models but has a well orchestrated score.

LA DONNA DEL LAGO (The Lady of The Lake)
Opera seria *in two acts by Gioacchino Rossini (1792–1868), libretto by Andrea Leone Tottola (d. 1831), based on the poem by Sir Walter Scott. First performance: Naples, Teatro San Carlo, 24 September 1819. First performance in U.K.: London, Haymarket, 18 February 1823; in U.S.A.: New York, 25 August 1829.*

ORIGINAL CAST. Isabella-Angela Colbran (title role), Andrea Nozzari (Rodrigo).

SYNOPSIS. The action takes place at the period when the Highlanders were ranged against James V of Scotland (Giacomo), who was planning to subdue the Highlands. Act I. Elena (soprano), daughter of the rebel leader Douglas of Angus, muses while crossing the lake, on her love for Malcolm (mezzo-soprano). Her father has, however, promised her to Rodrigo (tenor). Uberto (tenor), who is in fact the King in disguise, is separated from a hunting party and she offers him hospitality. He soon falls in love with her and takes away with him the mistaken impression that she returns his feelings. Elena is about to be married to Rodrigo when Malcolm arrives with forces to repel the Royal army, which is advancing. The Highlanders swear to forget their private differences in the common cause. Act II. Elena disillusions Uberto about her love for him and he gives her a ring which he promises will obtain anything for her from the King. They are surprised by Rodrigo, who challenges Uberto to a duel and loses. Subsequently the rebels are defeated, and Douglas is captured. Elena then realizes Uberto's identity: the King releases Douglas, and gives Elena in marriage to Malcolm.

■ Rossini composed this score with his customary speed. The music is not only spontaneous and original, but is also extremely complex in structure, with many novel touches foreshadowing the themes and cadences of lyrical romantic opera.

OLIMPIE (Olympia)
Opéra lyrique *in three acts by Gaspare Spontini (1774–1851), libretto by Michel Dieulafoi and Charles Brifaut, based on the play by Voltaire. First performance: Paris Opéra, 22 December 1819.*

SYNOPSIS. The temple of Diana at Ephesus. Antigone, King of Asia Minor, and Cassandre, King of Macedonia, successors to Alexandre Magnus, having been enemies for some time, have made peace. Cassandre is rumoured to have brought about Alexandre's death; he now loves one of Antigone's slaves, by the name of Améneide, who is in reality Alexandre's daughter, Olympie. He asks her to marry him. Presiding over the nuptials is the priestess Arzane, who is really Statira, Alexandre's widow. She is horrified when she recognizes the man she believes to have assassinated her husband. Cassandre tells mother and daughter that on the day of Alexandre's death, he saved them, but Statira does not believe him. The crowd acclaims Olympie as Queen. Antigone now wishes to marry her, while his followers hunt for Cassandre. Olympie is torn between love for Cassandre and respect for the law. Eventually Antigone confesses as he dies that he alone was responsible for the murder of Alexandre. Cleared of suspicion, Cassandre is finally permitted to marry Olympie. Statira gives her daughter to his safe-keeping; the throne which was formerly her husband's is now Olympie's, and the soldiers hail her as Queen.

■ The original version of *Olympie* ended with the death of the princess, the suicide of Statira and the appearance of Alexandre, who received them among the immortals. In Spontini's version the dramatic element of the plot was substantially reduced. Despite that, this opera, of which the composer was particularly fond, is the one that best reflects his musical temperament.

DIE ZWILLINGSBRÜDER (The Twin Brothers)
Singspiel *in one act by Franz Schubert (1797–1828), libretto 'adapted from the French' Les deux Valentins by Georg Ernst von Hofmann. First performance: Vienna, Kärntnertortheater, 14 June 1820.*

SYNOPSIS. The conventional plot springs from a promise made by a village mayor to marry his daughter Lieschen to his neighbour, Franz Spiess. Since Franz is due to go to war, with his twin brother Friedrich, the wedding is postponed. Some eighteen years go by, and the girl marries someone else. The twins return, each having lost an eye and in poor physical shape. Although Friedrich has retained his gentle nature,

Carl Maria von Weber conducting Der Freischütz *at Covent Garden, London.*

Franz has become hot-tempered and both have been ruined by the war. Neither knows of the other's homecoming. The course of the action is fairly predictable. Friedrich sings a beautiful aria greeting his native land once again, while Franz provides a touch of drama, insisting that the old promise should be honoured. There is, however, a happy ending.

■ Although the text is modest enough, the music has many happy moments. The overture contains hints of the type of music to be found in some of Schubert's later symphonies. The aria which is now regarded as the finest, although neglected by contemporary critics, is 'Der Vater mag wohl immer Kind mich nennen'.

DIE ZAUBERHARFE (The Magic Harp)
Musical comedy in three acts by Franz Schubert (1797–1828), libretto by Georg Ernst von Hofmann. First performance: Vienna, Theater an der Wien, 19 August 1820.

■ This opera was not a success and the composer destroyed it, except for the overture *Rosamunde*.

LALLA ROOKH (NURMAHAL, or DAS ROSEN-FEST VON CASCHMIR)
Festspiel by Gaspare Spontini (1774–1851), libretto by Carl Alexander Herklots, based on the fourth episode of

Thomas Moore's Oriental Tales. *First performance: Berlin, Royal Palace, 27 January 1821.*

■ Originally conceived as a play with music, it was later refashioned as an opera and staged in 1822 with the title of *Nurmahal*.

PRECIOSA
Romantic play in four acts by Pius Alexander Wolff with incidental music by Carl Maria von Weber (1786–1826); based on the novel La Gitanilla *from* Novelas Exemplares *by Cervantes (1547–1616). First performance: Berlin, (Königliches) Opernhaus (later Staatsoper), 14 March 1821. First performance in U.K.: London, Covent Garden, 28 April 1825; in U.S.A.: New York, Franklin Theater, 9 March 1840.*

SYNOPSIS. The scene is Spain. A young nobleman falls in love with a beautiful gipsy and joins her band in order to follow her. When it is discovered that Preciosa is actually of noble birth herself there are no social obstacles to their marriage.

■ When he composed *Preciosa*, Weber was entering on a tranquil period, after the stormy years of his youth. He was married to Carolina Brandt and was Royal Kapellmeister in Dresden. The opera was highly successful in Germany and until 1890, 115

The soprano Isabella Colbran (1785–1845), who married Rossini and created many of his major soprano roles. Portrait by Schmidt. Milan, Museo Teatrale alla Scala.

performances were given in Berlin alone. It is, however, seldom performed nowadays.

LE MAÎTRE DE CHAPELLE, or LE SOUPER ÌMPRÉVU (The Unexpected Dinner)

Opéra-comique in one act by Ferdinando Paër (1771–1839), text by Sophie Gay founded on Le Souper Imprévu, ou Le Chanoine de Milan *by Duval, 1796. First performance: Paris, Théâtre Feydeau, 29 March 1821. First performance in U.K.: London, Covent Garden, 13 June 1845; in U.S.A.: (selections only) New York, Chinese Museum, 1 August 1849; (complete work) 25 June 1852.*

SYNOPSIS. The action takes place in the house of Barnaba (bass), the *maestro di cappella* of a small village near Milan, in 1797. Geltrude (soprano), the French cook, rails against her master because he has not only unexpectedly invited Benedetto (tenor), his disagreeable nephew, to dinner but, as if that were not enough, has also announced his intention of making her join him in singing his opera *Cleopatra*. Geltrude frightens the two men by telling them that the French are attacking the village and urges her master to show his courage. Barnaba and Benedetto agree that the

best thing to do in the circumstances is to hide in the cellar. When Geltrude admits that she has been fooling them, Benedetto announces himself ready to display his bravery, which has not been very evident until then. Barnaba, for his part, sends him to the priest to beg a bottle of wine and takes advantage of his absence and of Geltrude's departure from the kitchen to sing a few snatches from his opera, imitating the bassoon and flute, doing a dance and dreaming of the day when, through this work, he will become rich and famous. He invites Geltrude to sing it with him, but she declares that she cannot understand Italian and pronounces all the words wrong on purpose. The composer persists, however, and when she finally manages to sing the music and pronounce the words correctly, Barnaba happily embraces her and they sing a final love duet.

■ Paër, despite being a difficult person who led a dissolute life, and notwithstanding the fame of his contemporaries, such as Rossini, was regarded abroad as one of the most accomplished composers of semiserious opera. *Le Maître de chapelle*, perhaps based on an incident in his own life, helped to establish his reputation. Paër was, in fact, maestro di cappella for many years to the courts of Parma, Vienna and Paris.

DER FREISCHÜTZ (The Free-shooter)

Romantic opera in three acts by Carl Maria von Weber (1786–1826), libretto by Friedrich Kind (1768–1843), based on the Gespensterbuch *by Johann August Apel and Friedrich Laun. First performance: Berlin, Schauspielhaus, 18 June 1821. First performance in U.K.: London, English Opera House (Lyceum), 27 July 1824; in U.S.A.: New York, 2 March 1825.*

ORIGINAL CAST included Caroline Seidler (Agathe), Johanna Eunicke (Aennchen), Heinrich Blume (Caspar), Carl Stümer (Max); conducted by the composer.

SYNOPSIS. Bohemia, around 1650. Act I. Max (tenor), a young forester, has missed every target in an archery contest with Kilian (baritone), who leads the peasants in a mocking chorus. Prince Ottokar's Chief Ranger, Cuno (bass), prevents a fight between the two men, but tells Max that unless he wins the shooting competition before the Prince on the morrow he will not win the hand of his daughter Agathe. Max does not feel as confident as he once did, and another forester, Caspar (bass), offers him a drugged drink with the advice that he can be sure of winning if he resorts to magic. The devil, Samiel (speaking part), watches as Caspar hands Max a gun and invites him to shoot at an eagle which he can hardly see. To Max's astonishment the bird falls at his feet and Caspar reveals that he has been using a charmed bullet. If Max wants more magic bullets, he must go in secret to the Wolf's Glen at midnight. Act II. Cuno's Lodge. A portrait of Cuno fell from its place in his house at the exact moment when Max shot the eagle. Agathe (soprano) has terrible forebodings and her friend Aennchen (soprano) tries

An entertainment by the Schubert Society at Atzenbrugg. At the piano Franz Schubert. Watercolour by Leopold Kuppelwieser. Vienna, Schubert Museum.

to soothe her. Max shows her the eagle he has killed, and refuses to be dissuaded from going to the Wolf's Glen, saying that he has to recover a deer that he has shot. In the Wolf's Glen Caspar offers Max's soul in return for his own and Samiel accepts. Caspar suggests that Samiel should use the seventh bullet which remains his to aim to kill Agathe. Max helps Caspar to mould the metal which is to be used for the seven magic bullets. While they pronounce the appropriate spells, a violent thunderstorm blows up and nightmarish visions cross the sky, including the Wild Hunt itself. As the seventh bullet is cast, Samiel himself appears. Act III. Max is successful in the contest, but his last bullet is the one that belongs to Samiel. Meanwhile, Agathe has dreamt that she was a dove shot by Max; her wedding bouquet has turned into a funeral wreath; her father's portrait has once again fallen down. Her friends try to calm her, saying that Max will win, that he will marry her and that all will be well. They help her put on her wedding dress. Accompanied by a Hermit, Agathe goes to watch the end of the contest in Prince Ottokar's presence. The Prince (baritone) sets the target as a dove fluttering among the trees. Agathe, remembering her dream, tries to stop Max from shooting, but the Hermit disturbs the bird and it flies to a tree behind

which Caspar is concealed. Max obeys the Prince and fires. Agathe faints, but it is Caspar who falls to the ground, fatally wounded. He dies cursing God and Samiel. Then the pact between Max and the devil is revealed. Ottokar wishes to banish the young forester, but the Hermit intercedes for him and suggests that if he proves honest and pious for a year, he may marry Agathe. The Prince agrees and the chorus sings praises to heaven.

■ Weber's librettist, Kind, was a leading light of a pseudo-romantic society known as the Liederkreis, and his plot was a combination of eighteenth-century nationalism and Klopstock's romanticism. Weber was more influenced by the latter, being especially attracted by the manifestations of nature, and this feeling is reflected throughout the score, particularly in the famous overture. Conceived as a *singspiel*, namely a mixture of song and the spoken word, *Der Freischütz* had its sources in some old, anonymous French stories which were rewritten by Apel and Laun. Beethoven, by that time deaf, had occasion to examine the score, which he described as 'devilry', not merely as regards its contents; and he wondered what those notes and orchestral combinations – so far removed from his conceptions of what constituted opera – would sound like. The première, in fact, was not very promising. The composer had to contend with the hostility of the supporters of Italian opera, who were faithful to the school of Spontini and who regarded this work as a real threat to their long supremacy. At the second production, at Vienna's Kärntnertortheater in October, the opera triumphed. With its synthesis of German traditions – heroic characters, savage nature and the supernatural – *Der Freischütz* came to be regarded as the archetype of German romantic opera. There were several adaptations, not all of them successful. Berlioz, for example, scored some of the spoken recitative and was much criticized for it. One last point to mention is that this opera exemplifies, in embryo, a feature that was to be fundamental to the operas of Wagner – the leitmotif, which occurs throughout the work, being associated with particular characters, situations and ideas.

ZELMIRA

Opera seria *in two acts by Gioacchino Rossini (1792–1868), libretto by Andrea Leone Tottola (d. 1831), inspired by Pierre Laurent Buirette de Belloy's tragedy of the same name. First performance: Naples, Teatro San Carlo, 16 February 1822. First performance in U.K.: London, 24 January 1824.*

SYNOPSIS. Polidoro, King of the island of Lesbos, is loved by his people, his daughter Zelmira, and his son-in-law, Ilo, a valiant Trojan prince. Ilo is forced to go abroad, and immediately Azorre, the ruler of Mitilene, takes advantage of his absence to avenge himself for having been refused the hand of Zelmira by her father. He invades Lesbos and goes in search of the old king in order to kill him. Zelmira hides her father in the royal tomb, and then, to allay suspicion, pretends to Azorre to desire her father's death for not having allowed her to marry Azorre. He is delighted and is completely deceived by this trick. He has the temple of Ceres burnt to the ground, believing the old king to be hidden inside. Antenore, who has coveted the throne of Mitilene, has Azorre murdered and himself conquers Lesbos until Ilo returns, defeats the usurper and restores Polidoro to the throne.

■ Belloy's tragedy already lacked excitement, and Tottola's translation and changes only rendered the libretto even weaker. However, Rossini's music made up for the unfortunate text and the opera was a success. The critics applauded the production of *Zelmira* as his masterpiece. In retrospect it is clear that the tedium of the libretto could not help but affect the creativity of Rossini and the score is in some parts fatally long-winded. The opera also poses technical challenges both for instrumentalists and singers.

SEMIRAMIDE

Melodramma tragico *in two acts by Gioacchino Rossini (1792–1868), libretto by Gaetano Rossi (1774–1855) based on Voltaire's* Sémiramis. *First performance: Ven-ice, Teatro La Fenice, 3 February 1823. First performance in U.K.: London, Haymarket, 15 July 1824; in U.S.A.: New Orleans, 1 May 1837.*

ORIGINAL CAST. I. Colbran, R. Mariani, F. Galli, L. Mariani, Sinclair.

SYNOPSIS. Act I. The temple of Belo in Babylon. Oroe (bass), High Priest, orders the temple doors to be opened. The satraps enter with their leader, Prince Assur (baritone), followed by the Babylonians and the Indians with their king, Idreno (tenor). Queen Semiramide (soprano) announces that the Oracle from Memphis will shortly designate a new king following the assassination of her husband, Nino. She is then prevented from speaking by a thunderbolt that puts out the altar flame and terrifies the crowd. Oroe interprets this omen to mean that the gods want vengeance for the late king's murder. Arsace (contralto), commander of the army, confides in Assur that he loves the Princess Azema. This angers Assur, for he also desires her and aspires to the throne. When Azema reveals her love for Arsace, Idreno is unable to hide the fact that he too loves her. At the Hanging Gardens of Babylon, Commander Mitrane reports to Semiramide the reply of the oracle of Memphis, a prediction of peace when Arsace returns and a forthcoming marriage. Semiramide easily misinterprets these words to signify approval of her own love for Arsace. She decrees that Idreno shall have Azema and announces, in front of Nino's tomb, that she herself will marry Arsace and bestow on him the crown. A thunderbolt interrupts the ceremony. The ghost of Nino (bass) appears, declaring that Arsace will indeed become king, when certain crimes have been atoned for. Act II. The royal palace. Together Semiramide and Assur, her accomplice in Nino's murder, recall their crime. Inside Nino's tomb Oroe tells Arsace the names of the regicides and that he is Nino's son, Ninias, who was believed dead. Oroe also instructs him to seek a sacrificial victim in Nino's vault. Arsace then confronts Semiramide with her horrendous crime and she admits her guilt, but Arsace finds himself unable to take revenge on the woman whom he now knows to be his mother. In Nino's tomb, Arsace has arrived to find a victim. Semiramide follows him, fearing that Assur may try to murder him and claim the crown himself. In the darkness, the son unwittingly strikes her down, mistaking her for Assur. On realizing what he has done, he wants to take his own life, but the people acclaim him as their king. Assur is arrested and Arsace takes Azema as his Queen.

■ Written within the space of only five weeks, *Semiramide* was Rossini's last opera for the Italian stage. It was received with little enthusiasm at its première in Venice. The public particularly disliked the first act, which it considered long and boring, but the critics immediately recognized its merits. Later in Naples and Vienna it was triumphantly received and became the subject of a novel by Joseph Méry – an unusual occurrence, for generally it is the literary work that inspires

La Dame Blanche *by Boïeldieu. Design for Act I. Paris, Bibliothèque de l'Opéra.*

the libretto and not vice versa. The libretto reflects the influence of Voltaire, who had succeeded in portraying the character of the Queen of Babylon with all of the power that history and legend have conferred upon it. The score is both majestic and lively; the thematic material is outstanding for its beauty and originality; and the first-act choruses are particularly noteworthy. Of all Rossini's *opere serie* composed before 1823, *Semiramide* is certainly the most ambitious and the richest in musical development.

JESSONDA

Opera in three acts by Louis Spohr (1784–1859), libretto by Eduard Heinrich Gehe after Antoine Marin Lemierre's tragedy La veuve de Malabar. *First performance: Cassel, 28 July 1823. First performance in U.K.: London, Prince's Theatre, 18 June 1840; in U.S.A.: Philadelphia, 15 February 1864.*

SYNOPSIS. The city of Goa, India. The old rajah, whom Jessonda had married against her will, has just died. In accordance with ancient law, she must be burnt alive on the funeral pyre with her dead husband. Nadori, a young Brahman who comes to tell Jessonda of her tragic fate, meets her sister, Amazili. He falls in love with her and promises to save Jessonda. Mean-

while Jessonda hopes to be freed by the Portuguese general, Tristan d'Acunha, to whom at one time she was betrothed, unaware that the besieging Portuguese and the Goans have signed a peace treaty and Tristan no longer has the power to free her. But when the pact is broken, because two spies set fire to the Portuguese ships, the General attacks the city and intervenes just in time to save Jessonda. Nadori takes her secretly to the temple, where she is reunited with Tristan, while Nadori wins the hand of Amazili.

■*Jessonda* was Spohr's greatest success and has also been performed many times in Germany in this century. The choruses of the Indian priests and the soldiers are particularly effective and the duet, *Schönes Mädchen* is considered one of Spohr's most beautiful compositions. For the first time he abandoned classical melodrama with its separate arias and recitatives, adopting a completely romantic form favouring continuity of action and music. *Jessonda* has taken its rightful place as an important work in the history of German opera.

EURYANTHE

Grand heroic-romantic opera in three acts by Carl Maria von Weber (1786–1826), libretto by Helmina

View of Covent Garden rebuilt after the fire of 1808.

von Chézy, based on the medieval romance l'Histoire de Gérard de Nevers et de la très vertueuse et très chaste Euryanthe de Savoye. *First performance: Vienna, Kärntnertor Theatre, 25 October 1823. First performance in U.K.: London, Covent Garden, 29 June 1833; in U.S.A.: New York, Metropolitan Opera House, 23 December 1887.*

ORIGINAL CAST. Henriette Sontag (Euryanthe), Thérese Grünbaum (Eglantine), Anton Haizinger (Adolar), Anton Forti (Lysiart).

SYNOPSIS. Act I. Louis VII (bass) celebrates the end of war and Count Adolar (tenor) praises the virtue of his betrothed Euryanthe of Savoy (soprano). The jealous Count Lysiart (baritone) expresses doubt that such virtuous women actually exist. Adolar challenges him to a duel, but Lysiart proposes a different kind of contest: if he fails to seduce Euryanthe, he will renounce all his possessions. King Louis tries to reason with him, but Adolar himself insists on the wager, stipulating that he too will give up everything if he loses. Meanwhile Euryanthe awaits the return of her betrothed and confides in Eglantine (mezzo-soprano),

daughter of a dispossessed noble, to whom Adolar offered hospitality. Eglantine secretly loves Adolar and succeeds in learning from Euryanthe a grievous family secret, the keeping of which is a sacred bond between Euryanthe and her lover: Emma, Adolar's sister, committed suicide by drinking poison from a ring after her lover was killed in battle, and her soul cannot find rest until some innocently accused person shall wet the same ring with tears. Act II. Lysiart despairs of success in his endeavour. Unexpected help arrives when Eglantine reveals Adolar's family secret and gives him the ring taken from Emma's tomb. The possession of this ring (and therefore the knowledge of Emma's suicide) will prove that a close bond exists between Lysiart and Euryanthe. Lysiart accuses Euryanthe before Adolar and the whole court of breaking her vow; he produces the ring and Adolar supposes that she gave Emma's ring as a love token to Lysiart. He surrenders Nevers to his rival and leads Euryanthe into the wilderness. Act III. Adolar decides not to kill her since she has shown herself ready to sacrifice her life for his and abandons her in the forest. In despair, she collapses; the king's hunting party discover her; she discloses Eglantine's shameful plot. She

Interior of the new Covent Garden.

faints when the king believes her and promises that justice will be done. Adolar learns from his faithful vassals that Lysiart is to marry Eglantine. As their wedding procession passes, Eglantine, who is still in love with Adolar and is dreading her marriage, raves about the conspiracy which has ruined Euryanthe. Adolar challenges Lysiart to a duel. Louis VII arrives with the news that Euryanthe has died of grief. Eglantine then triumphantly confesses her deceit. Lysiart kills her and is arrested. Suddenly Euryanthe revives and the two lovers are at last reunited. Emma too has now found rest, for the innocent Euryanthe had wept over the ring.

■ The story is based on the same legends as Boccaccio's *Gerardo di Nevers* and Shakespeare's *Cymbeline*. According to Hugo Wolf, Euryanthe is 'a practical manual for composers of opera'. After the enormous triumph of *Der Freischütz*, Weber was commissioned to write this work by the director of the Kärntnertor Theatre of Vienna. *Euryanthe*, too, enjoyed a great success. Conceived as a 'Grand Opera', this heroic-romantic work was praised by Beethoven, but severely criticized by Schubert as antimusical. In fact the only weakness of *Euryanthe* is its unwieldy libretto.

DIE VERSCHWORENEN, ODER DER HÄUSLICHE KRIEG (The Conspirators, or The Domestic War)

Singspiel *in one act by Franz Schubert (1797–1828), libretto by Ignaz Franz Castelli (1781–1862) after the* Lysistrata *of Aristophanes. Composed 1820; published 1823. First performance: Vienna, Musikvereinsaal, 1 March 1861 (concert); Frankfurt, 29 August 1861 (opera). First performance in U.K.: London, Crystal Palace, 2 March 1872; in U.S.A.: New York, 16 June 1877.*

SYNOPSIS. Bastiano, Major Leopold Gschwandtner's orderly, meets his beloved Linda. He then gives Barbara, the Major's wife, a letter announcing the return of the troops for a short period of leave. The women are tired of being left alone and rebel at the idea of seeing their men for such brief periods. To induce them to give up their visions of military glory, they decide to go on strike and to refuse to sleep with their husbands. To their amazement, they see that the men intend to behave in exactly the same way towards them (because the plot has been overheard). The men even insist that their ladies should accompany them in the next campaign. An armistice is eventually signed: a complete surrender by the men, who promise never again to go to the wars.

■ The libretto, written by Castelli, a friend of Beethoven and Weber, was first published in 1823 together with other works intended to provide Austrian composers with good texts, the lack of which they had much lamented. Schubert particularly liked *Die Verschworenen* and wrote the score in a very short time. Though only a single act, its qualities of balance and homogeneity place it among Schubert's finest works.

L'AJO NELL'IMBARAZZO (The Tutor Embarrassed)

Opera buffa *in two acts by Gaetano Donizetti (1797–1848), libretto by Jacopo Ferretti, based on a comedy by Giovanni Giraud (1807), previously set to music by Guarnaccia, Celli, Mosca and Pilotti. First performance: Rome, Teatro Valle, 4 February 1824. First performance in U.K.: London, Haymarket, 28 July 1846.*

SYNOPSIS. The story makes fun of the strict upbringing of children in very religious families. Don Giulio (baritone) requires that his sons, Enrico (tenor) and Pipetto (bass), be brought up in total ignorance of diversions, and women in particular, until the age of 25. Enrico, however, has already married a pretty neighbour called Gilda (soprano), by whom he has a son. Pipetto makes advances to old Leonarda (mezzo-soprano) the housekeeper, who is senile and takes him seriously. Don Gregorio (buffo), the tutor, can do nothing to prevent Gilda being mistaken by Leonarda for his mistress, when she is discovered in his room. The confusion is eventually sorted out and Don Giulio entrusts Pipetto's education to his elder brother.

■ This work, sometimes presented as *Don Gregorio*, was the culmination of a more auspicious period for Donizetti than the preceding one during which he had failed to gain the public's favour. A new version was given at the Teatro Nuovo in Naples on 26 April 1826. This is the first important *opera buffa* by the composer and was immediately taken up by many Italian and foreign theatres.

DON SANCHE, ou LE CHÂTEAU D'AMOUR (Don Sancho, or The Castle of Love)

Opéra-féerie *in one act by Franz Liszt (1811–86), libretto by Emmanuel Guillaume Théaulon de Lambert and De Rancé. First performance: Paris, Opéra, 17 October 1825. First performance in U.K.: London, 1977.*

■ The lost score was rediscovered in 1903 by Jean-Philippe Chantavoine. This is Liszt's only opera, written when he was just twelve.

GIULIETTA E ROMEO (Romeo and Juliet)

Opera *in two acts by Nicola Vaccai (1790–1848), libretto by Felice Romani (1788–1865). First perfor-*

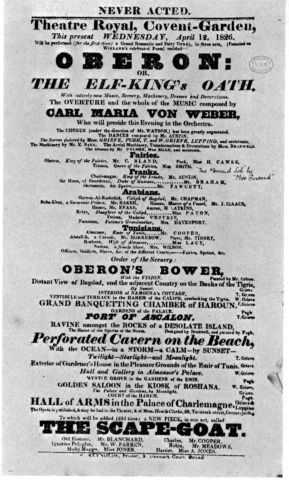

Play-bill for the first performance of Weber's Oberon *at Covent Garden, London, 12 April 1826. London, Victoria and Albert Museum.*

mance: Milan, Teatro della Cannobiana, 31 October 1825. First performance in U.K.: London, 10 April 1832.

ORIGINAL CAST. Giovanni Battista Verger, Giuseppina Demeri, Adele Cesari, Raffaele Benedetti, Luigi Biondini.

■ Another production of the famous tragedy of the lovers from Verona. The last part is of particular merit; in 1832 thanks to Maria Malibran, it was incorporated into Bellini's *Capuleti e i Montecchi*, in which the great singer was renowned in the part of Juliet.

LA DAME BLANCHE (The White Lady)

Opera *in three acts by François Adrien Boïeldieu (1775–1834), libretto by Eugène Scribe (1791–1861), based on two novels,* Guy Mannering *and* The Monastery, *by Sir Walter Scott. First performance: Paris, Opéra-Comique, Salle Feydeau, 10 December 1825. First performance in U.K.: London, Drury Lane, 9 October 1826; in U.S.A.: New York, 24 August 1827.*

ORIGINAL CAST. Rigaud (Anna), Henry (Gaveston), Ponchard (George Brown), Boulanger (Jenny), Féréol (Dikson), Desbrosses (Marguerite).

SYNOPSIS. Act I. The setting is Scotland and the year 1759. Dikson (tenor) and his wife Jenny (soprano) are tenants on the estate of Avenel. They offer hospitality to a stranger, an officer (tenor) in the King's infantry, who tells them that his name is Georges Brown and that he knows nothing of his childhood – he has only memories of servants, a young girl companion and a lady who nursed him back to health. Dikson relates the history of the castle of the counts of Avenel. The last count, who supported the Stuarts, fled after the battle of Culloden and took refuge with his family in France, where he is said to have died. Gaveston (bass), the count's former steward, who had been entrusted with the management of the castle, has decided to auction the estate the next day to meet the demands of the creditors. Gaveston hopes to buy the castle himself, but Dikson has organized the local landowners to agree to buy the property and hold it for its rightful owner. Jenny then mentions the White Lady of the castle, who appears when the Avenels are in misfortune. She is horrified when her husband reveals that he once asked the White Lady for 2,000 Scottish pounds in return for his soul. She has commanded him to appear at the castle that night. Georges takes his place, looking forward to the adventure. Act II. A large Gothic hall in Avenel Castle. Anna (soprano), an orphan who was brought up by the Avenels and is now Gaveston's ward, tells Marguerite (soprano), the old nurse, that the countess told her where she could find the Avenel treasure. Marguerite wishes that Julien, the Avenel heir, would return and marry Anna. Gaveston ridicules the legend of the White Lady and, when Georges arrives determined to find her, thinks that he is mad. Anna has decided to give the Avenel money to Dikson so that he can be sure of outbidding Gaveston and appears to Georges disguised as the White Lady. She is surprised to see Georges instead of Dikson, but commands him to bid against Gaveston on the morrow and to trust the White Lady for funds. At the auction, Georges recognizes Anna as the girl who once healed his wounds and she tells them that the White Lady has sent her. He successfully outbids Gaveston and promises to return with the money. Act III. In the castle, Anna and Marguerite are looking for the statue of the White Lady (which is where the money is concealed). Gaveston is then informed that Georges Brown is really Julien of Avenel; Anna overhears this and despairs for her happiness since she, a penniless orphan, cannot hope to marry a count. Marguerite finds the statue of the White Lady and in the presence of all, Anna (disguised again as the ghost) hands Georges the money and declares his true identity. Georges says that he will renounce all unless he can marry her, and the tenants express their satisfaction with their new count and countess.

■ Byron's poetry and Scott's novels were very popular in France at that time. The theatre also reflected public

Miss Mary Anne Paton in the role of Reiza in the first performance of Weber's Oberon.

taste with the appearance of Scottish landscapes, ruined castles, mysterious apparitions, romantic scenery and visions. La Dame Blanche, Boïeldieu's masterpiece, marked a turning point in French opéra-comique, inaugurating its heyday in the nineteenth century. Boïeldieu composed this work after an eight-year stay in Russia. He had come to realize that his early works showed a poor grasp of technique and he tried to remedy this failing. The music of La Dame Blanche is light, easy, graceful and limpid; it enjoyed a huge success. Boïeldieu here displayed a fluent melodic talent and for decades this opera was the backbone of the major French theatres: in 1826 alone it was performed 150 times, and on 16 December 1862 it had its 1,000th performance.

ADELSON E SALVINI

Opera semiseria by Vincenzo Bellini (1801–35), libretto by Andrea Leone Tottola. First performance: Naples, Teatro del Conservatorio di S. Sebastiano, 12 December 1825.

■ Adelson e Salvini, Bellini's first opera, was defined by himself at the end of the manuscript as 'a play, alias a muddle', which does indeed aptly describe this work. Set against the background of Naples, the plot concerns Lord Adelson and the painter Salvini, both of whom are courting the beautiful countess Fanny. The

Sketch for Bishop's Aladdin. *London, Victoria and Albert Museum.*

opera was well received at its first performance, which earned Bellini the commission to write *Bianca e Fernando* (see below, 1826).

OBERON, or THE ELF KING'S OATH

Romantic opera in three acts by Carl Maria von Weber (1786–1826), libretto in English by James Robertson Planché, based on Sotheby's translation of the poem Oberon *by Christoph Martin Wieland (1733–1813). First performance: London, Covent Garden, 12 April 1826. First performance in U.S.A.: New York, 9 October 1828.*

ORIGINAL CAST. Mary Anne Paton (Reiza), John Braham (Huon), Lucia Elizabeth Vestris (Fatima), John Fawcett (Sherasmin), Charles Bland (Oberon), Harriet Cawse (Puck), Mary Anne Goward (Mermaid), conducted by the composer.

SYNOPSIS. Act I. Oberon (tenor) has told Titania that they will not meet again until they find a faithful couple. Puck (soprano) tells Oberon that Charlemagne

has given Huon of Bordeaux the task of travelling to Baghdad, to 'kill the man on the Caliph's left hand and to kiss the Caliph's daughter by way of betrothal'. Oberon resolves to help the knight (tenor) and his squire Sherasmin (baritone). Transporting them to Baghdad, he gives them also a horn that makes men dance, or summons assistance, and a cup which burns the lips of any impure man who tries to drink from it. Meanwhile the Caliph's daughter, Reiza (soprano), reflects that she loves the knight she has dreamt about and is telling her attendant, Fatima (soprano), that she would die rather than marry her father's chosen husband for her, when report reaches her that a mysterious stranger has come to rescue her. Act II. Huon arrives just in time to prevent Reiza's marriage and the horn helps them to overcome the Caliph's guard and to kill Reiza's intended husband. Oberon congratulates Huon on his success and Sherasmin makes advances to Fatima. The two couples set sail for Greece. Puck, however, tells the sea spirits to cause a storm, the ship is wrecked and the survivors separated. Reiza is kidnapped by pirates, who leave Huon on an island. Oberon orders Puck to release him after seven days and to

Beverly Sills and Marilyn Horne in Rossini's Le Siège de Corinthe *at La Scala, Milan.*

bring him to Tunis. Act III. In Tunis Fatima and Sherasmin, now slaves of the Emir of Tunis, sing of their love for each other, but Fatima laments her separation from Reiza. Huon appears, through Puck's magic, and Fatima discovers that a beautiful woman fitting Reiza's description has been brought to the Emir. The Emir's wife is annoyed about this and invites Huon to kill her husband and to take her as a wife. When he persistently refuses she calls the Caliph and pretends that Huon has tried to attack her. Huon is sentenced to death despite Reiza's pleading; at the moment when the pyre is to be lit, the sound of the magic horn causes the slaves to dance and the pyre to disappear. Oberon and Titania appear and Oberon thanks Huon and Reiza for their proof of fidelity. In Charlemagne's court Huon's return is greeted with acclaim.

■ Though lacking the dramatic intensity of *Der Freischütz*, this last opera of Weber contains pages of his finest music. The libretto, on the other hand, is mediocre. During that early period of Romanticism, fanciful and fabled themes attracted many writers and composers. Wieland's poem, from which the libretto is taken, was in turn based on a medieval poem *Huon de Bordeaux*. The characters Puck and Oberon were introduced from Shakespeare as a means of enlivening the tale. Commissioned directly by the management of Covent Garden, *Oberon* is a *singspiel*, that is, a composition in which sung and spoken parts alternate. Weber began this opera in January 1825, but had to suspend work because of worsening ill health. Though not fully recovered, he returned to work; he continued with the score in Paris, and then in London, where he was engaged for twelve concerts. In March 1826 when rehearsals began, there were sharp disagreements between the composer and some of the singers, who did not fully understand the spirit of the opera. Consequently a complex series of changes had to be made with the result that, as the rehearsals progressed, the opera began to take on quite a different character from the original one. For example, the now famous overture had to be revised so many times that the final version was ready only a few days before the première. *Oberon* was received with enthusiasm by the public, but not by the critics. Partly they disliked the ingenuousness of the text; partly they made unfair comparisons with *Der Freischütz*, Weber's masterpiece, which had prompted Covent Garden to commission *Oberon*. But can an artist be expected to create more and more beautiful masterpieces? In any case the English critics felt that Weber had not exerted himself as much for London as he had for Berlin. Weber was saddened by these observations and planned to take up the ill-fated work again, when his death intervened. Later critics have done full justice to *Oberon*, yet, apart from the overture, it is very rarely performed.

ALADDIN
Fairy opera by Henry Rowley Bishop (1786–1855), libretto by George Soane. First performance: London, Drury Lane, 29 April 1826. First performance in U.S.A.: Philadelphia, 12 November 1830.

SYNOPSIS. The story is taken from the oriental tale of 'Aladdin and His Wonderful Lamp'.

■ *Aladdin* was commissioned by Elliston, manager of Drury Lane, as competition for Weber's *Oberon* at the rival Covent Garden. Weber's opera was highly successful, whereas *Aladdin* was a complete failure and had to be withdrawn after a few performances.

BIANCA E GERNANDO
Melodramma in two acts by Vincenzo Bellini (1801–35), libretto by Domenico Gilardoni after the play by Carlo Roti, Bianca e Fernando alla tomba di Carlo IV duca di Agrigento. First performance: Naples, Teatro San Carlo, 30 May 1826.

ORIGINAL CAST. Henriette Méric-Lalande

Giovanni Battista Rubini as Gualtiero in the first performance of Bellini's Il Pirata.

Sketch by Karl Friedrich Schinkel for Spontini's Agnes von Hohenstaufen, *1827. Berlin, Nationalgalerie.*

(Bianca), Giovanni Battista Rubini (Gernando), Luigi Lablache (Filippo).

SYNOPSIS. The dukedom of Agrigento has been usurped by Filippo, who has imprisoned Duke Carlo and spread a rumour that he has died. Gernando, the Duke's son, has been exiled and his daughter, Bianca, a widow with one baby son, believing Filippo's protestations of devotion to her, is prepared to marry him. Gernando returns in disguise as 'Adolfo'. He pretends that he saw Gernando killed in a duel in Scotland, and offers his services to Filippo. The usurper is deceived and orders him to murder the old Duke. Gernando at first thinks that his sister has betrayed the family, but they are reunited and together find their father's prison. A rebellion against Filippo breaks out and Carlo is restored to the throne.

■ Bellini's second opera, and the first to be publicly performed, was originally entitled *Carlo d'Agrigento*. For the first performance the censor required the title to be changed to *Bianca e Gernando* to avoid any possible reference to the late Bourbon King Fernando. The result was sufficiently favourable for Barbaja, the famous impresario, to commission another opera from Bellini for La Scala. Hearty approval came from Donizetti who, after attending the dress rehearsal, wrote 'it is beautiful, beautiful, beautiful, and especially from one who is writing an opera for the first time'. Subsequently changes were made to the text (with a contribution from Felice Romani) and to the music by Bellini himself, and it was presented in its new form at the inauguration of the Teatro Carlo Felice in Genoa on 7 April 1828. *Bianca e Fernando* never became part of the repertory; there were a few performances in Italy in the nineteenth century, and abroad it was only performed in Barcelona in 1830.

LE SIÈGE DE CORINTHE (The Siege of Corinth)
Tragédie lyrique in three acts by Gioacchino Rossini (1792–1868), libretto by Giuseppe Luigi Balocchi (1776–1822) and Louis Alexandre Soumet, based on the tragedy Anna Erizo *by Cesare Della Valle. First performance: Paris, Opéra, 9 October 1826. First performance in U.K.: London, Haymarket, 5 June 1834; in U.S.A.: New York, 6 February 1835.*

ORIGINAL CAST. Cinti, Fremont, L. Nourrit, Adolfo Nourrit, Dérivis, Prevost.

SYNOPSIS. Act I. Corinth, the Senate. A council of war, presided over by the governor of the city, Cléomène (tenor), decides to hold out to the end against the invading Turks. A young officer, Néocle (tenor), asks Cléomène for the hand of his daughter Pamira (soprano) in marriage, but she declares that she is in love with an enemy soldier, whom she knows as Almanzor. Scene 2. The Square. Led by Mahommet II (bass), the Muslims defeat the Greeks. Cléomène is

Portrait of Donizetti. Nuremberg, German National Museum.

heart. As the opera ends, the flames rise from the burning city of Corinth, signalling its destruction.

■ *The Siege of Corinth* is a revision of *Maometto II*, which Rossini had composed in 1820 on the text by Cesare Della Valle. It is rich with magnificent arias, including '*L'heure fatale approche*', sung by Pamira in the third act. The finale is remarkable not only for its musical achievements but because it constituted an innovation which other nineteenth-century composers of opera were to follow.

AGNES VON HOHENSTAUFEN
Opera in three acts by Gaspare Spontini (1774–1851), libretto by Ernst Raupach. First performance: Berlin, 28 May 1827 (the first act only). First complete performance: Berlin, Königliches Opernhaus (later Staatsoper), 12 June 1829.

■ This is Spontini's last opera. It was written during his Berlin period, when he was director of theatres, and was described by the composer and the librettist as an historical-romantic opera. Also from this period are Spontini's *Lalla Rookh (Nurmahal)* and *Alcidor*.

IL PIRATA (The Pirate)
Opera seria in two acts by Vincenzo Bellini (1801–35), libretto by Felice Romani (1788–1865), based on the three-act mélodrame, Bertram, ou Le Pirate, *by Raimond, in turn based on a play by Charles Robert Maturin. First performance: Milan, Teatro alla Scala, 27 October 1827. First performance in U.K.: London, King's Theatre, 17 April 1830; in U.S.A.: New York, 5 December 1832.*

ORIGINAL CAST. Giovanni Battista Rubini (Gualtiero), Antonio Tamburini (Ernesto), Henriette Méric-Lalande (Imogene).

SYNOPSIS. The story is set in the thirteenth century in and around the Sicilian castle of Caldora. With the victory of the Angevins, Imogene (soprano), daughter of a follower of Manfred of Swabia and beloved of Gualtiero (tenor), also a supporter of the Swabians, has been forced to marry Ernesto (baritone), Duke of Caldora, a powerful Angevin baron, to save her imprisoned father from death. Gualtiero, now the leader of a band of pirates, has been defeated in a sea battle by Ernesto's forces. Act I, Scene I. He and his men are swept ashore near the castle of his enemy and Imogene during a storm. Imogene compassionately offers them hospitality without recognizing their leader. Scene II. The castle of Caldora. When Gualtiero realizes the identity of his hostess, he tells her who he is. He reminds her that he had become a pirate and fought against the Angevins out of love for her, hoping that she would wait until his side had won to marry him. The heartbroken Imogene explains that she had to give way to Ernesto's blackmail and marry him in order to save her father's life. Gualtiero wants to challenge the

brought before the victorious leader by Mahommet's confidant, Omar. Pamira discovers that the man she knew as Almanzor is in fact Mahommet. He offers peace to the city out of love for her. Cléomène curses her for her love. Act II. After the Turkish victory Pamira and Ismène (mezzo-soprano), her confidante, are in Mahommet's pavilion. As Pamira prepares for her marriage to Mahommet, she struggles with conflicting sentiments of love and duty. Néocle, a prisoner, comes to tell them that Corinth has rebelled. The battle is clearly visible from the Turkish camp and when Pamira hears her father calling her from the walls she decides to return to her own people. Mahommet furiously orders that the city be razed to the ground. Act III. Pamira and Néocle have managed to escape and are hiding among the graves of the Corinthians. The Greeks have lost and can expect nothing but death. Néocle intercedes with Cléomène, who pardons his daughter. She repents her guilty passion and swears to be faithful to Néocle. Meanwhile the Turks advance. Mahommet tries to take Pamira prisoner. Rather than surrender to the enemy, she plunges a dagger into her

Drawing by Du Fauget for the first performance of Rossini's Le Comte Ory. *Left, Adolphe Nourrit in the part of Count Ory and (right) disguised as a hermit, with Jawurek in the part of Isolier.*

Duke to a duel. Ernesto returns triumphant to the castle, having won the battle against the pirates. He reproves his wife for not being as happy as he is over the victory. Act II. Ernesto is informed that Gualtiero is on the island. He discovers him in his wife's chamber and draws his sword, but in the ensuing duel Ernesto is killed. Enraged at the death of their leader, the assembled knights of Caldora condemn Gualtiero to death. He mounts the scaffold and Imogene goes mad with grief.

■ The opera is based on Maturin's tragedy *Bertram* (1816), but the title presumably comes from Scott's *The Pirate* (1821). Bellini was commissioned by the famous impresario Barbaja on the strength of the success of *Bianca e Gernando* (or *Bianca e Fernando*) in Naples. *Il Pirata* was the first of many successful collaborations between Bellini and Felice Romani. In Milan in 1827 there were some extraordinarily gifted singers who enjoyed immense popularity, not only Lalande, but Rubini, for whom the difficult and exhausting role of Gualtiero had been expressly written. The première was at La Scala, the last production

of the autumn season, and it was a triumph. During the same year La Scala gave fifteen more performances. The following year *Il Pirata* began to make the rounds of the European theatres. The text was translated into French and German. This is Bellini's longest opera and has certain characteristics not found in most of his later works: a dramatic Donizetti-like quality expressed through the predominance of the spoken recitative over the aria (though there is no lack of purely lyrical passages); and certain of Imogene's romances and the whole of the final mad scene presage Norma's famous aria *Casta Diva*, which is similar also in its orchestration. The opera opens with a long prelude, which introduces the stormy atmosphere of the first scene.

LE CONVENIENZE E LE INCONVENIENZE TEATRALI (The Conventions of the Theatre)
Opera in one act by Gaetano Donizetti (1797–1848), libretto by the composer, based on two famous farces by Semeone Antonio Sografi (1794). First performance: Naples, Teatro Nuovo, 21 November 1827.

SYNOPSIS. Luigia (soprano), seconda donna, makes a fuss during a rehearsal in a small opera house about her part. When her mother, the formidable Mamm'Agata (baritone), arrives, she sets about obtaining for her daughter comparable prominence to the prima donna, Corilla (soprano). At last, Corilla walks out; the impresario (bass), in despair, accepts Mamm'Agata's assurances that she herself can take the role, and all look forward, with trepidation to the evening's rehearsal.

■ A short, very amusing opera which pleased the public even recently in a series of performances.

LA MUETTE DE PORTICI, or MASANIELLO (The Dumb Girl of Portici)

Melodramma *in five acts by Daniel Auber (1782–1871), libretto by Eugène Scribe (1791–1861) and Germain Delavigne. First performance: Paris, Opéra, 29 February 1828. First performance in U.K.: London, Drury Lane, 4 May 1829; in U.S.A.: New York, 15 August 1831.*

ORIGINAL CAST. Cinti Damoreau, Nourrit, Bernard Dabadie, Noblet.

SYNOPSIS. The action takes place at Portici and Naples in 1647. Act I. In the gardens of the palace of the Duke of Arcos there are festivities for the marriage of Alfonso (tenor), son of the Duke, and the Spanish Princess, Elvira (soprano). Alfonso tells his friend Lorenzo (tenor), how much he regrets having to abandon Fenella (dancer), a dumb girl whom he had seduced, so that he can marry Elvira. Fenella escapes from her captivity and with gestures tells her story to Elvira, who offers her protection. During the marriage, Fenella recognizes the bridegroom as her former lover, and indicates as much to Elvira. The newly married bride disowns her husband. Act II. A picturesque spot near Portici. As the fishermen prepare their nets, Masaniello (tenor), Fenella's brother, is deeply concerned that his sister has not been seen for a month. Fenella suddenly appears on the cliff top and runs into her brother's arms. She explains as best she can what happened to her, without disclosing the Duke's identity. Masaniello, together with the other peasants, promise revenge for Fenella. Act III. A square in Naples. Elvira forgives Alfonso, but she does not forget her promise to protect Fenella and sends Selva (bass), an officer, to find her. Selva forces Fenella to follow him, driving back Masaniello, who tries to defend her, and who now realizes the identity of his sister's seducer. Act IV. Masaniello's hut. Portici is in revolt, but Masaniello, the instigator of the rebellion, now regrets the excesses of the mob. When two strangers ask for refuge, he willingly agrees and even though he recognizes them as Alfonso and Elvira, he supplies them with a boat to escape. Act V. The rebels have occupied the palace, and Masaniello is proclaimed King. The Duke mounts a victorious counter-attack, however, and Masaniello is slain by his own men just as

he saves Elvira's life once again. Fenella is overcome with grief at her brother's death and begging Elvira to be reconciled to Alfonso, throws herself from the balcony of the palace while Vesuvius begins to erupt.

■ Between 1828 and 1880 *La Muette* was performed 500 times in Paris alone. It was one of the biggest hits of the Paris Opéra and is Auber's most famous opera. It was also very popular abroad, especially in Germany, where at least six translations of the text can be found. When it was performed in Brussels on 25 August 1830, it gave the signal for the outbreak of a popular revolt, which led to the independence of Belgium from the Dutch. The libretto was also translated into English, Danish, Polish, Croat, Italian, Swedish, Norwegian and Slovenian. At the London opening in 1829 the opera appeared under the title of *Masaniello*; whilst in 1832 at the Carneval of Trieste (for which the score was slightly modified by Callas and Donizetti), it was called *Il Pescatore di Brindisi*. Both *La Muette* and *Fra Diavolo* are still performed today. An unusual aspect of this work is that the main character is performed by a mime or a ballerina. Of the many operas written by Auber, *La Muette* is one of his few serious subjects and the only one which the critics found to have a persuasive dramatic content. According to Wagner, we have for the first time an accurate rendering of the instrumentation, clear characterization of the choruses finally integrated with the action, impassioned melodies and a search for strong dramatic effects. A reason given – despite Auber's denial – to explain the difference between *La Muette* and Auber's other works was that the more exquisite melodies were inspired by Neapolitan songs. It was also suggested that a special tension was produced by Auber's association with the Paris Opéra for the first time, and by the particular climate of latent revolution in France during the years immediately preceding the Revolution of 1830. None of these explanations is completely satisfactory. The fact remains that with *La Muette* Auber created the model for all subsequent *grand opéra* by fully assimilating the themes of the true romantic melodrama.

DER VAMPYR (The Vampire)

Opera in two acts by Heinrich Marschner (1795–1861), libretto by Wilhelm August Wohlbrück. First performance: Leipzig, 29 March 1828. First performance in U.K.: London, Lyceum, 25 August 1829.

SYNOPSIS. Lord Ruthven (bass), the Vampire, is brought back to life by Aubry (tenor) and asks the devil, his master, to grant him more time to live. He obtains three years on condition that he obtains for the devil three virgin brides. Two of them, Ianthe and Emmy (sopranos), are easy prey, whereas Malwina

Cover of the monthly Il Teatro Illustrato *for February 1882, showing the operas being performed in the principal Italian houses during Carnival; at La Scala,* Guglielmo Tell.

IL TEATRO ILLUSTRATO

PREZZI D'ABBONAMENTO:

ranco di porto nel Regno . . . Anno L. 6 — Sem. L. 3
lessandria, Susa, Tunisi, Tripoli. » » 7 — » 3 50
nione post. d'Europa e Amer. Nord » » 8 — » 4 —
merica del Sud, Asia, Africa . . . » » 10 — » 5 —
ustr., Chili, Bol., Panama, Parag. » » 12 — » 6 —
Un numero separato Cent. 50 in tutta Italia.

Anno II. — Febbrajo 1882. — N. 14.

Edoardo Sonzogno
EDITORE
Milano. — Via Pasquirolo, N. 14.

AVVERTENZE.

Gli abbonati annui ricevono in dono, nel corso dell'anno, QUAT-
TRO COMPOSIZIONI MUSICALI, oltre ad un'elegante Copertina
per riunire in volume le dispense dell'annata.

Prezzo delle inserzioni nella copertina Cent. 50 per ogni linea
o spazio di linea.

157

(soprano), faithful to her beloved Aubry, is not deceived by Ruthven's flattery despite the fact that her father, Davenaunt (bass), wants her to marry him. Aubry begs Davenaunt in vain to postpone the marriage. Aubry is forced to reveal Ruthven's true nature at the risk of his own life in order to save Malwina. Just as the wedding is about to take place, the period of time allotted to Ruthven expires, and, struck by lightning, he sinks into hell.

■ Marschner composed this opera in Leipzig after moving there from Dresden, where he had been *Musikdirector* of Italian and German opera. *Der Vampyr* was an immediate success in Germany and abroad – in London it was given 60 times consecutively. It earned Wagner's esteem and in 1833 he contributed to it an aria of his own composition. The subject is taken from *The Vampire* by J. W. Polidori (attributed to Byron) and from a play by Charles Nodier, Pierre François Adrien Carmouche and Achille de Jouffroy which was performed in Paris in 1820.

LE COMTE ORY (Count Ory)

Melodramma giocoso in two acts by Gioacchino Rossini (1792–1868), libretto by Eugène Scribe (1791–1861) and Charles Gaspard Delestre-Poirson. First performance: Paris Opéra, 20 August 1828. First performance in U.K.: London, Haymarket, 28 February 1829; in U.S.A.: New York, 22 August 1831.

ORIGINAL CAST. L. Cinti-Damoreau, Mori, Javurek, A. Nourrit, Levasseur, E. B. Dabadie.

SYNOPSIS. In and around the castle of Formoutiers; about 1200. The men have gone to the Holy Land on a Crusade. The young Count Ory (tenor), disguised as a hermit, makes the most of the situation with the help of his friend Raimbaud (baritone). He is determined to

Gioacchino Rossini, contemporary lithographs.

gain entrance to the castle and pay court to the Count of Formoutiers's sister, Adèle (soprano). Alice (soprano), a young peasant girl, and Ragonde (contralto), custodian of the castle, are among the many who consult the 'hermit' whom they believe to be a fortune-teller of great wisdom. Isolier (mezzo-soprano), the Count's page, arrives as well and not recognizing Ory, confides in him his love for the young Countess Adèle. When Adèle herself arrives to see the hermit, he tells her of the page's love, but advises her to keep well away from him. Ory is invited to the castle and all seems to be going well for him when he is unmasked by his tutor. The ladies return in dismay to the castle. Act II. A room in the castle. As the outraged ladies talk over Ory's deception, they hear calls for help from some poor pilgrim sisters who say they have fled from Ory and require shelter. When left alone, they prove to be Ory and his men in disguise. Isolier recognizes them, however, and decides with the Countess to turn the tables on his enterprising master and rival. In a darkened room Ory, deceived by the voice of the Countess, who is hiding behind the sofa on which Isolier is seated, pays court to the page mistaking him for Adèle. At the sound of the trumpets, announcing the return of the Count de Formoutiers and Ory's father, Ory and his companions are forced to flee by a secret door. Adèle goes to meet her brother, and the other ladies receive their husbands. Adèle decides that she will marry the faithful Isolier, who has succeeded in thwarting the insidious Count Ory.

■ Based on a comedy by Scribe which, in the form of an ancient ballad, tells the story of Ory, the seducer of an abbess and her nuns, the libretto expands the original text to achieve the necessary length. Scribe's displeasure with the results led to the withdrawal of his name from the showbill of the first performance. Actually the text has much stylistic merit. The overture and some arias were taken from *Il Viaggio a Reims* (1825) to supplement the rest of the score, written expressly for *Le Comte Ory*. Its incisive melodic quality caught the notice of the critics and the public. Its humour, unlike that of *Il Barbiere di Siviglia* (1816), is more contained and aristocratic, but, though it lacks the same verve, it is undoubtedly one of Rossini's masterpieces. *Le Comte Ory* was given a triumphant reception in France and French composers frequently used it as a model for their own compositions. In Italy it did not achieve the success it deserved, partly owing to a bad translation, which forced Rossini to make untimely cuts in the score. He then personally supervised a new translation and the necessary musical changes. But this effort failed as well and Rossini concluded: 'if they like it in France, let's leave it to the French; the Italians have different tastes.'

LA FIANCÉE

Comic opera in three acts by Daniel Auber (1782–1871), libretto by Eugène Scribe (1791–1861). First performance: Paris, Opéra-Comique, 10 January 1829. First performance in U.K.: London, Drury Lane,

Performance of Rossini's Guglielmo Tell *at La Scala, designed by Salvatore Fiume and produced by Sandro Bolchi.*

4 February 1830; in U.S.A.: New York, 21 August 1829.

■ *La Fiancée* was warmly received in France and also abroad, where it was often performed until about 1850. The last performance in Paris was in 1858.

LA STRANIERA (The Stranger)
Opera seria *in two acts by Vincenzo Bellini (1801–35), libretto by Felice Romani (1788–1865). First performance: Milan, Teatro alla Scala, 14 February 1829. First performance in U.K.: London, 23 June 1832; in U.S.A.: New York, 10 November 1834.*

ORIGINAL CAST. Henriette Méric-Lalande (Alaide), Caroline Unger (Isoletta), Domenico Reina (Arturo), Antonio Tamburini (Valdeburgo).

SYNOPSIS. The action takes place in Brittany in and around the castle of the Signore di Montolino in the fourteenth century. Act I, Scene I. The castle of the

Signore di Montolino (bass) is the scene of the marriage of Isoletta (mezzo-soprano) and Arturo (tenor). Isoletta sadly tells Valdeburgo (baritone) that Arturo has fallen in love with a mysterious veiled woman, Alaide (*La Straniera*) (soprano), who lives in a hut near the castle. Scene II. Inside *La Straniera*'s hut. Arturo has joined Alaide and confesses his love for her, and she admits hers for him, but begs him never to come again or a terrible misfortune will befall them both. Scene III. A forest in the vicinity; in the distance Alaide's hut. Arturo meets Valdeburgo, who asks him on behalf of everyone to return to Isoletta, but Arturo requests that first Valdeburgo should meet *La Straniera* and if he considers her unworthy of him, then Arturo will abandon her forever. Valdeburgo recognizes her as his own sister and embraces her. Then he begs Arturo never to see her again, for he knows her secret which prevents her from ever marrying Arturo. Scene IV. Near the hut in a place overlooking the lake. Arturo is consumed with jealousy on hearing from Osburgo (tenor) that *La Straniera* and Valdeburgo plan to run away together and he challenges

Valdeburgo to a duel. Valdeburgo is wounded and falls into the lake. *La Straniera* arrives too late and reveals to Arturo that Valdeburgo is her brother. Griefstricken, he plunges into the lake to search for the wounded man whilst *La Straniera*, found by some of the local inhabitants alone with Arturo's bloody sword, is accused of double homicide. Act II, Scene I. The large courtroom of the Hospitallers, in whose jurisdiction the events have happened. First Arturo and then Valdeburgo appear during the trial to exonerate *La Straniera*, who refuses to defend herself, or even to lift her veil. Valdeburgo allows only the Prior to see her face; utterly amazed, he orders her immediate release. Scene II. Alaide's hut. Valdeburgo persuades Arturo to return to Isoletta. He invites Valdeburgo, as a favour, to his wedding. Scene III. Isoletta's room in the castle. Arturo swears eternal love for her. Preparations for the wedding are begun. Scene IV. In front of the church of the Hospitallers. Arturo greets Valdeburgo and noticing the veiled woman leaves Isoletta at the altar. Isoletta throws down her wreath; *La Straniera* picks it up for her and unveils herself. Arturo and Isoletta are married, but Arturo suddenly unsheathes his sword and cries that he will live or die with *La Straniera*. The Prior then reveals that Alaide is Queen Agnès of France, who was sent away from court, but has now been recalled to the throne. Arturo realizes the impossibility of his love and kills himself; Isoletta falls on his dead body.

■ This opera is based on the novel *L'Etrangère* by Charles Victor Prévôt d'Arlincourt (1789–1856). Bellini wrote it presumably at Moltrasio on Lake Como, where he was the guest of his mistress Giuditta Turina Cantù. He received the commission from the impresario Barbaja, who had already procured him *Il Pirata*, also for La Scala. The plot unfolds in that atmosphere of romance, mystery and legend so dear to the audiences of that era and which Romani captured so well, though it did not suit his literary talents. Though not an altogether well-balanced work, owing partly to a mediocre libretto, *La Straniera* displays that lyrical, non-dramatic inspiration characteristic of most of Bellini's works. It enjoyed a considerable success in Italy and abroad. During the nineteenth century it was frequently performed, outside Europe as well. The libretto was translated into German, Danish, Hungarian and Swedish.

LA ZAIRA

Tragedia lirica *in two acts by Vincenzo Bellini (1801–35), libretto by Felice Romani (1788–1865). First performance: Parma, Teatro Ducale, 16 May 1829.*

■ Set in the Far East and based on Voltaire's tragedy *Zaïre* (1732), the opera was performed at the inauguration of the Teatro Ducale, Parma. The première was a resounding failure, but Bellini incorporated material from *La Zaira* into *I Capuleti e i Montecchi*, his immensely successful opera of a year later.

ELISABETTA AL CASTELLO DI KENILWORTH (Elizabeth at the Castle of Kenilworth)

Opera seria *in three acts by Gaetano Donizetti (1797–1848), libretto by Leone Andrea Tottola, based on the novel by Sir Walter Scott. It is also known by the title* Il Castello di Kenilworth. *First performance: Naples, Teatro San Carlo, 6 July 1829.*

GUILLAUME TELL (William Tell)

Opera *in four acts by Gioacchino Rossini (1792–1868), libretto by Etienne de Jouy (1764–1846) and Hippolyte Bis (1789–1853) from Friedrich Schiller's play. First performance: Paris, Opéra, 3 August 1829. First performance in U.K.: London, Drury Lane, 1 May 1830; in U.S.A.: New York, 19 September 1831.*

ORIGINAL CAST. Cinti-Damoreau, Nourrit, Levasseur, Dabadie, Dabadie, Mori, Prévost.

SYNOPSIS. Act I. A village in the Alps. Guillaume (baritone) reflects on the oppressive Austrian domination of Switzerland. A fisherman in his boat sings; Hedwige, Guillaume's wife (soprano), and his son Jemmy (soprano) are at work. The shepherds celebrate the engagements of two girls, while Melchthal (bass) reproaches his son Arnold (tenor) for not being married. Arnold replies that it is because he is in love with Mathilde (soprano), daughter of the Austrian governor Gessler, who owes her life to him. Tell helps a shepherd Leuthold (bass) to escape from Gessler's troops after he had killed a soldier who tried to abduct his daughter. The soldiers set fire to the village when they do not find Leuthold, and take Melchthal as hostage. Act II. A mountain valley by the lake of Lucerne. The mountaineers return home at sunset. Mathilde and Arnold declare their love for each other. She is unable to persuade him to join the Austrians and in this way gain glory so that she could marry him. Tell brings Arnold the news that his father has been killed. Arnold swears that he will fight with the patriots and Tell rouses the Swiss with a strong call to arms. Act III, Scene I. A deserted, rustic place. Arnold tells Mathilde of his intentions and she promises to love him always. Scene II. The market square near Gessler's castle: the tyrant summons the citizens to bow down before a pole (bearing his hat on the top) which he has had erected. Tell and Jemmy, who refuse to obey, are recognized in the crowd and accused of helping Leuthold to escape. Tell is ordered to shoot an apple from his son's head. He hesitates but Jemmy encourages him and promises to stand still. Tell lets fly his arrow, which goes straight to the target accompanied by cheers from the crowd. He proudly explains that he meant to shoot Gessler had he missed the apple and hurt Jemmy. Gessler has father and son arrested, but the boy is spared and given in custody to Mathilde. Act IV. Arnold's house. Arnold and the conspirators prepare for war. Mathilde arrives with Jemmy, and the news that Tell has escaped. Jemmy gives the signal for the revolt by setting fire to the house. A storm breaks over the lake and the sky darkens. Gessler manages to reach

Lithograph by Godefroy Engelmann for the third act of Auber's Fra Diavolo, *1830. Paris, Bibliothèque de l'Opéra.*

safety in his boat, but dies from an arrow shot by Tell. The conspirators rejoice that the Altdorf fortress has fallen. Switzerland is free once again.

■ *Guillaume Tell* is based on the play by Schiller. The libretto, written by de Jouy, regular poet of the Paris Opéra, had to be revised by Hippolyte Bis, but the result was colourless and banal. Rossini took five months to write the score in 1828 – considerably longer than was usually necessary. When the opera was performed a year later, it was given a disastrous reception by the public. This was not the Rossini they knew, with his repertoire of bravura pieces. And yet this is precisely what makes *William Tell* great. The setting and the atmosphere are brought to life by the music and it is a thoroughly romantic work, foreshadowing later developments in this field. Other composers of that period, like Bellini, Donizetti and even Berlioz – not usually an admirer of Rossini – immediately perceived the greatness and originality of the work. There are in fact no *crescendos* or *cabalette* or the usual finales with the typical cadenzas, but rather a search for a totally

new style, rich with pathos, idyllic moments and high dramatic tension. Another innovation was the use of Swiss folk songs, which many other composers were to take up in the nineteenth and twentieth centuries. Among the most significant passages, apart from the celebrated overture, are Mathilde's romance, *Sombre forêt* (Act II), Tell's aria to his son, *Sois immobile* (Act III) and the magnificent final chorus. Rossini wrote *William Tell* when he was 37 and with it opened the way for a new era of romantic opera, just as he had set the style for comic opera with his *Barbiere di Siviglia*. Grand opera in Italy and France owed much to his example. After *William Tell*, Rossini composed no more operas.

FRA DIAVOLO, ou L'HÔTELLERIE DE TERRACINE (The Inn at Terracine)

Comic opera in three acts by Daniel Auber (1782–1871), libretto by Eugène Scribe (1791–1861) and Germain Delavigne. First performance: Paris, Opéra-Comique, 28 January 1830. First performance

Zoé Prévost in the part of Zerlina in the first performance of Auber's Fra Diavolo. *Drawing by A. Lacauchie, engraved by Danois. Paris, Bibliothèque de l'Opéra.*

in U.K.: London, Drury Lane, 1 February 1831; in U.S.A.: New York, 17 October 1831.

ORIGINAL CAST. Chollet, Féréol, Prévost, Boulanger.

SYNOPSIS. Matteo (bass), an innkeeper, wants his daughter Zerlina (soprano) to marry a rich farmer, although she loves Lorenzo (tenor). Lord Rocburg (tenor) and his wife Lady Pamela (mezzo-soprano) arrive at the inn after being attacked by robbers, who stole their jewels; they managed, however, to keep their money. A reward of 1,000 ducats is offered for the return of the jewels and the capture of the robbers, and Lorenzo sets out to win it. The leader of the robbers is Fra Diavolo (tenor), who turns up at the inn calling himself Marchese di San Marco. He makes up to Lady Pamela to find out where she has concealed her money. Lorenzo recovers the jewels and kills twenty of the band: Fra Diavolo vows to avenge his companions. During the night, he tries to frame Zerlina in a compromising situation with Milord but finds himself caught in a trap. Lorenzo, richer by 1,000 ducats, can now marry Zerlina.

■ The text is based on the exploits of the legendary Sanfedist, Michele Pezza, known as Fra Diavolo. The libretto, however, presents the hero more as a gentleman thief than a political figure. The traditional *opéra comique* included long spoken passages, and the earlier performances of *Fra Diavolo* were given in this form. Later Auber changed these passages to sung recitatives. Although this is by far Auber's most famous *opéra comique* and is perhaps preferred by the general public over *La Muette de Portici*, *Fra Diavolo* is not substantially different from Auber's other *opéras comiques*. The music's sparkle and charm and its lack of profundity are characteristic. The influence of Rosini – for whom Auber felt unbounded admiration – is evident, as in all Auber's works. The libretto, written under the direction of Eugène Scribe (whose friendship with Auber led to their collaboration for approximately 40 years), was, after its enormous Parisian success, translated into almost all the European languages. The Public's enthusiasm for *Fra Diavolo* did not begin to diminish until this century, although arias such as the famous *Romance favorite* remain as popular as ever. Today *Fra Diavolo* is performed almost exclusively in France.

I CAPULETI E I MONTECCHI (The Capulets and the Montagues)

Tragedia lirica *in two acts by Vincenzo Bellini (1801–35), libretto by Felice Romani (1788–1865), derived from Shakespeare's* Romeo and Juliet. *First*

performance: Venice, Teatro La Fenice, 11 March
1830. First performance in U.K.: London, 20 July
1833; in U.S.A.: New Orleans, St Charles Theater, 4
April 1837.

ORIGINAL CAST. Giuditta Grisi, Giulia Grisi,
Caradoili Allan, Bonfigli, conducted by the composer.

SYNOPSIS. Verona in the thirteenth century. Act I,
Scene I. In the Capulet palace. Capellio (bass) tells his
friends – Guelph supporters – to prepare themselves to
receive a proposal of peace from the Montecchi
(Ghibellines). He hates Romeo (mezzo-soprano),
head of the Montecchi, for the murder of his son, and
promises his daughter, Giulietta, in marriage to
Tebaldo (tenor) if he will assassinate Romeo. Romeo,
who loves and is loved by Giulietta (soprano) in secret,
presents himself to Capellio as the ambassador of the
Montecchi: he requests a truce between the families to
be sealed by Giulietta's marriage to Romeo. Capellio
disdainfully refuses any such proposal and announces
that his daughter is soon to marry Tebaldo. Scene II.
Giulietta's room. In despair, Giulietta contemplates
her wedding with Tebaldo. Romeo enters, but he is
unable to persuade her to elope. He escapes as
Giulietta leaves with her father for the marriage. Scene
III. The wedding guests arrive at the Capulet palace.
Romeo mingles with them in disguise and tells Lorenzo
(bass), the Capulet doctor, who has sympathized with
the lovers' plight, that he intends to rescue Giulietta by
force. During the fighting, Romeo declares his love for
Giulietta to her father, who is appalled and the

*Giuditta Pasta as Norma in a miniature by Luigi
Bianchi.*

*Opposite page,
below: a print of
the Teatro La
Fenice, Venice, in
1721.*

*Interior of the
Teatro La Fenice,
Venice, in the first
half of the
nineteenth century.*

Capulets foil his attempt to abduct the bride. Act II, Scene I. Giulietta's room. Not knowing how to extricate herself from her marriage with Tebaldo, Giulietta follows Lorenzo's advice and drinks a sleeping potion which will give her the appearance of death. She will then be taken to the tomb of the Capulets, where Romeo, advised of the plan by Lorenzo, will be waiting when she awakens. Capellio, however, arrests Lorenzo on suspicion and prevents this information from reaching Romeo. Scene II. Outside the palace. Romeo and Tebaldo are about to fight a duel, when they hear that Giulietta has been discovered dead. At the news, the two put down their weapons. Scene III. The Capulet tomb. Romeo believes Giulietta to be dead and poisons himself. Giulietta awakes to see him dying beside her and in her grief falls dead on the body of her beloved. Capellio leads his men in to capture Romeo, but he finds only the lifeless corpses of the young lovers.

■ Bellini wrote this opera to vindicate himself for the failure of *Zaira* in Paris and borrowed parts of *Zaira* for his work. He succeeded in full and *I Capuleti e i Montecchi* was a tremendous success. Bellini, however, had begun to show signs of ill health. It is interesting to note that because of the limited time available to him, he used Romani's libretto for Nicola Vaccai's *Giulietta e Romeo* (1825). For this reason it was customary for many years (beginning with a performance in Bologna in 1832 up until December 1895, when the original version was given in Naples) to replace the last part of *I Capuleti e i Montecchi* with Vaccai's version. The exquisitely moving character of the story was exactly the sort of subject to stimulate Bellini's talents, which here reached sublime melodic heights, particularly in the final duet and in Giulietta's romance *Oh! Quante volte!* After its triumphant Venetian première, it was performed in all the major Italian and European theatres with celebrated singers like Malibran and Ronzi.

ANNA BOLENA (Anne Boleyn)

Opera seria *in two acts by Gaetano Donizetti (1797–1848), libretto by Felice Romani (1788–1865). First performance: Milan, Teatro Carcano, 26 December 1830. First performance in U.K.: London, Haymarket, 8 July 1831; in U.S.A.: New Orleans, November 1839.*

ORIGINAL CAST. Giuditta Pasta, Orlandi, Giovanni Battista Rubini, Galli.

SYNOPSIS. Enrico (bass), King of England, neglects his Queen, Anna (soprano), for Giovanna Seymour (mezzo-soprano), lady-in-waiting. He recalls Lord Riccardo Percy (tenor), whom he had exiled so that he could marry Anna, in order to make a case against the Queen for treason. Anna is unable to stop her former lover protesting his continued love for her and he is only just prevented by the page Smeton (contralto) from running himself through with his sword. Enrico

Opera lovers. Lithograph from the nineteenth century, Milan, Municipal Print Collection.

arrests all three of them. Giovanna begs Anna to confess and take advantage of the King's offer to spare her life. She refuses, but forgives Giovanna for having taken Enrico's love from her. Smeton's lies to the Court, made in order to save Anna, are taken as conclusive proof of her guilt. Giovanna refuses to become Queen and asks the King for mercy on Anna. Anna's brother Rochefort (bass) and Percy are condemned with her. Anna's senses are disturbed by memories of Percy's love and she prays for God's blessing on the King's new wife.

■ The première of *Anna Bolena* was a triumph, partly because of the exceptional cast. This work confirmed Donizetti's place among the most important composers of the day and gave him the opportunity to reveal the dramatic aspect of his lyrical muse. It was also his first opera to be performed all over Europe. In Paris it received a good reception despite competition with Bellini's *La Sonnambula*. After appearing for years on each season's play bills, it disappeared from the repertory. When it was revived at La Scala in 1957 with Callas in a production by Luchino Visconti, it achieved another triumphant success.

LA SONNAMBULA (The Sleepwalker)

Melodramma *in two acts by Vincenzo Bellini (1801–35), libretto by Felice Romani (1788–1865). First performance: Milan, Teatro Carcano, 6 March*

1831. First performance in U.K.: London, Haymarket, 28 July 1831; in U.S.A.: New York, 13 November 1835.

ORIGINAL CAST. Giuditta Pasta (Amina), Giovanni Battista Rubini (Elvino), Luciano Mariani (Rodolfo), Elisa Taccani (Lisa), Lorenzo Biondi (Alessio).

SYNOPSIS. The story takes place in a Swiss village at an unspecified time. Act I, Scene I. The village square; on one side Lisa's inn, on the other Teresa's mill; 'in the background, gentle hills'. The villagers arrive to celebrate the marriage of Elvino (tenor), a rich landowner, and Amina (soprano), an orphan adopted by the mill-owner's wife, Teresa (mezzo-soprano). Lisa, the innkeeper (soprano), is consumed with jealousy, because she wanted to marry Elvino herself, and she takes no notice of Alessio (bass), who is devoted to her. When Elvino arrives, he presents Amina with a wedding ring worn by his mother. Their love duet is interrupted by the unexpected arrival of a nobleman. He is Count Rodolfo (bass), the son of the deceased lord of the village, who has been absent from the town for so many years that no one recognizes him. Keeping his identity secret, he pays many elegant compliments to Amina and Elvino jealously rebukes him. He scoffs at the villagers' tale of a local ghost – a woman who appears on misty nights. Scene II. A room at the inn. Rodolfo flirts with Lisa, who is delighted, when Amina appears in the room, sleepwalking, and lies down on a couch. Lisa hides while Rodolfo, disconcerted, is uncertain whether or not to wake the girl, and leaves her. The villagers arrive to pay their respects to the Count, but find no one in his room but Amira asleep. No one believes Amina's explanation of innocence, except Teresa, and Elvino in despair repudiates her. Act II, Scene I. A shady valley between the village and the castle. Some villagers report that the Count considers Amina is speaking the truth about the sleepwalking, but Elvino refuses to believe the story. He cannot, however, forget his love for her. Scene II. Teresa's mill. Lisa has made the most of Amina's misfortunes and is about to wed Elvino when Teresa accuses her of infidelity and produces Lisa's handkerchief which was found in Rodolfo's room. Elvino suspects himself betrayed for the second time and rejects this marriage as well. Suddenly, to everyone's amazement, Amina appears on the edge of the roof, above the mill race. No one dares to speak lest the disturbance should cause Amina to lose her balance and fall. When she comes down singing pathetically about her love for Elvino, he realizes that Rodolfo's explanation was correct and again puts the wedding ring on her finger. Then he awakens her and the village resumes its celebrations for the wedding.

■ *La Sonnambula* is the first of Bellini's three great operas. Duke Litta of Milan had commissioned him to write an opera for the Teatro Carcano. Initially the subject was to have been based on Victor Hugo's *Hernani*, but when Bellini heard that Donizetti was pres-

enting *Anna Bolena* that same season, he decided not to compete with a composer of Donizetti's stature on a similar type of historical subject. He therefore chose as his theme a rustic idyll. Romani was engaged to write the libretto, based on Eugène Scribe's ballet-pantomime *La Somnambule, ou L'Arrivée d'un Nouveau Seigneur*, which Romani and Bellini modified considerably. Much of the opera was composed at Moltrasio, where Bellini was the guest of Giuditta Turina. The first performance was accompanied by a ballet, *Il Furore d'Amore*, and the score was dedicated to the musician Francesco Pollini. It success was overwhelming and was followed by frequent performances in Italy and abroad, including Paris, London and New York. The famous London production of 1833 at Drury Lane had Malibran singing in English; Bellini was called to the footlights and deliriously applauded. Subsequently, during the first decades of the twentieth century, *La Sonnambula* declined in popularity because its pastoral subject was considered out of date. Today it has regained its fame and is performed all over the world. In this work Bellini achieved the full mastery of his melodic and lyrical expression with those famous arias which have been called 'the longest and sweetest ever created by man's ingenuity'; for example, Elvino's cavatina *Prendi, l'anel ti dono* and Amina's romance *Ah, non credea mirarti*, masterpieces of their type. *La Sonnambula* unfolds with admirable musical coherence in a gentle pastoral mood without dramatic or tragic incidents. The orchestration is extremely simple and, though this has at times been judged a fault, it is perfectly suited to this type of composition.

ZAMPA, ou LA FIANCÉE DE MARBRE (Zampa, or The Marble Betrothed)
Melodrama in three acts by Ferdinand Hérold (1791–1833), libretto by A. Honoré Joseph Mélesville (1787–1865). First performance: Paris, Opéra-Comique, 3 May 1831. First performance in U.K.: London, Haymarket, 19 April 1833; in U.S.A.: New York, 12 August 1833.

SYNOPSIS. Act I. A hall with a marble statue. In the town of Milazzo, the joyful preparations for the forthcoming wedding of Alphonse (tenor) and Camille (soprano) are interrupted by the arrival of Zampa (tenor) with his corsairs. Although of noble birth, Zampa is now a cynical and arrogant pirate, and a seducer of women, who has been in love with Camille for a long time. To win her, he does not hesitate to furnish proof that her father is his prisoner and that if she refuses to marry him, he will take revenge by killing her father. As the pirates carouse, Zampa notices a statue at the far end of the room which bears a disturbing resemblance to a young girl, Alice de Manfredi, who died after he had seduced and abandoned her. He is disturbed by the resemblance, but behaves in his usual blustering manner and places a ring on the statue's finger, declaring with a sneer that she is his wife until the next day. Act II. The countryside near

Performance of Meyerbeer's Robert le Diable *at the Opéra, Paris. Colour lithograph by J. Arnout. Paris, Bibliothèque de l'Opéra.*

Camille's house. After a simple rustic chorus sung by women gathered round an altar, Zampa once again declares his love for Camille. When he has departed Camille meets Alphonse, who confesses that Zampa is none other than his brother. Though Alphonse had contemplated killing him to have Camille back, he cannot bring himself to do it. Thus it seems that the ill-omened marriage between Camille and Zampa will take place. Act III. Camille's room. A departing boatman sings a sad adieu to his village. Alphonse and Camille resolve to elope and depart. Zampa tries to follow them, but in the dark the statue of Alice confronts him, seizes him by the arm and drags him over a cliff.

■ Despite Berlioz's trenchant criticisms of this opera, it was a huge success in Paris. Of all Hérold's works, *Zampa* is by far the most famous. In the space of a few years it was performed throughout Europe and cemented the composer's success. The romantic character and panache of the protagonist, coupled with the genuine merits of the melodic invention, made this opera a particular favourite in France as well as in Germany.

ROBERT LE DIABLE (Robert the Devil)
Opera in five acts by Giacomo Meyerbeer

(1791–1861), libretto by Eugène Scribe (1791–1864) and Germain Delavigne. First performance: Paris, Opéra, 22 November 1831. First performance in U.K.: London, Drury Lane, 20 February 1832; in U.S.A.: New York, 7 April 1834.

ORIGINAL CAST. Nourrit, Levasseur, Dorus-Gras, Cinti-Damoreau, Taglioni.

SYNOPSIS. Palermo in the thirteenth century. Robert, Duke of Normandy (tenor), learns from the minstrel Raimbaut (tenor) that he is supposed to be the son of Princess Bertha and the devil. Outraged, he is about to kill Raimbaut, but his foster-sister Alice (soprano), who is betrothed to Raimbaut, intercedes for him. She warns Robert to be on his guard against his friend Bertram (bass), but cannot give any reason. (He is, in fact, the devil.) Robert, who is in love with Isabella, Princess of Sicily (soprano), is invited to participate in a tournament for her hand in marriage. He impresses everyone with the magnificence of his equipage, but he soon loses it in gambling. The Princess pities him and supplies new armour, but he fails to attend the tournament because he has been decoyed into a nearby wood by someone who looked like his main rival for Isabella's hand. It was, in fact, Bertram. Robert is dismayed to hear that he has lost Isabella's hand by default and Bertram suggests that he go to the ruined convent of St Rosalie and cut a magic branch that will give him irresistible power. At midnight at a diabolic orgy, attended by the ghosts of nuns who broke their vows, Robert commits the sacrilege of opening a tomb to remove the magic branch. The next day he uses the branch to gain entrance to Isabella's apartments and causes everyone to fall into a deep sleep. He attempts to take her away with him, but before the magic takes effect she finds the strength to reprove him for his disloyalty. Much affected by Isabella's words, Robert breaks the branch and the spell is lifted; he is arrested. Bertram helps him to escape and is about to compel him to sign in return a contract of eternal loyalty, when Alice arrives with the news that Isabella has forgiven him. Bertram tries to frighten him by revealing his true identity (as the fiend and his father), but Alice produces his mother's will in which she begged him not to be deceived, as she had been. Midnight sounds and Robert is released from evil to hasten to Isabella, while Bertram disappears back to Hell.

■ *Robert le Diable* represents an important phase in Meyerbeer's career. It is the first opera of his French period and it initiates his prolific collaboration with Scribe, whose librettos provided the elaborate plots and romantic situations so appropriate to Meyerbeer's

The French bass Nicolas Prosper Levasseur in the role of Bertram in the first performance of Meyerbeer's Robert le Diable, *1831. Engraving by Maleuvre. Milan, Museo della Scala.*

music – eclectic in style but rich in pathos and emotion. The current vogue for ostentation and pomposity, as expressed in *grand opéra*, found its most prestigious interpreter in Meyerbeer. One could almost identify the merits and defects of grand opera with those of Meyerbeer: a stage spectacle rich with sensational effects supported by an exceptional technical ability; a search for pleasing melodies; an emphasis on choruses and the orchestra. The opera was enormously successful and established Meyerbeer as one of the most popular composers of his time. Certain arias like *Nonnes qui reposez* from the third act, when Bertram invokes the evil spirits to help him conquer Robert, or the duet *Oh, toi que j'aime* from the fourth act, sung by Isabella and Robert, reveal an exceptional dramatic talent. In 1968 this work was revived in Italy on the occasion of the Florence May Festival.

NORMA

Tragedia lirica in two acts by Vincenzo Bellini (1801–35), libretto by Felice Romani (1788–1865), based on Alexandre Soumet's tragedy Norma, ou

The soprano Sabina Heinefetter, the first to sing Adina in Donizetti's L'Elisir d'Amore.

L'Infanticide. First performance: Milan, Teatro alla Scala, 26 December 1831. First performance in U.K.: London, Haymarket, 20 June 1835; in U.S.A.: Philadelphia, 11 January 1841.

ORIGINAL CAST. Giuditta Pasta (Norma), Giulia Grisi (Adalgisa), Domenico Donzelli (Pollione), Vincenzo Negrini (Oroveso).

SYNOPSIS. Gaul at the time of the Roman occupation. Act I, Scene I. The sacred forest of the Druids; in the middle is the oak tree of Irminsul and at its foot is the Druids' stone altar. Oroveso (bass) leads the Druids in expressions of hatred of the Roman invaders. They depart. Pollione (tenor), the Roman proconsul, appears and confides to his friend Flavio (tenor) that he has forsaken the Druid high priestess Norma (soprano), by whom he has had two sons, for Adalgisa (mezzo-soprano), another priestess. He recounts a dream warning him of Norma's vengeance. The two Romans leave as the Gauls return for the sacred rites; Norma, intending to avert further battles which might endanger Pollione's life, announces that Irminsul does not yet call the Gauls to war and that Rome will fall eventually because of its own internal weaknesses. She then invokes the chaste goddess of the moon, *Casta Diva*, for peace. When the others have departed Adalgisa returns to the clearing to meet Pollione, who persuades her to run away with him to Rome. Scene II. Norma's dwelling. Adalgisa confesses to Norma that she has a lover. Norma gently forgives her for breaking the sacred vow of chastity until she discovers that Adalgisa's lover is none other than the man who has just entered, Pollione. In fury, she calls down a curse upon them. Pollione leaves hurriedly at the sound of the temple gong calling the Gauls together. Act II, Scene I. Norma's dwelling. Norma finds that she cannot bring herself to kill her two children. Clotilde (mezzo-soprano) calls Adalgisa (whom Norma expects to be Pollione's new wife) and Norma entrusts her children to her. Adalgisa, however, no longer wishes to marry a man who has behaved so badly and offers instead to go to him and beg him to return to Norma. The two priestesses affirm their love for each other. Scene II. A lonely spot near the Druids' forest. Oroveso counsels patience to the warriors. Scene III. The temple of Irminsul. Norma waits hopefully until Clotilde reports that Adalgisa has been unable to influence Pollione. In a rage, Norma strikes the sacred gong to summon her people, and declares that Irminsul desires the extermination of the Romans. They reply with the impetuous fury of warriors, and demand a victim for sacrifice. At that moment Pollione is caught in the temple and is brought to Norma. She is about to sac-

Fiorenza Cossotto (Adalgisa) and Montserrat Caballé (Norma) in Bellini's Norma *at La Scala in December 1972.*

Scene from the last act of Bellini's La Sonnambula. *Engraving by P. Oggioni.*

rifice him when she stops and asks to be alone with him. She enjoys bringing him to his knees in an effort to save the life of Adalgisa, but when she recalls the people it is her own life that she offers as the victim – a priestess who has broken her vows. At first no-one believes her confession but she is adamant and, surrendering her children to her father, she prepares to mount the sacred pyre. Pollione recognizes her supreme nobility of spirit and they are reunited in death.

■ Most of the music for *Norma* was written at Blevio on Lake Como, where Bellini was the guest of Giuditta Pasta, who was to sing Norma at the première. Apparently she and Romani, the librettist, inspired Bellini to work. Incredible as it may seem, *Norma*, awaited by the Milanese as the most important event of the season, was a disastrous failure at its première. Pacini observed that he saw Bellini 'shed a few tears', and Bellini wrote to his friend and biographer Florino that he was greatly discouraged. Possibly one of the main reasons for the fiasco was the introduction of certain innovations to the traditional form of Italian opera, the most important of which was undoubtedly the replacement of the 'finale primo', or the great choral scene at the end of the first act, with a splendid but simple trio. However, at the second performance *Norma* was extraordinarily successful and was then warmly received throughout Italy. But the most favourable reaction came from outside Italy and in particular London where, directed by Bellini himself

and the title-role sung by Malibran, it was greeted with a frenzy of delight 'such as we have not seen for a long time' at Covent Garden. Another memorable production was in 1859 at Verona (with the Marchisio sisters) when the hymn '*Guerra! Guerra!*' brought the public to its feet. *Norma* has been translated into almost every language and continues to be performed all over the world. It is generally considered Bellini's masterpiece and one of the most important developments in the history of opera. If Bellini lacked truly vigorous dramatic sense, nevertheless in *Norma* he achieved a particular static solemnity which, combined with the absolute purity of the melodies, reminds certain critics of Greek tragedy. The lyricism of *Norma* has always been much esteemed, but reservations exist regarding the inadequate and simple orchestration. It was suggested that Bizet should re-orchestrate the score, but he felt that this was not possible. In Wagner's opinion, 'The poetry of *Norma* reaches the heights of Greek tragedy; and the closed forms of Italian opera, which Bellini ennobles and elevates, provide a contrast to the solemn and grandiose character of the whole. All the passions, so remarkably transfigured by the melody, are set against a majestic background from which they do not waver, but take shape within a large clear framework that unintentionally reminds us of Gluck and Spontini.' And further '. . . I admire in *Norma* the rich melodic vein expressing the most intimate passions with a sense of profound reality; a great score that speaks to the heart, a work of genius.'

DONZELLI   GRISI   PASTA

Nor. Trema per te fellone - Pei figli tuoi per me...
Adal. Che ascolto? ah, Pollione! - Taci t'arretra ...
...ahimè!

Norma

Domenico Donzelli (Pollione), Giulia Grisi (Adalgisa) and Giuditta Pasta (Norma) in the first performance of Bellini's Norma. *Milan, Museo Teatrale alla Scala.*

L'ELISIR D'AMORE (The Elixir of Love)

Opera comica *in two acts by Gaetano Donizetti (1797–1848), libretto by Felice Romani (1788–1865), based on Eugène Scribe's libretto* Le Philtre, *written in 1831 for Auber. First performance: Milan, Teatro della Cannobiana, 12 May 1832. First performance in U.K.: London, Lyceum, 10 December 1836; in U.S.A.: New York, 18 June 1838.*

ORIGINAL CAST. Sabina Heinefetter (Adina), Giuseppe Frezzolini (Dulcamara), Henri Bernard Debadie (Belcore), B. B. Genero (Nemorino).

SYNOPSIS. The story takes place in a village in the Basque country. Act I. On Adina's farm. Young girls and harvesters are resting under the trees. Adina (soprano) is reading them the story of Tristan, whose unrequited love for Isolde is resolved by a love potion. Shy young Nemorino (tenor), who loves Adina, utters a sigh. She takes no notice of his attentions; she admits that she is fickle and capricious and seems to prefer the attentions of the arrogant Belcore (baritone), sergeant of the garrison. The village square. A quack doctor, Dulcamara (bass), offers Nemorino a remedy in a little bottle which he claims will cure all ills and pains, restore youthful vigour to the old and guarantee love

for the young. Recalling the story of Tristan, Nemorino's hopes are rekindled. The doctor guarantees that the elixir will make Adina fall at his feet within 24 hours (just enough time for the doctor to make his departure). The ingenuous Nemorino is so sure of the medicine's potency that his behaviour towards the girls changes completely. He laughs and jokes in Adina's presence, paying little attention to her, almost as though she no longer interests him. Surprised and vexed, Adina decides out of spite to accept Belcore's proposal of marriage, which means that they must be married immediately, for the garrison must leave town the next morning. Everyone is invited to the wedding celebration – friends, peasants and Doctor Dulcamara. Plunged into despair once again, Nemorino begs Adina to wait at least 24 hours (time for the elixir to take effect), but she is adamant. Act II. At the farmhouse, preparations for the wedding are under way in great haste. Nemorino accepts Belcore's proposal that he enlists in order to receive 20 crowns, with which he can buy a second bottle of elixir. Meanwhile, there is talk in the village that Nemorino's uncle has died and left him a large legacy. Knowing nothing of this, Nemorino is suddenly surrounded by the village girls, from which he immediately concludes that the elixir has begun to take effect. Adina is overcome with jealousy as she realizes that, even without his inheritance, she is really in love with Nemorino. She discovers the lengths to which he has gone to win her and buys back his enlistment paper in order to release him. For his part, he is moved to notice the single tear on her cheek which indicates that his love is returned ('*Una furtiva lagrima*'). Doctor Dulcamara does a roaring business as the success of the elixir is the talk of the village, and everyone celebrates the happy couple's wedding.

■ *L'Elisir d'Amore* was commissioned by the Teatro della Cannobiana to replace a work which another composer had failed to submit in time. Donizetti was given only fourteen days, seven of which were taken up by the librettist preparing the text. The result was a sensational success, which ran for 32 consecutive nights. *L'Elisir* is a perfect example of nineteenth-century comic opera. Together with *Don Pasquale* and *Il Barbiere di Siviglia*, it is considered the highest achievement of its kind. It has been a constant favourite and continues to be performed regularly, especially in Italy. The score overflows with charming melodies from which Donizetti's sense of humour emerges clearly. Laughter changes to a smile and behind the smile is sadness, as in the famous '*Una furtiva lagrima*'. A version in Piedmontese dialect by 'Anaclet como d'Alba' was given at the Teatro Rossini in Turin in the autumn of 1859.

IL FURIOSO ALL'ISOLA DI SAN DOMINGO (The Madman of the Island of San Domingo)

Opera semiseria *in two acts by Gaetano Donizetti (1797–1848), libretto by Jacopo Ferretti, based on an episode from* Don Quixote *by Cervantes. First perfor-*

Final scene of Bellini's Norma *at La Scala in 1976–77. Produced by Mauro Bolognini; sets by Mario Ceroli; costumes by Gabriella Pescucci.*

mance: Rome, Teatro Valle, 2 January 1833. First performance in U.K.: London, Lyceum, 17 December 1836.

SYNOPSIS. Cardenio (baritone), a madman, wanders about the island of San Domingo, where he is looked after by Bartolomeo Mergoles (bass) and his daughter Marcella (soprano), and terrifies the inhabitants, especially Kaidamà (buffo). The reason for his madness is the infidelity of Eleonora (soprano), his wife, whom he had left behind when he went to seek their fortune. During their searches for him both Cardenio's brother Fernando (tenor) and Eleonora are shipwrecked on the island. Several tragedies are narrowly avoided before Eleonora can convince him of her sincere repentance; Cardenio regains his sanity and forgives his wife.

■ This work was highly successful in Italy and abroad. Within six years it was performed in 70 theatres. *Il Furioso* was written during a particularly unhappy period in Donizetti's life, when he was in poor health and financial difficulties. The libretto is only indirectly based on Cervantes's *Don Quixote* (Part I, Chapter XXVII), for Ferretti actually used a five-act play by an unknown writer also entitled *Il Furioso nell'Isola di San Domingo*, which was based on *Don Quixote*.

BEATRICE DI TENDA

Tragedia lirica *in two acts by Vincenzo Bellini (1801–35), libretto by Felice Romani (1788–1865). First performance: Venice, Teatro La Fenice, 16 March 1833. First performance in U.K.: London, 22 March 1836; in U.S.A.: New Orleans, 21 March 1842.*

ORIGINAL CAST. Giuditta Pasta (Beatrice), Anna Del Serre (Agnese), Alberico Curioni (Orombello).

SYNOPSIS. The action takes place in the Castle of Binasco in the year 1418. Act I, Scene I. The Castle of Binasco. Filippo Maria Visconti, the debauched Duke of Milan (baritone), reveals his love for Agnese del Maino (mezzo-soprano), a lady-in-waiting to his wife, Beatrice di Tenda (soprano), whom he had married for her great wealth and power. He dislikes the deference shown to his wife, and has tired of her, so he plots with Rizzardo (tenor), Agnese's brother, to try to get rid of her. Beatrice's cousin Orombello (tenor) confides in Agnese that he loves Beatrice, but because she is herself secretly in love with Orombello, Agnese decides to take revenge on both Orombello and Beatrice, for their supposedly adulterous union. She hands some compromising letters, written by Orombello to Beatrice, over to the Duke. Scene II. In the garden, Filippo accuses Beatrice of intrigue and adultery. She demands

Allegory from the first half of the nineteenth century celebrating the triumphs of Vincenzo Bellini and Maria Malibran.

justice. In a remote part of the castle, Beatrice flatly rejects Orombello's advances, but they are discovered together by Filippo and Agnese. Act II. The Gallery in Castle Binasco. Before the judges, Beatrice protests her innocence and Orombello, who had confessed under torture to a crime they did not commit, takes heart and retracts his statement. Agnese repents her evil deeds and begs Filippo to pardon them, but the sound of Beatrice's supporters demanding her release is enough to resolve Filippo to order their executions. Scene II. A vestibule leading to the scaffold. Beatrice walks courageously to her death; Orombello joins her in pardoning Agnese, who confesses her guilt and remorse.

■ *Beatrice di Tenda* was written by Bellini following a period of inactivity that began after the success of *Norma* in 1831, and lasted until the end of 1832. There was a project in 1832 for an *Oreste*, but this did not materialize. Bellini composed the score for *Beatrice* with his customary haste and the result was a disastrous first night. He wrote later that every time he had to compose an opera in a hurry the result was never up to expectations (not a great deal less, however, if Bellini was able to write of *Beatrice* that 'the opera was in no way inferior to her sisters'). The subject – the heroine unjustly accused and executed by her husband for adultery – is based on historical fact. It had already been used in a tragedy by Tibaldi Flores (1825) and a ballet by Monticini (1832). The opera's unfavourable reception in Venice provoked a serious disagreement between Bellini and Romani, and this led to the dissolution of their partnership, which had seen the birth of Bellini's finest operas. Each held the other responsible for *Beatrice*'s failure and in the end even Bellini's

friendship with his mistress Giuditta Turina was destroyed. The opera subsequently gained the public's favour and was performed extensively in Italy and abroad; the libretto was translated into German and Hungarian. Today, however, it is rarely seen.

PARISINA

Opera seria *in three acts by Gaetano Donizetti (1797–1848), libretto by Felice Romani (1788–1865), based on the poem by Lord Byron. First performance: Florence, Teatro della Pergola, 17 March 1833. First performance in U.K.: London, 1 June 1838; in U.S.A.: New York, 22 October 1850.*

ORIGINAL CAST. Domenico Cosselli (Azzo), Gilbert Duprez (Uga), Ungher (Parisina).

SYNOPSIS. Azzo d'Este (baritone), Duke of Ferrara, has, after the death of his first wife, married the beautiful Parisina (soprano). He suspects that she is unfaithful to him with his son by his first wife, Ugo, whom she had loved before he forced her to marry him. She tries to keep their love secret, but she is much disturbed when she has to crown Ugo the victor of a tournament. That night Azzo hears her murmuring his son's name in her sleep and resolves to revenge himself upon them. They try to escape, but Ugo is caught and executed. Parisina falls lifeless on his body.

■ The story is taken from a well-known event that ended in bloodshed and sorrow for the dukedom of Ferrara at the time of Nicolò III (1425). Extremely favourably received, *Parisina* has been rarely performed in the present century.

HANS HEILING

Romantic grand opera in a prologue and three acts by Heinrich Marschner (1795–1861), libretto by Eduard Devrient. First performance: Berlin, 24 May 1833.

SYNOPSIS. The story is taken from a legend. Harz Mountains in the sixteenth century. Hans (baritone), son of the Queen of the Spirits (soprano) and of a mortal father, abandons his supernatural form and assumes human shape to love a girl, Anna (soprano). When she discovers his true identity, however, she leaves him for Konrad (tenor). Hans then disappears forever, promising never to return to the land of men.

■ Acclaimed by the public all over Germany and especially in Copenhagen, *Hans Heiling* brought its composer an honorary doctorate from the University of Leipzig. The young Wagner conducted the opera in Vienna and Magdeburg and it exerted a certain influence on him.

TORQUATO TASSO

Opera seria in three acts by Gaetano Donizetti (1797–1848), libretto by Jacopo Ferretti. First performance: Rome, Teatro Valle, 9 September 1833. First performance in U.K.: London, 3 March 1840.

The Swedish soprano Jenny Lind in Bellini's La Sonnambula.

SYNOPSIS. The story recounts the love of Torquato Tasso (baritone) for Eleonora (mezzo-soprano), sister of the Duke of Ferrara (bass). The two lovers are betrayed by court intrigues contrived by the courtier Don Gherardo (buffo) and the Duke's secretary Roberto (tenor). The Duke orders Tasso to be confined for seven years in a madhouse and when he is finally freed, to be crowned as a great poet, he is horrified to hear that Eleonora had died five years before.

■ The opera appeared under the title of *Sordello il Trovatore* in Naples in 1835 and continued to be performed until 1881. In the libretto Ferretti tried, in so far as was possible, to make Tasso speak his own verses.

LUCREZIA BORGIA

Opera seria in a prologue and two acts by Gaetano Donizetti (1797–1848), libretto by Felice Romani (1788–1865), based on the tragedy by Victor Hugo (1833). First performance: Milan, Teatro alla Scala, 26 December 1833. First performance in U.K.: London, Her Majesty's Theatre, 6 June 1839; in U.S.A.: New Orleans, 1843.

ORIGINAL CAST. Henriette Lalande (Lucrezia Borgia), F. Pedrazzi (Gennaro), L. Mariani (don Alfonso), Marietta Brambilla (Maffio Orsini).

SYNOPSIS. The early sixteenth century. Prologue. A feast is in progress at a Venetian palace. Maffio Orsini (contralto) recounts how after the battle of Rimini, where he was saved by Gennaro (tenor), he met an old man who prophesied that there would be a death among his friends at the hand of the infamous Lucrezia Borgia. Among those present is Gennaro (tenor), who is ignorant of his mother's identity and has only a letter in which she begs him never to search for her. While Gennaro sleeps on a sofa, a masked woman bends over him to kiss him: his companions identify her, to his horror, as Lucrezia Borgia (soprano). Act I. Ferrara. Gennaro and his friends have arrived with a delegation from Venice. Lucrezia's fourth husband, Alfonso (baritone), becomes jealous when he sees the attention the Duchess pays to Gennaro. His friends have also noticed these attentions and tease Gennaro, who has refused to join them at a festivity at the Negroni palace, that he has succumbed to the Duchess's charms. He denies this and to show some proof he scratches out the first letter of her name on the crest, so that only the word 'orgia' remains. The Duke orders his arrest and Lucrezia demands immediate death for the offender. She relents and changes her mind, however, when she finds that Gennaro is the culprit. She administers an antidote to his poisoned drink and arranges his escape by a secret door. Act II. At the last minute Gennaro decides to accompany his friends to the Princess Negroni's. When the ladies have withdrawn, a servant offers the young Venetians drinks. Suddenly the lights are extinguished and funereal music is heard. Lucrezia

Portrait of Vincenzo Bellini. Nuremberg, German National Museum.

torgia da Romano, Nizza di Grenata, Giovanna I di Napoli and Elisa da Fosco. The main reason for censorship was the Borgias' papal connections. Donizetti also introduced, for the first performance, a change in the placement of the orchestra which then became traditional – though with some modifications. The strings, which had been scattered among the other instruments, were grouped in the centre near Donizetti who, assisted by the first violinist, conducted the performance.

MARIA STUARDA (Mary Stuart)

Opera seria *in three acts by Gaetano Donizetti (1797–1848), libretto by Giuseppe Bardari after Schiller. Because of censorship the first performance was given under the title of* Buondelmonte *with a revised libretto by Pietro Salatino and the composer. This version was presented in Naples at the Teatro San Carlo on 18 October 1834. It appeared under its original title – but with considerable changes – in Milan at La Scala with Malibran on 30 December 1835. First performance in U.K.: London, St Pancras Town Hall, 1966; in U.S.A.: New York, 1964.*

SYNOPSIS. The story is concerned with the last days of Mary Queen of Scots ('Maria', soprano) and takes place in the Palace of Westminster and the castle of Fotheringay in 1587. Leicester (tenor), the last of Maria's lovers, makes the most of his favoured position with Elizabetta (soprano), the Queen of England, to arrange a meeting between the two Queens. Maria tries to humble herself and to ask the Queen's pardon, but she is provoked beyond endurance and hits out with insults to Elizabetta. She is condemned and Cecil (bass) confirms that her hasty decision made in anger was correct. Maria prepares for death calmly, and prays for her friends before going to the scaffold.

enters with an armed guard and all the doors are locked. She comments that the wine was poisoned in revenge for their insults to her name. Too late she recognizes Gennaro, who refuses the proffered antidote and dies as she declares that she is his mother.

■ This opera was initially given a cool reception despite a first-rate cast. When it appeared at the Théâtre-Italien in Paris on 27 October 1840, Victor Hugo went to court to withdraw his permission as author and won his case. The only way to continue performing the opera was to change the setting, costumes and period. Thus Lucrezia became *La Rinnegata* and the setting became a Turkish city. Later an agreement was reached with Hugo which allowed *Lucrezia Borgia* to return under its original title. To satisfy Lalande, Donizetti had to write for the first performance a final cavatina which he intended to drop later on. More and more changes were made to the original libretto, mainly because of political censorship. Alternative titles included *Alfonso, Duca di Ferrara, Eus-*

I PURITANI DI SCOZIA (The Puritans of Scotland)

Melodramma serio *in three acts by Vincenzo Bellini (1801–35), libretto by Count Carlo Pepoli (1796–1881). First performance: Paris, Théâtre-Italien, 25 January 1835. First performance in U.K.: London, Haymarket, 21 May 1835; in U.S.A.: Philadelphia, 22 November 1843.*

ORIGINAL CAST. Giovanni Battista Rubini (Arturo), Antonio Tamburini (Riccardo), Luigi Lablache (Giorgio), Giulia Grisi (Elvira).

SYNOPSIS. The seventeenth century during the Civil War between the supporters of Cromwell and the Stuarts. Act I, Scene I. A rampart of a Puritan fortress near Plymouth. It is the morning of the day of the marriage of Elvira (soprano), the daughter of Lord Gualtiero Valton (bass), the commander, to Lord Arturo Talbo (tenor), a Royalist. Sir Riccardo Forth (baritone) confides to Sir Bruno Roberton (tenor) his sorrow that he is not the intended bridegroom, for he loves Elvira. Scene II. Elvira's apartment. Sir Giorgio

Costumes for Sir Giorgio (first sung by Louis Lablache) and Elvira (first sung by Giulia Grisi) in Bellini's
I Puritani *(1835). Paris, Bibliothèque de l'Opéra.*

Valton (bass) tells his niece that nothing must stand in the way of her marriage with Arturo. Scene III. The Armoury is crowded with guests bringing wedding gifts, which include a voluminous white veil for the bride. As they set off for the ceremony, Lord Valton gives Arturo a safe-conduct to leave the fortress and entrusts Elvira to him. He cannot himself take part in the ceremony because he has to escort an unknown lady, believed to be a Stuart spy, to London. Left alone with her, Arturo discovers that she is Enrichetta di Francia (soprano), widow of the late King. He does not hesitate to help her to escape by using his pass and disguising her in Elvira's wedding veil. Riccardo challenges Arturo as they leave but when he sees that the veiled lady is not Elvira but the prisoner he lets them pass, in the hope of winning Elvira by disclosing Arturo's betrayal and flight on his wedding day. When Elvira learns that Arturo has fled with another woman, she loses her reason and her friends prepare to track down the fugitives. Act II. In the fortress, Giorgio describes Elvira's madness before she appears, singing of her sorrow and with affecting gestures and words,

imagining her wedding day. Sir Giorgio, who has guessed Riccardo's part in the escape, convinces him that for Elvira's sake he must not pass sentence of death on Arturo. They decide to fight and die together, loyal to the Puritan cause. Act III, Scene I. A storm rages and Arturo risks his life to see Elvira once more. From the windows comes the voice of Elvira singing a love song that he had taught her. He lets a party of Puritans pass by before he steps under Elvira's window to take up the song. She comes out and they embrace, but Arturo realizes to his horror from her behaviour that her wits have gone. He refuses to leave her, although he knows that the Puritans will capture him and sentence him to death. Scene II. Arturo is about to be executed when a general pardon to all Cavalier prisoners is announced, following Cromwell's decisive victory. Elvira's sanity is restored and the young couple are finally brought together.

■ *I Puritani* was Bellini's last opera and the one to which he devoted the most time and attention. He wrote it for Paris, where the theatre-going public was more accustomed to a varied musical diet from all over Europe and where Rossini, for many years a resident, was considered by all to be the greatest Italian composer. In addition to these considerations, the libretto presented its own problems. Unlike the librettos which his friend Romani used to provide, this one required complicated scenic and musical adaptations and Bellini was obliged to spend a great deal of time on it. Pepoli had been engaged to write a libretto based on François Ancelot and X. B. Saintine's play *Têtes Rondes et Cavaliers* (in its turn based on Sir Walter Scott), but he was not equal to the task. The discontented Bellini reminded him that 'a play set to music must make the audience cry, shudder with horror and die singing'. Nevertheless, the première was a sensational success and during the mad scene 'the whole theatre was reduced to tears', whereas '*Suoni la tromba e intrepido*' (Act II) produced an explosion of patriotic fervour: 'the women all waved their handkerchiefs and the men tossed their hats in the air'. Bellini, however, was unable to enjoy the full extent of his opera's success, for he died worn out from work at Puteaux on 24 September 1835. *I Puritani* is still performed all over the world, though not frequently because of its strenuous demands on the singers, in particular the tenor role, which was apparently written expressly for the extraordinary voice of the tenor Giovanni Battista Rubini. Considered one of Bellini's most successful operas, *I Puritani* contains numerous pages of unsurpassed lyric beauty, like the stupendous and affecting mad scene. Bellini here displays an assimilation of other European schools of music with the almost total absence of recitative and a meticulous care for orchestration. It represents a completely new approach to traditional Italian opera, but at the expense of the dramatic coherence, which, in striking contrast to *Norma*, is considered weak.

LA JUIVE (The Jewess)
Opera in five acts by Jacques Fromental Elie Halévy (1799–1862), libretto by Eugène Scribe (1791–1861). First performance: Paris, Opéra, 23 February 1835. First performance in U.K.: London, Drury Lane, 29 July 1846; in U.S.A.: New York, 16 July 1845.

ORIGINAL CAST. Marie Cornélie Falcon, Dorus-Gras, Adolphe Nourrit, Levasseur.

SYNOPSIS. Constance, in the fifteenth century. Act I. A Square. Prince Léopold (tenor), a general in the Imperial army, goes by the name of Samuel and has taken work in the shop of the goldsmith Eléazar, the Jew (tenor), in order to make advances to his daughter Rachel (soprano). He is recognized by one of his soldiers, Albert (bass), but swears him to secrecy. The City Provost Ruggiero (baritone) announces a public holiday in honour of Prince Léopold's victory over the Hussites, but then he orders the arrest of Eléazar, who has been found working, and urges that he and his daughter should be sentenced to death. Cardinal de Brogni (bass), supreme head of the Council, however, remembers Eléazar from years ago and intervenes for their release. Rachel happily responds to 'Samuel's' serenade and invites him to their Passover meal, assuming him to be a fellow Jew. Both she and Eléazar are amazed that 'Samuel' can prevent their arrest during the riot which breaks out when they leave the shop. Act II. Eléazar's house. The Passover is being celebrated; 'Samuel', surreptitiously drops the unleavened bread without eating it. Princess Eudoxia (soprano), the Emperor's niece and Léopold's wife, interrupts the meal with a request for a gold chain for her husband. Léopold is full of remorse about his infidelity and so admits, when Rachel questions him, that he lied to her because he loved her; he is not a Jew and, when surprised with her by Eléazar, he further confesses that he is already married and cannot marry her, Eléazar furiously curses him. Act III. During the festivities in the Emperor's garden to celebrate Léopold's victory, Eléazar and Rachel arrive to deliver the chain and hear Eudoxia offer it to Léopold, addressing him as her husband. Rachel rips it from his neck and declares that she – a Jewish girl – and Léopold are lovers; Léopold does not deny it. Brogni denounces all of them for breaking the laws of Heaven and condemns them to death. Act IV. The Anteroom to the Council Chamber. Eudoxia entreats Rachel to spare Léopold by revealing his innocence and Rachel finally agrees. The Cardinal tells Eléazar that he can save his daughter by becoming a Christian, but Eléazar refuses. Moreover, he reminds Brogni that when the Cardinal's house in Rome was on fire, a Jew carried his daughter (whom the Cardinal has never seen again) to safety. Despite Brogni's entreaties, Eléazar will reveal no more. Act V. A dais overlooking the square. Ruggiero reads the death sentence to Rachel and Eléazar. (Léopold has been absolved by Rachel's confession and his sentence commuted.) Rachel is offered the choice of accepting Christianity rather than death, but she refuses indignantly. As she falls dead on the scaffold, Eléazar reveals to Cardinal Brogni that she was his long lost daughter.

■ *La Juive*, considered Halévy's masterpiece, introduces an historical subject of religious conflict. A pupil of Cherubini, Halévy took as his model grand opera, using epic themes. Though the score is somewhat reminiscent of Gluck, *La Juive* fulfils the demands of its epoch as a work of dramatic intensity and strong emotions. Among the best pages are Eléazar's entreaty in Act II and the dramatic duet between Eudoxia and Rachel in Act IV. Halévy wrote certain arias expressly for the more prestigious singers. For the character of Eléazar he had in mind the particular abilities of the tenor Adolphe Nourrit, and for Rachel, the exceptional talents of the soprano Marie Cornélie Falcon. The Paris Opéra prepared an unprecedented stage setting for *La Juive*, which won over the Paris public by the third performance. The set for the execution scene was indeed impressive. The famous Franconi Circus arranged to send twenty horses for each performance.

The Armoury in the first part of Bellini's I Puritani *at the Théâtre-Italien, Paris, in 1835. Contemporary lithograph.*

MARINO FALIERO

Opera in three acts by Gaetano Donizetti (1797–1848), libretto by Emanuele Bidera, based on the plays by Lord Byron (1821) and Delavigne (1820). First performance: Paris, Théâtre-Italien, 12 March 1835. First performance in U.K.: London, 14 May 1835; in U.S.A.: New York, 15 December 1843.

SYNOPSIS. The opera concerns the story of the Doge Marin Faliero, whose wife was publicly lampooned by Michele Steno. The punishment fixed for Steno by the Council of Forty did not seem sufficiently severe to the Doge. He considered himself insulted and decided to overthrow the government. But his plot was discovered and he was condemned to death.

■ In 1834 Donizetti was asked to compose an opera for the Théâtre-Italien in Paris. It was his first work for the French stage and not an overly felicitous occasion, for just at that time Bellini was enjoying the success of his *Puritani*. Written between *Lucrezia Borgia* and *Belisario*, *Marino Faliero* is not one of Donizetti's best operas.

LUCIA DI LAMMERMOOR

Opera in three acts by Gaetano Donizetti (1797–1848), libretto by Salvatore Cammarano (1801–52), based on the novel The Bride of Lammermoor *by Sir Walter Scott. First performance: Naples, Teatro San Carlo, 26 September 1835. First performance in U.K.: London, Her Majesty's Theatre, 5 April 1838; in U.S.A.: New Orleans, 28 December 1837.*

ORIGINAL CAST. Fanny Tacchinardi-Persiani (Lucia); Luigi Duprez (Edgardo); Domenico Cosselli (Lord Ashton); Gioacchini (Arturo Bucklaw); Porto-Ottolini (Raimondo).

SYNOPSIS. The story is set in Scotland at the end of the sixteenth century. Act I. 'The Departure.' We are in the garden of Ravenswood castle, which once belonged to the Ravenswood family, but now is wrongfully held by the Ashtons. Lord Enrico Ashton (baritone) is troubled because his political activities have weakened his position and he needs to make some strong alliances. His sister Lucia (soprano) must make up her mind to marry Arturo Bucklaw (tenor),

Costume for Rachel (first sung by Cornélie Falcon) in Halévy's La Juive *(1835). Paris, Bibliothèque de l'Opéra.*

but she refuses, giving the reason that her mother has just died. Normanno (tenor), Captain of Enrico's guard, suspects that Lucia is in love with a man whom she meets secretly each day in the castle park. He is perhaps the stranger who one day saved Lucia's life by killing a maddened bull. Their suspicions are confirmed and it seems that the man is in fact Sir Edgardo of Ravenswood. Enrico is furious because of the feud between their families. That night Lucia, accompanied by Alisa (mezzo-soprano), waits for Edgardo in the park by a fountain. Alisa is anxious and begs Lucia to put an end to a friendship which can only bring her sorrow. When he arrives, he tells her that before he leaves for France he wants to try to make a reconciliation with the Ashtons by asking for her hand as a pledge of peace. Knowing her brother's feelings, she tries to dissuade him and begs him to postpone this plan. They exchange rings as a solemn vow of their secret engagement. Act II. In order to force Lucia to comply with his wishes, Enrico shows her a forged letter from Edgardo to another woman. Lucia reluctantly accepts marriage to Arturo. The festivities

begin. Lucia, pale and dazed, signs the contract. At that moment, Edgardo forces his way through the crowd and in despair accuses Lucia of infidelity; he curses the Ashton family. Drawing his sword, he throws himself on Enrico and Arturo, but Raimondo (bass), the chaplain, separates them. Act III. Enrico arrives on horseback at the tower of Wolf's Crag, the present residence of the Ravenswoods. As a storm rages, he asks Edgardo for satisfaction for the insults to his sister. Edgardo accepts the challenge and they agree to a duel at dawn near the burial ground of the Ravenswoods. In the meantime, at the castle the bride and groom have retired while the wedding festivities continue. Suddenly Raimondo interrupts the general merriment to announce that Lucia has gone completely mad and killed Arturo. She enters the hall, no longer recognizing anyone, and, as in a delirium, she enacts an imaginary wedding ceremony with Edgardo. Edgardo, unaware of what has happened, goes to the place appointed for the duel, determined to let himself be killed as he has nothing more to live for. He hears a deathbell and learns of Lucia's madness and death. He throws himself on his sword.

■ The libretto does not deviate much from Scott's novel, which alludes to incidents concerning the Stair family (the Ashtons) and Lord Rutherford (Edgar of Ravenswood). The events that inspired Scott's novel date back to 1689 at the time of the struggle between the supporters of William III of Orange and those still loyal to James II. In the libretto the time is fixed at the end of the sixteenth century. Donizetti wrote the score in 36 days. It is a work of major importance in the field of *opera seria* and initiated Donizetti's period of maturity. The first performance enjoyed an exceptional public and critical success. It is still performed successfully today. Considered Donizetti's masterpiece of *opera seria*, *Lucia* is also one of the finest romantic pre-Verdian operas. Its mad scene ('*Ardon gli incensi*') is the most famous of its kind in all opera, requiring great technical virtuosity for the difficult vocal writing.

BELISARIO
Opera in three acts by Gaetano Donizetti (1797–1848), libretto by Salvatore Cammarano (1801–52). First performance: Venice, Teatro La Fenice, 4 February 1836. First performance in U.K.: London, 1 April 1837; in U.S.A.: Philadelphia, 29 July 1843.

SYNOPSIS. The story is divided into three parts, entitled Triumph, Exile and Death. It recalls the deeds of the Roman general Belisario, who fell into disgrace at the court of the Emperor Justinian. Belisario returns triumphant to Byzantium after the Italian campaign. The senate applauds him, whilst his wife Antonina invokes divine revenge on him for having tried – so she wrongly believes – to have his own children put to death. His enemies take advantage of his wife's wrath to induce her to make false accusations of treason against Belisario to the Emperor. Belisario is sen-

The Salle Favart which, with the Salle Ventadour and the Salle Feydeau, was used by the Théâtre-Italien in Paris between 1815 and 1876 and where the works of Rossini, Bellini, Donizetti and Verdi achieved memorable triumphs.

tenced to be blinded and exiled. And so, blind and outlawed, he is accompanied and consoled by his daughter. In the third act Alamiro, a young captain of the Barbarians, leads his men to the walls of Byzantium to avenge the injustice done to Belisario. The young man is recognized by Belisario as the son who was believed dead. Belisario is mortally wounded in battle and dies before his wife's eyes. She has discovered the falsity of the accusations and informs the Emperor. Filled with remorse and despair, she too dies.

■ Donizetti returned to Venice with *Belisario* after an absence of seventeen years. It was warmly received, but cannot be considered to be among his greatest successes.

LES HUGUENOTS
Opera in five acts by Giacomo Meyerbeer (1791–1864), libretto by Eugène Scribe (1791–1861) after Émile Deschamps (1791–1871). First performance: Paris, Opéra, 29 February 1836. First performance in U.K.: London, Covent Garden, 20 June 1842; in U.S.A.: New Orleans, 29 April 1839.

ORIGINAL CAST. Julie Dorus-Gras (Marguerite), Marie Cornélie Falcon (Valentine), Adolphe Nourrit (Raoul), Nicholas Levasseur (Marcel), Serda, Dupont.

SYNOPSIS. The story takes place in France in August 1572. Act I. To comply with the King's wishes – that the bitter religious hostilities cease – the Catholic Count de Nevers (baritone) invites to a banquet at his château in Touraine the Huguenot Raoul de Nangis (tenor) with fellow Catholics. A toast of love is suggested and Raoul begins with a vow to an unknown girl whom he had defended from an attack in the street by some young men. A young woman comes to speak with the Count. Raoul recognizes her as the unknown lady whom he now loves and assumes that she is the Count's mistress. She is, in fact, Valentine de Saint-Bris (soprano), who has been sent by the Queen to beg the Count to free her from her promise of marriage. Urbain (mezza-soprano), the Queen's page, invites Raoul to meet a lady who wishes to remain anonymous and he leaves blindfolded for the mysterious meeting. Act II. The gardens of Chenonceaux. To consolidate the peace, Marguérite de Valois (soprano) wants Valentine (whose father, de Saint-Bris, is a Catholic leader) to marry Raoul. Valentine is happy, for she admired Raoul's courage and has fallen in love with him. When Raoul's blindfold is removed, Marguérite offers to receive him at court if he will marry Valentine. The Count de Saint-Bris (baritone) presents his daughter to

Interior of the Salle Ventadour, Paris.

Raoul who, believing her to be Nevers' mistress, refuses to marry her. The Catholics are incensed. Act III. Paris. The wedding of Valentine and Nevers is about to be celebrated. Raoul's servant, Marcel (bass), gives Saint-Bris a note from his master challenging him to a duel. Valentine overhears a plot to ambush Raoul at the duel and warns Marcel, who calls his followers. Before the duel begins, fighting breaks out between Catholics and Huguenots until the arrival of the Queen quells the disturbance. Raoul now realises the truth about Valentine's meeting with Nevers. Act IV. Paris, the house of the Count de Nevers. Raoul questions Valentine, but he is forced to hide when Saint-Bris and Nevers arrive. Saint-Bris wants to exterminate the Huguenots, but Nevers will not take part in the conspiracy and is arrested. The Catholics are to wear white scarves and at the tolling of a bell they will begin the massacre of the Huguenots. Priests bless their swords. When the bell begins to ring, Raoul, who has heard the terrible plan from his hiding place, frees himself with difficulty from Valentine's embrace and runs to warn his fellows. Act V, Scene I. Raoul calls the Huguenots, who have gathered to celebrate the marriage of the King and Queen, to arms. Scene II. A Huguenot churchyard. Marcel lies wounded and Raoul, nearby, is determined to await death beside him. Valentine appears with the news that Nevers has been killed and that the Queen is prepared to pardon him if he will give up his faith. Raoul refuses and Valentine, deeply affected, resolves to accept the Protestant faith of her beloved. They die together, killed by her father's men.

■ The story is based on the massacre of the Huguenots in Paris on the night of St Bartholomew, 24 August 1572. This is one of Meyerbeer's most beautiful operas and it enjoyed a huge success. Singers of outstanding talent have performed its very demanding roles, like the American Lillian Nordica, the Australian Nellie Melba, the Italian Sofia Scalchi, the Polish brothers De Reszke. Meyerbeer was an innovator of lyric opera, the creator and best exponent of grand opera, and in his *Huguenots* we find the merits and defects of all his finest productions: pages of true poetry and fine dramatic insight contrast with sheer romantic and spectacular stage effects.

I BRIGANTI (The Brigands)
Melodrama by Saverio Mercadante (1795–1870), libretto by Jacopo Crescini, based on Schiller's tragedy Die Räuber. *First performance: Paris, Théâtre-Italien, 22 March 1836. First performance in U.K.: London, 2 July 1836.*

SYNOPSIS. The story is set in seventeenth-century Bohemia in the castle of Moor. Act I. Mourning for the supposedly dead Prince Maximilian is over and his son Corrado is to succeed him and marry his cousin Amelia. Amelia, however, loves Ermanno, Corrado's brother, whom everyone believes to be dead, but who is in fact the leader of a band of brigands. Amelia meets him by chance in a cloister, where she has gone to pray. Corrado surprises them and challenges his brother to a duel. Act II. Ermanno and his brigands storm the castle and release Maximilian, whom Corrado had shut away in a tower so that he could usurp the title. In a duel Ermanno is forced to kill his brother. Instead of choosing to live in the castle with his father and to marry Amelia, however, he chooses to return to the brigands and to put right the wrongs inflicted on the weak.

■ Despite Mercadante's best efforts, the opera lacks originality, the characters are poorly delineated and the numerous incidents never reach the level of true drama. Nonetheless, when it first appeared, *I Briganti* was well received, partly for its superb orchestration and fine presentation.

DAS LIEBESVERBOT, oder DIE NOVIZE VON PALERMO (The Ban on Love)
Opera in two acts by Richard Wagner (1813–83), libretto by the composer, based on Shakespeare's Measure for Measure. *First performance: Magdeburg, Stadttheater, 29 March 1836.*

SYNOPSIS. The plot hinges on the classic theme of a dishonest governor who takes advantage of the Duke's absence to condemn his rival to death unjustly. In response to the entreaties of the condemned man's sister, he promises a pardon if she will give herself to him. She agrees but devises a scheme whereby her place will be taken on the appointed night by the governor's rejected mistress. Their plan succeeds, but the governor breaks their agreement by ordering the execution all the same. At this point the Duke returns and the scandalous affair is exposed. The condemned man is pardoned. The governor is also pardoned and is compelled to marry his former mistress.

■ The opera had a single, unfortunate performance which was a complete failure. As a result many singers moved to Königsberg with Wagner, among them Minna Planer, the soprano who was to become his wife. The *Ban on Love* differs somewhat from Shakespeare's comedy. It contains themes, such as the contrast of darkness and light and the freedom of love, which were to become of prime importance in Wagner's later works. Stylistically the influence of many composers is evident, from Gluck to Bellini to Auber, but Wagner's characteristic use of Leitmotiv is already present.

IL CAMPANELLO DELLO SPEZIALE, o IL CAMPANELLO DI NOTTE (The Chemist's Bell, or The Night Bell)
Opera buffa in one act by Gaetano Donizetti (1797–1848), libretto by the composer, based on a French vaudeville La Sonnette de Nuit *by Léon Lévy Brunswick, Mathieu-Barthélemy Troin and Victor Lhérie. First performance: Naples, Teatro Nuovo, 1 June 1836. First performance in U.K.: London, Lyceum, 30 November 1837; in U.S.A.: New York, Lyceum, 7 May 1917.*

Joan Sutherland in Donizetti's Lucia di Lammermoor *at the Metropolitan Opera House, New York (1961).*

SYNOPSIS. The story is set in Naples in the house of Don Annibale Pistacchio (bass), a middle-aged chemist. A party is in progress to celebrate his marriage to the beautiful Serafina (soprano). Enrico (bass), cousin and former suitor of Serafina, prepares his revenge. Don Annibale must leave the next morning at five o'clock for Rome, where he is awaited by a notary who has advised him that, if he does not appear, he will lose his right to an inheritance. Don Annibale is therefore in a hurry to conclude the celebrations, but Enrico makes sure that even when the guests have left Annibale is constantly interrupted and stopped from enjoying his wedding night with his bride. The door bell rings over and over again as Enrico appears in one disguise after another to buy medicines. (There was a Neapolitan statute forbidding chemists from refusing to answer emergency calls, on pain of imprisonment.) Enrico is first disguised as a French nobleman who, returning from a party, requests some medicine for an upset stomach; then as a singer who has lost his voice and insists on telling the whole lengthy story; and then someone arrives with such a complicated prescription that a great deal of time is needed to prepare it. By now it is five o'clock and Don Annibale must leave for Rome.

■ Also known as *Il Campanello*, this opera was composed in only a week (to save an impresario from bankruptcy) during one of the saddest periods in Donizetti's life. He had recently lost his father, his mother, a daughter and his wife. The opera was highly successful in Italy and abroad and is still performed.

LE POSTILLON DE LONGJUMEAU (The Coachman of Longjumeau)

Opera buffa in three acts by Adolphe Adam (1803–56), libretto by Adolphe de Leuven and Léon Lévy Brunswick. First performance: Paris, Opéra-Comique, 13 October 1836. First performance in U.K.: London, St. James's, 13 March 1837; in U.S.A.: New York, 30 March 1840.

SYNOPSIS. On his wedding night, the coachman Chappelou (tenor) is persuaded to sing to the guests. His song is heard by the Marquis de Corcy, Director of the Paris Opéra (tenor), who offers him a job at the Opéra if he will leave Longjumeau and come to Paris immediately. Chappelou reluctantly agrees and asks his friend Bijou (baritone) to break the news to his bride Madeleine (soprano). She is furious. In Paris, Chappelou becomes principal tenor (his stage name is Saint-Phar) and Bijou has become leader of the chorus. Madeleine has inherited a fortune, and passes as a great lady, called Madame de Latour. Both Saint-Phar and the Marquis fall in love with her and Saint-Phar arranges for Bijou to dress up as a priest and to marry them. Madeleine locks Bijou up and a real priest celebrates the ceremony – to Saint-Phar's horror, for he has not forgotten Madeleine – and when the Marquis accuses him of bigamy, Madeleine has to reveal her identity to save the day.

■ It was customary to alternate the spoken parts, or recitative, with the arias. *Le Postillon* is a light-hearted opera, often vulgar and in some instances trivial; it is considered Adam's masterpiece. It brought him international fame despite the fact that his most popular opera in France was *Le Chalet* (1834), which is today completely forgotten. With the fall of the Second Empire, this type of *opera buffa*, of which Adam was a master, rapidly declined in popularity and so *Le Postillon* has been rarely performed this century even in France.

ZHINZA TSARYA (A Life for the Tsar)

Melodrama in five acts by Mikhail Ivanovich Glinka (1804–57), libretto by Baron Georgy Fedorovich Rozen. First performance: St Petersburg, Impe Theatre, 9 December 1836. First performance in U.K.: London, Covent Garden, 12 July 1887; in U.S.A.: (concert version) New York, 14 November 1871; stage performance: San Francisco, 12 December 1936.

ORIGINAL CAST. Petrov, Stepanova, Leonova, Vorobeva. Conductor: C. Cavos.

SYNOPSIS. Act I. The Village of Domnin. Antonida (soprano), a peasant girl, greets her fiancé, Bogdan Sobinin (tenor), newly returned from the front line of the Russian defences against the Polish invasion. Everyone rejoices at the Russian victory, but Ivan Susanin (bass), Antonida's father, expresses his concern for his country's future. 'For how long', he asks, 'can the Russians withstand the Poles while the succession of the Tsar is disputed and they are without a ruler?' As long as the country is in danger Susanin will oppose his daughter's wedding. Sobinin announces, however, that the new Tsar has been elected: Mikhail Romanoff, their landlord, and so his own wedding can now take place. Act II. The Polish camp. News of the election arrives during the celebrations of a Polish festival and the officers decide to advance immediately into Russia. Act III. Susanin's dwelling. There are preparations to celebrate Antonida's forthcoming marriage. Vanya (contralto), an orphan adopted by Susanin, sadly reflects that he is too young to fight against the Poles and that his sister will soon be leaving home. Polish soldiers burst in and order Susanin to take them to the Tsar. Susanin pretends to obey, but secretly charges Vanya with the task of warning the Tsar, while he delays the soldiers by leading them on a false trail. In parting from Antonida, he advises her not to delay the wedding until his return. Act IV. Before a monastery. Vanya rides his horse to death in his haste to warn the Tsar of the danger. Meanwhile the Polish soldiers, led by Susanin, camp for the night in a forest. Susanin knows that he does not have long to live since the Poles have guessed his trickery, but he is certain that Vanya will have completed his mission by dawn. He thinks of his daughter for the last time and prepares himself for death. Act V. The Square of the Kremlin. The exultant crowd acclaims the Tsar and the liberation of Russia from the invaders. The Tsar praises the loyalty of Antonida, Sobinin and Vanya, who stand weeping for the dead hero.

■ 'I could not become an Italian composer and, remembering my homeland with nostalgia, I gradually began to think of composing like a Russian.' With these words from his *Memoirs*, Glinka sums up his past and his basic understanding of a new Russian music. *A Life for the Tsar* was composed two years after his return from travels in Germany, Switzerland and Italy, which lasted from 1830 to 1834. This opera represents a reconciliation between the musical cultures of Europe and Russia, stimulated probably by Glinka's knowledge of the Russian writers Pushkin and Gogol, whose considerable influence on cultural life aimed at the creation of a national style. At its première *A Life for the Tsar* was enthusiastically received by the St Petersburg public in the presence of the Tsar, who gave the signal when to applaud. It may be said to mark the birth of Russian opera.

PIA DE'TOLOMEI

Opera in two acts by Gaetano Donizetti (1797–1848), libretto by Salvatore Cammarano (1801–52), based on

A print caricaturing the Act II sextet from Donizetti's Lucia di Lammermoor.

a short poem by Bartolomeo Sestini (1822), in turn derived from Dante's Purgatorio, Canto V. First performance: Venice, Teatro Apollo, 18 February 1837.

SYNOPSIS. This is a free adaptation of the story of a character made famous by Dante. Pia is confined to the Maremma in Tuscany by her husband, Nello, who gives her no reason for his decision. He believes the accusation of adultery made against her by his nephew Ghino. On his death-bed Ghino confesses that he acted out of jealousy because his attempts to seduce her were unsuccessful. Nello is too late to save her. She forgives him and begs him to end the feud of their families.

■ Received with limited enthusiasm, *Pia de' Tolomei* has been rarely performed.

IL GIURAMENTO (The Oath)
Opera is three acts by Saverio Mercadante (1795–1870), libretto by Gaetano Rossi (1820–86). First performance: Milan, Teatro alla Scala, 10 March 1837. First performance in U.K.: London, 27 June 1840; in U.S.A.: New York, 14 February 1848.

ORIGINAL CAST. Schoberlechner, Tadolini, Donzelli, Castellan, Balzar.

SYNOPSIS. Elaisa (soprano) and Bianca (mezzo-soprano) are rivals in love for Viscardo (tenor). Bianca is already married, however, to Manfredo (baritone), who orders her to take poison to expiate her adultery. Elaisa, who is indebted to Bianca, saves her by substituting a sleeping drug for the poison. When he sees Bianca apparently lifeless, Viscardo is convinced that Elaisa has murdered her. Just as Bianca revives, he kills Elaisa.

■ *Il Giuramento* is considered Mercadante's best work and is the only one of his numerous operas which is still performed today. Despite the succession of dramatic situations, its characters lack originality. There are nonetheless lyrical moments such as the aria 'Ma negli estremi istanti' (Elaisa) at the end of the third act. It remained popular for a long time and was performed at the Teatro Valle in Rome in 1839 and at the Comunale in Bologna in 1840 with the title *Amore e Dovere*. The libretto is based on the prose drama *Angelo* by Victor Hugo (1835) with certain changes in the characters and places; e.g., Hugo's setting of Padua in the sixteenth century is changed to Syracuse in the fourteenth century.

ROBERTO DEVEREUX, CONTE DI ESSEX
Opera in three acts by Gaetano Donizetti (1797–1848), libretto by Salvatore Cammarano (1801–52), based on François Ancelot's tragedy Elisabeth d'Angleterre. First performance: Naples, Teatro San Carlo, 29 October 1837. First performance in U.K.: London, 24 June 1841; in U.S.A.: New York, 15 January 1849.

Cover of the score of Glinka's A Life for the Tsar *from an edition of 1906 designed by Vassily Kandinsky.*

SYNOPSIS. The story unfolds in London at the end of the sixteenth century. Roberto Devereux, Earl of Essex (tenor), is accused of treason by his enemies. Elizabetta (soprano), the Queen, who still loves him, will not accept the death sentence passed by the House of Lords. She suspects that Essex is unfaithful to her, but she does not know with whom. Essex denies this, but he in fact returns the love of Sara (mezzo-soprano), the wife of his friend Nottingham (baritone), and, when they meet, he throws down the Queen's ring (given to him with a promise that if it was returned Elizabetta would grant his wish) and accepts Sara's embroidered scarf as a love token. Essex is condemned, despite Nottingham's defence, and the Queen is furious to hear that the scarf (which she recognizes) was found next to his heart, when he was searched. She accuses Essex and shows the scarf to Nottingham, who curses his former friend. Sara contemplates taking the ring to the Queen, but Nottingham delays her. Essex waits in vain for a reprieve, while the Queen waits for him to send the ring. When Sara brings it, she at last recognizes her rival and her royal pardon is given at the moment when the cannon signalling the execution is fired.

■ This opera proved to be a huge success and was performed regularly until 1882. Though one of Donizetti's lesser works, it has continued to generate interest. It has been much performed recently, mainly in England and America. A complete recording was made in 1970.

LE DOMINO NOIR (The Black Domino)
Comic opera in three acts by Daniel Auber (1782–1871), libretto by Eugène Scribe (1791–1861). First performance: Paris, Opéra-Comique, 2 December 1837. First performance in U.K.: London, Covent Garden, 16 February 1838; in U.S.A.: New Orleans, November 1839.

■ One of Auber's most successful and highly regarded operas. It was received enthusiastically by the Parisian public and ran for some 1,000 performances in Paris until 1882. It is still given today in France and elsewhere. So great was its popularity that the libretto was translated into almost every European language.

ZAR UND ZIMMERMANN (Tsar and Carpenter)
Comic opera in three acts by Albert Lortzing (1801–51), libretto by the composer based on a play by A. Honoré Joseph Mélesville, Jean Toussaint Merle and Eugène Cantiran de Boirie (1818). First performance: Leipzig, Stadttheater, 22 December 1837. First performance in U.S.A.: New York, 13 January 1857; in U.K.: London, Gaiety, 15 April 1871.

SYNOPSIS. The story concerns Peter the Great (baritone), Tsar of Russia, who has come to work in the naval dockyards at Saardam to learn the secrets of shipbuilding. He is wrongly identified by the Burgomaster, Van Bett (bass), and manages to escape while a fellow Russian – a deserter from the army, Peter Ivanov (tenor) – enjoys the Burgomaster's festivities in honour of the Tsar.

■ This is perhaps Lortzing's most famous opera and was a great success in Germany. His model for melody was Mozart and he wrote with a simple charm and a fine sense of humour. Lortzing was principally a man of the theatre (being an actor himself) and paid great attention to the dramatic effect of his librettos, with a particular flair for comedy in which he had experimented as an actor.

BENVENUTO CELLINI
Opera in three acts by Hector Berlioz (1803–69), libretto by Léon de Wailly and Auguste Barbier (1822–1901). First performance: Paris, Opéra, 10 September 1838. First performance in U.K.: London, Covent Garden, 25 June 1853; in U.S.A.: New York (concert performance), 1965.

SYNOPSIS. The events begin in Rome on the last day of the Carnival of 1532. Benvenuto Cellini (tenor) is in love with Teresa (soprano), daughter of the Pope's treasurer, Balducci (baritone), who has been promised in marriage to the Pope's sculptor, Fieramosca

A caricature of Hector Berlioz conducting (1846).

(baritone). Cellini plans to elope with Teresa that night disguised in a white monk's habit. Fieramosca overhears the plan and disguises himself similarly. Teresa is confused as to which is Cellini and a scuffle ensues; Cellini stabs Fieramosca's bravo and escapes, leaving the other white monk – Fieramosca – to be arrested. The Pope has ordered Cellini to cast the statue of Perseus before the morning and Cellini and Teresa have only just exchanged vows of love when Fieramosca and Teresa's father arrive to accuse him of murder. The Pope's envoy, Cardinal Salviati (bass), calls to see the completed statue. Cellini successfully casts the statue, throwing all his other work into the mould to have enough metal, and all are amazed at the beauty of his creation.

■ Composed between 1834 and 1837, *Benvenuto Cellini* was a dismal failure at its première. It was later performed successfully in Weimar in 1852 and in London in 1853 and on several occasions after Berlioz's death, but it was never part of the permanent repertory. Its failure was partly due to the inconsistency of the libretto. '*Benvenuto Cellini*', wrote F. d'Amico, 'springs literally from a dual romantic motif: Hoffmann's *Salvator Rosa*, which provided Berlioz with more than one dramatic situation, and the Italian Renaissance setting, which lends a picturesque and exotic flavour. Herein lies the originality of this opera: a setting that provides more than just a backdrop.'

IL BRAVO

Melodrama in three acts by Saverio Mercadante (1795–1870), libretto by Gaetano Rossi (1820–86) and M. M. Marcello. First performance: Milan, Teatro alla Scala, 9 March 1839.

ORIGINAL CAST. Balzar, Benciolini, Castellan, Donzelli, Polonini, Quattrini, Marconi, Schoberlechner, Tadolini, Villa.

SYNOPSIS. The action takes place in Venice. Foscari (bass), a nobleman, is in love with Violetta (soprano) and has Maffeo, her guardian, murdered. Pisani (tenor) returns incognito from exile in order to arrange for Violetta and himself to elope together. He obtains shelter from Il Bravo (tenor), the Venetian government's hired assassin. Teodora (soprano) repents having abandoned her daughter, Violetta, as a child and pays Il Bravo to abduct her. In order to be alone with her daughter, Teodora dismisses the other guests attending a ball, and mother and daughter are joyfully reunited. Then Il Bravo reveals that he is Violetta's father and that he was compelled to undertake his dreadful employment to save the life of his father, who is imprisoned in the Piombi. He discloses to Teodora that he has been ordered to kill her since she has offended the Venetian nobility by sending them away from her reception. Teodora wrests the dagger from him and kills herself just as a messenger arrives to tell Il Bravo that his father has died and he is now released from his terrible pledge. Violetta is at last able to leave Venice with Pisani.

■ The libretto is based on the novel by James Fenimore Cooper (1789–1851), with some changes in the names and in the plot, and on the play *La Vénitienne* by A. Burgeois.

OBERTO, CONTE DI SAN BONIFACIO (Oberto, Count of St Boniface)

Opera in two acts by Giuseppe Verdi (1813–1901), libretto by Temistocle Solera (1815–78) (originally by Antonio Piazza, but revised by B. Merelli and Solera). First performance: Milan, Teatro alla Scala, 17 November 1839.

ORIGINAL CAST. Antonietta Ranieri-Marini (Leonora), Mary Shaw (Cuniza), Lorenzo Salvi (Riccardo), Ignazio Marini (Oberto). Conductor: Cavallini.

SYNOPSIS. The Castle of Bassano, where Cuniza is living. Young Count Riccardo (tenor) arrives to marry Cuniza (mezzo-soprano). In the past, he deceived his friend Oberto (bass), Count of San Bonifacio, by seducing his daughter Leonora (soprano), and when Oberto discovers this treachery, he persuades Leonora to tell Cuniza. Mortified by Leonora's story Cuniza decides to give up Riccardo and insists that he marry Leonora. Oberto is not satisfied with this revenge. He challenges Riccardo to a duel and is killed. Riccardo goes into voluntary exile. There is nothing left for Leonora, who has witnessed the duel, but to enter a convent.

■ This is Verdi's first opera, possibly incorporating material composed for another project on the subject

Costumes for Madeleine (first sung by Zoé Prévost) and Chappelou (first sung by Jean-Baptist-Marie Chollet) in Adam's Le Postillon de Longjumeau, *Paris, Opéra-Comique, 1836. Paris, Bibliothèque de l'Opéra.*

of *Rocester*, which was never performed. Commissioned by Bartolomeo Merelli, it enjoyed a degree of success and earned the young Verdi a new contract for three more operas. The libretto and the score were bought for publication by Giulio Ricordi. He paid a thousand Austrian lire to Merelli and the same to Verdi, a good fee for that time. He had perceived in Verdi a distinctly new approach from that of Donizetti: the dramatic sense characteristic of the mature Verdi was already in evidence.

LA FILLE DU REGIMENT (The Daughter of The Regiment)
Opera in two acts by Gaetano Donizetti (1797–1848), libretto by Jules Henri Vernoy de Saint-Georges and Jean François Bayard. First performance: Paris, Opéra-Comique, 11 February 1840. First performance in U.S.A.: New Orleans, 6 March 1843; in U.K.: London, Her Majesty's Theatre, 27 May 1847.

ORIGINAL CAST. Marie-Julienne Boulanger (Marquise), Juliette Bourgeois (Marie), Blanchard (Duchesse), Henry (Sulpice), Mécène Marié de L'Isle (Tonio).

SYNOPSIS. The story is set in Switzerland. Act I. The fields near a village, while fighting carries on down the valley. The Marquise de Birkenfeld (soprano) stops here briefly before returning to her castle. Sulpice (bass), sergeant of the Savoyard soldiers, arrives with Marie (soprano), the young vivandière, 'la fille du régiment', found in a battlefield and raised among the soldiers. A young Swiss named Tonio (tenor) has been following the troops out of love for Marie and is arrested as a spy. Marie intervenes and relates how this young man, with whom she is now in love, saved her from falling over a precipice. The regiment declare that she can only marry a grenadier and Tonio enlists. When Sulpice hears that the Marquise wants an escort to Birkenfeld, he recounts that years ago a Captain

The producer Margherita Wallmann directs a scene from Donizetti's La Fille du Régiment *with Mirella Freni at La Scala during the 1967–68 season.*

The Teatro San Carlo in Naples from a mid-nineteenth-century engraving.

Roberto, with that same surname, entrusted Marie to his soldiers before he died. The Marquise declares that Marie must be her niece and decides to take her to the castle with her. Marie is delighted to have found her family, but sad to leave the regiment, and especially Tonio. They depart amid general consternation. Act II. A salon in the castle. Marie, elegantly dressed, receives Sulpice, who scarcely recognizes her. Notwithstanding the luxury, Marie dislikes having to learn so many tiresome things, like dancing and singing. She tells the Marquise that she prefers fanfares to the mawkish love songs that she must now sing. Tonio, now an officer, arrives with the regiment and they repeat their vows of love. The Marquise has however arranged that Marie should marry the Duke of Krakentorp and confides to Sulpice that she is in fact Marie's mother. Marie is very moved and feels that she cannot, as a good daughter, refuse her mother's wish. In the face of Marie's and Tonio's evident misery, however, the Marquise relents and allows their marriage.

■ This is Donizetti's first French opera and one of his most popular. It was enormously successful in France,

Italy, and other countries. 600 performances had been given at the Opéra-Comique by 1875 and it still appears there frequently even today. *La Fille du Régiment* is a light melodrama, very similar in spirit to Donizetti's other comic operas. After its Paris debut, it appeared for the first time in Italy at La Scala on 30 October of the same year.

UN GIORNO DI REGNO, ossia IL FINTO STANISLAO (King for a day, or The false Stanislaus)
Opera in two acts by Giuseppe Verdi (1813–1901), libretto by Felice Romani (1788–1865), based on a comedy by Pineux Duval. First performance: Milan, Teatro alla Scala, 5 September 1840. First performance in U.K.: London, St Pancras Town Hall, 21 March 1961; in U.S.A.: New York, Town Hall, 18 June 1960.

ORIGINAL CAST. Luigia Abbadia (Giulietta), Raffaele Ferlotti (Cavalier di Belfiore), Antonietta Marini (Countess del Poggio), Agostino Rovere (La Rocca), Lorenzo Salvi (Edoardo), Raffaele Scalese (the Baron).

SYNOPSIS. In order to escape his enemies Stanislaus, King of Poland, asks Cavalier di Belfiore (baritone) to impersonate him. Belfiore plays the part even with his own former mistress, the Countess del Poggio (soprano), who fortunately does not recognize him. He is then caught up in a whole series of amorous intrigues at court involving the courtiers and guests from the castle. News finally arrives that the King is safe and he rewards Belfiore with the title of Marshal. Belfiore then reveals his identity and marries the Countess del Poggio.

■ Verdi was in no frame of mind to write an amusing opera. In the space of two years his wife and two children had died. This was probably why *Un Giorno di Regno* lacked conviction and proved unsuccessful. Another reason was probably Romani's libretto. Romani had worked successfully with Donizetti and Bellini, but he was limited to the simple Arcadian taste, which was now out of fashion. Subsequent rewriting by Temistocle Solera did not improve matters.

SAFFO (Sappho)
Opera in three acts by Giovanni Pacini (1796–1867), libretto by Salvatore Cammarano (1801–52). First performance: Naples, Teatro San Carlo, 29 November 1840. First performance in U.K.: London, Drury Lane, 1 April 1843; in U.S.A.: Boston, May 1847.

SYNOPSIS. Greece at the time of the 46th Olympiad. Faone (tenor) believes that Saffo (soprano) has betrayed him and in revenge decides to marry Climene (mezzo-soprano), daughter of Alcandro (baritone), priest of Apollo. When Saffo discovers that Faone has married someone else, she is filled with despair and destroys Apollo's altar, where she has gone to pray. She repents this sacrilege, however, and offers to expiate her crime by throwing herself from the sacred rock. The oracle agrees, but at the same time it is discovered that Saffo is Alcandro's daughter, whom all had believed had been drowned. The priest pleads in vain with the priests of the oracle to change the decision which deprives him of the daughter he has just found.

The last scene of Act II of Verdi's Nabucco *at the Hoftheater, Stuttgart. From an engraving in the* Leipziger Illustrierte Zeitung, *1845.*

Faone is also in despair because he did not realize Saffo's love until too late; he desires only death. The people watch as Saffo is escorted by the priests of the oracle to the clifftop; Faone has to be restrained from following her to his death.

■ Composed in only twenty days, *Saffo* is Pacini's most successful opera. His music has charm, but is sometimes only superficial. He began composing in the style of Rossini, but broke away from this with *Saffo*.

LA FAVORITE (The Favourite)
Grand Opera in four acts by Gaetano Donizetti (1797–1848), libretto by Alphonse Royer, Gustave Vaëz and Eugène Scribe, based on Baculard d'Arnaud's play Le Comte de Comminges *(1764). First performance: Paris, Opéra, 2 December 1840. First performance in U.K.: London, Drury Lane, 18 October 1843; in U.S.A.: New Orleans, 9 February 1843.*

CAST. Rosine Stoltz (Leonore), Gilbert L. Duprez (Fernand), P. Barroilhet (Alphonse XI), N. P. Lavasseur (Balthazar). Conductor: F. A. Haberneck.

SYNOPSIS. Castille, 1340. Act I. At the Monastery of St James of Compostela the novice Fernand (tenor) is troubled by the presence of a woman whom he meets coming out of church. He confesses his disquiet to the abbot, Father Balthazar (bass), and decides to give up the monastic life despite the abbot's warnings. Fernand, blindfolded, comes ashore on the island of St León. When Inez (soprano) removes the blindfold, he urges her to tell him the name of the lady who returns his love but always receives him so mysteriously. Inez reveals nothing. The lady is actually Leonore of Gusman (soprano), mistress of King Alphonse of Castille (baritone), who has abandoned the Queen for her. Fernand persists in asking Leonore who she is and asks her to marry him. She replies that it is not possible and begs him not to try to see her again. As a last farewell, she gives him a letter which will launch his career in the army. Inez arrives in haste to announce the unexpected arrival of the King. Fernand deduces only that Leonore must be a lady of high birth but decides to gain honour and glory in order to win her. Act II. The gardens of the Palace of the Alcazar. Festivities are about to commence to celebrate a victory over the infidels. Fernand has particularly distinguished himself in battle by saving the King's life and is to be publicly thanked and rewarded for his valour. Leonore begs the King for her freedom; she can never marry him and can no longer tolerate her difficult and humiliating situation. But the King refuses. During the celebrations, he intercepts a note addressed to Leonore and resolves to discover from her the identity of the writer. (It is Fernand.) Father Balthazar brings a message from the Pope, in which he severely criticizes Alphonse's conduct towards the Queen and his relationship with an adventuress. To everyone's horror, he then delivers the papal excommunication on Alphonse. Leonore rushes away

in despair. Act III. Unaware of what has happened, Fernand arrives exultant at having earned the King's confidence. The King thanks him for everything and asks how he may repay him. Fernand asks to be allowed to marry Leonore. She enters at that moment and learns to her amazement that the King is favourable to her marriage with Fernand. Alphonse wants the marriage to take place immediately. Despite Leonore's desire to marry Fernand, she does not wish to deceive him and sends Inez to tell him about her relations with the King. Alphonse arrests Inez before she can accomplish her mission. While preparations for the wedding continue, Alphonse confers decorations and titles on Fernand. The courtiers make unflattering remarks, believing that Fernand is playing along to help the King placate the Pope. Leonore arrives and, seeing Fernand's untroubled state, believes that he has generously accepted the situation. After the ceremony some unpleasant insinuations are made about Fernand, and some men refuse to shake his hand. Fernand does not understand and as his anger mounts, Balthazar acquaints him with the facts. Fernand is appalled and believing that he has been deceived by Alphonse and Leonore, he breaks his sword, tears off his decorations and departs with Balthazar. Act IV. Outside the church of St James of Compostela. Fernand (in a monk's habit) prays at the tombs. A pilgrim arrives and falls exhausted next to Fernand. He recognizes her as Leonore who has come to ask his forgiveness. At first he is tempted to spurn her, but when he hears the truth, he proposes that they go away together to a place where they are not known. But it is too late. Leonore is worn out and, hearing Fernand's words of forgiveness, dies in his arms.

■ This opera was supposed to be performed in three acts at the Théâtre de la Renaissance with the title *L'Ange de Nisida* (*The Angel of Nisida*). But with the closure of that theatre, the performance was transferred to the Opéra and Donizetti, in collaboration with Scribe, added a fourth act and changed the title to *La Favorite*. Despite a decidedly second-rate libretto, this is Donizetti's greatest achievement after *Lucia di Lammermoor*, in tragic opera. Nonetheless the first three acts fall far short of the fourth, which has moments of true inspiration. The opera's success was enormous and has never diminished. By 1904 it had been performed no less than 650 times at the Paris Opéra alone.

LES DIAMANTS DE LA COURONNE (The Diamonds of the Crown)
Opera comica in three acts by Daniel F. E. Auber (1782–1871), libretto by Eugène Scribe (1791–1861) and Jules H. Vernoy de Saint-Georges. First performance: Paris, Opéra-Comique, Salle Favart, 6 March 1841. First performance in U.K.: London, Princess's Theatre, 2 May 1844; in U.S.A: New York, 14 July 1843.

■ One of Auber's most successful comic operas, *Les*

The second scene of Act IV of Verdi's Nabucco *at La Scala, Milan, during the 1966–67 season, in a production by Franco Enriquez with sets by Nicola Benois.*

Diamants was performed in many European and non-European countries throughout the nineteenth century. It has however never been included in the permanent repertory.

LE COMTE DE CARMAGNOLA (Count Carmagnola)

Opera in two acts by Ambroise Thomas (1811–96), libretto by Eugène Scribe (1791–1861). First performance: Paris, Opéra, 19 April 1841.

ORIGINAL CAST. Prosper Dérivis and Julie Dorus-Gras.

■ The story is based on the same historical incident as the eponymous novel by Alessandro Manzoni. In fifteenth-century Venice the Senate accused the commander of the Venetian troops – then waging war against Milan – of treason and wrongfully sentenced him to death. The celebrated French librettist gave his own interpretation to the story, adding amorous intrigues to complicate the plot. In spite of this Thomas produced a charming and brilliant score, trying hard to make a success of his second debut in Paris, this time at the Opéra. But *Le Comte de Carmagnola* was withdrawn after only eight performances and hardly ever again performed.

NABUCCO

Opera in four acts by Giuseppe Verdi (1813–1901), libretto by Temistocle Solera (1817–78). First performance: Milan, Teatro alla Scala, 9 March 1842. First performance in U.K.: London, Her Majesty's Theatre, 3 March 1846; in U.S.A.: New York, Astor Opera House, 4 April 1848.

ORIGINAL CAST. Giuseppina Strepponi (Abigaille), Giovannina Bellinzaghi (Fenena), Corrado Miraglia (Ismaele), Giorgio Ronconi (Nabucco), Prosper Dérivis (Zaccaria).

SYNOPSIS. The story is set in Babylon and Jerusalem. Act I. The Hebrews have been defeated by the Babylonian armies of Nabucco (baritone). The High Priest Zaccaria (bass) tries to raise their spirits by disclosing his trump card: he has taken prisoner Nabucco's daughter, Fenena (soprano). However, Ismaele (tenor), nephew of the King of Jerusalem, falls in love with her. As he tries to free her, the slave girl Abigaille (soprano) and Nabucco arrive. Zaccaria wants to have Fenena put to death, but Ismaele prevents him. The Hebrews curse Ismaele as a traitor to his people. Act II. Nabucco is away and Fenena is acting as Regent. Abigaille plots to kill her and usurp the throne, whilst Fenena is converted to Judaism by Zaccaria. Abigaille is about to achieve her aim by taking advantage of false reports of Nabucco's death. Suddenly the King returns and, much to the Jews' horror, he proclaims himself god. Act III. Abigaille finally succeeds in dethroning Nabucco and rules with savage cruelty. She decides that the Hebrew prisoners must be sacrificed; Fenena too must die for having been converted to the enemy's religion. As they await death, the Hebrews intone *Va Pensiero*. Act IV. To regain the throne Nabucco allies himself with the Assyrians and they march on Babylon. He arrives in time to save his daughter. Abigaille kills herself, but before dying she asks Fenena's pardon and intercedes with Nabucco to allow Fenena to marry the faithful and devoted Ismaele.

■ The title of Verdi's third opera was originally *Nabucodonosor*, which was soon abbreviated to *Nabucco*. The work was an important turning point in the composer's career. Deeply saddened by family deaths and the disastrous reception of *Un Giorno di Regno*, he had resolved to write no more operas, but Bartolomeo Merelli, impresario at La Scala, still retained faith in his ability, and eventually persuaded him to set Solera's libretto. The opera was an immediate success, and Verdi's name rapidly spread to all parts of Italy. On its first revival at La Scala, in the autumn of 1842, *Nabucco* received an almost unprecedented 57 performances. One of the most notable aspects of the opera was its bold use of the chorus as an active protagonist in the drama, and Verdi was soon named 'papà dei cori' by his adoring Milanese public. Though the work owes a good deal to Rossini's later French operas, and in particular to *Moïse*, it firmly established Verdi as an original voice in Italian opera – a voice which spoke directly and passionately to the Italian people. The chorus *Va pensiero* still remains one of Verdi's most famous and best loved melodies.

LINDA DI CHAMOUNIX
Opera in three acts by Gaetano Donizetti (1797–1848), libretto by Gaetano Rossi (1774–1855), after A. P. d'Ennery and Gustave Lemoine, La grâce de Dieu. *First performance: Vienna, Kärntnertortheater, 19 May 1842. First performance in U.K.: London, Her Majesty's Theatre, 1 June 1843; in U.S.A.: New York, Palmo's Opera House, 4 January 1847.*

ORIGINAL CAST. Eugenia Tadolini (Linda), Marietta Brambilla (Pierotto), Napoleone Moriani (Carlo di Sirval), Felice Varesi (Antonio), Prosper Dérivis (The Prefect), Agostino Rovere (Marquis of Boisfleury). Conductor: Gaetano Donizetti.

SYNOPSIS. Haute-Savoie and Paris, about 1760. Act I. In a modest farm house a tenant farmer, Antonio (baritone) and his wife Maddalena (soprano), are worried that they will be evicted. The landlord's brother, the Marquis of Boisfleury (baritone), promises to help them by offering to educate their daughter Linda (soprano) at his château. Antonio and Maddalena are very grateful for the offer, unsuspecting of the Marquis's less than honourable intentions. Linda returns from Mass, singing with Pierotto (contralto), a young

orphan, and with other children. She is greeted by Carlo (tenor), a painter from another town, who is paying court to her, but is in fact the Viscount of Sirval, nephew of the Marquis. He dares not reveal his identity lest it should create a barrier between them. The Prefect (bass) tells Antonio and Maddalena that it would be inadvisable for Linda to stay with the Marquis and suggests that she go away for a while, perhaps to stay with one of his brothers in Paris. Linda, Pierotto and other young Savoyards, leave for Paris to look for work. Act II. Paris. After the death of the Prefect's brother, Linda has gone to stay with Carlo in a splendid apartment. Although he wants to marry her, he has to obtain the permission of his mother, who is opposed to the match. When Linda hears some singing in the street, she recognizes Pierotto, whom she has not seen since they first arrived in Paris. Meanwhile Carlo's mother has nearly succeeded in persuading him to marry a very rich girl. An old beggar comes to Linda's door: it is her father, but she does not immediately recognize him. Then, when she tries to embrace him, he pushes her contemptuously away, believing that she is Carlo's mistress. When Pierotto tell her that Carlo is to marry another, her mind begins to wander. Act III. The square of Chamonix. The young Savoyards are returning home with their season's earnings. Carlo arrives looking for Linda, having rejected the arranged match desired by his mother. She has now agreed that Linda and Carlo should marry. Carlo meets Linda's parents and reassures them about their daughter's conduct in Paris. Linda and Pierotto arrive, and Linda, exhausted from the trip, is still unbalanced. She does not recognize anyone, but Carlo succeeds in restoring her sanity with a song that he used to sing. Linda returns to a new life, and amid much emotion and embracing the opera ends joyfully for one and all.

■ This is the first opera composed by Donizetti for the Court of Vienna. It was so successful that the Emperor appointed him Court Composer and Master of the Imperial Chapel, positions once held by Mozart. The Empress Maria Carolina presented Donizetti with a scarf on which she personally had embroidered in gold, 'The Empress of Austria to Donizetti on the evening of 19 May 1842 for the opera *Linda*'. The work was not translated into German until 1849, when it was performed in Vienna.

RIENZI, DER LETZTE DER TRIBUNEN (Rienzi, the last of the Tribunes)
Opera in five acts by Richard Wagner (1813–83), libretto by the composer, based on the novel by Edward George Bulwer Lytton (1803–73), inspired by an anonymous chronicle from fourteenth-century Italy. First performance: Dresden, Hofoper, 20 October 1842. First performance in U.K.: London, Her Majesty's Theatre, 27 January 1879; in U.S.A.: New York, Academy of Music, 4 March 1878.

ORIGINAL CAST. Wilhelmine Schröder-Devrient

Richard Wagner surrounded by his friends. Drawing by E. B. Kietz, 1841.

(Adriano), Henriette Wüst (Irene), Joseph Tichatschek (Rienzi), Wilhelm Dettmer (Colonna), Michael Wächter (Orsini).

SYNOPSIS. Rome in the fourteenth century was divided by family rivalries. The Orsinis try to abduct Irene (soprano), Rienzi's sister, whilst Rienzi is away. Adriano Colonna, who loves Irene, succeeds in thwarting the attempt with the help of his family and the populace. When Rienzi returns, a revolt breaks out and Adriano, though of noble birth, sides with the people. Rienzi now rules Rome and a plot to kill him is foiled. But the Orsinis and Colonnas, unwilling to relinquish the power that they have exercised for centuries, incite the people. The Pope excommunicates Rienzi. Thus Rienzi finds himself isolated; the populace rise up against him and Adriano tries in vain to save him. The crowd storm the Campidoglio and set it on fire. Rienzi dies in the flames together with the young lovers, Irene and Adriano.

■ *Rienzi* was written in the hopes of having it performed in Paris, but despite the influential patronage of Meyerbeer, it was not accepted there. This youthful effort by Wagner has all the pomp and splendour of grand opera: romances, marches, parades, duets, ballets and a spectacular finale with the Campidoglio in flames. Received with much enthusiasm in Dresden, *Rienzi* fared badly after that and has been rarely performed in this century. Although it does not begin to approach the style and dramatic strength of the mature Wagner, it contains some admirable pages, as well as its famous overture.

RUSLAN I LYUDMILA (Ruslan and Lyudmila)
Fairy opera in five acts by Mikhail Glinka (1804–57), libretto by the composer and Valeryan Shirkov, from the poem by Alexander Pushkin (1799–1837). First performance: St Petersburg, Imperial Theatre, 9 December 1842. First performance in U.K.: London, Lyceum, 4 June 1931; in U.S.A.: New York, Town Hall, 26 December 1942.

CAST. Osip Afanasevich Petrov, A. M. Stepanova. Conductor: C. Albrecht.

SYNOPSIS. The story is set in the ninth century in pagan Russia. Act I. Castle of the Grand Duke of Kiev. At the court of the Grand Duke Svetosar (bass), his daughter Lyudmila (soprano) is about to marry Ruslan (baritone), but both the warrior Farlaf (bass) and the Tartar Prince Ratmir (contralto) want to marry Lyudmila and intend to kill Ruslan. Lyudmila is sad at the prospect of leaving her father and he consoles her. Suddenly darkness descends and a ghost abducts Lyudmila. Svetosar promises his daughter in marriage to whoever can bring her back safe. Ruslan, Farlaf and Ratmir set about finding her. Act II. The cave of the magician Finn. Ruslan arrives to consult the magician who reveals that Lyudmila has been carried off by the dwarf Chernomor (tenor). He then tells Ruslan the sad story of his love for Naina (mezzo-soprano) who, having won his affections with her magic arts, turned into a witch. Meanwhile, Farlaf meets the witch Naina and accepts her offer to help him find Lyudmila. As Ruslan continues his search, he finds himself in a field strewn with corpses and confronts an enormous head whose breath produces a tremendous wind. He runs the head through with his lance and underneath he finds a sword, the weapon with which he can kill the dwarf Chernomor. Act III. Naina's castle. Gorislava (soprano), in love with Ratmir, has been made a prisoner by the witch's magic spells. Ratmir arrives at the castle but does not meet Gorislava. He too is brought under Naina's powers by means of a slave girl's dance. All three seem as if hypnotized. Finn, however, breaks the spell and Ratmir and Gorislava once again embrace. Act IV. Chernomor's castle. The unhappy Lyudmila, a prisoner of Chernomor, cries over her unhappy fate. The dwarf cheers her up by organizing a feast with oriental dances. Ruslan bursts in and as Lyudmila is cast into a deep sleep by Chernomor, he and the dwarf engage in a fierce battle. Ruslan overcomes his opponent by cutting off his beard, the source of his powers. Picking up the sleeping Lyudmila, he sets off for Kiev. Act V. On the road to Kiev, Farlaf and Naina abduct Lyudmila once again. Farlaf brings her to Kiev claiming that he has saved her, but he is unable to rouse her. Only Ruslan can wake her and a celebration is held for the reunited couple.

■ *Ruslan i Lyudmila* confirmed Glinka's position as a great national composer. Although the writing of the libretto and the score took a considerable time – Pushkin was supposed to see the completed text but he died before this was possible – the finished work was a remarkable accomplishment. Though *Ruslan* makes a definite break with traditional western music (certainly more so than *A Life for the Tsar*) the influence of many composers is evident, from Mozart to Bellini to Donizetti. Popular themes are used in the plot, which is interwoven with reference to legend and fairy tales, and influenced by exotic and oriental elements. The music borrows extensively from the vast heritage of Russian, Georgian, Turkish, Arabian and Finnish folk music. In his exploration of oriental themes, Glinka was a forerunner of these melodic and colourful aspects which Moussorgsky, Borodin and Rimsky-Korsakov were to make an essential part of the new style of Russian music. Glinka's approach was considered extremely innovative when it was first presented in the first half of the nineteenth century – a middle course between the revolutionary and the provocative. Nevertheless, between 1842 and 1846 *Ruslan* was performed 56 times.

DER FLIEGENDE HOLLÄNDER (The Flying Dutchman)

Opera in three acts by Richard Wagner (1813–83), libretto by the composer, based on Heinrich Heine's Memoirs of Herr von Schnabelewopski. *First performance: Dresden, Hofoper, 2 January 1843. First performance in U.K.: London, Drury Lane, 23 July 1870; in U.S.A.: Philadelphia, Academy of Music, 8 November 1876.*

ORIGINAL CAST. Wilhelmine Schröder-Devrient (Senta), Michael Wächter (the Dutchman), Karl Risse (Daland), Reinhold (Erik). Conductor: Richard Wagner.

SYNOPSIS. The flying Dutchman (baritone) is a sea captain who vowed that he would round the Cape of Good Hope in a raging storm; he did so but the devil condemned him to sail the seas until the Day of Judgement unless he can find a girl who will love him faithfully until death. Every seven years he is allowed to leave his ship to seek such a woman, and a term of seven years has just finished as the opera begins. Act I. A storm drives the ship of Daland, a Norwegian sea captain (bass), into a bay some way from his home. A steersman (tenor) sings himself asleep with a sea song before the ghostly ship of the Dutchman moors alongside. Daland is much impressed by the Dutchman's wealth and agrees to the stranger's suggestion that he should marry his daughter. The weather clears and the ships set sail. Act II. In Daland's house, Senta, his daughter (soprano), and her friends spin and sing; she sings the legend of the Dutchman, a picture of whom hangs on the wall. Erik (tenor), her admirer, begs her to forget such a fancy, which has scared the other girls, and asks her to return his love. He relates how he has dreamt of her father's return in a ghostly ship, accompanied by a stranger, with whom he then saw Senta walking arm in arm. Senta laughs and turns her gaze once more at the portrait. Her father appears with the Dutchman. Senta immediately declares her love for

Act IV of Glinka's Ruslan and Lyudmila *at the Bolshoi Theatre, Moscow, 1868.*

Sketch by Boris Bilinsky (1930) for the first scene, Act I, of Glinka's Ruslan and Lyudmila.

him, and Daland congratulates them. Act III. A sailors' chorus from Daland's ship indicates that the crew are merrymaking and they taunt the ghostly spectres on the Dutchman's ship for not doing likewise. The challenge is taken up by the Dutchman's crew with a wild chorus that terrifies the sailors and their girls. Senta is pursued by Erik, who chides her for her faithlessness. The Dutchman overhears them and, fearing that she may be faithless to him also, resolves to leave. Erik and his friends prevent her from following him. The Dutchman declares who he is and puts to sea. Senta rushes to the clifftop and, confirming her loyalty once and for all, throws herself into the sea. The Dutchman's ship vanishes. There is a final tableau of the lovers, in each other's arms and now redeemed, rising to heaven.

■ In the summer of 1839 the ship bringing Wagner from Königsberg to London was caught in a terrible storm and thrown up onto the Scandinavian coast. The dazzling light of the tempest and the roar of the sea made a deep impression on Wagner, conjuring up an image of the condemned Dutchman aboard his spectral ship sailing the seas, in desperate search of salvation. The fable of the Flying Dutchman, taken up by Heine, was a traditional tale from the fifteenth century

among sailors of the north, possibly an unconscious reworking of the legend of the wandering Jew, which in its turn was derived from the myth of Ulysses. The three legends have as a common element a basic aspiration of the human soul: to achieve eternal peace. The original idea for this romantic opera was undoubtedly inspired by Wagner's dramatic sea voyage, together with the recollection of the Nordic legend.

Wagner wrote the libretto in Paris in 1841 and composed the music in six weeks in the spring of 1842 at Meudon, where he had retired from the noise and the distractions of the city. The opera contains Wagner's main themes: a curse, redemption and the desire for death as the only inner certainty – themes which remain fundamental to his operas from *Tristan* to the *Ring of the Nibelung* to *Parsifal*. The *Leitmotif* appears for the first time: a leading motif identifying a character, an idea or a sentiment. Though contained within arias, duets and ballads, *leitmotif* in the *Dutchman* has not yet been fully absorbed into the main body of the music such as we find in Wagner's later works.

DON PASQUALE
Opera buffa *in three acts by Gaetano Donizetti*

Scene from Act I of Glinka's Ruslan and Lyudmila *at the Bolshoi Theatre, 1957.*

(1797–1848), libretto (signed Michele Accursi) by Giovanni Ruffini (1807–81), a reworking of the libretto by Angelo Anelli for Ser Marcantonio *by Stefano Pavesi. First performance: Paris, Théâtre-Italien, 3 January 1843. First performance in U.K.: London, Her Majesty's Theatre, 29 June 1843; in U.S.A.: New Orleans, 7 January 1845.*

ORIGINAL CAST. Giulia Grisi (Norina), Mario Tamburini (Ernesto), Antonio Tamburini (Doctor Malatesta), Luigi Lablache (Don Pasquale).

SYNOPSIS. The action takes place in Rome. Act I. A room in Don Pasquale's house. The rich and elderly Don Pasquale (bass) is furious with his nephew and heir, Ernesto (tenor), because he is unwilling to accept a marriage of convenience which his uncle has arranged with a rich, sedate woman. The young, handsome Ernesto is in love with an equally young and attractive widow, Norina (soprano), whose unpardonable sin is a lack of money. Don Pasquale wants neither to see nor hear of her and threatens to disinherit his nephew. Doctor Malatesta (baritone), a friend to both lovers and Don Pasquale, decides to help them obtain the old man's consent. He arrives on a visit and pretends to take his side on hearing about Ernesto's behaviour. He artfully proposes that Don Pasquale should punish his nephew by taking a wife for himself, and proposes his very own sister, Sofronia, who is

supposed to possess all the qualities necessary to make his old age pleasant. Don Pasquale is delighted with this proposal and begs his friend to introduce him to Sofronia. Malatesta instructs Norina, who is to play the part of the fictitious sister, on how to charm Don Pasquale when she meets him and then, when the marriage contract has been signed – a false one, of course – to drive him mad with her capriciousness. Act II. Don Pasquale's house. Don Pasquale is completely won over by Sofronia's sweetness and good graces and asks to proceed immediately with the marriage. Another friend, disguised as a notary, is summoned for the contract. Now Ernesto, having made up his mind to leave, arrives to say goodbye. Informed of his uncle's marriage, he is horrified to see Norina. The Doctor quickly enlightens him about their plan. Now that the contract has been signed and countersigned, Norina begins to play the second part of her act. She puts on a display of extravagance and loose morals. She pretends to redecorate the house, she summons jewellers, dressmakers, and hairdressers, whilst Don Pasquale accumulates a pile of bills. Act III. Don Pasquale's presumed wife is insatiable. She wants to be entertained and prepares to go to the theatre. Don Pasquale attempts to stop her but she slaps him. As she leaves, she purposely drops a note from Ernesto in which he arranges to meet her that evening in the garden. Don Pasquale sends for Malatesta. Having got him into this situation, the Doctor must now get him out. They meet

The final scene of Wagner's Der fliegende Holländer *from the* Leipziger Illustrierte Zeitung *on the day after the opera's first performance, 1843.*

with Sofronia, and Malatesta tells her that on the following day Norina, Ernesto's future wife, is coming to the house. Sofronia announces that she will not tolerate such an indignity and walks off, but she is afraid of being deceived and therefore asks to attend the wedding. Don Pasquale agrees to everything to ensure Sofronia's departure. Then the plot is revealed. Don Pasquale becomes angry, but so great is his joy at being freed from the nightmarish Sofronia that he consents to Norina's and Ernesto's marriage.

■ Donizetti wrote *Don Pasquale* when he was at the height of his career. The Théâtre Italien in Paris asked him to prepare an *opera buffa* and Donizetti was reminded of Angelo Anelli's libretto which had been written some ten years previously for Stefano Pavesi's *Ser Marcantonio*, a now forgotten work. Ruffini was

living in exile in Paris because of his association with Mazzini's movement and he wrote librettos for a living. He accepted the task of re-working Anelli's text. But Ruffini and Donizetti did not get on and Ruffini refused to sign the finished libretto. It appeared with the initials M.A., those of Michele Accursi, another Mazzini exile, a friend of Donizetti and his theatrical agent in Paris. Donizetti took only eleven days to compose *Don Pasquale* in November 1842, but the instrumentation and the various adjustments required by the individual singers took rather longer. The success of *Don Pasquale* was overwhelming and soon afterwards it was performed all over the world with equal success. The critics also praised it warmly. It was Donizetti's last great success and of his 66 operas, it remains one of the most popular. It has never passed out of the repertory. *Don Pasquale* and *L'Elisir*

Original cast of Wagner's Der fliegende Holländer: *Michael Wächter (The Dutchman), Reinhold (Erik), Risse (Daland), Wilhelmine Schröder-Devrient (Senta), E. Wächter (Mary).*

Act III of Wagner's Der fliegende Holländer *at the Bayreuth Festival in 1956; produced by Wolfgang Wagner.*

d'Amore are not only considered Donizetti's comic masterpieces, but, together with the *Barbiere di Siviglia*, they constitute the three crowning delights of nineteenth-century comic opera.

I LOMBARDI ALLA PRIMA CROCIATA (The Lombards at the First Crusade)
Opera in four acts by Giuseppe Verdi (1813–1901), libretto by Temistocle Solera (1817–78), based on the poem by Tommaso Grossi (1790–1853). First performance: Milan, Teatro alla Scala, 11 February 1843. First performance in U.K.: London, Her Majesty's Theatre, 12 May 1846; in U.S.A.: New York, Palmo's Opera House, 3 March 1847.

ORIGINAL CAST. E. Frezzolini (Giselda), C. Guasco (Orante), P. Dérivis (Pagano, the hermit), G. Severi (Arvino), T. Ruggeri (Viclinda). Conductor: G. Panizza.

SYNOPSIS. The end of the eleventh century. Act. I. 'The Vendetta.' Two brothers, Pagano (bass) and Arvino (tenor), loved the same woman, Viclinda (soprano). She preferred Arvino and, on the day of their marriage, Pagano tried to kill him. For this he was exiled, but now, after many years, he returns to Milan dressed as a penitent and a reconciliation takes place between him and Arvino, Viclinda and their daughter Giselda (soprano). Pagano is still hoping to be revenged on his brother and gathers a band of ruffians, led by Pirro (bass), to attack the family house and kill Arvino. The plan misfires, however, when Pagano kills his father, not his brother, in the confusion. In remorse, he tries to commit suicide, but is prevented and exiled once again. Act II. 'The Man in the Cave.' Acciano (bass), the tyrant of Antioch, prays to Allah for help against the Crusaders. His son Oronte (tenor) is in love

with one of the Christian prisoners, Giselda, and wishes to be converted to Christianity, to the delight of his mother Sofia (soprano), who has herself been secretly converted. Pagano, meanwhile, has become a hermit living in solitary retreat. His former follower, Pirro, does not recognize him when he comes to beg forgiveness for having become a Moslem. He now offers to betray Antioch. This enables the Crusading Lombards, led by Arvino, to capture Antioch. In the harem Sofia tells Giselda that Acciano and Oronte have been killed. The Lombards enter and Giselda curses the god who allowed such a war; her father is so incensed at her lack of faith in the holy crusade that he tries to kill her. Pagano, who has not been recognized, saves her, pleading that she is merely 'a poor mad girl'. Act III. 'The Conversion.' The valley of Jehoshaphat outside Jerusalem. Oronte is not dead. Disguised as a Crusader, he meets Giselda and they swear their eternal love. They leave the Crusaders' camp. Arvino laments that he should have had such a daughter and he is further incensed when he hears that Pagano has been seen nearby. Oronte, mortally wounded, and Giselda take refuge in Pagano's cave. Oronte is baptized before he dies in the arms of his beloved Giselda. Act IV. 'The Holy Sepulchre.' Giselda, now reconciled to her father, has a vision of Oronte among the angels. In the battle for Jerusalem Pagano is mortally wounded. Brought into Arvino's tent, he discloses his identity. Arvino forgives him and carries him in his arms to the entrance of the tent. From there they can see the Crusaders' flags flying on the conquered city.

■ A romantic taste for the medieval and its ballads characterizes Verdi's first experiment with a widely popular type of opera. *I Lombardi* was then revised for presentation in Paris on 26 November 1847 (under the title of *Jérusalem*) and in Constantinople in 1851. The revisions were no great improvements, but they allowed Verdi to establish a relationship with a more mature public and to confront the problems of grand opera, a particularly useful exercise for his future development.

MARIA DI ROHAN, o IL CONTE DI CHALAIS

Opera in three parts by Gaetano Donizetti (1797–1848), libretto by Salvatore Cammarano (1801–52), based on a play by Lockroy, Un Duel sous le Cardinal de Richelieu. *First performance: Vienna, Kärntnertortheater, 5 June 1843. First performance in U.K.: London, Covent Garden, 8 May 1847; in U.S.A.: New York, 10 December 1849.*

ORIGINAL CAST. Eugenia Tadolini (Maria), Carlo Guasco (Riccardo of Chalais), Giorgio Ronconi (Enrico of Chevreuse). Conductor: Gaetano Donizetti.

SYNOPSIS. The opera is divided into three parts: Unfortunate Consequences of Duels; Not Love But Gratitude; Senseless Revenge. The action takes place in Paris around 1630. Enrico of Chevreuse (baritone) is imprisoned for having killed a nephew of Cardinal Richelieu in a duel. Maria of Rohan (soprano), a lady-in-waiting to the Queen and secretly married to Enrico, asks Riccardo, Count of Chalais (tenor), to intercede for Enrico with the King, whose favour Riccardo enjoys. Maria leads Riccardo to believe that she is related to Enrico, but does not reveal that he is her husband. Riccardo, who is in love with Maria, promises to help her. Soon afterwards a valet announces that the King has pardoned Enrico of Chevreuse, and Maria is unable to contain her great joy, which arouses general surprise. Armando of Gonde makes some malicious insinuations and Riccardo challenges him to a duel. Enrico, just released from prison, offers to be his second. Rumour has it that Richelieu has been dismissed and so Enrico feels that he can disclose his secret marriage. Before the duel Riccardo writes a letter to Maria – fearing that he may be killed – in which he expresses his feelings. Maria arrives unexpectedly and Riccardo locks the letter away in a box. She informs him that Richelieu has returned to power and may exact revenge for Riccardo's having obtained Enrico's freedom from the King. Enrico arrives at this moment and Maria hides in another room. Enrico has come for Riccardo as it is nearly time for the duel. Riccardo, however, lingers with Maria and the time passes rapidly. A friend comes to tell him that Enrico has taken his place in the duel and has been wounded. Riccardo hastens to Enrico's side. He is informed that

Act II of Wagner's Der fliegende Holländer *at the Bayreuth Festival in 1969; produced by August Everding with sets by Josef Svoboda.*

A scene from Donizetti's Don Pasquale *at the Salzburg Festival, 1971. Production and sets by Ladislav Stros.*

Richelieu's guards are searching his house. He quickly returns home, anxious about the letter, but it is gone. On the Cardinal's instructions the letter is handed over to Enrico. Enrico is enraged and does not believe Maria's declarations of innocence, nor, on Riccardo's arrival at that moment, Riccardo's word of honour that he never touched Maria. Enrico wants a duel and the two men set off, but Enrico returns shortly afterwards to report that Riccardo has killed himself to escape from Richelieu's guards.

■ This work was immensely successful, but has now disappeared from the repertory. It was revived in Bergamo in 1957.

THE BOHEMIAN GIRL
Opera in three acts by Michael William Balfe (1808–70), libretto by Alfred Bunn (1796/7–1860). First performance: London, Drury Lane, 27 November 1843; in U.S.A.: New York, 25 September 1844.

SYNOPSIS. Set in Germany, the story tells of a Polish nobleman, Thaddeus, and his beloved Arline, daughter of Count Arnheim, who was kidnapped as a child by gypsies and brought up by them. Arline is accused of stealing a jewel, but all of a sudden she is recognized by her father, the governor of Pressburg, who is so happy to have found his daughter that he agrees to give her in marriage to Thaddeus, despite the fact that he is a political exile.

■ The text is based on *La Gypsy*, a ballet-pantomine by J. H. Vernoy de Saint-Georges performed in 1839 and taken from the novel *La Gitanilla* by Cervantes (1614). It is Balfe's most famous work and was undoubtedly the most popular English opera of the first half of the nineteenth century and the only one to have a resounding success abroad. Its arias (among them, *I dreamt that I dwelt in marble halls*) were well known in England for a long time and it was continually in the repertory, with frequent performances at Drury Lane and Covent Garden. The libretto was translated into Italian (*La Zingara*), German, French, Swedish, Croat and Russian. Balfe composed the score during one of his periodic visits to England from Paris, where he had settled. The first performance was a huge success; then in 1869 it was given at the Théâtre Lyrique in Paris as *La Bohemienne* in a French version, which included various new pieces by the composer, expanding the opera to five acts. Balfe was awarded on that occasion the Legion of Honour by Napoleon III.

MEDEA
Opera in three acts by Giovanni Pacini (1796–1867), libretto by Benedetto Castiglia. First performance: Palermo, Teatro Carolino, 28 November 1843. First performance in U.S.A.: New York, 27 September 1860.

SYNOPSIS. The scene is Corinth. Medea has sacrificed her kingdom and family for Giasone, who she fears will abandon her to marry Creusa, daughter of Creonte, the King. In despair and anger she declares that Creonte's family will suffer terrible punishments. Because of Medea's impiety, the judges and priests grant Giasone's request to dissolve his marriage and have Medea sent into exile. She appears resigned, but before leaving she wishes to speak with Giasone and requests that she at least be allowed to take her children with her. But Creonte intervenes and commands her to leave immediately. But in the end, after desperate entreaties, she is allowed to see her children for the last time. Whilst everyone is celebrating, Medea enters the temple with her children. Soon afterwards she comes out with a bloody dagger in her hand, having killed Creusa and her children. Outside the temple, amid the general uproar, Medea kills herself.

■ *Medea* belongs to Pacini's post-Rossini period when he made an individual contribution to the development of Italian opera by introducing, among other things, a more diffuse and deeply felt melodious quality. In general he lacked judgement in his choice of librettos, which almost always adhered to the current fashion.

ERNANI

Opera in four acts by Giuseppe Verdi (1813–1901), libretto by Francesco Maria Piave (1810–76), based on Hernani, ou l'Honneur Castillan *by Victor Hugo (1802–85). First performance: Venice, Teatro La Fenice, 9 March 1844. First performance in U.K.: London, Her Majesty's Theatre, 8 March 1845; in U.S.A.: New York, Park Theater, 15 April 1847.*

ORIGINAL CAST. Sofia Löwe, Carlo Guasco, Antonio Superchi, Antonia Selva.

SYNOPSIS. Spain and Aix-la-Chapelle, 1519. Act I. Ernani (tenor), outlawed by the King of Spain, Don Carlo (baritone), has become a bandit. He loves Elvira (soprano) and hopes to abduct her from the castle of Don Ruy Gomez de Silva (bass), to whom she is betrothed. She returns Ernani's love. The King, also in love with her, discovers Ernani in her rooms. Silva arrives and challenges the intruders to a duel but, on recognizing the King, he regains his composure and demands punishment for Ernani. The King assists Ernani's escape by passing him off as his messenger. Act II. Ernani's revolt has failed and, disguised as a pilgrim, he takes refuge at Silva's castle on the very day of Elvira's wedding. Silva, instead of turning him over to the King, feels bound by the traditional rules of hospitality, and his desire to have personal revenge on Ernani, to offer him protection. The King carries off Elvira as a hostage when Silva refuses to reveal Ernani's hiding place. Silva allows the King to take Elvira but then challenges Ernani to a duel. Ernani refuses to fight, but agrees that his life is forfeit to Silva, once he has been revenged on the King. He leaves a horn with Silva; he will kill himself when the old man blows it. Act III. Aix-la-Chapelle. Charlemagne's tomb. The King has hidden in the tomb because he suspects that conspirators will meet there to plot against his life and he plans to identify them. Meanwhile the Electors are discussing the succession of the Holy Roman Empire. Silva and Ernani are among those who draw lots for the privilege of killing the King and Ernani refuses to yield the right to Silva, even when Silva offers to give back the horn. Cannon shots announce that Don Carlo has been elected Emperor. The plotters are caught, but the King, after Elvira's intercession, pardons them in exchange for their loyalty. As final proof of his benevolence, he gives permission for Ernani to marry Elvira. Act IV. The guests are celebrating the young couple's wedding at a sumptuous dinner. At the height of the festivities Ernani's horn is sounded three times. Ernani begs for his life, but Silva does not even relent when Elvira adds her pleas. Ernani stabs himself and Elvira, grief-stricken, falls senseless on his body.

■ The fame of Victor Hugo's play, published in 1830, was already widespread and it was taken as the model for French Romanticism. Verdi was fully aware of the responsibility involved in adapting such a famous work and proposed to Piave all the principal changes that were made to the original text. Nevertheless, Hugo regarded the opera as a travesty of his play. To heighten the effect of the romantic content Verdi sought to counterbalance the soprano, tenor and baritone voices and inserted dramatic choral passages such as the particularly thrilling *Si ridesti il leon di Castiglia*, destined to become one of the *Risorgimento*'s most popular songs.

I DUE FOSCARI (The two Foscari)
Opera in three acts by Giuseppe Verdi (1813–1901), libretto by Francesco Maria Piave (1810–76), based on the play by Lord Byron (1788–1824). First performance: Rome, Teatro Argentina, 3 November 1844. First performance in U.K.: London, Covent Garden, 10 April 1847; in U.S.A: Boston, 10 May 1847.

SYNOPSIS. Venice, 1457. The elderly Doge, Francesco Foscari (baritone), is called upon to preside over a meeting of the Council of Ten, supreme court and executive of the State, in the trial of his son Jacopo (tenor) for treason. Jacopo had been discovered to have been in correspondence with the Sultan and the Genoese, while in exile in Crete for a previous charge of murder. Jacopo's wife, Lucrezia Contarini (soprano), is furious when she hears that the Ten have condemned him to further exile, for she is sure of his innocence. The Doge commiserates with her, but declares that his duty to the State demands that he should not show mercy on his son. Act II. Jacopo sees visions in his prison and does not recognize Lucrezia when she comes to visit him. They are both dismayed when the Doge also enters, confirming that he can do nothing to relieve the sentence. Loredano (bass), the sworn enemy of the Foscaris, brings Jacopo news that he must set out immediately for Crete. The Ten, in session with the Doge, refuse to mitigate the punishment on Jacopo despite his pleas and those of Lucrezia and their children. Act III. A carnival crowd disperses when they see Jacopo's prison galley approach. Jacopo bids farewell to Lucrezia and collapses as he boards the ship. News is brought to the Doge of a confession which clears his son's name, but Lucrezia announces his death. The Ten demand the Doge's resignation, on the grounds of his old age, infirmity and great sorrow; at first the old man refuses, but then acquiesces. He dies as the bells ring in the new Doge. Loredano exults in the Foscaris' doom.

Play-bill for Balfe's The Bohemian Girl *at the Philharmonic Theatre, London, 1875. London, Victoria and Albert Museum.*

■ Verdi realized that the opera was not a complete success and in 1848 he wrote to Piave that because of its uniformity it 'seemed more like a funeral' than a dramatic work. Yet when Byron's play had been proposed to Verdi as a text for an opera he replied, 'It is an estimable subject and highly suitable, full of passion and perfect for setting to music.' In any case Verdi was to profit from this experience when he came to write *Simon Boccanegra*, another study of the conflict between the interests of the State and family affections.

ALESSANDRO STRADELLA

Opera in three acts by Friedrich von Flotow (1812–83), libretto by Wilhelm Friedrich Riese, based on a comédie mêlée de chant *by the French writers P. A. A. Pittaud de Forges and P. Duport. First performance: Hamburg, Stadttheater, 30 December 1844. First performance in U.K.: London, Drury Lane, 6 June 1846; in U.S.A.: New York, 29 November 1853.*

SYNOPSIS. The plot unfolds towards the end of the seventeenth century. The first act is set in Venice, the second and third acts in a village near Rome. Act I. Alessandro Stradella (tenor) is in love with Leonora (soprano), pupil of the rich Venetian Bassi (bass). She returns Alessandro's affections, but her tutor wants to arrange a rich marriage. Stradella arrives in a gondola at Palazzo Bassi and persuades Leonora to run away with him. They succeed thanks to a band of masqueraders, friends of Alessandro, who step between the two fugitives and Bassi's servants who are supposed to obstruct the escape. Act II. The marriage of Alessandro and Leonora is about to take place. The wedding party sets off for the church. Barbarino (tenor) and Malvoglio (bass), two suspicious characters, appear, hired by old Bassi to kill Stradella and kidnap the girl. The festivities begin and the two hired assassins mingle with the guests. Act III. Barbarino and Malvoglio are no longer willing to kill Alessandro, for they have been won over by his charm and beautiful voice. Bassi arrives and on learning of their change of heart he increases his offer by so much that the two cannot refuse. But when they hear Stradella sing a romance about the repentance of a culprit, they are so moved that they fall to their knees and beg forgiveness.

■ This work had been presented on 4 February 1837 at the Palais Royal as a *comédie mêlée de chant* with arias by Flotow. The libretto and score were then expanded into an opera in 1844. The story is freely based on the life of the famous seventeenth-century composer and singer, and the opera had a wide success in Germany. *Alessandro Stradella* and *Martha* are the only operas by Flotow that have remained in the repertory.

GIOVANNA D'ARCO (Joan of Arc)

Opera in a prologue and three acts by Giuseppe Verdi (1813–1901), libretto by Temistocle Solera (1817–78), based on the play Die Jungfrau von Orleans *by Friedrich Schiller (1759–1805). First performance: Milan, Teatro alla Scala, 15 February 1845.*

SYNOPSIS. France. The English are about to launch an attack which seems irresistible. Carlo VII (tenor), the King of France, places his sword beneath a miraculous picture of the Madonna. Giovanna (soprano) comes regularly to pray for her country's safety. She encourages Carlo, begging him not to abandon the country's defences and declaring herself ready to put on armour and go into battle. Giacomo (baritone), suspicious that his daughter's 'visions' are sent not from Heaven but from Hell, is horrified to see her leaving with the King. Victory follows the French offensive; Giovanna admits that she has fallen in love with Carlo. Giacomo accosts his daughter outside Rheims Cathedral and accuses her of blasphemy, and a thunderclap appears to attest the truth. Giovanna does not understand her father's accusations. She is imprisoned and handed over to the English. Giacomo suddenly realizes, when he hears her vindicate herself in a delirium, that he has been mistaken and she is released.

Freed, she returns to the battle. France and her King are saved, but Giovanna is killed.

■ This was the worst period in Verdi's life which is apparent not only from the music, but also from the suggestions that he made to Solera for the libretto, which turned out to be highly complicated and improbable. According to the critics, *Giovanna d'Arco* is a 'crude imitation of the finale of *Aida*'. Verdi had other things on his mind. Informed by Ricordi that he was

THE BOHEMIAN GIRL

A picture postcard of Balfe's The Bohemian Girl. *London, Enthoven Theatre Collection, Victoria and Albert Museum.*

being swindled by the impresario Marelli, Verdi broke with La Scala. As a result his works did not appear in that theatre for many years.

UNDINE

Romantic opera in four acts by Albert Lortzing (1801–51), libretto by the composer, inspired by a short story by Friedrich de La Motte Fouqué. First performance: Magdeburg, 21 April 1845. First performance in U.S.A.: New York, 9 October 1856.

SYNOPSIS. The story takes place in 1452 in a fishing village and the palace of Duke Henry. The knight Hugo von Ringstetten (tenor) is about to marry Undine (soprano). Undine believes that she is the daughter of Tobias (bass) and Martha (contralto), an old fisherman and his wife, but in reality she is a water-sprite and was put in place of their real daughter by the Prince of the Waters. Undine is radiant with happiness, unable to control her joy. As she prepares for the wedding ceremony, she remarks on the delicate beauty of Hugo's scarf and asks where it came from. Berthalda (mezzo-soprano), a young noblewoman, gave it to him. On learning this, Undine is disturbed, but Hugo comforts her affectionately, whilst the villagers collect to celebrate the marriage. Meanwhile Kühleborn (baritone), Prince of the Waters, wins the confidence of Veit (tenor), Hugo's groom, and joins the festivities. He also expresses his doubts about the future happiness of the two young people, foreseeing a renewal of Hugo's passion for Berthalda. He vows to bring Undine back to the Kingdom of the Waters and tells her that she must return to the water when Hugo ceases to love her. Undine and Hugo leave for Berthalda's castle, where they are to live. Undine has confessed to Hugo her true nature and that she may keep her soul for as long as he continues to love her. Should his love cease, she will turn into a water-sprite once again and return to her natural home. Kühleborn also belongs to Berthalda's court and he poses as the King of Naples' ambassador. Berthalda, who is in love with Hugo, is pleased at his return, but when she learns of his marriage she announces that she has accepted an offer of marriage to the King of Naples. During a celebration she asks Kühleborn to sing. He tells the story of how the daughter of a poor fisherman and his wife falls into the water and is rescued by a nobleman, who raises her as his own child in his palace. He then introduces Tobias and Martha to Berthalda and tells her that she is their daughter. Berthalda is furious and orders Kühleborn's arrest. Then she has her father's strong-box brought in, confident of finding proof of her noble origins. She opens the document and on reading it, she faints. Kühleborn has spoken the truth and she must now leave court immediately. On the shores of a lake Berthalda succeeds in convincing Hugo that he has been bewitched by Undine and she regains his love. They are caught by Undine, who reminds Hugo of his promise. He rejects her, no longer wanting anything to do with her, a girl without a soul. Kühleborn appears unexpectedly in the middle of the ominously swollen lake. He now has the proof that he wanted: creatures with a soul are more cruel than those without. Undine returns to her kingdom, yet she will never forget her experiences on earth. Time passes and Hugo becomes more restless. Undine has appeared to him in a dream and promised to return at midnight. He has covered all the palace fountains with rocks so that she cannot appear from the water. Veit, however, in despair over the loss of his young mistress and Berthalda's and Hugo's imminent marriage, removes the rocks to allow Undine's return. When midnight strikes, she emerges veiled from the fountain. Hugo is irresistibly drawn to her even though he knows that to approach her means death. Undine removes her veil and opens her arms. Thus united the two disappear into the water. From out of the waves Kühleborn appears on a rock and at his feet are Hugo and Undine radiant with happiness.

■ *Undine* is a romantic opera with a fluent melodic line and brilliant orchestration. Though more skilfully constructed than E. T. A. Hoffmann's opera *Undine* of 1816, it does not achieve the same imaginative boldness because of its excessive sentimentality.

ALZIRA
Opera in a prologue and two acts by Giuseppe Verdi (1813–1901), libretto by Salvatore Cammarano (1801–52), based on Alzire, ou les Américains *by Voltaire (1694–1778). First performance: Naples, Teatro San Carlo, 12 August 1845.*

ORIGINAL CAST. Arati (Alvaro), Coletti (Guzmano), Ceci (Ovando), Fraschini (Zamoro), Benedetti (Ataliba), Tadolini (Alzira), Salvetti (Zuma), Rossi (Otumbo).

SYNOPSIS. Peru, middle of the sixteenth century. Alvaro (bass), the Spanish Governor of Peru, has been captured by the Incas. He is about to be put to death when their leader Zamoro (tenor), presumed dead after being taken prisoner by Alvaro's son Guzmano (baritone), appears. Zamoro releases Alvaro, but swears vengeance on the Spaniard for having captured his beloved, Alzira (soprano), and her father Ataliba. Act I. Alvaro resigns in favour of Guzmano, who asks Ataliba for Alzira's hand, as a pledge of a Spanish peace with the Incas. Alzira refuses and Guzmano surprises her with Zamoro. Despite his father's pleas, Guzmano sends Zamoro to execution but, hearing that the Incas are about to attack Lima, he relents, swearing that they will meet shortly in battle. Act II. The Incas have lost the battle and Zamoro has been captured. Guzmano frees Zamoro when Alzira reluctantly agrees to marry him. Zamoro hears of her supposed treachery and returns to Lima on the day of their wedding. He stabs Guzmano, who nobly orders his soldiers not to execute him but to let him marry Alzira.

■ *Alzira* was written during Verdi's early period and is one of his few failures. In later years he called it 'really ugly'. In fact it was never again performed. Verdi composed *Alzira* reluctantly. The score was supposed to have been ready by the winter of 1844–45, but was delayed because of Verdi's ill-health. The first notes did not appear until the Spring of 1845. Another delay occurred because the soprano Tadolini was expecting a child and, as she was forty, it was feared that she might lose her voice. In fact everything went very well – for Tadolini, not for *Alzira*.

TANNHÄUSER UND DER SÄNGERKRIEG AUF WARTBURG (Tannhäuser and the Song Contest at the Wartburg)
Romantic opera in three acts by Richard Wagner (1813–83), libretto by the composer. First performance: Dresden, Hofoper, 19 October 1845. First performance in U.K.: London, Covent Garden, 6 May 1876; in U.S.A.: New York, Stadt Theater, 4 April 1859.

ORIGINAL CAST. Anton Mitterwurzer, Dettmer, Joseph Alois Tichatschek, Wilhelmine Schröder-Devrient, Johanna Wagner. Conductor: Richard Wagner.

SYNOPSIS. The story is set in Thuringia at the beginning of the thirteenth century. Act I. In the Venusberg, Venus (mezzo-soprano), surrounded by her court of nymphs, bacchantes and fauns, holds in her power the knight and poet Tannhäuser (tenor). Satiated with pleasures, he repulses Venus and begs her to set him free. She threatens him in an attempt to dissuade him, saying that the world will never forgive him, but when he pronounces the name of the Virgin Mary she vanishes. Tannhäuser finds himself in a valley near the castle of Wartburg. A shepherd (soprano) sings of Spring's return and he falls to his knees in prayer as a group of pilgrims pass by on their way to Rome. A horn sounds the arrival of the Landgrave Hermann (bass), accompanied by his noblemen, who recognize Tannhäuser. They invite him to return (after his year's absence) with them to the castle where, he is reminded by Wolfram von Eschenbach (baritone), the Landgrave's niece, Elisabeth (soprano), loves and waits for him. Act II. The Hall of Minstrels in the Wartburg. Elisabeth greets Tannhäuser. A song contest is announced for which the prize is Elisabeth's hand in marriage. The Landgrave proposes love as the theme. Silence falls and Wolfram, the first contestant, rises and sings of the true value of spiritual love. When Tannhäuser's turn comes, he impetuously sings a hymn to Venus in praise of sensual passion. All are outraged and the men draw their swords upon him. Elisabeth intervenes, despite her distress, appealing to their Christian forgiveness, and Tannhäuser, deeply repentant, accepts the Landgrave's command to seek atonement by joining the pilgrims bound for Rome. Act III. The Valley of the Wartburg. Wolfram and Elisabeth have waited in vain for Tannhäuser's return. Her strength failing and near death, Elisabeth appeals to the Madonna to pardon Tannhäuser, whom she has not seen among the returning pilgrims. Wolfram, left alone, prays to the Evening Star to protect her. Tannhäuser appears, in rags and exhausted. He tells Wolfram in despair that the Pope has refused to absolve him, saying that his soul would be saved only when the Pope's staff sprouts leaves once again. Disheartened

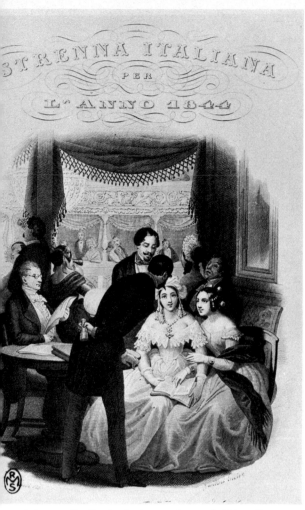

A box at La Scala during an interval. From Strenna Italiana, *1844.*

ter von der Vogelweide, Wolfram von Eschenbach, Biterolf and many others. Elisabeth possibly represents the glorious Princess Elisabeth of Hungary, the subject of an old German poem, *The Miracle of the Roses*. Both these stories had been told and embellished by various Romantic poets. Wagner incorporated them in a new work that asserts the theme of redemption and presents the conflict between the spirit and the senses. Venus is not just the goddess of sin, but the source of eternal beauty, whereas Elísabeth represents pure love bringing redemption through sacrifice and death. *Tannhäuser* is a work of extraordinary ardour and musical richness. It was given a lukewarm reception in Dresden; then the first scenes were changed for a performance at the Paris Opéra with the addition of a 'bacchanal', a concession to contemporary taste for the ballet. Perhaps the unusual placement of the ballet at the beginning of the first act explains the opera's failure at its Paris première on 13 March 1861. Success was not long in coming, however, and today *Tannhäuser* is considered one of Wagner's most important early works. Among its most famous pieces is the splendid overture, which presents many of the themes that are developed in the course of the opera.

ATTILA
Opera in a prologue and three acts by Giuseppe Verdi (1813–1901), libretto by Temistocle Solera (1817–78), based on the play Attila, König der Hunnen *by Zacharias Werner (1768–1823). First performance: Venice, Teatro La Fenice, 17 March 1846. First performance in U.K.: London, Her Majesty's Theatre, 14 March 1848; in U.S.A.: New York, 15 April 1850.*

SYNOPSIS. Prologue. Odabella (soprano) is taken prisoner by Attila (bass), who has killed her father. She swears vengeance. Attila rejects an offer of peace from the Roman consul Ezio (baritone), and decides to march on Rome. Foresto (tenor), who is in love with Odabella, leads the survivors of Attila's latest outrage. Act I. Foresto manages to meet Odabella, and accuses her of infidelity; she denies the charge, and tells him of her plans to murder Attila. Meanwhile, Attila is troubled by dreams, but manages to dismiss them from his mind. He is met at the gates of Rome by Leo (bass), a Roman bishop; recognizing Leo from his dream, Attila falls terrified to the ground. Act II. Ezio's camp. A treaty has been arranged between the Huns and the Romans, and Ezio is invited to a banquet given by Attila. Foresto meets Ezio and together they plot to murder Attila. At the banquet, Foresto's attempt to poison Attila is foiled by Odabella, who wishes to kill him with her own hands. Attila decides to marry Odabella in gratitude for her help. Act III. Foresto and Ezio plan another attack on Attila. Odabella appears, is again accused by Foresto, but again protests her desire for vengeance. Attila confronts all three conspirators and is finally stabbed by Odabella.

and resigned to eternal damnation, Tannhäuser calls on Venus and a vision of dazzling and enticing beauty appears. Wolfram tells him that Elisabeth has prayed for him and at the sound of her name, Tannhäuser rejects the vision once again. A procession approaches bearing Elisabeth's coffin. Penitent and redeemed, Tannhäuser embraces her corpse and dies. As the sun rises, pilgrims from Rome carry in the Pope's staff which has, miraculously, burst into leaf; the clear voices of the pilgrims hail the miracle of salvation: 'Let it be known in every land that God has forgiven him!'

■ The subject of *Tannhäuser* was taken from history and legend. The character Tannhäuser actually existed. Born around 1205, he was a *minnesinger*, a German lyric poet and musician. A legend grew up around him, that of the nobleman, repentant of his life of dissipation, who goes to Rome to ask Pope Urban IV for absolution and instead is censured. Wagner juxtaposed another legend concerning the poetic contest at the Wartburg in which the most famous poet-knights of the early thirteenth century took part: Wal-

■ Verdi made good use of his reputation as a patriotic

composer, which he had earned with *Nabucco, I Lombardi* and *Ernani*. But he continued to explore new techniques and worked extensively on the character of Attila. Werner's play was sent to him by Count Mocenigo together with a personal comment on Madame de Staël's writings on Germany, which Verdi studied with passionate interest. Verdi expected miracles from his librettist Solera. The result is rather uneven and merits Rossini's remarks, which the critics dug up for the occasion, 'Verdi composes with a helmet on his head'. And in the same vein, some French critics remarked, 'It is more like a fanfare from the *bersaglieri* than a true opera.'

LA DAMNATION DE FAUST (The Damnation of Faust)

Légende dramatique *in four acts and ten scenes by Hector Berlioz (1803–69), libretto by the composer and G. Almire Gandonnière, based on Gérard de Nerval's translation of Goethe's* Faust. *First performed as a concert: Paris, Opéra-Comique, Salle Favart, 6 December 1846. First performance in U.K.: Liverpool, 3 February 1894; in U.S.A.: New Orleans, 1894.*

CAST. G. Roger, H. Leon, Durlot-Maillard. Conductor: Hector Berlioz. Text modified and adapted for the stage by Raoul Gunsbourg and given in this new form for the first time at the Casino de Monte Carlo, 3 February 1893. Conductor: Raoul Gunsbourg.

SYNOPSIS. Act I. Hungary. The veranda of a pavilion with windows looking out onto meadows and to one side, a hill dominated by a fortress. At dawn Faust (tenor), an elderly philosopher weighed down by his years, observes the awakening of the happy village. He hears the peasants singing and the soldiers marching to war (the famous Rakoczy march). He only feels more disconsolate and incapable of emotion. Act II, Scene I. Faust's study. Unable to bear his solitary life any longer, Faust decides to poison himself. He is about to do so when he is restrained by the sound of church bells celebrating Easter and in the same instant by the appearance of Méphistophélès (baritone), who offers him youth with all its pleasures. Scene II. Faust asks Méphistophélès to prove his powers. And so Faust finds himself in Auerbach's tavern in Leipzig in the midst of a merry crowd of soldiers and students. But soon Faust is once again overcome with boredom. Scene III. Faust has magically regained his youth and is transported in his sleep to a wood on the banks of the Elbe. Marguérite (soprano) appears and he falls instantly in love. Act III. The stage is divided in two: on one side is Marguérite's room; on the other, a road. With Méphistophélès's help Faust enters the room as Marguérite undoes her plaits and sings the ballad of the King of Thule. Faust steps out and, declaring his love, he seduces her. Méphistophélès carries Faust off. Act IV, Scene I. Marguérite's room. Distraught with love, Marguérite despairs over her lost peace of mind as she vainly waits for Faust. Scene II. Forest and caves. The

aged Faust is once again tired of life's pleasures and asks Nature for peace. Méphistophélès, afraid of losing Faust's soul, informs him that Marguérite is in danger. Still in love with him, she had given her mother a sleeping draught each night in order to wait for him, thus causing her mother's slow death. Now she has been discovered and will be sentenced. Faust begs Méphistophélès for his help and Méphistophélès agrees in exchange for Faust's soul. Scene III. Faust and Méphistophélès, mounted on Vortez and Giaur, rush headlong on an infernal course into an abyss. Scene IV. Hell. Exultant, Méphistophélès boasts of his victory to the assembled princes of darkness, while Faust is put to the flames. Scene V. Heaven and Earth. Marguérite has repented and accepted her punishment, refusing Méphistophélès's help. She ascends to Heaven amid a chorus of angels singing God's praises; a choir of seraphim dry the tears from her face.

■ Berlioz first thought of writing an opera based on Goethe's *Faust*, which had impressed him deeply, in the autumn of 1829 at the time of his overriding passion for a Shakespearian actress, Harriet Smithson, who was to become his wife. This period produced the cantata for chorus and orchestra entitled *Eight Scenes from Faust Opus 1*, which constitutes the embryo of the new score (dedicated to Liszt) that Berlioz was to write in 1845. A year later it was performed under the title *La Damnation de Faust*. The public's reaction was decidedly negative; on 12 December the second performance, prepared with great care, was a total failure and Berlioz was left with a debt of about 10,000 francs. He was profoundly affected by the failure, cut off, as it were, from the operatic world. Several decades later the work became a sensational success and it remains the only popular opera written by Berlioz. *La Damnation* began as a series of symphonic-vocal pieces and was first performed as a concert. In the 1880s Raoul Gunsbourg adapted it for the theatre, eliminating those parts too difficult to execute on the stage and changing the order of the scenes to make the sequence of events more easily understandable to the public. After its première at Monte Carlo the opera continued to be performed successfully in this revised form. Nevertheless, even after Gunsbourg's reforms, the only truly theatrical part is the third act (a trio with Marguérite, Faust and Méphistophélès), which is understandable because Berlioz was not writing for the theatre. For this reason the concert version is more effective, more closely aligned with the composer's intentions. Precisely because of this mid-way position between a theatrical piece and a concert, *La Damnation* is musically very varied and each scene very different. The first act, with its complex orchestration and fine preparation, ends with the famous Rakoczy march. (When Berlioz was asked why he had set the action in Hungary, he replied, 'Because I wanted an orchestral piece with an Hungarian theme, just as I would have chosen a setting anywhere in the world if there had been any reason musically for doing so.') The second act is less lively, more melancholic; the third, as we have already noted, has a definite theatrical quality;

The Teatro alla Scala, Milan, from a painting of 1852.

Drawing for the first production of Wagner's
Tannhäuser. *Dresden 1845.*

and the fourth act, the actual damnation of Faust (which departs from Goethe's version, in which Faust is saved), is like a solemn and macabre epilogue, in which Berlioz expresses his turbulent Romanticism.

MACBETH
Opera in four acts by Giuseppe Verdi (1813–1901), libretto by Francesco Maria Piave (1810–76), based on Macbeth *by Shakespeare. First performance: Florence, Teatro alla Pergola, 14 March 1847. First performance in U.K.: Glyndebourne, 21 May 1938; in U.S.A.: New York, Niblo's Gardens, 24 April 1850.*

ORIGINAL CAST. Marianna Barbieri-Nini (Lady Macbeth), Felice Varesi (Macbeth), Angelo Brunacci (Macduff), Niccola Benedetti (Banquo).

SYNOPSIS. Scotland. A chorus of witches greet Macbeth (baritone) and Banquo (bass), the former as thane of Cawdor and King of Scotland, the latter as the father of Kings. Immediately news arrives that Macbeth has been created thane of Cawdor by King Duncan. Lady Macbeth reads a letter describing these events and, when she hears that Duncan plans to stay with the Macbeths at Dunsinane that night, she decides to persuade Macbeth to murder him while he sleeps, and thus make the prophecy come true. The murder is done, and Banquo, who goes to wake the King, awakens the castle with shouts of horror. Act II. Duncan's sons have fled, taking upon themselves the suspicion of parricide. Macbeth, now King of Scotland, plots to murder Banquo and his son, Fleance, to defeat the rest of the prophecy. During a banquet, he hears that

Fleance has escaped (although Banquo has died) and sees terrible visions of Banquo at the feasting table. Lady Macbeth cannot restrain his agitation. Act III. Macbeth consults the witches again, who warn him he is safe until 'Birnam Wood' comes to Dunsinane, and from all but a man not born of woman. Lady Macbeth, incensed by the thought of Banquo's descendants ruling in Scotland, vows to help him to exterminate their enemies. Act IV. Duncan's son, Malcolm (tenor), leads the English army to Birnam Wood, where they camouflage their numbers with branches. Lady Macbeth, troubled by nightmarish visions, walks in her sleep, to the consternation of her maid and doctor. Macbeth hears of her death as the English army approaches; he is killed by Macduff (baritone), who tells him that he 'was from his mother's womb untimely ripp'd'.

■ *Macbeth* underwent a series of changes and revisions. After the première in Florence it appeared in St Petersburg in 1855 under the title of *Sivardo il Sassone*. It was then given in Paris at the Théâtre-Lyrique in 1865 in a new version by Verdi, considerably revised to meet French taste, translated by Nuittier and Beaumont and with a revised libretto by Andrea Maffei (1798–1885), a mediocre poet but a well-known translator. Considered one of Verdi's most expressive and forceful operas, *Macbeth* is seen today as a monumental step forward musically, but very uneven as dramatic art. Piave did not in fact succeed in portraying the complexity of Shakespeare's characters, nor did Maffei, in the later version, help Verdi to establish a rapport with the subtle and intricate personalities of the characters. Thus we have some of Verdi's finest pages and others of the most remarkable ingenuousness and, in the final analysis, mediocrity. An example of the latter is the witches' scene, which Shakespeare conveys with a vivacity and strong evocative sense that is quite lost in the opera. The most outstanding feature is the orchestration, which was a notable improvement in Verdi's technique and a valuable experience for later works.

I MASNADIERI (The Robbers)
Opera in four acts by Giuseppe Verdi (1813–1901), libretto by Andrea Maffei (1798–1885), based on the tragedy Die Räuber *by Friedrich Schiller (1759–1805). First performance: London, Her Majesty's Theatre, 22 July 1847; in U.S.A.: New York, 31 May 1860.*

SYNOPSIS. The beginning of the eighteenth century, Germany. Carlo (tenor) and Francesco (baritone) are the sons of Massimiliano Moor (bass). Carlo ran away from home and joined a band of robbers, but he has now begged his father's forgiveness in a letter. This has been intercepted by his younger brother, who sees a chance of gaining the inheritance, and Carlo receives a forged reply refusing him forgiveness. In despair he swears to lead the brigands and serve them faithfully. Meanwhile Francesco forges another letter, from which it appears that Carlo is mortally wounded and bids Amalia (soprano), his betrothed, to marry Francesco instead. Massimiliano and Amalia are dismayed and the old man swoons, apparently lifeless. Act II. Amalia prays by the tomb of Massimiliano and refuses to marry Francesco; she hears from Arminio (tenor) that neither Carlo nor Massimiliano is dead. Carlo's band is surrounded by soldiers. Act III. Amalia flees to the forest where the brigands are hiding. Arminio brings food for Massimiliano, who is concealed in a nearby tower, but mistakes Carlo for Francesco and runs off. Carlo discovers his father who, almost dead, does not recognize his son. Carlo hears of Francesco's evil deeds and vows vengeance. Act IV. Francesco has had a nightmare in which he was damned at the Last Judgement. The robbers attack the castle but fail to capture him. Massimiliano blesses Carlo as his saviour. Carlo, unable to admit the disgrace of his shameful life to Amalia, kills her rather than ask her to share it with him.

■ The opera was not well received by its English audience and Verdi was accused of having failed to reach in his music the dramatic heights of Schiller's tragedy. It is quite true that the violence and passion of the original text do not emerge with comparable power in the opera. In February of the following year it was produced in Italy (at the Teatro Apollo, Rome), and here, too, it was greeted with criticism rather than praise. It is one of Verdi's less successful compositions.

MARTHA, oder DER MARKT VON RICHMOND (Martha, or Richmond Market)

Opera in four acts by Friedrich von Flotow (1812–83), libretto by Wilhelm Friedrich Riese, taken from ballet-pantomine Lady Henriette, ou La Servante de Greenwich by J. H. Vernoy de Saint-Georges, set to music by Flotow, together with Burgmüller and Deldevez (performed in Paris on 21 February 1844). First performance: Vienna, Kärntnertor Theater, 25 November 1847. First performance in U.K.: London, Drury Lane, 4 July 1849; in U.S.A.: New York, Niblo's Gardens, 1 November 1852.

ORIGINAL CAST. Anna Zerr, A. Ander, K. J. Formes.

SYNOPSIS. The action takes place in England in 1710, in the time of Queen Anne. Act I. Lady Harriet (soprano) is bored, despite attempts by Nancy (contralto) and the other maids of honour to amuse her. Her cousin, Sir Tristram (bass), who is an unsuccessful suitor of hers, comes to visit her. Outside in the street they hear bands of young girls passing on their way to the annual market in Richmond to find jobs. They sound so happy that Lady Harriet suggests to Nancy that they dress up as working girls and join in, and she persuades her cousin to accompany them. They are in Richmond Square dressed as country people, where there is a large gathering of bailiffs and farm-workers; Plunkett (baritone), a well-to-do farmer, is also there with his friend Lionel (tenor). Lionel had grown up in

Above, the song contest from Wagner's Tannhäuser *Act II at the 1965 Bayreuth Festival with scenery by Wieland Wagner.*
Below, the bacchanal from Tannhäuser *Act I at the 1961 Bayreuth Festival with scenery by Wieland Wagner.*

the home of the Plunkett family, after being entrusted to their care by his dying father. Nothing is known of this father except that he left behind a precious ring with the instruction that if his son ever found himself in trouble, he should hand it over to the Queen. Plunkett offers a place to Harriet, who has assumed the name of Martha, and to Nancy, who is calling herself Julia. For a joke they accept their earnest, but then find themselves forced to follow Plunkett and Lionel, and pledged to a year's work! Sir Tristram tries to protest but is rudely shoved aside. Act II. A room in Plunkett's

La Damnation de Faust *by Hector Berlioz as performed at the Paris Opéra and produced by Maurice Béjart.*

■ This is Flotow's most successful and popular opera and it is still performed. Closely related to the most fluent examples of the *Opéra-Comique*, it has an eclectic style and Franco–Italian influences.

ESMERALDA

Opera in four acts by Alexander Dargomizhsky (1813–69), libretto by the composer, based on a translation of the libretto that Victor Hugo had written in 1836 based on his novel Notre-Dame de Paris *(1831) and intended for the composer L. Bertin. First performance: Moscow, Imperial Theatre, 17 December 1847.*

SYNOPSIS. Medieval Paris is reconstructed in an imaginary atmosphere which is romantic and picturesque. Esmeralda is a reserved young gypsy girl possessed of a rich inner sensibility. She earns her living as a dancer and fortune-teller and lives amongst the worst rabble in the city, lying beggars and tramps, in the district known as Cour des Miracles. All who know her fall automatically in love with her and amongst her lovers are Quasimodo, a deformed hunchback of Herculean strength, and Frollo, a speculator. This latter, who is in a position to blackmail Quasimodo, puts pressure on him to capture Esmeralda. The attempt fails owing to the intervention of Phébus de Châteaupers, a captain of archery. Esmeralda truly loves her rescuer, but for Phébus the whole thing is just an enjoyable adventure. He does however arouse the jealousy of Frollo, who murders him. Esmeralda is

farmhouse. The girls are asked to do the spinning and make the supper, but soon show how unskilled they are. Feelings of attraction begin to grow between Nancy and Plunkett and between Harriet and Lionel. When they are retiring for the night Sir Tristram arrives with his carriage and the two girls escape. Act III. A hunting horn is heard at the inn where Plunkett is drinking with some other farmers. The Queen is passing by with her retinue on horseback. Plunkett goes out to watch and recognizing Nancy tries to approach her, but her friends prevent him. Lionel too recognizes Harriet and goes up to kiss her hand, but she makes a great show of repulsing him, moved by shame at loving a farmer. Lionel wants to exercise his rights as master, but at Harriet's protests he is promptly arrested. Before being taken away he gives Plunkett the ring to be handed over to the Queen. Act IV. Plunkett's house. Harriet and Nancy arrive. Harriet had taken the ring herself to the Queen and Lionel has been restored to his title and possession as the Earl of Derby, of which his father had been unjustly stripped. With some difficulty Harriet succeeds in obtaining forgiveness for treating the young man badly. While Plunkett proposes to Nancy, Harriet offers her heart and hand to Lionel. It all ends with a celebration in Lady Harriet's garden, during which they re-enact the scene of the Richmond market, with the two girls dressed up once more as country girls.

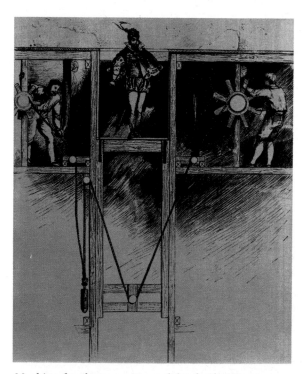

Machine for the apparition of the devil in La Damnation de Faust *by Berlioz. From* Vom Fels zum Meer, *1882.*

Prologue of Verdi's Attila *performed at La Scala during the 1974–75 season; produced by Lamberto Puggelli with sets by Paolo Breghi and costumes by Luisa Spinatelli.*

accused of the murder and, despite the support of the people in the Cour des Miracles, is condemned. Frollo is careful not to exculpate her, but Quasimodo obtains proof of his guilt and murders him by hurling him from a tower of the cathedral. Then he too dies in the criminals' cemetery, clutching the lifeless body of Esmeralda in his arms.

■ This is a mediocre opera, as Dargomizhsky himself realized some twenty years later. However it was the first attempt to use crowd scenes in a Russian opera – an idea adopted later on with great success. But at that time it was the reason why the Imperial Theatre made the composer wait a full eight years before staging the opera, which had in fact been completed in 1839. Dargomizhsky was discouraged and his work for the theatre slowed down. The first performance was not a success and the opera was only repeated on the three successive evenings. After that it was performed sporadically over the next thirty years.

IL CORSARO (The Corsair)
Opera in three acts by Giuseppe Verdi (1813–1901), libretto by Francesco Maria Piave (1810–76), based on the poem by Lord Byron (1788–1824). First performance: Trieste, Teatro Grande, 25 October 1848.

PRINCIPAL PERFORMERS. Marianna Barbieri-Nini, Carolina Rapazzini, Gaetano Fraschini, Achille de Bassini, Giovanni Volpini, Giovanni Petrovitch.

SYNOPSIS. Corrado (tenor) leaves his beloved, Medora (soprano), while he leads an expedition of pirates against the Moslems. In the harem of Seid, Pasha of Coron (baritone), Gulnara (soprano), his favourite wife, is summoned to a feast to celebrate Seid's expected victory over the pirates. Corrado, disguised as a dervish, enters the Turkish camp. The pirates' attack misfires, however, and Corrado is captured. Gulnara has fallen in love with him and, when her pleas for his life have no effect on Seid and when Corrado refuses to kill his captor in his sleep, she stabs Seid herself. Corrado agrees to escape with her, although she now knows that he loves another. Medora, meanwhile, has heard of the abortive attack and is dying. Corrado throws himself into the sea in despair.

■ For a while Verdi had pondered over the parallel between Corrado and Garibaldi and the underlying

Ilva Ligabue and Boris Christoff in Verdi's I Masnadieri *at the Opera, Rome, December 1972.*

theme of patriotism, represented in this case by the war between the Greeks and the Turks. But when he got to know the libretto better, he abandoned the idea. In addition, he was beginning to harbour a deep dislike for the publisher Francesco Lucca, who had commissioned him to write the opera. It was written very hastily while he was in Paris.

LE VAL D'ANDORRE (The Vale of Andorra)

Lyric drama in three acts by Jacques Fromental Elie Halévy (1799–1862), libretto by J. H. Vernoy de Saint-Georges (1801–75). First performance: Paris, Opéra-Comique, 11 November 1848. First performance in U.K.: London, St James's Theatre, 7 January 1850; in U.S.A.: New York, 15 March 1851.

SYNOPSIS. The action, which takes place in the time of Louis XIV, centres round a group of men who are due to enlist in the army. The only way out for those unlucky enough to have been chosen by lot lies in paying a large sum of money to Captain Hilarion. A country girl, Rose, steals some money from a widow, Thérèse, in order to help Stéphane (a hunter with whom she is in love) avoid his military service. A second love affair involves a young peasant, Saturnin, and Giorgette, a wealthy heiress and landowner. Thérèse accuses Rose of theft and the charge is brought before the judges. Thérèse, who has meanwhile discovered Rose to be her own daughter, is condemned to exile for refusing to repeat her charges against the girl. The blow of separation between the women is softened by consolations of an amorous nature. Rose marries Stéphane, while Saturnin finds happiness with Giorgette.

■ In this work Halévy demonstrates again his versatility and his undisputed fascination with 'Grand Opera'.

As usual the action is complicated, as in all Halévy's operas, but the music contains some excellent passages where the melodic style and the harmony are woven over a foundation of delightful musicality. These are the qualities which Hector Berlioz singled out when reviewing the opera for the 'Journal des Débats' on 14 November 1848. He wrote: 'The *Val d'Andorre* at the Opéra-Comique is one of the most generous, spontaneous and heartfelt works that I have ever seen.' The public also gave this opera a warm welcome.

POLIUTO

Opera in three acts by Gaetano Donizetti (1797–1848), libretto by Salvatore Cammarano (1801–52), based on the tragedy by Corneille, Polyeucte *(1640). Posthumous first performance: Naples, Teatro San Carlo, 30 November 1848. First performance in U.K.: London, Covent Garden, 20 April 1852 (as* I Martiri*); in U.S.A.: New Orleans, 24 March 1846 (as* I Martiri*).*

ORIGINAL CAST. C. Baucardé (Poliuto), E. Tadolini (Paolina), F. Colini (Severo), T. Rossi (the Governor Felice), M. Arati (Callistene).

SYNOPSIS. Mytilene, capital of Armenia: 257 A.D. Poliuto (tenor) is to be baptized as a Christian. His wife, Paolina (soprano), suspects his secrecy and follows him to the Christians' hiding place. Nearco (bass), their leader, warns her not to reveal what she now knows lest she may endanger her husband's life. The new proconsul, Severo (baritone), arrives in Mytilene; Paolina is amazed since she only married Poliuto when she had heard Severo was dead. Her father Felice (tenor), the governor of the city, tells Severo of his daughter's marriage. Callistene (bass), high priest of Jove, arranges that Poliuto should overhear the meeting of the two former lovers, when Paolina begs Severo to leave her in peace; only the news of Nearco's capture stops Poliuto taking action against his wife, whom he suspects of betraying him. To save Nearco Poliuto reveals his conversion and, despite Paolina's pleas, he is also arrested. Callistene rejoices in the martyrdom of the Christians. Paolina is so moved by her husband's unshakable faith that she resolves to share his martyrdom.

■ Written in 1838 to be performed at the San Carlo in Naples, the opera was stopped by the Neapolitan censorship on the grounds that the subject matter was 'too sacred'. In Paris, Scribe prepared a French translation with the title *Les Martyrs* and as such it was staged at the Opéra on 10 April 1840. The principal roles were sung by Duprez and Dorus-Gras. *Les Martyrs* was translated into Italian as *I Martiri* and staged in Lisbon on 15 February 1843, and then in other countries. In Italy the translation was published under the title *Paolina e Poliuto* and the German translation which came out in Austria in 1841 was called *Die Römer in Melitone*. The original work had been requested by the French tenor Nourrit, who counted on using the role of Poliuto to regain the admiration of the public, which he

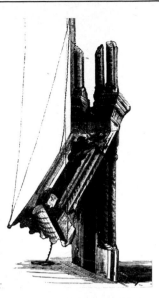

*From the top left:
machine for producing
wind noises, for making
the moon appear, for
making buildings
collapse, for producing
the sound of thunder;
and a cross-section of the
stage seen from behind.*

felt he had lost. The fact that the opera was rejected by the censor affected the already tottering sanity of the tenor, who was never able to sing it. The original version was only performed in public seven months after the death of the composer, and in the same theatre for which it had been written ten years previously. The opera was revived in 1960 at La Scala in Milan with outstanding performances by Maria Callas and Corelli, and was a resounding success.

LA BATTAGLIA DI LEGNANO (The Battle of Legnano)

Opera in four acts by Giuseppe Verdi (1813–1901), with a libretto by Salvatore Cammarano (1801–52). First performance: Rome, Teatro Argentina, 27 January 1849. First performance in U.K.: Cardiff, 31 October 1960.

ORIGINAL CAST. T. de Giuli Borsi, Gaetano Fraschini, Filippo Colini.

SYNOPSIS. Lombardy. Twelfth century during the invasion of Federico Barbarossa. Act I. A league of Lombard towns was formed to meet the enemy and Rolando (baritone) is delighted to meet his old comrade Arrigo (tenor), now the leader of the Veronese, who he had thought had been killed. Lida (soprano), Rolando's wife, and formerly in love with Arrigo, spurns the attentions of Marcovaldo, a German prisoner of war. When Arrigo reproaches her for being unfaithful to him she explains that she was convinced he was dead. Act II. Rolando and Arrigo ask the people of Como to join the League, but the citizens rely on their treaty with Barbarossa (bass), who then appears with a huge army. Act III. Arrigo joins the band of the Death Riders who have sworn to expel the invaders from Italy. Lida writes him a letter declaring her love, which is intercepted by Marcovaldo who, to revenge himself on Lida, hands it to her husband. Rolando, who has meanwhile asked Arrigo to care for Lida and his children if he – as the leader of the Death Riders – should be killed, is furious with jealousy. He surprises them together, but he does not kill Arrigo, who has to leap from the window in order to take part in the battle as a Death Rider. Act IV. Mortally wounded and reconciled to Rolando, Arrigo dies among the rejoicing after the glorious victory over Barbarossa.

■ It is generally considered that *La Battaglia di Legnano* represents a stage in Verdi's progress towards more structured and psychologically complex operas, such as *Luisa Miller*. It is a solid, well-balanced composition, although the subject matter gives rise to a rather grandiloquent and forced tone. The opera was very successful. After it, Verdi retired to Sant'Agata and from then on produced fewer works but employed greater care. Perhaps he was also enraged by the censor, who once again wanted to change place-names and characters. One curious revival occurred in October 1960, when the opera, retitled *The Battle*, was staged in Cardiff and set in the period of Nazi-occupied Italy.

DIE LUSTIGEN WEIBER VON WINDSOR (The Merry Wives of Windsor)

Comic-fantastic opera in three acts by Otto Ehrenfried Nicolai (1810–49), with libretto by S. H. Mosenthal (1821–77) after Shakespeare. First performance: Berlin, Hofoper, 9 March 1849. First performance in U.K.: London, Her Majesty's Theatre, 3 May 1864; in U.S.A.: Philadelphia, 16 March 1863.

SYNOPSIS. Act I. The ageing John Falstaff is simultaneously courting several ladies, who get together to play a trick on him. They invite him to a flirtatious assignation at the home of Mistress Ford (Frau Fluth) while her husband is away. However, they warn the latter by an anonymous letter. He arrives in a rage and the seducer is compelled to seek safety by hiding in a laundry basket. Act II. Not realizing that he is talking to the husband himself, the conceited Falstaff tells him of his adventure-cum-misadventure, increasing the jealousy and suspicion of the man who believes himself to be betrayed. At a second rendezvous, again frustrated by the stormy arrival of Ford (Fluth), Falstaff only escapes with the greatest of difficulty, comically clad in the clothes of an old maidservant. Act III. Mistress Ford lets her husband into the joke she has plotted together with her friends and together they decide to teach Falstaff a harsher lesson. They invite him to meet them in Windsor Forest, where instead of a tender lover he finds a band of elves who chastise him.

■ This is Nicolai's masterpiece. He died very young, a few months after the first performance. The opera, which unites the best elements of German romanticism with Italian tradition, enjoyed a huge success right from its first appearance. Even today it still forms part of the repertoire of many German-speaking theatres on account of its wit, irony and genuine comedy, as well as the freshness of its melodies and its brilliant orchestration.

LE PROPHÈTE (The Prophet)

Opera in four acts by Giacomo Meyerbeer (1791–1864), with a libretto by Eugène Scribe (1791–1861). First performance: Paris, Opéra, 16 April 1849. First performance in U.K.: London, Covent Garden, 24 July 1849; in U.S.A.: New Orleans, 1 April 1850.

ORIGINAL CAST. Pauline Viardot-Garcia, Jeanne Anais Castellan, Gustave Roger.

SYNOPSIS. Holland at the time of the Anabaptists. Act I. Jean of Leyden (tenor) and Berthe (soprano) love each other and ask the Count Oberthal (bass) for consent to their marriage. The latter falls in love with Berthe, withholds his consent and orders her to go to his castle. Berthe obeys, but makes Jean's mother, Fides accompany her. Act II. The Anabaptists, learning of this abuse of power, invite Jean to join them and prophesy that he will be crowned. Berthe manages to

Cover of the vocal score of Verdi's Luisa Miller.

exploited by such outstanding tenors as the Pole Jean de Reszke and the Italians Caruso and Martinelli.

LUISA MILLER

Opera in three acts by Giuseppe Verdi (1813–1901), with a libretto by Salvatore Cammarano (1801–52), drawn from the tragedy Kabale und Liebe *by Friedrich Schiller (1759–1805). First performance: Naples, Teatro San Carlo, 8 December 1849. First performance in U.K.: London, Sadler's Wells Theatre, 3 June 1858; in U.S.A.: Philadelphia, 27 October 1852.*

PRINCIPAL PERFORMERS. Marietta Gazzaniga, Teresa Salandri, Settimio Malvezzi, Achille De Bassini.

SYNOPSIS. The Tyrol, eighteenth century. Act I. Miller (baritone) doubts the honourable intentions of the stranger with whom his daughter Luisa (soprano) has fallen in love. Wurm (bass), whose love has been rejected by Luisa, reveals that the stranger is Rodolfo (tenor) son of the Count of Walter (bass). The Count, when he hears from Wurm about his son's love affair, is furious because he has arranged a marriage for him with Federica (contralto), who is both wealthy and in love with him. Rodolfo is unable to pacify his father and further hurts Federica's pride by explaining his true feelings. Miller then tells his daughter Rodolfo's true identity; when Rodolfo arrives, he admits this but swears to marry Luisa despite his father's opposition. Walter then appears, insults Luisa and arrests the father and daughter. Rodolfo threatens to make known the disreputable way in which his father, with Wurm's aid, had attained nobility and power – a threat which makes Walter order Luisa's immediate release. Act II. Walter and Wurm persuade Luisa to sign a letter in which she declares that she loves Wurm, not Rodolfo, in order to save her father's life, and they compel her to tell this lie to Federica. Rodolfo's reaction to the letter is to challenge Wurm to a duel, but Walter takes the opportunity to obtain his son's agreement to the match with Federica. Act III. On the day of the marriage, Miller, freed from prison, discovers that Luisa plans to commit suicide; he suggests that instead they should leave the country forever. Rodolfo appears and asks Luisa whether she really wrote the letter and, when she confirms this, he offers her a flask, from which he has just drunk, and from which she drinks; in despair, he tells her that it was poison. Luisa then reveals the truth and dies. Rodolfo manages to kill Wurm before himself collapsing dead beside her.

■ Written in 1783 and published in the following year with the title *Luise Millerin*, Schiller's tragedy is a typical cloak and dagger drama. Verdi, who was far from insensitive to such gloomy and dramatic stories, nonetheless succeeded in giving a new, more delicate conception to the character of Luisa, by regarding her with a certain amount of psychological subtlety. This is the reason why the opera is considered Verdi's first mature work. Indeed, at the time it was written it was

escape and tries to rejoin her fiancé, but the Count forces her to return by threatening to kill Fides, who is still in his power. Act III. In the camp of the Anabaptists. The rebels are gathered together with Jean, who has become their prophet, and decide to attack the castle. Oberthal's son is also there, hiding amongst the crowd. He is recognized and about to be put to death when he is saved by Jean, who learns from him that Berthe has escaped again. Fides also manages to escape and she and Berthe curse the Anabaptists for leading her son astray. Berthe swears she will kill their prophet. Act IV. Three Anabaptists betray their prophet, who is now besieged in a castle at Munster. Berthe, on learning that Jean and the prophet are one and the same person, commits suicide. Jean, rather than surrender, sets fire to the gunpowder and blows up the castle, killing himself and Fides, who has pardoned him, and the enemies who had come to capture him.

■ The story is based on a historical episode drawn from the Anabaptist revolt: the coronation in Munster in 1535 of Jan Neuckelszoon, Jean of Leyden in the opera. *Le Prophète*, like other operas by Meyerbeer, revolves around strong theatrical situations and a choral conception that is often realized at the expense of individual characterization. The opera had enormous success up to the beginning of this century and was said to signify the beginning of a second period in the style of the great musician, a new milestone. This judgement was later modified but contains a germ of truth. Luisa Miller is a middle-class heroine and that is undoubtedly a new departure. Moreover, one must remember that the opera was composed in 1849. The hopes and enthusiasms of the great European revolutionaries were largely extinguished, and tyranny was reconsolidating its hold. There is no longer much room for the optimistic impulse which had gripped people and transformed the choruses of Verdi's earlier operas into patriotic symbols. People turned back to feelings of a personal nature, and yet one cannot truly say of Verdi that he turned back. On the contrary, this first delicate and refined treatment of a female character is the master's starting point from which he subsequently focused on the personality of Violetta.

CRISPINO E LA COMARE (Crispino and the Fairy)

Lighthearted melodrama in three acts by Federico (1809–77) and Luigi (1805–59) Ricci, with libretto by Francesco Maria Piave (1810–76). First performance: Venice, Teatro San Benedetto, 28 February 1850. First performance in U.K.: St James's, 17 November 1857; in U.S.A.: New York, 24 October 1865.

ORIGINAL CAST. Carlo Cambaggio (Crispino Tacchetto), Giovannina Pecorini (Annetta), Luigi Rinaldini (Fabrizio), Luigi Ciardi (Mirabolano), Giuseppe Pasi (Contino del Fiore), Angelo Guglielmi (Don Asdrubale), Giovannina Bordoni (Lisetta), Paolina Prinetti (la Comare).

SYNOPSIS. Act I. A square in Venice. While Crispino (buffo), a poor shoemaker, is sitting on a bench outside his shop, Don Asdrubale (bass), the landlord, lies in wait for Annetta (soprano), Crispino's wife, who is unsuccessfully trying to sell newspapers to earn a bit of money. The shoemaker is enraged by Don Asdrubale's arrogance, but remembers his debts to him and runs off in despair with the intention of throwing himself down a well. Annetta manages to disentangle herself from Don Asdrubale's grasp and runs away. Crispino, meanwhile, is just about to jump down the well, when a woman suddenly comes out of the shadows and stops him. She is a fairy (mezzo-soprano) and would like to help Crispino. He will become rich and famous if he pretends to be a doctor. If he does not see her beside the pillow when visiting a patient, the latter will be cured. Amid general merriment Crispino begins his profession. Act II. Bortolo, a builder who has fallen from a roof, is brought into the local pharmacy. Doctor Fabrizio (baritone) has given him up for lost. Crispino, not seeing the fairy, announces that he will recover, and after complicated operations and to the amazement of the onlookers the builder does recover. Act III. A square in Venice with Crispino's house grandly rebuilt. Lisetta (soprano), the niece of Don Asdrubale, falls seriously ill. Crispino intervenes and coming into the room sees the fairy close to Asdrubale. He declares then that Lisetta will recover but that her uncle will die.

The latter soon after suffers a heart attack, whereas Lisetta is cured. But the cobbler inevitably gets carried away by his successes, his reputation and his wealth. One day, as he is quarrelling with his wife, the fairy appears; Crispino chases her away with insults, saying that he no longer needs her help. She hits him on the shoulder and he falls in a faint into a chair, and then tumbles down into an underground room, where she reveals to him that she is Death and that his moment has come. Crispino repents and so moves her with his pleas for pardon that she allows him to return to his family. Soon after Crispino finds himself back, surrounded by his wife and children and some friends, recovering from his strange fainting fit. Seeing how happy Annetta is to see him safe, Crispino promises to change his way of life.

■ *Crispino e la Comare* is certainly the best opera written by the Ricci brothers. Its theatrical merit is probably due to the combination of their qualities: Luigi was imaginative and inventive while Federico made up for a certain lack of inspiration with a great technical ability and a careful style. It is interesting to note that Luigi attributed all the best parts to his brother Federico, and vice versa. The opera is extremely enjoyable and well-balanced both from the point of view of the text and stage action and of the music. The latter is imbued with the characteristic melodic vivacity of the Neapolitan School and is not lacking in genuine harmonic invention and very tasteful instrumentation.

LA TEMPESTA (The Tempest)

Opera in three acts by Jacques Fromental Elie Halévy (1799–1862), with a libretto by Eugène Scribe (1791–1861) translated into Italian by Pietro Giannone from the play by Shakespeare (1611). First performance: London, Her Majesty's Theatre, 8 June 1850.

Machinery for the appearance of the swan in Wagner's Lohengrin, *1882.*

Scene from the 1867 Munich production of Wagner's Lohengrin.

■ The libretto of this opera, which only deals with a part of the Shakespeare play, was originally written to be set to music by Felix Mendelssohn-Bartholdy.

GENOVEVA

Opera in four acts by Robert Schumann (1810–56) with a libretto by Robert Reinick, drawn from the tragedies by Friedrich Hebbel and Ludwig Tieck. First performance: Leipzig, Stadttheater, 25 June 1850. First performance in U.K.: London, Drury Lane, 6 December 1893.

ORIGINAL CAST. Adèle Rémy, M. Vergnet, M. Auguez, Eléonore Blanc, M. Challet.

SYNOPSIS. Act I. Count Siegfried leaves his wife Genoveva in the custody of the faithful Golo while he goes off to join the army of Charles Martel, who is fighting the Saracens. Golo falls in love with her, and taking advantage of a fainting fit, kisses her. Margareta, a witch and Golo's nurse, watches this scene, and in order to gain her revenge for being sent away from the castle, offers to help him woo Genoveva and arouses the hostility of the Court against her. Act II. Golo confesses his love to Genoveva but is firmly rejected. On the advice of Margareta he uses a trick to persuade Drago to enter Genoveva's room secretly.

He tells him that in the bedroom he will find proof that she is betraying Siegfried. Meanwhile Margareta publicly heaps accusations on the girl. The people of the castle, egged on by Golo, go into her room and discover Drago, who is killed, while the supposedly unfaithful wife is dragged off to prison. Act III. In Strassburg. Siegfried is wounded. Margareta rushes off to cure him and then invites him into her hut. There he can watch the past and the future in a magic mirror. He refuses, but Golo arrives to tell him what has happened at the castle and to warn him of his wife's betrayal. To gain proof of this Siegfried looks into the mirror and sees Genoveva holding out her arms to Drago. Full of fury, he breaks the mirror with his fist and rushes off to the castle. Drago's image rises from the splinters of the mirror, threatening Margareta and bidding her to reveal the deceit she has practised. Act IV. Siegfried's men are taking Genoveva into the forest, where she is to be executed. The unhappy lady prays to the Virgin Mary; the wicked Golo still does not give up and tempts her to save her life by running away with him. But Genoveva refuses again. The soldiers are about to kill her when the sound of hunting horns is heard in the forest announcing the arrival of Siegfried. He now knows the truth and hastening to save his wife carries her back in triumph to the castle. Hindulfus, the Bishop of Treves, gives his blessing to the reunited couple.

■ *Genoveva* was the only work that Schumann wrote for the theatre. The choice of libretto was not a happy one. Written by the painter and poet Reinick at the instigation of Schumann himself, it was altered many times by the composer and remains nonetheless a somewhat weak text. The composer had instructed Reinick, when choosing from his two sources, to favour Hebbel's work, adhering especially closely to the dramatic qualities of this text, centred on the figure of the treacherous Golo and his violent passions, whereas the composer's score is at its best when dealing with the tender description of the unlucky heroine. The overture and the duet between Golo and Genoveva are especially memorable amongst the more beautiful passages of the work, but on the whole it is weighed down by an excessive number of scenes and episodes where the apparent but superficial variety is underlaid by a somewhat conventional uniformity. The first performance, which was followed by only two repeat performances, was a great disappointment to Schumann, who had placed great hopes in this composition and believed that it signified a turning-point in his artistic output. After the tragic death of the composer, *Genoveva* had a certain amount of success and was more highly thought of than previously.

LOHENGRIN

Romantic opera in three acts by Richard Wagner (1813–83) with his own libretto. First performance: Weimar, Hoftheater, 28 August 1850. First performance in U.K.: London, Covent Garden, 8 May 1875; in U.S.A.: New York, Stadt Theater, 3 April 1871.

ORIGINAL CAST. Carl Beck, Hoder, Rosa von Milde, Feodor Milde, Fastlinger. Conductor: Franz Liszt.

SYNOPSIS. Antwerp, early tenth century. Act I. King Henry the Fowler of Germany (bass) has come to the city to collect an army to fight the Hungarians who have invaded Germany. He finds that the succession to the dukedom is disputed by Frederick of Telramund (baritone), whose wife is Ortrud (mezzo-soprano), and Elsa (soprano), the daughter of the late duke. Elsa's brother, the rightful heir, has mysteriously disappeared and Frederick and Ortrud accuse Elsa of murdering him to gain the title. The King orders that the truth be determined by single combat between Frederick and a champion of Elsa's cause. No knight comes forward to fight for her, however, and she prays that a dream she has had of a knight protector may come true. Despite the derision of her enemies, at the sound of the herald's trumpets a swan-drawn boat sails down the river, bearing a knight (Lohengrin, tenor) who offers to champion her cause. She promises to wed him if he is victorious and he asks her to swear never to try to find out his name. He defeats Frederick ignominiously. Act II. Although banished, Frederick and Ortrud plot in Antwerp to bring about Elsa's downfall. Ortrud pleads with Elsa for forgiveness and Elsa agrees to do what she can to mitigate their sen-

tence. The wedding procession begins and Elsa is about to enter the cathedral when Ortrud denounces Lohengrin as a black magician. Vehemently, Elsa denies this, but a suspicion has been instilled in her mind, which Frederick's repeated accusations do nothing to allay. Act III. In the bridal chamber, Lohengrin and Elsa sing of their love, but she interrupts the idyll by asking the forbidden question. At this moment Frederick and his henchmen break in, but Lohengrin kills him at one blow and the others flee. Then, in sorrow, he tells Elsa that he must leave her presence when he has answered her question. On the river bank, the King musters the army and the people invite Lohengrin to lead them. He refuses, asking for judgement on his murder of Frederick and telling of Elsa's falseness in breaking her promise. He reveals that he is a Knight of the Holy Grail, and the son of Parsifal, and that having told them this secret he has to return to Monsalvat, where the Grail is kept. He bids Elsa farewell and the swan reappears. Ortrud then announces that the swan is in fact Elsa's brother, transformed by her evil witchery and that if Elsa had kept her oath to Lohengrin, he could have broken the spell on her brother. Lohengrin prays that this may yet be done. The swan is transformed once more into Elsa's brother, the rightful duke, and it is in his arms that Elsa collapses as she watches her husband depart on the boat, now drawn by the white dove of the Holy Grail.

■ The drafting of this opera took Wagner from 1845 to 1848. He drew upon a multitude of sources, but the basic nucleus can be traced back to a poem written towards the mid-thirteenth century by a Thuringian ballad-singer and elaborated a little later by an anonymous poet from Bavaria. Other elements of the drama come from *Parsifal* by Wolfram von Eschenbach, from *The Knight of the Swan* by Konrad von Würzburg and from *Young Titurel* by Albrecht von Scharfenberg, all from the thirteenth century. It has been held that Wagner wanted to portray, in the person of Lohengrin, the solitude of the artist and the lack of understanding he meets in the world around him. Lohengrin, according to the composer's own statement in the *Mitteilung an meine Freunde*, personifies the miraculous and difficult attempts made by the artist to enter the world of humanity. An attempt which demands in return absolute loyalty, like that which was demanded unsuccessfully from Elsa when she was forbidden to learn the origins of her husband. The fluent vocal line of the opera explains its immense popularity especially in Latin countries. In any case it is beyond doubt that *Lohengrin* marks an important step in the progress towards the completion of the reforms that Wagner had been pursuing for some time. There is a very obvious effort to break away from the closed aria, and to arrive at a recitative which, above all in the character of Ortrud, reaches the highest points of expressiveness.

STIFFELIO

Opera in three acts by Giuseppe Verdi (1813–1901)

Wagner's Lohengrin *Act I, in the 1968 Bayreuth Festival production directed by Wieland Wagner.*

with a libretto by Francesco Maria Piave (1810–76) drawn from the play Le Pasteur *by Eugène Bourgeois and Emile Souvestre (1806–54). First performance: Trieste, Teatro Grande, 16 November 1850. First performance in U.S.A.: New York, 4 May 1863.*

ORIGINAL CAST. Marietta Gazzaniga, Gaetano Fraschini, Filippo Colini, Rainieri Dei, Francesco Reduzzi.

SYNOPSIS. The action takes place in the castle of Stankar in Germany at the beginning of the nineteenth century. A Protestant pastor, Stiffelio (tenor), who is being persecuted for his beliefs, takes refuge in the home of Count Stankar (baritone), and marries his daughter Lina (soprano). She is unfaithful to him, during his absence, with a nobleman, Raffaele (tenor). Stankar threatens to kill Raffaele in order to vindicate the family honour, but Stiffelio declares that it is the duty of a good Christian to pardon, and he accepts the repentance of his young wife.

■ The opera had its problems with the censor, who declared it blasphemous, cut out a scene in which Stiffelio quotes the Gospel, and wanted places and names to be changed. Moreover, the public did not like the story, which was later reworked into *Aroldo* (produced in 1857, see p. 229).

L'ENFANT PRODIGUE (The Prodigal Son)

Opera in four acts by Daniel Auber (1782–1871), with a libretto by Eugène Scribe (1791–1861). First performance: Paris, Opéra, 6 December 1850. First performance in U.K.: London, Drury Lane, 19 February 1851; in U.S.A.: New York, 2 June 1851.

■ This is Auber's only opera on a biblical subject. It was performed a number of times in the nineteenth century with moderate success (the libretto was translated into English, Italian and German), but was never performed after the end of the century.

LA DAME DE PIQUE (The Queen of Spades)

Opera in three acts by Jacques Fromental Halévy (1799–1862), with a libretto by Eugène Scribe (1791–1861). First performance: Paris, Opéra-Comique, 28 December 1850.

■ The opera, whose title refers to the well-known story by Pushkin, tells the story of a young man, Hermann, who is obsessed by the idea of seizing from an old lady a secret about a game of cards. After causing the death of the old lady, the young man is haunted by nightmares and goes mad. (See the opera by Tchaikovsky, produced in 1890.)

RIGOLETTO

Opera in three acts by Giuseppe Verdi (1813–1901), libretto by Francesco Maria Piave (1810–76), based on the verse drama Le Roi s'amuse *by Victor Hugo (1832). First performance: Venice, Teatro La Fenice, 11 March 1851. First performance in U.K.: London, Covent Garden, 14 May 1853; in U.S.A.: New York, Academy of Music, 19 February 1855.*

SYNOPSIS. Mantua during the Renaissance. Act I. At the court of Mantua no woman is safe from the lust of the licentious duke (tenor) and no husband from the acid tongue of his hunchback jester Rigoletto (baritone). Rigoletto mocks Ceprano, husband of the duke's latest fancy, to the courtiers' amusement. They are interrupted by a procession taking Count Monterone (bass) to execution because he had bitterly attacked the duke for ravishing his daughter. He curses Rigoletto. The courtier Marullo (tenor) plans to play a joke on the jester by stealing the girl whom Rigoletto keeps locked up in his house and whom everyone supposes to be his mistress. They do not know that the duke has already noticed the girl, who is in reality Rigoletto's daughter, Gilda (soprano), and that he has gained admittance to the house to declare his love. Sparafucile (bass), a professional assassin, accosts Rigoletto, offering his services if he should ever need

them. Gilda does not tell her father about the visit of the Duke, whom she believes to be a student. The courtiers arrive to break into the house and Rigoletto, thinking that they are stealing into Ceprano's palace and not his own, agrees to help them. He puts on a mask, which is actually a blindfold, and waits while the courtiers climb into the house and carry off Gilda. In despair and too late he realizes that he has been tricked, and that Monterone's curse is being fulfilled. Act II. In the Ducal palace the courtiers tell the Duke of their exploit and laugh over their success. He is delighted to find that Gilda is in the palace, while his court mocks Rigoletto, who dares not show his grief too openly. A page requests the Duke's attendance on the Duchess, and meets with the reply that he is occupied. As Rigoletto suddenly guesses where Gilda may be found, the girl herself runs into his arms, distraught and sobbing. Even the courtiers are abashed when they discover that she is his daughter and leave them together. Gilda tries to stop her father from swearing vengeance on the man she still loves, although she now realizes that he has ruined her. Act III. By the riverside, at night. A thunderstorm is beginning. In a disreputable inn, Sparafucile explains to his sister Maddalena (mezzo-soprano) that they are to be paid for the dead body of her next customer who, unknown to her, is the Duke. Outside Gilda and Rigoletto watch their victim arrive and make advances to Maddalena ('*La donna è mobile*'). Gilda now recognizes that her lover fully deserves the fate Rigoletto has planned for him. She agrees to precede him to Verona, travelling in a youth's clothes, where he will join her, fleeing Mantua for ever. Maddalena sends her admirer into the bedroom and argues with her brother about murdering him, for she likes him too well. They resolve to kill their next visitor and substitute one body for another. So when Gilda returns, desperate to save her lover's life, she walks into the trap. Sparafucile puts her almost lifeless corpse in a sack and hands it over to the jester when he comes to savour his revenge. Through the night can be heard the Duke's voice repeating his love song, and Rigoletto knows he has been deceived; in horror he opens the sack and discovers who has been actually assassinated. Gilda revives to beg his forgiveness before she dies, and he then collapses senseless over her corpse. Monterone's curse has been fulfilled.

■ The Venetian censorship would not allow the opera to be performed as it insulted a sovereign ruler. That was indeed the case in Victor Hugo's original, but Verdi transformed Francis I of France into the Duke of Mantua. This was not enough, however. According to the censors, the curse was a wicked deed, the amorous adventures were told in too free a manner, etc. ... Verdi had to rework the libretto completely and spent no small effort in trying to maintain at least the fundamentals of the original stage action. At any rate he managed to put even this experience to good use. He had to devote himself with much greater care to the individual, the protagonist, the intensity of whose dramatic situation becomes the true unifying thread holding the action together. This marks a real step forward as regards the dramatic conception and involves an enormous effort to make the music correspond to the deep turbulent feelings of the jester. This first opera in the 'popular trilogy', followed by *Il Trovatore* and *La Traviata*, oversteps the traditional limits of opera. The protagonist here is no gentleman, but a deformed and grotesque jester, and Verdi had to make the utmost of his psychological aspects, both directly and in contrast with the other commoner in the story, the assassin Sparafucile, just as the study of Gilda's personality is valid in itself and effective in contrast with the Duke of Mantua. As far as the critics were concerned, Verdi's psychology still seemed 'childish' and crude in comparison with the magnificence of Wagner. It was Stravinsky who corrected this judgement and turned it in favour of the Italian composer. He saw 'more genuine inventiveness' in *Rigoletto*. In reality, Verdi tried to go beyond the classical division of opera into arias, recitatives and duets, with the aim of achieving a continuity which only Boito could subsequently give him in his marvellous arrangements of Shakespeare's plays.

SAPHO (Sappho)

Opera in three acts by Charles Gounod (1818–93), libretto by Emile Angier. First performance: Paris, Opéra, 16 April 1851; first performance in U.K.: London, Covent Garden, 9 August 1851.

SYNOPSIS. Ancient Greece. Sapho (mezzo-soprano), taking part in a singing contest for the opening of the Olympic games, is acclaimed by the audience when she wins against Alcée (baritone), a strong rival. Phaon (tenor), the lover of Glycère (soprano), now falls in love with the poetess. The island of Lesbos is ruled by a tyrant, Pithéas, and Phaon instigates a plot to overthrow him. When Glycère discovers this, she threatens Sapho that if she does not give up Phaon, she will give the names of the conspirators to Pithéas. She also warns Phaon that his life is in danger and that he should escape while there is still time. He begs Sapho to accompany him, but she dares not for fear of Glycère, who loses no opportunity to malign her. Phaon curses her inconstancy and takes Glycère away with him. Sapho, in despair, laments her lost love and then throws herself over a precipitous cliff into the sea.

■ In this first opera of Gounod's, the celebrated Pauline Viardot took the role of Sapho at its first performance. The music, although containing passages rich in colour and sensitivity, is on the whole not very dramatic, and the opera had little success when it first appeared. Nonetheless, *Sapho* marks an important moment in Gounod's career. It was, in fact, thanks to his meeting with Viardot that he turned to the theatre and it was no accident that this opera was composed while he and his mother were guests at the singer's farm at Brie. A new edition of *Sapho*, in four acts and with some changes in the score, was performed at the Paris Opéra on 2 April 1884.

LE JUIF ERRANT (The Wandering Jew)

Opera in five acts by Jacques Fromental Elie Halévy (1799–1862), libretto by Eugène Scribe (1791–1861) and Jules Henri Vernoy de Saint Georges (1801–75). First performance: Paris, Opéra, 23 April 1852.

SYNOPSIS. The subject is the legend of the wandering Jew, who was condemned to wander the world forever. In 1190, the Jew (Ashavérus) saved his granddaughter, Irène, from bandits in Flanders and entrusted her to Théodora, a poor ferrywoman. Théodora sets out for Constantinople to return the baby to her father, the Emperor Baudouin. News of his death reached her, however, when she had only reached Bulgaria and she decided to stay there. During those years, Théodora's brother, Léon, becomes increasingly attached to the girl, whom he believes to be his sister. She is kidnapped, taken to Constantinople and is about to be sold into slavery to Nicéphore, the next emperor, when Ashavérus reappears to reveal the truth about her Imperial ancestry. She is proclaimed Empress. The senators demand that she marry Nicéphore, but she refuses because, when she sees Léon and Théodora kneeling before her, she secretly confesses to Léon that she returns his love. Nicéphore then plots to murder Léon, but Ashavérus rescues him; he has a vision of the Last Judgement, before the Angel of Death appears, commanding once again, 'Marche! Marche! Marche toujours!'

■ Halévy here gives full rein to his taste for fanciful opera as he had already done in *La Juive*, although the legendary character of Ashavérus is set within a historical context. Its dominant characteristics are splendid scenic effects, rich orchestration and a highly effective dramatization of the story. This opera did not have the success of *La Juive*, despite a certain similarity in subject matter.

SI J'ÉTAIS ROI (If I Were King)

Opéra comique in three acts by Adolphe Adam (1803–56), libretto by Adolphe Philippe d'Ennery and Jules Brésil. First performance: Paris, Théâtre Lyrique, 4 September 1852. First performance in U.K.: Newcastle, 20 February 1893; in U.S.A.: New York, 29 November 1881.

■ Often presented during the nineteenth century in France, it was also performed in many foreign countries. Today it is almost totally forgotten, but is still occasionally staged in France.

IL TROVATORE (The Troubadour)

Opera in four acts by Giuseppe Verdi (1813–1901), libretto by Salvatore Cammarano (1801–52), based on the Spanish tragedy, El Trovador, *by Antonio García Gutiérrez (1812–84). First performance: Rome, Teatro Apollo, 19 January 1853; first performance in U.K.: London, Covent Garden, 10 May 1855; in U.S.A.: New York, 2 May 1855.*

Title-page of the first edition of the score of Verdi's Rigoletto, *showing the quartet in the last act.*

ORIGINAL CAST. R. Penco (Leonora), Goggi (Azucena), C. Baucardé (Manrico), G. Guicciardi (Count Di Luna).

SYNOPSIS. The action takes place in Spain at the beginning of the fifteenth century. Act I, Scene I. Ferrando (bass), Captain of the Guard commanded by Count Di Luna, tells his men a story. Many years ago, when the Count was still a young child, his brother was thought to be bewitched by an old gypsy. She was hunted down and burnt at the stake, but her daughter, Azucena, exacted a terrible revenge: one night, the brother disappeared and a half-burnt child's skeleton was found on the very spot where the old gypsy had been executed. Scene II. Leonora (soprano), a lady-in-waiting to the Princess of Aragon, is in love with Manrico (tenor), a troubadour who serenades her. Walking in her garden, she hears his voice in the distance and rushes to meet him, only to find Count Di Luna (baritone), who is also in love with her. Manrico appears, the two men defy each other and prepare to fight a duel. Act II, Scene I. The gypsy camp. Manrico, injured in the duel, has been nursed back to health by Azucena (mezzo-soprano), whom he believes to be his mother. Azucena, like Ferrando, returns to the terrible events of the past, but gives a further twist to the story: she did, indeed, steal Di Luna's brother, but in her distress she mistakenly cast her own son onto the flames. In spite of this, she insists that Manrico is still her son. News arrives that Leonora, believing Manrico dead, is about to enter a convent; Manrico rushes off to prevent her. Scene II. Di Luna and his men are already

at the convent and attempt to abduct Leonora. Manrico arrives and rescues her. Act III, Scene I. Di Luna's camp. Azucena has been caught and is questioned by Di Luna. Her identity as the old gypsy's daughter is discovered, and she is sentenced to be burnt at the stake. Scene II. Manrico is about to marry Leonora when news arrives of Azucena's capture; he leaves hurriedly with a rescue party. Act IV, Scene I. Manrico has also been captured by Di Luna and Leonora hears his voice from a prison window against the chant of the *Miserere* for the Dead. She begs Di Luna to save her lover, offering herself in exchange. Di Luna agrees to the bargain, but Leonora secretly takes poison from a ring. Scene II. The prison cell. Manrico tries to comfort Azucena with thoughts of their former life. Leonora arrives to tell Manrico of his freedom, but, guessing the price she has had to pay, he angrily rejects it. The poison soon takes effect, and Leonora dies reconciled to him, in his arms. Di Luna appears and, seeing that he has been tricked, orders Manrico's immediate execution. As the head rolls from the block, Azucena triumphantly announces that Di Luna has killed his own brother: her final words are, 'Mother, you are avenged!' (*Sei vendicata, o madre!*)

■ The second opera in the 'popular trilogy' is without doubt the most conventional from the point of view of the plot; yet it was welcomed by a public well used to gloomy drama. The music is of a very high order, at least in its capacity to dramatize the personalities of the characters. Choruses are used less effectively, having an almost totally decorative function. The libretto was completed by Leone Emanuele Bardare, as Cammarano died suddenly (when still young), leaving largely uncompleted notes. Perhaps it is for this reason that the network of events does not fit well round the figure of the hero; yet despite these defects, Verdi wrote some of his most beautiful music for the troubadour and Leonora, and they are rightly the most famous and celebrated passages in the work. The gypsy's final scene is also extremely effective.

LA TRAVIATA (lit. The Wayward Woman)
Opera in three acts by Giuseppe Verdi (1813–1901), libretto by Francesco Maria Piave (1810–76), based on the novel, La Dame aux Camélias *by Alexandre Dumas the younger (1848). First performance: Venice, Teatro La Fenice, 6 March 1853; first performance in U.K.: London, Her Majesty's Theatre, 24 May 1856; in U.S.A.: New York, Academy of Music, 3 December 1856.*

ORIGINAL CAST. Fanny Salvini Donatelli (Violetta), Lodovico Graziani (Alfredo), Felice Varesi (Germont). Conductor: G. Mares.

SYNOPSIS. Paris, middle of the nineteenth century. Act I. At the home of Violetta Valéry (soprano), a beautiful and celebrated courtesan, a supper party is in progress. Gaston (tenor) introduces his friend, Alfredo Germont (tenor), as the man who came every day

Set of costume designs for Verdi's Rigoletto.

during her recent illness to enquire after her health. Alfredo sings a toast, to which she replies in praise of love. As the guests go off to dance, Violetta collapses in a fit of coughing. She tells them it is nothing, but Alfredo lingers and declares his love for her. She laughs at his ardour, declaring that she has only a few months to live, but she is touched and dismisses him with the injunction that he may return when the camelia she has given him has faded. The guests leave and she remains alone, considering Alfredo's invitation to love, until she resolves to forget him and to continue her present life of feverish gaiety. Act II, Scene I. At Violetta's country house. For several months she has been living in blissful happiness here with Alfredo. Alfredo surprises Annina (mezzo-soprano), the maid, on her return from Paris and she reluctantly tells him that her mistress ordered her to supervise the sale of her property, to pay for the life she is now leading. Alfredo leaves for Paris immediately to stop this. In his absence, Violetta receives a visit from his father, Giorgio Germont (baritone), who tells her

that she is ruining his son and that his liaison is the reason why his daughter cannot be married. He begs her to give him up and tries to make her admit that their love affair cannot last. In despair, she sacrifices herself to Germont's wishes, asking only to be embraced as a daughter and to choose how to break the news to Alfredo. Alfredo returns to find her distracted. She frantically confesses her love for him and leaves. At the moment Alfredo reads the note in which she announces that they must part, his father reappears to offer consolation and to ask him to come home. Angrily rejecting these suggestions, Alfredo notices an invitation for that evening from Flora, one of Violetta's former friends, and he concludes that this is where he will find her. Scene II. At Flora's, gypsies dance and tell fortunes. Violetta arrives on the arm of her former protector, Baron Duphol (baritone), who gambles with and loses to Alfredo. Violetta begs Alfredo to leave, but he forces her to explain her behaviour: in desperation, she says that she no longer loves him. At this, Alfredo calls the guests to witness that he pays his

The Imperial Palace in Halévy's Le Juif errant. *From* Illustrierte Zeitung *of Leipzig, 1852.*

debts in full and throws his winnings in her face. Giorgio Germont, who has followed him to Paris, enters to rebuke and disown his son for such shameful conduct. The Baron challenges Alfredo to a duel. Act III. Violetta's bedroom. Violetta's health has declined and her money is almost spent. She tells Annina to spend half of what little remains on the poor. Then she rereads Giorgio Germont's letter explaining that Alfredo now knows the whole truth and that they will both soon return to ask her forgiveness. '*È tardi*' (too late), she cries. Then Annina runs in excitedly with Alfredo close behind. They sing once more of their love and their future together while Giorgio Germont realizes how much his demands have cost her. Reconciled to both father and son, Violetta dies.

■ A year after its first performance, when *La Traviata* was being performed at the Teatro San Benedetto in Venice, Verdi moved the action back to the seventeenth century to satisfy public preference. This third and last opera of his 'popular trilogy' is one of the richest in psychological insight in the history of Romantic theatre. The opera faithfully reproduces the French novel although changing the names of the main characters. (Violetta, in the novel which Dumas based on a true story, was called Marguérite Gautier, and Alfredo was Armand Duval.) This did not prevent the opera from attracting, alongside its exceptional success, all the criticisms which had already been heaped on the novel: a high-living prostitute who sacrifices herself for love, and who appears to be the victim of society, was not at all in line with contemporary morality, which, at most, could have tolerated her redemption. But Verdi was no longer tempted by the strong tones that an expiation would have demanded. Since *Luisa Miller* he had been attracted to subtle characterization. This new direction shows in the music from the start. The composer does not use the usual overture, but a prelude (and another leading into Act III) which sets the mood of the drama. Once again, as in *Rigoletto*, the main character towers over the others, but in this case it is not only a question of artistic choice, but is also partly autobiographical. Verdi's mistress, Giuseppina Strepponi, was, in fact, seriously ill and the composer, already once widowed, feared deeply for her life. Even the niceties and moral preoccupations of Germont can be compared to the nasty rumours that circulated about Strepponi, who before going to live with Verdi (whom she married after they had lived together for many years), had been the mistress of the singer Moriani, by whom she had had two sons.

L'ÉTOILE DU NORD (The Star of the North)
Opera in three acts by Giacomo Meyerbeer (1791–1864), with a libretto by Eugène Scribe (1791–1861). First performance: Paris, Opéra-Comique,

16 February 1854; first performance in U.K.: London, Covent Garden, 19 July 1855; in U.S.A.: New Orleans, 1 April 1855.

SYNOPSIS. A Russian peasant girl, Katherine, dresses as a man and enlists in her brother's place in the Tsar's army. She takes the opportunity to do a service to the Tsar, Peter the Great, by informing him of a plot that is being hatched against him. The Tsar falls in love with the girl and marries her.

■ In this opera Meyerbeer uses several fragments of an earlier *singspiel*, *Ein Feldlager in Schlesien*, which he had written especially for the soprano Jenny Lind, known as the Swedish Nightingale. This opera-ballet was chosen for the inauguration of the Berlin Royal Theatre on 7 December 1844. The same work was then rewritten and its name changed to *Vielka*. (*L'Etoile du Nord* had its first Italian performance in Milan at the Teatro alla Cannobiana on 30 April 1856.)

ALFONSO UND ESTRELLA
Opera in three acts by Franz Schubert (1797–1828), with a libretto by F. von Schober. First performance: Weimar, 24 June 1854. Composed between September 1821 and February 1822.

SYNOPSIS. Mauregato has unlawfully seized the throne of Troila, who has fled to the mountains with a few loyal subjects and his son Alfonso. The life of the usurper is tormented by the memory of his past misdeeds; his only joy is his daughter, the lovely Estrella. During a hunting expedition she loses her way in the woods and by chance meets Alfonso. The two young people fall in love, but Estrella has a suitor. He is the evil Adolfo, Mauregato's general, who on the strength of his military glory asks for her hand in marriage. He is refused and, incensed at being rejected, plots against the throne. Alfonso returns as liberator and is welcomed as the lawful heir. He can now marry Estrella, while old King Troila magnanimously pardons all past wrongs. Only Adolfo ends up in prison and the opera finishes amidst general rejoicing.

■ The libretto is rather poor. Both the subject matter and the style are conventional, but Schubert was able to clothe the scanty literary merits of the text with marvellous music. Especially in the finale of Act I one can see how perfectly the composer has mastered the drama of the situation. The opera is full of beautiful melodies which anticipate some of the themes of German opera in the following decades.

LES VÊPRES SICILIENNES (The Sicilian Vespers);
performed in Italy as *I Vespri Siciliani*
Opera in five acts by Giuseppe Verdi (1813–1901), with a libretto by Charles Duveyrier and Eugène Scribe (1791–1861). First performance: Paris, Opéra, 13 June

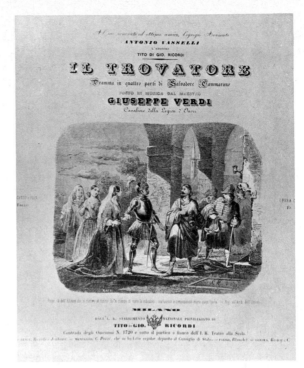

Title-page of the score of Verdi's Il Trovatore. *Milan, 1853.*

1855; first performance in U.K.: London, Drury Lane, 27 July 1859; in U.S.A.: New York, 7 November 1859.

ORIGINAL CAST. S. Cruvelli, L. Guéymard, L. H. Obin, S. Sannier.

SYNOPSIS. Sicily, thirteenth century. Act I. In the great square in Palermo. The French have occupied Sicily. Hélène of Austria (soprano), who has lost a brother when he was executed by the French governor, Montfort (baritone), causes the Sicilians to erupt in a riot which the governor's appearance is, however, enough to quell. She is in love with Henri (tenor), a young Sicilian, who joins her on his release from prison, and proudly refuses Montfort's proposal that he should fight for the French. Act II. Hélène and Henri have met a fanatical Sicilian patriot, Procida (bass), to discuss an uprising. Henri is arrested by Montfort's troops when he insultingly refuses to accept his invitation to a ball. Procida successfully whips up Sicilian hatred of the invaders by arranging for French troops to break up a wedding party. Act III. Montfort discovers that Henri is his own long lost son (by a woman he wronged). On the strength of this, he persuades Henri to attend a masked ball, at which a long ballet (half an hour) is performed, and which Procida and Hélène attend to assassinate the governor. Henri saves his father's life and the rebels are arrested. Act IV. In the fortress where the rebels have been imprisoned. Henri attracts Hélène's pity when he explains his relationship to Montfort; but Procida does not forgive

Pier Luigi Pizzi's sketches for La Traviata, *performed in the Arena at Verona in the summer of 1970.*

him for betraying their cause. Montfort offers to pardon his friend if Henri will address him as father. As the prisoners approach the scaffold, Henri agrees and his wedding to Hélène is announced. Act V. Procida plans to ambush and slaughter guests at the wedding. Hélène refuses to marry Henri when she realizes the inevitable bloodshed, but Montfort brooks no opposition to his arrangements and orders the bells to be rung for the ceremony. The Sicilians launch their attack.

■ Translated into Italian by A. Fusinato and E. Caimi, this opera was performed at the Teatro Ducale in Parma on 26 December 1855 and at La Scala, Milan, on 4 February 1856 under the title *Giovanna di Guzman*. Verdi was not very happy with the original libretto; on the other hand the French theatre did not seem very keen on a score so far removed from the music of Meyerbeer's type, which was then all the rage in Paris. The composer felt especially that the love story was too unrelated to the historical context, and this was not in keeping with his conception of lyric opera where the political and personal themes should be united in the characters' actions. But despite this the opera was exceptionally successful and indeed Verdi received an invitation, which he declined, to settle in Paris.

RUSALKA
Opera in three acts by Alexander Dargomizhsky (1813–69), with the composer's own libretto drawn from the dramatic poem by Alexander Pushkin (1832). First performance: St Petersburg, Imperial Theatre, 16 May 1856; first performance in U.K.: London, Lyceum Theatre, 18 May 1931; in U.S.A.: Seattle, 23 December 1921.

ORIGINAL CAST. Petrov, Bulachova, Leonova.

SYNOPSIS. It tells the story of Natasha, a miller's daughter. She is seduced and abandoned by a prince, who has left her with child. In despair she throws herself into the river Dnepr and is transformed into a *rusalka*, a water-nymph. The miller goes mad and the prince in the meantime marries another. A few years later Natasha sends her little daughter, also a nymph,

Verdi's Il Trovatore Act II, *in the production given at La Scala, Milan, in the 1966/67 season. Scenery by Nicola Benois, directed by Luchino Visconti.*

Verdi's La Traviata *Act II at Covent Garden in London, directed by Luchino Visconti.*

in search of her father. The prince is drawn by an irresistible force towards the river, where the child tells him that her mother has never forgotten him, but loves him still and awaits him. The mad miller arrives and throws the prince into the water.

■ After travelling in Europe in 1844–45, Dargomizhsky decided to write an opera of a national character. However, it took him ten years, perhaps because of his discouragement following *Esmeralda*, or because of the genuine difficulties of staging, or perhaps simply because of his long researches in the field of national folklore. *Rusalka* was performed in 1856 with little success, but nonetheless was occasionally revived, also abroad, and is now firmly in the repertoire of the Soviet Union. In comparison with *Esmeralda*, the composer has further developed a form of melodic recitative, which constitutes the original element in the opera. Pushkin's text is much more closely respected here than in Dvořák's version (produced in 1901, see below).

I PROMESSI SPOSI (The Betrothed)
Opera in three acts by Amilcare Ponchielli (1834–86), with a libretto by Emilio Praga (1839–75). First performance: Cremona, Teatro della Concordia, 30 August 1856; first performance in U.K.: Edinburgh, 23 March 1881.

■ Taken from the novel by Alessandro Manzoni, the opera was written in 1855. It had a reasonable success, which did not however cross provincial boundaries. The triumph of Petrella's *I Promessi Sposi* in 1869 encouraged Ponchielli to revise his own youthful opera of the same name. He was helped and assured of success by the more authoritative libretto of Emilio Praga. The revised version was performed in Milan, at the Teatro dal Verme, on 5 December 1872, and was so well liked that the publisher Ricordi commissioned Ponchielli to write another, this time for La Scala. It was to be *I Lituani* (1874), with a text by A. Ghislanzoni.

TUTTI IN MASCHERA (All in Masks)
Opera in three acts by Carlo Pedrotti (1817–93), with a libretto by Marco Marcelliano Marcello inspired by Carlo Goldoni's comedy L'impresario delle Smirne. First performance: Verona, Teatro Nuovo, 4 November 1856.

SYNOPSIS. Abdalà, a rich Turkish impresario passing through Venice, wants to take a group of musicians from the Fenice with him to Damascus. Vittoria, the company's leading lady, is the only one reluctant to accept the offer because she does not want to leave her lover, the Cavaliere Emilio. But when another singer, Dorotea, through a misunderstanding, accuses her of being her rival in the affections of Don Gregorio, whom Dorotea herself loves, Vittoria declares herself ready to go, to Emilio's dismay. But he has discovered

a note in which Abdalà has invited an unknown lady to meet him at a masked ball at the Fenice. Emilio, fearing that the unknown lady may be Vittoria, decides to attend the ball dressed as a Turk, hoping to be taken for Abdalà. Vittoria falls into the trap and thinking that she is talking to the wealthy impresario, begs him to release her from the contract since her one desire is to stay with Emilio, whom she truly loves. Thus the two lovers make their peace and the company leaves for Damascus without Vittoria.

■ Amongst Pedrotti's many operas in a light-hearted vein, this one was unanimously considered his best and was performed many times at the Athénée in Paris under the title *Les Masques*. It includes many effective passages, both comic and spectacular. An instance of its humour is the moment when Don Gregorio announces pompously his departure for Damascus, where his talent and his skill will at last find their true reward. Spectacular effects include the masked ball and the festival chorus of the carnival.

SIMON BOCCANEGRA
Opera in a prologue and three acts by Giuseppe Verdi (1813–1901), with a libretto by Francesco Maria Piave (1810–76), based on the play by Antonio García Gutiérez (1812–84). First performance: Venice, Teatro La Fenice, 12 March 1857; first performance in U.K.: London, Sadler's Wells Theatre, 27 October 1948; in U.S.A.: New York, Metropolitan Opera House, 28 January 1932.

ORIGINAL CAST. Leone Giraldoni (Boccanegra).

SYNOPSIS. Genoa, in the fourteenth century. Prologue. Two plebeians, Paolo (baritone) and Pietro (bass) agree to support Simon Boccanegra (baritone), a popular naval hero, in his bid for the dogeship of the city, an office traditionally held by aristocrats, one of whom, Fiesco (bass), is Doge at present. Fiesco is mourning the death of his child, Maria, who loved Boccanegra and had borne him a daughter. The child has disappeared. Fiesco hates Boccanegra for what he did to Maria and swears that only the re-appearance of his granddaughter will soften his enmity. Boccanegra is acclaimed as Doge by the citizens. Act I, Scene I. Twenty-five years later. Boccanegra's daughter Amelia (soprano) has been brought up, believing herself an orphan, by the patrician enemies of Boccanegra, among whom is Fiesco, who has assumed the name of Andrea. She has fallen in love with Gabriele Adorno (tenor). Boccanegra, while trying to persuade her to marry his supporter Paolo, rapturously discovers her identity. He naturally wishes to please her and accepts her refusal of the marriage. Paolo and Pietro resolve to kidnap her. Scene II. A meeting of the Council, over which the Doge presides, is interrupted by a riot caused by Adorno's murder of an unidentified plebeian who had tried to abduct Amelia and whose last words had seemed to implicate the Doge. Adorno is only prevented from knifing Boccanegra by Amelia's

The soprano Montserrat Caballé in Les vêpres siciliennes *at the Metropolitan Opera House, New York, in 1974.*

intervention. Boccanegra calls for peace between the warring factions ('*Piango su voi, sul placido raggio del vostro olivo*') and leads a chorus in which Paolo has to join, cursing those who organized the kidnap. Act II. Paolo tries to blackmail Fiesco (still unrecognized under his assumed name) and Adorno into poisoning the Doge. They indignantly refuse to behave so basely, although Adorno easily believes that Boccanegra has seduced Amelia. Amelia fails to convince him that this is untrue and once again shields her father from her lover's attack. When Adorno discovers their true relationship he is mortified; the Doge offers him Amelia as his bride. Adorno, who realizes that Paolo has now carried out his threat to poison the Doge, swears to suppress the patricians' rebellion which has just broken out. Act III. The disturbance has been put down and Paolo sentenced to death for treason. Boccanegra begins to feel the effect of the poison and reflects on the carefree happiness of his life at sea. When Fiesco takes the opportunity to announce his true identity and to take revenge, Boccanegra reveals that Amelia is the granddaughter who can reconcile them. He dies, to be succeeded as Doge by his new son-in-law, the patrician Adorno.

■ As Piave's libretto was not very successful, Verdi asked Boito many years later to rewrite it. However, this former Bohemian from Milan did not succeed greatly in improving the story, which is in itself mediocre. The new version was put on at La Scala on 24 March 1881. Actually the original libretto was more Verdi's doing than Piave's. The composer had forwarded a rough copy in prose to the Fenice in August 1857. Piave's only task was to turn it all into verse. The score is decidedly better. In the character of Boccanegra the composer has succeeded in conveying the drama of a man of passionate feelings who suffers because of the fickleness of the people. Boccanegra has to endure both betrayal and insults to his conduct, which he sincerely believes is of the purest integrity. He is capable, thanks to his intrinsic honesty, of reappraising and changing his opinions, but this does not help him avoid an unjust fate. It was difficult to create a character so unswerving who is yet buffeted by constant changes of mood. Nonetheless, Verdi has succeeded in creating in him one of his most effective characters and in portraying the suffering of his humane spirit.

AROLDO

Opera in four acts by Giuseppe Verdi (1813–1901), with a libretto by Francesco Maria Piave (1810–76), remodelling Stiffelio *(1850). First performance: Rimini, Teatro Nuovo, 16 August 1857.*

ORIGINAL CAST. Marcellina Lotti, Giovanni Pancani, Carlo Poggiali, Giovanni Battista Cornago, Gaetano Ferri. Conductor: Angelo Mariani.

SYNOPSIS. The action takes place in 1200. Aroldo, a Saxon knight (tenor), returns from a crusade and is angry because his wife Mina (soprano) no longer wears the ring he gave her. While her husband was away, Mina had been the mistress of a roving knight, Godvino (tenor), who had been a guest of her father Egberto (baritone). The hermit Briano (bass), Aroldo's friend, tells him of the deceit. Aroldo goes off to be a hermit. The years pass and a storm shipwrecks Mina and Egberto near the hermitage. Aroldo and his wife recognize each other, she begs his forgiveness. The old crusader pardons her and they return to live together again.

■ Verdi had often thought of rewriting *Stiffelio*, much of whose music he felt he could put to better use. Piave insisted that the rebel priest of the earlier work should become a crusader, but Verdi did not at first agree. However, he finally admitted that the poet was right. During the final rehearsals Verdi found the conductor Mariani worried that the orchestral musicians were not, according to him, playing the storm scene well. Verdi defended them saying that the scene itself was at fault and rewrote the music in one night. Then everyone was satisfied.

LE MÉDECIN MALGRÉ LUI (The Doctor in spite of himself)
Opéra comique *in three acts by Charles Gounod (1818–93), with a libretto by Jules Barbier (1825–1901) and Michel Carré (1819–72) taken from the comedy by Molière (1666). First performance: Paris, Théâtre-Lyrique, 15 January 1858; first performance in U.K.: London, Covent Garden, 27 February 1865; in the U.S.A.: Cincinnati, 20 March 1900.*

SYNOPSIS. Sganarelle, a woodcutter and doctor's assistant, is quarrelling with his wife, Martine, and beats her soundly. Then he takes to the bottle while she plans to play a trick on him in revenge. When a servant of their wealthy neighbour, Géronte, comes to look for a doctor in order to ask him to attend Géronte's daughter, Lucinde, who has been suddenly struck dumb, Martine informs him that Sganarelle is just the doctor he needs. He is eccentric, she says, and needs a beating before he will work. So the servant thrashes the drunken woodcutter until he agrees to visit Lucinde. Her lover, Léandre, then explains to the audience that Lucinde is only pretending to be dumb to avoid being married off by her father to a rich suitor. Sganarelle appears in a doctor's outfit and at first shows more interest in Jacqueline, the maid, than in Lucinde. He impresses Géronte with a hilarious display of nonsense Latin and quickly diagnosing that Lucinde's dumbness is caused by an impediment of the tongue. Soon his reputation attracts all the neighbours, including Léandre, who asks his assistance in persuading Géronte to accept him as a son-in-law. Sganarelle passes him off as his apothecary and Géronte is amazed that when he has taken Lucinde's pulse-rate, she suddenly begins to speak. He soon begs Sganarelle to stop the interminable flow, however, because she only says that she wants to marry Léandre. Lucinde and Léandre elope and Sganarelle narrowly avoids execution for his part in her abduction when news comes that Léandre's rich uncle has died, bequeathing enough to make him most acceptable to Géronte. Sganarelle forgives his wife but instructs her to treat him – a doctor – with more respect in future.

■ Gounod tastefully reproduced in this opera the customs of the seventeenth century. There are many good moments in the score, such as the duet between Sganarelle and Martine or the sextet during the consultation, and some ingenious musical tricks such as Sganarelle's 'couplets de la bouteille'. Here the sonorous, imitative effect is made by a sustained rhythmic device played on horns, bassoons, clarinets and flutes. The opera established Gounod's position as a composer for the theatre and was received with a fair amount of interest in London, where it was performed with the title 'The Mock Doctor'.

IONE, or L'ULTIMO GIORNO DI POMPEI (Ione, or The Last Days of Pompei)
Opera in four acts by Errico Petrella (1813–77), with a libretto by Giovanni Peruzzini based on the novel by E. G. Bulwer Lytton. First performance: Milan, Teatro alla Scala, 28 January 1858; first performance in U.K.: London, Bijou Theatre, 28 June 1876; in U.S.A.: New York, 6 April 1836.

ORIGINAL CAST. Albertini-Boucardé, Carmelina Poch, Ricciardi, Carlo Negrini. Conductor: Cavallini.

SYNOPSIS. Pompei, A.D. 79. Ione (soprano) loves Glauco (tenor), a rich Greek, but she is loved by the Egyptian Arbace, high priest of Isis, who plots with the inn-keeper Burbo, to steal her from Glauco. Burbo knows that Ione's young Thessalian slave, Nidia, is secretly in love with Glauco and tells her that he can give Glauco a love potion to make him forget Ione and fall in love with her. Unfortunately the potion has the different effect of depriving Glauco of his senses: Ione begs Arbace for assistance and prays to Isis. Arbace takes advantage of the situation to try to seduce her. They are observed by Nidia, who, wanting to put right the wrong she has unintentionally committed, calls Glauco, and he, mad with jealousy, tries to murder the priest. He is condemned to the arenas for sacrilege. He is pardoned, however, while the first tremors of an earthquake begin, and Vesuvius erupts. Glauco and Ione run to the sea to save themselves while Nidia, in despair that her love is not reciprocated, remains behind to die.

■ The first performance of *Ione* at La Scala was a complete fiasco. Several unfortunate circumstances contributed to this, such as the hasty staging by the impresario Marzi. The costumes were second-rate and the scenery appalling. The eruption of Vesuvius was portrayed by a few fireworks let off in the wings. On 10 July of the same year *Ione* was put on at Padua. For this performance the famous funeral march had to be abandoned because the band who were meant to play it had left for the battle-field. Nonetheless, the public accorded Petrella a real triumph. However, a performance on 9 November 1858 at the Teatro San Carlo in Naples was again a huge failure.

First scene of Verdi's Simon Boccanegra *Act I, staged at La Scala, Milan, in the 1975/76 season; designed by Ezio Frigerio and directed by Giorgio Strehler.*

ORPHÉE AUX ENFERS (Orpheus in the Underworld)

Opéra-Féerie in four acts by Jacques Offenbach (1819–80), with a libretto by Hector Crémieux and Ludovic Halévy (1833–1908), reworked by the authors in four acts in 1874. First performance: Paris, Bouffes-Parisiens, 21 October 1858; first performance in U.K.: London, Haymarket Theatre, 26 December 1865; in U.S.A.: New York, March 1861.

SYNOPSIS. This is a comic-satiric version of the myth of Orpheus and Eurydice. Orphée is a violin-teacher and Eurydice is no paragon of fidelity. Amongst her admirers is Pluton, who disguises himself as Aristée, a manufacturer of honey, and Jupiter, who changes into a fly in order to pass through a keyhole to be near her. When Eurydice dies, Orphée, who loathed her, is compelled to behave like the legend and to fetch her back from the underworld. There Orphée sees all sorts of strange things – gods doing the cancan, defying Jove by singing the *Marseillaise* and dancing a minuet. He is about to leave with Eurydice when Jupiter gives him a hefty kick that makes him turn round. She is lost to him forever, to his delight, and is enthusiastically welcomed back to the underworld with a wild bacchanale.

■ The opera was badly received on the first night, but the critics' outrage at the parody of classical legend, and of Gluck's *Orfeo e Euridice*, attracted attention. As a result, it quickly became a huge success. A revival, fifteen years later, was also very successful: the disillusioned society of the Second Empire, aware of the fragility of the régime, were avid for amusement and to laugh at themselves. While in the drawing rooms real or presumed allusions to people and situations were sought in the plot, in the street the most popular tunes such as the cancan and the *galop* were sung. The rhythm of the latter seemed 'to express in a whirl the entire century, government, institutions, customs and laws' (Sarcey). The excellent collaboration of Offenbach and the librettists Crémieux and Halévy thus launched a popular new musical genre, the operetta, which brought characters and musical styles 'down to earth', while Grand Opera in France was in decline.

DER BARBIER VON BAGDAD (The Barber of Bagdad)

Opera in two acts by Peter Cornelius (1824–74), with his own libretto drawn from the 'Thousand and One Nights', a plot already used in two singpiels *by G. André (1780) and Hattasch (1793). First performance: Weimar, Hoftheater, 15 December 1858. Conductor: Franz Liszt. First performance in U.K.: London, Savoy Theatre, 9 December 1891; in U.S.A.: New York, Metropolitan Opera House, 3 January 1890.*

SYNOPSIS. The young Nureddin (tenor) is love-sick for Margiana (soprano), daughter of the Cadi. His childhood friend, Bostana (mezzo-soprano), promises to arrange a meeting for him with her, on condition that he calls her favourite barber for the occasion, the talkative Abul Hassan (bass). He detains Nureddin with incessant gossip, but at last the young man manages to get away to keep his assignation. Abul follows him secretly to the Cadi's house. The lovers are interrupted by the unexpectedly early return of the Cadi (tenor) from the mosque. Nureddin hides in a chest. Abul fears that the young man has been killed and makes a terrific din, calling the Caliph (baritone) to come and investigate in person. Nureddin is found in the chest and the Cadi has to give way to pressure from the Caliph. So the two young people obtain consent to marry, while the Caliph, entranced by Abul's amazing stories, takes him into his service.

■ This was Cornelius's first opera. His friend Liszt, who held the post of theatrical conductor, had it performed at Court. But owing to a series of intrigues and boycotts it was not a success and had to be withdrawn. It was for this reason that Liszt had to give up his post. It was never again performed during the composer's lifetime, but on 11 February 1884 at Karlsruhe *Der Barbier von Bagdad* was revived, reorchestrated by Felix Mottl and then became quite popular. It was again revived in 1925 at the Metropolitan Opera House in New York. It is very vivacious and is considered one of the best nineteenth-century German comedies after Wagner's *Meistersinger von Nürnberg*. There is a noteworthy intermezzo based on the muezzin calling the faithful to prayer.

UN BALLO IN MASCHERA (A Masked Ball)

Opera in three acts by Giuseppe Verdi (1813–1901), with a libretto by Antonio Somma (1809–65), inspired by Gustave III, ou Le Bal Masqué *by Eugène Scribe (1791–1861). First performance: Rome, Teatro Apollo, 17 February 1859; first performance in U.K.: London, Lyceum Theatre, 15 June 1861; in U.S.A.: New York, Academy of Music, 11 February 1861.*

ORIGINAL CAST. Eugenia Julienne-Déjean, Zelinda Sbriscia, Leone Giraldoni, Gaetano Fraschini, P. Scotti. Conductor: E. Terziani.

SYNOPSIS. Boston during the last years of the seventeenth century. Act I. Riccardo of Warwick (tenor), Governor of Boston, is giving an audience to his ministers and officials. Among those present are Samuel (bass) and Tom (bass), who are plotting to kill him. He receives a list from his page Oscar (soprano) of those invited to the next grand masked ball. Amelia (soprano), wife of Renato (baritone), Riccardo's faithful secretary, is amongst the list of guests. Riccardo nurtures a secret love for Amelia, which causes him much grief since she is the wife of his most trusted friend, who is just now all the dearer to him for uncovering the plot against his life. Meanwhile a judge (tenor) arrives with an order for the expulsion of the black woman Ulrica (contralto), who is accused of witchcraft. Oscar, the page, defends her and Riccardo, who would like to know the truth, goes to visit her disguised as a sailor. When they arrive at the witch's hovel, Ulrica is predicting honour and riches to the sailor Silvano (bass). A

Some caricatures of Verdi by M. Delfico: the selection of singers, studying a new score, rehearsals for Simon Boccanegra, *Verdi chasing away the hecklers.*

servant tells her quietly that Amelia is on her way, and the woman asks them all to leave so that she can welcome the girl alone. Amelia asks for a cure for a love which is frightening her. Ulrica says she could make such a potion from a herb that grows near a scaffold and which is picked at night. Riccardo has overheard. Ulrica predicts that he will die at the hand of a friend, the first one to shake his hand. Those present mock the prophecy, but no one wants to shake Riccardo's hand. Renato arrives, however, and shakes his hand in a joyful and spontaneous way, knowing nothing of the prediction. Act II. Amelia has come to the field near the scaffold where the herb grows. Riccardo finds her and they declare their mutual love and sadness. At the sound of footsteps Amelia veils herself. Renato appears and tells Riccardo that the plotters are nearby, waiting to murder him. Riccardo escapes in time but the plotters try to tear the veil off the girl. Amelia shows her face to avoid a fight. The plotters are highly amused and Renato is in despair at the betrayal. Act III. Amelia begs in vain to be pardoned. Sure that a

sad end awaits her, she gives her little son a final kiss. Renato joins the conspiracy to kill Riccardo. They draw lots to decide who will kill Renato. Amelia picks the fatal paper, on which Renato's name is written. Oscar brings the invitation to the ball. Amelia hands him an anonymous note for Riccardo, putting him on his guard and telling him to flee. Meanwhile Renato discovers from Oscar what costume his victim will be wearing, and during the ball he stabs him. The other guests try to kill the murderer, but Riccardo speaks up for him, confessing his own guilty love and clearing Amelia completely. He grants Renato promotion and an order to transfer to England, pardons those implicated in the conspiracy and dies.

■ Scribe's play had as its protagonist not an American governor, but a Swedish king, Gustavus III. In the original draft the libretto had kept the characters just as the French writer had portrayed them. But the censorship intervened heavily, forbidding attacks on rulers. First there was the Bourbon censorship in Naples, then the Papal censorship in Rome. The Vatican did not perhaps have the problem of a ruler as such, but it certainly did not like a story dealing with a Catholic monarch such as the King of Sweden. Faced with the Neapolitan censorship, Verdi reacted firmly. Faced with the Papal censorship, he consented to change the scene from Stockholm to Boston and to change the King to the Count of Warwick, Governor of Boston. The first complete, uncensored performance took place much later, in 1958 at the Paris Opéra. Verdi took great care over the libretto and came to regard it as partly his own. He used the plot to capture elegance and nobility of feeling even in tragedy and passion. And for the first time he felt some interest in humour, which was later going to burst forth in his old age with *Falstaff*. His concern for the setting 'coincides', according to Mila, 'with a very great concern for the instrumentation and ever-deepening interest in melodic recitative'.

FAUST

Opera in five acts by Charles Gounod (1818–93), with a libretto by Jules Barbier (1825–1901) and Michel Carré (1819–72), from Faust *by Goethe. First performance: Paris, Théâtre-Lyrique, 19 March 1859; first performance in U.K.: London, Her Majesty's Theatre, 11 June 1863; in U.S.A.: Philadelphia, 18 November 1863.*

ORIGINAL CAST. Caroline Miolan-Carvalho (Marguérite), Barbot (Faust), Reynald (Valentin), Balanqué (Méphistophélès). Conductor: Deloffre.

SYNOPSIS. Act I. Faust's study. Now an old man, Faust (tenor) thinks back sadly of his solitary life deprived of youth and love. He is about to take poison when he is distracted by the sound of girls' singing in the street. Using magic formulae, he calls up the devil and Méphistophélès (bass) appears, dressed as a knight, to offer Faust youth and pleasure in exchange for his soul. When Faust hesitates, Méphistophélès shows him a vision of a beautiful girl, Marguérite (soprano), and Faust signs the pact. Transformed into a handsome knight, he leaves with Méphistophélès in search of pleasure. Act II. A market place on a holiday (*Kermesse*). Valentin (baritone), Marguérite's brother, is off to war and entrusts his sister to Siebel (mezzo-soprano), a student who is in love with her. Méphistophélès arrives and interrupts Wagner (bass), who is giving a toast, by predicting his death in battle, that any flower picked by Siebel will wither, and Valentin's death at the hand of a man he knows. He withdraws when the youths cross their swords in front of him. When Marguérite approaches, Faust asks her permission to accompany her home, while Siebel is kept at a distance by Méphistophélès. The girl modestly refuses and goes off alone, but Méphistophélès assures Faust that she will be his. Act III. Marguérite's garden. Siebel picks flowers for Marguérite, but they shrivel in his hand, as the devil had predicted. By sprinkling them with holy water he revives them, however, and places a bunch near the porch. Méphistophélès and Faust arrive with a casket of jewels with which he replaces Siebel's humble gift. Marguérite returns and thinks over the strange events of the *Kermesse* as she spins, singing an old ballad. She notices Siebel's flowers and then the casket, which entrances her. Decking herself in the jewels she admires herself and shows them to her neighbour Marthe (mezzosoprano). Faust and Méphistophélès reappear and while the latter successfully courts Marthe, Faust declares his love for Marguérite. After they have parted Marguérite opens the casement, thinking herself alone, and calls to Faust to return quickly. Méphistophélès laughs as Faust rushes to answer her prayer and they fall into each other's arms. Act IV. In a church. Méphistophélès prevents Marguérite, now pregnant with Faust's child, from praying and predicts eternal damnation for her. To the soldiers' chorus, Valentin returns and hears Méphistophélès singing a mocking serenade to Marguérite. He smashes the guitar and turns on Faust with a sword: in the duel, he is killed by a thrust directed by Méphistophélès. Act V. Walpurgis Night on the Brocken and the Harz Mountains. Méphistophélès shows Faust a wild orgy in which the most famous courtesans of history take part. Faust demands to be taken back to Marguérite. He finds her in prison awaiting execution for the murder of her son during a fit of the madness to which she has now succumbed. He tries to persuade her to escape with him, but she recoils from the devil and, calling for Divine mercy, dies. A choir of angels accompanies her soul to Heaven while Faust kneels and prays.

■ The opera, inspired by Goethe's play, centres round the person of Marguérite and is sometimes performed in Germany under the title *Margarethe*. From 1839, when he was in Rome, Gounod had made clear his intention of setting *Faust* to music and over the next twenty years wrote those themes that the various episodes of Faust suggested to him. In 1857 Barbier took on the task of writing the libretto together with Carré, who had already written a 'fantasy-drama' on Faust, which Gounod had seen performed at the *Gymnase* in 1850. While it was being sketched out, however, the director of the Opéra-Comique and the artists of the Lyrique demanded various cuts. Gounod has written some of his best music in this opera, expressing the tenderness and the sufferings felt by Marguérite's delicate soul. Amongst the most beautiful moments are Faust's meeting with her and the ballad of the King of Thule. *Faust* was very well received by the public, and following this success Gounod transformed it from an 'opéra-comique' into a Grand Opera, as he had always intended it and as it stands today, introducing recitatives instead of spoken passages, which were in use at the Théâtre-Lyrique. For a London performance in 1864 Valentin's prayer was inserted into the prelude and in 1869 the ballet was added to Act V. Other parts, such as the soldiers' chorus, had been written for the unfinished *Ivan the Terrible*, while the theme for Marguérite's prayer to Heaven derives from the *Dies Irae* of a *Requiem* written in 1842.

J. Chéret's poster for Offenbach's Orphée aux enfers, *1858. Paris, Bibliothèque de l'Opéra.*

DINORAH, or LE PARDON DE PLOËRMEL

Opera in three acts by Giacomo Meyerbeer (1791–1864), with a libretto by Jules Barbier (1825–1901) and Michel Carré (1819–72). First performance: Paris, Opéra-Comique, 4 April 1859; first performance in U.K.: London, Covent Garden, 26 July 1859; in U.S.A.: New Orleans, 4 March 1861.

ORIGINAL CAST. M. J. Cabel, J. B. Faure, C. L. Sainte-Foy, Bareille, V. A. Warot.

SYNOPSIS. Brittany. Dinorah (soprano), mad with grief at being deserted on her wedding day, wanders in the countryside in search of her lover, the goatherd Hoël (baritone). She falls asleep in the cottage where Corentin lives. Hoël tells Corentin (tenor) how a terrible storm had destroyed his home on the day of his wedding and that, because he had not wanted to force a life of hardship on his bride, he had set off to look for a treasure of which he had been told by a sorcerer. Corentin joins in the search. Since the elves who guard the hoard will kill anyone who tries to steal it, neither of them wants to be the first to touch it. When Dinorah appears and Hoël runs away imagining that she is a ghost, Corentin tries to persuade her to touch the treasure. She faints, however, and Hoël is in time to revive her. The sudden shock of recognition has the fortunate effect of obliterating from her mind the memory of her desertion and of the year of separation that has passed. Hoël hastens to convince her that nothing has happened and resolves to abandon the treasure. The happy couple make their way back to the church at Ploërmel for their postponed wedding.

■ Although *Dinorah*, earlier entitled *Le Pardon de Ploërmel*, does not have the historical character which was most congenial to Meyerbeer, he wrote it with taste and elegance, and reinforced the somewhat fragile libretto and musical structure with haunting arias rich in charm, such as *Dors, petite, dors tranquille* in Act I, and the famous *Shadows Aria* of Act II.

RITA, or LE MARI BATTU (Rita, or The Beaten Husband)

Opéra-comique in one act by Gaetano Donizetti (1794–1848), with a libretto by Gustave Vaëz. First performance posthumously: Paris, Opéra-Comique, 7 May 1860; first performance in U.S.A.: New York, Hunter College, 14 May 1957.

ORIGINAL CAST. Warot (Beppe), Barielle (Gasparo), Caroline Faure-Lefebvre (Rita).

SYNOPSIS. Rita (soprano), landlady of a Swiss inn, married a sailor called Gasparo (baritone), who beat her on the day of their wedding, deserted her and fled to Canada. When she heard that he had been shipwrecked, she married Beppe (tenor), who is now the one to be beaten. Gasparo returns to check on a rumour that Rita has died and Beppe seizes the opportunity to try to get out of his marriage. They draw straws to decide who is to take her, for Gasparo wants to marry a Canadian girl. Then Gasparo tears up his marriage contract, advises Beppe on how to beat wives and leaves Rita to enjoy new-found domestic harmony.

■ The opera was composed in 1841 and is also known as *Deux hommes et une femme* (Two Men and a Woman). It had a less rapturous welcome than Donizetti's better-known works. In Italy it was only performed once in 1876 in Naples.

BÉATRICE ET BÉNÉDICT

Opera in two acts by Hector Berlioz (1803–69), with a libretto by the composer, based on Shakespeare's play Much Ado About Nothing. *First performance: Baden-Baden, Théâtre Bénazet, 9 August 1862; first performance in U.K.: Glasgow, 24 March 1936; in U.S.A.: New York, Carnegie Hall, 21 March 1960.*

■ *Béatrice et Bénédict* is closely related to the Italian comic opera, and was Berlioz's last work. It was immediately a resounding success. The libretto was soon translated into German. The opera is not part of the normal Berlioz repertoire either in France, where it was first performed, at the Opéra-Comique, on 4 June 1890, or in other countries.

LA FORZA DEL DESTINO (The Force of Destiny)

Opera in four acts by Giuseppe Verdi (1813–1901), with a libretto by Francesco Maria Piave (1810–76), based on Don Alvaro o la Fuerza del Sino *by Angel de Saavedra, Duke of Rivas (1791–1865). First performance: St Petersburg, Imperial Theatre, 10 November 1862; first performance in U.K.: London, Her Majesty's Theatre, 22 June 1867; in U.S.A.: New York Academy of Music, 24 February 1865.*

ORIGINAL CAST. C. Barbot, C. Nantier-Didiée, E. Tamberlick. L. Graziani, A. De Bassini, G. F. Angelini.

SYNOPSIS. Spain and Italy in the eighteenth century. Act I. Don Alvaro (tenor) loves Donna Leonora di Vargas (soprano), daughter of the Marquis of Calatrava (bass). The Marquis has forbidden the marriage of

Scene from Verdi's Un ballo in maschera, *performed at the Teatro San Carlo in Naples, 1859.*

his daughter to a half-caste, so the lovers have decided to elope. Their escape is unsuccessful and although Alvaro protests Leonora's innocence, the old man does not believe him. Alvaro throws his pistol on the floor and it accidently goes off and kills the Marquis, who curses Leonora before he dies. Act II. Leonora, in her search for Alvaro, is dressed as a youth. One day she lodges at an inn near Hornachuelos where she recognizes her brother, Don Carlo (baritone), also in disguise as a student, and hears him swear to seek out his sister and kill her seducer. A gypsy girl Preziosilla (mezzo-soprano) guesses that he is not what he says he is, but asks no questions. In anguish, Leonora flees to the monastery of the Madonna of the Angels. She is brought by Fra Melitone (baritone) to the Father Superior (bass), to whom alone she reveals her real name. The Father Superior promises not to disclose her secret (Chorus *La vergine degli Angeli*). She becomes a hermit in a lonely mountain cave nearby, protected by a holy curse on all who infringe her rights of solitary retreat. Act III. The war between Spain and Napoleon breaks out in Italy. Don Alvaro, under a false name, enlists in the Spanish army, in the neighbourhood of Velletri. He is sure that Leonora must be dead. In battle he saves the life of a fellow-countryman, Carlo (under an assumed name), and they seal a pact of brotherhood, without realizing each other's identity. When Don Alvaro is wounded he hands him a sealed envelope with instructions to destroy it without looking inside. Don Carlo discovers that it contains a portrait of Leonora and realizes that the man who saved his life is Alvaro. He challenges him to a duel to the death as soon as his wound is healed. They have barely picked up their swords when a patrol arrives and separates them. A new day begins in the camp, and soldiers and camp followers begin their daily round. Act IV. Monastery of the Madonna of the Angels. The poor are waiting in the cloisters to be given a free meal, distributed by brother Melitone. They compare him unfavourably to the kind Father Raffaele, the name Don Alvaro has assumed. Don Carlo manages to trace him and challenges him once again to a fight to the death. Alvaro reluctantly lets himself be provoked and fatally wounds his adversary. To obtain absolution for him, he calls upon the hermit in the nearby cave. At first the hermit refuses, but Alvaro suddenly recognizes Leonora, and guiltily explains that the dying man is none other than her own brother. Carlo stabs her as she administers the last rites and the Father Superior himself gives her absolution as she dies in Alvaro's arms at last.

■ Verdi was unhappy with the libretto and wanted it to be rewritten. Since Piave was ill, the task was given to Antonio Ghislanzoni (1824–93), a strange man and successively a doctor, singer, journalist and writer. He was a witty man and said that at the end of the opera the corpses 'piled up too much' (in fact in Piave's version Don Alvaro also died); he preferred to let one character live on. It is his version which is performed today. The first performance of the new version was given at La Scala in Milan on 27 February 1869, staged by Verdi himself, who found fewer problems and greater satisfaction in this second version. At St Petersburg he had had to battle with secret intrigues on the part of jealous musicians and difficulties caused by the illness of Barbot, which had delayed the opening for a year. But in Milan it had a considerable success.

FERAMORS

Opera in two acts by Anton Rubinstein (1830–94), with a libretto by Julius Rodenberg, based on Lalla Rookh *by Thomas Moore. First performance: Dresden, Hoftheater, 24 February 1863.*

SYNOPSIS. An oriental tale of the Princess of Hindustan Lalla Rookh, who is promised in marriage to the King of Bokhara. On the journey she falls in love with Feramors, a young singer. Her grief when she has to leave him changes to joy when she discovers that he is none other than the King himself.

■ *Feramors* is Rubinstein's most pleasing opera. Its ballet music and choruses are still played in concerts. The oriental atmosphere attracted the composer, but the dramatic aspect is weak and the melodic material is treated very conventionally.

DIE LORELEY

Opera in four acts by Max Bruch (1838–1920), on a text by Emanuel Geibel. First performance: Mannheim, Hoftheater, 14 June 1863.

■ The libretto was originally written for Mendelssohn, who did not live to complete the work.

LE PÊCHEURS DE PERLES (The Pearl Fishers)

Opera in three acts by Georges Bizet (1838–75), with a libretto by Eugène Cormon (Pierre Etienne Piestre)

Rehearsals for Verdi's Un ballo in maschera *under the direction of Franco Zeffirelli. Designed by Renzo Mongiardino, it was performed at La Scala in 1972.*

and Michel Carré (1819–72). First performance: Paris, Théâtre-Lyrique, 30 September 1863; first performance in U.K.: London, Covent Garden, 22 April 1887; in U.S.A.: Philadelphia, 23 August 1893.

ORIGINAL CAST. Morini (Nadir), Guyot, Ismael (Zurga), Léontine de Maesen (Leïla).

SYNOPSIS. Act I. A beach on the island of Ceylon, in Antiquity. The fishermen prepare for the fishing season. They have elected Zurga (baritone) as their King. He welcomes Nadir (tenor), a friend whom he has not seen since the time when they vowed to renounce their love for the same girl. They promise each other eternal friendship now that the pangs of love no longer worry them. The old villagers bring in the priestess who has been chosen to sing on the clifftop to placate the anger of Brahma, while the fishermen are diving. Sworn to chastity and heavily veiled, she is not immediately recognized by the two men as Leïla (soprano), the very girl who was the cause of their rift. Leïla impresses Nourabad (bass), the High Priest, by telling him that she once saved a stranger's life and shows him the necklace with which she was rewarded. Then, thinking herself alone, she takes off her veil to sing. Nadir hears her voice and recognizes her; he declares his renewed love for her, which she returns. Nourabad finds them together and Zurga, furiously jealous, condemns them both to death. A storm breaks overhead, a portent of the wrath of the sea god. Leïla unsuccessfully pleads with Zurga for Nadir's life, and then asks him to give her necklace to her mother. The King recognizes it as the one given to the girl who saved his life, as a child. To repay this debt, he resolves to help the lovers. He sets the village on fire to distract the fishermen and despite the fulminations of Nourabad, Leïla and Nadir escape.

■ Bizet was harshly criticized when *Les Pêcheurs de Perles* first appeared. He was accused of being too much influenced by both Wagner and Verdi. Berlioz was one of the very few to recognize immediately the opera's worth and he declared it to be a genuine expression of Bizet's own personality. The score is full of charming melodies, but is also given substance by the composer's striking grasp of drama and by his great ability to evoke an atmosphere and character in musical terms.

LES TROYENS (The Trojans)

Poème lyrique *in two parts (*La prise de Troie *and* Les Troyens à Carthage*) and five acts by Hector Berlioz (1803–69), with a libretto by the composer based on* Virgil's Aeneid. *First performance: Paris, Théâtre-Lyrique, 4 November 1863 (when, however, only Part Two was performed). Performance of the entire opera on two evenings, 6 and 7 December 1890 in German at the Hoftheater in Karlsruhe. First performance in U.K.: Glasgow, 18–19 March 1935; in U.S.A.: Boston, 27 March 1955. And in Berlioz's original version: London, Covent Garden, 17 September 1969.*

ORIGINAL CAST. M. Charton-Demeur and Maujauze; conductor: Hector Berlioz.

SYNOPSIS. Act I. The Trojans rejoice that the Greeks have lifted their ten-year siege of Troy and departed, leaving behind a huge wooden horse. Cassandre (soprano), daughter of King Priam (bass), alone does not share the general belief that Troy has triumphed; she tells her betrothed, Chorèbe (baritone), that she has dreamt of her dead brother, Hector, and of rivers of blood in the streets. Priam and Hécube, his queen (mezzo-soprano), lead the hymns of thanks for deliverance; Enée, son of Vénus and Anchises (tenor), reports to them that the High Priest, Laocoön, has been devoured by snakes when he tried to destroy the horse, expecting it to be a Greek trick; they interpret this to be a sign that the gift is a sacred object. Priam commands that the horse be brought into the city and not even the clash of arms inside it dissuades the citizens from dragging it in. Act II. Scene I. In his palace, Enée is awakened by the ghost of Hector (bass), who tells him that the Greeks, hidden in the horse, have taken Troy. He orders him to lead the Trojans who remain to found an empire in Italy. Panthée (bass) brings some of the Trojan treasure he has saved and Chorèbe calls Enée to arms. Scene II. Before the altar of Vesta-Cybele, Cassandre tells the Trojan women of Enée's vision and his rescue of the treasure. She exhorts them to commit suicide rather than fall into Greek slavery; scorning the few who refuse to kill themselves, she stabs herself as the enemy soldiers enter. The other women follow her example, dying with the word 'Italie' on their lips, and the soldiers recoil in horror, realizing too late that the spoils of war have now escaped them. Act III. Didon's palace, Carthage. The Carthaginians give thanks for their prosperity and Didon (mezzo-soprano) accepts their choruses of loyalty. Anna (contralto) notices her sister's sadness, however, and suggests that she remarry, but Didon swears to be true to her husband's memory. Iopas (tenor) announces that some Trojans have been shipwrecked on the coast; no sooner has Ascagne (mezzo-soprano), Enée's son, told Didon that they are bound for Italy, than Narbal (bass), her minister, brings the news of a Numidian invasion. At this point, Enée comes forward and offers Trojan assistance, which Didon gratefully accepts. Act IV. After a pantomime of the Royal Hunt and Storm, in an African forest, the scene changes to Didon's garden by the sea. Narbal is anxious that Enée's fate is to desert Didon and that Carthage will suffer from the queen's passionate love for him, but Anna foresees only happiness in their love for each other. Enée tells Didon how

T. Laval's poster for Gounod's Faust *at the Théâtre-Lyrique, 1859.*

Scene One of Act II of Verdi's La forza del destino *at La Scala in the 1965/66 season; directed by Margherita Wallmann, costume and set designs by Nicola Benois.*

Andromaque has so far forgotten Hector as to marry her captor, Pyrrhus. They sing of their love for each other, but Mercure (bass), the messenger of the Gods, appears suddenly in the moonlight and repeats 'Italie' three times. Act V. Scene I. A sailor's song sounds from the Trojan fleet riding at anchor in the bay. Trojan captains complain that they prefer their present easy life to that of campaigns. Enée despairs that his destiny compels him to desert Didon. His resolve not to leave without a last farewell is shaken by a vision of the spectres of his father, brothers and sister, and he orders the Trojans to depart immediately. Didon, unable to prevent him, curses his faithlessness. Scene II. Didon prepares for death. Scene III. The Carthaginians have built a pyre to burn what the Trojans left behind. Narbal and Anna are unable to stop Didon

climbing it and throwing herself on a sword. She has a vision of triumphant Imperial Rome as her subjects proclaim endless enmity on the descendants of Enée.

■ The opera springs partly from Berlioz's passion for Virgil and partly from his interest in tragedy. This interest was met by the events of the second and fourth Books of the Aeneid, which had been translated into a Shakespearian kind of verse. An important element is the mime, with its Gluck-like solemnity. In *Les Troyens* the composer stuck faithfully to the conception, followed by Aeschylus and the other Greek writers of tragedy, of portraying several dramatic stories together. These are linked together by a very clear thread and one follows on the other, the difference between Berlioz and the Greeks being that they

Verdi's La forza del destino *at the Metropolitan Opera House, New York, in 1964.*

produced trilogies, whereas he only uses two stories. In the opera we find grand outbursts of passion with which the composer brings the feelings of the ancient characters to new life. The fourth act is very famous, influenced, so it is said, by Purcell's *Dido and Aeneas*, while the short prologue to Part Two, written by the composer just before the first performance, is hurried and of little worth.

MIREILLE

Opera in three acts by Charles Gounod (1818–93), with a libretto by Michel Carré (1819–72) from a romance in Provençal verse, Mireio, *by Fréderic Mistral (1859). First performance: Paris, Théâtre-Lyrique, 19 March 1864 (five-act version) and 15 December 1864 (three-act version); first performance in U.K.: London, Her Majesty's, 5 July 1864; in U.S.A.: Philadelphia, 17 November 1864.*

SYNOPSIS. During a Provençal spring, Mireille (soprano), the beautiful daughter of the wealthy Ramon (bass), loves and is loved by a poor young man, Vincent (tenor). Mireille's *confidante*, the sorceress Taven (mezzo-soprano), warns her that her father intends to marry her to a very rich man called Ourrias (baritone). Mireille confesses her love to her father and he replies that he will never let her marry Vincent. Ourrias is jealous of Vincent and wounds him badly, leaving him for dead. He is sorry for his misdeed too late; he drowns in the Rhône. Taven heals Vincent, however, and when Mireille hears of this she goes on a pilgrimage to Saintes-Maries-de-la-Mer. The journey under the burning sun exhausts her, however, and she dies in the arms of Vincent, to her father's despair.

■ The definitive, new version in three acts, in which Vincent and Mireille are reunited, was performed on 15 December 1864. Gounod wrote this opera in the Provence, at Saint-Rémy, in the space of two months, where he felt he was in spiritual contact with Mistral, the Provençal poet, who lived nearby. The real inspiration of this delicate, fragile music is the Provence. Although the librettist has left very little of Mistral's poem, the music recaptures the legendary charm of Provence and incorporates ancient and medieval songs.

LA BELLE HÉLÈNE

Opéra-bouffe in three acts by Jacques Offenbach (1819–80), with a libretto by Henri Meilhac (1813–97) and Ludovic Halévy (1833–1908). First performance: Paris, Théâtre des Variétés, 17 December 1864; first performance in U.K.: London, Adelphi Theatre, 30 June 1866; in U.S.A.: Chicago, 14 September 1867.

SYNOPSIS. Act I. Ancient Greece. Hélène (soprano), who is presiding over a feast, notices Paris (tenor), dressed as a shepherd and unknown to everyone except Calchas (baritone), and is struck by his beauty. Paris wins a competition 'of things of the mind'. Hélène, who knows that Vénus has promised her as first prize to the winner, is deeply moved. Act II. Hélène, looking very serene, tells Paris that she can never love him since she is married to Menelaus. Agamemnon (bass), from Argos, arrives to play a game of goose. Calchas cheats, is discovered and chased out by the whole group, leaving Hélène alone. Paris gains access to her apartment, dressed as a slave, and they are discovered kissing by Menelaus. Excuses are useless. Act III. Hélène is at the seaside at Nauplia. She tries to forget the affair like any good bourgeois wife, but Vénus has other ideas. She is offended by the lack of respect Menelaus has shown for her wishes and she launches a whole epidemic of marital betrayals in Sparta. Agamemnon and Calchas urge Menelaus to placate the goddess. Menelaus has, meanwhile, written to Cythera, Vénus's home, begging her for peace. A priest of Vénus arrives and advises Menelaus to allow his wife to visit Cythera in order to sacrifice to Vénus. Hélène sets sail with the envoy who reveals at the last minute that he is none other than Paris.

Giuseppe Verdi in St Petersburg for the opening of La forza del destino.

formance in U.K.: London, Covent Garden, 22 July 1865; in U.S.A.: New York, Academy of Music, 1 December 1865.

ORIGINAL CAST. Belval, Castelmary, Marie Battu, Emile Naudin, Joseph Warot, Marie Sasse.

SYNOPSIS. Act I. Lisbon, King's Council Chamber. Don Diégo (bass) tells his daughter Inès (soprano) that the king has decided to marry her to Don Pédro (bass), President of the Royal Council, since it is assumed that Vasco da Gama (whom she loves) has been drowned in a shipwreck during his expedition. The Council meets to consider whether to send help to the survivors. Opportunely, Vasco (tenor) himself appears to tell of his adventures and to hand in a petition showing the possibility of rounding the Cape of Storms beyond which lie rich and still unknown lands. As proof of his assertions he presents two prisoners belonging to a strange race from that land, Sélika (soprano) and Nélusko (bass). The Grand Inquisitor (baritone) accuses Vasco of heresy and has him and the two slaves imprisoned. Act II. A prison of the Inquisition. Vasco dreams of his journeys and his beloved Inès. Sélika, the slave-girl, wakes him tenderly and protects him from Nélusko, who loves her and wants to kill him. When Vasco awakes, Sélika shows him a secret route to reach her homeland beyond the Cape of Storms. Vasco embraces her gratefully just as Inès and Don Pédro enter with a pardon, which she has obtained by consenting to marry Don Pédro. She is not convinced by Vasco's repeated assurances that he still loves her and his despair is increased when he learns that Don Pédro is to lead the next expedition. Act III. Aboard Don Pedro's flag-ship, Inès, Sélika and the other women are resting while Don Pédro consults the charts. Nélusko, who has the task of pilot and who has already wrecked

■ The opera with the soprano Hortense Schneider in the title role, unsurpassed in brilliant roles of this kind, was an outstanding success and received seven hundred performances. The satire and parody on the conventions of Meyerbeer's theatrical writing gave rise to much discussion and amusement; there were some who even expressed anger at the send-up of Homer's Iliad. The opera remains Offenbach's masterpiece. According to Corte-Pannain, 'a marvellous perfection of form and content, a satisfying realization of all the intimate details required by the subject, maximum tension in the most harmonious and complete aesthetic eurhythmics'. As proof that its success was not due solely to the time it was written, it has been recently revived with as much success as it had received nearly a hundred years before.

L'AFRICAINE (The African Maid)
Opera in five by Giacomo Meyerbeer (1791–1864), with a libretto by Eugène Scribe (1791–1861). First performance: Paris, Opéra, 28 April 1865; first per-

Lithograph of the first performance of Gounod's Faust *on 19 March 1859 at the Théatre-Lyrique. Paris, Bibliothèque de l'Opéra.*

Scene from Les Troyens *by Berlioz in the 1969 Covent Garden production in London.*

two of the ships, steers dangerously close to a reef. An unknown ship, flying the Portuguese flag, overtakes them and Vasco himself boards Don Pédro's vessel to warn them of the danger. Don Pédro ignores his advice and orders that he be executed, but a storm blows up and a force of Sélika's African tribe overrun the ship, capturing and killing the Portuguese. Act IV. Madagascar. A beach with temples and palaces. Grand celebrations are being held to honour the return of Sélika (who, it turns out, is queen of the island) and of her faithful Nélusko. Selika promises that the law of her ancestors must be obeyed and that death is the penalty for a stranger who sets foot on the island. She pretends, however, that Vasco is her husband, to save his life, and the High Priest calls down the blessing of the gods on the couple. Vasco embraces her but, as he promises to stay with her for ever, he hears Inès grieving for her lost love. Act V. Scene I. In Sélika's gardens. Inès and Vasco are found together. Sélika is furious, but Vasco reassures her by saying that he will

not break his word and that Inès, being Catholic, can never marry him as he has married Sélika. Sélika, however, perceives the strength of love which binds them and suppressing her own love, she frees them and orders them to return to their ship. Scene II. Sélika makes her way to a headland where the manchineel tree grows. The odour of this tree is poisonous and to breathe it is certain death. Hearing the guns which announce the ship's departure, she sends Vasco a final greeting *D'ici je vois la mer immense*, and refuses Nélusko's desperate attempts to move her from the place of death. He then joins her in death and they die as an invisible choir sings that all are equal in death.

■ The opera is a free rendering of the story of Vasco da Gama, the Portuguese navigator who was the first to round the Cape of Good Hope. Meyerbeer worked on it for over twenty years. Begun in 1838, it was first of all set aside for *Ein Feldlager in Schlesien* (1844), which inaugurated the Royal Theatre in Berlin. Then it was taken up and set aside several times until 1860, when a second complete version was written. Rehearsals began in Paris in 1863 but were cut short by the composer's death on 2 May 1864. The opera was revised by François-Joseph Fétis and staged the following year when, despite its phenomenal length (about six hours), it was a great success and acknowledged to be the composer's masterpiece, combining elements of grand Romantic opera, Italian melodrama and French taste. *L'Africaine* is the most typical of the Grand Operas (of which genre Meyerbeer was one of the creators and most famous exponents). As for the 'sixteen beat' notes which are often discussed, they come, according to the musicologist G. Giacomelli, straight from a march-prelude for fife and drum which has been played since time immemorial in Holy Week processions at Cagliari.

TRISTAN UND ISOLDE

Music drama *in three acts by Richard Wagner (1813–83), with a libretto by the composer. First performance: Munich, Hoftheater, 10 June 1865; first performance in U.K.: London, Drury Lane, 20 June 1882; in U.S.A.: New York, Metropolitan Opera House, 1 December 1886.*

ORIGINAL CAST. Ludwig Schnorr von Carolsfeld (Tristan), Malvina Schnorr von Carolsfeld (Isolde), Zottmayer (Marke), Heinrich (Melot), Mitterwurzer (Kurwenal). Conductor: Hans von Bülow.

SYNOPSIS. Isolde's tent of tapestries and curtains on the deck of Tristan's ship, crossing from Ireland to Cornwall. Tristan (tenor) is taking Isolde (soprano), daughter of the king of Ireland, to be married to his uncle, King Marke of Cornwall (bass). From the top of the rigging a sailor sings a song about an Irish girl travelling westward. The princess orders her attendant Brangäne (mezzo-soprano) to bring Tristan to her to renew the act of homage he made to her before setting sail. Tristan's faithful groom, Kurwenal (baritone), laughs that his master need pay homage to no-one, since he killed Morold, the Irishman whom Isolde loved. Isolde angrily reacts to this story by telling Brangäne that she once had Tristan's life in her hands. A wounded man who said his name was Tantris once came to her to have his wounds healed. She discovered by matching the splinter from Morold's wound to the stranger's sword that he was in fact the Tristan who, having killed the man she loved, sent her his severed head. She had been about to stab him in revenge when his beseeching gaze restrained her. Instead she had cured him with magic potions and kept silent. When he recovered he departed, promising never to see her again. He broke his word, however, by returning under his real name to request her hand in marriage for the King of Cornwall. She cannot help revealing her passionate love for the knight, whom she now considers has betrayed her. To avenge herself, she resolves that they shall both take poison. Kurwenal announces that the coast of Cornwall is in sight and Isolde begs him to

A lithograph by V. Katzler caricaturing Marie Geistinger in the role of Hélène and Josephine Gallmeyer as a ballerina in Offenbach's La belle Hélène. Milan, Museo teatrale alla Scala.

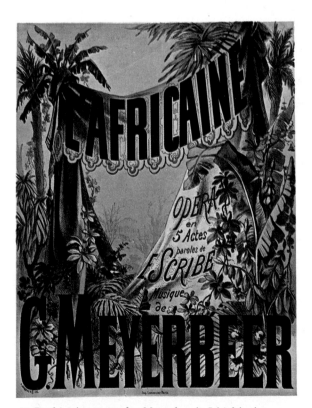

A. Barbizet's poster for Meyerbeer's L'Africaine. Paris, Bibliothèque de l'Opéra.

Sketches for the scenery of Tristan und Isolde *by Richard Wagner, based on ideas of the composer.*

in the distance. Isolde, now married to Marke, is impatiently waiting for Tristan with Brangäne: when the torch by her door is put out, Tristan will know that it is safe to approach. Brangäne suspects a plot, however, by King Marke's knight Melot (tenor) and it is Isolde who finally extinguishes the light. Tristan throws himself into her arms, and they sing a hymn to the night, praying for it to be guardian of their love. Brangäne, who is keeping watch at the top of a tower, warns them that it is nearly dawn but the lovers ignore her. Their ecstasy is broken by Brangäne's scream and by Kurwenal, who runs in to warn Tristan that the hunting party is approaching. Melot had arranged the hunt to trap the lovers. Marke reproaches first his nephew and then his wife. Isolde promises Tristan that she will follow him wherever he leads. Tristan allows himself to be wounded by Melot. Act III. Outside Tristan's castle at Kareol in Brittany, Kurwenal watches over the wounded knight while a shepherd's lament tells them that no ship has yet appeared on the horizon. Tristan wakes, cursing the light and complaining that Isolde is remaining in the realm of daylight, and falls back in a faint on his couch. When the shepherd's pipes sound the arrival of Isolde's ship, he tears off his bandages in delirious joy and rises to meet her. Isolde holds him in her arms as he dies. Meanwhile King Marke and Melot have landed from another ship. Kurwenal, fearing an attack, kills Melot and in the fighting also receives a fatal wound; he collapses at Tristan's side. King Marke intended to pardon the lovers, having learnt how Brangäne tricked them, but he has arrived too late. Isolde sings a lament for Tristan (*Liebestod*: 'Mild und leise wie er lächelt') and falls dead on his corpse.

■ The text was completed in Zurich in 1857. The musical score was written between 1857 and 1859, first in Switzerland, then in Venice, 'city of a hundred deeply solitary spots', where the composer had gone broken-hearted after ending his affair with Mathilde Wesendonk. Wagner found the subject of *Tristan* in the thirteenth-century German poem by Gottfried von Strassburg, which was an elaboration of an ancient Celtic legend. Only the central characters and the basic story of the ancient poem survive in the music drama, for the sense of magic and enchantment felt by the audience right from the opening bars of the prelude can only be explained by two fundamental and simultaneous experiences undergone by the composer during the years in which he was sketching out his great opera. At this time Wagner had found in the writings of Schopenhauer a confirmation of his own ideas. He declared that he had found the only 'possibility of hope' in the thoughts of that philosopher, which are permeated by the idea that in life there is no place for will (and who also believed that the 'focal point' of existence lies in erotic desire). They were also the years of his passionate love for Mathilde, wife of a Swiss industrialist, Otto Wesendonk, in whose country house near Zurich he had stayed as guest from the summer of 1857 to the summer of 1858. Mathilde was delicate and sensitive and wrote poems, some of which were set to music by Wagner and became the *Wesendonk*

call Tristan. When the knight arrives, Isolde accuses him of cowardice, saying she has only cured him in order to gain her revenge when his strength should be fully restored. Tristan offers her his sword so that she can erase his insult by his death, but Isolde refuses, proposing that they should drink together a cup of reconciliation. Tristan understands that the cup is drugged, but he does not flinch. They drink and neither dies because Brangäne has substituted a love potion for the poison. They embrace in ecstasy as shouts announce that the ship has reached Cornwall. Act II. Gardens in front of King Marke's castle on a summer night. The hunting horns of the royal hunt can be heard

Wieland Wagner's staging of Wagner's Tristan und Isolde, *Bayreuth, 1963. Above right, Act I; left, Act II; below, Act III.*

Lieder, whose thematic material flows into the sonorous river of *Tristan*. His love for this woman grew as it became less possible to satisfy and left deep wounds in his heart. These two experiences (his encounter with the philosophy of Schopenhauser and his love for Mathilde) are, so to speak, the roots from which grows the story of the drama. *Tristan und Isolde* is the story of a love which can only realize itself by abandoning the will to live, and by uniting the lovers in a world of non-existence. The summit of this ideal is reached in the great love duet in Act II and the deep aspiration for death. It is, according to Thomas Mann, the most inspired love story ever written, with its belief in night-time as truth, and its view of day-time as illusion. And in these conceptions it is closely related to Romantic thought and feeling. The marked chromaticism used to express the longing for love and for death, which is a prelude to the break-up of tonality, and the continual ebb and flow of the music make it the most revolutionary opera of the late Romantic period and the starting-point for modern music.

THE BARTERED BRIDE (Prodaná Nevěsta)
Comic opera in three acts by Bedřich Smetana

(1824–84), with a libretto by Karel Sabina (1813–77). First performance: Prague, Provisional Theatre, 30 May 1866; first performance in U.K.: London, Drury Lane Theatre, 26 June 1895; in U.S.A.: Chicago, Haymarket, 20 August 1893.

ORIGINAL CAST. Eleonora von Ehrenberg (Mařenka), Josef Kysela (Vašek), František Hynek (Kečal), Vojtěch Šebesta (Micha), Jindřich Polák (Jeník).

SYNOPSIS. Act I. A Czech village on a holiday in Spring. Everyone is merry except the lovely Mařenka (soprano) and the young man she loves, Jeník (tenor), because her parents want her to marry someone wealthier. No one knows anything of Jeník's antecedents. Kečal (bass), the village marriage broker, persuades Mařenka's parents that Vašek (tenor), the younger son of Tobias Mícha, a rich landlord from a distant village, would be a suitable son-in-law, but Mařenka refuses him, saying that she has just become engaged to Jeník. Act II. A Czech inn. Vašek, who stammers, arrives in the village and when Mařenka realizes that this is the bridegroom her parents intend for her she tells him that his intended bride is temperamental and that she

Ludwig and Malvina Schnorr von Carolsfeld, the first Tristan and Isolde in Wagner's opera, Munich 1865.

might even murder him. She suggests that he marry another, much prettier girl instead and he promises to do so. Kečal then invites Jeník to give up Mařenka in exchange for money and Jeník reluctantly agrees, stipulating that the bridegroom should be Tobias Mícha's son. Kečal gathers the village together to witness Jeník signing a document renouncing Mařenka and everyone is horrified to hear that he has bartered her for money. Act III. The village square. Vašek cannot find the girl who gave him such good advice but a travelling circus distracts him and he quickly falls for a ballerina called Esmeralda (soprano). He even agrees to help them in an awkward situation by dressing up as a dancing bear – the real performer is so drunk that the performance could not otherwise go on. Mařenka is mortified to hear that Jeník has given her up and decides to do as her parents wish; Vašek is delighted to find that the girl he likes is actually Mařenka. Disaster is averted when Tobias Mícha arrives and recognizes Jeník with amazement as his long-lost eldest son. Then Jeník shows the contract with Kečal's promise to hand over 700 florins to him when Mařenka marries Tobias's son. The general merriment is not much disturbed by the news that a bear is

roaming free, because it turns out to be Vašek in costume!

■ The writing of the opera was begun in May 1863 and finished in March 1866. After the first performance, which Smetana himself conducted, he continued to add new arias and make changes to the score until he arrived at the final version in three acts in 1870. On 25 September of that year it was performed for the first time in its new version. Despite the lengthy period of its composition and the changes and modifications which generally damage the compactness of a work, a marvellous unity of style is maintained throughout *The Bartered Bride*. In fact the laborious rewriting achieved a perfect balance between originality and the underlying traditional element of the music. The way in which the country atmosphere is depicted both in the joyfulness of the holiday and in the intimate village problems, gives it some claim to be considered his masterpiece. It is certainly one of the greatest Czech operas, and demonstrates the composer's ability to write convincing music in the popular idiom of his country.

MIGNON

Opéra-comique *in three acts by Ambroise Thomas (1811–96), with a libretto by Michel Carré and Jules Barbier, based on Goethe's* Wilhelm Meister's Lehrjahre *(1796). First performance: Paris, Opéra-Comique, 17 November 1866; first performance in U.K.: London, Drury Lane, 5 July 1870; in U.S.A.: New Orleans, 9 May 1871.*

ORIGINAL CAST. Celestina Galli-Marié (Mignon).

SYNOPSIS. Act I. In the courtyard of a German inn, Philine (soprano) and Laerte (tenor), members of an acting company, watch an old musician, Lothario (bass), whose mind often wanders, and Wilhelm Meister (tenor), a student on his travels, protect a pretty girl from ill-treatment by a gypsy. The girl is Mignon (mezzo-soprano) who gives them both flowers for their trouble; Meister gives his to Philine when she comes down to meet him. Mignon tells Meister that she is the gypsy's servant and that she can remember nothing of her childhood; the young man decides to pay the gypsy enough money to free her. She is extremely grateful and already jealous that he should appear to prefer Philine to her. Act II. Scene I. In Philine's boudoir in a castle where Laerte and Philine are to play *A Midsummer Night's Dream*, Mignon and Meister enter the room while Philine is preparing for the performance and Mignon pretends to fall asleep in order to observe the others closely. When they have left she dresses herself in one of the actress's costumes much to the scorn of Philine and her admirer. Meister, fearing further embarrassments, decides that he cannot travel with her. Scene II. In the park, Lothario comforts Mignon, who rashly wishes aloud that the castle would burn down with everyone in it. The play ends and Meister comes out into the garden with the actors; he is obviously sorry to have been cruel to Mignon, so

Philine sends her inside to pick up the flowers which Meister had given her (the bouquet that Mignon herself gave to Meister). As she enters the conservatory, it bursts into flames (for Lotario took her at her word) and Meister rescues her. Act III. The Cipriani castle. Meister has brought Lotario and Mignon, who has been very ill, to Italy. It becomes apparent that this is the very castle from which Mignon was kidnapped as a child and that Lotario, whose wits have recovered in these familiar surroundings, is her father.

■ In the revitalization of French music which took place in the middle of the nineteenth century, Ambroise Thomas played a noteworthy part. He was an excellent teacher, director of the Paris Conservatory from 1871 as successor to Auber, and as such led the way to a new lease of life in French music for the theatre by his interest in great literature. As well as theorizing, he set Shakespeare's *A Midsummer Night's Dream* to music in 1850 and when Gounod's *Faust* appeared in 1859, he too looked for inspiration to the work of the great German poet. And so he wrote *Mignon*, inspired by Goethe's *Wilhelm Meister*. It was followed by *Hamlet* in 1868 and *Françoise de Rimini* in 1882. *Mignon* is undoubtedly Thomas's best opera. Even in its tragic moments the music is shot through with a grace and charm that make it intensely attractive. It is also interesting to note that Thomas changed the tragic end of Goethe's drama to give full rein to his own predilection for non-tragic conclusions. *Mignon* is Thomas's only opera still in the repertoire of many opera houses throughout the world.

DON CARLOS

Opera in five acts by Giuseppe Verdi (1813–1901), with a libretto by François-Joseph Méry (1798–1865) and Camille Du Locle (1832–1903) drawn from the tragedy by Friedrich Schiller (1759–1805). First performance: Paris, Opéra, 11 March 1867; first performance in U.K.: London, Covent Garden, 4 June 1867; in U.S.A.: New York, Academy of Music, 12 April, 1877.

ORIGINAL CAST. Marie-Constance Sass, Pauline Gueymard, J. B. Faure, L. Henri Obin, R. Morère, A. Castelmary. Conductor: F. G. Hainl.

SYNOPSIS. France and Spain in 1560. Act I. Don Carlos (tenor), the Infante of Spain, meets Elisabeth de Valois (soprano) at Fontainebleau and falls in love with her. The princess returns his feelings but the news that the King of France has promised her hand to Carlos's father, Philip II of Spain (bass), makes their love impossible. Act II. In the cloisters of the monastery of San Yuste, the monks pray at the tomb of Charles V. Don Carlos confides his unhappiness to his friend Rodrigo (baritone), who implores him to accompany him to Flanders where they are hoping to end the wars. Carlos entrusts to Rodrigo a farewell message for Elisabeth, now the Queen of Spain. He would like to see her one last time before leaving the

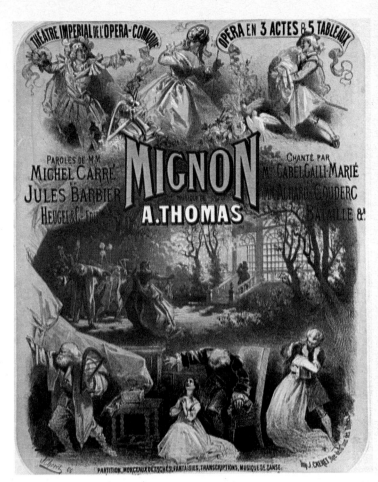

J. Chéret's poster for Mignon *by Thomas at the Opéra-Comique in 1866. Paris, Bibliothèque de l'Opéra.*

country. When they meet, she is faithful to Philip in spite of her feelings. Carlos has no sooner gone than Philip arrives and finding the Queen unattended, he puts the blame on Elisabeth's one French lady-in-waiting and sends her back to France. When he is alone with Rodrigo he voices his suspicions of a possible love affair between Elisabeth and his son. Act III. Scene I. The Queen's gardens in Madrid during a ball. Don Carlos has been asked to a meeting with a veiled lady. Thinking it is Elisabeth he declares his love, but it is actually the Princess Eboli (mezzo-soprano), who is in love with him. When she realizes his mistake she decides on revenge. Rodrigo tries unsuccessfully to calm her. He asks Carlos to give him all the incriminating documents he has. Scene II. An auto da fé. In the square of Our Lady of Atocha a group of heretics are brought to the stake. Some Flemish deputies, led by Don Carlos, interrupt the royal procession to ask the King to put an end to the persecutions in Flanders. The King orders their arrest and Don Carlos threatens him with a sword, but Rodrigo manages to restrain him. Act IV. Scene I. In his study, Philip reflects on the burdens of his life when the Grand Inquisitor (bass) enters. He demands that Don Carlos should be

Teresie Rückaufova as Mařenka in Smetana's The Bartered Bride, *1866. Prague, Smetana Museum.*

Adelina Patti in Gounod's Roméo et Juliette.

sacrificed and that Rodrigo should be handed over to the Inquisition, saying that he fears rebellion. Philip finally agrees. Elisabeth then enters in great anxiety – one of her jewel-cases has disappeared. She sees the casket on Philip's desk: it has been stolen by Princess Eboli to obtain revenge on the Queen, for in it is a portrait of the Infante, enough proof to the King that he is being betrayed. The Queen swoons when he accuses her of infidelity. Eboli confesses to her what she has done and moreover that she has been Philip's mistress and she announces her decision to retire to a convent. Scene II. In the prison where Don Carlos is held, Rodrigo tells him that he will not be condemned since the incriminating papers have been found on himself. Carlos does not believe him, but a sudden shot fired by a servant of the King hits Rodrigo and kills him. When the King comes to free his son, the people acclaim the Infante, yet they bow before the Grand Inquisitor, and the authority of the Church. Act V. Elisabeth is in the cloisters of the monastery of San Yuste, praying at the tomb of Charles V for Don Carlos's safety. Carlos arrives to say a last farewell to her before leaving to fight for freedom in Flanders. Philip and the Grand Inquisitor find them together and assume that they are guilty. Carlos is about to be arrested when the gates of the tomb of Charles V open wide and the Emperor leads Carlos into the cloisters.

■ *Don Carlos* is the third work to be commissioned from Verdi by the Paris Opéra, coming after the newly rewritten *Lombardi*, now called *Jérusalem*, and *Les Vêpres Siciliennes*. It has the richness and clarity typical of French lyric drama. In it Verdi reaches peaks of dramatic effect. From the point of view of instrumentation also the composer shows himself to have been influenced by current European ideas. He was commissioned to write *Don Carlos* in 1850 at the suggestion of Alphonse Royer and Gustav Vaëz, but he did not begin to work on it until 1865, keeping his promise to have it ready for the Paris Exposition of 1867. He conceived it in five acts out of respect for French custom, but was not particularly happy with this arrangement. So when it had also been performed in Italy at Bologna (at the Teatro Communale on 27 October 1867) in a translation by A. de Lauzières, he returned to work on it. In 1883 he finished a new version with a revised libretto by Zanardini in four acts. The opera was performed in this form at La Scala in the following year. The tenor aria, *Io la vidi e il suo sorriso*, was all that remained of the former first act. But Verdi was still not content and once again he revised it, restoring it to its former size while keeping many of the new ideas and changes. This final edition was not as successful as the second version. One of the reasons for this almost universal judgement may well be found in the fact that, in order to satisfy the demands of Grand Opera, Verdi had to insert a number of secondary episodes. These may well increase the spectacular effects, but at the same time they make the story rather confused and long-winded.

ROMÉO ET JULIETTE
Opera in five acts by Charles Gounod (1818–93), with a libretto by Jules Barbier (1825–1901) and Michel Carré (1819–72) after the tragedy by Shakespeare. First performance: Paris, Théâtre-Lyrique, 27 April 1867; first performance in U.K.: London, Covent Garden, 11 July 1867; in U.S.A.: New York, 15 November 1867.

ORIGINAL CAST. Caroline Miolan-Carvalho (Juliette), Michot (Roméo), Daram (Stefano).

SYNOPSIS. Act I. A hall in the Capulet house. A large ball is taking place. Roméo (tenor), of the Montague family, enemies of the Capulets, slips in with a mask to meet Rosaline, to whom he has taken a fancy. However, he sees Juliette (soprano) and they fall in love at first sight. Juliette's cousin, Tybalt (tenor), swears he will avenge the insult done to his family. Act II. A balcony at the Capulets' house. Roméo secretly enters the garden, helped by his valet, Stéphano (soprano), in order to see Juliette again. During their meeting some of the Capulet servants try to kill Roméo, but he manages to escape. Resuming their meeting, the two young people decide to marry secretly in spite of the hatred that divides their families. Juliette says she will let Roméo know the place and date of their wedding through her confessor, Frère Laurent, who will be the one to marry them. Act III. Frère Laurent's cell. The Frère (bass) marries the young lovers in spite of the possible consequences. Soon after, Stéphano sings a mocking serenade near the Capulets' house which provokes a quarrel between the Capulet supporters and those of the Montagues. Roméo tries to separate the combatants and at first refuses the challenge of Juliette's cousin Tybalt, because of his love for her. When he sees that his friend Mercutio (baritone) is killed, however, he avenges him by killing Tybalt. Juliette's father (bass) hears Tybalt's dying words accusing Roméo, and the Duke of Verona banishes him. Act IV. The Capulets' house. Roméo has spent the night with Juliette and now says a last farewell to her. Juliette's father tells her in the presence of Frère Laurent that Tybalt's dying wish was that she should marry Count Paris. Frère Laurent manages to help Juliette remain silent in her despair. When left alone with her, Frère Laurent proposes a wild plan that he

Scene from the first performance of Verdi's Don Carlos, *with the* auto-da-fé. *Contemporary lithograph.*

will give her a potion to send her into a deep sleep so that everyone except Roméo will believe her to be dead. In the Capulet chapel everything is now ready for Juliette's wedding to Count Paris, but as Juliette approaches the altar, she falls down as though dead. Act V. The Capulets' tomb. Roméo has not received Frère Laurent's message. He assumes that Juliette is really dead and enters the tomb secretly to see her again. Over her body, he drinks poison. When Juliette awakes, she embraces Roméo and begs him to flee with her. Roméo in despair tells her of his terrible mistake. Juliette stabs herself with Roméo's dagger.

■ This celebrated story of the lovers of Verona had already been set to music by various composers, not least of whom were Berlioz (*Romeo et Juliette*) and Bellini (*I Capuleti e i Montecchi*). The subject was just of the kind to stimulate Gounod and to suit his melodic sensitivity and yet, except for certain lyrical passages, the opera is perhaps excessively theatrical. However, when it appeared in Paris it received warm praise and many repeat performances, firstly at the Théâtre-Lyrique until the end of 1873 and then at the Opéra.

LA JOLIE FILLE DE PERTH (The Fair Maid of Perth)

Opera in four acts by Georges Bizet (1836–75), with a libretto by J.-H. Vernoy de Saint-Georges and Jules Adenis after the novel by Sir Walter Scott (1828). First performance: Paris, Théâtre-Lyrique, 26 December 1867; first performance in U.K.: Manchester, 4 May 1917.

SYNOPSIS. Act I. Perth, Scotland. The eve of St Valentine's Day. Henri Smith (tenor), an armourer, is in love with Catherine Glover (soprano). He gives refuge to a gypsy, Mab (soprano), and conceals her when Catherine arrives, to avoid an awkward situation; he gives Catherine a little enamelled gold rose and declares his love for her. A stranger, in fact the Duke of Rothsay (baritone), enters the shop and begins to flirt with Catherine. Mab stops Henri hitting him for his impertinence, but her sudden appearance causes Catherine to suspect that she is Henri's mistress. She throws the gold flower on the ground (and Mab picks it up) before she leaves. Act II. The Duke leads a drinking song and confides to Mab his plan to abduct Catherine. At midnight Henri serenades Catherine but she does not appear and another admirer, Ralph (bass), watches the Duke's men put Mab, wearing Catherine's clothes, into a litter and take her away. He informs Henri that Catherine has gone to the castle but immediately finds he was mistaken because Cathcrine herself appears on her balcony. Act III. The Duke is gambling with friends until a masked lady enters, when all withdraw. She puts out the light before taking off her mask, so the Duke never knows he has been deceived. He steals the gold rose from her. Catherine and her father arrive to announce the formal betrothal of Catherine and Henri; Henri rejects her, pointing to the gold rose on the Duke's coat. Act IV. In his shop,

Henri, miserably, refuses to believe Ralph's protestations of Catherine's innocence; he agrees to fight a duel to prove her virtue. Catherine herself convinces him at last of her innocence and he resolves to let himself be killed, to prove it conclusively. Mab then appears with a chorus of young lovers to tell Catherine the happy news that the Duke has stopped the duel. She finds that Catherine has lost her senses and it is only the sound of Henri's voice singing his serenade that restores them.

■ Bizet was trying to satisfy contemporary fashion in every way in this opera, to the extent of seeming quite reactionary and arousing the opposition of all those who expected him to produce something unusual. Verdi's influence is the most strongly felt, yet this is Bizet's only opera to be warmly received when staged. It is the only time that he was ever present at a successful reception of one of his works.

MEFISTOFELE

Opera with a prologue, four acts and an epilogue by Arrigo Boito (1842–1918), with a libretto by the composer based on Goethe's Faust. *First performance: Milan, Teatro alla Scala, 5 March 1868; first performance in U.K.: London, Her Majesty's Theatre, 6 July 1880; in U.S.A.: Boston, 16 November 1880.*

SYNOPSIS. Prologue. In the heavens Mefistofele (bass) wagers with the Lord that he can win Faust's soul. Act I. Scene I. It is Easter Sunday and a large crowd has gathered to watch the Elector's procession. Faust (tenor) with his pupil, Wagner (tenor), watch the dancing in the square. Dusk falls and Faust is worried that he is being followed by a sinister grey friar. Scene II. In his study Faust opens the Gospel, but is startled by the reappearance of the friar, who throws off his disguise and reveals his identity as Mefistofele. Faust accepts his offer of one moment of perfect joy in return for his soul after death. Act II. Scene I. Faust, who is young again and has assumed the name of Enrico, is paying court to a charming girl called Margherita (soprano). He persuades her to give a sleeping draught to her mother so that the two of them can meet later. Scene II. On the Brocken. Mefistofele has brought Faust to watch the Witches' sabbath, but Faust is upset by a vision of Margherita in chains with a red sign on her neck. Act III. In a prison. Margherita has gone mad and in her delirium she sings of her misdeeds. She is accused of poisoning her mother and drowning the baby she had by Faust. Faust arrives with Mefistofele, who agrees to rescue Margherita, but she refuses to take the Devil's help. In a brief moment of lucidity she begs for mercy and falls dead. A heavenly choir announces her salvation. Act IV. In Greece on the banks of the river Peneios. Faust wants to meet Elena to bring about a fusion of Greek beauty and German wisdom, between the Classical and Romantic spirits. Elena sings of the Fall of Troy and touched by Faust's admiration, promises him her love. Epilogue. In Faust's study. Old and tired, he realizes with disillusion the emptiness of what Mefistofele has given him and

Watercolour by Echter of Quaglio's designs for the first performance of Wagner's Die Meistersinger von Nürnberg *at the Munich Hoftheater, 1868.*

that his death is fast approaching. He prays to God and protects himself from Mefistofele's temptations with the Gospels. He dies repentant, while Mefistofele, defeated, sinks into the ground.

■ The first performance of *Mefistofele* ended in a barrage of whistles, and for many years afterwards the composer would only sign with an anagram of his name: Tobia Gorrio. After this fiasco, Boito revised, rewrote and cut the score. The first version was actually unbearably long (five and a half hours) and repeat performances were subdivided into two evenings. After the composer's modifications it was performed with success at the Teatro Comunale in Bologna on 4 October 1875, and from then on was considered one of the masterpieces of lyric opera. To perform *Mefistofele* in the Italian theatrical climate of the day was undoubtedly a controversial and unexpected thing to do, and it drew down a chorus of protests on the composer's head from the worlds of theatre and of music. Boito's daring lay in breaking with the enclosed and isolated musical traditions current in Europe. He wanted to draw the attention of everyone to the fact that there was a fine musical culture on the other side of the Alps, which had given birth to Beethoven, Cho-

pin, Schumann and now Wagner. The choice of subject was already a break with tradition – a libretto after a German literary masterpiece. Many years were spent preparing the text and writing the music, with frequent interruptions to do other work or follow other interests. The libretto, written by Boito himself, creates the atmosphere of Goethe's drama better than other attempts to turn it into a lyric opera. Boito remained essentially a poet, more admired for his ideas by the literary world than by other musicians. As music it is often a series of reflex movements and compromises: a construction of the intellect. Within the opera, however, there are moments of rare beauty and pathos where the music is truly lyrical. In Gounod's *Faust* the composer has accentuated the character of Margherita, and Berlioz in *La Damnation de Faust* had been most concerned with the lively, colourful episodes in Goethe's poem. Boito combines these elements with a philosophical interpretation. Thus philosophical concepts are brought into the Italian melodrama which had hitherto not entered the story, such as the antithesis between good and evil, virtue and sin, Heaven and Earth, Satan and God. The best criticism on Boito is still that of Benedetto Croce, which appeared in 1904.

Wieland Wagner's design for Die Meistersinger von Nürnberg, *Act III. Bayreuth, 1958.*

HAMLET

Opera in five acts by Ambroise Thomas (1811–96), with a libretto by Jules Barbier and Michel Carré after Shakespeare. First performance: Paris, Opéra, 9 March 1868; first performance in U.K.: London, Covent Garden, 19 June 1869; in U.S.A.: New York Academy of Music, 22 March 1872.

ORIGINAL CAST. Faure, Gueymard, M. B. Nilsson, Castelmary.

SYNOPSIS. The action keeps closely to Shakespeare's tragedy. Hamlet, Prince of Denmark, hears the ghost of his dead father telling him the truth about his death – that his own brother murdered him in order to marry the Queen (thereby becoming Hamlet's stepfather) and to usurp Hamlet's place on the throne of Denmark. Hamlet swears revenge, and the better to conceal his purpose, he pretends to be mad, and drives Ophélie, whom he loves and who loves him, to despair and suicide. The king, however, realizing that Hamlet knows his secret, tries to have him murdered. He first poisons a drink for him (which kills the Queen instead, when she drinks it by mistake) and then he arranges a duel for Hamlet with Laerte (Ophélie's brother), in which the tip of Laerte's rapier is poisoned. Both are mortally wounded but Hamlet stabs the king with the poisoned blade as he dies.

■ After the success of *Mignon*, Thomas wanted to write a really committed opera and chose a subject from Shakespeare according to the contemporary fashion for setting famous works of literature to music. Even though the libretto is not first-rate, with its interludes of dancing and ballet (e.g. *La Fête de Printemps*) typical of Grand Opera, the music is excellent, especially on account of the composer's great skill at making the most of the vocal parts. Hamlet's part was changed from tenor to baritone and is one of the most dramatic baritone roles in the history of opera, while the soprano parts have often been the vehicles in which great dramatic singers (in the part of the Queen) or coloraturas (Ophélie) have reached the peaks of their success. The opera received a rapturous welcome and people of the time considered it 'the most important French opera since Halévy'. The instrumentation is more careful than in Thomas' other works (for example, the rhythmic use of the saxophone in the graveyard scene). This is one of the last examples of Grand Opera and, after *Mignon*, can rightly be considered the composer's best lyrical work.

DALIBOR

Tragic opera in three acts by Bedřich Smetana (1824–84), with a libretto by Joseph Wenzig. First performance: Prague, Municipal Theatre, 16 May 1868;

first performance in U.K.: Edinburgh, King's Theatre, 20 August 1964; in U.S.A.: Chicago, Sokol Hall, 13 April 1924.

SYNOPSIS. Prague, fifteenth century. Dalibor (tenor), a knight, has attacked the castle of the Burgrave of Ploskovice to avenge his friend, Zdeněk, the minstrel (who had been brutally murdered), and burnt it down, killing the Burgrave. Milada (soprano), the Burgrave's sister, asks the King, Vladislav (baritone), for justice, but when she sees Dalibor for the first time at his trial and hears his noble self-defence, she relents and begs instead for mercy for him. Vladislav nevertheless imprisons him. Milada joins those followers of Dalibor who want to rescue him and devises a plan by which she gains access to the prison, dressed as a youth assisting the old jailer, Beneš (bass). She successfully penetrates the dungeon and explains her purpose to the knight. He is much moved and accepts from her a violin on which he can amuse himself and also give the signal for the rescue attempt to begin. Beneš discovers that he has been tricked and Vladislav is compelled by his judges to alter the sentence on Dalibor to the death penalty. The guards surprise Dalibor at the moment he is about to give the signal, the rescue attempt misfires and both he and Milada are killed.

■ The first performance took place on the occasion of the laying of the foundation stone of the present

Act II of Wagner's Die Meistersinger von Nürnberg *in the New York Metropolitan Opera House production.*

National Theatre of Prague. *Dalibor* is Smetana's only tragic opera. It was taken from a well-known medieval Czech legend. The character of Dalibor may be taken to symbolize the nation itself and his life is the struggle

for liberty. Although the first performance was well received, the opera soon disappeared from the stage, much to Smetana's disappointment.

DIE MEISTERSINGER VON NÜRNBERG (The Mastersingers of Nuremberg)
Opera in three acts by Richard Wagner (1813–83), with a libretto by the composer. First performance: Munich, Hoftheater, 21 June 1868; first performance in U.K.: London, Drury Lane, 30 May 1882; in U.S.A.: New York, Metropolitan Opera House, 4 January 1886.

ORIGINAL CAST. Franz Betz, Franz Nachbaur, K. Heinrich, G. Hölzel, K. Schlosser, Mathilde Mallinger. Conductor: Hans von Bülow.

SYNOPSIS. Nuremberg towards the middle of the sixteenth century. Act I. In the church of St Katherine it is almost the end of the evening service in which the congregation celebrate the eve of the feast of St John. While the faithful throng the church, a young knight, Walther von Stolzing (tenor), is struck by the beauty of Eva (soprano), the jeweller Pogner's daughter, and going up to her asks with gentleness and concern if she is engaged to be married. He learns that, although she is not yet engaged, her father intends to marry her to the winner of a competition, to be held the next day by the Mastersingers. Eva has the option of refusing him, but she may only marry a Mastersinger, at any rate. She cannot hide her sudden affection for Walther and confides 'You or no one'. Magdalene (mezzo-soprano), her companion, boldly suggests that Walther should himself take part in the competition and she asks her boyfriend, David (tenor), apprentice to Hans Sachs, to teach him how to be a Mastersinger. The women leave and the lad begins a confused explanation of the complicated rules to be observed by singers who wish to create a 'Mastersong' and gain admittance to the guild. The Mastersingers arrive for a meeting and as soon as the session is open the young knight begs to be admitted to their ranks. 'Do you know the rules?' they ask him. 'What school do you come from?' Calmly he replies that he has been taught by breezes, waterfalls, birds and the lovely poetry of Walther von der Vogelweide. Beckmesser (bass-baritone), a pedantic clerk who wants to marry Eva, is delighted to be 'marker' with the task of noting all the competitors' faults. Walther sings a passionate hymn to Spring, but his song is not in accordance with the rules. With malignant glee, Beckmesser noisily chalks up on his slate all his rival's mistakes and Walther is rejected. Hans Sachs, the cobbler-poet, is the only one to admire the bold imagination of the poem, but his intervention is of no help. Act II. A lovely summer evening creeps over the old streets of Nuremberg. Magdalene is annoyed to hear that David's tuition did not assist Walther to sing to the Masters' liking. Pogner (bass) repeats his intention to give Eva in marriage only to a Mastersinger. Hans Sachs is sitting outside his shop, musing over the knight's free singing, which has deeply moved him. Eva approaches him and under the pretext of discussing

Scene 2, Act II of Verdi's Aida *at La Scala in 1975/76; sets and costumes by Lila de Nobili, directed by Franco Zeffirelli.*

shoes with him, she plays on his affection in order to find out what Walther did wrong. She confuses the Mastersingers' rules with Sachs's own opinion and leaves him crossly. Walther then arrives and Sachs overhears his plans for elopement. He opens his shop just as they are about to leave and a moment's hesitation is enough to stop this rash project because Beckmesser arrives to serenade Eva. The lovers hide behind a huge lime-tree. The clerk has decided to sing a lute serenade under Eva's window, but Sachs's presence puts him off and he pretends instead to ask the shoemaker for an opinion on his song. Meanwhile Magdalene, dressed as Eva, has appeared at a window. Sachs agrees to give Beckmesser an opinion and adds that he will signify each mistake by banging hard with his hammer on the sole he is mending. A grotesque serenade begins, accompanied by resounding hammer blows from Sachs and the noise wakes up the neighbours. David interrupts, thinking the serenade is addressed to Magdalene and has a scuffle with the clerk, which is the sign for other apprentices to have a brawl. Eva and Walther, hiding behind the tree, try once more to escape, but they are prevented and sep-

arated by Sachs. When the horn of the nightwatchman (bass) is heard, however, the streets empty as though by magic. Once more calm reigns under the full moon. Act III. Scene I. Sachs is sitting in his shop, deep in meditation, and barely hears David's apologies for his part in the previous night's disorders. Walther enters and tells of a dream he has had. Sachs writes down the words, gives him sound advice and from the dream they make a magnificent master song. They both go out and Beckmesser arrives to collect his shoes. He finds Walther's song in Sachs's handwriting and thinking that it must be a poem by the celebrated cobbler-poet himself, which Sachs composed to compete with him for Eva, he decides to steal it. Sachs notices that the poem has been stolen, but allows Beckmesser to keep it, as he will only make a fool of himself by singing it. Beckmesser is satisfied and has scarcely left, when Eva enters, pretending she has an ill-fitting shoe. Walther, Magdalene and David also arrive and the scene ends with a superlative quintet. Scene II. The tournament is about to begin in a field beside the river Pegnitz outside the city. One by one the artisans' guilds arrive to be cheered by the crowds and at last the Mastersingers appear. Beckmesser is the first to sing, but everyone laughs at the grotesque nonsense that he makes of his song. He is furiously embarrassed and calls Sachs a traitor and a liar. Then Sachs explains the true story of the composition, and invites Walther to sing the poem as it was originally intended. The crowd immediately acclaim it and the Mastersingers offer him the crown and Eva's hand in marriage. Still mindful of the insults he suffered at his first attempt, the young man wants to refuse the rank of Mastersinger, but Sachs rebukes him with affectionate severity and explains that the young couple should not despise the traditions of art. Walther is duly admitted as a Mastersinger, but Eva takes the crown off Walther's head and places it on Sachs instead; the Masters acclaim him as their chief, amidst general joy and celebration.

■ *Die Meistersinger von Nürnberg* is the only comedy amongst Wagner's output. According to the composer it makes a jolly, bourgeois antithesis to the aristocratic drama of *Tannhäuser*. In both cases the nucleus of the story is a singing contest, but the context and spirit are entirely different in each case. In contrast to the noble, tormented medieval knights of *Tannhäuser*, one has the good-natured, quarrelsome, sentimental town craftsmen of sixteenth-century Nuremberg. The finale is dramatic in one opera, but gay and festive in the other. The association of singers in Nuremberg was the most famous of many such associations which existed in Germany at that time, especially since one of its members was Hans Sachs, the famous shoemaker and poet, born in 1494. Wagner found the essential elements for his comedy in a 'Nuremberg Chronicle' written by Wagenseil in 1694; in particular the ceremonial, the competition sessions and the bizarre poetry and rigid rules that accompanied them. Onto this foundation the composer grafted a fable which was purely the fruit of his imagination. Within the context of middle-class town life the opera symbolizes the eternal conflict between the need for change, with Walther, the singer of unfettered inspiration as its helmsman, and the conservative forces of a too strongly held critical tradition, personified in Beckmesser (the 'marker'). In this latter character one can discover the features of the Viennese critic Eduard Hanslick, the major exponent of anti-Wagnerism. Hans Sachs is the wise mediator, guardian of tradition and at the same time aware of the need for artistic renewal. This happiest of Wagner's operas is nonetheless permeated by a thread of melancholy resignation. Some people maintain that Hans Sachs's renunciation of his love for Eva symbolizes Wagner's separation from Mathilde Wesendonk, who inspired *Tristan und Isolde*. In this opera the composer has demonstrated his outstanding mastery of harmonic, contrapuntal and instrumental writing. His technique reaches extraordinary peaks of virtuosity in the overture, in the fantastic brawl of Act II, in the quintet in Act III and in the finale. For this reason, according to Massimo Mila, the opera can be considered 'a monument of knowledge and of musical doctrine, a tribute of

Rehearsing a scene from Verdi's Aida *at the Arena of Verona in 1974, directed by Roberto Guicciardini.*

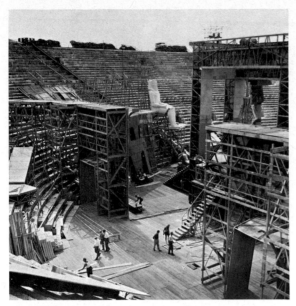

Constructing the set for the Triumph Scene in Aida *Act II in the Arena at Verona in 1974.*

homage to the highest tradition of German art by a composer who, because of his revolutionary restlessness, had seemed until then to be a dilettante genius rather than a legitimate heir to Johann Sebastian Bach'.

WILLIAM RATCLIFF
Opera in three acts by César Antonovich Cui (1835–1918), libretto by A. N. Plesceev, after a tragedy by Heinrich Heine (1822). First performance: St Petersburg, Maryinsky Theatre, 26 February 1869.

SYNOPSIS. The action takes place in Scotland in an atmosphere of ghosts and crime. In a castle on the eve of the wedding of Mary MacGregor and Douglas, Mary's father warns Douglas that a student who had been a guest in the castle years before had fallen in love with Mary and sworn that she should never belong to anybody but himself. His name was William Ratcliff and he has already twice murdered Mary's bridegrooms on the eve of her wedding. Douglas goes fearlessly to meet Ratcliff and finds him at the fatal spot where the two previous murders had taken place. Douglas overcomes him in a duel, but spares his life when he recognizes in him one who had once saved his life. Mary is obsessed with the memory of Ratcliff and discovers that her mother and Ratcliff's father had been lovers, but had not been able to marry. They were caught together after each had married another, and MacGregor had murdered Ratcliff's father and Mary's mother had died of grief. At the climax of the tragedy Ratcliff comes in wounded and Mary greets him lovingly, but in a spasm of madness the young man kills MacGregor, Mary and himself with his sword.

■ The composition of *William Ratcliff* took ten years. In it one can clearly see the contradictions of Cui's position within the Group of Five. The subject is far from anti-Romantic and the music reveals clearly the influences of French music, Schumann and Wagner.

RUY BLAS
Opera in four acts by Filippo Marchetti (1831–1902), libretto by Carlo d'Ormeville (1840–1924) after the play (1838) by Victor Hugo. First performance: Milan, Teatro alla Scala, 3 April 1869; first performance in U.K.: London, Her Majesty's Theatre, 24 November 1877; in U.S.A.: New York, 14 October 1874.

SYNOPSIS. The action takes place in Spain towards the end of the seventeenth century. Ruy Blas, a young man of humble origins, has become the valet of Don Sallustio, a courtier who has fallen into disgrace with the Queen, because, having seduced one of her ladies-in-waiting, he then refused to marry her. Don Sallustio wants to be revenged on the Queen, and when his cousin, Don Cesare, refuses to help, he decides to use his valet instead. He presents him to the Queen as Don Cesare and she becomes his mistress. Ruy Blas is raised to the rank of minister and wins popular support by his wise reforms. At this point, Don Sallustio decides to tell the Queen of the trick and entices her to a lonely villa with a false message purporting to come from Ruy Blas. To save her honour and eliminate every trace of his own guilt, Ruy Blas murders Don Sallustio and commits suicide.

■ The opera, which was performed at La Scala in the same season as *La Forza del Destino* first appeared there, went almost unobserved because of this other significant event. However, it had great good fortune after being performed at the Teatro Pagliano in Florence. In two years alone it was sung in sixty other theatres, and compared in popularity to *Rigoletto*. Although *Ruy Blas* lacks continual dramatic inspiration, it is noteworthy on account of the effective local colour, and in this sense is a precursor to the operas of Catalani and Puccini.

IL GUARANY
Opera in four acts by Antonio Carlos Gomes (1836–96), libretto by Antonio Enrico Scalvini (1835–81) after the novel by José Martiniano de Alencar. First performance: Milan, Teatro alla Scala, 19 March 1870; first performance in U.K.: London, Covent Garden, 13 July 1872; in U.S.A.: San Francisco, 1884.

SYNOPSIS. Cecilia (soprano), daughter of Don Antonio de Mariz (bass), Portuguese Governor of the Spanish territory of Guarany, is the object of the attentions of both Don Alvaro (tenor) and Gonzales (baritone). Her father wants her to marry Don Alvaro, but she has fallen in love with Pery (tenor), a native prince. Gonzales tries to capture Cecilia with the help of two Spanish adventurers, Ruy Bento (tenor) and Alonso (bass). He promises in reward to show them the site where he has discovered a silver-mine. The situation becomes desperate when some ferocious Aimoré Indians seize Cecilia and threaten to kill Pery. Don Antonio rescues them, but the Indians, organized by Don Gonzales, launch a last attack on the castle. Don Antonio sets fire to what remains of his castle while Cecilia, supported by Pery, watches the dreadful catastrophe in safety.

■ This opera with its spontaneous melodies and an action rich in theatrical effects, won a warm welcome when it appeared at La Scala. It is modelled on Verdi's melodramas and adds to this a rich exotic flavour. Gomes's fame and fortune were increased by Verdi's approving judgement when he talked about *Il Guarany* in terms of 'true musical genius' and 'exquisite workmanship'; and also by the patronage of the Emperor Don Pedro II of Brazil, who attended the triumphal performance of the opera at Rio, together with the composer. Some years before his triumph at La Scala, the Brazilian composer had had a great success in Milan with two musical comedies, *Se sa minga* (1867) and *Nella Luna* (1868), but in his later operas he was influenced by Wagner's style and he did not succeed in recapturing the melodic originality or the spectacular quality of *Il Guarany*.

AIDA

Opera in four acts by Giuseppe Verdi (1813–1901), libretto by Antonio Ghislanzoni (1824–93) based on a fragment by François Auguste Mariette, enlarged by Camille Du Locle (1832–1903) in collaboration with Verdi. First performance: Cairo, Opera House, 24 December 1871; first performance in U.K.: London, Covent Garden, 22 June 1876; in U.S.A.: New York, Academy of Music, 26 November 1873.

ORIGINAL CAST. Anta Pozzoni, Eleonora Grossi, Pietro Mongini, Francesco Steller, Medini. Conductor: Giovanni Bottesini.

SYNOPSIS. Memphis and Thebes at the time of the Pharaohs. Act I. Scene I. Hall in the Royal Palace at Memphis. The advancing Ethiopian army are threatening the Nile valley and the city of Thebes. The High Priest, Ramfis (bass), has consulted the gods to find out who should lead the Egyptian army against the enemy. This honour has fallen on Radamès (tenor). He does not yet know this, but he is longing to be chosen so as to impress the Ethiopian slave, Aida (soprano), whom he secretly loves. Radamès is himself loved by Amneris (mezzo-soprano), the King of Egypt's daughter, who has guessed his love for Aida. The King (bass) arrives with his Court and announces officially that Radamès will lead the Egyptians. Aida, daughter of the Ethiopian King, Amonasro, is desperately torn between love and patriotism. Scene II. The temple of Vulcan. During a grand ceremony in the temple, Radamès receives the sword from the hands of Ramfis and is blessed for

war and victory. Act II. A room in the apartments of Amneris. The Egyptians return victorious. The Princess tricks Aida by telling her the false news that Radamès is dead and discovering from the girl's misery that she returns Radamès's love, Amneris then discloses her lie and that she – the princess of Egypt – is the rival of a mere slave for the hero's love. Aida is about to retort that she too is a princess when she recalls the danger and simply pleads for mercy. Amneris is unrelenting. Scene II. Near a gate in the city of Thebes. Radamès returns triumphant at the head of his troops with his war chariots, banners and spoil. Amneris herself crowns him victor. He asks the King to spare the lives of the prisoners, among whom is Amonasro (baritone). Aida recognizes her father, but he begs her not to reveal who he is. The priests demand death for the Ethiopians or at least that Aida should be retained and all the others are to be set free. The King agrees and gives Amneris's hand in marriage to Radamès. He and Aida choke back their grief at this sudden decision. Act III. The banks of the Nile. The wedding is approaching and Amneris goes to pray in the temple of Isis. Amonasro realizes that his daughter could influence Radamès and could persuade him to tell her the route the Egyptian army will take on the next campaign. So Aida persuades her lover to escape Amneris's wrath by fleeing and he tells her that the Napata pass is still unguarded. Amonasro, who has overheard their conversation, comes out from his hiding-place and declares that he will cross that pass with his army. Radamès is horrified that he has unwittingly betrayed his country when Ramfis and Amneris appear. Amonasro hurls himself onto the princess, but she is protected by Radamès, who then confesses that he has betrayed the precious information and gives himself up as a prisoner to the priests. Act IV. Scene I. In the Pharaoh's palace. Amneris, who still loves Radamès, begs him to give up Aida in return for a pardon. He refuses because he wants to atone for his treachery. Amneris is appalled that the priests condemn him to be buried alive. Scene II. Above: The Temple of Vulcan, and below: the crypt in which Radamès must die. When the stone has been sealed, the condemned man discovers that Aida is waiting there for him. While Amneris weeps in despair in the temple above, the two lovers embrace and wait for death, singing their last supreme song of love and of farewell to life.

■ *Aida* was commissioned by Ismail Pasha, the Egyptian viceroy; not, as has been thought, for the inauguration of the Suez Canal, but for the opening of the Khedive's new opera house. The two dates were almost identical, but the opera was almost a year late in being performed. Scenery and costumes had to come from Paris and the French capital was besieged by the Prussians and therefore cut off. In *Aida* Verdi wanted to show that he was capable of great variety, moving from grandiose crowd scenes to individual characters, from mass emotions to intimate drama. These demands compelled him to take great pains, on the one hand over the tremendous diversity of situations and to reconcile very widely differing sections; and at the same time to look for maximum co-operation from the singers, who had not only to come to grips with their own individual parts, but also to enter into the spirit which gives life to every aspect of the opera. For the European performances, the Italian one in particular (which took place at La Scala six weeks after the one at Cairo), the composer took it upon himself to oversee every aspect of the production, from the arrangement of the solo instruments to the design of the scenery. In comparison with Verdi's earlier works, where the vocal element was the absolutely over-riding feature, *Aida* represents a change of scheme, the use of the orchestra being much more incisive and significant. It is no longer a case of what Mila called 'the vulgarity of traditional accompaniments', but an opera 'full of Italian sunlight'. Verdi felt the need to challenge the Wagnerian ascendancy, nor could he yet be influenced by it since the German composer's works only reached Italy in the years that followed. Verdi already knew a few of the scores, but although he found them fascinating he felt himself to be a long way removed from the ideas of the German master. Yet sixteen years were to pass before he could bring himself to write another opera, *Otello*.

THE STONE GUEST (Kamyeny Gost)

Opera in three acts by Alexander Dargomizhsky (1813–69), libretto based on the play by Pushkin (1830). First performance, posthumously: St Petersburg, Maryinsky Theatre, 28 February 1872.

ORIGINAL CAST. Petrov and Kommissarzevsky.

SYNOPSIS. The action takes place in Spain. Act I. Scene I. The outskirts of Madrid in the evening. Don Juan (tenor), with his servant Leporello (bass), has returned secretly from exile to meet Donna Laura (mezzo-soprano). He has been condemned for killing the Commander and he goes to the monastery where the murdered man's widow Anna (soprano) comes every evening to pray. She arrives, veiled, and Don Juan promises himself that he will seduce her. Scene II. Supper at the home of Donna Laura, an actress. The guests take leave and the lady of the house talks to her new lover, Don Carlos (baritone). She confesses to him that she has loved Don Juan, who arrives on the scene as though she had evoked him. A duel ensues and Don Carlos is killed. Act II. In the cloister near the Commander's tomb, Don Juan, dressed as a monk, goes up to Donna Anna and confesses his love for her. She is very disconcerted by the unsuitability of such a conversation in such a place, but invites the man – who has introduced himself as Diego de Calvido – to come to her house the next day. Don Juan promises her to behave honourably. Alone with Leporello, Don Juan gives vent to his delight to the point of jokingly asking the Commander's statue to Anna's house the next day. The statue accepts with a nod of the head. Act III. Anna's bedroom. The seducer has almost won his battle and has even revealed his true identity. She has

almost forgiven him when there is a banging on the door. The statue enters, and, as Anna faints, it clasps Don Juan in a fatal grip.

■ Dargomizhsky had given up writing for the theatre after his bitter experiences with *Esmeralda* and *Rusalka*. But he was encouraged to write a grand opera by the enthusiasm of the Group of Five, who used to meet in his house. *The Stone Guest*, based on Pushkin's version of *Don Juan*, was still unfinished at the composer's death. It was orchestrated by Rimsky-Korsakov, while Cui completed the unfinished sections. It was fairly successful, and has been regularly performed in Russian theatres. There have also been some recent revivals in other parts of the world, such as that at the Florentine 'Maggio musicale' of 1956. The opera remains significant on account of a certain form of melodic recitative already attempted by the composer in earlier operas and perfected in this one. For this reason the work has had a considerable influence on Russian musicians.

DJAMILEH

Opéra comique in one act by Georges Bizet (1838–75), libretto by Louis Gallet, based on the poem Namouna *(1832) by Alfred de Musset. First performance: Paris, Opéra-Comique (Salle Favart), 22 May 1872; first performance in U.K.: Manchester, 22 September 1892; in U.S.A.: Boston, Opera House, 24 February 1913.*

SYNOPSIS. The story is set in Egypt. Haroun (tenor), a rich and bored young man of the world, changes his mistress every month. Each time he charges his secretary, Splendiano (baritone), to buy him a new one at the market. Djamileh (mezzo-soprano) would be fated to the same end and would have been cast off if she had not fallen in love with Haroun. She arranges with the secretary to be offered to Haroun again in disguise. By this combination of cunning, love and devotion, the slave-girl conquers Haroun's heart.

■ Like all Bizet's operas, *Djamileh* is set in a strange land and has a rich, oriental colour. In it we can detect a foretaste of what Bizet will later become. The opera was not successful and was criticized for being too 'Wagnerian'; after eleven performances its run was ended. It did not return to Paris until 27 October 1938.

THE MAID OF PSKOV (Pskovityanka) revised as IVAN THE TERRIBLE

Serious opera in four acts by Nicolay Rimsky-Korsakov (1844–1908), libretto by the composer from a play by Lev Alexandrovich Mey (1822–62). First performance: St Petersburg, Maryinsky Theatre, 13 January 1873; first performance in U.K.: London, Drury Lane, 8 July 1913.

SYNOPSIS. Russia, end of the sixteenth century. The free city of Pskov lives in terror of suffering the same fate as Novgorod, whose inhabitants had rebelled against the Tsar, Ivan the Terrible. Two old nurses, Vlassievna (contralto) and Perfilievna (mezzo-soprano), discuss the rumour that the Princess Olga, who has been brought up by the Governor of Pskov, Prince Youry Ivanovich Tokmakov, as his daughter, is in fact of more exalted birth. Olga (soprano) comes to meet her lover, Michael Toucha (tenor), and tells him that she fears that she is to be betrothed to an old friend of Prince Tokmakov, the Boyar Matouta. Toucha leaves when the Prince (bass) and the Boyar (tenor) walk into the garden, talking over the imminent arrival of the Tsar. The Prince offers his friend the hand of Olga in marriage, revealing, however, that she is his niece (his sister's daughter by an unknown father). Suddenly the alarm bell sounds, warning the citizens of Ivan's approach. In the main square, Tokmakov persuades all but Toucha to greet their Tsar in peace and not to oppose him with arms. Ivan (bass) is therefore received with hospitality, but it is not until he sees Olga that he shows any signs of relenting from his ruthless purpose of subduing the city. Summoning the Prince, he learns of Olga's mysterious parentage and promises to leave the city in peace, taking Olga with him. In a nearby forest Olga and Toucha are surprised together by Matouta's servants, as they plan to elope. In his tent, Ivan recalls his love for Olga's mother and, when the girl is brought in, he soon forgives her. Father and daughter talk, but when Toucha launches an attack in the camp to rescue her, Olga is shot in the confusion and dies – 'sacrificed for the city'.

■ The composer found inspiration for the opera at the country house of his friend Lodygenski in proximity to nature and the Russian countryside. Work was then interrupted and only completed when he was living with Mussorgsky, whose influence may be felt throughout the work and especially in the characterization. From the original story of Olga, *The Maid of Pskov* eventually became the story of the conflict between Pskov and the Tsar.

LE ROI L'A DIT (lit. The King has Commanded it)
Opéra comique in three acts by Léo Delibes (1836–91), libretto by Edmond Gondinet. First performance: Paris, Opéra-Comique, 24 May 1873; first performance in U.K.: London, Prince of Wales Theatre, 13 December 1894.

SYNOPSIS. A series of circumstances has led to the belief at the court of Louis XIV that the Marquis of Montecontour has a son, whereas he actually has four daughters. The Marquis is commanded to present his son at court, so he passes off a peasant as his own offspring. The boy takes advantage of the situation to create all manner of trouble for the Marquis. Finally the Marquis devises a plan to get rid of the young nuisance and the King consoles him for 'the loss of a son' with a dukedom.

■ This was Delibes's first attempt to write a full-scale opera. He had previously written over a dozen operet-

tas. It was very successful in Paris and was also performed abroad. In 1898 it was reduced to two acts by Philippe Gille.

SOROCHINSKY FAIR (Sorocinskaja Jarmarka)
Comic opera in three acts by Modest Mussorgsky (1839–81), libretto by the composer, based on a story by Gogol. The opera is unfinished. Begun in 1873, Mussorgsky completed the Prelude, the Market scene in Act I, a large part of Act II, a scene adapted from the symphonic piece A Night on the Bare Mountain, *an instrumental dance (the hopak at the end of Act III) and two songs. First private performance: St Petersburg, Comedy Theatre, 30 December 1911, on the occasion of the 30th anniversary of the composer's death. First public performance: Moscow, Free Theatre, 21 October 1913. First performance in U.K.: London, Fortune Theatre, 17 February 1934; in U.S.A.: New York, Metropolitan Opera House, 29 November 1930.*

SYNOPSIS. In the village of Sorochinsky, during the fair. Cherevik (bass) does business while his daughter Parassia (soprano) admires the clothes and ornaments on show. She wants him to buy her something, but he is too busy talking to listen to her. Gritzko (tenor) pays court to Parassia, while an old gypsy (bass) tells of a devil in the neighbourhood who casts spells upsetting people's affairs and stealing cattle and horses. Cherevik notices Gritzko's attentions to his daughter and intervenes, but finding that he is the son of an old friend, he gives him permission to marry Parassia. To celebrate the event they go together to the inn where Khivria (mezzo-soprano), Cherevik's peevish wife, joins them. She tells everyone off and refuses her consent to the match. Evening falls and the square empties. The gypsy promises to help Gritzko if he will sell him some cattle. On the way home Parassia meets Gritzko and they embrace tenderly. Act II. Cherevik's cottage. Khivria continues to scold her husband, and finally chases him out of the house. As soon as she is alone, she dresses up and lays the table, to prepare for her lover, the foolish son of the local priest (tenor). The two are dining together when Cherevik returns, accompanied by his friends. Khivria just has time to hide her lover in the attic and to whisk away the remains of the meal. As they drink, the guests tell the story of the devil who appears in the village in the guise of a pig. They have hardly said it when a pig's head appears at the window and there is general panic. The priest's son rushes down from the attic and tries to hide under Khivria's skirt. But it is not the devil – it is the gypsy who, followed by the local young people, is playing a trick on them. The priest's son's presence is discovered amongst general laughter and Khivria's 'affair' is revealed. Act III. The village square. Parassia comes out of her house looking at herself in a little mirror, finds herself pretty and – feeling happy – does a little dance. Cherevik joins her. Gritzko asks again to marry her and despite Khivria's further attempts to prevent the marriage, this time her husband does not allow her to interfere. Everything is thus resolved and the engaged pair kiss while the other young people dance a hopak round them.

■ As the opera was still in a fragmentary state, in 1917 the Russian composer Cesar Antonovich Cui (1835–1918), who like Mussorgsky had been one of the Group of Five, undertook to rewrite it. It was again rewritten in 1923 by Nikolay Cherepnin, who took charge of the first complete performance at Monte Carlo. This version is more faithful to Mussorgsky's harmonic and melodic language, which was an ingenious and faithful interpretation of Russian folk melodies and also, in this opera, of Ukrainian song.

BORIS GODUNOV

Opera in a prologue and four acts by Modest Mussorgsky (1839–81), libretto by the composer, based on the play by Pushkin (1826) and on the History of the Russian Empire *by Nikolay M. Karamzin (1829). First performance: St Petersburg, Maryinsky Theatre, 8 February 1874; first performance in U.K.: London, Drury Lane, 24 June 1913; in U.S.A.: New York, Metropolitan Opera House, 19 March 1913.*

SYNOPSIS. The action takes place in Russia between 1598 and 1605. Prologue, Scene I. Outside the monastery at Novedevichy, where Boris Godunov (bass) is in retreat, a crowd of Russian peasants pray for guidance. The Tsar Feodor has died (his heir Dimitri was killed in mysterious circumstances many years ago) and Boris has been called upon by the people to be his successor. Scene II. In the Kremlin Square Boris is crowned. Act I. Scene I. A cell in the monastery at Chudov. The old monk Pimen (bass) has finished writing the chronicle of his times while the novice Grigory (tenor), who shares his cell, is asleep. When Grigory wakes, he tells of his dream, which Pimen takes to signify great ambition. He encourages Grigory to carry on his own work of a historian and not to hanker for the worldly life outside the monastery. He tells him the story of the Tsarevich's murder and Grigory calls for human and divine vengeance on the murderer. Scene II. An inn on the Lithuanian border. The innkeeper sings a happy song as she does her mending. Missail (tenor) and Varlaam (bass), renegade friars, arrive, followed by Grigory, who has run away from the monastery and is trying to cross the border in disguise. The border guards have orders to apprehend him and suddenly burst into the inn to search it. The official (bass) is illiterate and makes Grigory himself read the description of the man they are looking for. He takes advantage of this to describe Varlaam's distinguishing features instead of his own, but his trick is discovered and he has to escape out of the window. Act II. Scene I. In the Tsar's apartments in the Kremlin. Xenia (soprano), Boris's daughter, is weeping for the death of her fiancé. The old nurse (contralto) tries to cheer her up with folk songs and a noisy dance; she is startled and terrified when Boris enters unexpectedly. Feodor (mezzo-soprano), his son, shows him on a map the frontiers of his realm. The Tsar is moved, but remorse for his past

crime tortures him. A boyar announces a visit from Prince Shuisky (tenor) and warns that the Prince is plotting against the Tsar. The Prince brings Boris news of an uprising started by someone who calls himself Tsarevich Dimitri. Boris is terrified, fearing that Dimitri has somehow survived and Shuisky tries to reassure him by retelling the story of how the Tsarevich's corpse was left in the church for five days, but showed no signs of decomposition. Boris imagines that the figures in the chiming clock are visions of the dead and he sinks to the floor, exhausted and sobbing with remorse. Act III. Scene I. In the castle of Sandomir in Poland. Princess Marina (mezzo-soprano) is being dressed and adorned by her maid. She is cynical and ambitious, and intends to seduce the pretender Dimitri, who is really the novice Grigory, in order to become one day the Tsarina of Russia. The Jesuit Rangoni (bass), her spiritual father, agrees to her plan, but makes her promise she will bring Russia back into the bosom of the Catholic Church. Scene II. In the garden by moonlight. Dimitri is waiting for Marina. Father Rangoni joins him and assures him of the princess's favours if he will do as he is advised. Marina appears and replies to Dimitri's passionate words with her own cold-hearted thirst for power. Dimitri is wounded by her cynicism, but she uses all her skill to seduce him. Father Rangoni, unseen, savours his triumph. Act IV. Scene I. A room in the Kremlin. The Duma is meeting to discuss the rebellion of the false Dimitri. Prince Shuisky tells them of the Tsar's hallucinations and his report is confirmed by the appearance of Boris himself. He falls into a state of delirium but orders the monk Pimen to be brought in. He tells of a recent miracle near the tomb of the murdered Tsarevich. Boris has another fit and sensing he is near to death summons his son. He points him out as his legitimate successor, begs him to rule justly, and dies. Scene II. The forest Kromy at night. The rebels have captured a boyar and subject him to mockery and ridicule. A simpleton (tenor) is robbed of his few alms while he is absorbed in prayer. Missail and Varlaam join the crowd in jeering at two Jesuits who sing the praises of Dimitri in Latin; Dimitri is acclaimed by the crowd as the new Tsar. The simpleton is left alone on the stage, lit up by gleams from the fires, bewailing the sad fate of Russia.

■ *Boris*, a masterpiece of Russian music, was begun in the autumn of 1868, on the advice of the historian V. Nikolsky, and finished in December of the following year. It was submitted to the literary committee of the Maryinsky Theatre of St Petersburg and rejected. It was considered too far removed from contemporary taste (both in Wagnerian drama, and in Italian–French melodrama), and the musical ideas of the talented innovator were too new and bold. With some cuts and the addition of the Polish scenes of Marina and Dimitri, the opera was once more submitted and once more rejected in 1872. But concert performances and performances of single scenes, which were put on by some of the singers of the Imperial Theatre, who had the right to choose their programmes, brought its orig-

The opening scene of Mussorgsky's Sorochinsky Fair, *performed by the Moscow Free Theatre, 1913. Moscow, Bakhruscin Theatrical Museum.*

inality and grandeur to the notice of the public. The opera was finally staged, conducted by Eduard Napravnik, with the baritone Ivan A. Melnikov as Boris, Julia P. Platonova as Marina, Daria Leonora as the innkeeper, Osip Petrov as Varlaam. The public was enthusiastic, but the critics were divided. After twenty-six performances in five years it was dropped and was then revived at the Moscow Bolshoi from 1888 to 1890. When Mussorgsky died, Rimsky-Korsakov took over the task of publishing the score and rewrote the orchestration (which in the original version presented some undeniable technical deficiencies), sometimes working in conflict with the composer's intentions. Despite a critical revision written by Paul Lamm and published in Russia in 1928, the opera is almost always performed in Rimsky-Korsakov's version. It was performed for the first time in Italy at the Teatro alla Scala on 14 January 1909. Diaghilev's company performed in it in Paris in 1908 with a famous interpretation by Chaliapin. It was conducted in New York in 1913 by Toscanini and also performed in the same year in London. A recent version by Shostakovich was written at the request of the Bolshoi Theatre of Moscow and published in Moscow in 1963.

DIE FLEDERMAUS (The Bat)

Operetta in three acts by Johann Strauss II (1825–99); original book and lyrics by Meilhac and Halévy (Le Réveillon, 1872), based on a German comedy by Roderich Benedix (Das Gefängnis, 1851), and adapted by Karl Haffner and Richard Genée. First performance: Vienna, Theater an der Wien, 5 April 1874. First performance in U.K.: London, Alhambra, 18 December 1876; in U.S.A.: New York, Stadt Theater, 21 November 1874.

ORIGINAL CAST included: Marie Geistinger (Rosalinde), Mme Charles Hirsch (Adele), Mme Rittinger (Orlofsky), Szika (Eisenstein), Rüdinger (Alfred), Lebrecht (Falke), Rott (Blind). Conducted by the composer.

SYNOPSIS. Vienna, in the second half of the nineteenth century. The house of Gabriel von Eisenstein, a wealthy man about town. His wife, Rosalinde (soprano), is surprised to hear the voice of an old admirer, Alfred, an opera singer (tenor), serenading her from the garden. He hides while the maid Adele (soprano) asks for the evening off to visit a sick aunt, which Rosalinde refuses to allow, flustered as she is by Alfred's appearance and the fact that her husband is to begin a short prison sentence that very evening. Adele bursts into tears, because in fact her sister, a ballet dancer called Ida (soprano), had secured her an invitation to a ball given by the wealthy Russian Prince Orlofsky. Alfred announces that he will return as soon as Eisenstein has gone to prison and Rosalinde changes her mind about needing Adele to help her in the house. Then Eisenstein (tenor) enters, blaming his lawyer, Dr Blind (tenor), for failing to extricate him from the mess in which he finds himself. His annoyance is dispelled when his friend Dr Falke (baritone) produces an invitation for him (and unknown to him for Rosalinde) to Prince Orlofsky's ball. So, although his wife thinks it strange, he leaves for prison in style – in evening dress! No sooner has he gone than Alfred takes his place at the supper table and in Rosalinde's arms. They are together when Frank, the prison governor (baritone), unexpectedly arrives – also in evening dress, for he too is to be a guest at Orlofsky's party – to escort his distinguished prisoner to his cell. Rosalinde avoids a compromising situation by persuading Alfred to pretend to be her husband and go to prison for her sake. Then she is free to dress herself, as Falke has instructed, as a Hungarian Countess and, well-

A. Krivsceni and E. Antonova of the Bolshoi in a scene from Mussorgsky's Sorochinsky Fair.

disguised, to leave for the ball. Act II. Prince Orlofsky's palace. The Prince (mezzo-soprano) sings of his boredom and begs Falke to amuse him. Falke, for his part, accepts the challenge by explaining that he has already arranged an entertainment. His plan is to obtain an elaborate revenge on Eisenstein for once leaving him after a party to walk home, in broad daylight, in fancy dress as a bat. The first diverting incident occurs when Eisenstein (under the assumed name of Marquis Renard) recognizes Adele; he is most embarrassed when she leads a laughing song mocking his confusion of a 'society' lady with a parlour maid. He is then introduced to the 'Chevalier Chagrin' (actually Frank) and their halting French exchanges cause much merriment, until the arrival of a masked Hungarian beauty quickly attracts his attention. He sets about charming her with his usual party trick – a chiming pocket watch. Rosalinde enjoys the game of parting her husband from his famous toy and reassures the company's doubts about her identity by singing a Czardas and Frischka with undeniably Hungarian spirit. Everyone sits back to enjoy a performance of the Imperial Ballet before joining in a chorus in praise of champagne, brotherhood and sisterhood. Realizing that it is six o'clock and time to report to the prison, the Marquis and the Chevalier hurry away. Act III. The prison. Frosch (speaking part) the jailer, is very tipsy and complains about the noise which his prisoner has been making and the nuisance of having to call a lawyer for him. Frank arrives, closely followed by Ida and Adele. They ask him to promote Adele's career on the stage and she sings a quick coloratura aria to prove her abilities. He bundles them into the only spare cell when another visitor rings the bell. It turns out to be Eisenstein, who is unnerved to hear that someone calling himself Eisenstein has been under lock and key all night. Frank leaves the room for a moment to greet a

further arrival and Eisenstein takes the opportunity to borrow Blind's wig and gown so as to be in a position to see the prisoner. The new arrival is Rosalinde, and Eisenstein takes a high moral tone when interviewing her with Alfred. Shortly, however, his own disguise is perceived and Rosalinde produces the incriminating chiming watch. As if by magic, all Prince Orlofsky's other guests arrive and they resume the chorus with a toast to champagne!

■ Johann Strauss II was the son of Johann Strauss I (1804–49), who had, with Lanner, popularized the Viennese waltz throughout Europe. The son followed in his footsteps as conductor and composer of dance music, but it is said to have been Offenbach, then the unchallenged king of Parisian operetta, who suggested to Strauss that he should try his hand at a work for the stage. It was certainly due to the persistent encouragement of Strauss's wife Jetty that this potential was realized. Although his first effort, *Die Lustigen Weiber von Wien (The Merry Wives of Vienna)* was abandoned when the leading lady withdrew, a second attempt *Indigo und die 40 Räuber (Indigo and the 40 Thieves)* enjoyed a great success. Friends immediately began to shower Strauss with compliments and advice, of which the most valuable was that he should look for a good librettist. His need must have been in the mind of the Viennese impresario, Steiner, when he bought, sight unseen, a text by Offenbach's own librettists, Meilhac and Halévy. It is not known whether they had offered Offenbach first refusal of *Le Réveillon*, a costume drama set in Paris on Christmas Eve, but it is known that Steiner was very disappointed when he read it. The publisher Gustav Levy suggested, however, that it could be adjusted for Viennese taste by two veteran collaborators: a 70-year-old recluse, Karl Haffner, and a man of the theatre, Richard Genée, his junior by 20 years. The brilliance of their success may be judged from the fact that Strauss was inspired to write in only 43 days a score which captures not simply the atmosphere of giddy hedonism in contemporary society but an excellently drawn gallery of characters. The orchestration surpasses anything he had previously written for subtlety and dramatic verve. The Czardas, for example, foreshadows the splendours of his other great operetta *Der Zigeunerbaron (The Gipsy Baron)*, with a truly Hungarian spirit. The score abounds in exquisite moments; notably the farewell trio in Act I when Rosalinde, Adele and Eisenstein all secretly look forward to their evening of delight; Adele's Act II laughing song ('*Mein Herr Marquis, ein Mann wie Sie*') (*My dear Marquis, a man like you*); and, of course, the Fledermaus waltz, set to the words which could be a motto for Strauss's whole life's work: *Glücklich ist, wer vergisst, was nicht mehr zu ändern ist* (Happy is he who forgets that which cannot be changed). Unfortunately, despite a brilliant première, the operetta was not immediately successful in Vienna, perhaps because of the recent Stock Exchange disasters (9 May 1873), and there were only 16 performances. It triumphed in Berlin, Hamburg and even Paris (no doubt to Offenbach's dismay) before it returned to be welcomed

Coronation scene from Mussorgsky's Boris Godunov *in the 1969 Covent Garden production.*

ecstatically by the Viennese. On 28 October 1894, it made history (for operetta) by receiving an evening performance at the Imperial Opera; and it has remained the supreme masterpiece and epitome of Viennese operetta ever since.

THE DEMON (Dyemoñ)

Serious opera in three acts by Anton Grigorevich Rubinstein (1830–94), libretto by Pavel Alexandrovich Viskovatov, based on the poem by Lermontov (1841). First performance: St Petersburg, Imperial Theatre, 25 January 1875; first performance in U.K.: London, Covent Garden, 21 June 1881; in U.S.A.: San Francisco, 17 June 1922.

SYNOPSIS. The demon, a mortal man with devilish characteristics, sadly contemplates the world below from the peak of Kazbec. Sick with boredom, he regrets his misspent youth and seeks a woman's love. He notices Tamara, dancing with some other girls on the eve of her marriage, and falls in love with her. He arranges for her future husband, Prince Sinodal, to be killed by brigands. To escape the demon's love Tamara shuts herself in a convent, but he pursues her even into the privacy of her cell. Here takes place the long love duet in which he celebrates his triumph. Sinodal, transformed into an angel, then appears and celestial voices call Tamara to Paradise. She frees herself from the arms of the demon and falls dead. She has gained redemption by the sacrifice of her life, and the demon is left despairing and alone.

■ *The Demon* was so successful at its first performance that the composer acquired the reputation of a national composer. It is still considered Rubinstein's finest opera. Even though the story, the pre-determined passions, the possibility of redemption, are all elements reminiscent of Wagnerian opera, the music has no link with that of the German composer.

CARMEN

Drama lyrique in four acts by Georges Bizet (1838–75), libretto by Henri Meilhac (1831–97) and Ludovic Halévy (1834–1908), based on the novel by Prosper Mérimée (1847). First performance: Paris, Opéra-Comique, 3 March 1875; first performance in U.K.: London, Her Majesty's Theatre, 22 June 1878; in U.S.A.: New York, Academy of Music, 23 October 1878.

ORIGINAL CAST included Célestine Galli-Marié (Carmen), Paul Lhérie (Don José), Joseph Bouhy (Escamillo), Margherite Chapuy (Micaela).

SYNOPSIS. Spain, about 1820. Act I. A square in Seville: on one side is a cigarette factory and opposite the dragoon guards barracks. Soldiers and passers-by stop in the square waiting for the cigarette girls to come out. Micaela (soprano), a country girl, is shyly looking for Don José (tenor), a dragoon corporal. Since he is not there, she leaves to return later. Don José arrives and at midday the factory girls return to work. Among them is a gypsy, Carmen (mezzo-soprano) who, with her eye on Don José, throws him a flower. He apparently remains indifferent, but afterwards he muses on her wild and reckless charm. Micaela returns with news of his mother and he promises to marry her as his mother would like. A quarrel has broken out in the factory and Carmen is arrested for wounding one of her companions. She is to be guarded by José and uses all her seductive powers to obtain her freedom. José hesitates at first, but then, completely under her spell, agrees to let her escape on their way to prison. Act II. The inn of Lillas Pastia. Carmen is dancing with two friends. The bullfighter Escamillo (baritone) enters, applauded by his admirers, and directs his admiration at Carmen, but she ignores his advances because she is expecting José to join her on his release from prison, where he has been held for letting her escape. The inn is full of smugglers. Remendado (tenor) and Dancairo (baritone) are planning a big expedition that night, but Carmen refuses to participate because José is expected any minute. He enters and they enjoy a brief time together before the retreat is sounded and he wants to return to barracks. Carmen invites him to run away with her to the mountains, where they will be completely free. Captain Zuniga (bass) comes in and orders José to return. The two men are about to fight when Dancairo and Remendado intervene, separate them and take the captain away. José is thus compelled by circumstances to leave the regiment and follow Carmen. Act III. The smuggler's headquarters in the mountains. José is weighed down with remorse at breaking his promises to his mother, and Carmen is already tired of him; she has thoughts of Escamillo. When she reads her fortune in the cards she sees death on every one, unlike her friends Frasquita (soprano) and Mercedes (soprano), who foresee rich and handsome lovers for themselves. Escamillo arrives and José picks a quarrel with him; Carmen has great difficulty in separating them. Micaela has watched the fight because she has come up to the hideout to persuade José to visit his mother, who is dying. José follows Micaela but threatens Carmen that he will catch up with her. Act IV. A square in Seville outside the bull-ring. The crowd applauds Escamillo, who is on his way to the bullfight with his new mistress, Carmen. Her friends warn her that José has been seen in the square. Carmen is not frightened and waits for her former lover. José begs her to return to him, but Carmen refuses scornfully and throws at his feet a ring he had given her. Shouts acclaiming Escamillo are heard from the bullring, and blind with jealousy Don José stabs Carmen to death. Then, sobbing, he allows himself to be arrested.

■ Neither the background nor the atmosphere of the opera has much in common with Mérimée's novel since the librettists have conveniently altered them to get rid of the crudely realistic features. In fact the Parisian theatre-going public did not care for stories of gypsies, thieves, cigarette-girls and smugglers, and especially

Photograph of the 1927 Moscow Bolshoi Theatre production of Mussorgsky's Boris Godunov.

when they ended in violence. Mérimée's Spain was softened by a lot of local colour, dances and brilliant choruses. One admirable character was introduced in the person of Micaela as a counter-balance to the brash and violent personality of Carmen. The latter is no longer a poor devilish gypsy girl whose husband has been killed by brigands. In the opera she is more of an elegant 'señorita' full of whims. Don José also is no longer a multiple murderer but a simple countryman. But despite these precautions there was an atmosphere of great tension on the evening of the first performance. The critics exploded in a storm and the opera was a failure. The libretto was criticized for immorality, for obscenity, for lacking a sense of theatre, for having broken with all the standards of good taste, and the music for belonging to so-called 'music of the future' and lacking in melody. The performances on the subsequent evenings were given before an almost empty hall. However, *Carmen* is Bizet's masterpiece; in it the composer uses his dramatic genius to overcome all the limitations of the libretto. While remaining within the traditional framework of *opéra-comique*, Bizet gives it a new vitality. He has left arias, songs, choruses, duets and recitatives intact, but has added a new dimension to conventional situations and feelings by endowing them with stronger and more realistic emotions, with passionate feelings and violent actions. The music is in keeping with these new features and is full of imagination. Certainly all the arguments about the sources of various themes are peripheral, as are those about the use of popular Spanish music. The opera was revived quite soon afterwards and was well received abroad and in the French provinces. It gathered momentum until its conclusive triumph in Paris eight years after the first performance.

On the evening of 23 December 1904 it was performed for the thousandth time in the same theatre; and on 29 June 1930 for the two thousandth time. *Carmen* has since toured the world, been translated into many languages and continues to be popular. It is very sad that Bizet, who died three months after the first performance, at the age of only 36, never knew how successful his work became. Indeed, the deterioration in his health and his last attack of illness were not unconnected with the opera's original failure.

DIE KÖNIGIN VON SABA (The Queen of Sheba)
Opera in four acts by Carl Goldmark (1830–1915), libretto by Salomon Hermann Mosenthal (1821–77). First performance: Vienna, Hoftheater, 10 March 1875; first performance in U.K.: London, Kennington Theatre, 29 August 1910; in U.S.A.: New York, Metropolitan Opera House, 2 December 1885.

SYNOPSIS. The text, based on the Bible, tells the story of the Queen of Sheba's visit to King Solomon. The King's favourite, Assad (tenor), who has been promised as bridegroom to Sulamith (soprano), daughter of the High Priest (bass), has fallen in love with the Queen (mezzo-soprano). Solomon (baritone) insists that his wedding go ahead despite this. The Queen will not admit in public that she returns Assad's passion, but her appearance at his wedding drives him to commit a sacrilegious crime in the temple. Solomon refuses the Queen's request to release him from prison and she leaves angrily. Sulamith retires to the desert to find peace, and when Assad is freed he goes to seek her. He is exhausted when he reaches her asylum and they can only sing of their future bliss before he dies.

■ This is Goldmark's first opera and it was very well received when it first appeared, making the composer's name famous. The music, which is uneven in quality, still remains interesting, with rich timbres and oriental-style melodies, and with well-assimilated Wagnerian harmonic influences. These elements make *Die Königin von Saba* one of this Hungarian composer's best works.

VAKULA THE SMITH (Kusnetz Vakula)
Opera in four acts by Peter Ilyich Tchaikovsky (1840–93), libretto by Yakov Petrovich Polonsky based on Christmas Eve *by Gogol (1832). First performance: St Petersburg, Maryinsky Theatre, 6 February 1876.*

■ This opera was rewritten by the composer in 1885 and performed with the title *Cherevichki* (The little Shoes) in Moscow on 31 January 1887. It is also known in Europe under the title *Oxana's Caprice*. It was the first work with which Tchaikovsky pronounced himself content. Originally the libretto had been written by Serov. The opera enjoyed great popularity in Russia, particularly as it makes frequent use of popular Russian and Ukrainian tunes.

Renato Guttuso's designs for the second act of Bizet's Carmen.

ANGELO
Opera in four acts by César Antonovich Cui (1835–1918), libretto by Victor Petrovich Burenin, based on Victor Hugo's play Angelo, tyran de Padoue *(1835). First performance: St Petersburg, Maryinsky Theatre, 13 February 1876.*

SYNOPSIS. The action takes place in Padua in 1549. Tisbe is a second-rate actress who is wrongly held to be the mistress of Malipiero, the Venetian Governor. In fact she loves Rodolfo (the assumed name of Ezzelino da Romano), who for his part is infatuated with Caterina Bregadin, a woman he met in Venice and whom he knows to be now married although he has no idea who her husband is nor where she lives. He discovers that she is Angelo's wife. Tisbe surprises Rodolfo and Caterina together and wants to take revenge on them but for her suspicion that Caterina once saved her mother. She resolves to protect Caterina from her husband's wrath at her adultery. She gives Caterina a sleeping-draught, instead of the poison which Angelo had prepared for her, and secretly removes her to her own house. Rodolfo imagines that Tisbe has poisoned her and murders her. He discovers that she had done what she did so that Caterina might be his.

LA GIOCONDA (The Joyful Girl)
Opera drammatica in four acts by Amilcare Ponchielli (1834–86), libretto by Tobia Gorrio (an anagram of Arrigo Boito, 1842–1918), based on Victor Hugo's play Angelo, tyran de Padoue *(1835). First performance: Milan, Teatro alla Scala, 8 April 1876; first performance in U.K.: London, Covent Garden, 31 May 1883; in U.S.A.: New York, Metropolitan Opera*

House, 20 December 1883. Second completed version: Milan, Teatro alla Scala, 12 February 1880.

ORIGINAL CAST. Marini-Masi, Biancolini-Rodriguez, Gayarre, Aldighieri, Maini. Conductor: Franco Faccio.

SYNOPSIS. The action is set in Venice in the seventeenth century. Act I. In the courtyard of the Ducal Palace, La Gioconda (soprano), a travelling singer, rejects the advances of Barnaba (baritone), a spy of the Council of Ten. In revenge he publicly accuses her blind mother, La Cieca (contralto), of witchcraft. The old woman would have been immediately killed by the crowd if Enzo Grimaldi (tenor), a Genoese prince (whom La Gioconda secretly loves), had not intervened to defend her. Although banished from Venice, he has returned in disguise, because he loves the Genoese wife, Laura Adorno (mezzo-soprano), of Alvise Badoero (bass), one of the chiefs of the Venetian State inquisition. Despite Enzo's efforts Alvise arrests La Cieca, but Laura obtains a pardon for her. La Cieca gives her a rosary as a token of her gratitude. Meanwhile, Barnaba, in an attempt to separate Enzo from La Gioconda, promises to help him elope with Laura. When La Gioconda finds out about Enzo and Laura and furthermore that Barnaba had informed the authorities, she decides to kill her rival. Act II. In order to put her plan into action La Gioconda hides in the ship on which Enzo and Laura intend to escape. She is about to stab Laura when she notices her mother's rosary and realizes that Laura must have been La Cieca's saviour. She resolves not to prevent the elopement and assists the lovers, when Alvise arrives, to escape. Laura and La Gioconda flee together while Enzo sets fire to the ship, dives into the water and

Bizet's Carmen *in the Paris Opéra production designed by Lila de Nobili.*

Rough sketch by Emile Bertin for Act IV of Bizet's Carmen, *performed at the Opéra-Comique in 1875. Paris, Bibliothèque de l'Opéra.*

swims to the shore. Act III. At the Ca' d'Oro in Laura's room. While a magnificent celebration is held in the reception rooms, Alvise accuses his wife of adultery and commands her to drink poison. La Gioconda manages to substitute a sleeping-draught for the poison and persuades Laura to drink it and pretend to be dead. After the ball (*Dance of the Hours*), Alvise raises a curtain and shows the horrified guests Laura lying on a bed as though dead. Enzo, masked, is among the guests but, when he sees Laura apparently dead, he gives himself away and is arrested. La Gioconda realizes that the only way to save the man she loves is to promise to love Barnaba in exchange for Enzo's life. Barnaba accepts the bargain and then profits by the general confusion to drag La Cieca away as a hostage. Act IV. Laura, still sleeping, is brought to a ruined palace in the Giudecca by some of La Gioconda's trusted men. The singer, who is in despair at her mother's disappearance and at having to give up Enzo, contemplates suicide. Enzo arrives, having escaped from prison with Barnaba's help, and although he knows about La Gioconda's generosity and sacrifices, runs off with Laura. When Barnaba comes to settle the bargain, La Gioconda pretends to consent but stabs herself. In his fury, he screams that he has killed her mother – but she can no longer hear him.

■ This is a typical example of popular grand opera, with strongly passionate and dramatic features, and melodies which are extremely memorable. It is perhaps Ponchielli's only opera which still deeply affects the public, especially the Italian public, and has stood the test of time. Because it is so spectacular it is very suitable for grandiose productions, such as those in the Arena in Verona. The libretto is very skilful and yet Boito was not happy with it and preferred to sign it with a pseudonym. The opera was a resounding success right from the first performance. Nonetheless, Ponchielli listened to certain observations from the critics and made numerous changes, stripping away much of the complexity of the story and the music. When it was performed in Rome (December 1877) and in Genoa (December 1879), the opera was very different from the original version. The final version was staged in Milan at the Teatro alla Scala on 12 February 1880.

DER RING DES NIBELUNGEN
(The Ring of the Nibelung)
A stage-festival play for three days and a preliminary evening by Richard Wagner (1813–83), text by the composer, inspired by the Nibelung saga. The Ring *comprises four operas: Prologue:* Das Rheingold; *Day*

I: Die Walküre; *Day II:* Siegfried; *Day III:* Götter-dämmerung. *First performance of the complete cycle: Bayreuth, August 1876.*

DAS RHEINGOLD (The Rhinegold)

One act. First performance: Munich, Hoftheater, 22 September 1869. First performance in U.K.: London, Her Majesty's Theatre, 5 May 1882; in U.S.A.: New York, Metropolitan Opera House, 4 January 1889.

ORIGINAL CAST. August Kindermann (Wotan), Franz Nachbaur (Froh), Heinrich (Donner), Vogl (Loge), Fischer (Alberich), Schlosser (Mime), Sophie Stehle (Fricka), Müller (Freia), Seehofer (Erda). Conductor: Franz Wüllner.

SYNOPSIS. The deep waters of the Rhine course slowly along their rocky bed, where the magic Rhinegold is guarded by the three Rhinemaidens, Woglinde (soprano), Wellgunde (soprano) and Floss-shilde (mezzo-soprano). They play in the waters, until the Nibelung, the dwarf Alberich (bass-baritone), appears. He has come up from the dark caves of Nibelheim, where the dwarves live. The Rhinemaidens tease him for his clumsiness and ugliness, and unthink-ingly arouse his desire for them. A shaft of sunlight suddenly catches the gold and they unwisely tell Alberich about the treasure's magic power. The man who possesses it and renounces love can forge a ring from it which will give him supreme power over the world. Alberich's desire turns to greed, and he curses love. To the Rhinemaidens' horror, he snatches their gold and climbs down to the bedrock. The light in the Rhine disappears. Gradually the shadow disperses and in the dawn a mountainous region is revealed. Lying asleep on the ground are Wotan (bass-baritone), the father of the Gods, and his wife, Fricka (mezzo-soprano). As they awaken their eyes are fixed in aston-ishment on Valhalla, a superb castle which has just been completed for the gods by the giants Fasolt (bass) and Fafner (bass). It was commissioned by Wotan, tired of his eternal wanderings, who had promised to give the giants in return Freia (soprano), the goddess of Youth. Wotan never intended to surrender her (since without her daily gift of apples the gods grow old) but meant to offer a different reward instead. He refuses to hand her over when the giants claim her. They are furious until Loge (tenor), the god of Fire, describes Alberich's Rhinegold. They are impressed by the story of his immense wealth and newly-acquired power, and accept the gold instead of Freia, whom they retain, nevertheless, as a hostage. As the goddess departs, the gods suddenly begin to look old. Wotan decides to accompany Loge to Nibelheim and to steal the gold. In the bowels of the Earth, Alberich has used the magic ring to enslave his fellow Nibelungs and he contemp-lates subduing the gods and giants too. Mime (tenor), his brother, has been compelled to make him a helmet (*the Tarnhelm*) which renders the wearer invisible or transforms him into any shape required. Alberich

boasts brazenly to Wotan and Loge about his powers and proves the effectiveness of the *Tarnhelm* by turn-ing himself first into a serpent and then, goaded on by Loge, into a toad, on which Wotan quickly places his foot. Thus he is trapped and the gods bring him, bound, up to their mountain. He is forced to hand over his treasure: the gold, the *Tarnhelm*, and, lastly, the ring – which Wotan quickly slips onto his finger. The dwarf in despair pronounces a terrible curse on the ring, before he goes: May it bring destruction on whoever possesses it. Fafner and Fasolt demand enough gold to hide the whole of Freia's body. Some chinks remain when all the gold is used, so Wotan hands over the *Tarnhelm*, but he refuses to surrender the ring. Erda (contralto), the all-wise earth goddess, rises from her slumber to warn him of the disasters which the ring will bring upon the gods. Wotan relents and Alberich's curse is imme-diately shown to be effective when Fafner kills Fasolt over the division of the spoils. Freia is released and the gods resume their youth. Donner (bass-baritone) calls up a storm, which dies down to leave an iridescent rainbow bridge leading across the valley of the Rhine to Valhalla, the gods' new home. The gods, totally enthralled, process slowly towards it, and only Loge heeds the laments of the Rhinemaidens below weeping for their lost gold.

DIE WALKÜRE (The Valkyrie)

Three acts. First performance: Munich, Hoftheater, 26 June 1870. First performance in U.K.: London, Her Majesty's Theatre, 6 May 1882; in U.S.A.: New York, Academy of Music, 2 April 1877.

ORIGINAL CAST. Heinrich Vogl (Siegmund), Bausewein (Hunding), August Kindermann (Wotan), Therese Vogl (Sieglinde), Sophie Stehle (Brünnhilde), Anna Kaufmann (Fricka). Conductor: Franz Wüllner.

SYNOPSIS. Wotan, father of the gods, bartered one of his eyes to Erda, the all-knowing Earth Mother, in exchange for some of her knowledge and she has also borne him nine warrior maidens, the Valkyries. Their task is to take the heroes from the battlefield to Val-halla and to wait on the gods. Wotan has also fathered a pair of twins by a mortal woman: Siegmund (tenor) and Sieglinde (soprano). They are known as the Wäl-sung twins (from Wälse, Wotan's other name). Wotan plans that Siegmund, a mortal with free will and not bound as he is by any promises or obligations to restore the ring to anyone, will be able to recover it from Fafner. The twins have, however, been separated when their mother was killed: Sieglinde was forced to marry Hunding (bass), while Siegmund was abandoned to fate. Act I. Siegmund, pursued by enemies, finds refuge in Hunding's hut. He finds only Sieglinde inside and, although they do not recognize each other, they feel immediately a bond of sympathy. Hunding returns and questions the stranger: he soon realizes that his guest is the man he himself has been pursuing and tells Siegmund that he may stay that night to rest, but that the next day they will fight a duel to the death. When Siegmund is alone, he reflects on his fate and recalls how his father had promised to give him a sword that would conquer in every battle. A sudden gleam from the fire momentarily illuminates a sword plunged up to the hilt in the trunk of the ash tree around which the hut is built. Sieglinde has, meanwhile, slipped a draught in Hunding's drink, which has put him in a deep sleep. She returns to tell her guest of her unhappy wedding day and of that mysterious stranger, blind in one eye, who had predicted that only a hero would be able to pull out the sword he thrust into the ash tree. The door swings open to let in brilliant moonlight and Siegmund knows that the woman and the sword belong to him. He extracts the sword and christens it Notung (daughter of necessity). Then, ecstatically happy to have found his sister at last, he leads her out and into the Spring night. Act II. A wild, rocky summit. Wotan (bass-baritone) orders Brünnhilde (soprano), his favourite Valkyrie daughter, to protect Siegmund from Hunding, who is chasing him. Fricka (soprano), guardian of marriage vows, demands that the Wälsungs' incestuous love should be punished through Siegmund's death. Wotan tries to argue that Siegmund – a mortal not bound by the gods' pacts – is needed to prevent Alberich from regaining possession of the ring (since, if he did, the gods would be annihilated). Fricka points out that Siegmund is not a free agent since he has Wotan's own sword. Wotan concedes defeat and orders Brünnhilde to follow Fricka's instructions and to ignore Siegmund. The gods leave and the Valkyrie watches the fugitives rest exhausted on the mountainside. While Sieglinde sleeps Brünnhilde appears to Siegmund and announces his imminent death and journey to Valhalla. He refuses to be parted from Sieglinde and threatens to kill her and himself as a last resort. Brünnhilde, moved by his love, resolves to disobey Wotan by helping them – as she was, after all, originally instructed to do. She watches Hunding and Siegmund fight, but as the latter is about to win, Wotan appears and shatters his sword. Hunding kills Siegmund. With a glance, Wotan kills Hunding and then sets off to pursue Brünnhilde and Sieglinde who have fled. Act III. The top of a rocky mountain. The Valkyries gallop to meet and discuss their adventures. Brünnhilde is the last to arrive and begs her sisters' help for Sieglinde. She knows that Sieglinde must be concealed from Wotan so that she can give birth to Siegmund's son, the hero who will refashion the fragments of his father's sword, Notung. They send Sieglinde to a forest on the edge of the world where Fafner guards his hoard. She has barely gone when Wotan arrives in a rage. He dismisses the Valkyries, except for Brünnhilde, who tries to excuse herself. Wotan strips her of her divinity and condemns her to a sleep, from which she will be awakened by the man whom she must marry. He does, however, surround the rock with a ring of fire so that only a hero can claim her as his own. Sadly he gives her a last greeting with a kiss, and then summons Loge to encircle the rock with flames. He draws back singing 'Whoever fears the point of my blade shall never pass through the fire.'

SIEGFRIED

Three acts. First performance: Bayreuth, Festspielhaus, 16 August 1876. First performance in U.K.: London, Her Majesty's Theatre, 7 May 1882; in U.S.A.: New York, Metropolitan Opera House, 9 November 1887.

ORIGINAL CAST. Georg Unger (Siegfried), Karl Schlosser (Mime), Karl Hill (Alberich), Amalie Materna (Brünnhilde), Franz Betz (Wanderer). Conductor: Hans Richter.

SYNOPSIS. Act I. In a cave in the forest Mime (tenor), the dwarf, is trying without success to weld a sword which Siegfried (tenor) cannot break. Mime has brought Siegfried up since Sieglinde died entrusting her child and the fragments of Notung (Siegmund's sword) to him. His sole intention has been to make use of Siegfried's strength and courage to kill Fafner (bass), who has transformed himself into a dragon, and guards the Rhinegold, the *Tarnhelm* and the ring in a lair in the depths of the forest. When Siegfried bursts cheerfully into the cave dragging behind him a bear he has captured in the forest, the dwarf is terrified. The boy laughs at him and breaks the latest sword into pieces. Then he questions him closely about his parents: Siegmund's and Sieglinde's flight, his father's duel with Hunding and how Notung was broken, his mother's death. He then asks Mime to refashion Notung. He leaves before a stranger, wrapped in a broad cloak and blind in one eye, enters. The Wanderer (bass-baritone) predicts to Mime that 'only a fearless man can temper the sword' and as he departs he also warns him to beware of such a fearless man. Mime realizes that he himself can never forge the sword and suggests the task to Siegfried, who does not seem to be afraid of anything, not even Fafner. Siegfried sets to work to mend Notung. Mime resolves to let Siegfried kill the dragon, and then to poison him so that he can get his hands on the treasure. Siegfried sings a joyful song as he forges Notung again and with the first blow of the recast weapon he splits the anvil in two. Act II. In the depths of the forest, Alberich (baritone) anxiously keeps watch on the cave in which Fafner (bass) guards the Rhinegold. The Wanderer warns Alberich to look out for Mime and reveals the dwarf's scheme. At first light, Mime brings Siegfried to the cave. The boy is not in the least scared and sends the dwarf away. The forest comes alive with birdsong. The gentle sounds suggest to his imagination the mother he has never known. He tries to imitate the song of a woodbird perched in the branches above, but he fails dismally and blows his silver horn instead. At the sudden blast of sound, Fafner wakes up. Siegfried is not frightened and plunges Notung into the dragon's heart. A drop of fiery blood from the monster burns his hand and the hero puts it to his mouth to soothe the pain. Suddenly he is able to understand the forestbird (soprano), which tells him first to find the *Tarnhelm* and the ring, which confer power over the world. This done, the bird warns him to be on his guard against Mime, who will now offer him a poisoned drink. Siegfried kills the dwarf and throws his body into the cave.

Marilyn Horne as Carmen and James McCracken as Don José in Carmen *Act I in the 1972 New York Metropolitan Opera House production.*

The forest begins to murmur again, and the bird relates how on a lonely rock, surrounded by fire, a beautiful woman sleeps, waiting for a hero to overcome the flames and to win her. Siegfried sets off with the bird as his guide. Act III. At the foot of the mountain where Brünnhilde is asleep, Wotan calls up Erda (contralto), the all-knowing, from the depths of the Earth and asks her about the future. He is disappointed by her ambiguous replies and sends her back to eternal sleep. When Siegfried appears, Wotan tries to bar his path to the summit, saying that Notung has once before been shattered by his spear. Siegfried gladly crosses his sword with his father's killer and breaks Wotan's spear – and with it the power of the gods. Unaware of the implications of this encounter, the hero now climbs to the summit. The sight of the Valkyrie combines with his desire for his mother to flood his heart with a new and powerful emotion; for the first time in his life he trembles with a strange terror. Brünnhilde wakes as he kisses her and greets the world in the radiant sunlight. Siegfried declares his passionate love for her and she, at first confused that she feels a human emotion unknown to the gods, finally acknowledges the supreme rapture of succumbing to her love for him. 'Norns break the threads of the gods' destiny. Let the twilight of the gods begin. Brünnhilde will live for the love of Siegfried.'

GÖTTERDÄMMERUNG (Twilight of the Gods)

Prologue and three acts. First performance: Bayreuth, Festspielhaus, 17 August 1876. First performance in U.K.: London, Her Majesty's Theatre, 9 May 1882; in U.S.A.: New York, Metropolitan Opera House, 25 January 1888.

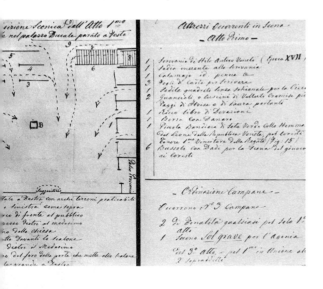

Plans and list of props required for the first performance of Ponchielli's La Gioconda *at la Scala in Milan on 8 April 1876.*

Lithograph for the first performance of Ponchielli's La Gioconda.

ORIGINAL CAST. Georg Unger (Siegfried), Eugen Gura (Gunther), Gustav Siehr (Hagen), Karl Hill (Alberich), Amalie Materna (Brünnhilde), Matilde Weckerlin (Gutrune), Luise Jaïde, Johanna Wagner, Josephine Schefzky, Federica Grün. Conductor: Hans Richter.

SYNOPSIS. Prologue. On the Valkyrie's rock, night. The three Norns (contralto, mezzo-soprano, soprano) weave the fates of men and of gods. The blackness of the night is lightened by the flames which encircle the peak. As they weave they murmur memories and prophecies. Suddenly the thread breaks; the Norns are terrified and sink down to rejoin Erda, the Earth Mother. As the sun rises, Siegfried (tenor) and Brünn-hilde (soprano) come out of a cave, where they have spent their first night together. The Valkyrie gives him Grane, her trusted horse, which once carried her into battle, and in exchange he gives her the ring. After a last passionate embrace he sets out on a journey along the Rhine. Act I. On the banks of the Rhine, in the Hall of the Gibichungs, where Gunther (baritone) and Gut-rune (soprano), the children of Gibich and Grimhild, reign advised by Hagen (bass), their half-brother. He is also Grimhild's son but his father was Alberich the dwarf, and he pursues his father's ambition to regain the ring. Hagen inflames Gunther's heart with desire for Brünnhilde and, although he does not reveal that

Joseph Hoffmann's sketches for Wagner's Der Ring des Nibelungen, *performed at Bayreuth in 1876:*
Das Rheingold;   Die Walküre *Act I;*
Siegfried *Act II;*   *closing scene of*
Götterdämmerung.

the Valkyrie is already Siegfried's bride, he does explain that Siegfried alone can pass through flames to win her. He suggests that Gutrune should mix a drugged drink which will affect Siegfried's memory by obliterating any previous loves in an all-consuming passion for the first woman he sees – Gutrune. To please her brother he will then agree to bring Brünnhilde down from the rock. So when Siegfried's boat lands at the shore Gutrune offers him the fateful cup to drink and he immediately begs her brother's permission to marry her. They quickly come to an agreement – he may wed Gutrune if he wins Brünnhilde for Gunther. Siegfried and Gunther swear to be blood-brothers. Meanwhile on the mountain Brünnhilde listens to the pleas of her sister Waltraute (mezzo-soprano), to return the ring to the Rhinemaidens in order to save Valhalla and the gods. Brünnhilde refuses to give away the symbol of her love. Siegfried's horn is heard approaching, but when he strides through the flames, Brünnhilde fails to recognize him because the Tarnhelm has given him Gunther's appearance. She tries in vain to resist him. Siegfried pulls the ring from her finger and orders her to go into the cave. He places Notung between them as a symbol of his fidelity to Gunther. Act II. Beside the Rhine, in front of the Hall of the Gibichungs, Hagen sees a vision of his father, who exhorts him to obtain the ring for the Nibelung again and to be faithful to his memory. Siegfried arrives, once more like himself, and relates his adventures. He reports that Brünnhilde and Gunther are following, and Hagen summons the Gibich warriors and vassals to welcome the bride and groom. Brünnhilde does not look up until she hears Siegfried's name: at this she stares amazed that he does not recognize her. Angrily she points to the ring on his finger. She declares that it was torn from her by the man who brought her through the charmed fire; Gunther suspects that Siegfried has betrayed him with Brünnhilde. Siegfried, however, swears by the blade of Hagen's spear that his ring was simply found among Fafner's treasure. Brünnhilde then swears by the same spear that her wrongs will be avenged. Brünnhilde, Gunther and Hagen plot to kill Siegfried during the boar hunt the next day. Hagen will spear him in the back, since Brünnhilde has admitted that that is the only place where Siegfried is not protected by her magic spells. Act III. The banks of the Rhine echo with horn calls as the hunt passes by. The Rhinemaidens plead with Siegfried to give back the ring, but not even their prophecy of his approaching death persuades him to listen to their pleas. Gunther and Hagen and the other huntsmen catch up with him and, while they rest, they ask Siegfried to tell them his story. He narrates as far as the death of Fafner and then his memory clouds over. Hagen gives him a drink – to refresh him: he does not know that it has been drugged with an antidote to the elixir of oblivion which Siegfried had drunk previously. Siegfried recalls, with growing emotion, his discovery of Brünnhilde and their exchange of vows. Gunther is amazed and suspects that Brünnhilde has told the truth. Just at that moment two ravens fly away to tell Wotan to prepare for the world catastrophe and as

Machinery to simulate the Rhinemaidens swimming in Das Rheingold, *for the Bayreuth production in 1876.*

Siegfried turns around to look at them Hagen spears him in the back. Siegfried's last words before he dies are a sublime greeting to Brünnhilde. The huntsmen lay his body on their shields and carry him back to the Hall. Gunther blames Hagen, in the presence of Gutrune, who is in despair, for the murder of Siegfried and Hagen kills him. As Hagen approaches Siegfried's corpse to take the ring, the hero's hand rises up defiantly. Brünnhilde has learnt the truth of Siegfried's dealings with the Gibichungs from the Rhinemaidens and now orders the vassals to prepare a funeral pyre for the hero. She claims the ring and places it on her finger. Then she sets fire to the wood and rides Grane into the flames. As the flames leap up, the Rhine overflows and the Rhinemaidens take the ring from Brünnhilde. Hagen makes a last attempt to grasp it and is drowned in the whirlpools, while the Hall crashes around him. The flames ignite the logs of the world

Ash-tree piled around Valhalla, where the gods are seen awaiting their doom. Alberich's curse on the gold has been fulfilled and Brünnhilde's supreme sacrifice for love has cleansed the world.

■ For the subject matter of *Der Ring des Nibelungen* Wagner drew freely on the poems of the Edda, a collection of ancient Norse songs dating back to the thirteenth century and containing myths and legends about the Germanic regions, and also on *The Nibelungenlied*, a medieval epic poem in German by an unknown author. In this latter, interwoven with the mythological strands, are some historical events referring to the Burgundian kingdom, which have been turned into legends. In Wagner's conception, however, there is no place for the historical elements. The events are placed at the beginning of the world and are given no precise date. The myth at the heart of *Der Ring* is

The Valkyries and Wotan in Die Walküre.

Scaffolding and magic lantern projection for the 'Ride of the Valkyries'.

The Ring *at the Bayreuth Festival of 1970. Directed and staged by Wieland Wagner. Scene Four of* Das Rheingold; *Anna Reynolds as Fricka and Thomas Stewart as Wotan in* Die Walküre *Act II; Jean Cox as Siegfried and Berit Lindholm as Brünnhilde in Scene Two of* Siegfried *Act III;* Götterdämmerung *Act II with the same singers as in the previous photo and Norman Bailey as Gunther.*

significant because of its original symbolism and because it touches the universal human problems; it has thus become an expression of the crises and contradictions which existed in nineteenth-century capitalist society. Thomas Mann has written that Wagner used myth – the language of a people still poetically creative – to create 'a work of art which turns to the idea of a world brotherhood, free from the illusion of power, or the domination of wealth, whose foundations are justice and love'. Wagner was occupied for more than twenty-eight years working on the cycle, starting in 1848 with the first sketch of the literary text of 'Siegfried's Death' (which became *The Twilight of the Gods*), and ending in 1876, the year in which the entire cycle was first performed in Bayreuth. Wagner wrote the texts in reverse order: *The Twilight of the Gods* was followed by *Young Siegfried* (1851) and finally by *The Valkyrie* and *The Rhinegold*. The definitive version was published in 1863. During this long period, the operas' philosophical meaning underwent basic changes. In the atmosphere of the 1848 Revolutions, which Wagner actively supported, the project had been conceived to illustrate Man's return from the capitalist system to primordial freedom; later it came to reflect the composer's conversion to the pessimistic ideas of Schopenhauer, which he adopted around 1854. It is illuminating to compare the first version, in which Siegfried and Brünnhilde enjoyed an apotheosis, rising from the flames to occupy Valhalla, which is a clear metaphor for a humanity which has achieved self-awareness and no longer requires divine guidance, with the final – very different – version. The redemption of the world through love (a recurring and fundamental theme in Wagner's work) is achieved at the end of *Götterdämmerung* with the annihilation of both men and gods: the final vision is one of primor-

dial, eternal Nature. The composition of the music followed the chronological sequence of the story. *Das Rheingold* was finished in 1854. In 1856 *Die Walküre* was finished and *Siegfried* was begun. This remained with only the first two acts until 1865. *Siegfried* was finished in 1869 and *Götterdämmerung* in 1874; parts of the latter were begun at the time the libretto was originally written. The whole cycle was first performed in its complete version in Bayreuth from 13 to 17 August 1876 for the inauguration of the Festspielhaus, a new theatre created by Wagner to put into operation the reforming ideals of drama which he had conceived and modified through the performances of his own operas. Karl Brandt, the most famous stage designer of the time, and the Viennese painter Joseph Hoffmann helped with the designs. They introduced many innovations. As a matter of interest, the gas lighting was linked to electric projectors and a magic lantern illuminated the Ride of the Valkyries.

The Ring of the Nibelung is one of the crowning glories of European culture. Both philosophy and music in the second half of the century were stimulated by this epic. It is the realization of the ideology of the *Wort-Ton-Drama* (Word-Tone-Drama) the *Gesamtkunstwerk*, the theory in which words, music and stage action, participating in equal measure, blend into one complete work, regardless of conventional structure. The

effect of the reforms on the drama, which had, after all, already been discussed in earlier centuries and put into practice in other ways from the days of Monteverdi onwards, fades to nothing in comparison with the revolution in the music. Freed now from the chains of the 'closed forms', the action flows along by means of the presentation, the return, the combinations and overlappings of the principal themes (leit-motif), each one of which suggests a person, a feeling or a situation. In this way an uninterrupted flow of musical texture is created, a never-ending melody based on the leit-motifs, which guide the listener through the drama where even words fail him, with their subtle but powerful allusions according to a scheme which is no longer purely musical, but, above all, dramatic. The continual modulations erase all sense of tonality and resolve into a chromaticism which is, in the words of Massimo Mila, 'very well suited to expressing such Romantic states of mind as aspiring towards the unattainable, or hope or regret, always outside present reality'. The history of musical language opens up at this moment towards a future crowded with new perspectives.

THE KISS (Hubička)
Opera in two acts by Bedřich Smetana (1824–84), with a libretto by Eliska Krásnohorská, based on a story by Karolina Světlá. First performance: Prague, Provisional Theatre, 7 November 1876. First performance in U.K.: Liverpool, 8 December 1938; in U.S.A.: Chicago, 1921.

SYNOPSIS. Lukáš (tenor), a widower with a young son, obtains permission to marry Vendulka (soprano) from her father, Paloucký (bass-baritone), but because they are both obstinate and hot-headed, trouble begins

at once. When Lukáš claims his first kiss from her, she refuses him because of the popular belief that a kiss given to a widower before the wedding brings grief to the dead wife. After trying temptations and threats without success, Lukáš angrily goes off to the inn to dance with other village girls (all of whom he kisses) and then returns to walk up and down provocatively with two of them under Vendulka's window. The girl is indignant at the insult and runs away to the woods. Both lovers begin to regret their behaviour, and their friends and relations carefully arrange a meeting. Vendulka opens her arms to Lukáš, but he insists on apologizing publicly before he seals their happiness with a kiss.

■ *The Kiss*, set in rustic surroundings like *The Bartered Bride*, lacks the gaiety which distinguishes Smetana's masterpiece. It is a gentle and melancholy meditation on life in a Czech village. It was immediately very successful and became, after *The Bartered Bride*, the composer's most popular and most performed work.

LE ROI DE LAHORE (The King of Lahore)
Opera in five acts and seven tableaux by Jules Massenet (1842–1912), libretto by Louis Gallet (1835–98). First performance: Paris, Opéra, 27 April 1877. First performance in U.K.: London, Covent Garden, 28 June 1879; in U.S.A.: New Orleans, December 1883.

SYNOPSIS. India at the time of Sultan Mahmud's attack in the eleventh century. Act I. Forecourt of the temple of Indra. Scindia (baritone), the King of Lahore's first Minister, is in love with Sità (soprano), the priestess, and he asks the high priest, Timour (bass), to

The Rhinemaidens in Wagner's Das Rheingold *at Bayreuth in 1876.*

release her from the vows that bind her to the sacred gods. This is refused. He knows that Sità has secret meetings at night with a man and she confesses her sacrilegious offence to him. Scindia, offended that she denies him her love, takes his revenge by denouncing her in public. Sità's lover turns out to be the King, Alim (tenor) himself, who is ordered to atone for his crime by fighting the invading Moslems. Act II. Fanfares and distant noises can be heard. Scindia announces that the army has been defeated and that the King has been mortally wounded – a divine judgement on his wickedness. Scindia usurps the throne while Alim is thus foully betrayed and imprisoned. He dies as Sità swears to love him for ever. Act III. The Garden of the Blessed in Indra's Paradise. The Blessed are waiting for Indra (bass) to speak when Alim appears. The god is so moved by Alim's story that he grants him the privilege of returning to life. The only condition is that Alim will

no longer be a king but a simple, ordinary man, and he will die at the same moment as Sità, the woman he loves. Act IV. The main square in Lahore. Alim awakes on the steps of the palace, in ordinary clothes. It is the day of Scindia's coronation. A grand procession moves toward the palace. Alim confronts Scindia and tries to kill him for his treachery, but escapes as Scindia denounces him as an impostor. Act V. Indra's sanctuary. Alim finds Sità in hiding: she has fled from the wedding chamber into which she had been forced. Scindia surprises them together, but Sità stabs herself and Alim dies with her as divinely ordained.

■ Massenet's first opera does not display his full maturity of expression, but it reveals the musical gifts that made him one of the most important musicians in French theatre in the second half of the nineteenth century. He built one of his most notable operas onto a dramatic libretto in which the guiding motive is passionate love. The most successful musical passages are those in which Alim awakens and where the scene in Paradise is introduced.

SAMSON ET DALILA
Opera in three acts and four tableaux by Camille Saint-Saëns (1835–1921), libretto by Ferdinand Lemaire, inspired by the episode in the Bible. First performance: Weimar, Hoftheater, 2 December 1877. First performance in U.K.: London, Covent Garden, 25 September 1893; in U.S.A.: New York, 25 March 1892.

ORIGINAL CAST. Von Müller (Dalila), Milde (the High Priest), Dengler (Abimelech), Ferenczy (Samson).

Karl Schlosser as Mime in Siegfried, *Bayreuth 1876.*

Amalie Materna as Brünnhilde in Der Ring des Nibelungen, *Bayreuth 1876.*

Georg Unger as Siegfried in Der Ring des Nibelungen, *Bayreuth 1876.*

Franz Betz as Wotan in Der Ring des Nibelungen, *Bayreuth 1876.*

SYNOPSIS. Act I. A public square in Gaza in Palestine around 1115 B.C. The Philistines cruelly oppress the Israelites, but Samson (tenor) tries to raise their morale by recalling the memory of the miraculous crossing of the Red Sea and encouraging them to put their complete trust in God. Gradually, he succeeds in giving them new hope. Abimelech (bass), the satrap of Gaza, scorns the effect which devotion to such a God will have. Samson is inspired by God to answer that provocation: he grasps Abimelech's sword and kills him. He warns the Philistines that their last hour is approaching. The High Priest of Dagon (baritone) curses the Israelites, but the Philistines seem to be prevented by a mysterious power from offering resistance to the rebellion. By the evening Samson and his warriors have occupied the city. They are at prayer together, when Dalila (mezzo-soprano), most seductive of Philistine women, enters with a group of beautiful maidens. They dance and she invites Samson to her house. Samson cannot resist her temptations. Act II. The valley of Sorek in Palestine at night-fall. Dalila nurses her hate for Samson, the enemy of her people, and quickly agrees to help the High Priest by finding out the secret of his extraordinary strength. Samson eventually arrives, torn between desire for the woman and awareness of his destiny as the liberator of his people. Gradually he succumbs to Dalila's wiles and confesses the secret of his strength. Thus he is easily captured by the Philistine soldiers when Dalila cries out in triumph that she has made him harmless by cutting off his hair while he slept. Act III. Scene I. The prison in Gaza. Samson in chains, blinded, his hair shorn off, laboriously turns the mill-wheel to which he has been tied. Other Jewish prisoners bewail his guilt and rebuke him for having betrayed them for a woman. Samson begs God to forgive him. Scene II. In the temple of Dagon. The High Priest is surrounded by Philistine princes. Dalila mocks Samson and invites him to participate in their sacred orgy. She laughs at him and reminds him how she enslaved him with her false promises. He is then led into the centre of the temple and compelled to kneel and humble himself before their god. Samson lets himself be led by a little boy between the two pillars that support the roof, but when the Chief Priest commands him to sacrifice to Dagon, he prays to the God of the Israelites to restore to him momentarily his former strength. With a colossal effort he pushes the columns apart and the temple collapses amidst the screams of the Philistines, crushing everyone beneath its rubble.

■ Although *Samson et Dalila* is considered to be Saint-Säens's best opera, and was performed on the initiative of Liszt at Weimar, it did not appear at the Paris Opéra for another sixteen years. It is Saint-Säens's second opera based on the Bible (the first, *Le Déluge*, had appeared in 1876). The pathos of the original story is not to be found in it. The characters are given a sentimentality which profoundly alters the Biblical tale. Dalila, whom the composer envisaged as the heroine of her race, dominates the story with the intensity of her irresistibly seductive nature, a quality

Poster for the 1881 Opéra-Comique production of Offenbach's Les Contes d'Hoffmann. *Paris, Bibliothèque de l'Opéra.*

which appears to be the central dramatic theme of the opera, the psychological justification for Samson's betrayal and the explanation of how the heroic will can succumb to feminine charm. In reality both Samson and Dalila are merely the habitual characters of Romantic melodrama. They do not have the historical dimension which, in the Bible story, makes them act out not only their own drama but also the drama of two races. Although their love duet in Act II is full of charm, it is expressed in exquisitely tender melodies which are inevitably inadequate both for the situation and for the characters. What compensates for the lack of fidelity to the episode in the Book of Judges is, above all, the musical merits of the score. The deficiencies in characterization and in background atmosphere are largely made up by the general qualities of this wonderful piece of workmanship. There are passages where the composition rises to peaks of undeniable beauty; for example, in the above-mentioned love-song of Act II. Here Saint-Säens's special preoccupation with form is very evident. He adopted the motto *L'art pour l'art*, and *Samson et Dalila* occupies a prominent place still in the operatic repertoire, on account of its clear-cut and well-balanced beauty, even if it lacks innovation or high grand ideals.

THE SECRET (Tajemství)
Opera in three acts by Bedřich Smetana (1824–84), libretto by Eliska Krásnohorská. First performance: Prague, Czech Theatre, 18 September 1878. First performance in U.K.: Oxford, 7 December 1956.

SYNOPSIS. Act I. Before the opera begins, Kalina (baritone) has been refused permission to marry Rose (mezzo-soprano) because he is not sufficiently prosperous. He is now a widower with one son, Vítek (tenor). Rose never married and bears a grudge against Kalina because Friar Barnabáš (baritone) once told her that Kalina passed up an opportunity of searching for a treasure, which she assumes would have given him enough wealth to ask for her hand. In the meantime, her brother Malina (bass) and Kalina have both become Aldermen, who divide the village into rival factions on every issue. Act I. After several displays of anger and rivalry, Malina and Kalina retire from the market place. An old workman brings Kalina a note he has discovered in Kalina's house and overhears Kalina tell Vítek that it contains the secret instructions as to how to find the treasure. Soon the news is all over the town. Act II. Kalina has travelled to a pilgrimage church in the hills where, according to the Friar's instruction, he will find the treasure. He falls asleep, and has visions of dwarves and gnomes, until pilgrims awake him with their singing. He discovers that his son Vítek is among them and has come to meet Blăzenka, Malina's daughter. He is furious and his son disowns him; then Kalina descends into the cave. Act III. In Malina's house, Blăzenka weeps for Vítek. Suddenly a knocking sound is heard at midnight and everyone but Rose hurries out of the 'haunted' room. Kalina emerges from behind the stove where he has followed the tunnel. It appears that Barnabáš meant that Rose herself was the treasure which Kalina could win, and as Vítek promises to marry Blaženka, a double betrothal brings the opera to an end.

■ This is Smetana's last opera but one, and by then he was completely deaf and in a desperate state of ill-health and poverty. Perhaps this is why, despite its comic subject-matter, *The Secret* is basically a sad work, whose main strands are Kalina's wounded pride, his lingering love for Rose, and the love of the two young people.

POLYEUCTE
Opera in five acts by Charles Gounod (1818–93), libretto by Jules Barbier (1825–1901) and Michel Carré (1819–72), based on the tragedy by Pierre Corneille. First performance: Paris, Opéra, 7 October 1878.

ORIGINAL CAST. Gabrielle Krauss (Pauline), Salomon (Polyeucte), Lasalle (Sévère).

SYNOPSIS. In Mytilene, the capital of Armenia, Pauline, daughter of the Governor Félix, has married Polyeucte out of deference to her family. Sévère, who was formerly engaged to her, but was believed to have

been killed in battle, returns, having distinguished himself in the campaign, and learns of her marriage to Polyeucte. Polyeucte, for his part, has been secretly converted to Christianity and, when he is compelled to go to the temple to sacrifice in honour of Sévère, he shuns the false pagan gods. Owing to the intervention of Pauline and Sévère, who in spite of everything admires his rival, he is saved from immediate execution, but Félix says that he will be thrown to the lions unless he rejects his faith. Encouraged by the pagan priest, Albin (bass), the Armenians vociferously demand the death of the Christians. Polyeucte refuses to renounce Christianity and his firm resolve wins Pauline to his side. Together they go to their martyrdom in the certainty that this terrible fate will unite them for ever.

■ *Polyeucte* was a disappointment to the Parisian public despite being well performed by Krauss, Salomon and Lasalle. Its lack of success stemmed not only from the libretto, which is an unsatisfying compromise

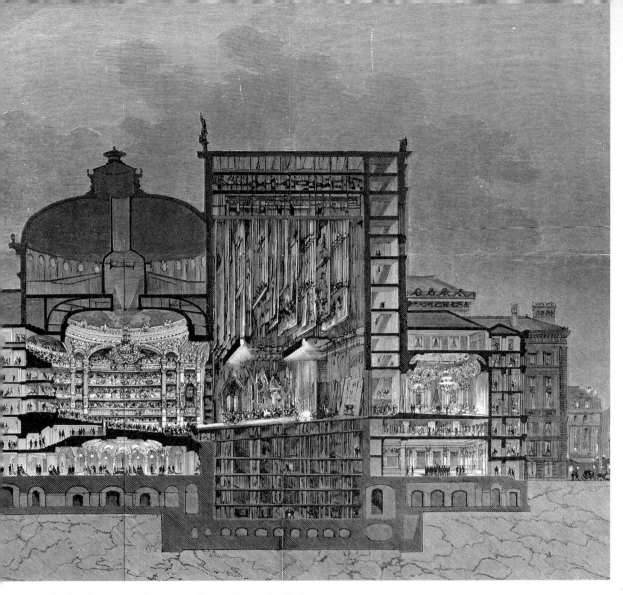

Longitudinal section of the new Opera House in Paris.

between opera and oratorio, but also from Gounod's music, which is often lacking in inspiration or ill-adapted to the religious and heroic qualities of Corneille's characters.

THE MERCHANT KALASHNIKOV (Kupec Kalashnikov)

Opera in three acts by Anton Grigorevich Rubinstein (1830–94), libretto by N. I. Kulikov, after Lermontov. First performance: St Petersburg, Imperial Theatre, 5 March 1880.

SYNOPSIS. The Palace of Ivan the Terrible. The Oprichniki, the Tsar's personal guard, have been informed that some delegates of the Zemstvo are to be received by the Tsar, to whom they will complain about their lot. The Tsar then appears and a solemn religious ceremony takes place. After he has received the delegates, Ivan chats in a relaxed way with his guards. One of them, a young man called Kiriheievich, turns out to

be in love. In the streets of Moscow the crowd disperse as the dreaded Oprichniki pass. When Aléna, the wife of the merchant Kalashnikov, comes out of her house to go to vespers, Kiriheievich seizes her, declaring his love for her. An old woman who has seen all this tells Kalashnikov on his return what has happened. He is in despair but resolves, despite his fears and doubts, to denounce Kiriheievich. The square in Moscow is thronged with a lively crowd. Ivan considers the arguments of Kiriheievich, who falsely accuses Kalashnikov of crimes, Aléna, who begs for mercy, and her husband, who stands in chains and asks for justice, and finally congratulates the courageous Kalashnikov for daring to challenge the Oprichniki. The opera ends with a chorus of the people surrounding Kalashnikov, as he comes out of prison.

■ The opera received a warm welcome but was quickly banned from the stage by the censor. Although the style is very mixed, it achieves great psychological depths in places (for example, Kalashnikov's arias and recitative in Act II). The tales of the clown are also very interesting as a faithful mirror of the soul of the Russian people.

IL FIGLIUOL PRODIGO (The Prodigal Son)

Opera in four acts by Amilcare Ponchielli (1834–86), libretto by Angelo Zanardini (1820–93). First performance: Milan, Teatro alla Scala, 26 December 1880.

ORIGINAL CAST. Francesco Tamagno, Anna D'Angeri, Edouard de Reszke, Federico Salvati.

SYNOPSIS. In the valley of Jessen, Ruben's tribe is celebrating Easter. The old man (bass) and his ward, Jeftele (soprano), are unhappy because his son Azaele is not with them. Amenofi (tenor), an Assyrian adventurer, tells them that his sister, Nefte (mezzo-soprano), was saved from a wild panther by Azaele. Azaele and Nefte are then given an enthusiastic welcome by everyone but Jeftele, who is engaged to Azaele and is jealous of Nefte. Nefte is grateful for the hospitality and tells of their pleasant life in Nineveh. Azaele decides to follow his friends despite the efforts of Jeftele and old Ruben to dissuade him. In Nineveh, in the hall of priests, near the temple of Ilia, a cruel custom requires a victim to be sacrificed every year to the river Tigris and Amenofi has decided that this year the victim will be Azaele. Nefte wants no part in her brother's plan, however, and tries to warn Azaele. In the large square in Nineveh the festival of Ilia is taking place. Amenofi and other young men provoke Azaele, who soon becomes a laughing stock. Meanwhile Jeftele and Ruben arrive in Nineveh. Jeftele is caught in the temple of Ilia and condemned to death. Amenofi postpones the execution until the next day and, when alone with her, declares his love, promising to do all he can to save her. Jeftele rejects him firmly. Azaele miserably compares those he thought were his friends with his father and Jeftele. When he sees Jeftele, he resolves to save her and claims that it was he who desecrated the temple. Ruben, Jeftele and Nefte try in vain to save him from the executioners who throw him into the Tigris. He escapes and begins a wandering life while his father goes mad. One Easter day he meets Jeftele, who persuades him to end his wanderings and to return to his father. On seeing his son, Ruben embraces him with emotion and regains his sanity.

■ This is the penultimate of Ponchielli's operas. It has a subtle oriental atmosphere, which was probably due to the influence of Verdi's *Aida*.

LES CONTES D'HOFFMANN (The Tales of Hoffmann)

A fantasy in three acts with a prologue and an epilogue by Jacques Offenbach (1819–80), libretto by Jules Barbier (1822–1901) and Michel Carré (1819–72), based on three stories by Ernst Theodor Amadeus Hoffmann (1776–1822). First performance: Paris, Opéra-Comique, 10 February 1881. First performance in U.K.: London, Adelphi Theatre, 17 April 1907; in U.S.A.: New York, Fifth Avenue Theater, 16 October 1882.

ORIGINAL CAST. Isaac, Talazac, Taskin, Grivot, Belhomme, Gourdon, Troy, Teste, Collin.

SYNOPSIS. Prologue: In Master Luther's beer-cellar at Nuremberg. Councillor Lindorf (baritone), the first of four incarnations of evil in the imagination of the poet Hoffmann (tenor), intercepts and steals a note which the beautiful opera-singer Stella (soprano) has sent to Hoffmann to arrange a meeting with him. The poet and his friend Nicklausse arrive. The students in the beer-cellar ask the poet if he has ever been in love and he starts to recount his fantastic adventures. Act I. In the work-room of the physicist, Spalanzani (baritone). Hoffmann has become his pupil in order to be near Olympia (soprano), whom he believes to be the scientist's daughter. In fact she is a mechanical doll constructed by Spalanzani with the assistance of his strange collaborator, Coppelius (bass-baritone). In vain the faithful Nicklausse tries to warn him; Hoffmann is in love and does not listen to reason. During a ball the poet declares his love to Olympia, who sings ('the nightingale in the grove') and dances divinely. She retires to her room. There is a sudden noise of breaking springs and machinery, and Coppelius, a reincarnation of Lindorf, enters with the shattered doll. Sadly, the poet realizes that he has been tricked. Act II. In Venice, a luxurious gallery on the Grand Canal; a barcarolle is heard ('sweet night of love'). Hoffmann is in love with Giulietta (soprano), who is under the influence of the demonic Dapertutto (bass-baritone). In order to please him she has already captured the reflection of her lover Schlemil (bass) and is preparing to do the same to Hoffmann. In vain, Nicklausse tries once again to get the poet to come to his senses, but he is deaf to all reason. He challenges Schlemil, who has the key to Giulietta's room, to a duel and kills him. Taking possession of the key, Hoffmann then finds that Giulietta has gone away with another lover. Act III. In Munich, in the house of the lute-maker Crespel (bass). This time Hoffmann is in love with Antonia (soprano), Crespel's daughter. The girl is rehearsing a song ('The little dove has flown') but her father scolds her and reminds her that the strain of singing could kill her as it did her mother. The villainous Dr Miracle (bass-baritone) arrives, the fourth incarnation of the evil genius of the poet. He conjures up the spirit of her mother to encourage Antonia to sing and then accompanies her on his violin. She cannot resist his diabolic persuasion and sings until she dies exhausted. Epilogue. Back in the beer-cellar (the scene of the prologue). Hoffmann has finished his stories and, convinced of Stella's deceit, he forgets her by drinking heavily.

■ The opera is a tribute to the German writer and composer, E. T. A. Hoffmann, whom Offenbach much admired. He died before the orchestration was finished and it was completed by Ernest Guiraud

Act I of Tchaikovsky's Eugene Onegin *in the Moscow Bolshoi Theatre production's first performance on 23 April 1881. Moscow, Theatre Museum Archives.*

(1837–92) and performed posthumously. This is Offenbach's most ambitious work and contains much that is pleasing and fresh. It contains the seeds of what was to become the new comic opera, which does away with the customary 'canaille' style and introduces lyric-dramatic characters that are alive and realistic.

THE MAID OF ORLEANS (Orleanskaya deva)

Opera in four acts by Peter Ilyich Tchaikovsky (1840–93), libretto by Vasily Andreevich Zhukovsky, based on the tragedy by Schiller. First performance: St Petersburg, Maryinsky Theatre, 25 February 1881.

■ In this opera Tchaikovsky turned from Russian subjects to a story that was dear to Western composers. However, he soon returned to Russian themes, which he found more congenial.

EUGENE ONEGIN

Opera in three acts by Peter Ilyich Tchaikovsky (1840–93), libretto by K. S. Shilovsky and Tchaikovsky himself, based on the poem by Pushkin (1831). First performance: Moscow, Imperial College of Music, 29 March 1879, performed by students at the College. First official performance: Moscow, Bolshoi Theatre, 23 April 1881; first performance in U.K.: London, Olympic Theatre, 17 October 1892; in U.S.A.: New York, Metropolitan Opera House, 24 March 1920.

SYNOPSIS. The action takes place in Russia at the beginning of the nineteenth century. Act I. Scene I. In the garden of Madame Larina's home. Madame Larina (mezzo-soprano) and nurse Filipevna (mezzo-soprano) are talking together whilst her daughters Tatyana (soprano) and Olga (contralto) can be heard singing. They are celebrating the end of the harvest. Olga, who is carefree and gay, is taking part in the celebrations whilst Tatyana, who is romantic and melancholy, remains a little apart. Lensky (tenor), Olga's fiancé, and his friend, Eugene Onegin (baritone), arrive to pay a visit. Onegin is a fashionable young man, well educated, blasé and egoistical, bored with the world in general. Nevertheless, Tatyana falls in love with him. Scene II. Tatyana's room, that night. Tatyana writes a long, passionate letter to Onegin, telling him how she feels and begging to meet him. Scene III. In the garden. Onegin arrives, courteous but cool, at the appointment. He dismisses her passionate declaration of love and he says he does not have a steady character. He therefore begs Tatyana to forget him. Act II. Scene I. A ball in Madame Larina's house for Tatyana's birthday. Monsieur Triquet (tenor), the dancing master, sings a song in honour of Tatyana. Onegin hears some gossip about the fact that he has danced with Tatyana, so he flirts with her sister and arouses Lensky's jealousy. They quarrel and Lensky challenges Onegin to a duel with pistols. Scene II. Beside an old mill at dawn the following morning. Lensky is accompanied by his friend Zaretsky (bass) and Onegin by his French servant. They seem to hesitate at the encounter in view of the friendship that had bound them together until the day before. But neither makes the first move towards a reconciliation. The seconds load the pistols and measure the distances. Lensky is killed at the first shot. Act III. Scene I. A sumptuous room in the palace of Prince Gremin (bass) in St Petersburg. There is a ball in progress and Onegin is amongst the guests. Six years have passed since the death of Lensky and Onegin has just returned from lengthy travels abroad, undertaken to get over his remorse. He sees Tatyana again, now the wife of Prince Gremiń, and falls madly in love with her. Scene II. Tatyana's drawing room. Following a request from

Onegin, Tatyana receives him. When faced by his passionate declarations of love, she resists the temptation to succumb and remains firm in her fidelity to her husband. She dismisses him once and for all.

■ This is undoubtedly Tchaikovsky's theatrical masterpiece. The music is fluent and spontaneous and typical of the composer, who had little sympathy with the Group of Five in Russia who were intent on creating a national music free from Western traditions. In fact, this opera may be said to contain all those European influences that were rejected by the Group: French, Italian and German. The most lively moments occur, however, when the composer uses rhythms that are typically Russian.

LIBUŠE
A 'festive' opera in three acts by Bedřich Smetana (1824–84), libretto by Joseph Wenzig. First performance: Prague, National Theatre, 11 June 1881.

SYNOPSIS. The Czech nation is governed by the princess Libuše (soprano), a descendant of the mythical Czech who led his people into Bohemia. She is much loved and respected for her wisdom and her ability to predict the future. She resolves an argument between two young and influential brothers Chrudoš (bass) and Šťáhlav (tenor) concerning the division of their paternal inheritance and orders it to be divided (following ancient custom) into two equal parts. Their dispute is aggravated by Krasava (soprano), a member of the princess's entourage, who loves Chrudoš, but pretends to love the other brother to arouse his jealousy. Chrudoš is not satisfied with Libuše's decision and insults her, scathingly declaring that it is not right that men should be governed by a woman. Hurt by this insult, Libuše chooses a simple, wise peasant, called Přemysl, to be her husband. Krasava repents of her foolish behaviour and confesses her love to Chrudoš, who is mollified by her despair and promises to be reconciled with Šťálhav. Přemysl founds the first Bohemian dynasty, which takes its name from him.

■ The first performance of *Libuše* was given to inaugurate the National Theatre in Prague and coincided with the marriage of Archduke Rudolf to Archduchess Stephanie. Smetana felt it was a great occasion and wanted to write 'an opera to celebrate memorable days'. His wish is still respected. *Libuše* is considered sacred by the Czech people and is still presented on all great occasions.

HÉRODIADE (Herodias)
Opera in four acts and seven tableaux by Jules Massenet (1842–1912), libretto by Paul Milliet, 'Henri Gremont' (Georges Hartmann) and Angelo Zanardini (1820–93), based on Hérodias *by Gustave Flaubert, published in 'Trois Contes' (1877). First performance: Brussels, Théâtre de la Monnaie, 19 December 1881.*

First performance in U.K.: London, Covent Garden, 6 July 1904; in U.S.A.: New Orleans, 13 February 1892.

ORIGINAL CAST. Marthe Duvivier (Salomé), Blanche Deschamps (Hérodiade), Edmond Verguet (Jean), Manoury (Hérode), André Grene (Phanuel), Charles Fontaine (Vitellius). Conductor Joseph Dupont.

SYNOPSIS. Salomé (soprano), who was left behind when her mother, Hérodiade (mezzo-soprano), went to marry Hérode, is a disciple of the prophet, Jean (tenor), with whom she is in love. Hérode (baritone) himself is fascinated by Salomé's beauty and openly desires her. Hérodiade means to profit by this passion to destroy Jean, who publicly attacks her depravity. Hérode sees in Jean and his followers the only effective Jewish opposition to the Roman domination of Proconsul Vitellius (baritone), which threatens his own power. Jean refuses to co-operate with him. When Hérode discovers his step-daughter's love for the prophet, Jean is thrown into prison. Salomé joins him there, determined to die with him. Jean no longer rejects her love since it has been purified by so much sacrifice. The guards take her away, however, to an orgiastic banquet in the palace. In desperation Salomé throws herself at the feet of Hérode and Hérodiade. Her mother recognizes her, but joins her too late in begging for mercy for Jean. The prophet has already been beheaded and Salomé kills herself before her mother's eyes.

■ *Hérodiade* is a passionate and violent opera and, as the critic Louis Gallet said, it bears strong similarities to Berlioz in its violent contrasts and to Verdi in the tremendous passion of the music. As Gallet points out, however, Massenet triumphs only 'when he is himself, when he uses his own natural ability and joyful youth to achieve the simplicity, richness and delicious sweetness that make him an incomparable charmer'.

THE SNOW MAIDEN (Snegurochka)
Opera (a Spring fairytale) in a prologue and four acts by Nicolay Rimsky-Korsakov (1844–1908), libretto by the composer, based on a comedy by Alexander N. Ostrovsky. First performance: St Petersburg, Maryinski Theatre, 10 February 1882; first performance in U.K.: London, Sadler's Wells Theatre, 12 April 1933; in U.S.A.: New York, Metropolitan Opera House, 23 January 1922.

SYNOPSIS. The Spring fairy (mezzo-soprano) does not want to put an end to winter. She confesses to the birds that she does not want to leave Snegurochka, the daughter she has had by old Winter (bass). They know that if Yarilo, the sun, ever catches sight of Snegurochka, she will die. Winter fears that Yarilo may instil in his daughter feelings of love that will melt her heart of ice. To protect her, he entrusts her to the Spirit of the Woods (tenor) and she is adopted by a peasant couple, Bobil (tenor) and Bobilicka (mezzo-soprano), who live at the entrance to the village of Tsar Berendey (tenor). Snegurochka settles into her new home, but she is not happy and, to distract her, Kupava (soprano), her best friend, invites her to her wedding and introduces her to Mizgir (baritone), her fiancé. He falls in love with Snegurochka and forsakes Kupava, who turns to the Tsar for help. Berendey questions the daughter of Winter, who replies that she does not love anyone and, not knowing how to reconcile the two young women, he invites them to the ball which marks the end of winter. Throughout the ball Snegurochka does not move, lost in her icy sadness. Kupava, however, accepts the love of Lehl (alto), a shepherd, who wants to marry her. In the evening, Mizgir declares his love to the daughter of Spring. She is so moved by this that she returns to the woods and begs her mother to bestow feelings of love on her. The Spring fairy appears carrying a garland of flowers for her daughter. The girl feels something stir inside her and goes to meet Mizgir. A new sensation, an emotion never felt before, persuades her to accept his proposal of marriage. When the wedding is about to take place Mizgir calls for the Tsar's blessing, but a ray of sun, a symbol of love, strikes the girl and she melts and disappears. The young man is desolate and so overcome with grief that he throws himself into the lake. As soon as the daughter of icy Winter has melted, the Sun begins to shine again.

■ Rimsky-Korsakov read Ostrovsky's work in 1874, but it was only later after reading it again that he asked the dramatist for permission to use the text. He set to work in the summer of 1880 and in around two and a half months the opera was finished. He was then living at Stelevo, in Russia, in the heart of the country, in a house with a huge garden. The richness of the countryside, the endless fields, the flowers and the forests, gave him something the creative urge, anxious as he was to capture something of the palpitating life that surrounded him. The opera achieved an immediate popular success. However, the critics were harsh and pointed to an excess of folklore and an almost total lack of dramatic sense. Despite this, the composer was satisfied with his work, so much so that in 1893, thirteen years after the first performance, he wrote a letter to his wife in which he described *The Snow Maiden* as his most successful opera, both from a musical and a theatrical point of view, which together made it a well proportioned work. The letter finished: 'Anyone who does not like *Snegurochka* has understood nothing of my music, nor of me.' In fact, the mythological background with its fairy-like delicacy and the fantastic interpretation of

Rimsky-Korsakov's The Snow Maiden *at the Bolshoi Theatre in 1893. Theatre Archives, Moscow.*

natural facts was extremely suitable for the composer, who in his music always touched the hearts of the people.

FRANÇOISE DE RIMINI

Opera in a prologue and four acts and an epilogue by Ambroise Thomas (1811–96), libretto by Jules Barbier (1825–1910) and Michel Carré (1819–72). First performance: Paris, Opéra, 14 April 1882.

SYNOPSIS. The story is taken from the life of Paolo Malatesta and Francesca da Rimini as told by Dante in the fifth Canto of the *Inferno*. Francesca, the wife of Gianciotto Malatesta, a nobleman of Rimini, is caught by her husband in the arms of Paolo, his brother, who is much younger and more handsome than he. Angry and jealous, Gianciotto kills them both. The librettists have, however, introduced innovations into the traditional story and have constructed a story within a story, by making Dante and Virgil appear in the prologue at the entrance to Hell.

■ This opera was the composer's last and in it he tried to resolve the differences between various contemporary musical trends (in particular there is much that is reminiscent of Wagner). At the first performance, it achieved a moderate success, but before long it was completely forgotten and this hurt the composer profoundly. From then on, in fact, he scarcely composed anything. Recently, the musical value of the opera has again been appreciated and, although it does not form part of the regular repertoire, it is now considered one of the composer's best works.

PARSIFAL

Sacred festival drama in three acts by Richard Wagner (1813–83). The libretto is by the composer. First performance: Bayreuth, Festspielhaus, 26 July 1882; first performance in U.K.: London, Covent Garden, 2 February 1914; in U.S.A.: New York, Metropolitan Opera House, 24 December 1903.

ORIGINAL CAST. Amalie Materna, Hermann Winkelmann, Theodor Reichmann, Carl Hill. Conducted by Hermann Levi.

SYNOPSIS. In Spain, on a mountain called Montsalvat, facing towards the kingdoms of the infidel stands the castle built by the devout knight, Titurel, to guard the Grail, the sacred goblet from which Christ drank at the Last Supper, and the Holy Spear, with which the Centurion wounded Christ on the cross. Titurel (bass), now very old, has handed his crown to his son, Amfortas (baritone). Amfortas, armed with the Spear, one day set off to destroy the castle of Klingsor, an evil magician, who intends to capture the Grail and break the power of the Holy Knights. He succumbed, however, to Klingsor's enchantment and let the Spear drop from his hand; Klingsor snatched it and wounded Amfortas with it as he was rescued by his fellows. It has

subsequently been revealed in a divine vision that the wound will only heal at the touch of the Spear and that the Spear can be recovered only by a 'pure fool'. The Knights of Montsalvat await this 'pure fool' while Amfortas feels his strength ebbing away. Act I. It is a grey dawn. In a glade at the foot of the rock, the knight Gurnemanz (bass) and two esquires watch a procession pass, taking Amfortas, on a stretcher, to a nearby lake where he hopes to find a cure for his wound. A strange woman, Kundry (soprano), whom the Knights know as their messenger but who, unknown to them, is sometimes bewitched by the forces of evil to serve Klingsor, brings a phial of balsam to soothe the King's suffering. When the procession has passed, Gurnemanz tells the esquires of the king's adventures in the castle of Klingsor and of his loss of the Spear. The tale is interrupted by the entrance of some Knights with a youth who has shot one of the sacred swans of Montsalvat. It is Parsifal (tenor). The young man, who understands little of himself or of the world, is deeply contrite. He does not know who his father is, nor does he know that his mother, Herzeleide, died of grief after losing her son. Gurnemanz, hoping that he may be the 'pure fool' promised to Amfortas, leads him into the castle to take part in the solemn ceremony of the Grail. In the Great Hall, Amfortas, reluctant because he considers himself unworthy, but comforted by the voice of Titurel and by an ethereal chorus of boys who are singing praises to the Lord, performs the sacred ceremony. The chalice shines in a ray of light when it is uncovered. He blesses the bread and the wine but the pain of the wound stabs and tortures him as he does so. Parsifal has understood nothing of the ritual and shows no sign of emotion. Gurnemanz chides him for his insensitivity and sends him away. Act II. In his enchanted castle, Klingsor (baritone) has watched these events in his magic mirror and realizes that Parsifal is indeed the 'holy fool' who can save Amfortas. He calls Kundry and orders her, against her will, to seduce Parsifal. When, from the top of the tower, Klingsor sees Parsifal approaching, the castle is magically transformed into a wonderful enchanted garden, full of flower-maidens who call to the young man and try to detain him. Kundry intervenes and reminds Parsifal of his mother, Herzeleide. Parsifal listens with growing emotion as she recalls his infancy protected by maternal love, a love which another woman can now give to him once again. Yet even as she gives him a lingering kiss, he feels the searing pain of Amfortas's bleeding wound. Suddenly he understands the guilt and the pain of the man who has sinned against the Grail and the blood of Christ. 'Amfortas', he shouts 'the wound! I feel it burning in my heart.' His cry makes Kundry uneasy and in her confusion she calls Klingsor. From the top of the tower he hurls at Parsifal the Holy Spear, but the weapon miraculously stops, suspended in mid-air. When Parsifal seizes it and traces the sign of the cross with it, the castle and garden vanish. Kundry falls unconscious to the ground. Act III. Near the mountain of the Grail. Many years have passed and it is the morning of Good Friday. Winter is giving way to Spring. Kundry attends Gurnemanz, who has gone into retreat as a hermit. She draws his attention to a Knight in black armour approaching them. When Gurnemanz says that arms should not be worn on Good Friday he silently takes off his helmet and his breast-plate, puts down the Holy Spear and kneels to pray. Gurnemanz recognizes the Spear and that Parsifal is indeed the saviour made pure by piety and trials, the 'pure fool' promised in the prophecy. He tells him that Titurel has recently died of grief. By the anxious reaction of Parsifal, the old man realizes that the youth is ready for his mission and in a simple, intimate ceremony ordains him king of the Grail. As his first sacred act, Parsifal baptizes Kundry and she bursts into tears. He shows her the wonderful awakening of nature, the Good Friday Spell, which announces the Resurrection and the pardon after the Passion, the day of supreme grief. To the sound of the bells of Montsalvat, the three of them move towards the castle of the Grail. In the Great Hall the knights watch over the body of Titurel. The agony of Amfortas has become unbearable. Parsifal approaches, touches him with the Spear and heals him. Then he himself uncovers the Grail, which radiates a glorious light while celestial voices proclaim salvation. Kundry sinks to the ground and dies, and a white dove appears above the knights, who kneel in adoration.

■ *Parsifal* was Wagner's last opera and he dedicated to it the last years of his life, from 1877 to 1882, although he had had the original idea and made the first drafts much earlier, in middle age. It was originally based on the *Parzival* of Wolfram von Eschenbach (c. 1160–1220) who, in turn, had based his idea on an old Breton legend. Wagner deviated a great deal from the original, if not in the action then in the spirit and the interpretation of the underlying motives which dominate the characters and pervade their actions. Once he has attained piety through the experience of sin, as suggested by Kundry's kiss, and through a long inner struggle, and has raised love to a feeling of universal compassion and rejected all egoism and passion, Parsifal can at last become the messenger of salvation. Because of this he is able to heal Amfortas's wound, to restore the Grail to its immaculate splendour and to present himself as the hero destined to redeem humanity. Guilt and the struggle against it are also a fundamental part of both Kundry 'the strongest and the most poetically striking female figure that Wagner has conceived' (Thomas Mann) and the tormented character of Amfortas. The mystic Christianity which pervades the opera (the reason, together with the 'pessimistic' solution of *Gotterdämmerung* for his definitive break with the philosopher Nietzsche) does not detract, despite the diversity of the subject matter and the natural evolution of the master's personality, from the substantial consistency of values in the whole of Wagner's work. Similarities have been pointed out between Siegfried and Parsifal, who have a similar innocence and mission, between Alberich and Klingsor, who are both willing to use tyranny and violence; and between Wotan and Amfortas, who are made impotent and prisoners by their own actions. Yet it may be suggested that, quite apart from these similarities of character and theme, the motif of redemption, which pervades the whole of Wagner's output, culminates in *Parsifal*. It is redemption which, through the rejection of power, of riches, of deceit and of violence, is the true leit-motiv of Wagner's work.

HENRI VIII

Opera in four acts by Camille Saint-Saëns (1835–1921), libretto by Léonce Détroyat and Armand Silvestre (1837–1901). First performance: Paris, Opéra, 5 March 1883; first performance in U.K.: London, Covent Garden, 14 July 1898.

SYNOPSIS. Henry VIII, King of England, is in love with Anne Boleyn, one of the Queen's maids of honour. Anne loves Don Gomez di Feria, the Spanish Ambassador, but since she wants to become Queen, she agrees to marry Henry. He rejects his rightful wife, Catherine of Aragon, and Parliament declares the English Church independent since Rome is against the sovereign's plans. However, Catherine has obtained a letter which proves that Anne and Gomez are in love. In order to get it back Anne goes to the retreat where Catherine is dying and pretends to repent. But the trick does not succeed. Henry and Gomez also try to get back the letter, but Catherine resists and throws the evidence in the fire. After Catherine's death, the king is still suspicious and now that the evidence has been destroyed he threatens to have Anne put to death if he should ever discover that she has deceived him.

■ The composition of the opera took some considerable time. Saint-Saëns was offered the libretto in Madrid during a visit there and he accepted it readily, even making note of a few modifications. Then he received another text by the same author, *Ines de Castro*, which did not suit him. After numerous postponements and after the authors had almost completely rewritten the libretto, *Henri VIII* was presented in Paris. It was a triumph, particularly for the French school. In the opinion of the critics it was 'a reflection rather than an inspiration, well worked out and compact'.

LAKMÉ

Opera in three acts by Léo Delibes (1836–91), libretto by Edmond Gondinet and Philippe Gille, based on the story by Pierre Loti, Le mariage de Loti (1880). First performance: Paris, Opéra-Comique, 14 April 1883; first performance in U.K.: London, Gaiety Theatre, 6 June 1885; in U.S.A.: Chicago, Grand Opera House, 4 October 1883.

ORIGINAL CAST. Van Zandt (Lakme), Talazac (Gérald), Cobalet (Nilakantha).

SYNOPSIS. The action takes place in India in the middle of the nineteenth century. Act I. A party of English people – Ellen, Rose (sopranos), their governess Mistress Bentson (mezzo-soprano) and two officers Frédéric (baritone) and Gérald (tenor) – break through the fence around the beautiful garden of Brahmin priest Nilakantha's temple. Curious about the air of mystery that surrounds Lakmé (soprano), the daughter of the Brahmin, Gérald stays behind after his companions have left. He is enchanted by her, and she, too, is attracted to him, but he slips away when her father (bass) arrives. Nilakantha vows to kill the man who violated the sacred ground. Act II. A market square. Nilakantha persuades Lakmé to sing in the town where the British garrison is stationed, because he is convinced that her voice will eventually force the intruder to give himself away and, once he has identified him, he will be able to take his revenge. That is what happens. Lakmé warns Gérald of the danger and urges him to run away with her to her retreat in the forest, but he refuses because he does not want to desert. Nilakantha identifies Gérald in the crowd that has formed to watch a religious procession, and stabs him. Lakmé is relieved to find that the wound is not very serious. Act III. In Lakmé's hut in the forest. Gérald awakes to find Lakmé beside him. She has brought him here to heal him with medicinal herbs. She explains that the distant sound is that of lovers singing as they go to drink from a fountain whose waters bring eternal love. She leaves him to fetch some water for them, and Frédéric appears. He persuades Gérald to return to the garrison. When Gérald hesitates to drink,

Lakmé realizes that he is troubled at having to choose between his duty and his love for her. She decides for him by eating a poisonous leaf and, after they have drunk and sworn eternal love, she reveals to the horrified officer that she is dying for him. Nilakantha surprises them, but his fury abates when he sees that his daughter has gone to a celestial life.

■ At the time of the composition of this opera there was a fashion for the mysterious Orient and Delibes followed it by composing an opera with an Oriental atmosphere. It is to the famous Bell song that the opera owes much of its popularity today. There is a good deal of Massenet's influence as well as all the vivacity and brilliance of operetta. It is the most famous of Delibes's operas. In 1895 it had already been performed 200 times at the Opéra-Comique in Paris and the 1,000th performance was in 1931. *Lakmé* has been performed all over the world and is still part of the French repertoire today.

MANON
Tragic opera in five acts and six tableaux by Jules Massenet (1842–1912), libretto by Henri Meilhac (1831–97) and Philippe Gille, based on the novel Histoire du chevalier des Grieux et de Manon Lescaut *by Abbé Prévost (1731). First performance: Paris, Opéra-Comique, 19 January 1884; first performance in U.K.: Liverpool, 17 January 1885; in U.S.A.: New York, Academy of Music, 23 December 1885.*

ORIGINAL CAST. Marie Heilbronn (Manon), Chevalier (Javotte), Molé-Truffier (Pousette), Remy (Rosette), Talazac (Des Grieux), Taskin (Lescaut), Cobalet (Lecomte), Grivot (Guillot). Conducted by Jules Danbé.

SYNOPSIS. The action takes place in France in 1721. Act I. In the courtyard of an inn at Amiens. Guillot de Morfontaine (tenor), an old roué, and de Brétigny (baritone) are dining with three actresses, Pousette, Javotte, Rosette (sopranos). The stage-coach from Arras arrives and a beautiful young woman descends from it – Manon Lescaut (soprano). She is met by Lescaut (baritone), her cousin, who is to take her to a convent school. As soon as Lescaut leaves her to look for her baggage, Guillot begins to boast to Manon of his riches and offers to elope with her. She is amused, but their conversation is interrupted by Lescaut, who chides her for allowing strangers to talk to her. He leaves her alone again, however, to play cards with some friends. The young Chevalier des Grieux (tenor), who is travelling to meet his father, is struck by Manon's beauty and comes over to her. They fall in love and she agrees to run away with him, suggesting that they use Guillot's carriage to do so. The old roué looks very foolish when their departure is discovered. Act II. Des Grieux and Manon's apartment in Paris. He is writing to his father to apologize for not meeting him and to announce his intention of marrying Manon.

A scene from Rimsky-Korsakov's The Snow Maiden *Act II at the Bolshoi Theatre, Moscow, in 1954.*

nary of Saint-Sulpice. The congregation praise the sermons of the Abbé des Grieux. The Count des Grieux tries in vain to persuade his son to give up the monastic life. Manon arrives while he is at prayer and is more successful, winning him over by her beauty. She persuades him to go away with her. Act IV. The Hôtel de Transylvanie, a gambling den in Paris. Manon persuades des Grieux to gamble what money he has left to win more. He plays cards against Guillot and wins. Guillot accuses him of cheating. The police arrest the two lovers. Act V. The road to Le Havre. The Count has obtained the release of his son, but Manon is to be deported as a common prostitute. Lescaut and des Grieux wait for the prisoners to pass. Lescaut has bribed the leader of the convoy for permission to have a brief word with his cousin, promising to take her straight back to the port. When Manon appears, exhausted and dishevelled, she throws herself in the arms of des Grieux. She is very weak and dies in his arms, reminding him of their love and begging his forgiveness.

■ *Manon* is perhaps the most famous of Massenet's operas. Despite its initial success, it was not well received by the critics and it was only after a few years that it became very famous. In 1952 it was performed in Paris for the 2,000th time. Musically, it can be considered Massenet's most complete opera. It includes, in fact, many different types of music, from the melodramatic to the comic, from the lyrical to the intimate and the tragic. The composer has here succeeded in producing the best of his art, reaching the height of French musical romanticism. In the refined melodic language he is in many ways a forerunner of Debussy and Ravel.

MAZEPPA
Opera in three acts by Peter Ilyich Tchaikovsky (1840— 1893), libretto by the composer and Victor Petrovich Burenin, based on the epic poem Poltava *by Alexander Pushkin. First performance: Moscow, Bolshoi Theatre, 15 February 1884; first performance in U.K.: Liverpool, 6 August 1888; in U.S.A.: Boston, Opera House, 14 December 1922.*

SYNOPSIS. The action takes place in the Ukraine at the beginning of the eighteenth century. Act I, Scene I. The garden of the villa of Kochubey (bass), the Minister of Justice. The military commander of the Ukraine, Mazeppa (baritone), a cossack, is a guest at the villa and Maria (soprano), the daughter of the house, is in love with him. Mazeppa is much older than Maria – he is her godfather – but she loves him because of a certain heroic air he has about him. She tells Andrei (tenor), who has been her companion since childhood, how she feels, and he goes away sadly because he now knows that his own love for her is unrequited. There is dancing and singing in honour of the guest and Mazeppa asks Kochubey for the hand of Maria. Surprised, Kochubey refuses. The commander then tells Maria's father that she has already promised herself to him. A

'The Good Friday Spell' in Wagner's Parsifal *during the performance at Bayreuth in 1882 with Amalie Materna (Kundry), Emil Scaria (Gurnemanz) and Hermann Winkelmann (Parsifal).*

Two men, who pretend to be soldiers, are admitted by the maid; they turn out to be Lescaut and de Brétigny. Angrily Lescaut asks des Grieux his intentions regarding his cousin. Des Grieux shows him the letter and Lescaut seems reassured. Meanwhile de Brétigny warns Manon that des Grieux's father plans to have him abducted that evening and offers to look after her himself. Manon is given the choice of telling her lover, and being forced to face a life of hardship with him, or living in luxury with de Brétigny. She sadly opts for the easier solution. While des Grieux despatches the letter to his father she recalls their tender love: '*Adieu, notre petite table*'. Although she asks him not to answer a knock at the door, des Grieux leaves the room to open it. There is the sound of a struggle and a coach departs with her lover inside. Act III, Scene I. In the Cours La Reine, Paris. Several people meet: Pousette, Javotte, Rosette, Guillot, de Brétigny, and Manon, who is gay and elegant. The Count des Grieux (bass), the father of the Chevalier, meets de Brétigny and discloses that his son has taken holy orders after being disappointed in love. Manon overhears the conversation and, without saying who she is, asks the Count for more news of his son, but he will not answer her questions fully. She ignores an entertainment which Guillot has arranged and resolves to visit des Grieux. Scene II. The Semi-

quarrel breaks out and Maria has to choose between her parents and Mazeppa. She hesitates briefly before choosing Mazeppa. They leave together while her parents curse the man who has stolen their daughter. Scene II. A room in Kochubey's home. Kochubey has discovered that Mazeppa is implicated in a conspiracy against the Tsar, involving the King of Sweden. Thinking that he has found a good way to punish the man who has seduced Maria, Kochubey sends Andrei to Moscow to tell the Tsar. Act II, Scene I. A dungeon of Mazeppa's castle. The Tsar did not believe the report against Mazeppa and has handed Kochubey over to the Ukrainian leader. Kochubey is tortured, but reveals nothing. He is condemned to death together with his follower Iskra (bass). Scene II. A room in Mazeppa's castle. The commander is worried because he does not know how to tell Maria of the imminent sentence on her father. She has noticed Mazeppa's strange behaviour and suspects that he is deceiving her. Mazeppa then tells her of the plot against the Tsar and asks her if she would prefer to see her father or her husband die. She does not reply and, not understanding the importance of the question, kisses him and assures him of her love. Mazeppa goes out asking her to forgive him. Her mother, Liubov (mezzo-soprano), finds her way into the castle and tells Maria that her father is about to be executed. They rush out to save him. Scene III. In a field where the gallows have been erected. Kochubey and Iskra are executed just before Maria and Liubov arrive. Overcome with grief, Maria faints. Act III. In the garden of Kochubey's house, now in ruins. After Peter the Great's victory at Poltava over Charles XII of Sweden, the Ukraine is devastated. Andrei, who tried to kill Mazeppa during the battle but did not succeed, is now looking for Maria. Mazeppa and his faithful retainer, Orlik (bass), have been betrayed by the King of Sweden and are now in flight. Andrei attacks Mazeppa, but he is fatally wounded by Mazeppa's pistol. Maria – a shadow of her former self and half demented – wanders in the garden, recalling childhood memories. She does not recognize Mazeppa, nor Andrei, who is dying, but she takes his head in her arms and rocks him, singing a lullaby. Mazeppa hurries away, leaving Andrei to die, while Maria, in her delirium, rocks him to and fro.

■ This opera was inspired by the historical character, Ivan Mazeppa, a cossack who tried to set up a Ukrainian state independent from Russia, by entering into an alliance with King Charles XII of Sweden. It began Tchaikovsky's return to Russian themes, which he had forsaken with the *Maid of Orleans*.

THE CANTERBURY PILGRIMS
Opera in two acts by Charles Stanford (1852–1924); libretto by Gilbert Arthur A'Beckett. First performance: London, Drury Lane, 23 April 1884.

■ This opera, taken from Chaucer's *Canterbury Tales* (c. 1390), has a lively plot based on life in England in the late Middle Ages. It contains rapid and brilliant sketches of character and skilful changes of scene. It was a resounding success in London. The composer made much use of Irish folklore and the characteristic elements of 'Merrie England'.

DER TROMPETER VAN SÄCKINGEN (The Trumpeter of Säckingen)
Opera in four acts by Viktor Nessler (1841–90), libretto by Rudolf Bunge based on the poem by Joseph Viktor von Scheffel (1854), which was inspired by a popular legend. First performance: Leipzig, Stadttheater, 4 May 1884; first performance in U.K.: London, Drury Lane, 8 July 1892; in U.S.A.: New York, 23 November 1887.

SYNOPSIS. The plot, which is set after the Thirty Years War, tells the story of the trumpeter, Werner Kirchhof, an ex-student of Heidelberg, who arrives at a castle on the Rhine. Here lives Maria, who is betrothed to the noble Damian and well known for her beauty. In a scene notable for its original wit and comedy, Werner teaches her to play the trumpet. Before long Maria can use her new skill to sound the alarm during an unexpected assault on the castle. In the battle that follows Werner is able to show his courage by defending her at great risk to his own safety, while her betrothed shows nothing but cowardice. Maria and Werner fall in love, but the idyll is destroyed by her proud father, who refuses to allow his daughter to marry a commoner. Werner is forced to leave and, on his travels, visits Rome, where his skills are appreciated by the Pope, who appoints him Choir Master at St Peter's. Two years later, in Rome, Werner and Maria meet again. When he hears of their romantic love affair, the Pope is moved and creates Werner the Marquis of Camposanto (a play on the meaning of Kirchhof, which means churchyard, like Camposanto). The young couple at last obtain her father's consent to their marriage.

■ The opera enjoyed an enormous success owing to the grace and expressiveness of the melodies and the balance between the romantic and the comic throughout the work.

LE VILLI
Opera in two acts by Giacomo Puccini (1858–1924), libretto by Ferdinando Fontana (1850–1919). First performance: Milan, Teatro dal Verme, 31 May 1884; first performance in U.K.: Manchester, 24 September 1897; in U.S.A.: New York, Metropolitan Opera House, 17 December 1908.

ORIGINAL CAST. Antonio d'Andrade. Conducted by Achille Panizza.

SYNOPSIS. Act I. A village in the Black Forest, in springtime. Having celebrated his engagement to Anna (soprano), Roberto (tenor) has to leave for Mainz to collect an inheritance from an aunt. Anna is sad and full of foreboding and Roberto is unable to comfort her. Act II. In Mainz Roberto met an adventuress and forgot Anna who, after waiting for him for months, has died of a broken heart. Her spirit has joined the Villi, the ghosts of girls who have died of grief after being forsaken in love, and who dance men to death in revenge. The scene is the village at midnight in winter. The Villi are dancing. Roberto returns and Guglielmo (baritone), Anna's father, appeals to Anna's ghost for revenge. She appears together with the Villi and Roberto, thinking she is alive, kisses her. She drags him into a wild dance until he falls dead at her feet. A *Hosanna* is heard in the distance.

■ *Le Villi* was inspired by a legend, probably of Slav origin, and was Puccini's first opera. It achieved a sensational success at the first performance and was praised by Verdi himself. At times both eclectic and conventional, the work is particularly noteworthy for its capable handling of dramatic situations.

MARION DELORME

Opera in four acts by Amilcare Ponchielli (1834–86), libretto by Enrico Golisciani, based on the play by Victor Hugo (1831). First performance: Milan, Teatro alla Scala, 17 March, 1885.

ORIGINAL CAST. Romilda, Pantaleoni, Francesco Tamagno, Augusto Brogi, Angelo Tamburlini, Adele Borghi, Angelo Fiorentini, Napoleone Limonta, Carlo Moretti. Conducted by Franco Faccio.

SYNOPSIS. After leading a worldly and dissipated life, Marion Delorme (soprano) has retired to live at Blois. The Marquis of Saverny (baritone), her former lover, rebukes her for forsaking those who love and admire her. Marion says that she now wants to live in solitude. From what she says Saverny realizes that she is in love, but he does not discover the name of the lucky man. When Saverny has gone, Didier (tenor) arrives and they sing a love duet. They are interrupted by the shouts of the Marquis, who is being attacked by robbers. The two rivals then meet, much to Marion's embarrassment.

In a square in Blois, a group of officers, among them Brichanteau and Gassé, talk with Lelio, a comic, about the latest news from Paris – the love affairs and duels. The biggest piece of news is Marion Delorme's retreat to Blois. Meanwhile the town crier announces that the King has strictly prohibited duelling. Saverny and Didier meet casually and a quarrel breaks out between them and suddenly turns into a duel. When the police arrive, Brichanteau suggests to Saverny that he pretend to fall dead; Marion arrives just as Didier is being arrested.

Laffemas and Saverny joke about the Marquis's feigned death, since he has changed his clothes and is now unrecognizable. Lelio's company of actors are staying in a nearby barn and Marion and Didier, who has escaped from prison, join them dressed as Spaniards. Saverny sees through their disguise and makes himself known to Didier, who is amazed since he thought he had killed him. Saverny tells Didier about Marion's stormy past, which greatly troubles Didier. Laffemas has also recognized Didier and devises a plan to bring him before Richelieu; he suggests that the actors give a performance for the Cardinal. Didier is now desperate and reveals his true identity; Laffemas orders him to be arrested as Saverny's assassin. At this point Saverny, too, drops his disguise and shows everyone that he is alive. Laffemas then orders his arrest also for having broken the King's decree. Although Marion obtains the King's pardon for Didier, Laffemas is unwilling to recognize its authenticity and declares his love for her, offering her Didier's release in exchange for her love. She rejects him indignantly. Meanwhile Saverny and Didier in goal together await sentence to be passed. A goaler tells Saverny that he has been ordered to let him escape. When the Marquis understands that Didier is not allowed to share the privilege he refuses the offer. Marion tries to persuade Didier to escape with her, but he only taunts her with her past. As the two men are about to be executed, Marion throws herself again at Didier's feet and begs his forgiveness. She finally obtains words of love from him. The two men are executed and Marion faints.

■ The libretto, which was based on a play by Hugo, was already known in Italy, since Bottesini and Pedrotti had earlier written operas on the same theme. The critics were not much impressed when the opera was first shown and this distressed Ponchielli a great deal. He died a few months later of pneumonia.

UNE NUIT DE CLÉOPÂTRE (A Night with Cleopatra)

Tragic opera in three acts and four tableaux by Victor Massé (1822–84), libretto by Jules Barbier (1825–1901), based on the short story by Théophile Gautier (1811–72). First performance: Paris, Opéra-Comique, 25 April 1885.

SYNOPSIS. A poor and unknown young man by the name of Mannassès, made bold by a burning passion for Cléopâtre, Queen of Egypt, performs a number of courageous deeds and manages to get himself noticed by her during one of her journeys on the Nile. He is granted one night of love with her in exchange for his death, a just punishment for such audacity. After a grand banquet, a sad epilogue to a brief dream, Mannassès poisons himself and dies. Just at that moment Mark Antony arrives with his soldiers and does not even cast a glance at his body.

■ From a highly exotic libretto, where elaborate taste for detail overwhelms the simplicity of the plot, Massé, a composer much influenced by Gounod, nevertheless produced a score that is well worked and effective, making fun of the exquisitely sensual music that was the indispensable ingredient of so much poetic decadence. We have confirmation of this in the minute descriptions of the countryside, the ancient temples and palaces, the legendary beauty of Cléopâtre and her wild and extravagant customs. All these elements are

The hall of the knights of the Grail in Wagner's
Parsifal, *Act I, produced by Wolfgang Wagner at the*
Bayreuth festival in 1975.

gently underlined by music which at times is sweet and
at others slightly caustic. Although a fluent writer of
melody with elegant taste, Massé is not ranked among
the leading figures of the French opera in the second
half of the nineteenth century. His opera has been
almost entirely forgotten. Only one of Cléopâtre's
arias (in the first scene of the second act), which still
seems fresh, is occasionally performed.

LE CID

Opera in four acts and ten tableaux by Jules Massenet
(1842–1912), libretto by Adolphe d'Ennery, Louis
Gallet and Edouard Blau, based on the tragedy by
Corneille (1637). First performance: Paris, Opéra, 30
November 1885; first performance in U.S.A.: New
Orleans, 23 February 1890.

ORIGINAL CAST. Fidès-Devriès (Chimène), Jean
de Reszke (Rodrigue), Edouard de Reszke (Don
Diègue), Pol Plançon (Gormas), Melchissédec (le
Roi).

SYNOPSIS. The action takes place in Spain at the time
of the *Reconquista* against the Arabs. To revenge an
offence against his father, don Rodrigue (tenor) kills
don Gormas (bass), the father of his betrothed,
Chimène (soprano). She asks the king (baritone) to
revenge her father's death, but as Rodrigue must fight
the Moors, his punishment is postponed. When he
returns victorious, he is acclaimed as the 'Cid' (master
warrior) by all. The king must have justice for Gormas's death and he orders the sentence to be given by
the girl who has suffered most by it – Chimène. After a
few heart-broken words, she pardons him. The 'Cid'
still feels guilty, but Chimène stops him from committing suicide. Saved by her love, the 'Cid' is then united
with her.

■ *Le Cid* is an imposing opera of love and glory, but is
not usually considered to be one of Massenet's best. As
well as the usual melodrama, there is a tendency to
indulge too much in popular tastes. It is also interesting
to note the influence of Verdi in this opera.

KHOVANSHCHINA (The Princes Khovansky)
'A National Music Drama' in five acts by Modest Mus-
sorgsky (1839–81), completed and orchestrated by
Rimsky-Korsakov (1883) and Shostakovich (1959);
libretto by the composer and Vladimir V. Stasov,
inspired by old chronicles of the schismatic 'Old Be-
lievers'. First performance: St Petersburg, Kononov
Theatre, 21 February 1886; first performance in U.K.:
London, Drury Lane, 1 July 1913; in U.S.A.:
Philadelphia, 18 April 1928.

SYNOPSIS. The plot is concerned with the struggle for
power between the representatives of old and new
Russia. The rebellion of the Streltsy, the corps of
archers led by Ivan Khovansky, has taken place (15
May 1682) and as a result Tsarevna Sophia has become
regent in the name of her children, Ivan and Peter. The
three main characters embody the ideological conflicts
of the struggle. Ivan Khovansky (bass), violent and
bigoted, leader of the Streltsy, represents the power of
the Boyars and the 'old' Russia. Dositheus (bass),
leader of the 'Old Believers', represents mystic Russia
and its uneuropeanized culture. Prince Galitsin (tenor)
may be identified with 'new' Russia and the western
influences. Mussorgsky's reflections on these characters are not moralistic: virtue and vice, religion and
superstition co-exist like the different sides of one
prism – the Russian spirit itself, which is the real subject of the opera. Act I. Dawn over Moscow. In the
Red Square a group of Streltsy discuss the deeds of the
night: they have beaten up a priest and drawn and
quartered a German. A letter writer (scrivener)
(tenor), crosses the square on his way to work. Shaklovity (baritone), a boyar, approaches him and, bind-
ing him with threats to secrecy, dictates an anonymous
letter, addressed to Tsarevna Sophia, accusing Ivan

Khovansky of stirring up trouble against the State, aided by the 'Old Believers'. Ivan Khovansky himself then arrives and announces to the crowd that he has been appointed the protector of Sophia's children. Emma (soprano), a young Lutheran, arrives, pursued by Andrew Khovansky (tenor), Ivan's son. He has killed her father and exiled her betrothed; now he claims her for himself. Martha (mezzo-soprano), a young widow, a mystic and 'Old Believer', who was once Andrew's mistress, defends her. Ivan Khovansky, who is charmed by Emma's beauty, orders his soldiers to take her to his palace – but rather than surrender her, Andrew is about to kill her when Dositheus, the leader of the 'Old Believers', appears. He invites them all to forget their differences and to fight together for the true orthodox religion. Ivan welcomes it, believing that he will be able to make good use of the alliance to further his own interests. Act II. In his summer residence, Prince Galitsin is reading a love letter from Tsarevna Sophia. He used to be her lover, but he no longer trusts her. Martha comes to tell his horoscope and predicts a future of disgrace and exile for him. Galitsin dismisses her curtly and orders his servant to have her drowned in the marshes. Then he reflects on her prophecies. He recalls that he fought the Poles for the lands they had usurped, and fought to strip the Boyars of their privileges; the reward for his efforts is to be disgrace. Khovansky enters unannounced to complain against Galitsin's interference in the government and they quarrel. Dositheus arrives and implores them to make peace in the name of old Russia. Galitsin refuses, but Khovansky accepts. Then Martha rushes in, having escaped from an assassin thanks to the intervention of the Petrovsky (the bodyguard of the Tsar, Peter the Great). The princes are alarmed by the unexpected presence of the Tsar's soldiers in Moscow and Shaklovity announces that the Tsar has proclaimed the Khovanskys traitors for plotting against the State. Act III. The Streltsy quarter opposite Belgorod. The 'Old Believers' march past, singing. Martha sings a popular lament about her past love. The drunken Streltsy are insulted by their women, who accuse them of being idlers. The scrivener reports that the Petrovsky are carrying out massacres on the outskirts of the Streltsy encampment. Khovansky refuses to lead the Streltsy in an attack, explaining that they must await the Tsar's orders. Act IV. Khovansky's residence. The Prince is seated at table, being entertained by singing and the dancing of Persian slaves. Proudly Khovansky ignores Galitsin's warning that his life is in danger. When Shaklovity invites him to the Tsarevna's Council, he is flattered and falls into the trap. He gets dressed, has a song sung in his honour and departs. As he goes, he is stabbed in

Klingsor's garden in Wagner's Parsifal *Act II, produced by Wolfgang Wagner at the Bayreuth festival in 1975.*

Poster by A. Chatinière for Henry VIII *by Saint-Saëns presented at the Opéra in 1883. Bibliothèque de l'Opéra Paris.*

Poster by A. Chatinière for Lakmé *by Léo Delibes, presented at the Opéra-Comique in 1883 Bibliothèque de l'Opéra, Paris.*

the back by Shaklovity. Meanwhile, in Moscow, Galitsin sets off with dignity on the road to exile. Martha brings the news to Dositheus that the Council has ordered the extermination of the 'Old Believers'. Andrew Khovansky learns that his father has been assassinated and has not been buried. He thinks he can still call upon the Streltsy to recover Emma, who has fled with the man she loves, but when the Streltsy approach, each of them carries an axe and a block for their execution. They have been condemned to death as Khovansky's accomplices. Martha hurries Andrew away to a hiding place. Peter the Great's guards arrive to announce that the Tsar has pardoned the Streltsy. Act V. A solitary retreat in the forest. It is night and Dositheus and his followers are preparing to sacrifice themselves on a pyre to testify to their faith. Sounds of trumpets can be heard from the advancing troops. The 'Old Believers', dressed in white and each holding a candle, advance towards the pyre. Martha comforts Andrew, who still calls for Emma. She reminds him of their past love, kisses him for the last time and pulls him onto the pyre as she sets it alight. Martha's song, which Mussorgsky called the 'requiem of love', heralds the arrival of the Petrovsky, who stop aghast at the sight of the flames.

■ This opera was left unfinished; the end of the second act and the final chorus of the 'Old Believers' existed only in sketches. It was orchestrated and completed by Rimsky-Korsakov, who was given the job by the publisher, Bessel. Although very valuable, Rimsky-Korsakov's version has been criticized as has his arrangement of *Boris*. He made some cuts to bring the score to a more suitable length but, more importantly, he sometimes altered the music itself, forcing the opera within the limits of his own aesthetics. After the first performance in 1886, which was repeated only eight times, the opera was performed again in 1891 at the Maryinsky Theatre, St Petersburg, with Chaliapin in the role of Dositheus. On 5 June 1913 it was performed at the Champs-Élysées, Paris, by the Diaghilev Company with revisions by Stravinsky and Ravel. A new version was prepared by Shostakovich and presented in Leningrad at the Kirov Theatre in 1960.

GWENDOLINE
Opera in two acts by Emmanuel Chabrier (1841–94), libretto by Catulle Mendès (1841–1909). First performance: Brussels, Théâtre de la Monnaie, 10 April 1886.

SYNOPSIS. The background to the plot is the war between the Saxons and the Danes. Harald, the Viking King, is in love with Gwendoline, the daughter of one of his prisoners, the Saxon leader, Armel. It is arranged that she should marry Harald on the understanding that she kills him in his sleep. But Gwendoline cannot go through with it and dies with him when Armel murders Harald.

■ This opera, both in its choice of a Nordic setting and the introduction of 'leit-motif', is the first tribute to

Post card of the early 1900's, depicting the final scene from Massenet's Manon.

Wagner by a French composer. However, Chabrier's Wagnerism is very personal and does not go beyond these external manifestations. Nevertheless, the work was rejected by the Paris Opéra as being too Wagnerian and was presented in Brussels at the Théâtre de la Monnaie, which from 1871 welcomed non-conformist works that were turned down by the Opéra. It met with an enthusiastic reception. With this opera Chabrier entered the ranks of professional composers, six years after he had left the ministry of the Interior.

OTELLO

Opera in four acts by Giuseppe Verdi (1813–1901), libretto by Arrigo Boito (1842–1918), based on the tragedy by Shakespeare. First performance: Milan, Teatro alla Scala, 5 February 1887. First performance in U.K.: London, Lyceum, 5 July 1889; in U.S.A.: New York, Academy of Music, 16 April 1888.

ORIGINAL CAST. Pantaleoni (Desdemona), Petrovich (Emilia), Tamagno (Otello), Maurel (Iago), Navarrini (Montano), Paroli (Cassio), Fornari (Roderigo). Conductor: Franco Faccio.

SYNOPSIS. The action takes place in Cyprus, a Venetian dominion, in the fifteenth century. Act I. The port, outside the castle of the Moor Otello (tenor), the Venetian governor of the island. It is evening and there is a violent storm at sea. A crowd of citizens and soldiers watch from the quayside as Otello's ship makes for port. Only the ensign, Iago (baritone), takes no part in the general concern for his master's safety. He hates Otello because Cassio (tenor) has been promoted over him and he plans his revenge. Otello finally reaches the harbour and triumphantly announces that the Turkish fleet has been defeated ('Esultate'). When he enters

A set from Tchaikovsky's Mazeppa *at the Bolshoi in 1884. Archives of The Theatre Museum, Moscow.*

E. Kibkalo in the part of Mazeppa and I. Petrov in the part of Kochubey, in the first act of Tchaikovsky's Mazeppa. *Moscow, Bolshoi 1966.*

the castle, the people light fires and drink to the victory. In the general jubilation, Iago begins to weave his plot. He insinuates to Roderigo (tenor), a Venetian who has confided in him that he loves Otello's wife, Desdemona, that Captain Cassio feels the same way about her. Then he manages to get Cassio drunk and sets the two men one against the other, and in the ensuing brawl, Cassio wounds Montano (bass), the former governor, who tries to separate them. Iago raises the alarm, exaggerating his account of the trouble and falsely informs Otello, who punishes Cassio by dismissing him. Iago rejoices in his victory. Desdemona (soprano) is attracted by the noise and, when they are alone, Otello and Desdemona sing a long and very beautiful love duet, while Venus shines in the sky ('*Già nella notte densa*'). Act II. A hall in the castle. A door in the centre leads out into the garden. Iago is continuing his plot. He suggests to Cassio that he asks Desdemona to speak to Otello on his behalf. In a monologue Iago expounds his cynical view of life '*I believe in a cruel god*' ('*Credo in un Dio crudel*'). He manages to sow the seeds of jealousy in Otello's mind, making him believe that there is a secret love affair between Cassio and Desdemona. When she comes in from the garden and tries to speak on behalf of the deposed Captain, Otello's jealousy is roused and he turns down the request. Again, Iago claims to have heard some compromising words from Cassio in his sleep ('*Era la notte, Cassio dormia*'). With the help of his wife, Emilia (mezzo-soprano), he has obtained a handkerchief that Desdemona had received as a present from Otello and he now claims to have seen it in Cassio's possession. For Otello this is proof. He kneels and swears a terrible vengeance 'Witness, yonder

marble Heaven' ('*Sí, pel ciel marmoreo giuro!*'). Act III. In the great hall of the castle. A herald has announced that a ship is due bringing ambassadors from Venice. Desdemona again asks for forgiveness for Cassio, but Otello asks her to show him the handkerchief he has given her. When she cannot show it, he accuses her of being a strumpet and sends her away. Alone, he bemoans his lost happiness 'Heav'n, had it pleased thee,' ('*Dio, mi potevi scagliare tutti i mali*'). He is disturbed by the arrival of Iago, who arranges for him to overhear his conversation with Cassio about a prostitute. He makes Otello believe they are talking about Desdemona and shows him Cassio playing with the handkerchief. Otello determines to kill Desdemona that night. Then the Venetian ambassadors announce that Otello is recalled to Venice and will be succeeded by Cassio. In front of everyone, Otello, now mad with rage, seizes his wife and throws her to the ground. Iago then proceeds with the final part of his plan by urging Roderigo to kill Cassio. Otello curses Desdemona; he collapses as the shouts of the crowd in praise of the Moor can be heard from outside. With a triumphant gesture Iago points to the inert body; 'Here is the lion' ('*Ecco il leone!*') he mocks. Act IV. Desdemona's bedroom. She prepares for bed, helped by her maid Emilia. Distressed by Otello's behaviour, which she cannot understand, Desdemona sadly recalls the story of one of her maids who was abandoned by the man she loved ('The Willow Song'). She has just finished praying ('*Ave Maria*') when Otello enters. He accuses her of having deceived him and in vain Desdemona protests her innocence. He smothers her. Emilia runs in with the news that Roderigo has been killed in his attempt to kill Cassio. Seeing Desdemona's body, she accuses Otello of killing an innocent woman, and she exposes Iago's plot. Iago escapes while Otello realizes his error. He stabs himself and, with his last breath, kisses his wife for the last time.

■ Verdi presented *Otello* to the public after almost sixteen years had passed since *Aida* during which he had composed only *The Manzoni Requiem*. During this period he had reflected at length on his experience and on the evolution of opera. He began to collaborate with Boito, who wrote the libretto for him with a 'continuous structure' which allowed the composer not to interrupt the development of the drama with arias, duets and recitatives. It was not an easy collaboration, but it was really as a result of the continual conflict and argument between them that the drama took shape. Boito had no intention of deviating from Shakespeare and he often asked if he had remained sufficiently faithful to the text. Yet clearly there was still alive in him the old formula of the *Scapigliatura*, of which he had been one of the foremost exponents: to blend together 'the three arts', that is music, literature and the visual arts (painting and sculpture – more appropriately, in the case of theatrical drama, the scenery, which in an opera such as *Otello* can only be suggestive). The quest for the combination of these different components, to form what, for the *Scapigliati*, was to

Mussorgsky's Khovanshchina *Act II in the Bolshoi production of 1912. Archives of The Theatre Museum, Moscow.*

be the 'complete art of the future', appears particularly effective when it is applied to the intensity and the psychological insights of Shakespeare. The same is true for *Falstaff*, Verdi's last opera, whilst his attempt at *Macbeth* turned out to be mediocre: although it has great value in Verdi's development, it did not succeed in capturing the true spirit of Shakespeare. Far from putting an end to the conflict dividing Verdians from Wagnerians, *Otello* showed that the old master had realized, during his years of meditation, that it was possible to learn from experiences different and sometimes opposed to those to which one has remained faithful throughout one's working life.

LE ROI MALGRÉ LUI (The King in Spite of Himself)
Opéra comique *in three acts by Emmanuel Chabrier (1841–94), libretto by Paul Burani (1845–1901) and Emile de Najac (1828–89), based on a vaudeville by François Ancelot. First performance: Paris, Opéra-Comique, 18 May 1887.*

ORIGINAL CAST. Max Bouvet, Delaguerrière, Lucien Fougère, Thierry, Adèle Isaac, Cécile Mézéray, Barnolt.

SYNOPSIS. The plot revolves around Henri de Valois who, before he became King of France, was King of Poland.

■ The third performance of the opera, on 25 May 1887, was interrupted because of a fire at the theatre. It only returned to the stage on the following 16 November, in a temporary setting. It is a comic opera – with a musical score that is interspersed with frequent passages of dialogue – in which Chabrier, usually considered to be one of the fathers of impressionism, uses his musical talents to the greatest originality, rejecting the contemporary French rules. Even though the audience and the critics did not immediately understand his originality, it was nevertheless Chabrier's most successful work. Like *Gwendoline* it was performed elsewhere in Europe. There have been more recent productions (1929 and later) with a simplified plot by Albert Carré.

LE ROI D'YS (The King of Ys)
Opera in three acts by Edouard Lalo (1823–92), libretto by Edouard Blau, inspired by a Breton legend. First performance: Paris, Opéra-Comique, 7 May 1888. First performance in U.K.: London, Covent Garden, 17 July 1901; in U.S.A.: New Orleans, 23 January 1890.*

SYNOPSIS. Outside the place of the King of Ys (bass), festivities are in hand to celebrate the wedding of his daughter, Margared (soprano), to Karnac (baritone), which will conclude the peace treaty between the two enemy countries. Margared and her sister, Rozenn (soprano), are both (unknown to each other) in love with Mylio (tenor), whose disappearance is a source of mystery. He unexpectedly returns one day and declares his love for Rozenn. When Margared hears of his return she wants nothing further to do with Karnac. In his indignation Karnac swears to take revenge, but Mylio takes up the challenge and offers to lead the armies of Ys to victory. He succeeds and claims Rozenn as his bride. This makes Margared mad with jealousy and in revenge she goes to Karnac with a plan to open the dyke which protects the city from the sea and so to drown the whole population of Ys. The statue of St Corentin (bass), the guardian saint of Ys, comes to life and tries to persuade Margared to give up this terrible scheme. While the marriage of Mylio and Rozenn takes place, Karnac breaks down the dyke. The people, terrified, takes refuge on a hill above the city. Margared, now repentant, takes refuge amongst them, but when the sea reaches the hill she confesses her guilt and calls upon St Corentin to protect them. She throws herself into the sea and the Saint performs a miracle: the water subsides and the sea retreats. The people kneel in prayer for the salvation of Margared's soul.

■ Lalo's opera was much acclaimed by critics and audience alike and is still very popular today in France.

DIE FEEN (The Fairies)
Opera in three acts by Richard Wagner (1813–83), composed in 1833 and 1834. Libretto by the composer, based on La donna serpente *(1762) by Carlo Gozzi. First performance: Munich, Hoftheater, 29 June 1888.*

SYNOPSIS. Prince Arindal of Tramond, the lucky husband of the sweet and mysterious Ada, must not ask for eight years who she is nor where she comes from. His curiosity overcomes him and when he learns that Ada is a fairy, his sons and his castle disappear with her. To recover his lost happiness, he must undergo difficult tests in order to break the spell that has turned Ada into stone. Taking up his arms, he faces the obstacles, overcomes them and manages to reach the sanctuary of the fairies. He frees his wife with his singing, but she can no longer become a woman. Then, by virtue of his love, Arindal too acquires immortality and is able to share with her in the joy of the fairy kingdom.

■ This opera was composed in Würzburg, where Wagner held the post of chorus master and second conductor. Following the taste for fantasy and romanticism of the early nineteenth century, this was the first of Wagner's operas and is typical of his formative period. He was obviously influenced by Weber, as well as by Beethoven, both in the text and the score. But, to the pure fantasy Wagner adds an authentic human touch, finishing the story with a catharsis, similar in some ways to a *Liebestod*, a theme which is fundamental to the development of his art.

THE JACOBIN
Opera in three acts by Antonín Dvořák (1841–1904), libretto by Marie Červinková-Riegrová. First performance: Prague, National Theatre, 12 February 1889. First performance in U.K.: London, St George's Hall, 23 July 1947.

SYNOPSIS. The opera is concerned with the story of a Jacobin who has returned from exile, where he had

V. Puckov in the role of Prince Andrew Khovansky and S. Strizhenov in the role of the scribe, in Mussorgsky's Khovanshchina *produced at the Kirov Academy of opera and ballet in Leningrad in 1960. Bakhuriscin theatrical museum, Moscow.*

been sent for political reasons. He tries to reinstate himself in the community, helped by his friend, the musician Benda.

■ When he wrote *The Jacobin* Dvořák was influenced by grand opera. It was a great success in Czechoslovakia and has been performed there many times.

EDGAR
Opera in four acts by Giacomo Puccini (1858–1924), libretto by Ferdinando Fontana (1850–1919), based on the drama in verse by Alfred de Musset La Coupe et les Lèvres. *First performance: Milan, Teatro alla Scala, 21 April 1889. First performance in U.S.A.: New York, Waldorf-Astoria, 12 April 1956.*

ORIGINAL CAST. Romilda Pantaleoni, Aurelia Cattaneo, Gregorio Gabrielesco. Conductor: Franco Faccio.

SYNOPSIS. Flanders, in 1302. Act I. Edgar (tenor) is torn between pure love for Fidelia (soprano) and sensual attraction for Tigrana (mezzo-soprano), a negress

ESCLARMONDE

Opéra romanesque *in four acts and eight tableaux by Jules Massenet (1842–1912), libretto by Alfred Blau and Louis de Gramont. First performance: Paris, Opéra-Comique, 14 May 1889.*

ORIGINAL CAST. Sybil Sanderson (Esclarmonde), Gibert (Roland), Taskin (Phorcas).

■ *Esclarmonde*, written for the Universal Exposition of 1889, can be called a grand and spectacular opera. The composer, who sometimes uses realism, as in *La Navarraise*, or mysticism, as in *Le Jongleur de Notre-Dame*), is in this opera much influenced by Wagner. Yet, although transformed by a variety of cultural and musical trends, Massenet speaks his own particular language and reveals a detached personality, of which the sweetness of the melodies is characteristic.

LORELEY

Azione romantica *in three acts by Alfredo Catalani (1854–93), libretto by Carlo d'Ormeville and A. Zanardini, based on the book by Depanis. First performance: Turin, Teatro Regio, 16 February 1890.*

ORIGINAL CAST. Virginia Ferni Germano, Leonora Dexter, Eugenio Durot, Enrico Stinco Palermini. Conductor: Edoardo Mascheroni.

SYNOPSIS. The action takes place on the banks of the Rhine around 1300. Act I. Walter (tenor), Duke of Oberwesel, is to marry Anna di Rehberg (soprano), niece of Rudolfo (bass), Margrave of Biberich, although he has sworn to love Loreley (soprano), a beautiful orphan who loves him passionately. Nevertheless, after consulting Hermann (baritone), who is secretly in love with Anna, Walter decides to leave Loreley and informs her of his decision to marry Anna. Loreley wanders in despair and humiliation on the banks of the Rhine, where according to legend, Alberich, the King of the Rhine, hears the laments of those who are unhappy and grants them their wishes. Loreley, therefore, asks Alberich for beauty to attract, a glance to conquer every heart, a voice to charm the soul, love to intoxicate and kill. He grants her every wish on condition that she agrees to marry him. She accepts and throws herself into the river, and after a while, she steps out transformed into a lovely enchantress with golden hair. Act II. A garden on the banks of the Rhine, in front of Rudolfo's castle. The wedding of Anna and Walter is about to begin and Anna is surrounded by her ladies-in waiting. Hermann warns her about Walter's previous infatuation, but Anna does not believe him, thinking that he is simply jealous. Loreley appears by the river and Walter is fascinated by her singing. Anna tries in vain to stop him from following her. When he has almost reached her, Loreley disappears into the water. Act III. The river bank at Oberwesel. Woodcutters and fishermen are talking about the appearance of a new enchantress from the Rhine, whom some of them have seen on a

abandoned as a baby by the gypsies and brought up by Fidelia's father. Frank (baritone), Fidelia's brother, loves Tigrana, but she is not in love with him. She is accused by the people of the village of scandalous behaviour and is defended by Edgar. Frank challenges his rival but is wounded. Edgar and Tigrana elope. Act II. Edgar joins a group of soldiers, among whom he recognizes Frank. The two become reconciled and Edgar confesses that he regrets having deserted Fidelia. Tigrana swears to obtain revenge for his desertion. Act III. The ramparts of a fortress near Courtray. Mass is being celebrated for Edgar, who is believed to have been killed in battle, but a monk appears who lists Edgar's crimes and his fellows are horrified. They realize then that the monk is himself Edgar. When Fidelia throws herself in his arms she is stabbed by Tigrana. The murderess is led away to execution while Edgar sobs over the corpse of his beloved.

■ In spite of the undoubted technical proficiency of the young Puccini, the opera was declared a failure by the critics and after the first performance it was only repeated twice. The failure was attributed largely to the subject matter, which was imposed upon the musician by the publisher, Ricordi, and was completely foreign to Puccini's taste. He revised the opera, still in 1889, reducing it from four to three acts. The new version was presented for the first time at Ferrara on 28 February 1892.

Francesco Tamagno, in the part of Otello in the final scene of Verdi's opera when it was first presented at La Scala, Milan, on 5 February 1887.

rock. Anna has died of grief, and her funeral procession passes by. Walter tries to approach the hearse, but Rudolfo curses him. In solitude, Walter contemplates throwing himself into the icy river. He suddenly notices Loreley on a rock and calls out to her reminding her of their love. She is touched and comes towards him. She is about to embrace him when the spirits of the air remind her that she has promised to be faithful to Alberich. She leaves Walter and returns to the rock, from where for evermore she will sing to lure sailors to their death. In despair Walter throws himself into the river.

■ *Loreley* is the revision of Catalani's first opera, *Elda*, which he had presented ten years before (1880), also at the Teatro Regio in Turin. In this second version he has clearly developed a personal style although he is still influenced by Ponchielli, Massenet and Wagner. The opera achieved great success and has occasionally been included in the repertoires of the world's major theatres.

CAVALLERIA RUSTICANA (Rustic Chivalry)
Opera in one act by Pietro Mascagni (1863–1945), libretto by Giovanni Targioni-Tozzetti (1863–1934) and Guido Menasci (1867–1925), based on a short story by Giovanni Verga. First performance: Rome, Teatro Costanzi, 17 May 1890. First performance in U.K.: London, Shaftesbury Theatre, 19 October 1891; in U.S.A.: Philadelphia, 9 September 1891.

ORIGINAL CAST. Gemma Bellincioni (Santuzza), Annetta Guli, Roberto Stagno (Turiddu), Gaudenzio Salassa, Frederica Casali. Conductor: Leopoldo Mugnone.

SYNOPSIS. It is dawn on Easter Day in a Sicilian village at the end of the nineteenth century. Before the curtain rises, Turiddu (tenor) can be heard singing a Sicilian love song to Lola (mezzo-soprano), the girl he loves and whom he had promised to marry before he left to do his military service. When he returned to the village, he found that she had married the carter, Alfio (baritone). He tried to console himself by courting and promising to marry another girl, Santuzza (soprano), but he has begun to see Lola again. When the curtain rises, a chorus of villagers comment on the beautiful day. Santuzza approaches Mamma Lucia (contralto), Turiddu's mother, and points out that, as she has been excommunicated, she cannot enter Mamma Lucia's house, but would like news of her son. He has not gone for the wine to Francofonte as his mother claims, but has been seen in the village. Their conversation is interrupted by Alfio's arrival. He, too, saw Turiddu near his home that morning. Santuzza stops Lucia from asking further questions, but when Alfio has gone she tells her that Turiddu has betrayed her and is now having an affair with Lola. Turiddu arrives and angrily refuses to answer Santuzza's questions. Their dramatic confrontation is interrupted by Lola's arrival on her way to church. She flirts with Turiddu and arouses Santuzza's jealousy. Turiddu follows her and pushes Santuzza violently away from him. Santuzza throws a curse after him and in her despair reveals Lola's infidelity to Alfio. The carter swears to take revenge. The action is interrupted by an intermezzo. Men and women come out of the church and Turiddu invites his friends to drink to 'the sparkling wine' (*'al vino spumeggiante'*). Alfio declines to take part and tersely makes his challenge. According to Sicilian custom, the two men embrace and Turiddu bites Alfio's ear as token of his acceptance of the challenge. Turiddu spares a last thought for Santuzza and asks his mother to look after her. He then asks for her blessing. Mamma Lucia has feelings of foreboding although she knows nothing of the duel. He leaves her and Santuzza comes to keep her company. There is a noise in the distance and suddenly a woman shrieks 'They have murdered Turiddu'. Santuzza collapses.

■ When a competition was announced in an issue of 'Teatro Illustrato' in July 1888 for 'an opera in one act – with a single scene or two at the most – on an idyllic, serious or humorous theme of the competitor's choice', Mascagni was engaged in drafting the first *Guglielmo Ratcliff*, at Cerignola where he was conductor of the orchestra and director of the Civic Theatre. The object of the competition was to encourage young Italian composers, and as well as a money prize, it carried with it a guarantee that the three winning entries would be staged at the Teatro Costanzi in Rome. Targioni, in a letter to the composer, suggested as subject a one-act drama by Giovanni Verga, based on his own short

Piero Cappuccilli in the part of Iago and Placido Domingo in the title role, in the production of Verdi's Otello, *presented at La Scala, Milan, in 1976.*

story. Mascagni replied that he had already thought of it in 1884 when he had seen Eleonora Duse in a dramatized version in Milan. The opera was drafted in a few months. In February 1890 Mascagni was called to Rome and told privately that *Cavalleria* had won. Later, the jury announced the result publicly in the 'Teatro Illustrato' together with the operas that had won the second and third prizes: *Labilia* by Niccolò Spinelli and *Rudello* by Vincenzo Ferroni. The resounding success that *Cavalleria* achieved at its first performance is an occasion to remember in the history of opera: 60 curtain calls on the first night. And within ten months this opera, by a composer unknown until a short time before, had taken its place in the European repertoire. The success was due, as Eduard Hanslick, the famous Austrian critic, said at the time, first and foremost to the revelation of a 'fresh, energetic and sincere talent' which was 'indisputably Italian' and 'modern European'. The great weight of passion expressed by the music of *Cavalleria*, in which melody dominates the score and gives ample scope to passionate singing, might be said to have typified opera of the 'Italian' as opposed to the 'German' school. The first-rate libretto, based on the short story rather than on the drama of Verga and constituting an almost unique example of the happy rapport that can exist between music and literature, contributed to the exceptional success of the opera. Moreover, *Cavalleria rusticana* fitted in with new European trends which were of both a spiritual, social and an aesthetic nature and pointed in the direction towards which painting and literature

had already been turning in other countries. Because of this, *Cavalleria*, born 'under the sign of realism', came to be considered a manifesto of musical *verismo*.

PRINCE IGOR (Knyaz Igor)

Opera in a prologue and four acts by Alexander Borodin (1833–87), completed by Rimsky-Korsakov and Glazunov. Libretto by the composer after a play by Vladimir Stasov, based on an anonymous ninth-century Russian poem 'The Song of Igor'. First performance, posthumously: St Petersburg, Maryinsky Theatre, 4 November 1890. First performance in U.K.: London, Drury Lane, 8 June 1914; in U.S.A.: New York, Metropolitan Opera House, 30 December 1915.

SYNOPSIS. Prologue. The square in the city of Putivl in the year 1185. The Polovtsians of Khan Kontchak (bass) are marching against the city and Igor Sviatoslavich, Prince of Seversk (baritone), has decided to go to fight them. Unexpectedly there is an eclipse of the sun, which is regarded as a bad omen, but Igor nevertheless leaves and takes with him Vladimir (tenor), his son by his first wife. Meanwhile, Skula (bass) and Eroshka (tenor), two ne'er-do-wells, who are not at all keen to take part in the attack, take advantage of the confusion to run away and join Prince Vladimir Galitsky (the brother of Igor's wife Yaroslavna), an irresponsible and pleasure-loving character. Act I, Scene I. Prince Galitsky's house. The guests, among whom are the two deserters, are rejoicing and talking about the gallantry of the Prince (bass), who has seized a girl for their pleasure. There is much drinking and it is suggested that Igor should be deposed in favour of Galitsky. He says that if he ruled he would never make anyone go without wine and pleasure. He refuses to assist a group of girls who protest that one of their number has been seized by his followers. Scene II. In the apartment of Yaroslavna (soprano), wife of Igor. She is anxious because she has no news of Igor and Vladimir. The girls, whose companion has been seized, beg her to intervene on their behalf against Galitsky and she soon exacts from him a promise to release the girl and mend his ways. Boyars announce that Igor's army has been defeated and Igor and Vladimir taken prisoner. The enemy is marching towards Putivl. Act II. The Polovtsian camp. Whilst a prisoner, Vladimir has fallen in love with Kontchakovna (mezzo-soprano), the daughter of Khan Kontchak. Ovlour (tenor), a Polovtsian soldier, who has been converted to Christianity, offers to help Igor escape, but Igor refuses such dishonourable conduct. Kontchak (bass), who admires Igor's frankness and dignity, offers him freedom in return for a promise of peace, but Igor insists that, if he were free, he would immediately begin a campaign against the Tartars. Polovtsian dances are performed to entertain him. Act III (usually omitted). The Polovtsian camp. Festivities are being arranged to celebrate the Tartar victory. Word spreads amongst the prisoners that Putivl has been taken by the enemy. Igor is urged by his companions to escape and defend the city. Vladimir is torn between love for Kontchakovna and love for his country. Whilst the Polovtsians dance and drink and finally fall asleep, Ovlour arranges for Igor to escape. Kontchakovna wakes the camp as Vladimir follows his father; the Khan stops his guards executing him and promises him his daughter in marriage. 'The generous young eagle will have a new nest and new happiness amongst the Polovtsians.' Act IV. The city walls of Putivl. Yaroslavna weeps for the plight of her husband and Russia. Suddenly she recognizes Igor galloping towards the city, accompanied by Ovlour. She is overjoyed to welcome him and they hurry to the citadel together. Eroshka and Skula see Igor and, fearing that he will punish them for desertion, climb the bell tower and ring the bells to announce his return. The people celebrate Igor's return and the two deserters are forgiven. Everyone is now confident that victory is near.

■ Borodin worked on *Prince Igor* from 1869 until his death, but he left it unfinished. It is the only opera he composed. He was a professor of chemistry, a profession in which he distinguished himself with a number of discoveries, and his tremendous love for music (he played the piano, the flute, the oboe and the cello) led him to compose whenever he could. He belonged to the 'Group of Five', which also included Mussorgsky, Balakirev, Rimsky-Korsakov and Cui. At his death a large part of the third act and the overture were still to be completed; only a small part of the orchestration had been finished. His friends, who had followed the various stages of the work very closely, undertook to complete it. Glazunov finished the third act and wrote out the overture, which he could remember perfectly, having often heard Borodin play it on the piano, although it had never been written down. Rimsky-Korsakov took the orchestration upon himself and remained faithful to the instructions received from the composer. The opera was very warmly received at the first performance and immediately became popular in Russia, despite some controversy over the work of the transcribers. Nevertheless, theirs remained the only edition for many years. In later editions the third act is often omitted – the one, in fact, that was the most incomplete in the original. The West was introduced to the score by the Polovtsian Dances, which were presented in Paris for the first time in 1909 by Diaghilev's *Ballets Russes*. The subject was very suitable for Borodin, who was interested both in Oriental and in Russian folk music, and both of these traditions are to be found in the score. Like all of his music, *Prince Igor* is simple and clear, but extraordinarily rich in the imagery of the countryside, fields, every-day life. It is also full of unrestrained humour and vitality, a characteristic typical of the enlightened optimism of this composer.

THE QUEEN OF SPADES (Pikovaya dama)

Opera in three acts and seven scenes by Peter Ilyich Tchaikovsky (1840–93), libretto by his brother Modest Ilyich Tchaikovsky, based on the tale by Pushkin (1834). First performance: St Petersburg, Maryinsky Theatre, 19 December 1890. First performance in U.K.: London, London Opera House, 29 May 1915; in U.S.A.: New York, Metropolitan Opera House, 5 March 1910.

ORIGINAL CAST. Nicolai Figner, Medea Figner, Dolina, Alexandrovna, Jakovlev. Conducted by Napravnik.

SYNOPSIS. The action takes place in St Petersburg around 1800. Act I, Scene I. A public park. Two officers, Tchekalinsky (tenor) and Surin (bass), meet and discuss their concern for their colleague, Herman. His passion for gambling takes him every evening into various gambling-houses in the city. He does not gamble, owing to lack of money, but he drinks too much. The two officers leave and Herman (tenor) and Count Tomsky (baritone) enter. Herman tells his friend that he is in love with a girl whose name he does not know. As other characters arrive, he finds out that she is Lisa (soprano), the fiancée of Prince Yeletsky (baritone). She is accompanied by her grandmother, a countess, who was once a compulsive gambler, nicknamed the 'Queen of Spades' (mezzo-soprano). She is said to know the secret of the three cards that always win. She has already shared this knowledge with two men and she knows that the third to ask her will cause her death. Herman longs to possess the secret, to become rich and marry Lisa. Scene II. Lisa's room. A party of her friends are singing and laughing. When they leave, she becomes melancholy. She is not sure that she will be happy with her fiancé. Herman sud-

The final duet in the first act of Verdi's Otello *at the Metropolitan Opera House, New York.*

denly appears at the window and declares his love for her. When the countess arrives, Herman hides but, as soon as she has gone, Lisa falls into his arms. Act II, Scene I. A reception room in a palace. A masked ball is in progress. Prince Yeletsky sings to please Lisa, while Herman dreams of the secret of the cards. A musical interlude is presented in which a shepherdess (Chloe) prefers a simple shepherd (Daphnis) to a rich lord. Lisa secretly passes Herman the key to the countess's palace and arranges to meet him that night. Scene II. The countess's room. Herman waits for the countess in her room. She returns and prepares for the night. Then she dozes in a chair. Herman comes out of his hiding place and begs the old lady to reveal the secret of the cards. In his excitement he draws a pistol. The shock kills her. In despair that he can never find the secret, he turns to find Lisa at the door. She drives him away, bitterly accusing him of preferring cards to her love. Act III, Scene I. Herman's room at the barracks. He reads a letter from Lisa in which she forgives him for his behaviour. The ghost of the countess appears to him and commands him to marry Lisa and the secret combination will be his: three, seven, ace. Scene II. On

the quay of the Neva. Lisa and Herman are reconciled, but when he makes as if to leave for the gambling house, she tries to restrain him. He pushes her aside and in despair she throws herself into the river and drowns. Scene II. A gambling house. Herman plays his final hand with Yeletsky. The three and the seven have already won, but instead of the ace, he now turns up the Queen of Spades. Before Herman's eyes the picture on the card becomes the grinning ghost of the countess and the young man, now utterly deranged, stabs himself.

■ The opera, which was composed in only 126 days, was greeted with much enthusiasm and has never ceased to be popular everywhere, particularly in Russia. The composer said of it, 'Either I am making a dreadful, inexcusable mistake, or the *Queen of Spades* is really my *chef d'oeuvre*'. The libretto sticks closely to Pushkin's story except for the conclusion. (In Pushkin's story the gambler goes mad and is put into a lunatic asylum, where he continues to repeat the names of the three cards.) It is the most dramatic and most elaborate of Tchaikovsky's operas.

The second act of Catalani's Loreley *at La Scala, Milan.*

L'AMICO FRITZ (Friend Fritz)

Lyric comedy in three acts by Pietro Mascagni (1863–1945), libretto by P. Suardon (real name Nicola Daspuro) (1853–1941) based on L'Ami Fritz *(1864) by Emile Erckmann and Alexandre Chatrian. First performance: Rome, Teatro Costanzi, 31 October 1891. First performance in U.K.: London, Covent Garden, 23 May 1892; in U.S.A.: Philadelphia, 8 June 1892.*

ORIGINAL CAST. Emma Calvé (Suzel), Fernando de Lucia, Synnemberg, Paul Lhérie (Fritz). Conductor: Rodolfo Ferrari.

SYNOPSIS. The action takes place in Alsace. Act I. Fritz (tenor), a middle-aged and wealthy landowner with a generous nature, cannot understand why people marry so much. He bets the Rabbi, David (baritone), one of his vineyards that he will never give up the bachelor life that he leads with his friends, Federico (tenor) and Hanezò (bass). At a party for his birthday however, he notices Suzel (soprano), the daughter of one of his tenants, and makes her sit beside him. As the party continues, David tells her that she will soon be the prettiest wife in Alsace. Act II. In an orchard, Fritz, who is staying in the country for a short holiday, helps Suzel to pick cherries ('*Tu sei bella, O stagion primaverile*'). David guesses that Suzel is in love with Fritz and by telling Fritz that the girl is about to marry a country boy, he gathers from Fritz's reaction that he returns those feelings. Upset by this news, and keen to overcome his unwelcome emotion, Fritz leaves with-

out a word of goodbye to Suzel; she is in despair as she does not understand his behaviour. Act III. Fritz cannot forget the girl he left so suddenly and listens unconsoled to the commiseration of Beppe (mezzo-soprano), a young gypsy he has befriended. David arrives to announce the arrival of Suzel's father, who has come to ask for his consent to the marriage, and Fritz shows his jealousy by opposing the match. When he learns from Suzel herself that she does not want the marriage, he finally declares his love for her. So David wins his bet and gives the vineyard to Suzel.

■ The opera appeared a year after the resounding success of *Cavalleria Rusticana*, which had brought unexpected fame to Mascagni, and it was awaited with great interest from the moment it was announced. It is among the best of his youthful output even though, as a reaction against the criticism that he had little knowledge of harmony and orchestration, he tried to blend together Italian, French and German elements without entirely succeeding in reaching an homogeneity of style. The story, set among the middle classes, seemed a less suitable subject for the composer than had been that of *Cavalleria Rusticana*.

LA WALLY

Opera in four acts by Alfredo Catalani (1854–93), libretto by Luigi Illica (1857–1919), based on the novel by Wilhelmine von Hillern, Die Geyer-Wally *(1875, dramatized in 1880). First performance: Milan, Teatro*

The composer, the conductor and the principal members of the cast in the first production of Cavalleria Rusticana *at the Teatro Costanzi, Rome, on 17 May 1890. Roberto Stagno, Leopoldo Mugnone, Pietro Mascagni, Gemma Bellincioni, Mario Ancona, Ida Nobili and Federica Casali.*

alla Scala, 20 January 1892. First performance in U.K.: Manchester, 27 March 1919; in U.S.A.: New York, Metropolitan Opera House, 6 January 1909.

ORIGINAL CAST. Pietro Cesari, Hericlea Darclée, Adelina Stehle Garbin. Conductor: Edoardo Mascheroni.

SYNOPSIS. The action takes place in the Tyrol around 1800. Act I. The square of Hochstoff, a Tyrolese village. The seventieth birthday of Stromminger (bass), the father of Wally (soprano), is being celebrated. Some huntsmen are putting on a display in his honour and among those present is Gellner (baritone), who is in love with Wally. The minstrel (soprano), Walter, a faithful friend of Wally's, plays his music and sings. Giuseppe Hagenbach (tenor) arrives from Sölden and tells of his exploits as a huntsman, but Stromminger, who dislikes him because he is the son of his old rival, provokes him and a quarrel breaks out, in which the old man would have come off worst, had Wally not intervened to separate them. When he hears that Wally has fallen in love with the young man, Stromminger declares that she must marry Gellner within the month. Her father will not listen to her protests and she leaves the village. Act II. The square in Sölden, where Wally is now living. It is a local holiday and people have come from neighbouring villages to celebrate, including Gellner, Hagenbach and the innkeeper Afra (contralto), his betrothed. Everyone considers Wally reserved, proud and unapproachable, and Hagenbach

bets his friends that he will manage to kiss her during the dancing. Ignorant of this, Wally agrees to dance with him. She accepts his advances and kisses him. When she realizes she has been the victim of a cruel joke, she swears she will get her revenge. She agrees to marry Gellner, who still adores her, if he will kill Hagenbach. Act III. Hochstoff. Wally regrets her anger too late, for Gellner was waiting for Hagenbach by a precipice and pushed him over the edge as he passed. In despair Wally calls for help. She descends on a rope into the ravine and rescues Hagenbach, who is brought up, injured and stunned, but alive. Wally hands him over to Afra. Then she goes off into the mountains. Act IV. Walter, who has followed Wally into the mountains, begs her to return to the safety of the valley, but she refuses and he goes back alone. Hagenbach, however, who has now realized that he loves Wally, comes in search of her. They embrace and dream of their future life together, but a blizzard surrounds them and they are buried by a sudden avalanche.

■ This is the fifth and best opera by Catalani. It is also his last, and was written the year before his death. The idea came to him on reading a novel, translated from the German, with the title 'La Wally dell'avvoltoio', in the literary section of the Milanese newspaper, 'La Perseveranza'. The work was completed in a few months and in *La Wally* is to be found everything that is typical of the composer's style – traditional Italian melodrama, a sprinkling of true poetry, romanticism and Wagnerian and French influences. Toscanini, a great admirer of Catalani and of *La Wally,* gave this name to one of his daughters. The publisher, Ricordi, said of the opera: 'rapid, interesting, vigorous and full of youth.' It was a great success and is still performed today all over the world.

WERTHER

Drame lyrique *in four acts by Jules Massenet (1842–1912), libretto by Edouard Blau, Paul Milliet and Georges Hartmann, based on* Leiden des jungen Werthers *by Goethe. First performance: Vienna, Hofoper, 16 February 1892. First performance in U.K.: London, Covent Garden, 11 June 1894; in U.S.A.: Chicago, 29 April 1894.*

ORIGINAL CAST. Ernst van Dyck (Werther), Franz Neidl (Albert), Mayerhofer, Marie Renard (Charlotte), Forster. Conductor: Hans Richter.

SYNOPSIS. The action takes place in Wetzlar near Frankfurt in 1780. Act I. In the garden of the house of the burgomaster. As the curtain goes up, the burgomaster (bass), a widower, is teaching his children a Christmas carol. He is interrupted by the arrival of his two drinking companions, Johann (bass) and Schmidt (tenor), who invite him to sup with them later. He refuses because, since his eldest daughter, Charlotte (mezzo-soprano), is about to leave for a ball that evening, he must stay and look after the family. The first guest to arrive is Charlotte's escort, Werther (tenor), a poetic young man of whom the burgomaster strongly approves. The vision of Charlotte dispensing a simple supper of bread and butter to her young brothers and sisters enchants Werther. The guests leave and Sophie (soprano), the second eldest daughter, despatches her father to the inn. She is surprised by the unexpected return of Albert (baritone), Charlotte's fiancé, who has been away. He is disappointed not to find Charlotte, but Sophie reassures him that he is not forgotten. When Charlotte and Werther are in the moonlight, he declares his love for her. The burgomaster calls out to his daughter that Albert has returned and Charlotte has to explain to Werther that she promised her dying mother to marry Albert. Werther runs off in despair, his idyll of love shattered. Act II. The square in Wetzlar. It is a holiday. Celebrations are in hand for the golden wedding of the village Pastor. Among the congregation are Charlotte and Albert, who have been married for three months. The friends Johann and Schmidt are celebrating in their own way and toast the health of the young couple. Werther, who watches from a distance, cannot hide his regret at being unable to marry her. Albert confides his happiness to Werther and suggests that he might find Sophie attractive. Werther, however, decides to speak to Charlotte. She begs him to stay away from her, at least for some time – until Christmas. Werther considers suicide the relief from so long a period of separation. Sophie gaily invites him to dance, but he violently refuses, saying that he intends to go away never to return. Sophie

bursts into tears, while Albert and Charlotte wonder what his sudden departure signifies. Act III, Scene I. A room in Albert's house, Christmas eve. Charlotte is re-reading the letters from Werther. She now realizes how much she misses him and she cannot disguise from Sophie that she is bitterly unhappy. Werther appears at the garden window. He is pale and distraught. Charlotte weeps as he recites some lines of Ossian which he had translated for her, and in a moment of weakness she allows him to kiss her. Then she frees herself from his embrace and hurriedly leaves the room, swearing never to see him again, and leaving him in the utmost despair. Albert arrives and suspects that Werther has visited Charlotte in his absence. A note is delivered from Werther asking to borrow Albert's pistols, for 'a long journey'. Albert tells his wife to hand them over to the servant; Charlotte, terrified by the idea that Werther might commit suicide, runs after him. Scene II. Werther's room. When Charlotte enters, he is lying on the floor, mortally wounded, but at the sound of her voice he revives. Charlotte confesses that she has loved him since their first meeting. Werther dies in her arms. In the distance, children can be heard singing the Christmas carol.

■ The idea of setting *'Leiden des jungen Werthers'* to music was suggested to Massenet by the publisher, Hartmann. There is no need to emphasize how the hyper-romantic theme of Goethe's text was perfectly suited to the sensitivity of Massenet. We also know that Massenet visited Wetzlar, the scene of the action, and was very moved by it, on a journey to Bayreuth which reinforced his love for Wagner's music. This is perhaps noticeable in the opera. As the librettist Milliet wrote 'When Christmas night descends on Werther, a clarity of forgiveness dissipates the shadows in which the world disappears and for him, as for Tristan, the spirits begin to sing in the silence where mortal voices have grown silent.' The opera was very successful in its day. Nowadays, however, Massenet's music is less appreciated, despite the admiration of Debussy. Saint-Saëns, a keen critic of the music of his colleagues, remarked that the music of *Werther* was the 'refinement', the 'crystallization', the 'condensation' of Gounod. A 'sugary cake', as G. Confalonieri says, but baked by a high-class confectioner.

I PAGLIACCI (The Clowns)

Opera in a prologue and two acts by Ruggiero Leoncavallo (1858–1919), libretto by the composer. First performance: Milan, Teatro dal Verme, 21 May 1892. First performance in U.K.: London, Covent Garden, 19 May 1893; in U.S.A.: New York, Grand Opera House, 15 June 1893.

ORIGINAL CAST. Stehle Garbin, Giraud, Maurel, Daddi, Roussel. Conducted by Arturo Toscanini.

SYNOPSIS. Prologue. Tonio (baritone), an actor in a company of strolling players, announces to the audience that the performance is about to begin. He says

appears on stage to meet Nedda, who is playing the part of Columbine. Canio, playing the part of Pagliaccio, Columbine's husband, bursts in and Harlequin runs away. Canio finds himself in his real life situation and becomes confused. His lines no longer belong to the play. Throwing himself at Nedda he asks her the name of her lover, and when she refuses to tell him, he stabs her. Silvio rushes onto the set to help Nedda and Canio kills him too. He then turns to the audience and murmurs 'The comedy is ended'.

■ Leoncavallo based this opera on an incident that had taken place in Montalto in Calabria, where his father was a judge, and he wrote it very quickly. It was acquired by Edoardo Sonzogno and immediately began a successful tour round the stages of the world. In the space of a few months it was performed in Vienna, Berlin, London, New York, Mexico, Buenos Aires, Stockholm and Moscow. It was considered a good example of *verismo* opera. Even today its success shows little sign of diminishing. Undoubtedly some of its popularity can be attributed to those operatic 'greats' who so loved to sing in it. These have included Caruso, Pertile, Galeffi, Ruffo and Tamagno. However, it met with quite a different fate at the hands of the critics. In 1893 Hanslick said there was a 'lack of taste'. In 1902 Bellaigue wrote that '*I Pagliacci* had horrified him'. Similarly in 1939 Domenico de Paoli called it 'a black chronicle whose amateurish and superficial score overflows with facile lyricism and crude effects'. Pannein was to write of 'debris of a past worn away by exhaustion' and of 'a culture without sinew'. However, the critics of today tend to look at it with fresh eyes. René Leibowitz speaks of a 'powerful work, of rare expressive intensity'.

Ugrinovic and F. Stravinski in the roles of the itinerant musicians in the first performance of Borodin's Prince Igor, *1890.*

that the drama, though presented by actors, is about real human beings with ordinary human feelings. Act I. A company of actors arrive in a village in Calabria and are greeted with enthusiasm by the inhabitants. Tonio holds out his hand to Nedda (soprano), the wife of the leader of the company, to help her down from the wagon, but he is pushed roughly aside by her husband Canio (tenor), who will not allow anyone near her. The actors move off towards the inn and Nedda is left alone, disturbed by her husband's words. She dreams of being as free as the birds in the sky. Tonio approaches and declares his love, which she scornfully rejects, and when he insists, she strikes him across the face with a whip. Tonio slinks away humiliated. He spies on her talking to Silvio (baritone), a villager, who is her lover and now asks her to go away with him. Unsure of herself, Nedda hesitates, but then promises to meet him after the performance. Their conversation is suddenly interrupted by Canio (whom Tonio has alerted). Silvio manages to escape without being recognized and Nedda refuses to reveal his name. It is almost time for the performance to start, so Canio must hide his anger behind the mask of a clown. Act II. The performance is about to begin and the expectant audience, Silvio among them, pass comments out loud. After a serenade, Beppe (tenor), dressed as Harlequin,

CRISTOFORO COLOMBO (Christopher Columbus)

Opera in three acts and an epilogue by Alberto Franchetti (1860–1942), libretto by Luigi Illica (1857–1919). First performance: Genoa, Teatro Carlo Felice, 6 October 1892. First performance in U.S.A.: Philadelphia, 20 November 1913.

ORIGINAL CAST. Giuseppe Kaschmann. Conducted by Luigi Mancinelli.

SYNOPSIS. Act I. In the courtyard of the convent of St Stephen at Salamanca. Some knights are among a large crowd waiting to hear whether the Council will approve the next enterprise planned by Christopher Columbus (Colombo). The reply is negative. When Colombo (baritone) appears in the doorway, he is mocked and roughly abused and he might have been physically injured if an officer of the Royal Guard, don Fernan Guevara (tenor), had not reminded the crowd that Queen Isabella was praying in the nearby church. Colombo goes over to the church as Isabella (soprano) comes out. She, too, is disappointed by the news and in a burst of enthusiasm she offers her diadem to Colombo to equip the expedition. Act II. At sea, on board the *Santa Maria*. There is an air of despair and despondency. Even Colombo doubts the success of his undertaking. Whilst three monks on the bridge conduct a prayer, Roldano (bass), Matheos (tenor), and others start a mutiny and threaten Colombo. He scans the horizon and sees lights; there are shouts of 'Land! Land!' Act III. Palos harbour. At the King's command Spanish knights are waiting for Colombo's return. Bobadilla (bass) arrives with a document in which don Alonzo Martin, commander of the 'Pinta', accuses Colombo of appropriating all the riches and proclaiming himself sovereign of the new land. Martin informs the King of Colombo's imminent arrival at Palos. The 'Pinta' is sighted and Colombo disembarks and kisses the ground, giving thanks to God. Isabella comes out of the church and warns him that a plot has been mounted against him. Despite Guevara's opposition, Colombo is arrested and put in prison. Epilogue. The royal chapel at Medina del Campo. Colombo, now old and in bad health, enters with Guevara, who wants to speak to the Queen about Colombo's wretched condition. Girls bring flowers into the crypt and pray for Isabella's soul. Colombo collapses when he hears of the Queen's death. He begins to ramble, talking of the sea, of his native city, his voyages, and the persecution he has suffered. He weakly tells Guevara that his last hour has come and falls to the ground. Guevara kneels in prayer beside his body.

■ It was Verdi who had suggested that Franchetti, a young composer from Turin, should be asked to set to music the libretto that won a competition arranged by the City of Genoa. The opera was intended to celebrate the fourhundredth anniversary of the discovery of America. However, the work presents considerable staging difficulties, especially in the second act, and this affected the early performances. In fact, through disagreement with the composer, Luigi Mancinelli left the task of conducting the orchestra at the third performance to the young Arturo Toscanini. The opera was later rearranged more than once. It was presented at La Scala, Milan, on 26 December 1892, before being produced in Germany and elsewhere.

I RANTZAU (The Rantzau Brothers)
Lyric opera in four acts by Pietro Mascagni (1863–1945), libretto by Giovanni Targioni-Tozzetti (1863–1934) and Guido Menasci (1867–1925). First performance: Florence, Teatro alla Pergola, 10 November 1892.

SYNOPSIS. While the brothers, Gianni and Giacomo Rantzau, are divided by a violent hatred, Luisa, the only daughter of Gianni, and Giorgio, the only son of Giacomo, are secretly in love. Their feelings are only revealed when Gianni wants Luisa to marry a man she does not like. She is disturbed by the prospect and falls seriously ill, while Giorgio, after a violent quarrel with his father, leaves home. In the hope of saving his daughter, Gianni decides to try and patch up his differences with his brother, but Giacomo takes advantage of the situation to impose humiliating conditions.

Although Gianni is prepared to submit, Giorgio rebels when he realizes that his father is being unjust. He manages to reconcile the two brothers and the young couple are able to marry.

■ In this opera the composer's inspiration seems to be curbed by the shabby atmosphere in which the action takes place, but some of the harmonic and rhythmic invention is pleasing and creates a lively effect.

IOLANTA
Opera in one act by Peter Ilyich Tchaikovsky (1840–93), libretto by Modest Ilyich Tchaikovsky, based on the Danish comedy Kong René's Datter *(King René's Daughter) by Henrik Hertz. First performance: St Petersburg, National Theatre, 24 December 1892. First performance in U.K.: London, Camden Festival 1968.*

SYNOPSIS. Provence, in the fifteenth century. Iolanta (soprano), the beautiful daughter of René (bass), King of Provence, is blind, but does not know that she is in any way different from her friends. The King refuses the conditions which Ebn-Hakia (baritone), a Moorish doctor, imposes if he is to cure her: namely that she should realize her disability and have the strength of will to combat it. Robert (bass-baritone), Duke of Burgundy, and his friend Count

The Polovtsian Dances from Borodin's Prince Igor *at the Bolshoi Theatre, Moscow.*

Vaudémont (tenor) come upon Iolanta while she sleeps in her father's garden. Although Robert is betrothed to her, he has never seen her and in fact loves another; Vaudémont, for his part, falls in love with her at first sight. When she awakes, she brings him refreshment. Then she picks him a white rose and he realizes that she cannot distinguish it from a red one and that she is blind. He describes the beauties of Nature around them and consoles her. They are discovered by the King and the doctor, who can now begin his treatment. René condemns the young knight to death if Iolanta fails to gain her sight, but when she has sworn to save his life, the King confides to Vaudémont that his threat was intended only to give her added determination to succeed. All ends happily with Robert released from his betrothal, and Iolanta, her vision now unimpaired, promised to Vaudémont.

■ This is Tchaikovsky's last opera and one of his most successful.

MADAME CHRYSANTHÈME
Comédie lyrique *in four acts and six tableaux by André Messager (1853–1929), libretto by Georges Hartmann and André Alexandre, based on the novel by Pierre Loti (1850–1923). First performance: Paris, Théâtre lyrique de la Renaissance, 30 January 1893. First performance in U.S.A.: Chicago, 19 January 1920.*

■ The story of the marriage between a lieutenant and a geisha affords the opportunity to evoke the atmosphere and customs of Japan. In this opera, Messager also shows himself to be an artist of taste and typically French refinement.

MANON LESCAUT
Lyric drama in four acts by Giacomo Puccini (1858–1924), libretto ('anonymous') by Giuseppe Giacosa, Luigi Illica, Giulio Ricordi and others, based on the novel by Abbé Prévost (1731). First performance: Turin, Teatro Regio, 1 February 1893. First performance in U.K.: London, Covent Garden, 14 May 1894; in U.S.A.: Philadelphia, Grand Opera House, 29 August 1894.

ORIGINAL CAST. Cesira Ferrani (Manon), Giuseppe Cremonini (Des Grieux). Conducted by Alessandro Pomé.

SYNOPSIS. France in the second half of the eighteenth century. Act I. Amiens, the courtyard of an inn. The young Chevalier des Grieux (tenor) is serenading some girls, when Manon (soprano) steps out of a stage-coach. She is on her way, accompanied by her brother, Lescaut (baritone), to a convent school. Manon and des Grieux fall in love, and when Edmondo (tenor) tells him that Geronte di Ravoir (bass), an old and wealthy official, has arranged for a coach in which to abduct her, they make use of it to elope together. Lescaut tries to console Geronte

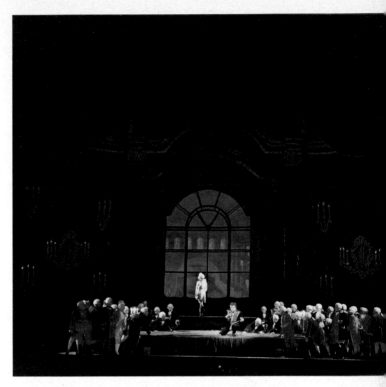

Tchaikovsky's The Queen of Spades *during the production at the Bolshoi Theatre, Moscow, in 1964. Sets by Vladimir Dmitrev, produced by Boris Pokrovsky.*

because he is certain he can persuade his sister to leave des Grieux for the wealth that a rich old man can offer. Act II. Geronte's luxurious apartment. Manon has left des Grieux and become Geronte's mistress. She looks back with regret on the time when she was poor but happy with des Grieux, and when her brother visits her she asks for news of him. Lescaut reports to des Grieux, whose fortunes have now been made at the gambling tables, where he may find Manon. They are reconciled in a passionate love scene. Geronte finds them together and leaves, threatening to get his revenge. Lescaut advises them to take the opportunity to escape immediately but Manon delays to collect the jewels that Geronte has given her. The Police arrive, summoned by the old man, and arrest her on charges of theft and prostitution. Act III. The harbour at Le Havre. Manon is to be deported to New Orleans. Des Grieux and Lescaut try in vain to obtain her release. After a roll-call the prisoners go on board. Des Grieux, who cannot bear to be separated from Manon, obtains the Captain's permission to follow her. Act IV. A desolate plain in North America. Having escaped from New Orleans, Manon and des Grieux are trudging along an endless road in the hope of finding an English colony. Manon is exhausted. Realizing that she is near to death, she sees her past life before her like a nightmare. Des Grieux goes to look for water and when he returns he finds her dying. She dies soon afterwards in his arms and, overcome with grief, he collapses over her body.

Tchaikovsky's The Queen of Spades *Act I during the Bolshoi Theatre production of 1891. Archives of The Theatre Museum, Moscow.*

■ Puccini decided to set to music the subject of Prévost's novel (just a few years after the resounding success of Massenet's *Manon* at the Opéra-Comique in Paris) and hotly defended his idea against those who pointed out the risks of such an immediate comparison. 'Massenet treated it (the subject) as a Frenchman, with refinement and grace. I shall treat it as an Italian, with desperate passion.' Thus was Puccini's judgement. He had very definite ideas on the libretto and was determined to put them into practice. Hence his tumultuous relationship with those who, one after the other, had a hand in the writing of the text. First of all there was Ruggiero Leoncavallo, who was still undecided whether to concentrate on theatre or composition. Then there was Marco Praga who, being a writer of prose, engaged a poet, Domenico Oliva, to help with the versification. Then came Giuseppe Giacosa, who was engaged by the publisher, Ricordi, and finally Luigi Illica. Five librettists, not to mention Ricordi, were too many and the opera was finally published more than three years after the work began, making no mention of the author of the text. It was Puccini's third opera after *Le Villi* and *Edgar* and the first in which he fully expressed his personality. It is dominated by a romantic spirit and an urgency of passion, which Puccini conveys with an abundance of melody not to be found in his later works. Indeed the very stylized characterization sometimes seems superfluous in the tremendous flood of melody. It has been said that des Grieux – 'the most feminine of Puccini's tenor heroes' – to whom the composer has given more arias and refrains than the heroine, could quite easily exchange his music with that of Manon 'without falsification of his essential character' (Mosco Carner). In the last act, the drama gives way completely to the music – which is amongst the most desperately tragic that Puccini ever composed. Here the action is largely static and entirely devoted to the death scene. Memorable among the

chorus scenes is the Le Havre Act when the various elements – the insolent comments from the crowd of onlookers, the roll-call of deportees, Lescaut's frantic agitation and the desperation of the two lovers – gradually combine to produce an atmosphere of telling power. At the première the audience greeted *Manon* with tremendous enthusiasm. The critics said that Puccini was 'one of the best, if not the best, of the young Italian operatic composers'. Its success – the most unqualified that Puccini had ever received at a première – formed the basis of his international fame and also assured him of economic prosperity.

FALSTAFF
Lyric comedy in three acts by Giuseppe Verdi (1813–1901), libretto by Arrigo Boito (1842–1918), based on Henry IV, Parts 1 and 2, and The Merry Wives of Windsor *by Shakespeare. First performance: Milan, Teatro alla Scala, 9 February 1893. First performance in U.K.: London, Covent Garden, 19 May 1894; in U.S.A.: New York, Metropolitan Opera House, 4 February 1895.*

ORIGINAL CAST. Vittorio Maurel (Falstaff), Emma Zilli (Alice), Adelina Stehle (Nannetta), Virginia Guerrini (Meg), Giuseppina Pasqua (Mistress Quickly), Edoardo Garbin (Fenton), Antonio Pini-Corsi (Ford), Vittorio Arimondi (Pistol), Pelagalli-Rossetti (Bardolph), Giovanni Parodi (Dr Cajus). Conductor: Edoardo Mascheroni.

SYNOPSIS. Windsor, during the reign of Henry IV. Act I. At the Garter Inn. Sir John Falstaff (baritone) is accused by Caius (tenor) of being a thief, but the fat knight objects at length and laughs at him. Falstaff then reveals to his two followers, Bardolph (tenor) and Pistol (bass), that he has a plan to rob two men of their money and their wives. He is referring to Page and Ford, and Bardolph and Pistol are to deliver letters to the two wives. They do not like his plan, declaring that they are men of honour and refuse to collaborate. Falstaff turns them out of the Inn and gives the job to his page. The two women Alice Ford (soprano) & Meg Page (mezzo-soprano) are highly amused to receive the letters and insulted to discover that they are identical. With their neighbour Mistress Quickly (mezzo-soprano) and Ford's daughter Nannetta (soprano), they decide to play a trick on their corpulent old admirer. Meanwhile, Bardolph and Pistol have told Ford (baritone) about Falstaff's plan; he is furious and plans his revenge. Young Fenton (tenor), who is in love with Nannetta, manages to snatch a kiss from her in the midst of the turmoil. Act II. As usual, Sir John is at the Garter Inn. Mistress Quickly comes in to tell that Alice Ford will see him between two and three that afternoon. When Mistress Quickly leaves, 'Signor Fontana' (Master Brook) arrives. He is, in fact, Ford in disguise and he offers gold to Falstaff if he will help him to capture the heart of Alice Ford. Naturally Falstaff accepts and bursts into song, for as he says, he already

The cast of the first performance of Massenet's Werther, *16 February 1892. Marie Renard in the part of Charlotte with a group of children; Ernst van Dyck as Werther; and Franz Neidl as Albert.*

has an appointment with the lady that very afternoon. Left alone for a moment, Ford vents his fury and jealousy. When Falstaff returns, they leave together. Mistress Quickly graphically describes the success of her mission to her friends. Nannetta is discovered sobbing because her father has promised her in marriage to old Dr Caius, and the three older ladies resolve to make sure that she marries Fenton, the man of her choice. They notice that it is already two o'clock and so Alice is left to receive Sir John on her own. The servants bring in a laundry basket. When Falstaff arrives, Alice keeps him at a proper distance. Mistress Quickly bursts in to announce the pre-arranged arrival of Meg

A sketch by E. Marchioro for Catalani's La Wally, *1921. Museo teatrale alla Scala, Milan.*

Page (mezzo-soprano), who, in her turn announces the unexpected arrival of Ford. Falstaff hides behind a screen. Ford, Fenton, Caius, Bardolph and Pistol enter. They search the room for Falstaff, but do not find him and then rush all over the house with no luck. As soon as they have left the room, Falstaff climbs into the laundry basket. The two young lovers hide behind the screen. Ford returns, hears the sound of a kiss from behind the screen and discovers Nannetta and Fenton. They run away; Bardolph then says he has seen Falstaff leaving by the stairs, so everyone follows him. Alice chooses this moment to ask her servants to empty the contents of the laundry basket out of the window into the Thames. She takes her husband by the arm and shows him the hilarious sight of Falstaff splashing around in the water. Act III. Outside the Garter Inn. Falstaff is enraged after his soaking. Mistress Quickly assures him that the servants were to blame, and that Alice Ford is longing to meet him. She suggests that they should meet at midnight by Herne the Hunter's Oak in the royal park and, in order that no one will recognize him, he should come disguised as the black huntsman. Falstaff and Mistress Quickly go into the Inn, and the other ladies plan the trick with Ford and other friends. They will foregather disguised as sprites and fairies to torment the fat knight, who will imagine they are the supernatural spirits who haunt the spot. Full of good humour, Ford secretly decides that the marriage between Nannetta and Caius will take place that night when everyone is in their nocturnal disguises. Mistress Quickly has overheard this, however, and she arranges a counter-plan. Scene II. At Herne's Oak, Windsor Park. Midnight. Falstaff, dressed as the black huntsman, is very frightened when he hears the 'song of the fairies'. Alice arrives and pretends to accept his declarations of love. Suddenly, Meg appears

The final scene in Leoncavallo's I Pagliacci. *Lithograph by A. Bonamore, published in Berlin.*

and says that there is a witch about; and a band of 'elves' throw themselves onto the fat man. They set about him, rolling him and pinching him. The thrashing ends when Falstaff recognizes Bardolph. Ford then comes forward, explains and forgives him. It is now the moment that Ford has chosen to bless his daughter's betrothal to Caius. He takes her by the hand and gives her to Caius. Alice presents a second couple who would like to share in the ceremonies. All unmask and Ford realizes too late that he has blessed the union of Caius and Bardolph (dressed like Nannetta as the Queen of the fairies) and that the other couple were his daughter and Fenton. What is to be done? 'All the world's a jest', is the conclusion.

■ With *Falstaff* Verdi bade his last farewell to the operatic stage. And he could not have done so in a more overwhelming fashion. Boito had written a continuous text that allowed the old maestro to develop his powers of expression as never before, giving the instruments roles that were almost equal to those of the characters and using the orchestra in an incomparable way. If Verdi's polemic statement: 'Look back, it will be a step forward', when taken too literally, had helped to retard the evolution of Italian opera, *Falstaff* acted indisputably as a major accelerating force.

HÄNSEL UND GRETEL

*Musical fairy story (*Märchenspiel*) in three acts by Engelbert Humperdinck (1854–1921), libretto by Adelheid Wette (sister of the composer), after the Grimm brothers' story in* Kinder- und Hausmärchen *(1812–14). First performance: Weimar, Hoftheater, 23 December 1893. Conductor: Richard Strauss. First performance in U.K.: London, Daly's Theatre, 26 December 1894; in U.S.A.: New York, Daly's Theater, 8 October 1895.*

SYNOPSIS. Act I. A room in a poor hut. The children, Hänsel (mezzo-soprano) and Gretel (soprano), are supposed to be helping around the house but they soon fall idle and sit beside the fire until their mother Gertrude (mezzo-soprano) shouts at them. In her annoyance, she knocks over the jug of milk which was the only food the family had. She sends them to gather strawberries in the wood. Their father Peter (baritone), a broom-maker, returns drunk as usual, but with lots of food, after a successful day's work. He is in a good mood, but grows anxious when he hears where the children have gone, for he knows that a wicked witch who cooks children in her oven lives in the wood. The parents rush off to look for them. Act II. In the wood. In the distance is the witch's house. The children have eaten all the strawberries that they picked despite what their mother said. They are afraid to return empty-handed, and when the Sandman (soprano) has dropped sand in their eyes, they say their prayers and fall asleep on the grass, watched over by their guardian angels. Act III. It is dawn. The Dew fairy (soprano) wakes up the children, and Gretel recounts her dream whilst Hänsel says he has never slept so well. The witch (mezzo-soprano), however, has created a little house made of marzipan and sugar in order to attract them. When they go up to it, she takes them prisoner and prevents them with her magic wand from escaping. Gretel is forced to lay the table whilst Hänsel is fattened up ready to be eaten. While the witch is not looking, Gretel grabs the magic wand and breaks the spell on Hänsel. Then they push the witch into the oven. The house crumbles and a row of flattened children appear and thank Hänsel and Gretel for breaking the enchantment. Peter and Gertrude find their children just in time to eat the witch, who has been baked into a huge, sweet cake, and to give thanks for the happy ending.

■ This opera was composed in the first place for the entertainment of the composer's family and the very first performance was at Frankfurt in a small private theatre. The composer later revised the opera and the new edition was much admired by Richard Strauss, who offered to conduct the first public performance. He wrote: 'Your opera has enchanted me. It is truly a masterpiece. I have not seen such an important work for a long time. I admire the abundance of melody, the finesse, the polyphonic richness of the orchestration ... all that is new, original, truly German.' Purely romantic, the work was especially pleasing to those who were tired of *verismo*. Humperdinck had studied with Wagner, but although there is much Wagnerian influence in *Hänsel and Gretel*, the score is both original and personal. He based a good deal of the musical material on popular songs and rhythms in order to make his work accessible to the ordinary people of his country. His opera started the fashion for musical fairy-stories, which were very popular in post-Wagnerian-Germany. It was a great success and has since been presented frequently throughout the world.

THAÏS

Comédie lyrique *in three acts and seven tableaux by Jules Massenet (1842–1912), libretto by Louis Gallet, based on the novel by Anatole France. First performance: Paris, Opéra, 16 March 1894. First performance in U.K.: London, Covent Garden, 18 July 1911; in U.S.A.: New York, Manhattan Opera, 25 November 1907.*

ORIGINAL CAST. Charles Delmas (Athanaël), Albert Alvarez (Nicias), Sybil Sanderson (Thaïs), Laure Beauvais (Albine), Delponget (Palémon). Conductor: Paul Taffanel.

SYNOPSIS. Egypt, in the fourth century A.D. Act I.

Scene I. The banks of the Nile. A refuge of the Cenobites. Athanaël (baritone) laments the corruption of the inhabitants of Alexandria and blames the beautiful courtesan, Thaïs (soprano). In his dream he sees her and, when he wakes, he decides to save her from sins. Scene II. The terrace of Nicias's house in Alexandria. Athanaël tells his friend Nicias (tenor) of his mission. Nicias laughs at the idea, but as he is expecting Thaïs that evening, he invites Athanaël to speak to her then. Thaïs tries to seduce Athanaël, who indignantly repulses her. Act II. Scene I. Thaïs's house. The courtesan is horrified at the idea of growing old. Athanaël persuades her to reflect upon her dissolute life and she almost allows herself to be converted. Yet in the end she refuses to give up her way of life. Scene II. In front of Thaïs's house. Athanaël is sleeping on the steps. His arguments have deeply affected Thaïs, and she now asks him what to do to gain salvation. He urges her to go to a convent where Albine (contralto) has gathered together young women who live in retreat. He offers to take Thaïs there on condition that she burns everything belonging to her past life. Thaïs agrees and leaves her house in flames as she walks away, dressed in a simple woollen tunic. Act III. Scene I. An oasis in the desert. Athanaël hands Thaïs over to the nuns at Albine's convent and takes his leave of her, sad at the thought of not seeing her again. Scene II. The banks of the Nile. The Cenobites' retreat. Athanaël

Enrico Caruso as Canio in Leoncavallo's I Pagliacci.

cannot forget Thaïs. Palémon (bass), an old Cenobite, reprimands him, urging him to resist the temptation of evil. Athanaël prays and goes to sleep. He dreams that Thaïs is dying, surrounded by the nuns. He gets up confused and determined to see her once again. Scene III. Athanaël arrives just in time to see her before she dies. She recognizes him and thanks him for saving her. In despair he talks to her of his love for her, but she no longer understands what he means by his sensual earthly love for, as she dies, her thoughts are of celestial forgiveness.

■ Though musically complex and eloquent, *Thaïs* is not so stylistically perfect as *Manon*. The most convincing passage today is the symphonic intermezzo, known by the name of 'Méditation' – a melodic violin solo supported by the harps. Let us also remember Athanaël's invocation *'Voilà donc la terrible cité'* and the famous duet. When it was first presented, the opera enjoyed considerable success.

GUNTRAM
Opera in three acts by Richard Strauss (1864–1949), libretto by the composer. First performance: Weimar, Hoftheater, 10 May 1894.

ORIGINAL CAST. Heinrich Zeller (Guntram), Pauline de Ahna (Freihild). Conducted by the composer.

SYNOPSIS. Medieval Germany. The guild of Champions of love, a secret society of Minnesingers, sends Guntram (tenor) to liberate the people oppressed by the tyrannical government of Duke Robert. Guntram saves the Duke's wife Freihild (soprano) from suicide and falls in love with her. The old Duke (bass), Freihild's father, and Duke Robert (baritone), to whom he has handed over the crown, invite Guntram to take part in a singing contest between the Minnesingers at court. Act II. A ball at the Duke's court. Guntram sings of the beauties of peace and good government, and of the horrors of war and cruelty. The Duke feels threatened by Guntram's words and challenges him to a duel and is killed. Guntram is imprisoned by order of the old Duke, but Freihild frees him. Act III. Friedhold (bass), an elderly member of the guild, urges Guntram to seek judgement from the other guild elders. But Guntram feels that it was not what he did that was wrong, since the fact that he killed an oppressor was right in itself, but what he felt, since he wished for the death of the husband of the woman he loved. He therefore, rejects the judgement of the guild and condemns himself to solitude.

■ *Guntram* was Strauss's first work for the stage. The fact that it was not successful was largely due to the very difficult part for the tenor. A new version, presented at Weimar in 1940, did not make it any easier. The score shows much Wagnerian influence, and the originality of the opera lies mainly in the dramatic conclusion to the third act, with its proud affirmation of individual conscience.

DONNA DIANA
Comic opera in three acts by Emil Nikolaus von Rezniček (1860–1945), libretto by the composer, based on the comedy El Lindo Don Diego *by Moreto (1654). First performance: Prague, National German Theatre, 16 December 1894.*

SYNOPSIS. Diana, the daughter of Don Diego, says that, like the goddess Diana, she will never take a husband. After a tournament, Don Diego invites her to choose a husband from among the winners: Don Cesare, Prince of Urgel, Don Luigi of Béarne and Gaston, Count of Foix. Don Cesare is in love with Diana, but she does not appear to return his affection. His servant, Perrins, advises him to behave in a similarly cool way himself, just as Perrins does towards Floretta, Diana's step-sister. During the ceremony when Diana's future husband is to be chosen, he is selected, but he refuses the golden crown, indicating that he shares her opinion regarding love and marriage. The deception works. Diana is offended by his coldness and decides to conquer him. During a reception, she manages to break down his resistance and humiliate him, but he quickly reassumes his former coolness. Meanwhile, Perrins and the other two suitors have chosen their wives, leaving Don Cesare and Diana to their reciprocal game of spite. Diana defiantly declares that she will marry Don Luigi, but Don Cesare simply congratulates her saying that he intends to marry Donna Laura. In the end Diana realizes that she loves Don Cesare and chooses him as her husband.

■ The success of the opera was immediate. It was first performed in Prague, where the composer held the post of director of music, and then spread quickly throughout the theatres of Germany. There is much Wagnerian influence both in the vocal and the instrumental parts. The comedy only comes out at times in the orchestration.

GUGLIELMO RATCLIFF (William Ratcliff)
Tragedy in four acts by Pietro Mascagni (1863–1945), text by Heinrich Heine (1822) in the translation by Andrea Maffei (1798–1885). First performance: Milan, Teatro alla Scala, 16 February 1895.

ORIGINAL CAST. Negri, Vidal, Pacini, De Grazia, Stehle, Rogers. Conducted by the composer.

SYNOPSIS. The action takes place in the north of Scotland, around 1820. Act I. Douglas (baritone), betrothed to Maria (soprano), the daughter of MacGregor (bass), arrives at MacGregor's castle. He says that he has been attacked by three brigands near the castle and was saved by an unknown cavalier. MacGregor tells him that many years before Maria had rejected the love of Guglielmo Ratcliff (tenor), who backs away in terror, but he hurls himself upon her and kills her. He then kills MacGregor, who has rushed up in a vain attempt to defend his daughter, and shoots himself.

■ The tragedy in one act, which was written by Heinrich Heine in three days in 1822, had already inspired the Russian composer, Cui, and would also be set to music by the Bohemian, Vavrinecz, and the Dutchman, Cornelis Dopper. It first attracted Mascagni's attention in his youth when he was a pupil at the Milan Conservatory. He had played the first draft of the opera on the piano for Hanslick, who liked it and predicted for it 'the success that it had not achieved in the version by Andrea Maffei at the Manzoni in Milan'. Puccini was also enthusiastic about this first work of Mascagni's, which was only produced after the great success of *Cavalleria Rusticana*. In many places it was practically rewritten, so much so that it can almost be considered a second version.

SILVANO

Opera in two acts by Pietro Mascagni (1863–1945), libretto by Giovanni Targioni-Tozzetti (1863–1934). First performance: Milan, Teatro alla Scala, 25 March 1895.

SYNOPSIS. The action takes place in a village on the Southern Adriatic coast. Matilde is waiting anxiously for the return of her fiancé, Silvano. Out of necessity he became a smuggler and has been in prison. During his absence Matilde has become the lover of Renzo, another sailor. Silvano returns during the celebrations for the launching of Renzo's new boat and they have a violent quarrel. Only Rosa, Silvano's mother, is able to separate them. Later Renzo slips into Matilde's house and threatens to kill Silvano is she will not agree to meet him on the rocks for one last time. Since she is afraid for Silvano, whom she still loves, she agrees. Silvano finds her there and threatens her with a pistol. When Renzo comes to defend her, Silvano shoots him and runs away.

■ This opera is not among Mascagni's best. In an attempt to follow current trends he presents episodes with crude realism, but he does not manage to achieve the dramatic charge of his early masterpiece, *Cavalleria Rusticana*, nor to match it in richness of melody.

DER EVANGELIMANN (The Evangelist)

Opera in two acts by Wilhelm Kienzl (1857–1941), libretto by the composer, based on the story by Leopold Florian Meissner (1894). First performance: Staatsoper, Berlin, 4 May 1895. First performance in U.K.: London, Covent Garden, 2 July 1897; in U.S.A.: Chicago, Great Northern Theater, 3 November 1923.

SYNOPSIS. Johannes Fredhofer, a teacher at the Benedictine Monastery of St Othmar, loves Martha, the daughter of the provost, and is jealous of his

Cesira Ferrani, who sang the name-part in Puccini's Manon Lescaut, *when it was first presented at the Teatro Regio, Turin, on 1 February 1893.*

has since challenged and killed her next two suitors. Douglas also receives a challenge from Ratcliff, inviting him to fight near the Black Rock. Act II. In an inn, Ratcliff explains to his friend, Lesley, how his better nature was destroyed when Maria refused him, and he is driven to kill anyone who sets eyes on her. He is followed by two mysterious figures, whose strange presence disturbs him every time they appear. Act III. Near the Black Rock two white shadows hold out their hands and disappear as Ratcliff arrives. On seeing him, Douglas recognizes Ratcliff as the cavalier who had saved him. In the duel that follows Douglas calls upon the spirits of Maria's former suitors to help him. Ratcliff falls, but Douglas refuses to strike him. Once he is alone, Ratcliff is again disturbed by the appearance of the ghosts. Act IV. While Maria is preparing for her wedding, Margherita (mezzo-soprano), her nurse, tells her the story of her own and Ratcliff's parents. Although Maria's mother, Elisa, and Ratcliff's father, Edward, had been in love, she had married MacGregor and he Jennifer Campbell. But they had not stopped loving one another. MacGregor had found Edward near the castle and had killed him, and Elisa died of grief. At this point in the story Ratcliff, pale and covered in blood, enters Maria's room. Maria is confused by his appearance and believes she is reliving her mother's story. She feels pity and love for him, but when she recovers she asks him to go. When she refuses to run away with him, Ratcliff goes mad. She

brother, Mathis, a chancellor at the same monastery, with whom the girl is in love. When he is not able to separate the two lovers he tells the authorities of their relationship and has Mathis expelled from the monastery. He then causes a fire, for which Mathis is blamed and sentenced to twenty years in prison. Magdalena, Martha's friend, meets him thirty years later. Mathis tells her that when he came out of prison and learned that Martha had been unable to get over her grief and had killed herself, he had become an evangelist preacher. Magdalena is looking after Johannes, who is stricken with remorse and near to death. She persuades the two brothers to meet. Although he does not recognize him, Johannes confesses his guilt to his brother, who absolves him and forgives him for what he has done.

■ Of the composer's operas *Der Evangelimann* was the only one to meet with lasting success. Besides the influence of the composers such as Schumann and Adolf Jensen, there is also much Wagnerian inspiration in the language and technique, to which Kienzl adds popular and intimate overtones.

LA COUPE ENCHANTÉE
Opera in two acts by Gabriel Pierné (1863–1937), libretto by Emmanuel Matrat, based on a comedy by La Fontaine and Champmeslé of 1688. First performance: Royan, 24 August 1895.

LA BOHÈME (freely translated: Bohemian Life)
Opera in four acts by Giacomo Puccini (1858–1924), libretto by Giuseppe Giacosa (1847–1906) and Luigi Illica (1857–1919), based on the novel Scènes de la vie de Bohème *by Henry Murger (1848). First performance: Turin, Teatro Regio. 1 February 1896. First performance in U.K.: Manchester, 22 April 1897; in U.S.A.: Los Angeles, 14 October 1897.*

ORIGINAL CAST. Cesira Ferrani (Mimi), Camilla Pasini (Musetta), Evan Gorga (Rodolfo), Tieste Wilmant (Marcello), Antonio Pini-Corsi (Schaunard), Michele Mazzara (Colline), Alessandro Polonini (Benoit/Alcindoro). Conductor: Arturo Toscanini.

SYNOPSIS. Paris, around 1830. Act I. In a garret on Christmas Eve. The poet Rodolfo (tenor) is looking at the snow-covered roofs, while his friend, the painter Marcello (baritone), works on a painting. It is cold and Rodolfo lights the stove with the manuscript of one of the drafts of his play. Two friends join them, the philosopher Colline (bass) and the musician Schaunard (baritone), who brings food and wine bought with money given to him by a patron. The four begin to feast when they are interrupted by the landlord, Benoit (bass), who has come to claim his rent arrears. His tongue loosened by the wine, Benoit boasts of his extra-marital affairs and the Bohemians, feigning indignation, throw him out. Marcello, Colline and Schaunard go to the Café Momus. Rodolfo, who

The soprano, Dorothy Kirsten, in the name-part of Puccini's Manon Lescaut *at the Metropolitan Opera House, New York.*

has to finish an article for his newspaper, stays behind. Mimi (soprano), a neighbour, knocks at the door and asks if he will light her candle. She has a sudden fit of coughing and faints: he helps her to recover. Then both candles blow out and Mimi drops the key to her door. As they search the floor in the dark (Rodolfo finds the key and hides it) their hands touch. He squeezes hers as if to warm it: '*Che gelida manina*'. They talk about themselves and quickly fall in love. From the courtyard, Rodolfo's friends call to him. The young lovers embrace and leave together. Act II. The Latin Quarter. In front of the Café Momus. Rodolfo and Mimi stop to buy her a bonnet, Colline buys a second-hand greatcoat from a dealer, Schaunard haggles over the price of a horn. In the crowd Musetta (soprano), who used to be Marcello's mistress, appears, accompanied by the elderly Alcindoro (bass). Musetta still cares for Marcello and invites him to return to her by singing a beautiful waltz – ('*Quando me'n vo*'). She sends Alcindoro to buy shoes and they embrace. A military parade passes by and the Bohemians slip away, leaving Alcindoro to pay the bill at the café. Act III. The Barrière d'Enfer (one of the Paris toll-gates). A February day at dawn. After quarrelling with Mimi, Rodolfo has settled in an inn where Marcello is also living. Marcello is painting the inn sign when Mimi comes up to him and, coughing badly, tells him that she suspects that Rodolfo has left her forever. Mimi hides when Rodolfo comes out and talks to his friend about his jealousy and about Mimi's poor health; he reveals that she is seriously ill. A fit of coughing gives Mimi away. The two lovers embrace and decide to separate only when Spring comes. Musetta then appears and quarrels with Marcello again. Act IV. The garret. Rodolfo and Marcello look back with regret on the days spent with Mimi and Musetta. Colline and Schaunard arrive and the four friends try to forget their sorrows by fooling around. Musetta suddenly arrives to say that Mimi is desperately ill and wants to return to Rodolfo for her last hours. The men carry Mimi into the room. Musetta sends Marcello to sell her ear-rings to buy medicine and goes out herself to look for a muff to warm Mimi's icy hands. Colline sells his old coat. Left alone, the two lovers recall their first meeting. The friends return and Colline says the doctor is on his way. Rodolfo thinks that Mimi is asleep until he notices the truth from his friends' faces. He throws himself, sobbing, over her lifeless body.

■ It took a long time to complete the libretto for *La Bohème* on account of Puccini's stormy relationship with the librettists, Illica and Giacosa. On more than one occasion they were on the point of giving up the task, saying it was impossible to do what the composer wanted. Puccini had begun to work on *La Bohème* in January 1893 (he said so himself during a controversy with Leoncavallo, who claimed sole rights to the subject) and he wrote the last note of the score on 10 November 1895, feeling as though 'his own youth died with the death of Mimi'. The audience reacted warmly at the first performance, especially at the end of the first act and in the final scene, but their enthusiasm fell far short of that with which *Manon Lescaut* had been received. The critics were divided and there were some who saw *La Bohème* as an 'unsuccessful' and 'deplorable decline'. In fact, because of the solid theatrical foundation, the perfect balance between the gay and the pathetic, the realistic and the impressionistic, the passionate lyricism and the clear characterization, *La Bohème* is probably Puccini's masterpiece and undoubtedly one of the most original creations for the operatic stage.

ZANETTO

Opera in one act by Pietro Mascagni (1863–1945), libretto by Giovanni Targioni-Tozzetti (1863–1934), and Guido Menasci (1867–1925), based on the one-act comedy Le Passant *by François Coppée (1869). First performance: Pesaro, Teatro Rossini, 2 March 1896. First performance in U.K.: London, 23 June 1896; in U.S.A.: New York, 4 January 1898.*

SYNOPSIS. The action takes place in Florence in the garden of the house of the well-known courtesan Silvia. She is worried that she cannot feel true love. She wishes to attract a young, strolling poet called Zanetto, who believes her to be of noble birth. She invites him to visit her, and when he says that he desires only to remain beside her, she is moved by the simplicity and spontaneity of his feelings. Gently she pushes him away, blessing through her tears the new sensation of the true love she feels.

■ When *Zanetto* first appeared the critics were perplexed. Only Ugo Oietti felt that the composer had written his 'most organic', most original, most 'continuous' opera. In fact, for Mascagni it marks a moment of rest, after ten years of intense activity. The choice of a poetic subject (based on a comedy in verse by Coppée performed for the first time in Paris in 1869 and translated by Emilio Praga in 1872) indicates Mascagni's desire to move into literary circles. There was nothing in the text, however, to arouse the composer's inspiration.

ANDREA CHÉNIER

Dramma di ambiente storico *in four acts by Umberto Giordano (1867–1948), libretto by Luigi Illica (1857–1919). First performance: Milan, Teatro alla*

Cover of a special edition of 'Illustrazione Italiana' with Verdi's Falstaff.

Scala, 28 March 1896. First performance in U.K.: London, Camden Town Theatre, 16 April 1903; in U.S.A.: New York, Academy of Music, 13 November 1896.

ORIGINAL CAST. Giuseppe Borgatti (Andrea Chénier), Mario Sammarco (Carlo Gérard), Evelina Carrera (Maddalena de Coigny).

SYNOPSIS. The action takes place in France between 1789 and 1794. Act I. In the ballroom of the Château de Coigny, the final preparations are in hand for a ball. Carlo Gérard (baritone), a servant, expresses his hatred for his aristocratic masters except the beautiful Maddalena de Coigny (soprano), the daughter of the house, with whom he is secretly in love. He pities his old father, who has been forced to work all his life for them. The guests arrive, among them Fléville (baritone), a novelist, Andrea Chénier (tenor) and the Abate (tenor). The Abate brings the latest disturbing news from Paris, but the company are immediately distracted by Fléville, who reads a Pastoral. Maddalena urges Chénier to read a poem and he recites *'un dí all'azzurro spazio'*, a denunciation of the injustices of the clergy and the nobility towards the ordinary people. He then begs Maddalena not to despise poetry and love. The festivities are interrupted by Gérard at the head of a band of peasants. The Contessa (mezzo-soprano) tells the major-domo (bass) to get rid of them and she dismisses Gerard before smoothing over the ugly scene with orders that the dancing should continue. Act II. In Paris. The terrace of the Feuillants and the Café Hottot. The Revolution is over. This is the age of the Terror. Chénier is constantly watched by an 'Incredibile' (tenor), a spy for the revolutionary Government, of which Gérard is a member. Chénier describes to his friend Roucher (bass) the picture he has of the unknown woman who has sent him several letters asking for protection. Roucher advises him to flee from Paris, but he refuses, at least until he has discovered who it is that is writing to him. Gérard, meanwhile instructs the Incredibile to find Maddalena and gives him her description. She turns out to be Chénier's correspondent and when the Incredibile sees her in conversation with Chénier, he runs off to inform Gérard. Gérard, not recognizing the poet, challenges Chénier, who seriously wounds him. When Gérard does recognize Chénier, he warns him that he is in danger. The Incredibile brings the police, but Gérard says he does not know the identity of his attacker. Act III. The Revolutionary Tribunal. A year later the Incredibile tells Gérard that Chénier has been arrested and that he should write out the bill of indictment. Gérard recalls his youthful feelings of patriotism, but allows lust and jealousy to overcome him. He has just signed the indictment *'Nemico della patria'*, when Maddalena appears as the spy had predicted, and implores him to save Chénier. At length she offers herself to Gérard if he will do all he can to save the poet and Gérard agrees. Although Chénier passionately defends himself before the Tribunal and Gérard bears witness that the indictment was false, Chénier is con-

Alberto Rinaldi in the part of Ford in Verdi's Falstaff, *presented at the Teatro della Pergola in Florence in May 1970.*

demned to death. Act IV. The courtyard of the prison of St-Lazare. Chénier awaits death and reads to Roucher his last poem, *'Come un bel dí di Maggio'*. Maddalena arrives with Gérard, who leaves her in order to make one final plea in their defence. Maddalena offers money and jewellery to the gaoler to be allowed to take the place of a female prisoner condemned to death. The two lovers can thus die together. The strength of their love makes them calm in the face of death. Gérard sobs in despair.

■ Of Giordano's operas, *Andrea Chénier* is the one which achieved the greatest success and even today it is often to be found in the repertoires of the world's greatest theatres. The critics often claim that Giordano's ability to take advantage of theatrical and vocal effects is here greater than his ability as an authentic composer. On almost all occasions the audience shows that it does not agree. The libretto had been prepared by Illica for Franchetti, who then decided not to use it.

Illica wanted to indicate his sources in a note which appears on the libretto: 'I had the idea of dramatizing the character for the musical theatre and took relevant historical details from H. de Latouche, Méry, Arsène Houssaye, Gauthier and J. and E. de Goncourt.' All the circumstantial details can be checked, as can the historical quotations and the precise references to the poetry and the life of the poet, Andrea Chénier, who was born in Constantinople in 1762 and died in Paris 1794. He joined the Club of the 'Feuillants', was investigated, arrested and then guillotined in the Place du Trône Renverseé. The opera was considered unstageable by A. Galli, Sonzogno's musical adviser, and was taken off the bill until Mascagni intervened, when the opera was reinstated. At this point, the tenor, Garulli, who was to have played the title-role, withdrew and the part had to be sung by a tenor whose reputation had already been damaged by earlier failures and who, therefore, had nothing to lose. It was a triumph and the tenor role has since attracted many great singers.

DER CORREGIDOR (The Magistrate)
Opera in four acts by Hugo Wolf (1860–1903), libretto by Rosa Mayreder-Obermayer, based on the story El sombrero de tres picos *by Pedro de Alarcón y Ariza (1874). First performance: Mannheim, Nationaltheater, 7 June 1896. First performance in U.K.: London, Royal Academy of Music, 13 July 1934; in U.S.A.: New York, Carnegie Hall, 5 January 1959.*

SYNOPSIS. Andalusia, 1804. Act I. Frasquita (mezzo-soprano), the wife of the miller, Tio Lucas (baritone), has attracted the attention of Don Eugenio de Zuniga (buffo tenor), the Magistrate, an impenitent womanizer. She takes advantage of this to ask him for an appointment for her nephew, but keeps him in his place when he tries to become too attentive. The magistrate sends a message to his wife, Doña Mercedes (soprano), saying that he has a lot to do and will have to spend the night working at the Town Hall. Act II. Tonuelo (bass) brings a message to Tio Lucas that he is required to give evidence at the Town Hall. When he has left, the magistrate arrives at the mill. He is soaked through and through because he has fallen in the brook, and while he dries his clothes by the fire, he makes advances to Frasquita. She half encourages him in order to get her nephew's appointment and half repulses him, until he threatens her with a pistol. She replies with a gun. He faints and she runs off to look for her husband, who in the meantime has realized that he has been tricked to keep him out of the way and has managed to make the Alcalde, the usher and the secretary drunk so that he can escape. Act III. Lucas and Frasquita miss each other in the dark. When he gets home, he finds Don Eugenio in his bed, where he has been put by a servant, and suspects that Frasquita had betrayed him. He remembers that Doña Mercedes is very beautiful and, dressed in the magistrate's clothes which were drying near the fire, he sets off to pay her a visit. When the Alcalde and his officials arrive, having recovered from their drunken stupor, they rush into

the bedroom and, assuming that it is Lucas in the bed, they grip hold of Don Eugenio. Frasquita arrives to point out their mistake and everyone rushes out to look for the miller. Act IV. At Don Eugenio's house, a maid tells them that her master has been in bed for more than an hour. Since they are shouting and carrying-on, the real Magistrate (dressed as the miller) and the Alcalde are manhandled by the police. Frasquita weeps to think that her husband is in bed with Mercedes. Yet it is not so, for she and the miller have agreed simply to punish their respective spouses. Lucas and Frasquita assure each other of their fidelity but Doña Mercedes leaves the Magistrate with the suspicion that he has been betrayed.

■ *Der Corregidor* was Wolf's first theatrical attempt (the second, *Manuel Venegas*, was not finished owing to his mental illness) and it shows traces of the fact that he was primarily a composer of *Lieder*. In fact, the opera is almost like a collection of pieces of chamber music. Some of the musical features are essentially theatrical, however, and even foreshadow later operatic solutions. Wolf also demonstrates here his ability of illuminating his characters, those bourgeois characters who live, in fact, in the world of his famous *liederbücher*.

JUNGFRUN I TORNET (The Maid in the Tower)
Opera in one act by Jean Sibelius (1865–1957), libretto by Rafael Hertzberg. First performance: Helsinki, National Theater, 7 November 1896.

■ The only opera by Sibelius, it was performed with little success for charity, under the direction of the composer. The work has never been published.

FERVAAL
Action dramatique in a prologue and three acts by Vincent d'Indy (1851–1931), libretto by the composer. First performance: Brussels, Théâtre de la Monnaie, 12 March 1897.

SYNOPSIS. The action takes place in the Midi and the Cévennes mountains at the time of the Druids. Fervaal, the only descendant of the chiefs of Cravann, has been brought up by the Druid Arfagaard. He renounces his love for Guilhen, daughter of the barbarian emir, who has nursed him back to health, in order to save his country. In a rage she vows to destroy it. The goddess Kaito had predicted to Arfagaard that from a broken vow and a death, a new order would emerge. Fervaal suspects that he is the chosen victim since he broke his oath to Guilhen. Unable to find death, however, he wanders on the mountain among the corpses of his warriors. Guilhen, herself nearly frozen by the cold, calls out to him, and Arfagaard tries to prevent him going to her. In the struggle, Fervaal stabs his master. Then he embraces his dying beloved and carries her to the mountain peak, as the dawn of Christianity begins to show its first light.

Verdi's Falstaff *at the Vienna Staatsoper.*

■ This is the first opera of note by D'Indy. Wagner's considerable influence is transformed by contact with French culture, the spirit which pervades it being very close to that of the dramatic symbolists. The theme is taken from a Celtic legend.

LA BOHÈME
Opera in four acts by Ruggiero Leoncavallo (1858–1919), libretto by the composer, based on the novel by Henry Murger (1848). First performance: Venice, Teatro La Fenice, 6 May 1897.

ORIGINAL CAST. L. Frandin, Rosina Storchio, R. Beduschi, R. Angelini-Fornari, Isnardon. Conductor: Alessandro Pomé.

SYNOPSIS. Paris 1837/38. Act I. Christmas Eve. Four friends meet at the Café Momus: the painter Marcello (tenor), the poet Rodolfo (baritone), the musician Schaunard (baritone), and the philosopher Colline (baritone). They are celebrating with Eufemia, Musette (mezzo-soprano), and Mimi (soprano), but as they are all broke, the bill is paid by an unexpected patron, the art-loving Barbemuche (bass). Marcello declares his love for Musette and succeeds in winning her attention. Rodolfo and Mimi are in love. Act II. During a party (which Musette has to give outside her house because the creditors have emptied it of its contents) a rich admirer, the Vicomte Paolo (baritone) suggests to Mimi that she comes to live with him. At first she hesitates, but then, weary of so much poverty, she accepts his offer. Soon afterwards Musette also leaves Marcello as she, too, is unable to bear a life of such misery and hardship – all that Marcello can offer is a continual struggle against the creditors. Act III. Mimi returns to Rodolfo, begging forgiveness and asking him to take her back, but he bitterly rejects her. Act IV. A year has passed and it is Christmas Eve again. Musette has returned to Marcello and the friends have gathered in Rodolfo's miserable attic to celebrate Christmas. Suddenly Mimi enters, seriously ill, and desiring only to be near Rodolfo when she dies. All the friends gather round her trying to help. She dies in the poet's arms.

■ Leoncavallo's opera was presented a year after Puccini's more successful opera. It was warmly received by the critics and public interest was aroused by the comparison between the two. The two *Bohèmes* were even performed at the same time in Milan, at the Teatro Lirico and the Dal Verme. After a while interest in Leoncavallo's opera waned and it was not revived even after it had been rewritten with the title *Mimì Pinson* and presented at the Teatro Massimo in Palermo in 1913.

L'ARLESIANA (The Maid of Arles)

Melodramma *in three acts by Francesco Cilea (1866–1950), libretto by Leopoldo Marenco (1831–99), based on the play* L'Arlésienne *by Alphonse Daudet (1872), which, in its turn, was based on a story by Daudet published in 1866 in* Letters from my Mill. *First performance: Milan, Teatro Lirico, 27 November 1897. First performance in U.S.A.: Philadelphia, 11 January 1962.*

ORIGINAL CAST. Tracey (Rosa), Ricci de Paz (Vivetta), Orlando (l'innocente), Enrico Caruso (Federico), Pasini (Baldassarre), Arisi (Metifio), Frigiotti (Marco). Conductor: Giovanni Zuccani.

SYNOPSIS. The action takes place in Provence. Act I. Outside Rosa Mamai's farm-house. An old shepherd, Baldassarre (baritone), is telling a story to Rosa's younger son, who is a little retarded. His patience is of great help to the child. Rosa (mezzo-soprano) is worried about her elder son, Federico (tenor), who has met a girl from Arles at the fair, with whom he has fallen in love and whom he now wants to marry. While Federico is away discovering more about her, Vivetta (soprano), Rosa's god-daughter, who is in love with him, finds out about his probable marriage and is grieved. Federico returns triumphantly announcing that the date of the wedding can be fixed. Meanwhile, Metifio (baritone), a horse-tender, tells Rosa that the girl whom Federico wants to marry has been his mistress. Her parents allowed it until Federico appeared on the scene. As proof he shows her two letters which he leaves with her so that she can show them to Federico. Federico is appalled and Rosa asks him never to speak of the girl again. Act II. Beside a pond. Rosa and Vivetta are looking for Federico, who has left home. Baldassarre finds him, and his little brother (mezzo-soprano) and the old man urge him to return and to consider his mother's grief. Rosa, however, realizes her son's misery and says that she is prepared to welcome the girl into her home. Federico is moved, but finds himself unable to accept the sacrifice, saying that he will try to overcome his infatuation and marry Vivetta. In tears, Rosa embraces him. Act III. In the farmhouse. Preparations are in hand for the wedding. While Federico assures Vivetta that he is completely over his affair,

Poster for the première of Massenet's Thaïs. *Victoria and Albert Museum, London.*

Poster for Puccini's La Bohème, *for the first performance produced by Adolfo Hohenstein in Turin, in 1896.*

SYNOPSIS. The action takes place at Sesto in Thrace, on the banks of the Hellespont. Ero, a priestess of Venus, has fallen in love with Leandro, the victor in the games held in honour of the goddess. Ariofarne, the archon of Thrace, who presides over religious ceremonies, is in love with Ero and asks her to yield to his desires. When she refuses, he swears to take his revenge. He orders her to be chosen as the priestess who, according to an ancient custom of the rites of Venus, is to be incarcerated in a tower, known as the Virgin's Tower, so that her purity may remain untarnished by carnal passion. Every night, regardless of the danger and defying the penalty of death, however, Leandro swims across the Hellespont to see her. One night, a violent storm breaks and he risks being discovered by Ariofarne, who has come with the priests to carry out a ceremony of propitiation to placate the raging sea. Leandro escapes by throwing himself into the sea and is dashed to death on the rocks. Ariofarne discovers that Ero has died of grief at her lover's death.

■ This opera, in which the chorus has the musically most important role, is more characteristic of oratorio than opera. It was performed for the first time in a concert version at the Norwich festival in 1896.

SADKO
Romantic opera in seven scenes (three or five acts) by Nicolay Rimsky-Korsakov (1844–1908), libretto by the composer and Vladimir I. Bielsky, based on an old anonymous Russian poem. First performance: Moscow, Solodovnikov Theatre, 7 January 1898. First performance in U.K.: London, Lyceum, 9 June 1931; in U.S.A.: New York, Metropolitan Opera House, 25 January 1930.

SYNOPSIS. Scene I. At a banquet of the merchants of Novgorod, two players on the *gousli*, a type of guitar, entertain. Najata (contralto) sings of the glories of old Kiev, but Sadko (tenor) irritates the merchants by suggesting that they lack the spirit of adventure. If he had as much money as they have he would not be content until his ships had sailed out of the lake into the open sea in search of unknown treasures. They laugh at him and continue their merrymaking. Scene II. At night. Sadko sings on the shore of lake Ilmen and the daughters of the sea appear. The Sea King's own daughter, Volkhova (soprano), falls in love with him and, before she leaves at dawn, makes him three promises as a token of her love: he will catch three golden fishes, he will journey to a far distant land and she will wait for him faithfully. Scene III. Lubava (mezzosoprano), Sadko's wife, is anxious lest Sadko may have left her and gone on an expedition. Scene IV. Morning, at the harbour. Sadko bets the assembled crowd of merchants that he can catch golden fishes in the lake. The catch does indeed contain three golden fishes, and the merchants agree that their wealth is forfeit. Sadko chooses to take only their ships and invites the adventurous among them to join him. Three foreigners describe their homelands for him – a Viking (bass), an

Metifio comes to collect his letters. Baldassarre has in fact already returned them, but Metifio has not seen them because he has spent the last two days in Arles. He says he has decided not to give up the girl. Federico is immediately furious with jealousy and attacks Metifio with a hammer. Baldassarre and Rosa separate them. They take Federico to his room and he seems to calm down. But that night, when everyone thinks he is asleep, he goes to the barn. Rosa and Vivetta try in vain to stop him, but in desperation he throws himself out of the window.

■ The enormous success of the opera made Cilea's name and also that of the famous singer, Enrico Caruso. Inspired by the same play by Daudet, Bizet had composed incidental music for *L'Arlésienne*, which was performed for the first time in Paris in 1872.

ERO E LEANDRO (Hero and Leander)
Opera in three acts by Luigi Mancinelli (1848–1921), libretto by Arrigo Boito (1842–1918). First performance: Madrid, Teatro Reale, 30 November 1897. First performance in U.K.: Norwich, 8 October 1896; in U.S.A.: New York, 10 March 1899.

The final scene of Puccini's La Bohème *at* La Scala, *Milan. Production and sets by Franco Zeffirelli.*

■ The plot of *Sadko* is taken from an old popular legend sung by the *shomorohi*, a type of minstrel composer. The idea of setting it to music came from Mussorgsky, but owing to pressure of work he left the task to Rimsky-Korsakov. Rimsky made his first draft in 1867, in the form of a symphonic poem, and in it was condensed the musical substance of the opera that was to be composed almost thirty years later. In the summer of 1894, the critic, Findeisen, wrote to the musician, suggesting an outline for a libretto. The range of the subject, the fantastic theme and the possibility of introducing the grandeur of the sea onto the stage by expressing the sounds of it, all captured the ardent imagination of the composer and he set to the work on the banks of a lake near Vetchacha, his family's summer residence. In writing the libretto, he was aided by the critic Stasov, and particularly by the writer-mathematician, Bielsky, who collaborated with him on a great many of his operas. In the summer of 1895, Rimsky worked exclusively on the score but, because of various hitches and his wish to make a number of modifications, it was not finished until the following summer. As R. M. Hofmann writes, in it is to be found 'the very essence of the nature and the genius of Rimsky-Korsakov. It is a combination of his profound love for the Russian people, his faith in his destiny, and his love of the fantastic.'

Indian (tenor) and a Venetian (baritone) – and Sadko resolves to set sail for Venice. Scene V. Twelve years have passed. Sadko is bound once again for Novgorod with a cargo of treasure. His ship is becalmed, and he remembers that he has not paid tribute to the King of the Ocean. The sailors throw pearls and gold overboard to no avail and Sadko realizes that he must sacrifice himself. He watches his ship sail away as he stands on a bare plank floating on the sea, strumming his *gousli*. Volkhova bids him descend to the seabed. Scene VI. At the Court of the King of the Ocean, he is presented to Volkhova's parents and the King celebrates his marriage to the Princess. Wedding guests dance to his *gousli*-playing, and cause such a disturbance that the waves cause several shipwrecks. Suddenly a legendary hero, dressed as a pilgrim, appears: he announces that Volkhova must immediately return to Novgorod, for she is to be transformed into a river. The old King's reign is over. Sadko and his bride set sail in a sea shell. Scene VII. The shore of lake Ilmen at dawn. Volkhova leaves Sadko asleep and becomes the river which joins the lake to the sea. When he awakes, he finds his wife Lubava standing beside him joyful at his return. He suspects that he has dreamed his adventures until he recognizes his ship sailing into the harbour and discovers that he is welcomed home as the wealthiest merchant in the city.

FEDORA
Opera in three acts by Umberto Giordano (1867–1948), libretto by Arturo Colautti (1851–1914), based on the play by Victorien Sardou (1882). First performance: Milan, Teatro Lirico, 17 November 1898. First performance in U.K.: London, Covent Garden, 5 November 1906; in U.S.A.: New York, Metropolitan Opera House, 5 December 1906.

A silver cigarette case which belonged to Giacomo Puccini on which is enamelled the scene from the third act of La Bohème.

Puccini's La Bohème *at the Théâtre de la Renaissance in Paris in 1899, with Soulacroix, Thévenet, Fraudaz, Leprestre and Ghasne.*

ORIGINAL CAST. Enrico Caruso, Delfino Menotti, Gemma Bellincioni. Conducted by the composer.

SYNOPSIS. The action takes place towards the end of the nineteenth century. Act I. St Petersburg, at the house of Count Vladimir. The servants are waiting for the Count, who is celebrating his last night as a bachelor. The following morning he will marry the rich princess, Fedora Romanov (soprano), thus recouping his finances. The Princess herself appears, worried because the Count has not met her at the theatre. His groom, Dimitri (contralto), runs off to look for the Count at his club, but at that moment he is brought in, wounded and accompanied by Grech (bass), a police officer. Grech conducts enquiries in order to reconstruct events. Cirillo (baritone), the coachman, says he accompanied the Count to the shooting gallery: then he heard two shots and someone rushed away, wounded and covered in blood. He called De Siriex, a French diplomat (baritone), and they discovered Vladimir, faint and wounded, inside the house. It is suspected that the old woman who lives in the house sent a letter to the Count that afternoon. But this letter cannot be found. Dimitri identifies a visitor who waited in the drawing room for some time but then suddenly left as Count Loris Ipanov (tenor). Vladimir dies, Grech announces that Loris Ipanov has disappeared. Act II. A reception at Fedora's house in Paris. Fedora has managed to make Loris fall in love with her in order to extract from him a confession that he is Vladimir's murderer. She writes a letter outlining what she thinks happened to Vladimir and accusing Loris, which Grech is to take to St Petersburg. She asks Grech to arrest Loris as he leaves her house. When Loris returns, however, he explains that for some time Vladimir had been his wife's lover and that he had discovered they were to meet even on the night before his marriage to Fedora. His proof consists of letters. Fedora is amazed

and all her feelings of love for the memory of Vladimir change to hatred. She is overcome with pity for Loris and, moved by his obvious devotion, stops him from leaving by confessing her love for him, thus compromising herself but preventing his arrest. Act III. In the garden of Fedora's villa in Switzerland. Loris and Fedora are happy together, but the plan that Fedora set in motion in Russia to revenge Vladimir's death has had tragic consequences for Ipanov's family. His brother has been arrested and has died in gaol, and his mother has died of grief. In the letter bringing this sad news to Loris, his friend, Borov (baritone), also tells him that the accusations against his brother were contained in a letter sent by a lady living in Paris. He only knows her Christian name but it would not be difficult to trace her. Loris swears he will get his revenge. In vain, Fedora begs forgiveness for that woman, but Loris is determined. Fedora poisons herself and Ipanov realizes too late that he was the cause of her suicide. She dies begging his forgiveness.

■ The opera was a great success, even outside Italy and particularly in Paris. It is Giordano's most successful work after *Andrea Chénier*. When he was eighteen years old and still at College, Giordano had been fascinated by Sardou's play on seeing Sarah Bernhardt in it at the Teatro Sannazzaro. He had asked the author for permission to set it to music at the time, but the reply had been: 'On verra plus tard'.

The four friends in La Bohème, *in a photograph sent by the cast to Puccini on the occasion of the 200th performance of the opera in Paris. Left to right: Fugère, Bouvet, Maréchal, Isnardou.*

IRIS

Melodramma *in three acts by Pietro Mascagni (1863–1945), libretto by Luigi Illica (1857–1919). First performance: Rome, Teatro Costanzi, 22 November 1898. First performance in U.K.: London, Covent Garden, 8 July 1919; in U.S.A.: Philadelphia, 14 November 1902.*

ORIGINAL CAST. Hariclea Darclée, F. De Lucia, Caruson, G. Tisci-Tamburini. Conducted by the composer.

SYNOPSIS. Act I. The action takes place in a village in Japan. Osaka, a young, wealthy rake (tenor), has fallen in love with Iris, a simple laundry girl (soprano), and he asks Kyoto, the owner of a tea-house (baritone), to abduct her. With this in mind they prepare a marionette show, the subject of which is the love of Dhia and Jor. Osaka sings the part of Jor, the son of the Sun God. Iris is attracted by his passionate song and joins the crowd to watch the show; she is seized and dragged away. Kyoto sends her father (bass), who is blind, some money together with a note to the effect that his daughter has gone of her own accord to the Yoshiwara, the district of ill-repute. The old man asks to be taken in search of Iris so that he can throw his curse upon her. Act II. After losing consciousness, Iris wakes up in Osaka's rich apartment and recognizes his voice as that of Jor. He tries in vain to conquer her, but she rejects his advances. Eventually he tires of her and leaves her to Kyoto, who dresses her up and shows her to the crowd. Her blind father is led to her and he curses and throws mud at her. In despair, she throws herself into a sewer. Act III. Iris's body is found at the bottom of the sewer by some rag-pickers, who try to remove her clothing and jewellery. Soon they realize that she is still alive and run away in terror. The light from the rising sun illuminates the last moments of Iris's life and seems to comfort her in her anguish. Flowers burst into bloom around her body. She ascends into the sky bathed in light and colour.

■ This opera first made its appearance at a time when there was a general thirst for freedom, a fact evident even in Hoenstein's typographical ornaments that decorate the score. It is in this historical perspective that the opera's great popularity should be viewed. Despite its enormous success with the public, it was received quite differently by the critics. Although the music contains melodic lines typical of Mascagni, and uses vocal means to express Illica's symbolism, the search for new expressive ideas and the effort to achieve consistency are very apparent.

MOZART AND SALIERI

Dramatic scenes in two acts by Nicolay Rimsky-Korsakov (1844–1908), text by Alexander Pushkin (1830). First performance: Moscow, Solodovnikov Theatre, 7 December 1898. First performance in U.K.: London, Albert Hall, 11 November 1927; in U.S.A.: Forest Park, Pa., Unity House, 6 August 1933.

Rimsky-Korsakov's Sadko *at the Bolshoi Theatre in 1898. Archives of The Theatre Museum, Moscow.*

SYNOPSIS. Salieri is in deep thought. He has given up everything for the sake of music, but now realizes that musical talent does not appreciate so much sacrifice and instead rewards a lazy, frivolous and unprincipled individual such as, in his opinion, Mozart. Mozart arrives in the company of a musician whom he had met in the street whilst he was massacring a good piece of music. He sits at the piano and improvises a short fantasy, full of sad presentiments. Salieri decides to kill Mozart, who has too much talent. He invites him to supper and secretly puts poison in the wine. When Mozart feels ill and takes his leave, Salieri is left alone and realizes the pointlessness of his crime: he has silenced his jealousy but he has also destroyed his faith in his own talent. Talent exists for its own sake, and certainly, thinks Salieri, Michelangelo would never have killed anyone out of envy; talent and breach of trust – he remembers the words that Mozart had spoken a short time before – have no chance of coexistence.

■ The idea of writing this opera came to Rimsky-Korsakov whilst reading Pushkin, his favourite poet. The second scene was written in the summer of 1897 as a kind of exercise and almost as a recreation. The result pleased him and he then decided to construct a full opera based on Pushkin's scenes. It is worth noting that Rimsky-Korsakov managed to adhere to the text without making any modifications, so great was his esteem for the poet. The slanderous and completely unjustified accusation that Salieri had poisoned Mozart out of professional jealousy was believed for a long time in the last century.

CENDRILLON (Cinderella)

Conte de fées *in four acts and six tableaux by Jules Massenet (1842–1912), libretto by Henri Cain (1859–1937), based on the fairy story* Cinderella *by Charles Perrault (1697). First performance: Paris, Opéra-Comique, 24 May 1899. First performance in U.K.: London, Little Theatre, 24 December 1928; in U.S.A.: New Orleans, 23 December 1902.*

ORIGINAL CAST. Julie Girardon (Cendrillon), Blanche Deschamps-Jéhin (Mme de la Haltière), Gmelen (le Prince), Bréjean-Gravière (la Fée), Jean Tiphaine (Noémie), Marie de Lisle (Dorothée), Lucien Fugère (Pandolfe), Dubose (le Roi).

SYNOPSIS. Act I. A drawing room in the house of Madame de la Haltière (contralto). Preparations are in hand for the Prince's grand ball, which Noémie (soprano) and Dorothée (mezzo-soprano), her two daughters, will attend, dressed in all their finery. As usual, her step-daughter, Lucy, who is known as Cendrillon (soprano), will not be included. When all is ready, the

Petrov in the second act of Rimsky-Korsakov's Sadko *at the Bolshoi Theatre, Moscow.*

family go to the ball. Left on her own at home, Cendrillon falls asleep. She dreams of fairies and sprites who enable her to attend the ball where she is beautiful and enjoys a great success. With her magic wand the fairy (la Fée – soprano), changes her poor dress into a magnificent ball gown and Cendrillon hurries away, but she must be back by midnight. Act II. The ball-room in the royal palace. The Prince (soprano) is miserable and stands alone. He has not managed to choose his future bride and he is not interested in the attentions of Cendrillon's two step-sisters. Cendrillon's unexpected

arrival arouses his excitement and, fascinated by her grace and beauty, he falls in love with her. On his knees he begs her to tell him her name. In reply, she tells him that she is his, but that he must never seek to know who she is. He tries in vain to detain her with tender words of love, but on the stroke of midnight she runs away, losing one of her glass slippers. The fairy prevents the Prince from following her. Act III, Scene I. A sitting room in Madame de la Haltière's house. Cendrillon returns after her flight from the ball and sits down weeping. When her step-sisters return, she pretends to be interested, and asks them what happened at the ball. They tell her bitterly of the scandalous arrival of an uninvited stranger and lead Cendrillon to suspect that the Prince doubts her innocence. Distressed by this, she resolves to run away to the farm where she and her father Pandolfe (bass) were happy after his first wife's death. Scene II. Beside an oak tree in the forest of the fairies, Cendrillon asks the fairy for comfort. The Prince arrives, happy to have found her and offers her his heart as proof of his sincerity. The fairies send them both to sleep. Act IV, Scene I. The balcony of Cendrillon's room. She was found unconscious in the wood and is recovering from a long illness. In reply to her question whether she said anything during her fever, Pandolfe replies that she spoke incoherent words about love and a shoe. The voice of a herald is then heard in the street, announcing that the Prince will personally receive girls so that they may try on the slipper lost by the mysterious stranger. Cendrillon realizes that it was not all a dream. Scene II. In the royal palace. A crowd gathers to watch the procession of girls. The Prince anxiously watches until at last the fairy arrives leading Cendrillon, who carries the heart, which the Prince had given her in the fairy wood. The crowd shouts excitedly and at last the Prince can embrace the girl he loves.

■ Although the opera contains an abundance of fluent melodic charm, it is overburdened with repetitive musical schemes. This attempt, implied in the choice of the libretto, to create a French opera similar to the German one that was enjoying much success at the time – *Hänsel and Gretel* by Humperdinck – was not entirely successful.

THE TSAR'S BRIDE (Tzarskaya Nevesta)

Drama in three acts by Nicolay Rimsky-Korsakov (1844–1908), libretto by Lev Aleksandrovich Mei (1822–62), with scenes added by I. F. Tumenev. First performance: Moscow, Solodovnikov Theatre, 3 November 1899. First performance in U.K.: London, Lyceum, 19 May 1931; in U.S.A.: Seattle, 6 January 1922.

SYNOPSIS. Grigor Griaznoy lives with Liubacha, a girl he has seduced and taken from her parents. He then falls in love with Martha, the boyar Lykov's beautiful fiancée. Griaznoy goes to a magician, Bomelius, to obtain a love potion for Martha. Liubacha overhears their conversation. She offers to give herself

Left: A sketch by Nicola Benois for Giordano's Fedora. *La Scala, Milan, 1955/56.*
Right: The cover of the score of Mascagni's Iris. *Ricordi Archives, Milan.*

to the magician if he promises to exchange the love potion for a slow and deadly poison. Knowing nothing of this Griaznoy gives the potion to Martha. The messenger of Ivan the Terrible announces that the Tsar has chosen Martha for his wife. Ivan's orders are carried out without question. Martha becomes the Tsarina, but she dies of a slow and mysterious illness. Griaznoy accuses Lykov of causing her death out of jealousy, but Lykov goes mad with grief. When Liubacha confesses, he kills her. The Tsar's guards arrest him.

■ Grigor Griaznoy, the leading character, is an *opritchniki*, that is a guard in the service of the Tsar with absolute power of life and death over all. The librettist, Tumenev, one of the composer's pupils, ignored the dramatic effect of the paradoxes and the arbitrary nature of the Tsar's power and concentrated on those aspects of the original work which were conventional (and in doubtful taste). Although Rimsky-Korsakov ranked this opera among his masterpieces, its only value lies in those melodies that are based on popular Russian songs.

TOSCA

Opera in three acts by Giacomo Puccini (1858–1924), libretto by Giuseppe Giacosa (1847–1906) and Luigi Illica (1857–1919), based on the play by Victorien Sardou (1887). First performance: Rome, Teatro Costanzi, 14 January 1900. First performance in U.K.: London, Covent Garden, 12 July 1900; in U.S.A.: New York, Metropolitan Opera House, 4 February 1901.

ORIGINAL CAST. Hariclea Darclée (Tosca), Enrico De Marchi (Cavaradossi), Eugenio Giraldoni (Scarpia). Conductor: Leopoldo Mugnone.

SYNOPSIS. Rome, June 1800. Act I. In the church of Sant'Andrea della Valle. Cesare Angelotti (bass), a consul of the fallen Roman republic, has escaped from the Castel Sant'Angelo. He takes refuge in the church, where his sister, the Marchesa Attavanti, has left him some clothes hidden in the family chapel. Mario Cavaradossi (tenor), a painter, is working in the church on a picture of Madonna. The sacristan points out its resemblance to the stranger who is often in the church (in fact, Marchesa Attavanti). When Cavaradossi is alone, Angelotti comes out of his hiding place and recognizes the painter as an old friend and Republican sympathizer. A commanding voice announces the arrival of Floria Tosca (soprano), a famous opera singer and Mario's mistress. Angelotti hides again. Tosca is suspicious of the whispers she had heard when she entered the church, thinking that Cavaradossi is deceiving her when he swears he was alone. Finally he manages to reassure her with a promise of a meeting that night at his villa. She is on the point of leaving when she recognizes the Marchesa Attavanti in the painting and once more before she leaves she shows her jealousy. Meanwhile Angelotti's escape has been discovered and a cannon is fired to raise the alarm. Cavaradossi decides to hide him in his villa outside the city and the two of them leave. The sacristan (bass) returns with the news of Napoleon's defeat. The church fills up for a Te Deum to be sung in thanksgiving. Scarpia (baritone), chief of police, enters. The discovery of a fan belonging to the Marchesa Attavanti and Cavaradossi's disappearance, as pointed out by the sacristan, persuade Scarpia that the painter, whom he knows as a Republican and Tosca's lover, is implicated in the escape. Tosca returns to alter the evening's arrangements and is surprised to find Cavaradossi no longer there. Scarpia suggests that the Marchesa's fan may explain his absence. Tosca

Girardon and Bréjean-Gravière in Massenet's Cinderella *at the Opéra-Comique in 1899. Bibliothèque de l'Opéra, Paris.*

leaves furiously for Cavaradossi's villa, where she expects to surprise him with the Marchesa, not noticing that she is followed by Spoletta (tenor), one of Scarpia's agents. During the Te Deum, Scarpia makes his plans – to send Cavaradossi to the gallows and to make Tosca his own. Act II. In his room at the Farnese Palace, Scarpia is eating supper. Through the open window sounds of a concert, in which Tosca is taking part, can be heard from another part of the palace. Cavaradossi is brought in, having been arrested by Spoletta. He denies that he is hiding Angelotti. Tosca enters, alarmed by the contents of a note she has received from Scarpia. Cavaradossi hardly has time to tell her to keep silent before he is led into the next room and tortured. Unable to stand his screams, she breaks down and reveals Angelotti's hiding place. Cavaradossi's outburst of anger at her betrayal is interrupted by news of Napoleon's unexpected victory at Marengo. His hymn to liberty ensures his execution, and he is led away under guard. Tosca prays (*'Vissi d'arte'*) and begs Scarpia to spare him; she is prepared to pay any price for his life. Spoletta returns to report that Angelotti has committed suicide, and when Scarpia demands Tosca as his mistress if she still wishes to save Cavaradossi, she nods her assent. Scarpia then appears to order a mock execution for Cavaradossi and signs a safe-conduct for Tosca and Cavaradossi. When he turns to embrace her, however, Tosca stabs him with a supper knife. She collects the safe-conduct from the dead man's fist, places two candles beside him and a crucifix on his breast. Act III. The battlements of Castel Sant'Angelo. At dawn Cavaradossi is brought from his cell. His last thoughts are for Tosca. (*'E lucean le stelle'* – When stars were brightly shining.) She appears unexpectedly and tells him that it will only be a

mock execution. They think of their future happiness together. The firing squad arrives and Tosca tells her lover to fall down as if dead. The shots are fired. When she runs over and lifts the cloak that the soldiers have thrown over his body, she finds that he is dead. Voices can be heard approaching. Scarpia's murder has been discovered and Spoletta and some soldiers rush in to arrest Tosca. She jumps onto the parapet and flings herself down with the cry, *'Oh Scarpia, avanti a Dio!* ('Scarpia, we will meet before God').

■ *Tosca* marks Puccini's incursion, on the one hand, into the field of verismo (insistence on realistic details, the quest for strong scenic effect, the emphasis on cruel or morbid aspects – one only needs think of Scarpia's motif) and, on the other hand, into the heroic and tragic dimension of grand opera: poles apart from the sentimental and intimate lyricism of *La Bohème*. The very rich musical invention (there are around sixty motifs, associated with situations and objects, running through the opera in a similar way to the Wagnerian *leit-motiv*) is forced to adapt itself to the rapid succession of events and an excited and disjointed dialogue. This adds to the dramatic power and it is not by chance that *Tosca* numbers amongst Puccini's most popular operas. The première took place in a highly tense and dramatic atmosphere. The hostility of certain artistic societies in Rome gave rise to the fear of disturbances and, a quarter of an hour before the singers went on stage, a voice – made plausible both by the disturbed political climate of the time and by the announcement of the Queen's presence – was heard to say that there would be an outrage during the performance. This probably had repercussions on the quality of the performance and it was received coolly and, in some cases, definitely unfavourably, by the critics. The reaction of the audience was very different. They declared it a resounding success and destined to survive.

LOUISE
Roman musical *in four acts and five scenes by Gustave Charpentier (1860–1956), libretto by the composer. First performance: Paris, Opéra-Comique (Salle Favart), 2 February 1900. First performance in U.K.: London, Covent Garden, 18 May 1909; in U.S.A.: New York, Manhattan Opera, 3 January 1908.*

ORIGINAL CAST. Marthe Rioton (Louise), Deschamps-Jéhin, Maréchal, Fugère. Conductor: André Messager.

SYNOPSIS. The action takes place in 'contemporary' Paris. Act I. A room in the attic of a poor tenement. Louise (soprano), the daughter of working-class people, is in love with Julien (tenor), a young, penniless poet. Louise's mother (contralto) catches them in conversation (she on the balcony of the house, he at the window of the attic where he lives) and quickly puts a stop to it, chastising her daughter for being in love with a Bohemian, a ne'er-do-well. Her father (baritone) agrees with his wife, but is more understanding and affectionate. Louise promises not to see Julien again. But as she is reading the newspaper to her father about spring in Paris she bursts into tears. Act II, Scene I. A street in Montmartre at dawn. The city is coming to life to the sounds of a slow orchestral prelude with the title 'Paris s'éveille'. People start to go about their business and the last noctambulist passes by, singing 'Je suis le plaisir de Paris', a symbol of carefree pleasure. Julien enters with a group of friends and hides when he sees Louise, who accompanies her mother on the way to work at the dressmaker's. As soon as her mother has gone, Julien goes over to her and tries to persuade her to come and live with him. Louise is torn between the desire to go with him and the affection that binds her to her father. Scene II. Inside the dressmaker's. Louise is preoccupied and does not take part in the chatter and singing of her companions. They tease her a little and then Julien's voice is heard outside serenading her. Louise feigns illness and goes out. Her companions watch her from the window going away with the young Bohemian. Act III. Louise and Julien are living in Montmartre. They call upon Paris to protect their love and their free and happy life. A group of Bohemians arrive, led by the leader of the fools (tenor), and in an absurd ceremony they crown Louise as the Muse of Montmartre. The jollity is interrupted by the arrival of Louise's mother, who begs her to return home just for

a little while. Her father became seriously ill after she left and is now dying and wants to see her. Louise is upset and, promising Julien she will return, follows her mother. Her mother assures him that she has no objection to this. Act IV. In the house of Louise's parents. Her father has now recovered, but he and his wife continue to keep Louise with them terrified of losing her again. She feels the call of Paris and desperately wants to return to the happy life she has left. She has a violent argument with her parents, who say that Julien has no intention of marrying her, but she refuses to be convinced. In the end the old man orders her from the house for ever. She escapes into the street while her father shakes his fist at the city that has taken from him what he held most dear.

■ In many ways the subject is similar to that of *La Bohème*, set to music by Puccini four years earlier, but the two operas have very little else in common. *Louise* is the most successful of the French naturalistic operas. It was an enormous success and became popular amongst all classes of Parisians. Its success is due to the fact that it brings together many different elements, among them musical simplicity, concrete realism, social awareness and the exaltation of peace and liberty, in a way that was pleasing to the anarchists. In many ways it was a daring piece of work: it was in fact very unusual to portray working-class people (workmen, dressmakers, street pedlars, etc.) in opera. On the stage the songs were often interspersed with trivial exclamations; the opera drew a very suggestive picture of Parisian life at the beginning of the century. All of this aroused a lively conflict between the hostility of the traditionalists and the enthusiasm of the forward-thinkers. The opera is also full of autobiographical references to the author's life in Montmartre and his socialist ideas. In particular the festivities in the third act are based on a similar occasion organized by Charpentier himself at Montmartre when a working-class woman was crowned Muse. All the music the composer had written for that occasion was incorporated in *Louise*. He later wrote the opera *Julien*, which was a continuation of Louise's story, but his success was not repeated.

The first act of Puccini's Tosca at Covent Garden, London, with Maria Callas. Produced by Franco Zeffirelli, sets by Renzo Mongiardino.

PROMÉTHÉE (Prometheus)
Tragédie lyrique *in three acts by Gabriel Fauré (1845–1924), libretto by 'Jean Lorrain', i.e. Paul Duval (1856–1906). Based on a previous treatment by Ferdinand Hérold (1791–1833). First performance: Béziers, the Arènes, 27 August 1900.*

ORIGINAL CAST. Edouard de Max (Prométhée), Cora Laparcerie (Pandore). Conductor: Charles Eustace.

SYNOPSIS. The classical myth is changed slightly by the introduction of a new character, Pandore, who loves the Titan Prométhée and tries to prevent him from taking the gift of fire to men. When Kratos, Bia and Héphaïstos chain him to the rock, she falls senseless to the ground and is presumed to be dead; she is laid in a cave and awakes to the sound of his lamentations. Hermès then offers her a casket full of the tears he sheds, a 'sweet burden' which, despite the protests of Prométhée, she bears away to earth.

■ This grandiose refurbishing of Aeschylus, Fauré's earliest stage-work, was given an open-air première in the bull-ring at Béziers. Anticipating a convention later adopted by Debussy, Stravinsky and others, Fauré introduces a mixture of sung and spoken passages. With chorus, corps-de-ballet, actors, singers and orchestral players (there were two orchestras of wind-instruments, and eighteen harps), the opera called for seven hundred performers in all and, although a rich patron, Castelbon de Beauxhostes, gave generous help, the difficulties of staging it were immense. The first performance was interrupted by a violent storm and it was postponed until the next day, when it was given before an audience of 10,000. The result was a triumph, repeated in the following year. In 1917 Roger Ducasse made a version suitable for production in a normal theatre. Prométhée is the most romantic and Wagnerian of Fauré's operas.

SKASKA O TZARE SALTANE (The Legend of Tsar Saltan; full title: The Legend of Tsar Saltan, of his son, the famous and mighty hero Prince Guidon Salanovich, and of the beautiful Swan Princess)

Fantastic opera in prologue, four acts and seven tableaux by Nicolay Rimsky-Korsakov (1844–1908), libretto by Vladimir Bielsky, after Pushkin (1832). First performance: Moscow, Solodovnikov Theatre, 3 November 1900. First performance in U.K.: London, Sadler's Wells, 11 October 1933; in U.S.A: New York, St James Theater, 27 December 1937.

SYNOPSIS. The Tsar Saltan (bass) chooses for his wife the youngest of three sisters, the beautiful Militrissa (soprano), who longs to give him a hero-son. The child, Guidon (2 mimes and a tenor), is born while the Tsar is on a campaign and Militrissa's elder sisters (soprano and mezzo-soprano) and their cousin Barbaricha (contralto), jealous of her fortune, take the opportunity to revenge themselves. They intercept a message from the Tsarina to her husband and send him news instead that she has given birth to a monster. The Tsar's reaction is terrible: mother and child are put in a barrel and flung into the sea. After many perils they reach a desert island. Guidon grows up to be a magician and saves the life of a swan, which in gratitude causes a marvellous city to spring out of the desolate land. Although he lives in luxury, the young hero is not happy. He wants to discover his father's identity and, with the aid of the swan, arrives secretly at Saltan's palace. The Tsar, hearing mariners' tales of the strange island, wishes to visit it, but he is dissuaded by the wicked sisters and Barbaricha, who have guessed the truth. When the swan turns into a princess (soprano), Guidon falls in love with her. He is acknowledged by

his father, while Militrissa forgives Saltan for his cruelty and even pleads for her sisters and Barbaricha.

■ *Tsar Saltan* is Rimsky-Korsakov's most symphonic opera and a masterpiece of fantasy. In the third act is the famous interlude known as 'The Flight of the Bumblebee'. The opera was composed during the summer of 1899, on the suggestion of Bielsky, to celebrate the centenary of Pushkin's birth.

ZAZÀ

Opera in four acts by Ruggiero Leoncavallo (1858–1919), libretto by the composer after a play by Charles Simon and Pierre Berton. First performance: Milan, Teatro Lirico, 10 November 1900. First performance in U.K.: London, Coronet Theatre, 30 April 1909; in U.S.A.: San Francisco, 27 November 1903.

ORIGINAL CAST. Rosina Storchio (Zazà), Eduardo Garbin, S. Samarco. Conductor: Ruggiero Leoncavallo.

SYNOPSIS. The action takes place in France, towards the end of the nineteenth century. Act I. Backstage at the Alcazar Theatre in Saint-Étienne. Zazà (soprano), a café singer, has had a triumphant success in music hall presented by the impresario Courtois (bass-baritone). She is the mistress of her stage partner Cascart (baritone). After the performance Bussy (baritone), a journalist, introduces a Parisian friend, Milio Dufresne (tenor), with whom she falls in love. He treats her coldly and tells Bussy he wishes to have nothing to do with theatre people – they are all light-minded, their acquaintance spells trouble. When she contrives to see him alone some evenings later he cannot resist her any longer. Act II. Zazà's house. For three months Dufresne has lived with Zazà, but has now told her that he must go to America for an indefinite stay. Cascart tells her that he has seen him with an elegant woman in Paris; he advises her to accept the fact and go back to the profitable career she had abandoned for this hazardous liaison. Maddened by rage and jealousy, she does not even listen, but sets off immediately for Paris. Act III. Dufresne's house. Milio, who has a wife (soprano) and small daughter, is very conscious of his duty to them. He knows that he must leave France altogether if he is to break off an affair that means so much to him. Scarcely have he and his wife left than Zazà is shown in, having passed herself off as a friend of Mme Dufresne. From a letter left open on a writing-table she suddenly realizes the true situation, and the discovery is made worse when Dufresne's daughter appears, friendly and excited. Knowing that she will never have the heart to destroy this family and ruin their happiness, Zazà leaves in despair. Act IV. Zazà's house. She has returned to Saint-Étienne, and although Courtois offers her an important contract, she refuses to go back to her work before seeing Milio once more. They meet, and the interview is stormy. Zazà tells him what she now knows and in the heat of their conversation provoked by his growing anger, pretends to have informed his wife of their love affair. In uncontrollable fury he heaps insults upon her, proclaiming his love for his wife and his disgust at a relationship founded on nothing but physical attraction. In the face of this, Zazà regains her dignity and assures him that his wife knows nothing; he can return to her without anxiety. Left alone, she gives way to grief and despair.

■ This was Leoncavallo's most successful opera, apart from *Pagliacci* and is often revived in Italy, especially as a vehicle for a singer with great dramatic gifts. Mafalda Favero was one of its foremost interpreters.

LE MASCHERE (The Masks)

Commedia lirica e giocosa *in three acts by Pietro Mascagni (1863–1945), libretto by Luigi Illica (1857–1919). Simultaneous first performances in six Italian cities: 17 January 1901. Conductor in Milan: Arturo Toscanini; in Rome: Pietro Mascagni.*

SYNOPSIS. Young Florindo is in love with Pantalone's daughter Rosaura, who returns his love but is intended by her father for Captain Spaventa. Brighella and Doctor Graziano's maid, Columbine, encourage the lovers and try to help. Brighella obtains for them a powder which, added to the wine, creates havoc among the guests at the wedding feast; everyone wanders about in a daze and the marriage-contract cannot be drawn up. Aided by Columbine and by Spaventa's

servant, Harlequin, the young couple attempt to postpone the wedding altogether. Harlequin promises to produce for them a portmanteau of documents compromising his master, which has, however, already fallen into the hands of Doctor Graziano who, with Brighella (disguised for the occasion as a policeman), denounces Spaventa as a cheat and a bigamist. At this, Pantalone surrenders and bestows his daughter on Florindo.

■ Mascagni was trying to 'go back to Cimarosa and Rossini' in this opera, and to create music that was 'easy, tuneful and light', to match the subject. It was favourably received in Rome, where he conducted it himself, especially at the second and subsequent performances, but failed in Milan, Turin, Genoa, Venice and Verona, where it was produced on the same night, partly, perhaps, because public expectations were too high after somewhat exaggerated advance publicity. However, its freshness and vitality, and the popular character of the score, led the critics to reconsider their verdict later.

RUSALKA

Operatic fairytale in three acts by Antonín Dvořák (1841–1904), libretto by Jaroslav Kvapil (1880–1940). First performance: Prague, National Opera House, 31 March 1901. First performance in U.K.: London, (John Lewis Musical Society), 9 May 1950; in U.S.A.: Chicago, 10 March 1935.

The second act of Puccini's Tosca *at La Scala in 1958, with Tito Gobbi and Renata Tebaldi in a production by Margherita Wallmann and designed by Nicola Benois.*

SYNOPSIS. Act I. On the shore of a lake, wood nymphs (two sopranos, contralto) sing and water nymphs dance to attract the attention of the Venerable Spirit of the Lake (bass). Rusalka (soprano), his favourite daughter, tells him, to his sorrow, that she wishes to marry a mortal prince (tenor). Unable to restrain her, he advises her to follow the instructions of the witch Ježibaba (mezzo-soprano). Nor can Ježibaba dissuade her, when she tells Rusalka that she will be unable to speak to the man she loves and if he proves faithless, she will wander by the lake forever in sadness, unless mortal blood is shed for her. Rusalka agrees to these conditions and helps her to cast the spell. She then sings to the moon of her great love for the Prince. He appears, drawn by some mysterious power, and falls in love with her, taking her away from the lakeside to his palace. Act II. Although the wedding festivities are beginning, the Prince is already bored with his silent bride, and favours a foreign Princess (soprano). A Forester (baritone) and a Kitchenboy (mezzo-soprano) discuss the turn of events. Despite the lament of the Spirit of the Lake, the Prince continues to flirt with the Princess and, as he passionately embraces her, Rusalka in a final frenzy of despair, throws herself between them. The Princess proudly withdraws and the Spirit of the Lake warns the Prince that he is now bound to Rusalka forever. Act III. Ježibaba reminds Rusalka that she may be saved from the curse if mortal blood is shed for her. She is resigned to her fate. The Forester and the Kitchen-boy beg the witch to release the Prince from her enchantment, but she frightens them away. Then the Prince, grief stricken, calls on Rusalka to forgive him. She rises from the waters and when he begs for death, allows him to kiss her, and their love is finally sealed as he dies in her arms.

■ Deriving from a popular fairytale, *Rusalka* was very successful with Slav audiences and is the best-known of the nine operas composed by Dvořák, still frequently performed in Czechoslovakia.

GRISÉLIDIS

Conte lyrique *in three acts and a prologue by Jules Massenet (1842–1912), libretto by Armand Silvestre (1837–1901) and Eugène Morand (1854–1928), based on the medieval legend. First performance: Paris, Opéra-Comique, 20 November 1901. First performance in U.S.A.: New York, 19 January 1910.*

ORIGINAL CAST. Lucienne Bréval (Grisélidis), Jeanne Tiphaine (Fiamina), Lucien Fugère (le Diable), Hector Dufranne (Marquis), Nicolas Maréchal (Alain). Conductor: André Messager.

SYNOPSIS. The Marquis de Saluce (baritone) has been called up for a crusade to the Holy Land and is forced to leave his son, Loys, and his beautiful, young wife, Grisélidis (soprano), behind. As he does not doubt her fidelity, he makes a bet with the Devil (bass-baritone) that the latter will not be able to impair her virtue. The Devil tries in vain to tempt her with a former suitor Alain (tenor) until he becomes so enraged about the bet that he kidnaps Loys. Disguised as a pirate, the Devil then invites Grisélidis aboard his ship to come and fetch the boy. At this point the Marquis returns and when the Devil refuses to return Loys, the desperate parents implore St Agnes, their protectress, for help. Whilst they are praying before her shrine, the triptych opens up and reveals the little boy, asleep at the Saint's feet.

■ The earliest known version of this romance occurs in *Le Fresne*, one of the *Lais* of the twelfth-century poetess, Marie de France. There is a version in Boccaccio's *Decameron* and Petrarch told the story in Latin, in which language it spread throughout Europe, Chaucer probably borrowing from him for the *Clerkes Tale* of 'pacient Grisilde'. From the musical point of view the opera, though by no means the best Massenet, has, besides a pleasing melodic line and a score well-suited to the text, a lyric quality that endows it with considerable charm.

FEUERSNOT (literally, 'fire-famine'; St John's Eve)

Singgedicht *in one act by Richard Strauss (1864–1949), libretto by Ernst von Wolzogen (1855–1934). First performance: Dresden, Königliches Opernhaus, 21 November 1901. First performance in U.K.: London, His Majesty's, 9 July 1910; in U.S.A.: Philadelphia (Metropolitan Opera), 1 December 1927.*

ORIGINAL CAST. Anny Krull (Diemut), Karl Scheidemantel (Kunrad). Conductor: Ernst van Schuch.

SYNOPSIS. It is St John's Eve, Midsummer, in Munich in the twelfth century. The children are collecting wood for the bonfires which traditionally mark the summer solstice. Diemut (soprano), the burgomaster's daughter, lets down a basketful on a rope from her balcony, then appears at the door. As she does so, Kunrad (baritone), a sorcerer and alchemist, emerges from the house opposite and, looking across at one another, they fall in love. He rushes over and kisses her on the mouth, to the stupefaction of the bystanders. When these have gone, he stays behind and begs her to admit him, but she, to punish him publicly for his impudence, invites him to get into the basket, pulls it half-way up and leaves him dangling. Everyone comes back to enjoy this spectacle but Kunrad utters magic words and all the fires in the town die out. With one leap, he then gains the balcony and harangues the crowd below. He reproaches them for failing to understand the irresistible, vital force of love and tells them that the 'dearth of fire' (i.e. *Feuersnot*) will continue until Diemut acknowledges it. They implore her to yield, which is what she wants to do in any case, and as he steps into her room the fires of St John are rekindled, while the townspeople rejoice at the lovers' union.

■ This opera when first seen created some sensation

for both the boldness of its subject and its many allusions to the difficult relations of Wagner and of Strauss himself with the public of Munich. (Diemut represents Munich, and the young sorcerer Strauss, Wagner being the master whose house and books he has inherited.) Musically, it is an odd medley of styles, influenced by Wagner and by contemporaries such as Mahler and Bruckner, while there are also foreshadowings of the composer's later and more considerable works.

LE JONGLEUR DE NOTRE-DAME (Our Lady's Juggler)

Miracle-play in three acts by Jules Massenet (1842–1912), libretto by Maurice Léna. First performance: Monte Carlo, Théâtre du Casino, 18 February 1902. First performance in U.K.: London, Covent Garden, 15 June 1906; in U.S.A.: New York, 27 November 1908.

ORIGINAL CAST. Nicolas Maréchal (Jean), Maurice Renaud (Boniface), Soulacroix (Le Prieur). Conductor: Léon Jéhin.

SYNOPSIS. The action is set in Cluny in the fourteenth century. Act I. It is market-day and Jean the juggler (tenor or soprano), about to go through his entertainment, sings the *Alleluia du vin* to attract the crowd. At this an angry Prior (bass) comes to the abbey door, and orders everyone to go away. Only Jean remains, crushed and confused. The Prior upbraids him for the blasphemous song, then, touched by his tears and his pleas for forgiveness, tells him the only way to gain the Virgin's pardon is to quit the juggling trade. Thinking about it, however, Jean prefers his freedom until Brother Boniface (baritone), the cook, shows him the comestibles he has bought and lets him help in preparing the monks' dinner, while the monks say grace and invite him to join them at table. Act II. In the abbey. Jean enjoys the free food and lodging of monastic life, but he envies the other monks' skills. After a canticle to the Virgin, the Prior, the poet-monk (tenor) and musician-monk (baritone) ask him to sing, but he refuses, because he knows no Latin songs and is ashamed that he can do nothing acceptable in honour of the Virgin. He proposes to leave, but they persuade him to stay and learn from them skills with which to praise his Creator. Brother Boniface convinces him that the Madonna welcomes everyone, even those as lowly and as ignorant of Latin as he is; their very lowliness endears them to her and she makes no difference between a juggler and a king: '*Fleurissait une rose*'. Jean sings a prayer to her as the curtain falls. Act III. The abbey chapel. The monks sing a hymn to the Madonna and file out; Jean, dressed in his habit, stays to ask if she will let him pay her homage with his juggling-tricks, in the only way he knows. He puts on his former costume and begins, unaware that he has been observed by the painter-monk (baritone) who thinks him mad and has gone to call the Prior. They return with Boniface, who restrains the Prior from interrupting Jean. As the monks argue fiercely about

humility and the propriety of Jean's behaviour a miracle occurs: the statue of the Madonna blesses Jean and smiles; a heavenly choir is heard singing in his praise. The brothers stand astonished and Jean, unaware of any miracle, apologizes to the Prior for his improvised performance. Then a halo shines about his head and he dies in the arms of the monks.

■ *Le jongleur de Notre-Dame*, although a minor opera, is an excellent example of the composer's art. It has all his usual melodic and lyric charm, even if the subject-matter is bizarre. The lyric and elegiac aspect of the score expresses, in fact, a pervading religious feeling rather than the actual drama and it is precisely because of this dissimilarity to his usual work that Massenet's *Jongleur* continues to appeal to modern audiences.

GERMANIA

Opera in a prologue, two acts and an epilogue, by Alberto Franchetti (1860–1942), libretto by Luigi Illica (1857–1919). First performance: Milan, Teatro alla Scala, 11 March 1902. First performance in U.K.: London, Covent Garden, 13 November 1907; in U.S.A.: New York, 22 January 1910.

ORIGINAL CAST. Enrico Caruso, Mario Sammarco, Amelia Pinto, Jean Bathory. Conductor: Arturo Toscanini.

SYNOPSIS. Prologue. This is set in an old mill where students who oppose the occupation of Germany, and her submission to Napoleon, run a clandestine printing-press. Ricke (soprano) is without news of her brother or her fiancé, Federico (tenor), but Carlo Worms (baritone) receives a letter saying Federico will soon be back and announcing the foundation of the patriotic student-union, the Tugendbund. Carlo has in fact betrayed his friend Federico by seducing Ricke, but she has repented, hates herself and is resolved to tell Federico everything until Carlo persuades her not to do so – their friendship will be ruined and a fatal duel would leave one less to fight for their country. Federico now arrives with tidings of Ricke's brother's death. There follows a general alert and the police arrive. Act I. A hut in the Black Forest, where Federico and Ricke are married by a Protestant pastor (bass). The students have scattered after their unsuccessful campaign against the French and Carlo appears, gaunt and weary, having escaped from the enemy. Learning that their wedding has just been celebrated, he insists on setting out again immediately, without staying to rest. Federico arranges to meet him in Königsberg, but when he goes out to set him on the road, Ricke, torn by remorse, decides that she cannot, after all, hide the truth. She scribbles a note and runs away. Federico returns and, by questioning her sister Jane (mezzo-soprano), discovers what has happened. Act II. The cellars of a secret society in Königsberg. Names are taken, signs exchanged, oaths sworn and reports made; many of the members are masked. Carlo is accused of dishonourable behaviour by one of those present, and when both remove their masks his accuser is revealed as Federico. He does not attempt to excuse himself: death in action will be his expiation. Epilogue. The plain of Leipzig after the battle. Ricke searches for Federico on the field and finds him dying. He asks who has won and then, on hearing the word 'Germany', he recognizes her. He tells her to forgive Carlo and to find his body. This she does, and covers him with the flag he had been clutching to his breast. She then returns to Federico, who dies in her arms, content in the victory.

■ The taste for resounding orchestral and spectacular stage effects betrays a German influence. Though of thoroughly romantic inspiration, there are touches of naturalism in this opera that link its composer with the new realist Italian school, and it was well received on its first appearance.

LOS AMORES DE LA INES (The Loves of Ines)
Zarzuela, or musical play, by Manuel de Falla (1876–1946), libretto by Emilio Dugi. First performance: Madrid, Teatro Comico, 12 April 1902.

■ One of the five zarzuelas written by Falla in collaboration with Amadeo Vives, a composer who specialized in this typically Spanish form of comedy with music. Ines was the only one to reach the stage, though fragments of another, La casa de Tocarme Roque (The Ramshackle House), were used as a basis for The Three-Cornered Hat.

PELLÉAS ET MÉLISANDE
Opera in five acts by Claude Debussy (1862–1918), on a text based on the play (1892) by Maurice Maeterlinck. First performance: Paris, Opéra-Comique, 30 April 1902. First performance in U.K.: London, Covent Garden, 21 May 1909; in U.S.A.: New York, 19 February 1908.

ORIGINAL CAST. Mary Garden (Mélisande), Gerville-Reache (Geneviève), Jean Perier (Pelléas), Hector Dufranne (Golaud), Felix Vieuille (Arkel), Viguié (the doctor), C. Blondin (Yniold). Conductor: André Messager.

SYNOPSIS. The action takes place in an imaginary period, in the imaginary kingdom of Allemonde. Act I, Scene I. Golaud (baritone), King Arkel's grandson, while hunting wild boar in the forest, finds a mysterious and lovely girl (soprano) weeping beside a well. She appears to remember nothing, but finally tells him her name, Mélisande. She agrees to accompany him and to marry him. Scene II. A room in King Arkel's castle. Geneviève (contralto), mother of the half-brothers Golaud and Pelléas (tenor), reads to the almost blind king (bass) a letter in which Golaud asks permission to bring home his bride, Mélisande. He will arrive in three days' time and look for a lamp to be lit on top of the tower to assure him that she is welcome. Arkel agrees, for Golaud is a widower with a small son, Yniold

Lithograph poster by Georges Rochegrosse for Charpentier's Louise at the Opéra-Comique, 1900. Paris, Bibliothèque de l'Opéra.

(soprano), and should remarry. Scene III. A stormy evening before the castle. Pelléas greets his brother and sister-in-law and Golaud asks him to accompany Mélisande while he goes to find his son. When Pélleas announces that he is leaving on the next day, the news makes her sad. Act II, Scene I. The park of the castle. Pelléas and Mélisande walk to an old fountain whose waters are said to cure the blind. Ignoring his warning, she plays with her wedding ring and it slips from her hand into the fountain. Scene II. A room in the castle. Golaud has had a fall while hunting and lies in bed wounded, tended by Mélisande. She complains of a feeling of foreboding and when he takes her hands to comfort her he notices that she no longer wears the ring. In explanation she tells him that she lost it in a cave on the seashore and he insists that she looks for it at once, taking Pelléas for protection, as it is night. Scene III. The cave. In the moonlight, three old beggars are lying on the ground. 'Do not let us wake them', says Pelléas, 'for they are sound asleep', but Mélisande hurries out very frightened. Act III, Scene I. The castle tower. Mélisande has let down her long hair and is singing at the window. Wonderstruck, Pelléas draws near to speak to her. As she leans out to give him her hand he is engulfed in her hair. They are surprised by Golaud, who reproves their childishness. Scene II. The vault beneath the castle. Golaud shows his brother the sinister and gloomy halls hewn out of the rock below the castle. They leave the place quickly. Scene III. Outside the vault. Golaud tells Pelléas he must avoid the company of Mélisande. Scene IV. Before the castle. Golaud, devoured with jealousy, forces himself to ask Yniold how Mélisande behaves with Pelléas when they are alone together. He lifts the child up to a window to watch them in the room. They are sitting without exchanging a word, the child reports, then, frightened, he bursts into tears. Act IV, Scene I. A corridor in the castle. Pelléas has made up his mind to leave and begs Mélisande for a last meeting at the fountain. They are discovered by an enraged Golaud, who drags Mélisande by her hair along the ground and, with no explanation, offers her violent insults. The old king, who is present, thinks Golaud must be drunk, but his protests go unheeded. Scene II. By the fountain. Yniold comes looking for a golden ball he has dropped and when he goes out the lovers appear, as if by previous agreement. They confess their love and embrace for the first and last time. Golaud has been spying on them from the shadows and now leaps forward, runs a sword through his brother and pursues his terrified wife. Act V. A room in the castle. The frail and youthful Mélisande is dying after the birth of a daughter. Desperate with grief, Golaud is nevertheless impelled to ask whether she betrayed him, with Pelléas; but she seems not to understand him, gazes sorrowfully at their child and dies without replying, as Arkel urges that she should be left in peace: 'the human soul is a very silent thing'.

■ Debussy's only opera, *Pelléas* is also his masterpiece. Maeterlinck's play had at last given the composer the text he was looking for, and he sketched out some of the characters in musical terms when it was first produced in 1892. Its symbolism echoed his own tastes, formed by the poetry of Verlaine and in the circle of Mallarmé, and he made of it something more like impressionism, or at least more expressive of impressionist values. He took eight years over the writing, from 1893 to 1901, and when it was finished the director of the Opéra-Comique, Albert Carré, was alarmed by the novelty of the language and the dramatic structure as a whole. His resident conductor, André Messager, appreciated its qualities and ensured its production; to him and to Georges Hartmann, the work is gratefully dedicated. The première was a tense occasion, for Maeterlinck had quarrelled both with Debussy and with the theatre because Mary Garden had been engaged to sing Mélisande instead of his wife, Georgette Leblanc. (He never saw a performance until 27 January 1920, in New York.) Excellent as was the cast on this first occasion, the novel style of the music outraged the audience. *Pelléas* was a failure, laughed at and hissed in the theatre and savaged in the press. But students and young composers such as Ravel, Dukas and Satie supported it wholeheartedly, as did Pierre Lalo, the influential critic of *Le Temps*. Their open championship, and Messager's firm stand, kept the opera on for fourteen nights and gradually the hostility died down. In other countries, too, it gave rise to impassioned and diverse dispute before its eventual enthronement among the accepted master-works. The difficulties it encountered seriously discouraged Debussy, and he never composed for the stage again.

ADRIANA LECOUVREUR
Opera in four acts by Francesco Cilea (1866–1950), libretto by Arturo Colautti (1851–1914), from the play (1849) by Eugenè Scribe and Ernest Legouvé. First performance: Milan, Teatro Lirico, 26 November 1902. First performance in U.K.: London, Covent Garden, 8 November 1904; in U.S.A.: New Orleans, 5 January 1907.

ORIGINAL CAST. Angelica Pandolfini, Edvige Ghibaudo, Enrico Caruso, Giuseppe De Luca, Sottalana, Giordani. Conductor: Cleofonte Campanini.

SYNOPSIS. The action is set in Paris in 1730. Act I. The greenroom of the Comédie-Française. The curtain is about to go up on a performance of Racine's *Bajazet* and Michonnet (baritone), the stage-director, is busy helping everyone with last-minute preparations. The Prince de Bouillon (bass), lover of the famous actress Mlle Duclos, comes in with Abate di Chazeuil (tenor).

Memento issued for the première of Mascagni's Le Maschere. *Ricordi Archives, Milan.*

Růžena Maturová in the title role and Bohumil Pták as the Prince in Dvořák's Rusalka *at the Czech National Theatre, Prague, 1901. Dvořák Museum, Prague.*

Václav Kliment as Vodnik the Spirit of the Lake in Rusalka, *Czech National Theatre, Prague, 1901. Dvořák Museum, Prague.*

Adriana (soprano) appears, in costume and trying over a speech. Michonnet then remains alone with Adriana and is about to confess his love for her, but she, unaware of it, confides her own love for an officer in the suite of Maurizio, Count of Saxony (tenor). This officer is, unknown to her, the Count himself, who now enters and professes his love for her. She gives him a bunch of violets. The Prince has intercepted a message which he supposes to have been written by his mistress, Mlle Duclos, in which she invites the Count of Saxony to a rendezvous at her villa, a villa which the Prince himself lent her. Out of spite, he invites the actors to sup there after the play. What he does not know is that the note was actually from his wife, who has for some time been receiving her own friends in this way. The Count accepts his invitation, which mentions 'a matter of politics', thinking of his claim to the throne of Poland. The Prince also invites Adriana and gives her a key to the villa so that she may come and go as she pleases. Act II. A room in the villa. The Princesse de Bouillon (mezzo-soprano) is waiting for Maurizio, with whom she is in love. He arrives, still thinking only of Poland, but as they talk she suspects that he is interested in another woman; to placate her he offers her the violets which Adriana had given him. When the Prince and his guests appear she hides in an adjoining room. Adriana discovers Maurizio's identity and agrees to help the lady whose name he does not disclose to escape by extinguishing the lights and giving her key to the Princesse, but, although neither sees the other properly, their exchanges reveal the fact that both of them love Maurizio of Saxony. Act III. A reception at the palace of the Prince de Bouillon. The Princesse welcomes the guests, hoping to pick out her

rival and, hearing Adriana's voice, tests her by saying that Maurizio has been wounded in a duel. The reaction to this confirms her suspicion that this is indeed the woman who helped her escape from the villa, and when Maurizio shortly afterwards appears, safe and sound, Adriana realizes, in her turn, that it must have been the Princesse who was there. After a ballet-entertainment there ensues a battle of words between the two, with the Princesse making pointed allusions to the Count's new friend and the actress showing the company a bracelet dropped by a 'society lady' in flight from a secret rendezvous. The Prince recognizes the bracelet as belonging to his wife who, in the general consternation, insolently presses Adriana to recite. She chooses the great speech from Racine's *Phèdre*, its culminating invective delivered straight to the Princesse herself. Act IV. Adriana's house. It is her birthday and friends come to offer their congratulations. A box arrives, as she thinks, from Maurizio, for it contains the violets, now faded. They were in fact sent by the Princesse, who has sprinkled them with poison. Adriana smells them and is at once taken ill. When Maurizio enters with the glad news that his claim to the Polish throne has been recognized, he asks her to marry him. Her happiness is short indeed; she becomes delirious and dies in his arms.

■ The French actress Adrienne Lecouvreur lived from 1692 to 1730 and was famous for her rôles in the plays of Corneille and Racine, and for her friendship with Voltaire. Cilea had already known success with his *L'Arlesiana*, and *Adriana*, too, had a favourable reception and soon became popular abroad. When performances grew less frequent he decided to revise and pare down the score and in this final version it was seen at the San Carlo in Naples in 1930, gaining new and definitive acceptance. It is widely regarded as his masterpiece.

L'ÉTRANGER (The Stranger)
Opera in two acts by Vincent d'Indy (1851–1931), libretto by the composer. First performance: Brussels, Théâtre de la Monnaie, 7 January 1903.

SYNOPSIS. The Stranger is a man who has sacrificed every affection to his own ideal, not understanding that human effort means nothing if it arises from mere egoism. He sails for ever on the sea, which he controls by means of an emerald that had once belonged to the Apostle Paul. Madeleine, the girl he loves, is puzzled by his apparently cold and insensitive attitude. She tries to make him jealous, and persuades him to reveal the secret of the emerald. Thus, however, its power is lost to him, and when she hurls it into the sea a great tempest blows up and capsizes the ship. No one dares to come to their aid. Bravely they face the storm, but sink beneath the waves.

■ There are echoes of Wagner in *L'Etranger*, the symbolism and mystery of *The Flying Dutchman*, and the romantic mysticism of *Lohengrin*. D'Indy may also have been thinking of Ibsen's *Brand*. Yet the music is not essentially affected by the ethical and psychological problems inherent in the plot, and the best passages occur in the second act, when he gives his creative faculty full play. Debussy disliked the work intensely, and called it 'a splendid lesson for believers in that crude foreign aesthetic that consists in the smothering of music under a mountain of realism'.

TIEFLAND (The Lowlands)
Opera in a prologue and two acts by Eugen d'Albert (1864–1932), libretto by Rudolf Lothar, based on the Catalan play Terra Baixa *(1896), by 'Angel Guimera'. First performance: Prague, Neues Deutsches Theater, 15 November 1903. First performance in U.K.: London, Covent Garden, 5 October 1910; in U.S.A.: New York, Metropolitan Opera House, 23 November 1908.*

SYNOPSIS. Pedro (tenor) is a simple shepherd for whom the world is a matter of good and evil, sheep and wolf. It is evil that overcomes him on his mountain as he sets a trap for the wolf which threatens his flock. The lowland man, Sebastiano (baritone), egotistic and domineering, has estates that extend as far as the eye can see and controls the very thoughts of all who work for him. He has a mistress, Marta (soprano), whom he once found starving by the roadside and later forced to yield to him; and he decides that Pedro is to marry her. As the wife of a poor shepherd she will be permanently and easily available to him, with no gossip to hinder his own marriage to a rich heiress. Marta, however, is deeply unhappy, constantly mocked by the other women and when Pedro learns the truth he kills Sebastiano as he would have killed the wolf. He then returns with his sheep to the mountains, and Marta, who wants to forget her sad and squalid past, goes with him.

■ This is the most popular and successful of d'Albert's operas and the only one to show marked German influence.

DIE NEUGIERIGEN FRAUEN (The Inquisitive Ladies)
Opera buffa in three acts by Ermanno Wolf-Ferrari (1876–1948), libretto by H. Teibler, translated from Italian text by Luigi Sugano based on the play Le Donne Curiose *by Goldoni (1707–93). First performance: Munich, Residenztheater, 27 November 1903. First performance in U.S.A.: New York, Metropolitan Opera House, 3 January 1912 (for the first time in Italian).*

ORIGINAL CAST. Paul Bender, Huhn, Tordek, Koppe, Friedrich Brodersen, Hermine Bosetti, Hans Breuer, George Sieglitz, conducted by the composer.

SYNOPSIS. A group of Venetian gentlemen have rented a house in which to meet safe from intrusion by their wives. The wives, however, wonder whether the men are not spending the time with other women.

Mary Garden, the original Mélisande, in Debussy's Pelléas et Mélisande.

Lithograph poster by Georges Rochegrosse for the first production of Debussy's Pelléas et Mélisande *at the Opéra-Comique, 1902.*

Colombina (soprano) manages to wheedle the address out of Florindo (tenor), and then to steal the key from Ottavio (bass). She and Beatrice (mezzo-soprano) try to gain admission, but Pantalone (bass-buffo) bars their way. Florindo and Ottavio arrive with a masked lady, whom Florindo recognizes as Rosaura, his betrothed. He gives her a terrible scolding for her lack of trust. The ladies then persuade Arlecchino (bass-buffo) to let them look in through the windows. Nothing is going on but an all-male supper-party, which they invade, with apologies. The men are furious at first, then calm down and everyone joins a light-hearted dance in honour of Florindo and Rosaura.

■ If the music of his first opera, *Cenerentola*, had perhaps overwhelmed the text, Wolf-Ferrari here keeps strictly to what suits Goldoni's dialogue, with a minimum of orchestral comment, that allows an unforced working-out of the plot. *Le donne curiose* was first heard in Munich, where the composer – Venetian-born, like Goldoni himself – was finishing his studies under Josef Rheinberger.

LE ROI ARTHUS (King Arthur)

Opera in three acts by Ernest Chausson (1855–99), libretto by the composer. First (posthumous) performance: Brussels, Théâtre de la Monnaie, 30 November 1903.

■ The only one of Chausson's operas ever to reach the stage. A projected production at Karlsruhe in 1900, though cited by some authorities, did not materialize. As in many of this composer's works, the text is based on a medieval legend.

SIBERIA

Opera in three acts by Umberto Giordano (1867–1948), libretto – originally entitled La donna, l'amante, l'eroina *(Woman, Courtesan, Heroine) – by Luigi Illica. First performance: Milan, Teatro alla Scala, 19 December 1903. First performance in U.S.A.: New Orleans, 13 January 1906 (in French).*

ORIGINAL CAST. Giovanni Zenatello, Rosina Storchio, Giuseppe De Luca, Antonio Pini-Corsi. Conductor: Cleofonte Campanini.

SYNOPSIS. Act I. The luxurious house given by Prince Alexis (tenor) to the courtesan Stephana (soprano). Dawn is breaking, but Stephana has not yet come home. Gléby, her lover and 'manager' (baritone), arrives to discuss business – of which the profits are largely his – and though the old servant Nikona (mezzo-soprano) swears she is ill in bed, he soon discovers the truth. Then Prince Alexis and some of his friends appear, wanting to play baccarat, and wait for Stephana. When she does eventually arrive, she slips into the house by a side door but is recognized by Vassili (tenor), Nikona's godson and a cavalry officer, who has fallen in love with her without knowing who she was – she told him she was a seamstress. She begs him to leave and forget her but they are exposed by the Prince, who heaps insults upon her: the two men fight and Alexis falls wounded. Act II. The frontier, with a column of prisoners crossing into Siberia. Stephana drives up in a sledge, produces a permit and asks to speak to convict number 107 – Vassili, sentenced for having wounded the Prince. She tells him she will follow him, abandoning the city and her way of life; having found love, she is resolved to find redemption too. Act III. The prison at the Transbaikal mines. Gléby has also been sent to Siberia and, at his own request, to this particular camp, where he can find Stephana. She refuses to escape with him through a disused well. While the prisoners celebrate Easter he tells everyone how he launched her on a prostitute's career. Stephana restrains Vassili from attacking him until she can endure it no longer and reveals what a greedy lying cheat of a 'manager' he was. The lovers attempt the escape, but Gléby sees them going into the well-shaft and raises the alarm. Stephana is shot and dies, declaring her love for Vassili.

■ A very successful work, especially in Italy, and with it Giordano also entered the regular repertoire of the Paris Opéra, the first Italian to do so since Verdi in

1870. A revised version was seen at La Scala on 5 December 1927.

JENŮFA (Její pastorkyňa) (Her Stepdaughter)

Opera in three acts by Leoš Janáček (1854–1928), libretto by the composer, after a story by Gabriela Preissová. First performance: Brno, Deutsches National-theater, 21 January 1904. First performance in U.K.: London, Covent Garden, 10 December 1956; in U.S.A.: New York, Metropolitan Opera House, 6 December 1924 (in German).

ORIGINAL CAST. Maria Kabeláčová, Leopolda Svobodová, Staněk-Doubravský.

SYNOPSIS. Act I. The mill belonging to Grandmother Buryja (contralto), a hot afternoon in summer. Her granddaughter Jenůfa (soprano) anxiously awaits the return of her cousin Števa (tenor), whom she loves and whose child she is carrying. He has had to go to the recruiting-office and she prays inwardly that they can be married, shuddering to think of her disgrace if he has joined the army and is unable to set matters right. Her grandmother scolds her for not doing her share of the work properly and Laca, Števa's stepbrother (tenor), shows that he is jealous of him. The old mill-foreman (baritone) enters, announcing that Števa has not been enlisted, then Števa himself appears, drunk, with some of his friends. He treats Jenůfa with scant courtesy, showing her a bunch of flowers given him by another girl and making her join him in a wild dance, which is interrupted by her stepmother, Kostelnička (soprano). She, ignorant of the implications, forbids any marriage until Števa has passed a year without drinking. Left alone with him, Jenůfa makes him swear to keep his promises, and he praises her delicate pink cheeks, but cannot convince her that he loves her. When he can no longer stand up and lurches off, Laca approaches and taunts her that Števa loves her only for her soft cheeks. His declarations of love are brusquely refused and he slashes her face with a knife. Realizing what he has done, he is horrified. Act II. A room in Kostelnička's house. Jenůfa's child has been born and her stepmother, whose pride and love for Jenůfa have been severely shaken, has kept her hidden indoors, telling people she has gone to Vienna to work as a maid. Now she has asked Števa to come and discuss things, but the interview is fruitless – he finally admits that he is engaged to marry the mayor's daughter, Karolka (mezzo-soprano). He promises only to keep the baby financially secure. When Laca arrives, delighted to find that Jenůfa has returned, Kostelnička tells him what has happened and foresees that he will not marry Jenůfa if he must also bring up Števa's son. So she tells him the baby is dead. While Jenůfa sleeps (Kostelnička gave her a narcotic drink), she takes the child away and explains on her return that Jenůfa was

Setting by Henry Moore for a production of Débussy's Pelléas et Mélisande *at Spoleto.*

delirious for two days and during that time the baby has died and been buried. Laca greets Jenůfa and she is much touched by his affection; yet a blast of icy wind blows upon the windows, which Kostelnička interprets as an omen. Act III. In the house. As Jenůfa and Laca prepare for their wedding her stepmother is a prey to remorse, and uneasy that the mayor and his wife, with Števa and Karolka, should be present; she seems to expect disaster. Indeed, just as she raises her hands to bless the bride and groom, a cry is heard – a child has been found under the newly melted ice. Jenůfa recognizes her dead baby, is accused of murder and with difficulty Laca saves her from the violence of the assembled guests. Then Kostelnička admits her guilt and makes as if to kill herself until she realizes that she must remain alive as a witness to Jenůfa's innocence and the mayor takes her into custody. Jenůfa, although horrified, forgives her on account of her motives and tries to send Laca away. When he refuses to leave her, his devotion shows her at last the depth of love.

■ *Jenůfa* is a turning-point in Janáček's career, marking the moment when, after experience in choral composition and earlier operatic works, he shakes off the German influence, conquers the confines of folk-lore and creates an entirely original idiom. The characteristically Czech, or Moravian, plot lends itself to innovation, including experiments in language: Janáček pays a great deal of attention to popular speech as well as melody, 'emphasizing the spoken and musical sense of the voices, the rhythm and spacing of phrases'. When the score was submitted to the Czech National Theatre early in 1903 it was criticized as 'lacking unity of styles', as 'striving after novelty' and being 'too primitive and atavistic'. After a triumphant première at Brno it was not performed again until 1916, when the doubts of the Prague Conservatoire, wedded as it was to tradition and disapproving Janáček's efforts to emerge from Wagner's shadow and establish a Slav musical world, were powerless to prevent its complete success. This was repeated two years later in Vienna and subsequently all over Europe, so that Janáček not only enjoyed international fame, but was also hailed as the leading composer in his own country.

MADAMA BUTTERFLY

Opera in three acts (originally two) by Giacomo Puccini (1858–1924), libretto by Giuseppe Giacosa (1847–1906) and Luigi Illica (1857–1919), based on David Belasco's play (1900) from a story by John Luther Long. First performance: Milan, Teatro alla Scala, 17 February 1904. First performance in U.K.: London, Covent Garden, 10 July 1905; in U.S.A.: Washington, 15 October 1906 (in English version by R. H. Elkin).

ORIGINAL CAST. Rosina Storchio, Giovanni Zenatello, Giuseppe De Luca. Conductor: Cleofonte Campanini.

SYNOPSIS. The action takes place in Nagasaki. Act I. Outside a house on the hill above the harbour. A Japanese wedding is to be celebrated between a Lieutenant in the U.S. Navy, Pinkerton (tenor) and the geisha Cio-Cio-San, Madam Butterfly (soprano). The house, with its sliding screens, is displayed by the marriage-broker, Goro (tenor), to the groom who, when the American consul Sharpless (baritone) arrives, makes it clear that he does not take the marriage seriously; for him, it is something to be forgotten when he tires of it. Sharpless warns him that Butterfly has taken the irreversible decision of renouncing her religion, unknown to her family. Butterfly enters with her friends and relations. The ceremony is held, but her uncle the Bonze, a Japanese priest (bass), denounces Butterfly for having deserted the religion of her ancestors. The guests are horrified and Pinkerton angrily drives them away and comforts the weeping Butterfly in a tender love-duet. Act II. Butterfly's house. Three years have passed since Pinkerton's departure. He promised to return 'when the robins nest' and still she waits patiently. Sharpless comes to read her a letter in which Pinkerton announces his marriage to an American wife, asking the Consul to tell Butterfly. Before he can do so, however, Goro appears with Prince Yamadori (baritone), a rich suitor who would like to marry Butterfly. Nothing Goro nor Sharpless can do will stop her refusing Yamadori scornfully, pointing out that her marriage is governed by U.S. law, and cannot be dissolved when the parties feel like it. Sharpless tries again to break the terrible news to her but she stops him excitedly when he suggests that her husband has forgotten her. She refuses to believe this and Sharpless eventually leaves. At that moment the harbour cannon is heard announcing the arrival of Pinkerton's ship. Butterfly and Suzuki, her maid (mezzo-soprano), in an ecstasy of happiness, decorate the house with petals before settling down to wait for Pinkerton to climb the hill. Act III. The dawn comes, but there is no sign of him. Sadly Suzuki persuades Butterfly to rest. The Consul appears and Suzuki learns that Pinkerton has brought his American wife Kate (mezzo-soprano) with him. Pinkerton, seeing in the house every sign of fidelity, realizes how badly he has behaved and in despair finds himself unable to face the woman he has so deeply wronged. When he has run down the hill, Butterfly appears, asks who the American lady is, and discovers the truth for herself. She wishes Kate every happiness and agrees to give up the child if Pinkerton will come himself in half an hour, to collect him. Alone, she contemplates her father's ceremonial hara-kiri dagger, which is inscribed 'Death with honour is better than life without honour', and kills herself. She crawls over to the child as her last strength ebbs away and Pinkerton finds them thus when he arrives a moment later.

■ *Butterfly* was Puccini's favourite among his own operas, his 'most deeply felt and imaginative invention'. It showed a return to psychological and intimate drama, to carefully observed motivation and the poetry of small, everyday things. The technical level,

Caricature by Enrico Caruso of himself as Maurizio and Lina Cavalieri in the title role of Cilea's Adriana Lecouvreur.

compared with that of *La Bohème*, is high, especially in its flowing melody, harmony and orchestral texture. There is more control in the use of *leitmotiv*, never pedantically attached to mere externals, but serving always to express meaning. Puccini, devoted to the subject and his heroine, immersed himself enthusiastically in the popular music of the life and religion of Japan, going so far as to learn the actual timbre of the Japanese female voice from the actress Sada Jacco, who was then touring in Europe. All this bore fruit. The exotic feeling that pervades much of the work miraculously escapes all the trace of affectation and perfectly matches the music. Authentic Japanese melodies, the employment of the pentatonic scale and some touches of instrumental exoticism, blend in a score that is pure Puccini. The action centres entirely on Butterfly herself, and on her tragic progress from initial happiness at the wedding, through the threat of isolation contained in the Bonze's curse and the theme of her father's dagger, to the dreamy ecstasy that opens the second act '*Un bel dí*': ('*One fine day*'), then the hopeless sorrow of '*Che tua madre*': ('*That your mother should take you on her shoulder*'), which she sings to her child, and the last farewell, '*Tu, tu piccolo iddio*' ('*Beloved idol*'), the most poignant moment of the opera. Pinkerton remains a contradictory character. His conduct is despicable yet, whether to justify Butterfly's affection or because of Puccini's own feeling for her, the first-act aria '*Viene la sera*' ('*Evening is falling*'), shows him in a romantic light, as does the later, anguished aria '*Addio, fiorito asil*' ('*Farewell, happy home*'). The rest of the cast, however, are little more than sketchily drawn. The first and only performance

of the original version, in two long acts with some over-emphasized and irrelevant detail, was shouted down by a hostile house at La Scala – a fiasco perhaps less owing to these faults, which were minor and easily remedied, than to organized demonstrations by opponents of Puccini. On 28 March 1904, in a new version at the Teatro Grande in Brescia, the curtain was dropped between Butterfly's vigil and the coming of dawn, thus dividing a lengthy act and refreshing the spectator. Puccini disliked the expedient, which in fact disrupts the continuity but the work has been given in three parts ever since. The huge success before the largely Milanese audience at Brescia was soon repeated in every major opera house in the world.

KOANGA

Opera in three acts by Frederick Delius (1862–1934), English libretto – later translated into German by the composer or his wife – by Charles Francis Keary from The Grandissimes *(1880), a novel by George Washington Cable. First performance: Elberfeld, Stadttheater, 30 March 1904. First performance in U.K.: London, Covent Garden, 23 September 1935 (in English).*

SYNOPSIS. The scene is a plantation on the Mississippi. Palmyra, a mulatto woman, spurns the overseer Simon Perez and loves Koanga, who is a prince in her own tribe. They cannot marry without the consent of the plantation-owner, Don José Martinez. This is given, but Perez abducts Palmyra during the wedding festivities and Koanga, after angry words with his master, runs away into the forest. Here he consults a voodoo witchdoctor and invokes plague on his oppressors. He finds Palmyra in time to save her from Perez and the two men kill each other. Seizing Koanga's dagger, she then kills herself.

■ The opera was not seen in the original English version until presented at Covent Garden. It was composed during the composer's residence on the Left Bank in Paris, in 1897.

RISURREZIONE (Resurrection)

Opera in four acts by Franco Alfano (1876–1956), libretto by Cesare Hanau, based on Tolstoy's novel. First performance: Turin, Teatro Vittorio Emanuele II, 30 November 1904. First performance in U.S.A.: Chicago, 31 December 1925.

ORIGINAL CAST. Elvira Magliulo, Angelo Scandiani, Mieli, Ceresoli. Conductor: Tullio Serafin.

SYNOPSIS. The action is set in Russia and Siberia, in the nineteenth century. Act I. In the country. Prince Dmitri Ivanovich Nekliudov (tenor), about to leave for the war, comes to take leave of his aunt Sofia Ivanovna (mezzo-soprano), whose attendant companion is Katiusha (soprano), his childhood playmate. He falls in love with her and they spend the night together

Costume-design (1953) by Jean-Denis Malclès for Adriana in Cilea's Adriana Lecouvreur.

since the subject appealed to him profoundly he at once commissioned Cesare Hanau, together with C. Antona Traversi, to prepare a libretto, and set to work on the music. He finished the first two acts in Paris within the year, the third in Berlin and the fourth in Russia, adding the finale in Naples in 1904. The première in Turin was a complete success, and the work was given in Europe and America with such singers as Mary Garden and Cervi Cairoli. The thousandth performance was celebrated at Naples in 1951. Though the accepted critical view is that the composer here ranges himself definitively with the Italian 'realists' – Puccini, Mascagni and Giordano – there are in fact indications of his future development in other directions: the extension of self-contained themes, for instance, and the presence of solo instrumental passages. *Risurrezione* is regarded as a youthful work, but also as Alfano's masterpiece.

AMICA
Dramma lirico in two acts by Pietro Mascagni (1863–1945), libretto by 'Paul Bérel' (Paul de Choudens); versified by Giovanni Targioni-Tozzetti. First performance: Monte Carlo, Théâtre du Casino, 16 March 1905.

SYNOPSIS. Savoy, about 1900. The farmer Camoine (baritone) wants to marry his maid, Maddalena (mezzo-soprano), and since his niece Amica (soprano), who lives with him, is an obstacle to this plan, he orders her to marry the shepherd Giorgio (tenor). She, however, loves Giorgio's brother Rinaldo (baritone), and refuses. Told she must obey or leave the house, she runs off with Rinaldo. Giorgio finds them and persuades Rinaldo to abandon her. Desperately trying to reach him, she falls into a ravine and is killed.

■ The poet and composer Arrigo Boito considered the opera the 'most powerful and characteristic' (*mascagnano*) that Mascagni ever wrote, though it lacks the spontaneity of his earlier works. The French libretto was translated into Italian by Giovanni Targioni-Tozzetti, in whose version it was sung at the Opera in Rome on 13 May 1905.

before he rejoins his regiment in the morning. Act II. The railway station of a small Russian town. Katiusha, pregnant, has been turned out of the house and is waiting anxiously for Dmitri, knowing that he will pass this way. At last she sees him with a prostitute, lacks courage to speak to him and turns away in misery. Act III. A prison in St Petersburg. After Dmitri's desertion and the death of her child, Katiusha, now a prostitute, has fallen into evil company and has become involved, though innocent herself, in a crime. There has been a cursory trial, she is condemned for murder and is to be sent to Siberia. Before she leaves, the remorseful Dmitri visits her in her cell and offers to marry her, but she is in abject despair and beyond all comfort. Act IV. On the road to Siberia. She has now recovered herself and is again the good and kindly Katiusha of the beginning, with a new purpose in life in trying to help her fellow-prisoners. Dmitri has returned and, wishing to marry her at any cost, obtains pardon and liberty for her. Yet she refuses, believing that only a total renunciation by them both can redeem their guilty past.

■ In 1902 the composer was in Paris to write two ballets for the Folies-Bergère and while there happened to see a dramatization of Tolstoy's *Resurrection* at the Odéon Theatre. This suggested an opera, and

SALOME
Musical drama in one act by Richard Strauss (1864–1949), based on the play by Oscar Wilde. German text by Hedwig Lachmann. First performance: Dresden, Königliches Opernhaus, 9 December 1905. First performance in U.K.: London, Covent Garden, 8 December 1910; in U.S.A.: New York, Metropolitan Opera House, 22 January 1907.

ORIGINAL CAST. Marie Wittich (Salome), Karl Burrian (Herod), Carl Perron (Jokanaan), Irene von Chavanne (Herodias), Rudolf Jäger (Narraboth) Conductor: Ernst von Schuch.

SYNOPSIS. Herod (tenor), Tetrarch of Judaea, is feasting with his court in the palace at Tiberias on the Sea of Galilee. From the terrace Narraboth, the Captain of the Guard (tenor), gazes at the Tetrarch's beautiful stepdaughter, Salome (soprano), with whom he is in love, and ignores the warnings of the Page (contralto) who loves and admires him. Salome comes out to look at the moonlight and to escape the noise and vulgarity of the banquet and hears the voice of Jokanaan (John the Baptist) (baritone), imprisoned by Herod in a cistern beneath a grill, announcing the coming of the Messiah. Fascinated, she asks to see him and when the guards refuse for fear of disobeying the Tetrarch's orders, she promises to love Narraboth if he will do what she asks. The prophet emerges and denounces Herod and his wife, Salome's mother, Herodias (mezzo-soprano) who has married her dead husband's brother. Salome is filled with desire for him. When he tells her to leave everything and seek the Son of Man, she only answers, 'Who is he, the Son of Man? Is he as beautiful as thou art?' and sings ecstatically of his beauty and of her desire to kiss his mouth. Narraboth, unable to bear it, kills himself, but she barely notices him. Jokanaan curses her when he realizes that she is the daughter of Herodias and descends once more to his dungeon. Herod comes out of the palace. His lust for Salome provokes a quarrel with Herodias, who demands the death of Jokanaan for his insults to her. Herod holds him in awe, considering him to be a holy man, and the Jews come forward to dispute for and against his teachings. In need of diversion, Herod begs Salome to dance. At first unwilling, she consents when Herod promises her anything she desires. The dance finished, she lies stretched out for an instant on the cover of the well, then throws herself into Herod's arms and demands the head of Jokanaan. His desire for her gives way to abhorrence, but he agrees at last. From the cistern, the executioner hands up the head on a silver dish and she seizes it in a frenzy of joy. He who has despised her love must now accept it; she who had craved for him can sate herself kissing his mouth as long as she pleases. Sick with horror, the King shouts to the guards to kill her and she is crushed to death beneath their shields.

■ The first performance of *Salome* was an interna-

Curtain by Laurenti for Wolf-Ferrari's Le donne curiose, *1967. Teatro La Fenice, Venice.*

tional triumph, despite the anxieties that had accompanied the production. The subject itself and its sickening finale, to say nothing of Salome's 'Dance of the Seven Veils', made the censor's intervention all too likely, and indicated Dresden as a more suitable location for the actual première than puritan Berlin or Catholic Vienna. (In Vienna Mahler might have ushered *Salome* into the world.) Casting, too, was fraught with problems. The intrinsic difficulties of the leading role, added to the composer's insistence on a voice that would not be drowned by the orchestra, caused the choice to fall on Marie Wittich, a sturdy Wagnerian soprano, as different from the lithe princess of Wilde's imagination as anyone could be. The famous dance was performed by a professional dancer. All the same, there were thirty-eight curtain-calls for singers, conductor and Strauss himself – 'in spite of old Wittich', as the latter confided to his friend and librettist, Hugo von Hofmannsthal. The brilliance and attack of the orchestral playing brought out to the full the intellectual content of the music, as in the magnificent interlude after the suicide of Narraboth and Jokanaan's return to the well, which describes the effect of the meeting on Salome – the revelation of a love 'more mysterious than the mystery of death'.

GREYSTEEL
One-act opera by Nicholas Comyn Gatty (1874–1946), libretto by his brother Reginald Gatty, based on a translation by Sir George Webbe Dasent of the Icelandic saga Gisli the Outlaw. *First performance: Sheffield, 1 March 1906, during the University Opera Week. First London performance: Crystal Palace, 24 May 1906.*

SYNOPSIS. The magic sword Greysteel belongs to Kol, a valiant warrior whose people have been captured and enslaved by a neighbouring clan; he himself is the slave of Ingjeborg, the beautiful daughter of Isi, their chieftain. Kol bears her no ill-feeling, however, and serves her faithfully, keeping the sword, his one treasure, sharp and shining against the day when he may use it once more. No ordinary weapon, it was forged by elves from tempered steel and its magical properties bring victory in battle. Ingjeborg is married to Ari, lord of Surnadale, where Kol, as part of her household, has accompanied her. She is wretchedly unhappy, for the marriage was not of her choosing, she is treated like a chattel by her husband and loves his brother Gisli, a man utterly unlike him. One day Surnadale is attacked by plundering Bearsarks from the North whose leader challenges Ari to single combat for all he has, his wife included. Ari disdains Kol's offer of Greysteel and is killed. When this happens Gisli, according to the law, at once inherits his possessions, including his wife. He must also still fight the Bearsark chieftain, but quickly despatches him, using the magic sword. A feast is held in celebration and Gisli and Ingjeborg liberate Kol, who may now take Greysteel against any enemy who threatens.

■ This was Gatty's earliest opera. It was revived in a longer, two-act version at Sadler's Wells Theatre, London, on 23 March 1938.

DON PROCOPIO
Opéra-bouffe in two acts by Georges Bizet (1838–75), based on a French translation by Paul Collin and Paul de Choudens of an Italian text by Carlo Cambiaggio. First (posthumous) performance: Monte Carlo, Théâtre du Casino, 10 March 1906.

SYNOPSIS. The story is set in the country house of Don Andronico in Italy, about 1800. Don Andronico (bass) has arranged to give his niece Bettina (soprano) to the rich old miser Don Procopio (baritone), and everyone combines to stop it. Bettina, her brother Ernesto (baritone) and Don Andronico's wife Eufemia (soprano) together make the old man believe that the bride intends to spend all his money and never give him a peaceful moment. Don Procopio, horrified at the prospect, makes innumerable excuses in order to get out of the engagement and Bettina, delighted, marries her beloved Eduardo (tenor), the young officer who has been courting her.

■ This opera was written in 1858 but did not come to light until discovered, almost thirty years later, among papers left by the composer Auber. The version performed in 1906 was in French, with recitatives by Charles Malherbe. The Italian original was heard for the first time on 6 February 1956, at the Municipal Theatre in Strasbourg. The text is condensed from *I pretendenti delusi* (*The Deluded Suitors*) by Luigi Previdali, of which Luigi Mosca had made an opera in 1811. It belongs to Bizet's student days in Rome and is an imitation of Italian *opera-buffa*, displaying links with Donizetti's *Don Pasquale*. Already, however, there is an evident technical skill and unusual liveliness of expression.

I QUATRO RUSTEGHI, or DIE VIER GROBIANE (The School for Fathers)
Operatic comedy in three acts by Ermanno Wolf-Ferrari (1876–1948), libretto by Giuseppe Pizzolato, from I Rusteghi *by Carlo Goldoni (1707–93) German version by H. Teibler. First performance: Munich, Hoftheater, 19 March 1906. First performance in U.K.: London, Sadler's Wells, 7 June 1946; in U.S.A.: New York, City Center, 1951.*

SYNOPSIS. Venice, about the end of the eighteenth century. Act I. Lucieta (soprano), daughter of Lunardo (bass), and Margarita (mezzo-soprano), her stepmother, together complain about her father's strictness. Carnival is nearly over and he will not allow her to take any part in it. Lunardo informs Margarita that he has bespoken an excellent marriage for Lucieta with Maurizio's son Filipeto (tenor), but that, as is only

Setting by Reinhardt Zimmermann for Janáček's Jenůfa *Act I in Stockholm, 1973.*

herself, attacks them with spirit, beginning with her own husband, Canciano, and then accusing the others of infecting him with their silly ideas. She takes full blame for the plot, but has no intention of making amends. The burden of her song is, 'I know too many old boors, too many old misers', and she wipes the floor with them. Riccardo goes off to talk to Filipeto's father Maurizio, who has sulked at home since his awful experience; Lucieta and Margarita beg Lunardo's pardon, thus affording him some slight satisfaction; the wedding is arranged without delay, and everything ends in a delightful supper-party.

■ The theatres of Munich and Berlin, notified that Wolf-Ferrari was working on this score, competed eagerly for the première. The composer was recognized as a gifted interpreter of Goldoni, a fellow-Venetian, among whose plays *I Rusteghi* was, understandably, one of the best loved; out of loyalty to their native city, however, the musician allowed himself some liberties with the dramatist, and his 'rusteghi' (literally churls) are less gruff than their originals. The opera has been compared to fine patterned lace, enriched with polyphonic passages, songs, repetitions and subtle instrumental melodies. The scenes for the bass voices, Canciano, Lunardo, and Maurizio, are especially colourful, with Simon's baritone in brilliant variation. Although the work as a whole may suggest an attempted musical echo of the eighteenth century, it is obvious that what Wolf-Ferrari had in mind – inevitably for an Italian composer of his time – was Verdi's *Falstaff*.

right and proper, there are to be no meetings between the engaged pair until the wedding day. These rigid notions are of course not good enough for either of them. Filipeto is equally anxious that he should not be made to marry a woman he has not even seen and calls on his aunt, Marina (soprano), to ask her for help. His uncle Simon (bass-baritone), whom he dreads, then arrives and sends him away. Shortly afterwards, Marina has another caller, Felice (soprano), accompanied by her husband Canciano (bass) and a visitor to Venice, Count Riccardo (tenor), and the women begin to plan how the young people can be given at least a glimpse of each other. Act II. The women meet at Lunardo's house and Felice explains her scheme. Since it is Carnival time, when in Venice nothing is impossible, Filipeto is to enter the house disguised as a woman, in the company of Count Riccardo. All goes swimmingly; the young couple look, and no sooner look than love. But now the old gentlemen make an untimely appearance. Filipeto and Riccardo hide, and the head of the household announces the betrothal. Maurizio goes off to fetch Filipeto, but discovers that he left home with Riccardo. In the ensuing discussion Canciano remarks that he always suspected the foreigner and Riccardo erupts indignantly. Filipeto is also found and the whole plot is uncovered. Lunardo is furious and orders all his guests to leave. The wedding is off! Act III. Lunardo, Canciano and Simon debate what should be done with such presumptuous women. They are joined by Felice who, instead of defending

MEDEA
Opera in three acts by Vincenzo Tommasini (1878–1950), libretto by the composer. First performance: Trieste, Teatro Verdi, 8 April 1906.

SYNOPSIS. The story, drawn from Euripides, is set in the ancient city of Corinth. Medea, wife of Jason, is devoured by jealousy. Her husband, whom she has helped in his great adventures and to whom she has borne two children, wishes to leave her and marry Glauce, the young and well-dowered daughter of King Creon. In revenge she resolves to use her magical powers to kill her rival and her own children besides, thus making Jason's life intolerable. She gives Glauce a poisoned veil, which kills both her and Creon, and afterwards she slays her children in the temple. Finally, cursing her husband, she throws herself into the flames.

■ *Medea* is a youthful composition, of no marked originality. The score demonstrates Tommasini's wish to absorb as much as he could of the musical culture of Europe, from Wagnerian drama to the 'impressionist' style, and, in addition, there are touches of German romanticism. His more mature works are influenced by French composers, Debussy in particular.

ARIANE (Ariadne)
Opera in five acts by Jules Massenet (1842–1912), libretto by Catulle Mendès (1842–1909), based on the Greek myth. First performance: Paris, Opéra, 31 October 1906.

ORIGINAL CAST. Lucienne Bréval (Ariane), Louise Grandjean (Phèdre), Lucien Muratore (Thésée). Conductor: Paul Vidal.

■ The story of Ariadne has inspired several operas including the *Arianna* of Monteverdi (1608; see above, p. 11), of which only a fragment survives; a work by Richard Strauss (1912); and another by Handel (1734). Massenet's *Ariane* is, however, among his minor achievements. It relies to a great degree upon an increasing variety of orchestral effects, alternating with the ecstatic, though somewhat facile, lyricism of the sung parts. There is a quality of easy and inventive spontaneity, but the opera is rarely performed.

STRANDRECHT (The Wreckers)
Opera in three acts by Ethel Mary Smyth (1858–1944). Text adapted from a Cornish drama, Les Naufrageurs *by Henry Brewster, and first produced in a German version by H. Decker and J. Bernhoff. Later translated into English by the composer and A. Strettell. First performance: Leipzig, Königliches Opernhaus, 11 November 1906. First performance in U.K.: London, Queen's Hall, 30 May 1908 (concert version). First staged in English as* The Wreckers: *London, Her Majesty's Theatre, 22 June 1909.*

SYNOPSIS. The people of a small Cornish village are in the habit of robbing and killing the unfortunate sailors wrecked on their coast; helped by the lighthouse-keeper, they lure ships on to the rocks by tampering with the light. Thirza (mezzo-soprano), wife of Pascoe the village headman and preacher (bass or baritone), is horrified by this practice. Lawrence, the lighthouse-keeper (baritone), and his daughter Avis (soprano) discover that someone is burning beacons to warn ships away from the dangerous reefs. A vessel is sighted and Avis watches to see if a warning beacon is lit, hoping to catch the culprit. Thirza and a fisherman, Mark (tenor), are in love. He has been lighting the beacons and she finds him about to start another fire. They decide to run away together after lighting their final warning. But Pascoe finds them together and falls into a swoon. Mark escapes, and when the crowd arrive, attracted by the fire, they accuse Pascoe. Avis, in love with Mark and jealous of Thirza – for she suspects their affair – claims that Pascoe was bewitched by his wife. Mark confesses and saves Pascoe from death, but when Avis tries to save him in turn by making out that he had spent the night with her, Thirza declares that he is her beloved and that it was she who helped him light the beacon. Although Pascoe tries to save his wife, the pair are left to drown in a cave.

■ The Wagnerian influence on Ethel Smyth is very clear in this opera; in the use of *leitmotiv*, for example, to heighten the dramatic effects. It is the first of her works on a specifically British subject.

KITEZH (Skazanye o nevidimom gradye Kiteže i dyeve Fevronye) (The Legend of the Invisible City of Kitezh and the Maiden Fevronia)
Opera in four acts and six tableaux by Nicolay Rimsky-Korsakov (1844–1908), libretto by Vladimir Bielsky. First performance: St Petersburg, Maryinsky Theatre, 20 February 1907. First performance in U.K.: London, Covent Garden, 30 March 1926 (concert performance); in U.S.A.: Ann Arbor, Michigan, 21 May 1932 (concert performance in English).

SYNOPSIS. Act I. A forest outside Kitezh the Less, on the outskirts of Great Kitezh. Here, across the Volga, lives Fevronia, the woodcutter's young sister. She is not unhappy in her solitary life; the forest animals respond to her gentle ways and she is content in their company. When Vsevolod (tenor), Prince of Kitezh, is wounded out hunting, she comes to his aid. He falls in

Left: Giovanni Zenatello as Pinkerton and Giuseppe De Luca as Sharpless in the original production of Puccini's Madama Butterfly *at La Scala, 17 February 1904. Right: Rosetta Pampanini as Butterfly.*

Music cover by Hohenstein for Puccini's Madama Butterfly.

love with her and asks her to be his wife. Ignorant of his true identity, she accepts and he leaves, promising to send attendants in a wedding procession to fetch her. Act II. A day of celebration in Kitezh the Less. Poiarok (baritone) the Prince's squire and gentleman, marshals the wedding procession; the drunkard Kutierma (tenor) bids Fevronia remember her lowly origins and the chorus joins in her unassuming reply. During a devastating Tartar raid Kitezh the Less is sacked and only she and Kutierma are left alive. The Tartar chieftains Bediai and Burundai (basses) force Kutierma to guide them to Great Kitezh, while Fevronia prays for its preservation. Act III, Scene I. The tragic news reaches Great Kitezh and Vsevolod leads the army against the enemy. His old father Yuri (bass) remains behind with the people to pray to the Virgin for victory and, as the bells begin and continue to ring, the city vanishes in a thick fog. Scene II. We are told in an interlude of the death of Vsevolod and his companions, and then see the Tartars gathered on the banks of Lake Yar, gazing across in astonishment to the site of the former city. Bediai is killed in a quarrel between the chieftains over the division of the spoils. In the night

Kutierma sees Kitezh reflected in the lake and his cry rouses the Tartars, who flee terror-striken at the marvel. Act IV, Scene I. Kutierma and Fevronia, now free, seek refuge in the forest, but he loses his way while she falls exhausted to the ground. Flowers spring up around her, as she dies. In her delirium she sees Vsevolod coming to take her to the invisible city. Epilogue: In eternity, the shining city lives again; its people, in fine raiment, resume the marriage festivities, and the Prince and Fevronia are united in the world beyond death.

■ *The Legend of the Invisible City*, first staged in 1907, was composed during 1903 and 1904. Unlike other operas of Rimsky-Korsakov, it is based on religious legend rather than on folk-tale, though the plot, turning on a miraculous event and the contrast of violence and brutality with faith and human feeling, suited his personal taste for myth and fable. It wonderfully catches the rhythm and melody of Russian folk-music, which is blended even more perfectly with the composer's invention than in his other works. The librettist, Bielsky, was a man of vast learning and wide reading who devoted himself entirely to Rimsky-Korsakov, sacrificing to their collaboration all prospect of literary fame on his own account. The story is an interweaving of several legends, so skilfully done that we can no longer tell them apart. Richard Hoffmann called the score 'one of the composer's greatest masterpieces and one of the highest peaks of Russian music'.

A VILLAGE ROMEO AND JULIET (Romeo und Julia auf dem Dorfe)

Opera in a prologue and three acts by Frederick Delius (1862–1934), libretto by the composer from a story by Gottfried Keller (1856). First performance, in German: Berlin, Komische Oper, 21 February 1907. First performance in U.K.: London, Covent Garden, 22 February 1910: (in English); in U.S.A.: Washington, 1972.

SYNOPSIS. Manz and Marti (baritones), two farmers near the Swiss village of Seldwyl, have after years of friendship come to violent dispute over a strip of land which lies between their holdings. Manz has a son, Sali (as a child soprano, as a man tenor), and Marti a daughter, Vreli (soprano), but these children are now forbidden to play, or even to speak, together. As the years pass, both the greedy rivals are ruined by their quarrel. Gradually, everything they have has been sold to pay for lawsuits – their land, their stock, their very chairs and tables – while, unknown to them, Sali and Vreli have continued to meet and are now in love. When Marti finds the lovers together one day, he attempts to drag Vreli away, but is knocked down by Sali. As a result he loses his reason and has to be put away. His house must now be sold in order to settle his debts. Briefly, the young couple are tempted to run off and join a troupe of vagabonds, but soon recollect that their love is very different from the light, unfeeling liaisons that obtain among wanderers. Gazing at the river, the same idea occurs to them both – why not let the water take them? They are homeless, friendless castaways, too poor even to be married and too loving to survive a separation; is not this the answer for them? If they cannot live, at least they can die together. They take a boat and sink it in midstream, going to their death with their arms round one another.

■ Written in 1901, this is Delius's most notable operatic work, well received when performed at Covent Garden on 22 February 1910. It is seldom given nowadays, but the intermezzo before the last scene, *The Walk to the Paradise Garden*, is a favourite orchestral piece.

ARIANE ET BARBE-BLEUE (Ariadne and Bluebeard)

Opera in three acts by Paul Dukas (1865–1935), libretto taken almost directly from the play by Maurice Maeterlinck (1901). First performance: Paris, Opéra-Comique, 10 May 1907. First performance in U.K.:

Giacomo Puccini, with Elsa Szamosi as Butterfly, Budapest 1906.

London, Covent Garden, 20 April 1937; in U.S.A.: New York, 29 March 1911.

ORIGINAL CAST. Georgette Leblanc and Felix Vieuille. Conductor: Franz Ruhlmann.

SYNOPSIS. Act I. Outside the castle. A clamorous crowd of peasants await the arrival of Barbe-bleue (bass) with his new, and sixth, wife, the beautiful Ariane (mezzo-soprano). They fear that she will meet the same fate as her predecessors, who have all inexplicably vanished. Ariane knows this history, but being brave as well as beautiful, she believes that Barbe-bleue loves her and that she can discover what has happened to his other wives and save them. He gives her a set of keys, six of silver and one of gold; the gold she must never use. The six keys open doors, beyond which she finds heaps of gems – amethysts, sapphires, pearls, emeralds, rubies, and diamonds. The diamonds alone dazzle her, for she has 'a passion for light'. There remains one further door, and the golden key will fit the lock. Unhesitatingly, she opens it, hears women's voices and glimpses a stairway leading downwards. At that moment Barbe-bleue enters, reproves her sternly for her disobedience and makes as if to drag her to the vault below. Ariane struggles and her cries reach the peasants outside the castle. When they rush in to rescue her, she tells them that she is in no further danger and begs them to leave, closing the gate behind them. Barbe-bleue, mortified, takes flight. Act II. Ariane and her nurse find the other wives in the vault, pale and terrified, in tattered clothes. They climb joyfully back into the sun and air. Act III. The wives have put on new clothes, and adorned themselves with flowers and jewels. When Barbe-bleue returns with his faithful negro guard, the peasants, who have remained outside to protect his wives, defeat him and bring him in, wounded and bound, to face his poor victims. The victims, however, seem to bear no malice. When Ariane cuts the ropes that bind him, the others bathe his wounds and when she calls upon them to follow her to freedom, for the way lies open, there is no enthusiasm. She and the nurse then take their departure and two of the wives shut the door behind them.

■ The composition of *Ariane*, interrupted by that of other music, was spread over several years. This is Dukas's only opera, and among the best things he ever wrote. The first performance was less than perfect, but there was progressive improvement on the following nights and the work was to enjoy some success, both abroad and especially in France.

ELEKTRA

Tragedy in one act by Richard Strauss (1864–1949), libretto by Hugo von Hofmannsthal (1874–1929), after Sophocles. First performance: Dresden, Königliches Opernhaus, 25 January 1909. First performance in U.K.: London, Covent Garden, 19 February 1910; in U.S.A.: New York, 1 February 1910.

ORIGINAL CAST. Anny Krull (Elektra), Ernestine Schumann-Heink (Klytämnestra), Margarethe Siems (Chrysothemis), Carl Perron (Orest). Conductor: Ernst von Schuch.

SYNOPSIS. The setting is the courtyard of the palace of the Atridae in Mycenae. Elektra (soprano), though of royal birth, is wild and unkempt, with the look of a hunted animal, and the serving women, as they draw water from the well, pass mocking comments on the indignities suffered by this disgraced daughter of Agamemnon. Only the youngest treats her with respect and she, when the women are recalled within, is whipped for her loyalty. Left alone, Elektra laments her wrongs, remembering her father and reliving the scene of his murder – how, when he came back as a hero from Troy, Klytämnestra (mezzo-soprano) surprised him in the bath-house and held him entangled in a net while Aegisth, her lover (tenor), stabbed him and she, his wife, gave the final blow with an axe. Imploring her dead father's aid. Elektra yields herself to a dream of vengeance and the triumphant ritual dance to follow. This vision is broken by the arrival of her younger sister Chrysothemis (soprano), whose only desire is to

marry, bear children and escape from the gloomy place. Chrysothemis says that their mother and Aegisth plan to incarcerate Elektra in a tower. Then a procession approaches – Klytämnestra on her way to the altar, with retinue, torches, knives and beasts for the sacrifice. Covered with jewels and amulets, but worn and bloated and supported by her confidante, she goes to beseech the gods for delivery from the guilty nightmares that haunt her sleep. The sight of Elektra infuriates her and she demands why her daughter should pollute the palace with her presence. But seemingly soothing words – 'Why rail against the gods? Are not you yourself a goddess?' – have their effect, and she leaves the attendants and comes to speak to her. She must know the remedy for the nightmares; she will offer any victim necessary. Elektra leads her on to speak of her son Orest (baritone), who has fled from home and who is in fact the avenging spirit of her dreams. She then threatens imprisonment unless Elektra tells her what offering to make, and the answer is an impassioned outburst – the Queen is herself the appointed sacrifice; when the axe falls there will be no more dreams, and the survivors will rejoice. The confidante comes out and whispers that two messengers have brought news of Orest's death and the Queen's terror gives way to exultation. Elektra sees that the duty of revenge now falls on her and since she is not strong enough to do the task single-handed, appeals to her sister. Chrysothemis, however, runs away in horror, pursued by her sister's curses. Frantically, Elektra begins to dig for the axe she has hidden and berates the messenger for having lived after his master's death.

From the 1907 New York production of Salome *by Richard Strauss.*

Grace Bumbry in the title role of Salome *by Richard Strauss: the Dance of the Seven Veils.*

therefore murdered her only love and with it her capacity for affection. Orest, in this view, is the one man who can take his father's place, so that her madness is focused on him as a substitute. For her the love between them is the means of vengeance and so of liberation; but absence has left him free from any such neurotic pressure and he returns merely as an executioner. He does not use the axe she has hidden, nor rejoins her after the killing (though in the ancient myth he is pursued by Furies for it and driven from home), and Elektra is thus left once more in hopeless solitude. Much as he admired Hofmannsthal, Strauss hesitated for a long time before he accepted the subject and the parallels with *Salome* worried him – between the two heroines, for example, and between Orest and Jokanaan. The musical invention, the larger orchestral structure and wider range of effects notwithstanding, is less bold than in the earlier work. From the dramatic standpoint the highlights of the score are the scene between Klytämnestra and Elektra when, to suggest the Queen's tormented character, the music passes from polytonality to extreme atonality; and the recognition scene, in which the protracted tension comes to a climax.

This marks her as one of the royal family and he guesses who she is. 'Orest lives', he tells her softly. Next, four old servants recognize him as the Prince and fall to their knees. 'Who are you?' Elektra exclaims, to be told, 'The dogs in the courtyard know me, and my sister does not.' Now she calls down blessings on him, mourning her present state and the beauty she has lost in the thirst for revenge. Orest, accompanied by his tutor, enters the palace and she is left to wait before the doors. An unearthly shriek from Klytämnestra brings Aegisth to the spot, and Elektra takes a torch to light him on his way. He, too, goes inside, then appears at a window, shouting for help. 'Agamemnon hears you!', is her response. Vengeance is accomplished. Like a bacchante, she begins the manic dance she has so long dreamed of, and falls lifeless to the ground, Chrysothemis throws herself upon her sister's body, then beats vainly on the palace doors.

■ *Elektra* was the first-fruits of the collaboration between Strauss and Hofmannsthal, and after the première objections were raised to the 'perverse and immoral' libretto. Yet, minor modifications apart, this sticks closely to Sophocles, whose text Hofmannsthal knew in the original Greek; what he had read of psychoanalysis (Rohde's *Psyche*, for instance, and *Studien über Hysterie* by Josef Breuer and Sigmund Freud), only led him to intensify what he had found there. Some critics nevertheless saw it as a purely psychoanalytical drama. The death of Agamemnon had transformed the young Elektra's natural love for him into an obsessive fixation; his murderers had

THE GOLDEN COCKEREL (LE COQ D'OR)
(Zolotoy Pyetushok)
Opera in three acts by Nicolay Rimsky-Korsakov (1844–1908), libretto by Vladimir Bielsky, from the story by Alexander Pushkin. First performance: Moscow, Solodovnikov Theatre, 7 October 1909. First performance in U.K.: London, Drury Lane, 15 June 1914; in U.S.A.: New York, 6 March 1918.

SYNOPSIS. In a short prologue the Astrologer (tenor with falsetto range) announces the performance of a legend, the lessons of which may be applied to real life. Act I. The throne-room in the palace of King Dodon. An enemy threatens the frontiers of the kingdom, so Dodon (bass), his two sons, Guidon (tenor) and Afron (baritone), his General Polkan (bass) and all his counsellors, consider the problem. No-one has sound advice to give until the Astrologer appears with the Golden Cockerel (soprano). This bird, he says, will crow a warning when danger threatens and thus safeguard the kingdom. Dodon, much reassured, promises to give the Astrologer the first thing he asks for. The Astrologer will take nothing then and there, but requests the King's offer in writing, so that he may take advantage of it later on. Dodon rejoices in the security that the Cockerel has brought him, and prepares for bed. He has not slept for long when the Golden Cockerel, facing eastwards, gives the alarm and the two princes depart with their armies, followed reluctantly by Dodon himself. Act II. A narrow mountain pass by moonlight. The princes and many of their soldiers have been slain; Dodon is in despair. Polkan, on seeing a tent in the mists, orders up a gun and is about to fire when the beautiful Queen of Shemakha (soprano) emerges from it and admits that she caused the princes' deaths. She proceeds to fascinate old Dodon by her voice and bearing, makes him dance and sing at her bidding, and then agrees to marry him on condition that General Polkan is whipped. Act III. The square in the capital. The people, in holiday attire, are expecting Dodon's return. When he arrives, in a superb chariot, with the Queen, the Astrologer comes forward and claims her as his reward – the first thing he asks for. Dodon refuses and strikes him with his sceptre, killing him. Then the Cockerel, to avenge his master, attacks the King and pecks him on the head so that he dies. The Queen vanishes and the populace are left lamenting Dodon's death as the curtain falls. The Astrologer, in a brief epilogue, begs the audience not to be alarmed: the opera was only a fairy-story and he and the Queen were the only real people in it.

■ *The Golden Cockerel* is a political satire depicting the Tsar declining from his majesty into foolishness. Completed in 1907, it aroused furious argument as the Imperial censorship, aware of its covert meaning, strove to keep it from the stage. Eventually a compromise was reached and two years later, after the composer's death, it was performed with Tsar and General reduced to General and Colonel and the Cockerel's famous song, 'Rule, and sleep easy in your bed', cropped to an inoffensive 'Sleep easy in your bed'. It

was a success, and was occasionally presented in forms other than the strictly operatic. On 24 March 1914, for example, the Paris Opéra gave it as a sumptuous 'pantomime', with the singers on stands at the side of the stage and the Russian Ballet to mime the story. Rimsky-Korsakov was 64 when he wrote it, and although he declared that his powers were gone, he produced a score that is entirely original and yet contains choruses and dances in the true Russian tradition. Most striking is the happy fusion of satire and fairytale, enriched with tunes that breathe his love for his country's native music.

PIERROT AND PIERRETTE
Lyrical music drama in two scenes by Joseph Holbrooke (1878–1958), libretto by Walter Grogan. First performance: London, Her Majesty's Theatre, 11 November 1909.

SYNOPSIS. It is a story based on the popular tale of Pierrot and Pierrette, who love one another dearly. All goes well until the arrival of the Stranger, personification of the power of evil, who induces Pierrot to go off with him to see the great world. Amid its debauches and corruption the unsullied happiness of his love for

The Tartars burn the city: Act II of Rimsky-Korsakov's The Legend of the Invisible City of Kitezh and the Maiden Fevronia, *Bolshoi Theatre, Moscow.*

Pierrette is forgotten. In the end the past proves stronger than mere material gratification and he returns to the sweetheart, who always knew he would come back and who, despite the Stranger's baleful influence, has waited faithfully.

■ Based on Grogan's allegorical fantasy, this was the first of Holbrooke's operas to reach the stage and he was himself the original conductor. Though not really successful, and now presented only occasionally in England and America, it has come to be considered one of his most charming works.

IL SEGRETO DI SUSANNA (Susanna's Secret)
Opera in one act by Ermanno Wolf-Ferrari (1876–1948), libretto by Enrico Golisciani; German version by M. Kalbeck. First performance: Munich, Hoftheater, 4 December 1909. First performance in U.K.: London, Covent Garden, 11 July 1911; in U.S.A.: New York, Metropolitan Opera House, 14 March 1911.

SYNOPSIS. The action is laid in Piedmont. Count Gil (baritone) thinks he has seen his wife Susanna (soprano) in the street, yet when he gets home there she is, seated at the piano, having, in fact run in just ahead of him. He can also smell tobacco and, since he never smokes, his suspicions are aroused. He can learn nothing from the servant, Sante (a silent role). Susanna says she has not been out. Repenting of his unworthy thoughts he is about to embrace her, when he smells the reek of tobacco once again, at which he accuses her of hiding something. 'Yes,' she says, 'I am but I shan't tell you what.' They quarrel and she takes refuge in her room, but soon comes out again to ask if he should not be going to the club. To the club he goes, and Susanna tells Sante to fetch the cigarettes she had gone out to buy. She is on the point of lighting up when her husband returns for a forgotten umbrella. Again he departs and at last she can smoke. The Count, determined to catch her lover, comes in through the window. Susanna's innocent secret is out; the husband apologizes, and promises to smoke himself in future, to keep her company.

■ Despite its modern subject, this little opera is modelled on the *intermezzi* of the seventeenth century. In 1911 Toscanini conducted it at the Teatro Costanzi in Rome, and it was very successful in New York and at Covent Garden. The unity of action, words and music led the conductor Felix Mottl to observe that, 'odd as it may seem, this is the most Wagnerian opera I know'.

DON QUICHOTTE (Don Quixote)
Comédie héroïque in five acts by Jules Massenet (1842–1912), libretto by Henri Cain (1859–1937), based on the play Le chevalier de la longue figure *(The Knight of the Doleful Countenance) by Jacques Le Lorrain, after Cervantes. First performance: Monte Carlo, Théâtre du Casino, 19 February 1910. First performance in U.K.: London Opera House, 18 May 1912; in U.S.A.: New Orleans, French Opera House, 27 January 1912.*

ORIGINAL CAST. Lucy Arbell (Dulcinée), Fédore Chaliapine (Don Quichotte), André Gresse (Sancho Panza). Conductor: Léon Jéhin.

SYNOPSIS. This is derived largely from Cervantes's novel though Le Lorrain makes Dulcinée a chambermaid and Don Quichotte a verbose preacher. The sensible Sancho has become a sort of apostle of socialism.

■ One of Massenet's later and certainly minor operas. The libretto is insignificant and musically it falls well below the level of his best work.

MACBETH
Opera in prologue and three acts by Ernest Bloch (1880–1959), libretto by Edmond Fleg (Flegenheimer), after Shakespeare. First performance: Paris, Opéra-Comique, 30 November 1910.

SYNOPSIS. The action takes place about the year 1030. Prologue. A desolate, windblown heath, the battlefield in the distance strewn with dead. The witches (soprano, mezzo-soprano and contralto) appear in the mist and make their veiled prophecies to Banquo (tenor) and Macbeth (baritone). Act I, Scene I. A hall in Macbeth's castle. We see that he is dominated, body and soul, by the ambitious and forceful personality of his wife (soprano). Fate brings the old King Duncan (tenor), with Malcolm (tenor) his son, to the castle. Scene II. The courtyard. Macbeth, ambitious for the crown, takes his dagger and kills Duncan. The psychological situation is admirably suggested in his dialogue with Lady Macbeth, by the drunken porter (baritone), the horrified chorus, and by the first signs of compunction in Macbeth himself. Act II, Scene I (suppressed since the 1938 revival at Naples). An assassin (bass) sent by Macbeth kills Macduff's wife (soprano) and children. Scene II. The banqueting-hall of the castle. Macbeth has also had Banquo murdered, because the witches hailed him as founder of a kingly line. Now, encouraged by Lady Macbeth, he boasts to his guests of his courage and ruthlessness when he suddenly sees Banquo's ghost and collapses in terror. His wife tries to distract him with caresses, but the spectre will not leave him and he falls raving to the ground. Act III, Scene I. The witches' cavern. Macbeth watches as they concoct their spells, and sees the ghosts of those he has murdered pass in an ever more menacing procession. Then the last apparition assures him that he is safe until

> *'Great Birnam wood to high Dunsinane Hill Shall come against him.'*

The words restore his hopes, though he remains

conscience-stricken, feared, and deserted by all. Scene II (the sleep-walking scene). Lady Macbeth, strength and resistance exhausted, sobs and cries out in her sleep, revealing her crimes and wickedness, and at last falls dead. The finale is scored for two choruses: one chorus hidden in leafy branches – the Birnam wood of the prophecy – and another of courtiers and terrified people. Macduff (bass) slays Macbeth in single combat and sets the crown on Malcolm's head.

■ *Macbeth* is Bloch's only opera, for although well received by critics and public, it was not particularly successful and he left France to write no more for the theatre. The first revival was on 5 March 1938 at the San Carlo in Naples. The librettist has condensed Shakespeare's complex tragedy into a few essential scenes and kept close to the text – often, indeed, with no alteration. Bloch, only twenty-five when he began the opera in 1904 (it was completed five years later), proved a magnificent Shakespearean interpreter. His music, neither forced nor rhetorical, gives powerful expression to the passion and drama of the original; and he shows with the utmost clarity the sombre figures of Macbeth and Lady Macbeth, with their victims, their ambition, their black deeds and their remorse.

LA FANCIULLA DEL WEST (The Girl of the Golden West)

Opera in three acts by Giacomo Puccini (1858–1924), libretto by Carlo Zangarini (1874–1943) and Guelfo Civinini (1873–1954) after the play The Girl of the Golden West *by David Belasco (1853–1931). First performance: New York, Metropolitan Opera House, 10 December 1910. First performance in U.K.: London, Covent Garden, 29 May 1911.*

ORIGINAL CAST. Emmy Destinn (Minnie), Enrico Caruso, Pasquale Amato. Conductor: Arturo Toscanini.

SYNOPSIS. A miners' camp at the foot of the Cloudy Mountains, during the Gold Rush of 1849. Act I. The Polka Saloon run by Minnie (soprano). The room is filled with gold miners drinking, gambling and quarrelling. In the distance the minstrel Wallace (baritone) is heard singing a ballad about the miners' homesickness. The customers include the sheriff, Rance (baritone). An agent of the Wells Fargo Transport Company informs him that the notorious bandit Ramerrez (tenor) and his men are roaming the neighbourhood. The sheriff starts a fight by declaring that he is in love with Minnie. She separates the men, and opening a Bible begins to read aloud from it when the post arrives: Rance receives a letter from one of Ramerrez's ex-mistresses, indicating his whereabouts. A stranger, who gives his name as Dick Johnson (but is in fact Ramerrez), enters. He remembers meeting Minnie before and they are at once strongly attracted to one another. Rance is jealous. One of Ramerrez's men,

Castro (bass), is brought into the saloon. Recognizing his chief, he pretends to give away the bandit's hiding place in order to draw away the sheriff and the miners. Left alone with Ramerrez, Minnie confides in him that the miners entrust their gold to her and tells him that she would risk her life rather then betray their trust. She invites him to continue their conversation in her cabin. Act II. Minnie's cabin. The opening scene is a domestic idyll with Minnie's servant, the squaw Wowkle (mezzo-soprano), her husband Jackrabbit (bass) and their baby. Minnie describes to Ramerrez the events which had brought her to the miners' camp and her love for her life in the Sierra. They declare their feelings for one another and when Rance and his men arrive to check she is all right in the snowstorm, Minnie claims to be alone. They tell her that Castro has proved to them that Johnson is Ramerrez. They depart and she, furious at being deceived, listens to the bandit's excuse for his way of life: that his father (the bandit leader before him) had left a large family to support when he died. She does not stop him rushing out, regardless of the danger which awaits him. He is shot. Minnie, taking pity on him, drags him back inside and hides him in the loft. She tells Rance that the bandit must have escaped, but a drop of blood falling from the loft betrays his presence. He is brought down into the room. Minnie desperately proposes that she should gamble his destiny on the outcome of a game of poker. If Rance wins, Johnson will be delivered up to justice and Minnie will be Rance's. If she wins, Johnson will go free. She cheats and wins. Act III. Dawn in the Great Californian Forest. The manhunt goes on. Johnson is captured by the miners and is about to be executed. Before being hanged, he begs that Minnie be left in ignorance of his ignoble fate and allowed to believe that he gained his freedom. Minnie rides up on horseback with a pistol in her hand. In an impassioned plea (*Fratelli, non v'è al mondo peccatore cui non s'apra una via di redenzione*) she reminds the miners that no sinner is beyond redemption and begs them to spare his life. Despite Rance's jealous protests, Johnson is freed. Bidding the crowd farewell, Johnson and Minnie set off together into the snowy forest.

■ In his operas Puccini constantly swung between psychological insight into pathetic heroines (*Bohème, Butterfly*) and the creation of powerful dramatic situations, heroic characters and lofty passions (*Tosca*). With *La fanciulla del West* he returns to the realms of grand opera, with a romantic plot, exotic setting and large crowd scenes. This time, however, the subject matter combines the classic triangle of two men and one woman, reminiscent in some respects of the situation in *Tosca*, with a Far West setting of daring modernity, designed to appeal to the American public. Highly dramatic situations like the discovery of Johnson, given away by blood dripping from the loft, and the poker game, are based on fact. Jake Wallace, the singer and banjo player whose song opens and closes the opera, really existed. The plot as a whole, despite the improbability of the characters and many of the details, belonged to a chapter of American history

Elektra: poster for the 'Richard Strauss Week' at Munich, 23–28 June 1910.

which was still very vivid in the public's mind. Of the main characters Minnie is the least convincing – beautiful and pure, yet a good friend of the brutish miners in the camp, a woman who preaches the power of love, yet cheats skilfully at cards and handles a gun with ease. Ramerrez-Johnson too is a highly gentlemanly bandit. What concerned Puccini, however, was that the opera should have a dramatically immediate impact and to this end the most sensational scenes in Act III (the manhunt in the forest and Minnie's final appearance on horseback armed with a pistol, like a Wild West Valkyrie), which do not occur in Belasco's play, were introduced into the libretto at the composer's suggestion. The rapid action, sudden changes of scene and rough characterization posed considerable musical problems and these, coupled with modest melodic invention, may account for the opera's limited popularity. Even so, some passages – for example Johnson's aria 'Ch'ella mi creda' in Act III – have become famous. Closer analysis of the score reveals masterly technical skill – for example, in creating the rough, primitive atmosphere of the gold-miners' camp, or in the use of realist devices to convey the characters' near-pathological tension at the moments of greatest suspense (the blood dripping from the loft, described by

spine-chilling arpeggios, or the card game). In his pursuit of new harmonic forms, sometimes completely obscuring the tonality, Puccini's debt to Debussy and to the Strauss of *Salome* is obvious, though recognizing these influences does in no way detract from the originality of his music. *La fanciulla del West* was a triumphant success with the New York audience. There were forty-seven curtain calls and between the second and third acts Puccini was crowned with a silver crown bearing the national colours of Italy and the United States. The critics, on the other hand, reacted more coolly and on the whole confined themselves to praising the composer's technical skill.

DIE KÖNIGSKINDER (The Royal Children)

Opera in three acts by Engelbert Humperdinck (1854–1921), text by 'Ernst Rosmer' (Elsa Bernstein). First performance: New York, Metropolitan Opera House, 28 December 1910. First performance in U.K.: London, Covent Garden, 27 November 1911.

ORIGINAL CAST. Farrar, Jadlowker, Goritz.

SYNOPSIS. The action takes place 'once upon a time' in an imaginary country. Act I. The wood and the witch's hut. The beautiful Goose Girl (soprano) is the wicked witch's prisoner. The King's son (tenor) meets her by chance in the wood, falls in love with her and offers to marry her, but the witch, by her magic spells, prevents the Goose Girl escaping. The Prince leaves, in the hope of the miracle which will allow them to meet again – a star must fall onto a certain lily as its petals unfold. The broom-maker, the fiddler and the woodcutter ask the witch who is to be king, as the old king has just died. The new ruler, declares the witch, will appear at noon. The fiddler also falls in love with the Goose-Girl and wishes to take her with him, but the witch refuses to let her go. A star falls onto the lily as it opens – the miracle which allows the Goose-Girl to escape. Act II. The town. The Prince, now King, agrees to look after the innkeeper's pigs in order to woo the Goose-Girl. As noon strikes she appears. The people mock her and refuse to accept her as Queen. The King, now a swine-herd, tries in vain to defend her and to convince the people that he is the dead king's son. Only the broom-maker's little daughter believes the young couple. Act III. Near the town. The King and Queen have been rejected by the people and are forced to sell their crowns to buy food. Destitute and scorned, they die in the snow in each other's arms. The people, led by the broom-maker's daughter, arrive, at last convinced of the royal children's true identity.

■ This is Humperdinck's most famous opera apart from *Hänsel und Gretel*. Again it is a children's opera with didactic intent. The original version consisted of a play with incidental music by Humperdinck and in this form it was first performed at Munich on 23 January 1897, with further performances in Vienna, Prague, Berlin, Riga, and New York. *Die Königskinder* was a universal success. The text was translated into English, Italian, Hungarian, French, Russian, Croatian and Swedish. The opera has had many performances all over the world and still features in the repertory of several opera houses.

DER ROSENKAVALIER (The Knight of the Rose)

'Comedy for music' in three acts by Richard Strauss (1864–1949), text by Hugo von Hofmannsthal (1874–1929). First performance: Dresden, Königliches Opernhaus, 26 January 1911. First performance in U.K.: London, Covent Garden, 29 January 1913; in U.S.A.: New York, Metropolitan, 9 December 1913.

ORIGINAL CAST. Carl Perron (Ochs), Margarethe Siems (Marschallin), Minnie Nast (Sophie), Eva von der Osten (Octavian), Karl Scheidemantel (Faninal), Fritz Soot (Italian tenor). Conductor: Ernst von Schuch.

SYNOPSIS. Vienna during the reign of the Empress Maria Theresa. Act I. The Feldmarschallin, Princess of Werdenberg (soprano), has taken advantage of her husband's absence to entertain her young lover Count Octavian Rofrano (mezzo-soprano) overnight. Her happiness is marred by her melancholy awareness that her beauty will soon fade. Startled by a commotion in the antechamber, she fears that her husband has come home early. It is, however, an unexpected visit from her cousin, the coarse, conceited Baron Ochs von Lerchenau (bass), who has come to beg her assistance in

Illustration for Rimsky-Korsakov's The Golden Cockerel. *Paris, Bibliothèque de l'Opéra.*

the matter of his betrothal to Sophie (soprano), daughter of a newly ennobled bourgeois, Herr von Faninal (baritone). Ochs forces his way past the footmen and enters the room before Octavian, now dressed up in some of the Marschallin's clothes, can slip away. True to form, he cannot resist flirting with this supposed chambermaid, while he asks the Marschallin to recommend a young nobleman to bear the traditional silver rose to his betrothed. She suggests her cousin Count Octavian as a candidate and shows Ochs his portrait. Ochs notices the resemblance to the chambermaid, but concludes that she must be the young nobleman's illegitimate sister. The Marschallin's levée opens: a crowd of tradesmen and petitioners enter – a notary, chef, milliner, scholar and animal seller, the intriguer Valzacchi (tenor) and his accomplice Annina (contralto), a noble widow and her three daughters, an Italian singer (tenor), a flute-player and a hair-dresser. Ochs discusses his matrimonial affairs with the notary and agrees to employ Valzacchi and Annina to discover anything they can about his future wife. Left alone, at last, the Marschallin is again overcome with melancholy and even Octavian's return does not cheer her. Instead she becomes more painfully aware that he will soon leave her for a younger woman. Octavian impatiently tries to reassure her but when he leaves the Marschallin realizes that they have not even kissed. She sends her little black page Mohammed after him with the case containing the silver rose for Sophie von Faninal. Act II. Herr von Faninal's palace. Preparations are being made to receive the Rosenkavalier. Sophie, attended by her duenna (soprano), awaits the arrival of her suitor in a state of tense excitement. Octavian enters and presents her with the rose. Love springs immediately between them. When Ochs arrives, Faninal does his best to follow the etiquette of the occasion, but Ochs ignores him and fondles Sophie lecherously. Then Ochs and Faninal discuss the finances of the marriage contract. Octavian swears to stop the marriage from taking place. This intrigues Valzacchi and Annina, who surprise him with Sophie and call Ochs to the scene. Octavian challenges him and wounds him with his sword. Ochs makes a dreadful fuss and calls for a doctor. Sophie firmly refuses to marry Ochs to her father's consternation. Octavian, determined to win Sophie, manages to procure the services of Valzacchi and Annina for himself. Ochs is left alone to recover. Annina hands him a note purporting to be from the Marschallin's chambermaid, 'Mariandel', agreeing to a rendezvous with him the next evening. Ochs is delighted at the prospect. Act III. A private room in the tavern chosen for the meeting of Ochs and the supposed maid. Valzacchi and Annina put the finishing touches to a trap for the Baron. Octavian, in women's clothes, gives them half their pay, leaves and returns soon after on the Baron's arm. Ochs dismisses the inn-keeper and waiters to cut down his costs and settles down to enjoy himself. Mariandel's resemblance to Octavian upsets him and he is further disturbed by mysterious noises and strange apparitions. Annina rushes in, veiled in crêpe and dressed in mourning, and claims that he is her husband and has abandoned her. Valzacchi, the innkeeper and the waiters encourage her and children burst in shouting 'Papa'. A police commissar (baritone) comes to investigate the uproar, ignores Ochs's protests that a misunderstanding has occurred and that he is simply dining with his betrothed Sophie von Faninal. Valzacchi has already alerted Faninal that his future son-in-law requests his presence, and father and daughter now appear to give the lie to the Baron's assertions. Meanwhile Octavian has explained the trick to the commissar. Then the Marschallin enters, summoned by one of Ochs's retinue. She immediately sums up the situation and, recognizing the commissar as her husband's former orderly, she dismisses him with the words that the affair was 'just a farce and nothing more'. Sophie overhears the phrase and realizes that this might also describe Octavian's love for her. The Marschallin, however, brings the young couple together again and while they express their youthful delight in one another she adds her voice to theirs (in a sublime trio), aware that her youth has passed and resigned to growing old. Taking Herr von Faninal's arm, she invites them all to return to Vienna in her coach. When they have left, Mohammed reappears to search for Sophie's handkerchief; the opera closes as he scampers back with it.

■ Strauss himself declared that *Der Rosenkavalier* would be an opera in the style of Mozart. By many critics it was regarded as a retrograde step after *Salome* and *Elektra* and a prime example of musical conservatism. In fact *Der Rosenkavalier* comes at the height of Strauss's creative activity. It is a work in which his entire musical personality, his strengths and weaknesses, can be seen as if through a magnifying glass. The Mozartian principle that 'the crudest situations and the most powerful sentiments must never free music of its obligation to be beautiful' is adapted to suit the composer of physical experiences, sensual realism and the exploration of pathological states of mind. The orchestra has a dominant role, at times even overwhelming Hofmannsthal's words. Certain passages are wholly modern in their composition, for example the high, polytonal chords played by flutes, celeste, harps and three solo violins to suggest the gleaming silver rose. When the opera was first performed there was much discussion about the use of Viennese waltz tunes, which were seen either as an anachronism or as a device intended to give *Der Rosenkavalier* a sense of timelessness. The charge of anachronism is hardly justified since the Viennese nobility of the day was fond of popular dances including the waltz, and the introduction of waltzes certainly gives the opera an unmistakably Viennese atmosphere. *Der Rosenkavalier* marks a further decisive step forward in Strauss's exploration of symphonic operatic technique. The characters' psychological development is clearly conveyed by the music. The waltzes, the intrigue and the lyrical élan of the opera appealed greatly to the public, which gave it a resounding welcome on its first night, marking the beginning of its triumphant success in opera houses all over the world.

THE CAPTAIN'S DAUGHTER (Kapitanskaya doka)
Opera by César Antonovich Cui (1835–1918); libretto by the composer, based on the story by Pushkin (1836). First performance: St Petersburg 1911.

SYNOPSIS. The adventures of young Griniov and his servant Savelich during the reign of Catherine the Great, at the time of Pugachev's rebellion (1773). Griniov is sent as a soldier to the Bielogorsky fortress and falls in love with Maria Ivanovna, the Commander's daughter. He fights a duel with his rival, the traitor Shvabrin. The rebel Pugachev takes over the fortress, but spares the lives of Maria and Griniov, because he recognizes in Griniov the young man who once gave him his fur jacket. Griniov is later accused of treachery because of his blameless dealings with the rebels, but in the end Maria obtains the Empress's pardon.

■ A fair example of Russian national opera, rarely performed despite some fine passages.

DÉJANIRE (Deianira)
Tragic opera in four acts by Camille Saint-Saëns (1835–1921), libretto by the composer and Louis Gallet (1835–98). First performance: Monte Carlo, Théâtre du Casino, 14 March 1911; first performance in U.S.A.: Chicago, 9 December 1915.

SYNOPSIS. Hercule falls in love with Jole and plans to marry her. His wife Déjanire, learning of his new passion, follows the advice of the centaur Nessus in order to win him back. She sends her husband the centaur's own tunic, understanding that he will return to her once he puts it on. The tunic is, however, soaked with blood poisoned with gall from the Hydra of Lerna and its effect is very different. Nessus in fact means to get his revenge on Hercule, who had mortally wounded him when the centaur attempted to carry off Déjanire. The tragic result is seen in the last act. Hercule and Jole prepare for their wedding before the Temple of Jupiter. Jole makes Hercule put on the fatal tunic while the crowd gathers round the sacred altar. As the ritual libations begin, he is seized by fearful agony. He begs the onlookers to throw him into the sea to cool the terrible burning of his flesh beneath the tunic. Finally, in the midst of the terrified crowd, he throws himself into the flames of a pyre, lit by a flash of lightning. He reappears transformed in the sky among the immortal gods.

■ Saint-Saëns first had the idea of turning *Déjanire* into an opera while writing incidental music for Gallet's play. The text needed major changes before it could be set to music. When, after Gallet's death, the Prince of Monaco and the directors of the opera asked Saint-Saëns for a new work, he decided to alter the libretto himself.

Gabriella Ravazzi as the Princess in Gian-Carlo Menotti's production of Rimsky-Korsakov's The Golden Cockerel, *Trieste 1974.*

L'HEURE ESPAGNOLE (Spanish Time)

Comédie musicale *in one act by Maurice Ravel (1875–1937), based on the comedy by Maurice Etienne Legrand (1873–1934), who wrote the libretto under the pen-name Franc-Nohain. First performance: Paris, Opéra-Comique, 19 May 1911; first performance in U.K.: London, Covent Garden, 24 July 1919; in U.S.A.: Chicago, 5 January 1920.*

ORIGINAL CAST. Vix (Concepción), Périer (Ramiro), Delvoye (Gomez), Coulomb (Gonzalve), Cazeneuve (Torquemada). Conductor: Ruhlmann.

SYNOPSIS. The shop of the clock-maker Torquemeda in eighteenth-century Toledo. The muleteer Ramiro (baritone) brings Torquemada (tenor) an old watch to mend. The watch-maker's wife Concepción (soprano) reminds her husband that he must check all the clocks in the town as he does every Thursday. Torquemeda leaves, asking Ramiro to await his return. This annoys Concepción, who is waiting for her young lover Gonzalve (tenor), so she asks Ramiro to carry one of two heavy Catalan clocks upstairs for her. Young Gonzalve (tenor) arrives meanwhile and recites poems to her and she tells him how much she had looked forward to his arrival. Ramiro meanwhile finishes his task and returns. Concepción persuades him to go back for the first clock and put the second one in its place. When the muleteer leaves the room she hides her lover inside this second clock. The situa-tion is complicated by the arrival of Inigo Gomez (bass), an influential banker, who is also an admirer. Concepción is clearly put out by his unexpected arrival. The muleteer returns with the first clock and, un-daunted, he continues his job, effortlessly lifting the second clock with Gonzalve inside it onto his shoul-ders. This time Concepción accompanies him. Gomez decides to play a trick on her and hides inside the remaining clock. Ramiro re-enters, followed by Con-cepción, who is annoyed with Gonzalve because his fine words do not match his actions. She complains that the clock now in her bedroom (containing Gonzalve) makes too much noise for her nerves and she asks patient Ramiro to fetch it. Gomez decides to make the most of the situation and to declare his love for Con-cepción. When his turn comes and he has been carried into the bedroom he is too fat to extricate himself from the clock. Exasperated by the situation and disap-pointed in her two lovers, Concepción decides to leave Gomez and Gonzalve shut up in their clocks and to retire with Ramiro, whose physical strength, patience and constancy she admires. The other two lovers finally manage to get out of the clocks, but they delay too long in the shop and are found there by Tor-quemada on his return. Their only way out is to pre-tend to be potential customers. Torquemada pretends to believe them and immediately sells them the two clocks, though he understands the situation perfectly well. The comedy ends with Torquemada telling his wife that they now have no clocks. Concepción replies that it does not matter as Ramiro will pass beneath her window every day to tell her the time.

■ Legrand helped in the adaptation of his comedy *L'heure espagnole* when he learned that Ravel wished to turn it into a comic opera. Although the comedy was well received, the opera had to wait longer for success. Finished in 1907, it was not performed until 1911 at the Opéra-Comique. The critics, despite some reserva-tions, did not condemn it outright, but the opera disap-peared from the French stage after a few performances and was not seen there again until 1938. It did not meet with real success until the year after when, on the second anniversary of the composer's death, it was included in a bill with *Daphnis et Chloé* and *Adélaide, ou Le langage des fleurs*. Franc Nohain's satire con-tained many attractive features, and while Ravel was usually more restrained in his choice of subject, he chose on this occasion a fairly risqué subject because of its dramatice potential. He attempts to animate objects – in the first scene, for example, clocks take on life as the grandfather clocks strike a series of different times. Ravel worked on the opera with great dedication, con-sidering that at that time he was worried about the health of his father, who died before the opera was performed, during a last desperate attempt by his son to take him abroad for treatment. Now that *L'heure espagnole* is an established favourite, it is easy to see that the critics in 1911 were mistaken in their attacks on the subject and in their failure to appreci-ate the delicacy of expression and musical magic. Ravel's refined sensibilities and balanced, well-chosen

Enrico Caruso as Dick Johnson, Emmy Destinn as Minnie and Pasquale Amato as the sheriff in the last scene of Puccini's La fanciulla del West *at its first performance at the Metropolitan, New York.*

Act I in the first performance of Puccini's La fanciulla del West.

harmonies raise the level of a comedy which in other hands might have become an undistinguished farce of doubtful taste.

LE MARTYRE DE SAINT SÉBASTIEN (The Martyrdom of St Sebastian)

Mystery in five scenes by Claude Debussy (1862–1918), with poetic text in French by Gabriele D'Annunzio (1863–1938). First performance: Paris, Théâtre du Châtelet, 22 May 1911.

SYNOPSIS. Rome in the early days of Christianity. First scene. The twin brothers Marcus and Marcellinus are tied to columns and about to be executed. They have repeatedly refused to sacrifice to the pagan gods and mean to bear witness to their Christian faith by their martyrdom. Their family weeps, while Sébastien, the captain of the archers, observes them closely. Suddenly Sébastien too raises his voice and proclaims his faith. The archers are dismayed, but the martyrs' family follow his example, declaring themselves believers. Second scene. Sébastien attends a ceremony at which seven sorceresses worship pagan divinities. He disrupts the proceedings by telling them about the Christian faith. Third scene. Sébastien has become the Emperor's favourite and receives promises of favours and honours, but he retains his faith and destroys the heathen idol the Emperor gives him. Fourth scene. On the Emperor's orders, Sébastien is to be shot by archers. They hesitate and Sébastien gently urges them to carry out their duty. When he dies, they weep for him in bitter remorse. The women lay the Saint's body on a litter. Fifth scene. Sébastien's soul floats up to heavenly bliss, in the midst of a host of martyrs and angels singing hosanna.

■ This work takes the form of a medieval mystery, divided into five scenes with a prayer-prologue, as was usual in the type of drama on which the opera is modelled. In the prologue the author describes the five scenes as five stained-glass windows, in that the story is deliberately fragmented and decorative. The prelude sets the tone which characterizes the whole work – orgiastic and pagan, yet at the same time mystical and Christian. Sébastien is represented by an ephebe, a role for dancer-reciter which was first taken by the ballet dancer Ida Rubinstein. Beside the characters with reciting roles there are singing parts – the *vox sola*, *vox coelestis*, *anima Sebastiani*, the voice of the Virgin, Erigone and the twins. The chorus has a substantial role. The opera caused a great scandal and was condemned in advance by the Archbishop of Paris. Although on the eve of the first performance D'Annunzio and Debussy signed a statement declaring their good faith and denying any sacrilegious intention, the opera was put on the Index. Whatever the intentions of poet and composer, the saint does in fact emerge as a profane figure.

D'Annunzio's poetry is written in archaic, stylized French. For Debussy this opera marked an important stage in the development of his expressive language. It is a work of prime importance, though hardly popular. In 1911 and 1917 there were plans to turn it into an opera proper, but nothing came of them.

ISABEAU

Dramatic legend in three parts by Pietro Mascagni (1863–1945), libretto by Luigi Illica (1857–1919). First performance: Buenos Aires, Teatro Coliseo, 2 June 1911; first performance in U.S.A.: Chicago, 12 November 1917.

ORIGINAL CAST. Farneti, Galeffi, Saludas, Da Ferrara, La Puma, Pozzi. Conductor: Pietro Mascagni.

SYNOPSIS. The action takes place once upon a time in an imaginary town. Part I. A contest is proclaimed in the castle of King Raimondo (bass). The knight who can inspire Princess Isabeau (soprano) with love will win her hand. Giglietta (mezzo-soprano), an old woodcutter, and her nephew Folco (tenor), a falconer, arrive at the castle bearing gifts for the Princess. The King's counsellor, Messer Cornelius (bass), wants to send them away, but Isabeau shows her pleasure at their tribute. A crowd gathers to watch the contest, at which Isabeau shows pity for only one of the competitors, a young stranger. This is Ethelbert d'Argile, the King's banished nephew. The people prepare to greet him as her spouse, but Isabeau refuses to accept him. On the advice of Cornelius, her father condemns her to ride naked through the streets of the city to make amends for her pride and her refusal to marry. Part II. The people request the King to issue an edict that anyone caught watching the Princess as she passes will be blinded. Doors and windows are barred as Isabeau, accompanied by her two maids, leaves the royal palace. She is covered only by her long hair. Folco, unaware of the edict, throws bunches of flowers down on her from a garden. He is attacked by the townspeople and Ethelbert saves him from their fury with difficulty. Part III. Giglietta begs Isabeau, who is full of remorse at being the involuntary cause of Folco's condemnation, to save him. Ethelbert reminds the princess that the people had asked for the edict for her sake, to defend her honour. Isabeau asks to be allowed to speak to the prisoner. He appears serene and happy to die with the vision of the princess in his mind. She offers to let him escape, and when he refuses she offers to marry him as she now loves him. Cornelius, who has overheard the conversation, opens the door of the prison and throws Folco to the angry crowd. When Isabeau, who has gone to give the King her decision, returns to find her beloved gone, she runs out to face death with him.

■ The opera was composed almost entirely between June and September 1910 in Luigi Illica's villa at Castellarquato, in close collaboration with the librettist. It was orchestrated in Milan, where Mascagni showed the score to Puccini, his former companion from their conservatory days. *Isabeau* was intended for the New York public, but for a number of reasons was transferred to South America after a dress rehearsal at the Teatro Carlo Felice, Genoa. In Italy it was performed simultaneously at La Fenice, Venice, and La Scala, Milan, after a dispute between the two theatres. Intended by Mascagni as an attempt to rejuvenate opera by means of a superfical 'D'Annunzianism', which was then all the rage, *Isabeau* was generally coolly received and far less successful than the author had hoped, in spite of some popularity with Argentinian audiences.

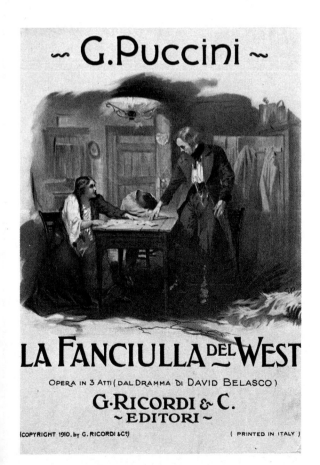

Title-page of the libretto of Puccini's La fanciulla del West, *published by Ricordi in 1910.*

CONCHITA
Opera in four acts and six scenes by Riccardo Zandonai (1883–1944), libretto by Maurizio Vaucaire and Carlo Zangarini, based on La femme et le pantin *by Pierre Louÿs (1898). First performance: Milan, Teatro Dal Verme, 14 October 1911 (Italian version by Carlo Zangarini); first performance in U.K.: London, Covent Garden, 3 July 1912; in U.S.A.: Chicago, 2 November 1912.*

ORIGINAL CAST. Tarquinia Tarquini, Schiarazzi, Zinolfi, Lucca. Conductor: Ettore Panizza.

SYNOPSIS. Conchita (soprano), a poor cigar-maker of Seville, rejects the advances of Mateo (tenor), a rich suitor, because she doubts his sincerity. Mateo offers money to her mother (mezzo-soprano) to alleviate their miserable living conditions, but Conchita runs away from home and earns her living as a flamenco dancer. Mateo tracks her down and offers her a rich villa to live in. To test him Conchita pretends to be found with a lover. Mateo reacts with great jealousy and she is finally convinced of his love for her and returns it.

■ The opera is remarkable for its elaborate orchestration and harmonies. It is clearly the work of a young composer, who knows, however, exactly what he wants to achieve. His youthful élan is combined with the poised reflective quality characteristic of the mature Zandonai, without diluting the lively romantic *verismo* of his theme.

I GIOIELLI DELLA MADONNA (The Jewels of the Madonna)

Opera in three acts by Ermanno Wolf-Ferrari (1876–1948), text by Enrico Golisciani and Carlo Zangarini. First performance: Berlin, Kurfürstenoper, 23 December 1911 (the German version is by H. Liebstöckl); first performance in U.K.: London, Covent Garden, 30 May 1912; in U.S.A.: Chicago, 16 January 1912.

SYNOPSIS. Naples. Act I. The festival of the Madonna is in progress, but the blacksmith Gennaro (tenor) does not join in the general rejoicing. He prays to the Madonna to free him from his unhappy love for Maliella (soprano), an orphan brought up by his mother, who has captured his heart. The girl meanwhile is clearly enjoying the festival. She shows off, dances and then leaves for the quay with Biaso (bass), the neighbourhood scribe. Rafaele (baritone), the leader of the Camorrists, arrives with his gang and woos her, declaring that for her he would even steal the jewels of the Madonna, at that moment being carried past in procession. Act II. The garden of the house of Carmela (mezzo-soprano), Gennaro's mother. Gennaro argues with Maliella when she announces her plan to leave home. He gives in and declares his love for her, but she shamelessly declares that she could only love a man who showed true courage and devotion to her – a man who could, for example, steal the jewels of the Madonna for her. Gennaro is furious and locks the gate to prevent her escaping. Then he sadly goes out. Rafaele arrives and serenades Maliella. They tell of their love for each other and she agrees to join him in his hide-out the next day. Gennaro returns, however: he has done as Maliella had asked and has stolen the jewels from the statue. She no longer repulses him and yields herself to his embraces. Act III. The Camorrists' headquarters. Rafaele enters and drinks a toast with his companions, for he has added another pearl, the beautiful Maliella, to his rosary of conquests. The girl now arrives and, in a trance, announces that she has given herself to Gennaro. When Rafaele realizes this he rejects her in disgust. He then sees that she is wearing the jewels of the Madonna and is appalled at the sacrilege. Gennaro enters, almost out of his mind. Maliella throws the jewels at his feet and runs away to drown herself. The Camorrists leave the den too, frightened that they will be mistaken for Gennaro's accomplices. Left alone, Gennaro gathers up the jewels, carries them to the Madonna's statue and places them at her feet, before stabbing himself.

■ Wolf-Ferrari here for once abandons Goldoni, though the opera is none the less Italian for that. The composer hardly ever departed from Italian subjects in his works, as if to compensate for the quirk of fortune which made him almost a foreigner, virtually unrecognized in his own country, but increasingly admired in Germany, where he was a great success with both critics and public. Like *Le donne curiose*, *I gioielli della Madonna* was most successful abroad. The opera was performed in New York with Arturo Toscanini conducting. The Metropolitan Opera invited Wolf-Ferrari to the first performances, so for once he was able to hear his work sung in Italian.

DIE BRAUTWAHL (The Marital Lottery)

Comic opera in three acts by Ferruccio Busoni (1866–1924), libretto by the composer from a story by E. T. A. Hoffmann. First performance: Hamburg, Staatsoper, 13 April 1912.

■ The first of Busoni's operas to be performed, written when he was living in Berlin, after his return to Europe from Boston.

THE CAULDRON OF ANWEN

Dramatic trilogy by Joseph Holbrooke (1878–1958), text by T. E. Ellis.

THE CHILDREN OF DON

Opera in three acts with prologue. First performance: London, London Opera House, 15 June 1912.

SYNOPSIS. The action is based on Celtic legend and takes place in an imaginary magic world. The children of the earth goddess manage to steal a magic cauldron from the druids and keep it for almost a thousand years.

DYLAN, SON OF THE WAVE

Opera in three acts. First performance: London, Drury Lane, 4 July 1914.

SYNOPSIS. Again based on a legend. The opera tells of the hero Dylan, who is killed by his cruel, treacherous uncle. The old man is in turn killed by the waves of the sea which flood his castle to avenge the hero's death.

BRONWEN

Opera in three acts. First performance: Huddersfield, 1 February 1929.

SYNOPSIS. The opera describes the adventures of Bronwen and her son Dylan – fair and handsome like Siegfried – in a magic, primitive world. The finale is dominated by an epic battle between British and Irish gods in which men also take part.

■ This trilogy, which belongs to the composer's mature period, was not a great success outside England although after the British premières there were some other performances of parts of the cycle. *Dylan* was performed in German at the Volksoper, Vienna, in 1923. The complete score of *Dylan* was published in 1910, before the London première, and *Bronwen* was first published in 1922. The trilogy is inspired by Celtic legends, and reveals the marked influence of Wagner and Strauss. Holbrooke's operas, though generally respected by the critics, have never found much favour with the public.

UNE ÉDUCATION MANQUÉE (An Unsuccessful Education)

Opera in one act by Alexis Emmanuel Chabrier (1841–1894), text by Eugène Leterrier and Albert Vanloo. First performance (in private with piano accompaniment): Paris, Cercle de la Presse, 1 May 1879. First public performance with orchestra: Paris, Théâtre des Arts, 9 January 1913; first performance in U.K.: London, St Pancras Town Hall, 14 March 1961; in U.S.A.: Tanglewood, 3 August 1953.

SYNOPSIS. The action takes place in a drawing room in the château of Count Boismassif during the reign of Louis XVI. The young count Gontran de Boismassif (tenor) arrives with his bride Hélène (soprano). Two elderly members of the family are given the task of telling the young couple how they are to behave after their wedding, a subject no-one has taught them. Gontran's grandfather simply sends a letter saying that in his day he managed very well without any kind of instruction. Hélène's aunt arrives, but she is an old lady and not much use. Luckily a storm springs up and drives the young couple into one another's arms. When at last Gontran's tutor Pausania (bass) arrives breathlessly to help his pupil he finds there is no longer any need for him.

■ Chabrier wrote this little opera while still working in the civil service before he devoted himself to music full-time.

PÉNÉLOPE

Opera in three acts by Gabriel Fauré (1845–1924), libretto by René Fauchois. First performance: Monte Carlo, Théâtre du Casino, 4 March 1913, with Bréval and Rousselière. Conductor: Jéhin.

■ Fauré's most important opera, dedicated to Saint-Saëns. As in all his operas, the subject matter is taken from ancient Greece. Musically speaking, it marks something of a break with Wagner and the romantic conventions which had previously had a considerable influence on the composer's output.

LA VIDA BREVE (The Brief Life)

Opera in two acts with four scenes by Manuel de Falla (1876–1946), text by Carlos Fernández Shaw. French version by Paul Milliet. First performance, in French: Nice, Théâtre de l'Opéra, 1 April 1913; first performance in U.K.: Edinburgh Festival, 1958; in U.S.A.: New York, Metropolitan Opera House, 7 March 1926.

ORIGINAL CAST. Lillian Grenville (Salud), David Devriès (Paco), Edouard Cotreuil (Salvador). Conducted by Miranne.

SYNOPSIS. Scene I. In a working-class house in Granada, the grandmother (mezzo-soprano) is feeding some birds. Her granddaughter Salud (soprano) is waiting for her lover Paco (tenor), who is late. When he arrives he is as affectionate as ever, but Salud's uncle, Salvador (baritone or *basso cantante*), comes home with the news that Paco is betrothed to a rich girl. The grandmother flies into a fury. Scene II. Night falls. Paco's forthcoming marriage is to be celebrated in the bride's house. Scene III. Salud watches from the street in front of the house where the celebrations are going on. She sings a song well-known to Paco to attract him. Scene IV. The patio of the house. Paco's new brother-in-law Manuel (baritone) congratulates the young couple. Salud and her uncle enter and explain in answer to Manuel's questions the story of her love for Paco. Paco denies everything. At his words Salud falls to the ground dead with grief while the grandmother and Salvador throw their curses upon him.

■ This was de Falla's first opera. It won the 1905 competition held by the Real Academia de Bellas Artes de San Fernando in Madrid, but the first performance was postponed. The manager finally managed to have it staged in Nice in April 1913. It was performed in Paris at the Opéra-Comique at the end of the same year (31 December 1913), but was not performed in Spain until 1914. It was a great success despite the feeble text. In Paris the music was particularly admired by such composers as Dukas, Albeniz and Debussy. It was also well received by the public and the critics.

L'AMORE DEI TRE RE (The Love of the Three Kings)

Tragic opera in three acts by Italo Montemezzi (1875–1952), libretto by Sem Benelli (1877–1949). First performance: Milan, Teatro alla Scala, 10 April 1913; first performance in U.K.: London, Covent Garden, 27 May 1914; in U.S.A.: New York, Metropolitan Opera House, 2 January 1914.

Roller's set for Act III of Der Rosenkavalier *by Richard Strauss, 1910. Paris, Bibliothèque de l'Opéra.*

ORIGINAL CAST. Luisa Villani (Fiora), Edoardo Ferrari-Fontana (Avito), Carlo Galeffi (Manfredo), Nazzareno De Angelis (Archibaldo). Conductor: Tullio Serafin.

SYNOPSIS. A remote Italian castle in the tenth century, forty years after a Barbarian invasion. Act I. Fiora, an Italian princess (soprano), was betrothed to Avito, an Italian prince, before she was forced to marry Manfredo (baritone), son of King Archibaldo (bass), the Barbarian conqueror of Italy. While Manfredo is on a campaign, the old King begins to suspect his daughter-in-law of infidelity. As he is blind, he is guided through the castle by one of his guards, Flaminio (tenor), another Italian, who deceitfully reassures him. On the night of Manfredo's return, the lovers meet as usual, but Avito is anxious and only escapes just before Archibaldo, on his own, enters. Fiora cannot convince him of her innocence (for his sense of hearing is acute), but she takes advantage of Manfredo's arrival to pretend that she was walking about the castle impatient to see him again. Act II. Manfredo is about to return to war and asks Fiora to wave to him from the battlements until he is out of sight. Fiora, touched by the simple request, feels a new emotion towards him stirring in her heart. Yet even as she waves, Avito invites her to embrace him. They declare their love passionately. Archibaldo hears their voices and approaches. Flaminio stops Avito from killing the old man, telling him to escape instead. Flaminio then has to greet Manfredo, who has noticed that Fiora stopped waving and has returned suspecting that all was not well, so that Fiora and Archibaldo are left together. Terrified and desperate, she taunts him, refusing to reveal her lover's name until he strangles

her. Manfredo hears what has occurred but forgives his wife for her great love although it was not for him. Act III. Fiora is laid out among flowers in the crypt of the castle, mourned by the men and women of the country, who knew her story and loved her. Avito returns and passionately kisses her, but he is seized by the chill of death, for Archibaldo has spread poison on her lips to discover her lover's identity. Manfredo, who does not want to live on, kisses Fiora and dies also. Archibaldo stumbles on the body of a man who he assumes was Fiora's lover and finds that it is his own son.

■ The opera enjoyed great success when performed at the Metropolitan, New York, with Toscanini conducting and with leading singers like the Spaniard Lucrezia Bori, the Italo-American Rosa Ponselle and the American Grace Moore playing the romantic role of Fiora.

Kobbé (9th edn., 1976) suggests that the title may be interpreted as the love of each of the three men for Italy (represented by Fiora), the conqueror and his heir are rejected in favour of one of her own countrymen, for whom she will sacrifice herself. More simply, it may describe Archibaldo's love for his son, Manfredo's unrequited longing for his wife, and the fulfilled passion of Avito and Fiora.

JULIEN, ou LA VIE DU POÈTE (Julian, or The Poet's Life)
Opera in a prologue and four acts by Gustave Charpentier (1860–1956), libretto by the composer. First performance: Paris, Opéra-Comique, 4 June 1913; first

Roller's costume designs for a soldier in Octavian's entourage and the Marschallin's notary in Der Rosenkavalier *by Richard Strauss, 1910.*

■ The enormous success of *Isabeau* gave Lorenzo Sonzogno the idea of a partnership between Gabriele D'Annunzio and Pietro Mascagni. At first, the composer was perplexed by the difficulties involved in setting to music the text, which the poet had completed previously. Attracted, however, by 'the beauty of the verse and the force of the tragedy', he managed to achieve a cordial working relationship with the poet, attempting to suit his music to the most subtle nuances of both content and form in the verse. Despite the fundamental weakness of its unusual length, the opera was most warmly received, when it first appeared, as a work of intense and passionate inspiration.

FRANCESCA DA RIMINI

Tragedy in four acts by Riccardo Zandonai (1883–1944), libretto by Tito Ricordi (1865–1933), after the tragedy by Gabriele D'Annunzio (1863–1938). First performance: Turin, Teatro Regio,

performance in U.S.A.: New York, Metropolitan Opera, 27 January 1914.

ORIGINAL CAST included Carré and Rousselière.

■ Intended as a sequel to the musical romance *Louise*, this opera failed to repeat the first work's considerable success.

PARISINA

Tragedia lirica *in four acts (reduced to three after the first performance) by Pietro Mascagni (1863–1945), text by Gabriele D'Annunzio (1863–1938). First performance: Milan, Teatro alla Scala, 15 December 1913.*

SYNOPSIS. Niccolò d'Este (baritone) had a son, Ugo (tenor), by his mistress Stella dell'Assassino (mezzosoprano), who was forced to leave the court when he married Parisina Malatesta (soprano). Ugo, though attached to his mother, who meets him secretly and tries to make him hate her rival, is won over by Parisina's beauty. While on a journey to the sanctuary at Loreto, Ugo saves Parisina from an attack by Slavonian pirates. She tries to withstand his passion, but in the end surrenders to him. Subsequently tortured by remorse, she imagines that she is pursued by the ghost of Francesca da Rimini and is reliving the events of her life. Niccolò learns of their relationship and catching them one night together sentences them to death. Stella hurries to see her son for the last time but he has already embraced Parisina and given himself up with her to the executioner.

Elisabeth Schwarzkopf as the Marschallin in Der Rosenkavalier *by Richard Strauss.*

19 February 1914; first performance in U.K.: London, Covent Garden, 16 July 1914; in U.S.A.: New York, Metropolitan Opera, 22 December 1916.

ORIGINAL CAST. Francesco Cigada, Linda Cannetti, Giuseppe Crimi, Raquelita Merly, Gabriella Besanzoni, Giuseppe Nessi. Conductor: Ettore Panizza.

SYNOPSIS. The action takes place in Ravenna and Rimini. Act I. A courtyard in the house of the Polentani in Ravenna. Guido, lord of the city, has arranged a marriage between his daughter Francesca (soprano) and Gianciotto Malatesta (baritone), who is lame. In order that the girl will not be put off by the truth, she is led to believe that she is to marry Gianciotto's brother, the handsome Paolo (tenor). As soon as Francesca sees Paolo she falls in love with him. Her sister Samaritana (mezzo-soprano) is filled with foreboding and tearfully begs her not to marry, but Francesca has made up her mind. Act II. Rimini is at war and the rival Guelphs and Ghibellines meet in battle (the Malatestas belong to the latter party). Paolo fights bravely on the tower. Francesca, anxiously following the course of the battle, has joined him there. In a pause in the fighting she reproaches him for the trick that was played on her. Fearing he has been wounded she takes his head in her hands. The enemy are driven away. Gianciotto enters and praises his brother's bravery: he has been elected Captain of the people and Commune of Florence.

Before Paolo departs all three drink a toast. Paolo and Francesca continue to gaze at one another beneath the eyes of her unwitting husband. Malatestino (tenor), brother of Gianciotto and Paolo, is carried in, wounded in one eye. He receives treatment, but longs for battle again. Act III. Francesca is reading the story of Lancelot and Guinevere. Her ladies dance and sing.

The slave Smaragdi (contralto) shows Paolo, who has returned from a long journey, into her apartment. Together they reread the story and their heads gradually move closer together. When Lancelot, in the tale, declares his love for Guinevere, they stop reading and embrace passionately. Act IV. Scene I. Malatestino is also in love with Francesca and tries to ensnare her, but she rejects him scornfully. She complains of the cries of a prisoner in a nearby dungeon, so Malatestino draws his sword and goes off to silence him. Gianciotto enters and Francesca complains to him about Malatestino's cruelty. Malatestino knocks at the door and Francesca leaves to avoid seeing him again. Gianciotto reproaches his brother, and Malatestino, grimly jealous at her behaviour, retaliates by revealing that Francesca and Paolo are lovers. Gianciotto demands proof. Malatestino bids him to wait until night. Scene II. Francesca lies in bed. She wakes from a nightmare that Paolo has been harmed and is comforted by her ladies, whom she then dismisses. Paolo enters. As they embrace, Gianciotto's voice is heard at the door. Paolo attempts to escape through a trap-door, but his coat is caught by a bolt, and he is forced back into the room.

The men fight. Francesca throws herself between them and is stabbed in the breast by Gianciotto, who deals Paolo a fatal blow as his wife falls into his arms.

■ Regarded as the model for twentieth-century Italian drama, *Francesca da Rimini* is one of the main achievements of Mascagni's leading pupil. Zandonai believed that orchestration was his strongest point and in this opera it is the superb orchestration which gives D'Annunzio's already powerful figures added life and force. Condemned for his 'Italian spirit' by the tribunals of the Hapsburg empire, the composer attached great importance to the national character of his work, ignoring the fashions of northern Europe. He concentrated on a restrained distribution of effects – the harmony elegant yet rich, the inspired melody never anything but graceful.

DER HEILIGE BERG (The Holy Mountain)
Opera in a prologue and two acts by Christian Sinding (1856–1941), libretto by Dora Duncker. First performance: Dessau, 19 April 1914.

■ The Norwegian composer wrote two operas. The other has never been produced in a public performance.

MÂROUF, SAVETIER DU CAIRE (Mârouf, the Cobbler of Cairo)
Opera in five acts by Henri Rabaud (1873–1949), libretto by Lucien Népoty, based on a story from the Arabian Nights in J. C. Mardrus's French version. First performance: Paris, Opéra-Comique, 15 May 1914; first performance in U.S.A.: New York, Metropolitan Opera, 19 December 1917.

SYNOPSIS. Act I. A poor cobbler's shop in Cairo. Mârouf (tenor or baritone) is sitting on a carpet, pondering how unlucky he is to have an old, bad-tempered wife, Fatimah (soprano). She once again finds him idle and asks for a cake for the evening. He has earned nothing that day, but luckily a friend, the pastry-cook Ahmad (bass), gives him a cake. It is not to his wife's taste, however, and in the end he decides he might as well eat it himself. Fatimah is furious and her shouts bring all the neighbours. The cadi (bass) arrives too and thinking that Mârouf has beaten his wife has him thrashed. Aching all over, Mârouf decides to take ship and leave home. Act II. Ali's shop in the city of Khaïtan. Mârouf's ship has been wrecked. Ali (baritone) finds him wandering on the shore, discovers that he is an old school friend and decides to help him. He spends a great deal of money on magnificent preparations, as if for the arrival of a very important guest. The Sultan (bass) and the Vizier (baritone), disguised as merchants, mingle with the crowd and try to work out who the stranger is. The vizier thinks he is a charlatan, but the Sultan, impressed by Mârouf's extravagance, introduces himself and invites him to dinner.

Act III. The Sultan's palace. In spite of the Vizier's protests, the Sultan of Khaïtan decides that Mârouf shall marry his daughter that day. In anticipation of the arrival of an imaginary caravan which is meant to bring the stranger's wealth, the Sultan orders the treasury to be opened to Mârouf, who generously distributes money to the rejoicing court and populace. The cobbler, rid of one wife, is afraid that the second may be worse. The charm and beauty of Princess Saamcheddine (soprano) so move him that he tells her his true story in a garbled fashion. As he recalls his unhappy past he swoons. The Princess helps him and kisses him, wondering what he means. Act IV. The harem. Days pass by, but no news of the caravan reaches the palace. The Princess, now in love with Mârouf, protects him and reassures the Vizier. Then she asks her husband to tell her the truth. He confesses that the caravan will never arrive. She persuades him to run away and at his insistence follows him, disguised as a boy. Act V. A plain near Khaïtan with a small garden and wretched peasant's hut. The two fugitives arrive and are sheltered by the peasant. Mârouf thanks him by helping with the ploughing. The plough uncovers a ring attached to a slab, which Mârouf barely manages to lift, uncovering a staircase. Saamcheddine is eager to explore it, but Mârouf dissuades her. They draw back quickly when the peasant arrives, to avoid sharing any treasure with him. In trying to close the hole the ring breaks and Mârouf gives it to the Princess. When she rubs it on her dress the peasant turns into the genie of the ring and the guardian of the treasure. Any wish Mârouf makes will be fulfilled. The promised caravan will arrive, saving him from execution and allowing the two to live happily ever after.

■ With an opening run of two hundred performances, *Mârouf* was the most successful of Rabaud's four operas. The libretto is based on a story from the *Arabian Nights*. The exotic subject matter gave plenty of scope for Rabaud's imagination and his taste for the colourful and the picturesque, which together with his refined style and elegant humour are the opera's outstanding qualities.

LE ROSSIGNOL (The Nightingale)
Opera in three acts by Igor Stravinsky (1882–1971), libretto by the composer and Stephan Mitusov from a fairy tale by Hans Andersen. First performance: Paris, Opéra, 26 May 1914; first performance in U.K.: London, Drury Lane, 18 June 1914; in U.S.A.: New York, Metropolitan Opera, 7 March 1926.

ORIGINAL CAST included the Diaghilev Company. Conductor: Pierre Monteux.

SYNOPSIS. Act I. A forest by the sea at night. A fisherman (tenor) is singing in his boat and is answered from the forest by the trilling of a nightingale. The chamberlain (bass), the bonze (bass) and courtiers (contraltos, tenors, basses) arrive, led by the cook (mezzo-soprano), to listen to the nightingale's marvellous song and invite her to sing it for the Emperor of China. They mistake the mooing of a cow and the croaking of frogs for the bird until their guide identifies its melodious voice for them. The nightingale (soprano) remarks that her voice sounds sweeter in the forest than in the palace: but the Emperor's will must be obeyed. The fisherman once again sings the bird's praises. The nightingale trustingly alights on the cook's hand to be taken to the Emperor. Act II. In the palace of porcelain the nightingale, perched on a stick held by a footman, starts to sing to the Emperor. He is deeply moved when he hears the goodness and purity of the song. The little bird will not accept the honours he offers, and flies away when it hears the song of a mechanical nightingale on the lid of a precious golden casket brought by three ambassadors from the King of Japan. The Emperor condemns the bird to eternal banishment and appoints the clockwork nightingale Singer of the Imperial Bedside Table. Act III. The Emperor's bedroom. The Emperor is lying ill, watched over by Death, who has stolen his royal regalia. The ghosts of his good and bad deeds appear to him and he longs for comfort. The nightingale comes and sings so sweetly that the ghosts are banished, and Death gives back the crown and standards. The melody continues till dawn when Death disappears. Once again the nightingale refuses any reward – it is enough to have seen the Emperor's tears, so it will return every night to sing to him. The courtiers enter, and are astonished to find the Emperor alive. In the distance the fisherman's voice proclaims that the song of the nightingale is the voice of heaven.

■ Stravinsky composed the first part of his delicate

Drawing by Léon Bakst showing Ida Rubinstein in Debussy's Le martyre de Saint Sébastien. *Paris, Bibliothèque de l'Opéra.*

score several years earlier than the rest. When he came to complete the opera, his greater musical maturity presented something of a problem and the contrast between the first act and the two succeeding acts might have detracted from the opera's unity. In fact, there is no abrupt change of style. The composer succeeded in writing a unified work, rich in feeling, humour, satire and fairy-tale elements. Andersen's tale already contained distinct comic touches and the composer made the most of these. The courtiers' entrance is grotesque; the rhythm of the mechanical nightingale's song is in marked contrast to the free melody of the real bird. In contrast with the subtle artful 'chinoiserie' the fisherman's airs are beautiful and profound, the nightingale's song delicate and technically perfect. The soft, clear atmosphere is only broken by the dark visions at the opening of the third act, where rhythms already familiar in Stravinsky after *The Rite of Spring* can be clearly heard.

Léon Bakst's costumes for Debussy's Le martyre de Saint Sébastien. *Paris, Bibliothèque de l'Opéra.*

THE IMMORTAL HOUR
Opera in two acts by Rutland Boughton (1878–1960), text by Fiona Macleod (pseudonym of William Sharp). First performance: Glastonbury, 26 August 1914; first performance in U.S.A.: New York, 6 April 1926.

SYNOPSIS. Dalua (baritone), the Lord of Shadow, is gifted with the fatal touch of death and has the power to know the thoughts of both mortals and immortals. He knows that Etain (soprano), princess of the fairies, has left her happy land of youth and of heart's desire to travel into the alien world of mortals in search of something nameless, some joy or new experience which she vaguely and obscurely senses is possible. Dalua also knows that the mortal king Eochaidh (baritone) has abandoned war and the struggle for power, the luxury and ceremonial of court, prompted by the wish for a new experience – the 'immortal hour'. Eochaidh has also asked the fairies to send him a girl more beautiful than any mortal so that he can win her love and make her his bride. Dalua decides to allow him to meet Etain, although the outcome can only be unlucky since marriage between a mortal and an immortal is impossible. He casts a spell which makes Etain forget all about her past. The two then meet and marry. After an idyllic year Etain has changed. She is anxious and troubled by dreams and confused memories of her past. During the festival to celebrate the first anniversary of their wedding, a stranger asks for a hearing. It is Midir, prince of the fairies, who had loved Etain in the land of youth and of heart's desire. He has come to take her back to her people. As soon as the stranger looks at Etain she suddenly remembers everything and follows him out of the palace as if in a trance, deaf to her husband's entreaties. This is Dalua's moment. At his fatal touch the king falls dead at the foot of his throne.

■ The opera was first performed in London in 1920. On 13 October 1922 it opened at the Regent Theatre, where it had a highly successful run of two hundred and sixteen performances.

MADAME SANS-GÊNE
Opera in three acts by Umberto Giordano (1867–1948), libretto by Renato Simoni (1875–1952) from the French comedy by Victorien Sardou and Emile Moreau. First performance: New York, Metropolitan Opera House, 25 January 1915, in Italian.

ORIGINAL CAST. Geraldine Farrar, Giovanni Martinelli, Pasquale Amato, Paul Althouse. Conductor: Arturo Toscanini.

SYNOPSIS. Act I. Paris, 10 August 1792. The day of the storming of the Tuileries. There is confusion in the laundry of Catherine Huebscher (soprano), a young and beautiful Alsatian woman, known as Madame Sans-Gêne because of her free and easy manner. Her customers include Fouché (baritone), the ambitious revolutionary, to whom she has taken a strong dislike. She prefers to serve a taciturn officer called Napoléon Bonaparte (baritone), who lives nearby. As Catherine is about to close the door, a wounded Austrian officer arrives and asks for help from his pursuers. Catherine hides him in her room. The man is Count Neipperg (tenor). Sergeant Lefebvre (tenor) arrives with a band of soldiers. He is Catherine's sweetheart and becomes suspicious when he finds the door closed. He discovers the wounded man, but understands Catherine's motives and tells the soldiers there is no one in the room. During the night Lefebvre himself helps Catherine arrange the Count's escape. Act II. The château of Compiègne, September 1811. Napoleon is at the height of his career. Madame Sans-Gêne has married Lefebvre, who has distinguished himself in the battle of Danzig and been made Marshal and Duke of Danzig. The scandals which Catherine's behaviour continues to provoke have annoyed the court, and the Emperor has ordered Lefebvre to obtain a divorce and take a wife more suited to his new position. The couple are in despair and are also concerned about the position of their friend Neipperg, whom Napoléon suspects of having relations other than political with his wife Marie Louise. At a reception Catherine makes a series of blunders. Two of the Emperor's sisters make fun of her and she soon loses her temper and rounds on them. A major-domo announces that the Emperor wishes to speak to Catherine. Act III. Napoleon coldly orders Catherine to get a divorce and leave a life for which she is not suited. She reminds him of the laundry days when he was just a young artillery officer, and the Emperor is moved. Then Count Neipperg is caught as he is about to enter the Empress's apartment. Napoleon is furious and orders his immediate execution. Madame Sans-Gêne intervenes, establishes the Count's innocence and saves him. Napoleon is much impressed by her intelligence and generosity. She leaves on the Emperor's arm to start the hunt, amid general astonishment.

■ The opera was a great success, but over the years has been performed less and less. It displays the same strong sense of theatrical power within an historical subject that had earlier been seen in the composer's *Andrea Chénier*.

FEDRA
Tragic opera in three acts by Ildebrando Pizzetti (1880–1968), text by Gabriele D'Annunzio (1909). First performance: Milan, Teatro alla Scala, 20 March 1915.

ORIGINAL CAST. Salomea Kruceniski, Anita Fanny, Eduardo di Giovanni, Edmondo Grandini, Giulio Cirino. Conductor: Gino Marinuzzi.

SYNOPSIS. Greece. In the palace of King Teseo (baritone), the mothers of the heroes who fought at Thebes are waiting for the arrival of the King, who is returning with the ashes of the dead. A (false) rumour that the King is dead spreads. Fedra (mezzo-soprano) is secretly pleased: she is in love with her stepson Ippolito (tenor) and hopes that her husband's death will remove all obstacles, and assure her union with the young man. Teseo, however, does return and his gifts for Ippolito include the beautiful slave Ippanoë (soprano). Fedra, jealous of the girl, at first flatters her, then resorts to threats; finally she drags her before the altar of Jupiter and stabs her through the heart. Ippolito, in his stepmother's room, asks the reason for the girl's death, but soon falls asleep, exhausted by a long ride. Fedra, unable to control her passion, kisses him on the lips. The kiss awakens the young man, who is horrified and rejects her advances. Fedra, mad with grief, resolves to kill herself, and vows to take revenge

on her stepson. When Teseo enters she tells him that Ippolito has tried to rape her. Enraged, the King calls on the god of the sea to kill his son. Soon afterwards he is called to the sea shore and is horror-struck to find Ippolito's corpse. He learns that his son was thrown from his horse and trampled to death. Fedra arrives. She has taken poison and confesses her guilt. Incoherently she declares that Ippolito is now hers at last, because after death no one can oppose her love. As if purified by grief, she throws herself dying on her stepson's body.

■ The opera was composed between 1909 and 1912 and was intended for the Teatro Costanzi, Rome, during the Carnival of 1913. However, it was not performed as the publisher decided to give precedence to Mascagni's *Parisina*, also with a text by D'Annunzio. After the première at La Scala, the critics described *Fedra* as an important operatic event. Since the end of the nineteenth century *verismo* operas and the nineteenth-century repertoire had held the field, in Italy at least, and Italian opera was dominated by realistic plots on contemporary themes rather than classical subjects. *Fedra* was an unexpected success, its heavy, sombre passions contrasting with the small-scale figures of everyday life.

Poster by G. Palanti for Mascagni's Isabeau. *Milan, Museo teatrale alla Scala.*

THE WIZARD

Opera with ballet in three acts by Joseph Holbrooke (1878–1958), text by the composer. First performance: Chicago, Opera House, Spring 1915.

THE BOATSWAIN'S MATE

Opera by Ethel Mary Smyth (1858–1944), libretto by the composer from Captains All *by W. W. Jacobs (1863–1943). First performance: London, Shaftesbury Theatre, 28 January 1916.*

SYNOPSIS. The former boatswain, Harry Benn (tenor), a self-confident and conceited man, is sitting under a tree outside the inn The Beehive one summer evening. He is hoping to persuade the landlady, Mrs Waters (soprano) to marry him and accept him as her permanent protector. Harry works out a plan. If he can persuade Travers (baritone), an ex-soldier whom he has just met, to enter the inn pretending to be a burglar, Mrs Waters will be frightened and shout for help. The boatswain will then rush in and pretend to save her. When Travers agrees, with the incentive of two sovereigns as a reward, the two men approach the inn. The 'burglar' enters the kitchen, making as much noise as he can, but Mrs Waters, hearing the din and suspecting burglars, is not at all frightened. She appears with a loaded gun in her hand. Travers hides in a cupboard and is locked in. After a series of further episodes, including a suspected murder, the landlady decides to get rid of Benn, and bestows her affections on the 'burglar' Travers, who becomes the new landlord of The Beehive.

■ This opera, by the first English woman to win international fame as a composer, is written in the spirit of a ballad. More natural in tone than the composer's earlier operatic works, it makes use of popular airs and displays a much less emphatic Wagnerian influence.

GOYESCAS

Opera in three scenes by Enrique Granados (1867–1916), libretto by Fernando Periquet y Zuaznabar. First performance: New York, Metropolitan Opera House, 28 January 1916; first performance in U.K.: London, Royal College of Music, 11 July 1951.

SYNOPSIS. The action takes place in a suburb on the outskirts of Madrid at the end of the eighteenth century. The toreador Paquiro (baritone) is loved by the beautiful Pepa (mezzo-soprano) but turns his attentions to Rosario (soprano), a lady of rank, who is loved in turn by a young officer, Fernando (tenor). At a ball the jealousies between the four break out. Soon there is a quarrel and Paquiro challenges Fernando to a duel in a wood near Rosario's house. Later Fernando rebuffs Rosario, doubting her fidelity and scorning her declarations of love. He is fatally wounded in the duel and dies in Rosario's arms.

■ Granados's last and most famous opera, *Goyescas* is a stage setting of his suite of piano pieces of the same name (1912). Granados was the pianist whose compositions (especially the two volumes of *Goyescas*, based on scenes and paintings by Goya) firmly established modern Spanish piano music. The opera was to have been performed in Paris but because of the outbreak of World War I had its première at the Metropolitan, New York. It was a triumphant success and won the composer an invitation to the White House. He died on the return voyage when the ship on which he and his wife were travelling was torpedoed by a German submarine.

ARIADNE AUF NAXOS

Opera in one act with prologue by Richard Strauss (1864–1949), text by Hugo von Hofmannsthal (1874–1929). First performance of first version: Stuttgart, Court Theatre, 25 October 1912, with Maria Jeritza, Hermann Jadlowker, Margarethe Siems, conducted by the composer. First performance of second version: Vienna, Hofoper, 4 October 1916, with Maria Jeritza, Selma Kurz, Lotte Lehmann. Conductor: Franz Schalk. First performance in U.K.: London, Covent Garden, 27 May 1924; in U.S.A.: Philadelphia, 1 November 1928.

SYNOPSIS. Prologue. Eighteenth-century Vienna. A room adapted for use as a theatre in the house of a *nouveau riche*. The music master (baritone) learns with dismay from the major-domo (speaking role) that in the entertainment which the master of the house is providing for his guests, the *opera seria* written by the composer, the music master's pupil, is to be followed by a *Commedia dell'Arte* farce. The young composer (soprano) enters, hoping to organize a rehearsal, but finds neither orchestra nor singers. Zerbinetta (soprano), the head of the troupe of comedians, emerges from her dressing room with an officer. The music master tells the composer about the plan for the two performances. The composer is outraged. The prima donna (soprano), fresh from the hands of her hairdresser, is furious. Meanwhile the master and his guests have finished dinner and the performers are told to be ready. The major-domo reappears with fresh instructions from his master. To save time, as there are to be fireworks afterwards, the two performances must be given simultaneously. The composer is utterly bewildered. The dancing master (tenor) tries to convince him that Zerbinetta, who is very expert at improvisation, will have no difficulty in adapting the *opera buffa* to the *opera seria*, if he will agree to cut the more long-winded parts of *Ariadne*. The composer, who cannot bear to mutilate his great work, tries to explain its loftier ideas to Zerbinetta, but she is unimpressed and uses all the tricks of seduction to give this passionate but inexperienced young man a glimpse of the true delights woman can offer. The composer is strongly attracted to her, but finishes the scene by declaring his faith in the power of music.

Montemezzi's L'amore dei tre re *at La Scala, Milan, in 1953, the fortieth anniversary of the first performance.*

The opera. A cave on the island of Naxos. Ariadne (the prima donna – soprano), abandoned by Theseus and inconsolable, is surrounded by nymphs (Naiade – contralto, Dryade – soprano, Echo – contralto). She laments her fate and calls on Hermes, the messenger of death. The comedians try to comfort her with their capers and by offering advice. They are joined by Zerbinetta, who sings the great aria *Grossmächtige Prinzessin*, a prodigious piece of vocal virtuosity, in which she expresses the essence of her amorous experiences – she swears to be faithful, but receives each new lover like a god. Harlequin (baritone) enters and makes advances towards Zerbinetta. She lightheartedly resists him and they withdraw. The nymphs announce the arrival of Bacchus (tenor), 'a charming boy, a young god'. Ariadne mistakes the newcomer for the messenger of death and offers herself to him. Bacchus, who is returning from the island of Circe and is still under the influence of a magic potion, believes she is the sorceress. Finally, in an extended duet, Ariadne, who has asked him to take her to the Underworld in search of Theseus, agrees to accompany him to Olympus. Zerbinetta appears again, and remarks on the inevitability of the outcome.

■ The first version of *Ariadne*, together with the incidental music for *Le Bourgeois Gentilhomme*, was conceived as a thank-offering to Max Reinhardt, the producer, for whom Hofmannsthal had adapted Molière's comedy. It was designed to replace the *divertissement* which ends the comedy and although not meant to last more than half an hour, the completed score was three times that length. The orchestra consisted of a small number of players, treated almost as soloists. After several attempts to stage it elsewhere, this version was performed at the Court Theatre, Stuttgart, where the many technical problems posed by the hybrid nature of the work (the need for two casts, the positioning of the orchestra in an ordinary playhouse, etc.) could be solved. However, it foundered because of its length as well as the disparity of style between the French comedy and German opera. One critic, Richard Specht, suggested the solution which the authors eventually adopted in the second version – making *Ariadne* independent of Molière and adding a sung prologue. Hofmannsthal had a very lofty view of his text and explained its deeper meaning in an article in *Neues Tageblatt* on 12 October 1912: 'The transformation which Ariadne undergoes in Bacchus' arms is the vital moment of the whole work. . . . The transformation is the life of life itself, the real mystery of nature as a creative force. Everything that wishes to live must rise above itself, be transformed . . . must forget. Ariadne was dead and is alive again, her spirit is truly

Stravinsky's Le rossignol *in the 1972 production at the Théâtre de la Ville, Paris.*

transformed. . . . Zerbinetta and her fellows see in Ariadne's experience all that they are capable of seeing: the exchange of one lover for another . . . the two spiritual worlds are ironically brought together in the end in the only way in which they can be brought together – in non-comprehension.' Strauss, who preferred to draw his inspiration from real people and feelings, had a different view. He regarded the characters in the text simply as projections of a literary idea. Hence his emphasis on Zerbinetta, the most vital character and the one given greatest musical prominence. (Zerbinetta's solo struck the librettist as 'vulgar'.) We can interpret *Ariadne* as an allegory of the two authors' collaboration, itself founded on mutual non-comprehension. The second version, an opera of undeniable charm, has been a regular success, less perhaps because of the quality of the music than because of the appealing formula of a play within a play and the contrast between the dynamic, realistic prologue and the static, allegorical opera.

SĀVITRI

Opera in one act by Gustav Holst (1874–1934), libretto by the composer. First performance: London, Wellington Hall, 5 December 1916. Conductor: Grunebaum. First performance in U.S.A.: Chicago, 23 January 1934.

SYNOPSIS. The action takes place in virgin forest in India at some unspecified time. The curtain goes up on an empty stage. A voice is heard calling Sāvitri (soprano), the wife of a woodcutter. She enters, remembering with apprehension a dream in which she had been warned of an impending disaster. She is afraid for her beloved husband, Satyavān (tenor), who has gone to cut down a tree. Death (bass) approaches the house, planning to carry off Satyavān, who has just returned and is comforting his wife. Her fears were wellfounded, for at the sight of Death her husband dies in her arms. Weeping, Sāvitri declares her eternal love for a husband who has loved her so much and is now gone for ever. She hears celestial voices, comforting and blessing her. They are, Death explains, the voices of those she has comforted and helped by the purity of her love. Eventually, Death takes pity on her pure selfdenial, offering to grant any wish except the return of her husband. Sāvitri asks for life, a happy and joyous life springing solely from the fulness of love; this for her can only mean one thing – Satyavān. Death is moved by her heartfelt prayer and, conquered by her love, returns Satyavān to her. Sāvitri sings gently to her husband.

■ The libretto is based on an episode from the *Mahā Bhārata*, the famous Indian epic poem, chosen because of Holst's interest in Indian civilization, particularly Sanskrit literature. The music was composed in 1908, but not performed until 1916. The opera was a great success and was later performed in the U.S.A. Nowadays it receives the occasional performance in England.

LA RONDINE (The Swallow)

Opera in three acts by Giacomo Puccini (1858–1924), libretto by Giuseppe Adami (1878–1946). First performance: Monte Carlo, Théâtre du Casino, 27 March 1917; first performance in U.K.: London, Fulham Town Hall, 9 December 1965; in U.S.A.: New York, Metropolitan Opera House, 10 March 1928.

ORIGINAL CAST included Gilda dalla Rizza, Ines Ferraris, Tito Schipa. Conductor: Gino Marinuzzi.

SYNOPSIS. Paris during the Second Empire. Act I. A party is being held in the fashionable house of the beautiful Magda de Civry (soprano), mistress of the banker Rambaldo (baritone). The poet Prunier (tenor), a drawing-room philosopher, comments mockingly that romantic love is once again in fashion, claiming society victims like an epidemic. The poet, who also fancies himself as a palmist, reads Magda's hand and predicts that she will fly away to sea like a swallow. Though she presses him he refuses to say more. A new guest arrives – young Ruggero Lastouc (tenor), who has come up from Montauban to meet Rambaldo. This is his first visit to Paris, and Lisette (soprano), Magda's maid, advises him to spend an evening at Bullier's café. Magda decides to go there too in disguise. Act II. Chez Bullier, the ballroom, frequented by students and *grisettes*. Magda, wearing Lisette's clothes, avoids unwelcome attentions by pretending to have a rendezvous. She sits down at a table with Ruggero, who fails to recognize his former hostess. Overcome by memories of her happiest years, when she lived in poverty dreaming of a great love, she surrenders herself to her growing passion for the young man. Act III. The terrace of a little house by the sea. Magda has abandoned the comforts of Paris to follow Ruggero to the Côte d'Azur. He wants to marry her and has written to ask his mother for her permission. Magda believes that her past makes her unfit to be his wife, so she discloses her true identity and leaves him for the 'gilded cage' of Paris and Rambaldo.

■ The idea of asking Puccini to write a light, sentimental operetta in the Viennese style came from Otto Eibenschutz and Heinrich Berté, directors of the Carl-Theater, Vienna. At first the composer was not interested, but he signed the contract in 1914 to spite the publishers Ricordi, with whom he had fallen out. As he was not happy with the original text by Alfred Maria Willner and Heinrich Reichert, he commissioned a revised version from Giuseppe Adami and set to work, again without much enthusiasm, completing the opera in 1916. The Monte Carlo audience gave the first performance a triumphant reception, but this was not repeated at subsequent revivals.

Despite its formal elegance *La Rondine* is the least convincing of Puccini's mature operas. This is partly because of its hybrid nature, which prevents it reaching the heights of expressive power, but also because of its failure to realize the comic potential of the characters Prunier and Lisette, who are only sketchily portrayed. Besides the waltzes, typical of the 'Chez Bullier' scene, Puccini added modern rhythms (tango, fox-trot and one-step) at various points in the score, in curious contrast to the Second Empire setting.

LODOLETTA

Dramatic opera in three acts by Pietro Mascagni (1863–1945), libretto by Giovacchino Forzano. First performance: Rome, Teatro Costanzi, 30 April 1917;

Act of Giordano's Madame Sans-Gêne *in the 1966–67 production at La Scala, Milan. Scenery and costumes by Giulio Coltellacci, producer Franco Enriquez.*

first performance in U.S.A.: New York, Metropolitan Opera House, 12 January 1918.

SYNOPSIS. The first two acts take place in a Dutch village, the third in Paris in 1853. The French painter Flammen, forced to flee from the police for political reasons, takes refuge in a Dutch village and meets a girl, Lodoletta, who has just recently lost her father. Flammen grows fond of her and paints her portrait. She falls in love with him and disregards the affectionate attentions of Giannotto, a young man from the village. The painter promises Lodoletta that he will not leave her, but when he is given permission to return to France he cannot resist the charms of the capital and leaves the village. Lodoletta follows him to Paris where, on New Year's Eve, Flammen is holding a party for his friends. He is tormented by memories of his past love, and cannot join in the merry-making. Lodoletta arrives at the house and, looking through a window, sees him. She is overcome with despair and exhaustion, and collapses dying in the snow. Flammen comes out into the garden. He understands too late what has happened and tearfully embraces the lifeless body.

■ The story is based on the novel *Two Little Wooden Shoes* (1874) by the English novelist Ouida, pen-name of Louise de la Ramée. The novel had already attracted the attention of Puccini, who commissioned an adaptation first from Roberto Bracco, then from Giuseppe Adami, but later abandoned the project. In the opera there is perhaps a certain lack of continuity between the first two acts, with their fresh, idyllic atmosphere reminiscent of *L'Amico Fritz*, and the third, in which the mood becomes more dramatic.

TURANDOT

Fable in two acts by Ferruccio Busoni (1866–1924), libretto by the composer based on Carlo Gozzi's play (1762). First performance: Zurich, Stadttheater, 11 May 1917; first performance in U.S.A.: New York, Little Orchestra Society 1967.

SYNOPSIS. Act I, Scene I. The walls of Peking in China. Prince Calaf (tenor) meets his faithful servant Barak (baritone), who has escaped from the disastrous war in which Calaf's father has lost his throne. Barak tells the Prince about events in the City: the Court is undergoing a crisis because Princess Turandot has decided that she will offer her hand to whoever can answer three riddles she asks; those who cannot

Franz Theo Reuter as the major-domo in the prologue of Ariadne auf Naxos *by Richard Strauss in a production at the Residenztheater, Munich, in 1937. Scenery and costumes by Ludwig Sievert, producer Rudolf Hartmann.*

answer are beheaded. Many have made the attempt, attracted by the cruel Princess's beauty. When Calaf sees her picture he too is bewitched and decides to try his luck. Scene II. The throne room in the royal palace of Peking. Truffaldino (high tenor), chief eunuch, is preparing the room for the next trial when the Emperor and his dignitaries will watch another suitor's attempts end (as usual) with his death. The contenders begin to arrive. The Emperor Altoum (bass) enters, followed by his ministers Pantalone (bass) and Tartaglia (bass). After publicly expressing his distress at the proceedings, he introduces the new suitor, Calaf, who refuses to reveal his name. When Turandot sees him she experiences a moment of emotion. The stranger solves her three riddles, but the Princess refuses to accept defeat and tries to kill herself. She is prevented and Calaf generously asks her a riddle himself: if Turandot can discover his name and the name of his family he will release her from her promise. Act II. Turandot's chamber. The Princess is puzzled by her feelings – she hates the man who has beaten her, but at the same time feels irresistibly drawn to him. Truffaldino is given the task of finding out the Prince's name, but he fails. Altoum learns the Prince's name, but will not reveal it to Turandot. He looks forward to her public humiliation. She asks her confidante Adelma for advice. Adelma, who was a princess before she became a slave, had once entertained Calaf as her guest and fallen in love with him. She offers to reveal his name in return for her freedom. Turandot eventually accepts the bargain, and, before her time runs out, answers the riddle. Calaf resigns himself to depart. At the last moment Turandot, now victorious, overcomes her pride and declares her love for him.

■ The atmosphere of the opera is one of fairy tale and whimsical fantasy, whereas in Puccini's *Turandot* (see p. 400 below) the mood is charged with passion and tragedy. Busoni's approach to everything – feelings and events – is ironical, and the irony is accentuated by the presence of the three stock comic characters Truffaldino, Pantalone and Tartaglia. The music is clearly inspired by oriental, Chinese and Arab themes.

ARLECCHINO, oder DIE FENSTER (Harlequin, or The Windows)

Theatrical capriccio in one act by Ferruccio Busoni (1866–1924), libretto by the composer. First performance: Zurich, Stadttheater, 11 May 1917; first performance in U.K.: (BBC broadcast) 1939; Glyndebourne, 25 June 1954; in U.S.A.: (semi-staged), New York, Carnegie Hall, 1951.

SYNOPSIS. The action takes place in Bergamo, Arlecchino's native town. In a little piazza Arlecchino (speaking role) is paying court to Annunziata (mimed role), wife of Ser Matteo (baritone), a pedantic tailor and keen reader of Dante's *Divina Commedia*. Arlecchino first disguises his actions by frightening Matteo with talk of barbarians invading the city, and later on

Helen Vanni as Ariadne in Ariadne auf Naxos *by Richard Strauss in the 1972 Glyndebourne production.*

appears disguised as a recruiting sergeant to sign him up, even offering to look after Matteo's house while he is away. Meanwhile Columbina (mezzo-soprano), Arlecchino's neglected wife, who boasts that she is always faithful to her husband in spite of everything, is unable to resist the advances of Leandro (tenor). Arlecchino knocks out Leandro with his wooden sword and runs away. But Leandro is not dead. Arlecchino calms down, gives his wife her freedom, and goes off with Annunziata. He is content to be free himself and to owe nothing to anyone. The moral of the opera is pointed out: Everything is new, everything goes on as before.

■ The subject was well suited to Busoni's sense of humour and his ironic treatment of outdated forms of Italian melodrama – for example, Leandro, the classic lover, who needs a guitar or lute before he can express himself. His serenade is in Italian, even in the original German text, to underline the irony (though Busoni was an Italian, he lived abroad all his life). Arlecchino, who does not sing at all in the opera (and at the first performance was played by the dramatic actor Alexander Moissi), is both a participant in the action and a commentator on events.

PALESTRINA

Opera in three acts by Hans Pfitzner (1869–1949), libretto by the composer. First performance: Munich, Residenztheater, 12 June 1917, with Karl Erb. Conductor: Bruno Walter.

SYNOPSIS. Rome and Trent, 1563. Act I. A room in Palestrina's house. Silla (mezzo-soprano), Palestrina's pupil, is trying out on his viol a piece different in musical style to his master's; he confesses his aspirations to Ighino (soprano). Cardinal Borromeo (baritone) enters, followed by Palestrina (tenor). The cardinal first rebukes the composer for teaching the young a new, perhaps sinful, art and gives vent to his irritation on the subject. He then commissions Palestrina to compose a Mass to close the Council of Trent. Palestrina feels old and tired: he is undergoing a religious crisis and refuses the task. He is so depressed that he even considers suicide. As he sits at his desk he sees a vision of the composers of the past who urge him to continue his work. They are followed by choirs of angels, intoning the *Kyrie eleison*, and finally his dead wife Lucretia (contralto) appears. Palestrina is filled with a feeling of peace and starts work feverishly. As dawn rises, and the voices die away, Silla and Ighino arrive for their lesson. They are amazed to find that a complete Mass has been composed. Act II. Trent, the great hall in the palace of Cardinal Madruscht (bass).

The prelates are engaged in fierce argument. The news spreads that Borromeo has had Palestrina thrown into prison for refusing to compose the Mass as ordered. The meeting begins with a prayer and a message of peace from the Pope, but business does not proceed smoothly. The participants discuss the rite of the Mass and Cardinal Borromeo tries to calm tempers. As noon strikes the stormy session ends. As soon as the legates have left, a fight breaks out between their Italian, German and Spanish servants. Soldiers burst in and open fire. Act III. Palestrina, visibly weaker and older, is again in a room of his house surrounded by five young singers and his faithful servant Giuseppe. His son, Ighino, kneeling by him, informs him that his Mass is about to be performed – when Silla was arrested he collected and kept the music Palestrina had composed that night, but it was eventually taken from him. Shouts of rejoicing can be heard from the street and the singers from the papal chapel come to report that the Mass has been a triumph. Pius IV (bass) in person congratulates Palestrina, and Cardinal Borromeo begs forgiveness from the composer. The old man is happy at his success but feels that his work is now ended. His pupil Silla has left for Florence to join the new Bardi school of music and though Ighino promises to be faithful to him he realizes that he has already given everything he can. At peace with himself, he gazes at the portrait of his wife, and then plays the organ to give thanks to God.

■ This opera, with its clear Wagnerian inspiration, found many admirers among conservative German music lovers who disliked the new trends displayed by Schönberg and Busoni. It was composed as a homage to Palestrina, whose *Missa Papae Marcelli* was said to 'have saved the art of counterpoint' in sixteenth-century church music. In recent years the Austrian singer Julius Patzak has been a leading interpreter of the title role.

THE MARRIAGE (Zenitba)
Unfinished comic opera in two acts by Modest Mussorgsky (1839–81), based on Gogol's comedy (1842). First full production: Petrograd, Musikzlnnaia Drama Teatr, 26 October 1917.

■ The opera was begun in 1864 and interrupted four years later (when Mussorgsky started work on *Boris*), with only the first act and part of the second completed. The first complete performance, revised by Rimsky-Korsakov, was given at Petrograd on 26 October 1917, but Rimsky-Korsakov had already given a concert performance of it in 1906, and on 1 April 1909 the Suvorin School of St Petersburg had produced a stage version with piano accompaniment. In 1923 it was performed in Paris with orchestration by Ravel. The action of the opera is based on characters rather than events – timid, unsure Podkolessin, the enterprising marriage-broker Fiokla, and the fiancée. Around these sometimes comic, sometimes pathetic, figures the composer creates a musical fabric perfectly in keeping with the character of each, in accordance with the musical ideals of the Russian Nationalist school of composers.

DUKE BLUEBEARD'S CASTLE (A Kékszakállú Herceg Vára)
Opera in one act by Béla Bartók (1881–1945), text by Béla Balázs. First performance: Budapest, Királyi Operház, 24 May 1918; first performance in U.K.: London, Rudolf Steiner Hall, 16 January 1957; in U.S.A.: New York, City Center, 2 October 1952.

ORIGINAL CAST. Olga Haselbeck (Judith), Oszkár Kálmán (Bluebeard). Conductor: Egisto Tango.

SYNOPSIS. The action takes place at a legendary time in an imaginary castle. The bard (speaking role) introduces the legend to the audience. Bluebeard (bass) and Judith (mezzo-soprano), his new wife, enter the hall of the castle, a large round room with seven doors and no windows. The scene is plunged in darkness. Bluebeard asks Judith to reflect on her decision to leave her family and give herself wholly to him, her secret husband. She remains firm in her resolve, and the two are isolated in their own enchanted world. Fired by curiosity and intent on letting light into his domain, she asks him for the key to the first of the seven doors leading off the hall. He gives it to her reluctantly, and she discovers a room full of shackles, knives and hooks, horrible instruments of torture, wet with blood. She asks for the key to the second door. This room too is full of sharp weapons – it is Bluebeard's blood-stained armoury. Meanwhile the hall gradually becomes lighter. Bluebeard unwillingly allows his wife to open the third room, the treasury, filled with gleaming jewels, again wet with blood. The fourth door opens onto a charming rose garden. Judith plucks one, but drops of blood drip from the stem. Her curiosity is still not satisfied and she wants to see more. The fifth door reveals an expanse of land, his kingdom, overhung by a deep, blood-red cloud on the horizon. Bluebeard desperately begs her not to open the two remaining doors, but to surrender to his love and to trust him; Judith will not listen. The sixth door opens onto a lake of tears. By now she understands the meaning of what she sees but, as if indifferent, she insists on opening the last door, sealing her doom. Three ghostly figures emerge, crowned and robed in fabulous jewels – Bluebeard's three former wives, transformed into incorporeal beings because they too wanted to see what Judith has now seen. Bluebeard tells Judith their story. He met the first in the morning and the dawn is sacred to her; the second at noon, so the afternoon is sacred to her; the third in the evening so the evening is dedicated to her. Now he has met Judith in the night. He dresses her in a crown and robe, and as she enters the seventh room, all the doors close. Bluebeard is left alone in the dark hall of his gloomy castle.

■ *Duke Bluebeard's Castle* is now regarded as the greatest masterpiece of Hungarian opera. It was not, however, an immediate success and when completed in 1911 was banned by the Hungarian Commission of Fine Arts. Bartók then retired from public musical life and devoted himself to the study of folk music. The opera was rediscovered in 1918 by the Italian conductor Egisto Tango, who realized its worth. After the defeat of the Magyar people in the First World War, Hungary underwent a political and economic crisis and nothing more was heard of the opera for several years. It was successfully performed in German (translation by W. Ziegler) in Frankfurt in 1922 and in Berlin in 1929. It was also performed in Hungarian in Florence on 5 May 1938 by a company from Budapest Opera as part of the annual May festival, the Maggio musicale. The opera, freely based on the fairytale *Barbebleue* by Charles Perrault (1628–1703), has only two characters. A significant departure from the original source is that the main character is no longer the traditional villain, and even commands our sympathy because of his extreme loneliness. *Bluebeard* represents the synthesis of all Bartók's musical experiences up to 1911. In it he combines the melodic forms of Hungarian folk music with more sophisticated artistic techniques. He was not completely free from the values inherited from the romantic tradition, and some critics believe that the folk music element inhibited his creative drive. There is a marked dualism between romantic and impressionistic influences on the one hand, and the search for a new musical language on the other. The orchestration is varied and complex, at times achieving a powerful expressive sonority. *Bluebeard* has been compared to Debussy's *Pelléas et Mélisande* (Kodaly described it as a 'Hungarian *Pelléas*'), and, at least in aesthetic purpose, the two operas have points of similarity.

IL TRITTICO (The Triptych):
IL TABARRO, SUOR ANGELICA, GIANNI SCHICCHI (The Cloak, Sister Angelica, Gianni Schicchi)
Triple bill by Giacomo Puccini (1858–1924). The three operas are independent and have no connecting theme. First performance: New York, Metropolitan Opera House, 14 December 1918.

ORIGINAL CAST. Claudia Muzio, Giulio Crimi and Luigi Montesanto (*Il Tabarro*); Geraldine Farrar, Flora Pernini (*Suor Angelica*); Giuseppe De Luca, Florence Easton, Giulio Crimi (*Gianni Schicchi*). Conductor: Roberto Moranzoni.

IL TABARRO
Libretto by Giuseppe Adami (1878–1946) from Didier Gold's one-act play La Houppelande *(1910).*

SYNOPSIS. Paris at the beginning of the twentieth century. A barge moored in the Seine. Giorgetta (soprano) is busy in the cabin while the stevedores finish unloading sacks from the barge and her husband Michele (baritone), the boat's owner, stands at the helm, watching the sunset. An organ-grinder plays a waltz. Michele, talking with his wife, sympathizes with Luigi (tenor), the youngest stevedore, who is penniless. The voice of a song-seller (tenor) is heard off stage. Frugola (mezzo-soprano), a rag-picker, appears, a bag of rubbish on her back. She and her husband, old Talpa (bass), set off home in the dark. Luigi, Giorgetta's secret lover, tired of his wretched life and unable to bear the torments of his secret love any longer, tells Michele that he plans to leave the barge as soon as it reaches Rouen. While Michele is below the two lovers sing a duet in which they express their guilt at their clandestine relationship and their eagerness to share a further brief hour of happiness together. They decide on the usual signal that all is clear for their meeting – Giorgetta will strike a match. Luigi leaves. Michele reappears and reminds his wife of their past happiness, when he used to wrap her tenderly in his great cloak. He mourns that she no longer loves him. Giorgetta, ill at ease, replies evasively. Michele broods on the reasons for the change in Giorgetta. He suspects that she has a lover and considers the three men who share their life but excludes them all – Talpa is too old, Tinca too drunk, and as Luigi is leaving it cannot be him. Michele lights his pipe. Luigi, watching from the bank, thinks this is Giorgetta's signal and hurries onto the barge. Michele guesses the truth. He forces the young man to confess and then strangles him, hiding the body under his cloak. Giorgetta, alarmed by the noises she has heard, appears again, but when she sees Michele alone pretends to be sorry for her earlier coldness and asks him to wrap her in his cloak as he used to do. Michele opens the cloak and to her horror shows her the face of her dead lover.

■ The original source for the text – a piece of Grand Guignol drama – probably accounts for the initially cool reaction *Il Tabarro* received from the critics, who felt that the subject matter was in bad taste. In fact Puccini himself was involved in preparing the libretto. He suggested cutting a subplot also ending in crime which occurs in Gold's play and emphasized the more romantic and richly emotional side of the story. The drama contains an introduction, a central part and a conclusion within the space of a single act, making the opera an effective and perfectly balanced whole. Above all *Il Tabarro* is a masterly study of atmosphere. Its fascination lies in its musical evocation of the river – the ghostly mists, the slowly moving waters, the oppressive monotony of the boatmen's lives. The harmonic language is evidence of Puccini's interests in new trends in contemporary music, but it is always functional, a means of expressing atmosphere or conveying character.

SUOR ANGELICA
Libretto by Giovacchino Forzano (1884–1970).

SYNOPSIS. The action takes place in a convent towards the end of the seventeenth century. Sister Angelica (soprano) has been forced to retire to the convent by her noble family to atone for the guilt of an illicit relationship, as a result of which she gave birth to a son seven years ago. Her aunt, the Princess (contralto), arrives and asks her to sign away her share of the family inheritance. In the course of their conversation she coldly informs Angelica that her little son is dead. Angelica is plunged into despair and takes poison, but when death approaches she is filled with remorse and calls on the Virgin Mary for salvation. A heavenly choir answers her. The Virgin appears, bathed in radiant light, gently leading a little child towards her as she dies.

■ Though technically flawless, *Suor Angelica* is the least successful of the *Trittico*. Its weakest point lies perhaps in the slender plot; the absence of dramatic situations and conflicts (apart from the powerful confrontation between Angelica and her aunt) fails to provide scope for the composer's musical imagination. It is only in the confrontation scene, which has been compared to the torture scene in *Tosca* – the torture is psychological here, but just as cruel – that Puccini reaches the heights of dramatic expression. The aunt, the only significant part for contralto voice in all Puccini's work, is one of the most original creations in his gallery of female characters. The same scene expresses in musical terms Angelica's transformation from a nun like all the others, as she appears in the first part of the opera, into a mother and a woman, an individual who has suffered. At the end her voice merges with the choir of angels. The miracle scene, though effective in purely theatrical terms, seems to lack genuine feeling.

GIANNI SCHICCHI
Libretto by Giovacchino Forzano (1884–1970), from an episode in Dante's Inferno.

SYNOPSIS. The action takes place in Florence in 1299. The relations of Buoso Donati, who has just died, are gathered round his bed. The rumour that he has left the whole of his sizeable fortune to the monks of Signa to make up for his misdeeds fills the relations with dismay. They interrupt their vigil and led by old Simone (bass) and Zita (mezzo-soprano), cousins of the dead man, search the house for the will. Rinuccio (tenor), Zita's nephew, finally discovers the document. Before handing it over to his aunt, he demands her permission for his marriage to Lauretta (soprano), daughter of Gianni Schicchi (baritone), a man despised by the Donati family because of his peasant origins. A reading of the will confirms their fears – Buoso has left everything to the monastery. Rinuccio persuades his family to send for Gianni Schicchi, a man well known for his cunning. When Schicchi arrives with his daughter Lauretta he is given such an unfriendly welcome that he prepares to leave again. Lauretta changes his mind by threatening to throw herself into the Arno if she is not allowed to buy her wedding ring, in the famous aria 'O mio babbino caro' ('O my beloved father'). Schicchi relents and works out a plan. He will pretend to be the dying Buoso Donati and dictate a new will to the notary. The relations agree to this enthusiastically and each secretly tries to bribe Schicchi to give him the best part of the inheritance. He agrees with each and sends for the notary. Dressed in Buoso's clothes, lying on the dead man's bed, he dictates a will which leaves the most prized possessions to himself. The relations are appalled, but cannot reveal the fraud as it involves them all, and the penalty for forgery according to an old Florentine law is exile and the loss of one hand. When the notary leaves, Schicchi chases Buoso's relations out of the house, which is now his, while Rinuccio and Lauretta embrace. Schicchi takes his leave of the audience. This, he tells them, is the trick that sent him to hell, but if they have enjoyed themselves as much as he has, let them grant him that there were extenuating circumstances!

■ In this opera modern comedy and ancient tradition are closely interwoven. The starting point for the story occurs in Canto XXX of the *Inferno*, in the circle where Dante places the falsifiers of words, persons and coins. This includes Gianni Schicchi who to win himself a mule:

'. . . lent his own false frame
To Buoso de' Donati, and made a will
In legal form, and forged it in his name.'

(Translation by Dorothy L. Sayers, Penguin) According to one tradition, the mule was his reward from the heir for impersonating Buoso, but in another version, which Puccini follows, Schicchi left himself the mule and a large legacy in the will. Details like the reference to the struggle between Guelfs and Ghibellines or to the resentment which old Florentine families felt towards urbanized peasants help to establish the opera's historical setting – a Florence which Puccini praises through Rinuccio ('*Firenze è come un albero fiorito;*' 'Florence is like a tree in blossom'). With this tribute to old Florence and the use of a plot and charac-

ters typical of the Commedia dell'Arte, some regard *Gianni Schicchi* as Puccini's most truly Italian opera. It is a comedy which, despite elements of cruelty and the macabre, sets out frankly to entertain, but manages to avoid all suggestion of routine. Instead it shows Puccini's remarkable ability to extend the range of his creative activity by adapting his style, formed in the mould of tragic opera, to a comic subject.

■ The idea of three one-act operas to be performed on one evening first came to Puccini just after he had completed *Tosca*. The original plan was that the three contrasting stories would be taken respectively from Dante's *Inferno*, *Purgatorio* and *Paradiso*. In the finished work only one episode is inspired by the Divina Commedia, though the intended contrast between the three episodes and their endings remains. (*Il Tabarro* is a sordid tale of despair, *Suor Angelica* a tragedy which leaves room for hope, *Gianni Schicchi* a comic opera). The three operas had very different fortunes. *Gianni Schicchi* was an immediate success and has been frequently performed, while the other two were neglected, and critics have only recently revised their adverse opinion of *Il Tabarro*. Puccini conceived *Il Trittico* as an indivisible whole and was at first unhappy to see it broken up, but he eventually admitted that the complete work was too long and resigned himself to separate performances.

DIE FRAU OHNE SCHATTEN (The Woman without a Shadow)

Opera in three acts by Richard Strauss (1864–1949), text by Hugo von Hofmannsthal (1874–1929). First performance: Vienna, Staatsoper, 10 October 1919; first performance in U.K.: London, Sadler's Wells Theatre, 2 May 1966; in U.S.A.: San Francisco, 18 September 1959.

ORIGINAL CAST. Maria Jeritza, Lotte Lehmann, Aagard Oestvig, Richard Mayr, Lucie Weidt. Conductor: Franz Schalk.

SYNOPSIS. Act I. An apartment in the Emperor's palace. The nurse (mezzo-soprano), crouching in the dark, is visited by a messenger (baritone) from Keikobad, King of the Spirits, who asks her if the Empress is still without a shadow. The Empress is a supernatural being, who was captured as a white gazelle by the Emperor. She is now happy as his wife, but must return to the world of spirits to which she belongs. The fact that she has no shadow is a symbol of the infertility (or inhumanity) of her love for the Emperor. The messenger announces that if the Empress has not found a shadow within three days she will have to return to her own world with the nurse (who is delighted) and the Emperor will be turned into stone. The messenger disappears. It is dawn and the

Emperor (tenor) narrates the story of how he first met his wife. He also mentions a falcon, which he injured and drove away because it struck the fairy gazelle's eyes with its wings. He leaves on a hunting trip. The Empress (soprano) awakes, sees the falcon hovering in the sky and hears its lament, 'The woman throws no shadow, and the Emperor will be turned into stone.' She begs the nurse to help her find a shadow. The nurse unwillingly obeys, telling her that they will have to descend to the wretched world of men. They arrive at the hut of Barak (bass-baritone), a poor dyer. He lives with his wife (soprano) and three lazy, deformed and violent brothers, the cause of frequent disagreements between husband and wife. Barak's wife loves him although she is unhappy with her life. In three and a half years of marriage she has not yet borne him a child. The nurse and the Empress enter, disguised as servants. The nurse wins the woman's confidence, flatters her and shows her visions of luxury and love. All this will be hers in return for her shadow and her renunciation of motherhood. Barak's wife agrees to the exchange and promises to deny her husband access to her bed. She hears Barak coming back and the nurse magically makes a meal appear – five little fishes, which sing a lament as they are fried on the fire; they are the spirits of the unborn children. The poor woman is terrified, but nevertheless continues with her bargain. The couple's bed is separated into two. Act II. The nurse and the Empress are again in Barak's hut. The nurse summons the apparition of a lover for the woman and urges her to be unfaithful to her husband. Barak, having done well at the market, returns home, followed by his brothers and a crowd of hungry children, to whom he gives food. The scene changes to the Emperor's falcon house, where the Empress should be staying. He sees her enter with the nurse, and realizes with desperate grief that she has been with earth people. He decides to kill her, but cannot choose an appropriate weapon. In the dyer's hut, the nurse puts Barak to sleep with a potion and again summons the apparition, which tries to possess the woman. She cries out and wakes Barak, who does not understand what is going on. She reproaches him for not paying attention to her. The Empress is increasingly disturbed at the situation she has brought about, and begins to feel pity for the man whose happiness she is destroying. She wonders whether this trickery is really the way to achieve dignity as wife and mother. Later she has a nightmare and sees the Emperor knocking at a door in the rock and entering a cave. She realizes that the closing of the door represents the sentence on her husband. She hears voices calling for 'the water of life'. The three days are almost over. Threatening clouds gather over Barak's hut, but the dyer is still cheerful and optimistic. His wife hysterically tells him that she has a lover, that she has renounced motherhood and that she has sold her shadow. Barak is incredulous at first, but then by the light of a fire lit by his brothers he sees that she has no shadow. A sword springs magically into Barak's hand, and he threatens to kill her. The Empress intervenes. She does not want the shadow if it means that blood will be shed. The woman, who has confessed to what she wished to do, not what she has done, is ready to die. The earth opens and swallows up the dyer and his wife. The Empress and the nurse leave in a boat, which has (again magically) appeared. Act III. Barak and his wife are in an underground cave, separated by a thick wall. Neither is aware of the other's presence nearby. She hears the voices of her unborn children, while he sings of his duty towards his wife. A voice calls them up a great staircase until they can see the rock of the Empress's dream. Meanwhile the magic boat has brought the Empress and the nurse to the rock. The nurse advises the Empress to avoid the judgement of Keikobad, who is waiting in the cave. She again tries to separate the dyer and his wife, but the messenger drives her away, condemning her to wander for ever in the world of men, which she detests. When the Empress enters the cave she refuses to drink the golden water which, the keeper of the gates of the temple tells her, would give her the woman's shadow. The Emperor appears to her in an alcove in the cave. He is turned to stone except for his eyes, which search for her desperately. But the Empress again refuses – she cannot save him if it means condemning two human beings. Her refusal works the miracle. Now she has a shadow and the Emperor comes back to life. Barak and his wife are reunited. The rejoicing voices of unborn children are heard from above.

■ *Die Frau ohne Schatten* is the most ambitious opera of the Strauss-Hofmannsthal collaboration, the richest in ideas and perhaps the most accomplished, despite the defects of overburdened symbolism and unnecessary characters. The theme – the union of man and woman in relation to a higher principle (Keikobad, God) and to human society – invites comparison with *Die Zauberflöte*, while its depth of introspection links it to *Tristan und Isolde*. Some critics have felt that Strauss has failed to convey the higher meaning of Hofmannsthal's text. Once the listener has grasped the complex system of symbols, however, the impact of the opera depends on Strauss's music, which fully develops and clarifies the subtleties of the text. The grandeur and delicacy of its orchestral texture, the mastery of symphonic technique and the vocal characterization reach levels rarely found in the composer's other operas. The Empress's awakening and entry in the first act, for example, are accompanied by a superb orchestral passage which for splendour, transparency and delicacy bears comparison with the best moments of *Salome* or the famous presentation of the rose in *Der Rosenkavalier*. Besides the Empress, there are outstanding vocal parts for Barak and his wife – the latter inspired by the composer's own wife, Pauline. *Die Frau ohne Schatten* was enthusiastically received at its first performance and won unanimous critical approval for the first time in Strauss's career.

LA LÉGENDE DE SAINT CHRISTOPHE (The Legend of St Christopher)
Sacred drama in three acts by Vincent d'Indy

Sketch for Puccini's Il tabarro *with notes by the composer.*

(1851–1931), libretto by the composer. First performance: Paris, Opéra, 6 June 1920.

SYNOPSIS. Act I. Auférus decides to serve the greatest power in the world. His first choice is the Queen of pleasure, but when she is defeated by the King of gold he leaves her court for his. Satan appears and melts this king's gold, so Auférus changes allegiance yet again. When the devil is forced by a vision to pay homage to the King of Heaven, Auférus sets out in search of this supreme king. Act II. Auférus's travels eventually lead him to Rome, but still he only meets with enigmatic replies. He returns home, and an old hermit advises him to look for God within himself. He takes up a post as ferryman at a river ford. One day, after he has refused passage to his former gods, he carries a young child across the river. A storm rises up, the weight of the child becomes almost unbearable, but he completes the task. As the storm subsides, the child tells him that he has just carried the King of Heaven, and he is re-named Christophe, the bearer of Christ. Act III. Christophe has been imprisoned by the worldly

powers, who condemn him to death. Satan desires his soul, and so sends the Queen of pleasure to tempt him. Christophe converts her to his religion, and when he is executed, she continues to preach the gospel in his name.

■ The subject is taken from the *Legenda Aurea* or *Legenda Sanctorum* by Jacopo da Varazze (1222–98). In structure it resembles a triptych, with each of the three acts in turn made up of three episodes linked by a narrative. It was composed during the period 1912–22, when D'Indy was director of the orchestral class at the Paris Conservatoire.

L'AVIATORE DRO (Airman Dro)

Tragic opera in three acts by Francesco Balilla Pratella (1880–1955), libretto by the composer. First performance: Lugo di Romagna, Teatro Comunale, 4 September 1920.

■ The composer was among those who signed the two manifestos of futurist music, and this opera reflects his beliefs.

DIE TOTE STADT (The Dead City)

Opera in three acts by Erich Wolfgang Korngold (1897–1957), text by Paul Schott. First performed simultaneously at the Stadttheater, Hamburg, and the Stadttheater, Cologne, 4 December 1920; first performance in U.S.A.: New York, Metropolitan Opera House, 19 November 1921.

IL PICCOLO MARAT (The Little Marat)

Lyric opera in three acts by Pietro Mascagni (1863–1945), libretto by Giovacchino Forzano (1884–1970) and Giovanni Targioni-Tozzetti (1863–1934). First performance: Rome, Teatro Costanzi, 2 May 1921.

ORIGINAL CAST. Lazaro, Dalla Rizza, Franci, Badini, Ferroni. Conducted by the composer.

SYNOPSIS. The action takes place in Paris during the French Revolution. Act I. Mariella (soprano), niece of the president of the revolutionary committee, nicknamed 'The Ogre' (bass), is attacked by a starving crowd as she takes food to her uncle. She is saved by a young stranger (tenor), who subsequently enrols in the Marats, the revolutionary guard. He is really the son of Princess de Fleury, an imprisoned aristocrat, whom he plans to save by winning the 'Ogre's' trust. Act II. The Prince is preparing his mother's escape with the help of a faithful carpenter (baritone), tired of revolutionary excesses, who promises to have a boat ready under the bridge near the prison. The Prince has confided to Mariella the truth about himself and his feelings, and his plan to save his mother. She cannot bear her uncle's ill-treatment any longer and decides to join the fugitives. The 'Ogre's' fury against some of the prisoners, including the Princess, explodes at a stormy meeting of the revolutionary committee. Act III. Helped by the Prince, Mariella ties her uncle to his bed as he sleeps. When he wakes the Prince threatens him with a dagger and forces him to sign an order freeing the Princess de Fleury and a safe-conduct for her and her companions. The 'Ogre' has to give in, but manages with his free hand to get hold of a pistol and wound the Prince. The carpenter strikes the 'Ogre' with a candlestick, and, with the Prince on his back, he flees with Mariella and the Princess.

■ Even before Giordano made his name with *Andrea Chénier*, the subject of the French Revolution had attracted Mascagni on several occasions. He postponed his plans for an opera set in the period until Ferdinando Martini advised him to read *Les noyades de Nantes* by Lenôtre and *Sous la Terreur* by Victor Martin, the book which provided the bulk of Forzano's plot. Mascagni was not happy with this text, however, and asked Targioni-Tozzetti to complete the libretto. The opera marks the composer's return to realism, with an emphasis on popular, sentimental airs. It was a great success at first, but has rarely been performed since.

PRINCE FERELON

Musical extravaganza in one act by Nicholas Comyn Gatty (1874–1946), libretto by the composer. First performance: London, Old Vic, 21 May 1921.

SYNOPSIS. A fairy story about a beautiful princess who rejects all suitors. The arrival of three new suitors is announced and the King, who is tired of his daughter's behaviour, tells her that this is her last chance – this time she must choose one of the three for her husband. If she cannot make up her mind the court will choose for her. On the appointed day, one of the Princess's ladies-in-waiting is preparing the throne room for the hearing when a handsome young man enters. He explains that he is Prince Ferelon and that he has come to ask for the Princess's hand in three different guises. This will give him three chances of success, since he truly loves her. The court enters. The Princess is sad because she knows that none of the suitors loves her and that they only want her for her riches and rank. The contest begins and the first suitor enters. It is Prince Ferelon dressed as a minstrel, accompanied by a group of singers. He offers the Princess a song composed for her. She admires the song, but rejects the suitor because love is something else. The second suitor enters – Prince Ferelon again, disguised as a fashion designer and followed by assistants and elegantly dressed models. He offers the Princess clothes and promises to design his most beautiful creations for her. This offer too is firmly rejected. The third suitor arrives – a strangely attired artist-poet with a *corps de ballet* which performs a lively dance. The Princess declares that such jollity is childish and rejects the offer. The King is furious and announces that one of the suitors will now be chosen by lot. The Princess is in despair because no one understands her problem. Prince Ferelon then openly declares his love for her and tells her he is glad that she rejected the worldly joys he offered – now he offers his heart alone. At last she is content, as this is the offer she has been waiting for. The King is pleased with her choice because the news that the suitor is Prince Ferelon has spread quickly. He orders the wedding celebrations to start at once.

■ The opera, also called *The Princess's Suitors*, won the Carnegie Award in 1922.

MÖRDER, HOFFNUNG DER FRAUEN (Murderer, Hope of Women)

Opera in one act by Paul Hindemith (1895–1963), text

tribution to the powerfully emotional artistic movement which flourished among the avant-garde in Germany after the First World War. In both text and music, the opera is violently expressionistic.

DAS NUSCH-NUSCHI
Erotic comedy 'for Burmese marionettes' by Paul Hindemith (1895–1963), text by Franz Blei. First performance: Stuttgart, Landestheater, 4 June 1921.

■ A violently polemical, anti-Romantic, anti-Wagnerian opera, which provocatively makes use of several famous themes – for example, one of King Marke's themes from *Tristan* is introduced during the castration scene.

LE ROI DAVID (King David)
Opera (dramatic psalm) in two parts by Arthur Honegger (1892–1955), text by René Morax. First performance: Mezières, Théâtre Jorat, 11 June 1921; first performance in U.K.: London, Royal Albert Hall, 17 March 1927; in U.S.A.: New York, 26 October 1925.

■ The text is based on the biblical texts, like other works by the composer. After the first performance it was performed in German at Winterthur on 2 December 1923, in a modified three-part concert version. Although not often performed, the stage version has also been adapted as a dramatic oratorio.

Giuseppe De Luca, the first interpreter of the title role in Puccini's Gianni Schicchi, *at the Metropolitan, New York, 14 December 1918.*

by the painter Oskar Kokoschka. First performance: Stuttgart, Landestheater, 4 June 1921.

SYNOPSIS. The night sky. A tower. The Man, white-faced, clad in armour, with bandaged forehead. Behind him a group of savage-looking men, with grey and red bands round their heads, long spears and torches. The Man is at their head, but at the same time in opposition to them. Meanwhile women enter from the left, led by the Woman – tall and strong, dressed in red, with flowing yellow hair. There is a dialogue between the men and the women about their mutual desire. A terrifying image of the Man emerges from their words. The men advance and the women huddle together, frightened. The Woman, leaping and crawling, approaches the Man. He furiously tears off her clothes and brands his mark on her flesh. She leaps on him with a knife, wounding him in the side. The men and women couple bestially on the ground. A coffin is lowered. The Man, moving slowly, is laid in it and placed in the tower. The Woman draws near to him. Gradually he recovers his energy and rises, while she falls to the ground. The men and women try to flee the Man, but he strikes them down like flies and makes off.

■ Like *Sancta Susanna* (1922) and *Das Nusch-Nuschi* (1921), this opera by the young Hindemith is a con-

KATYA KABANOVA
Opera in three acts with six scenes by Leoš Janáček (1854–1928), libretto by the composer, based on V. Červinka's translation of The Storm *by Alexander Ostrovsky (1859). First performance: Brno, 23 November 1921; first performance in U.K.: London, Sadler's Wells Theatre, 10 April 1951; in U.S.A.: Cleveland, Karamu House, 26 November 1957.*

SYNOPSIS. The action takes place during the second half of the nineteenth century in the little Russian town of Kalinov on the banks of the Volga. Act I. Boris (tenor) tells his friend Kudryash (tenor) of his unhappiness – he loves Katya (soprano), Tichon Kabanov's wife, and his family life is spoilt by his relationship with his Uncle Dikoy (bass), with whom he must keep on good terms if he is to receive his grandfather's inheritance. Katya enters with her husband (tenor) and Marfa (contralto), known as Kabanicha, her mother-in-law, who scolds her son for loving his wife more than her. She warns him that Katya will take a lover if she is always treated so gently. Katya too is unhappy, for she mourns for her youth and feels oppressed by her stepmother's tyranny. She is disappointed in her husband, who does not understand her and refuses to take her with him on his imminent journey. There is a further

Puccini's Suor Angelica *at La Scala, Milan, in 1962. Scenery and costumes by Ardengo Soffici.*

confrontation between mother, son and wife before Tichon eventually departs. Act II. Varvara (mezzo-soprano), a ward in the Kabanov household, gives Katya the key to the garden where Katya, after much hesitation and filled with foreboding, agrees to meet Boris. Their meeting takes place while Varvara and Kudryash stand guard. Katya is at first silent and withdrawn, but eventually allows herself to declare her love for Boris. They embrace passionately and swear eternal love. Act III. Tichon has returned, and Katya, tormented by remorse, interprets the approach of a violent storm as a warning from Heaven. She confesses everything to her husband. After bidding Boris farewell she gazes on the waters of the Volga and then throws herself into the river. Kabanicha accepts the neighbours' condolences, as the corpse is laid out.

■ The opera, composed between 1919 and 1921, represents one of the peaks of Janáček's career. It is rich in moments of powerful drama, harshly realistic episodes in a strong declamatory style alternating with evocative passages of typically Slav lyricism. The clearly delineated characters include, besides Katya, the figure of Kabanicha, her mother-in-law, the symbol of an old peasant society clinging rigidly to ancient traditions. The drama centres around Katya's struggle against this old woman. Her final desperate gesture is not just a protest in the name of her own freedom but also an accusation against the remorseless moral pressure exerted by the society around her, which has driven her to the deed. This aspect was underlined by Max Brod who, after hearing the opera, expressed his admiration to the composer for his moral principles, which had led him to 'confront the question of a life without compromise'.

LA LEGGENDA DI SAKUNTALĀ (The Legend of Sakuntalā)

Opera in three acts by Franco Alfano (1876–1954), libretto by the composer. First performance: Bologna, Teatro Comunale, 10 December 1921.

ORIGINAL CAST included Concato, Piccaluga. Conductor: Tullio Serafin.

SYNOPSIS. The action takes place in India at an unspecified time. Act I. Dawn in a dark, silent forest. A hermitage. As the hermit Durvāsas (bass) knocks for admittance, the sounds of the royal hunt can be heard in the distance. When the King (tenor) enters, the hermits beg him not to kill the sacred gazelle he is hunting. By sparing it, he wins the hermits' friendship and they ask for his protection until the return of their leader Kanva (bass), who disappeared long ago. As the hermits know, Kanva foretold that the King would fall in love with the beautiful Sakuntalā (soprano), who lives in the hermitage and was brought up by Kanva. As soon as the King sees her, he falls in love and disguises himself as a pilgrim to enter the hermitage. He learns that Sakuntalā is of royal origin. In the end she surrenders to his passion. Act II. Near the hermitage two of Sakuntalā's friends, Priyamvada (mezzo-soprano) and Anusuya (soprano) are preparing garlands for the religious ceremonies. Durvāsas knocks at the hermitage door, but no one answers because of the rule that only Sakuntalā, who is not there, should open it. In a rage the hermit curses her and prophesies that when the King meets her again he will not remember loving her unless she shows him the ring he gave her. When Sakuntalā learns what has happened she is distressed, but Kanva, who has returned, comforts her. He knows about her love for the King and prophesies that she will become a mother. He suggests she visit the court. The forest is lit up by the sunset. Act III. The interior of the royal palace, with a bed in the centre of the stage. The King is sad amid the splendours of his court, and is entertained with dancing and amusements. An attendant announces the arrival of the hermits with a veiled woman. As prophesied, the King does not remember anything and the hermits explain the reason for their visit. Sakuntalā removes her veil, but the King still does not remember her. She cannot find his ring and leaves in despair. Meanwhile the guards bring in a fisherman who has found the ring on the river-bed. The King's memory returns and he sends for Sakuntalā. But she has thrown herself into the nymphs' pool and disappeared in a cloud of fire. A brilliant light illuminates two hermits who lay a new-born child covered with a veil at the King's feet. Everyone bows down before the heir.

■ *La leggenda di Sakuntalā* is taken from the play *Sakuntalā*, the masterpiece of the fifth-century Indian lyric and dramatic poet, Kālidāsa. Alfano's first real success and regarded as one of his best works, it has been performed in many theatres in Italy as well as in Italian in Buenos Aires and Montevideo and in German in Düsseldorf (1924) and elsewhere. The adaptation of the original Indian legend presented some difficulties, and during the Second World War the only complete score of the opera was destroyed. The composer had to re-write it from an incomplete score for voices and piano. The new version was performed at the Rome Opera on 9 January 1952 as *Sakuntalā*. The opera is rich in chromatic harmonies and its orchestration and technique show the composer's search for new means of expression and a more modern symphonic style. In the 1952 score the influence of Strauss is apparent and there are also echoes of Puccini, especially in the melodious use of the voice.

THE LOVE FOR THREE ORANGES (Ljubov k trem Apelsinam)
Opera in four acts and ten scenes with a prologue by Sergei Prokofiev (1891–1953), libretto by the composer from Carlo Gozzi's comedy (1761). First performance: Chicago, Opera House, 30 December 1921; first performance in U.K.: Edinburgh, August 1962.

Sketch by Wakhevitch for Puccini's Gianni Schicchi, *1967. Paris, Opéra-Comique.*

Viorica Ursuleac (the Empress), Hildegarde Ranczak (Barak's wife) and Elisabeth Höngen (the nurse) in Act I of Die Frau ohne Schatten *by Richard Strauss, performed at the Nationaltheater, Munich, in 1939. Scenery and costumes by Ludwig Sievert. Producer Rudolf Hartmann.*

ORIGINAL CAST included Nina Koshetz and Hector Dufranne. Conducted by the composer.

SYNOPSIS. Prologue. The curtain is down. Highbrows, wits, romantics and low-brows are arguing about the best form of entertainment. Ten announcers chase them from the stage and promise the audience a new genre – *The Love for Three Oranges*. The herald (bass) announces the start of the performance. Act I. A room in the King's palace. The King of Clubs (bass) is in despair because his son, the prince (tenor), is suffering from melancholy and will only be cured if he can be made to laugh. Pantaloon (baritone) suggests that feasts and theatrical entertainments may do the trick, and the jester Truffaldino (tenor) promises to arrange everything. The King instructs his prime minister Leandro (baritone) to organize the entertainment. Pantaloon is worried as he knows that Leandro is plotting against the prince's life. The stage darkens and a backdrop covered with cabbalistic signs is lowered. Thunder and lightning. The magician Tchelio (bass), the King's protector, and Fata Morgana (soprano), Leandro's protector, appear, and Fata Morgana beats the magician at cards. The King's palace again. Leandro is telling his accomplice Clarissa (contralto), the King's niece, about his plan for killing the prince, by subjecting him to extremely boring readings every day. They catch the black slave Smeraldina (mezzo-soprano) eavesdropping, but forgive her when she tells

them that if Fata Morgana is present at the festivities their success will be assured, as no one ever laughs in her presence. Act II. The prince's room. Truffaldino makes him get dressed for the festivities. The great court of the royal palace. The jester tries his best, but the presence of Fata Morgana, disguised as an old beggarwoman, stops anyone laughing. Truffaldino picks a quarrel with her and knocks her down so that she falls head over heels. At this the prince bursts out laughing. But the wicked fairy gets her revenge by pronouncing that the prince will set off in search of three oranges and fall in love with them. The prince leaves with Truffaldino, blown away by a pair of bellows worked by the devil Farfarello (bass). Act III. A desert. Truffaldino and the prince are on their way to the castle of the witch Creonte, the owner of the three oranges. They are helped by the magician Tchelio, who gives them a magic ribbon for Creonte, who has taken the form of a gigantic cook, and watches over the oranges. Creonte's castle. The cook threatens them with a ladle, but is pacified by the gift. The prince creeps stealthily into the kitchen and takes the three oranges. A desert. It is night-time, and the prince is sleeping. Truffaldino is thirsty and cuts open two of the oranges, which by now have grown to an enormous size. Two beautiful Princesses, Linetta (contralto) and Nicoletta (mezzo-soprano), step out, but die of thirst before Truffaldino can help them. Terrified he runs away. The prince wakes up and cuts open the third orange. The beautiful princess Ninetta (soprano) emerges and is saved from dying of thirst with the help of the spectators, who produce a bucket of water from one of the boxes. The prince hurries off to fetch his father, but when he returns to marry Ninetta he finds that Smeraldina has turned the princess into a rat and taken her place. The King insists that the prince marries her instead. Act IV. The magician and Fata Morgana are quarrelling in front of the cabbalistic curtain. The spectators manage to shut Morgana away. The throne room. To everyone's disgust a rat is found sitting on the throne, but Tchelio changes her back into Ninetta. Smeraldina, Leandro and Clarissa are condemned to death and try to flee from Fata Morgana, but they fall through a trap door. There is general rejoicing for the young couple.

■ The opera was first performed at the Chicago Opera, then under the direction of Mary Garden, with a French text by Janacopoulos. It was not a great success at first and caused some bitterness between Prokofiev and Igor Stravinsky, who had a low opinion of the work. Four years later *The Love for Three Oranges* had its first performance in Russia, and again had a mixed reception. Prokofiev wrote in his autobiography: 'Some critics tried to guess whom I was making fun of – the audience, Gozzi, the operatic form or those who do not know how to laugh.' The composer's intentions seem to have been misinterpreted. The richly varied and imaginative music is meant to bring out the fairy tale element in Gozzi's comedy. The opera makes use of different groups, each representing an attitude or state of mind (highbrows, wits, romantics, low-brows), who gradually take part in the action and provide a psychological interpretation of it. Prokofiev later composed a suite based on *The Love for Three Oranges* which was more successful than the opera and immediately became popular. This suggests that criticism of the opera was mainly directed at the novelty and far-fetched symbolism of some of its scenes.

GIULIETTA E ROMEO

Tragedy in three acts by Riccardo Zandonai (1883–1944), libretto by Arturo Rossato (1882–1942), from Shakespeare's play and earlier stories by Luigi da Porto and Matteo Bandello. First performance: Rome, Teatro Costanzi, 14 February 1922.

ORIGINAL CAST. Gilda Dalla Rizza, Miguel Fleta, Carmelo Maugeri, L. Nardi. Conducted by the composer.

SYNOPSIS. The action takes place in Verona and Mantua. Act I. The supporters of the Montagues and Capulets are fighting. A young man wearing a mask intervenes to stop them and confronts Tebaldo (baritone), a Capulet. The town crier (bass) announces that a patrol is on the way and the opposing factions quickly disappear. The masked man hides nearby. Giulietta, a Capulet (soprano), appears at a window and the young man, who is Romeo, a Montague (tenor), addresses her passionately. Their situation is unbearable since they have declared their love although their families are bitter enemies. Giulietta lets down a silken ladder. Romeo climbs up and stays till dawn. Act II. Tebaldo interrupts the dancing of the Capulet girls, Giulietta among them. He has found out about Romeo's visit and reproaches Giulietta. He reminds her of her duty to her family and to her father, who has decided that she must marry the Count of Lodrone. Giulietta swears that she will never do it. Gregorio (tenor) enters, wounded, to report that there has been another fight and that Romeo was one of his assailants. This is untrue, as Romeo is in fact hiding in the garden. He emerges from his hiding place and Tebaldo challenges him to a duel. Tebaldo is mortally wounded and Giulietta helps her lover escape. He

The last scene of Act II of Die Frau ohne Schatten *by Richard Strauss, 1939. Munich, Nationaltheater.*

leaves behind his bloody sword. Act III. Romeo is at an inn in Mantua waiting for his servant to bring news from Verona. A singer (tenor) enters and sings a lament for Giulietta's death. Romeo refuses to believe it until his servant (tenor) arrives and confirms that Giulietta has died on the eve of her wedding with Lodrone. Romeo returns to Verona. When he sees Giulietta's body in the burial chamber he takes poison. Giulietta, who only had taken a sleeping draught in order to escape marriage, recovers. She collapses with grief beside her dying lover.

■ In *Giulietta e Romeo* the influence on Zandonai of Puccinian *verismo* is clear, though the composer displays a more modern sensibility in his handling of many situations, particularly in his use of the orchestra. It has been suggested that the opera is most successful while the drama is still developing and before it reaches its tragic climax. This is quite in keeping with Zandonai's natural temperament as a lyric rather than a dramatic composer.

SANCTA SUSANNA
Opera in one act by Paul Hindemith (1895–1963), text by the composer, based on the play by the Expressionist poet August Stramm. First performance: Frankfurt, Opernhaus, 26 March 1922.

SYNOPSIS. A nunnery church on a May night. Susanna and Klementia are praying in front of the altar, above which hangs a large crucifix. Susanna is in the grip of an ecstatic delirium, which at times seizes Klementia too. The saint hears a woman's voice and through a window sees a frightened girl who gathers up courage to tell them that she has lain with her young lover beneath the wisteria. The young man arrives and takes her away. Klementia remembers how thirty or forty years before as a young woman she one night discovered a naked nun at the altar, embracing the crucifix. This nun was walled up alive for her sins. At this Susanna strips and approaches the crucifix. Klementia reminds her of her vows of poverty, chastity and obedience. Other nuns enter. The opera ends as the naked woman stands near the altar while her fellow nuns address her as Satan.

■ This youthful work by Hindemith reflects his early artistic aims. It displays much of the new objectivism then prevalent among the German avant-garde. The opera is perhaps more important as a polemical reaction against romanticism than for its intrinsic musical worth. It is a good example of those Expressionist works which, despite certain excesses, attempted to counteract the threatening and oppressive mood of contemporary Germany.

AMADIS
Opera in a prologue and four acts by Jules Massenet (1842–1912), libretto by Jules Claretie (1840–1913) based on Amadis de Gaula, *a romance of chivalry by the fifteenth-century Spanish writer Garcia Ordóñez de Montalvo. First performed (posthumously) at Monte Carlo, Théâtre du Casino, 1 April 1922.*

SYNOPSIS. Amadis, the natural son of King Périon, is abandoned with his mother Elisène to the mercy of the waves. He escapes death by a lucky chance and is taken by King Langrines to his father's court. Here he meets Floriane, daughter of Lisuarte, King of Brittany. They fall in love. Amadis now embarks on a series of extraordinary adventures in honour of Floriane, ranging from the discovery of his parents, with the help of a ring, duels with giants and fights in enchanted castles to the freeing of the oppressed – all classic themes of chivalry. Finally after many adventures, and after a misunderstanding between the two has been resolved, Floriane and Amadis are married.

■ Although clearly a minor work, *Amadis* shows how well suited the late Romantic music of Massenet is to a text based on the legends of chivalry (in this case the romance is drawn from the Breton Cycle). Love is portrayed as the highest emotion, which transports the lover beyond reality to a world where he can act freely without restrictions. As regards the music, the orchestra closely follows the development of events on stage and this perfect match gives rise to intensely lyrical and dramatic passages for the singers.

LA BELLA ADDORMENTATA NEL BOSCO (Sleeping Beauty)
Fairy tale in three acts by Ottorino Respighi (1879–1936), libretto by Gian Bistolfi based on Charles Perrault's story. First performance: Rome, Teatro Odescalchi, 13 April 1922.

SYNOPSIS. All the animals of the forest are celebrating the princess's birth. The wicked fairy, who has not been invited to the feast, arrives and angrily predicts that the princess will be pricked by a spindle and die. The witch disappears and a chorus of stars calm the frightened animals. The prophecy is fulfilled. One day an old man with a spindle appears before the young princess. As she has never seen a spindle before, she touches it and falls asleep. Life slows down around her and the doctors vainly try to rouse her. The blue fairy tries to help the King and Queen in their grief by making everyone fall into the same deep sleep as the princess. Only the spiders remain, spinning their webs. Prince Aprile arrives, kisses the princess and wakens her and all around her. The well-known fairy tale ends, as it began, with general rejoicing.

■ The opera, first performed in 1922 but composed between 1907 and 1909, had a long and successful initial run before being performed all over the world. In 1934 the composer revised the score for production in Turin, replacing the dance of the marionettes with

Janáček's Katya Kabanova *at the Berlin Komische Oper. Scenery by Rudolf Heinrich.*

a children's dance, but leaving the singers in the orchestra pit as in the original version. Once again it was a great success.

RENARD (The Fox)

Burlesque ballet in one act with voice parts by Igor Stravinsky (1882–1971), text by the composer after Russian folk-tales, translated into French by Charles Ferdinand Ramuz (1878–1947). First performance: Paris, Opéra, 3 June 1922; first performance in U.K.: London (B.B.C.) 1935; in U.S.A.: New York, 2 December 1923.

SYNOPSIS. The cock (tenor) waits on his perch for the fox's arrival. The fox (tenor) enters dressed as a nun and invites the cock to confess his sins, but the cock ignores him. The fox now appeals to the cock's emotions, making out that he has returned from the desert and is hungry and thirsty; again to no avail. The fox cunningly returns to the subject of confession and tells the cock he must ask forgiveness for all his sins – forty wives are far too many, and he even fights the other cocks in the hen-run for more. The fox continues to scold until he manages to grab the cock. The cock struggles frantically and cries out wildly as the fox starts to pluck him; the noise attracts the cat (bass) and the goat (bass), who chase the fox away. When the two rescuers have left, the fox returns, however, and continues his plucking. The cat and goat come back and strangle him. The opera ends with a procession of all the animals.

■ The first performance of the ballet was conducted by Ernest Ansermet (1883–1969), at that time conductor with Diaghilev's famous *Ballets russes*, with choreography by Nijinska and scenery and costumes by M. Larionov. It is a chamber work, with a small number of vocal and instrumental parts compared with the large-scale operas of the nineteenth century. It is a reaction against the spirit of such operas, and particularly against the Wagnerian approach. The different elements – musical, literary and choreographic – are almost independent of one another and the work achieves unity through the free interplay of these individual elements.

MAVRA

Opera buffa in one act by Igor Stravinsky (1882–1971), text by Boris Kochno (born 1903) after Pushkin's poem The Little House at Kolomna *translated into French by J. Larmanjat. First performance: Paris, Opéra, 3 June 1922; first performance in U.K.: London (B.B.C.), 27 April 1934; in U.S.A.: Philadelphia, 28 December 1934.*

ORIGINAL CAST included Slobodskaya, Sadovène, Rosovska, Skoupevsky.

SYNOPSIS. A village in Russia. Parasha (soprano) is talking to her lover, a hussar called Vassily (tenor), at the window of her house; they are trying to arrange a meeting. When he has left, her mother (contralto) enters, complaining that, since her old servant died, she has had no-one to help in the house. Parasha goes to look for a new maid. Left alone, her mother mourns for the dead servant and her skills. When a neighbour (mezzo-soprano) arrives, she repeats her complaints to her. Parasha returns with a new maid, Mavra, a good-looking, strong, healthy girl recommended by an acquaintance and apparently suitable for the job. The mother leaves her daughter and the new cook alone in the house so that Parasha can give her instructions. In fact 'Mavra' is the enterprising Vassily in disguise. Their happy reunion is interrupted by the mother's return. She leaves again with her daughter, planning to return secretly to spy on her new servant. To her amazement when she returns she finds the cook shaving. There is total confusion. The mother faints at the sight of this suspicious character. The neighbour gives chase to Vassily, who jumps out of the window and runs away, while Parasha calls after him in vain.

■ *Mavra* marks a particular stage in Stravinsky's continual exploration of musical style. It came soon after *Pulcinella*, which incorporates themes by Pergolesi, and marks the beginning of the composer's return to musical models from the past. Yet at the same time it includes elements of Russian and gypsy music and even jazz, which distinguish it from similar works which simply pay tribute to nineteenth-century European opera. Another original feature is the unusual orchestral balance, with its predominance of woodwind and brass instruments (tuba, clarinets, trumpets and trombones). The subject is typical of the Russian folk-tale tradition. In addition to the use of Pushkin as a source, the event which leads to the uproarious finale – the discovery of the 'maid' shaving – has a popular, realistic flavour quite unlike the tone of eighteenth- and nineteenth-century *opera buffa*. In this respect *Mavra* is the last work of the composer's 'Russian' period. The scoring is deliberately energetic, even aggressive, in keeping with the racy tone of the plot. The opera displays a new appreciation of elements drawn from earlier models of European opera, apparent mainly in the sentimental passages, where themes and techniques derived from the Italian-inspired melodrama of Glinka can be heard. This also explains the overall structure, which consists entirely of arias without recitative. *Mavra* was not a great success, mainly because of inadequate staging and the circumstances in which it was performed. An opera of this type, rich in delicate nuances and with a small cast, was not really suited to the enormous stage of the Paris Opéra and Larionov's splendid scenery was too different in style from the sensational Diaghilev ballet *Renard*, performed on the same evening as the opera. *Mavra* demands the dedicated, attentive audience of a concert hall rather than of a traditional opera.

ALKESTIS
Opera in two acts by Rutland Boughton (1878–1960), text based on Gilbert Murray's English version of Euripides' tragedy Alcestis. *First performance: Glastonbury, 26 August 1922.*

SYNOPSIS. In the palace of Admetus, King of Pherae in Thessaly, there is universal mourning for the imminent death of the beautiful young queen Alkestis. For nine years the god Apollo had served in Admetus's household as punishment for killing the Cyclops who made Zeus's thunderbolts. The young King treated him well, so when Apollo left he made the Fates agree that when the time came for Admetus to die he could escape death if a close relation was willing to take his place. The moment of his death has come much sooner than anyone expected. His wife Alkestis has offered to take his place, not wishing to leave her own children fatherless and believing she will be serving the people well by saving the life of their good and respected King. But as the hour of her death approaches, Admetus is tortured by remorse and despair. Alkestis is carried out into the open, dressed in her burial robes and surrounded by her family and subjects. She begs her husband not to marry again and give her children a stepmother. Then she dies and is carried back into the palace. A tall stranger now enters. It is Herakles, passing through Pherae on his way to perform another of his labours, who seeks hospitality from his friend Admetus. Admetus, despite his grief, makes every effort to show hospitality and conceals his wife's death from Herakles. In the evening, when the hero goes to rest, the funeral procession carries Alkestis to her tomb. Herakles meanwhile learns the truth from a slave who has remained in the palace to attend him. Horrified at the news he determines to make amends for the further pain he has caused by his presence. Impressed by the extraordinary devotion Alkestis has shown in offering up her life for her husband, he decides to confront Death at the tomb and prevent him carrying her soul off to the Underworld. Admetus returns from the burial ceremony in a state of inconsolable grief. Herakles now enters accompanied by a veiled woman, to whom all eyes turn. She is revealed as Alkestis, whom Herakles has saved from Death.

DEBORA E JAELE
Dramatic opera in three acts by Ildebrando Pizzetti (1880–1968), libretto by the composer after the Book of Judges. *First performance: Milan, Teatro alla Scala, 16 December 1922.*

ORIGINAL CAST. Elvira Casazza, Giulio Tess, Anna Gramegna, Umberto di Lelio, Giovanni Azzimonti. Conductor: Arturo Toscanini.

SYNOPSIS. The subject is taken from the Old Testament, Book of Judges, Chapters IV and V. Act I. The tribes of Nephthali, Zebulun and Issachar are gathered in a square in Kedesh waiting for Deborah (soprano), the prophetess of Israel, to speak. They are ready to fight Sisera (tenor), the cruel King of Canaan, but want the prophetess to advise them about strategy and predict the outcome of the battle. She tells them they will win if they attack the enemy in the open. Jaele (soprano), wife of the spy Hever (baritone), is falsely accused of returning Sisera's love. Deborah takes up Jaele's cause, and sends her on a special mission to Sisera: it is she who must persuade him to lead his army into the open field, where Barak (bass) Commander of the Jewish forces, will overcome him. Act II. The terrace of Sisera's palace at Harosheth. Sisera, contradicting his cruel reputation, punishes the servant of one of his captains for abducting two young slaves from their parents. Hever betrays his own people by advising Sisera to ambush them where they can easily be defeated, but Sisera, disliking this traitorous behaviour, has him arrested. A veiled woman enters. It is Jaele, whom Sisera has loved for a long time. She advises the King to lead his people to Mount Tabor, where she tells him there are only a few hundred Israelites. Her trickery is soon discovered. She admits her guilt and asks Sisera to pass judgement over her, but instead of punishment, he declares his love. She is moved by his words, and is attracted towards him, but, on the point of relenting, she hears a lullaby sung by the mother of children killed by Sisera's soldiers. Mindful of her duty, she returns to Israel. Act III. The Israelites win the battle as prophesied. All their enemies are killed, except Sisera, who takes refuge in Jaele's tent. The prophetess Deborah orders her to give him up to the people, but she kills him herself rather than allow him to fall into the hands of his victorious enemies.

■ *Deborah and Jaele*, composed between 1915 and 1921, is generally regarded as Pizzetti's masterpiece. It is a good illustration of his conception of music drama, based on an exact and balanced relationship between text and music, a reaction against both *verismo* and post-romantic opera.

BELFAGOR

Comic opera in two acts with prologue and epilogue by Ottorino Respighi (1879–1936), text by Claudio Guastalla, from the comedy by Ercole Luigi Morselli, itself based on a well-known story by Machiavelli. First performance: Milan, Teatro alla Scala, 26 April 1923.

ORIGINAL CAST. Stabile, Sheridan, Merli, Azzimonti, Azzolini, Ferrari, Gramegna. Conductor: Antonio Guarnieri.

SYNOPSIS. Prologue. A small piazza in a little Tuscan town, with a church, parish priest's house and apothecary's house. Baldo (tenor) tells Candida, his loved one (soprano), of his imminent departure. Their conversation is interrupted by the arrival of her father, Mirocleto, the apothecary (bass). Belfagor, an arch-fiend (baritone), appears before him. He has come to earth to find out whether it is true that marriage leads men to perdition and persuades Mirocleto to give him his daughter in marriage with a gift of a hundred thousand ducats. Act I. Baldo and Candida talk together in her father's shop until dawn. He leaves and Candida's mother, Olimpia (mezzo-soprano), and sisters Fidelia

Sketch by Gianni Ratto for Prokofiev's The Love for Three Oranges.

and Maddalena (sopranos), come downstairs to go to Mass. Belfagor enters and introduces himself as Ipsilonne, a rich merchant friend of Mirocleto. The women leave, but the two sisters manage to return and their father catches them kissing the stranger in an attempt to win him. Ipsilonne chooses Candida, however, and declares his love for her to the disappointment of her sisters and her own despair. Act II. A month later. The marriage has been celebrated, but all is not well for the arch-fiend. Candida rejects him while he has fallen in love with her. On the evening of a feast day Baldo returns and demands an explanation. When Candida learns of his return she runs away from the matrimonial home. Ipsilonne miserably returns to being a devil while his comrades ruthlessly dismantle Mirocleto's house. Epilogue. Baldo and Candida seek help from the parish priest. Belfagor, disguised as a beggar, is pretending to be asleep on the church steps. He declares that Ipsilonne has gone away because he has satisfied his desires with Candida and does not wish to spend the rest of his life with the daughter of an apothecary. Baldo chases him away, but is filled with doubt and refuses the priest's attempts to comfort him. In despair Candida falls to her knees and prays for a miracle to convince Baldo of her innocence. Miraculously the bells of the little church start to ring on their own. Belfagor realizes he has lost and prepares to return to Hell.

■ The text was begun by Ercole Luigi Morselli and completed by Claudio Guastalla. Respighi started work on the score in May 1921 and finished it in May the following year. The theme – the devil's attempt at marriage – had appealed to many authors, but Guastalla's version provided Respighi with a subject well suited to his musical personality and versatility. It gave him scope for a whole range of moods – fantastic and realistic, unashamedly comic and delicately expressive. *Belfagor* is regarded as Respighi's most spontaneous opera. He was certainly influenced in his choice of text and subject matter by his successful collaboration with Guastalla, but he was also passionately interested in astrology and a keen collector of diabolical tales.

THE PERFECT FOOL
Comic opera in one act by Gustav Holst (1874–1934), text by the composer. First performance: London, Covent Garden, 14 May 1923; first performance in U.S.A.: Wichita, 20 March 1962. Conductor of the first performance: Eugène Goossens.

SYNOPSIS. The action takes place once upon a time in an enchanted country. An ancient prophecy says that the princess 'shall marry the man who does the deed no other man can do'. Her many suitors include an old wizard, who has prepared a magic potion which will restore him to youth before her eyes. The perfect fool enters with his mother, and she cunningly substitutes water for the wizard's potion, pouring the latter down her son's throat. It has been predicted of the perfect fool that: 'He wins a bride with a glance of his eye; with a look he kills a foe. He achieves where others fail, with one word.' The fool does not take part in the ensuing contest for the princess's hand, but she eventually notices him and as soon as their eyes meet she falls in love. In revenge, the wizard sets fire to a wood to prove his power, but a look from the fool is enough to shrivel him up and put out the fire. The princess only has eyes for the fool and asks if she may become his wife. The fool now does what no other can do: he says 'No' – and promptly falls asleep again.

■ This opera, with its folk-tale plot, is something of a caricature of Italian, French and German opera – the princess's suitors sing snatches from *La Traviata*, quarrel in phrases and tunes from Wagner's operas and strike attitudes from Gounod's *Faust*. The music is agreeable, often original and well-suited to the witty text. The opera was a great success at first in London, although it is not often performed now.

PADMÂVATÎ
Opéra-ballet in two acts by Albert Roussel (1869–1937), libretto by Louis Laloy, after an event in thirteenth-century Indian history. First performance: Paris, Opéra, 1 June 1923; first performance in U.K. (concert version): London, Coliseum, 1969.

SYNOPSIS. Ratan-sen (tenor), King of Chitoor, is married to Padmâvatî (contralto). The Queen's beauty is such that a Brahmin (tenor) falls in love with her and tries to tempt her, but without success since she is as virtuous as she is beautiful. The rejected suitor is driven from the kingdom. In revenge he asks the Mogul Sultan of Delhi, Alauddin (baritone), for help and takes him to Ratan-sen's palace. The Sultan also falls in love with Padmâvatî and declares that if she is not given to him, he will destroy the city. The people, angered by the Brahmin's behaviour, tear him to pieces. Inevitably war breaks out. The city is besieged and Ratan-sen is mortally wounded in the fighting. The wounded king, in a desperate effort to save his people, commands Padmâvatî to surrender to Alauddin, but she refuses indignantly and, as the enemy army advances to take Chitoor, stabs her dying husband in the heart. She orders his funeral pyre to be built, and throws herself into the flames at the moment when Alauddin arrives to claim his prize.

■ The subject came to Roussel during his extensive travels in the East. While avoiding an affected 'oriental' style, he enriches the music with some strikingly original features and achieves rare modal and harmonic freedom. He also revived the old tradition of the opéra-ballet, in which dancing and singing are of equal importance.

EL RETABLO DE MAESE PEDRO (Master Peter's Puppet Show)
Opera in one act by Manuel de Falla (1876–1946),

libretto by the composer, based on an episode from Cervantes's Don Quixote *(part II, Chapters XXV–XXVI). First concert performance: Seville, Teatro S. Fernando, 23 March 1923. First full performance: Paris, Princess de Polignac's palais, 25 June 1923. First performance in U.K.: Clifton, 14 October 1924; in U.S.A.: New York, 29 December 1925.*

ORIGINAL CAST (Paris). Dufranne, Salignac, Garcia, Periso. Conductor: Vladimir Golschmann.

SYNOPSIS. Don Quixote (bass) is watching a puppet show given at an inn. While Master Peter (tenor) works the puppets, the boy's voice tells the story. In Charlemagne's palace, Don Gayferos is happily playing cards, forgetting about his wife Melisendra, who has been captured by the Moors at Saragossa. This behaviour annoys the Emperor, who has been like a father to Melisendra, and he reprimands Gayferos and sends him off to rescue his wife. Gayferos leaves for Saragossa. In the palace of Marsilio, the Moorish king, Melisendra is anxiously awaiting her husband's arrival. Meanwhile Marsilio punishes a Moor who has tried to take advantage of her. Don Gayferos finds his wife on an unguarded balcony of the palace. He helps her climb down and they escape together. The alarm is given and Marsilio and some of his knights give chase. Don Quixote from the beginning of the show has identified closely with the action and even joined in, at first by expressing indignation at Melisendra's imprisonment and the lack of rescuers. Now, thinking it his duty to help the fugitives, he draws his sword and begins to fight the puppets representing the Moors. No-one can stop him and he does not calm down until he has destroyed the puppet show. Then he cheerfully explains that he intervened to save two innocents – obeying the rule that knights errant should always be ready to help the weak. He offers a prayer to Dulcinea, and Master Peter looks ruefully at his decimated puppets.

■ Originally De Falla wanted even the 'human' characters in the action to be represented by puppets and on a number of occasions his intentions were carried out. However, he later allowed masked singers and mimes to take the parts. The orchestra is very small and the harpsichord plays an important part.

HOLOFERNES
Opera seria *in three acts by Emil Nicolaus von Reznicek (1860–1945), libretto by the composer, based on the play* Judith *by Friedrich Hebbel (1840). First performance: Charlottenburg (Berlin), Hoftheater, 27 October 1923.*

SYNOPSIS. Nebuchadnezzar, encouraged by his victories, sends his trusted general Holofernes to besiege the city of Bethulia. The people are exhausted by the siege and ready to surrender from hunger. The beautiful widow Judith reproaches them for their lack of faith and urges them to wait until the next day before giving in. Then, richly dressed and accompanied by her maid, she leaves for the enemy camp. Holofernes is won over by her charms. To provoke him, she tells him she hates him, though in fact she too is moved and tells her maid of her feelings. Yet, faithful to her plan to free her people, she enters Holofernes's tent, submits to his desires and cuts off his head while he sleeps. When she returns to Bethulia and shows the people their enemy's head she is welcomed with general rejoicing as their saviour. She does not share their joy and kills herself rather than bear the enemy's child.

■ This opera is based on a famous episode from the Apocrypha (Book of Judith). The composer enters fully into the spirit of the tragedy, underlining the dramatic quality of the action with powerful and intense music, which bears comparison with Strauss. The composer's own libretto also helps to make *Holofernes* a convincing and unified opera.

NERONE
Tragic opera in four acts by Arrigo Boito (1842–1918), libretto by the composer. First performance (after the composer's death): Milan, Teatro alla Scala, 1 May 1924.

ORIGINAL CAST. Aureliano Pertile, Rosa Raisa, Luisa Bertana, Carlo Galeffi, Marcello Journet, Pinza. Conductor: Arturo Toscanini.

SYNOPSIS. Act I. A cemetery on the Appian Way. It is night-time. Simon Mago (baritone) and Tigellino (bass) are digging a trench in which Nerone (tenor) is to bury the urn containing the ashes of his mother Agrippina, whom he has murdered. Nerone arrives, tortured by feelings of guilt over his deed, and comforted only by comparing himself with Orestes. Simon Mago has persuaded the Emperor that his sense of guilt will be eased if the ashes are given proper burial, but Nerone is still afraid of the people's reaction. The mysterious appearance of a ghostly figure, bearing a torch and wearing a necklace of snakes, causes Nerone and Tigellino to take flight. It is Asteria (soprano), who is in love with Nerone and follows him everywhere, hoping to attract him. Simon Mago promises to help her, though he really plans to make use of her madness. Simon Mago discovers the burial place used by the Christians. Fanuèl (baritone), a Christian leader, confronts him while Rubria (mezzo-soprano) runs to warn their fellow Christians that their tombs have been discovered. Simon asks Fanuèl to teach him how to perform miracles, but Fanuèl indignantly refuses. A large procession comes from Rome to welcome Nerone. Act II. The temple of Simon Mago. When the ceremony is over, the priest and his acolytes prepare the temple for Nerone's arrival, staging a scene in which Asteria will appear disguised as a goddess of the dead. As Nerone is superstitious and gullible, Simon Mago hopes to get him completely in his power in this way. The Emperor discovers the deception and orders his guards to destroy the temple altar. He cruelly orders the magician to throw himself from a tower of the circus on the next festival to show the people if he can fly. To avoid being unmasked the priest agrees, but works out a plan to save himself. Act III. The orchard of a lonely house. Fanuèl is talking to a group of the faithful. As a mysterious figure approaches in the semi-darkness, everyone except Fanuèl and Rubria runs away. It is Asteria, wounded and bleeding, who warns Fanuèl and Rubria to escape, because Simon Mago is attempting to buy his freedom by betraying the Christians. Simon arrives and hands Fanuèl over to the guards. Rubria is left behind and makes plans to save him. Act IV. The entrance to the circus. There is confusion as one spectacle ends and the next begins. Simon is plotting to set fire to Rome to distract Nerone and the audience from the spectacle and gives himself a chance to escape. Asteria has agreed to light the fire because she hopes it will save the lives of many Christians as well as Simon. Tigellino reveals the plot to Nerone, but the Emperor is unconcerned and declares that if Rome burns he will have the glory of rebuilding it. Rubria, veiled as a priestess of Vesta, demands in the name of the goddess that the Christians be saved, but is herself condemned to the same fate. Nerone orders Simon to be thrown from the top of the tower. Clouds of smoke, and cries of terror indicate that the fire has started. There is chaos as people take flight. In the vaults beneath the circus, where the dead bodies are thrown, Asteria and Fanuèl, who escaped amid the confusion caused by the fire, see Simon Mago's corpse and find Rubria wounded. She confesses to Fanuèl her hidden love for him, and that she is a Vestal who had embraced Christianity without giving up the worship of Vesta. Fanuèl forgives her. As the flames spread, the vault of the circus collapses, burying Rubria and the other Christians.

■ Boito spent many years composing *Nerone*, sometimes breaking off work on it for years at a time. The idea for the opera first came to him while he was still writing *Mefistofele*. The libretto was eventually published in 1901, but the musical score did not appear during his lifetime and was completed after his death by Tommasini and Smareglia, on Toscanini's instructions. As in *Mefistofele*, the text is more successful than the music, though in *Nerone* the composer maintains a more powerful dramatic intensity. Once again he aims to give artistic and lyrical force to the antithesis of good and evil, in this case the contrast between the pagan world and the dawning of Christianity.

ERWARTUNG (Expectation)
Monodrama in four scenes for soprano and orchestra by Arnold Schönberg (1874–1951), text by Marie Pappenheim. First performance: Prague, Neues Deutsches Theater, 6 June 1924; first performance in U.K.: London, Sadler's Wells Theatre, 4 April 1960; in U.S.A.: Washington, D.C., 28 December 1960. First performed by Marie Gutheil-Schoder. Conductor: Alexander von Zemlinsky.

SYNOPSIS. Scene I. The edge of a wood by the light of the moon. A woman (soprano) is on her way to meet her lover. She senses a hidden threat in the still night air, but summons up her courage and enters the wood. Scene II. A road between tall trees in total darkness. The woman feels mysterious presences in the darkness, touching her and holding her back. She thinks that she hears weeping. A rustling noise and a bird's cry fill her with terror. She starts to run and stumbles over what she takes to be a lifeless body, but it is only a tree trunk. Scene III. A clearing lit by the moon, with tall grass, ferns and huge yellow toadstools. The woman takes breath and tries to calm herself. She stops to listen, imagining she hears her lover calling. Immediately she regrets that the night is so short. Then she is again overcome by the fear that a hundred hands are catching hold of her, while huge staring eyes watch her in the dark. Scene IV. A moonlit road. A path leads away from the road towards her rival's house. The woman is exhausted, her face and hands covered with scratches. As she goes towards the trees, looking for a place to rest, her foot strikes against something. It is the bleeding body of her murdered lover. She cannot believe what she sees. Deliriously she covers the lifeless body with kisses, reproaching her lover bitterly for his infidelities in a frenzy of incoherent and inexpressible memories. Finally morning separates the lovers for ever.

■ *Erwartung* was Schönberg's first composition for the theatre. He was so struck by the text which he had commissioned from the young poet Marie Pappenheim that he composed the score in a fortnight in a state of feverish excitement. When it was first performed one critic described the opera as 'the highly concentrated summing up of everything produced since Wagner, almost a critical essay, in sounds not words, which by the force of its intentions and creative vision, makes rational explanation impossible'. The music, written during Schönberg's atonal period, forms a continuous flow with sudden bursts and flashes of sound which vanish without continuity or development, broken only by a pause when the woman makes her fearful discovery. The vocal part is a recitative, interspersed with explosions of melodic sound. Theodor Adorno remarked that in *Erwartung*, as in the whole of Schönberg's expressionist phase, 'the seismographic registering of traumatic shocks becomes the technical law of musical form, musical language is polarized – at one extreme producing an almost physical sense of shock, while at the other rigidly holding back the unyielding experience of anguish'.

HUGH THE DROVER, or LOVE IN THE STOCKS
Ballad opera in two acts by Ralph Vaughan Williams

Stravinsky's Le renard *at the Théâtre de la Ville, Paris, 1972.*

(1872–1958), text by Harold Child (1869–1945). First performance: London, Perry Memorial Theatre, Royal College of Music, 4 July 1924. First professional performance by the British National Opera Company at Her Majesty's Theatre, 14 July 1924, with Tudor Davis and Mary Lewis. First performance in U.S.A.: Washington, 21 February 1928.

SYNOPSIS. The action takes place in England at the beginning of the nineteenth century. Mary's father, the Constable (bass), wants his daughter (soprano) to marry the rich but oafish John the Butcher (bass-baritone). She falls in love, however, with Hugh the Drover (tenor), who is regarded with suspicion by the townspeople because he loves the freedom of the countryside, animals and the open road. John continues to press his suit with Mary's father, convinced that his wealth will prove irresistible. The two men fight a boxing match to decide which shall marry Mary, and Hugh wins. Then John accuses Hugh of being a Napoleonic spy. Hugh is locked into the village stocks. None of Mary's stratagems to release him are successful and Hugh has to spend the night there, and endure the taunts of John and his friends. In the morning, however, Mary appears with her father's key to the stocks and unlocks them. The lovers are about to escape, when Mary's absence is noticed at home, and the villagers are surprised to find her sitting beside Hugh – in the stocks! John declares that he cannot marry one who behaves in this undignified way, but Mary's friends sympathize with her. A Sergeant

(baritone) arrives to take the suspected spy away, but he recognizes Hugh as an old comrade and cheerfully releases him. Instead, he marches off with John, determined to 'make a man' of him. Hugh and Mary happily set off together for the open road.

■ Although the character of John the Butcher has been criticized as a dull creation arousing neither sympathy nor dislike, the opera as a whole has great delicacy. Mary is a surprisingly passionate character for an English opera and the music underlines this throughout. The opera, composed between 1911 and 1914, has never been a great international success.

DIE GLÜCKLICHE HAND (The Lucky Hand)
Drama with music in four scenes, for baritone, chorus of male and female voices and orchestra, by Arnold Schönberg (1874–1951), text by the composer. First performance: Vienna, Volksoper, 14 October 1924; first performance in U.S.A.: Philadelphia, Academy of Music, 11 April 1930. Conductor of first performance: Fritz Stiedry.

SYNOPSIS. Scene I. A fabulous monster, lying on the man's back, grips his neck between its teeth. The chorus (six men and six women, whose green faces can just be seen in the darkness) urge the man (baritone) to believe in reality, not dreams, to renounce the unobtainable and to distrust the appeal of the senses. The man and the monster disappear in the darkness. Scene II. In front of a radiant sun the man and the woman (silent role) reveal their love. He brushes her hand with his to tell her of his happiness. The master appears (the symbol of cold earthly reality), and the woman follows him, deserting the man, who does not notice and exclaims triumphantly that she will be his for ever. Scene III. The man, armed with a sword, climbs up a rock in which there are two caves. In one there is a workshop where several workers are busy. Taking no notice of their threatening attitude, he splits the anvil in two with a single blow of the mallet and draws a diadem decorated with previous stones from a piece of gold. Ignoring the workers' hostility and scorn he throws them the jewels, laughing. In the other cave, the woman is begging the master to give her back a strip of stuff torn from her dress. When the master leaves, the man tries to win the woman again, but she runs away and, as she climbs up a crag, rocks (which turn into the monster) fall and bury him. Scene IV. The man is again trapped by the monster (the anguish inherent in all human life) while the chorus comments upon his agonizing and hopeless quest.

■ The short text for *Die glückliche Hand* dates from 1910, but the score was not completed until three years later. The opera – a complicated allegory about the isolation of the individual (the artist) in an industrial society – is important both musically (Theodor Adorno regarded it as perhaps Schönberg's most significant work) and as theatre. Musically it can be described as an 'insatiable superimposition' of different but simultaneous layers of rich sound which create a totally new quality of tone colour. The alternate use of *Sprechgesang* and singing also produces a highly original effect. As a theatrical work *Die glückliche Hand* is intended – as the author's detailed stage directions show – to establish certain essential relationships between all stage elements (speech, gesture, colour) which are governed by precise measurements of length, fullness and intensity in the same way as sounds. Schönberg laid particular emphasis on the symbolism of colours (as in Kandinsky's theories) which change in relation to the music.

INTERMEZZO
Bourgeois comedy in two acts with symphonic interludes by Richard Strauss (1864–1949), text by the composer. First performance: Dresden, Staatsoper, 4 November 1924; first performance in U.K.: Edinburgh, King's Theatre, 9 September 1965; in U.S.A.: New York, Lincoln Center, 11 February 1963.

ORIGINAL CAST included Lotte Lehmann, Joseph Correck. Conductor: Fritz Busch.

SYNOPSIS. Act I. The conductor Robert Storch (baritone) is leaving for Vienna. Christine, his wife (soprano), complains about the disadvantages of being married to a famous man, and reminds her husband that she comes from a much superior family. Left alone, she welcomes the attentions of the young Baron Lummer (tenor) and goes dancing with him, but soon realizes that he is after her money. A letter addressed to Storch arrives. Christine opens it and reads with horror a message which shows beyond a doubt that the writer, one Mieze Meier, is on intimate terms with her correspondent. Christine is furious and sends her husband a telegram stating that she will never see him again. Act II. The telegram reaches Storch while he is playing cards with his friends, including the conductor Stroh (tenor), for whom the letter was really intended. Sending Stroh ahead to explain the mistake to Christine, Storch returns home, but his wife, though convinced of his innocence, receives him coldly. It is bound to end like this sometime, she tells him. Robert at last gives vent to his feelings, and Christine immediately realizes that she could never live without him. The couple are reconciled and Christine remarks that theirs is a 'truly happy' marriage.

■ *Intermezzo* is based in detail on an episode from the married life of Strauss and his wife Pauline. After the composer had failed to get Hofmannsthal or Bahr to collaborate on the text with him, he decided to write it himself, encouraged by Bahr. This combination of circumstances produced the musical richness and psychological depth which makes *Intermezzo* a near-perfect opera. The 'musical conversation' style of the scenes themselves, with the skilful use of *parlando*, conveys the tragic-comic twists of the plot while the interludes probe more deeply into the characters' psychology and true feelings.

THE CUNNING LITTLE VIXEN (Příhody Lišky Bystroušky)
Opera in three acts and nine scenes by Leoš Janáček (1854–1928), libretto by the composer from a story by R. Těsnohlídek. First performance: Brno, 6 November 1924; first performance in U.K.: London, Sadler's Wells, 1961; in U.S.A.: New York, Mannes College of Music at Hunter College, 1964.

SYNOPSIS. Act I. A forester (bass-baritone) captures the vixen Bystrouška (soprano) and tries unsuccessfully to educate her in the ways of men. She attempts to stir up a revolt in the hen-run, breaks through her rope and escapes to the wood and her former freedom. Act II. The forester tries to capture her again, with all the bitterness of an abandoned lover. The vixen in fact reminds him of Terynka, a wild, free gypsy girl whom he had loved in youth and who has since been courted unsuccessfully by the schoolmaster (tenor), and is to marry Harašta (bass), a poultry-vendor and a free man like her. The vixen has meanwhile moved into the home of an old Badger (bass) and married a fox (soprano), by whom she is expecting cubs. Act III. Harašta shoots the vixen after a battle of wits over his chicken

Raymond Ellis in Holst's The Perfect Fool *at Covent Garden, London.*

basket. Her death echoes the loss of Terynka, and the cycle seems to be complete. In the early spring, however, the forester again finds himself in the clearing where he had captured Bystrouška. In a daydream, he sees a little vixen cub staring at him just like its mother, and with her love for life; he reaches out for it, but grasps instead a little frog. He suddenly realizes Nature's power of renewal and becomes at peace with the world.

■ This work is one of the most important Czech operas of this century. Drawing on Czech folk songs, the composer created a very effective and individual style. The opera is one of his most lyrical and melodious compositions.

I CAVALIERI DI EKEBÙ (The Knights of Ekebù)
Opera in four acts by Riccardo Zandonai (1883–1944), text by Arturo Rossato, based on the novel Gösta Berling *by Selma Lagerlöf (1858–1940). First performance: Milan, Teatro alla Scala, 7 March 1925.*

ORIGINAL CAST. Franco Lo Guidice, Elvira Cassazza, Fanelli, Autori, Franci, Walter, Tedeschi and Laura. Conductor: Arturo Toscanini.

SYNOPSIS. Ekebù in Sweden. The priest Gösta Berling (tenor) has been stripped of his office and sent away from his presbytery because he drinks too much. When he is thrown out of an inn and reproached by Anna (soprano), the girl he loves, he feels ready to die. The 'commander' (mezzo-soprano), the woman who owns the ironworks and castle of Ekebù, offers him work with the 'Knights', a group of stray ex-soldiers, half adventurers, half bohemians. Gösta publicly tells Anna during a Christmas show that he loves her and they embrace. Sintram (bass) hints that the 'commander' has sold the knights' souls to the devil; she is driven out. She later returns, sick, when the knights have already decided to ask her back. She forgives everyone and before dying leaves her possessions to Gösta and Anna. The knights return to their usual work.

■ This is perhaps Zandonai's most interesting score and was a great success. It was performed in Stockholm in 1928 to celebrate the seventieth birthday of Selma Lagerlöf, on whose novel the text is based.

L'ENFANT ET LES SORTILÈGES (The Child and the Enchantments)
Fantaisie lyrique *in two acts by Maurice Ravel (1875–1937), text by Colette (1873–1954). First performance: Monte Carlo, Théâtre du Casino, 21 March 1925. First performance in U.K.: Oxford, 3 December 1958; in U.S.A.: San Francisco, 19 September 1930.*

ORIGINAL CAST. Gauley, Orsoni, Dubois-Lauger, Bilhon, Lafont, Warnéry, Mathilde, Baidarott. Conductor: Victor de Sabata.

SYNOPSIS. Act I. Inside an old Norman house, with low ceiling and a warm and welcoming atmosphere. The main character, a child aged six or seven (mezzo-soprano), is trying to do his homework. He longs to do all the things that are forbidden – pull the cat's tail or stand his mother in the corner. His mother (contralto) now enters and discovers that he has not even begun his homework. As a punishment he is only allowed a cup of sugarless tea and a piece of dry bread. Left alone, the child flies into a temper – he smashes things, tears the wallpaper, pulls the cat's tail and tries to hurt the squirrel in the cage. Finally he sinks exhausted into an armchair. Now the enchantments begin. The armchair breaks into an old-fashioned dance with a Louis XV chair (soprano). The other pieces of furniture, like the armchair, express their scorn for the child. The grandfather clock (baritone) complains that he has lost his balance, and all the other objects join in. Fairy-tale figures step out of the torn wallpaper – shepherds and shepherdesses with their sheep and goats dance to soft music and mourn that they will never be together again. The child weeps. A princess (soprano) steps out from the pages of his torn book to comfort him gently, though even she scolds him. As he listens she disappears and her place is taken by an alarming old man (tenor) with a Greek 'Pi' on his head who spouts a string of problems to be solved. He is Arithmetic. Meanwhile the moon rises. The cat (mezzo-soprano) goes to meet the tom cat (baritone) and together they sing a dramatic love duet. Act II. It is night in the garden. All the animals there have a grudge against the child and fling reproaches and threats at him. Then they leave him alone, breaking into weird conversations and wild complicated dances with such careless enthusiasm that they wound a squirrel (mezzo-soprano). The child tenderly takes care of the little animal and tries to comfort it. He bandages up its wounded paw with a ribbon. When the animals see the child's good deed, they are amazed at his unexpected kindness. Finally they take him safely home to his mother and leave him with her. The enchantments are over and the child is back in the real world. The opera ends as he calls for his mother.

■ Colette had for some time been seeking a composer to set her text to music and approached Ravel at the suggestion of a mutual friend. Their partnership was not easy because Ravel encountered many difficulties,

Stage design by Nicola Benois for the second scene of Manuel de Falla's El retablo de Maese Pedro.

both in the text, which he asked the writer to change several times, and in the staging. The work, which was originally to have been called *Ballet pour ma fille*, might never have been finished without the help of Raoul Gunsbourg, then director of the Monte Carlo theatre, who set the composer a deadline. There was uproar at the first performance and the opera provoked further controversy when it was put on in Paris in 1926. It was not fully appreciated until it appeared in New York, London and Brussels. Since then it has been seen all over the world. The composer's original fears about the difficulties of staging have proved well founded. The child's part has to be played by an adult and the wires needed to move and control the enormous furniture and furnishings rather spoil the intended effect of an enchanted world. However, the magical and fantastic nature of the music itself is completely effective, creating an opera which breaks traditional rules and remains unique of its kind. Ravel's imaginative power is apparent in the continual switches between the tender and the ironic, and in the succession of vignettes which show a miniaturist's love of exact detail. Ravel lived in his parents' house as a bachelor until their death and in this opera he displays a touching concern for what goes on within domestic walls. *L'enfant et les sortilèges* is a moving yet simple tale in which the composer uses the delicate shades of his art to express his affection for the characters of Colette's fairy tale.

IL DIAVOLO NEL CAMPANILE (The Devil in the Belfry)

Opera in one act by Adriano Lualdi (1887–1971), libretto by the composer, based on Edgar Allan Poe's story. First performance: Milan, Teatro alla Scala, 22 April 1925.

ORIGINAL CAST. Elvira Casazza, Gaetano Arsolini, Rorri, Baracchi, Menescaldi and de Oliveira as the devil (mimed role). Conductor: Vittorio Gui.

SYNOPSIS. The action takes place at an unspecified date in an imaginary town which is dominated by the continual chiming of countless clocks. The most important is the clock on the tower in the main square, which has a large sign at the top reading 'The infallible'. The intrigues between young lovers and the wives of elderly husbands are regulated by the clocks. However, one day the devil gets into the clock tower and throws time into confusion. The little town goes mad. Everything happens at breakneck speed – the old men find out about their young wives' affairs, there are escapes, pursuits and fights. Finally the devil leaves, but by then the townspeople have learned to live disorderly lives.

■ Lualdi always preferred comic subjects and parody. He revived the forms and styles of eighteenth-century Italian drama, though the influence of Wolf-Ferrari and the use of technical innovations give his work a more up-to-date flavour. The rather fanciful score for *Il diavolo nel campanile* is one of the most typical examples of his work.

DOKTOR FAUST

Opera in two prologues, one interlude and three scenes by Ferruccio Busoni (1866–1924), libretto by the composer based on the old Faust legends and Marlowe's Doctor Faustus *(1588). First performed after the composer's death: Dresden, Staatsoper, 21 May 1925. First performance in U.K. (concert version): London, Queen's Hall, 17 March 1937; in U.S.A.: New York, 1 December 1964. Conductor of the first performance: Fritz Busch.*

SYNOPSIS. The action takes place during the first half of the sixteenth century. First prologue. Faust's study in Wittenberg. The doctor (baritone) receives a visit from three students, who offer him the gift of a book and a key which will give him power over the forces of Hell. Second prologue. Faust performs the prescribed ritual at midnight. He takes off his girdle, makes a magic circle on the floor and enters it with the key and book. He questions the infernal spirits which appear in tongues of flame, but the first five disappoint him. The sixth promises him things he has long desired and materializes as Mephistopheles (tenor), who agrees to give Faust everything he wants until his death, if Faust will become his slave for eternity. Faust at first refuses to sign the pact, but Mephistopheles reminds him that he has many debts, that the brother of a girl he had seduced has sworn to kill him and that the Church authorities suspect him of sorcery because of his activities as an alchemist. Faust signs. Interlude. In the cathedral Marguérite's brother (baritone), the soldier who has sworn to kill Faust, is kneeling in prayer. He asks God to let him meet the man who seduced his sister. Mephistopheles misleads some soldiers to mistake him for a wanted bandit. They attack and kill him. Scene I. Celebrations are in progress in the park of the Duke's palace at Parma. Faust arrives, preceded by his reputation as a man who can perform wonders. By conjuring up various illusions, he fills the courtiers with amazement and makes the Duchess (soprano) fall in love with him. The Duke (tenor) is jealous and tries to poison him, but Mephistopheles warns him in time. Faust flees and the Duchess follows him in a trance. Scene II. An inn at Wittenberg. Faust is talking with students and mentions his adventure with the Duchess of Parma. Mephistopheles enters, bringing news of the Duchess's death. He throws the corpse of a new-born child on the floor to show Faust's guilt, then turns it into a bundle of straw and sets fire to it. The figure of a beautiful woman emerges from the smoke – it is Helen of Troy. She disappears as Faust approaches. The students who had given him the book and key appear and ask for them back, but Faust tells them he has destroyed them. They tell him his death is near. Scene III. Faust wanders in the snow-covered streets of

Wittenberg. He sees Wagner (baritone), his former pupil and now rector, being congratulated by his students. Then he sees his own house and hears voices warning him of the coming judgement. Desperately he tries to perform some action which will redeem him. On the church steps he sees a beggar woman with a child: she is the Duchess of Parma, carrying her dead child; the ghost of Marguérite's brother stands in the church doorway and the crucifix has Helen of Troy's face. Faust makes a last desperate effort to redeem his sins. He covers the dead child with his cloak, makes a circle with his girdle, enters it and speaks the magic words. He dies, but a youth bearing a green branch rises from his cloak and walks away.

■ The opera was unfinished when the composer died and it was completed by Philipp Jarnach. The text is not based on Goethe's play, but on the same sources that the poet drew upon – the character of Faust in an old puppet play and Marlowe's *Doctor Faustus*. The opera is Busoni's last and finest achievement, a full, mature work which the composer had planned all his life.

L'ORFEIDE

Trilogy by Gian Francesco Malipiero (1882–1973), libretto by the composer. Each part is independent: La morte delle maschere *(The Death of the Masks), prelude;* Sette canzoni *(Seven songs), seven dramatic expressions;* Orfeo, *or* L'ottava canzone *(Orpheus, or The eighth song), epilogue. First performance: Düsseldorf, Stadttheater, 30 October 1925.*

ORIGINAL CAST. Stuck, Waldmeier, Bouquoi, Bara, Ludwik, Redensbeck, Backstein, Faber, Roffmann, Barleben, Schilp, Fassbaender, Ullrich, Senff-Thiess, Grahl, Thiess, Dobski, Bruggermann, Schoemmer, Putz, Nettesheim, Ries. Conductor: Harthmann.

SYNOPSIS. *La morte delle maschere.* A theatre impresario introduces the typical mask characters of the *commedia dell'arte* to the audience. Suddenly a masked man bursts in, chases away the impresario and shuts all the mask characters up in a cupboard. He condemns them to death for representing events far removed from real life. In their place he brings in new opera characters taken from life who represent and sing of human matters. One by one the characters who are to appear in the *Sette canzoni* file past, and are introduced by the masked man, Orfeo (tenor). *I vagabondi*: A woman guiding a blind man is bewitched by the singing of a minstrel (baritone) and follows him, forgetting about her companion. When he realizes what has happened he sadly gropes his way off. *A vespro*: One evening a friar notices a woman deep in prayer as he is about to lock up the church. Indifferent to her troubles he makes her leave. *Il ritorno*: An old mother (soprano) beside herself with grief mourns for her son, whom she believes to be dead. The young man returns, but she does not recognize him and to his distress spurns him. *L'ubriaco*: A young man is running away from his mistress's house where he has been caught by her husband. He bumps into a drunk (baritone) and knocks him down. The husband mistakes the drunk for the lover and gives him a terrible beating. *La Serenata*: Inside a house a girl is weeping over a relative who has died. She does not hear her lover (tenor) sing his serenade, but he has only to enter the house to understand her plight. *Il campanaro*: A bell-ringer (baritone), sounding the alarm to warn people of a terrible fire, sings a merry song, unconcerned by what is going on. *L'alba delle Ceneri*: A hearse passes by a group of penitents who invite people to pray. A band of mask-characers enter dancing, but a symbolic figure (baritone) representing death appears, and puts them to flight. As the penitents move away, two masked girls join the group. *Orfeo*, or *L'ottava canzone*: The epilogue shows a theatre full of people, including the king and queen. An actor (baritone) portrays Nero's cruelty. At this the old men are indignant, but the children laugh and applaud. Orfeo appears and sings a soft, gentle song which puts the audience to sleep, all except the queen, who is delighted by the singer and leaves with him.

■ In the first part of this work Malipiero expresses his belief that the theatre must abandon the academic forms of the past and face reality. The seven episodes which form the second part are called *canzoni* (songs) because they are based on simple *arioso* melodies, without obbligato accompaniment or recitative. Like songs, they are a melodic elaboration of a brief moment from life. The words are taken from old Italian texts, mainly from the Renaissance period. The third part returns to the original theme of the conflict between the theatre and reality, ironically highlighting the difficulties of trying to free the theatre from traditional forms. Despite his earlier declarations, Orfeo resumes a conventional style, though his audience falls asleep. The opera has proved highly controversial.

WOZZECK

Opera in three acts and fifteen scenes by Alban Berg (1885–1935), libretto by the composer adapted from the play Woyzeck *by Georg Büchner (1836). First performance: Berlin, Staatsoper, 14 December 1925. First performance in U.K.: London, Covent Garden, 22 January 1952; in U.S.A.: Philadelphia, 19 March 1931.*

ORIGINAL CAST. Leo Schützendorf (Wozzeck); Sigrid Johannson (Marie), Fritz Soot (the drummajor), Martin Abendroth (the doctor), Gerhor Witting (Andres), Waldemar Henke (the captain). Conductor: Erich Kleiber.

SYNOPSIS. The action is set in Germany in about 1836. Act I, Scene I. The Captain's room. The captain (buffo tenor) is being shaved as usual by Wozzeck (baritone), his batman. He chats about the meaning of life and alows himself to moralize, commenting on the fact that Wozzeck lives with Marie and has an illegitimate son by her. Wozzeck listens for a while, but then declares that he has no time to be moral since he does not even have enough to eat. Scene II. The open countryside with the town in the distance. Wozzeck and his comrade-in-arms Andres (lyric tenor) are gathering wood. Wozzeck has hallucinations and sees the landscape before him turn into terrifying images. Meanwhile distant drums signal that it is time to return to barracks. Scene III. Marie's room. Marie (soprano) is standing at the window watching the soldiers, including the drum-major (dramatic tenor), pass by. She gets into an argument with her neighbour Margret (contralto), who criticizes her way of life. As Marie is rocking the child, Wozzeck arrives, still disturbed by his visions in the wood. He utters incoherent phrases and then runs away. Scene IV. The doctor's study. Wozzeck, still in an agitated state, arrives at the doctor's study from Marie's house. For a pittance he has agreed to act as a guinea-pig for the doctor's strange experiments with special diets. His incipient madness begins to become apparent. Scene V. In front of Marie's house. The drum-major, who has been courting Marie for some time, now propositions her directly and she fatalistically gives in. Act II, Scene I. Marie's room. Marie is trying on a pair of earrings when Wozzeck enters and jealously demands an explanation. She pretends to have found them. Wozzeck calms down, gives her his pay and leaves. Left alone, she thinks about her infidelity. Scene II. In the street Wozzeck meets the doctor and the captain, who hint at Marie's behaviour until he is convinced that she has been unfaithful. Scene III. In front of Marie's house. Wozzeck, disturbed by the doctor's and the captain's insinuations, has a violent quarrel with Marie. Scene IV. A beer garden. Wozzeck sees Marie and the drum-major dancing in a group of soldiers and young people. While two drunken workmen and Andres sing popular songs, Wozzeck is seized by a desire to kill. When the fool (tenor) approaches him, murmuring 'I smell blood', he wildly repeats the words 'blood, blood.' Scene V. The barrack room. Wozzeck tells Andres of his torment. The drum-major enters and insults Wozzeck, mentioning Marie. They fight briefly, and Wozzeck is knocked to the ground. Act III, Scene I. Marie's room. While the child sleeps Marie reads the gospel story of Mary Magdalen and offers a heart-felt prayer to heaven. Scene II. Wozzeck and Marie are walking in the wood by a pond. She wants to go home but he will not let her. Calmly at first, then with increasing agitation, he accuses her and then cuts her throat. He returns to the inn. Scene III. The inn. As the dancers dance the polka Wozzeck tries to make love to Margret, but she sees bloodstains on his clothes and he rushes from the room. Scene IV. The wood near the pond. Wozzeck is looking for the knife. On finding it he throws it into the pond, but thinking he has not thrown it far enough wades in to retrieve it and to wash himself. Even after the water has reached his neck, he

continues to walk further in. The doctor and the captain pass by, but hurry away when they hear strange sounds. Scene V. In front of Marie's house. The child (treble) is playing with a wooden horse. His friends tell him that his mother is dead, but he does not understand and goes on playing.

■ The genesis of *Wozzeck* was long drawn out. Though the first performance took place on 14 December 1925, Berg had first conceived the opera in May 1914 when he saw a performance of Georg Büchner's *Woyzeck*. He was deeply impressed and decided to set the play to music. He therefore began the far from easy task of adaptation, eventually producing an opera in fifteen scenes rather than the original twenty-five. In 1921 the score was complete and orchestrated, but it was not performed until 1925. Even then the opera ran into difficulties and was banned under Nazism as decadent. It has since been frequently performed in the musical capitals of the world. It is interesting to note the extent to which Berg abandons traditional operatic form, made up of arias, recitatives, etc., and instead uses instrumental forms as the basis of each scene. The structure of the score is as follows: Act I, Scene I, suite; Scene II, rhapsody and hunting song; Scene III, military march and lullaby; Scene IV, passacaglia; Scene V, *Andante affettuoso (quasi Rondo)*; Act II, Scene I, sonata movement; Scene II, fantasy and fugue; Scene III, largo; Scene IV, scherzo; Scene V, martial rondo (the act as a whole may be regarded as a symphony divided into movements); Act III, Scene I, invention on a theme; Scene II, invention on one note; Scene III, invention on a rhythm; Scene IV, invention on a chord of six notes; (orchestral interlude; invention of a key); Scene V, invention on a quaver figure. The orchestra is rarely used to the full – only in fact during the symphonic interludes played when the curtain is down. As Berg pointed out, it is best to listen to *Wozzeck* not by following the musical structure scene by scene, but by becoming involved in the action, and following the characters' psychological stage as the music faithfully mirrors all the morbid and irrational changes in the characters.

PAUL ET VIRGINIE

Unfinished opera by Erik Satie (1866–1925), text by Raymond Radiguet (1902–23) and Jean Cocteau (1889–1963).

■ The opera is based on Bernardin de Saint-Pierre's popular pastoral novel (1787).

JUDITH

Biblical opera in three acts by Arthur Honegger (1892–1955), libretto by René Morax after The Book of Judith *in the Apocrypha. First performance: Monte*

Carlo, Théâtre du Casino, 13 February 1926. First performance in U.S.A.: Chicago, 27 January 1927. Conductor of the first performance: Arthur Honegger.

SYNOPSIS. The story is based on the deeds of the biblical heroine, Judith. When Judith realizes that her town Bethulia is about to surrender to the enemy, led by the Assyrian Holofernes, she decides to sacrifice herself to save it. She goes to the Assyrian camp, makes Holofernes fall in love with her and becomes his lover. As soon as he is overcome by wine, she cuts off his head and leaves the camp. Her people recover their courage and finally defeat their enemies. Judith gives thanks to God, and puts on a veil as a sign of mourning for the dead.

■ Morax's stage version of the story of Judith is one of many literary and musical adaptations inspired by the episode, from the Middle Ages onwards. Both writer and composer were concerned with an accurate portrayal of the biblical events and the ancient world in general. Their original intention was to produce a play, and a play with incidental music was in fact first performed on 13 June 1925 in the theatre at Mezières, in Switzerland. Later the musical content was expanded and the text cut accordingly. The first performance of the full operatic version in Monte Carlo was warmly received and there were many further performances elsewhere. The libretto has been translated into several languages.

Cover for Ravel's L'Enfant et les Sortilèges.

TRE COMMEDIE GOLDONIANE (Three Plays by Goldoni)
Three one-act operas by Gian Francesco Malipiero (1882–1973), texts by the composer based on plays by Carlo Goldoni (1707–93). First performance: Darmstadt, Hessisches Landestheater, 24 March 1926.

ORIGINAL CAST. Stephanova, Albrecht, Liebel, Kapper, Calloni, Holzin, Etzel, Wogt, Hoffmann, Röhrig, Lahn, Kuhn, Delarde, Barczinsky, Bischoff, Schumacher, Müller-Wischin. Conductor: Joseph Rosenstock.

LA BOTTEGA DEL CAFFÈ (The Coffee Shop)

SYNOPSIS. The action is set in Venice during the eighteenth century. Don Marzio (baritone), a confirmed gossip, is sitting in a small square at a table outside Ridolfo's café. Eugenio (tenor) emerges from the gambling den opposite, which is run by Pandolfo (bass). He persuades his friend Ridolfo (tenor) to lend him money to pay off his gambling debts to 'Count Leandro' – in fact a swindler called Flaminio (baritone). Meanwhile Placida (mezzo-soprano) arrives, disguised as a beggar woman, to spy on her husband, 'Count Leandro', who is a frequent visitor of Lisaura (mimed part), a dancer of doubtful reputation. As the 'count' leaves Lisaura's house he offers Eugenio money to go on playing. Eugenio thinks he is down on his luck, but eventually accepts. Meanwhile Pandolfo tells Don Marzio that he always wins because he has rigged a pack of cards. Eugenio now returns, having won at last, and celebrates his luck by inviting everyone to supper. As they set off, Placida, furious at seeing her husband with Lisaura, attacks him, but he roughly pushes her away. Eugenio is eager to help her, but his wife Vittoria (mimed part), who has been listening to Don Marzio's gossiping, scolds him for his dissolute life. Meanwhile the guards arrive. Don Marzio has tipped them off about the gambling den and the rigged cards, and they make straight for the gamblers. While the two couples, Leandro and Placida, and Eugenio and Vittoria, are reconciled, Pandolfo is arrested and Don Marzio is thrown out of the café as a scandalmonger and spy.

L'Enfant et les Sortilèges by Maurice Ravel. Costume designs by Paul Colin for Arithmetic and the Chinese cup. Paris, Opéra, 1939. Right, sketches by François Geneau for the dragonflies. Paris, Opéra, 1958.

SIOR TODERO BRONTOLON (Sior Todero, The Grumbler)

SYNOPSIS. The scene is Venice in the eighteenth century. Todero's bedroom. Todero (baritone), a surly old miser, discovers Nicoletto (baritone), Desiderio's son, in intimate conversation with the maid Cecilia (soprano). He angrily turns them out. Then he calls Desiderio (baritone) and tells him that he would like his granddaughter Zanetta to marry Nicoletto, because this match would allow him to save on the dowry. Finally he informs his own son, Pellegrin, Zanetta's weak father, reminding him that he is master in the house. His daughter-in-law, Marcolina (soprano), is, however, made of sterner stuff and tells him that her daughter will marry as she (and not her grandfather) wishes. Then, learning that Nicoletto and Cecilia are in love, she arranges their wedding without telling the old man. To make amends Zanetta chooses to marry Meneghetto Ramponzoli, who is so rich that he does not expect a dowry. Instead he gives the old miser a purse of gold, an argument Todero finds so convincing that he withdraws his objections.

LE BARUFFE CHIOZZOTTE (Quarrels in Chioggia)

SYNOPSIS. The comedy is set in Chioggia, a small town near Venice, during the eighteenth century. Pasqua (mezzo-soprano) with her daughter Lucietta (soprano) and Libera (mezzo-soprano) with her daughters Checca and Orsetta (sopranos) are making lace outside their house in a little square. Toffolo (tenor) (known as Marmottina) is Checca's sweetheart, but he ignores her and courts Lucietta instead. Checca is furious and reminds Lucietta that she is Titta-Nane's sweetheart. This starts a quarrel, which is stopped by their mothers. Checca is not satisfied and tells Titta-Nane (tenor) and his brother Beppe (tenor), Orsetta's sweetheart, what has happened. The men start fighting, brandishing knives and throwing stones, one of which strikes Toni (bass), Lucietta's father, who was not even involved. The fighting becomes general and is only stopped by the arrival of the law, in the person of Isidoro (baritone), who threatens to send everyone to prison. He is so touched, however, by the girls' tears that he promises to pardon everyone if they will make up their quarrel. The girls embrace their own sweethearts and invite Isidoro into Toni's house for a drink. Suddenly some trivial incident sparks off a scuffle among the women. They start shrieking and gesticulating, while Isidoro looks on mournfully.

■ The trilogy, with the central figures of Don Marzio, Todero and Isidoro, round whom a host of colourful characters revolve, is a recreation of the atmosphere of eighteenth-century Venice. The three acts are freely adapted from Goldoni's comedies of the same names, with elements from other of his plays. Toffolo's song in *Le Baruffe Chiozzotte* is part of a sixteenth-century Venetian poem. The dialogue is partly in Italian, partly in Venetian dialect. Malipiero cut Goldoni's plays down to their essentials and set the action to music with a lively, supple symphonic structure, keeping the spoken recitative quite distinct. He does not attempt a colourful portrayal of the setting, since his aim is to make his characters real and convincing and in this way to convey a sense of time and place. In the three operas he shows us different aspects of Venetian life at the time – street life, family life and the life of the people.

TURANDOT

Opera in three acts by Giacomo Puccini (1858–1924), libretto by Giuseppe Adami (1878–1946) and Renato Simoni (1875–1952), based on Carlo Gozzi's fairy-tale drama (1762). First performance: Milan, Teatro alla Scala, 25 April 1926. First performance in U.K.: London, Covent Garden, 7 June 1927; in U.S.A.: New York, Metropolitan Opera House, 16 November 1926.

ORIGINAL CAST. Rosa Raisa, Maria Zamboni, Michele Fleta. Conductor: Arturo Toscanini.

SYNOPSIS. Legendary times, in Peking. Act I. A square in front of the Imperial Palace. In front of a large crowd a Mandarin (baritone) pronounces the death sentence on a Persian prince who has failed to answer three riddles put to him by Princess Turandot (soprano), daughter of the Emperor Altoum (tenor). Turandot has vowed that she will only marry a suitor of noble blood who can solve her three riddles and she has decreed that anyone who fails will be beheaded. Meanwhile in the crowd Timur (bass), exiled King of Tartary, and his faithful companion, the slave girl Liù (soprano), meet Calaf (tenor), Timur's son, believed dead in battle. The unsuccessful suitor is led to the scaffold. The crowd take pity on him and call for mercy. Calaf too is shocked by Turandot's cruelty, but when she appears on a balcony and silently gestures for the Persian Prince to die, he falls hopelessly in love with her and can only think of winning her. Three courtiers, Ping (baritone), Pang (tenor), and Pong (tenor), try in vain to dissuade him, and so do his father and Liù (who is secretly in love with him). Calaf comforts Liù, but then he sounds the gong which is the signal that another suitor wishes to undergo the trial. Act II, Scene I. A sumptuous pavilion in the Imperial Palace. Ping, Pang and Pong (figures based on the mask characters of the Commedia dell'Arte) lament the pitiful state of China due to Turandot's cruelty. They dream of retiring to the countryside, far away from the Princess, and hope that she will finally discover true love. Act II, Scene II. A courtyard inside the palace. Before the Emperor, seated on his throne at the top of a monumental staircase, and all the court, Turandot tells of the historic events which are the cause of her terrible vow. Thousands of years before, her ancestress Lo-u-ling was dishonoured and killed by a barbarian king. The cruel trial her suitors have to undergo is her revenge for that crime. Calaf is invited to withdraw, but he refuses firmly and the contest begins. He solves the riddles one by one (the answers are: hope, blood and Turandot) and wins. Turandot is humiliated and begs her father to save her from becom-

ing a foreigner's slave, but the Emperor declares that his oath is sacred. Calaf offers to release her if she can discover his name and origin before dawn. Act III, Scene I. A garden of the Imperial Palace. In the quiet of the night the voices of heralds can be heard, proclaiming Turandot's decree: no-one is to sleep until the unknown Prince's name has been discovered. Calaf is certain of victory, already imagining the kiss which will awaken Turandot's love at dawn (aria *Nessun dorma*). The courtiers try to draw his secret from him with threats and promises. Timur and Liù, who were seen with Calaf, are brought before Turandot by guards. Liù declares that she alone knows the Prince's name. Fearing that she will reveal the secret under torture, she seizes a dagger and kills herself. Left alone with Turandot, Calaf first reproaches her for her coldness and cruelty, then kisses her on the mouth. The kiss seems to break a spell and she suddenly realizes that she has loved him from the start. Calaf now reveals his name. Scene II. In front of the assembled court, Turandot announces that she has discovered the unknown Prince's name – it is love.

■ When Puccini died on 29 November 1924, he left *Turandot* unfinished, ending with Liù's death. At Toscanini's suggestion, the score was completed by Franco Alfano (1876–1954), an established composer, whose successful works included *Risurrezione* (1904) and *La Leggenda di Sakuntala* (1921). But at the La Scala première, the performance ended, as Puccini himself seems to have anticipated, after Liù's aria, *Tu che di gel sei cinta*. Toscanini then turned to the audience and said, 'The opera ends here, because the composer died at this point.' Puccini chose his subject matter, suggested to him by Renato Simoni, an authority on Gozzi, almost by chance. The story was fairly well known and had been set to music several times already. A few years before, in 1917, Busoni's *Turandot* had been performed in Zurich (p. 370). However, as work advanced Puccini gradually came to believe that he was creating an original and perhaps unique opera. Six months before his death he confessed to Adami, 'I think about *Turandot* every hour and every minute, all the music I have written before seems a joke and is no longer to my taste.' *Turandot* is indeed the most mature and accomplished of all Puccini's works. It is also a recapitulation of all his creative experiences, bringing together the four sides of his art: the lyrical and sentimental element, personified by the gentle, devoted Liù, the most touching character in the opera and the most typical of Puccini; the heroic, represented by Calaf and Turandot; the comic and grotesque with the three mask characters, who introduce a blend of serious drama and commedia dell'arte reminiscent of Strauss's *Ariadne auf Naxos*, and the exotic, achieved by avoiding precise historical references and incorporating authentic Chinese themes into the score. Puccini also makes greater use than elsewhere of pentatonic motifs common in non-European musical traditions. Compared with his other operas, the harmonic language contains more features drawn from contemporary music, including extreme dissonances, polyton-

Sven-Erik Vikström (the captain), Anders Näslund (Wozzeck) and Arne Tyren (the doctor) in Berg's Wozzeck in Stockholm.

Berg's Wozzeck at Covent Garden, London, 1952.

ality and surprising vocal and orchestral effects. In terms of the plot, it is interesting to observe how Puccini's sympathy for the character of Liù led the action into a serious *impasse*. Liù's death and the procession to carry her body away are the most powerful moments in the opera, and make the happy ending seem out of place. Puccini was faced with the problem of establishing some link between Liù's sacrifice and the humanizing of Turandot, but death prevented him from solving it.

LES MALHEURS D'ORPHÉE (The Misfortunes of Orpheus)
Opera in three acts by Darius Milhaud (1892–1974), libretto by Armand Lunel. First performance: Brussels, Théâtre de la Monnaie, 7 May 1926. First performance in U.K.: London, St Pancras Town Hall, 8 March 1960; in U.S.A.: New York Town Hall, 29 January 1927.

ORIGINAL CAST. Thomas and Bianchini. Conductor: de Thoran.

SYNOPSIS. A lyrical and magical updated version of the legend of Orpheus and Eurydice. The action takes place in the Camargue. Orpheus (baritone) is an animal healer, Eurydice (soprano) a gypsy. Act I. Orpheus is a good, innocent man who loves the wild, natural countryside and is the animals' friend, seeking them out in their lairs and nursing them. His friends, the wheelwright, the basket-maker and the blacksmith, are worried about him and scold him. Orpheus reassures them. He tells them he will soon be getting married – to the gypsy girl Eurydice, who has just arrived with her family. Eurydice enters. She has run away from her family because they do not want her to marry Orpheus. Act II. Eurydice is struck down by a mysterious illness and Orpheus tries in vain to cure her. His friends the fox, the bear and the wild boar try to help him, but in vain. Eurydice dies, entrusting Orpheus to the animals' care. They carry her off, followed by Orpheus. Act III. Orpheus is at home when Eurydice's sisters arrive, seeking vengeance for her death. One is armed with scissors, one with a stick, one with a whip. Orpheus does not try to defend himself. He wishes to die and only the animals understand his torment. However, when he dies even the sisters realize his innocence and their chorus ends with the words, 'He loved her too much'.

■ The opera, with a small orchestra of fifteen players, is one of Milhaud's characteristic *opéras-minutes*, or short chamber operas, and was dedicated to the pianist and organist the Princesse de Polignac. It has often been performed in Europe and America, and is generally regarded as a little masterpiece, combining the composer's most lyrical style with moments of sublime inspiration.

KING ROGER (Król Roger)
Opera in three acts by Karol Szymanowski (1882–1937), libretto by the composer and Jaroslaw

Iwaszkiewicz. First performance: Warsaw, 19 June 1926. First performance in U.K.: (B.B.C. broadcast) 1955; (staged version) London, New Opera Company at Sadler's Wells Theatre, March 1975.

SYNOPSIS. Act I. In a Byzantine church, choirs led by the Archbishop (bass) intone Gregorian chants and the music reaches a gorgeous climax as King Roger (baritone) enters with his Queen, Roxane (soprano). Edrisi (tenor), an Arab scholar, warns the King that the faithful wish him to condemn the teachings of a mysterious 'shepherd' who has appeared in the countryside. The Queen pleads for him, and, when the Shepherd (tenor) himself comes in, he impresses the King so much that he is invited to come to the palace that evening. Act II. The palace. The King is attracted by the Shepherd's colourful music and dancing, until he claims to have been sent from God; he entrances Roxane, but the King firmly orders the guards to put him in chains for blasphemy. The fetters break, however, and laughing he leads his followers – Roxane among them – out into the hills. Roger tears off his crown and follows, as a pilgrim now, not as a King. Act III. Edrisi and the King approach the ruins of a Greek temple. Roxane greets her husband and endeavours to explain the mysteries of the Shepherd's faith – how he exists in every living thing as a life force. At last transformed into Dionysus, the Shepherd presides over a riotous dance of bacchantes, into which Roxane disappears. The King watches a new day dawn, his awareness enhanced by the mystic experience.

■ The opera was inspired by the deeds of King Roger II of Sicily celebrated in an anonymous German poem of the twelfth century. The composer wrote it between 1920 and 1924 and his cousin Iwaszkiewicz collaborated on the text. The opera skilfully introduces medieval tunes and recreates a religious atmosphere around them. The first act is the most successful. The other themes in the score help to build up an atmosphere of sensual mysticism and an evocation of the pagan world.

HÁRY JÁNOS
Opera in five parts, with a prologue and an epilogue, by Zoltán Kodály (1882–1967), libretto by Béla Paulini and Zsolt Harsányi, based on a poem by János Garay. First performance: Budapest, 16 October 1926. First performance in U.K.: London, Camden Town Hall, 1967; in U.S.A.: New York, Juilliard School, 18 March 1960.

■ Kodály's first opera, a military folk tale based on Hungarian folk tunes. The title refers to an old soldier who lived at the time of the Napoleonic wars. The opera was an enormous success in Hungary.

CARDILLAC
Opera in three acts by Paul Hindemith (1895–1963), *libretto by Ferdinand Lion, based on E. T. A. Hoffmann's story Das Fräulein von Scuderi (1818). First performance: Dresden, 9 November 1926 (with the same title as Hoffmann's story). First performance of completely revised version in four acts: Zurich, Stadttheater, 20 June 1952. First performance in U.K.: (concert version of original) London, Queen's Hall, 18 December 1936; (staged version) London, New Opera Company at Sadler's Wells, 1970; in U.S.A.: Santa Fé, 1967.*

ORIGINAL CAST (of revised version) included Brauen, Lechleitner, Jungwirth, Hillenbrecht. Conductor: Hans Zimmerman.

SYNOPSIS. Paris in the last decade of the seventeenth century. Act I, Scene I. A square in front of the shop of the jeweller Cardillac (baritone). It is night-time. Guards arrive to investigate the most recent of a series of murders. A crowd gathers, alarmed at this latest mysterious crime and the prescribed punishment is announced for the murderer, when he is discovered. Dawn. The jeweller opens up shop. The prima donna from the opera, the Lady (soprano), and her Cavalier (tenor) enter. He eagerly courts her, but she prefers to talk about the recent crimes – apparently a piece of Cardillac's jewellery has been stolen from each of the victims. She demands the most beautiful object from Cardillac's shop as the price of her surrender. The young man confides in Cardillac and admires his work, particularly a magnificent golden belt which he wants to buy. The jeweller refuses to sell it until the Cavalier insists. Scene II. The Lady's bedroom. The Cavalier enters and conquers her heart with his valuable gift. Suddenly a masked man slips in through the window, kills the young man and escapes with the belt. Act II. In the jeweller's shop. A gold merchant (tenor) who suspects that Cardillac is the murderer brings gold, but Cardillac refuses it as impure. An Officer (bass) who loves Cardillac's daughter (soprano) enters and asks for her hand. Cardillac happily consents: 'How could I love,' he asks, 'what was not truly mine?' The Officer buys a chain and Cardillac follows him, in cloak and mask, out into the street. Darkness falls. Act III [added in 1952]. The stage of the Académie Royale, with the wings on the right, the stage itself on the left. Lully's opera *Phaéton* is being performed. While the prima donna is on stage, declaring her love for Phaéton (tenor), the gold merchant comes on through the wings. He warns her of the danger she is putting herself in by wearing the belt, but she is fascinated by the strange situation. As the opera continues the Officer enters and then, unnoticed, Cardillac. The audience applauds as the opera finishes. The singer sees the jeweller and stares at him as if bewitched, for as an artist herself she understands his plight. She goes up to him, offers him the golden belt and embraces him. The Officer, who has been watching secretly, seizes it and runs away. Cardillac, ignoring the singer's call, rushes wildly in pursuit. Act IV. A square with a café. The gold merchant watches the Officer enter with the belt, followed by Cardillac, who attacks him. After a fierce fight, Cardillac escapes. The Officer's arm is wounded and the gold merchant, who intervened to help him, is found holding the belt and a dagger. Cardillac returns with his daughter. The gold merchant accuses the jeweller of the murder but the Officer declares that the gold merchant was his attacker. Cardillac confronts the crowd, and admits that he can identify the criminal. They threaten to burn his workshop unless he gives them this information. He confesses, to save his works, and they tear him to pieces. His daughter and the Officer arrive too late to save him.

■ Hindemith's free adaptation of Hoffmann's story was completed and set to music in 1926. But in 1952 he completely revised the opera, adding new characters and extra scenes, and enlarging it to four acts by adding the act (Act III) which includes the performance of part of Lully's *Phaéton*. In *Cardillac* the music does not define or share in the characters' emotional states, nor does it follow closely the highly dramatic text: at times it is even deliberately detached from the meaning of the words, in a continuous flow of clear, neo-classical polyphony. The separation of the opera's two levels – the music, which is dominant, and the text – has been described as *Musikoper*, a term specially created for this work, which accurately reflects this stage of the composer's development. During this period he favoured a strictly impersonal and objective style, laying particular emphasis on immediate and mechanical effects. Even so the music of *Cardillac* and other compositions of the period are far from impersonal or inexpressive. In the later version the composer chose to revise the score in the light of his new aesthetic ideas.

THE MAKROPULOS AFFAIR (Věc Makropulos)

Opera in three acts by Leoš Janáček (1854–1928), libretto by the composer based on a play by Karel Čapek. First performance: Brno, 18 December 1926. First performance in U.K.: London, Sadler's Wells Theatre, 12 February 1964; in U.S.A.: San Francisco, 19 November 1966.

SYNOPSIS. In a law suit, the famous opera singer Emilia Marty (soprano) shows surprising personal knowledge of events which occurred one hundred years previously. After a succession of dramatic events, she admits her strange history. Born 337 years ago, she was given a recipe for an elixir of eternal life. Since that time she has lived under a number of pseudonyms (always with the initials E. M.), but has become increasingly tired and bored of her interminable existence. At the end of the opera, she burns the formula and, as the paper disintegrates, she sinks dying to the ground.

■ Described by the composer as a 'modern historical opera', *The Makropulos Affair* is really a fairy tale. It dates from the period after the First World War when Janáček created works full of violent dramatic contrasts, sometimes fully expressionist in character.

ANGÉLIQUE
Farce in one act by Jacques Ibert (1890–1962), text by Nino. First performance: Paris, Théâtre Bériza, 28 January 1927. First performance in U.K.: London, Fortune Theatre, 20 February 1950; in U.S.A.: New York, 8 November 1937.

ORIGINAL CAST. Bériza. Ducruz, Warnery, Marvini.

SYNOPSIS. France at an unspecified date. Angélique (soprano), whose violent character belies her name, is married to Boniface (baritone), the owner of a china shop, a hen-pecked little man who always loses out to his domineering wife in their frequent quarrels. Finally he takes the advice of his friend Charlot (baritone) and puts her up for sale, hoping that some passer-by who knows nothing of her true nature will fall in love with her. She is persuaded to go along with the scheme by the prospect of a brilliant future. Three purchasers immediately show up – an Italian (tenor), an Englishman (tenor) and a Negro (bass). All three fall in love with Angélique at first sight, but each brings her back after a short period, battered and bruised by the beating she has given him. Poor Boniface is in despair at the failure of his scheme and begs the devil to take his horrible wife away. The devil (tenor) miraculously appears, seizes Angélique and bears her off. Delighted at their freedom, Boniface and Charlot celebrate her disappearance with their friends and neighbours, and with the three buyers who have come to claim their money back, but nevertheless join in the general rejoicing. But unbelievably the devil reappears. He wants nothing to do with this woman, who has turned Hell into 'a real Hell' and stirred up the damned. Boniface tries to hang himself when he sees her, but Angélique stops him – she has become a good, obliging and submissive wife and promises him eternal love. Boniface doubtfully accepts her offer and embraces her while the neighbours rejoice. As the curtain falls, Boniface appears and announces that his wife is still for sale.

■*Angélique* is one of the most successful French operas of the first half of the twentieth century. The farcical plot owes something to the popular medieval folk legend of the devil Belfagor. The composer skilfully adapts his style to this type of farce, using new means of expression to recreate features of the *opera buffa* of the Rossini school. The influence of Offenbach has also been noted, particularly in the use of theatrical devices (refrains, humorous ensembles, duets, etc.), and there are similarities with a certain type of French operetta (for example the works of Charles Lecocq). The text was quickly translated into several languages and the opera was an immediate success when first performed. It has been seen all over the world and is still a repertory piece – a richly comic, well-constructed farce.

JONNY SPIELT AUF (Johnny strikes up)
Jazz opera in two acts by Ernst Křenek (born 1900),

libretto by the composer. First performance: Leipzig, Opernhaus, 10 February 1927. First performance in U.S.A.: New York, Metropolitan Opera House, 19 January 1929.

SYNOPSIS. Act I. The action takes place in the present day. The scene shows a plateau overlooking a glacier. Max (tenor), a fine musician but a difficult introvert character, meets Anita (soprano), a beautiful singer. They spend a few days of love and happiness together until Anita has to leave for Paris, where she is to sing in one of his operas. He watches her preparations for departure unhappily. In Paris, among the guests in Anita's hotel is Daniello (baritone), a charming violinist and owner of a valuable violin which is a great temptation to Jonny (baritone), a young black musician in the hotel band. When she returns from the theatre Jonny tries to seduce her, but she is rescued by Daniello, who tries to get rid of the young man by offering him a thousand francs. Offended, Jonny steals Daniello's violin and hides it in Anita's banjo case. Yvonne (soprano), Jonny's sweetheart, quarrels with the hotel manager over Jonny's behaviour and is given the sack. Anita immediately employs her and prepares to leave with her, although Daniello, who has meanwhile become her lover, begs her to stay. For Anita, their brief affair is over and she leaves him. When the violinist realizes that his violin is missing he has the hotel turned upside down in the search. Realizing that his pleas to Anita are in vain, he takes his revenge by giving Yvonne the ring which Anita had given him with the instruction to hand it to Max when they arrive. Meanwhile Jonny has to give up his job and follow the two women to avoid losing the violin. Act II. Max is nervously awaiting Anita's return. When she arrives late, she seems distracted and takes no notice of his state of mind. Yvonne gives him the ring and Max thinks he understands everything and runs away. Jonny then climbs in through the window and tells Yvonne about his theft of the violin. His confession upsets her and confused by conflicting feelings, she tells Anita about the ring, which explains the reason for Max's disappearance. He has made his way to the plateau intending to kill himself, but he hears an invisible chorus (the mysterious voice of the glacier) and its words restore his faith in life. He also hears Anita's voice, singing his song, and this gives him a sense of infinite peace and serenity. He decides to return to the hotel and to the woman he loves. Meanwhile, Daniello has also arrived at the hotel and immediately recognizes the sound of his violin (which Jonny is playing). He informs the police, who chase Jonny to the station (he hopes to escape to Amsterdam), where he meets Anita, on her way to America with Max. When Jonny realizes that the police are after him, he puts the violin case among Max's suitcases and Max is arrested for the theft. Only Yvonne, who knows the whole truth, can save him. Daniello tries to stop her explaining the situation, but he falls under a train and is killed. Finally Jonny confesses that he stole the violin. Max, now free, can join Anita on her journey to America, a journey to the New World which symbolizes his new-found faith

in life. Jonny, violin in hand, climbs to the top of the station. The station clock transforms into a globe, and Jonny plays while sitting astride it. Below him people dance the Charleston.

■ With this opera Křenek achieved international success. The critic Porena has written of it: 'The musical techniques mark a transition between the composer's impetuous youthful style and the rather palely correct operas of 1930 and thereabouts. Jazz elements blend with shades of Puccini to create a general effect which is both pleasing and pungent.' The opera was performed in fifteen European and American cities, including Moscow and New York, always with great success.

THE KING'S HENCHMAN
Opera in three acts by Deems Taylor (1885–1966), text by Edna St Vincent Millay (1892–1950). First performance: New York, Metropolitan Opera House, 17 February 1927.

SYNOPSIS. The action is set in England during the Middle Ages. King Edgar wants to marry Princess Aelfrida, but as he has never met her he sends Aethelwold to look at her and propose to her on his behalf if she is beautiful. When Aethelwold sees her, he falls in love and marries her. He tells the King that she is very ugly and unworthy of his love. But when the King arrives, he realizes that he has been deceived and demands an explanation. In remorse Aethelwold kills himself in the presence of his wife and King.

■ When the Metropolitan Opera in New York commissioned an opera from him, Deems Taylor set off for Paris. He spent the whole of 1926 there and worked with Edna St Vincent Millay on the libretto. The opera was enthusiastically received and won the composer a further commission from the Metropolitan (*Peter Ibbetson*, 1931). *The King's Henchman* is now rarely performed in repertory, although its melodious, picturesque music is of some interest.

BASI E BOTE
Opera in two acts and three scenes by Riccardo Pick-Mangiagalli (1882–1949), libretto by Arrigo Boito (1842–1918). First performance: Rome, Teatro Argentina, 3 March 1927.

ORIGINAL CAST. Mariano Stabile, Ada Sassone-Soster, Amalia Bertola, Alessio de Paolis, Fernando Autori.

SYNOPSIS. The action takes place in Venice and involves the traditional Italian mask-characters. Pantalon dei Bisognosi (bass) wants to marry his young ward

Rosaura (mezzo-soprano) for her dowry. Florindo (tenor) is in love with Rosaura and she with him. Columbina (soprano) and Arlecchino (baritone), Rosaura's and Florindo's servants respectively, who are also in love, help their employers to avoid the old man's watchful eye. They are finally discovered, but escape in the general confusion. Poor Pierrot (mimed role), Pantalone's servant, comes out worst and is arrested for theft. Old Pantalone is taken ill because of the beating he has received, so Arlecchino pretends to call a doctor and himself appears in disguise. He removes Pantalone's glasses and stuffs his ears with cotton wool, making him so blind and deaf that he does not know what is going on. With the help of the notary, Tartaglia (tenor), Florindo and Rosaura are married. The old man even adds his signature, under the impression that he is signing his own marriage contract. Arlecchino and Columbina are married in the same way. When Pantalone finds out that he has been cheated, he is furious but calms down when Florindo presents him with a casket of ducats. Meanwhile, Pierrot has escaped from prison disguised as a chimney sweep. The opera ends with general rejoicing.

■ This was Pick-Mangiagalli's first opera, though he had previously composed a number of ballets. An

The singers take a curtain call at the end of Puccini's Turandot *at the Bolshoi Theatre in Moscow in 1964. On the left, Birgit Nilsson.*

elegant composer to whom inspiration came easily, he came under various influences from impressionism to the German symphonic style. Technically skilled, he hardly ever achieved a truly personal mode of expression.

SCHWANDA THE BAGPIPER (Švanda Dudák)

Opera in two acts by Jaromir Weinberger (1896–1967), text by Miloš Kareš and Max Brod, based on the folk tale by Tyl (1808–56). First performance: Prague, Czech National Theatre, 27 April 1927. First performance in U.K.: London, Covent Garden, 11 May 1934; in U.S.A.: New York, Metropolitan Opera House, 7 November 1931.

SYNOPSIS. Babinsky (tenor), a romantic robber, persuades the bagpiper Schwanda (baritone) to make Queen Ice-heart (mezzo-soprano) fall in love with him by means of his music. He succeeds, but when the queen learns that he is married she condemns both him and his wife Dorotka (soprano) to death. They are saved by Babinsky, who steals the executioner's axe, and by Schwanda's piping, but a rash promise sends him to Hell. Babinsky rescues him by beating the Devil (bass) in a game of cards. He wins back Schwanda's soul and Schwanda returns to the world of the living, still playing his pipes. Babinsky pretends that Dorotka no longer remembers him and that she has grown old and ugly. Schwanda disbelieves him and all ends happily as he discovers her to be still young and beautiful.

■ This is the only important Czech opera of the inter-war years to repeat Smetana's great popular success. It is a lively piece, but has been criticized for its sometimes rather forced effects.

OEDIPUS REX

Opera-oratorio in two parts by Igor Stravinsky (1882–1971), text by Jean Cocteau (1889–1963) after Sophocles, translated into Latin by Jean Daniélou (1908–74). First performance: Paris, Théâtre Sarah Bernhardt, 30 May 1927. First performance in U.K.: London, Queen's Hall, 12 February 1936; in U.S.A.: Boston, 24 February 1928. Conductor of the first performance: Igor Stravinsky.

SYNOPSIS. Part I. Thebes is stricken by a plague. The people ask Oedipus (tenor), their King, to save them from this terrible scourge. Creon (bass-baritone), the king's brother-in-law, who has been sent to consult the oracle of Apollo, returns. He tells the people that the god has said that Thebes will be saved when the death of the old King Laius, murdered many years before, has been avenged. Oedipus swears that the murderer will be found and condemned to death, whoever he may be. He sends for Tiresias (bass). The

Birgit Nilsson as Turandot in Puccini's opera at La Scala, Milan, in 1964.

composer's life, when he was developing the neo-classical style which eventually culminated in *The Rake's Progress. Oedipus Rex* is already clearly conceived as a series of 'closed' pieces, with the symmetrical formal structure of eighteenth and nineteenth-century models. The opera-oratorio is rich in symbolism, intellectually conceived. The legendary figures acquire their tragic dimension by their composure in the face of their destiny. The score underlines this approach, rhythmically organized with a continuity of style, quite unlike the *barbarie* of the composer's earlier operas. The different groups of instruments interact without blending into one another, so that the music has something of the pure, refined tone of chamber music. The solutions Stravinsky offers in this work to the problems of modern opera are perhaps rather feeble, when set against Prokofiev's bold experiments, or Schönberg's courageous and rewarding innovations. Adorno rightly spoke of 'the contradiction between the claim to greatness and nobility on the one hand and on the other . . . . . . the unremittingly weak musical content.' Only Stravinsky's gifts manage to turn Oedipus into a tragic and fully human figure.

soothsayer is unwilling to answer the questions, but finally reveals that the murderer is himself a king. Oedipus, angered by the implications of that, accuses Creon of conspiring with Tiresias to oust him. Part II. Jocasta (mezzo-soprano), previously Laius's wife, now married to Oedipus, calms the people. She tells them that the oracles have been wrong before – they said the old king would be killed by his own son, but in fact he was murdered by an unknown traveller. Her words deeply disturb Oedipus as he himself has killed an old man in the way Jocasta has just described. A shepherd (tenor) and a messenger (bass-baritone) now arrive. The messenger announces that Oedipus's supposed father, Polybus, is dead. He also reveals that Oedipus had been abandoned on a hillside, found there by the shepherd and adopted by Polybus. He is really Laius's son. Appalled, Oedipus and Jocasta begin to understand the tragic train of events: Oedipus had killed the old king without knowing who he was. Finally Oedipus realizes the terrible truth; he has murdered his father and married his father's wife: his own mother. Jocasta hangs herself. Oedipus, overcome with grief, blinds himself with a gold pin so that he can no longer see the light of day. He appears before the people, who sympathize with his horrible suffering. They bid him a moving farewell.

■ On the subject of the opera's Latin text, Stravinsky commented that it was a pleasure 'to set to music a stylized, almost ritual, language of such a high standard that it finds its own level. One no longer feels governed by the sentence, by the strict meaning of words.' The opera is one of the finest works from this period of the

HIN UND ZURÜCK (There and Back)
Sketch with music in one act by Paul Hindemith (1895–1963), libretto by Marcellus Schiffer after an English revue sketch. First performance: Baden-Baden, 15 July 1927. First performance in U.K.: London, Sadler's Wells Theatre, 14 February 1958; in U.S.A.: Philadelphia, 22 April 1928.

SYNOPSIS. Emma, who is totally deaf, is busy doing her embroidery in the living room when her niece Helen comes in. Soon afterwards Robert, Helen's husband, arrives. He has taken time off work to celebrate his wife's birthday and bring her a present. The maid brings a letter for Helen. Embarrassed, she tells her husband that it is from her dressmaker, but when he becomes suspicious she confesses that it is from her lover. He flies into a rage, seizes a pistol and wounds her fatally. The doctor, accompanied by a nurse who reels off names of medicines, declares there is no hope. At this point a sage with a long white beard appears and philosophizes as follows: 'Seen from above, it does not matter whether human life runs from the cradle to the grave, or whether man first dies and then is born again. So let us reverse destiny and you will see that there is the same strict logic and that everything will be as before.' With geometrical symmetry the action starts again and events are repeated in reverse order. Robert re-enters through the window, the doctor and nurse re-appear, Helen gets up and the conversation takes place the other way around. (Helen first saying that the letter is from her lover, then from the dressmaker). Finally Robert gives his wife a birthday present. The opera ends with the aunt sneezing – she has been present throughout, but totally oblivious to everything going on around her.

This work, described as a sketch, comes between Hindemith's *Cardillac* and *Neues vom Tage* and belongs to the period of 'Neue Sachlichkeit', when the composer developed the theory of a return to 'workaday music' (*Gebrauchsmusik*) as a reaction against the problems posed by expressionism. Based on a libretto by Marcellus Schiffer, writer of revues and *chansonnier*, the opera has the witty, provocative, ironic feel of Berlin cabaret. It is based on an extremely simple idea – the action which reaches its climax and then flows back to its opening scene with geometrical symmetry. The short opera – perhaps influenced by the fashion for cinema montage, here reflected in the second half of the reversed sequence of events – might seem to be intended solely as a grotesque and entertaining parody of the theatre. In fact, it has a more serious and biting polemical aim, as a criticism of post-First-World-War German society and its institutions, not least the family, with Helen and Robert as the modern couple. The geometrical structure of the text seems to have stimulated Hindemith's rich contrapuntal inventiveness. In setting the circular sequence of events to music he uses a cabaret ensemble which, besides a harmonium behind the scenes for the sage's monologue, combines two piano duets and six wind instruments (trombone, trumpet, bassoon, alto saxophone, clarinet and flute).

The result is a style of music which is deliberately elusive, sometimes harsh but never uncontrolled, a perfect accompaniment for Schiffer's text, coupled with an artfully sarcastic use of vocal resources.

LA CAMPANA SOMMERSA (The Sunken Bell)
Opera in four acts by Ottorino Resphighi (1879–1936), libretto by Claudio Guastalla, based on Gerhart Hauptmann's play Die versunkene Glocke *(1896). First performance: Hamburg, Stadttheater, 18 November 1927. First performance in U.S.A.: New York, Metropolitan Opera House, 24 November 1928.*

SYNOPSIS. The 'silver' meadow, home of the good witch of the woods (mezzo-soprano), the elf Rautèndelein (soprano), the faun Ondino (baritone), nymphs and gnomes, is threatened on every side by the encroachment of man. The people of the valley make a bell, but the faun breaks a wheel of the cart used to move it. This leads to a series of misfortunes for the blacksmith Enrico (tenor), who is hurt trying to save the bell when it sinks to the bottom of the lake. Rautèndelein falls in love with him and wants to join him in the land of men. Magda (soprano), Enrico's

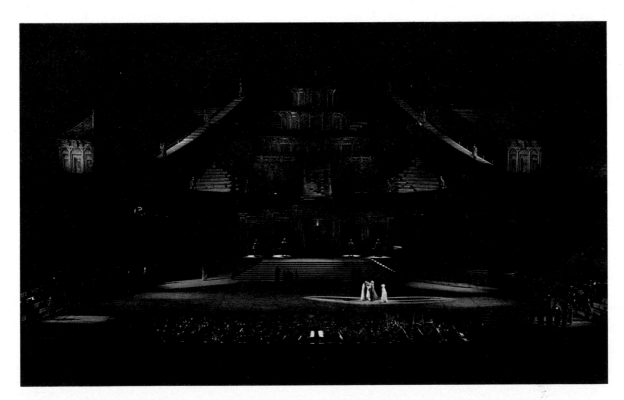

Puccini's Turandot *in the Roman Arena at Verona in 1969. Produced by Luigi Squarzina, designed by Pier Luigi Pizzi.*

wife, and their two children hear of the accident and seek help. Her quiet love is not enough for him and when the elf kisses his eyes he sees a new exciting world. He goes to live with Rautèndelein and undertakes a huge project in a mountain workshop – the building of a temple for better humanity. The priest (bass) wants Enrico to return – his children are on their own now as Magda has drowned herself in the lake. The tolling of the sunken bell can be heard and Enrico, grief-stricken, rejects Rautèndelein. He cannot live without her and the witch allows him to see her one last time before he dies. Rautèndelein appears, reproaches him for leaving her, then kisses him and stays at his side while he dies, invoking the sun.

■ *La Campana Sommersa* was a universal success, despite the whimsicality and perhaps illogicality of the story. Originally Respighi planned to use a German text, as the publisher in charge of the negotiations with Hauptmann wanted the première to take place in Germany as it eventually did.

LE PAUVRE MATELOT (The Poor Sailor)
Opera in three acts by Darius Milhaud (1892–1974), libretto by Jean Cocteau (1889–1963). First performance: Paris, Opéra-Comique, 16 December 1927. First performance in U.K.: London, 1950; in U.S.A.: Philadelphia, 1 April 1937.

SYNOPSIS. The action takes place in a seaport in the present day. Act I. A dance tune, the *javanaise*, played on a pianola sets the mood – the poor houses round the harbour, the narrow, busy streets, the shops and bars frequented by the poor seafolk. The wife (soprano) is faithfully awaiting the return of her sailor husband (tenor), who had gone away fifteen years before. She runs a small bar near a wine shop owned by a friend of the sailor (baritone) who loves her and wants to marry her, yet even her father (bass) cannot persuade her to accept him. It is night-time. The sailor appears at the end of the street. He first visits his friend to find out if his wife has waited for him. The friend immediately wants to tell the wife because he knows how happy she will be, but the sailor will not let him. He plans to stay the night with his friend and then visit his wife as a stranger the next morning to test her love. Act II. The sailor calls on his wife, who does not recognize him. He tells her that he has news of her husband, who is on his way home, poor and burdened with debts, which will have to be paid somehow. She is delighted and scarcely listens to him. The sailor spins a far-fetched tale about the Queen of America, who, he says, fell in love with the sailor but he rejected her out of loyalty to his wife. The friend brings back a hammer he has borrowed and pretends not to know the guest. Act III. During the night the woman rises and silently going over to the sailor strikes him twice with the hammer. Then she takes a string of pearls from his pocket, planning to use it to pay her husband's debts. She wakes her father and

together they prepare to throw the body into the water-tank. The pianola again begins its melancholy tune, and the wife sings of her husband's return home.

■ The opera was the result of Milhaud's collaboration with Jean Cocteau. Between 1918 and 1920 the so-called 'Groupe des Six' formed round Cocteau and Erik Satie, composed of Louis Durey, Germaine Tailleferre, Georges Auric, Arthur Honegger and Francis Poulenc as well as Milhaud. Their aim was a renewal of music through a return to pure musical expression and an openness to new ideas and techniques, rejecting both the Wagnerian inheritance with its literary and philosophical, post-Romantic undertones and the impressionism of Debussy. The three short acts, inspired by sailors' ballads and old, traditional *complaintes* (lamentations), form one of the freshest and most vivid operas of a versatile composer. It was enthusiastically received and has been performed all over the world.

ANTIGONE
Opera in three acts by Arthur Honegger (1892–1955), libretto by Jean Cocteau (1889–1963). First performance: Brussels, Théâtre de la Monnaie, 28 December 1927. First performance in U.S.A.: New York, 16 April 1969.

SYNOPSIS. The tragedy of Antigone, daughter of Oedipus and Jocasta, king and queen of Thebes. After Oedipus blinded himself as a punishment for killing his father and unknowingly marrying his own mother, his daughter Antigone, child of their incestuous love, accompanied him to Colonus. However, she returns to Thebes to bury her brother Polynices, who had waged war on his own city to become king. He has been left without burial on the orders of Creon, tyrant of Thebes. Antigone defies him, is shut up in a cave and kills herself. Haemon, Creon's son, who loves her and cannot live without her, follows her example.

■ The libretto follows Sophocles's great tragedy *Antigone* fairly closely. It was written in 1922, the same year as Honegger's incidental music, but was not turned into a proper opera until 1927. It is not one of the composer's best known works and is not often performed.

DER ZAR LÄSST SICH PHOTOGRAPHIEREN (The Tsar Has His Photograph Taken)
Comic opera in one act by Kurt Weill (1900–50), text by Georg Kaiser. First performance: Leipzig, Neues Theater, 18 February 1928. First performance in U.K.: B.B.C. radio broadcast, 2 December 1978.

SYNOPSIS. The Tsar (baritone) is visiting Paris, where an old anarchist is plotting to assassinate him.

Stage design by Caspar Neher for Hindemith's Cardillac. *Venice, 1948.*

The latter manages to persuade the Tsar to visit the studio of a well-known lady photographer, Angèle (soprano), where, however, he finds waiting for him a member of the anarchist group, the false Angèle (soprano). The Tsar is a smooth operator – he showers her with compliments, and even wants to take her photograph. In the absurd situation which develops, the conspirators are obliged to abandon their plan and run away to escape discovery and arrest.

■ Weill's short opera is a satirical attack on the aims, methods and achievements of anarchist conspiracies. It follows the principles of *Zeitoper*, but has more obvious similarities with the silent cinema in its far-fetched situations and lively humour.

L'ABANDON D'ARIANE (The Desertion of Ariadne)
Opéra-minute in five scenes by Darius Milhaud (1892–1974), libretto by Henri Hoppenot. First performance: Wiesbaden, 20 April 1928. First performance in U.S.A.: Urbana, Ill., 6 March 1955.

SYNOPSIS. The action takes place on the island of Naxos and is a free satirical adaptation of the legend of Ariadne. Ariane (soprano) tries to avoid the amorous advances of Thésée (tenor), who is loved by Phèdre, Ariane's sister. Dionysus (baritone) manages to pair off Thésée and Phèdre, and allows Ariane to rise up into the skies to accompany Diane.

■ The opera is the second of a group of *Opéras-minutes* in one act. The others are *L'Enlèvement d'Europe*, performed at Baden-Baden in 1927, and *La Délivrance de Thésée*, performed at Wiesbaden in 1928. In these short pieces the composer skilfully uses such devices as bitonal writing, the spoken chorus and percussion to convey his lyrical yet ironic mood.

FRA GHERARDO
Dramatic opera in three acts by Ildebrando Pizzetti (1880–1968), libretto by the composer. First performance: Milan, Teatro alla Scala, 16 May 1928. First performance in U.S.A.: New York, Metropolitan Opera House, 21 March 1929.

ORIGINAL CAST. Antonin Trantoul, Florica Cristoforeanu, Aristide Baracchi, Edoardo Faticanti, Salvatore Baccaloni, Giuseppe Nessi, Ines Minghini Cattaneo. Conductor: Arturo Toscanini.

SYNOPSIS. The action takes place over a number of years in twelfth-century Parma. Gherardo (tenor), a rich weaver who has given everything to the poor for the love of God, cannot resist Mariola (soprano), an orphan girl who loves him. He spends the night with her, but in the morning sends her away because he regards her simply as a temptation he must escape to give himself to God. He leaves the town to atone for his sin. Nine years later, now a friar and known as a holy man, he returns to Parma and incites the people to drive out the corrupt authorities. He meets Mariola, now ruined and poor, but still in love with him, and learns from her that she gave birth to his child, which died in infancy. Filled with remorse, he asks her to forgive him for the wrong he has done her. He is arrested on a charge of heresy and the bishop and governor (baritones) tell him that he can only save his own and Mariola's lives if he publicly confesses his sins. Mariola in desperation plans to free him and calls together his followers. The people riot in the main square of Parma. The friar is brought in front of the crowd, confesses his guilt and retracts the doctrine he has been teaching. Unable to stifle the voice of his conscience, he suddenly changes his tone and hurls abuse at the authorities for their corruption. Mariola, who has sadly heard him recant from among the crowd, rejoices when he recovers his dignity and so is discovered. The governor orders her arrest, but a woman, mad with grief because her son has been killed in the rioting crowd, stabs her in the back. Mariola dies and Fra Gherardo is led unresisting to the stake.

■ The opera, written between 1925 and 1927 and based on an episode from the *Chronica* of Fra Salimbene da Parma (1221–87), is a further development of Pizzetti's style, based on sung recitative. It contains all the psychological, moral and religious torment which Pizzetti transfigured and raised to new and pure heights in his mature work *Assassinio nella Cattedrale* (see p. 478 below).

DIE ÄGYPTISCHE HELENA (The Egyptian Helena)

Opera in two acts by Richard Strauss (1864–1949), text by Hugo von Hofmannsthal (1874–1929). First performance: Dresden, Staatsoper, 6 June 1928. First performance in U.S.A.: New York, Metropolitan Opera House, 6 November 1928.

ORIGINAL CAST. Elisabeth Rethberg, Maria Rajdl, Kurt Taucher. Conductor: Fritz Busch.

SYNOPSIS. The powerful sorceress Aithra (soprano), daughter of an Egyptian king, is beloved of Poseidon. She learns from the Omniscient Sea Shell (contralto) that Menelas (tenor) means to murder Helena (soprano), whose abduction was the cause of the Trojan war. Aithra wrecks their ship and having distracted Menelas by the illusion that the Trojans, led by Helena and the dead hero Paris, are outside, she gives Helena a drink to wipe out all memories of past evils. Then she explains to Menelas that, while he and the Greeks have been fighting at Troy, the real Helena was sleeping in Egypt. Menelas accepts her story and joyfully embraces his wife in whom he now finds every quality he dreamed of; together they succumb to the sorceress's charms and travel to a land where the Trojan war is unknown. Yet he believes that he has killed Helena (as part of Aithra's illusion) outside Aithra's palace. Altair (baritone) and Da-Ud (tenor), his son,

two Arab chiefs, invite Menelas to hunt with them. Both father and son openly admire Helena, to Menelas's growing jealousy. During the hunt, he kills Da-Ud. Helena has meanwhile discovered the antidote to Aithra's drug and gives it to herself and her husband to drink. They are reunited – no longer as shadows and images of themselves – and the appearance of their daughter Hermione suggests a happy future.

■ *Die Ägyptische Helena* deals in a serious manner with a theme dear to Strauss – trust and illusion in marriage. Helena has a fine aria, 'Zweite Brautnacht! Zaubernacht, überlange' at the beginning of the second act. Strauss also prepared a revised version of the opera, which was first performed at Salzburg in 1933.

DIE DREIGROSCHENOPER (The Threepenny Opera)

Musical drama in a prologue and three acts by Kurt Weill (1900–50), libretto by Bertolt Brecht (1898–1956), freely adapted from John Gay's eighteenth-century ballad opera The Beggar's Opera (see p. 35 above). First performance: Berlin, Theater am Schiffbauerdamm, 31 August 1928. First performance in U.K.: London, Royal Court, 9 February 1956; in U.S.A.: New York, Empire Theater, 13 April 1933.

ORIGINAL CAST included Lotte Lenya.

SYNOPSIS. London in about 1900. Prologue. Beggars, thieves and prostitutes are plying their trades during the annual fair in Soho, to the strains of a ballad singer. Act I. The fence, J. J. Peachum (bass) is selling or hiring out costumes and accessories to beggars to arouse the pity and generosity of the public. His daughter Polly (soprano) marries the robber Macheath (Mack the knife, baritone), whose gang provides them with stolen furniture. The priest arrives and the guests include the commissioner of police, Tiger Brown (bass). Polly goes to tell her family that she is married. They are furious because Macheath is a criminal and decide to hand him over to the police, certain that they will find him at a brothel in Tonbridge. Act II. Macheath decides to hide in the marshes at Highgate to escape from Peachum. He bids Polly farewell, after instructing her how to run the gang in his absence. Meanwhile, Mrs Peachum (soprano) has bribed the prostitutes, offering them a reward to give up Macheath as soon as he arrives. So Pirate Jenny (mezzo-soprano) calls Mrs Peachum and Constable Smith when Macheath has arrived and he fails to escape. He is taken to prison, though he pays fifty guineas not to be handcuffed. Brown's daughter Lucy (soprano), whom Macheath has pretended to marry, arrives, very upset, not least because she has learned that Polly is planning to visit the prison. There is a jealous scene between the two girls. Macheath denies that he has married Polly, who is dragged away by her mother, and with Lucy's help he escapes. Peachum

Stravinsky's Oedipus Rex *at La Scala, Milan 1968–69. Lajos Kozma as Oedipus and Marilyn Horne as Jocasta. Designed by Pier Luigi Pizzi, produced by Giorgio de Lullo.*

gers rarely arrive on horseback, if the downtrodden dare to resist.'

■ *Die Dreigroschenoper* is a political and social opera expressing the ideas developed further in *Mahagonny*. It directly involves the audience and forces them to reflect on existing social conditions. The music draws on cabaret, jazz, melodrama and folk music, and openly takes sides rather than simply providing an accompaniment. The orchestra, despite the use of cello and flute, is predominantly a jazz ensemble. The opera, which consists of twenty-two distinct pieces (and in this respect looks back to the past), is a *singspiel* in the true sense, consisting of spoken dialogue and sung parts – ballad tunes, recitative, simple airs, and dance rhythms like the foxtrot and the shimmy. Some think the music much better than the text, which is perhaps not one of Brecht's most successful. *Die Dreigroschenoper* won both enthusiastic acclaim and violent abuse.

LE PREZIOSE RIDICOLE (Literally: The Ridiculous Smart Women)

Opera in one act by Felice Lattuada (1882–1962), text by Arturo Rossato (1882–1942), based on Molière's comedy Les Précieuses Ridicules *(1659). First performance: Milan, Teatro alla Scala, 9 February 1929. First performance in U.S.A.: New York, Metropolitan Opera House, 10 December 1930.*

ORIGINAL CAST. Mafalda Favero, Ebe Stignani, Jan Kiepura, Salvatore Baccaloni, Faticanti. Conductor: Gabriele Santini.

SYNOPSIS. The action takes place in a suburb of Paris in 1650. La Grange (tenor) and Croissy (baritone), two young gentlemen in love with Madelon (soprano) and Cathos (mezzo-soprano), respectively daughter and niece of Gorgibus, are annoyed by the behaviour of the girls, who have firmly rejected them. Madelon and Cathos are foolish, vain creatures, concerned only with their looks and with frivolous pastimes. La Grange plans to obtain his revenge by sending Mascarille, his foppish servant, to make fools of them and teach them a lesson. Meanwhile Gorgibus (bass), who approves of both matches, scolds the girls for their frivolity and threatens to send them to a convent. Mascarille arrives in a sedan chair, disguised and accompanied by a crowd of servants. He introduces himself to the girls, who are impressed by the fine display and compete for his favours, but only succeed in making themselves ridiculous. Then the 'Vicomte de Jodelet' (baritone), in reality Croissy's valet, arrives and pretends to be a great hero. The girls are overcome with delight and call everyone in, introducing the young men as their fiancés. During the celebrations La Grange and Croissy appear, unmask their servants and shame Madelon and Cathos at making such fools of themselves. They lock themselves in their rooms, after

arrives at the prison to collect the reward for the robber's arrest. He discovers that Macheath has escaped and blames Brown, threatening to organize a disturbance among the beggars at the Queen's coronation, if Brown does not take immediate and strong action. Act III. Pirate Jenny again betrays Macheath to the Peachums as he has been found with another prostitute, Suky Tawdry. Mrs Peachum hurries off to denounce him while her husband organizes the threatened disturbance. Brown arrives, hoping to arrest them all, but the beggars are not there and arresting Peachum would only make things worse. Meanwhile Polly visits Lucy Brown and they are grumbling about Macheath's behaviour when Mrs Peachum arrives to tell them that he has been arrested and is about to be hanged. Polly hurries to the prison for a last farewell. Macheath tries unsuccessfully to scrape together enough money to bribe a policeman and get away. He asks everyone's forgiveness and sets off for the gallows. At the last minute a royal messenger rides up; the Queen pardons Macheath, gives him a castle, makes him a peer and sends her best wishes to the couple. Peachum comments: 'Unfortunately real life is very different, as we know. Messen-

receiving a scolding from Gorgibus. Only Marotte (soprano), the servant of the *précieuses ridicules*, is amused by the revelations.

■ The opera was a great success in Italy. All Lattuada's operas, including this seventeenth-century comedy, conform to the post-Verdi, romantic realist tradition, with hints of a more modern approach in certain details, particularly effects of orchestral colour.

SIR JOHN IN LOVE

Opera in four acts by Ralph Vaughan Williams (1872–1958), text selected by the composer from Shakepeare's The Merry Wives of Windsor *(1600–1601). First performance: London, Perry Memorial Theatre at the Royal College of Music, 21 March 1929. First performance in U.S.A.: New York, Columbia University, 20 January 1949. Conductor of the first performance: Malcolm Sargent.*

■ The opera, yet another account of the adventures of Sir John Falstaff, is in the form of a romantic comedy. It won a considerable success, but is not generally considered one of the composer's best works. It must, however, have been a difficult task to follow in Verdi's footsteps and set this subject to music. Nor did Vaughan Williams possess, among his many great gifts, the ability to create the rapidly changing rhythms which are so necessary here. In his opera, Falstaff takes on a lyrical personality which is somewhere between an idle good-for-nothing and an unlucky hero.

THE GAMBLER (Igrok)

Opera in four acts by Sergei Prokofiev (1891–1953), libretto by the composer from the story by Dostoievsky (1866). First performance: Brussels, Théâtre de la Monnaie, 29 April 1929 (with a French text and entitled 'Le Joueur'). First performance in U.K.: Edinburgh, 30 August 1962; in U.S.A.: New York, 85th Street Playhouse, 4 April 1957.

SYNOPSIS. Alexey Ivanovich (tenor) is the youthful tutor to the two small children of a retired Russian General (bass), who lives in Roulettenburg with his stepdaughter, Pauline (soprano), in the expectation of an inheritance from an old aunt, known as Babulenka (mezzo-soprano). They are all gripped by a passion for gambling and are horrified when Babulenka herself arrives to find out what the experience is like. She has soon gambled away the fortune which she brought with her and leaves, warning Pauline not to marry a French Marquis (tenor) who has made advances to her. Meanwhile the General's mistress, Blanche (contralto), has left him for another, Prince Nilsky (tenor). Alexey, angered by Pauline's suggestion that she might

marry a wealthy Englishman, Mr. Astley (baritone), has a run of luck at the tables and brings his winnings back to her. His amazing success haunts his mind as she throws the money in his face and leaves him.

■ Prokofiev wrote this opera in just five and a half months, from October 1915 to March 1916. By writing the libretto himself, he hoped to remain as faithful as possible to the dialogue and the spirit of Dostoievsky. As far as the music was concerned he tried to compose for this lively and dynamic work a suitably lively score, and succeeded to the extent that it was labelled 'futuristic'. Eleven years later, on going back to the manuscript, he found it too longwinded and reduced its length. This is the version that was used in its first performance at Brussels.

NEUES VOM TAGE (News of the Day)

Comic opera in three parts by Paul Hindemith (1895–1963), libretto by Marcellus Schiffer. First performance: Berlin, Kroll Theater, 8 June 1929. First performance in U.S.A.: Santa Fé, 12 August 1961. First performance of the new version in two acts: Naples, Teatro San Carlo, 7 April 1954.

SYNOPSIS. Act I. Sitting room in Edward and Laura's house. Although they are only just back from their honeymoon a trivial incident gives rise to such a fierce quarrel between Edward (baritone) and Laura (soprano) that they decide to divorce. When Mrs Pick (contralto), the reporter, arrives, she agrees with their decision. The Civil Law Court. The bureaucratic obstacles are so many and of such a kind that the young couple decide to follow the advice of two other couples, Elli (soprano) and Ali (tenor), and Olli (contralto) and Uli (bass), who have quickly divorced and are now planning to remarry, swapping partners. Edward and Laura decide to go to the 'Universe' Agency. The Agency Offices. All the typists are in love with the glamorous Hermann (tenor), who is chosen by the Baron (bass) (President of the Agency) to resolve Edward's and his wife's problem. A Museum. A Hall with a statue of Venus. Laura and Hermann have a date here to fake a love scene to help on the divorce. Edward considers that the young man is doing his part with too much enthusiasm. He hurls the statue to the ground in order to interrupt things. Bathroom in a hotel. When Laura, now separated from her husband and living in a hotel, comes in to have a bath, she finds Hermann there. She is very shocked. Mrs Pick photographs the scene and calls in witnesses, but Laura weeps with embarrassment. The Baron comes in and dismisses the 'over-literal' Hermann. Everyone leaves and Laura can have her bath in peace. Act II. On the right, Laura's hotel room, on the left a prison cell where Edward is being held on account of his act of vandalism. Both of them regret everything and finally she goes and embraces her husband in his cell. The Baron decides to exploit the situation by making the two of them act out their story in one of his theatres. Offices of the 'Universe' Agency. Hermann, who is upset, finally accepts a new assignment from the same two unhappy couples, who now want to divorce their new partners. Then everyone goes to see the show. Edward and Laura's little bedroom. While they are getting ready, a new quarrel very nearly breaks out, but finally they make their way on to the stage. The Universe Theatre. The audience comes in, the young couple repeat their quarrel with comic exaggeration. At last they have fulfilled their bargain and can be alone and left in peace. They want nothing more to do with acting, the Baron can look for a new Edward and a new Laura. Advertisements and news items light up on the back-cloth and everyone reads aloud the 'News of the Day'.

■ Hindemith wanted to show a satirical and caricatured portrait of daily life, in the same spirit as Weill (*Die Dreigroschenoper*) and Schönberg (*Von Heute auf Morgen*). The music of *Neues vom Tage* is a successful amalgamation of jazz and neo-classical themes. But the use of *musikoper* (i.e. the discrepancy between the music and the action) makes the opera less comprehensible and less unified. In fact it was written shortly after *Cardillac* and contains something of the style of the earlier work, although here the musical language is less adept at expressing the theoretical convictions embodied at this point in Hindemith's work. Sometimes the conjunction of the music and the words is a purely decorative one, in which the two have no affinity; this is especially true in certain lyrical passages, as if purposely to emphasize that beauty is independent of emotive qualities. When this technique is not employed to excess, there are indeed pages which are both intense and, despite the composer's intentions, passionate.

THE NOSE

Opera in two acts by Dmitri Shostakovich (1906–75), libretto by J. Preis from the story by Nicolai Gogol. First performance: Leningrad, Maly Theatre, 12 January 1930. First performance in U.S.A.: Santa Fé, 11 August 1965; in U.K.: London, New Opera Company at Sadler's Wells Theatre, 4 April 1973.

SYNOPSIS. Kovalev, an official, wakes up one morning to discover with surprise and irritation that his nose has gone. While the poor chap is in despair, his barber is equally surprised when at breakfast he finds the runaway nose in his bread. In fear and trembling he goes to throw it into the river to get rid of something that he sees as incriminating. Meanwhile Kovalev has gone out in search of his nose. He meets it in the street dressed up as a high official, but soon loses sight of it. Even the police get interested in the search for the spiteful nose. Heart-rending appeals appear in the papers, but all in vain. One day it is at last brought home to its rightful owner. A surgeon is urgently called

to sew it back into place, but difficulties arise and the operation fails. Kovalev despairs more and more of getting his nose back in its rightful place. But one fine day, as unpredictably as it had gone, the rebellious nose comes home and calmly goes back to its place.

■ This amusing piece of satire by Gogol already contained many separate little episodes and dramatic effects. The number of characters is considerably increased in the libretto (about 70!) and because of this the composer has been unable to give them sufficient musical characterization. *The Nose* was written between 1927 and 1928, when Shostakovich was just over twenty, and so is a youthful work. He wrote it with great energy, almost as a musical joke, and it is perhaps too much dominated by caricature.

VON HEUTE AUF MORGEN (From Day to Day)

Opera in one act by Arnold Schönberg (1874–1951), libretto by 'Max Blonda' (pseudonym of Gertrud Kolisch Schönberg). First performance: Frankfurt, Städtische Bühnen, 1 February 1930.

SYNOPSIS. Husband (baritone) and wife (soprano) arrive home one night after a party. He still retains in his head the fascinating image of his wife's friend (soprano), indulges in fantasies, and reacts with a certain amount of irritation to his wife. She is taking care of the child (recited part) and begs her husband to lie down and rest, reminding him of his next day's work. He insists on turning the conversation back to the friend. He praises her wit, her charm, her modernity, and in his thoughts he compares the prosaic effect of conjugal embraces to the sinful intoxication that a kiss from those lips would give him. His wife remarks crossly that it is easy for a woman to keep her charm if she does not have to worry about a husband, children, the home and the cooking. On the other hand she herself can't be completely insignificant since at the party the singer (tenor), who was the evening's celebrity, had sat next to her looking at her with shining eyes and had spoken to her in such a witty and gallant way. She accuses her husband of being dazzled by any woman's fashionable appearance. The husband rejects the comparison between the friend – a woman of the world – and his wife – an excellent housewife – as absurd. Each accuses the other of discouraging and undervaluing their true worth under the shackling influence of domestic routine. The wife, unseen by her husband, begins to change her image. She alters her hair-style, her clothes and her make-up and suddenly appears in a sophisticated négligé. He rediscovers her beauty and charm, flirts with her and shows his jealousy of the singer. She pays no attention to him, but wants to dance, to drink toasts. She talks of clothes and admirers. In her (pretended) excitement she wakes the baby, but refuses to attend to it, and her husband has to feed it, just as he has to pay the gas bill when the collector arrives. The telephone rings. It is the singer phoning from a night-club where he is with the friend, asking the wife to join him. The husband is at his wit's end with jealousy and unhappiness and fears that his infatuation with the up-to-date woman, the modern woman, has caused him to lose his life's companion. Once again the wife changes her clothes and reverts to her former self: a calm and efficient housewife. The singer and the friend arrive, but their witticisms and charm cannot break the new bond which links husband and wife. The guests leave, disappointed not to have found a couple who are truly free and modern. The husband comments that the others are governed by fashion, while they themselves are governed by love. The opera ends with a word from the child 'Mummy, what does "modern men" mean?'

■ Schönberg's decision to write a comic opera (whose text was written by his wife under a pseudonym) is partly explained by the influence of Berlin's cultural climate in the twenties. *Von Heute auf Morgen*, which occupied Schönberg in 1928 and 1929, is however basically in keeping with the rest of his works. Apart from poking fun at modernity, the theme of the opera is the relationship between what is external and what is internal, between appearance and reality. This theme is central to his other major operas, such as *Moses und Aaron*. The score contains amongst other things a parody on forms of music prevalent at the time, such as the waltz and jazz, and a skilful quotation from Wagner. It is, moreover, a consistent example of dodecaphonic technique and illustrates the composer's more conciliatory attitude towards the public in his maturity. The opera had, however, very little success and is one of his least performed works.

AUFSTIEG UND FALL DER STADT MAHAGONNY (Rise and Fall of the City of Mahagonny)

Opera in three acts by Kurt Weill (1900–50) on a text by Bertolt Brecht (1898–1956). First performance: Leipzig, Neues Theater, 9 March 1930. First performance in U.K.: London, Sadler's Wells Theatre, 16 January 1963; in U.S.A.: New York, 23 February 1952.

SYNOPSIS. Leokadia Begbick (mezzo-soprano), Fatty (tenor), and Trinity Moses (baritone) are being hunted by the police for bankruptcy and procuring. They make their way in the back of a lorry towards the Gold Coast to seek fortunes. The vehicle breaks down in a desolate spot and they can't decide whether to proceed on foot. Leokadia proposes that they should build a new city on that spot. And that is how Mahagonny, the paradise of gold-seekers, comes into existence. Jenny (soprano) and six other girls soon arrive to bring cheer to the citizen-clients. Fatty and Trinity Moses organize propaganda for the new city. People begin to flock in immediately, including four friends – Bill (baritone), Jake (tenor), Jim (tenor) and Joe (bass), who have grown rich in Alaska doing some heavy tree-felling. Leokadia offers them the girls and Jim chooses Jenny. But crisis comes to golden Mahagonny. Leokadia is already thinking of slinking out when Fatty warns her that they are still 'wanted' by the police and that the city is surrounded. So Leokadia stays where she is. Meanwhile Jim is clearly fed up with the many prohibitions existing in Mahagonny. The danger of a tornado causes panic to break out. Jim uses the anarchy to establish new laws; from now on anything is to be allowed in Mahagonny. Act II. Everyone is agitated about the imminent disaster when the tornado suddenly changes direction. Since Jim's laws are still in force, everyone goes wild with joy. (So much so that Jake almost dies of indigestion.) A great boxing match is announced in which Joe will fight Trinity Moses. Jim is the only one to bet on his friend, but he loses and he is 'cleaned out'. The city has now become the scene of the most incredible debauchery. Jim gets drunk, cannot pay his debts and is thrown into prison. Jenny leaves him. Act III. The trial of Jim is under way. The judge, who is quite willing to be bribed, is Leokadia herself; Trinity Moses appears for the prosecution and Fatty will assume the defence. The charge against Jim is the gravest known in Mahagonny: he has not paid his bill! However, a whole series of aggravating circumstances weigh in alongside the main charge: Jim has in fact seduced Jenny, the prostitute, has disturbed the public peace and has caused the death of his friend Joe by pushing him into the match against Trinity Moses. He is taken to the electric chair and he invites everyone to think seriously about the point of the goings-on in Mahagonny. A fire envelops the city and the people walk around as though crazy, with a series of contradictory placards. As they await the final destruction, they all sing about the death of Jim and the death of the city.

■ A first version, in the form of a one-act *singspiel* had already been performed at Baden-Baden in 1927, three years before the final version was staged. Then Brecht and Weill thought of extending it. When it was performed at Leipzig the public was up in arms; they considered it to be totally subversive. It is no accident that the repeat performances were continually broken up by the Nazis. When the latter were in power, *Mahagonny* was prohibited and in 1938 the scores of it were destroyed. (This included the one kept in Vienna, as soon as Hitler's troops had occupied Austria.) Only the original copy was saved, and this was rediscovered after the war.

WIR BAUEN EINE STADT (We Build a City)

Children's opera in one act by Paul Hindemith (1895–1963), libretto by Robert Seitz. Composed in 1930.

SYNOPSIS. A group of children build a city which they hope will be 'the loveliest in the world'. They all get together and work hard, knowing that if they do so it will soon be finished. Each one contributes his skill and his own tools, carrying sand and rocks. The people

GUILLAUME II.

EMPEREUR D'ALLEMAGNE

Sa Majesté

MOZAFFER-ED-DINE

SHAH de PERSE

Sa Majesté

ALEXANDRE III

EMPEREUR DE RUSSIE

Design by Luciano Damiano for Weill's Der Zar lässt sich photographieren. *Milan, Museo teatrale alla Scala.*

who live in it come from every part of the world and by every means of transport: a blacksmith, a dentist, a confectioner, Mr Fränkl, with his dog, Mrs Mayer with her parrot and other people 'whose names we do not know'. 'And what will you do in the city?' asks the teacher, so the children begin playing, at shopkeepers, at ticket-collectors, at paying visits. Night falls, the children sleep and thieves come and steal things. However, the police keep watch and put them in prison. The city is well-governed and the traffic carefully controlled. Even the Mayor and Councillors are children – 'since adults have no place here'.

■ This little children's opera was conceived in the same spirit as *Gebrauchsmusik* (utility music): that is to say, music for everyone's use and for everyone to participate in directly. In fact the composer has written a score that can be performed very freely and used by children to give them some musical education. One can add, if required and if possible, other singing numbers, instrumental numbers or dances. The opera was composed in 1930 and it also gives expression to the ideals of those times, when a machine age was hopefully seen as the foundation of a new world built on reason and technology.

FROM THE HOUSE OF THE DEAD (Z mrtvého domu)
Opera in three acts by Leoš Janáček (1854–1928),

libretto by the composer, based on the novel by Dostoievsky (1862). First performance: Brno, 12 April 1930. First performance in U.K.: Edinburgh, 28 August 1964.

SYNOPSIS. Act I. Courtyard of a Siberian prison on the river Irtysh. One freezing winter dawn the inmates come out of their cells, and a political prisoner, Alexander Petrovich Goryanshikov (baritone) arrives. He irritates the Commandant (baritone) by his appearance and manner, and is ordered to be flogged. Then the guards push the convicts off to work. Those who remain listen to Luka (tenor) as he recalls how he stabbed a tyrannical major while serving in the army. Goryanshikov is dragged across the stage afer receiving his punishment. The other prisoners stop working to watch him. Act II. A year has passed. Easter. The prisoners are working on the banks of the Irtysh. Goryanshikov is teaching Alyeya (soprano), a young Tartar with whom he has formed a close relationship, to read. Skuratov (tenor) relates how he was imprisoned for shooting a man who was going to marry the girl he loved. Townspeople arrive to watch the convicts perform two plays, 'Kedril and Don Juan' and 'The Beautiful Miller's Wife', in celebration of the holiday. When the curtain falls the wretched prison life begins again. Alyeya is wounded by a fellow prisoner who has picked a quarrel with him. Act III. The prison sick-bay. Luka is dying. While Goryanshikov is visiting Alyeya, Shapkin (tenor) tells how he was imprisoned by means of a trick, and Shishkov (bass) tells how he went mad with jealousy and killed his wife. Luka dies, and Shish-kov suddenly recognizes him as his former rival; he curses the body. The Commandant informs Goryan-shikov that he has been pardoned. Goryanshikov kisses Alyeya affectionately and leaves. The other convicts set free a caged eagle, symbol of the human spirit's unconquerable freedom.

■ The libretto was originally written in a mixture of Czech, Russian and various Slav dialects. Then the producer O. Zitek put it all into Czech. It was Janáček's last work, written in 1927 and 1928, and it was completed after his death by D. Zitek (text) and Chlubna and Bakala (music). *From The House of the Dead*, in which the real protagonist is the mass of convicts, represents the peak of dramatic expression achieved by the composer.

CHRISTOPHE COLOMB (Christopher Columbus)
Opera in two parts and twenty-seven scenes by Darius Milhaud (1892–1974), libretto by Paul Claudel (1868–1955). First performance: Berlin, Staatsoper, 5 May 1930, with German text by R. S. Hoffmann. First performance in U.K.: London, Queen's Hall, 16 January 1937; in U.S.A.: New York, Carnegie Hall, 6 November 1952 (both concert versions).

SYNOPSIS. The action takes place from the mid-fifteenth century to the first few years of the sixteenth century. Part I. The narrator (actor) starts reading the book of the life of Columbus, while the chorus mur-murs comments in the background. On the stage we see an inn at Valladolid, and Columbus (baritone) arrives, a poor old man, with his mule. A kind of trial begins, reviewing his actions concerning the discovery of America. Prosecution and Defence expound their case. Four ladies, embodying Envy, Ignorance, Vanity and Avarice, lead four quadrilles of dancers until a cloud of doves ('colombes' in French) clears the stage. Now we see Queen Isabella (soprano) as a child sur-rounded by her young maids-of-honour in her garden. The Sultan Miramolin gives her a dove in a cage, and Isabella puts a ring on its foot and releases it. Colum-bus is now a boy in Genoa, dreaming of the travels of Marco Polo; a voice bids him turn his attention to the sea. The narrator picks up the story: Columbus has reached the Azores. On the screen we see Columbus in Lisbon: he is married and involved in business deal-ings, but he has not given up his dream. He presents his plan to the King (bass): a wise man and a scientist refute his assertion that the earth is round and that it is possible to find the East by sailing West. Isabella is in her chapel: on the screen appear representations of the glorious events of her reign. The Queen receives Col-umbus. In the port of Cadiz preparations are afoot to equip the Pinta, the Niña and the Santa Maria. The narrator describes the demon gods of precolumbian America, angered because they know their rule will soon be ended. Columbus and his ships are on the high seas; the crew rebels, wishing to return and give up the expedition; but Columbus asks them to sail on west-wards for three more days. A dove appears and land is sighted. Part II. The narrator picks up the story: Col-umbus returns to Spain in triumph, but the King and his advisers look at him with mistrust. The King sum-mons three wise men to give him counsel; when a servant attracts more notice than his master, they say, it is time to bury him. The hold of a ship: Columbus is bound in chains to the foot of the mainmast, a tempest is raging and the captain asks Columbus to help them. Columbus prays and calms the elements, but by so doing he has tempted divinity. The stage darkens: Col-umbus's conscience. On the screen are seen hordes of slaughtered Indians, Negro slaves in chains, sailors asking payment for their lives, the wife and mother he has abandoned, the 'other self' of Columbus reproving him for not having fulfilled the task appointed him by the divinity. The narrator continues: Columbus is back in Spain, a messenger comes from Queen Isabella, whose sufferings will soon be over, to tell Columbus that she wishes that he too might forget past suffering and receive his reward at last; the Queen's funeral procession crosses the stage. On the screen we see again the garden, Isabella as a child, her young maids-of-honour, Miramolin; the scene glows with silvery light. Isabella remembers the dove that flew away and never returned, she thinks of her friend Columbus and sends for him. He is not to be found in any of the palaces or grand houses of Spain, but in the humble inn at Valladolid. He sends his old mule to the Queen, and on this animal, splendidly caparisoned, the Queen rides into the Kingdom of Heaven, over a carpet depicting America. In the background can be seen the Earth rotating: a dove flies forth from the globe.

■ The opera is the first of Milhaud's South American trilogy, which includes *Maximilian* (1932) and *Bolivar* (1950). It is a religious allegory represented by a suc-cession of scenes that are bound neither by time nor space, and through music that is written on different tonal levels to express the contemporaneousness of the events. To link the scenes the composer makes use of a narrator, cinematographic projection and a chorus. It is certainly the most mature of his choral works. 'In *Christopher Columbus*', writes Paul Collaer, 'we have the whole of Milhaud. It represents the synthesis of all his previous work, and all the sensitivity he poured into the other dramas. *Christopher Columbus* is his greatest achievement.'

DER JASAGER (The Man who says Yes)
Didactic opera in two acts by Kurt Weill (1900–50), libretto by Bertolt Brecht (1898–1956), based on a fifteenth-century Japanese Noh drama. First perfor-mance: Berlin, 24 June 1930.

SYNOPSIS. The preamble states, 'the most important thing to study is agreement. Many people agree when they really do not mean it. Many people are never consulted and many others agree with false conclusions.' Act I. The boy does not come to school and his teacher visits his home to find out why not. He himself is preparing an expedition to cross the mountains and to find a wise man. When he arrives at the boy's house he finds that the reason for his absence from school is his mother's illness. The woman promises to take care of herself and wants the boy to accompany the teacher's expedition. The teacher warns him that he should not go, as it is dangerous, but the boy insists, saying that he can ask the wise man for a cure for his mother. Act II. The boy, the teacher and three older students are on their way. The boy does not feel well. According to an old tradition, which must be respected, anyone who does not complete the journey must be thrown into the valley. Must they all turn back or will the young boy submit to his destiny? The boy says that he will, on condition that the teacher takes the medicine back to his mother. In this way he carries out his duty to the group.

■ Weill had written: 'An opera for schools must not only be a musical work, but must also concern itself with intellectual and moral matters.' It was precisely the morality of this story, seemingly an attack on Prussian discipline, which turned the public and the critics against the the opera, particularly as it was intended to be a didactic one. A new finale in which the boy would answer 'no' was proposed, but never set to music. Weill had already written *Zaubernacht* (1921) and *Recordare* (1924) for young people and also, together with Hindemith, the cantata *Der Lindberghflug* (1929). The opera was due to be performed at the Festival of Baden-Baden, but was withdrawn after a disagreement between Brecht and the organizing committee. It was intended to be useful in three ways: an education for young composers, an education for young performers and an educational experience of a scholarly kind. Albert Einstein was one of the chief admirers of *Der Jasager*, but the Nazis attacked it violently and interrupted performances. Its first performance took place at the Prussian Academy of Church and Synagogue Music and was conducted at the composer's express wish by a student called Kurt Drabeck.

LA VEDOVA SCALTRA (The Cunning Widow)

Lyric comedy in three acts by Ermanno Wolf-Ferrari (1876–1948), libretto by Mario Ghisalberti (born 1902) based on a comedy by Carlo Goldoni (1707–93). First performance: Rome, Opera, 5 March 1931.

SYNOPSIS. The action takes place in Venice in the eighteenth century. It is primarily a description of the national characteristics of four gentlemen who are competing for the love of a beautiful widow, Rosaura (soprano). She plays off one suitor against another, just as Arlecchino (baritone) does, but cannot choose between them. Finally she decides to bestow her hand on the one who demonstrates the greatest constancy. She designs a test: she disguises herself as a woman who is evidently easily conquered and in this way receives tokens of love from the French Monsieur le Bleau (tenor), the fiery Spaniard Don Alvaro (bass) and even from the formal English Milord Rubenif (bass). Count Bosconero (tenor), the Italian, alone rejects her advances. So Rosaura gives back the tokens which her trick has won for her and marries the Italian.

■ This light-hearted, colourful subject appealed strongly to Wolf-Ferrari's taste and refinement. Several passages from the opera are often performed separately.

TORNEO NOTTURNO (Night Tournament)

Seven nocturnes for the stage by Gian Francesco Malipiero (1882–1973), libretto by the composer. First performance: Munich, Nationaltheater, 15 May 1931.

ORIGINAL CAST. J. Bölzer, H. Rehkemper, A. Gerzer, J. Tornau, E. Feuge, W. Härtl, G. Langer, C. Sendel, H. Fichtmüller, A. Wagenpfeil, J. Betetto. Conductor: K. Elmendorff.

SYNOPSIS. The opera is made up of seven scenes, which the composer has called nocturnes, each with its own title. Through these brief episodes we watch the never-ending struggle between Mr Despair (tenor), a sad man doomed to failure, and Mr Heedless (baritone), a man who knows how to grab life's pleasures as they come along. The first nocturne is called 'The Serenade', and in it a beautiful girl named Aurora (silent part) hears Mr Heedless singing a happy song and, enraptured by it, falls into his arms. A sudden impulse of regret makes her run away. Mr Heedless tries to detain her and after a short struggle she falls lifeless to the ground. Mr Despair, who had tried unsuccessfully to defend her, throws himself in anguish onto her body. In the second nocturne, 'Torment', which takes place during a storm, Mr Heedless seduces a naïve girl and persuades her to leave her old mother. Mr Despair watches this wicked action, but is powerless to prevent it. 'The Forest': Mr Despair finds the girl in a forest and tries without success to free her from the charm of Mr Heedless, who treats her badly. 'The Good Time Inn': Two courtesans attempt to console Mr Despair in the inn, but Mr Heedless arrives and captivates the women with his insidious songs. Mr Despair attacks him in a burst of rebellious rage, but the other man flings him to the ground – to everyone's amusement. 'The Burnt-out Hearth': Mr Despair escapes to his dark and deserted home to find that his sister has been seduced by Mr Heedless. She is trying to keep him with her, but Mr Heedless pushes her away and goes off, throwing her some money. 'The Castle of Boredom': In a castle a jester (baritone) and a juggler are trying in vain to amuse the old Lord and his no-longer-young wife. Mr Heedless arrives bringing with him a new feeling of vitality and winning the heart of the Lady. Mr Despair attacks Mr Heedless, but is captured by the servants and taken to prison. 'The Prison': Mr Heedless is also brought to the prison, accused of seducing the Lady of the Manor. Taking advantage of the dark, Mr Despair kills him. Soon after, the Lady arrives to set free her lover, but Mr Despair manages to trick her into the cell while he himself escapes. The call-boy (speaking part) introduces himself to the audience and declares that neither the death of his rival nor his new-found liberty has calmed Mr Despair's soul. Men are dominated by tormenting passions that nothing can appease.

■ *Torneo Notturno* is considered to be Malipiero's masterpiece. It follows on the lines of the Seven Songs (the second part of the Orfeo trilogy) with its almost total abolition of recitatives and its inclusion of songs. With its unique essence and perfection of form, it constitutes the peak of the composer's ambitions in the theatre.

AMPHION

Mélodrame in one act by Arthur Honegger (1892–1955), text by Paul Valéry (1871–1945). First performance: Paris, Opéra, 23 June 1931.

ORIGINAL CAST included Ida Rubinstein (Amphion), Charles Panzera (Apollon).

SYNOPSIS. Amphion, son of Jupiter and Antiope, is a man beloved by the gods and especially loved by Apollon (baritone), who gives him his lyre. At first Amphion touches the divine strings too roughly, but on a second attempt he releases music whose sound, as though by magic, makes stones move by themselves and group into architectural forms. This is the legend of the birth of architecture. He builds Thebes and a Temple to Apollon, where the Muses are themselves transformed into columns. A veiled woman prevents the people carrying him into the temple as a god and instead leads him away with her. She throws the lyre into a deep pool and leaves him; the only man unable to enjoy his work of creation. Silence falls.

■ The literary text is an original work by the famous French poet, who explained during a discussion of the opera in 1932 how he had wanted to create a work in which literature and music were inseparably linked. He wanted to avoid a chaotic mixture of dance, mime, songs and symphonic passages which would 'have detracted from its dramatic unity, and he declared that in Honegger he had found a firm support. The music certainly does fit perfectly with the classical austerity of the text, reinterpreting it in a modern idiom with a sense of balance such as he has not always achieved in his other works. The work was only moderately successful when it first appeared (choreographed by Massine in decors by Alexandre Benois) and even now it is not often included in the repertoire.

IL FAVORITO DEL RE (The King's Favourite)

Burlesque in three acts by Antonio Veretti (born 1900), libretto by Arturo Rossato. First performance: Milan, Teatro alla Scala, 17 March 1932.

ORIGINAL CAST. Tassinari, Falliani, Menescaldi, Di Lélio. Conductor: Franco Ghione.

SYNOPSIS. The action takes place in an unspecified kingdom in an unspecified world. While Argirolfo (tenor), the King's favourite, is happily seated at a banquet, a queue of his creditors arrives. The guests flee, and the creditors, failing to get their money, carry off half the house. Argirolfo and his wife Lalla (soprano) work out a plan. Each of them will wring the heart of one of the Royal Couple by announcing the death of the other and then ask for money for the funeral. A real muddle arises from this and the King (bass) and Queen (mezzo-soprano) quarrel. Finally both Argirolfo and Lalla have to pretend to be dead. Then the King promises a thousand denari to whoever can sort out the mystery and explain to him who died first. Argirolfo 'recovers' miraculously and explains the trick. He is pardoned.

Facing page, above: The Salle Montansier, Rue de Richelieu, home of the Paris Opéra until, following the attempt on the life of the Duc de Berry, it was razed to the ground by order of the Archbishop of Paris, and a new home was found in the Rue Le Peletier (bottom).
Above: the present-day Opéra.

■ The plot is the same as that of Weber's *Abu Hassan* and comes from the Arabian Nights. Like most of Veretti's early compositions, the score shows the marked influence of Pizzetti, although there are also indications of a more modern style.

LA DONNA SERPENTE (The Snakewoman)
Fairy-tale opera with a prologue and three acts by Alfredo Casella (1883–1947), libretto by Cesare Lodovici, based on the tale by Gozzi (1762). First performance: Rome, Opera, 17 March 1932.

ORIGINAL CAST. Laura Pasini, Antonio Melandri, Giovanni Inghilleri. Conducted by the composer.

SYNOPSIS. The action takes place in the Caucasus in a legendary era when the fairies ruled. Prologue. The fairies' garden. There is great excitement in the fairy kingdom because Miranda (soprano), the daughter of the fairy King Demogorgon (baritone), has asked permission to live among the mortals and marry Altidor (tenor), King of Teflis. Demogorgon cannot refuse because she has two powerful allies, the wizard Geonca (bass) and the high priest Checsaia, but he imposes certain conditions. Miranda must spend nine years and a day with her husband without telling him her true identity and when she has done this, Altidor must swear never to curse her, whatever happens. She must then provoke him by terrible deeds and if Altidor still keeps his word she may become mortal and stay with him. If Altidor breaks his oath, however, Miranda will turn into a snake and remain so for two hundred years and then return to the fairy kingdom. Miranda accepts the conditions and departs. Act I. Desert and rocks. After nine years and a day of happy marriage, gladdened still more by the birth of two children, Altidor was told of Miranda's true identity, but she and the children have disappeared. Altidor and his old tutor Pantùl (baritone) search desperately for them in the desert. His people beg him to return to Teflis, his own country, which is threatened by an invasion of Tartars, and try unsuccessfully to convince him that Miranda is really a cruel witch. Pantùl falls asleep. Suddenly the desert is transformed into the palace garden. Miranda appears and warns Altidor that if he wants to be reunited with her he must remain in the desert and undergo the hardships and difficulties which she will send him, without ever cursing her. Act II, Scene I. Desert and rocks. Togrùl (bass), a faithful minister, insists that Altidor should go home. Some nurses arrive bringing the King news of his children and further pleas from his wife to be strong and not to give way. She appears with the children on top of a rock, accompanied by a violent earthquake. Soldiers keep Altidor, who wants to reach her, at a distance. The flames of a funeral pyre leap up and Miranda orders the soldiers to throw the children onto it. Altidor and Togrùl try to rush forward, but stand petrified. Altidor is very upset, but does not curse Miranda. Scene II. A drawing room in the Royal Palace at Teflis. Altidor's sister, Armilla (soprano), a noted warrior, has defeated King Morgone with her Amazons and warriors. A messenger announces that the Tartars are at the gates of the city and the inhabitants are starving. Badur (baritone), a traitor, has not brought the necessary supplies of food and the country's destiny seems to be sealed. Altidor arrives, blaming himself for neglecting his country in its hour of danger; then Badur reports that the enemy troups are led by Miranda. Altidor cannot restrain himself from cursing her. Miranda appears and tells him of the penalty she must suffer unless he redeems her by an act of exceptional courage. She has saved the population from being betrayed by Badur, who has poisoned the new supplies, by withdrawing them from use. She turns into a snake and glides away. Act III, Scene I. The Royal Palace in Teflis. While the populace celebrate their victorious return from the war against the Tartars, Altidor is sad. Farzana (soprano), a fairy, arrives to tell him that Miranda is on the peak of a Caucasian mountain and that Altidor must overcome enormous challenges to free her. His people and ministers try to dissuade him, but he sets off and they all follow him. Scene II. Among the rocks is a level place with a tomb. Three monsters appear one after the other and the King kills each of them. Miranda calls him from the tomb, but a wall of fire rises up to prevent him from going further. He hurls himself unhesitatingly into the flames and subdues them. The tomb disappears and in its place stand Miranda's palace, Miranda herself and her children.

■ 'By avoiding the temptations of verismo and above all by concerning himself little with the drama, but greatly with the music, Casella has given us a kind of anthology of his best styles in *La Donna Serpente*, modelling himself both on the comic tradition of *Falstaff*, on the seventeenth-century taste for spectacular opera and on his favourite predecessors in Italian musical history.' (M.Mila.)

THE SPINNING-ROOM OF THE SZEKELYS (Szekely Fono)
Opera in one act (A Scene from Transylvanian Village Life) by Zoltán Kodály (1882–1967), libretto by Bence *Szbolcsi. First performance: Budapest, Hungarian Opera Theatre, 24 April 1932.*

SYNOPSIS. One winter's evening in a spinning-mill in a Magyar village. A young widow (contralto) takes her leave tearfully of her lover (baritone), who has to leave the country after some unspecified brush with authority. A little girl warns him that the police are looking for him and he manages to escape. A group of girls and the neighbour (contralto) come to console the widow and they begin to sing a little tune to which she responds by singing a melancholy song. The little girl returns to report that the lover is safe and the widow cheers up. They happily sing 'The tale of Coccodè'. This is interrupted by the appearance of a noisy group of boys and the widow proposes that they play the game of 'Ilona Görög', a lively performance of a love story in which a young man, Laszlo (tenor), pretends to his mother that he wishes to die of love for the beautiful Ilona (soprano). The widow takes the part of Ilona's mother and two young lovers (chosen from those present) take the two main parts. The arrival of a mummer (baritone), masked as a 'big-nosed flea', puts an end to the merriment, for he is disliked and mistrusted by all. Suddenly the voice of the lover is heard and he arrives, escorted by the police and an old woman. Several men are brought before her until she identifies the 'flea' as the culprit. The police lead the prisoners away and the widow is left alone to express her despair until the lover returns unexpectedly, explaining that the muddle has at last been sorted out, and that he is free. Serenity returns and the two exchange vows of love.

■ The opera is an amalgam of songs, choruses and national dances, in which there is no fundamental dramatic theme. The story is in fact conceived as a kind of web of events suggested by the subjects of the folksongs themselves. Moments of pure dance also form part of the composition, and folk-lore traditions make up the major part of the text.

MARIA EGIZIACA (Mary of Egypt)
Mystery in three episodes by Ottorino Respighi (1879–1936), libretto by Claudio Guastalla. First performance: (concert version) New York, Carnegie Hall, 16 March 1932; (staged version) Venice, Teatro La Fenice, 10 August 1932.

SYNOPSIS. At the port of Alexandria, Maria (soprano) is standing on the shore looking thoughtfully out to sea. She begs a sailor (tenor), who sings nostalgic songs, to take her away with him. She also begs a pilgrim (baritone), from whom she has discovered that the ship is bound for Soria in the Holy Land, to persuade the sailor to take her on board. She has no money, but will pay with love. The pilgrim is shocked, but the sailors agree. When they arrive at Soria, Maria wants to follow the crowd into the temple. The pilgrim tells her that she should purify her sinful body before

Weill's Aufstieg und Fall der Stadt Mahagonny *at the Hamburg Staatsoper in 1962, designed by Caspar Neher.*

entering the temple. An angel appears to her as she is about to protest. She repents and the heavenly messenger instructs her to retire to a hermitage in the desert. In the last episode the Abbot Zosimo (baritone), who has withdrawn during Lent into the desert, notices a hole dug by a lion during the night. He interprets this as a divine sign. Maria, now an old lady, arrives and accepts that this grave is her last test. She puts her whole and final trust in the Virgin.

■ Respighi took his inspiration for this opera from the 'Lives of the Holy Fathers' by D. Cavalca, from where he also partly acquires the simplicity of the tale. The simplicity is also due, however, to the fact that the composer intended his work for the concert hall and not for the stage. It was in fact first performed in a concert version in New York with neither scenery nor props.

LA FAVOLA D'ORFEO (The Story of Orpheus)
Chamber opera in one act by Alfredo Casella (1883–1947), libretto by Corrado Pavolini, based on the play by Angelo Poliziano (1480). First performance: Venice, Teatro Goldoni, 6 September 1932.

■ The opera, inspired by the myth of Orpheus, is a well-balanced and harmonious example of a typically Italian vocal style which derives from the seventeenth century and which 'never offends sobriety, proportion nor the proper limits of expression' (M.Mila). It

includes some melodies by Germi which had been presented at the Ducal Court in Mantua on 18 July 1472.

DIE SIEBEN TODSÜNDEN DER KLEINBÜRGER (The Seven Deadly Sins of the Petty Bourgeoisie)
Ballet chanté in a prologue and seven scenes by Kurt Weill (1900–1950), text by Bertolt Brecht (1898–1956). First performance: Paris, Théâtre des Champs-Elysées, 7 June 1933. First performance in U.K.: London, Savoy Theatre, 1933; in U.S.A.: New York, City Center, 4 December 1958.

ORIGINAL CAST included Lotte Lenya (Anna I) and Tilly Losch (Anna II).

SYNOPSIS. Anna comes from a Louisiana family: Mother (bass), Father (tenor I) and two brothers (tenor II and baritone). She is sent out into the world to earn enough money for them to build a house on the Mississippi. She has, like all of us, two sides to her nature: Anna I (soprano), the practical realist, and Anna II (dancer), her dreamy, idealistic counterpart. Each scene takes place in a different American city and represents one of the Cardinal Sins: sloth, pride, anger, gluttony, lust, avarice and envy. In capitalist society these sins take on a significance which is the opposite of their original meaning. Thus sloth prevents progress on the social ladder, pride prevents a woman from undressing, anger compels one to oppose injustice when it goes against one's own interests, lust makes a woman go with a man who pleases her instead of one who can pay, and so on. Anna I, who stands for the rational being, urges Anna II, who is the instinctive urge, to submit herself to this law. Once Anna I has overcome her sister's moral scruples and accepted the rules of the game imposed by society, they succeed in earning enough money to realize their ambition and build a house for their family.

■ The work, with its condemnation of the alienating effect of society, was the last joint effort of Kurt Weill and Bertolt Brecht and is now recognized as one of their most successful. It has many features reminiscent of their earlier collaborations, but the music may be said to contribute more to the dramatic climaxes than previously, without, however, reducing the impact of the words. Even a concert hall version can thus be followed with interest.

ARABELLA
Lyrical comedy in three acts by Richard Strauss (1864–1949), libretto by Hugo von Hofmannsthal (1874–1929). First performance: Dresden, Staatsoper, 1 July 1933; first performance in U.K.: London,

Covent Garden, 17 May 1934; in U.S.A.: New York, Metropolitan Opera House, 10 February 1955.

ORIGINAL CAST included Viorica Ursuleac (Arabella), Alfred Jerger (Mandryka), Margit Borkor (Zdenka). Conductor: Clemens Krauss.

SYNOPSIS. Last day of Carnival in Vienna in 1860. Graf Waldner (bass), a retired officer up to his ears in debt, lives in an elegant hotel in Vienna with his wife, Adelaide (mezzo-soprano) and two daughters, Arabella (soprano) and Zdenka (soprano). His one hope is to find rich husbands for his daughters, but as he does not have the money to present both girls in society, Zdenka has been brought up as a boy. Arabella has several suitors, but she is waiting for 'true love' (she has noticed an interesting stranger outside the hotel) and rejects Matteo (tenor). Zdenka, however, loves him and as she cannot give herself away, she gives vent to her feelings by writing him passionate letters, which she signs with her sister's name. The Count is harassed by his creditors and worried because none of his old friends have replied to his requests for money. His troubles are over, however, when the nephew of one of them, Mandryka (baritone), appears in answer to his letter, offering him plenty of money and requesting Arabella's hand in marriage. Act II. Arabella is introduced to Mandryka at a ball and she recognizes him as the interesting stranger. They realize straightaway that they were made for one another. She begs him to leave her alone for an evening to make the most of her unattached youth for the last time. Mandryka then overhears Zdenka giving Matteo a letter, assuring him of Arabella's love and giving him a key which, she says, is the key to Arabella's bedroom.

Arabella has by then left the ball and Mandryka suspects the worst of her. Act III. Matteo awaits Arabella in the hotel foyer and cannot understand why she rejects his advances. When Mandryka and her parents arrive, she is unable to convince them of her innocence until Zdenka appears with her hair down and in a nightdress, to explain that she gave Matteo the key to her own room and now only wants to throw herself into the Danube. Matteo turns his affection from one sister to the other, but Arabella bids Mandryka goodnight, asking only for a glass of water to calm her nerves. He does not grasp her reference to the story of the Croatian custom by which village brides offer their bridegrooms a glass of water (as a symbol of chastity) until she descends the stairs to proffer him the drink. Then they understand each other and they embrace.

■ Although the opera is weighed down by intrigues and incidents from the dramatic point of view, Strauss reaches the high point of his art in the duets for Arabella and Zdenka, and for Arabella and Mandryka, and in Arabella's and Mandryka's arias, which are full of unbearably voluptuous anticipation. The only reality of these characters is that of the flesh; their only certainty, the certainty of their desire, and they live in a world of decadence and decay. But for this reason Strauss's music brings out in them something which is both genuine and absolute.

LA FAVOLA DEL FIGLIO CAMBIATO (The Fable of the Changeling)
Opera in three acts and five scenes by Gian Francesco Malipiero (1882–1973), libretto by Luigi Pirandello (1867–1936). First performance: Brunswick, Landestheater, 13 January 1934.

ORIGINAL CAST included Lotte Schrader, Gusta Hammer, Albert Weikenmeier. Conductor: Hans Simon.

SYNOPSIS. In a Sicilian village, a mother (soprano) is weeping at her tragic lot; the witches have stolen her little boy and replaced him with a deformed idiot. Her friends comfort her and take her to the house of a sorceress, Vanna Scoma (contralto). She tells the mother that the baby is being well cared for in a palace and advises her not to look for him. Years pass. The customers in the village café are commenting on the arrival of a Prince (tenor) who has come to the village to recover his health, when a half-witted young man (tenor) known as 'Son of the King' begins to announce amidst general hilarity that he is of royal descent. The mother then declares that she has recognized the newly arrived Prince as her long-lost son. Two ministers (baritones) report to the Prince that the King is ill and the people in revolt. Vanno Scoma declares that the King is already dead and that the Prince must go home immediately. He, however, has noticed that the mother has been watching him closely and asks her her name. She merely replies that she once had a son who looked like him and who was snatched away from her. 'Son of the King' suddenly attacks him. He manages to avoid the blow, but when the ministers insist that he departs, he proposes that, since he is tired of life at Court and the mother insists that the deformed boy is the rightful heir to the throne, they accept 'Son of the King' as their ruler. When the poor idiot has the crown on his head he will seem like a real King. For his own part, he will be poor but happy with the woman who claims him as her son.

■ *The Fable of the Changeling* occupies a well-defined position in Malipiero's vast output for the theatre, since it marks the beginning of a new style, based mainly on the adoption of a 'sung narrative' which he develops in his later works. Musically speaking the style is compact yet not heavy. The mother's songs and lamentations are the core of the music and are so intense and authentic that the static nature of the drama goes unnoticed in performance.

KATERINA ISMAILOVA/LADY MACBETH OF MTSENSK (Ledi Makbet Mtsenskago Uezda)
Opera in four acts (nine scenes) by Dmitri Shostakovich

(1906–75), libretto by the composer in collaboration with A. Preis, based on a story by Nikolay Leskov (1865). First performance: Leningrad, Maly Theatre, 22 January 1934; first performance in U.K. (concert version): London, Queen's Hall, 18 March 1936; in U.S.A. (concert version): Cleveland, 31 January 1935. First performance of revised version: Leningrad, January 1963; in U.K.: London, Covent Garden, 1963; in U.S.A.: San Francisco, 1964.

SYNOPSIS. Russia, 1865. Act I. Zinovy Borisovich Ismailov (tenor), a wealthy merchant and the son of Boris (High Bass), has married Katerina (soprano), who is young and beautiful, but has no dowry. She does not love her husband and is plunged into the solitary, boring life of the Ismailov household and has to put up with her dictatorial father-in-law. Zinovy engages a new servant, Sergei (tenor), who is handsome and cheeky and has a reputation as a ladykiller. Zinovy has to leave home to repair a dam and Boris compels him to make Katerina kneel and swear to be faithful during his absence. While he is away, however, she makes passionate love to Sergei. Act II. Old Boris lusts after Katerina himself, but discovers her affair and, at his orders, Sergei is severely beaten. Katerina takes revenge by poisoning her father-in-law. Sergei suggests that it would be easier for them if they could marry and enjoy the family money, so she kills her husband when he returns, and she and her lover hide the body in the cellar. Act III. Katerina and Sergei contemplate their crimes during their wedding festivities. A drunken beggar demands more wine from the cellar and the body is discovered. The police stop the bride and groom from escaping and arrest them. Act IV. Sergei and Katerina are among the convicts on the road to Siberia. Sergei has tired of this affair, which has ruined his life, and turns his attentions to Sonetka (contralto), a young convict girl. Katerina loves him as much as before and is mad with grief and jealousy. She throws herself and her rival off a bridge. The other prisoners march on indifferent to their fate.

■ The first performances were received with mixed reactions by the public, although there was no doubt of the opera's importance. The criticisms were mostly of an ideological or political kind. Shostakovich had treated Leskov's story very freely. Whereas the writer viewed Katerina as being cruel without justification, and makes her a murderess greedy for wealth and revenge, the composer tried to locate the drama in its social setting and to give it a social interpretation. In fact, he wrote 'Katerina is a beautiful, intelligent young girl, who is being smothered in the world of vulgar commerce. She has a husband but no happiness – the murders she commits are not so much real crimes as a revolt against her circumstances and against the sordid and sickening atmosphere in which middle-class merchants of the nineteenth century lived.' For Shostakovich, as a convinced communist, the story of Katerina is an attempt to express anti-bourgeois subject matter, but his efforts were not appreciated. The overall initial success, whose repeat performances

lasted for nearly a year, was cut short by an article in 'Pravda' on 26 January 1936, in which the work was accused of betraying the simplicity and concreteness of language and was therefore to be considered as 'the negation of opera'. The opera was fully rehabilitated after Stalin's death, once Zdanov (the probable author of the Pravda attack) had disappeared from the political scene.

LA FIAMMA (The Flame)
Melodrama in three acts by Ottorino Respighi (1879–1936), libretto by Claudio Guastalla, based on the play The Witch *by Hans Wiers Jenssen. First performance: Rome, Opera, 23 January 1934. First performance in U.S.A.: Chicago Opera, 2 December 1935.*

ORIGINAL CAST. Giuseppina Cobelli, Aurora Beradia, Angelo Minghetti, Carlo Tagliabue, A. Martucci, A. Cravcenco, L. Parini, M. Sassanelli, A. Prodi.

SYNOPSIS. The Byzantine era: seventh century. Act I. The villa of Exarch Basil near Ravenna between the sea and a pine forest. Eudossia (mezzo-soprano), Basil's mother, and Silvana (soprano), his second wife, are at work alongside their attendants. Silvana finds her mother-in-law overpowering and dislikes life at court. Chatting with one of the maids, she tells of her desire to leave the claustrophobic life of the palace. Screams are heard and Agnese (mezzo-soprano), a witch, protesting her innocence but pursued by a ferocious crowd, begs help from Silvana. She hints that she knows something about Silvana's mother and Silvana hides her. The maids announce the joyful news that the Exarch's son, Donatello (tenor), is coming home. He recognizes Silvana as the woman who once helped him and took him to the home of the dreaded Agnese. Eudossia is greeting her grandson when the witch hunt, led by an Exorcist, demands where to find Agnese. She is discovered and dies at the stake, cursing her accusers. Act II. Inside the ancient walls of Theodoric's palace at Ravenna, Donatello is chatting with the maids. Among them is Monica (soprano), who is sent away when she confesses her love for him. Basil (baritone) is alone with his wife and tells her that his attraction to her began when Agnese bewitched him. When he goes, she uses the power inherited from her mother to conjure up Donatello. He appears and they give way to their love. Act III. Scene I. In Donatello's room. Eudossia interrupts the two lovers. When Basil arrives, Silvana confesses her love for Donatello to him. Upon hearing this, he dies and his mother accuses Silvana of witchcraft. Scene II. In the basilica of San Vitale the people await the trial with excitement. Silvana defends herself against the accusation and Donatello supports her. However, Eudossia will not relent. Donatello then asks Silvana to swear on the cross, but she realizes that if he asks this then he too

Die Dreigroschenoper by Kurt Weill. Left, Vanessa Redgrave in Tony Richardson's 1972 London production; right, Domenico Modugno in the 1973 Italian production directed by Giorgio Strehler.

does not believe in her, and she refuses. She is condemned to die at the stake.

■ Respighi asked Guastalla to choose a subject set in the Byzantine world and advised him to consult Diehl's 'Byzantine Figures'. But the librettist's initial plan, to write a text dealing with the Empress Theodora, miscarried and in its place he concocted this story set in Ravenna, famous for the mosaics of San Vitale, instead of Constantinople. The composition was a particularly arduous task, because Respighi set himself extremely high standards and was never satisfied with his efforts; to the extent that he continued to make alterations even when rehearsals were under way. According to his wife, Elsa, he worked with especial enthusiasm on this opera, took an interest in every aspect of it and suggested to Guastalla how the Acts should be arranged as well as words for the choruses and what metrical rhythms to use. All this care brought about the desired effect; the opera is outstanding for its dramatic expressiveness and for its clever combination of elements of passionate and spiritual emotion, and sinister menaces of witchcraft. It was an immediate success with both public and critics, and has been performed all over the world.

CECILIA
Mystery in three episodes and four scenes by Licinio Refice (1883–1954), libretto by Emidio Mucci. First performance: Rome, Opera, 15 February 1934.

SYNOPSIS. Preparations are in full swing in the house of the noble Valerio family for the arrival of Cecilia

(soprano), who is to marry Valeriano (tenor). A rumour spreads among the slaves that the bride is Christian. Tiburzio (baritone), Valeriano's brother, comes in before the bridegroom; the crowd cheer Valeriano, who is followed shortly afterwards by Cecilia with her wedding attendants. The couple are finally left alone and Valeriano tells Cecilia of his love for her. Although she returns his feelings, she admits to another, greater, love because of which she cannot yield to Valeriano. He cannot understand her. An angel appears to defend her purity. She takes Valeriano to the catacombs, where a series of miracles converts him. The bishop, Urbano (bass), baptizes him and with divine blessing their happiness is now complete. In the last episode, Valeriano and Tiburzio have been killed and Cecilia is on trial. Amachio (baritone), the Roman prefect, tries to persuade her to forsake her oath, and then tortures her with fire, but her burns are healed by a shower of roses. She is finally brutally murdered by a soldier. Her house is made into a temple.

■ The opera has no great value either as music or as literature. The score is confused and over-emphatic, especially in the second episode and even the finale is rather long-winded. *Cecilia* owed its success to the splendid performance by Claudia Muzio. It was also performed in other countries and Refice died while he was conducting it in Rio de Janeiro.

IL DIBUK (The Dybbuk)
Dramatic legend in a prologue and three acts by Lodovico Rocca (born 1895), libretto by Renato

Simoni, based on the Yiddish work by Shalom An-ski. First performance: Milan, Teatro alla Scala, 24 March 1934; first performance in U.S.A.: Detroit, Masonic Temple, 6 May 1936.

ORIGINAL CAST. Oltrabella, Costa Lo Giudice, Paci, Bettoni, Wesselowsky, Palombini. Conductor: Franco Ghione.

SYNOPSIS. The end of the nineteenth century in Poland. In the prologue, Reb Sender the Jew (baritone) and his friend Nissen (bass) strike a strange bargain: if one has a son and the other a daughter, they will wed them. This is what is now about to happen to Hanan (tenor), Nissen's son, and Leah (soprano), Sender's daughter, who have fallen in love. However Sender does not approve of Hanan and has found another husband for his daughter. Hanan dies of grief and Leah cannot forget him. On the day of her wedding, a messenger in the crowd relates the mystical story of the dybbuk: the soul of anyone who dies in despair and cannot find peace in death enters the body of the beloved. When, in the middle of the feast Leah calls out disconnected phrases and rejects her husband, the messenger declares that the dybbuk has arrived, and that Hanan's soul has entered Leah. The next day Sender takes her to the rabbi and asks him to free his daughter from the dybbuk, but the attempt fails. Sender then repents and Hanan's spirit leaves the body of his beloved. When she is left alone to rest, his ghost appears to the unconscious girl, holding out its arms and calling imploringly to her. Leah dies while the chorus announces that the lovers are united for ever.

■ Il Dibuk was composed in 1929–30, but it only achieved success in 1933 during a competition organized by La Scala. Here the opera stood out amongst the 180 compositions which were entered. The anti-Semitic prohibitions of 1938 did not stop several revivals of the opera.

PERSÉPHONE

Melodrama in three parts by Igor Stravinsky (1882–1971), libretto by André Gide (1896–1951). First performance: Paris, Opéra, 30 April 1934; first performance in U.K.: London, Queen's Hall, 28 November 1934 (concert version); in U.S.A.: Boston, Symphony Hall, 15 March 1935.

SYNOPSIS. Eumolpos (tenor), a priest in the temple at Eleusis, calls on Demeter as she gets ready to accompany her daughter Persephone on the unhappy journey which it is her fate to undertake. Persephone (narrator) has the gift of keeping Spring eternally around her, but the priest has noticed a narcissus amongst the flowers which surround her. This flower symbolizes the kingdom of the dead and when she looked at it she suddenly had a vision of the after-life. The nymphs beg her to chase away such thoughts, but

Persephone decides to go down into the Underworld and there tries to comfort the wandering souls of the dead. They explain to her that their life is only seemingly real. Eumolpos comments on the inescapability of death and invites Persephone to become Queen of this sad Kingdom and give up the idea of returning to Earth. She is unprepared for such a fate and grieves at the idea of losing her Eternal Springtime, but the priest explains to her that ever since she left Earth it has been plunged into Winter's cold. From now onwards the land will only be fertile through the efforts of mankind and Persephone will return every year to bring Spring, so that the seed which lives in the ground can germinate with the return of the new season.

■ This opera was composed at the request of Ida Rubinstein, and conducted by Stravinsky himself with choreography by K. Joos. Gide's text was inspired by the Homeric 'Hymn to Ceres'. Perséphone is really a secular oratorio, whose sections are linked by dances. The recitative with its musical accompaniments is the dominating feature, interspersed with shreds of singing and passages of mime. The role of Persephone is partly mimed, partly spoken and partly danced. The only solo singing role is that of Eumolpo who explains the story, with comments of the chorus. The choral melodies, more than any other aspect of the composition, are the most perfect outcome of Stravinsky's researches in which he has aimed at achieving something which is original, modern and complete in itself, within a classical, traditional framework.

NERONE (Nero)

Opera in three acts and four scenes by Pietro Mascagni (1863–1945), libretto by Giovanni Targioni-Tozzetti (1863–1934), based on a comedy by Pietro Cossa (1872). First performance: Milan, Teatro alla Scala, 16 January 1935.

ORIGINAL CAST. Lina Bruna Rasa, Margherita Carosio, Aureliano Pertile. Conductor: Pietro Mascagni.

SYNOPSIS. The action takes place in Rome in the first century A.D. In an inn in the Suburra district, the innkeeper, Mucrone, discusses with his customers – Petronius, a gladiator, Nevius, a mimic actor, and Eulogius, a slave-trader – the topics of the day. These include Nero's corruption and the expansion of the new sect of Christians. Nero himself arrives in disguise, accompanied by his friend Menecrates. He is pursuing a Greek slave-girl called Egloge, who has sought refuge in the inn and with whom he has fallen in love. Nero is left alone and gets drunk. Atte, a freed-woman and imperial concubine, who sincerely loves him, reproaches him for his dissolute ways. When she learns of his passion for Egloge, she threatens to murder the slave-girl and, as the Emperor pays no heed to her threats, she poisons the girl during a banquet. While

Nero recovers from his grief, a rebellion in Rome forces him to flee, with Atte and two other freed slaves. One of these, Faonte, offers him shelter in his hut, where they are discovered by the centurion Icelus. Before he can bring the Emperor to the Senate, however, Nero commits suicide. Atte has already killed herself.

■ This opera, which appeared in 1935 after a silence of fourteen years, was awaited with great expectation. It was written in a few months although it had been Mascagni's intention to set Cossa's 'comedy' to music ever since 1895, the time of *Ratcliff*. Despite the composer's assurances that he wanted to keep faithfully to the author's conception, the character of Nero is quite different in Targioni-Tozzetti's version to the original play. The librettist has emphasized Nero's cynical and sensual characteristics at the expense of his artistic aspirations and talents.

ORSÉOLO

Dramatic opera in three acts by Ildebrando Pizzetti (1880–1968), libretto by the composer. First performance: Florence, Teatro Comunale, 4 May 1935.

ORIGINAL CAST. Franca Somigli, Bergamini, Augusto Beuf, Luigi Fort, Giulietta Simionato. Conductor: Tullio Serafin.

SYNOPSIS. The story takes place in Venice in the middle of the seventeenth century. A Senator tells Marco Orséolo (bass), the State Inquisitor and Head of the Ten, that his enemy Rinieri Fusinér (tenor) accuses him of abducting his sister Cecilia. He defends himself indignantly against the charge and his son Marino (tenor) admits that it was he who seized the girl, who drowned while trying to escape. His father is furious and orders him to leave the city. That evening, while Orséolo attends a ball with his daughter Contarina (soprano), Rinieri confronts him publicly, insults him and then disappears. During the ball, without Rinieri's knowledge, his brothers Alvise (baritone) and Delfino (tenor) capture Contarina and take her to a fisherman's hut. When Rinieri finds out he orders them to release her immediately. Orséolo threatens to arrest the abductors but Contarina for her part, was favourably impressed by Rinieri's noble appearance and tells her father that, if he is arrested, she will swear that she had fallen in love with him and followed him of her own accord. Her father disowns her and she retires into a convent. Rinieri is about to leave for the war against the Turks and confesses to Contarina that he loves her; although she returns his love, she resolves to dedicate her life to the expiation of her sins. Rinieri returns with a delegation bringing Marino's sword to his father and reporting his death in battle. He offers also other personal belongings of his son. The old man refuses them with dignity, saying that he cannot take them from an enemy. At that moment the sword snaps inexplicably –

which, according to an ancient legend, is a sign that God demands peace. Orséolo gives up all ideas of revenge and Rinieri begs Contarina, who has meanwhile returned home, to accept his love. She remains firm, however, in her decision to lead a life of sacrifice and renunciation.

■ *Orséolo*, like *Vanna Lupa* and *Cagliostro*, is to be counted among Pizzetti's secular works, but like the rest of his output, can be said to be dominated by a strong moral sense.

DIE SCHWEIGSAME FRAU (The Silent Woman)

Comic opera in three acts by Richard Strauss (1864–1949), libretto by Stefan Zweig (1881–1942) from the comedy Epicoene *by Ben Jonson (1609). First performance: Dresden, Staatsoper, 24 June 1935; first performance in U.K.: London, Covent Garden, 20 November 1961; in U.S.A.: New York, City Opera, 7 October 1958.*

SYNOPSIS. Sir Morosus (bass), an old sea dog, lives on a pension and, since miraculously escaping from an exploding ship, cannot bear noise. He is looked after by his garrulous Housekeeper (contralto). Henry (tenor), his nephew and sole heir, comes to live in the house with a group of friends who are artists in an Opera Company. They create immense confusion. Morosus considers the theatre to be a dishonourable profession and throws out his unwanted guests, disinherits his nephew and tells his barber (baritone) to find him a silent, obedient wife. The barber, who takes Henry's part, brings a shy, silent woman called Timida to Morosus. (She is really Henry's wife, the singer Aminta, soprano.) After a mock wedding Timida changes into a fearsome chatterbox. In despair, Morosus wants to divorce her, but a fake tribunal, suddenly improvised by the Company, refuses to do so. In the end Henry and Aminta confess their tricks to Morosus and after a thundering fit of anger he finds inner peace through a reconciliation with the two young people.

■ *Die schweigsame Frau* is one of the musically richest of Strauss's operas and one of the most highly elaborate in its formal structure. Quick and brilliant dialogues reminiscent of eighteenth-century opera buffa overflow into group scenes without a break. The brass, together with a frenzy of percussion, give an effective portrayal of the crazy atmosphere which upset Morosus in his home. The opera received a triumphant welcome from the public and the critics, but was banned by Hitler after its third performance, since Zweig, who wrote the libretto, was a Jew.

PORGY AND BESS

Opera in three acts by George Gershwin (1898–1937),

libretto by Du Bose Heyward and Ira Gershwin, based on a novel by Du Bose Heyward, called Porgy. *(The author and his wife Dorothy had already made it into a play.) First performance: Boston, 30 September 1935. First performance in U.K.: London, Stoll Theatre (by all-Negro American touring company), 9 October 1952.*

ORIGINAL CAST. Anne Brown (Bess), Todd Duncan (Porgy), Warren Coleman (Crown), Eddie Matthews (Jake), Abbie Mitchell (Clara), Bubbles (Sporting Life).

SYNOPSIS. The story takes place in Catfish Row, the negro quarter of Charleston, South Carolina, in the recent past. Act I. A quarrel breaks out during a game of dice and Crown (bass), a burly and violent porter working at the docks, kills his friend Robbins and has to flee. Bess (soprano), who was his girl, is left alone and is protected by Porgy (baritone), a lame beggar, who has always been in love with her. At night the people of Catfish grieve for Robbins and collect money for his funeral. Act II. Bess, living with Porgy, makes him very happy. One day when the people of Catfish have gone for a picnic to the island of Kittiwah, leaving Porgy behind, Crown meets Bess again and persuades her to go off with him. After a few days Bess returns, ill and terrified, to Porgy. He welcomes her back, cares for her and promises to protect her from Crown, whom, although she finds him irresistible she knows to be a bad influence on her; besides, she declares that she now loves Porgy. During a storm, the women pray for their men at sea. Crown returns and livens up the atmosphere with a bright jazz tune before agreeing to set out to rescue one of the fishing boats. He swears to come back soon to collect Bess. Act III. During the night the women weep for their dead. Crown appears, goes to Porgy's house, and calls for Bess, but Porgy stabs him to death. Then Porgy expresses the joy of a poor cripple who has suffered many insults and jeers. He is arrested, and spends a week in prison, but refuses to confess to his crime and, through lack of evidence, he is eventually released. Bess is alone during his absence and a little drug-peddler called Sporting Life (tenor) takes advantage of this to persuade her to follow him to New York, tempting her with false promises of a better life. When Porgy gets home the neighbours tell him what has happened. Instead of being discouraged, however, he sets off to New York to look for his girl.

■ The opera is based on the very successful play by Du Bose and Dorothy Heyward, which opened in the New York Theatre Guild on 10 September 1927 and ran for 367 performances. The opera was produced in New York on 10 October 1935 (shortly after the Boston première), but it was not at first successful. Later revivals, however, broke all previous Broadway records by having more than 400 consecutive performances. This approval extended to Europe and even to the Soviet Union, where it was performed in Leningrad on 26 December 1955. (This was incidentally the first time during the cold war that an American Theatre Group was received in the U.S.S.R.) The orchestra is composed traditionally, with the addition of some typical instruments of national folk music. Percussion and banjo are used in an interesting way because the opera draws on the folk idiom, popular rhythms, jazz melodies and Negro spirituals. *Porgy and Bess* is thus a major departure from the European model and well deserves its reputation as the first and foremost American opera.

CYRANO DE BERGERAC
Serious opera in four acts and five scenes by Franco Alfano (1876–1954), libretto by Henri Cain (1859–1937), based on Edmond Rostand's play (1897). First performance: Rome, Teatro Reale, 22 January 1936.

ORIGINAL CAST included Maria Caniglia, Luccioni, de Paolis.

SYNOPSIS. The story takes place in Paris around 1640. Cyrano is a penniless young nobleman from Gascony who has an enormous nose. He is secretly in love with his cousin Roxane. When he discovers that she loves a fellow soldier called Christian, who lacks the courage to declare his love, he sacrifices himself for the sake of his friend's happiness. One night he imitates Christian's voice and asks Roxane for a kiss. She agrees and Christian slips into Cyrano's place. After Roxane and Christian are married, Cyrano and Christian leave for the war and Cyrano writes a love letter for his friend to Roxane. She is moved by the passion which is so clearly expressed in the letter and arrives at the camp to give her loving husband an embrace. Christian, however, has been fatally wounded in battle and as he dies he asks his friend to tell his wife who really wrote the letter. Cyrano does not have the heart to disillusion the young wife in her love for her dead husband. Fifteen years later, Cyrano is fatally injured by an enemy and taken to the convent where Roxane has been living ever since she lost Christian. Here he speaks to her in phrases which are so ardently and passionately loving that she realizes the truth and becomes aware that it was really Cyrano's spirit that she had always loved in Christian. Cyrano dies in her arms.

■ The opera belongs to the composer's late period. When first performed in Rome, it was sung to a libretto by Cesare Meano and Filippo Brusa which was a translation from Cain's French text, adapting the words to the rhythmic demands of the music. It was first performed in French at the Opéra-Comique in Paris on 29 May of the same year. Both performances were a success, but the opera was not subsequently taken into the repertoire. The composer had previously been accused of 'frenchifying' Italian opera, but in this work he tried to reconcile the two genres by adopting a more typically 'Italian' style while attending to the instrumentation with great care.

GIULIO CESARE (Julius Caesar)

Opera in three acts and seven scenes by Gian Francesco Malipiero (1882–1973), libretto by the composer, based on the tragedy by Shakespeare. First performance: Genoa, Teatro Carlo Felice, 8 February 1936; first performance in U.S.A.: (concert version) New York, Carnegie Hall, 13 January 1937.

ORIGINAL CAST. Giovanni Inghilleri, Ettore Parmeggiani, Alessandro Dolci, Apollo Granforte, Gino Vanelli, Sara Scuderi, Maria Pedrini. Conductor: Angelo Questa.

SYNOPSIS. Act I. Caesar (baritone), followed by a procession, is on his way down a street in Rome to celebrate Lupercalia. A fortune-teller (baritone) comes up to him and warns him to beware the Ides of March. Brutus (baritone), Cassius (baritone) and Casca (tenor) discuss the crowd's acclaim and express their fear that Caesar will be offered an emperor's crown. At night the three meet in Brutus's garden, along with other conspirators, and repeat their fear and concern for the danger that Caesar's popularity brings to the safety of the Republic. Brutus's wife Portia (soprano) begs her husband to tell her what is happening. Act II, Scene I. Meanwhile in Caesar's palace his wife Calpurnia (soprano) is terrified by her prophetic dreams. She begs her husband not to go out, especially as he has had unlucky auguries during the propitiating sacrifices. He decides to stay at home, but when Cassius, Brutus and the other conspirators arrive he is afraid of being called a coward and goes with them. Scene II. In the Senate House on the Capitol the conspirators have arranged that Casca should be the first to strike Caesar. Metellus Cimber (baritone) prostrates himself before Caesar and asks mercy for his exiled brother. Caesar is unmoved and Casca stabs him in the neck, while the other conspirators also leap at him. Brutus is the last to strike him and Caesar falls at the feet of Pompey's statue. Mark Antony (tenor) is prepared to be killed also by the conspirators, but they spare him. He shakes their hands and then begs pardon of Caesar's memory for striking a bargain with his murderers. He asks Brutus for permission to bury Caesar and speak to the people. Act III, Scene I. Caesar's burial takes place in the Forum. Brutus speaks first and explains to the people why he was compelled to kill Caesar. When it is Mark Antony's turn to speak, he manipulates the crowd's feelings skilfully, and when he announces that it was Caesar's will that all his possessions should go to the people, there is an outburst of hatred against the conspirators. Meanwhile in the street some citizens meet the poet Cinna (tenor) and, mistaking him for the conspirator of the same name, pursue him with the intention of killing him. Scene II. The two opposing sides are facing each other on the battlefield. On one side are Octavian and Mark Antony, on the other Brutus and Cassius. The battle begins. Cassius comes on followed by Pindarus (tenor), whom he asks to climb a hill to survey the scene and report on it. From there Pindarus sees Brutus surrounded and assumes that he has been taken prisoner. Cassius cannot bear the idea of defeat and kills himself. Brutus does the same. Mark Antony's and Octavian's victorious troops sing hymns to the glory of Rome.

■ In writing *Giulio Cesare* Malipiero has discovered new musical forms very far removed from the method of writing in 'panels', and capable of expressing a continuous theme, which is both changing and yet contains a logic throughout its uninterrupted flow. Malipiero himself called this a 'period of lyricism'. It lasted from 1935 to 1941 and since it coincided with a period of cultural obscurantism in Italian society it seems likely that the composer wanted to protect himself as far as possible from controversy.

IL CAMPIELLO (A Venetian Square)

Opera buffa in three acts by Ermanno Wolf-Ferrari (1876–1948), libretto by Mario Ghisalberti, based on a comedy by Carlo Goldoni (1756). First performance: Milan, Teatro alla Scala, 12 February 1936.

ORIGINAL CAST. Malfalda Favero (Gasparina), Ines Adami Corradetti (Lucieta), Nardi (donna Cate Panciana), Margherita Carosio (Gnese), Tess (Orsola), Luigi Fort (Zorzeto), Antori (Anzoleto), Salvatore Baccaloni (the knight Astolfi), Zaccarini (Fabrizio), Giuseppe Nessi (Donna Pasqua Polegano). Conductor: Gino Marinuzzi.

SYNOPSIS. The story takes place in Venice, in the middle of the eighteenth century. Act I. A small square with several houses and an inn. The Neapolitan cavalier Astolfi (baritone), who is very refined but penniless, is paying court to an affected young lady called Gasparina (soprano), but he also has an eye on Lucieta (soprano), who is in love with Anzoleto (bass) (a travelling salesman), and on Gnese (soprano), who loves Zorzeto (tenor). The old women of the square also worm their way into the tangle of love affairs. They are Orsola (mezzo-soprano) (Zorzeto's mother), Pasqua (tenor) and Cate (mezzo-soprano). Astolfi offers Lucieta a ring, which she refuses so as not to break her pledge to Anzoleto. Her mother, Donna Cate, however, accepts it. But the faithless Neapolitan begins paying more attention to Gasparina. Act II. Astolfi invites everyone to lunch. Gasparina declines as she does not want to descend to the level of 'the populace'. So she stays at home with her uncle, Fabrizio (bass), who is angry at the continual noise and endless brawls that take place in the square. Fabrizio takes a liking to the amorous knight, for he, too, is from Naples. He does not mind that Astolfi is penniless since he is keen to marry off his niece. A new quarrel breaks out, but luckily ends in a great ball where all the principal characters come together. Act III. Fabrizio has had enough of the noisy square and finally decided to move house. Meanwhile a furious quarrel breaks out between Zorzeto and Anzoleto (bass) after a series of

Respighi's La fiamma, *sets and costumes by Salvatore Fiume.*

misunderstandings, and Astolfo only manages to restore the peace, in his usual way, by inviting everyone to a good 'tuck-in' at the inn. Here he announces his forthcoming marriage to Gasparina. The girl bids an emotional but refined farewell to the square and also to her beloved city, which she must now leave to follow her husband to far-off Naples.

■ Wolf-Ferrari retired to a house on the outskirts of Rome to write *Il Campiello*, and not even his closest friends could find him. He felt greatly at ease in the Roman Spring and he was especially happy to be at last working for an Italian theatre, La Scala. These are the two elements which combined to produce the particular balance between melancholy and vicaciousness which is the hallmark of this opera, one of the composer's most successful works. He himself remembered this time as one of his most happily fertile periods. 'When I was 26,' he wrote, 'I became a child to write *Le donne curiose*, and now at 60 I do the same for *Il Campiello*. A real child I was, I am, I always will be.' And it certainly is with child-like gusto that he manages, while sticking remarkably closely to the text, to convey the bustling and unconventional brilliance which characterize this comedy of Goldoni. Its plot is simple and direct and is brought to life above all by the rapid succession of quarrels and their sudden transformation into moments of precarious peace.

NOTTURNO ROMANTICO (A Romantic Night)
Opera in one act and two scenes by Riccardo Pick-Mangiagalli (1882–1949), libretto by Arturo Rossato

(1882–1949). First performance: Rome, Opera, 25 April 1936.

ORIGINAL CAST. Aurelio Marcato, Pia Tassinari, Nini Giani, Giuseppe Monacchini, Saturno Meletti. Conductor: Tullio Serafin.

SYNOPSIS. The scene is set in a villa on Lake Como in 1825. A grand party is taking place in the house of Contessa Clotilde (mezzo-soprano). Elisa (soprano) her niece, loves, and is loved by, the patriot Aurelio Fadda (tenor), a former lover of Clotilde. Count Zeno (baritone) gets to know about the love affair between Elisa and Aurelio and tells Clotilde about it. Burning with jealousy, she decides to take revenge. Aurelio arrives inconspicuously amongst all the guests, and gives Elisa a love token of a medal containing his mother's portrait. Clotilde interrupts their conversation and, after sending her niece out, she reproaches Aurelio for betraying her. She pretends to accept his excuses and after promising to help him escape she denounces him to Zeno. Elisa is suspicious and tries to dissuade Zeno from doing anything, but he has decided to wait for Aurelio in the square and shoot him as a traitor. When Elisa hears the gunshot she falls to the ground in a faint.

■ In 1936, the year in which *Notturno Romantico* received its first public showing, Riccardo Pick-Mangiagalli was made Director of the Milan Conservatory, a post which he continued to occupy until his death. He was of Bohemian origin and took Italian nationality. He began his career as a concert pianist, but despite many successes he devoted himself almost entirely to teaching and composition.

THE POISONED KISS, or THE EMPRESS AND THE NECROMANCER
Romantic extravaganza in three acts by Ralph Vaughan Williams (1872–1958), libretto by Evelyn Sharp, based on the tale 'The Poison Maid' from Richard Garnett's collection 'The Twilight of the Gods' (1888). First performance: Cambridge, 12 May 1936. First performance in U.S.A.: New York, City Opera, 21 April 1937.

SYNOPSIS. The adolescent love between the wizard, Dipsacus (bass), and the Empress Persicaria (contralto) was soon transformed into deep resentment. After many years their respective, innocent, children also become involved in this old hatred. The wizard accustoms his daughter, Tormentilla (soprano), to withstand ever increasing doses of poison from a very early age onwards, so that her kisses will be poisonous, whereas the Empress has seen to it that her son, Amaryllus (tenor), has become immune to poison. When the two youngsters meet, they fall in love instantly, without being aware of each other's identity. The complicated romance between Amaryllus and Tormentilla brings the wizard and the Empress

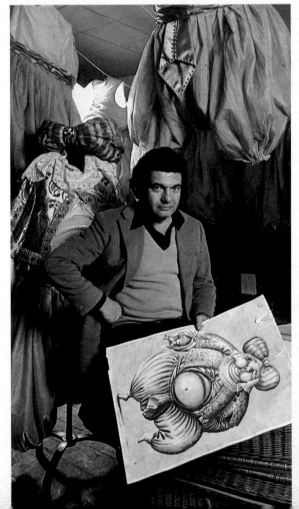

Behind the scenes at La Scala, Milan. Facing page: the main area of the theatre workshop; a corner of the shoemaking and wardrobe departments. Above left: some idea of the immensity of the stage: twenty-seven metres high, thirty-five metres deep and thirty metres wide. Above: inside the lighting-control room. Below: the view from the royal box.

together in a dramatic meeting, during which love prevails. So the story ends with three marriages, because in the meantime Amaryllus's jester and Tormentilla's maidservant have also become infatuated with each other.

■ The opera was a failure in spite of some fine lyrical songs and ensembles, because it is half way between operetta and musical comedy without being truly one or the other.

DAS DUMME MÄDCHEN (The Backward Maiden)
Lyric comedy in three acts by Ermanno Wolf-Ferrari (1876–1948), libretto by Mario Ghisalberti, based on the comedy by Lope de Vega (1562–1635). First performance: Mainz, 1937.

SYNOPSIS. The palace of Ottavio (baritone) in Madrid in the first half of the seventeenth century. Ottavio has two marriageable daughters, Nise and Finea (sopranos). Nise is very gifted, Finea is backward – at the age of 20 she still is unable to read. A young man called Liseo (bass) wants to marry her, but when he discovers this flaw in her personality he begins to pay court to Nise, who in her turn is loved by Lorenzo (tenor). When Lorenzo discovers that Finea's dowry is the larger, he starts to pay his attentions to her. Love wakes the young girl up and she overcomes her backwardness. Now Liseo turns to her again, but she knows how to hold him at bay be pretending to be backward once more. It all finishes with a spate of marriages since the servants follow their masters' example.

■ The first Italian performance of the opera took place at La Scala in Milan during the 1938–39 season, conducted by Umberto Berrettoni.

LUCREZIA
Drama in one act and three scenes by Ottorino Respighi

Gershwin's Porgy and Bess *at its first performance in Boston, 30 September 1935. The production was directed by Rouben Mamoulian and designed by Serge Soudeikine, with Todd Duncan and Anne Brown as* Porgy *and* Bess.

Another scene from the first production of Porgy and Bess, *1935.*

Gershwin's Porgy and Bess *in the 1942 Broadway production.*

weapon. They go to Rome to stir up the people against Tarquinio's family and annihilate them.

■ The opera is unfinished and was not revised by the composer, who had begun to work on it only in the year before his death. His wife Elsa collected the drafts of the score and wrote in the missing parts. For this reason it is hard to evaluate it.

(1879–1936), libretto by Claudio Guastalla. First performance: Milan, Teatro alla Scala, 24 February 1937.

ORIGINAL CAST. Maria Caniglis, Ebe Stignani, Ettore Parmeggiani. Conductor: Gino Marinuzzi.

SYNOPSIS. The year 509 B.C. A Roman camp under the walls of Ardea, a small town near Rome. Several patricians are arguing about the virtue of their wives, each one asserting that his own wife is the most devoted. Collatino (tenor) suggests a bet: if each man goes to his own home to discover the truth the facts will undoubtedly prove himself to be the winning husband. Collatino does indeed win the bet, as we are told by a narrator, but this victory is the forerunner of grief. Sesto Tarquinio (baritone) sees Collatino's wife Lucrezia (soprano) and falls in love with her. The next evening he goes to Collatino's village, introduces himself to his friend's wife as a passing traveller, and asks for hospitality. During the night he uses a trick to get into her bedroom, declares his love to her and overcomes her resistance. Lucrezia tells her husband, her father and her friend Bruto (tenor) what has happened and then, calling for revenge, she stabs herself rather than live on after suffering such shame. Bruto pulls the dagger from her body and, together with all the others present, swears to kill Sesto Tarquinio with that very

AMELIA AL BALLO (Amelia goes to the Ball)
Opera buffa *in one act by Gian Carlo Menotti (born 1911), libretto by the composer. English version by George Mead. Preview: Philadelphia, Academy of Music, 3 March 1937. First performance: New York, Metropolitan Opera, 1 April 1937. First performance in U.K.: Liverpool, 19 November 1956.*

ORIGINAL CAST. Muriel Dickson, John Brownlee.

SYNOPSIS. A cheerful prelude gives a first taste of the humour and subtle irony which pervade the whole work. The story takes place in Amelia's room, where feverish activity is going on as the curtain rises. Amelia (soprano) is being helped by two maids (mezzo-sopranos) to get ready for the first ball of the season. The confusion is increased by the presence of a friend (contralto) who is waiting impatiently for her. At last, when Amelia is ready, her husband (baritone) rushes in demanding to talk to her in private. The friend leaves and the husband produces a letter which leaves him in no doubt that she has a lover. She denies this feebly and rather absently, all her concentration being directed towards going out as soon as possible. Finally, to put an end to the argument, and after obtaining a promise that he will then escort her to the ball, she tells him that the man who signs himself 'Bubu' is their neighbour (tenor), the one with the moustache, the tenant on the third floor. Amelia thinks she can go at last, but her husband feels differently and rushes up the stairs. After a few minutes of vexation while she realizes that once shots are fired they will never be able to leave, Amelia decides to warn her lover, who slides down a rope into her bedroom. He embraces her, but she does not have time for such behaviour. He suggests that they run away together, but Amelia refuses for that particular evening. When the husband returns in an even greater rage at not having found his rival, 'Bubu' hides, but he is soon discovered. When the husband tries to shoot him his pistol jams. An argument starts up between the two men, but gradually changes into an exchange of explanations and finally of friendly confidences, the lover telling of his burning passion and the husband of his lost love. Meanwhile Amelia is trembling with irritation at the waste of time until she can no longer control her impatience. She seizes a vase and hurls it at her husband's head. He falls to the ground unconscious. Amelia screams, people come running, the police arrive led by a Commissioner, who questions everyone. Amelia gives a most unexpected version of the events. According to her, the lover is a stranger who came to their flat to rob them and struck the husband, who had caught him red-handed. In amazement the lover tries to defend himself, but naturally no-one believes him and he is taken away under arrest. The wounded man is taken to hospital and at last Amelia is free to go to the Ball. She gladly agrees to be escorted by the Commissioner.

■ *Amelia goes to the Ball* was Menotti's first successful opera. His most notable characteristics are already in evidence: a marked talent for lyricism, a style of writing music which makes an intelligent use of his American experiences and of the influence of music which is modern, if not avant-garde, and yet traditional; a well-planned libretto which offers sure opportunities for the music to achieve certain effects, and a very keen sense of the theatre. The opera's success was instantaneous and the young composer became known worldwide. Critical opinion is divided on its musical merits. It is the first and so far the only opera that Menotti has written in Italian.

THE SECOND HURRICANE
Opera for children by Aaron Copland (born 1900), libretto by Edward Denby. First performance: New York, Henry Street Music School, 21 April 1937.

■ This is a spectacular entertainment in operatic form for use in schools of music.

IL DESERTO TENTATO (The Desert of Temptation)
Mystery in one act by Alfredo Casella (1883–1947).

Text by Corrado Pavolini. First performance: Florence, Teatro Vittorio Emmanuele, 6 May 1937.

ORIGINAL CAST. Maria Melone, Gabriella Gatti, Carmelo Maugeri. Conductor: Antonio Guarnieri.

■ The opera is a symbolic encounter between the 'pure' heroes, the aviators, and the 'barbaric' ones, the native warriors. It was intended to be a triumphant celebration of the Italian occupation of Ethiopia.

THE MAN WITHOUT A COUNTRY
Opera in two acts by Walter Damrosch (1862–1950), libretto by Arthur Guiterman, based on a tale by Edward Everett Hale (1863). First performance: New York, Metropolitan Opera, 12 May 1937.

ORIGINAL CAST. Traubel and Carron. Conductor: Walter Damrosch.

SYNOPSIS. Philip Nolan is a young officer from New Orleans in the United States Army. He is charged as a Separatist, is tried and would have been acquitted had he not, exasperated by a tedious cross-examination, unwisely exclaimed, 'Oh to Hell with the United States of America, I hope I have heard the end of them!' The Court condemns him to 'the immediate enjoyment of his wishes'. He is put on board a warship about to embark on a long patrol where no-one is ever to speak, either to him or in his presence, about the United States, nor may he have access to any book or newspaper which might contain even a passing mention of his country. In this way 'the man without a country' spends more than fifty years, in one ship after another and always kept far from his homeland. This cruel punishment finally transforms the man 'without a country' into an ardent patriot. During a battle, stepping in for an officer who is wounded, he bravely secures victory when all hope had been abandoned. For this exploit he is reinstated, but the document ordering his release never arrives. He dies clasping the United States flag, while a sympathetic officer tells him the story of America during the half century from 1810–60, a highly eventful period in the life of the newly-formed country.

■ This is the fourth of the composer's five operas. Damrosch was responsible for introducing the music of many European composers, from Brahms and Tchaikovsky to Sibelius, into America.

LULU
Opera in a prologue and two acts by Alban Berg (1885–1935), libretto by the composer, based on the plays Der Erdgeist *(1893) and* Die Büchse der Pandora *(1901) by Frank Wedekind. First performance:*

Zürich, Stadttheater, 2 June 1937. First performance in U.K.: London, Sadler's Wells (by Hamburg company) 3 October 1962; in U.S.A.: Santa Fé, 7 August 1963.

ORIGINAL CAST. Nuri Hadzič (Lulu). Conductor: Denzler.

SYNOPSIS. The story is set around 1930. Prologue. A ring-master (bass) is on stage, dressed in a red overcoat and white trousers with his whip in his hand, announcing the show to the audience while the curtain is still down. His best and most dangerous number is 'Lulu, the real, wild, beautiful beast, tamed by the human race'. Act I, Scene I. A painter's studio. Lulu (soprano) is having her portrait painted and with her are the painter (tenor), Dr Ludwig Schön (baritone), the editor of a major newspaper, and his son Alwa (tenor). Lulu has been the mistress of Dr Schön who had picked her off the street, but now, at his desire, she has become the wife of old Dr Goll. Ludwig and Alwa Schön leave and Lulu is alone with the painter. He is overcome by desire for her, throws himself at her feet and embraces her. The aged Dr Goll arrives just at that moment and in his distress dies of a heart attack. While the painter rushes off to find a doctor Lulu recovers from her initial dismay to realize that now she is both free and rich. Scene II. Lulu's house. She is now married to the painter, but is annoyed at the news she has received in a letter from Dr Schön. In it her former lover tells her that he is going to marry a virtuous woman. An old swindler called Schigolch (bass), a wandering musician, now comes onto the stage. He is hoping to take Lulu's money by pretending to be her adoptive father. When Schön arrives Schigolch sensibly disappears. Schön has come to say his last goodbye to Lulu, but she flies into a rage and their quarrel is only brought to an end by the arrival of the painter. Schön is furious and when Lulu leaves, he tells the painter all about her dissolute life, and the fact that he himself has bought every one of the pictures that the painter has sold in the last few years, to allow Lulu a life of luxury. The painter goes off, but soon afterwards a big splash is heard. He has killed himself in the bath with a razor. Scene III. Theatre dressing-room. Lulu is now a famous and admired dancer. She is getting ready to go on stage when Alwa and a prince come in, both of them madly in love with her. Lulu goes off to do her act, but soon after comes back and pretends to feel ill. She has seen Schön's fiancée in the stalls and does not want to sing or dance for her. Old Schön comes in and his former love revives at the sight of her. When she threatens to run away with the prince (tenor), the doctor has no alternative but to break off his engagement. Act II, Scene I. A large sitting room in the Schön house. Lulu is now Mrs Schön, but she keeps the doctor in a constant state of torment and jealousy, since she will not give up the company of her old friends. Now Schigolch, the ring-master, Rodrigo, a student of gymnastics (contralto) and the Countess Geschwitz (mezzo-soprano) arrive to see Lulu, all of them being madly in love with her. They hide, however, when Alwa comes in. Thinking that he is alone with his stepmother, he throws himself at her feet. Schön comes in, unnoticed, and in despair at seeing his son

Mario Vellani-Marchi's sketch for Wolf-Ferrari's Il campiello, *1949.*

too conquered by Lulu, he confronts her with a pistol. Lulu reproaches him with having wasted her youth and in the quarrel that ensues she gets hold of the gun and kills Schön. Now there is a filmed intermezzo. The film of the trial is shown on a screen and Lulu is convicted of the murder of her third husband. Then she is seen suffering from cholera, in a pauper's hospital, from which the Countess Geschwitz helps her to escape. Scene II. The same stage-set as in the previous scene, but many years later. Lulu comes in with her friends; Alwa, Schigolch, the student of gymnastics and Rodrigo. Soon they all go out with one excuse or another except Alwa, who declares his love to her again when he is alone with her. She is sitting on a divan and she replies cynically, 'This is still the same sofa that your father bled to death on'. Act III, Scene I. (Left unfinished at Berg's death.) Paris. A secret gaming-house. Lulu is now one of the Marquis Casti-Piani's prostitutes and he wants to sell her to an Egyptian. To escape this fate she disguises herself and flees to London with Alwa, the Countess Geschwitz and Schigolch. Scene II. (Entirely the composer's music.) A garret in London. Lulu now does absolutely anything to earn money for herself and her friends. On Christmas Night, Alwa is dying and Lulu goes off with a client. He is Jack the Ripper. Shortly afterwards a scream is heard from the room where they went. Jack the Ripper comes out smeared in Lulu's blood and murders the Countess Geschwitz as well, when she stands up to him calling on the name of her beloved Lulu.

■ *Lulu* kept Berg completely occupied from 1928 until his death in 1935; the only thing he wrote during those years, apart from the opera score, were the concert aria *Der Wein* (Wine) and, just before he died in 1935, a concerto for violin and orchestra. However, Act III was never completed (as has already been noted). In 1934 Berg himself arranged a suite of five symphonic pieces from the opera, which he called the 'Lulu Symphony'. He completed this arrangement in a very short space of time and on 11 December 1935, after a preview in Berlin, it was first performed in Vienna, only a few days before his death, which occurred on Christmas Eve. The theme of the opera is Lulu herself, seen as a personification of all the evil perpetrated in the world in the name of sex, which itself is seen as a wild and infernal power. But whereas in Wedekind's plays all the images and situations are painful and hopeless, in Berg's opera there are some glimpses of life and optimism. The music also contains this dual element; it is the music of bitterness and disillusion, but there are moments which are deeply lyrical, especially for Lulu herself, as though to redeem her tragic and devilish character. Musically speaking, *Lulu* is directly related to *Wozzek* as though it were a deepening of that work.

Its main features are: the instrumental patterns, which are directly reminiscent of *Wozzek*, the use of the orchestra, rich in subtleties and moods, and the dodecaphonic language, which is used with greater care and consistency than in *Wozzek*. Berg's dodecaphony is very far removed from the raw idiom of Schönberg, and is constantly linked with the lyrical elements which characterize the composer's music.

CARMINA BURANA (Songs from Beuern)

Scenic cantata in three parts by Carl Orff (born 1895), subtitled Cantiones profanae cantoribus et choris cantandae, *with mediaeval texts (dating from the first half of the thirteenth century) taken from the collection of that name, formerly in the monastery of Benediktbeuern in Bavaria (Codex Latinus 4660 of Beuern) and now in Munich. First performance: Frankfurt, Staatsoper, 8 June 1937. First performance in U.S.A.: San Francisco, 3 October 1954.*

■ The cantata opens with a prologue in which a chorus sings to Fortune, who holds the human race in her power and distributes favours and troubles as regularly as the lunar phases succeed one another. Those who have been wounded are given sympathy and those who at present reign supreme are warned that sooner or later they will fall. Part I is entitled *Veris laeta facies* (The glad face of Spring). The season is celebrated by choruses singing of her coming and her gifts. The baritone solo urges his companion to love and loyalty and tells her to be as happy as Spring and her youth bid her. This part ends with a dance and with some choral singing whose theme is the love games that boys and girls play together. In Part II, *In taberna* (At the inn), the baritone reflects bitterly that his life on earth is as fragile as a leaf. Man loves to play and willingly accepts the exertions of love, but then loses himself in vice. Now the chorus intervenes to tell how all the people playing in the inn are only trying to do down whoever is out of luck. Part III, *Amor volat undique* (Love flies everywhere). The solo soprano tells how a girl, when she is alone, weeps just like a boy who cannot obtain a kiss from his beloved; how different if they are left alone together in a room! The girl ends up in the arms of her lover even if her modesty makes her hesitant and uncertain at first. The cantata ends with a chorus in honour of Venus (*Ave formosissima*) and a return to the opening chorus to Fortune.

There are dance and mime parts in this Cantata. Orff is considered to have opened up a new phase in his work with this composition, so as to repudiate his earlier works. Later on *Carmina Burana* became part of the trilogy entitled *Triumphs*, which also included *Catulli Carmina* and *Trionfo d'Afrodite*, see pp. 444 and 464 below.

MARIA D'ALESSANDRIA (Mary of Alexandria)

Opera in three acts and four scenes by Giorgio Federico Ghedini (1892–1965). Libretto by Cesare Meano. First performance: Bergamo, Teatro della Novità (Donizetti), 9 September 1937.

ORIGINAL CAST. Serafina di Leo (Maria), Antenore Reali (the father), Nino Bertelli (the son), Andrea Mongelli (Dimo), Baracchi (guardian of the fire and fourth shepherd), Coda (the gaoler Bebro), Pozzoli (Euno and third shepherd), Mercuriali (Nemesio, the deacon Silverio and Mahat), Arbuffo (Misuride and first shepherd), Ticozzi (the blind woman and second shepherd). Conductor: Giuseppe Del Campo.

SYNOPSIS. The story is set in the fourth century. A rowing boat leaves Alexandria with a group of pilgrims bound for Palestine. Maria (soprano), a notorious prostitute searching for a better fate in another country, joins them. Among the pilgrims is a converted courtesan called Misuride (soprano) with her father (baritone) and her son (tenor). When the son sees Maria by the gleam of the lighthouse light, he is dazzled by her beauty. Soon the boat comes to a halt, since most of the pilgrims and the crew are enjoying themselves with Maria in the hold. The son is upset and the father, who wants to attack her for her sinful conduct, is locked up. Maria orders the men to go on rowing but she heads the boat towards the wealthy city of Byzantium. Meanwhile a violent storm blows up. The father has freed himself from the hold and aims a huge bow at Maria; the son leaps to protect her and it is he, not she, who is wounded. Maria is profoundly moved and, going down on her knees, she takes him in her arms and prays to God. In a deserted and rocky landscape, the shepherds discuss the storm which wrecked a large ship during the night, when Maria appears between the rocks, dragging a lifeless body. It is the son who saved her from certain death and whom she now wants to give a proper burial. She calls on her Saviour, but cannot find rest. A voice from heaven, the son's voice, promises her salvation and tells her that she will join her Saviour. He urges her to walk into the desert, to repent, and to wait for her last hour. She agrees and sets off full of hope.

■ This is Ghedini's first work for the stage (apart from *Gringoire*, which was not performed) and, although it is influenced by Wagner and Pizzetti, it contains an original poetic and dramatic vision, which is evident even more clearly in his subsequent works, where those influences are absent.

RIDERS TO THE SEA
Opera in one act by Ralph Vaughan Williams (1872–1958), text by John Millington Synge (1904). First performance: London, Royal College of Music, 1 December 1937. First performance in U.S.A.: Cleveland, 26 February 1950.

SYNOPSIS. A fisherman's cottage on the west coast of Ireland. Maurya (contralto), an old woman, battles against a hard fate and against the wind and the sea. The sea has robbed her of a husband and four sons; her daughters Cathleen and Nora (sopranos) discover that a fifth has recently been drowned. The old mother has an omen that her youngest and last remaining son, Bartley (baritone), will also be claimed by the elements. Neighbours bear his corpse into the cottage. With dignity and resignation she expresses her grief; no more can be taken from her, and she has nothing more to fear from the sea and the storms.

■ *Riders to the Sea* is considered to be the composer's best opera. He uses many folk songs for colour and immediacy, at the same time maintaining an overall, unifying dramatic tension. In this grief-stricken tragedy, Vaughan Williams makes marvellous use of a chorus of women and keeps the instrumentation down to the bare essentials, letting the sound of wind alone conclude the piece.

MARGHERITA DA CORTONA
Legend in a prologue and three acts by Licinio Refice (1883–1954), libretto by Emidio Mucci. First performance: Milan, Teatro alla Scala, 1 January 1938.

ORIGINAL CAST. Augusta Oltrabella, Giovanni Voyer, Tancredi Pasero, Tatiana Menotti. Conductor: Franco Capuana.

SYNOPSIS. Margherita (soprano), a young girl who is as poor as she is beautiful, leaves home because her stepmother treats her badly. She becomes the mistress of Arsenio (baritone), a wealthy young nobleman. He is killed while hunting, and the blame for his death falls on the two brothers of Chiarella (soprano), a shepherdess whom Arsenio had seduced before he met Margherita. Margherita returns to her father, but everyone is encouraged by the stepmother to reject her. Only the noble Uberto (tenor) offers to help her. He takes her to Cortona, where she leads a life of such penitence and sacrifice that she gains a reputation for holiness. One day she learns that it was Uberto who killed Arsenio. A procession files past, taking Chiarella and her brothers to be hanged, and Margherita goes to meet it and offers her own life to save theirs. Uberto tries to pretend that she is mad, but the judge's response (bass) is to free the three convicts. The people rejoice and acclaim her as a saint. The nobles rally to Uberto and civil war breaks out. Peace is restored when Margherita comes out of church transfigured and bearing a large cross. She is pardoned by her father and retires to a life of solitude and prayer. Chiarella is left to comfort and help the people.

■ This is Refice's best work for the theatre, and yet unfortunately traces of D'Annunzio's influence are not enough to counteract the over-exuberance and second-rate aestheticism. In fact the opera does not rise much above most Italian works of that period, even in its best moments.

JEANNE D'ARC AU BÛCHER (Joan of Arc at the Stake)

Dramatic oratorio in a prologue and eleven scenes by Arthur Honegger (1892–1955), libretto by Paul Claudel (1868–1955). First performance: Basel (concert version) 12 May 1938. First performance in U.S.A.: (concert version) New York, 1 January 1948; (stage version) San Francisco, 15 October 1954.

ORIGINAL CAST. Ida Rubinstein, Jean Périer, Serge Sandoz, Charles Vaucher, Ginevra Vivante, Berthe de Vigier.

SYNOPSIS. The action takes place in France during the 100 Years' War. Prologue. A chorus laments the sad fate of France in the hands of the enemy, and a voice announces that a young girl will come to free her. Scenes: Jeanne (speaking part) is seen on a pyre with a fire burning at her feet. St Dominic (speaking part) descends from Heaven to comfort her by showing her the book where the angels have recorded all the insults that men have flung at her. Jeanne relives her trial, where the judges wear animal masks: the President is a pig, the Chancellor an ass and the judges are sheep. She is condemned to die at the stake for heresy and witchcraft. St Dominic explains to her that they are all in the power of the devil and explains why she is being put to death. The Kings of France, Burgundy and England arrive and play at cards with Death, accompanied by their wives, Stupidity, Pride, Greed and Lust, and by their footmen who, as umpires of the game, share out the money they have gained by handing over Jeanne to the Duke of Bedford. The death knell is sounded and once more Jeanne hears the voices of St Margaret (soprano) and St Catherine (contralto), while the chorus of people celebrate the marriage between the giant Heurtebise (good French bread) and Madame Botti (good French wine) and then go off en masse to see the King of France passing on his way to his coronation in Rheims. Meanwhile Jeanne remembers her childhood, when her 'voices' urged her to help her country and when, with love to strengthen her, she undertook to help her King win back his throne. She is afraid of the fire, but the Virgin (soprano) comforts her, and she feels she can bear the flames with joy, since she herself is a flame of France. In the end her chains snap and she ascends to Heaven, while the crowd proclaims her innocence.

■ Claudel's poetry delineates a vision of the mediaeval world based on the mysterious and magic features which were so much part of the spiritual climate in Joan's time. The allegory is given plenty of scope and an element of magic derives from the fact of having Joan on the pyre right from the beginning and reliving her childhood from the pyre, as well as her struggle against the English, her trial, and her conviction. Critics agree that in this opera Honegger has achieved a true fusion of his previous musical experiences and has given a wonderful musical expression to the mystical, lyrical and dramatic aspects of the poetry. It is not a lyric opera in the traditional mould. In fact some parts are sung, some recited (including the heroine's part) and, generally speaking, only the celestial and allegorical characters rather than the real people have a truly vocal role.

MATHIS DER MALER (Mathias the Painter)

Opera in seven scenes by Paul Hindemith (1895–1963), libretto by the composer. First performance: Zurich, Stadttheater, 28 May 1938. First performance in U.K.: 15 May 1939 (concert version); in U.S.A.: Boston University, 17 February 1956.

ORIGINAL CAST. Stig, Hellwig, Funk, Baxevanos, Mosbacher. Conductor: Denzler.

SYNOPSIS. Prelude: *Engelkoncert* (Concert of Angels). Scene I. Monastery of St Anthony at Mainz. Mathis (baritone) is painting a fresco and wondering whether he is really fulfilling God's will with his art. The chief of the rebellious peasants, Hans Schwalb (tenor), bursts through the gate with his daughter, Regina (soprano). They are being pursued by the Confederate army headed by Sylvester von Schaumberg (tenor) and beg for refuge, amazed to find someone who can live quietly and dedicate his life to art in a world so full of trouble and injustice. Mathis listens as Schwalb explains why the peasants are right to rebel against those who abuse them. The painter agrees to help them and offers his horse, on which they depart, not long before Sylvester arrives in search of them. Mathis admits that he helped them escape, but maintains that he is answerable for his action only to the Cardinal Archbishop of Mainz, Albrecht von Brandenburg. Scene II. Mainz. A hall in the Cardinal Archbishop's palace. The Cardinal (tenor) hears the arguments of both Catholics and Protestants. Lorenz von Pommersfelden (bass) and Wolfgang Capito (tenor) are among the Catholics and a rich merchant of Mainz, Riedinger (bass), and his daughter Ursula (soprano) are among the Lutherans. Mathis comes in and Ursula, who is in love with him, rebukes him for his long absence. Schaumberg then comes in. He recognizes Mathis and accuses him publicly of helping Schwalb escape. Mathis declares that he supports the oppressed, and although Pommersfelden wants to have him arrested, the Cardinal refuses and allows him to leave his service and to go freely into the world. Scene III. Riedinger's house. Wolfgang Capito, the Cardinal's adviser, has come to Riedinger's house to remove certain prohibited books. He placates the merchant by reading him a letter from Luther urging the Cardinal to marry and to change his archbishopric into a principality. Capito suggests that a marriage between the Cardinal and Ursula would be financially advantageous to the state and Riedinger begs his daughter to accept the offer in the cause of her religion. Ursula is dismayed and when Mathis arrives she declares her love for him fulsomely. Mathis replies that he has decided to renounce love and art and to join the peasants in their

Berg's Lulu *at the Spoleto* Festival dei due Mondi *(Festival of Two Worlds), 1974; directed by Roman Polanski.*

campaign. Ursula then tells her father that she will do whatever her faith requires of her. Scene IV. A square in Königshofen, a village captured and sacked by the rebels. They take the Count and Countess Helfenstein (contralto) prisoner. The Countess flees to a chapel, while her husband is killed; then the peasants destroy a painting of the Virgin in the chapel and drag the Countess outside. Mathis, outraged at their excesses, defends her and is knocked down. Schwalb and Regina arrive in time to rebuke the mob for using unnecessary violence while the enemy is approaching. In the ensuing battle, the peasants are defeated and Schwalb is killed. The Truchsess von Waldburg (bass), commander of the League's army, and Sylvester want to take Mathis prisoner, but the Countess intercedes on his behalf. He is left alone with Regina, who weeps over her father's corpse, to consider the futility of his life of action. Scene V. The Cardinal's study in Mainz. Capito tries to persuade the Cardinal to join the Lutherans and to marry a rich wife. The Cardinal is surprised to find that Ursula is his proposed bride. He asks her to explain how she came to agree to the proposal. She replies that she is willing to sacrifice her life for her faith, and much impressed by her fervour he is strengthened in his own faith. He dismisses Capito, blesses Ursula and resolves to withdraw from the world. He gives permission for the Lutherans to acknowledge

their faith openly. Scene VI. A wood in the Odenwald. Mathis consoles Regina, who still mourns for her father. While she sleeps he has a vision in which he sees himself as St Anthony tempted by luxury (the Countess), wealth (Pommersfelden) lust and martyrdom (Ursula), knowledge (Capito) and military glory (Schwalb). This vision vanishes and St Paul (Pommersfelden), with features resembling the Cardinal, appears and urges him to return to his painting, for in that way he can best serve God and achieve his vocation. Scene VII. Mathis's studio in Mainz. Mathis is exhausted after a long bout of work and Ursula watches over Regina, who is near to death, while she considers the painter's inspired creativity since his experience of the war. Ursula wakes Mathis and Regina dies beside him. Interlude: 'Entombment'. It is nearly morning when the Cardinal appears to take his final leave of Mathis. Mathis also feels the need to put away the symbols of his life's work, and to remain alone with his memories of his art and its achievements.

◼ *Mathis der Maler* is possibly Hindemith's greatest work. It is an attempt to recreate the life of the great, mysterious painter, Mathias Grünwald, and to pay homage to his masterpiece, the Isenheim altar-piece in the Alsatian town of Colmar. Against a background of civil war, the characters in the opera appear at moments of high tension and decision; they are always alone, despite the blazing fires and furious battles, and Mathias is the most solitary of them all. He is the artist whose peace of mind is shattered by the world outside, who can see beauty but no longer knows if he can or should struggle to achieve it. This is the symbolic significance of the first scene (where the painter, painting his frescoes in the monastery, confronts Schwalb driven to despair by war and suffering, who is amazed that anyone can still find time to paint). This conflict between art and life is sustained through a very skilful musical structure where counterpoint is combined with deep expressiveness. Hindemith has moved a long way from his original expressionist sources of inspiration and has also moved beyond the period of the *Neue Sachlichkeit*. Now he returns to a contrapuntal style which has its origins in Bach. In recovering the melodies and harmonies of the tonal system and despite calling himself the most resolute adversary of dodecaphony, Hindemith has worked out a plan which is equally rigid and limiting. Music is now like a system of planets, containing within itself an infinite series of sounds. 'We cannot turn back from the world which has been created for us. Every path leads us there.' These words, uttered by Mathis and the Cardinal at the end of the sixth scene, are indicative. They show us how for Hindemith music was the image of that universal harmony that unites man to the Cosmos. His task then is to sketch out eclipses and geometrical, celestial paths as in Kepler's view of world harmony. (See his five-act opera *Die Harmonie der Welt*, p. 477 below.) *Mathis der Maler*, which was very successful at its first performance in Zurich in 1938, was taken as a cultural and political statement against National Socialism, which had forced Hindemith into exile.

FRIEDENSTAG (The Day of Peace)
Opera in one act by Richard Strauss (1864–1949), libretto by Joseph Gregor (1888–1960). First performance: Munich, Nationaltheater, 24 July 1938. First performance in U.S.A.: Los Angeles, 2 April 1967.

ORIGINAL CAST. Viorica Ursuleac (Maria), Hans Hotter (Commandant), Ludwig Weber (Holsteiner). Conductor: Clemens Krauss.

SYNOPSIS. The story takes place inside the besieged, fortified city of Breda on 24 October 1648 (the day of the Westphalian Peace). The people are exhausted and want to surrender but a message from the Emperor allows them no alternative but to hold out to the death. The Commandant (baritone) decides to blow up the citadel and die with it, but his wife Maria (soprano) refuses to leave him. The fuse to set fire to the gunpowder is all ready when three cannon shots are heard. It is the signal for peace: the Thirty Years' War is over. The Commandant suspects a trick and receives the Holsteiner (bass), the general of the besieging army,

with a drawn sword. Only Maria's timely intervention averts a tragedy and, as the generals embrace, all sing a chorus in praise of peace.

■ *Friedenstag* is a theoretical look at the differing reactions mankind can have towards war, but it suffers from the poor quality of its libretto. Stefan Zweig rewrote the main scene, but even this contribution does not redeem it, and the subject matter was foreign to the composer's temperament. The resulting score is one of Strauss's least vital and most conventional. Despite being well received by the German public, the opera has since been rarely performed.

DAPHNE
Bucolic tragedy in one act by Richard Strauss (1864–1949), libretto by Joseph Gregor (1888–1960). First performance: Dresden, Staatsoper, 15 October 1938. First performance in U.S.A.: (concert version) New York, Brooklyn, 7 October 1960; (staged version) Santa Fé, 29 July 1964.

ORIGINAL CAST. Margarete Teschemacher (Daphne), Torsten Rolf (Apollo), Martin Kremer (Leukippos). Conductor: Karl Böhm.

SYNOPSIS. While a feast is being prepared in her village in honour of Dionysus, the young Daphne (soprano), daughter of Gaea and Peneios, is absorbed in her contemplation of nature, and at sunset she begs the sun to stop in its tracks and let her go on looking at the trees, the flowers and the stream. She does not care for the shepherd Leukippos (tenor), who loves her. Her mother Gaea (contralto) rebukes her for rejecting him. Apollo (tenor) appears (unrecognized in human form) and Peneios asks Daphne to look after him. The god is so struck by her beauty that he calls her 'sister'. Then he finds that he has fallen in love with her. Daphne does not guess who he is and she is confused and frightened.
The shepherds gather to celebrate the festival. Leukippos (dressed as a girl) invites Daphne to join the maidens. Apollo is jealous and reveals the disguise of Leukippos, before showing himself as the Sun. Apollo kills Leukippos with an arrow, but then, bitterly remorseful when confronted with Daphne's despair, who feels herself responsible for the shepherd's death, he begs pardon from Dionysus for interrupting his rites and for meddling in mortal affairs. He begs Zeus to change the girl into one of the trees she loves so well, and Daphne sings while she is transformed into a laurel, of whose branches wreaths for victors and heroes will be made.

■ *Daphne* is rarely performed, but like Strauss's other late lyrical works, it has a classic stature which transcends time and space. Its most beautiful pages are the symphonic interlude accompanying Apollo's kiss and Daphne's last song as she turns into a laurel.

RE HASSAN (King Hassan)

Opera in three acts and four scenes by Giorgio Federico Ghedini (1892–1965), libretto by Tullio Pinelli. First performance: Venice, Teatro La Fenice, 26 January 1939.

ORIGINAL CAST. Tancredi Pasero (King Hassan), Cloe Elmo (Moraima), Giovanni Voyer (Hussein), Irene Minghini Cattaneo (Jarifa). Conductor: Fernando Previtali.

SYNOPSIS. The story is set in Spain in the fifteenth century. In the Alhambra Palace at Granada. Hussein (tenor) accuses his father Hassan (bass) of being too old to lead his people with the necessary vigour during a period as difficult as the present. Hassan believes that his son covets the throne. Hussein feels estranged from his father who, he says, never loved him, and he adds that his mother Jarifa, who has been repudiated by the King, has continually spurred him on to get possession of the throne. The Spanish ambassador, Count Fernando Gonzales (tenor), reminds Hassan that he is obliged to pay a tribute to the King of Spain. Only when this is done will King Ferdinand be able to forgive the injuries endured at the hands of the Arabs. Hassan replies scornfully that he will never pay. This means war – the first war against the Christians for two hundred years. The crowd surges angrily round Hassan's palace shouting that they want no more battles, massacres or violence. The alcalde of Granada is wounded, the city falls, and Hussein, Moraima, his wife (mezzo-soprano), and Jarifa (mezzo-soprano) are among the prisoners. Hassan accuses the alcalde of betrayal and condemns him to death. Meanwhile in King Ferdinand's palace Don Alvaro (baritone) makes Hussein a proposition from the Catholic King: that in exchange for his freedom he should fight against King Hassan. He would be provided with arms and men to win back the Kingdom, provided he handed over Granada to Spain. As a token of good faith, the King asks for Hussein's son. At first Hussein is unwilling to take the boy from his mother, but Jarifa cleverly whets his ambition and he accepts the King's bargain. King Hassan and his retinue enter an arid plain. All his most trusted men are dead and he has decided to send for his son. When the latter arrives, covered in dust and filth, he offers to abdicate in his favour, but Hussein can gain no joy from this prospect, since in the meantime his wife, Moraima, has died from grief at being separated from her son. An officer announces that King Ferdinand is on his way.

■ The opera was written in 1937 and 1938 and a new version was performed in Naples at the Teatro San Carlo on 20 May 1961.

DER MOND (The Moon)

Opera in two acts by Carl Orff (born 1895), libretto by the composer, based on a tale by the Grimm

brothers. *First performance: Munich, Nationaltheater, 5 February 1939. A new version was performed in the same theatre on 26 November 1950. First performance in U.S.A.: New York City Opera, 16 October 1956.*

LA PULCE D'ORO (The Golden Flea)

Opera in three acts and four scenes by Giorgio Federico Ghedini (1892–1965), libretto by Tullio Pinelli. First performance: Genoa, Teatro Carlo Felice, 15 February 1940.

ORIGINAL CAST. Iris Adami-Corradetti, Irma Colasanti, Alessandro Grande, Afro Poli, Mattia Sassanelli, Ubaldo Toffanetti. Conductor: Franco Capuana.

SYNOPSIS. A young tramp (tenor) arrives at a country inn. He talks a lot and is very self-confident. All the people there – Olimpio (baritone), the inn-keeper, and his wife Fortuna (contralto), their daughter Lucilla (soprano) and the customers – are struck by a tiny golden cage that a young man shows them. The new arrival, whose name is Lupo Fiorentino, claims that he keeps a golden flea in the cage which has come from a mysterious distant country, and which can turn anything that it bites into gold, except food. Old Verna (bass) is incredulous and the others are fascinated. Lupo opens the cage to demonstrate, but the flea escapes and soon afterwards Lucilla screams that she has been bitten. After discussing the matter they decide that Lupo Fiorentino had better watch over the girl while she sleeps in a sack. Olimpio places himself outside the door to make sure that nothing happens to Lucilla and that the boy does not disappear with his precious flea. During the night everyone makes wild plans about getting rich by possessing the amazing flea. Lupo Fiorentino comes downstairs in the dark and is about to leave when Olimpio hits him over the head with a club and he falls to the ground. Thinking that he is dead, Olimpio and the others carry him into the street. Old Verna wants to tell the police of the crime, but Olimpio ties him to a table. Just then Lupo Fiorentino staggers in, covered in blood-stains, thinking he has been struck for seducing the girl, and saying he wants to marry her. She is quite happy about this idea and the two go off together. The story of the flea will remain a mystery: was it true or did Lupo invent it to get near Lucilla?

ROMEO UND JULIA

Opera in two acts and six scenes by Heinrich Sutermeister (born 1910), libretto by the composer, based on Shakespeare's tragedy (in Schlegel's translation). First performance: Dresden, Staatsoper, 13 April 1940. Conductor at first performance: Karl Böhm.

■ This is the Swiss composer's first work for the stage and in places, betrays the influence of Verdi's late works.

VOLO DI NOTTE (Night Flight)

Opera in one act by Luigi Dallapiccola (1904–75), libretto by the composer, based on the novel Vol de Nuit *(1931) by Antoine de Saint-Exupéry. First performance: Florence, Teatro della Pergola, Maggio musicale, 18 May 1940. First performance in U.K.: Glasgow, 29 May 1963; in U.S.A.: Palo Alto, California, 1 March 1962.*

ORIGINAL CAST. Maria Fiorenza (Mme Fabien), Francesco Valentino (Rivière), Antonio Melandri (radiotelegraphist), Pauli (Pellerin), Baldini (Leroux), Vincenzo Guicciardi (Robineau). Conductor: Fernando Previtali.

SYNOPSIS. The story takes place in the office of a flying company at Buenos Aires airport around 1930.

The Director, Rivière (bass-baritone), who plans dangerous night flights, is waiting for three aeroplanes to return. Meanwhile he chats with an old squadron leader, Leroux (bass), and tells him that he has renounced the pleasures of life in order to discover new means of communication. The plane from Chile arrives safely, having escaped a cyclone. But bad news comes from the Patagonian plane. We learn, via the radiotelegraphist, that he is in difficulties due to bad weather conditions. Fabien, the pilot, signals that he is in danger as he only has enough petrol for half an hour's flying. Simone Fabien (soprano), his wife comes in, anxious at her husband's lateness. The radiotelegraphist again makes contact with Fabien and receives his desperate messages until at last the aeroplane plunges into the sea. Meanwhile the third plane has landed (from Paraguay) and the news of Fabien's death speads around the airport. The workmen protest against the dangers of the night flights and pour into Rivière's office, demanding an end to them. Coldly and calmly he orders a plane to leave for Europe. One must not stop because of an accident, he says, not even a tragic one, for the future of flying is at stake. The men are overwhelmed by Rivière's relentless will and withdraw slowly, pronouncing his name with respect. Having won his painful battle, Rivière returns to his work as usual.

■ *Volo di Notte* is Dallapiccola's first work for the stage. The theme is the dramatic confrontation between man and technical progress. The score is influenced by Schönberg's expressionism, but also maintains links with Dallapiccola's earlier polyphonic and monodic compositions. He first wrote a preparatory study for the music called *Tre laudi* (1936–37). This was the first time dodecaphonic music was used in Italian opera.

SEMYON KOTKO

Opera in five acts by Sergei Prokofiev (1891–1953), libretto by the composer, based on a tale by V. Katayev, with whom he collaborated. First performance: Moscow, Opernyi Teatr Stanislavsky, 30 June 1940.

SYNOPSIS. At the end of the first world war, a young farmer called Semyon Kotko goes home to his native village in the southern Ukraine. Everything has been changed and upset by the war, and power is in the hands of the Soviet, who establish order in accordance with the revolutionary principles. Remenyuk and a sailor called Tsaryov, the Soviet's representatives, divide the land and cattle equally between the people. Semyon has his share and, fortified by this new wealth, he asks Thatchenko, a rich land-owner, for the hand of his daughter Sonia, whom he loves. But her father wants a better match for her and consents unwillingly. Meanwhile a German detachment arrives to attack the village. They hang Tsaryov and, urged on by Thatchenko, who hopes in this way to get rid of the young man as a future son-in-law, they burn down Semyon's house. Semyon however escapes from the flames and together with Remenyuk he organizes a group of resistance fighters to liberate the country. He returns in time to prevent Sonia's marriage to Klembovski, a rich man her father had found for her.

■ The wealth of this opera lies mainly in Prokofiev's ability to express the contrast between the calm, happy life of a remote little Ukrainian village and the cruel events which succeed one another with tragic brutality. However *Semyon Kotko* was the start of the misfortunes which beset Prokofiev's professional life. It was accused of formalism, as Shostakovich's *Lady Macbeth of Mtsensk* had been.

L'OMBRA DI DON GIOVANNI (Don Giovanni's Shadow)

Opera in three acts and four scenes by Franco Alfano (1876–1954), libretto by E. Moschino. First performance: Milan, Teatro alla Scala, 2 April 1941. A revised version was performed on 28 May 1941 during the Maggio musicale fiorentino, entitled Don Juan de Mañara.

■ The opera marks Alfano's return to the stage after a period of writing exclusively symphonic music. A characteristic feature is the role of the chorus, which at times takes a leading part in the dramatic unfurling of the story.

I CAPRICCI DI CALLOT (The Fantasies of Callot)

Opera in a prologue and three acts by Gian Francesco Malipiero (1882–1973), libretto by the composer. First performance: Rome, Opera, 24 October 1942.

SYNOPSIS. The Carnival is announced by four pairs of masked dancers. Giacinta, a dressmaker, gets ready to take part by sewing herself a magnificent dress, which she hopes will stun her fiancé Giglio, a penniless actor. The Carnival is in full swing in a Roman street. Amongst the masked figures are also a little old man and a charlatan, who first play a joke on the two lovers and end by celebrating their marriage at a sumptuous feast.

■ The opera is considered by the critics to be a successful combination of Malipiero's sense of the unreal and fantastic with E. T. A. Hoffmann's *Prinzessin Brambilla* and with the 24 etchings *Balli di Sfessani* by Jacques Callot (1592–1635). In the words of Domenico de Paoli, 'the music is an irresistible, uninterrupted melody which goes from voice to instrument and back to voice and bounces back to the orchestra, not altogether unlike the "panels" of his first period, but with a close counterpoint between the music and the story in which each supports the other whilst maintaining its own autonomy. The music is often used to emphasize the story and, above all, to give character to the solo parts.'

CAPRICCIO
Conversation piece for music in one act by Richard Strauss (1864–1949), libretto by Clemens Krauss (1893–1954). First performance: Munich Nationaltheater, 28 October 1942. First performance in U.K.: London, Covent Garden (by Bavarian State Opera) 22 September 1953; in U.S.A.: Santa Fé, 1 August 1958.

ORIGINAL CAST. Viorica Ursuleac (Madeleine),

Friedenstag *by Richard Strauss at the Munich Nationaltheater in 1938; sets and costumes by Ludwig Sievert, produced by Rudolf Hartmann.*

Horst Taubmann (Flamand), Hans Hotter (Olivier), Georg Hann (La Roche), Walter Höfermayer (Count), Hildegard Ranczak (Clarion). Conductor: Clemens Krauss.

SYNOPSIS. A château on the outskirts of Paris about 1775. The beautiful widowed Countess Madeleine (soprano) listens in her drawing-room to a string sextet (used also as an overture to the opera) which the composer Flamand (tenor), her protegé, has dedicated to her. Flamand and the tragic poet Olivier (baritone), his rival for the Countess's love, observe her reactions to the music from a window. Dozing in an armchair is the impresario, La Roche (bass), who is going to stage Olivier's tragedy in the castle theatre for the Countess's birthday. A short discussion arising from Gian Battista Casti's play *Prima la Musica e poi le Parole*, takes place between the composer and the poet, each defending the superiority of his own art form. La Roche interrupts to put forward the claims of the theatrical performance. The Count (baritone), brother to the Countess, has a part in the forthcoming tragedy and rehearses the main scene with the famous actress Clairon (mezzo-soprano), with whom he is in love. (His declaration of love is actually a translation of a poem of Ronsard's, *Je ne sçaurois aimer autre que vous*.) Flamand is seized by inspiration and sets the poem to music, while Olivier takes advantage of this to declare his love to Madeleine. Flamand returns to sing the sonnet at the harpsichord and declares his own love as soon as Olivier is called away for rehearsals. The Countess is agitated, but escapes his pressing demands by promising her answer next morning at eleven o'clock. A dancer's performance offers the opportunity to revert to their discussion of priority among the arts. The Impresario introduces two Italian singers, who perform a duet to words by Metastasio. La Roche announces that the entertainment to be presented for the Countess will be a sublime allegory entitled 'The Birth of Pallas Athene'. Everyone is highly amused and rude about it at first and the Countess elicits from La Roche that it is to be followed by a heroic-dramatic spectacle, 'The Fall of Carthage'. The Impresario makes a heated defence of theatre, which requires characters of more passion, and music of greater drama, than either Olivier or Flamand can produce. The Count suggests that Flamand and Olivier should accept the challenge by writing an opera about the arguments of all those then present in the château, and that the characters should be the people now in the room. It is a moment of intense emotion; the frontiers between reality and theatre have been broken down. All the guests leave for Paris and the servants clear up. The prompter, who has been asleep, wakes up and almost convinces the butler that without him there could be no theatre. The Countess, elegantly dressed, comes into the empty room. She has made a date with both Flamand and Olivier for the next morning, at the same time and in the same place, but she has not yet decided what answer to give them. 'If I choose one, I lose the other. Can one win without losing?' Supper is announced.

■ The idea underlying *Capriccio*, Strauss's last opera, may have been first suggested to him by Stefan Zweig who, in January 1934, had called his attention to a strange libretto. 'First the music and then the words', written by Casti for an opera by Mozart's rival Salieri (see p. 94 above). The idea was adopted and abandoned several times until it finally found fruition in a collaboration between the composer and the conductor Clemens Krauss. The opera is especially noteworthy for the clear audibility of the text – in itself quite a good one – which was partly written by Strauss himself. The need to understand the words during the performance of an opera was in fact a problem that obsessed Strauss throughout a large part of his working life. The Countess is the centre of the opera; she represents a personification of opera, a source of inspiration and a synthesis of poetry and music. In this way the choice facing Madeleine is exactly that of the operatic composer and in her honour he has collected together fragments from his favourite operas.

CATULLI CARMINA (Poems of Catullus)
Scenic cantata in three sections by Carl Orff (born 1895), text taken from poems of the Latin poet Gaius Valerius Catullus (87–54 B.C.). First performance: Leipzig, Stadttheater, 6 November 1943. First performance in U.S.A.: (concert version) Los Angeles, June 1955; (staged) Katonah, New York State, 26 June 1964.

SYNOPSIS. Old people are sceptical about the love affairs and the vows of eternal fidelity in which the young indulge. They tell them to think twice and make them listen to the songs of Catullus. Now the stage play starts. Scene I. Catullus and Lesbia sing hymns to life and love. Catullus rests his head in Lesbia's lap and goes to sleep. Soon the lovers appear and Lesbia leaves Catullus to join them. When the poet wakes up he despairs at Lesbia's sudden betrayal, after she had sworn shortly before that she would never leave him. Catullus is consoled by his friend Caelus. Scene II. The poet is sleeping near Lesbia's house. He dreams of Lesbia's embrace and, remembering her loving promises, hopes that they will not prove to be false. While he is pondering on this, he notices Lesbia flirting with Caelus. He curses her ingratitude and that of all women. Scene III. Catullus meets a beautiful girl called Ipsitilla and begs her to invite him to her house. Ammiana comes along and charges him ten thousand sesterces for the rendez-vous. He chases her away and sets out once more to look for Lesbia amongst the whores and lovers. She calls to him, but he forces himself not to listen to her and with a great effort, sends her away. although he still loves her and only her. He will never be able to cease loving Lesbia despite all her faults, but her behaviour makes it impossible for them to marry. Lesbia rushes into her house in despair. This is the end of the stage play. The boys and girls continue to swear eternal faithfulness and undying love to each other, having stopped watching the performance a long time before. The old people are depressed and complain sadly.

■ This opera is the second part of the Trilogy *I trionfi*, which also includes *Carmina Burana* and *Trionfo d' Afrodite* (see pp. 437 and 464).

THE GAMBLER (Igrok)
Opera by Dmitri Shostakovich (1906–75), libretto based on Dostoievsky.

■ The opera dates from 1943, but is incomplete and has never been performed. This is most probably due to the composer's discouragement at the criticisms which were made of his opera *Lady Macbeth*. For the plot see Prokofiev's opera, p. 412.

PETER GRIMES
Opera in a prologue, epilogue and three acts by Benjamin Britten (1913–76), libretto by Montagu Slater, based on George Crabbe's poem The Borough *(1810). First performance: London, Sadler's Wells Theatre, 7 June 1945. First performance in U.S.A.: Berkshire Festival, Tanglewood, Mass., 9 August 1946.*

ORIGINAL CAST. Joan Cross (Ellen Orford), Peter Pears (Grimes), Edith Coates (Auntie), Minnie Bower and Blanche Turner (Nieces), Valetta Jacopi (Mrs Sedley), Owen Brannigan (Swallow), Edmund Donleevy (Ned), Roderick Jones (Balstrode), Morgan Jones (Boles). Conductor: Reginald Goodall.

SYNOPSIS. This story is set in The Borough, a small fishing-town in East Anglia. The time: around 1830. The moot hall. At the end of the inquest on Peter Grimes's apprentice, Swallow (bass), the magistrate, brings in a verdict of accidental death, but advises Grimes (tenor) to take on no more boy apprentices. Grimes is by no means satisfied, and would like to be fully exonerated of all suspicion. Only Ellen Orford (soprano), the schoolmistress, remains to comfort him. Act I, Scene I. The beach and street. Grimes discovers how hard it is to work his boat single-handed. Ned Keene (baritone) tells him he has found him a new apprentice, an orphan from the workhouse, and Ellen, against the villagers' general opinion, offers to go with Carter Hobson (bass) to fetch him. A storm blows up and all the fishermen hasten to haul their boats and their nets into shelter. Captain Balstrode (baritone) suggests that Grimes would be well advised to leave the Borough but the fisherman replies that he will shut the mouths of the gossips with money. Scene II. Inside The Boar, towards evening. The storm is still raging, and the inn is crowded. Grimes enters, distraught, and

Malipiero's I capricci di Callot *at the Opera in Rome, 1942.*

everyone thinks he is drunk when he sings a visionary aria about the mystery of the heavens and of life. The fisherman and Methodist Boles (tenor) inveighs against him and calls him a child-murderer. Ellen arrives with the boy who is to be Peter's new apprentice, describing the terrible journey they have had. Without giving him time to warm himself, Peter grabs the boy and takes him home through the storm. Act II, Scene I. On the beach, some weeks later. Ellen and the new apprentice are sitting on the beach while the Sunday service takes place in the church. The boy's clothes are torn and his body is covered in bruises. They are joined by Peter, who has heard that there is a shoal of fish and wants to set sail at once. Ellen insists that he should allow the boy to rest at least on a Sunday, and a quarrel ensues. When the congregation come out of the service they soon hear that Ellen has quarrelled with Grimes, and in great indignation the men of the town decide to visit Grimes's hut to see what is going on. Scene II. The interior of Grimes's hut, an upturned old boat. Grimes tries awkwardly to comfort the sobbing boy. Then he hears the procession of townsmen approaching and hastily bundles him and all the tackle out of the back door, which leads directly to the cliff-

top. The boy, terrified and hampered by the tackle, loses his footing and falls to his death. The villagers enter only to find the hut empty and tidy. Act III. The beach and street at night. There is a dance at the moot hall. Neither Grimes nor his apprentice has been seen for several days, and it is thought that they are both out fishing, but Mrs Sedley (mezzo-soprano), a rich widow and a gossip who prides herself on having a nose for scandal, overhears Balstrode tell Ellen that the boat has returned. Ellen is horrified to recognize the sweater she had knitted for the apprentice as the one washed up on the beach. On the basis of this information, Mrs Sedley rouses Swallow (who is enjoying the company of one of Auntie's 'nieces' at The Boar) and orders a search, which takes the terrifying form of a manhunt for Grimes, the outsider of the community. Ellen and Balstrode find Grimes soaked and exhausted, wandering half-deranged in the fog. Balstrode quietly advises him to take the boat out to sea and sink it. He helps Peter to push the boat out, and then takes Ellen away. It is dawn. The town is stirring, lights come on in the windows. People make their way to work. Someone says that a boat is sinking out at sea, but nobody takes any notice.

■ With this opera Britten gained international recognition as a composer. In London, *Peter Grimes* was hailed with great enthusiasm, the more so as it was first performed in 1945 (to mark the reopening of the Sadler's Wells Theatre), and people felt that at last it was possible to devote themselves to the things they had for so long had to neglect. The opera was commissioned by the Koussevitzky Music Foundation, and to this day it remains one of Britten's most powerful operas, as well as the work that re-established English music on an international level. The musical language incorporates elements of diverse origins. Preludes and interludes have since been adapted to form a suite entitled *Four sea interludes from Peter Grimes*.

THE MEDIUM
Opera in two acts by Gian Carlo Menotti (born 1911), libretto by the composer. First performance: New York, Barrymore Theater, 8 May 1946 (private performance); first performance in U.K.: London, Aldwych, 29 April 1948. From 18 February 1947 it was often performed together with The Telephone.

SYNOPSIS. The action takes place in the present, in the U.S.A. Act I. Madame Flora (Baba), (contralto), helped by her daughter Monica (soprano) and by the mute Toby, lives by tricking people with her supposed gifts as a medium. A séance is about to begin: Baba pretends to go into a trance, while Monica, garbed in floating white veils, appears in a bluish light for Mrs Nolan (mezzo-soprano), who has lost a daughter, and then, concealed behind a curtain, imitates the gentle laughter of a little girl, which sounds to the Gobineau couple (soprano and baritone) like the laughter of their dead child. The séance comes to an end when Flora leaps up with a sudden shriek: a frozen hand has clutched her by the throat. She orders her clients to leave and then accuses Toby of playing a cruel joke on her. Monica calms her, but again she hears childish shouts and laughter. Monica soothes her by singing a sweet lullaby. Act II. Monica and Toby are playing quietly together. Flora bursts in, drunk, accuses Toby again and whips him furiously. The clients return, but Flora no longer wants to keep up the pretence and offers them their money back. They refuse it, saying that their visions were quite real. Then she forces Toby to leave also, in spite of Monica's pleas. She falls asleep. Toby creeps back into the room, but finding the door to Monica's room is locked, he hides. Baba stirs in her sleep and then awakes to see a curtain fluttering. She grasps a pistol and fires: a red bloodstain spreads over the curtain and the lifeless body of Toby falls to the floor. Flora cries that she has killed the ghost and Monica beats wildly on the door to be let in.

■ Composed at the request of the Alice M. Ditson Foundation of Columbia University, the opera was an enormous success and Menotti himself directed a film version.

WAR AND PEACE (Voina y Mir)
Opera in five acts and thirteen scenes by Sergei Prokofiev (1891–1953), libretto by the author in collaboration with Mira Mendelson, based on the novel by Tolstoy. First performance: (original version) heavily cut, Moscow, 7 June 1945; (first eight scenes only) Leningrad, Maly Theatre, 12 June 1946. First performance in U.K.: (concert version) Leeds Festival 1967; (staged version) London Coliseum (Sadler's Wells Company) 1972; in U.S.A.: N.B.C. TV, New York, 1957.

SYNOPSIS. The story is set in Russia at the beginning of the nineteenth century. Part I. Natalya Rostova (Natasha) (soprano) catches the attention of the young widower Prince Andrei Bolkonsky (baritone) when he visits the estate of her father Count Rostov (bass). He is introduced to her again by his friend, the wealthy and unconventional Pierre Bezukhov (tenor) at a ball in St Petersburg. His father, the old Prince Nikolai (bass-baritone), opposes the match and the marriage is postponed for a year while Andrei leaves Natasha to make sure of her love for him. Pierre's wife Hélène (mezzo-soprano) provides her brother Anatol (tenor) with an opportunity to turn Natasha's head with the promise of elopement. Anatol celebrates his success before leaving his gipsy girl and friends to collect Natasha. Her cousin Sonya (mezzo-soprano), however, has divulged the secret to their hostess, old Maria Akhrosimova (contralto), who stops the scheme. Pierre tries to comfort Natasha, declaring that, were he young enough and free, he would beg for her hand. She, in despair, asks him to explain everything to Andrei, and to ask for his forgiveness although their engagement is over. Pierre berates Anatol for his infamy, denouncing his (and his own wife's) immorality, and concludes that their whole society is futile. Part II. 25 August 1812. Borodino. Andrei bitterly recalls his love for Natasha when he meets Pierre, who has come to watch the battle. They part, thinking they will never meet again. Prince Kutuzov (bass), commander-in-chief of the Russians, invites Andrei to join his staff, but Andrei prefers to serve in the front line. Napoleon (baritone) contemplates the outcome of the battle and the fate of Moscow. Kutuzov orders the retreat and the city is set on fire by its citizens before they leave; the Rostovs have fled, with the wounded. Pierre is arrested as an incendiary and Napoleon reflects on the strength of the Russian resistance. Andrei was among the wounded at Borodino and is close to death when Natasha discovers him in a peasant hut far from Moscow. They recall their love for each other, and their first meeting, before he dies in her arms. The French have begun a retreat from Moscow in midwinter, taking with them their prisoners, including Pierre. The convoy is attacked by Russians and Pierre hears that, while victory is theirs and Natasha is safe, Andrei is dead. Kutuzov arrives and a chorus greet him with a final great acclamation of the Russian spirit.

■ The opera was first given in concert form in Moscow, at the Writers' Club, on 16 October 1944. The first stage performance in 1946, covered only the first eight scenes. The definitive version, greatly enlarged, was a posthumous performance in 1955. It is a work of great breadth and admirably synthesizes Tolstoy's intent to show the struggle of the Russian people against the invader and at the same time the private life of the main characters.

THE RAPE OF LUCRETIA

Opera in two acts by Benjamin Britten (1913–76), libretto by Ronald Duncan, based on Le viol de Lucrèce *by André Obey (1931) and on passages from the works of Livy, Shakespeare, Nathaniel Lee, Thomas Heywood and F. Ponsard. First performance: Glyndebourne, 12 July 1946; first performance in U.S.A.: Chicago, 1 June 1947.*

SYNOPSIS. The action is narrated by a Male Chorus (tenor) and a Female Chorus (soprano). Rome is ruled by the Etruscan upstart Tarquinius Superbus (baritone), who is on a campaign and making merry and discussing with his generals Collatinus (bass) and Junius (baritone) their bet of the night before, when they had paid a surprise visit to their wives in Rome. Only Lucretia, the wife of Collatinus, was found virtuously at home. Junius is furious with jealousy and taunts Tarquinius that not even he would try to dishonour such chastity. The King furtively leaves the tent and rides to Rome. He finds Lucretia (soprano) quietly spinning with her attendant Lucia (soprano) and nurse Bianca (contralto). Tarquinius is offered hospitality for the night. Act II. During the night he enters Lucretia's bedroom, threatens her at sword point and rapes her. The following morning she sends a messenger to summon Collatinus. After telling her husband how she has been raped, she stabs herself. The Chorus draws from the story a Christian moral.

■ *The Rape of Lucretia* had great success; it had been performed eighty times by October 1946. In this opera for the first time Britten drastically reduced the number of participants: it is scored for fifteen orchestral players and eight singers. By this pioneering approach Britten aimed to solve the problems attached to staging expensive operas.

Carl Seydel (Monsieur Taupe) in Capriccio *by Richard Strauss at the Munich Nationaltheater, October 1942; sets and costumes by Rochus Gliese, directed by Rudolf Hartmann.*

THE BETROTHAL IN A MONASTERY (Obrucenie v monastyre)

Opera in four acts by Sergei Prokofiev (1891–1953), libretto by the author in collaboration (for the part in verse) with Mira Mendelson, based on Sheridan's The Duenna. *First performance: Leningrad, Kirov Theatre, 30 November 1946; first performance in U.K.: B.B.C., 1963 (recording of Stanislavsky Theatre, Moscow); in U.S.A.: New York, Greenwich Mews Playhouse, 1948 (as* The Duenna*).*

SYNOPSIS. Seville, in the eighteenth century. Don Jerome (tenor), wealthy and highly respected, has a daughter and a son: Louisa (soprano) and Ferdinando (baritone). He concludes a business agreement to sell fish in the city with old Mendoza (bass), by promising him his daughter in marriage. Louisa, however, loves Antonio (tenor), a handsome but impoverished young man, while her duenna, Margaret (contralto), has her eye on Mendoza. Ferdinando, for his part, loves Clara d'Almanzo (mezzo-soprano), who returns his love. From these sentiments the plot unfolds. Louisa and her duenna together hatch a plan and Louisa manages to escape from home in disguise as Margaret. She runs into Clara, herself in the midst of an elopement with Antonio, and which she half-heartedly wants to stop by seeking refuge in the Convent of St Catherine. In order to avoid Mendoza's attentions Louisa pretends to be Clara and asks Mendoza to take a love letter to Antonio for her. The old man, unaware of the deception, returns with the youth, after first paying a call at Don Jerome's house, where he met the duenna and took her for Louisa; (by flattery, Margaret enticed him to propose their elopement). The plot speedily thickens:

all' meet at a monastery, where a duel between Antonio and Ferdinando, who have also been deceived, is narrowly averted. At Don Jerome's house that evening, everything is explained. The four young people have contrived to marry in accordance with their own wishes, and the old father has to accept that, while his daughter married a pauper, his son has married a fabulously rich girl, and gives his blessing to them both.

■ This is one of Prokofiev's best operatic works: in it the composer gives expression to both his lyrical and humorous gifts. Mira Mendelson, who collaborated with him on the text, became his wife after the composer's divorce from Lina Ljubera.

L'ORO (Gold)

Opera in three acts by Ildebrando Pizzetti (1880–1968), libretto by the composer. First performance: Milan, Teatro alla Scala, 2 January 1947.

ORIGINAL CAST. Antonio Annaloro, Mercedes Fortunati, Cesare Siepi, Eraldo Coda. Conductor: Ildebrando Pizzetti.

SYNOPSIS. The story takes place in an indeterminate period, presumably close to the present day. Giovanni dei Neri (tenor), a rich landowner, has revolutionized his farming methods, thereby causing discontent among the farm workers. The most discontented of them go in a group to Giovanni, but they are reassured when he tells them that he is acting for the good of all. Shortly afterwards Martino (bass or baritone), a servant, arrives with information that traces of gold have been found nearby. The news travels swiftly and the peasants ask Giovanni's help in locating the gold. Christina (soprano), however, the wife whom Giovanni had married abroad and who has borne him a son who is dumb, is oppressed with gloomy forebodings and urges her husband to leave the place. The peasants are angry; they are suspicious of one another and above all they doubt the loyal collaboration of their employer. Christina begs Giovanni to give up this dream of easy riches, but he confides to her that he has found a cave full of gold, although he does not want to blow up the rock for fear of being buried beneath the rubble. The peasants seize Martino, demanding to know whether Giovanni has found gold. As his employer rushes to his assistance, a blast is heard: Christina has blown up the cave, to prevent gold fever from causing fighting and bloodshed among the people. Giovanni in despair decides to leave: meanwhile a group of peasants arrive carrying Christina, who has been fatally injured by a falling rock. At the sight of his dying mother, her son is so profoundly shocked that he recovers his power of speech. Christina dies serenely, in the knowledge that her sacrifice has brought amity among the peasants, who decide to return to work in the fields.

■ Pizzetti worked on this opera from 1939 to 1942. The novelty of the work consists in the portrayal of a social drama that takes place in the present day, but is much closer in spirit to works set in the past than might at first appear. The seed of this opera can already be found in *Lena* (1905), which is also inspired by a peasant theme.

THE TELEPHONE, or L'AMOUR À TROIS

Opera buffa in one act by Gian Carlo Menotti (born 1911), libretto by the composer. First performance: New York, Hecksher Theater, 18 February 1947; first performance in U.K.: London, Aldwych, 29 April 1948.

SYNOPSIS. The story is set in Lucy's apartment. Ben (baritone) is about to go away, but first he calls on Lucy (soprano) to bring her a gift, an abstract sculpture. 'Just what I've always wanted,' says Lucy in her careless, empty-headed way. Ben is on the point of saying something more important to her when the telephone rings: it is one of Lucy's girl friends, and she settles down for a long gossip. Eventually Ben seems to have an opportunity to broach the subject, but he is again foiled by the telephone ringing. This time it's a wrong number. Ben is growing anxious about the time he is wasting, since he must soon leave, but Lucy simply picks up the telephone to check the time. Ben makes another attempt to make his speech, but once again he is interrupted by the telephone: this time it is George who is ringing to complain to Lucy about some piece of

Costume designs for the first production of Britten's Peter Grimes *at Sadler's Wells, London, 1945.*

gossip. Lucy is in tears, and goes to get a handkerchief. Ben is on the point of cutting the wires in sheer exasperation when the telephone 'as if crying for help', shrills once more, and Lucy comes running to its rescue. She is still so upset at George's remarks that she simply has to unburden herself to her friend Pamela. She is so carried away by the conversation that she doesn't notice that Ben has left until she finally puts the phone down. But the telephone rings again: this time it is Ben who, in desperation, had been driven to making his proposal by telephone. 'Take a note of my number and call me every day,' concludes Lucy.

■ Performed together with *The Medium*, in accordance with the old custom of coupling a comic opera together with a tragic opera, both were an immediate and resounding success, further confirmed by the 211 performances given on Broadway at the Barrymore Theater, in the space of seven months starting in May the same year.

LES MAMELLES DE TIRÉSIAS (The Breasts of Tiresias)

Opéra bouffe in a prologue and two acts by Francis Poulenc (1899–1963), libretto by Guillaume Apol- linaire *(1903). First performance: Paris, Opéra-Comique, 3 June 1947; first performance in U.K.: Aldeburgh, 16 June 1958; in U.S.A.: Brandeis University, Mass., 13 June 1953.*

ORIGINAL CAST. Denise Duval, Paul Sayen, Emile Rousseau, Robert Jeanbeat. Conductor: M. Erte.

SYNOPSIS. A character in the part of the Theatre Director (baritone) explains to the audience that in this opera the author has resolved to reform modern habits, reminding woman of her sacred duties of submission and fertility. The story begins. It takes place in Zanzibar, where Thérèse (soprano) complains to her husband (tenor) about the life she leads: she always has to take care of the home and the children, and moreover must continually go on bearing children, so that her job is never ending. She declares that she wants to do something more important: to be a general or a politician. Determined to deny her womanhood, she opens her blouse and out fly two balloons, representing her breasts. She feels a beard sprout on her chin, strikes a masculine pose and changes her name to Tirésias. The husband in his turn is obliged to dress as a woman and Tirésias leads him through a crowd which has gathered to watch a fight between two drunks, who end by killing one another. His wife's arrogant manners soon weary the husband and, his patience at an end, he tears off his woman's clothes and declares that if his wife no longer wants to bear children then he, with his own special method, will produce as many as he wants all by himself. The onlookers are astounded and even the two drunks revive to watch the strange happening. Within a very short time the husband brings 40,000 children into the world, some of them already fully grown and therefore able to earn money. A policeman is very worried about this state of affairs: if he cannot put a stop to this man's magic arts there will soon be too many mouths to feed and the economy of Zanzibar will be grievously affected. In the presence of all the people he seeks the advice of a fortune-teller, but her answers appear to be an attack on his sterility and he finds himself almost strangled by her, but for the intervention of the husband, who discovers that she is none other than Thérèse. She repents her folly and begs her husband's forgiveness, while various pairs of lovers declare that everyone needs to love, to be loved, and to bring children into the world.

■ From this surrealist drama written by Apollinaire in 1903 (apart from the Paris performance in 1947, performed only once in Milan in 1963) Poulenc has created a real and very French comic opera, in which the lively text (full of double meanings and racy expressions) is matched by a subtly sensual score, based on a highly effective harmonic language.

ALBERT HERRING
Opera in three acts by Benjamin Britten (1913–76), libretto by Eric Crozier (born 1914), based on a short story by Guy de Maupassant: Le rosier de Madame Husson *(1888). First performance: Glyndebourne, 20 June 1947; in U.S.A.: Tanglewood, 1949.*

ORIGINAL CAST. Joan Cross (Lady Billows), Peter Pears (Albert), Frederick Sharp (Sid), Nancy Evans (Nancy), Betsy de la Porte (Mrs Herring). Conducted by the composer.

SYNOPSIS. The action takes place in Loxford, a picturesque market town in Suffolk, in the spring of 1900. Act I, Scene I. The breakfast room in the house of Lady Billows (soprano), an austere and virtuous lady who takes it upon herself to be the guardian of the town's morals. A committee of local notables is meeting to elect a May Queen, a contest organized by Lady Billows with the intention of combating the town's moral decadence. Painstaking research reveals, alas, that no girl is worthy of the honour, and it is therefore decided to elect a 'May King' in the person of young Albert Herring (tenor), a boy as 'pure as new-mown hay', who has been brought up very strictly by his mother, a greengrocer. Scene II. Mrs Herring's shop. The committee members come to announce their decision. When they have left, the mother (contralto) rejoices. The young man himself is reluctant to accept the honour, but when he objects his mother sends him to

his room in disgrace. Act II, Scene I. The vicarage garden. A table is laid for the banquet that is to follow the May Queen festival. Sid (tenor), a friend of Albert's, has added a good measure of rum to Albert's lemonade for a joke: speeches are made, and Albert is presented with his prize money of £25. Scene II. Mrs Herring's shop. Albert returns home rather fuddled, singing. He overhears Sid and Nancy (soprano) saying how sorry they are for him that he is so much under his mother's thumb. With sudden resolve he sets out with his prize money to find out what he has been missing. Act III. Mrs Herring's shop. The next afternoon everyone is talking of Albert's disappearance, and every search has been in vain. In a lane outside Loxford his coronet of orange blossom has been found, all trampled and dirty. It seems certain that the young man must be dead, but just then Albert arrives, grubby and dishevelled. He has spent three pounds on beer, whisky, rum and gin. Unperturbed by the hail of rebukes he says that it is his mother who is to blame for the repressive upbringing she had given him. The young people cheer him, but the committee and the authorities retire in indignation, while his mother has a fit of hysterics.

■ By exchanging the setting from Normandy, where Maupassant's story takes place, to Suffolk in the Victorian age, where the opera is set, the story has lost some of its verve; it has, however, been skilfully adapted, in word if not in spirit. Like Britten's other operas, *Albert Herring* is scored for a very small orchestra: only twelve instruments. The work was written for the English Opera Group, a group started by Britten himself with the aim of overcoming the organizational and financial problems involved in the production of both new operas and operas in the classical repertoire. With this work, which was applauded by both public and critics alike, Britten once again showed his talent for composing for the theatre by his skilful character portrayals aptly underlined by the various orchestral instruments. *Albert Herring* has also been acclaimed abroad, and not only in the English language.

DANTONS TOD (Danton's Death)
Opera in two acts by Gottfried von Einem (born 1918), libretto by the composer and Boris Blacher, based on the play by Georg Büchner (1835). First performance: Salzburg Festival, 6 August 1947; first performance in U.S.A.: New York City Opera, 9 March 1966.

ORIGINAL CAST. Paul Schöffler, Joseph Witt, Maria Cebotari, Julius Patzak. Conductor: Ferenc Fricsay.

SYNOPSIS. The action takes place in Paris in 1794. Act I, Scene I. The Gambling Rooms. Hérault de Séchelles (tenor) is playing cards with some ladies. Danton (baritone) talks to his wife Julie (mezzosoprano) and Deputy Camille Desmoulins (tenor).

Title-page by Steinberg of the score for Menotti's The Telephone.

The three politicians are concerned about Robespierre's autocratic tendencies and the excesses of the Reign of Terror. It would fall to Danton to oppose the majority of the Assembly who want to prolong the revolution, but he is sceptical about his real chances of changing the present course of events. Scene II. In the street, a private quarrel between Simon (bass), a theatrical prompter, and his wife (contralto) leads to a riot; a young aristocrat (tenor) who was passing by is in danger of being strung up by the mob because he has a handkerchief and addresses a citizen as 'Monsieur'. Robespierre (bass), member of the Committee of Public Safety, harangues the mob, pandering to them with a speech about the power of the people. Danton later reproaches him and Robespierre realizes that he must rid himself of such idealist collaborators as Danton and Desmoulins. Scene III. The two men are arrested and Desmoulins's wife Lucile (soprano) runs after them. Act II. The square in front of the Conciergerie prison. A crowd is arguing about the rights and wrongs of these arrests. Desmoulins cries out through the bars that he does not want to die and begs for his wife while Danton awaits his fate with resignation. Lucile arrives, demented with grief, and sings

with them a beautiful trio, soon drowned by the protests of other prisoners. Scene II. Before the Revolutionary Tribunal, Danton and his friends are accused by Herrmann (baritone), the President, of consorting with aristocrats. Fired by Danton's speech, some of the mob take their side, and disorder ensues. Danton publicly denounces the danger of impending dictatorship. The prisoners are taken away. Scene III. In the Square of the Revolution men and women await the arrival of the tumbrils of condemned men. Whatever the public reaction at the trial, the sentences were predetermined. Danton and his companions arrive singing the *Marseillaise*, but their voices are drowned by the shouting of the mob. When it is all over and the square is empty but for the executioners clearing up, Lucile arrives and sits weeping on the steps of the guillotine.

■ The opera was well received at the Salzburg Festival, not least because it came at the right moment: the Hitler dictatorship had not long come to an end. With this success, von Einem obtained a place on the organizing committee of the Festival. Büchner's text, which consisted of twenty-nine scenes, has been condensed into the six of the opera without betraying the original. In 1950 the composer made a new version of the work.

LE BACCANTI (The Bacchanal)
Opera in prologue, three acts and five scenes by Giorgio Federico Ghedini (1892–1965), libretto by Tullio Pinelli, based on the Bacchae *by Euripides. First performance: Milan, Teatro alla Scala, 21 February 1948.*

ORIGINAL CAST. Augusta Oltrabella (Agave), Piero Guelfi (Dionysus), Antonio Annaloro (Pentheus), Nino Carboni (Cadmus). Conductor: Fernando Previtali.

SYNOPSIS. Thebes is corrupted by the orgiastic and licentious behaviour that has accompanied the new religion, the cult of Dionysus. Even the prophet Tiresias (bass) is caught up in the new trend, and Agave (soprano), the queen herself, with her daughters and handmaidens has abandoned her mantle of royalty to follow the Bacchantes and Maenads in the streets of the city. Some follow suit, others flee. Pentheus (tenor), son of Agave, returns and is angered at what he finds. He demands to be taken before Dionysus (baritone) and tears the crown of vine-leaves from his head. The old King Cadmus (bass) tries to restrain him. Dionysus emerges laughing. Pentheus wants to call on the army to stop the Maenads from destroying everything. Dionysus exhorts him not to cause bloodshed; he himself will accompany him to confront the Maenads at Mount Cithaeron. When they reach the place, Dionysus incites the Maenads to be revenged on the man who has insulted their god. Pentheus calls out to his mother, but she does not recognize him. In the third Act, in a square in Thebes,

Jean Giraudeau, Reine Auphan and Michel Roux in Poulenc's Les mamelles de Tirésias *at the Opéra-Comique in Paris, 1972; sets and costumes by Jean-Denis Macles, produced by Louis Ducreux.*

Cadmus, supported by some elders, announces that he has had difficulty in collecting the pieces of Pentheus's body, which had been torn to shreds by the Maenads. Bacchantes and Maenads enter the square, led by Agave, who carries a thyrsus on which the head of Pentheus is impaled. At a shout from Cadmus the dance of jubilation is stopped. The old King commands Agave to come to her senses and realize what has happened. She slowly comes to grips with reality again, and swoons in horror. Dionysus appears, his thirst for vengeance still unslaked. He condemns Agave to wander the face of the earth until her death, and Cadmus to be turned into a dragon. In vain the Thebans plead to the god to have mercy.

■ Written between 1941 and 1943 and therefore a work of the composer's full maturity, in the *Baccanti* 'the spirit of Euripides' tragedy lives again in the magic of the sound and the voices, the Dionysian exaltation springs from the sound and fury of Ghedini's own musical genius'. (Piero Santi)

DOWN IN THE VALLEY
Folk opera by Kurt Weill (1900–50), libretto by A. Sundgaard. First performance: Bloomington, University of Indiana Theater, 15 July 1948.

THE STORY OF A REAL MAN (Povesto'o nastojaščem čeloveke)
Opera in four acts by Sergei Prokofiev (1891–1953), libretto by Mira Mendelson, after B. Polevoj. First per-

formance: Leningrad, Kirov Theatre, 3 December 1948.

■ A minor work by the composer of *The Love for the Three Oranges.*

IL CORDOVANO (The Cordoban)
Opera in one act by Goffredo Petrassi (born 1904), based on a play by Miguel de Cervantes, translated by Eugenio Montale. First performance: Milan, Teatro alla Scala, 12 May 1949.

ORIGINAL CAST. Emma Tegani, Dora Gatta, Jolanda Gardino, Franco Corena. Conductor: Nino Sanzogno.

SYNOPSIS. Donna Lorenza (soprano), the beautiful young wife of Cannizares (bass), is at home complaining of her husband's jealousy to her niece Cristina (soprano) and her neighbour Hortigosa (contralto). The two women persuade Lorenza to overcome her scruples and take a lover. Hortigosa promises that she will arrange everything, not forgetting Cristina's requirements. Thus it comes about that she smuggles a young man into the house hidden in a large rolled-up rug (a Cordoban rug). While Cannizares is inspecting the rug, the young man slips into Lorenza's bedroom and makes love to her. Lorenza gives voice to her happiness, singing the young man's praises. Cannizares at first thinks it is just a joke, but then unsuspectingly enters his wife's bedroom. She greets him by throwing a large basin at his head, and in the confusion the young man manages to escape. A watchman (baritone) comes running to see what all the noise is about; musicians and dancers enter, pretending to celebrate the reconciliation of the couple, but really celebrating the illicit union that will endure happily. Cristina complains aside that Hortigosa has not kept her promises to her too.

■ The opera faithfully follows the comic interlude by Cervantes entitled *The Jealous Old Man* (1615), itself an adaptation for the theatre of one of his own short stories. It is one of Petrassi's more complex and significant operas, with a wealth of allusion and psychological perception matched by the music.

LET'S MAKE AN OPERA!
Entertainment for young people in two parts (and three acts) by Benjamin Britten (1913–76), libretto by Eric Crozier (born 1914). First performance: Aldeburgh, 14 June 1949; first performance in U.S.A.: St Louis, 1951.

■ Part I. The subject is the rehearsal of an opera (*The Little Sweep*) by adults and children. Progress is discussed and parts are learned: the audience is also required to learn a part.

Britten's Albert Herring, *performed at Aldeburgh in 1962.*

THE LITTLE SWEEP
Part II of the children's opera Let's Make an Opera!

SYNOPSIS. The story, which is set in 1810, concerns the encounter of Sam, an eight-year-old apprentice sweep, with a group of children who live at Iken Hall in Suffolk. The children manage to set him free from his sweep-master, Black Bob.

■ Despite its lightheartedness, the opera conveys pity and indignation for the wretched condition of the boy sweep, condemned to an apprenticeship akin to slavery through the poverty of his parents. The practice of using small boys to sweep the most difficult and dangerous narrow sections of chimneys was still very common in England at the beginning of the nineteenth century. The cast numbers thirteen in all: seven children and six adults, a mixture of professionals and amateurs. Britten and Crozier had the brilliant idea of augmenting the number of amateurs by audience participation. The audience has to sing four pieces in the course of the opera: *The Sweep's Song* as an overture, *Sammy's Bath* and *The Night Song* as interludes between the scenes, and *Coaching Song* which forms the finale. But first the audience has to rehearse, and this is done in the first part, which was later revised by Crozier, who divided it into two acts to demonstrate the stages in the production of an opera: the conception, the words and the music. The orchestra is reduced to a bare minimum, as in Britten's other operas: in this case, four strings, piano and percussion (for only one player).

ANTIGONAE
Tragic play with music in one act by Carl Orff (born 1895), based on the tragedy by Sophocles (497–406 B.C.), translated by Friedrich Hölderlin. First performance: Salzburg, 9 August 1949.

ORIGINAL CAST. Res Fischers, Hermann Uhdes, Maria Ilosvay, Lorenz Fehenberger, Ernst Hafliger, Helmut Krebs, Joseph Greindl, Benno Kusche. Conductor: Ferenc Fricsay.

SYNOPSIS. Creon (baritone), King of Thebes, has forbidden, on pain of death, the burial of the body of Polynices, son of Oedipus, who had tried to occupy the city. His brother, Eteocles, had defended the city, and the two brothers had killed one another. Their sisters, Antigone (soprano) and Ismene (mezzo-soprano) are grief-stricken and in despair at the decree that forbids them to bury their rebel brother. Antigone decides to defy the wrath of Creon, but while burying Polynices she is caught by the watchman (tenor) and he drags her before the King. She declares that no human law can be above the law of love and charity. Creon condemns her to death even though Haemon (tenor), his son, who is betrothed to her, and Ismene try to persuade him to change his cruel decision. Creon remains unmoved until the soothsayer Tiresias (tenor) prophesies that if Creon perseveres in forbidding the burial of Polynices, great misfortunes will fall on his house. This causes Creon too late to decide that Antigone must be spared. A messenger (bass) announces that Creon has found his son Haemon clasping the corpse of Antigone in his arms. She has stabbed herself in despair. The tragic chain of events is to continue: Haemon kills himself, and when Creon brings the body of his son from Antigone's prison, blaming himself for his death, a messenger announces that his wife, Eurydice (soprano), has also committed suicide.

■ The opera is characterized by a sombre and monotonous orchestration: the orchestra has no strings other than the double bass, but includes a variety of percussion instruments. The voices are used perfectly to follow the rhythms of speech.

BILLY BUDD
Opera in one act by Giorgio Federico Ghedini (1892–1965), libretto by Salvatore Quasimodo (1901–68) based on the novel by Herman Melville, published posthumously in 1924. First performance: Venice, Teatro La Fenice, 8 September 1949 for the 12th International Festival of Contemporary Music.

For synopsis, see the opera of the same name by Benjamin Britten, p. 460.

■ The same theme was set to music by Benjamin Britten in 1951. Ghedini had conceived it as a 'stage oratorio'; it was later performed as a one-act opera.

THE OLYMPIANS

Opera in three acts by Arthur Bliss (1891–1975), libretto by J. B. Priestley. First performance: London, Covent Garden, 29 September 1949.

CAST. Margherita Grandi (Diana), Edith Coates (Mme Bardeau), James Johnston (Hector), Glynne (Lavette), Franklin (Mars). Conductor: Karl Rankl.

■ It tells the story of the gods of Olympus, no longer acknowledged and now reduced to poverty, living as strolling players. Each year, however, for one single night they are returned to their glorious past.

THE CONSUL

Musical drama in three acts by Gian Carlo Menotti (born 1911), libretto by the composer. First performance: Philadelphia, Shubert Theatre, 1 March 1950; first performance in the U.K.: London, Cambridge Theatre, 7 February 1951.

ORIGINAL CAST. Patricia Neway (Magda), Marie Powers (the Mother), Gloria Lane (the Secretary), Maria Marlo (the Foreign Woman), Cornell MacNeill (Sorel), Leon Lishner (Secret Police Agent) and Andrew McKinley (Magician). Conductor: Lehman Engel.

SYNOPSIS. Time: the present; a European city. Act I. Scene I. John Sorel (baritone) is a patriot fighting to free his country from a police régime. He returns to his apartment wounded after the police had interrupted a secret meeting, but manages to flee just in time when they come to arrest him. He tells his wife Magda (soprano) to visit the consulate of the country to which he wants to go, and to obtain the necessary papers for herself, their son and her mother (contralto). John will send any message to them through Assan, the glass-cutter. Scene II. Magda is in the waiting room at the consulate. Many people are waiting to see the Consul, but despite the pathetic nature of their cases the Secretary (mezzo-soprano) officiously keeps everyone out, distributing questionnaires and forms to be filled in. Among the applicants is a magician (tenor), who little by little involves everyone in his tricks, creating an atmosphere of unreality. Act II. Scene I. A month has passed and still Magda has no news of her husband. Nor, despite her numerous attempts, has she managed to speak to the Consul. Then at last the signal comes: a stone shatters a window pane, and Magda at once summons Assan (baritone). A secret agent (bass) who suddenly appears and questions Magda, regards Assan with suspicion. When they are alone, Assan informs the two women that John is still in the mountains, but refuses to cross the frontier until he is assured that his family will be able to join him. To add to their sorrows, the baby dies in his sleep while his grandmother is singing him a lullaby. Scene II. Some days later Magda is once more at the Consulate. The same people are

still waiting, and the magician has hypnotized them so that they are dancing round like automatons, much to the irritation of the Secretary. At last it is Magda's turn, but the Secretary asks for further documents: in her desperation, Magda breaks into a passionate tirade against a bureaucracy which lets men suffer and die because of its red tape. The Secretary is moved by her plea and finally agrees to let her see the Consul as soon as his 'important visitor' has left. This visitor is the Secret Police Agent; when she recognizes him Magda faints. Act III. Magda is at the Consulate. Assan hurries in to inform her that John knows that the baby has died and that her mother is dying, and has decided to return so that she will not be left alone. Magda writes to beg him not to return because he would certainly be arrested. Assan leaves, followed shortly by Magda. John arrives in search of his wife, followed by the secret agent, and, despite the Secretary's protests that they are violating the Consulate rules, he is allowed to go with them of his own accord. In desperation, the Secretary promises to help and telephones Magda. Scene II. Magda has returned home, intent on taking her own life to prevent John from running the risk of arrest for her sake. She shuts the doors and windows and turns on the gas. Through her confused thoughts, nightmare figures seem to surround her, while the telephone rings in vain that would have told her of John's arrest and the futility of her own suicide.

■ The opera was a resounding success: it remained in repertory at the same theatre for eight months and won the Pulitzer prize and the Drama Critic Award, was translated into twelve languages and performed in twenty countries.

L'ALLEGRA BRIGATA

Six tales in an opera in three acts by Gian Francesco Malipiero (1882–1973), libretto by the composer. First performance: Milan, Teatro alla Scala, 4 May 1950.

ORIGINAL CAST. Tatiana Menotti, Emma Tegani, Gino Penno, Renato Capecchi. Conductor: Nino Sanzogno.

SYNOPSIS. The story is on two levels. In a puppet theatre in a park, Dioneo (tenor) and Violante (soprano) are exchanging vows of love. They are surprised by the friends who compose the 'allegra brigata'; among them is a former lover of Violante's, Beltramo (baritone), whose jealousy is aroused at the sight of Dioneo. He tries to pick a quarrel, but his friends manage to calm him down and Lauretta (soprano), to ease the tension, suggests that each one in turn should tell a story. Violante begins with the story of Panfilia, who is in love with an admirable young man, but whose father forces her to marry another. She sickens with grief and is on the point of death. On the stage of the puppet theatre Panfilia (soprano) is seen on her deathbed; her young lover (tenor) comes to see her for the last time, and when he finds that she is already dead he falls lifeless at her side. So the story ends, and all the listeners have tears in their eyes at such a sad tale. Now it is Oretta's (mezzo-soprano) turn, and she tells the second story. A young painter (tenor), a guest in a monastery, receives a lady in his cell. He goes out of his cell for a moment and takes the candle with him, leaving her in the dark. Hearing a sudden crash, he hastens back to his cell and finds that she has bumped into some shelves and knocked down some pots of paint. She is covered with paint from head to foot, and he fails to recognize her. Taking her for the devil, he starts to yell, whereupon the monks come running and the lady has to escape through the window. The young man faints, and the little curtain falls. Now it is Dioneo's turn to tell a story. His is the tale of a gentleman, Alfonso da Toledo (tenor), who encounters a beautiful lady called Laura in Avignon, and makes a tryst with her, after he has given her all the money he has, a thousand florins. Left penniless, he has to sell his clothes and his weapons. Intrigued by his behaviour, a man (baritone) asks how he came to be reduced to such a condition. Alfonso confides to the stranger, who is none other than Laura's husband, how he came to be in his present plight. The man goes home, forces his wife to hand over all the money, and then kills her. Simplicio is the next to tell a story. He relates the adventure of Ferrantino degli Argenti of Spoleto (baritone). Caught in a storm, he seeks shelter in the house of Canon Francesco da Todi (baritone). When Francesco returns and finds him in the kitchen with his pretty young maid Caterina (mezzo-soprano), he tries to drive him out, but Ferrantino has no intention of leaving and goes so far as to draw his sword. Francesco goes off to denounce the young man before the Signoria; Ferrantino locks him out so that he cannot get into the house again and then, after Caterina has served him with food and drink, he takes her off to the bedroom. When Francesco's guests arrive, he shouts to them that they have come to the wrong house. Francesco returns and beats on the door in vain: nobody takes any notice of him. During the telling of this tale, Beltramo has turned aside in vexation; he goes up to Violante to reproach her for her heartlessness. Simplicio, grasping the situation, calls him to one side and calms him down; then he invites Lauretta to tell them a cheerful tale. She relates the story of a beautiful married lady (soprano) who has a rather odd brother, given to wandering about at night fighting his own shadow. While the lady's husband is away, her young lover (tenor) decides to come and visit her by night; in order not to arouse suspicion, he disguises himself as the lady's brother. The lovers are together when the mad brother arrives, and taking the young man for his own shadow, attacks him with his sword. The clash of swords brings the servants running to the scene, and they are astounded to find a man of flesh and blood instead of a shadow, but while the mad brother is laughing and the servants' attention is distracted, the young man manages to flee. So ends Lauretta's story, and the friends then play blind man's buff. After this they ask Beltramo to tell his story. He is at first reluctant, but eventually he tells

the tale of Eleonora (soprano), a beautiful lady who amused herself by mocking others. One day Pompeo (tenor), a young suitor, comes to call on her. When Eleonora hears her husband (baritone) returning, she hides Pompeo in a chest under a pile of garments. The husband shows his wife his new acquisition: a fine and very sharp sword. She urges him to show the quality of the blade by slicing through the garments on the chest with a single blow. He is about to do as she suggests, but she stops him in time. When he leaves, Pompeo emerges from the chest, more dead than alive with fright. The young man decides to be revenged on Eleonora, and spreads the rumour that he is gravely ill. On the stage of the puppet theatre we see Pompeo in bed; his sister Barbara (mezzo-soprano) enters, accompanying Eleonora, who has come to visit the supposedly dying young man. No sooner is she alone with him than Pompeo flings off the covers and pounces on her, tearing off her cloak. Scantily clad, she attempts to defend herself, but Pompeo forces her to lie down beside him, then he calls Barbara, who brings in several people. Pompeo tells them that he has taken a miraculous medicine which has cured him instantly. Eleonora tries in vain to hide, burying her face under the pillows, but they all recognize her. Soon everyone hears about it, including Eleonora's husband, who kills Pompeo. When the little curtain falls, Dioneo criticizes the husband for his jealousy, but Beltramo turns on him and kills him as Pompeo had been killed. The play within a play is over, and there is general dismay.

■ The opera, composed in 1943, depends on the contrast between the puppet-like performance of the secondary stories, and the real tragedy that is enacted in the foreground.

BOLIVAR
Opera in three acts by Darius Milhaud (1892–1974), based on the play by Jules Supervielle (1936). First performance: Paris, Opéra, 10 May 1950.

ORIGINAL CAST. Janine Micheau, André Bourdin, Hélène Bouvier, Marcelle Croisier. Conductor: André Cluytens.

SYNOPSIS. The action takes place in various localities in Venezuela, Peru and Colombia during the first thirty years of the nineteenth century. Bolivar (baritone) lives in San Mateo, in Venezuela, together with his young wife Maria Teresa (soprano) and the slaves Nicanor (tenor) and Précipitation (contralto). While out riding, Maria Teresa is taken ill and dies. Bolivar is grief-stricken and swears that he will never marry again. To honour the memory of his wife he frees the two slaves. A group of farmers arrive who are outspoken against the harshness and abuse of power shown by the Spanish rulers. Bolivar tries to defend them before the governor, then, realizing that peaceful intervention is useless, leads them to revolt. Caracas: The city is thrown into confusion by an earthquake. A

Giulio Coltellacci's design for the first production of Petrassi's Il Cordovano *at La Scala in Milan, 1949.*

monk (baritone), playing on the terror of the people, tries to win them back to the Spanish cause. Bolivar drives him out, succours the wounded, and encourages the survivors to rebuild their ruined houses. Among the crowd is Manuela (soprano), who admires Bolivar's courage and self-denial. The town hall. News is brought that the independents led by Bolivar have defeated the Spaniards at Taguanés and will shortly arrive. They are acclaimed by the people; Manuela and other girls lead Bolivar in triumph. Bolivar is won over by Manuela's charm. Act II. Bolivar has lost the battle of La Puerta, and is now preparing to defend the capital. Manuela wants to follow him, but he does not wish it and asks Nicanor (tenor) to take care of her. General Bovès (bass), the victor of La Puerta, arrives. He questions Manuela and compels her, along with other women related to the rebels, to attend a ball. Spanish officers in their splendid uniforms make a macabre contrast with these women dressed in mourning. Outside the prisoners are being shot. The women can no longer bear their humiliation and start wailing and calling upon their dead. Bovès drives them out and they flee for their lives. Bolivar is crossing the Andes, and his soldiers are weary and demoralized. They are joined by Manuela. When they reach the summit and see the great plain stretching out below them, they are filled with enthusiasm and confident that they will be victorious. Bolivar has realized his dream of liberating South America from Spanish rule. At Lima there is an official reception, when the most important men in the land pay homage to him. In his honour, Upper Peru is renamed the Bolivar Republic. He is offered the crown of Great Colombia, but refuses it out of respect for his democratic ideals. There are those who plot against him, however, unjustly accusing him of setting up a dictatorship. In the course of yet another attempt on his life, he only just escapes, but faithful Nicanor is killed. By now Bolivar is sick and weary and draws up his political will, in which he pictures a federation of free states. Then, comforted by a vision of his beloved Maria Teresa, he dies.

■ The opera, completed in 1943, pays homage to the South American hero Simon Bolivar and at the same time is an act of faith in freedom, with particular reference to the freedom of a Europe that was suffering the ravages of war. Milhaud had stayed in Brazil during 1917–18, devoting himself to the study of the folk music that he incorporates, in his own personal style, in many of his works. *Bolivar* is the third opera of a trilogy (*Cristophe Colomb*, 1930; *Maximilian*, 1932) dedicated to famous characters linked with the history of South America. It is the most ambitious opera from the period spent by the composer in the United States (1940–47), but was only moderately successful in Paris. On 25 April 1953 it was performed in Naples, Teatro San Carlo, with the same cast as for the world première.

THE JUMPING FROG OF CALAVERAS COUNTY

Opera in one act by Lucas Foss (born 1922), libretto by Jean Karsavina, based on a story by Mark Twain. First performance: Bloomington, University of Indiana, 18 May 1950.

SYNOPSIS. A stranger with a large moustache (bass) challenges the jumping frog, called Daniel Webster, belonging to Smiley (tenor). While the boys start to lay bets, the stranger fills Daniel's gullet with lead pellets. In the square the stranger courts Lulu (mezzo-soprano), which makes the local boys jealous. Needless to say, Daniel loses the race and, after the stranger has gone off with all the money, the trick is discovered. The frog is set free, and the stranger is brought back and forced to return the money and shown up for the trickster he is. Then Lulu gives her smiles once more to Smiley.

■ This, Foss's first opera, shows him to be a brilliantly talented composer.

IL PRIGIONIERO (The Prisoner)

Opera in a prologue, one act and four scenes by Luigi Dallapiccola (1904–75), libretto by the composer, based on La Légende d'Ulenspiegel et de Lamme Goedzac *by Charles de Coster (1827–79) and on* La torture par l'espérance, *one of the* Contes cruels *(1883) by Philippe Auguste Villiers de l'Isle-Adam. First performed in concert form on the R.A.I., 1 December 1949. First performance: Florence, Teatro Communale, for the 13th Florentine Music Festival, 20 May 1950. First performance in U.K.: (concert version), London, 1954; London, New Opera Company at Sadler's Wells, 27 July 1959; in U.S.A.: New York City, Juilliard School, 15 March 1951.*

ORIGINAL CAST. Magda Laszlò (the mother), Scipio Colombo (the prisoner), Mario Binci (gaoler and Grand Inquisitor), Mariano Caruso (a priest), Gian Giacomo Guelfi (another priest), Luciano Vela (Fra Redemptor). Conductor: Hermann Scherchen.

SYNOPSIS. The action takes place in Saragossa, around 1570. Prologue. Against a black background, spotlights pick out the white face of the mother (soprano). She expresses her forebodings and relates a dream which haunts her every night: the dread spectre of Philip II coming towards her and gradually turning into the symbol of death. Scene I. A horrible cell in the dungeons of the Inquisition in Saragossa. It is dark. The prisoner (baritone) is lying on his pallet, and his mother is beside him. He speaks of the tortures he has undergone, and tells her how his faith and hope were restored when one evening the gaoler called him 'brother'. The gaoler (tenor) enters and the mother leaves. Scene II. The gaoler continues to call the prisoner 'brother'. He tells him that revolt has broken out in Flanders and describes the deeds of the Beggar Army (the Flemish patriots). He speaks with increasing fervour until finally the prisoner is aroused from his torpor and exclaims, weeping: 'Thank you, brother, you have given me fresh hope.' When the gaoler leaves, the prisoner realizes that the door is ajar. There is a long corridor outside, and the prisoner stumbles

along it. Scene III. Beneath the dungeons. The prisoner is dragging himself along, in dread of being discovered at every step. A 'Fra Redemptor' (torturer) and two other priests (bass and baritone), who are having a theological discussion, pass by, too busy to notice him. An interlude engulfs the listener. Scene IV. The prisoner reaches a garden beneath a starry sky. A great cedar dominates the middle of the garden, and in his elation at being in the open air the prisoner flings his arms around the tree trunk. But two great arms reach out and clasp him: it is the Inquisitor, who was also his gaoler, and who now gently reproves him for having tried to escape his just punishment. The prisoner understands that he has been subjected to the ultimate torture: the illusion of freedom. He allows himself to be led to the pyre, laughing like a madman and repeatedly uttering the word Liberty almost to himself.

■ The idea of an opera with the theme of human liberty as its subject first came to Dallapiccola in 1939, when the Fascist racial laws had come into operation. The year before he had already started work on the *Canti di prigionia* as a 'realizeable form of protest' against the racist measures. But the composition of *The Prisoner* could be started only in 1944, the year of the liberation of Florence. The work was completed early in 1948. Although set against the historical background of the war of liberation in Flanders, the opera is meant as an act of homage to the resistance against the Nazi régime and as a denunciation of all dictatorships. In addition to the four scenes, the score includes two sung interludes and one symphonic interlude. For the second of the two sung interludes the composer recommends the use of mechanical aids, loudspeakers etc., to achieve an overwhelming volume of sound. The opera was well received by the public in Florence, but the Italian critics were rather negative and considerable controversy ensued. There was reaction not only to the twelve-note row technique in the composer's melodies and the harsh harmonies, but also to the ideological implications of the libretto. The opera was hailed as a masterpiece abroad, however, and was soon widely performed.

MORTE DELL'ARIA (Death from the Air)

Tragic opera in one act by Goffredo Petrassi (born 1904), libretto by T. Scialoja. First performance: Rome, Teatro Eliseo, 24 October 1950. Conductor: Fernando Previtali.

SYNOPSIS. The Inventor (tenor), to the dismay of the sceptical onlookers, intends to launch himself from the top of a high metal tower to prove the efficacy of a parachute-garment he has invented. At the last moment, however, he hesitates, and the spectators can see that he has realized that his flight cannot succeed. Nevertheless he will not give up the experiment; declaring that he is ready to die sooner than relinquish his longing to trust to the air, he flings himself off the tower and is dashed to pieces on the ground. The photographer (tenor) and reporters hurry to send the news. The observer (baritone) on the tower scatters flowers over the dead man. The chorus sings a sad farewell.

■ The opera was inspired by a real-life incident which occurred in Paris at the beginning of the century, recorded by a few photographs in an old album. The story, with its obvious similarity to the myth of Icarus, finds lofty expression in Petrassi's remarkable music.

DIE VERURTEILUNG DES LUKULLUS (The Condemnation of Lucullus)

Opera in two acts and twelve scenes by Paul Dessau (born 1894), libretto by Bertolt Brecht (1898–1956). First performance: Berlin, Staatsoper, 17 March 1951. Conductor of first performance: Hermann Scherchen.

SYNOPSIS. An imaginary trial of the Roman general after his death. The judges' robes are worn, not by magistrates, but by the shades of a baker, a prostitute, a schoolmaster, a fishmonger: poor folk who during their earthly existence had been victims of the wars of Lucullus. All the merits the general can boast are not judged sufficient to justify or compensate for the crimes he has committed. So he is condemned to the void.

■ This is the only opera of Dessau's that has ever been performed. It includes several spoken passages, and the text is easy to understand. The original title was *Das Verhör des Lukullus (The Interrogation of Lucullus).* Its performance was keenly opposed for political motives, connected with the cold war.

THE PILGRIM'S PROGRESS

Morality in a prologue, four acts and an epilogue by Ralph Vaughan Williams (1872–1958), libretto by the composer based on the Allegory by John Bunyan (1678). First performance: London, Covent Garden, 26 April 1951.

SYNOPSIS. The story, in several episodes, of the journey of the soul (the Pilgrim) from the City of Destruction (the earthly world) to the Golden Gate of the Celestial City (the hereafter).

■ Bunyan (1628–88) was a Nonconformist preacher, imprisoned for twelve years for preaching without a licence. The music follows the stages of his book, with alternating moods of serenity and menace, irony and power. One episode, 'The Shepherds of the Delectable Mountains', had already been performed in London on 11 July 1922. It was subsequently incorporated in the opera.

COMEDY ON THE BRIDGE (Veselohra na mostĕ)

Broadcast opera in one act by Bohuslav Martinu (1890–1959), libretto by the composer, from the play by Vaclav Kličpera. First given on Radio Prague, 18 March 1937. First performance in U.S.A.: N.B.C. Television Network, New York, 29 May 1951.

SYNOPSIS. The action takes place on a bridge between two villages that are at war with one another, at a date unspecified. Returning from enemy territory, where she has been to bury a brother killed in battle, young Popelka is stopped on the bridge by a sentry who prevents her from entering her own village. She is frantic, thinking that her sweetheart, Sykos, and her mother will be worried and looking for her. Bedron the hop-grower is also stopped, on his way back from a secret mission, and starts paying court to Popelka. While he is kissing her, Sykos arrives and reproaches her for her frivolous behaviour. The trio are joined by Bedron's wife Eva who, when Sykos tells her what has been going on, jealously upbraids her husband. Lastly the village schoolmaster arrives, busy trying to solve a riddle. As the truce seems to be over, the five confide their secrets to one another, when suddenly news is brought that their side has been victorious. Bedron is praised for carrying out his mission, Popelka discovers that she has buried the body of an unknown man and that her brother is alive, and the schoolmaster solves his riddle.

■ This brilliant one-act opera won the Premio Italia in 1949 and was broadcast by the RAI in 1950. It was performed for the first time in Italy at the Fenice in Venice on 19 September 1951. The music combines a wide variety of influences, from the eighteenth century to the melodies and rhythms of Czech folk music.

THE RAKE'S PROGRESS

Opera in three acts and an epilogue by Igor Stravinsky (1882–1971), libretto by Wystan Hugh Auden (1907–73) and Chester Kallman. First performance: Venice, Teatro La Fenice, 11 September 1951; first performance in U.K.: Edinburgh (by Glyndebourne Opera), 25 August 1953; in U.S.A.: New York, Metropolitan Opera House, 14 February 1953.

ORIGINAL CAST. Rounseville (Rakewell), Elisabeth Schwarzkopf (Anne), Otakar Kraus (Shadow), Raphael Arié (Trulove), Jennie Tourel (Baba), Hughes Cuénod (Sellem). Conducted by the composer at the first performance.

SYNOPSIS. England in the eighteenth century. Act I, Scene I. The garden of Trulove's house in the country. A suspicious character, Nick Shadow (baritone), announces that young Tom Rakewell (tenor) has come into a huge inheritance. Tom bids a fond farewell to his sweetheart Anne (soprano), and sets off happily for London in the company of Nick, an odd fellow, who offers his services free for a year and a day. Scene II.

be sold by auction to pay his debts. Sellem (tenor), the auctioneer, starts to sell his goods. Baba stops him; she tells Anne, who has returned, that Tom still loves her and that she alone can save him from the shameful life he is leading. Baba herself goes back to the circus and the applause of the crowd. Scene II. By an open grave in a churchyard. The truth is at last revealed to Tom: Nick is the devil, and is after Tom's soul rather than his money. Tom asks if he can gamble his last chance on a game of cards. Thanks to miraculous good luck and the memory of his sweetheart, he succeeds in guessing the three cards drawn from the pack. Enraged, Nick condemns Tom to madness, then sinks from sight into a grave. Final scene. Tom wakes up in Bedlam, believing that he is Adonis and that Venus will soon come to visit him. He has gone mad. Faithful Anne comes to comfort him, and letting him believe that she is Venus, she rocks him to sleep with a lullaby. Then she leaves with her father. Tom wakes after she has gone, raves of his sweet Venus who has lovingly cradled and forgiven him, calls on her and on Orpheus, then sinks back, dead. The moral of the story is pointed by all the characters in an epilogue.

■ The première was given in Venice by the Teatro alla Scala for the Biennale, during the 14th International Festival of Contemporary Music. Stravinsky first got the idea for the opera from Hogarth's engravings, in which the eighteenth-century artist depicts the story of a rake with a calligraphic morality very close in feeling to the traditional forms to which the composer then subscribed. With the help of Kallman's experience of theatre, Auden transposed these pictures into a subtle, colourful libretto, faithfully recreating the spirit of the originals. Stravinsky called the libretto 'one of the finest ever written'. There is an obvious similarity to models such as Mozart's *Don Giovanni*. But whereas Da Ponte's libertine has an ebullient and demonic vitality, Tom Rakewell is a passive character, who does not lead his servant astray but is led astray by his servant, and this characterization certainly corresponds to Stravinsky's expressed aim. Only Anne is a positive character. The rake can only express intentions: *I wish I had money* (Act I), *I wish I were happy* (Act II), *I wish it were true* (Act II). Partly in response to the very measured sound of the English libretto, the composer has recreated a predominantly eighteenth-century sound in this opera. Auden himself said that the right sound for the opera would depend on 'a small orchestra, few characters, a small chorus. In short, "chamber music", as – for example – in *Così fan tutte*.' Hence the use of recitative and arias accompanied by the small orchestra with one solo instrument, derived directly from Bach (for example Anne's aria in the third scene of Act I, supported by the bassoon melody). It might seem surprising that the composer of *Petrouchka* should make such limited use of percussion in this opera: it is in fact scored only for timpani, and with classical restraint. But even in 1935, in his *Chronicles of my life*, Stravinsky wrote: 'I have the distinct feeling that in my compositions of the last fifteen years I have not been followed by the majority

Opening scene of Dallapiccola's Il prigioniero; *sets and costumes by Ita Maksimovna, produced by Günter Rennert.*

Mother Goose's brothel in London. Tom, surrounded by trollops and merry-makers, embarks on a life of debauchery. Scene III. Trulove's garden. Anne has not heard from her sweetheart; unknown to her father, she sets off for London to find Tom and help him. Act II, Scene I. Tom's house in London. Tom is bored; he has one amorous adventure after another, but he is not happy. To show the world that he doesn't give a fig for morals or conventions, he agrees to Nick Shadow's proposal that he should marry Baba the Turk (mezzo-soprano), a rich but monstrous bearded lady who appears at fairs. Scene II. Outside Tom's house. Tom and Baba, now married, arrive in a sedan-chair. Anne is heartbroken to see how low Tom has sunk; her words disturb him deeply, although he does not show it. Anne flees, Baba steps out of the sedan-chair and shows her long beard to the crowd, who applaud her. Scene III. Tom's house. The young man has become disgusted with the monstrosity he has married, and stops her talking by covering her face with his wig. Nick Shadow gives him a strange machine that is supposed to make bread out of stones and Tom flings himself wholeheartedly into this folly. Act III, Scene I. Tom's house. As might have been expected, the young rake has gone bankrupt. He disappears and all his possessions are to

Menotti's The Consul, *produced at the* Festival dei due Mondi *(Festival of Two Worlds) in Spoleto in 1972.*

of my listeners. They expected something else of me . . . they are used to the language of these other works (*Firebird*, *Les Noces*, in addition to those already mentioned) . . . they cannot or will not follow me along the path of my musical thought.' It was certainly puzzling that this composer, who in his early years would with each new composition deviate from the style and pattern of his previous work, should draw even closer – even as early as 1919 when he was writing the ballet *Pulcinella* – to a stricter, neo-classical form – he who had shocked Paris and the critics of all Europe with the audacious rhythm and harsh sounds of *The Rite of Spring*. The truth was that, whilst he inveighed against what he called the 'reactionaries of the avant-garde', he could or would not accept the new and almost necessary Schönbergian language, and it was not until the 1950's, after *The Rake's Progress*, that he approached the atonalism and serialism of the Viennese school. The composer's own particular style at the time was, however, appropriate to this opera, in which his unique creative gifts meet the exacting demands of the whole tradition of opera.

LA STORIA DI UNA MAMMA
Musical tale in one act by Roman Vlad (born 1919), libretto by Gastone da Venezia, based on the story by Hans Christian Andersen (1805–75). First performance: Venice, 7 October 1951.

SYNOPSIS. The mother (soprano) tries to snatch her son back from death. To this end she submits to sac-

rifices, but at the end must bow to the will of God. Death takes her child into the Unknown, and the mother can only pray.

■ Conceived as an opera for radio, a concert version was also written, as well as a version for piano and voice.

BILLY BUDD
Opera in a prologue and four acts by Benjamin Britten (1913–76), libretto by E. M. Forster and Eric Crozier, based on the novel by Herman Melville, published posthumously in 1924. First performance: London, Covent Garden, 1 December 1951; first performance in U.S.A.: N.B.C. Television, 19 October 1952.

ORIGINAL CAST. Peter Pears (Vere), Theodor Uppman (Budd), Frederick Dalberg (Claggart), Geraint Evans (Mr Flint), Michael Langdon (Ratcliffe), Hervey Alan (Mr Redburn), Anthony Marlow (Red Whiskers), Inia Te Wiata (Dansker). Conducted by the composer.

SYNOPSIS. On board H.M.S. *Indomitable* in the summer of 1797. This was the year of the famous mutinies, such as the *Spithead* and *Nore* mutinies, and living conditions on board British warships were particularly hard for the crews. Their resentment was more than justified. The authorities, fearing the consequences of the French Revolution, were concentrating all their energies on the fight against France. The *Indomitable* is on her way to rejoin the fleet in the Mediterranean. Like many ships in those days, she is short-handed and so, when she crosses a merchant ship (significantly named the *Rights o' Man*) a party is sent to board her, and Billy Budd (baritone) is among the men pressganged into service with the Royal Navy. Billy is a nice-looking, ingenious lad, liked by all except John Claggart (bass), the master-at-arms. Claggart persecutes the boy relentlessly and malevolently. He is sadistic and depraved, and tries everything to corrupt Billy and destroy him; he tries to incite him to mutiny, then accuses him before Captain Vere (tenor). The captain is an honest man, highly esteemed by both officers and crew. He guesses at the truth and calls Claggart and Billy into his cabin. Billy stammers painfully, as he always does when he is excited or upset, and feels that he has been trapped and ignominiously betrayed. In his frustration he is unable to restrain himself, and strikes Claggart a blow. Claggart falls dead. The captain knows that Billy is not really to blame, but in accordance with the law he has to assemble a drumhead court, and Billy is condemned to death. The sentence is carried out at dawn, by hanging.

■ This work is probably unique in the history of opera in that it has no female roles. It was commissioned by the Arts Council of Great Britain and a version in two acts was subsequently given at Covent Garden on 9

January 1964. The same subject was also set to music by Federico Ghedini (see p. 453).

BOULEVARD SOLITUDE

Lyrical drama in seven scenes by Hans Werner Henze (born 1926), libretto by Grete Weil after the play by Walter Jockisch based on the Histoire du Chevalier des Grieux et de Manon Lescaut *by A. F. Prévost (1731). First performance: Hanover, Landestheater, 17 February 1952; first performance in U.K.: London, New Opera Company at Sadler's Wells, 25 June 1962; in U.S.A.: Santa Fé, 2 August 1967.*

ORIGINAL CAST. Sigrid Claus, Walter Buckov, Theo Zilliker. Conductor: Johannes Schüler.

SYNOPSIS. Scene I. French railway station entrance hall, today. Two students, Armand (tenor) and Francis (baritone), are sitting at a small table in the café. Seated nearby is Manon (soprano), with her brother Lescaut (baritone), who walks over to the bar. Manon and Armand get into conversation; she is being escorted by her brother to a convent school in Lausanne, but she feels lonely and does not want to leave. Armand is also lonely, so Manon decides to follow him to Paris. Lescaut does not detain his sister. Scene II. An attic in Paris. Armand and Manon are in financial straits because Armand's father has stopped sending money. Armand asks Manon to borrow from Francis. While Armand is getting dressed, Lescaut enters. He has found an elderly rich man who is ready to be Manon's

protector: all she needs to do is to appear at the window and give a sign. Armand reappears and says goodbye to Manon, promising to return shortly; her brother brings pressure to bear on Manon, and she agrees to accept the proposition. Scene III. Drawing room in the house of Lilaque *père* (tenor). Manon is writing a letter to Armand, telling him that she wants to see him again. Lescaut enters and tears it up. He demands money but Manon has none, so he breaks open the safe and takes the contents. Lilaque arrives, his suspicions aroused, and when he discovers the robbery he throws Manon and Lescaut out. Scene IV. The University Library. Francis tells Armand that Manon and Lescaut have been forced to leave Lilaque's house. Armand protests that Manon could never commit such a crime and Francis leaves him. Armand continues dreaming of Manon as he reads Catullus. He finds that she has sat down beside him and they declare their love as the chorus chant the words of the Latin poet. Scene V. A bar of ill repute. Armand is addicted to cocaine. Lescaut and Lilaque *fils* (baritone) enter in search of Manon. The younger Lilaque has fallen in love with her, and Lescaut assures him that his sister will not reject him. While Armand, under the influence of cocaine, imagines that he is Orpheus come to save Eurydice, Manon, who has entered the bar, goes off with Lilaque. Armand receives a note from Manon inviting him to call on her the next day (while Lilaque *fils* is out of the house). Scene VI. A bedroom in the house of Lilaque *fils*. Armand must leave because Lilaque *fils* might return at any moment, and sadly he makes ready to part from Manon. He notices a modern painting on the wall, which Manon and Lescaut, who are urging him to hurry, ridicule, but Lescaut rips it out of its frame with a view to selling it later. Lilaque *père* arrives unexpectedly, and Armand and Lescaut hide in the bedroom while Manon makes herself agreeable to him. The old man asks no better and insists on entering the bedroom. Manon tries in vain to stop him. In the bedroom he discovers not only the stolen painting, but also Armand and Lescaut. He orders the maid to summon the police and tries to prevent them from escaping. At this point Lescaut produces a pistol and shoots him, pressing it into his sister's hand as he runs away. Lilaque *fils* enters to find his father dead and Armand and Manon horror-struck. Scene VII. Outside a prison. Armand is waiting for Manon to be transferred to another prison. There is now no hope that she will be saved, and Manon, under prison escort, avoids looking at Armand as she passes. He is left alone in the square.

■ The musical eclecticism that was to be even more pronounced in *Re cervo* is already present in a creative and innovative way in *Boulevard Solitude*. Henze's score brought twelve-tone music to the masses by showing that it was not merely some intellectual experiment, while the mood of the music, the subtle tonalities, the skilful use of harmony and voices (ranging from the spoken word to Puccini-like arias) make this opera an imaginative work of great beauty. *Boulevard Solitude*, composed in Paris in 1950 and 1951, succeeds in evoking the *ambiance* and cultural

Fernand Léger's design for Milhaud's Bolivar, *1950. Paris, Bibliothèque de l'Opéra.*

milieu of those years. The story is never treated from a moral standpoint and leaves comment and description to the music; the result is obtained by a combination of the most heterogeneous elements of opera and ballet. The opera, which was enthusiastically received, succeeds with its dissonances and tender passages, in conveying the alienation created between Armand and the world and in showing, in the character of Manon, an example of the difficulty of living and loving in a world dominated by money, greed and lack of understanding.

AMAHL AND THE NIGHT VISITORS

Opera in one act by Gian Carlo Menotti (born 1911), libretto by the composer, inspired by the famous painting Adoration of the Magi *by Hieronymus Bosch. Commissioned by the National Broadcasting Company of New York, it was broadcast on 24 December 1951. First stage performance: Bloomington, University of Indiana, 21 February 1952. First performance in U.K.: on B.B.C. TV, 1967.*

ORIGINAL CAST. Chet Allan (Amahl), Rosemary Kuhlman (Mother). Conductor: Thomas Schippers.

SYNOPSIS. It is evening. Amahl (treble), a crippled twelve-year-old boy, is playing his shepherd's pipe outside the open doorway of their poor hut, and his mother (soprano) calls to him to come indoors. The boy enters and tells his mother that he has seen a comet with a fiery tail; she is sad and anxious, and pays no attention to her son's 'fantasies'. The two settle down for the night when there is a knock at the door; Amahl goes to open it, but does not dare to say who is there. His mother goes to the door herself and finds the three Wise Men standing outside, Kaspar (tenor), Melchior (baritone) and Balthasar (bass), great Eastern Kings clothed in dazzling splendour. They tell of their journey and how they are following the comet which will lead them to a newborn child. Shepherds gather round and bring food for the noble guests. During the night the mother tries to steal some gold, but she is caught in the act. The poor woman explains that she had given way to temptation out of her longing to make a gift to her crippled child. The Kings are filled with compassion and tell her she can keep the gold, since the Child they seek has no need of gold. He will build His Kingdom on love, not on riches. While the shepherds sing, Amahl, who possesses only his crutch, offers it as a gift to the unborn King. He hands it over and realizes that he can walk without it. The miracle astonishes everyone and the Kings give thanks. The mother reluctantly lets Amahl follow the three Wise Men on their journey.

■ The opera, which was a well deserved success, was repeated for thirteen consecutive years on Christmas Eve. The first performance in Italy was in Florence on 9 April 1953, on the occasion of the Florentine *Maggio musicale*, conducted by Leopold Stokowski and sung by Alvaro Cordova and Giulietta Simionato.

PROSERPINA Y EL EXTRANJERO (Proserpina and the Stranger)

Opera in three acts by Juan José Castro (1895–1968), libretto by Omar del Carlo. First performance: Milan, Teatro alla Scala, 13 March 1952.

CAST. Elisabetta Barbato, Giangiacomo Guelfi, Giulietta Simionato, Cloe Elmo, Rosanna Carteri, Mirto Picchi, Giacinto Prandelli. Conductor: Juan José Castro.

SYNOPSIS. In a quarter of ill repute in Buenos Aires, Proserpina has just been brutally treated for the umpteenth time by Porfirio Sosa, the lover who has brought her here, taking her from her mother who lives on a farm in the pampa. Porfirio has been arrested for this and all his other unsettled accounts with the law. Marcial Quiroga, a sinister local character, has designs on Proserpina, who is now alone: he would not mind having her as his mistress, and she could earn money for him too. But his plans are foiled by the arrival of a stranger who takes lodgings in the same house. The stranger intervenes to protect Proserpina, and she is able to leave with her mother, who comes to take her home again to the pampa. Her mother wants to find a respectable husband for her, but Proserpina is obsessed by the memory of the stranger. She runs away to Buenos Aires again and flings herself into his arms. Suddenly the stranger, mindful of something, pushes her away as the shade of his dead wife appears. He

The 1966 Deutsche Staatsoper of Berlin production of Dessau's Die Verurteilung des Lucullus.

comes from a distant world that nobody knows. He has suffered greatly, perhaps too much. Porfirio returns from prison, thirsting for revenge, having been told by Marcial of Proserpina's love-affair. Porfirio and Marcial kill the stranger. Proserpina gathers up the stranger's few belongings and goes away, while Porfirio tries in vain to make her stay.

■ In 1952 *Proserpina and the Stranger* won the prize offered by La Scala, Milan, to honour the fiftieth anniversary of the death of Giuseppe Verdi.

LEONORE 40/45
Opera semiseria *with a prologue and prelude and two acts by Rolf Liebermann (born 1910), libretto by Heinrich Strobel. First performance: Basle, Stadttheater, 26 March 1952.*

ORIGINAL CAST included Schemionek, de Vries, Olsen. Conductor: Krannhals.

SYNOPSIS. The story develops between 1939 and 1947 in France and Germany. During the prologue, Emile (baritone), a guardian angel living on earth, tells us that we are about to see a love story enacted, and that he will only intervene when needed by the participants. In 1939 Alfred (tenor), a German living with his father on the French border, is listening to Beethoven's *Fidelio* on the radio when the programme is interrupted to announce that the country is mobilizing for war: he must leave. In the house opposite, a Frenchwoman, Germaine (contralto), asks her daughter Yvette (soprano) for news of the political situation. Her husband had been killed in the First World War, and she declares that only through peace and goodwill will men be able to solve their problems. Yvette, on the other hand, is convinced that France is in the right, and she is excited by these events. Two years later, in occupied Paris, Yvette and Alfred meet at a concert. They get to know one another and fall in love. In August 1944, however, Alfred has to leave Paris with the retreating German army. Yvette wants to hide him in her house, but he refuses to allow her to run such a risk; they bid farewell as the people of France celebrate their liberation. At this point Emile appears, explaining that it is time for him to intervene in order that the story should have a happy ending. The war is over and Yvette has lost trace of her fiancé and is desperately searching for him. Emile approaches her and, to test her love, tells her that Alfred must be punished for his part in the German atrocities. Yvette defends him and eventually the angel leads her to Alfred, arranging for her to be taken on by the factory where he is employed. After a time, Yvette and Alfred decide to get married and present themselves before a tribunal that symbolizes the machinery of bureaucracy. The judges declare that it is impossible to arrange a marriage between two persons whose countries are enemies. At this point the guardian angel appears again: to the strains of *Fidelio*,

Stravinsky's The Rake's Progress *in its first production at the Teatro La Fenice in Venice, 1951.*

he says that, like Leonora, the heroine of the Beethoven opera, Yvette has won love by her faith, and he joins the two young people in matrimony.

■ The opera received a mixed reception by both public and critics. It is the embodiment of Liebermann's liking for drama constructed on two levels: the realistic level and the surrealist-symbolic level. On the one hand the opera represents a condemnation of war and tyranny, and on the other it extols the new music, symbol of a renewed and free humanity.

DIE LIEBE DER DANAE (The Love of Danaë)
Opera in three acts by Richard Strauss (1864–1949), libretto by Joseph Gregor (1888–1960). The score was finished in 1940. First performance: Salzburg Festival, 14 August 1952; first performance in U.K.: London, Covent Garden, 16 September 1953; in U.S.A.: Los Angeles, 5 April 1964.

ORIGINAL CAST included Annelies Kupper, Paul Schoeffler, Josef Gostic. Conductor: Clemens Krauss.

SYNOPSIS. Act I. Pollux (tenor), King of Eos, is deeply in debt. He wants to marry his daughter Danae (soprano) to Midas (tenor), King of Lydia. Pollux's four nephews – the husbands of Semele (soprano), Europa (soprano), Alcmene (mezzo-soprano) and Leda (soprano), four beautiful women who have all been loved by Jupiter – set off for Lydia. In her dreams, Danae is visited by Jupiter (baritone) in the form of a shower of gold. When she awakes she swears that she will only accept the man who brings her the pleasures of love as well as gold. Midas, dressed simply as a messenger and calling himself Chrysopher, tells Danae that her suitor is arriving and accompanies her to the harbour to welcome him. Jupiter has taken the place of Midas, and when he steps off the ship Danae recognizes him as the object of her golden dreams, and swoons. Act II. Jupiter explains to the four queens that his precautions in making love to Danae have been taken to avoid the jealousy of Juno. He warns Midas that the gift of the golden touch was given on condition of absolute obedience. When Midas touches Danae she is turned to gold. Jupiter appears, and Midas proposes that the statue be allowed to choose between the King of the gods and the humble donkey-driver he once was himself. Danae chooses the human love of the poor mortal, and life flows through her veins again. Act III. Midas, now deprived of his riches and power, reveals to Danae his pact with Jupiter. Danae blesses the poverty which has united her with the man she loves. Jupiter wants to win Danae back, and disguising himself as a vagabond, he appears before her. Danae cannot be tempted by his offer of riches, and when Midas returns to their simple hut, she throws herself into his arms.

Britten's Billy Budd. *London, December 1964.*

■ The virtuosity of the score and the splendour of the orchestration cannot conceal the tedious and inconsistent passages in an opera which has never secured a place in the operatic repertory. Yet there is one passage of real beauty in the prelude to the third act, when Jupiter tries for the last time to win back the love of Danae. Based on a quotation from the Marschallin's theme in *Der Rosenkavalier*, this passage expresses Strauss's own melancholy renunciation of those pleasures of life that only youth can enjoy. The opera was completed in 1944 and the composer, by then eighty years old, was able to attend a dress rehearsal, given especially for him in Salzburg in 1944. But no public performance took place during the next eight years.

TRIONFO D' AFRODITE (Triumph of Aphrodite)
Scenic cantata by Carl Orff (born 1895), text by the composer after verses by Catullus, Sappho and Euripides. First performance: Milan, Teatro alla Scala, 13 February 1953; first performance in U.S.A.: Houston, 2 April 1956.

ORIGINAL CAST included Nicolai Gedda, Elisabeth Schwarzkopf. Conductor: Herbert von Karajan.

SYNOPSIS. The recurrent theme in the collection of lyrics of which the cantata is composed is love, and the names of Hymen and Venus, the god of marriage and the goddess of love and beauty, often recur in the songs which are enacted upon the stage. The scene opens with youths and girls joking together during a wedding ceremony, exchanging questions and answers. The chorus exhorts the bride to submit to her husband and

to the laws of love, an exhortation repeated several times in the course of the opera. Then follow songs extolling the happiness that follows marriage, describing the ceremony and the dialogue between bride and bridegroom. Love overwhelms all who submit to the laws of Aphrodite, and the chorus calls on Venus and the Muses to let joy reign, adding that man and woman must be in harmony, for only from such a union can children be born who will build a healthy society. Then comes praise for the bride and her loving husband. She for her part must not deny him, or he will seek elsewhere. The opera ends with a final song in praise of the bride and groom.

■ *Trionfo d' Afrodite* is part of a trilogy of scenic cantatas entitled *Trionfi* (Triumphs), together with *Carmina Burana* and *Catulli Carmina* (see pp. 437, 444 above). Two of the songs are among Sappho's most famous verses: the song in which the bride is compared with the moon that sheds its light over all the earth, and the song praising the excellence of the bridegroom.

GLORIANA
Opera in three acts by Benjamin Britten (1913–76), libretto by William Plomer, based on Lytton Strachey's Elizabeth and Essex *(1928). First performance: London, Covent Garden, 8 June 1953; first performance in U.S.A.: Cincinnati, 8 May 1956.*

ORIGINAL CAST included Joan Cross (Elizabeth) and Peter Pears (Essex). Conductor: John Pritchard.

SYNOPSIS. Act I. Scene I. The Earl of Essex (tenor) is

pacing nervously up and down outside a tilting-ground, waiting to hear if his rival, Lord Mountjoy (baritone), has been defeated. But Mountjoy is victorious, and enters bearing his victor's prize. Essex insults him and provokes a duel. The Queen (soprano) arrives, surrounded by her court. She chides the combatants and bids them be reconciled. Scene II. In her apartments Queen Elizabeth talks with her minister, Sir Robert Cecil, and assures him that she is wedded to the State. Just then the Earl of Essex enters, and at the Queen's request he sings her a sweet Elizabethan lyric, accompanying himself on her lute. Then he turns to the Queen and begs her to send him to Ireland to overthrow her enemy Tyrone. The Queen declares she can refuse him nothing, and then dismisses him. The act ends with the Queen praying for strength and grace to fulfil her high office. Act II. Scene I. One of the Queen's Progresses. The citizens of Norwich receive her with a gorgeous Masque performed in her honour. Scene II. The garden of Essex's house. Mountjoy meets Lady Penelope Rich (soprano), Essex's sister, and while they sing of their love for each other, cannot help overhearing Essex telling his wife Frances (mezzo-soprano) of the obstacles to his appointment in Ireland. A quartet evolves in which Mountjoy and Penelope add their pleas for patience and caution to his wife's, for they will surely outlive the old Queen and decide her successor. Scene III. During a ball at Whitehall Palace, the Queen notices that Lady Essex is wearing an ostentatiously elaborate gown. She orders an energetic dance to be played and then commands the ladies to change their linen – a ruse by which she removes the dress from Lady Essex and reappears wearing it herself. The astonished Court witnesses her humiliation of Frances, her rival for Essex's love. Elizabeth leaves, but soon returns to announce that Essex will lead her armies against Tyrone and the act ends in a chorus praising his valour and wishing him well. Act III. Essex has been defeated in Ireland and returned with his unruly army. He bursts into Elizabeth's presence before she has finished dressing, when she is without her wig, firstly to beg her pardon and then to complain of his enemies not only in Ireland but also at home. She accuses him of betrayal, which he angrily denies, then she recalls sadly their past intimacy. He departs and she accepts Cecil's advice to keep him under close supervision. Scene II. A blind ballad singer (bass) informs the passers-by of Essex's imminent fall from favour and the City Crier (baritone) proclaims the Earl a traitor. Scene III. Whitehall Palace. Cecil warns the Council that the Queen will hesitate to sign the death warrant. They bring in a verdict of guilty and the Queen dismisses them. She receives a petition from Lady Essex, to whom she promises safety for Essex's children whatever happens to their father, and from Lady Rich, whose pride provokes her to sign the warrant immediately. In the conclusion episodes from the Queen's last days are conjured up, before the final death scene is presented.

■ Commissioned by the Arts Council of Great Britain

to celebrate the Coronation of Queen Elizabeth II, *Gloriana* was first performed at a gala attended by Her Majesty at Covent Garden. It was not well received then, but has since come to be regarded as one of Britten's finest achievements, especially as regards the choral writing, which is often separately performed.

DER PROZESS (The Trial)
Opera in two acts and nine scenes by Gottfried von Einem (born 1918), libretto by Boris Blacher and Heinz von Cramer, based on the novel by Franz Kafka (1925). First performance: Salzburg Festival, 20 August 1953; first performance in U.S.A.: New York, City Opera, 22 October 1953.

ORIGINAL CAST. Antonio Annaloro, Elena Rizzieri, Fernando Piccinni. Conductor: Artur Rodzinski.

SYNOPSIS. Act I. 1919. Josef K. (tenor) is sleeping in his room. He wakes up and rings his bell. To his surprise two individuals enter his room and tell him that he is being arrested. They do not tell him on whose orders he is being placed under arrest nor of what crime he is accused. Shortly afterwards the inspector (baritone) tells Josef that he is under arrest, but can continue to go to his job at the bank. In Fräulein Bürstner's room, Josef K. first talks to the landlady of the boarding-house, apologizing for the disturbance caused by his visitors that morning, and then tells Fräulein Bürstner (soprano) what has happened. She offers to help him at his trial, since she is about to qualify as a lawyer. On his way home that night Josef K. has strange encounters and has the feeling that he is being persecuted by everyone. The trial – the charges, the cross-questioning, the persons present – is something of a farce. Josef K. is appalled, and denounces the injustice and corruption. Act II. A lobby in the hall. Willem (baritone) and Francesco (bass) are to be flogged by order of the tribunal. Josef K. tries to stop the flogging. A passer-by on the staircase tells him that he must present himself immediately at the Court and warns him that he had better obey or he will make things worse for himself. Josef K's uncle (bass) introduces him to a lawyer who might be able to help him, but the lawyer says there is not much he can do in view of Josef K's truculent manner before the tribunal. Leni (soprano), the lawyer's secretary, tries to attract Josef K.'s attention and offers to help him. At the bank Josef K. is unable to do his work because he is worried about the trial. A manufacturer, a bank client of Josef K.'s, advises him to go to the painter Titorelli (tenor), who has important connections and paints the portraits of the judges. Titorelli tells him that his intervention would only procure him a pretence of acquittal, because nobody ever secures a real acquittal. And without a real acquittal, the trial can be reopened at any moment. The best thing would be to ask for a postponement, that way you never get condemned. 'Nor do you get acquitted,' replies Josef K. and takes his leave. While he is waiting for somebody in the cathedral, he is warned by the prison chaplain that his trial is going against him. The cathedral is in darkness, Josef K. cannot find the way out; two men step out of the darkness beside him and lead him like automatons. One of the men takes out his dagger, the other removes Josef K.'s jacket and opens his shirt. It all takes place in silence and darkness.

■ The opera was well received at the Salzburg Festival and was praised by the critics, but when it was performed in the United States in the autumn of the same year, it was given a cool reception. Kafka's story does not really lend itself to operatic interpretation, and in the opinion of the critics von Einem's music was not always suited to the text.

PARTITA A PUGNI (Boxing Match)

Concert drama in an introduction and three rounds by Vieri Tosatti (born 1920), libretto by the composer. First performance: Venice, Teatro La Fenice, 8 September 1953.

ORIGINAL CAST included Rolando Panerai, Agostino Lazzari. Conductor: Nino Sanzogno.

SYNOPSIS. The scene is set in a suburban sports centre in modern times. An important boxing match is about to begin. Palletta (baritone), so-called because of his stocky build, is the favourite. The two contestants enter the ring, Palletta swaggering and his opponent (tenor) looking hesitant and scared. The referee starts the fight, and at first Palletta is on the attack; the crowd yells at him to let his adversary have it. His opponent is on the defensive, parrying the blows with increasing difficulty. In the third round the boxers break the rules and are separated; the opponent takes advantage of Palletta's momentary inattention to land him a hard blow which knocks him out for the count. The referee (spoken role) declares that Palletta is beaten, and there are angry catcalls from the crowd.

■ *Partita a pugni* is an adaptation of a play by L. Conosciani. In this opera the composer displays his own particular vivacity and an inventiveness that inclines to satire and paradox, but he does not completely accept the tradition of conventional operative language. The opera is Tosatti's most enduring success. He has consistently endeavoured to take music out of its isolation by associating it with other forms of expression (such as words). *Partita a pugni*, quite apart from its unusual subject, thus has the quality of a bitter farce, with a tight and coherent treatment.

THE TENDER LAND

Opera in three acts and three scenes by Aaron Copland (born 1900), libretto by Horace Everett. First performance: (original version) New York, City Opera, 1 April 1954; (revised version) Oberlin, Ohio, 20 May 1955.

SYNOPSIS. The story takes place in the Mid-West of America in June around the year 1930. Laurie Moss (lyric soprano), over-protected by her mother (contralto) and her grandfather (bass), is about to graduate from High School when Martin (tenor) and Top (baritone), two casual labourers of doubtful morals, turn up at the farm. Laurie falls in love with Martin, and they plan to run away together the morning after the graduation ceremony, which is to be followed by a party in Laurie's honour at the Moss house. Top, however, succeeds in convincing Martin that their nomad existence will not suit Laurie and is not the life for a married man. So the two lads sneak away before dawn. Disillusioned and bored, Laurie also leaves home to escape from her mother's protectiveness and make her own way in life. The mother transfers all her protectiveness to Laurie's younger sister, so the cycle begins all over again.

■ The opera was commissioned by Rodgers and Hammerstein for the thirtieth anniversary of the League of Composers. Copland does not enjoy the same popularity abroad as in the United States. It is rather strange that this should be so, since he is to be considered the most representative American composer in his involvement with the music of our century.

DAVID

Opera in five acts and twelve scenes by Darius Milhaud (1892–1974), libretto by Armand Lunel, based on the First and Second Books of Samuel and the Book of Kings. First performance: (concert version) Jerusalem, 1 June 1954; (staged version): Milan, Teatro alla Scala, 2 January 1955. First performance in U.S.A.: (concert version) Los Angeles, Hollywood Bowl, 22 September 1956.

ORIGINAL CAST. Anselmo Colzani, Italo Tajo, Carlo Badioli, Maria Amadini, Marcella Pobbe, Nicola Rossi Lemeni, Jolanda Gardino. Conductor: Nino Sanzogno.

SYNOPSIS. Act I. The Lord God orders the prophet Samuel (bass) to choose Saul's successor from among the sons of Jesse (baritone). The one ordained is David (baritone), poet and warrior: Samuel anoints him with the holy oil. In the King's tent Saul (baritone) is sad and asks David to soothe him with song. From the camp of the Philistines can be heard the sound of arms and the voice of Goliath (bass) challenging the Israelites to choose a champion to fight him. Saul promises his daughter Michal (soprano) in marriage to the man who will accept the challenge. David, armed with a sling, fights and slays the giant. Saul is glad of the victory, but in his heart he is envious of David. During the celebrations he tries to kill him, but Michal persuades David to flee. Act II. David is encamped on the edge of the forest. During the night he makes a sortie into the camp of Saul and takes his spear and the jug of water from beside the sleeping King, who is forced to acknowledge David's generosity, for he could have killed him in his sleep. He begs David's forgiveness and asks him to return. The ghost of Samuel, who is now dead, appears to warn Saul that the Lord has turned from him and given the crown of Israel to David. Shortly after this, Saul and his son Jonathan (tenor) are killed in battle. Act III. David is seated on the throne of Israel, surrounded by his six wives, each with a small child. Michal enters, lamenting the deaths of her father and brother; David, who has always loved her, comforts her and makes her his Queen. The Kingdom of David is growing ever more powerful, in accordance with the will of the Lord. It is time the Kingdom had a worthy capital, and David chooses the Jesubite stronghold of Zion; here Jerusalem, city of peace, is to be built. Act IV. Inside the stronghold of Zion the Ark of God is borne into the Tabernacle. David, barefoot and humbly clad, dances in front of the Tabernacle. Michal rebukes him, but her pride will be punished by God with sterility. David has meanwhile taken Bathsheba from her husband Uriah and the Lord punishes his wrongdoing by the death of their firstborn son. Then a second child is born, Solomon, who is to be David's most beloved son. Absalom, another of David's sons, wanting to succeed his father, causes a rebellion of the tribes. David subdues the rebels, and Absalom, his head caught in the boughs of a tree in the forest, is killed. Act V. David is old, and is comforted by the young slave girl Abishag. The moment has come for the prophecy to be fulfilled and for Solomon (child alto) to succeed to the throne of Israel. As David prepares to leave life on earth, surrounded by his weeping women, Solomon is anointed by the fountain of Gihon and the people acclaim him as their King and sing the praises of David, founder of Jerusalem.

■ Composed for the King David Festival, on a commission from the Koussevitsky Foundation. It is one of the composer's most demanding operas, and contains passages of unsurpassed lyric and dramatic richness. To underline the immediacy of the Bible story, in its relevance to the tragic events of our own time, Milhaud has introduced, along with the chorus of Hebrews who comment on the scenes being enacted, a 'chorus of 1954 Israelis', who stress the analogy between the present-day situation and that in the past.

A DINNER ENGAGEMENT
Opera in two scenes in one act by Lennox Berkeley (born 1903), libretto by Paul Dehn. First performance: Aldeburgh, 17 June 1954.

■ This opera, a very modern comedy, relates the matchmaking manoeuvres of the Earl (baritone) and Countess (soprano) of Dunmore, who are in reduced circumstances, to marry off their daughter Susan (soprano) to a prince (tenor). The marriage does in fact take place, but not at all as they had planned it.

PENELOPE
Opera semiseria in two acts by Rolf Liebermann (born 1910), libretto by Heinrich Strobel. First performance: Salzburg, Festspielhaus, 17 August 1954. Conductor: Georg Szell.

■ This is a modern variation of the ancient legend of Ulysses and Penelope. The opera is on two levels, the characters of Greek mythology intermingling with today's to tell a modern episode set in the Second World War: a woman, believing that her husband has been killed, marries again, but then hears that he is still alive. She goes to meet him, only to find that he has now really died. She hurries home, only to find that her second husband has hanged himself. The music contains passages that are truly moving, as for example in the scene between Penelope and Ulysses.

THE TURN OF THE SCREW
Opera in a prologue and two acts by Benjamin Britten (1913–76), libretto by Myfanwy Piper, based on the short story by Henry James (1898). First performance: Venice, Teatro La Fenice, 14 September 1954; first performance in U.K.: London, English Opera Group at Sadler's Wells, 6 October 1954; in U.S.A.: Boston, 1961.

ORIGINAL CAST. David Hemming * Olive Dyer, Arda Mandikian, Jennifer Vyvyan, Joan Cross, Peter Pears. Conducted by the composer.

SYNOPSIS. Act I. Prologue. The Prologue (tenor), to piano accompaniment, sets the scene. From a sheet of paper, now yellowed with time, he reads how a governess had been engaged by their guardian in London to take charge of two orphan children. The guardian was constantly occupied with business matters, travelling and social engagements, and had made the condition that the governess should never bother him with any problems relating to the children, but should handle everything herself. Bly, a country house in East Anglia. Scene I. *The Journey*. The governess (soprano) excitedly anticipates her new charges. Variation I; Scene II. *The Welcome*. The children, Miles (treble) and Flora (soprano), anxiously question the housekeeper, Mrs Grose (soprano), about the new appointment and welcome her by showing her around the beautiful house and grounds. Variation II; Scene III. *The Letter*. The Governess is horrified to receive a letter dismissing Miles from school, but as Mrs Grose cannot throw any light on the reasons, she resolves to do nothing. Variation III; Scene 4. *The Tower*. The

Fenneker's sketch for the first production of Orff's Trionfo d'Afrodite, *1953.*

Governess is astonished to see the figure of a man standing high up on a tower of the house. Variation IV; Scene V. *The Window.* She sees the man again through a window and, when she describes him, Mrs Grose immediately recognizes him as Peter Quint, the former butler, whom she had feared. From what she says the Governess gathers that he had seduced her predecessor, Miss Jessel, and had gained a strong influence over Miles. Both Quint and Miss Jessel have since died. The Governess resolves to protect the children, while not disturbing their guardian. Variation V; Scene VI. *The Lesson.* She begins to suspect Miles's innocence, even in the strange rhymes he sings to remember Latin words. Variation VI; Scene VII. *The Lake.* The Governess, sitting with Flora by the lakeside, sees Miss Jessel and hurries away. Variation VII; Scene VIII. *At Night.* Quint's voice (tenor) calls Miles out into the garden, promising 'all things strange and bold', while Miss Jessel (soprano) waits for Flora. Together they entice the children, until the Governess and Mrs Grose discover them and bring them both back indoors. Act II. Variation VIII; Scene I. *Colloquy and Soliloquy.* Miss Jessel accuses Quint of betraying her, but the ghosts join to sing 'The ceremony of innocence is drowned'. The Governess ruminates on her predicament; she feels lost and in despair. Variation IX; Scene II. *The Bells.* Outside church, she is appalled to hear the children making fun of the *Benedicite.* Miles asks to be allowed back to school and questions whether the guardian would agree with her decision to protect him herself, in isolation. She worries that he and Flora are still more under the influence of the ghosts than of herself. She decides to leave. Variation X; Scene III. *Miss Jessel.* On her return to the school room, she sees Miss Jessel at her desk, 'waiting for the child'. The Governess writes to the guardian. Variation XI; Scene IV. *The Bedroom.* She asks Miles if there is nothing he can explain to her about his expulsion, but the boy swiftly blows the candle out. Variation XII; Scene V. *Quint.* Quint advises Miles to steal the letter, before it is sent. Variation XIII; Scene VI. *The Piano.* While Miles plays the piano for the enjoyment of the housekeeper and the Governess, Flora is able to slip away. Variation XIV; Scene VII. *Flora.* The little girl is found by the lakeside and angrily turns from the Governess's persistent questioning saying that she knows nothing about Miss Jessel. Mrs Grose takes her away, while the Governess realizes that she has failed. Variation XV; Scene VIII. *Miles.* The housekeeper, leaving Bly with Flora, tells the Governess that she had heard terrible things from her during the night. Alone with Miles, the Governess begins to question him about Quint. The boy hears Quint's voice urging him not to betray their secrets, but the Governess insists and, as he utters the name, Peter Quint, he collapses in her arms. The Governess triumphantly claims him as her own, only to discover that her battle with Quint has cost the boy's life.

■ In relation to James's story, the libretto has two important changes: the central character is no longer the governess, but the two children, and the ghosts materialize, whereas in the story they only appear, but do not speak. The plot is broken up into sixteen short yet effective scenes. The scheme of the opera consists of a Theme and fifteen variations: each variation is connected with the scene that follows. The work has its roots in the instrumental tradition of the English Renaissance, as is later confirmed by the magisterial ground-bass in the final scene. The title has a double meaning: the first, that the presence of a child in stories of this kind is a 'turn of the screw', in the sense that it increases the horror; the second, in connection with the Theme, which 'turns' through the fifteen variations of the interludes between the scenes. In this, as in many other operas composed by Britten after a certain stage in his career, the orchestra is reduced to only thirteen instruments, which nevertheless convey a wealth of expression. The first performance was very favourably received, and subsequent performances have repeatedly confirmed the success of this opera.

TROILUS AND CRESSIDA
Opera in three acts by William Walton (born 1902), based on Troylus and Cryseyde *(c. 1380) by Geoffrey Chaucer, adapted by Christopher Hassall. First perfor-*

Sylvia Fisher in Britten's Gloriana *at Sadler's Wells in London, October 1966.*

mance: London, Covent Garden 3 December 1954. First performance in U.S.A.: San Francisco, 7 October 1955.

SYNOPSIS. Troy in the twelfth century B.C. Act I. War is raging between Greeks and Trojans. The young Trojan Troilus (tenor) is in love with Cressida (soprano/mezzo-soprano), a widow, daughter of the Trojan High Priest Calkas (bass), who has deserted to the Greeks. Act II. Pandarus (tenor) arranges that Troilus meets Cressida at a supper party at his house. They are forced because of a storm to spend the night there. In the morning, Diomede, Prince of Argos (baritone), a commander of the Greeks, makes a proposal to the Trojans: in exchange for Cressida, whose father wants to have her back, and whose beauty has entranced him, he will return Antenor (baritone), a Trojan captain whom they have captured. Troilus is unable to prevent the exchange and gives Cressida a scarf in token of his undying fidelity to her, promising to send her a letter. Cressida does not love Diomede and waits in vain for Troilus to send letters. Calkas has, however, arranged for them to be intercepted before they reach Cressida, who eventually yields to his arguments and gives Diomede the scarf in token of her favour. Taking advantage of a truce, Troilus crosses to the Greek camp and finds Cressida hailed as future Queen of Argos. He attacks Diomede, but Calkas falsely deals Troilus a mortal blow, and Cressida, heartbroken, takes her own life.

■ In Walton's opera, Cressida is not the young woman – ready to take other lovers besides Troilus – that we find in Chaucer. Here she is faithful unto death. Hassall's libretto intelligently paints her portrait, and the whole work is pervaded by a sad irony. With its recurring themes, *Troilus and Cressida* is a music-drama closer in feeling to Schubert than to Wagner. Its fine romantic music is characteristic of all Walton's work.

LA FIGLIA DI JORIO (The Daughter of Jorio)
Pastoral tragedy in three acts by Ildebrando Pizzetti (1880–1968), libretto by the composer, based on the tragedy by Gabriele D'Annunzio (1863–1938). First performance: Naples, Teatro San Carlo, 4 December 1954.

ORIGINAL CAST. Clara Petrella, Mirto Picchi, Gian Giacomo Guelfi, Maria Luisa Malagrina, Maria Teresa Mandalari, Anna Maria Canali, Saturno Meletti, Gerardo Gaudiosi, Plinio Clabassi. Conductor: Gianandrea Gavazzeni.

SYNOPSIS. The story is set in Abruzzo. Preparations are being made in the house of Lazaro di Roio (baritone) for the marriage of his son Aligi (tenor) to Vienda di Giave (mime). Aligi appears, still heavy with sleep and troubled by strange forebodings; Vienda drops the piece of bread handed to her by her mother-in-law, and this too is seen as a bad omen. Suddenly among the guests appears Mila (soprano), the daughter of Jorio, an old sorcerer. She asks for protection from some reapers who, knowing her reputation as a prostitute, would like to possess her. Aligi moves to throw her out, but an angel appears behind her, as if to protect her, and as the angel holds up a cross the reapers hastily leave in confusion. Lazaro has been hurt in the stampede, and falls to his knees. Aligi falls in love with Mila, and goes to live a pure life with her in a cave. Ornella (soprano), Aligi's sister, comes to beg her brother to return home. Mila realizes that she must give the young man up for his own good. Lazaro di Roio also comes, and tries to rape Mila when she is alone. Aligi rushes in and Lazaro, beside himself with passion, orders the two peasants who have accompanied him to bind his son and drag him away; then he flings himself upon Mila, but at the crucial moment Aligi, who has been set free by Ornella, comes back. He throws himself on his father and stabs him to death. The next day, in Lazaro's house, the mourners are weeping over the body of the murdered man. Aligi has been sentenced to death for his crime. His mother makes him drink a sleeping draught to stun his senses, so that he will feel less terror before the execution. Meanwhile Mila arrives and declares that she alone is responsible for the crime; she says that with her magic arts she caused Aligi to think he had killed his father, but insists that in fact the crime was committed by herself. Aligi, stupefied by the potion he has drunk, believes her and curses her. The mob calls for Aligi to be set free and prepare the pyre to burn Mila; she goes to the stake with serenity, knowing that she has saved her love. Only Ornella understands her sacrifice and weeps for her.

■ This is one of Pizzetti's most successful operas. We find here that perfect fusion of words and music that characterizes the better operas of this composer. Another important element is the use of the chorus, which gives the opera the quality of a 'dramatic madrigal'.

THE SAINT OF BLEECKER STREET

Music-drama in three acts and five scenes: words and music by Gian Carlo Menotti (born 1911). First performance: New York, Broadway Theatre, 27 December 1954; first performance in U.K.: B.B.C. Television, 1967.

SYNOPSIS. Bleecker Street, in the Italian quarter of New York. Annina (soprano), a rich girl, has intense religious visions and the stigmata appear on her hands. She lives with her brother Michele (tenor), who wants to keep her away from what he considers the hysterical superstition of their neighbours. They regard her as a saint, with power to cure their disabilities. Annina has the support of a priest, Don Marco (bass). During a wedding party, Annina and Don Marco reprove Desideria (mezzo-soprano), Michele's mistress, for her immoral conduct; Michele accuses them of bigotry and Desideria, beside herself, says that Michele will not marry her because he is in love with his own sister. Michele kills her and runs into hiding. Some months later, Annina and Michele meet. He implores her to leave the city with him, but she refuses and begs him to give himself up. She tells Don Marco that she wants to become a nun before she dies. During her initiation ceremony Michele reappears, still hoping to influence his sister. Annina is so weak that she cannot hear him: the ceremony continues, and as Annina draws her last breath, Don Marco raises her lifeless arm and places the consecrated ring on her finger.

■ Like *The Consul*, *The Medium* and others of Menotti's operas, this work has its roots in the reality of daily life, the particular and limited reality of a colony of Italian immigrants with all their human and sometimes obscene passions, their fanatical superstitious kind of religion. In this opera, however, realism and daily life do not always attain to drama, but tend to be reduced to a highly coloured and violent chronicle. Nevertheless the opera was well received by the public, who filled the Broadway Theatre for a hundred consecutive evenings.

THE MIDSUMMER MARRIAGE

Opera in three acts by Michael Tippett (born 1905), libretto by the composer. First performance: London, Covent Garden, 27 January 1955.

Milhaud's David *at La Scala in Milan, 1954. Sets and costumes by Nicola Benois, produced by Margherita Wallmann.*

ORIGINAL CAST. Joan Sutherland, Leigh, Dominguez, Lewis, Lanigan. Conductor: John Pritchard.

SYNOPSIS. Act I. *Morning*. A sanctuary in a hilltop clearing at dawn, on midsummer day. Mark (tenor), a young man of unknown parentage, is to marry Jenifer (soprano). Their friends celebrate with dancing, but King Fisher (baritone), Jenifer's father and a businessman, tries to stop the proceedings, assuming that they mean to elope. Each of the lovers goes in search of that part of him/herself which he/she feels he/she lacks – Jenifer towards masculine reason and assertion, Mark toward instinct. They reappear half-transfigured in ecstasy. Act II. *Afternoon*. Jack (tenor), a mechanic, and Bella (soprano), King Fisher's secretary, affirm their love which requires no deep philosophical and psychological adjustment to be strong and tender. A series of ritual dances takes place. Act III. *Evening and Night*. The celebrations have continued and everyone is rather tired, until King Fisher announces the arrival of Madame Sosostris (contralto), a clairvoyante, to give her opinion in opposition to the traditional rites of the Ancients, who rule in the sanctuary. A heavily veiled figure is carried in and she declares that Mark and Jenifer are in love, and ready to accept one another. King Fisher tears the veil off her to reveal a huge flower-bud, whose petals open to reveal the couple. They face King Fisher. He dies. The dancers begin a ritual fire dance and the lovers withdraw into the flower, which bursts into flames, before they are seen again as their normal selves in the light of a new dawn.

■ Tippett's first opera. Inspired by Mozart's *The Magic Flute*, the music is deeply-felt and often very beautiful.

IL CAPPELLO DI PAGLIA DI FIRENZE
(Literal translation: The Florentine Straw Hat)

Music-farce in two acts and five scenes by Nino Rota (born 1911), libretto by the composer and his mother Ernesta, based on the comedy by Labiche: Le Chapeau de paille d'Italie. *Composed in 1946. First performance: Palermo, Teatro Massimo, April 1955. First performance in U.S.A.: Santa Fé, 1977.*

SYNOPSIS. At the house of Fadinard (tenor), a wealthy young man, there is feverish preparation for the celebration of his marriage to Elena (light soprano), daughter of the farmer Nonancourt (bass). Unfortunately on the way home Fadinard's horse has completely ruined – by eating it – the straw hat of Anaide (soprano), who was out walking with her lover, Lieutenant Emilio (baritone). The couple follow Fadinard: if he does not remedy the damage done by his horse, Anaide will be in serious trouble with her jealous husband. The excellent quality of the straw hat makes it difficult to find a similar one, as there are only a few of its kind on the market. A whole merry-go-round of adventures and misunderstandings now begins, from the milliner's shop to the house of Anaide's husband, whose suspicions are thus confirmed, and the postponement of Fadinard's wedding. Vézinet (tenor), a deaf old uncle, unwittingly solves the complicated situation: he gives Elena a hat identical to the one Fadinard is trying so hard to find. With the hat in her possession, Anaide can mock her jealous husband, Fadinard persuades the father of his betrothed to consent again to the marriage, and the wedding procession is once again under way.

■ The opera has been performed in Italy and abroad; in Milan, at the Piccola Scala, it was included in the programme for two consecutive seasons. This *divertissement*, which had already been used in the cinema by René Clair, is a perfect vehicle for an endless number of jokes. The witty and graceful music accords perfectly with the lively text.

IRISCHE LEGENDE (Irish Legend)

Opera in five scenes by Werner Egk (born 1901), text by the composer, based on W. B. Yeats's The Countess Cathleen *(1892). First performance: Salzburg, Festspielhaus, 17 August 1955.*

CAST. Borkh, Klose, Lorenz, Böhme, Frick. Conductor: George Szell.

THE FIERY ANGEL (Ognennyj Angel or L'Ange de Feu)

Opera in five acts and seven scenes by Sergei Prokofiev (1891–1953), libretto by the composer, based on the novel by Valery Bryusov (1908). First performance: (concert version) Paris, Théâtre des Champs-Elysées, 25 November 1954; (staged version) Venice, Teatro La Fenice, 14 September 1955. First performance in U.K.: London, New Opera Company at Sadler's Wells, 27 July 1965; in U.S.A., New York, City Opera, 22 September 1965.

ORIGINAL CAST. D. Dow, R. Panerai, M. Borriello, A. Annaloro, E. Campi, G. Carturan. Conductor: Nino Sanzogno.

SYNOPSIS. Act I. Germany, sixteenth century. A room in a poor inn. Ruprecht (baritone), returned from long voyages to America, hears a woman's screams; he bursts into the next room and finds Renata (soprano), a young woman, distressed by some invisible danger. When she has calmed down, she tells her story: ever since she was a child, she has been visited by an angel, Madiel. When she became a young woman, and offered him her love, the angel disappeared, but promised that he would return in mortal guise. Renata subsequently thought she recognized him in Heinrich, the Count who became her lover. Now he has abandoned her, and she is tormented by terrible visions. Ruprecht decides to help her to find Count Heinrich. A fortune-teller (mezzo-soprano) predicts bloodshed. Act II. Cologne. Renata, with the help of Ruprecht, has turned to witchcraft to find her lover. Jacob Glock (tenor), the Jew who provides her with occult writings, proposes that they visit Agrippa von Nettesheim (tenor), a magician. Agrippa, however, parries Ruprecht's requests, saying he is only a scholar. Act III. Outside Heinrich's house. Renata has tracked down her Heinrich but he has again rejected her. She presses Ruprecht, convinced that he was deluded to imagine Heinrich was Madiel. Heinrich then appears, shining like an angel, and Renata changes her mind. But by then a duel has been arranged between Heinrich and Ruprecht. On the banks of the Rhine, Ruprecht is wounded in the duel and succoured by his friend Mathias (baritone). Renata swears that she loves him and she seems to join him in his delirium. A doctor (tenor) arrives, and promises to save him. Act IV. Square in Cologne. Renata leaves Ruprecht, believing her love for him to be sinful, and enters a convent. The young man recovers in an inn, where Mephistopheles (tenor) and Faust (baritone) are staying. The devil mocks the innkeeper in a macabre and grotesque scene, then asks Ruprecht to take him round the city, and the young man eventually agrees. Act V. A convent. There has been no peace in the convent since

Renata was accepted as a novice. The Mother Superior (mezzo-soprano) and the Inquisitor (bass) interrogate her, and she tells them of her visions: all the nuns gradually fall victim to a diabolical anguish, groaning and suffering convulsions. After scenes of wild hys

Britten's The Turn of the Screw *at La Scala, Milan, in 1969. Designed by Virginio Puecher and Ugo Mulas.*

teria, Renata is sentenced to be burnt at the stake for witchcraft.

■ After his unsuccessful *Love for Three Oranges*, Prokofiev devoted himself with passion to *The Fiery Angel*: although beset by economic difficulties, he lived in solitude for eighteen months in a small Bavarian village, neglecting almost all other work. The composing of the opera took from 1922 to 1925. So much effort contrasts strangely with the complete oblivion into which the opera was to fall. The second act was performed only once, in concert form, in 1928. Then the score was lost, and only found again by chance in Paris in the archives of a publishing house. Although Prokofiev was still alive in 1952, the year when the score was found again, the first performance of the opera was given posthumously. Indeed, the composer himself had made no effort to get it performed, and the one attempt, by the Berlin Municipal Opera, came to nothing for no apparent reason. Brought to the stage for the Festival of Venice, it had been televised the previous year, 25 November 1954, in concert form, from the Théâtre des Champs-Elysées in Paris, and is now universally considered one of Prokofiev's masterpieces, in which he has successfully treated a subject that was, for him, unusually complex and tortuous.

LA GUERRA (The War)
Music-drama in one act by Renzo Rossellini (born 1908), libretto by the composer. First performance: Naples, Teatro San Carlo, 25 February 1956.

ORIGINAL CAST. Olivero, Pobbe, Gueli, Di Palma, Meletti, Clabassi. Conductor: Oliviero De Fabritiis.

SYNOPSIS. Modern times. A city in a country dominated by foreign rule, Marta (mezzo-soprano), a paralysed old woman, lives with her daughter Maria (soprano) in a semi-basement. The two women anxiously await the return of Maria's younger brother Marco (spoken role), who had had to flee three years ago to escape the army of the invader. The postman (bass), a neighbour, who brings Maria news of the enemy's retreat in face of the army of Liberation, warns her that she will be in grave danger once the invaders have been driven out. He refers to her relationship with Erik (tenor), an officer in the enemy army. That evening, while Marta is asleep, Erik secretly enters the house and begs Maria to go with him; she is expecting a child and cannot decide what to do. Erik has to leave to take charge of his troops. Marta, who has overheard what they were saying, implores Maria not to leave her. An air-raid warning sounds, and the basement is quickly crowded with people come to take shelter. The drama ends with the return of Marco, now blind. He is left with the body of his mother, who dies with the effort of going to meet him. Maria disappears and rejoins Erik. The crowd jubilantly celebrate their regained liberty.

■ Renzo Rossellini, the composer of several sound tracks for the cinema and brother of the famous neorealist director, Roberto, only began writing for the theatre in his maturity. With this drama of very contemporary mood and subject-matter, he shows how themes that lend themselves to film treatment can be equally well expressed by using the resources of the operatic stage.

L'IPOCRITA FELICE (The Happy Hypocrite)
Opera in one act by Giorgio Federico Ghedini (1892–1965), libretto by F. Antonicelli, based on Max Beerbohm's The Happy Hypocrite. *First performance: Milan, Piccola Scala, 10 March 1956.*

ORIGINAL CAST. Tito Gobbi, Giuseppina Arnaldi, Anna Maria Canali, Graziella Sciutti, Antonio Pirino. Conductor: Antonino Votto.

SYNOPSIS. London in the eighteenth century. Mankind, sad and weary, asks the story-teller (tenor) for a story, and he tells the tale of Lord Inferno (baritone). In a garden in London an open-air entertainment is being given. Lord Inferno is attending the play, accompanied by his mistress Gambogi (mezzo-soprano). On the stage is Cupid, in the guise of a dwarf (soprano), and then the leading actress enters, the beautiful Jenny Mere (soprano). The dwarf shoots his arrows and runs off gleefully. Lord Inferno is struck by one of Cupid's arrows and falls in love with Jenny. But she will have nothing to do with him, declaring that she will marry only a man with the face of a saint, whereas Lord Inferno has a face that shows only too clearly the vain, worldly life he has led. From a mask-maker, Aeneas, Lord Inferno procures another face that will cover his ugliness. He is thus transformed into Lord Paradise, and this time Jenny, who has also been struck by one of the dwarf's arrows, returns his love. They marry and live in happiness, but Gambogi is jealous and one day strips the mask off her lover's face. He confesses his deceit to Jenny, and begs her forgiveness, but through the miracle of love Jenny now sees Lord Inferno's own face as more beautiful than it was before. Gambogi is foiled, and the opera ends with an invitation to believe in love, the only ray of hope in life.

DER STURM (The Tempest)

Opera in three acts and nine scenes by Frank Martin (1890–1974), based on Shakespeare's The Tempest. *First performance: Vienna, Staatsoper, 9 June 1956.*

SYNOPSIS. A ship carrying Antonio, Duke of Milan, Alonso, King of Naples, and Ferdinand, the King's son, is shipwrecked in a violent tempest off the coast of

Marie Collier in Walton's Troilus and Cressida, *April 1963.*

an island. The storm had been unleashed by the magic arts of Prospero, Antonio's brother, who had been deposed twelve years before by Antonio with the help of Alonso, and left with his daughter Miranda to perish at sea. But Prospero and Miranda had been cast ashore on this island, where the wicked witch Sycorax has been banished. Prospero had set free various spirits imprisoned by the witch, including Ariel and Sycorax's son Caliban, a monstrously ugly creature. Ferdinand, thought by his father to have been drowned, meets Miranda, falls in love with her, and obtains Prospero's consent to marry her. At Prospero's command, Ariel frightens Antonio and Alonso to the point that they repent their evil-doing. Alonso is reunited with his son, Prospero is reconciled with his brother and, abandoning his magic arts, prepares to sail away with the others and leave the island to be ruled by Caliban.

■ In the opera, which faithfully follows the version made by Schlegel from Shakespeare's play, the lyric passages alternate with *singspiel* and spoken dialogue, and the dramatic scenes with comic and elegiac scenes. The appearances of Ariel are accompanied by comment from the chorus, the role itself being performed by a dancer.

KÖNIG HIRSCH (King Stag/Il Re Cervo)

Opera in three acts by Hans Werner Henze (born 1926), libretto by Heinz von Cramer, based on Carlo Gozzi's fairy story Il re Cervo *(1762). First performance: (original version) Berlin, Städtische Oper, 23 September 1956; (renamed* Il Re Cervo) *Cassel 1963. First performance in U.S.A.: Santa Fé, 4 August 1965.*

ORIGINAL CAST. Pilarczyk, Konya, Neralis, Junwirt, Krebs. Conductor: Hermann Scherchen.

SYNOPSIS. Act I. In an imaginary kingdom somewhere in the South, the Governor (bass-baritone) tries to seize power from the King (tenor), still a young lad, by arranging for him to be abandoned in the forest. Brought up by the forest animals, the King returns after some years and regains his throne. Two speaking statues, Truth and Wisdom, help him. It is time the King took a wife, and the two statues (contraltos) point out the virtues and defects of all the girls who parade before him. He falls in love with one maiden (soprano) and, fearful lest the statues advise against his love, he smashes them. The Governor accuses the maiden of wanting to kill the King, and she is condemned to death. The King realizes that it is his duty to save her; he pardons her and then, renouncing his kingdom, returns to the forest to live close to nature and in search of peace. A parrot (ballerina) who accompanies him will put him in touch with the world of nature. Act II. Hoping to kill the King, the Governor organizes a hunt in the forest. The parrot and Nature defend the King, who is changed into a stag, but a message from the parrot to the King is intercepted by Checco, the young dreamer (tenor), who reveals the King's new shape and so the hunters chase the stag. The whole forest protects the King stag and drives the hunters away. The King's metamorphosis is only apparent, however; time passes and he feels once more the call of the world of men, and is unable to be at peace within himself. Understanding that he must accept the limitations of the human condition, he returns to the city to live among men, and to seek the love of a woman. Act III. The Governor has meanwhile made himself King, but fearful that the real King might return, he lives in a continual state of fear and apprehension. With the return of the legitimate King the situation is brought to a head and the Governor is killed by the same assassin he had hired to kill the King. And so justice and happiness win the day: the King, restored to the form of a man once again, marries the maiden he loves.

■ *King Stag*, written in Italy, is an act of homage to Italy and the Italians and, as the composer said himself, to 'beautiful Naples, city of kindness and sunshine, and her inhabitants, who are so enigmatic that one thinks one will never understand them'. Influenced by the avant-garde twelve-tone technique from Schönberg to Webern, Henze has always taken up an intermediate position with regard to the more extreme and severe forms, preferring to incorporate avant-garde elements within a musical framework that has its roots in Berg and Stravinsky, and is sometimes coloured by shades of jazz or popular music. The score of *King Stag* exemplifies this approach: the music has a fundamentally modern structure, but there are also explicit concessions to a non-operatic language, influenced by popular and traditional Italian songs and tunes. The opera, which might content neither the traditionalist nor the avant-garde listener, has nevertheless been warmly received, even though applause and opposition both continued for half an hour at the première.

DIALOGUES DES CARMÉLITES (Dialogues of the Carmelites)

Opera in three acts and twelve scenes by Francis Poulenc (1899–1963), libretto by Emmet Lavery, based on the drama by Georges Bernanos, inspired by the novel Die Letzte am Schafott *(1931) by Gertrud von Le Fort and a scenario of Rev. Fr Bruckberger and Philippe Agostini. First performance: Milan, Teatro alla Scala, 26 January 1957. First performance in U.K.: London, Covent Garden, 18 January 1958; in U.S.A.: San Francisco, 20 September 1957.*

ORIGINAL CAST. Virginia Zeani, Gianna Pederzini, Scipio Colombo, Nicola Filacuridi, Leila Gencer, Gigliola Frazzoni, Eugenia Ratti, Vittoria Palombini, Fiorenza Cossotto, Alvinio Misciano, Antonio Pirino, Arturo La Porta, Michele Cazzato, Carlo Gasperini. Conductor: Nino Sanzogno.

SYNOPSIS. The story is set in Paris in 1789. The Marquis de la Force (baritone), in a room in his palace, is waiting for his daughter Blanche (soprano) and at the same time trying to calm his son the Chevalier (tenor), who is anxious lest the tumult of the crowd upset his sister's already precarious balance of mind. Blanche enters and it is clear that she is agitated and troubled: she announces her intention to retire to a convent where she will find peace. Some time later, pale rumours of events reach the Carmelite convent where Blanche has retired and has adopted the nun's habit. She has become friendly with Constance (soprano), although reproving her for her frivolous character. One day Constance tells Blanche that she knows, by miraculous intuition, that they will die together. Blanche is agitated and forbids Constance to speak of death. Meanwhile the Prioress (contralto), who is gravely ill but unable to face impending death with serenity, confesses her anguish to her companions. Blanche sees her own drama reflected in the Mother Superior's and is profoundly disturbed; Constance takes a very different attitude, declaring that a person should not die thus locked in egoism. Some days later the convent is attacked by the mob. The Sisters decide to stay and accept martyrdom. Only Blanche, who had initially seemed to accept the idea of sacrifice, flees and returns home. The Sisters are arrested and sentenced to death: one by one they mount the scaffold with dignity, singing the *Salve regina*. When it is Constance's turn, Blanche suddenly rushes out of the watching crowd towards the guillotine. Transfigured by a mysterious joy, that has driven out all her fear, she sings a hymn of glory to God and is ready to face her martyrdom.

■ The idea for this opera was suggested to Poulenc in 1953 by the publisher Ricordi; in June 1956 he delivered the score to the publisher. Poulenc has retained the beautiful, feminine qualities of Bernanos' work, while refraining from trying to penetrate the labyrinth of philosophical arguments that are woven into the original. The story itself stems from a novel by Gertrud von Le Fort, which in its turn was inspired by historical fact: the execution of sixteen Carmelite nuns from Compiègne on 17 July 1794 in Paris.

UNA DOMANDA DI MATRIMONIO (A Wedding Proposal)

Comic opera in one act by Luciano Chailly (born 1920), libretto by Claudio Fino, based on the comedy by Anton Chekhov. First performance: Milan, Piccola Scala, 22 May 1957.

ORIGINAL CAST. Luigi Alva, Renato Capecchi, Eugenia Ratti. Conductor: Nino Sanzogno.

SYNOPSIS. Lomov (tenor), a shy and awkward peasant, who suffers from a nervous tic, decides to ask the wealthy Chabukov (baritone) for the hand of his aged daughter, Natalya (soprano), not because of his love for her, but for practical reasons. The conversation

Prokofiev's The Fiery Angel *at the Paris Opéra, 1965.*

with Chabukov is almost disastrous, because he thinks that Lomov is asking him for money, but the moment he understands that Lomov wishes to propose to his daughter, he is delighted and leaves the couple to themselves. However, their first meeting turns into a fierce row (Natalya being unaware of the reason for Lomov's visit) about the ownership of a field situated between their properties. After Lomov has left angrily, Natalya is told by her father what the reason was of Lomov's visit. She has him recalled immediately, suddenly overwhelmed with love for the only man who is interested in her. They meet again. Having calmed down, she asks him to declare himself. He is too shy to find the courage to do so. She tries to make superficial conversation about hunting to make him feel at ease. But this harmless subject results in a second row about the quality of their hounds and Natalya's father intervenes and insults the poor Lomov to such an extent that the latter goes away. When calmed down, the father tries desperately to persuade the couple to marry immediately before another row intervenes. Both are very happy. However, the moment the hounds are mentioned, the row starts again and the father says philosophically 'Here begins marital happiness'.

■ *Una Domanda di Matrimonio*, the second theatrical composition of Luciano Chailly, demonstrates his personal style and has an immediate impact. It was very favourably received and there were 200 performances in its first 20 years.

MOSES UND ARON (Moses and Aaron)

Incomplete opera in three acts by Arnold Schönberg (1874–1951), text by the composer after the Book of Exodus. *First given in a concert performance: Hamburg Radio, 12 March 1954. First staged performance: Zurich, Stadttheater, 6 June 1957. First performance in U.K.: London, Covent Garden, 28 June 1965; in the U.S.A.: Boston, 2 November 1966.*

SYNOPSIS. Act I. Scene I. The Calling of Moses. Moses (bass-baritone, *Sprechstimme* role) is praying by the Burning Bush, and out of the Bush the Voice of God (represented by six solo voices and speaking chorus) answers him, telling him to enlighten the chosen people of Israel, free them from the slavery of Egypt and lead them to the Promised Land. Moses is filled with dismay, for he fears he has not the gift of eloquence (*'Ich kann denken . . . aber nicht reden'*). But the voice tells him to go down into the wilderness, where he will meet his brother Aron; Aron will know the words for Moses, just as Moses knows the thoughts of God. Scene II. Moses meets Aron in the desert. Moses reveals to his brother the mission to which they have both been called. Aron (tenor) submits to the will of God, but doubts whether the people can love an invisible God, a God they cannot visualize (*'Unsichtbar! Unvorstellbar!'*). Scene III. Moses and Aron bring God's Message to the people. Meanwhile the people are growing agitated. A young girl (soprano) says she has seen Aron, in a strange exalted state, going away into the wilderness. A young man (tenor) says he has seen him appear in a cloud of light. Another man (baritone) maintains that he has heard that a God has commanded Aron to go and meet Moses. The people, spurred on by the Priest (bass), argue and conjecture about the nature of this new God, and are torn between hope and scepticism. The hubbub increases, and finally Moses and Aron appear. Scene IV. Moses recounts the incomprehensible virtues of God; Aron rouses the people's pride in being chosen and their longing for freedom. But who can hope for salvation from a God who is eternally invisible? (*'Anbeten? Wen?'* – 'To worship? Whom?'). The doubters grow scornful. Moses is exhausted and disheartened, but Aron takes up his rod and performs the first miracle (*'Das Wort bin ich und die Tat'*): he casts the unbending rod (*das Gesetz*/the Law) to the ground and it turns into a serpent (*die Klugheit*/discretion). The people begin to fear the new God, but they fear Pharaoh even more. Aron insists that they are ill and the crowd are terrified when he shows them the hand of Moses diseased with leprosy; suddenly the leprosy vanishes and the hand looks healthy once more. (*'Erkennet euch auch darin'* – 'Discover therein your likeness'). The people rejoice, crying that a God who can cure leprosy can defeat Pharaoh. They demand to set out immediately for freedom, across the wilderness. The Priest asks them how they will survive. Aron replies with another miracle: water in a pitcher is turned into blood – the blood of the Hebrews, the chosen people who, like the Nile, are the lifeblood of the country; then the blood becomes water again, the water of the Nile, in which Pharaoh will perish. Then Aron, in the name of the Lord God, promises to lead his people to the land of milk and honey. The people, won over by Aron's eloquence and the miracles he performs, fall to their knees and worship the new God. Through Him, mightier than the Egyptian gods, they will be free. Interlude. An invisible chorus, speaking and singing, asks anxiously where Moses can be. It is now some time since he was last seen. (*'Wo ist Moses? Wo ist sein Gott? Wo ist der Ewige?'*.) Act II. Scene I. Aron and the Seventy Elders before the Mountain of Revelation. For forty days the people have been waiting at the foot of Mount Sinai for Moses to come down with the tablets of the Law. Uncertainty breeds unrest. The Seventy Elders and the Priest are in agreement: they can wait no longer. Aron tries to calm them (*'Wenn Moses von dieser Höhe herniedersteigt . . . soll mein Mund euch Recht und Gesetz vermitteln'*), but the people are in revolt. Scene II. They want to tear Moses to pieces, to *see* his Omnipresent God or to return to the worship of their old images of Gods. The Elders beg Aron to intervene, and his only recourse to prevent the slaughter of the priests is to offer the people their forms of worship. He tells them to bring gold, which he fashions into a golden calf. Scene III. The Golden Calf and the Altar. Before this statue he tells the people that God is in everything that exists. This gold in itself is immutable; only its form is changed. In this symbol they may worship themselves. Meanwhile processions of offerings, food and animals throng the stage as the sacrifice is prepared. An animal is garlanded and led to the altar. Then the dance of the slaughterers begins, the Dance round the golden calf or 'Tanz der Schlächter'. The animal is quartered and the pieces of meat thrown to the crowd.

An invalid woman (alto), brought before the golden calf, rises from her stretcher, cured. Beggars (6–8 altos and 6–8 basses) offer their poor rags to the golden calf; old men (tenors) sacrifice their last moments of life to it. . . . The chiefs of the tribes (tenors and basses), led by the Ephraimite (baritone), gallop around it to join in the homage to the idol; a youth who speaks against their idolatry and still believes in the one true God is brutally beaten to death. (*'Rein sei der Ausblick zur Ewigkeit!'*). The frenzy intensifies as the people become drunker and wilder. The Elders praise the Gods of sense and spirit and the revels culminate in the sacrifice of four naked virgins (two sopranos, two altos), who are stabbed before the altar by priests armed with long knives. As dancing, rape, destruction and suicide sweep the stage and music resounds from all directions, Moses comes down from the mount. Scene IV. His cry of anguish is heard in the distance. Once on stage, his wrath is terrible indeed. Furiously he orders the destruction of the golden calf. Scene V. Moses and Aron. The two brothers face one another alone. (*'Aron, was hast du getan?'*.) Aron replies that he has worked marvels for eyes and ears to witness and counters Moses's intransigence by objecting that the tablets of the Law are themselves only an image, a tangible expression of thought. Moses is seized by doubt, destroying the tablets, and asks God to take the mission away from him. He falls to the ground in despair, while on the horizon can be seen a column of fire which shows the way to the Promised Land. Aron

sings of image and ideas as one as he glimpses the Infinite showing not Himself but The Way. For the people this God is still stronger than the Egyptians. Moses, not believing that God can be encompassed, despairs (*'O Wort, du Wort, das mir fehlt'*). Act III. (not set to music). Moses has asserted his authority and had Aron bound, accusing him of seducing the people from the true God for his own glorification. He reaffirms his faith in an inexorable God, the head of a chosen people unlike the other peoples of the earth, who are slaves to vain ambitions and ephemeral pleasures. When asked if Aron should be killed, Moses tells the warriors to free him: God will show whether he is to live. (*'Gebt ihn frei, und wenn er es vermag, so lebe er'*.) As soon as his chains are loosened, Aron falls dead. Moses's final words reassure the people that even alone in the wilderness they will be one with God.

■ *Moses und Aron*, the apex of Schönberg's artistic and spiritual evolution, was left unfinished at his death. He had begun the text, which is complete, as far back as 1926. The work, originally conceived as a cantata, finally became an opera-oratorio in three acts. The music for the first two acts was mostly written between 1930 and 1932 and resumed shortly before the composer's death in 1951. Schönberg never wrote the music for the third act. The explanation often given for this is the advent of Nazism and Schönberg's emigration to the United States. The deeper reason was probably the difficulty of expressing the philosophical contradiction of the theme – the inevitable distortion of a visionary's uncompromising ideals by the attempts to communicate them to the people.

It is no coincidence that Moses's closing words bewail his inarticulacy. It is as if the work itself were declaring the impossibility of its own completion. Schönberg himself, although he seems at least to have planned the music for the final act, wrote in 1951 of the possibility of performing the opera either by staging the first two acts (omitting the third altogether or else agreeing 'that it is possible for the third act to be spoken, in case I cannot complete the composition') or by limiting the performance to the 'Dance round the golden calf' (Act II, Scene III). The 'Dance' was in fact performed separately in Darmstadt, on 29 June 1951, and was enthusiastically received. The score is at once one of the most complex and one of the most lucid ever written by Schönberg. Based on a single twelve-note series, it demands a full symphony orchestra, a very large chorus, a group of six solo voices in the orchestra and numerous soloists. Apart from more traditional singing techniques, there is also a wide use of *Sprechgesang* ('Speech-song' or 'notated' speech). The characterization of the main vocal roles is particularly significant. Moses, who understands thought but lacks eloquence, and who in the Bible is a stammerer, speaks throughout the opera in *sprechgesang*. Aron, his spokesman, his voice, sings lyrically but conventionally, which ultimately carries the danger of distorting the lofty nature of Thought.

Act II, Scene Four of Poulenc's Dialogues des Carmélites *at La Scala, Milan 1957.*

DIE HARMONIE DER WELT (The Harmony of the World)

Opera in five acts by Paul Hindemith (1895–1963), libretto by the composer. First performance: Munich, Prinzregententheater, 11 August 1957.

SYNOPSIS. The central character in the opera is the great astronomer and astrologer Johannes Kepler (1571–1630), who aimed to reconcile Science and Religion as part of the cosmic harmony. The complementary character is General Wallenstein (1583–1634) who believed in the stars and their influence. The opera, in fourteen scenes, depicts the two main characters searching for harmony in the cosmos while the Thirty Years War is raging. Kepler stands for 'contemplative man': he seeks the order that governs the world in the laws that underlie the ceaseless movement of the planets. Wallenstein is the 'virtuous man of action': he seeks an earthly harmony, a kingdom that unites all Europe. The opera ends with a final scene of baroque grandeur, a celestial apotheosis, in which all the characters, transformed into zodiacal symbols, shine in the firmament. Kepler is the Earth, Emperor Rudolf II is the Sun, Wallenstein becomes Mars, Susanna, Kepler's wife, becomes Venus, and his mother Katherina is the Moon.

■ As in Hindemith's mature style, the music of this opera is full of linear complexity and rhythmic energy.

Even in his later years, however, Hindemith continued to keep aloof of recent developments in music, including the then prevailing twelve-tone technique, and remained a confirmed advocate of tonality and traditional vocal and instrumental practice. In this allegory, with its mystical and medieval flavour, he has nevertheless given powerful expression to his beliefs in a universal cosmic order.

VANESSA

Opera in four acts by Samuel Barber (born 1910), libretto by Gian Carlo Menotti (born 1911). First performance: New York, Metropolitan Opera House, 15 January 1958.

ORIGINAL CAST. Eleanor Steber (Vanessa), Rosalind Elias (Erika), Regina Resnik (The old Baroness), Nicolai Gedda (Anatol), Giorgio Tozzi (Doctor), George Cehanovsky (The Major-Domo), Robert Nagy (A Footman). Conductor: Dimitri Mitropoulos.

SYNOPSIS. The action takes place in a country mansion in Scandinavia around 1905. Vanessa (soprano), a woman of great beauty, has been waiting twenty years for her lover's return – she waits in vain, for he is dead. Anatol (tenor), a handsome young man who is in fact her lover's son, arrives at the house. He falls in love with Erika (mezzo-soprano), Vanessa's niece, but at length is rejected by her. Eventually it is Vanessa and Anatol who marry and leave for a life together in Paris. It is then Erika's turn to wait in the castle for her lover's return.

■ The first performances were notable for Menotti's production (he is himself a composer of opera) and for the costumes and sets of Cecil Beaton. Together with the mature craftsmanship which the music showed these performances helped establish Barber as one of the leading American composers of the fifties. The opera was awarded the Pulitzer Prize in 1958.

ASSASSINIO NELLA CATTEDRALE (Murder in the Cathedral)
Tragic opera in two acts and an interlude by Ildebrando Pizzetti (1880–1968), libretto by the composer based on Murder in the Cathedral *by T. S. Eliot (1935). Translated by Alberto Castelli. First performance: Milan, Teatro alla Scala, 1 March 1958.*

ORIGINAL CAST. Nicola Rossi-Lemeni (Becket), Aldo Bertocci, Enrico Campi, Gabrella Carturan, Antonio Cassinelli, Adolfo Cormanni, Dino Dondi, Leyla Gencer, Silvio Maionica, Mario Ortica, Rinaldo Pelizzoni, Lino Puglisi, Marco Steffenoni, Nicola Zaccaria, Conductor: Gianandrea Gavazzeni.

SYNOPSIS. Act I. The story is set in Canterbury, in December 1170. Tommaso Becket (bass), Archbishop of Canterbury and champion of the independence of the church from the state, has just returned to Canterbury after seven years' exile in France, brought about by disagreement with King Henry II. He is welcomed with affection by the faithful, who are at the same time fearful lest his return should signal further troubles and hardship. In his study, he is visited by four tempters (2 tenors and 2 basses). The first urges him to his old carefree life as one of the king's favourites; the second exhorts him to take up political power again; the third suggests that he lead the common people in revolt and overthrow the monarchy; the fourth, more crafty and astute, tempts him with the thought of martyrdom. Tommaso prays to God to save him from these temptations, and after he has prayed he appears calmer and more serene. Interlude. The Archbishop, preaching in the Cathedral on Christmas morning, tells the faithful that true happiness lies only in submission to the will of God, and that he is ready to accept what comes from God's hands, even martyrdom. The orchestral section which follows is a commentary on the sermon and the progress of the drama. Act II. Four knights (2 tenors and 2 basses) arrive asking to see the Archbishop. They accuse him of betraying the king, but withdraw when he defends himself against the charge. At the hour of Vespers, the priests (tenor, baritone, bass) and the faithful, feeling that some catastrophe is imminent, want to bar the doors. Becket will not allow this, saying that the House of God must always be open. The four

knights return and demand that Becket should make an act of submission to the king. When he refuses they kill him with their swords. They tell the terrified congregation that the assassination was the only way to resolve the conflict between the Church and the monarchy. A chorus of the faithful sing a hymn to 'Blessed Thomas'.

■ This is one of Pizzetti's last operas, yet the logical sequel to his work from *Fedra* (1915) to *Figlia di Jorio* (1954). These three operas have one feature in common: they are all works of great breadth, inspired by noble vision and dominated by an intense religious feeling. Pizzetti's skill in catching the general sense of Eliot's poem, telescoping and condensing the action and interpreting it musically, made the première a considerable success.

MARIA GOLOVIN
Opera in three acts by Gian-Carlo Menotti (born 1911), libretto by the composer. First performance: Brussels, American Pavilion of the World Fair, 20 August 1958. First performance in the U.S.A.: New York, Martin Becket Theater, 5 November 1958.

ORIGINAL CAST. Franca Duvel, Patricia Neway and Herbert Handt. Conductor: Peter Herman Adler.

SYNOPSIS. The action takes place in a small frontier town, about 1919. Maria Golovin (soprano) is awaiting her husband's return from a prisoner-of-war camp, and comes to spend the summer with her son Trottolo and Dr Zuckertanz (tenor), his tutor, in the villa of Donato (bass-baritone), a young blind man, who lives with his mother (contralto) and their maid Agata (mezzo-soprano). Donato, sensitive and protected, spends his time making small bird-cages. He is at once attracted to Maria and she, because she is lonely and sorry for the unhappy young man, becomes his mistress. They are not happy, however, because Donato is jealous, possessive and neurotic. The tension increases when an escaping prisoner (baritone) forces himself on the household. Maria stays too long at a party and, on her return, the enraged Donato grabs a gun to shoot her. His mother guides his arm away, but he thinks he has killed Maria. He sprinkles flowers where he thinks Maria lies.

■ The music of this intense drama is 'the most subdued that Menotti has ever written, without excesses, sweetly modulated, sparingly and appropriately orchestrated' (Abbiati), but it was nevertheless greeted with criticism as well as applause. The climax is cruelly calculated and very characteristic of the composer's sense of drama – feelings are exposed in all their ambivalence and irrationality.

LA VOIX HUMAINE (The Human Voice)
Tragédie-lyrique in one act by Francis Poulenc (1899–1963), after Jean Cocteau's play of 1930. First

Schönberg's Moses und Aron *in the 1973 Paris Opéra production; sets by Günther Schneider-Siemssen, costumes by Hill Reihs-Gromes, produced by Gérôme.*

■ The idea for this opera was given to Poulenc by his friend and publisher Hervé Dujardin and it was created specifically for the singer Denise Duval. Poulenc follows the Cocteau text exactly with all the interruptions and volte-faces of the original, but the score does not quite achieve the tension that the drama suggests. Although the music is subordinate to the words, the composer nevertheless shows a penetrating insight into feminine psychology and the *état d'âme* previously explored in his full-scale opera, *Les dialogues des Carmélites*. By using only a single character, Poulenc has attempted an unusual theatrical form – a solo opera.

A HAND OF BRIDGE
Opera in one act by Samuel Barber (born 1910), libretto by Gian Carlo Menotti (born 1911). First performance: Spoleto, Teatro Caio Melisso, 17 June 1959.

ORIGINAL CAST. Patricia Neway, Ellen Miville, William Lewis, René Miville. Conductor: Robert Feist.

SYNOPSIS. Four people – Geraldine, Sally, Bill and David – sit around a small green table, each more preoccupied with personal problems than with the card game. Between bids, they speak briefly to each other or to themselves, sometimes fatuously, at other times with genuine feeling. As the game ends, the curtain falls.

■ The opera, performed at The Spoleto Festival of Two Worlds, shows the subtle romanticism and talent for irony which characterizes all Barber's dramatic work.

performance: Paris, Opéra-Comique, 6 February 1959. First performance in U.S.A.: New York, Carnegie Hall, 23 February 1960; in U.K.: Edinburgh International Festival, 30 August 1960.

SYNOPSIS. Elle and Lui are parting lovers saying farewell over the telephone. We hear only the voice of Elle, who moves from moments of profound tenderness to intense passion and even violent emotion; Lui, on the other end of the line, remains invisible throughout. His presence is suggested only by the pauses in the woman's speech. Sometimes they break off, but neither has the courage to terminate this last, desperate leave-taking. Uncertainties, doubts, protests, assumed indifference, dark despair . . . each phase is quickly banished by the next. At last, Elle, exhausted, flings herself onto the bed, hanging onto her last slender link with her lover. Gripping the receiver she reveals her attempted suicide, and implores him to go. The drama ends with her muffled sobs as the abandoned receiver falls to the floor.

LA PROCEDURA PENALE (The Penal Process)
Opera in one act by Luciano Chailly (born 1920), libretto by Dino Buzzati. First performance: Como Festival, 30 October 1959.

SYNOPSIS. In an aristocratic salon in Milan, the Countess Mauritia Delormes serves tea to her friends. She is anguished by one of the usual problems of the hostess – to know which of her guests prefer milk or lemon in their tea. Conventional conversation prevails: the weather, the most fashionable book and the engagement of an aristocrat who has 'gone to the dogs' after an affair with a model. Titti underlines naively the most stupid points of the conversation with her extraordinary pronunciation. The twins interrupt often without a reason. Paolo sings an elegy in the style of Kurt Weill on the woes of being a widow. As one subject passes to another, the atmosphere changes, becoming tense and pregnant with suspense. A few moments later Giandomenico discovers that the Countess is implicated in a desperate crime. A short period of darkness. And then a change of characters and situation. The guests are now judges, the salon is a law-court and the hostess the accused. Everyone treats the guilty woman with relentless cruelty; they destroy her alibi. They wish to see her dead. In the end they condemn her to something worse: she is made to live in her false society with the same friends for the rest of her life.

Darkness back again. The scene and characters as before. The frivolous and mundane conversation starts all over again and the cruel interlude is forgotten. In this cold atmosphere, amongst these inexpressive, petrified faces, there remains only one question: milk or lemon in one's tea?

■ Chailly and the librettist Buzzati worked together on four operas and one ballet. According to most critics *Procedura Penale* is the most effective product of their collaboration.

LA NOTTE DI UN NEVRASTENICO (A Night in the Life of a Neurotic)
Dramma buffo in one act by Nino Rota (born 1911), text by Riccardo Bacchelli (born 1891). First performance: Milan, Piccola Scala, 8 February 1960. Conductor: Nino Sanzogno.

SYNOPSIS. The *nevrastenico*, or neurotic (bass-baritone), who is obsessed with the need for silence, is about to spend a night in a hotel. To ensure quietness, he has taken not only his own room, but the two adjoining rooms as well, nos 80 and 82. As he looks forward to an undisturbed rest, his precautions turn out to prove in vain. For there is a fair in town and the hall-porter (bass) has carelessly let no. 80 to a *commendatore*, a citizen of some standing (tenor), and no. 82 to two clandestine lovers (light soprano and tenor). The *commendatore* drops a shoe, and the sound is magnified by the acoustics of the reinforced concrete. From no. 82 the rapturous cries of the lovers can be heard. Bells ring and hotel staff come running from every side. The *nevrastenico* stands up for his rights and the intruders are driven out. When at last he seems to have some silence and expectation of sleep, he forfeits them yet again; obedient to his instructions, the room waiter (tenor) faithfully arrives at six in the morning to wake him with hot coffee.

■ This opera, though unpretentious and slight, received international interest with the award of the 1959 R.A.I. Premio Italia prize. The comic plot is enhanced by one of the most invaluable fundamentals of opera: simplicity, together with elegant lyricism, a characteristic of all Rota's music for stage and screen.

IL DOTTORE DI VETRO (The Glass Doctor)
Radio opera in one act by Roman Vlad (born 1919),

libretto by M. L. Spaziani (born 1924). First performance on the third programme of the R.A.I., 26 February 1960.

ORIGINAL CAST. Franco Calabrese, Mario Borriello, Agostino Lazzari, Teodoro Rovetta, Jolanda Giadrino, Elena Rizzieri. Conductor: Ettore Gracis.

SYNOPSIS. Isabella (soprano), the daughter of Panfilo (bass), has been promised to a rich elderly doctor (baritone). She loves Tersandro (tenor), a young man who gains employment with the doctor in order to try to dissuade him from the marriage. To this end he convinces him that love has made him fragile and turned him into glass. The doctor arrives at Panfilo's house in a basket packed with straw. His host embraces him, and the doctor swoons for fear of shattering into pieces. Isabella, who is aware of the plot, plays her part by fussing anxiously over the old man. He regains his senses and, certain that he must must be dead, insists that he is surrounded by devils. Panfilo begins to think that the doctor is not a suitable bridegroom for Isabella after all; it comes to his mind that he might marry his daughter to Tersandro, an eligible young man! The doctor's assistant at once reveals his true identity, and the young couple are soon wed.

■ Written for the 1959 Premio Italia, *Il dottore di vetro* exists in both a broadcast and a stage version. In the latter form it was given on 4 October 1965 at the Berlin Festwochen.

A MIDSUMMER NIGHT'S DREAM
Opera in three acts by Benjamin Britten (1913–1976), libretto adapted from Shakespeare by Benjamin Britten and Peter Pears. First performance in the U.K.: Aldeburgh, 11 June 1960. First performance in the U.S.A.: San Francisco, 10 October 1961.

■ Britten's view of the Dream is an interplay of three planes of experience; three quite differently peopled worlds. The world of the fairies is evoked by the haunting counter-tenor of Oberon, the mysterious and magical sound of string instruments, harp and celesta and the chantings and carollings of the fairies. The world of the lovers is warmer and more natural, but still at times highly nervous – as in the famous quarrel quartet in Act II, perhaps the most truly operatic music Britten ever wrote. The world of the rustics is very much an earthy world of humour tinged with sadness – lumbering rhythms, march tunes and the joke-within-a-joke of the play-within-a-play (Pyramus and Thisbe).

INTOLLERANZA 1960
Opera in two acts by Luigi Nono (born 1924), adapted from an idea of Angelo Maria Ripellino (born 1923)

Pizzetti's Assassinio nella cattedrale *performed outside the Basilica of Sant'Ambrogio in Milan, July 1966.*

using texts by him, Brecht, Sartre, Fučik and Mayakovsky. First performance: Venice, Teatro La Fenice, 13 April 1961. Produced by Vaclav Kaslik; designs and projections by Emilio Vedova. First performance in the U.S.A.: Boston, 22 February 1965.

ORIGINAL CAST. Petre Munteanu (The Emigrant), Catherine Gayer (The Woman), Italo Tajo (The Tortured Man). Conducted by Bruno Maderna.

SYNOPSIS. An emigrant miner (tenor) torn by homesickness runs away, abandoning the woman he loves (soprano). She does not understand his feelings and becomes his enemy. Alone and unknown, he accidentally becomes involved in a political demonstration, is arrested and, after torture and brain-washing, finally sent to a forced labour camp. After all the institutionalized brutality and pointless suffering, he still finds among his fellow-prisoners love and fellow-feeling, despite what the 'system' has tried to eradicate from the hearts of men. At the end of the opera, the land is covered by a purifying flood that symbolically sweeps everything away. Brecht's *An die Nachgeborenen* (To the Newborn) is the closing chorus, and there is here a faith in new understanding amongst men and new meaning to life.

■ The opera, dedicated to Arnold Schönberg, has been altered several times and is now entitled *Intolleranza 1971*. At the first performance, and subsequently in Cologne, it gave rise to fierce controversy both because of its political content and because of its avant-garde musical language. The music requires an orchestra of eight instruments, a large chorus, fifty solo singers and several narrators. Both electronic sound and pre-recorded voices are also relayed during the performance and various moving images are projected onto the stage, sometimes superimposed or juxtaposed. With this opera Nono aimed at a work of universal appeal that would be linked with the expressionist theatre of the twenties (Ernst Toller and Friedrich Wolf) and contemporary American theatre (Arthur Miller and Eugene O'Neill). Its message, in Nono's words, is 'The arousal of a man's conscience, an emigrant-miner who seeks a reason, a human basis for living beyond the restrictions of poverty. He has to survive intolerance and torture, in order to rediscover a fellow-feeling between himself and other men. There remains the present certainty that man needs and can find the brotherhood of man.' This opera, in its several versions, has exerted considerable influence on the younger generation of opera composers in Italy and elsewhere.

THE LONG CHRISTMAS DINNER

Opera in one act by Paul Hindemith (1895–1963), libretto by the composer after the one-act play by Thornton Wilder (born 1897). First performance: Mannheim, 17 December 1961 (in the German translation by the composer, entitled: Das lange Weihnachtsmahl*). First performance in the U.S.A.: New York, Juillard School of Music, 13 March 1963.*

SYNOPSIS. The Bayard family dining room. A long table is festively laid for Christmas dinner. To right and left there are two doors, standing respectively for life and death, the one adorned with fruit and flowers, the other with black velvet draping. The action covers a span of ninety years: ninety Christmas dinners. At the outset the house is new, and sitting at the table are the infirm Mama Bayard, her son Roderick and his wife Lucy. The old woman recalls past times and the conversation is affable and conventional. When Cousin Brandon enters we realize that five years have passed. While the conversation continues, Mama Bayard's wheelchair gradually slides towards the black door and then disappears. Yet the conversation continues almost the same as before as if little had happened: time passes. A nurse enters with a perambulator: the baby is Charles, the couple's son. Then comes his little sister Genevieve. Once again, the years pass and Roderick falls ill: by now the man of the family is young Charles, about to marry Leonora Banning. The father dies. A child is born to the new young couple, but his life journey from the door of life to the black door is very short. Brandon and Lucy disappear also and Genevieve is overcome with grief. Twins are born: then another child. Cousin Hermengard comes to live with the family and it is she who, after further episodes, sad and happy, alternating as before, is left alone at the end. She tells the audience that she plans to build a new house for the next generation.

■ *The Long Christmas Dinner* was Hindemith's last work for the theatre and like the few other works composed in his final years it is more introspective, philosophical and spiritual than the lyrical works of his middle years. The work lasts only an hour and Hindemith approached not only Wilder, but also Edith Sitwell, Eugène Ionesco and Peter Ustinov as possible librettists for a companion piece. Neither Wilder's *Hiawatha*, about a night train-journey, nor any other project was forthcoming.

KING PRIAM

Opera in three acts by Michael Tippett (born 1905); libretto by the composer. First performance: Coventry, Coventry Theatre, 29 May 1962.

ORIGINAL CAST. Marie Collier, Josephine Veasey, Margreta Elkins, Richard Lewis, Forbes Robinson. Conductor: John Pritchard.

■ The opera is inspired by the story of the last King of Troy and his death as the city burns. The composer himself has stated that the subject is the 'mysterious nature of moral choice'. The work is one of the most successful of Tippett's compositions.

LA ATLANTIDA (Atlantis)

Scenic cantata in a prologue and three acts by Manuel de Falla (1876–1946), completed by Ernest Halffter, based on the poem (1877) by Jacinto Verdaguer y Santalo, adapted by the composer. First performance in concert form: Barcelona, 24 November 1961. First stage performance: Milan, Teatro alla Scala, 18 June 1962. First performance in U.S.A.: New York, Philharmonic Hall (Lincoln Center) by the Metropolitan Opera Company, conducted by Ansermet, 29 September 1962.

SYNOPSIS. Prologue. Christopher Columbus as a boy is shipwrecked on an island. Here he meets an old man who tells him the mythical story of the oceans and the sinking of Atlantis, the Kingdom of the Titans. Spain is the only remaining trace of this continent, and it is there that the treasure of the lost kingdom can be found. Act I. *The Burning of the Pyrenees*. On the mountains of Spain Hercules finds the dying Queen Peirene, driven out of her kingdom by the monster Geryon, which has set fire to the forests and departed in the direction of Cadiz. Hercules swears to avenge her. Act II. *Hercules and the triple-bodied Geryon*. Geryon cleverly persuades Hercules to go to Atlantis. *The Orchard of the Hesperides*. He journeys to the garden of the Hesperides, where the tree of golden apples grows, tended by the seven daughters of Atlas. It is guarded by a dragon. *Hercules and the Dragon*. Hercules slays the dragon. The Hesperides also die, knowing what their fate would be at the hands of Hercules. The gods turn them into the constellation of the Pleiades. *The Sons of Atlas in the Temple of Neptune*. The Titans rebel against the god. *Alcides and the Sons of Atlas*. Hercules makes headway among the Titans and returns to Cadiz to fight Geryon. *The Straits of Hercules*. Hercules stands where Gibraltar is today and considers how to fight the Titans. *The Voice of God*. God condemns the Sons of Atlas who have revolted. *The Sinking*. Atlantis is destroyed, sunk beneath the ocean, while the Titans try to climb up to heaven with an enormous tower until the archangel with a sword of fire causes it to collapse. *Ne plus ultra*. The Titans are destroyed and Hercules sets the columns of rock as the impassable limit of the sea. Act III. *The Pilgrim*. Columbus looks out from the clifftop at the ocean and the columns of Hercules. *The Dream of Isabella*. The queen dreams of a dove that drops her wedding ring into the sea: islands filled with flowers rise from the waters. The dove makes a garland of the flowers and lets the garland fall on Isabella's head. She helps Columbus to realize his dream by equipping the ships to sail into the unknown. *The Caravels*. Their sails filled with the wind, the ships cross the Atlantic like

Closing scene of Manuel de Falla's Atlantida *at La Scala, Milan 1962.*

birds. *The salve Regina*: in the silence of the unexplored sea the sailors are heard singing their hymn of praise to the Virgin. *The Supreme Night*. While his men sleep, Columbus searches the heavens for omens. *Finale*. Land is sighted, echoing with songs of praise as if it were a great cathedral symbolizing Spain and Christianity triumphant.

■ Falla had begun work on this opera in 1928, then he had put it aside and returned to it from time to time; the cantata was still incomplete at his death and was finished by his pupil Ernest Halffter. There are considerable difficulties in staging the opera because of the large number of characters required both for singing and mimed roles. The chorus plays an important role, and is divided into 'action chorus' and 'narrative chorus'.

DON PERLIMPLIN, or IL TRIONFO DELL'AMORE E DELL'IMMAGINAZIONE (The Triumph of Love and Imagination)

Radio-opera in one act (Introduction, prologue and 9 scenes) by Bruno Maderna (1920–73), adapted by the composer from the comedy by Federico García Lorca (1899–1936), translated by Vittorio Bodini. First performance: R.A.I., 12 August 1962. Flute soloist: Severino Gazzelloni. Conductor: Bruno Maderna.

SYNOPSIS. This is a fairy tale in dialogue which tells the story of the aged husband of Belisa, Don Perlimplin, who kills the young knight of the red cloak, Belisa's lover. The knight of the red cloak turns out to be none other than Don Perlimplin himself – or perhaps his *alter ego*.

■ This, Maderna's first opera, was written especially for radio, and uses many of the techniques developed by Berio and Maderna in the R.A.I. in Milan. It is a music-comedy in which all the characters (Belisa, the housekeeper Marcolfa, the sister-in-law, two 'folletti' and the speaker chorus) have speaking roles. Only Belisa sings – just two pieces. Don Perlimplin is impersonated by a flute which converses with the other actors, substituting musical phrases and interjections for the words of the text – passionate, tender, questioning, doubting, in flurries and arabesques of great virtuosity inspired by Gazzelloni's unique talent. The orchestra consists of two violins, viola, cello, 2 double basses, 5 saxophones, in addition to a small band of woodwind and brass, percussion, marimba, vibraphone, mandoline, electric guitar, harp, piano, solo flute and tape. Belisa's song is for three voices, effected by over-dubbing and one voice on tape. Of the three 'blues' contained in the score, the last (*Dark rapture crawl*) featured in the *Divertimento* composed by Maderna with Luciano Berio in 1959. Lorca has been a frequent inspiration for contemporary composers – from Wolfgang Fortner to Poulenc.

PASSAGGIO

Mise-en-scène *for orchestra, 28 soloists and two choruses, by Luciano Berio (born 1925), text by Edoardo Sanguineti (born 1930), composed in 1962.*

SYNOPSIS. This work has no real plot. It is an allegorical stage representation of a message which is revealed through a series of dramatic representations of an existential situation. *Passaggio* is about the 'passage' of the central character (soprano) through tragic moments in contemporary life; the composer and the librettist have spoken of a 'profane passion', as if the work represented a kind of secular 'way of the cross'.

Passaggio is one of Luciano Berio's first works for the theatre; when it appeared, the public found it very disturbing, as the composer had intended. The aim was not to write a simple melodrama with a comforting structure, but a real, unsentimental problematic issue: they had to create therefore an *'opera aperta'*, and indeed the sets in *Passaggio* are so vague and so ill-defined that the audience has to supply them with meaning. In this respect it can be said that *Passaggio* represents a new and revolutionary concept of opera which, apart from its intrinsic validity, is still a part of the cultural scene today.

ORESTIA

Trilogy of operas by Darius Milhaud (1892–1974), based on the tragedies by Aeschylus, translated and adapted by Paul Claudel (1869–1955). The trilogy consists of: Agamemnon, *composed in 1913; first performance: Paris, 16 April 1927;* Les Choéphores *(The Libation Bearers), in seven sections; first performance: Paris, 8 March 1927 (concert version); Brussels, Théâtre de la Monnaie, 27 March 1935 (staged version); first performance in U.S.A.: New York. 16 November 1950 (concert version);* Les Euménides, *composed between 1917–22; first performance, Antwerp, 27 November 1927. First complete performance: West Berlin, April 1963.*

SYNOPSIS. Keeping faithfully to the classical myth, *Agamemnon* tells the story of Clytemnestra's vengeance on her husband Agamemnon, who had sacrificed their daughter Iphigenia to his ambition. Agamemnon returns victorious from the war, surrounded by his soldiers, his ships laden with prisoners and the spoils of war. Clytemnestra greets him with apparent joy, but once inside the palace she kills him, and herself announces it to the chorus.

Les Choéphores is the drama of Orestes, driven by fate to avenge his father by killing his mother and her lover Aegisthus. The Furies, the avengers of matricide, torment him, for he is stained with the blood of unnatural crime.

In *Les Euménides*, Athene and Apollo plead the cause

The first Metropolitan Opera House in New York.

The new New York Metropolitan Opera House in the Lincoln Center.

Inside the new Metropolitan Opera House. The first General Manager, Rudolf Bing, in front of the auditorium; facing page, below, the stage during preparations for a production.

of Orestes before the gods who, whilst they do not revoke the decrees of fate, at least allow religious and social considerations to overcome them: it is the beginning of a new order, and pity takes the place of vengeance. For Orestes, victim of Fate, the Furies are changed into the Eumenides, well-meaning divinities.

■ The three scores, composed over many years, show the music gradually gaining prominence over the text. While the first opera is a musical setting of the final episode in the spoken drama of *Agamemnon, Les Choéphores* combines declamation, the alternation of one voice with fragments of other voices, the 'scandito' chorus and an accompaniment of 16 percussion instruments, which is highly dramatic and effective. In *Les Euménides* there is, by contrast, hardly any speech at all, yet there is a deeper unity of inspiration and spirituality.

MONSIEUR DE POURCEAUGNAC
Comedy in music by Frank Martin (1890–1974), after Molière. First performance: Geneva, Grand Théâtre, 23 April 1963.

SYNOPSIS. The story is set in Paris in the seventeenth century. Julie loves Eraste, who loves her in return, but her father, Oronte, intends to marry her to a gentleman from Limoges, Monsieur de Pourceaugnac, an absurd and fatuous man with pretensions to nobility. From the moment he reaches Paris he is the unsuspecting victim of a series of cruel jokes perpetrated by Eraste, who makes him out to be a madman, and invents false creditors, false lovers and false wives. The poor man is eventually arrested, and finally flees the city, accused of having violated Julie. Eraste pretends to save her, and Oronte at last agrees to their marriage.

■ This opera, in which the composer's preference for the forms of French impressionism is apparent, is also a happy blend of the most advanced features of contemporary musical language.

LE DERNIER SAUVAGE (The Last Savage)
Opéra bouffe in three acts; words and music by Gian Carlo Menotti (born 1911). First performance: Paris, Opéra-Comique, 21 October 1963. First performance in U.S.A.: New York, Metropolitan Opera, 23 January 1964.

SYNOPSIS. The action takes place partly in Chicago and partly in India, and the main character is a young woman, Kitty (coloratura), who has a passion for anthropology. Accompanied by her millionaire parents, she goes to India, where the family find themselves faced with a reality that they try in vain to

understand; there are endless misunderstandings and they confuse the fake with the authentic, which gives rise to a series of comic situations. The son of a Maharajah falls in love with Kitty, but she refuses to marry him until she has found the 'abominable snowman' in the Himalayas – the last savage. To satisfy her curiosity, the prince arranges for a stable boy, Abdul, to dress up as the 'snowman' and it is this poor peasant whom Kitty eventually marries.

■ Although commissioned by the Paris Opéra, it was first presented at the Opéra-Comique because its subject was considered more suitable to that theatre. The opera is an amusing satire on the customs of a certain level of American society; the music is brilliant, highly inventive and with immediate appeal. Technically most accomplished, it makes few demands on the listener. It is also traditional, as the composer himself explained: 'In my other operas you can tell that I am aware of the trends of contemporary music. In *Le Dernier Sauvage* I chose to ignore them completely.'

LABORINTUS II
Opera scenica by Luciano Berio (born 1925), for chamber orchestra, electronic music, contralto, two sopranos; spoken text from passages from the Vita Nova, Convivio, *and* Divina Commedia *by Dante and from the works of T. S. Eliot, Ezra Pound, Edoardo Sanguineti, Biblical and other texts. Composed between 1963 and 1965 at the request of the ORTF for the seventh centenary of Dante's birth, it was first performed by Legrand and Bancomont (sopranos), Meunier (contralto), Sanguineti (spoken role), and the Ensemble Musique Vivante conducted by Luciano Berio.*

■ In this opera (to use the word in its widest sense) the composer rejects not only the traditional 'languages' of which opera consists (sung words, music, stage actions and choreography), but also the traditional structuring and purpose of the text, as had been the case, albeit in different ways, in *Passaggio*. Berio himself wrote that *Laborintus II* 'can be treated as a representation, a story, an allegory, a document, a dance, etc. . . . and can therefore be performed in schools, theatres, on television, in the open, etc.' It is thus an 'OPERA APERTA', whose end result is not objective and predetermined by the composer but extremely subjective and dependent on the spectator as well as the conductor and the producer. Umberto Eco wrote of *opera aperta* that 'The end result is an interpretation as well as a performance, so that with every performance the opera is new.' The structure of *Laborintus II* (which owes its title to an earlier poetic collection by Edoardo Sanguineti entitled *Laborintus*) is a montage of various 'concrete' sounds juxtaposed not for continuity but disjointedly, so that formal structures are challenged throughout. The work is not concerned with a particular aspect of

and Chester Kallman based on *The Bacchae by Euripides*. *First performance: Salzburg Festival, 6 August 1966. First performance in U.K.: London, Coliseum, 1974; in U.S.A.: Santa Fé, 1967.*

SYNOPSIS. The action takes place near the royal palace in Thebes and on Mount Citheron. The chorus relates that Cadmus (bass) has abdicated in favour of his grandson Pentheus (baritone) and wishes happiness to the new King. When a voice offstage announces that the god Dionysus has come to Boeotia, they rush off to welcome him. Cadmus, Tiresias, an old blind prophet (tenor), Agave (Pentheus's mother) and Beroë (Pentheus's nurse) (mezzo-soprano) argue about whether Dionysus has truly come to Thebes, before Tiresias goes off to join the followers of the god – the Bassarids – on Mount Citheron. The captain of the Guard (baritone) rebuffs Agave's flirtations, and reads a royal proclamation forbidding the cult of her sister Semele, who is said to have been ravished by Zeus and given birth to Dionysus. Pentheus then extinguishes the flame on the altar to Semele and declares that anyone who lights it again does so on pain of death. When they hear the music of the Dionysiac revels, Agave and Autonoë follow it as if in a trance. Pentheus sends the Captain to arrest everyone on the mountain and confides to Beroë that he has abandoned polytheism and taken vows of chastity and abstinence. The Captain brings in some prisoners in a state of trance including Tiresias, Autonoë, Agave and a stranger, but Pentheus cannot even make his mother recognize him. His questions to the stranger receive only enigmatic replies, so he sends him for torture. The stage darkens; an earthquake shakes the city walls, the flame on Semele's altar shoots up and the prisoners flee back to Mount Citheron. The stranger promises Pentheus that he can show him, in his mother's mirror, what is happening on the mountain. Pentheus, fascinated and repelled, agrees to look in the mirror. Intermezzo: the scene reveals Pentheus's frustrated desires and secret imaginations, in a parody of the eighteenth-century French courtly entertainment set in Arcadia, as the theme of the Judgement of Calliope. The characters of the opera adopt names from Latin mythology. Pentheus, spellbound by the vision, is persuaded to go, dressed as a woman, to Mount Citheron to see the revels for himself. Dionysus ignores Beroë's pleas to spare his life. Pentheus is discovered in hiding by a group of Maenads, led by Agave. He is torn to pieces. Cadmus and the Captain watch the return of the Bassarids to Thebes. Agave, holding Pentheus's head, demands news of her son. In horror, she is eventually brought to realize what she has done. Dionysus orders Thebes to be burnt and Cadmus and his daughters to go into perpetual exile. Agave admonishes the god to remember that Tartarus awaits even him. The opera ends as the chorus worship the strange statues of Dionysus and his mother Semele, now deified.

■ The composer, who belongs to the avant-garde of modern music, has found in the mythical symbolism of Euripides's tragedy the vehicle for his own lyrical

Die Bassariden by Henze at the Salzburg Festival, 6 August 1966. Designed by Filippo Sanjust.

present-day life, political argument for example, although it rejects both verbal and musical conventional language. In Berio's text there are in fact various linguistic codes, from ancient to modern Italian, from Latin to English, that are often used more for their semantic properties than purely for their sound. The choice of literary texts, however, is certainly not haphazard, since it underlines the artful affectation of the music. Among the more interesting and contrasting musical collages should be mentioned the 'jam' session – jazz improvisation with drums, double-bass, clarinet – and a whole section of electronic music. Orchestral music disappears almost completely, and instead we have the words of the *Convivio*: 'music is all relative . . .'. Towards the end of the opera, the spoken chorus 'mixes' the words of a text by Sanguineti like a linguistic 'cocktail', arranging and rearranging them until they are whispering them, and the opera concludes with an impalpable heart-beat.

DIE BASSARIDEN (The Bassarids)

Opera seria *in one act with an intermezzo by Hans Werner Henze (born 1926), libretto by W. H. Auden*

drama. The result is a grandiose work in which the philosophical argument of the libretto between rationality and irrationality (the conflict which opposes Pentheus to Dionysus) is reflected in harsh musical contrasts. The opera was a great success at its first performance.

ANTONY AND CLEOPATRA
Opera in three acts by Samuel Barber (born 1910), text by Franco Zeffirelli, based on the play by Shakespeare. First performance: New York, Metropolitan Opera, 16 September 1966.

ORIGINAL CAST. Leontyne Price (Cleopatra), Justino Diaz (Antony), Rosalind Elias (Charmian), Belén Amparàn (Iras), Jess Thomas (Octavius Caesar), Mary Ellen Pracht (Octavia), Ezio Flagello (Enobarbus), John Macurdy (Agrippa). Conductor: Thomas Schippers.

SYNOPSIS. Act I, Scene I. The curtain rises on a set called the empire. Romans, Greeks, Hebrews, Persians and Africans implore Antony to leave Egypt and to return to Rome. Scene II. Cleopatra's palace in Alexandria. Antony confides to Enobarbus his intention to break with Cleopatra. When he tells the queen of his decision, she tells him to leave at once. Scene III. The Roman Senate. The Romans put pressure on Antony to confirm his loyalty to the Empire by marrying Octavia, sister of Octavianus. Scene IV. Cleopatra's palace. The queen pines for Antony and asks for mandragora to sleep out his absence. Scene V. Rome. Antony marries Octavia, on the understanding that his military duties will often keep him away from her. Scene VI. In Alexandria Cleopatra is grief-stricken when she hears of Antony's marriage. Scene VII. On board a Roman galley; Octavianus, Lepidus and Enobarbus together with Antony. While Antony is sleeping, Enobarbus reveals the general's intention to return to his Egyptian mistress, while the chorus describe the first time she appeared before him. When he wakes from his dreams, Antony cannot suppress his cry: 'I shall return to Egypt.' Act II, Scene I. In Rome, Octavia learns of Antony's infidelity. Octavianus, angered at the double betrayal of his wife and of Rome, decides to wage war on Antony. Scene II. The garden of Cleopatra's palace. While a soothsayer is predicting the future, Enobarbus brings the news that the Roman legions are drawing near. Cleopatra declares that together with her army she wishes to share the fate of her lover. Scene III. In Antony's camp, bad omens are interpreted by the soldiers as a sign that Hercules, the god whom Antony loves, is deserting him. Scene IV. A battlefield. Antony has been defeated and he urges his followers to seek mercy from Octavianus. Scene V. Octavianus appears and shows that he has no pity for his rival. Scene VI. Antony has taken refuge in Cleopatra's palace. After a violent scene, she leaves to go to her tomb monument, but sends a messenger to

tell Antony that her last thoughts were of him. Scene VII. Enobarbus prepares to take his own life. Scene VIII. Antony's tent. Believing Cleopatra to be dead, Antony implores the standard-bearer Eros to kill him. Eros turns the sword on himself instead, and Antony commits suicide. As he is dying he is carried to Cleopatra's monument. Act III. The tomb. Antony dies in Cleopatra's arms. Octavianus arrives; he wants to take the captive queen to Rome in triumph, and warns her not to choose suicide. Cleopatra, however, dies from the poisonous bite of an asp smuggled past the guards in a basket of figs.

■ The opera was performed at the inauguration of the new Metropolitan Opera House in New York. Franco Zeffirelli also produced and designed the sets. The choreography was by Alvin Ailey.

ULISSE (Ulysses)
Opera in a prologue and two acts by Luigi Dallapiccola (1904–75), libretto by the composer, inspired by Homer's Odyssey. First performance: Berlin, Deutsche Oper, 29 September 1968.

Justino Diaz as Antony in the first performance of Barber's Antony and Cleopatra, *16 September 1966, which opened the new Metropolitan Opera House in New York; produced by Franco Zeffirelli.*

ORIGINAL CAST. Erik Soeden (Ulisse), Catherine Gayes (Nausicaa), Jean Maderra (Circe/Melanto), Victor von Halem (Alcinoo), Hildegaard Hildebrecht (La Madre).

SYNOPSIS. Prologue. Ulisse (baritone) refuses the gift of eternal youth from Calypso (soprano) and sails away. Symphonic interlude describing the wrath of Poseidon. Shipwrecked on the island of Scheria, Ulisse meets Nausicaa (light soprano), who leads him to the court of her father Alcinoo (bass-baritone). Act I. Scene I. In a room in the palace, Demodoco (tenor) sings of the return of the Greeks from Troy and of the disappearance of Ulisse, when the hero himself enters. Ulisse cannot restrain his tears; he reveals his name and relates his adventures as follows: Scene II. He sailed towards the land where the lotus-eaters live. They seduced a number of his companions to leave the ship and eat the flowers of oblivion, never to return. Scene III. For a year Circe (mezzo-soprano) detained Ulisse and when he set sail once more, the enchantress predicted that he would never find peace. Scene IV. He met his mother Anticleia (dramatic soprano) in Hades, and from the seer Tiresia (tenor) he learnt that his return to Ithaca would bring bloodshed. Scene V. His tale is told, and Alcinoo offers him an escort to take him to Ithaca. Act II. Scene I. Penelope's suitors have failed in an attempt upon the life of Telemaco (counter-tenor), Ulisse's son. A stranger comes to the island and begs the hospitality of the swineherd Eumeo (tenor). He questions Telemaco at length, without revealing his identity. Scene II. Ulisse is moved when he hears the song of Penelope (soprano). Scene III. Antinoo (baritone) makes the handmaid Melanto (mezzo-soprano) dance with Ulisse's bow. Telemaco, whom the suitors had thought to be dead, returns with the stranger, who to their amazement takes and draws the bow: this action reveals his identity since Ulisse alone is capable of drawing the bow. He shoots the suitors. Symphonic interlude. Epilogue. Ulisse, pursued by the Furies, has set sail on another journey and realizes sadly that he has never found what he was seeking. Suddenly struck by a mystic realization, he exclaims: 'God! My heart and the sea are no longer alone!'

■ From both ancient and modern texts, from Homer, but also from Dante and Pascoli, the composer has worked out a personal interpretation of the character of the Greek hero and his eternal search for peace, which he discovers finally in the sense of the divine.

L'IDIOTA (The Idiot)
Opera in three acts by Luciano Chailly (born 1920), libretto by Alberto Loverso, based on the novel by Dostoievsky. First performance: Rome, Opera, 18 February 1970.

■ *L'Idiota*, an opera of great importance, closely fol-

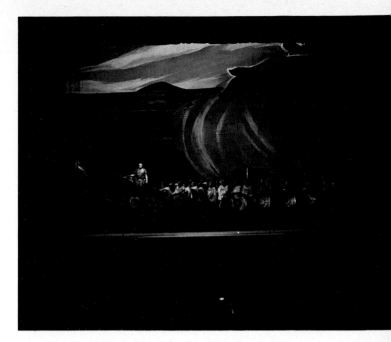

Act II, Scene Two of Dallapiccola's Ulisse *at La Scala, Milan 1969; sets and costumes by Farulli, produced by Sellner.*

lows the story of the novel. It has often been re-staged in France, Germany and Italy and is considered to be the greatest theatrical achievement of its author.

DER BESUCH DER ALTEN DAME (The Visit of the Old Lady)
Opera in three acts by Gottfried von Einem (born 1918). libretto based on the tragische Komödie *of the same name by Friedrich Dürrenmatt (born 1921). First performance: Vienna, Staatsoper, 23 May 1971.*

ORIGINAL CAST. Christa Ludwig (Claire Zachanassian), Eberhard Wächter (Ill). Conductor: Horst.

SYNOPSIS. In the small Swiss town of Güllen all the inhabitants, led by the burgomaster, are gathered at the station to await the arrival of the fabulously wealthy Claire Zachanassian (mezzo-soprano), who has been away from her home town for more than forty years. Her extraordinary riches could mean new life to the town, which is in a sorry plight. Many place their trust above all in the companion of her youth, Alfred Ill (baritone), with whom the inexperienced young girl was known to have had a love affair. The lady arrives, incredibly old, caked in make-up, covered with jewels and followed by her seventh husband, quantities of luggage and a coffin. A banquet is held in her honour, and it is learned that she is indeed willing to donate an enormous sum of money, on condition that the people hand over to her the body of Alfred Ill, the man who had seduced her, made her pregnant and refused to acknowledge his son, after a complaisant judge had heard the evidence of two hired drunks. Thus abandoned, the girl had finished up in a brothel. The judge is now the lady's butler and the two false witnesses, blinded and castrated, are travelling in her suite. After much hesitation, the townspeople, avid for money, vote in favour of killing the seducer, and deliver the body to her. She is appeased, and leaves with her strange suite, taking the coffin and its macabre contents with her; she will bury Alfred's body in her garden in Capri. The old lady has gone, and the inhabitants of Güllen have their money: they noisily demonstrate their satisfaction.

■ *Der Besuch der alten Dame* is a drama about the hypocrisy of the modern world, where a crime for greed is passed off as an act of justice. It has a rich score, with complex contrapuntal tessitura and a strictly tonal system. The veins of irony and grotesque humour are underlined by mechanical Stravinsky-like rhythms, or by Puccini-type melodies in the part of the lady, or the chromatic stammering insults of the two castrati. 'These features combine to make us consider the score as an autonomous creation rather than the illustration of a text, and our attention is focussed precisely where the music is at its most intense: on the orchestra' (Paolo Isotta).

TREEMONISHA
Opera in three acts by Scott Joplin (1868–1917), libretto by the composer. Composed in 1908. First partial performance: Atlanta, Morehouse College, January 1972, by the Atlanta Symphony conducted by Robert Shaw. Subsequent arrangements and orchestration by Gunther Schuller for the Houston Grand Opera, with dances created by Louis Johnson.

ORIGINAL CAST. Carmen Balthrop, Betty Allen, Curtis Rayam, Willard White.

SYNOPSIS. A plantation in Arkansas, a few miles from the Red River. Act I. A September morning 1884. The charlatan-magician Zodzetrick (tenor) is trying to sell a 'miraculous' rabbit's paw to Monisha (soprano), but her husband Ned (baritone) prevents her from buying it because it is too expensive. Treemonisha (contralto) arrives and chases the charlatan away, saying that he has already done enough harm by spreading superstition among the simple local folk. Remus (tenor) tells him that he is unlikely to gain her favour since she is famous for miles around for her attempts to fight superstition. Treemonisha organizes a dance for the harvesters, led by Andy (tenor) and suggests that they gather twigs to make garlands. Monisha intervenes, to say that they must not tear the leaves off a particular tree because it is sacred. She reveals, much to everyone's surprise, that Treemonisha was found beneath it, when she was about three years old. Treemonisha, like the others, had considered herself to be the daughter of Monisha and thanks her for loving her like a mother. Then she and her friend Lucy (soprano) go into the wood. Parson Alltalk (bass) comes to the threshing-floor and leads a prayer meeting. Then Lucy returns in distress, announcing that Zodzetrick and his partner Luddud (baritone) have kidnapped Treemonisha. Ned, Remus and the young men go off in search for her. Act II. In the woods, afternoon. Zodzetrick and Luddud arrive with Treemonisha at their hideout, where other charlatan-magicians are gathered. They accuse her of aiming to destroy their living by fighting superstition. While they are deliberating, eight bears appear, but they do not harm her and simply play in the glade. The charlatans resolve to throw her into a huge wasps' nest. They are terrified, however, by the sudden appearance of a masked figure and run away. It is in fact Remus, who has played on their superstition by dressing up as the devil. Remus and Treemonisha embrace. On their way home, they encounter some cotton planters. Act III. Ned and Monisha's hut, evening. Ned is trying to comfort his wife when Remus and Treemonisha arrive, and they celebrate her escape. Zodzetrick and Luddud have been caught, but Treemonisha is content to let them go with a good scolding. The planters ask her to be their leader and she accepts when both men and women have indicated their hearty support for her. She gives her first order: everyone must dance.

■ Appropriately called 'the sleeping beauty of American music', *Treemonisha* remained only a name for over sixty years: the name of an opera – it was said – that one of the ragtime greats, a father of jazz, Scott Joplin, had composed 'out of a craze for greatness' but without managing to get it published. The truth of the matter was rather different: Joplin himself had published *Treemonisha* in 1911 in Harlem; then he became ill with syphilis. The disease, which was to bring about his death in 1917, prevented him from making any serious endeavour to get his opera performed. It was rediscovered in 1970 by Vera Brodsky Lawrence while researching with a view to publishing the complete works of the composer, and published in the following year by the New York Public Library. An evocative blend of ragtime (the country dance, the song of the planters and the final dance), of passages that suggest ballet (the playing of the bears), and a central structure that derives from European opera – perhaps Italian opera, popular in the United States at the beginning of this century as well as a splendid use of the chorus and the fantasy of Weber – *Treemonisha* had woken from her long sleep to become an unprecedented success of the Afro-American stage.

LORENZACCIO
Romantic melodrama in five acts, twenty-three scenes

and two off-stage, by Sylvano Bussotti (born 1931) with acknowledgements to the play of the same name by Alfred de Musset (1834). Text by the composer. First performance: Venice, Teatro La Fenice, 7 September 1972.

ORIGINAL CAST. Forster-Durlich, Jacobeit, Kenklies, Genersch, Hering, Stuckmann. Conductor: Gianpiero Taverna.

SYNOPSIS. Set in Renaissance Florence, the plot concerns the murder of the dissolute tyrant Alessandro dei Medici by his cousin Lorenzo and the latter's justification of his deed. In one scene a game of chess is being played, the winner to become Duke of Florence and the chessmen being represented by living characters. Alfred de Musset and George Sand also appear on the stage and talk with Florentine courtiers about art, and later on Musset recites some of his verses. Some characters undergo strange transformations: a page turns into Eros, a citizen's daughter into a noblewoman and later into Death, and George Sand into Lorenzo's aunt.

■ This extraordinary opera, which was composed between 1968 and 1972, and performed in 1972 at the 35th Festival of Contemporary Music in Venice, is one of the most interesting of the works by this Florentine composer. It is a work of great breadth and originality in which all the features of opera are filtered through the composer's own poetic imagination. Bussotti has a particular place within the avant-garde, having developed his own highly personal poetic sound, nowhere more evident than in this opera.

RECITAL I (For Cathy)

Opera by Luciano Berio (born 1925) for voices, orchestra, harpsichord and pianoforte, with text by Berio, and references to texts by Mosetti and Sanguineti. Translation by Cathy Berberian. First performance: Lisbon 1972, with Cathy Berberian (soprano), H. Lester (pianoforte and harpsichord soloist), London Sinfonietta conducted by Luciano Berio.

SYNOPSIS. At the beginning, the central character sings the Monteverdi aria *Lettera amorosa* to herself, first accompanied by an invisible harpsichord, then by the orchestra. Monteverdi's music becomes distorted and a spoken monologue ensues, alternating with snatches of the classical repertoire by the singer, this time accompanied by solo violin. At this point the musical mood degenerates into night-club music, while the violinist plays fragments of Tchaikovsky's violin concerto. The pianist arrives late on stage and the singer's role gradually becomes a spoken role. She mimes a lecture claiming that ritual is the only form that gives meaning to sound and gesture in opera; five musicians enter, dressed in *commedia dell'arte* costumes, who, with snatches of Bach and other composers, change and interchange roles and instruments. In the final section the principal singer embodies the classical lyrical-tragic role of opera.

■ This is a highly elaborate opera from the point of view of form. *Recital I* is 'played' on several levels: from a normal recital for voice and piano accompaniment to complex passages by the chamber orchestra. The most interesting feature of *Recital I* is the impossibility of placing it in any one musical tradition: being thus unconfined, it is a work of great musical fertility, and confirms the importance of this composer as an international leader of the musical avant-garde.

SATYRICON

Opera in one act by Bruno Maderna (1920–73), libretto taken from the novel by Petronius Arbiter (first century A.D.). First performance: Nederlandse Operastichting Amsterdam, 16 March 1973. Conductor: Bruno Maderna.

SYNOPSIS. The action on-stage is centred solely upon the supper of Trimalcione, a wealthy and vulgar Roman gourmandizer. The opera opens with a vainglorious speech by Fortunata, Trimalcione's wife, who boastfully displays the riches of her husband. Trimalcione in his turn makes a kind of verbal will and testament, desiring a large statue to be erected in his memory on his tomb; his speech ended, he subsides with a series of very loud belches. Abinna, who symbolizes Money, sings the praises of wealth and tells the story of a matron of Ephesus who, faithful to her husband while he was alive, lost no time after his death in betraying him near his very tomb and even defiled his corpse. At this point Fortunata tries to seduce the philosopher Eumolpo; Trimalcione is outraged and publicly taunts his wife, saying that he had taken her off the streets and made an honest woman of her but that he regrets the day he married her, when he could have married an heiress; the very thought of that is enough to get Trimalcione very worked up and while insisting that he does not want to boast, he displays and brags about his own riches. The opera concludes with Criside's admonishment to be ever mindful of fate, the unpredictable mistress of all men.

■ This work by one of the most important exponents of the New Music, confirms the importance of the repeated essays by the avant-garde to enter the world of opera. Indeed modern composers are successfully exploring the infinite possibilities of this field of music, and the relationship between music and literature; in *Satyricon*, for example, in the scene in which Fortunata appears we have snatches of different types of music, from cabaret to Kurt Weill to 'folk'. In this connection we should also mention the several passages taken from Wagner, Bizet, Verdi, which help to recreate musically the atmosphere of burlesque *pastiche* which is the main feature of Petronius's satire.

Maderna's Satyricon *at the Piccola Scala in Milan; sets and costumes by Ulisse Santicchi, directed by Giulio Chazalettes.*

DEATH IN VENICE
Opera in two acts by Benjamin Britten (1913–76), libretto by Myfanwy Piper, based on a short story (1913) by Thomas Mann. First performance: 16 June 1973 at the Maltings, Aldeburgh. First performance in U.S.A.: New York, Metropolitan Opera, 1974.

ORIGINAL CAST. Peter Pears (Aschenbach), John Shirley-Quirk (Traveller etc.), James Bowman (Voice of Apollo).

SYNOPSIS. It is the story of Aschenbach (tenor), an elderly writer who becomes fascinated, while staying in Venice, by the beauty of a Polish boy, Tadzio (dancer). Despite the spread of plague in the city, he stays as long as the Polish family – he cannot at first bring himself to warn them of the disease lest they leave. In the end it is they who depart and Aschenbach who dies, confusing the image of Tadzio with the sweet harbinger of death.

■ Britten's last opera follows the original Mann story closely, endowing it with a strong mythological significance.

AL GRAN SOLE CARICO D'AMORE (In the Glorious Sun of Fulsome Love)
Opera in two parts by Luigi Nono (born 1924), texts adapted by the composer from Rimbaud, Gorky, Brecht, Pavese, Michel, Tania Burke, Sanchez, Haydée Santamaria, South-Vietnamese guerillas, Marx, Lenin, Gramsci, Dimitrov, Che Guevara. First performance: Teatro alla Scala, Milan, April 1975. First performance in U.K.: Edinburgh Festival, 8 September 1978.

ORIGINAL CAST. Paoletti, Goranceva, Fabbri, Ricagno, Jankovic, Basiola, Davia, Socci. Conductor: Claudio Abbado.

SYNOPSIS. The action revolves around several women revolutionaries, symbolically linked in the character of the Mother who sums up their destinies in love and warfare. The guiding theme of the Paris Commune holds together the threads of a tapestry of different evidence and testimonies; it is linked with other episodes (at other times and in other places, up to the immediacy of the present day) that share the same revolutionary nature and tension: the Russian revolu-

Britten's Death in Venice *at Covent Garden, London 1973.*

Act II of the first production of Nono's Al gran sole carico d'amore, *Milan, April 1975. Designed by David Borovsky, directed by Juri Ljubimov.*

tions of 1905 and 1917, workers' revolts, the Latin-American struggles for liberation and the Vietnam war.

■ With this opera, Nono and his collaborators (Ljubimov, Borovskij, Jakobson, Abbado and Pestalozza) have attempted to put into practice an idea that had already been theoretically expressed: the need for a new type of musical theatre (the sub-title for the libretto is in fact 'For a new musical theatre'). The opera is thus a very ambitious enterprise, and only time will tell whether or not it is a success. From the stylistic point of view, we can say that Nono has remained faithful in his music to his earlier position: a rejection of the pseudoscientific objectivity resulting from post-Webern structuralism, and free also of the various mysticisms and irrationalities of neo-Dada. The music is complex and varied in its approach, from solo singing to chorus, from orchestra to electronic means. It was conceived from the start as a dramatic language matched visually by scenery, costumes and choreography, and by the way in which the space is used on stage.

KABALE UND LIEBE (Intrigue and Love)
Opera in two acts by Gottfried von Einem (born 1918), libretto by Lotte Ingrish, based on the tragedy by Friedrich Schiller (1784). First performance: Vienna, Staatsoper, 25 February 1977.

ORIGINAL CAST. Anja Silja, Brigitte Fassbaender, Walter Berry. Conductor: Christoph von Dohnányi.

■ The libretto, by the composer's wife and based on the Schiller drama that had furnished the subject of Verdi's *Luisa Miller*, is a modified and very much lighter version of the original. The orchestra is greatly reduced in size. There is no chorus, and the instruments are used to differentiate the characters: the cello and horn for Ferdinand, the oboe for Lady Milford, the trumpet for the President. The opera was well received by the critics, who acknowledged the composer's great instinct for the stage, and saw the work as a perfect synthesis between theatre and opera.

OPERA
Performance in three acts by Luciano Berio (born 1925), libretto by the composer. First performance: Santa Fé, 1970. New version, with modified text and orchestration: Florence, Teatro della Pergola, May 1977.

SYNOPSIS. The action is on three alternating levels. The story of the sinking of the Titanic (transatlantic liner which sank on 12 April 1912 after colliding with an iceberg on its maiden voyage) alternates with scenes in the terminal ward of a hospital and scenes from the myth of Orpheus. These three themes are interwoven, each serving as a commentary upon the other, overlapping, and each in turn coming into prominence. They combine to form a kind of meditation, a dream or a 'morality' on the theme of death and of the human condition in the face of unjust violence.

■ The three points around which *Opera* revolves are characterized by a great variety of unusual modes. The myth of Orpheus, given in the English version of the verses of Alessandro Striggio, is sung at the beginning of the first two acts, where a soprano accompanied by pianoforte is learning an aria that she will sing with the orchestra at the beginning of the third act. Titanic and Terminal are characterized by a variety of vocal passages. There is frequent use of musical references and snatches from works of the composer himself as well as of other composers. *Opera*, Berio writes, 'is often also a kaleidoscope, a parody of easily recognizable kinds of music. The accumulation of many different musical, vocal and scenic modes – that is to say different modes of theatre – is the reason for the title, which is not necessarily meant to suggest a parody of melodrama, but rather the plural of "opus".'

NAPOLI MILIONARIA
Opera in three acts by Nino Rota (born 1911), libretto by Eduardo De Filippo (born 1900). First performance: Spoleto, Teatro Caio Melisso, 22 June 1977.

SYNOPSIS. Reproducing with some alterations Eduardo De Filippo's famous comedy which had appeared in 1945, it tells the story of a Neapolitan family at the end of the second world war, when the city was under Allied occupation.

■ Although given a mixed reception by the critics, this opera contains music of high technical quality. It includes echoes of famous songs ('Funiculí funiculà') that lend a touch of local colour, as well as echoes of jazz to suggest the American army of occupation.

INDEXES

Index of Operas

Page numbers in *italic* refer to the illustrations

501

Index of Composers, Librettists and Literary Sources

Composer's names are set in **bold** type. Page numbers in *italic* refer to the illustrations

Maderna, Bruno, *contd.*
  Orfeo, 10
  Satyricon, 491; *492*
Maeterlinck, Maurice
  Ariane et Barbe-Bleue, 346–7
  Pelléas et Mélisande, 332–3
Maffei, Andrea, 312
  Macbeth, 208
  I Masnadieri, 208–9
Maffei, Scipione
  La Fida Ninfa, 39–40
Mahā Bhārata, 368
Malipiero, Gian
  L'Allegra Brigata, 454–5
  I Capricci di Callot, 442–3; *445*
  La Favola del Figlio Cambiato,
    422
  Giulio Cesare, 428
  L'Orfeide, 10, 396
  Torneo Notturno, 417
  Tre Commedie Goldoniane,
    398–400
Mancinelli, Luigi
  Ero e Leandro, 320
Mann, Thomas
  Death in Venice, 492
Manzoni, Alessandro
  I Promessi Sposi, 228
Marcello, Benedetto
  Arianna, 34–5
Marcello, Marco Marcelliano
  Tutti in Maschera, 228
Marchetti, Filippo
  Ruy Blas, 256
Marenco, Leopoldo
  L'Arlesiana, 319–20
Mariani, Tommaso
  Livietta e Tracollo, 44
Marie de France
  Le Fresne, 330
Mariette, François Auguste
  Aida, 257
Marlowe, Christopher
  Doctor Faustus, 395
Marmontel, Jean François, *73*
  Céphale et Procris, 76
  Démophoon, 100
  Didon, 90
  Le Huron, 68–9
Marschner, Heinrich
  Hans Heiling, 173
  Der Vampyr, 156–8
Martin, Frank
  Monsieur de Pourceaugnac, 486
  Der Sturm, 473
Martin, Victor
  Sous la Terreur, 378
Martinu, Bohuslav
  Comedy on the Bridge, 458
Mascagni, Pietro, 340, 362; *303*
  Amica, 340
  L'Amico Fritz, 302, 370
  Cavalleria Rusticana, 298–9,
    302, 313; *303*
  Guglielmo Ratcliff, 299, 312–13,
    426
  Iris, 323; *325*
  Isabeau, 356–7, 361; *365*
  Lodoletta, 369–70
  Le Maschere, 329; *333*
  Nerone, 425–6
  Parisina, 361, 365
  Il Piccolo Marat, 378
  I Rantzau, 306
  Silvano, 313
  Zanetto, 315
Massé, Victor
  Une Nuit de Cléopâtre, 289–90
Massenet, Jules, 286, 298
  Amadis, 384
  Ariane, 344

Cendrillon, 324; *326*
Le Cid, 290
Don Quichotte, 350
Esclarmonde, 297
Grisélidis, 330
Hérodiade, 282
Le Jongleur de Notre-Dame,
  297, 331
Manon, 286–7, 308, 312; *293*
La Navarraise, 297
Le Roi de Lahore, 275–6
Thaïs, 311–12; *319*
Werther, 304; *309*
Massinger, Philip
  The Prophetess, 25
Matrat, Emmanuel
  La Coupe Enchantée, 314
Maturin, Charles Robert
  Bertram, 154–5
Maupassant, Guy de
  Le Rosier de Madame Husson, 450
Mayakovsky, 480–1
Mayr, Johann Simon, 121
  Ginevra di Scozia, 112, 118
  Lodoïska, 112
Mayreder-Obermayer, Rosa
  Der Corregidor, 317
Mazzolà, Caterino
  The Adventurers, 92
  La Clemenza di Tito, 106–8
Meano, Cesare
  Maria d'Alessandria, 436–7
Méhul, Etienne Nicolas
  Joseph en Égypte, 122; *123*
Mei, Lev Alexandrovich
  The Maid of Pskov, 258
  The Tsar's Bride, 324–5
Meilhac, Henri
  La Belle Hélène, 240–1
  Carmen, 264–5
  Manon, 286–7
  Le Réveillon, 261–4
Meissner, Leopold Florian
  Der Evangelimann, 313–14
Mélesville, A. Honoré Joseph, 184
  Zampa, 165–6
Melville, Hermann
  Billy Budd, 453, 460–1
Menasci, Guido
  Cavalleria Rusticana, 298–9
  I Rantzau, 306
  Zanetto, 315
Mendelson, Mira
  The Betrothal in a Monastery,
    447–8
  The Story of a Real Man, 452
  War and Peace, 446–7
Mendès, Catulle
  Ariane, 344
  Gwendoline, 292–3
Mendouze, R.
  Anacréon, 119
Menotti, Gian Carlo
  Amahl and the Night Visitors, 462
  Amelia al Ballo, 433
  The Consul, 454, 470; *460*
  La Dernier Sauvage, 486
  A Hand of Bridge, 479
  Maria Golovin, 478
  The Medium, 446, 449, 455, 470
  The Saint of Bleecker Street, 470
  The Telephone, 448–9; *451*
  Vanessa, 477–8
Mercadante, Saverio
  Apoteosi di Ercole, 139–40
  Il Bravo, 185
  I Briganti, 180–1
  Il Giuramento, 183
Merelli, Bartolomeo
  Oberto, conte di San Bonifacio,
    185–6

Mérimée, Prosper
  Carmen, 264–5
Merle, Jean Toussaint, 184
Méry, François-Joseph
  Don Carlos, 247–9
Messager, André
  Madame Chrysanthème, 307
Metastasio, Pietro, 34, 53, 63, 64,
    68, 72
  Achille in Sciro, 45, 57
  Adriano in Siria, 44
  Alessandro nelle Indie, 48–9, 53,
    60, 64
  Antigono, 52–3
  Artaserse, 36, 50–1, 57, 62
  Attilio Regolo, 57
  Catone in Utica, 37, 48
  Ciro riconsciuto, 53
  La Clemenza di Tito, 106–8
  Il Demetrio, 40, 52
  Demofoonte, 45, 52, 56–7, 100
  Didone Abbandonata, 56
  Egeria, 65
  Ezio, 40, 50, 57–8
  Impressario delle Canarie, 93
  L'Isola disabitata, 82
  Issipile, 58
  Lucio Silla, 74
  L'Olimpiade, 42–4, 48, 90
  Il Re Pastore, 60, 78–9
  Semiramide Riconosciuta, 36,
    51–2, 57, 65
  Il Sogno di Scipione, 73–4
  Zenobia, 60
Meyerbeer, Giacomo, 193, 226
  L'Africaine, 241–3; *243*
  Dinorah, 235–6
  L'Étoile du Nord, 224–5
  Ein Feldlager in Schlesien, 242
  Les Huguenots, 179–80
  Le Prophète, 214–15
  Robert, le Diable, 166–7; *166,
    167*
Meziers-Riccoboni, M. J. Laboras
  de
  Sophie, ou le Mariage Caché, 110
Migliavacca, Giovanni Ambrogio
  Armida, 61–2
Milhaud, Darius
  L'Abandon d'Ariane, 409
  Bolivar, 416, 455–6; *461*
  Cristoforo Colomb, 416, 456
  David, 466–7
  La Délivrance de Thésée, 409
  L'Enlèvement d'Europe, 409
  Les Malheurs d'Orphée, 401
  Maximilian, 416, 456
  Orestia, 484–6
  Le Pauvre Matelot, 408
Milliet, Paul
  Hérodiade, 282
  La Vida Breve, 359
  Werther, 304
Minato, Niccolò
  Serse, 17, 49
Mistral, Fréderic
  Mireio, 240
Mitusov, Stephan
  Le Rossignol, 363–4
Molière
  Amphitryon, 100
  Les Fêtes de l'Amour et de Bac-
    chus, 19
  Le Médecin malgré lui, 230
  Monsieur de Pourceaugnac, 486
  Les Précieuses Ridicules, 411
Moniglia, Giovanni Andrea
  L'Hipermestra, 17
  Semiramide, 19
Montemezzi, Italo
  L'Amore dei tre re, 359–60; *367*

Monteverdi, Claudio
  Arianna, 11–12, 13, 344
  Il Ballo delle Ingrate, 12–13
  Il Combattimento di Tancredi e
    Clorinda, 13
  L'Incoronazione di Poppea,
    14–16
  Orfeo, 9–10, 11, 13; *10*
  Il Ritorno di Ulisse in Patria, 14
Moore, Thomas
  Lalla Rookh, 237
  Oriental Tales, 141
Morand, Eugène,
  Grisélidis, 330
Morax, René
  Judith, 397–8
  Le Roi David, 379
Moreau, Emile
  Madame Sans-Gêne, 364
Morelli, S.
  Sallustia, 37–9
Moreto,
  El Lindo Don Diego, 312
Moretti, Ferdinando
  Cleopatra, 102
  Ifigenia in Aulide, 99
Morselli, Ercole Luigi,
  Belfagor, 387–8
Mortellari, Michele
  Lucio Silla, 74
Mosca, Luigi, 148
  L'Italiana in Algeri, 130
Moschino, E.
  L'Ombra di Don Giovanni, 442
Mosenthal, Salomon Hermann
  Die Königin von Saba, 265
  Die lustigen Weiber von
    Windsor, 214
Mosetti, 491
Mozart, Wolfgang Amadeus, 68,
    76, 77, 92, 184, 194; *83*
  Apollo et Hyacinthus, 67
  Ascanio in Alba, 73
  Bastien und Bastienne, 58, 70–2
  La Clemenza di Tito, 106–8; *103,
    104*
  Così fan Tutte, 102–4; *101*
  Don Giovanni, 78, 97–9, 459; *95,
    97, 98*
  Die Entführung aus dem Serail,
    83, 85–7; *80, 81*
  La Finta Giardiniera, 77–8
  La Finta Semplice, 72
  Idomeneo re di Creta, 83–4
  Lucio Silla, 74–6, 79
  Mitridate rè di Ponto, 72–3, 79
  Le Nozze di Figaro, 94–6, 98, 99,
    104, 133; *91, 93*
  L'Oca del Cairo, 87–8
  Il Re Pastore, 60, 78–9
  Der Schauspieldirektor, 93–4
  Il Sogno di Scipione, 73–4
  Lo Sposo Deluso, 88–9
  Thamos, König in Aegypten, 76
  Zaïde, 82–3, 86
  Die Zauberflöte, 108–10, 376,
    471; *105–7*
Mucci, Emidio
  Cecilia, 424
  Margherita da Cortona, 437
Murger, Henry
  Scènes de la Vie de Bohème, 314,
    318
Musset, Alfred de, 491
  La Coupe et les Lèvres, 296
  Namouna, 258
Mussorgsky, Modest, 194, 259
  Boris Godunov, 260–1; *263,
    265*
  Khovanshchina, 290–2; *296*
  The Marriage, 372

Sources of Illustrations

Collections, Theatres and Institutions

Bayreuther Festspiele Bildarchiv: 193, 197, 198, 199, 208, 209, 219, 245, 252, 272, 273a, 274, 275, 276, 287, 290, 291. Civica Raccolta Stampe Bertarelli, Milan: 24, 122, 129, 136, 152, 157, 164, 167, 183, 217, 223, 244, 293a, 310, 352. Biblioteca Nazionale, Florence: 6, 9. Bibliothèque Nationale, Paris: 18, 73, 109. Bibliothèque de l'Opéra, Paris: 19, 22, 26d, 49, 59, 64, 66, 74, 111, 115, 123, 139, 145, 161, 162, 166, 175, 176, 177, 178, 186, 235, 238, 241b, 243b, 247, 249, 267, 277, 292, 326, 332, 336, 353, 360, 361, 363, 364, 398, 418, 461, 479. Bildarchiv der Öst. Nationalbibliothek, Vienna: 30, 309a. Bundesdenkmalamt, Vienna: 88. Covent Garden London: 266b. Deutsch Bücherei, Lipsia: 189, 224. Ente Autonomo Teatro Scala, Milan: 159, 321a, 429, 459, 462. Fairfax Murray Collection, London: 20. Germanisches National-museum, Nuremberg: 154, 174. Hamburgische Staatsoper: 421. Kunstsammlung, Weimar: 137. Metropolitan Opera House, New York: 98, 181, 253, 270, 301, 314. Musée Carnavalet, Paris: 138. Musée de l'Opéra, Paris: 51, 246. Museo Civico, Turin: 38. Museo San Martino, Naples: 71, 94. Museo Teatrale della Scala, Milan: 26s, 47, 54, 71, 79, 85, 91, 97, 103, 104, 107a, 108, 127, 134, 163a, 167, 170, 179, 207, 215, 222, 243a, 271b, 303, 309b, 315, 325as, 340, 346, 365, 377, 387, 394, 399cd, 415, 435, 489. Museum Bedricha Smetany, Prague: 248s, 334. Musiksammlung der Öst. Nationalbibliothek, Vienna: 27. Nationalgalerie, Berlin: 135, 153. Nationalmuseum, Stockholm: 15 (Tessin-Harleman), 34, 83. National Portrait Gallery, London: 42/43, 55. Opéra-Comique, Paris: 381. Salzburger Festspiele: 487, Schubert Museum, Vienna: 143. Teatro La Fenice, Venice: 341. Teatro dell'Opera, Rome: 89. Theater Collection, Cambridge: 35as. Theater Museum, Monaco: 16, 23, 75, 106, 107. Victoria & Albert Museum, Einsthoven Theatre Collection, London: 148, 149, 150, 202, 203. Villa Verdi, S. Agata di Busseto: 233.

Photographic Agencies and Photographers

Ansa: 355. Arborio Mella: 11, 21, 31, 63, 185, 335. Auerbach, London: 361. Bernard: 368, 391, 452. Beth Bergman: 105. Blauel: 23, 75, 106. Cegani: 237. Giancarlo Costa: 14, 46, 70, 86, 115, 146, 147, 155, 166, 195, 205, 319, 341, 353, 360, 361, 364, 381, 399s, 409. Culver Pictures: 356as, 433s. Carlo Dani: 108, 136, 271bd. Ludovico De Cesare: 80, 401d. De Gregorio (Ricciarini): 419. Deutsche Fotothek, Dresden: 12, 17, 32, 33, 37. Di Biasi: 188, 256. Zoë Dominic, London: 242, 453, 464, 469, 473. Dufoto: 212. Frank Durand: 98, 181, 270. Enar Merkel Rydberg: 401s. Lionello Fabbri: 95, 337, 439, 460. Farabola: 348, 375, 445. Freeman R. John, London: 173. Gay Garnett: 371. Greth Geiger: 120. Giacomelli, Venice: 39, 131, 463. Giraudon, Paris: 99, 138, 185. M. L. Keep: 248d. Erich Lessing (Magnum): 187, 227, 263, 318, 484b, 485. Giorgio Lotti: 405, 407, 430, 431. Raymond Mander & Joe Mitchenson: 35b, 100, 393. Marchiori: 316. Marzari: 26s, 163a, 207. Louis Melançon: 229, 253, 314, 484c. Novosti: 194, 196, 261, 262, 265, 281, 283, 286, 293b, 294, 295, 296, 297, 305, 306, 308, 323, 324, 349. Paris Mach: 210a, 475. Petazzi: 321b. Erio Piccagliani: 78, 81, 121, 130, 151, 168, 171, 191, 211, 226b, 231, 239, 254, 302, 307, 329, 367, 369, 380, 406, 411, 449, 456, 468, 470, 472, 477, 481, 483, 492, 493b. G. B. Pinaider: 9. Publifoto: 488. Mauro Pucciarelli: 266a. Rampazzi: 38. Rastellini: 424d. Ricordi: 325ad, 333, 357. Houston Rogers: 327. Bruno Salmi: 54, 71a, 79, 91, 103, 127, 143, 167, 170, 179, 243a, 309b, 325ad, 333, 365, 394, 415, 435, 489. Scala: 6. Vernon Smith: 240. Sohlmans Musiklexikon: 93, 200, 343, 385. Syndacation International: 493a. Studio Giovetti, Mantua: 10. Tomsich (Ricciarini): 8, 71b. Unifix: 424s. Vaudamm Studio, New York: 433d. Roger Viollet: 180. Archivio fotografico Mondadori: 7, 39, 62, 67, 69, 77, 78, 101, 102, 113, 114, 118, 119, 120, 128, 132, 133, 142, 158, 162, 163b, 168, 169, 172, 184, 188, 210, 212, 213, 216, 225, 226a, 236, 237, 241a, 348d, 251, 255, 256, 271a, 273b, 279, 298, 299, 311, 313, 316, 320, 321b, 322b, 339, 344, 345, 347, 352, 356, 357, 370, 379, 382, 383, 387, 399, 405, 407, 424, 430, 431, 432, 433d, 443, 447, 451, 484a.